Handbook of Drug Use Etiology

The writings, opinions, and thoughts expressed in this volume are the personal views of the contributing authors and do not necessarily reflect those of the funding agencies, governmental bodies, American Psychological Association, or foundations providing support for the research contained herein. We are collectively grateful for the provision of financial resources to conduct the research studies described herein. Without such generous support, we would be grabbing at straws and ultimately possess no more than a fractured and incomplete understanding of the processes involved in drug use etiology.

Handbook of
Drug Use
Etiology

Theory, Methods,
and Empirical
Findings

Edited by

Lawrence M. Scheier, PhD

American Psychological Association

Washington, DC

Published by
American Psychological Association
750 First Street, NE
Washington, DC 20002
www.apa.org

To order
APA Order Department
P.O. Box 92984
Washington, DC 20090-2984
Tel: (800) 374-2721; Direct: (202) 336-5510
Fax: (202) 336-5502; TDD/TTY: (202) 336-6123
Online: www.apa.org/books/
E-mail: order@apa.org

In the U.K., Europe, Africa, and the Middle East, copies may be ordered from
American Psychological Association
3 Henrietta Street
Covent Garden, London
WC2E 8LU England

Typeset in Berkeley by Circle Graphics, Inc., Columbia, MD

Printer: Sheridan Books, Ann Arbor, MI
Cover Designer: Minker Design, Sarasota, FL
Technical/Production Editor: Dan Brachtesende

The opinions and statements published are the responsibility of the authors, and such opinions and statements do not necessarily represent the policies of the American Psychological Association.

Library of Congress Cataloging-in-Publication Data

Handbook of drug use etiology : theory, methods, and empirical findings / edited by Lawrence M. Scheier.
   p. cm.
  Includes bibliographical references and index.
  ISBN-13: 978-1-4338-0446-5
  ISBN-10: 1-4338-0446-8
  1. Drug abuse—Etiology—Handbooks, manuals, etc. 2. Drug abuse—Psychological aspects—Handbooks, manuals, etc. 3. Drug abuse—Social aspects—Handbooks, manuals, etc. I. Scheier, Lawrence M.

RC564.15.H358 2010
362.29—dc22
                  2009005416

British Library Cataloguing-in-Publication Data
A CIP record is available from the British Library.

Printed in the United States of America
First Edition

To my daughters Kyley Johnna Ann and Shane Jodie Ann, your lives have definitely brought me great joy. I am a better person for having the opportunity to rear you. In the spirit of your teenage years, replete with hormones, gym workouts, numerous tennis and soccer matches, spirited debate regarding the meaning of life, and pensive meals together, I leave you with these musical lyrics to ponder:

> And so I cry sometimes when I'm lying in bed
> Just to get it all out, what's in my head
> And I, I am feeling a little peculiar
> And so I wake in the morning and I step outside
> And I take a deep breath and I get real high
> And I scream from the top of my lungs
> What's goin' on?
>
> And I try, oh my God, do I try
> I try all the time in this institution
> And I pray, oh my God, do I pray
> I pray every single day for a revolution!

—"What's Up?", by Linda Perry (1992),
lead guitarist and vocalist for
the band Four Non-Blondes[1]

[1] Perry, L. (1992). *What's up?* On *bigger, better, faster, more!* [CD]. Santa Monica, CA: Interscope Records. © 1992 Sony/ATV Harmony, Stuck In The Throat Music. All rights administered by Sony/ATV Music Publishing LLC, 8 Music Square West, Nashville, TN 37203. All rights reserved. Used by permission.

Contents

Contributors

Michael G. Ainette, MA, Albert Einstein College of Medicine, Bronx, NY

Aaron Alford, PhD, MPH, Battelle Centers for Public Health Research and Evaluation, Arlington, VA

Susan L. Ames, PhD, University of Southern California, Alhambra

Judy A. Andrews, PhD, Oregon Research Institute, Eugene

James C. (Jim) Anthony, PhD, Michigan State University, East Lansing

R. Gabriela Barajas, MA, Columbia University, New York

Lula A. Beatty, PhD, National Institute on Drug Abuse, National Institutes of Health, Bethesda, MD

Peter M. Bentler, PhD, University of California, Los Angeles

Dana Bishop, MEd, Tanglewood Research Inc., Greensboro, NC

Gilbert J. Botvin, PhD, Weill Medical College of Cornell University, New York

Michael J. Brondino, PhD, University of Wisconsin—Milwaukee

Jeanne Brooks-Gunn, PhD, Columbia University, New York

Karren Campbell, PhD, Pacific Institute for Research and Evaluation, Calverton, MD

Nancy D. Campbell, PhD, Rensselaer Polytechnic Institute, Troy, NY

Felipe González Castro, MSW, PhD, Arizona State University, Tempe

Duncan B. Clark, MD, PhD, Western Psychiatric Institute and Clinic, Pittsburgh, PA

Richard R. Clayton, PhD, University of Kentucky, Lexington

Kevin Conway, PhD, National Institute on Drug Abuse, National Institutes of Health, Bethesda, MD

James Derzon, PhD, Centers for Public Health Research and Evaluation, Battelle, Arlington, VA

Susan C. Duncan, PhD, Oregon Research Institute, Eugene

Terry E. Duncan, PhD, Oregon State University, Corvallis

Linda Dusenbury, PhD, Tanglewood Research, Inc., Greensboro, NC

Susan T. Ennett, PhD, University of North Carolina at Chapel Hill

Daniel P. Evatt, MA, University of Illinois, Chicago

Michael Fendrich, PhD, University of Wisconsin—Milwaukee

Brian P. Flaherty, PhD, University of Washington, Seattle

Kim Fromme, PhD, University of Texas at Austin

Margo Gardner, PhD, Columbia University, New York

Meg Gerrard, PhD, Dartmouth Medical School, Lebanon, NH

Frederick X. Gibbons, PhD, Dartmouth College, Hanover, NH

Meyer D. Glantz, PhD, National Institute on Drug Abuse, National Institutes of Health, Bethesda, MD

Justin E. Greenstein, MA, University of Illinois at Chicago

Kenneth W. Griffin, MPH, PhD, Weill Medical College of Cornell University, New York

Joel W. Grube, PhD, Pacific Institute for Research and Evaluation, Berkeley, CA

William B. Hansen, PhD, Tanglewood Research, Inc., Greensboro, NC

Deborah S. Hasin, PhD, Research Foundation for Mental Hygiene, Inc./New York State Psychiatric Institute, New York

Susan Haws, MPH, University of North Carolina at Chapel Hill

Timothy Heeren, PhD, Boston University, Boston, MA

Adrienne Heinz, MA, University of Illinois at Chicago

Ralph W. Hingson, ScD, MPH, National Institute on Alcohol Abuse and Alcoholism, National Institutes of Health, Bethesda, MD

Hyman Hops, PhD, Oregon Research Institute, Eugene

Andrea M. Hussong, PhD, University of North Carolina at Chapel Hill

Adi Jaffe, MA, University of California, Los Angeles

Kimberly A. Jochman, PhD, PPD, Inc., Austin, TX

Timothy P. Johnson, PhD, University of Illinois at Chicago

Valerie L. Johnson, PhD, Rutgers, The State University of New Jersey, Piscataway

Jon D. Kassel, PhD, University of Illinois at Chicago

Hila Katz, BA, New York State Psychiatric Institute/Columbia University, New York

Wendy Kliewer, PhD, Virginia Commonwealth University, Richmond

Marvin D. Krank, PhD, University of British Columbia Okanagan, Kelowna, British Columbia, Canada

Adam M. Lippert, MA, Pennsylvania State University, University Park

Flavio F. Marsiglia, PhD, Arizona State University, Phoenix

Julia A. Martinez, MA, University of Missouri—Columbia

P. Gayle Nadorff, MA, University of Connecticut, Storrs

Tanya Nieri, PhD, University of California, Riverside

Robert J. Pandina, PhD, Rutgers, The State University of New Jersey, Piscataway

Amee B. Patel, MA, MSEd, University of Texas at Austin

Mary Ann Pentz, PhD, University of Southern California, Alhambra

Elizabeth A. Pomery, MA, Iowa State University, Ames

Lawrence M. Scheier, PhD, LARS Research Institute, Inc., Las Vegas, NV

Kenneth J. Sher, PhD, University of Missouri—Columbia

Scott J. Smith, PhD, LMSW, Oakland University, Rochester, MI

Leslie B. Snyder, PhD, University of Connecticut, Storrs

Alan W. Stacy, PhD, Claremont Graduate University, Claremont, CA

Steven Sussman, PhD, University of Southern California, Alhambra

Dawn L. Thatcher, PhD, University of Pittsburgh, Pittsburgh, PA

Yonette F. Thomas, PhD, National Institutes of Health, Bethesda, MD

Jennifer C. Veilleux, MA, University of Illinois at Chicago

Margaret C. Wardle, MA, University of Illinois at Chicago

Helene Raskin White, PhD, Rutgers, The State University of New Jersey, Piscataway

Reinout W. Wiers, PhD, University of Amsterdam, Amsterdam, The Netherlands

Thomas A. Wills, PhD, University of Hawaii at Mahoa, Honolulu

Michael R. Winter, MPH, Boston University, Boston, MA

Scott T. Wolf, PhD, University of Missouri—Columbia

Preface

Words are like everything else in life by virtue of the fact that they have a beginning. Tracing words back to their linguistic roots falls under the purview of etymology, which emphasizes word origins and their integration into the fabric of our linguistic experience (Liberman, 2005). Consulting etymological books is like combing through a vast archaeological dig replete with historical layers annotating the various lexical roots of words. A quick glance at the title of this handbook shows three linguistic elements worth mentioning. First is the word *handbook,* which is perhaps a gross misnomer given the book's hefty size. Owing to its stout nature and breadth of coverage, it could aptly be titled *compendium* or *digest.* When one thinks of a handbook, the image of an easily portable reference book or pocket guide comes to mind. Be that as it may, there is a certain scholarly recognition that comes along with publishing a handbook, providing the book with a much loftier stature that resonates well in academia. Among many considerations, the contents of this handbook represent a synopsis or compilation of findings. In this respect, the resulting use of *handbook* is thus appropriate given that the contents provide a ready reference threading or weaving a fabric of understanding between vast pools of knowledge.

The term *drug use* also represents an intriguing concept and may fall under a modicum of scrutiny. I raise this point because all youth drug use is considered illegal, and therefore one might argue that the term *abuse* is more appropriate for the title. This represents an interesting polemic, and one that may eventually position us in the middle of certain political crosshairs. How laypeople and even scientists or addiction experts readily distinguish between *use* and *abuse* may not be so apparent. One could make the argument that *abuse* resonates well when considering the consequences of drug use: what we believe drug use does to the individual, its disruptive influence on the individual's family, and its devastation of the fabric of our society. The tension in this semantic dichotomy arises (i.e., political crosshairs) because each and every day we all witness underage youth smoking cigarettes and even some youth drinking surreptitiously on weekends or sharing a marijuana "blunt."

Coupled with these observations, there is a modicum of tolerance in our society for the beginning stages of drug use and a general awareness that many youth get their first experience with alcohol in the home, through religious ceremony, or with older siblings. As a whole, society is somewhat acquiescent to the nature of adolescent experimentation, considering drug use normative and part of the trials and tribulations of adolescent growth. This makes formulating the conceptual focus of the handbook difficult because we need to realize there is a very faint—if not thin—line that exists between use and abuse

(Newcomb, 1992). As Newcomb (1992) pointed out, a simple pharmacological model suggests that consumption practices dictate abuse, and there is no further need to consider other extraneous predictors in this equation. Readers can quickly dismiss this model as an oversimplification, knowing full well that even consumption has multiple faces. Some youth, for instance, will smoke cigarettes infrequently and not consider their behavior as connoting "use," whereas other youth will smoke more regularly, leading to abuse if not addiction.

Simplification or not, readers must also recognize that a significant body of behavioral science research has shown that behavior is the best predictor of behavior (Bentler & Speckart, 1981; Epstein, 1979). Thus, we must pick and choose our best medicine in an effort to discern or qualify the object of our scrutiny. That said, the authors of this volume are concerned for the most part with the early stages of behavior and with addressing the conditions of risk, those that arise within the individual from biogenetic susceptibility, those that are encountered in social interactions between individuals, those that resonate from deeper stores of learning experiences, and those that reflect the large social institutions capturing our collective behaviors. This focus on progenitors is what distinguishes use from abuse and provides utility to the handbook.

Turning then to the final component of the title—*etiology*—we gain a better foothold in the construction of this volume, borrowing strength from linguistic origins. Etymology traces the origin of the word *etiology* to the Latin *aetiologia* as in "statement of causes" and the Greek *aitiologia*, which comes from the word *aitia*, or "cause." Further inspection shows that the modern English word *cause*, defined in *Webster's Seventh New Collegiate Dictionary* (1967) as "something that occasions or effects a result," has its linguistic roots in the Latin *causa*. Major synonyms include *determinant, reason, antecedent*, and *occasion*. Were it not for the complexity of human behavior and the fact that cause and effect are not so direct, observable, and relatively easy to discern, we would complete the etymological discussion. However, there is more to this linguistic digression than catches the roving eye.

Mackie (1980) suggested that cause is the cement of the universe, allowing us to inspect the origin of being. In a related vein, British philosopher Karl Popper (1963) reminded us that the search for cause or origins in either words or experiences is linked inextricably to the search for meaning and truth. Popper suggested that the need to know (*epistēmē*) lurks behind the search for all cause and fuels our search for truth and the nature of all being. He went on to elaborate that the process of obtaining true knowledge is to rid ourselves of false prejudices and to strip our minds of ignorant "cocksureness"; in other words, we should engage ourselves in a process of mental purging and cleansing. (Socrates considered this a state of amnesia or *anamnēsis*.)

The notion that everything has a cause is pervasive in our logico-deductive thinking. It is not uncommon to hear scientists query, "What caused that?" and to frame models of behavior in terms of an "irreducible cause." One of the more evolved states of deductive thinking is readily seen in the work of physicists: searching for the ultimate cause of the universe and casting this singular event in a physical beginning (i.e., the big bang). This logical positivist focus on regressing backward in time to the origination point from which all matter and thus life began is evident in the fallacy of our everyday thinking: People tend to think of things as singular in their expression even though we live in a pluralistic world in which most events have multiple causes. When it comes to discussing drug use etiology, one may be tempted to believe that there is a single identifiable cause of the problem when, in fact, if a thousand people are using a drug, there are a thousand different reasons or pathways that in some fashion led to this use. It remains to be seen whether readers concur with this position after digesting the contents of the handbook (*digest* being perhaps a more appropriate reflection of the book's girth).

This discussion of causation and etiology also highlights a somewhat different concern. As with any science, there seems to be a need for conceptual integration and model building leading toward the goal of a unified theory (Barrow, 2005; Davies, 1992). Notwithstanding, linking parts into a unified whole is considerably more difficult in the study of drug use etiology. Suffice it to say that there is no single irreducible cause of drug use; rather, it reflects a skein of numerous forces operating at the intersection of self and society. This "interactional" view owes its pedagogical roots to Vygotsky (1978), a Russian barrister, writer, and developmental psychologist. It was Vygotsky who painstakingly preached that we should not reduce human behavior down to the level of psychological atoms but rather emphasize the virtues of what makes us uniquely human as an affair with social context. At the very least, the handbook is artistically colored by social constructivism, building a picture of the self that is drawn from social experiences, paying tribute to the space between people as much as to the space within. We can also draw similar parallels to social constructivism from the German philosopher Georg Wilhelm Friedrich Hegel (1807/1967). Hegel felt that humans' unique position in the fiefdom of animals is that we are "other directed," responding to social cues that help augment our own self-regard (which he termed *a struggle for self-recognition*).[1]

The confluence of Vygotsky's (1978) and Hegel's (1807/1967) philosophical positions is the point at which we recognize that drug use is at once social by nature and solipsistic by action. Drug use enhances social interactions and satisfies many social needs, while at the same time the act of consumption is primarily done for the drug's individual effects (i.e., the "felt" experience). In many respects, the study of drug use etiology is a philosophical quagmire, treading a fine line in any discourse regarding humans' individual natures and their collective self. From its inception as part of an individual's behavioral repertoire, drug use begins as a volitional act with the self usually acting in full control, regulating not only mode of ingestion but also rate and quantity of consumption. To push Hegel's view even further, the earliest stages of drug use (and here I touch on etiology in its purest sense) is other directed—brought about by peer pressure, conformist tendencies, and the intrinsic social valuation of praise and recognition by a peer reference group. Drug use is part of the social construction of an individual whose outward "looking-glass self" deems its use as necessary and sufficient to obtain peer approval.[2]

---

[1] Lerner (1991) outlined a model specifying organism–context relations, which he theorized are the essential components of development. The basic premise behind the model is that genes in and of themselves do not precipitate structural or functional change, but rather that there is an interaction between intraorganism and extraorganism (contextual) factors that promulgates change. Essentially, this linkage provides the framework for the developmental contextual view (Lerner, 1986), which has also been termed the *dynamically interactive view* (Lerner, 1978). The model argues for reciprocal exchanges linking contextual variation with individual differences in the expression of behavior (see also Dannefer & Perlmutter, 1990; Lerner & Kauffman, 1985; and Nesselroade & von Eye, 1985, for additional mention of reciprocal systems in development and von Bertalanffy, 1968, for a more complete discussion of systems theory as it applies to psychology).

[2] Further explication of the social interactional or contextual view of drug use etiology is presented later in several chapters that make up a section of this volume addressing drug use etiology and social influences. A good overview of this perspective with an emphasis on social processes contributing to drug use can be found in Hops, Andrews, Duncan, Duncan, and Tildesley (2000). Further analysis of social influences is outlined in Ouellette, Gerrard, Gibbons, and Reis-Bergan (1999). Historically speaking, Deutsch and Gerard (1955) outlined one of the first social influence models that distinguished between descriptive norms, which elaborate what youth think their friends are doing and approve of, as opposed to "injunctive norms," which capture what their friends would want them to do.

At some point in the natural progression of things, however, pressures from the peer group fade, and the value of social conformity and self-recognition becomes less influential as drug use progresses toward a more protracted and involved state. At some point in this progression, the self loses control, creating a new juncture at which recreational or experimental consumption transforms into more compulsive use. Here again, we can see the relevance of mind–body dualism, connecting the social experience and psychological manifestations of drug use with physical consequences usually marked by such hallmark characteristics as physiological tolerance and pangs of withdrawal. It is not uncommon for users to describe the magical effect of certain drugs characterized by a kaleidoscope of social experiences (i.e., Ecstasy) or the synesthesia resulting from drug-induced changes in mental chemistry (e.g., LSD, peyote, psilocybin, and other mind-altering hallucinogenic compounds) that reinforce continued use. The highly woven fabric of drug use experiences, the multitude of causes, and the myriad consequences all make it even more difficult to conceptualize an empirical science built on a single cause.

One way to opt out of this conundrum is to avoid writing a book that identifies the cause of drug use and rather seek a more optimal vantage point that deftly coalesces statements about the multiple causes of drug use. Although this may create a less defined picture of the problem, it weaves a more compelling fabric of understanding with the ultimate goal of chronicling a compendium of causes. In many respects, the handbook takes a major step in this direction, taking a long, hard look at the major domains of risk that have curried favor in the past and asking whether this information is mere opinion or true knowledge. Furthermore, the handbook addresses whether this information has been useful (i.e., whether it has solved any problems) by advancing efforts at prevention and treatment.

Readers may notice some other features as they venture forward. For instance, the handbook highlights the main issues in drug use etiology without having to be drug specific. When asked to contribute, many chapter authors initially asked whether they should limit their focus to alcohol or cigarettes or include more than one drug. This was relatively easy to answer in light of the accumulation of evidence supporting the gateway, or "stepping stone," hypothesis (Kandel & Chase, 2002). Studies on the developmental progression of drug use have informed us that experimental drug use most commonly involves an invariant sequence consisting of alcohol, cigarettes, and marijuana. The sequence then progresses to involvement with hallucinogens, cocaine, pills, opiates, and other illicit substances including club drugs. There are so many permutations connecting drug pathways that identification of a single prominent canalization of drug behavior is rendered at the very least elusive. The end result is that contributors have focused on drugs that are consistent with their scholarly and substantive interests, resulting in a book whose thematic orientation is topical, attending to the diverse nature of drug use.

A NOTABLE GAP IN THE FIELD

Despite the centrality and importance of research on drug use, particularly to prevention science, there is a paucity of published books that attend to etiology. More than 20 years ago, the National Institute on Drug Abuse (NIDA) published the *Etiology of Drug Abuse: Implications for Prevention* (Jones & Battjes, 1985) as part of its continuing efforts to inform the public through its Research Monograph Series. Other books that come to mind have attended to etiology but have usually heralded a single theoretical perspective or linked their substantive focus to a single innovative analytic method (i.e., readers may want to consult Beschner & Friedman, 1979; Galizio & Maisto, 1985; Kandel, 1978; and Newcomb & Bentler, 1988, for historical references). The emphasis on addressing a single pressing question (i.e., the gateway hypothesis) or spelling out multiple theories of addiction diminishes the full breadth of studies on drug use etiology. Something else that crops up and is worth mentioning comes from perusing the table of contents of NIDA's 56th Research Monograph (Jones & Battjes, 1985). Interestingly, the monograph proffers a series of substantive concerns that remain the focus of drug etiology research even today. We are as concerned and charged today with finding the causes of drug use as we were 30 years ago.

THE MAKINGS OF A CRISIS

It is clear that drug use etiology research has benefited from an infusion of capital applied in myriad ways, including expenditures for basic science, treatment, prevention, and increased epidemiological monitoring and surveillance. Along with this financial windfall, NIDA has underwritten increasing numbers of well-thought-out and scientifically rigorous studies aimed at elucidating the causes and consequences of drug use and abuse. In just the 2 decades between 1980 and 2000, the budget at NIDA has grown from $73 million in total expenditures ($37 million on research grants) to $696 million ($529 million on research grants alone). The budget request for 2009 exceeds $1 billion and reached this appropriation plateau through congressional action in 2005 (NIDA, 2008). Historically, fueling this rapid increase was the presidential National Commission on Marihuana and Drug Abuse, which met in 1972 and reconvened again in 1974 to develop a second report. The commission was a first of its kind, pooling resources from the government, addiction experts, and drug scholars nationwide. It kicked off a campaign that would eventually position the United States as a worldwide leader in the War on Drugs. The decision to seat a commission and follow its recommendations with legislative activity was catapulted into the limelight by the Vietnam conflict and the social renaissance that kindled the historic 1960s era. Interestingly, the architects of the commission report dutifully acknowledged that the country needed to come to grips with the causes of the nation's drug problem.

Sensitization to the drug problem in the United States can trace some portion of its historical roots to the "morphinomania" of the 19th century (morphine is named after Morpheus, the Greek god of dreams). An ever-widening circle of cultural influences brought on by rapid trans-Atlantic transportation systems coupled with advances in pharmaceutical chemistry created a changing landscape of drugs of abuse including the introduction of opium poppy cultivation. From this prodigious poppy seed (fruit pod) comes the analgesic derivatives morphine, codeine, noscapine, papaverine, and thebaine, the latter involved in the production of semisynthetic morphine analogues like oxycodone (Percodan) and hydrocodone (Vicodin). This epochal event was then followed by concerns over alcohol that culminated in legislative efforts to regulate consumption through a constitutional amendment (Musto, 1999). What is important from a historical point of view is that the public outcry and legislative preoccupation over drug abuse has not really abated. A little more than 3 decades following the National Commission on Marihuana and Drug Abuse, we are witnessing a continuation of the response to illicit drug use in the form of the National Youth Anti-Drug Media Campaign, a social marketing campaign to deter youth from using drugs. The campaign (now using the popular and catchy phrase "above the influence"), which began airing to the public in 1999, uses various media channels to modify social norms, beliefs, and attitudes toward drug use among youth and to impress on parents the need to monitor their children as an effective form of social control. Public service announcements using both television and radio and various forms of print media, billboard advertising, movie theater trailers, and Internet Web sites provide a forum for youth to learn that drug use is not normative; can be quite toxic, even lethal; and can cause serious physical harm (Hornik, 2006).[3] More recently, in 2002 the campaign invoked the Marijuana Initiative, hoping to amplify the government's response to the steady increase in reported marijuana use by our nation's youth. The initiative increases the flood of advertising materials that emphasize the negative consequences of marijuana use.

Another side to the etiology coin needs attention. As a result of the United States' continued pursuit of a concerted public health agenda and various legislative mandates to monitor drug use trends, we have become more informed about who is using what drug and how much they are using. Both the Monitoring the Future study (Johnston, O'Malley, Bachman, & Schulenberg, 2007) and the National Household Survey on Drug Use (in 2000, renamed the National Household Survey on Drug Use and Health; Substance Abuse and Mental Health Services Administration [SAMHSA], 2008) collectively provide a clearer picture of drug use trends among youth at two critical junctures, between the ages of 12 and 17 and the early period of young adulthood (18–25 years of age). We do, in fact, have a means to gauge whether the emphasis on interdiction, social marketing media campaigns, and reliance on school- and community-based prevention have effectively and collectively reduced drug use. Even more important, we are able to use epidemiological surveillance data to better plan and design various prevention initiatives, infusing more science into the political arena. Thus, we have added an important tool to the armamentarium that provides the first line of defense in the oft-cited War on Drugs.

There are additional factors influencing the surge in attention paid to drug use etiology. The government now has a more formal mandate to combat drug use (and abuse), evidenced primarily by the Executive Office's National Drug Control Strategy (Office of National Drug Control Policy, 2007) and stemming directly from the formation of the Office of National Drug Control Policy (ONDCP). ONDCP was created in 1988 as part of the Omnibus Drug Initiative Act introduced by House Representative Thomas S. Foley and later voted into legislation by Congress as the Anti-Drug Abuse Act of 1988. This law represents one of the largest concerted efforts to align the capital and human resources needed to fight our nation's War on Drugs. From a historical point of view, nothing of this magnitude had been attempted since the National Prohibition Act of 1919 (also called the Volstead Act), leading to enforcement of the 18th constitutional amendment, and likewise since implementation of the Harrison Narcotic Act of 1914. The Harrison Narcotic Act provided a steady hand of government regulation over narcotic sales, preparation, distribution, and use previously unheralded in the United States' history of dealing with addiction. Later formulated as the Federal Controlled Substances Act of 1970, it classified and

[3] Evaluation findings produced by ONDCP can be downloaded from http://www.mediacampaign.org/publications/index.html; the youth Web site http://www.freevibe.com; the NIDA Web site, http://www.drugabuse.gov/DESPR/Westat/; and a site developed by campaign personnel, http://www.theantidrug.com. The ONDCP has another Web site containing published information regarding the campaign at http://www.whitehousedrugpolicy.gov.

severely restricted heroin and morphine (among many narcotic substances) as Schedule II substances in an effort to combat addiction.

Amid increased expenditures and greater attention paid to drug use and abuse, there is the growing sense that maybe all the efforts have not netted any substantial dividends. That is, various monitoring registries have shown that more people (including youth 12–17 years of age, young adults 18–25 years, and older adults) are enrolled in treatment today than ever before (SAMHSA, 2004, 2006). Coupled with this bothersome fact, the sheer number of youth acknowledging that they have tried or experimented with drugs has achieved seemingly historical proportions (Johnston et al., 2007; SAMHSA, 2008). To put this in perspective, heavy alcohol use, defined as five or more drinks on the same occasion on each of 5 or more days in the past 30 days, increases dramatically when examining use patterns for youth between the ages of 12 and 14 (0.5%), 15 and 17 (4.5%), and 18 and 20 (13.4%). These numbers have remained fairly consistent over the past decade. Incidence data also paint a compelling picture of the dire problems caused by drug use. In 2007, 2 million youth initiated marijuana use, 1 million started smoking cigarettes daily, and another 8% of the youthful population between the ages of 12 and 17 were diagnosed with either substance dependence or abuse.

Added to this, we have made little progress in the past decade or so, despite billions of dollars expended, in reducing national smoking rates (Centers for Disease Control and Prevention, 2007), per capita levels of ethanol consumption (Lakins, LaVallee, Williams, & Yi, 2007), or alcohol-related traffic fatalities (National Highway Traffic Safety Administration, 2008). Returning then to the original intention in compiling the handbook, perhaps it is time to take an unsullied look at the causes of drug use, and use this information to develop a concerted societal response to the problem. This is precisely what the National Commission on Marihuana and Drug Abuse attempted back in 1972, and because the societal problem appears visible on the radar screen again, the door has been left open.

SEARCHING FOR THEMATIC INTEGRATION

As with any book of this size and scope, my editorial prerogative forced me to make some hard and fast decisions, particularly considering the goals of the handbook, its target audience, and the sheer weight of a volume that would identify all of the risk and protective factors or major domains of influence on drug use etiology. This latter effort represents a Herculean task, and it would probably take a lifetime to synthesize the complete works into a single volume. However, over the past few years we have witnessed the emergence of several prominent themes that have maintained staying power as the field progressed from its infancy to later and more advanced developmental stages. Thus, one task I faced involved paring down the number of themes or domains of influence that have received the lion's share of empirical scrutiny to a manageable set and using these domains of influence as beacons to help illuminate the path toward the eventual emergence of an integrated conceptual model. This book therefore represents more of a synthesis than a concerted exploration of new theory. Although the handbook may seem to struggle with the major conceptual, methodological, and theoretical problems that have surfaced in the field, it also shies away from belaboring the need for a unified model when all the evidence seems to point to multiple-influence models of drug use etiology. This is an important strength given the present state of knowledge in the field and shows the book has some added currency with respect to historical relevance. It is also worth noting that by choosing certain domains of influence to serve as the backbone for the volume, other pressing domains that have received more recent attention have been disregarded. For example, the handbook pays only limited attention to the biological foundations of drug use. Other chapters attend more carefully to genetic influences in drug susceptibility, elucidating familial substance use liability and the role of genetics in the continuum that includes use, abuse, and dependence.

Understandably, inclusion of the many important domains of influence at the biological and social levels would help present a more comprehensive picture of drug behaviors. A broader view of etiology would then better inform public policy. Notwithstanding, this volume covers the psychological and psychosocial causes of drug use, in essence treating the drug-using person as a functioning social human being. Granted, there may be cellular or trans-synaptic responses at the organismic level that dictate addiction severity (i.e., dependence) as well as pharmacological factors that shape the withdrawal process. These and related models of behavior certainly deserve further scrutiny under a similar scholarly rubric. However, the focus of this book rests with the human being interactively constructing the social features of his or her world. In sum, even with the ability to reduce or boil down the complexity of drug use etiology to a few domains of influence, scientists should not disregard the real problems that confront the field. Regardless of the increased expenditures on research, prevention, and treatment, there is still a crisis in drug use etiology, owing to the absence of a unified theory or even a skeletal framework harboring an integrated conceptual model. It is hoped that this volume will direct readers in the right direction to begin sketching out that model or at least testing its veracity against sample data.

ONE FINAL NOTE

Before you turn the page and begin to read the handbook, there is one last issue worth discussing. Philosopher Immanuel Kant spearheaded a movement by debating the merits of rational thought as a means of discovering truth. His "critical theory" proposed that doubt, negation, and contradiction were a surefire means to test the validity of scientific propositions and satiate the thirst for knowledge. Despite the antithetical nature of his approach when contrasted with the logical positivistic foundation of modern science, Kant moved mountains when it came to pure thinking and encouraged philosophers to refrain from spouting off theories about reality when they could root their notions of man in experience (or analytic propositions) and sensation.

At the close of his classic philosophical treatise *Critique of Pure Reason,* Kant (1781/1998) posed three questions that drove his intellectual inspection of life. The questions that he felt bound our interest in human reason were "What can I know?" "What should I do?" and "What may I hope?" Together, these questions transcended the typical philosophical and often trying banter regarding the questions of being and rationality, attending instead to the ultimate question of human potentiality: What are we to become? The study of drug use is one of the many important tools in recognizing the path we will take toward addressing this timeless concern. If science is to play a useful role in the pursuit of self-awareness, then it must reconcile the problems of drug use and abuse within society. Toward this end, the handbook puts the stamp of imprimatur on the collective wisdom proffered by its contributors. With regard to Kant's first pressing question—"What can I know?"—the handbook focuses on the reasons, causes, and determinants of early drug use. We simplify things by building a needed repository of information, organized thematically, and addressing the most pressing issues in the field.

The handbook also provides a vehicle for addressing "What should I do?" by tapping a reservoir of information that can inform prevention. Hopefully, the last page of this handbook is the first page of a companion volume that rigorously examines drug prevention. Only when the two disciplines sew together a harmonious fabric of understanding will we be able to make any headway toward eradicating youthful drug use. The book also takes an important step toward resolving Kant's third question, "What may I hope?" We can hope that the information bound in these pages is read. The legislative activity that put into motion the War on Drugs is the voice of reason by the people and for the people. This book represents the voice of science, which has a cause to bear in examining one of the most important and debilitating problems in all history, the problem of youth drug use.

References

Anti-Drug Abuse Act of 1988, Pub. L. 100-690, 102 Stat. 4181 (1988).

Barrow, J. D. (2005). *Theories of everything: The quest for ultimate explanation.* London: Vintage Books.

Bentler, P. M., & Speckart, G. (1981). Attitudes "cause" behaviors: A structural equation analysis. *Journal of Personality and Social Psychology, 40,* 226–238.

Beschner, G. M., & Friedman, A. S. (Eds.). (1979). *Youth drug abuse: Problems, issues, and treatment.* Lexington, MA: Lexington Books.

Center for Disease Control and Prevention. (2007, November 9). Cigarette smoking among adults—United States, 2006. *Morbidity and Mortality Reports Weekly, 56,* 1157–1161.

Controlled Substances Act, Pub. L. 91-513, 21 U.S.C. 801 et seq. (1970).

Dannefer, D., & Perlmutter, M. (1990). Development as a multidimensional process: Individual and social constituents. *Human Development, 33,* 108–137.

Davies, P. (1992). *The mind of god: The scientific basis for a rational world.* New York: Simon & Schuster.

Deutsch, M., & Gerard, H. B. (1955). A study of normative and informational influences upon individual judgment. *Journal of Abnormal and Social Psychology, 51,* 629–636.

Epstein, S. (1979). The stability of behavior: On predicting most of the people much of the time. *Journal of Personality and Social Psychology, 37,* 1097–1126.

Galizio, M., & Maisto, S. (Eds.). (1985). *Determinants of substance abuse: Biological, psychological, and environmental factors.* New York: Plenum Press.

Harrison Narcotic Act of 1914, ch. 1, 38 Stat. 785 (1914).

Hegel, G. W. F. (1967). *The phenomenology of mind* (J. B. Baillie, Trans.). New York: Harper & Row. (Original work published 1807)

Hops, H., Andrews, J. A., Duncan, S. C., Duncan, T. E., & Tildesley, E. (2000). Adolescent drug use development: A social interactional and contextual perspective. In A. J. Sameroff, M. Lewis, & S. M. Miller (Eds.), *Handbook of developmental psychopathology* (2nd ed., pp. 589–605). New York: Kluwer Academic/Plenum.

Hornik, R. (2006). Personal influence and the effects of the National Youth Anti-Drug Media Campaign. *Annals, 608,* 282–300.

Johnston, L. D., O'Malley, P. M., Bachman, J. G., & Schulenberg, J. E. (2007). *Monitoring the Future national survey results on drug use, 1975–2006. Vol. I: Secondary school students* (NIH Publication No. 07-6205). Bethesda, MD: National Institute on Drug Abuse.

Jones, C. R., & Battjes, R. J. (Eds.). (1985). *Etiology of drug abuse: Implications for prevention* (NIDA Research Monograph 56, a RAUS Review Report, DHHS Pub. No. [ADM] 85-1335). Rockville, MD: National Institute on Drug Abuse.

Kandel, D. B. (Ed.). (1978). *Longitudinal research on drug use: Empirical findings and methodological issues.* New York: Wiley.

Kandel, D. B., & Chase, M. (Eds.). (2002). *Stages and pathways of involvement in drug use: Examining the gateway hypothesis.* Oxford, England: Cambridge University Press.

Kant, I. (1998). *Critique of pure reason* (N. K. Smith, Trans.). London: Palgrave MacMillan. (Original work published 1781)

Lakins, N. E., LaVallee, R. A., Williams, G. D., & Yi, H. (2007). *Surveillance Report #82: Apparent per capita alcohol consumption: National, state, and regional trends, 1970–2005.* Bethesda, MD: National Institute on Alcohol Abuse and Alcoholism, Division of Epidemiology and Prevention Research. Retrieved January 9, 2008, from http://www.niaaa.nih.gov/Resources/Database Resources/QuickFacts/AlcoholSales/consum01.htm

Lerner, R. M. (1978). Nature, nurture and dynamic interactionism. *Human Development, 21,* 1–20.

Lerner, R. M. (1986). *Concepts and theories of human development* (2nd ed.). New York: Random House.

Lerner, R. M. (1991). Changing organism-context relations as the basic process of development: A developmental contextual perspective. *Developmental Psychology, 27,* 27–32.

Lerner, R. M., & Kauffman, M. B. (1985). The concept of development in contextualism. *Developmental Review, 5,* 309–333.

Liberman, A. (2005). *Word origins . . . and how we know them.* New York: Oxford University Press.

Mackie, J. L. (1980). *The cement of the universe: A study of causation* (2nd ed.). Oxford, England: Oxford University Press.

Webster's seventh new collegiate dictionary. (1967). Springfield, MA: G. & C. Merriam.

Musto, D. F. (1999). *American disease: Origins of narcotic control* (3rd ed.). New Haven, CT: Yale University Press.

National Highway Traffic Safety Administration. (2008). *Traffic safety facts: Research note. 2007 traffic safety annual assessment—Alcohol-impaired driving fatalities* (DOT HS 811 016). Washington, DC: National Center for Statistics and Analysis. Retrieved November 19, 2008, from http://www-nrd.nhtsa.dot.gov/Pubs/811016.PDF

National Institute on Drug Abuse. (2008). *Fiscal year 2009 budget information.* Bethesda, MD: Author. Retrieved October 3, 2008, from http://officeofbudget.od.nih.gov/ui/2008/NIDA.pdf

National Prohibition Act, ch. 85, 41 Stat. 305 (1919).

Nesselroade, J. R., & von Eye, A. (Eds.). (1985). *Individual development and social change: Explanatory analysis.* San Diego, CA: Academic Press.

Newcomb, M. D. (1992). Understanding the multidimensional nature of drug use and abuse: The role of consumption, risk factors, and protective factors. In M. Glantz & R. Pickens (Eds.), *Vulnerability to drug abuse* (pp. 255–297). Washington, DC: American Psychological Association.

Newcomb, M. D., & Bentler, P. M. (1988). *Consequences of teenage drug use: Impact on the lives of young adults.* Beverly Hills, CA: Sage.

Office of National Drug Control Policy. (2007). *National Drug Control Strategy.* Retrieved July, 2008, from http://www.whitehousedrugpolicy.gov/publications/policy/ndcs07/ndcs07.pdf

Ouellette, J. A., Gerrard, M., Gibbons, F. X., & Reis-Bergan, M. (1999). Parents, peers, and proto-types: Antecedents of adolescent alcohol expectancies, alcohol consumption, and alcohol-related life problems. *Psychology of Addictive Behaviors, 13,* 183–197.

Popper, K. (1963). *Conjectures and refutations: The growth of scientific knowledge.* London: Routledge Classics.

Substance Abuse and Mental Health Services Administration, Office of Applied Studies. (2004). *The DASIS report: Adolescent treatment admissions: 1992 and 2002.* Rockville, MD: Author.

Substance Abuse and Mental Health Services Administration, Office of Applied Studies. (2006). *Treatment episode data set (TEDS): Highlights – 2005* (DHHS Publication No. [SMA] 07-4229). Rockville, MD: Author.

Substance Abuse and Mental Health Services Administration, Office of Applied Studies. (2008). *Results from the 2007 National Survey on Drug Use and Health: National findings* (DHHS Publication No. SMA 08-4343). Rockville, MD: Author. Retrieved from http://ncadistore.samhsa.gov/catalog/productDetails.aspx?ProductID=17911

Von Bertalanffy, L. (1968). *General systems theory.* New York: Braziller.

Vygotsky, L. S. (1978). *Mind in society: The development of higher psychological processes* (M. Cole, V. John-Steiner, S. Scribner, & E. Souberman, Eds.). Cambridge, MA: Harvard University Press.

Acknowledgments

Constructing a book of this magnitude and scope would not have been possible without editorial guidance and assistance. I am indebted to the support provided by the American Psychological Association's Books Department, particularly acquisitions editor Susan Reynolds; the production staff, spearheaded by Jennifer Macomber; and the wonderful technical editing and generous personal support provided by Ron Teeter and Kathie Baker. As any editor knows full well, the initial brush strokes on the papyrus canvas are truly bound into a coherent volume only with the publisher's incredible support.

In the very early stages of scratching out the outline for this book, I recollected a professional experience that had been somewhat influential in my thinking. I had attended a National Institute on Drug Abuse site visit for a P50 center grant as one of several investigators with a program project bundled in the center. The center served as a repository of scientific brainpower and gathered the resources of several etiology and prevention researchers under one roof. The center review team was spearheaded by Richard Clayton, a sociologist by training and a person who had amassed a distinguished career in etiology and prevention. At one point during the review process, he addressed a room full of psychologists and said, "I am extremely impressed with your overall contribution and productivity. However, I feel compelled to state that with all these psychologists on your team it would be prudent if you had a sociologist in your group to round things out."

Many years later now, and after some consideration (consternation?), I felt it only fitting to invite Richard Clayton to write the introduction to a book written collaboratively and predominantly by psychologists. For whatever it is worth, Richard Clayton is a sociologist operating in a psychologist's world. His introduction to this handbook is a wonderful means to showcase the balance required between knowledge of the individual emphasized by psychologists and the seemingly embedded social nature of our existence heralded by sociologists. Only a sociologist could synthesize such a broad, powerful, and sweeping view highlighting the powerful social institutions that help shape our lives and perhaps contribute in some fashion to behaviors like drug use.

Inside the cavernous halls of academe, I owe a great deal to Michael D. Newcomb, PhD, who mentored me at the right time in my life and showed me that all good things come from the heart. He also taught me to trust my intellectual intuition, follow my imagination, and use my own experiences as lampposts to guide me in the night. I wish Michael well in his own journeys. There are many other mentors who have helped to shape and sculpt my professional aspirations and ambition. Although I remain silent in tribute to them, they know who they are. I was fortunate enough to have two parents with equal investment in keeping me on the straight and narrow path. I remain indebted to them for the gift of life. I have two teenage daughters, Kyley Johnna Ann and Shane Jodie Ann, who keep me focused and believe in me, a debt of love that I can never repay. Each and every day of my life, I bear the responsibility of creating for them a drug-free existence, a charge that I am willing to bear. Finally, I want to thank the formidable group of contributors who made this handbook possible. They accepted the challenge of synthesizing the past, present, and future of drug use research into scholarly chapters. The book is a tribute to their wisdom, their commitment to understanding the seemingly intractable nature of drug use, and their dedication to scholarly pursuits. I am honored to have been able to work so closely with each contributor, to nurture new friendships, and to be able to provide a lasting format for our collective wisdom.

Handbook of Drug Use Etiology

Introduction

Richard R. Clayton

A principal metaphor used by Lawrence M. Scheier, the editor of this volume, to frame the issues that are woven in, on, over, around, and through the etiology of drug abuse is *road map.* Think about it. A road map shows the traveler where all of the roads are—the interstate highways, the beltways around the cities, and the smaller, usually two-lane roads that were used by citizens before the interstate highway system became a reality. A road map also shows the traveler where the towns and cities are located and provides mileage indicators showing how far it is from one town to the next.

In his Concluding Remarks, Scheier uses another, even more powerful metaphor, that of the Iditarod dog sled race, which began as a medical mission of mercy from Anchorage, Alaska, in 1925 to deliver serum for treatment of an outbreak of diphtheria in Nome. That journey covered almost 1,000 miles of snow-covered frozen tundra. Scheier likens the topographical, weather, physical, emotional, and other challenges of the Iditarod to the intellectual odyssey of untangling the etiology of drug use. He etches into our minds a clear picture of the Iditarod, consisting of endless, desolate tundra that extends for miles and miles and miles without any hint of a signpost or weathered trail to follow. Likewise, he also depicts the journey of drug use etiology canvassing similar territory with researchers encountering similar challenges requiring inner strength and scholarly fortitude. I also believe that such intellectual journeys are often lonely, but this handbook is empirical testimony to the scientists, theorists, and scholars who

have, like skilled cartographers, done an excellent job of mapping the complex topography of the etiology of drug use and identifying the signposts and sometimes weathered trails. In fact, the substance abuse field may more accurately reflect the wisdom of Yogi Berra, who, when describing how to reach his house, allegedly said, "When you come to a fork in the road—take it!" There have been many forks in the road, some branches of which have led us to our desired destination and some of which have required us to go back and take a different (and perhaps less traveled) road. What is encouraging is the extent and strength of the evidence obtained from all these travels about different pathways to understanding drug use etiology.

Use of tobacco, alcohol, and other drugs is well recognized as a complex, multivariate, and multi-determined behavior. As a field of scientific inquiry, we have made a rather broad assumption, with some evidence, that there may be common causal factors and pathways to use of different drugs. The etiology of drug use requires a focus on pathways to initial use and on trajectories of use that may or may not include the emergence of dependence and trajectories of desistence that include cessation and relapse. What is ultimately needed in the field is a synthesis of theories and methods derived from at least three major domains: (a) life-span development, including possible sensitive and especially vulnerable periods; (b) individual-level biopsychosocial and behavioral mechanisms that will ultimately involve testing similar hypotheses across species; and (c) physical and

I am deeply grateful to Lawrence M. Scheier for helping to flesh out many of the ideas that surface in this chapter. Although the materials presented are solely my own opinions, they do reflect communication back and forth that helped to conceptualize several distinct problems of the field. In this respect, the introduction is truly a collaboration of minds, melding together diverse professional interests and ideology.

social environments (levels of nested contextual factors, including family, peers, neighborhood, schools, community, society, and culture) and how these relate to life-span development and biopsychosocial and behavioral mechanisms. The interactions of individual differences, nested contextual factors, and developmental pathways may over time result in new ways to look at the critical transition from no use to use and trajectories of use for different drugs, perhaps leading to dependence or to eventual desistence.

In this respect, this handbook is impressive, and without a doubt makes a significant contribution. Lawrence M. Scheier has done an incredible job of herding intellectually giant cats in producing it. It is full of insightful papers that reflect well the growth, breadth, and depth of the knowledge base concerning the etiology of drug use. The handbook is organized into 10 parts that individually address the major themes of drug use etiology. Together, they present a masterful and comprehensive review of the many historical markers and significant milestones on the drug use etiology road map. The selection of these 10 parts makes the handbook an exciting addition to the literature on drug use and increases its utility for readers from various walks of life. Basic science researchers will find some familiarity in the various digests of risk and protective factors. Treatment providers and those working with youth in the trenches will find the chapters on prevention and family systems quite relevant and appropriate sources of information. Those interested in biopsychosocial and genetic models of drug behaviors will also find selections to earmark. Moreover, additional sections attend to intrapsychic and dispositional factors in drug use etiology and to larger macro forces that impinge on people's daily lives. The section addressing race and culture is insightful if not forward thinking, pushing the field to seek parsimony and clarity on its inevitable journey. The section on modeling provides a solid handle for epidemiologists seeking an interface between statistics and real-world applications. In this respect, the handbook should find good company in a wide range of scientific disciplines. In this introduction, I do not take the reader through an exhaustive review of each chapter; rather, I highlight certain points made in the chapters as informative road signs that will enhance the journey. My intention here is to provide readers with a more

firm position of their respective location and enable them to derive a sense of where the field seems to be going.

CREATING A ROAD MAP FOR DRUG USE ETIOLOGY

To begin, the chapters and the large and scientifically rigorous research reviewed throughout are witness to the critical role that the National Institute on Drug Abuse (NIDA) has played in leading the field to intellectual heights that no one could have dreamed of in the early to mid-1970s when this institute was in its earliest days. Thomas and Conway (chap. 1) paint a clear picture of NIDA's vision, describing it as both ambitious and far reaching. The chapter does a wonderful job of unfolding the federal road map, carefully plotting topographical twists and curves along the way. This inside bird's-eye view helps shape the different ideological currents that influence drug research and comes from years of shepherding grants as they progress from innovative ideas to actual science. Along with peer review, this is the critical way the government mines scientific minds and molds the federal drug abuse research portfolio.

Like most substantive areas of inquiry, the history of the field of drug use etiology reflects attempts to deal with what is perceived as an emergent threat to public safety and health. As Campbell (chap. 2) notes, the early focus in the field was primarily on opiates and addicts, not youth or drug use in the general population, as may be the case today. She captures the essence of the history of studies of the etiology of drug use in her title, "Multiple Paths to Partial Truths." The field benefited immensely from the establishment of two public health narcotics hospitals in the mid-1930s in which social and behavioral science researchers conducted ground-breaking research while basic scientists explored the biopsychosocial and behavioral roots of drug addiction. The chapter explores the influence of these early centers and tracks various changes in public policy regarding drug use and addiction. The confluence of policy initiatives and public health mandates eventually led to NIDA's formation. The remainder of the chapter explores the central themes that have concerned NIDA over the past 3 or 4 decades of investigation.

Glantz (chap. 3) examines some of the touchstone issues that must be addressed in theories of substance abuse dependence problems. He highlights the importance of definitions and phenotypes to address the heterogeneity in substance abuse dependence problems. Like most substantive areas of inquiry, the history of the field of drug use etiology reflects attempts to deal with what is perceived as an emergent threat to public safety and health. One of the strengths of this chapter (and integral to the handbook) is discussion regarding the plausibility of an integrated conceptual model of drug use etiology. It is perhaps legitimate and bona fide to begin sketching the boundaries of a unified theory given the accumulation of findings amassed to date. At least the faint lines of a conceptual model that tethers the major risk and protective factors to existing psychological theory can help decode and sort through the massive reservoir of data examining drug use that we have available.

EPIDEMIOLOGY AND THEORY

Research on the nature, extent, correlates, causes, and consequences of drug use, abuse, and dependence has grown enormously, both in its breadth and depth, since the establishment of the Special Action Office for Drug Abuse Prevention in the Executive Office of the White House in the early 1970s and the establishment of the National Institute of Alcohol Abuse and Alcoholism and NIDA in the mid-1970s. This handbook and the excellent comprehensive reviews it contains are empirical evidence of the impressive progress made in understanding not only changes in the epidemiology of drug abuse over time but also the complex architecture of factors that account for individual and population group differences in drug use and abuse.

Two of the chapters in this handbook provide an excellent introduction and overview of what is known about the epidemiology of drug abuse. Epidemiology is concerned with monitoring the incidence and prevalence of diseases. It is like a mechanical counter at a New York subway turnstile, clicking with every person who enters and leaves. Strategic decisions are often made in the inner circles of our nation's capital on the basis of the sheer number of

people we think experience drug problems. We also monitor on a daily basis the surfacing of new drugs that have damaging health consequences (e.g., black tar heroin, crack cocaine). In some respects, epidemiologists build repositories of information that help clarify and perhaps quantify whether our political, legislative, social, and scientific efforts successfully mitigate the social problems we face.

In chapter 4, Griffin focuses on a number of critical developmental transition events that may influence onset of drug use in early adolescence (pubertal timing, school transitions), progression and the peak of drug use during late adolescence and emergent early adulthood (employment outside the home, college attendance), and the decline in drug use that often occurs in young adulthood (employment status; marriage, cohabitation, and divorce; pregnancy and parenthood). Trajectories of use of various drugs do not occur in a vacuum; they are necessarily related to the significant developmental transitions identified and described by Griffin. In addition, simultaneous use of multiple drugs, often in pharmacologically sophisticated ways, may be the norm rather than the exception.

Chapter 5 by Scheier is an erudite and intellectually stimulating discussion of the evolution of social–cognitive theories that have had enormous influence on the field. The chapter begins with a refreshing discussion of theory, reminding readers of the need to make connections (axiomatic statements) that help uncover relationships rather than dissect processes in a search for irreducible knowledge of causation. We should quickly recognize that lacking any true theory, we would be harbingers of scientific nihilism, and this book would fall apart at the seams. A common thread among the theories covered in the chapter is that the causes of drug use reside primarily inside the individual and emphasize cognition, beliefs, and perceived self-efficacy. I do not know anyone who would disagree about the importance of cognitive maps and decision-making algorithms in explaining drug use. Whatever lack of attention there is to theories that address the environment—and contextual influences—is made up by the inclusion of a section in the handbook that amply covers macro-level influences in much greater detail. The editor probably saw the handwriting on the wall and made wise choices. The focus in chapter 5 is also interesting because it is located proximal to chapters on epidemiology that emphasize population groups and macro-level processes rather than individual-level decision making as essential facts in drug use etiology.

Chapter 6 by Anthony notes that epidemiology and etiology are integrally connected and may go hand in hand. Anthony provides excellent examples of public health issues other than drug use to highlight the etiologic significance of causes of incidence and causes of cases. Anthony emphasizes that the rubric of mechanisms "pushes us beyond the more basic question of whether a cause–effect relationship is present toward the questions about how a cause–effect relationship surfaces" (p. 116). Anthony's use of examples of research conducted by his investigative group, illustrating the application of basic epidemiological principles, their connection to etiologic and policy questions, and the political arithmetic of epidemiology, makes this chapter especially enlightening and worth reading.

COGNITIVE AND AFFECTIVE INFLUENCES

The four chapters in Part III of the handbook build on the conceptual and theoretical foundation established by Scheier (chap. 5) and expand and amplify the constructs with thorough reviews of an extensive empirical literature. As a whole, this section draws us closer to the historical roots of psychological study, emphasizing the cornerstone features of learning theory including motivation, reinforcement, and the "glue" that binds stimulus to response (Bolles, 1972). Wills and Ainette (chap. 7) provide a carefully crafted discussion of the dimensions of temperament, emphasizing that self-control (behavioral and emotional) is key to understanding how temperament (planful compared with more impulsive) is related to substance abuse. They have also tied this relationship to the dual-process model that has relevance for the neurobiological bases of self-control and substance abuse. One of the more illuminating qualities of this chapter revolves around the authors' inclination to conceptualize temperament and self-control processes in an epigenetic framework, providing a developmental flavor that can link early

forms of behavior with later regulatory functions and drug use.

Patel and Fromme (chap. 8) review the extensive literature on outcome expectancies and discuss the activity of expectancies as both mediators and moderators. This is a conceptual framework that has provided a useful bridge linking the alcohol, tobacco, and illicit drug research communities and their quest for common etiologic pathways. The chapter deftly showcases the theoretical underpinnings of modern expectance theory, highlighting the seminal work of Edward Tolman (1932). Briefly, Tolman arrived on the scene at a time when "habit strength" was the main feature of stimulus–response learning experiments. He emphasized the concept of mental processes by arguing that rats pursued solving a maze because of an expectation (belief) of what was in the goal box (food), not because of some elemental biological drive. His crafty experimental studies essentially paved the way for a Cartesian renaissance in psychology, underscoring the importance of self-referent thinking. His work is a vital part of the arguments used in outcome expectancy theory and has found a home in modern expectancy arguments regarding the role of beliefs in drug consumption.

In chapter 9, Stacy, Ames, Wiers, and Krank marshal the evidence linking the associations that exist among attitudes, beliefs, expectancies, and proscriptive norms. They also discuss the neural substrates of cues and decision making with reference to the opponent process model (see Koob & LeMoal, 1997) and the downward spiral of hedonic dysregulation. As they point out, motivation operates at many different levels, and the type of reflective, controlled, and deliberative thinking we customarily associate with explicit self-reported cognitions may only be one part of the cognitive machinery that drives drug choices. Their alternative view involves theories of spontaneous cognitive processes (also called implicit associative memory). The type of tasks used in studies of spontaneous associations or implicit memory rely more on automatic, unintentional processing, providing a gauge of thinking that exists beneath the radar of consciousness and mere self-perception. The two-system distinction in fact fits well with Kahneman's (2003; Kahnemann & Tversky, 1979) claim for a default system of information processing.

Affect and emotional distress come in many shapes and forms, including anxiety, depression, neuroticism, and related factors, that contribute to psychopathology, including poor impulse control, rebelliousness, hostility, and aggressiveness. A Freudian would bundle these psychic disturbances as ego-dystonic experiences, suggesting disharmony in the mental world. Although a bulk of the handbook favors cognitive models of drug use etiology, there is certainly room for exploring the role of affect. Chapter 10 by Kassel et al. offers compelling insight into the fine line between diffuse mood, emotion, and the evaluative features of affect, with specific indications as to how they relate to drug use initiation. Several important themes emerge from this chapter, including a specific unveiling of reasons for affect–drug use linkages (does affect influence drug use and does drug use influence affect?), the many faces of affect (i.e., the iceberg lurking beneath cognition), and the notable absence of any consensus regarding why affect motivates drug use. It is refreshing, however, that as we thumb through the pages of a handbook emphasizing cognition, we finally get to read about feelings.

USE, ABUSE, AND LIABILITY

As a nice segue to Part IV, Thatcher and Clark (chap. 11) provide a stimulating discussion, one conclusion of which states, "The available research has demonstrated that childhood manifestations of psychological dysregulation—including conduct problems, deficits in executive functioning, and irritability—have been definitely shown to predict accelerated alcohol and other drug use during adolescence and the onset of [substance use disorders]" (p. 219). The chapter provides insight into brain voxels, neurocircuitry, and neuroimaging techniques that can help pinpoint with greater precision the neuroanatomical substrates of substance use disorders. We are also introduced to the concept of linking brain maturation (gray matter pruning) and various markers or deficiencies (P300 amplitude waves) to behavioral performance associated with substance use disorders.

Chapter 12 by Sher, Wolf, and Martinez is a conceptual masterpiece painting a wonderfully clear picture of how etiology can inform the distinction

between normal drinking and disordered drinking. In particular, Sher et al. tie their chapter to the strong literature on allostatic and incentive sensitization, craving and motivation, and loss of control. One of the finer points of this chapter is the concept of "goading the drinker," that is, the precise mechanisms or risk processes that drive increases in consumption for the benefits of consumption. Being able to draw this fine distinction is an important component of understanding why users accelerate their alcohol or drug use in spite of negative consequences.

Hasin and Katz (chap. 13) take a broad-brush approach and begin by reviewing a host of environmental factors followed by an extended discussion of more intermediate factors before delving into putative genetic factors for the etiology of substance use. This is one of the most thorough and balanced treatises on the topic available. As the chapter details, information on mu-opioid receptor genes, serotonin transporter protein synthesis, and synaptic modulation, among many advances in genetics, will eventually pan into broad-spectrum genomic screens that can augment the work of prevention.

Hingson, Hereen, and Winter (chap. 14) use data from the National Epidemiologic Survey of Alcohol Related Conditions to raise a number of important issues about measurement and the prevalence and severity of alcohol use and dependence. The specific focus of the chapter is age at onset of drinking and transition to alcohol use disorders, or what Sher and his colleagues have labeled *disordered drinking*. Here again, the fine-tooth comb used to discern states of drinking is part and parcel of the need to separate risk factors along the basis of their ability to predict early stages of alcohol (and drug) use from more disordered consumption patterns.

RACE, ETHNICITY, AND CULTURE

The chapters in Part V raise important questions about the predominant approach to research in health disparities. *Race* and *ethnicity* refer to complex and heterogeneous phenomena, and analyses that are based on the current demographic classification mechanism may mask the fact that race is more a social construction than a biological or genetic construction (see Fernander, 2007, and also Moolchan et al., 2007). There is also significant confounding of race and ethnicity with socioeconomic status (see LaViest, 2005) and, as shown by Gardner, Barajas, and Brooks-Gunn later in chapter 22, where one lives may be as important if not more important than race in explaining population group differences in drug use. This type of fine-grained analysis that can discern the various contributions of racial identity, socioeconomic factors, and contextual influences (e.g., neighborhood) is now coming of age (see, e.g., Murray et al., 2006) and helping scientists to grapple with difficult concepts such as culture.

Chapter 15 (Marsiglia and Smith) is organized around commonly identified risk factors that operate at different levels (community, family, school, individual, and peer) and has a strong emphasis on acculturation and ethnic self-identity throughout. Exploring the reasons for health disparity and race-based differences in vulnerability introduces us to meaningful explanations that go beyond the question of whether race is skin deep. Chapter 16 (Castro and Nieri) is perhaps the most compelling and thorough exegesis of all of the constructs related to culture. *Culture* is a broad catchall that attempts to address the traditions, customs, beliefs, and attitudes that constitute people's worldviews (*Weltanschauung*). The precise communication channels used for cultural knowledge diffusion may in some cases increase protection and in other instances convey risk. In light of this, the authors identify the most important concerns for the field, suggesting that theory is the starting point for all good measurement and conceptualization. In turn, the study of identity, cultural or otherwise, requires "innovative yet rigorous approaches . . . in its total temporal and systemic context" (p. 315). Only with these complementary pieces in place can we obtain a much richer understanding of the role of acculturation as it accounts for high-risk behaviors in minority populations.

In chapter 17, Beatty describes in detail the efforts and initiatives used by NIDA to enhance the human capital capacity for conducting research examining disparities in drug abuse rates and to examine the heterogeneity in drug use both within and between racial and ethnic minority groups. Knowing that race is more than skin deep leads us back to the position that we need to focus more closely on what specific

cultural elements foster vulnerability. Toward this end, Gibbons, Pomery, and Gerrard (chap. 18) systematically describe a program of research (the Family and Community Health Study) testing the influence of discrimination on substance use among African American adolescents on the basis of the prototype–willingness model, an expansion of the theory of reasoned action. Using data collected in Iowa and Georgia, they describe the results of their test of the prototype–willingness model and the mediators and moderators of the relationship between perceived discrimination and substance use.

PEER AND FAMILY INFLUENCES

In terms of contextual influences on drug use, the field has a tendency to treat each context separately. Cook (2003), however, made a compelling case for studying multiple contexts simultaneously. This marriage of perspectives is most useful in the study of peer and family influences, which follows next in the handbook. One might arguably state that our knowledge of peer and parent influences is quite rudimentary, limited to suppositions that behavioral similarity between adolescents and their peers or parents is what dictates uptake of drug use. Theory alone dictates the importance of the "looking-glass self" (Mead, 1934) that permeates youth development. More important, crystallization of identity and the hallmark challenges of adolescence steadfastly highlight referent others (Brown, 1990). Having a reference group embodies the other directedness and affair with social context that elaborated by both Hegel and Vygotsky (see the Preface) but still begs the question "How do peers influence drug use?" Added to this is the reality that peers play second fiddle to parents in certain areas of functioning, so parent influences must be addressed as well.

Kliewer's chapter (chap. 19) on family processes is organized around "three distinct pathways through which parents and families affect adolescent behavior: coaching (messages parents relay to their children), modeling (parents' own behaviors), and family context (features of the family environment that either support or inhibit behavior)" (p. 336). She notes the dearth of research on the emotional tone and content of parent–child communication and that coaching and modeling have not been studied simultaneously. Other gaps in the knowledge base are how parental modeling of coping processes (e.g., appraisal, coping behavior, efficacy evaluation) is related to adolescent coping processes and drug use and the lack of attention paid to parents' own emotion regulation coping skills. Simply put, we have been so focused on cognitive skills and affect regulation among adolescents, we have failed to notice that some parents are seriously narcissistic, deficient, and sometimes drug impaired in their own ability to deal with life's challenges. These factors and the dimensions of family context identified and discussed by Kliewer may be the most critical elements and mechanisms in what appears to be intergenerational transmission of drug use patterns and clustering of drug abuse and other problem behavior in families.

The drug research field, as with most if not all other academic disciplines, has a tendency to assume homogeneity and lump people, places, or experiences together when the empirical heterogeneity we observe should lead us to split them. When the now-infamous Woodlawn study children were followed up on in their teens and later as adults, the finding was that father absence was less important as a predictor of subsequent drug use than was mother aloneness (Ensminger, Juon, & Fothergill, 2002; Kellam, Ensminger, & Simon, 1980; Kellam, Ensminger, & Turner, 1977). As long as there was another adult in the household, regardless of role, the probability of drug use was lower, close to the probability of drug use found for those raised in two-parent homes. Like most other fields of scientific inquiry, the drug research field has a tendency to reify the conventional wisdom when a more in-depth examination would reveal a very different picture of reality. What is even more interesting about these findings from a public policy perspective is that they emerged at the same time as then Assistant Secretary of Labor Daniel Patrick Moynihan was announcing that the problem with the Black family in the United States was the absence of a male role model. He may have identified a social fact, but he may also have failed in its interpretation.

The overlap between the two chapters examining peer influence on adolescent and emerging young adulthood drug use is surprisingly relatively small.

Pandina, Johnson, and White (chap. 20) provide an excellent review of a number of relevant theories (social learning theory, peer-cluster theory, primary socialization theory, and the social development model). The chapter emphasizes the importance of selection and socialization: "Adolescents originally select friends who are like themselves in terms of shared behaviors and attitudes. Friends continue to influence one another as a result of continued associations and reciprocal reinforcement of behaviors that define, or at least characterize, relationships" (p. 388). The chapter then continues with an extensive discussion of peer-led programming designed to help change the norms or at least perception of the norms. Chapter 21 by Andrews and Hops extends the review of evidence on selection and socialization processes introduced by Pandina et al. and provides a thorough review of the mediators of peer influence on drug use and an extensive list of factors that may serve as moderators of the relationship (e.g., from environmental and contextual factors to biological and genetic factors).

ENVIRONMENTAL INFLUENCES (SCHOOL, NEIGHBORHOOD, CENSUS)

With deep roots in early sociological studies, there is a strong emerging body of literature on the importance of neighborhood effects and drug use, partly as a result of new interest in the "built environment" and partly because of the work of Krieger, Chen, Waterman, Rehkopf, and Subramanian (2005); results from the Project on Human Development in Chicago Neighborhoods (Sampson, 2003; Sampson, Raudenbush, & Earls, 1997); and the groundbreaking work of Steinberg, Blatt-Eisengart, and Cauffman (2006). Even before these timely and important studies, John B. Calhoun's (1962) impressive experimental studies of overpopulation and the resulting attention to social density as opposed to spatial density laid the groundwork for collaboration between psychology and urban sociology. Calhoun's work paved the way for scientists to realize that crowding and pressure from social interactions promulgated certain deviant behavior (in his experiments, forced crowding among rats instigated infanticide, hyper-aggression, and anomalous sexual behavior). Before

Calhoun's infamous "behavioral sink" experiments, it was the French sociologist Emile Durkheim (1893/1997) who reinforced the need to focus on social life in modern times. Durkheim made famous the term *social anomie* as a reflection of disaffection from social institutions. Modern-day renditions of Durkheim's position are encountered in social control theory, which emphasizes the role of strain caused by disorganized and rundown neighborhoods, limited economic resources, high crime, failed schools, and social chaos, all of which encourage detachment from conventional institutions and a movement toward deviant opportunities as a way of reducing personal disaffection.

What follows in chapter 22 is an incredibly rich review of the literature on neighborhood effects on substance use presented by Gardner, Barajas, and Brooks-Gunn. It is organized around adolescents and adults; around different approaches to measuring neighborhood influence, the links between neighborhood socioeconomic status (SES), and substance use outcomes; and the processes through which neighborhood SES might influence adolescent and adult substance use outcomes. All of this is overlaid with the literature organized around individual-level designs, nested designs, experimental or quasi-experimental designs germane to relocation projects, and natural experiments driven by exogenous shocks. Gardner et al.'s suggestion of a curvilinear relationship between neighborhood SES and substance use outcomes is an example of balanced and critical appraisal of the conceptual, methodological, and substantive findings in this arena of research.

One of the more unsettling points Gardner et al. raise in their chapter suggests that affluence may be on equal footing with poverty in stimulating drug use (e.g., Luthar, 2003). A devout emphasis on achievement (i.e., peer conformity) and the concomitant isolation from parental controls leave many affluent youth home alone with limited supervision. This "preppy" syndrome, along with a culture of materialism (i.e., a poverty of affluence), has been cited as a cause of drinking and drug use among more fortunate high-SES families. As Luthar (2003) suggested, the root cause of adolescent angst is not risk as normally conceptualized, stemming from poverty, neglect, and inefficient parenting skills, but rather as associated

with the pressures of peer conformity, inconsistent caregiving, and poorly connected neighborhoods that produce emotionally bereft homes (Buss, 2000; Luthar & Becker, 2002). In this respect, chapter 22 is a significant contribution to this volume and to the field writ large. The information reaches across numerous disciplines and reinforces the strengths of the ecological view. To wit, in chapter 6, Anthony refers to a beautiful example of how the presumed relationship of race to crack use largely vanished when crack use was examined among African Americans and Whites living in the same neighborhood (Lillie-Blanton, Anthony, & Schuster, 2002; see also LaViest, Thorpe, Mance, & Jackson, 2007).

Ennett and Haws (chap. 23) note that schools are both peer-oriented social systems and formally organized institutions with adult governance, although little of the research on school influences explicitly acknowledges these dual functions. As part of their governance and pedagogic practices, schools have rules and regulations that impart messages to youth about personal conduct and create a social norm regarding acceptable behavior. The authors examine school influence through the eyes of six theoretical approaches (social contagion theory, social network theory, theory of health-promoting schools, integrated theory of delinquency and drug use, social development model, and primary socialization theory). It is interesting that although there is some overlap in the theories reviewed by Ennett and Haws and those reviewed in previous chapters, there are also some marked differences. The authors then engage in a very stimulating discussion of the similarities within and differences among schools by focusing on intraclass correlation coefficients and the complexity of nested hierarchical data and multilevel models. The field has now evolved to the point to which it is possible to understand and disentangle the effects of schools as peer social systems and as formal institutions to understand trajectories of drug use. This has major implications for evaluations of school-based and curriculum-driven prevention programming.

Fendrich, Lippert, Johnson, and Brondino (chap. 24) describe a study conducted among adults residing in 44 unique census tracts in Chicago using propensity score matching procedures to adjust for selection bias. There was evidence that the adjustment made a difference in estimates of the impact of neighborhood on drug use (marijuana and cocaine). A potentially unique feature of this study was the use of biological information taken from hair, urine, and saliva drug tests to augment self-report data on drug use. There is speculation in the chapter that because those in high-risk neighborhoods are more likely to be exposed to cocaine, prevention interventions should perhaps be targeted at the neighborhood level.

Movies like *Blow* and *The French Connection,* among many others, feature drug use as a glamorous means to obtain status, success, and financial freedom. However, the downside of drug trafficking is long prison terms and loss of freedom for the perpetrator if caught. It is only fitting then to include in this section a chapter that examines the different ways in which the media influence (or portray) substance use. Chapter 25 by Snyder and Nadorff highlights the importance of the media as etiological influences on substance abuse because of their potential reach and penetration into the segmented population groups of most concern. The chapter also addresses a different type of connection—one that proposes a mechanism for how people dispel fears that the media will affect them (the third-person hypothesis) with another mechanism that suggests people regard their private and interior world as somewhat distinct from everyone else's. Even if we accept the notion that our worlds are unique, special, and private, this still begs the question of why media moguls believe mass marketing and communication can influence youth drug use. In spite of some success, particularly with regard to tobacco and alcohol, there is a relatively limited evidence base for media effects on use of specific illicit drugs, and the observed effect sizes of media campaigns have been relatively modest (see Palmgreen, Donohew, Lorch, Hoyle, & Stephenson, 2001; Palmgreen, Lorch, Stephenson, Hoyle, & Donohew, 2007).

Grube (chap. 26) provides a thorough yet succinct review of the efficacy of a variety of environmental interventions that emphasize preventing drinking and drinking problems among youth. A public health (i.e., policy-driven) approach for regulated products (i.e., particularly tobacco and alcohol) that influences the environmental opportunities and challenges for

both drinking and consequences of drinking may be a good model for future work on the etiologic and ecological factors influencing use of prescription drugs. The chapter goes to great lengths to clarify the different intervention types (e.g., dram shop liability vs. taxation and price regulation) and provides a wonderful digest of empirical findings.

It is encouraging to see the coverage of SES as an etiologic factor. The evidence from public health is that SES is one of the most potent predictors of both problem behaviors and disparities in health care between poor and more affluent individuals (see Adler & Newman, 2002; Chen, Matthews, & Boyce, 2002). Yet we currently face turbulent economic times in which the fine line distinguishing poverty and wealth is hard to see. Notably, the individual-level and macro-level measures of the various dimensions of SES have their genesis in the 1950s and 1960s. Given the technological changes in how we communicate, changes in the distribution of wealth, and the increasing gaps in indices of wealth between the top and bottom rungs on the SES ladder, one item on the drug use etiology agenda might be using more current and relevant measures of SES.

STATISTICAL MODELS OF DRUG USE ETIOLOGY

Some might question the logic behind including statistical models of drug use as a discrete section of the handbook. In other words, statistics is not regarded as a major influence and therefore does not comport with an earlier argument made by the editor in his Preface that he winnowed down the handbook to a discussion of the major influences. However, we would be remiss to avoid recognizing that recent innovations in statistical modeling have enabled the field to marshal its resources and carve out more precise explanatory models of influence. In fact, statistical modeling benefits us considerably by allowing us to pare away the poorly fitting models and purify the remaining knowledge base. The section should also have a somewhat calming influence on those whose interests rest with causation and resolving chicken-and-egg questions about drug use. Statistical models framed around strong methodological designs can go a long way toward providing fertile answers and addressing simultaneously causal inference.

Flaherty (chap. 27) shows how latent class analysis can inform drug use etiology, specifically outlining methods to statistically aggregate classes of users on the basis of their response profiles. In contrast to a fixed-effects model, in which parameter estimates have to fit all the sample respondents, a latent class model searches for the most meaningful way to sift through item response profiles (e.g., answers to questions on a survey) and create homogeneous subgroups. These groups may entail users versus nonusers, classification on the basis of various risk exposure, or individual differences in consequences of drug use (i.e., abuse vs. dependence symptoms). The end result is that we are able to push a great deal of information through a statistical sieve and gain a more refined understanding of etiological processes. In the example provided, examining methamphetamine use among youth participating in the National Survey of Drug Use and Health, we get to see how, based on their use of other drugs, discrete classes of users yield information about who is most likely to use methamphetamine.

Chapter 28 by Terry Duncan and Susan Duncan is a veritable primer on latent growth curve modeling. The chapter is a clear treatise, systematically covering all of the essential issues and questions required to develop a working knowledge of latent growth curve modeling. The chapter moves from the simplest models and constructs to topics of increasing complexity and relevance because the field is asking and attempting to address research questions that were not even thought of 10 or 20 years ago. The field has moved in a relatively short period of time from using simple descriptive statistics such as correlation, partial correlation, multiple regression, and fixed effects analysis of variance to being able to track changes over time for individuals nested in multiple levels of contexts. Although not specifically discussed by either Jaffe and Bentler (chap. 29) or the Duncans, more widespread use of ecological momentary assessments and data collected multiple times a day over lengthy periods of time will provide increased incentives for improvements in analytic techniques (see Colder et al., 2006; Weinstein, Mermelstein, Hankin, Hedeker, &

Flay, 2007). In addition, the field will have multilevel data extending upward into increasingly larger environmental contexts. The future will also include data from multiple levels extending downward into biological, molecular, and genetic domains, and these types of variables will not necessarily be collected synchronously. Scientists will, however, need to be able to connect everything to changes in individuals over time that are closer to happening in nanoseconds than at baseline, end of treatment, or during the intervention, and at numerous later fixed points in time. The future will require innovations in missing data algorithms as we move from relatively modest numbers of data collection points (fewer than 10) to hundreds of data collection points. If any or all of us think the road that the field of drug use etiology has traveled thus far has been difficult to navigate, the road ahead will be even more challenging, but equally and perhaps even more exciting.

Chapter 29 (Jaffe and Bentler) provides a historical review of the pre–structural equation modeling era, the early years of structural equation modeling, the use of LISREL and EQS, and the growth of the use of structural equation modeling in drug use etiology. The chapter traces the historical development of drug use etiology research and neatly weaves in a story about the prescient efforts of Sewell Wright, one of the fathers of population genetics. Wright helped promote path analysis (a precursor to modern structural equation modeling) on the basis of his need to separate genetic influences across generations (these were truly recursive models!). What began as a stated need in genetics soon benefited behavioral scientists, who were able to blend the sophistication of matrix algebra with modifications in path analysis to create covariance structure analysis.

The drug abuse field has benefited enormously from investments by NIDA from its earliest days to the present in statistical modeling and exploration of more efficient and effective ways of analyzing the complex nexus of predictors of change in drug use trajectories. Because of this institutional commitment, Peter Bentler has devoted significant energy to techniques to drive the drug use etiology field and has thus had a huge impact on the field. The long and short of these innovations is that we are able now to engage a more rigorous level of theory testing using causal multivariate frameworks. It is true that progress on improved analytical techniques has decidedly outpaced developments in measurement of key variables and theory development. This gap between theory and statistical capacity will continue to hold back developments in the etiology of drug use.

FACTORS INVOLVED IN CESSATION

There is only one chapter in this section, chapter 30 by Fromme and Jochman on "maturing out of substance use," with much of the focus on alcohol. The literature has shown that the developmental period of emerging young adulthood is a time when various forms of drug use seem to peak, with cigarette use as a possible exception. Fromme and Jochman organize their chapter around role incompatibility theory and, like other chapters, selection and socialization processes. The evidence is reviewed concerning a host of role transitions that often occur during this critical developmental period (e.g., marriage, pregnancy and parenthood, employment, changes in the composition of social networks, gender and race, personality factors, expectancies). This is an excellent review of the literature, although the number of references to illicit drugs is somewhat limited. Some might take issue with the chapter's subtitle, "The Other Side of Etiology." Notwithstanding, etiology is not just about the initiation and progression of use of drugs but is equally germane for understanding the correlates, predictors, and causes of desistence and cessation, lapse, and relapse. Surely, if we knew the factors predicting cessation and somehow bundled this as part of prevention, we could perhaps accelerate youth's disinclination to use drugs.

CREATING A BRIDGE BETWEEN ETIOLOGY AND PREVENTION: POLICY AND PRACTICE IMPLICATIONS

The road maps covered in previous sections in this volume contain huge amounts of useful information for someone interested in voyaging through the states of drug use etiology. The bridge metaphor in the title for this section is therefore quite appropriate. Etiology and prevention science (and epidemiology;

see chap. 6) are integrally connected. The bridge connecting them is constantly in use and crowded with the traffic of ideas. Within this flow, we learn that prevention programming is designed to produce change in etiologically relevant mediators. The assumption is that the prevention program will yield changes in the mediators that will lead to positive outcomes on drug use.

A movie about a man who built a baseball diamond in the middle of several cornfields located in Iowa is the source of a common saying, "If you build it, they will come." In the last scene of the movie, it is dusk and the lights are on at the baseball field, and a long line of cars stretches into the distance on the road leading to the field. Chapter 31 by Pentz captures the stream of ideas flowing through the empirical findings and conceptual models presented in the previous sections of the handbook. Her work thoroughly illustrates the dilemma of translating research into practice and practice into research. One of the great problems encountered in bringing applied science to practice is the complete underutilization of the knowledge base regarding what works. For example, Ringwalt et al. (2002) found that fewer than 30% of schools that were eligible to receive prevention funding for evidence-based prevention programs were actually using an evidence-based program (see chap. 32). Pentz provides a good primer on the nomenclature and classifications being used in translational research using the integrative transactional theory as the architecture for her chapter. The integrative transactional theory suggests that 17 risk factors can be clustered into intrapersonal, social situational, or environmental contexts of influence on adolescent drug use. In this excellent review, she identifies 10 steps in a model of translation from research to practice and back. This chapter has implications that extend far beyond prevention science research. The results from efficacy and effectiveness trials and the replication of those results in further real-world settings at the community level by community-based professionals and citizens are the true tests of return on society's investments in science. The same is true for the process from bench to bedside to patient to community and back that is at the heart of clinical and translational research in medicine. It is obvious that there are still miles left on the drug use etiology journey, and many places on the road map that are still barren, without signs or directions. Dissemination and translation research is in its infancy, and Pentz has done a good job of introducing discipline into this emerging subdiscipline. As she notes, "This type of translation, and the translation of practice back into research on multiple health risk behaviors, is an area ripe with opportunities for new research" (p. 593).

Chapter 32 (Hansen et al.) consists of an interesting meta-analysis of data (288 effect sizes were calculated) from 25 of the prevention programs that are included in the National Registry of Evidence-based Programs and Practices.[1] The authors conducted the analyses "to summarize the measured impact of these programs for reducing substance use and to identify critical features of programs that may account for their success" (p. 597). All of the programs included in this meta-analysis were deemed successful at the outset. They were classified on a number of dimensions and metrics that putatively differentiate the more successful (efficacious) program elements from the less successful. Although the authors identify some of the program components that are associated with greater program effectiveness, the conclusion is that the most important rate-limiting factors include the resources and support available for their implementation. One bottom-line factor is that the impact of these programs on individual-level drug use outcomes is generally modest. Even so, the authors caution that communities choosing strategies that are "negatively correlated with effectiveness [shift] the burden of proof that these strategies represent good community choices to those who would advocate their adoption" (p. 614).

Another plausible interpretation is that the assumptions about salient etiologic factors underpinning these programs may be seriously skewed toward the single level (individual) rather than multiple levels (including various contexts measured independently of the individual-level factors) and that the trajectories of intraindividual change may be measured too grossly (one time a year) to detect situational-specific and more proximal influences on use. The fact is that we have tended to create or build entire black-box programs without much a priori knowledge of whether the essential components of the prevention program are of roughly equal value. Therefore, we are left with comparing those who in the experimental condition with those in the control condition, not knowing which of the components of the intervention were important. As the authors of chapter 34 appropriately note, in the most widely cited results from the trial of Life Skills Training (see Botvin et al., 1995), those who received 60% or more of the lessons had significantly better results than those in the control condition. However, the 25% to 33% of youth in the experimental schools who received fewer than 60% of the lessons were not any different on drug use outcomes from those in the control condition. One could argue that those exposed to fewer than 60% of the lessons may be exactly those youth often referred to as being at higher risk of drug use. And, even for those who received 60% or more of the lessons, Botvin and his colleagues are not able to tell potential adopters of the program which of the lessons had more or less impact or whether some of the lessons had minimal impact. Perhaps we need new approaches to creating prevention programs, approaches that involve determining that each component is of roughly equal potency at the outset so that when comparing the black box to no box, we are really examining the effect of a robust program. Collins, Murphy, Nair, and Strecher (2005) argued for a multiphase optimization strategy as an alternative approach to achieving program optimization and evaluation. Together with componental and dismantling strategies, the end result will be to find out which component yields the "biggest bang for the buck."

Recognizing the influence of social constructivist thinking on this handbook, it is only fitting then that we also examine the possibility that problems in the way in which people cognitively construct the world are linked somehow to drug use. In chapter 33, Sussman shares a prevention view of how errors in judgment that take shape as misperceptions, incon-

[1] The registry accessible at http://nrepp.samhsa.gov was created in an effort to evaluate the efficacy of mental health and substance use interventions. An independent group of evaluators rate programs on a variety of stringent scientific criteria. This effort sponsored by the U.S. government is part of an overall program of knowledge diffusion and support efforts to provide state-of-the-art technical information on what programs work and for whom in a manner readily accessible to the public.

gruities, fallacies, and distortion play a role in promulgating drug use and misuse. As an added benefit, Sussman then creates a conceptual bridge spanning the cognitive processing limitation view and a meaningful discussion of prevention strategies. Included in this discussion is a virtual unpacking of different prevention modalities that can effectively counteract the myriad cognitive information errors that promote drug use.

As Botvin and Griffin note in chapter 34, a large proportion of prevention science research has focused on mediators that are central to social learning theory, problem behavior theory, and the risk and protective factors identified by Hawkins, Catalano, and Miller (1992). The central part of chapter 34 is a review of the results of small-scale efficacy trials; effectiveness trials with minority youth; large-scale effectiveness trials; and independent research testing the school-based, curriculum-driven intervention Botvin and his colleagues have been studying for almost 2 decades, Life Skills Training. There is an extensive discussion of the protective effects of competence skills, diffusion of innovations theory, and the real-world relevance of implementation fidelity, adaptation, adaptation versus fidelity, and institutional support structures. The authors assume that the most important etiologic mediators (social psychological factors), if changed, may produce positive results on drug use. Notably, these mediators exist almost exclusively at the individual level, inside the person. Although the research designs used to evaluate Life Skills Training involve schools that are randomized to treatment conditions, there is little explicit recognition of the potential influence of macro-level environmental or contextual factors or the extraindividual factors that exist in the schools themselves and in the community environments in which they are located. Rest assured, however, that with the other portions of the handbook in tow, future studies will blend these ideas into a more formative prevention platform.

In his Concluding Remarks chapter, Scheier does an outstanding job of covering every important signpost on the journey through drug use etiology covered in this handbook. At the very outset, in the Preface, he ruminated about definitions of causality, essentially arguing that cause is concerned with

knowing "where we come from." By the end of this handbook, he has taken us all on a very long journey and is now more concerned with where we are going. In truth, the handbook serves as a sort of road map, showing readers that we are moving in the right direction. As editor, Scheier has striven diligently to provide a bird's-eye view of the multiple theoretical and conceptual roads that the field can take in the coming years. His view of the future of drug use etiology is both inspiring and challenging.

References

Adler, N. E., & Newman, K. (2002). Socioeconomic disparities in health: Pathways and policies. *Health Affairs, 21,* 60–76.

Bolles, R. C. (1972). Reinforcement, expectancy, and learning. *Psychological Review, 79,* 394–409.

Botvin, G. J., Baker, E., Dusenbury, L., Botvin, E. M., & Diaz, T. (1995, April 12). Long-term follow-up results of a randomized drug abuse prevention trial in a White middle-class population. *JAMA, 273,* 1106–1112.

Brown, B. B. (1990). Peer groups and peer cultures. In S. S. Feldman & G. R. Elliott (Eds.), *At the threshold: The developing adolescent* (pp. 171–196). Cambridge, MA: Harvard University Press.

Buss, D. M. (2000). The evolution of happiness. *American Psychologist, 55,* 15–23.

Calhoun, J. B. (1962). Crowding into the behavioral sink. *Scientific American, 206,* 139–148.

Chen, E., Matthews, K. A., & Boyce, W. T. (2002). Socioeconomic differences in children's health: How and why do these relationships change with age? *Psychological Bulletin, 128,* 295–329.

Colder, C. R., Lloyd-Richardson, E., Flaherty, B. P., Hedeker, D., Segawa, E., & Flay, B. R. (2006). The natural history of smoking: Trajectories of daily smoking during the freshman year. *Addictive Behaviors, 31,* 2212–2222.

Collins, L. M., Murphy, S. A., Nair, V. J., & Strecher, V. J. (2005). A strategy for optimizing and evaluating behavioral interventions. *Annals of Behavioral Medicine, 30,* 65–73.

Cook, T. D. (2003). The case for studying multiple contexts simultaneously. *Addiction, 98*(Suppl. 1), 151–155.

Durkheim, E. (1997). *The division of labor in society* (J. P. Smith, Trans.). New York: Free Press. (Original work published 1893).

Ensminger, M. E., Juon, H. S., & Fothergill, K. E. (2002). Childhood and adolescent antecedents of substance use in adulthood. *Addiction, 97,* 833–844.

Richard R. Clayton

Fernander, A. F. (2007). Racially classified social group tobacco-related health disparities: What is the role of genetics? *Addiction, 102*, 58–64.

Hawkins, J. D., Catalano, R. F., & Miller, J. Y. (1992). Risk and protective factors for alcohol and other drug problems in adolescence and early adulthood: Implications for substance abuse prevention. *Psychological Bulletin, 112*, 64–105.

Kahneman, D. (2003). A perspective on judgment and choice: Mapping bounded rationality. *American Psychologist, 58*, 697–720.

Kahnemann, D., & Tversky, A. (1979). Prospect theory: An analysis of decisions under risk. *Econometrica, 47*, 263–291

Kellam, S. G., Ensminger, M. E., & Simon, M. B. (1980). Mental health in first grade and teenage drug, alcohol, and cigarette use. *Drug and Alcohol Dependence, 5*, 273–304.

Kellam, S. G., Ensminger, M. E., & Turner, R. J. (1977). Family structure and the mental health of children. *Archives of General Psychiatry, 34*, 1012–1022.

Koob, G. F., & LeMoal, M. (1997, October 3). Drug abuse: Hedonic homeostatic dysregulation. *Science, 278*, 52–58.

Krieger, N., Chen, J. T., Waterman, P. D., Rehkopf, D. H., & Subramanian, S. V. (2005). Painting a truer picture of U.S. socioeconomic and racial/ethnic health inequalities: The public health geocoding project. *American Journal of Public Health, 95*, 312–323.

LaViest, T. A. (2005). Disentangling race and socioeconomic status: A key to understanding health disparities. *Journal of Urban Health, 82*, 26–34.

LaViest, T. A., Thorpe, R. J., Jr., Mance, G. A., & Jackson, J. (2007). Overcoming confounding of race with socioeconomic status and segregation to explore race disparities in smoking. *Addiction, 102*(Suppl. 2), 65–71.

Lillie-Blanton, M., Anthony, J. C., & Schuster, C. R. (2002, February 24). Probing the meaning of racial/ethnic group comparisons in crack cocaine smoking. *AMA, 269*, 993–997.

Luthar, S. S. (2003). The culture of affluence: Psychological costs of material wealth. *Child Development, 74*, 1581–1593.

Luthar, S. S., & Becker, B. E. (2002). Privileged but pressured: A study of affluent youth. *Child Development, 73*, 1593–1610.

Mead, G. H. (1934). *Mind, self, and society*. Chicago: University of Chicago Press.

Moolchan, E. T., Fagan, P., Fernander, A. F., Velicer, W. F., Hayward, M. D., King, G., et al. (2007). Addressing tobacco-related health disparities. *Addiction, 102*, 30–42.

Murray, C. J. L., Kulkarni, S. C., Michaud, C., Tomijima, N., Bulzaccelli, M. T., Iandiorio, T. J., et al. (2006). Eight Americas: Investigating mortality disparities across races, counties, and race-counties in the United States. *PLoS Medicine, 3*, 1513–1524.

Palmgreen, P., Donohew, L., Lorch, E. P., Hoyle, R. H., & Stephenson, M. T. (2001). Television campaigns and adolescent marijuana use: Test of sensation seeking targeting. *American Journal of Public Health, 91*, 292–296.

Palmgreen, P., Lorch, E. P., Stephenson, M. T., Hoyle, R. H., & Donohew, L. (2007). Effects of the Office of National Drug Control Policy's marijuana initiative campaign on high sensation-seeking adolescents. *American Journal of Public Health, 97*, 1644–1649.

Ringwalt, C. L., Ennett, S., Vincus, A., Thorne, J., Rohrbach, L. A., & Simons-Rudolph, A. (2002). The prevalence of effective substance use prevention curricula in U.S. middle schools. *Prevention Science, 3*, 257–265.

Sampson, R. J. (2003). The neighborhood context of well-being. *Perspectives in Biology and Medicine, 46*, S53–S64.

Sampson, R. J., Raudenbush, S. W., & Earls, F. (1997, August 15). Neighborhoods and violent crime: A multilevel study of collective efficacy. *Science, 277*, 918–924.

Steinberg, L., Blatt-Eisengart, I., & Cauffman, E. (2006). Patterns of competence and adjustment among adolescents from authoritative, authoritarian, indulgent, and neglectful homes: Replication in a sample of serious juvenile offenders. *Journal of Research on Adolescence, 16*, 47–58.

Tolman, E. C. (1932). *Purposive behavior in animals and men*. New York: Century.

Weinstein, S. M., Mermelstein, R. J., Hankin, B. L., Hedeker, D., & Flay, B. R. (2007). Longitudinal patterns of daily affect and global mood during adolescence. *Journal of Research on Adolescence, 17*, 587–600.

PART I

CREATING A ROAD MAP FOR DRUG USE ETIOLOGY RESEARCH

THE EPIDEMIOLOGY OF DRUG ABUSE: HOW THE NATIONAL INSTITUTE ON DRUG ABUSE STIMULATES RESEARCH

Yonette F. Thomas and Kevin Conway

Drug abuse epidemiologic research focuses on understanding the nature, extent, consequences, and etiology of drug abuse across individuals, families, age groups, gender, communities, and population groups. Epidemiologic research plays a critical public health role by providing an estimate of the magnitude, impact, and risk of drug abuse and related problems on a population and by laying the foundation for developing strategies to prevent drug abuse, plan and evaluate drug abuse services, and suggest new areas for basic, clinical, and treatment research (chap. 6, this volume, provides further insight on the strengths of epidemiological research).

The natural history of drug use, abuse, and addiction can be observed most efficiently and validly in epidemiologic studies. The population-based approach provides specific advantages when compared with research relying on convenience samples, such as clinical samples, by reducing the potential for selection bias in observed associations while enhancing generalizability. There are, however, some notable limitations to epidemiologic research. Large sample sizes can pose difficulties in terms of time and cost to obtain intensive and detailed measures, particularly over extended periods of time. The observational nature of epidemiologic drug abuse research can limit experimental control and manipulation of variables under study. However, underused applications in epidemiologic study design, such as nested case control studies, enable integration of focused intensive measurement in the context of epidemiologic research. It is possible to draw epidemiologically informative samples, based on specific characteristics,

for recruitment into laboratory-based research. Although collaboration between laboratory-based and epidemiologic research is becoming more widespread in other areas of health research, it is less common in drug abuse research.

The National Institute on Drug Abuse (NIDA), through its Division of Epidemiology, Prevention, and Services Research and directly through that division's Epidemiology Research Branch, encourages innovative research that incorporates the strengths of epidemiologic and laboratory-based designs. Recent advances in health science research have recognized the influence of behavioral, social, psychological, and genetic factors across the spectrum of diseases, including drug abuse and addiction. For diseases with a substantial environmental component, however, individually or in combination, these factors are not sufficient to explain or predict disease patterns. Therefore, to better understand the epidemiology of drug abuse and its consequences within and across populations, NIDA encourages research on the interactive influence of environmental, social, and cultural factors on the initiation and progression of drug use among population groups. This handbook provides a sweeping panorama of the most recent empirical studies that attest to this focus. The institute has funded many of the studies described in this book and continues to look on this highly innovative research as state-of-the-art science with tentacles reaching deep into the social problem of drug abuse.

Novel conceptualization and measurement of environmental, social, and cultural contexts that arise from theoretically grounded research are important to the advancement of drug abuse research. Ultimately, the successful identification of specific genes and related biological and physiological systems and other etiologic processes of complex diseases like addiction depend on precise, quantitative measurements of personal environmental exposures to evaluate their impact on disease risk. Increased understanding of how genetic, biological, social, cultural, and contextual phenomena interact to influence behavior will inform prevention and treatment for individuals at risk for drug abuse and addiction. In this chapter, we outline two major areas of focus in drug abuse research and discuss their role in the furtherance of the scientific enterprise.

DRUG ABUSE EPIDEMIOLOGY

Epidemiologic methodology has historically been the foundation for developing an understanding of the nature and extent of drug abuse, for developing strategies to prevent drug abuse, and for providing scientific support for other types of basic, clinical, and treatment research. The focus over the past 2 decades has been on the furtherance of an understanding of the natural history of drug abuse in the population, including its courses and consequences, clues to causation, and identifiable targets for intervention. Merikangas (2000, 2002) provided an excellent description in which, using the traditional epidemiologic triangle, she depicted drug abuse as the result of a complex dynamic interaction among characteristics of the host, environment, and agent–vector (see Figure 1.1).

Despite the multifactorial etiology of drug abuse depicted in Figure 1.1 and conceptualized in several broad theories of drug abuse, drug abuse research has focused and continues to focus largely on individual risk factors at the expense of understanding the interaction of broader and interrelated factors. When multiple contributive factors have been considered, the emphasis has commonly been on simple additive models of predispositional factors, and these models have typically concentrated on factors from a single domain—that is, the biological, the behavioral, or the environmental. Comprehensive reviews have been written to identify empirically derived risk and protective factors for drug problems. Hawkins, Catalano,

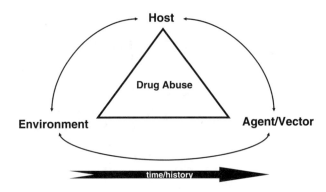

FIGURE 1.1. Epidemiologic triangle. From "Genetic Epidemiology of Substance-Use Disorders" (p. 537), by K. R. Merikangas, in H. D'haenen, J. Ben Boer, and P. Wilner (Eds.), *Textbook of Biological Psychiatry*, 2002, New York: Wiley. Copyright 2002 by John Wiley and Sons. Adapted with permission.

and Miller (1992), for example, identified 17 major factors that influence drug abuse risk, of which 4 were listed as broad contextual factors (laws and norms favorable toward behavior, drug availability, extreme economic deprivation, and neighborhood disorganization). There is also evidence linking the number of risk factors with the magnitude of risk, whether additively (Bry, McKeon, & Pandina, 1982), multiplicatively (Newcomb, Maddahian, Skager, & Bentler, 1987), or interactively (Glantz, Weinberg, Miner, & Colliver, 1999). Subsequent refinements of these models have included protective factors, with the argument that their interaction with risk dictates vulnerability (e.g., Griffin, Scheier, Botvin, & Diaz, 2000; Scheier & Newcomb, 1991; Scheier, Newcomb, & Skager, 1994). By and large, reviews of factors associated with drug abuse etiology have concentrated on individual-level factors, at the relative expense of social and environmental influences.

Of the various risk factors for drug abuse, family history has been identified as the most potent and consistent risk factor for drug use disorders (Merikangas, 2002). Indeed, there is compelling evidence for this statement from a range of genetic epidemiologic studies, including family studies, twin studies, and adoption studies (see also chap. 13, this volume). For example, results from family studies have shown that drug use disorders run in families (Bierut et al., 1998; Merikangas et al., 1998). The results from twin and adoption studies have demonstrated that much of the familial clustering of drug use disorders can be explained by genetic factors (Cadoret, Troughton, O'Gorman, & Heywood, 1986; Kendler, Karkowski, Neale, & Prescott, 2000) and that such genetic factors may confer risk generally across the various classes of illicit drugs (Kendler, Jacobson, Prescott, & Neale, 2003). More important, genetic epidemiologic studies of drug abuse have yielded results that are compelling in terms of consistency, magnitude of relative risk, and coherence of the public health message.

Gender-Specific Differences

Research has indicated that there are significant gender-specific differences in biological factors in drug abuse and related risk behaviors, antecedents and consequences of drug abuse, and responses to prevention and treatment. NIDA (and the National Institutes of Health more generally) encourages investigators, wherever possible, to include adequate numbers of both male and female participants in their studies to make meaningful gender comparisons. Researchers are also encouraged to design studies to explore gender differences in the nature and extent of drug-using behaviors, including sexual risk behavior associated with injecting and noninjecting drug abuse; in the pathways and determinants of initiation, progression, and maintenance of drug abuse; and the behavioral and social consequences of drug abuse.

Drug Abuse and HIV/AIDS

HIV/AIDS and drug abuse are frequently referred to as twin epidemics, and whenever possible, it is essential that epidemiologic studies address this interrelationship. NIDA responded swiftly to the epidemics of the 1980s with a resounding emphasis on these problems and established several lines of funding earmarked for HIV/AIDS research. Clearly, the interrelationship of HIV/AIDS and drug abuse is one compelling reason (injection drug users are at much higher risk of contracting HIV/AIDS). Investigators are encouraged to incorporate appropriate measures and examine factors critical to understanding transmission risks for HIV/AIDS and other sexually transmitted diseases, hepatitis C and B, and tuberculosis. Disparities in these risks across different population groups are also a central concern to NIDA. The aim is to promote integrated approaches to understanding

and addressing cofactors and interactions among individuals and their environments that contribute to the continuum of problems related to drug abuse, including HIV/AIDS.

Racial and Ethnic Variations

Research has shown that minority groups, particularly African Americans and Hispanics, are in some instances less likely to use illicit drugs, but that such groups tend to be overrepresented among those who suffer from co-occurring and adverse health, behavioral, and social consequences related to drug use (e.g., HIV/AIDS, premature births, intentional and unintentional injuries, violence, crime, unemployment, school dropout). Figure 1.2 depicts this phenomenon. Further epidemiologic research is needed to inform prevention and intervention strategies aimed at reducing and eliminating drug-related health disparities, as well as services research on access, utilization, and retention of racial and ethnic minority populations in drug abuse treatment. Part V of this handbook (chaps. 15–18) examines more carefully the concept of racial health disparity, exploring in some detail the conceptualization of race, culture, and ethnicity as they apply to drug use and abuse. NIDA encourages research in these aspects through its Prevention Research Branch and Services Research Branch. Within epidemiology, however, a focus on identifying risk factors and consequences that are unique to, vary with time and circumstances in, or are more prevalent in subpopulations in socioeconomically disadvantaged and medically underserved rural and urban communities continues to bear fruit.

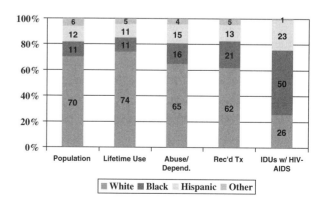

FIGURE 1.2. Consequences of drug abuse and addiction disproportionately affect minority populations.

Methodological Innovation

Advances in the field of drug abuse epidemiology will require innovations in statistical, epidemiologic, sociologic, and genetic epidemiologic designs to meet challenges in the rapidly evolving drug abuse field. NIDA encourages methodological innovations that address transitions in stages and trajectories of drug abuse, intergenerational transmission of drug abuse, and heterogeneous pathways to and consequences of drug abuse. In particular, emphasis is geared toward approaches that facilitate nested case-control and case-cohort designs that efficiently combine the advantages of epidemiologic samples with more intensive laboratory-based and biological measures. Moreover, several innovations in measurement involve real-time measures of drug abuse (experience sampling methods) and associated risk factors through the use of handheld devices and secondary analyses of existing epidemiologic data sets that contain high-quality information about drug abuse.

SOCIAL EPIDEMIOLOGY OF DRUG ABUSE

Converging trends in geography, epidemiology, and sociology have refocused attention on the various influences of the social and physical environment on health (Berkman & Kawachi, 2000). Cross-disciplinary dialogue on concepts, methods, and evidence about the influences of the social environment on individual risk and health and behavior are critical to this approach. Medical sociologists, social epidemiologists, and other social scientists have long since advised that understanding adverse health behaviors and preventing them requires focus not just on individual attributes and behaviors but on the further influences on health of the environment in which the individual lives. There is a large literature on this subject, and readers may catch a glimpse in various publications (e.g., Adler, Boyce, Chesney, Cohen, & Folkman, 1994; Berkman & Kawachi, 2000; Berkman & Syme, 1994; Lin, Munsie, Hwang, Fitzgerald, & Cayo, 2002; Miech & Hauser, 2001; Monroe & Steiner, 1986; Sewell & Armer, 1966; Yen & Kaplan, 1999). However, work in this area "depends on the resolution of multiple methodological challenges (e.g., dealing with nested levels of aggregation, simultaneity bias, and differential selection)" (Singer & Ryff, 2000, p. 8) to avoid problems related to the ecological fallacy. The National Research Council committee, which was charged with articulating future directions for behavioral and social sciences research at the National Institutes of Health, advised that the National Institutes of Health should conduct "more extensive research on [how] the collective properties of social environments" affect health behavior and health outcomes (Singer & Ryff, 2000, p. 8). This emphasis underscores the need for continued focus on the interaction of individual behavioral and genetic factors with those of the individual's social environment— for example, familial structure and patterns, social networks and supports, neighborhood and/or community when assessing health behavior in general, and adverse health behavior such as drug abuse in particular.

Diverse factors account for the variations in the etiologies of drug abuse among individuals and population groups with different predisposing or protective factors and comorbid conditions and the multiple patterns in which these factors occur. Many of these factors emanate from or are reinforced by norms and behaviors of family members and other significant players, intervening processes such as collective socialization, and peer group influence, as well as social and institutional processes (Burton & Jarrett, 2000; Hawkins et al., 1992; Sampson, Morenoff, & Gannon-Rowley, 2002). In other words, the social environment is something of a sphere that encompasses the many factors interacting with individual characteristics and resulting in diversity. Yen and Syme (1999) defined *social environment* as inclusive of "the groups to which we belong, the neighborhoods in which we live, the organization of our workplaces, and the policies we create to order our lives" (p. 1). These authors went on to clarify the environment as being "the result of the continuing interaction between natural and man-made components, social processes, and the relationships between individuals and groups" (p. 1). Similarly, Berkman and Kawachi (2000) pointed to the social environment's influencing behavior by changing norms and enforcing patterns of social control, those that are either health promoting or health damaging.

The need to examine the interaction of individual factors with familial, biologic, and socioenvironmental factors and the accumulation of effects of these interactions over time and across generations is important to the furtherance of drug abuse epidemiologic research. There is a definite need to focus and extend drug abuse research to include an examination of the interaction of individual susceptibility and social and biologic environments, both as main effects and as effect modifiers, and the accumulation of risk and how these determinants differentially impose risk across time and generations (chap. 3 of this volume considers these "touchstone" issues). Conceptions of how social group, neighborhood and community, culture (familial, group), or environment influence drug abuse remain unfocused if only individual-level risk factors are addressed.

Berkman and Kawachi (2000, p. 6) defined *social epidemiology* as "the branch of epidemiology that studies the social distribution and social determinants of states of health." In this chapter, we define the social epidemiology of drug abuse as the study of the interaction of individual susceptibility with social environment, genetic environment, and neighborhood environment (both as main effects and as effect modifiers) and how these determinants differentially impose risk across time and generations. This definition can, therefore, be dichotomized as interactivity (Newcomb & Bentler, 1986) and cumulative risk–history (Wallace, 1994).

As readers will find out from digesting this handbook, drug abuse is more accurately characterized by diversity and complexity, with myriad causes and consequences. Because drug abuse has untoward effects on many other facets of functioning (cognitive impairment, social problems, and medical complications, to name a few) and because as a society we seem focused on its eradication, it is significant that it be treated as an adverse health behavior. As a good deal of this handbook spells out more carefully, the focus of our empirical studies has been on the identification of biopsychosocial factors that contribute to resilience and drug abuse resistance and moderating effects of social and environmental contexts on the expression of biological or genetic predisposition. This multilevel perspective is driven by the realiza-

tion that different social conditions can result in different levels of genetic influences on drug-abusing behavior and foster a wide range of consequences. In addition, new perspectives on drug abuse include multilevel approaches such as the impact of collective properties and healthy communities as risk or protective factors—that is, neighborhood and community-level variables—that entail more incisive looks at the effects of residential instability, collective efficacy, or social cohesion or other aspects of locally shared environments as contributors to drug-abusing behaviors (Lynch, Kaplan & Salonen, 1997; Petronis & Anthony, 2000; Sampson, Raudenbush, & Earls, 1997). The conceptualization of drug abuse and its consequences as the social epidemiology of drug abuse facilitates the examination of the interaction of individual factors with familial, biologic, and socioenvironmental factors and the accumulation of effects of these interactions over time and across generations.

Specifically, it is important to recognize that the field of social epidemiology may prove particularly useful when conceptualizing the meaning of the environment. Along these lines, it has been argued that advances in epidemiology require the embracing of new paradigms of thought that involve interdisciplinary collaboration and consideration of influence across multiple levels. Susser and Susser (1996; Schwartz, Susser, & Susser, 1999), for example, proposed a research paradigm termed *eco-epidemiology* that encourages movement away from the traditional risk factor approach and toward a paradigm that "addresses the interdependence of individuals and their connection with the biological, physical, social, and historical contexts in which they live" (Schwartz et al., 1999, p. 25). This approach involves the simultaneous consideration of multiple levels of organization, time dimensions, and dynamic processes. Although the eco-epidemiology paradigm falls short of recommending methodological approaches to realize this shift, we propose that bridging social epidemiology with genetic epidemiology will be a particularly fruitful methodological approach in this regard. Notwithstanding, readers will be invigorated reading this handbook, which approaches history and the blending of diverse disciplines with an even hand.

LINKING SOCIAL AND GENETIC EPIDEMIOLOGY IN DRUG ABUSE RESEARCH

The methodological tools of genetic epidemiology and the conceptualizations of social epidemiology are natural partners that, if aligned, have great potential to advance the drug abuse field. Linking social and genetic epidemiology is one way to interface the influences of individuals, families, and community in a manner that is conceptually driven and empirically tested within methodologies that are specifically suited to ascertain familial transmission and heritability. In many ways, the guiding principles of social epidemiology naturally complement the methods of genetic epidemiology, particularly family studies that extend across multiple generations.

Despite significant progress in genetic epidemiology of drug abuse, further advancement in this area involves wrestling with significant conceptual and methodological issues surrounding genetic and environmental influences on human disorders. Peltonen and McKusick (2001) commented that

> most common human diseases represent the culmination of lifelong interactions between our genome and the environment. Predicting the contribution of genes to complex disorders is still a challenge, and determining the interactions between genes and the environment during any disease process is a daunting task. (p. 1)

In particular, there has been considerable discussion about the difficulties of teasing apart the role of genetics, environment, and their interplay in drug use disorders and other psychiatric disorders (Merikangas, 2002; Merikangas & Risch, 2003). Drug use disorders are particularly clear examples of human disorders that pose great challenges because they, although being familial and heritable, do not follow Mendelian patterns of inheritance; probably involve multiple genes, each exerting small effects; require environmental exposure for a genetic liability to be expressed; and may develop in the absence of known genetic risk. And although the quest persists for the reliable detection of risk-conferring genes for drug use dis-

orders, success in this endeavor and in the identification of Gene × Environment interactions will hinge in part on the conceptualization of the environment. Indeed, Merikangas (2002) argued for the "development of richer conceptualization of environmental factors that may be important mediators of expression of genetic risk for mental disorders through integration of the tools of genetic epidemiology, behavioral neuroscience, developmental psychology and neuroscience" (p. 542). We propose that social epidemiology be added to the list of essential disciplines that can enrich this critical discussion.

Several genetic epidemiologic research designs are especially well suited for linkages with social epidemiology, including family studies, twins-reared-apart studies, adoption studies, and migrant studies. First, the basic family study of drug use disorders involves identifying individuals (i.e., probands) with a drug use disorder (i.e., drug abuse or drug dependence) and then determining the presence or absence of the disorder among relatives. Family studies often extend across several generations for a comprehensive ascertainment of the disorder in the pedigree, by way of direct interviews with relatives or family history reports about relatives. The rate of the disorder in the relatives of the probands is then contrasted with the rate of the disorder in relatives of controls, yielding the relative risk that represents the "familiality" of the drug use disorder. As noted in the review by Merikangas (2002), this relative risk approaches eightfold in some family studies. Second, the twins-reared-apart design is particularly informative and powerful because of its unique ability to separate genetic from environmental sources of variance. In this design, monozygotic twins (who share 100% genetic material) are adopted away into different family environments, thereby offering an opportunity to examine the influence of environmental factors (which vary between the twins) on the expression of traits that are suspected to have a genetic component. Grove et al. (1990), for example, examined drug abuse in monozygotic twins separated at birth and determined that the heritability of drug abuse was $h = 0.45$. Third, adoption designs are also quite informative in elucidating genetic and environmental factors. Like the twins-reared-apart design, individuals are adopted away from birth parents and into new family environments. Genetic risk for a disorder is ascertained by gathering information about the disorder in birth parents, and the presence of the disorder in birth parents constitutes genetic risk in the adopted-away offspring.

The work of Cadoret, Yates, Toughton, Woodworth, and Stewart (1995; Langbehn, Cadoret, Caspers, & Troughton, 1998) has shown that adopted-away offspring of drug abusers are at heightened risk for drug problems and that environmental influences may moderate this risk. Fourth, the migrant study is a very powerful approach to identifying the influence of cultural factors that confer risk or protection for drug use disorders. A migration study of drug abuse would examine the impact of a significant change in residence (e.g., across a physical boundary such as a border) on a drug-related outcome, by virtue of comparing the rate of the outcome among individuals who migrate to that of matched individuals who remain in the original residence. Because migration often involves a dramatic change in many environmental domains (e.g., family, culture, politics, economics), this design offers many opportunities to examine the impact of such changes on drug-related outcomes.

Although such designs offer the potential to examine the effects of several domains of influence that are central to social epidemiology—history, cohort, culture, community, and family—such opportunities have not been actualized. Clearly, there are numerous practical and economic reasons for this because these study designs are difficult and time-consuming endeavors that involve considerable interdisciplinary collaboration. Nevertheless, many genetic epidemiologic studies are ideally suited for understanding the mediators that link risk-conferring factors (i.e., genetic liability) with disorder phenotype because such processes unfold over time within individuals who are nested within families, communities, and other levels of influence. Although the field of genetic epidemiology is not alone in the relative inattention to causal processes of drug use disorders relative to the identification of risk factors, the methodological tools inherent to genetic epidemiology are particularly appropriate for examining such processes through a multilevel perspective that ranges from genetic liability to macro-level dynamics. The con-

cepts of social epidemiology can be used to maximize the potential of such genetically informative designs, and in doing so can advance the science of drug abuse epidemiology in an iterative manner that is balanced conceptually and empirically.

FUTURE RESEARCH

Theoretical orientations from diverse disciplines provide context for assessing the collective properties of community environments on drug-abusing behavior. Researchers continue to search for collective characteristics that shape individual and group outcomes and continue to question "why some groups versus others" and "why some communities versus others." Although many societal characteristics have been identified as being responsible for certain variations in group-level outcomes, relevant, driving, and empirically identifiable questions remain. For example, how do socioenvironmental and microecological conditions together influence drug-abusing behavior? What is understood about the mechanisms and processes by which social structure affects drug-abusing behavior? Specifically, then, we encourage drug abuse researchers to further and more deeply explore the interplay of social interactions, social environment, structural context with individual behavioral characteristics, and heritability.

Further drug abuse studies should examine the interaction of individual and social environmental factors on drug use, abuse, and dependence. Studies should consider both immediate and cumulative (life course and transgenerational) effects of interactions among drug-abusing behaviors, environments, and genes. Such studies should draw on current research on the effects of social environmental factors on health and disease in general. In the process, key research questions are as follows: Can the environment as culture be meaningfully disaggregated into measurable components? Which aspects or dimensions of the social environment—society, social institution, small group, dyad—should be included and measured and at what level of analysis? What are the independent and related effects of community factors, familial factors, and biologic factors on drug use, abuse, and dependence? What are the mechanisms through which area characteristics affect drug use, abuse, and dependence? What is the collective impact of neighborhood factors such as residential stability or instability, collective efficacy, social cohesion, or other aspects of locally shared environments on drug use, abuse, and dependence in different population groups?

Innovative methodologies that enable the exploration of individual susceptibility, environmental influences, and heterogeneity of drug abuse phenotypes as interwoven mechanisms promise a new generation of drug abuse research. A focus on individual susceptibility should be achieved using longitudinal research that controls for temporal sequencing and identifies putative causal factors and pathways to drug abuse, as well as the natural history of drug abuse. In the process, there needs to be an integration of laboratory-based measures that cannot be obtained in field research. Unfortunately, laboratory and clinical research are often conducted in isolation from epidemiologic research, and epidemiologic evidence is often not incorporated into laboratory and clinical research—for example, natural history and drug use patterns. Because much of what we know about drug abuse liability is based on volunteer samples, nesting laboratory-based measures within longitudinal population-based studies seems critical. In addition, epidemiologic evidence can be used to inform selection of participants for laboratory-based research. As well, drug abuse research must take greater advantage of innovations in epidemiologic study design, that is, nested case-control studies, case cohort studies, and selected sampling from cohort studies.

In focusing on environmental influences, new research should emphasize using and paralleling prevalence estimates from national surveys such as the National Survey on Drug Use and Health, formerly the National Survey on Drug Abuse; the Monitoring the Future study; the Youth Risk Behavior Survey; the National Comorbidity Survey; the National Survey of Parents and Youth; the National Longitudinal Survey of Youth; and others with community-level research. It is known that national surveys miss relatively rare drug use (e.g., heroin), are subject to regional variation, capture pockets of drug use, reflect emerging trends in drug use, and disregard high-risk groups not living in permanent households. It is further known that drug use is invariably a local phenomenon with considerable variation across communities. In addition, although national surveys can provide important information about trends in prevalence of drug use, they provide little information about factors that lead to differences in drug use outcomes across communities. Therefore, research targeted at understanding interactions of individual and social environmental influences with community-level factors require particular attention.

Extending drug abuse research into the study of interactions across domains of risk factors—gene–environment, individual susceptibility–social environment, neighborhood environment as an effect modifier—provides great promise for the next generation of drug abuse research. Such approaches will further our understanding of the interactions between individual vulnerability and social environmental influences that affect transitions between stages of drug use, ranging from opportunities to use drugs to the development and possible remission of drug dependence. However, this requires the innovative use of epidemiologic methods that characterize the nature and extent of drug abuse in population groups and explicate causal pathways with the goal of reducing the negative public health impact of drug abuse.

References

Adler, N. E., Boyce, T., Chesney, M. A., Cohen, S., & Folkman, S. (1994). Socioeconomic status and health: The challenge of the gradient. *American Psychologist, 49,* 15–24.

Berkman, L. F., & Kawachi, I. (Eds). (2000). *Social epidemiology.* New York: Oxford University Press.

Berkman, L. F., & Syme, S. L. (1994). Social networks, host resistance, and mortality: A nine-year follow-up study of Alameda County residents. In A. Steptoe & J. Wardle (Eds.), *Psychological processes and health: A reader* (pp. 43–62). Cambridge, England: Cambridge University Press.

Bierut, L. J., Dinwiddie, S. H., Begleiter, H., Crowe, R. R., Hesselbrock, V., Nurnberger, J. I., et al. (1998). Familial transmission of substance dependence: Alcohol, marijuana, cocaine, and habitual smoking: A report from the collaborative study on the genetics of alcoholism. *Archives of General Psychiatry, 55,* 982–988.

Bry, B. H., McKeon, P., & Pandina, R. J. (1982). Extent of drug use as a function of number of risk factors. *Journal of Abnormal Psychology, 91,* 273–279.

Burton, L. M., & Jarrett, R. L. (2000). In the mix, yet on the margins: The place of families in urban neighborhoods and child development research. *Journal of Marriage and the Family, 62,* 1114–1135.

Cadoret, R. J., Troughton, E., O'Gorman, T., & Heywood, E. (1986). An adoption study of genetic and environmental factors in drug abuse. *Archives of General Psychiatry, 43,* 1131–1136.

Cadoret, R. J., Yates, W. R., Toughton, E., Woodworth, G., & Stewart, M. A. (1995). Adoption study demonstrating two genetic pathways to drug abuse. *Archives of General Psychiatry, 52,* 42–52.

Glantz, M. D., Weinberg, N. A., Miner, L. I., & Colliver, J. D. (1999). The etiology of drug abuse: Mapping the paths. In M. D. Glantz & C. R. Hartel (Eds.), *Drug abuse: Origins and interventions* (pp. 3–45). Washington, DC: American Psychological Association.

Griffin, K. W., Scheier, L. M., Botvin, G. J., & Diaz, T. (2000). Ethnic and gender differences in psychosocial risk, protection, and adolescent alcohol use. *Prevention Science, 1,* 199–212.

Grove, W., Eckert, E., Heston, L., Bouchard, T., Segal, N., & Lykken, D. (1990). Heritability of substance abuse and antisocial behavior: A study of monozygotic twins reared apart. *Biological Psychiatry, 27,* 1293–1304.

Hawkins, J. D., Catalano, R. F., & Miller, J. Y. (1992). Risk and protective factors for alcohol and other drug problems in adolescence and early adulthood: Implications for substance abuse prevention. *Psychological Bulletin, 112,* 64–105.

Kendler, K. S., Jacobson, K. C., Prescott, C. A., & Neale, M. C. (2003). Specificity of genetic and environmental risk factors for use and abuse/dependence of cannabis, cocaine, hallucinogens, sedatives, stimulants, and opiates in male twins. *Archives of General Psychiatry, 160,* 687–695.

Kendler, K. S., Karkowski, L. M., Neale, M. C., & Prescott, C. A. (2000). Illicit psychoactive substance use, heavy use, abuse and dependence in a U.S. population-based sample of male twins. *Archives of General Psychiatry, 57,* 261–269.

Langbehn, D. R., Cadoret, R. J., Caspers, K., & Troughton, E. P. (1998). Genetic and environmental risk factors for the onset of drug use and problems in adoptees. *Drug and Alcohol Dependence, 69,* 151–167.

Lin, S., Munsie, J. P., Hwang, S., Fitzgerald, E., & Cayo, M. R. (2002). Childhood asthma hospitalization and residential exposure to state route traffic. *Environmental Research, 88,* 73–81.

Lynch, J. W., Kaplan, G. A., & Salonen, J. T. (1997). Why do poor people behave poorly? Variation in adult health behaviors and psychological characteristics by stages of the socioeconomic life course. *Social Science & Medicine, 44,* 809–819.

Merikangas, K. R. (2000). Genetic epidemiology of drug use disorders. *Trends in Neuroscience, 2,* 55–62.

Merikangas, K. R. (2002). Genetic epidemiology of substance-use disorders. In H. D'haenen, J. Ben Boer, & P. Wilner (Eds.), *Textbook of biological psychiatry* (pp. 537–546). New York: Wiley.

Merikangas, K. R., & Risch, N. (2003). Will the genomics revolution revolutionize psychiatry? *American Journal of Psychiatry, 160,* 625–635.

Merikangas, K. R., Stolar, M., Stevens, D. E., Goulet, J., Priesig, M., Fenton, B., et al. (1998). Familial transmission of substance use disorders. *Archives of General Psychiatry, 55,* 973–979.

Miech, R. A., & Hauser, R. M. (2001). Socioeconomic status and health at midlife: A comparison of educational attainment with occupation-based indicators. *Annals of Epidemiology, 11,* 75–84.

Monroe, S. M., & Steiner, S. C. (1986). Social support and psychopathology: Interrelations with preexisting disorder, stress, and personality. *Journal of Abnormal Psychology, 95,* 29–39.

Newcomb, M. D., & Bentler, P. M. (1986). Substance use and ethnicity: Differential impact of peer and adult models. *Journal of Psychology, 120,* 83–95.

Newcomb, M. D., Maddahian, E., Skager, R., & Bentler, P. M. (1987). Substance abuse and psychosocial risk factors among teenagers: Associations with sex, age, ethnicity, and type of school. *American Journal of Drug and Alcohol Abuse, 14,* 413–433.

Peltonen, L., & McKusick, V. A. (2001, February 16). Genomics and medicine: Dissecting human disease in the postgenomic era. *Science, 291,* 1224–1229.

Petronis, K. R., & Anthony, J. C. (2000). Perceived risk of cocaine use and experience with cocaine: Do they cluster within US neighborhoods and cities? *Drug and Alcohol Dependence, 57,* 183–192.

Sampson, R. J., Morenoff, J. D., & Gannon-Rowley, T. (2002). Assessing "neighborhood effects": Social processes and new directions in research. *Annual Review of Sociology, 28,* 443–478.

Sampson, R. J., Raudenbush, S. W., & Earls, F. (1997, August 15). Neighborhoods and violent crime: A multilevel study of collective efficacy. *Science, 27,* 918–924.

Scheier, L. M., & Newcomb, M. D. (1991). Psychosocial predictors of drug use initiation and escalation: An expansion of the multiple risk factors hypothesis using longitudinal data. *Contemporary Drug Problems, 18,* 31–73.

Scheier, L. M., Newcomb, M. D., & Skager, R. (1994). Risk, protection, and vulnerability to adolescent drug use: Latent-variable models of three age groups. *Journal of Drug Education, 24,* 49–82.

Schwartz, S., Susser, E., & Susser, M. (1999). A future for epidemiology? *Annual Review of Public Health, 20,* 15–33.

Sewell, W. H., & Armer, J. M. (1966). Neighborhood context and college plans. *American Sociological Review, 31,* 159–168.

Singer, B. H., & Ryff, C. D. (Eds.). (2000). *New horizons in health: An integrative approach.* Washington, DC: National Research Council, National Academies Press.

Susser, M., & Susser, E. (1996). Choosing a future for epidemiology: II. From black box to Chinese boxes and eco-epidemiology. *American Journal of Public Health, 86,* 674–677.

Wallace, J. M. (1994). Race differences in adolescent drug use: Recent findings from national samples. *African-American Research Perspective, 1,* 31–35.

Yen, I. H., & Kaplan, G. A. (1999). Neighborhood social environment and risk: Multilevel evidence from the Alameda County study. *American Journal of Epidemiology, 49,* 898–907.

Yen, I. H., & Syme, S. L. (1999). The social environment and health: A discussion of the epidemiologic literature. *Annual Review of Public Health, 20,* 287–308.

CHAPTER 2

MULTIPLE PATHS TO PARTIAL TRUTHS: A HISTORY OF DRUG USE ETIOLOGY

Nancy D. Campbell

The emergence and growth of research on drug abuse in general—and specifically on the causes of drug abuse—has been influenced by many different historical currents. Over the past 200 years, some of the more salient historical moments include the Temperance movement, which instilled tremendous interest in the causes and treatment of alcoholism in the 19th century. In addition, ritual smoking of opium among Chinese laborers turned public attention to nonmedical uses of opiates in the late 19th century. The nation's preoccupation with opiate use, primarily morphine and heroin, began in the early 20th century and intensified after World War II. Later in the 20th century, the Vietnam conflict instilled focused governmental attention on poppy derivatives including heroin. The 1960s counterculture created interest in psychedelic drugs, including LSD; marijuana and amphetamine use also dramatically increased during this period. Cocaine was popularized among the Hollywood jet set in the 1970s and soon found a new outlet in the crack cocaine that ravaged our nation's urban poor in the 1980s. Alcohol and stimulants have long been popular among college students; since the 1990s, club drugs, including flunitrazepam (Rohypnol), ketamine, gamma-hydroxybutyric acid (GHB), and methylenedioxymethamphetamine (Ecstasy), have found a niche in U.S. drug culture. Health problems associated with nicotine and cigarette inhalation have long stimulated interest in the causes of youthful smoking.

This chapter encapsulates the institutional history that has fueled the growth of research on drug use etiology over the past century. The first section of the chapter examines research on drug addiction before the U.S. government's decision in 1973 to create the National Institute on Drug Abuse (NIDA). Although the National Institute on Mental Health (NIMH) had made research on drug and alcohol dependence part of its portfolio since 1948, formation of NIDA and its sister institute the National Institute on Alcohol Abuse and Alcoholism in 1970 significantly contributed to the emergence of etiology as a subfield. Despite shifting political emphases across different presidential administrations, the missions of NIDA and the National Institute on Alcohol Abuse and Alcoholism have remained focused on the causes, consequences, and prevention of drug and alcohol abuse. The chapter also traces key historical influences that helped distinguish drug use etiology as a separate scientific discipline and contextualizes the different conceptual and methodological perspectives that have shaped this field within broader social and political forces. Any historical dissection of the sources of drug use etiology must address the social roots of drug and alcohol use, the normative influences that have driven the field to embrace concepts such as use and abuse, and legislative activity designed to shape social norms.

THE EARLY YEARS

Before the inception of NIDA, coordination of drug abuse research had been handled primarily by NIMH. The NIMH was formed in 1948 as an outgrowth of the U.S. Public Health Service's Division of Mental Hygiene (Grob, 1991). The NIMH also interacted with a quasi-governmental Committee on Drug Addiction and Narcotics, which had been formed by

the National Research Council, an organ of the
National Academy of Sciences. The Committee on
Drug Addiction and Narcotics originally arose in the
early 1920s from a committee created by the New
York City Bureau of Social Hygiene (funded by the
Rockefeller Foundation and addressed later in this
chapter). The Committee on Drug Addiction and
Narcotics had a dual mission: to find a nonaddicting
analgesic to replace heroin and morphine and to
find a cure for the condition (Acker, 1995, 2002).
The committee's efforts were not solely focused on
etiology, but also included prevention as part of its
broad mission. In 1965, the committee renamed itself
the Committee on Problems of Drug Dependence,
the coveted name today encompassing a large, interdisciplinary professional association consisting
largely of substance abuse researchers. NIDA eventually absorbed some of the functions of this committee, which coordinated the efforts of the Addiction
Research Center at the U.S. Public Health Service
narcotic hospitals in Lexington, Kentucky, from
1935 to 1974 when the Addiction Research Center
became the intramural research branch of NIDA
(Campbell, 2007). Although the institutional history
of substance abuse research presents a tangled web
of mergers and acquisitions, the field has been a productive and lively specialization that has led to the
formation of multiple subfields.

PAST AND PRESENT MODELS
OF DRUG USE ETIOLOGY

Several recent reviews have noted the Herculean
task required to organize and integrate the diverse
models created by drug use etiology researchers
(Petraitis, Flay, & Miller, 1995; Scheier, 2001).
Models have proliferated partly on the basis of the
drug in question and the population under study.
The variegated state of the field also reflects the
push or pull of prevention, which can influence
elaboration of etiology in many different ways. A
prevention theme guided by a cognitive–behavioral
approach, for instance, might bias the focus of etiology toward behavioral skills or cognitive determinants. A prevention theme molded around family
systems theory might herald the importance of
interpersonal relations and family dynamics. The

diversity of models, theoretical approaches, and
conceptualizations of drug use is perhaps the most
significant challenge faced by etiology researchers.

First-generation drug policy historians agree that
one underlying historical current revolves around
the linkage between who uses drugs and under what
circumstances. For example, drug policy historians
support the notion that social learning cycles and
changes in medical practice bear at least as much
responsibility for drug use trends as do changes in
state or federal government policy (Courtwright,
2001; Musto, 1999). Knowing why certain drugs
were prohibited or subject to government regulation
requires knowing who used them and in what circumstances. For instance, Americans were voracious
consumers of a bewildering variety of patent medicines in the 19th century, but most made judicious
use of habit-forming drugs (McTavish, 2004). Before
the 20th century, members of the medical profession were considered the main cause of morphine
addiction. Morphine, a principal alkaloid of opium,
was isolated by German pharmacists early in the
19th century. The invention of the hypodermic
needle propelled the spread of morphine addiction
in the 1860s and 1870s. One hypodermic syringe
in the hands of a doctor who possessed few other
remedies to treat cholera or dysentery was an efficient route to overmedication.

Over the course of time, large numbers of White
middle- and upper-class women became the majority of morphine addicts in the 19th century
(Courtwright, 2001). The social status and racial
and ethnic makeup of these individuals protected
them from being labeled as social deviants. By contrast, Chinese laborers or members of the White ethnic working class who developed a drug habit were
considered deviant. The earliest restrictions of habit-
forming drugs were in response to the importation of
Chinese smoking opium in the 1890s. It is notable
that mainstream society regarded the use of smoking
opium to relax after work differently than the so-
called medical use of morphine by members of the
leisure class.

As these few examples show, construction and
specification of etiological models change with shifts
in the demographics of drug-using populations and
cultural attitudes toward patterns of use. Opiate

addiction (including morphine and heroin) offers an example of how ideas about causation shift when social conventions depict certain forms of drug use as deviant. Once opium trickled down to the working classes and nonmedical use became the norm, the "opium problem" was labeled a form of deviance deserving punishment, not pity. By 1910, heroin had overtaken morphine as the nation's drug of choice when it came to nonmedical use. Injection as a route of administration had displaced heroin sniffing, opium smoking, and pharmaceutical morphine use (i.e., cough syrup) as the primary pattern of drug abuse in the United States by the 1940s (Courtwright, 2001). Fast forward to the period shortly after World War II, and one notes the public outcry about juvenile delinquency and, especially, male adolescent heroin addiction. Later in this chapter, I revisit this particular cohort of adolescents, who became the focus of epidemiologically based studies to better understand the late-1960s heroin epidemic.

In general, models of causation and consequence are shaped by prominent historical events and to some degree reflect cultural parameters. These currents of influence suggest two things: First, a historical review of the field needs to consider how specific research agendas took shape in relation to broad social changes that manifested in the transformation of social norms and public policy; second, explanatory models grappling with the causes of drug use at the individual or group level require contextualization within the circumstances in which drug and alcohol use and abuse take place. Causal factors investigated as determinants depend on the social constructions present at the time—particularly those that dominate the public view of drug use. Consider that the Motion Picture Production Code of 1930 prohibited depictions of narcotics use, but for many decades to some cigarette smoking and alcohol consumption were commonplace in Hollywood films. Changes in social norms particularly affecting television and sports venues produced social norms that restricted advertising of alcohol and tobacco products. Social rituals and cultural incorporation of drug use reduces the social burden or stigmas associated with use. When members of a group engage in drug-using rituals and behaviors that are perceived as abusive or deviant, new social norms and policies are

typically invoked (Courtwright, 2001; Gusfield, 1996; Valverde, 1998).

DRUG USE ETIOLOGY FROM A SOCIAL WORLDS PERSPECTIVE

The current fund of knowledge on drug use etiology represents an accumulation of findings that have been produced and refined over an extended period of time. The consolidation and institutionalization of this knowledge yielded what is called a *social world,* defined as a universe of mutual discourse and a set of affiliative mechanisms that form the basic building blocks of collective action (Clarke, 2005; Weiner, 1981). Affiliative mechanisms can take the form of journals or scientific publications, conferences, peer review, and scientific collaboration. When it comes to social organization of knowledge, Knorr-Cetina (1999) suggested that different subfields or disciplines exhibit different epistemic cultures. Epistemic communities gain cultural authority to enhance their credibility in several ways, by the production of scientific evidence and the construction of consensual interpretations. Like any other knowledge-based field or discipline, the social processes of drug use etiology reflect an epistemic culture or a universe of mutual discourse that is exemplified through conferences, scientific meetings, and journal publications.

WHAT CAUSES SUBSTANCE ABUSE? HISTORICAL ANTECEDENTS OF DRUG USE ETIOLOGY

One of the earliest substantive considerations of etiology was funded by the Rockefeller Foundation as part of a study conducted by the New York City Bureau of Social Hygiene. Charged with learning what was known about narcotic addiction in hopes of preventing or curing it, the bureau's Committee on Drug Addiction reviewed data from 4,000 studies produced in the period between the 1850s and 1925. The result of this primitive meta-analytic review was published in a hefty tome called *The Opium Problem* (Terry & Pellens, 1928). The thicket of theories, definitions, and models of addiction that had arisen by the early 20th century had rendered attempts to define the etiology, pathology, symptomatology, and prognosis of drug addiction impossibly complex. In this respect, *The Opium Problem* was a response to the lack of information on addiction with an eye cast toward discovering how to prevent or cure narcotic addiction. The volume reflected the basic tenor of the committee chair, physician Charles E. Terry, who established the first municipal morphine maintenance clinic in the country. Terry and members of the committee represented the first line of defense in the struggle to respond to the unintended consequences of the Harrison Narcotic Act of 1914. The Harrison Narcotic Act provided legislation that required physicians and pharmacists to register with the U.S. Department of the Treasury but was broadly interpreted as prohibiting physicians from maintaining their patients on narcotics (Courtwright, 2001, p. 2). A byproduct of this legislation required that addicts register at morphine maintenance clinics. However, by 1922 most of the clinics had ceased operations. In the end, zealous enforcement of the newly enacted legislation resulted in overcrowded prisons and jails, where addicts were forced to kick the habit in the absence of medical assistance.

Terry and Pellens (1928) found that the state of knowledge regarding etiology was at best inconclusive and fractionated and reflected poor science. Drug addiction affected people from all walks of life, and drawing random samples of addicts rarely reflected a true cross-section of the populations involved in narcotic addiction. This led Terry and Pellens to write,

> T[he] prison physician, the alienist [psychiatrist], and the medical head of a private sanatorium handle very different types [of drug users,] and it is quite apparent that studies of such selected groups elicit very different conclusions as to the relative influence of causative factors. (p. 94)

Statements about drug use causation depended on where studies were conducted and which populations of addicts were studied. These and other observations encouraged Terry to outline a model of etiology reflecting the composition of the diverse addictive populations. He classified three types of

users, including those with *iatrogenic addiction* or dependence consequent to medical treatment; those affected by *social contagion,* resulting from what was termed *vicious associations* encountered within the rapidly forming urban underworld; and those with the psychological or psychopathological traits said to predispose individuals to a drug habit. These categories corresponded to the causal notions that prevailed at the time among both professionals and lay individuals alike.

The Physician's Role in Iatrogenic Addiction

Sometime in the latter portion of the 19th century, the increasingly visible problems associated with addiction stimulated several state boards of health and local governments to commission studies of narcotic use. Private philanthropic foundations and charitable organizations also supported this cause, providing funds to study factors that promoted narcotic habits. These collective studies primarily identified physicians and pharmacists as the primary culprits perpetrating narcotic habits. A study commissioned in 1871 by the State Board of Health of Massachusetts listed several prominent causes of drug abuse, including injudicious and unnecessary prescribing by physicians, overwork, a vicious mode of life, desire for stimulation, ease with which opium could be procured, and overuse of soothing syrups during infancy and childhood (Oliver, 1871). Seven years later, the Michigan State Board of Health also identified physicians as the primary cause of addiction, along with dosing of infants and children and use of opiates for relief of painful menstruation and disease of the female organs (Marshall, 1878). The State Board of Health in Iowa concluded that drug addiction arose primarily from the carelessness of physicians (Hull, 1885). Until the early 20th century, most etiological studies emphasized the role of the physician in spreading drug habits to middle- and upper-class patients.

Historically, iatrogenic opiate addiction was clearly a major vector for the chief consumers of opiates, who were primarily drawn from the wealthier and more respectable classes. Other causal factors commonly mentioned were physical and mental pain, insomnia, overwork, and the nervous strains and stresses of modern life. Pain and obstetrical and gynecological problems were cited to account for the preponderance of women among the opiate users of the 19th century. Terry was convinced that the primary cause of drug addiction was iatrogenic. He used the public health apparatus to deliver free treatment in Jacksonville, Florida, from 1912 to 1920 (Musto, 1999). In 1921, Terry became the executive director of the New York City Bureau of Social Hygiene and head of the Committee on Drug Addiction. Using this professional platform, he sought to educate physicians about the causes and extent of the problem and to more systematically study the causes and consequences of addiction. However, the federal government prosecuted physicians who prescribed narcotics, based on the theory that restricting access to opiates would encourage addicts to quit and limit production of new addicts. Slowly but surely, this would lead to a complete eradication of morphine and heroin addicts. This belief was based on declines in morphine addiction that followed recognition of the iatrogenic route as a primary driver of the narcotic habit (Courtwright, 2001). However, additional scrutiny would soon show that physicians were not solely responsible for the practice of heroin sniffing and injecting.

Vicious Associations: The Rise of Social Contagion as an Explanation

Even with the tremendous emphasis placed on iatrogenic addiction, convicted criminals rarely attributed their narcotic habits to physicians. In 1914, the year the Harrison Narcotic Act was passed, only 20 out of 1,000 inmates at the Manhattan City Prison reported iatrogenic reasons for their addiction (Lichtenstein, 1914). The inability of members belonging to the working or "sporting" class to trace their habits back to doctors created the need for new theories of causation (Keire, 1998). What eventually arose was an explanation based on analyses of criminal populations and illicit drug markets that reinforced the importance of differential association and peer influences. Reliance on peers and social contacts as an explanation of drug use represented the first stab at a theory of social contagion. It was not long before the seedy, economically disadvantaged,

urban centers rife with prostitution, illegal vice, gambling, and other nefarious activities gained prominence as cauldrons of social deviance. Although the broader shift of narcotics use from the respectable to the working classes was initiated before the passage of the Harrison Narcotic Act, the implementation and enforcement of the act hastened and consolidated these processes.

The contagion theory soon gained momentum in various professional and academic communities. A study of drug cases at Bellevue Hospital found that most addicts took their "first step through being unfortunate enough to meet and associate with addicts" (Bloedorn, 1917, p. 117). Hubbard (1920) interviewed addicts registered at the New York City Narcotic Clinic and reported that 70% of cases were young workers who attributed their habit to "bad associates" and "evil environments." Few among the 7,000 cases treated at Riverside Hospital and the Workhouse Hospital in New York City were truly iatrogenically addicted (Hubbard, 1920). At that time, prominent scholars of the narcotic problem reported that etiological factors were contingent on race, ethnicity, and social class. Addicted persons from the middle and upper classes continued to be depicted as innocently addicted by negligent physicians. In contrast, addicts drawn from the poor and working classes were characterized as indulging in "vicious association." At that time, there was little effort to clarify the predisposing social, environmental, and psychological factors from demographic factors influencing narcotic addiction.

The New York City Bureau of Social Hygiene Committee on Drug Addiction recommended the institution of a federal research program to generate and apply systematic knowledge of the causes and consequences of narcotic addiction. Members of the committee found no available theory compelling enough to garner support. The committee urged the federal government to embark on empirical research that would yield findings that could be generalized across many groups and would serve to remedy the inexact state of knowledge pervasive in the field (Terry & Pellens, 1928). In 1929, the committee merged with a committee of the National Research Council and embarked on a quest to find a non-addicting analgesic (Acker, 2002). Operating under the auspices of the National Academy of Sciences from 1939 to 1976, this newly formed committee recognized that finding the defining root of the drug problem was a major challenge. Among the many pressing concerns facing members of the committee was the realization that not everyone using drugs became addicted or habituated. Psychological models, therefore, would need to develop an individual difference perspective regardless of which model was used to account for addiction.

Emergence of Psychopathology in Drug Use Etiology

The federal government tentatively entered the research arena in the mid-1920s. Lawrence Kolb (1925a, 1925b, 1925d) advanced a psychiatric theory of addiction while working at the federal Hygienic Laboratories in Washington, DC (forerunner of the National Institutes of Health). He too was intrigued by the observation that not everyone who initiated narcotic use ended up an addict. Was there something abnormal about addicts before they became addicted, or did the use of narcotics turn them into psychopaths and neurotics? Kolb was convinced that psychopathological traits predisposed certain individuals to the serious deterioration that resulted from regular indulgence in narcotics. However, he observed that thousands of people took narcotics and experienced nothing beyond drowsiness or pain relief. Thus, Kolb reasoned that people regarded as normal did not obtain "positive pleasure" from drugs. In contrast, those who enjoyed drug effects must be abnormal, defective, or suffering from hidden mental conflicts. The use of drugs afforded a moment of relief; continued need for relief instigated a habitual physiological dependence. Although Kolb's language of psychopathology is now generally regarded as obsolete, he advanced the first widely accepted diagnostic criteria for narcotic addiction. His classification system divided addicts into two broad classes—the vicious, who were addicts that got high, and the medically or accidentally addicted, who did not experience euphoria (Kolb, 1925c, 1925d). Kolb then created six categories within these two classes, each corresponding to clinical assertions regarding etiology. It was important that the problem of addiction was not

cast as a criminal issue emphasizing police interdiction, but rather as a public health problem.

Kolb believed that even vicious or psychopathic addicts struggled with a sense of inadequacy and used narcotics to prop themselves up so as to appear adequate to the demands of modern life. In this view, people characterized as abnormal would become more and more restless and unhappy if the underlying sense of unease and fundamental emotional conflicts that were the root cause of their addictions went unaddressed. Kolb and his protégé, Robert H. Felix, developed a formal diagnostic characterization from countless hours spent with addicts residing at the newly opened U.S. Public Health Service Narcotic Farm located in Lexington, Kentucky. This institution was one of two federally sponsored drug treatment facilities that operated from 1935 to 1976. Felix worked in the small research unit at Lexington until he became the founding director of the NIMH in 1948. The laboratory then changed its name to the NIMH Addiction Research Center, which 25 years later became the intramural research program of NIDA. Around the time of World War II, Kolb and Felix relocated from Lexington to Washington, DC, where they lobbied for and ultimately founded the NIMH. This new federal institution would then become a wellspring of theoretical development that influenced drug use etiology studies from that point in time forward.

MALIGNANT FAMILIAL ENVIRONMENTS

Oddly, in the context of our prevailing focus on gateway drugs, including cigarettes, alcohol, and marijuana, it was heroin that first trickled down to youth. The 1951 crisis over adolescent heroin addiction and juvenile delinquency represented a formative historical moment, one later recognized as the first modern drug epidemic (DuPont, 1973; DuPont & Greene, 1973; Hughes, Barker, Crawford, & Jaffe, 1972). The NIMH funded a group of addiction researchers and social psychologists to study drug use among urban youth subcultures. This effort resulted in the publication of a classic book titled *The Road to H: Narcotics, Delinquency, and Social Policy* (Chein, Gerard, Lee, & Rosenfeld, 1964). This book represented the first real empirical work to distill the facts regarding pathways to heroin use and focused on identifying factors predisposing a person to heroin abuse. *The Road to H* was based on ongoing studies conducted in three of the five boroughs of New York City between 1949 and 1954. In writing *The Road to H*, social psychologist Isidor Chein and colleagues produced the first thorough scientific compilation of drug use etiology (emphasizing heroin), including information on family configuration (e.g., father absence and maternal dominance), degree of neighborhood cohesion (e.g., relative level of social disorganization), economic or status deprivation, and a host of psychological constructs they labeled *neurotic character disorders.*

The Road to H (Chein et al., 1964) provided evidence of a shift in narcotics use then underway from adults to youth and from White to African American and Spanish-speaking populations. Heroin addiction in the 1950s was seen as the outcome of a particular form of psychopathology consisting of a weak ego structure, defective superego, inadequate masculine identification, unrealistic orientation to the future, and distrust of major social institutions. Addicts were depicted as maladjusted: Unable to form relationships based on proper social roles, they could not tolerate anxiety or frustration without acting out. Chein et al. (1964) identified a pattern of "disturbed family relationships" revolving around a domineering mother and an absent father. Chein et al. reported that more heroin-addicted youth compared with nonaddicted youth from similar socioeconomic circumstances grew up in homes characterized as inadequate or deficient, leading these authors to believe that opiate use was functional for those who grew up in "malignant familial environments" considered the primary cause of opiate addiction. Chein et al. (1964) rooted opiate addiction in a constellation of neurotic behaviors by stating,

> We have reason to believe that, even if there were no sanctions against opiate use, we would regard or learn to regard the people who become opiate addicts as seriously disturbed in their relationships with themselves, with their families, and in the complexities of their

relationships with what is loosely called "reality." . . . In short, we have reason to be concerned with opiate addiction because of its human significance as an indicator of trouble within the individual and, because of the endemic nature of opiate addiction, as an indicator of trouble within many individuals in our society. (pp. 364–365)

The Road to H (Chein et al., 1964) soon became a recognized road map delineating poverty and economic deprivation in urban racially inhabited communities as central causes of addiction. A major milestone was the authors' careful blending of epidemiology with social psychology as an explanatory framework for addiction. From a historical point of view, several factors pushed *The Road to H* to the front line of knowledge regarding adolescent drug use. First, the growth of social psychiatry and the strengthening of epidemiological models expanded the nation's conceptualization of juvenile delinquency, which included a broad range of what would now be called "problem behaviors." The national fervor over juvenile delinquency was not limited to heroin addiction but also concerned smoking cigarettes and marijuana, drinking, and participating in gang activities. There was increased pressure on the government to examine more closely the structural determinants of juvenile delinquency. Within a short amount of time, social theorists argued that social strain created differential opportunity structures (Cloward & Ohlin, 1960; Merton, 1938). The rifts created by perceived social injustice, including barriers to economic opportunity, were major factors contributing to delinquent subcultures (Cohen, 1955; Sutherland, 1939). Youth were wandering the streets with limited chances to pursue any meaningful financial fortune in a climate of postwar affluence. These conditions combined to create fertile grounds for what sociologist Emile Durkheim (1951) called *anomie,* characterized by an aimlessness or lack of purpose that signaled the breakdown of social structures designed to regulate desire and appetite. Durkheim saw the driving force of human insatiability as not unlike the structure of addiction: "The more one has, the more one wants, since satisfactions received only stimulate instead of filling needs" (p. 248). Sociologists like Robert K. Merton (1938) soon tethered Durkheim's concept of anomie to social strain theory. According to Merton, deviant behavior represented a gap between aspirations and people's differential access to legitimate means to satisfy them.

By the late 1950s, research began increasingly to focus on drug use during the period of late adolescence. The overall emphasis at this point in time highlighted parental and familial factors, peer influences, and the role of low self-esteem as determinants of heroin use. On the basis of the work of Chein and others, these and other factors were seen as a more global response to a wider range of stressors. Notably, even with the number of studies already conducted emphasizing heroin addiction among adults and youth, the field of drug use etiology did not take shape as a separate discipline because of the absence of stable links between epidemiology and etiology. NIMH was beginning to actively fund studies of the psychosocial characteristics of drug abusers in attempts to pin down mental health precursors. At the same time, epidemiological models and improved data collection methods were growing in strength. For instance, Ball, Chambers, and Ball (1968) accessed thousands of patient records from the U.S. Public Health Service narcotic hospitals in Lexington, Kentucky, and Fort Worth, Texas. They then summarized the current knowledge of associations between marijuana use and opiate addiction that emerged on the basis of extensive studies conducted in the mid-1960s.

Another major study that reinforced epidemiological models was the Hughes et al. (1972) study of heroin use in Chicago in 1949–1950. This study stemmed from the data collection efforts underway at the Illinois Drug Abuse Program, which was directed by Jerome H. Jaffe (who went on to serve as advisor on drug abuse issues to the Nixon White House). Patrick Hughes et al. (1972) claimed that the incidence and prevalence of heroin addiction "followed the course of contagious diseases, fluctuating from periods of epidemic spread on the one hand to relatively quiescent periods on the other" (p. 995). This study furnished a great deal of information on the "Natural History of a Heroin Epidemic" and led researchers at Illinois Drug Abuse Program and elsewhere to model addiction using an epidemiological framework. The epidemiological view painstakingly argued against the view that addicts are "diseased individuals," an emphasis considered impractical in policy circles (Hughes et al., 1972). These studies involved retrospective accounts of heroin addicts who had initiated drug use as adolescents in the postwar wave. Hughes et al. had found empirical support for identifying the crest of an epidemic said to be peaking again by the late 1960s. Interest in initiation or onset of use arose out of the federal government's need to make reasonably accurate claims regarding the number of individuals likely to transition from one stage of use (onset) to other, more serious stages. The emerging focus on stages and sequences in the epidemiological models of the mid-1970s differed from the previously dominant focus on relapse (Ball & Chambers, 1970). By shifting the focus of research earlier in the cycle of drug use, the stage was set for the conceptualization of etiology.

THE SOCIOLOGY OF DEVIANCE

One of the earliest conceptual tools used to formulate models of drug use etiology was forged during the 1930s in the Department of Sociology at the University of Chicago. During this time, Edwin Sutherland (1939) elaborated the theory of differential association to explain how individuals learn criminal behavior through interactions with others already involved in criminal patterns. Differential association provided a theoretical platform for later models emphasizing peer influence in drug initiation (Akers & Cochran, 1985; Oetting & Beauvais, 1987). One of Sutherland's colleagues, Herbert Blumer, developed the theory of symbolic interaction to account for the ways in which people enact social norms on the basis of the meanings they attribute to things such as drugs and the interpretations they form in the course of social interaction. Like alcohol, a drug can act as a social lubricant and ease interpersonal tensions. This connotes a social meaning to drugs and proscribes their normative use. The work by Sutherland and Blumer opened doors for several other researchers to generate applications of sociological models to account for drug use. In particular, two graduate students at the University of Chicago created new avenues for sociology to begin synthesizing models of addiction and drug use etiology. Bingham Dai's doctoral thesis addressed "Opium Addiction in Chicago" (1937/1970), and Alfred Lindesmith examined "The Nature of Opiate Addiction" (1937; later published as *Opiate Addiction* in 1947). Critical of the concept of anomie, Lindesmith took issue with the sociological assumption that drug addicts, chronic drunkards, or mentally disabled people rejected social norms or retreated from social convention (Lindesmith, 1947; Lindesmith & Gagnon, 1964). Rather than attribute drug involvement to the absence of normative beliefs and poor adherence to social conventions, Lindesmith relied on ethnographic accounts as the basis for his argument that drug users merely adhered to different social norms. The use of intensive field interviews and ethnographic techniques opened doors for sociologists to see firsthand how norms and conventions were formed among deviant subcultures.

Howard S. Becker was a student of Blumer who extended Lindesmith's field methods to learn more about marijuana use. Marijuana was unusual in that it did not produce the same physiological dependence encountered with opiates (Acker, 2002; Becker, 1998). A jazz pianist, Becker inhabited a milieu in which drinking and smoking marijuana were widely practiced. His 1951 dissertation and subsequently published article "Becoming a Marihuana User" (Becker, 1953) formed the core of his classic book *Outsiders: Studies in the Sociology of Deviance* (Becker, 1963). Becker proposed that drug use could easily be fashioned as commitment to a career; even though it was considered deviant, it still reflected a concerted choice on the user's part. The negative connotations attached to drug careers arose because "almost all research in deviance deals with the kind of question that arises from viewing it as pathological. That is, research attempts to discover the 'etiology' of the 'disease'" (Becker, 1963, p. 22). He also proposed a model of *drug progression,* in which he suggested "patterns of behavior develop in orderly sequence" (p. 23). The concept of the deviant career was a sequential model consisting of clearly delineated steps that individuals took along the way to forming habitual patterns of drug use.

ETIOLOGY GAINS A FOOTHOLD IN INTERDISCIPLINARY ALCOHOL STUDIES

As this brief overview shows, no single historical thread weaves together the story of drug use etiology. Rather, a more complex picture emerges in which contributions from various disciplines (e.g., medicine, sociology, and behavioral science) interlock. Various efforts to understand the causes of alcohol and drug use were developing at the same time, but lack of a central repository or concerted funding mechanism hampered collaboration and unification of the field. At the same time as Kolb (1925c, 1925d) outlined his classification system for drug users, similar efforts were underway to create a more refined picture outlining patterns of alcohol use and factors contributing to alcoholism. The Yale Laboratory of Applied Physiology engaged in interdisciplinary studies of alcohol use as early as the 1930s (Roizen, 1991). This effort led to the establishment of the Yale Center of Alcohol Studies in 1943 and the formation of the Research Council on Problems of Alcohol, both of which opened the door to professional education on alcoholism. The first modern treatment program based on the disease concept was implemented through the Yale Plan Clinics starting in 1944. Etiology was a principal focus of many alcohol studies in the 1940s, and this was further exemplified by several "susceptibility tests" that were proposed to effectively detect drinking propensities (Landis, 1945; Williams, 1947). In 1962, the Yale Center relocated to Rutgers, the State University of New Jersey, where it has continued to serve as a premiere training and research center.

The federal consolidation of alcohol research has an interesting history that can be traced back to several climatic events. Marty Mann, a recovering alcoholic who endorsed the disease concept of alcoholism, founded the National Committee for Education on Alcoholism. This organization operated as part of the Yale Plan until political differences that arose toward the end of the 1940s forced the two groups to part ways. Renamed the National Council on Alcoholism, Mann relocated the organization to the New York Academy of Medicine. Mann and Bill W., founder of Alcoholics Anonymous, lobbied Congress for the formation of the National Institute on Alcohol Abuse and Alcoholism, which Richard M. Nixon signed into law on New Year's Eve, 1970. Up until that point, there was limited public funding for research on alcohol and alcoholism through NIMH. Within a few short years, in 1976 the research agenda at the National Institute on Alcohol Abuse and Alcoholism expanded to include behavioral and biomedical studies of etiology.

The formation of an alcohol etiology subfield preceded the drug use etiology subfield by perhaps a decade. The faster consolidation of research in alcohol etiology arose in part because alcoholism was thought to reflect a broader public mandate, and consumption and related problems such as drunk driving were more visible. There was also a traditional focus on the causes of drinking that was a holdover from the Temperance movement. By contrast, drug use and abuse appeared more varied; there was no clearly defined set of problems arising from abuse, and there was less information available on drug use etiology. Although many different disciplines including sociology, psychology, nursing, and medicine had taken an interest in drug use etiology, there had been no major political movement like Temperance or Alcoholics Anonymous to address drug problems. Whereas the "opium problem" had become a problem of the poor working class, drug control policy had not experienced the same level of popular support that led to passage of the National Prohibition Act of 1919 (also known as the Volstead Act). Added to this, the multidisciplinary flavor of and focus on multiple drug use hampered efforts to establish etiology as a subfield within any one academic or scientific discipline.

CONDITIONS FOSTERING THE EMERGENCE OF DRUG USE ETIOLOGY

Overall, research on drug and alcohol use and abuse grew out of several academic and scientific disciplines, each of which maintained its own theoretical views. During the emergent stages of drug use etiology, researchers shared little information beyond their focus on *drugs*, a term that lacks distinctive

clarity and continues to hold many different meanings. As scientists and scholars initiated studies that were eventually recognized as drug use etiology, they borrowed and exchanged certain methodologies, research design strategies, and theoretical perspectives in an effort to learn more about the causes of drug-taking behaviors. Up to this point, most etiology researchers adopted the suggestion that drug use represented a form of deviant behavior. The field was thus dominated by a sociological emphasis on environmental or structural influences (i.e., poverty, urban blight) as primary factors in narcotic addiction. Only psychoanalytic models emphasizing the fractured ego and the disruption of early infantile relations contrasted with this view. From 1950 through 1970, and consistent with the growing emphasis on studying lives over time, a spate of new studies on drinking and drug use as multiple or co-occurring problem behaviors integrated epidemiological information and a developmental life course perspective. One of the capacities central to the emergence of etiology as a separate field was the emphasis on longitudinal studies. George Vaillant's (1966a, 1966b, 1966c, 1966d) study of New York opiate addicts discharged from the U.S. Public Health Service narcotic hospitals in Lexington, Kentucky, was groundbreaking in its use of longitudinal follow-up. Vaillant mined the data obtained from the Core City Sample in search of insights regarding the etiology of alcoholism (Glueck & Glueck, 1950; Vaillant, 1983). His work was one of several longitudinal studies funded by NIMH and then later receiving funding from the Alcohol, Drug Abuse, and Mental Health Administration (Bachman, Kahn, Mednick, Davidson, & Johnston, 1967).

As the use of longitudinal follow-up methodology grew, diverse theoretical orientations and different perspectives on life course events paved the way for some dissension and open debate regarding the origins of drug use and related problem behaviors. Two basic camps arose, one camp arguing that drug behaviors can best be understood from the identification of unique predictors, and a second camp viewing drug use as one of many related problem behaviors sharing common predictors (Jessor, Graves, Hanson, & Jessor, 1968; Jessor & Jessor, 1977). Social psychologists Richard and Shirley

Jessor fashioned what would eventually be termed the common factor model based on problem behavior theory (PBT). PBT provided a systems view to account for precocious sexual activity, marijuana use, alcohol use, or youthful cigarette smoking collectively as problem behaviors. The common factor model was based more on the co-occurrence or interrelationships of many behaviors and was not bound by any particular sequence or unfolding of these behaviors. Coming at the tail end of the 1960s social revolution, the Rocky Mountain Cohort study was the first of several longitudinal studies to grapple with identifying theoretically meaningful predictors of drug and alcohol use. In many respects, the historical context of the social and political forces during the 1960s led to the inclusion of measures of self-esteem, alienation, and social criticism (Scheier, 2001). Inclusion of these variables responded to the academic community's consideration of and receptivity toward social anomie (Merton, 1957) and social learning theory (Rotter, 1954). Funded in its earliest stages by NIMH, the study included racially diverse youth from a community located in southwestern Colorado (including Native American Indians). Later, with the addition of a longitudinal component, the study became known as the Rocky Mountain cohort study (Jessor & Jessor, 1977). Since its inception, the study has spanned a considerable portion of the life span of and even extended data collection on the original cohort beyond young adulthood (Jessor, Donovan, & Costa, 1991).

PBT integrated three explanatory systems of psychosocial influences: the personality, the perceived environment, and the behavior system. These systems were used to account for a dynamic state called *proneness,* which captured the level of likelihood that a problem behavior would occur within any one or all of the explanatory systems (Jessor et al., 1991). Proneness reflected the interaction of the three systems and went considerably beyond more limited demographic models or the reliance on addictive personality as a means to account for behavior (Jessor et al., 1991). Although *risk and protective factors* has become the current lingua franca in the field of drug use etiology, Jessor et al. (1991) saw their theoretically relevant measures as interchangeable with the broad catchall of risk and protection.

More important, PBT located causality at the systemic social-structural level rather than rooting it within the problematic individual. PBT eventually broadened its umbrella to include prediction of a wide range of behaviors and linked early involvement in problem behavior with risk for increased morbidity and mortality. One of PBT's strengths was its reliance on a more expansive social-psychological framework and its willingness to consider a wide range of functional components linked with a syndrome of problem behaviors.

In a recent oral history interview between Jessor and myself, he noted that PBT was "motivated by the need to account for intergroup differences with the same ideas used to explain intragroup differences." He went on to say,

> I wanted at that time to take the challenge of not only saying why there was more Indian drunkenness than Anglo drunkenness, but I wanted to be able to say why some Indians are sober while many others are drunk, and vice versa. [This is] clearly a central issue in social science in general. So much of social science [emphasizes] differences between men and women, between minorities and majorities, between Americans and others, but that kind of emphasis on group mean differences eludes much of what is going on because there is always variation within any group. To not talk about the variation within the group, and just to talk about variation between groups, seemed to me to be misleading. . . . I needed a set of concepts that would describe and capture variation at the societal or group level and at the same time account for individual variation within groups. (R. Jessor, personal communication, June 5, 2007)

The attempt to capture and account for both group and individual variation had become especially pressing in the social context of widespread adolescent experimentation with drugs in the late 1960s, which involved a far broader range of substances than previously observed during the heroin epidemic of the early 1950s. Reaching into the middle classes, this nation's second major encounter with drugs in the mid-20th century occurred at a time of social protest and political turmoil. Perceptions of rampant marijuana smoking, casual pill use, and popular experimentation with hallucinogens—in addition to heroin use and abuse by troops in Vietnam—compelled a concerted federal response.

INSTITUTIONALIZATION OF RESEARCH ON DRUG ABUSE IN THE 1970S

Drug use etiology arose out of a productive convergence between epidemiology, sociology, psychiatry, and psychology. Despite the groundbreaking epidemiological work accomplished by Chein et al.'s (1964) *The Road to H* and Ball and Chambers's (1970) *The Epidemiology of Opiate Addiction in the United States,* such perspectives were not fully incorporated into the field of drug abuse until after the inception of NIDA (Richards & Blevins, 1977; Rittenhouse, 1977). The perceived need for epidemiological studies was high during the Nixon administration because of the public and congressional concern that large numbers of heroin-addicted servicemen would be returning to the United States from Vietnam. The public relations nightmare of returning war veterans possessing intractable heroin habits spurred the Nixon administration to take a hard look at the various funding mechanisms that proliferated throughout the health, education, and welfare apparatus during the 1960s. The administration's first action was to consolidate drug treatment, prevention, and research efforts under the auspices of the White House Special Action Office for Drug Abuse Prevention. Under the direction of Jerome H. Jaffe, the new agency was given a 4-year mandate to produce visible short-term gains. The Nixon-era reforms took drug abuse research, education, and prevention out of NIMH hands and placed these functions under the control of the Special Action Office for Drug Abuse Prevention. After 4 years, the Special Action Office for Drug Abuse Prevention phased into NIDA, which was created by legislative action in the fall of 1973. NIDA's initial congressional budget and activity was slated to begin in 1974 under the direction of Robert DuPont.

One of Jaffe's historically prescient moves at the Special Action Office for Drug Abuse Prevention was to recruit sociologist Lee Robins to study the problem posed by returning war veterans. Jaffe gained the full cooperation of the Department of Defense (Jaffe, 1987, p. 595). Issued in May 1974, Robins's first report to the Special Action Office for Drug Abuse Prevention was titled *The Vietnam Drug User Returns,* and it documented that the rate of opiate and marijuana use by Vietnam veterans decreased rapidly on return. Shortly after Robins's initial study, NIDA produced a research monograph titled *Young Men and Drugs,* which concluded that military service—and specifically service in Vietnam—was not an important causal factor in the increase in heroin use documented among young men between the late 1960s and early 1970s (O'Donnell, Voss, Clayton, Slatin, & Room, 1976). The authors of this comprehensive study concluded that

> those who were exposed to drug use in the military or in Vietnam may have begun to use drugs earlier than they otherwise would have done, but not many more began to use than would have been expected to do so without experience in the military. When the focus is on men who were in Vietnam in 1970 and 1971, drug use rates are high. However, when the focus is broadened to encompass all of the young men in the sample, the effects of military service on drug use are invisible, and the effect of service in Vietnam is little more than a ripple in a stream. (O'Donnell et al., 1976, p. 124)

Research efforts driving the study of *Young Men and Drugs* combined a natural history approach with epidemiological data assessing incidence, prevalence, correlates, and determinants for nine classes of psychoactive drugs. In addition to the natural history approach, the study that led to *Young Men and Drugs* explored the historical question of whether there had indeed been an epidemic of drug use in the late 1960s among young men. As O'Donnell et al.

(1976) outlined their project, they noted that their multiple foci "implied different and to some extent contradictory considerations in the research design" (p. 2). *Young Men and Drugs* illustrates an important point about the type of studies that could be accomplished during the mid-1970s. Research responded to competing demands issuing from multiple spheres, and thus the study bears the mark of a time when the concept of epidemic was new. O'Donnell et al. introduced the notion that there were "periods of experimentation" or "periods of risk" during which young men were likely to initiate drug use. They showed spikes in three classes of illicit drug use in 1969—marijuana, psychedelics, and stimulants—before the rise in opiate use. Here the traditional distinction between licit and illicit drugs mattered for the interpretation of the study. Despite more young men initiating drinking and cigarette smoking earlier in the study period, it was the 1969 rise in illicit drugs that drew the attention of the founding director of NIDA, Robert DuPont, and became an important topic popularized by the media. This interest translated directly into the construction of alcohol, tobacco, and marijuana as gateway drugs, a topic more thoroughly discussed in the next section.

Using its vast resources to fund national databases and create sustainable longitudinal studies, NIDA represented a relatively stable, centralized funding source that could underwrite studies outside either the criminal justice or the mental health systems. The agency's primary goal was to discover the causes of drug abuse and translate this information into effective prevention and treatment programs. One of its first centralized activities having to do with causation was a conference that examined the merits of longitudinal research. The conference was spearheaded by sociologist Denise B. Kandel, and it showcased people who eventually gained national and international prominence as drug use etiology researchers (Kandel, 1978). The event marked an important milestone in the consolidation of drug use etiology as a professional subfield. Participants identified common themes and empirical findings that touched on the predictors of socially problematic drug and alcohol use. One of the more compelling observations to come from this conference was the integral role played by

alcohol as a gateway to heavier and more protracted drug use.

The gateway hypothesis was developed around a series of empirical findings suggesting that drug involvement proceeds in an invariant hierarchical manner. Partly on the basis of Guttman scaling models, several empirical studies confirmed that use of drugs higher in the sequence (i.e., marijuana) was always predicated on use of certain drugs (alcohol or cigarettes) appearing earlier in the sequence (Kandel, 1975; Kandel & Faust, 1975; Kessler, Paton, & Kandel, 1976). This eventually gave way to the idea that drug involvement could be patterned in a stage-sequential manner and used to predict involvement with later drugs. One side effect of the gateway model was that alcohol was always implicated as the starting point in the sequence. By the 1980s, there was growing recognition that any distinction between alcohol and drug research, and therefore between alcohol and drug use etiology, was artificial and not supported by a growing body of empirical findings. Sociologists Richard Clayton and Christian Ritter acknowledged that the two fields could be represented as "strikingly similar yet quite different or strikingly different yet quite similar" (Clayton & Ritter, 1985, p. 69). What precipitated the distinction between the funding and focus of the alcohol and drug research institutes was based more on their separate histories and the need to chart epidemiological trends using different methods and metrics.

COMING OF AGE: DISTINGUISHING ETIOLOGY FROM EPIDEMIOLOGY

Continued emphasis on the epidemiology of drug use took shape following two NIDA conferences organized in 1974 and 1976 (Richards & Blevins, 1977; Rittenhouse, 1977). At this point in time, etiological research was still largely subsumed by epidemiological research. Conference participants lamented the lack of overlap between studies of licit drugs, notably alcohol, and the illicit drugs that were the focus of their research (i.e., marijuana). Both conferences emphasized the blending of epidemiological methods with developmental models and heralded the rich data provided by longitudinal studies. The NIDA conferences also sparked immediate interest in studies that monitor drug trends using nationally representative surveys. The first of these was the Monitoring the Future study, which grew out of the Youth in Transition study, a longitudinal study tracking the causes and consequences of high school dropout. Extensive descriptive data on drug use and trends among thousands of high school seniors were collected by researchers at the University of Michigan's Survey Research Center (Bachman, 1986; Johnston, Bachman, & O'Malley, 1977).

One other important large-scale survey that monitors drug trends is the National Household Survey on Drug Abuse, which has since been renamed the National Survey on Drug Use and Health. Like the Monitoring the Future study, the National Survey on Drug Use and Health predates the inception of NIDA, which was mandated to continue household surveys and has done so uninterrupted since 1974. The household surveys were initiated in 1971 under the auspices of the National Commission on Marihuana and Drug Abuse (Miller et al., 1983). The survey has become the responsibility of the Substance Abuse and Mental Health Services Administration since 1992, when NIDA became a part of the National Institutes of Health and ceased responsibility for treatment, prevention, and service delivery. The National Survey on Drug Use and Health and its predecessor the National Household Survey on Drug Abuse is one of the primary sources of information on drug use trends among U.S. civilians age 12 and older. A comparable survey of military personnel both here and abroad is conducted annually by the Research Triangle Institute under contract to NIDA (Bray, Guess, Mason, Hubbard, & Smith, 1983; Burt, Beigel, Carnes, & Farley, 1980). The number of persons surveyed as part of the National Survey on Drug Use and Health in any given year can exceed 67,000. Monitoring the Future, which surveys more than 45,000 youth annually, represents a counterpart to the household survey but provides a more refined look at drug use trends for secondary school youth in Grades 8, 10, and 12, the critical and vulnerable years in adolescence in which risk for drug initiation is highest.

NIDA's massive epidemiological tracking studies began in 1975 and have been conducted annually ever since (Bachman, Johnston, & O'Malley, 1984).

Lloyd Johnston must have anticipated the growing distinction between epidemiology and etiology in the late 1980s, which led him to emphasize the importance of etiologic studies "insofar as they are any different from epidemiological studies" (Johnston, 1991, p. 57). Although both national surveys have helped to amass a considerable database outlining current and past trends in youthful drug use, they lack the distinctive capacity to offer information on the prediction of behavior. Neither survey uses longitudinal methodology, thus limiting their ability to monitor change at the individual level (however, Monitoring the Future recently added a small longitudinal component to track a cohort of youth past adolescence). Added to these concerns, both surveys contain a limited repository of information detailing risk and protective factors commonly regarded as determinants of drug use. Even with these limitations, both the National Survey on Drug Use and Health and the Monitoring the Future study provide extremely important information on who is using what drug and whether drug use patterns change in relation to social influences. Pressing questions about what are the optimal determinants of drug use, and whether conditions of risk remain stable over time or fluctuate on the basis of age, race, gender, or structural factors such as poverty, remain unresolved even with the best of epidemiological information at our fingertips.

FROM STAGES AND SEQUENCES TO THE COMPLEX, MULTIVARIATE MODELS OF THE LATE 20TH CENTURY

As mentioned briefly, during the 1980s drug use etiology was dominated by two conceptual models: Kandel's developmental progression model and Jessor and Jessor's PBT (Clayton & Ritter, 1985). In 1975, Kandel published an influential article in the journal *Science* titled "Stages in Adolescent Involvement in Drug Use." Her seminal work on developmental stages of drug use and the natural progression of drug use eventually gained the moniker *gateway hypothesis*. Shortly thereafter, NIDA director DuPont made this term part of common parlance in public policy and popular discourse by publishing *Getting Tough on Gateway Drugs*

(DuPont, 1984). DuPont advocated for the inclusion of alcohol, tobacco, marijuana, and even cocaine as gateway drugs. His efforts fueled an antidrug parents' movement that enjoyed its heyday during the Reagan administration's Just Say No campaign.

Essentially, three propositions are embedded in the gateway hypothesis (Kandel & Jessor, 2002). First, there is the widely replicated finding depicting a developmental sequence that individuals who become involved with drugs move through in an invariant fashion. Second, use of a drug earlier in the typical sequence is associated with increased risk or likelihood of use of a drug that appears later in the sequence. The third proposition is typically used to support claims that using a drug earlier in the sequence somehow *causes* the use of a drug later in the sequence. This last proposition is the part of the gateway hypothesis invoked most often in public discourse and policy debates and in defense of drug prevention programs. Science-based prevention efforts typically seek to prevent the initiation of drugs early in the sequence so as to prevent use of those that typically appear later in the sequence. Kandel and Jessor (2002) took issue with the third proposition, finding no evidence to support it.

> There is no compelling evidence that the use of a drug earlier in the sequence, in and of itself, causes the use of a drug later in the sequence or, for that matter, that it causes the use of any other drug or, indeed, any other behavior. The difficulty of establishing causality is, of course, intrinsic to much of social science. Making a causal claim is difficult in the absence of carefully controlled experimental designs. Even more important, perhaps, is the difficulty of ruling out alternative inferences that can explain the association between the initiation of an earlier drug and the initiation of a later drug in the developmental sequence. At this time, the causal interpretation of the Gateway Hypothesis is still without scientific foundation. (pp. 365–366)

Given the difficulties of establishing true causality in the social sciences, Kandel and Jessor have been

careful to use the term *association* rather than *causation*. Nevertheless, the gateway hypothesis was fruitful for theory building in the etiology field because it offered a clear and well-defined perspective regarding drug progression. One pressing concern that remains a focus of research today is to identify which factors predict movement from one stage to another (Collins, 2002; Graham, Collins, Wugalter, Chung, & Hansen, 1991).

During the mid-1980s, the etiological field was acknowledged to be coming of age. In 1984, NIDA undertook its first explicit review of the field, compiling a research monograph titled *Etiology of Drug Abuse* (Jones & Battjes, 1985). As part of this process, Jessor outlined a mission to improve the fields' stature, including

> the capability to bring to bear empirical data, collected at the same time, in explaining shifts and changes in trends of adolescent drug use; the shared awareness . . . that drug use is not an isolated behavior but one that covaries with and is embedded in a complex of other behaviors; the accumulation of detailed information about the natural course of development of drug use beyond adolescence and the establishment of the age of highest risk for onset of use; the growing consensus that early onset of drug use has reverberating implications for later patterns of use and abuse; and, of course, the remarkable increase in methodological sophistication ranging from long-term, follow-up designs, to systematic process and outcome evaluation of interventions, to analytic models relying on life tables and hazard functions. (Jones & Battjes, 1985, p. 257)

Then complex forms of etiology research arose to muddy the waters by turning to nonlinear modeling systems to account for drug behaviors. Thus, in contrast to the simple (x) stage-sequence model, which captured the sequential nature of the progression that was essential to the gateway hypothesis, the common factor model arose as a way of incorporating multiple common risk factors that instigated drug involvement (Jessor & Jessor, 1977). The notion of vulnerability to a syndrome or proneness to deviance arose to account for the rich set of common risk factors implicated in a wide range of problem behaviors (Donovan & Jessor, 1985; Donovan, Jessor, & Costa, 1988; Jessor, Chase, & Donovan, 1980). PBT was further refined by situating drug abuse as one of a cluster of problem behaviors that included truancy, delinquency, unhealthy eating, excessive television viewing, reckless driving, and risky sexual behavior. Richard Jessor offered a personal view of his involvement in what eventually became a historic study:

> In our questioning we tried to map a comprehensive picture of an individual's life. So we asked questions about values, beliefs, and orientations, whether they did community work and went to church, and we asked about family and context and their dreams. We did this with their names so they knew we were interested in them as individuals, whereas so much of the drug research was to go into a group and say, we don't want your name so you can answer honestly, and what we want to know is how much drugs you use and where you did them and so on, which is a way of devaluing the individuality of a person. Whereas we told them from the very beginning we're interested in them as individuals, we want to follow their lives, we want to understand the whole perspective that they have and where we can see them as complex individuals who are moving on a trajectory through time. (R. Jessor, personal communication, June 5, 2007)

Jessor's PBT model (Jessor & Jessor, 1977) set the tone for using complex feedback systems possessing multiple layers and providing for interactions that condition relations between systems. Recent attempts to "organize" complex systems have produced the first attempts to pull multiple theories under a single roof. Flay's theory of triadic influence (Flay & Petraitis, 1994) provides an example of this type of organizational synthesis. The theory of triadic influence is a developmental systems theory that integrates genetic and environmental factors to predict drug use. It incorporates a high degree of association between health beliefs and social behaviors, allowing for mutual influences between them (Flay, Petraitis, & Hu, 1995). In a very poignant review article, Petraitis et al. (1995) outlined the core constructs, underlying assumptions, and characteristics of the models that made up the prevailing paradigm in the etiology field over the last 2 decades of the 20th century. Using the metaphor of a puzzle, Flay et al. (1995) set out to clarify, organize, and integrate the multivariate theories that seek to explain experimental substance use.

Researchers have increasingly sought to model complex and multivariate interactions across multiple levels and scales. The field has evolved sophisticated statistical modeling techniques such as structural equation modeling to test causal hypotheses (Newcomb & Bentler, 1988) and model dynamic growth curves depicting trajectories of behavior over time (Curran, Stice, & Chassin, 1997). Structural equation models represent an essential tool to help the field grapple with models positing multiple influences. The technique also permits positing latent variable constructions to encompass unobserved processes (i.e., family influence construed by multiple indicators of family relations, monitoring, and discipline). Other refinements in the use of structural equation modeling techniques with drug use survey data include parameter estimation with nonlinear forms, using small samples, and minimizing bias often encountered with missing and unbalanced data.

One of the most striking characteristics of a more mature field of drug use etiology is the exponential growth of complex multivariate models since the mid-1980s. The search for a unified or integrative theory to organize the current body of knowledge central to the field of drug use etiology continues with the current volume. Yet no dominant theory has emerged; few of the basic contentions within the field have been resolved. One way to conceptualize the numerous models designed to explain the emergence of socially problematic drug use is that they are cognitive in nature, primarily based on attitudes, beliefs, and decisions that are proximal to drug-using behavior. The health belief model, pioneered within the U.S. Public Health Service in the 1950s, explains drug use through perceptions of risks, costs, and benefits of use (Becker, Drachman, & Kirscht, 1974; Maiman & Becker, 1974; Rosenstock, 1974). The phenomenological orientation of the health belief model and its emphasis on perceived severity of risk and barriers to care provided a foothold for psychology to examine motivational features of drug use from a slightly different perspective. Similarly, social learning theory developed highly psychological constructs like self-efficacy (Bandura, 1977, 1986), which helped tether drug prevention to the role of cognitive–behavioral skills (Botvin, Baker, Dusenbury, Tortu, & Botvin, 1990; Botvin, Baker, Renick, Filazzola, & Botvin, 1984; for a review, see Botvin, 1996). Models that emphasize distal explanatory factors such as future aspirations or orientations tend to integrate the strengths of cognitive–affective theories, social learning theories, and intrapersonal constructs. (Petraitis et al., 1995, contains an excellent comparative overview of the strengths and weaknesses of the major etiological theories that emerged by the late 20th century.)

Contention over proximal versus distal factors is by no means confined to the academic world. A movement to base prevention and intervention programs on science emerged in the 1990s. Schools and communities sought to teach children and adolescents to resist peer pressure, increase self-esteem, and develop health-promoting rather than health-compromising behaviors. The prevention field focused on reducing risks and fostering resilience by teaching specific skills. Gradually, a focus on positive youth development, positive action, and health promotion has emerged. Despite many attempts to bridge the gap between research and practice, the impracticality of etiological theories remains a complaint of those tasked with developing science-based prevention programs (Flay et al., 1995). Etiology researchers recognize that no single problem behavior necessarily causes the others, but translating this recognition into predictive models and prevention programs has proved complex.

DOGMA VERSUS DISCOURSE: THE NATURE OF EPISTEMIC SHIFTS

The shift toward conceptualizing cause in terms of multiple risk and protective factors led to methodological innovation and change in research practices. Shifts in the conceptual practices and specialized languages of specific sciences exemplify what sociologists and historians of science mean by the lexical shifts that signal what Kuhn (1962) called *paradigm shifts*. Foucault (1970) attended to the discursive shifts that led up to the broader epistemic shifts that redefine the very conditions of possibility of all knowledge. In many respects, claims for scientific knowledge "reflect in their very form the agency and intentionality of their makers" (Keller, 1992, p. 95). This same sense of agency has been operative for drug use etiology researchers who constantly cross-fertilize, refine, and retool the perennial cultural assumptions made about drug addicts as social deviants. Many of the historical constructs cited in this chapter endure even as new discourses arise.

Various critical theoretical enterprises have arisen to remind scientists that their objects and subjects are socially constructed (Berger & Luckmann, 1966; Hacking, 1999). The objects and subjects of study of any particular arena are coproduced through the conceptual practices in which researchers engage, the institutions that fund their work, and, in the case of drug use etiology, the perception of the public and legislative policy toward those whom they study. The social processes by which paradigm shifts take place must be contextualized within broader epistemic changes that shift the boundaries of the populations that are perceived to be using drugs and alcohol problematically. In the larger field of drug abuse research, the succession of one paradigm by another follows changes in which certain drugs were prioritized as social problems. Changes in research agendas also follow shifts in the actual and perceived populations who use particular drugs in problematic fashion. Transformations in the conceptual and methodological approaches of those who study socially problematic drug use occur in tight relationship to the material and institutional supports for such study. Funding or resource allocation is perhaps an easier way to glimpse these changes. The resources now available to NIDA and other National Institutes of Health institutes for HIV/AIDS heralds a new emphasis, which became more obvious once researchers and policymakers recognized that intravenous drug use was a major transmission vector in the United States. This is an example of how historically and culturally specific understandings shape perceptions of which risks or protections are salient—and thus which social problems deserve public support. The study of drug use etiology has long been a public science and is thus responsive to the broader politics of substance abuse.

Historically over the past century, there have been many shifts in what the public perceives of as problematic with regard to drug use. There have been shifts in the populations from which drug users come, and their choice of drugs has changed quite rapidly. A wide range of etiological theories has been advanced to make sense of these changes, to lodge causal claims where possible, and to model complex social processes. Yet adolescent drug use has become endemic in many parts of the world, assuming different shapes and patterns in different social structures. Meanwhile, the field of drug use etiology has witnessed a bewildering succession of models and methods, concepts, and empirical findings, not one of which supplies more than the "partial truths" of which Terry and Pellens (1928) spoke nearly a century ago. That lesson of history may be taken either as a cautionary tale or as a stimulus to further integration between the multiple research arenas that together make up the social worlds of drug and alcohol abuse research.

From my perspective as a historian of science who studies the forms that knowledge production concerning drug use and abuse has taken in different times and places, this chapter illustrates multiple ways in which historical and social forces shape ideas about what problems are worth studying and how we go about selecting from the many phenomena we consider problematic. Drug use etiology as a subfield reflects numerous currents from sociology, psychology, epidemiology, medicine, and related health sciences. The field has made numerous knowledge claims, and these claims reflect the

mark of time and place; the history of their production is the tale I have tried to tell in this chapter. When does drug use become socially problematic? Whose drug use becomes socially problematic? Studying how objects and subjects of knowledge are shaped into problematic concerns was the province of Michel Foucault, who studied the history of systems of thought and the systematicity of the discourses through which we produce facts and the effect of fact production on our thinking. Foucault trained his gaze on the empirical and theoretical study of the social and human sciences, which brought into focus the figure of humans as their object and subject of study. It is perhaps fitting to close with the question of what the figure of the drug user offers to the field of drug use etiology. The field emerged from epidemiological and criminological studies of deviance, and it did so to make sense of changes in social relations and material conditions that both widened and intensified the use of illicit drugs. Thus, the facts that issue forth from drug use etiology have played a role as shapers of the dominant ideology of drug use. More important, the facts that underlie the episteme of the field are also like soft molding clay, with various cutting tools crafting a concerted history reflecting the culturally dominant constructions of drug use and abuse.

References

Acker, C. J. (1995). Addiction and the laboratory: The work of the National Research Council's Committee on Drug Addiction, 1928–1939. *Isis, 86,* 167–193.

Acker, C. J. (2002). *Creating the American junkie: Addiction research in the classic era of narcotics control.* Baltimore: Johns Hopkins University Press.

Akers, R. L., & Cochran, J. E. (1985). Adolescent marijuana use: A test of three theories of deviant behavior. *Deviant Behavior, 6,* 636–655.

Bachman, J. G. (1986, April). *"Youth in Transition" to "Monitoring the Future": A tale of two longitudinal studies of youth in the United States.* Paper presented at the 70th annual meeting of the American Educational Research Association, San Francisco, CA.

Bachman, J. G., Johnston, L. D., & O'Malley, P. M. (1984). *Monitoring the Future: Questionnaire responses from the nation's high school seniors, 1982.* Ann Arbor, MI: Institute for Social Research.

Bachman, J. G., Kahn, R. L., Mednick, M. T., Davidson, T. N., & Johnston, L. D. (1967). *Youth in transition:*

Vol. 1. Blueprint for a longitudinal study of adolescent boys. Ann Arbor, MI: Institute for Social Research.

Ball, J. C., & Chambers, C. D. (1970). *The epidemiology of opiate addiction in the United States.* Springfield, IL: Charles C Thomas.

Ball, J. C., Chambers, C. D., & Ball, M. J. (1968). The association of marijuana smoking with opiate addiction in the United States. *Journal of Criminal Law, Criminology, and Police Science, 59,* 171–182.

Bandura, A. (1977). Self-efficacy: Toward a unifying theory of behavioral change. *Psychological Review, 84,* 191–215.

Bandura, A. (1986). *Social foundations of thought and action: A social cognitive theory.* Englewood Cliffs, NJ: Prentice Hall.

Becker, H. S. (1953). Becoming a marihuana user. *American Journal of Sociology, 59,* 235–242.

Becker, H. S. (1963). *The outsiders: Studies in the sociology of deviance.* New York: Free Press.

Becker, H. S. (1998). *Tricks of the trade.* Chicago: University of Chicago Press.

Becker, M. H., Drachman, R. H., & Kirscht, J. P. (1974). A new approach to explaining sick-role behavior in low income populations. *American Journal of Public Health, 64,* 205–216.

Berger, P. L., & Luckmann, T. (1966). *The social construction of reality: A treatise on the sociology of knowledge.* Garden City, NY: Anchor Books.

Bloedorn, W. A. (1917). Studies of drug addicts. *U.S. Naval Medical Bulletin, 11,* 64–69.

Botvin, G. J. (1996). Substance abuse prevention through life skills training. In R. D. Peters & R. J. McMahon (Eds.), *Preventing childhood disorders, substance abuse, and delinquency* (pp. 215–240). Newbury Park, CA: Sage.

Botvin, G. J., Baker, E., Dusenbury, L., Tortu, S., & Botvin, E. M. (1990). Preventing adolescent drug abuse through a multimodal cognitive–behavioral approach: Results of a 3-year study. *Journal of Consulting and Clinical Psychology, 58,* 437–446.

Botvin, G. J., Baker, E., Renick, N. L., Filazzola, A. D., & Botvin, E. M. (1984). A cognitive–behavioral approach to substance abuse prevention. *Addictive Behaviors, 9,* 137–147.

Bray, R. M., Guess, L. L., Mason, R. E., Hubbard, R. L., & Smith, D. G. (1983). *Worldwide survey of alcohol and non-medical drug use among military personnel, 1982* (RTI/2317/01-01F). Research Triangle Park, NC: Research Triangle Institute.

Burt, M. A., Biegel, M. M., Carnes, Y., & Farley, E. C. (1980). *Worldwide survey of non-medical drug use and alcohol use among military personnel.* Bethesda, MD: Burr Associates.

Campbell, N. D. (2007). *Discovering addiction: The science and politics of substance abuse research.* Ann Arbor: University of Michigan Press.

Chein, I., Gerard, D. L., Lee, R. S., & Rosenfeld, E. (1964). *The road to H: Narcotics, delinquency, and social policy.* New York: Basic Books.

Clarke, A. E. (2005). *Situational analysis: Grounded theory after the postmodern turn.* Thousand Oaks, CA: Sage.

Clayton, R. R., & Ritter, C. (1985). The epidemiology of alcohol and drug abuse among adolescents. *Advances in Alcohol and Substance Abuse, 4,* 69–98.

Cloward, R., & Ohlin, L. (1960). *Delinquency and opportunity.* New York: Free Press.

Cohen, A. (1955). *Delinquent boys.* New York: Free Press.

Collins, L. M. (2002). Using latent transition analysis to examine the Gateway Hypothesis. In D. B. Kandel (Ed.), *Stages and pathways of drug involvement: Examining the gateway hypothesis* (pp. 254–269). New York: Cambridge University Press.

Courtwright, D. T. (2001). *Dark paradise: A history of opiate addiction in America.* Cambridge, MA: Harvard University Press.

Curran, P. J., Stice, E., & Chassin, L. (1997). The relation between adolescent and peer alcohol use: A longitudinal random coefficients model. *Journal of Consulting and Clinical Psychology, 65,* 130–140.

Dai, B. (1970). *Opium addiction in Chicago* (Doctoral dissertation, University of Chicago, 1937). Montclair, NJ: Patterson Smith.

Donovan, J. E., & Jessor, R. (1985). Structure of problem behavior in adolescence and young adulthood. *Journal of Consulting and Clinical Psychology, 53,* 890–904.

Donovan, J. E., Jessor, R., & Costa, F. (1988). The syndrome of problem behavior in adolescence: A replication. *Journal of Consulting and Clinical Psychology, 56,* 762–765.

DuPont, R. L. (1973). *Perspective on an epidemic.* Unpublished manuscript, Washington Center for Metropolitan Studies.

DuPont, R. L. (1984). *Getting tough on gateway drugs.* Washington, DC: American Psychiatric Press.

DuPont, R. L., & Greene, M. H. (1973, August 24). The dynamics of a heroin addiction epidemic. *Science, 181,* 716–722.

Durkheim, E. (1951). *Suicide: A study in sociology* (G. Simpson & G. A. Spaulding, Trans.). New York: Free Press.

Flay, B. R., & Petraitis, J. (1994). The theory of triadic influence: A new theory of health behavior with implications for preventive interventions. *Advances in Medical Sociology, 4,* 19–44.

Flay, B. R., Petraitis, J., & Hu, F. B. (1995). The theory of triadic influence: Preliminary evidence related to alcohol and tobacco use. In J. B. Fertig & J. P. Allen (Eds.), *Alcohol and tobacco: From basic science to clinical practice* (pp. 37–57). Bethesda, MD: U.S. Government Printing Office.

Foucault, M. (1970). *The order of things.* New York: Random House.

Glueck, S., & Glueck, E. (1950). *Unraveling juvenile delinquency.* New York: Commonwealth Fund.

Graham, J. W., Collins, L. M., Wugalter, S. E., Chung, N. K., & Hansen, W. B. (1991). Modeling transitions in latent stage-sequential processes: A substance use prevention example. *Journal of Consulting and Clinical Psychology, 59,* 48–57.

Grob, G. N. (1991). *From asylum to community: Mental health policy in modern America.* Princeton, NJ: Princeton University Press.

Gusfield, J. R. (1996). *Contested meanings: The construction of alcohol problems.* Madison: University of Wisconsin Press.

Hacking, I. (1999). *The social construction of what?* Cambridge, MA: Harvard University Press.

Harrison Narcotic Act of 1914, ch. 1, 38 Stat. 785 (1914).

Hubbard, S. D. (1920). *The New York City narcotic clinic and differing points of view on narcotic addiction* [Monthly Bulletin]. New York: Department of Health.

Hughes, P. H., Barker, N. W., Crawford, G. A., & Jaffe, J. H. (1972). The natural history of a heroin epidemic. *American Journal of Public Health, 62,* 995–1001.

Hull, J. M. (1885). *The opium habit: Third annual report of the Iowa State Board of Health.* Des Moines: Board of Health of the State of Iowa.

Jaffe, J. H. (1987). Footnote in the evolution of the American national response: Some little known aspects of the first American strategy for drug abuse and drug traffic prevention (Inaugural Thomas Okey Memorial Lecture). *British Journal of Addiction, 82,* 587–600.

Jessor, R., Chase, J. A., & Donovan, J. E. (1980). Psychosocial correlates of marijuana use and problem drinking in a national sample of adolescents. *Journal of Public Health, 70,* 604–613.

Jessor, R., Donovan, J. E., & Costa, J. A. (1991). *Beyond adolescence: Problem behavior and young adult development.* New York: Cambridge University Press.

Jessor, R., Graves, T. D., Hanson, R. C., & Jessor, S. L. (1968). *Society, personality, and deviant behavior: A study of a tri-ethnic community.* New York: Holt, Rinehart, & Winston.

Jessor, R., & Jessor, S. L. (1977). *Problem behavior and psychosocial development: A longitudinal study of youth.* New York: Academic Press.

Johnston, L. D. (1991). Contributions of drug epidemiology to the field of drug abuse prevention. In C. L. Leukefeld & W. J. Bukoski (Eds.), *Drug abuse prevention intervention research: Methodological issues* (National Institute on Drug Abuse Research Monograph 107, DHEW Pub. No. ADM 91-1761, pp. 57–80). Washington, DC: U.S. Government Printing Office.

Johnston, L. D., Bachman, J. G., & O'Malley, P. M. (1977). *Drug use among American high school students, 1975-1977* (DHEW Publication No. [ADM] 78-619). Rockville, MD: National Institute on Drug Abuse.

Jones, C. L., & Battjes, R. J. (Eds.). (1985). *Etiology of drug abuse: Implications for prevention* (National Institute on Drug Abuse Research Monograph 56, DHEW Pub. No. ADM 85-1335). Washington, DC: U.S. Government Printing Office.

Kandel, D. B. (1975, November 28). Stages in adolescent involvement in drug use. *Science, 190,* 912–914.

Kandel, D. B. (1978). *Longitudinal research on drug use: Empirical findings and methodological issues.* Washington, DC: Hemisphere/Wiley.

Kandel, D. B., & Faust, R. (1975). Sequences and stages in patterns of adolescent drug use. *Archives of General Psychiatry, 32,* 923–932.

Kandel, D. B., & Jessor, R. (2002). The gateway hypothesis revisited. In D. B. Kandel (Ed.), *Stages and pathways of drug involvement: Examining the gateway hypothesis* (pp. 365–372). West Nyack, NY: Cambridge University Press.

Keire, M. L. (1998). Dope fiends and degenerates: The gendering of addiction in the early twentieth century. *Journal of Social History, 31,* 809–822.

Keller, E. F. (1992). *Secrets of life: Essays on language, gender, and science.* New York: Routledge.

Kessler, R. C., Paton, S. M., & Kandel, D. B. (1976). Reconciling unidimensional and multidimensional models of patterns of drug use. *Journal of Studies on Alcohol, 37,* 632–647.

Knorr-Cetina, K. (1999). *Epistemic cultures: How the sciences make knowledge.* Cambridge, MA: Harvard University Press.

Kolb, L. (1925a). Drug addiction in its relation to crime. *Mental Hygiene, 9,* 74–89.

Kolb, L. (1925b). Pleasure and deterioration from narcotic addiction. *Mental Hygiene, 9,* 699–724.

Kolb, L. (1925c). Relation of intelligence to etiology of drug addiction. *American Journal of Psychiatry, 5,* 163–167.

Kolb, L. (1925d). Types and characteristics of drug addicts. *Mental Hygiene, 9,* 300–313.

Kuhn, T. S. (1962). *The structure of scientific revolutions.* Chicago: University of Chicago Press.

Landis, C. (1945). Theories of the alcoholic personality. In *Alcohol, Science, and Society* (Lecture 11, pp. 129–142). New Haven, CT: Quarterly Journal of Studies on Alcohol.

Lichtenstein, P. M. (1914). Narcotic addiction. *New York Medical Journal, 14,* 962–966.

Lindesmith, A. (1937). *The nature of opiate addiction* (Doctoral dissertation, University of Chicago, 1937).

Lindesmith, A. (1947). *Opiate addiction.* Bloomington, IN: Principia Press.

Lindesmith, A., & Gagnon, J. (1964). Anomie and drug addiction. In M. Clinard (Ed), *Anomie and deviant behavior: A discussion and critique* (pp. 158–188). New York: Free Press.

Maiman, L. A., & Becker, M. H. (1974). The health belief model: Origins and correlates in psychological theory. *Health Education Monographs, 2,* 336–353.

Marshall, O. (1878). *The opium habit in Michigan: Sixth annual report of the State Board of Health, Michigan.* Lansing, MI: State Board of Health.

McTavish, J. R. (2004). *Pain and profits: The history of the headache and its remedies in America.* New Brunswick, NJ: Rutgers University Press.

Merton, R. K. (1938). Social structure and anomie. *American Sociological Review, 3,* 672–82.

Merton, R. K. (1957). *Social theory and social structure* (Rev. ed.). New York: Free Press.

Miller, J. D., Cisin, I. H., Gardner-Keaton, Harrell, A. V., Wirtz, P. W., Abelson, H. I., & Fishburne, P. M. (1983). National survey on drug abuse: Main findings, 1982 (DHHS Pub. No. ADM 83-1263). Washington, DC: U.S. Government Printing Office.

Musto, D. F. (1999). *The American disease: Origins of narcotics control* (3rd ed.). New Haven, CT: Yale University Press.

National Prohibition Act, ch. 85, 41 Stat. 305 (1919).

Newcomb, M., & Bentler, P. (1988). *Consequences of adolescent drug use: Impact on the lives of young adults.* Newbury Park, CA: Sage.

O'Donnell, J. A., Voss, H. L., Clayton, R. R., Slatin, G. T., & Room, R. G. W. (1976). *Young men and drugs: A nationwide survey* (National Institute on Drug Abuse Research Monograph 5, DHEW Pub. No. [ADM] 76-311). Washington, DC: U.S. Government Printing Office.

Oetting, E. R., & Beauvais, F. (1987). Peer cluster theory, socialization characteristics, and adolescent drug use: A path analysis. *Journal of Counseling Psychology, 34,* 205–213.

Oliver, F. E. (1871). *The use and abuse of opium: Third annual report of the State Board of Health of Massachusetts.* Boston: State Board of Health of Massachusetts.

Petraitis, J., Flay, B. R., & Miller, T. Q. (1995). Reviewing theories of adolescent substance use: Organizing pieces in the puzzle. *Psychological Bulletin, 117,* 67–86.

Richards, L. G., & Blevins, L. B. (1977). *The epidemiology of drug abuse: Current issues* (National Institute on Drug Abuse Research Monograph 10, DHEW Pub. No. [ADM] 77-432). Washington, DC: U.S. Government Printing Office.

Rittenhouse, J. D. (1977). *The epidemiology of heroin and other narcotics* (National Institute on Drug Abuse Research Monograph 16, DHEW Pub. No. [ADM] 76-311). Washington, DC: U.S. Government Printing Office.

Robins, L. (1974). *The Vietnam drug user returns* (Special Action Office Monograph, Series A, No. 2). Washington, DC: U.S. Government Printing Office.

Roizen, R. (1991). *The American discovery of alcoholism, 1933-1939* (Doctoral dissertation, University of California, Berkeley). Retrieved November 27, 2002, from http://www.roizen.com/ron/disshome.htm

Rosenstock, I. M. (1974). Historical origins of the health belief model. *Health Education Monographs, 2,* 328–335.

Rotter, J. B. (1954). *Social learning and clinical psychology.* New York: Prentice-Hall.

Scheier, L. M. (2001). Etiologic studies of adolescent drug use: A compendium of data resources and their implications for prevention. *Journal of Primary Prevention, 22,* 125–168.

Sutherland, E. (1939). *Principles of criminology* (3rd ed.). Philadelphia: J. B. Lippincott.

Terry, C. E., & Pellens, M. (1928). *The opium problem.* New York: Bureau of Social Hygiene.

Vaillant, G. E. (1966a). A twelve-year follow-up of New York narcotic addicts. I. The relation of treatment to outcome. *American Journal of Psychiatry, 122,* 727–737.

Vaillant, G. E. (1966b). A twelve-year follow-up of New York narcotic addicts. II. The natural history of a chronic disease. *New England Journal of Medicine, 275,* 1282–1288.

Vaillant, G. E. (1966c). A twelve-year follow-up of New York narcotic addicts. III. Some social and psychiatric characteristics. *Archives of General Psychiatry, 15,* 599–609.

Vaillant, G. E. (1966d). A twelve-year follow-up of New York narcotic addicts. IV. Some characteristics and determinants of abstinence. *American Journal of Psychiatry, 123,* 573–584.

Vaillant, G. E. (1983). *Natural history of alcoholism.* Cambridge, MA: Harvard University Press.

Valverde, M. (1998). *Diseases of the will: Alcohol and the dilemmas of freedom.* Cambridge, England: Cambridge University Press.

Weiner, C. L. (1981). *The politics of alcoholism: A social worlds analysis.* New Brunswick, NJ: Transaction Press.

Williams, R. J. (1947). The etiology of alcoholism: A working hypothesis involving the interplay of hereditary and environmental factors. *Quarterly Journal of Studies on Alcoholism, 7,* 567–587.

CHAPTER 3

TOUCHSTONE ISSUES FOR THEORIES OF SUBSTANCE ABUSE–DEPENDENCE ETIOLOGY

Meyer D. Glantz

One of the hallmarks of a maturing scientific field is that it uses the information it has gained to sharpen the focus of the questions it asks, to articulate and explore the tacit undemonstrated assumptions in its approaches, and to identify the defining phenomena that a comprehensive theory must account for. Research has led to notable advances in our understanding of the etiology and nature of substance use problems. However, not only has this research made progress in determining answers to questions about the development of substance use problems, it has also made great progress in asking better, more heuristically useful questions. A *touchstone* was originally a black stone used to assay the purity of gold and silver. The metal in question would be rubbed on the touchstone, and the resulting streaks would be compared with those left by a sample of known purity. In contemporary usage, a touchstone refers to a test of the validity of a concept. The field of substance use problems etiology has reached the stage at which it is reasonable to expect proposed theories to address certain questions and touchstone issues. Although it is not possible to present all of the touchstone issues in this chapter, I describe some of the major ones. A theory of the etiology of substance use problems should at least be congruent with and account for relevant, replicated, empirical research findings in the field. Ideally, a comprehensive theory should also address each touchstone issue and be consistent with or at least able to account for the gen-

erally accepted findings associated with the touchstone issues.

DEFINING THE TERMS

An important first step is to define certain central terms. The study of etiology is the search for the origin or cause of a condition or disorder, the attempt to answer the questions "Why?" "How?" and "Under what circumstances?" Usually, the purpose of the inquiry is to gain the information necessary to control the occurrence of the condition. A primary goal of understanding the determinants of individuals' vulnerability to a condition is to anticipate who is at greater risk and to mitigate that susceptibility, which requires identifying those factors that increase or decrease risk of the condition and that influence the persistence, severity, and course of the disorder. Etiology and vulnerability are not interchangeable concepts, and even a substantial understanding of one does not guarantee an understanding of the other. In addition, even an in-depth depiction of vulnerability to and the etiology of a disorder are not necessarily equivalent to a comprehensive explication of that disorder. The influences that determine the onset and development of a condition may be different from those that determine its persistence and subsequent course over time, recovery, relapse, and so forth. For the most part, *etiology* and *vulnerability* are not controversial terms. However, there is much less

The viewpoints expressed in this chapter do not necessarily represent those of the National Institutes of Health or the U.S. Department of Health and Human Services. I thank Lisa Dierker, Zili Sloboda, Ralph Tarter, Kevin Conway, David Shurtleff, Wilson Compton, and Marvin Snyder for thoughtful discussions that contributed to my formulation of the ideas contained in this chapter. The views expressed in this chapter do not necessarily represent their views.

agreement about what constitutes the defining characteristics of substance use problems, and this is a cardinal touchstone issue.

DEFINING THE PROBLEM

The most important definition for a theory of substance use problem etiology is a specification of the essential qualities of substance use problems, including a comparison with and differentiation from similar and related conditions (Glantz & Colliver, 2002). This is not merely a semantic issue. One of the biggest obstacles to progress in researching the etiology of substance use problems is the lack of a fully explicated, consensually accepted, empirically supported definition of the phenomenon and, in particular, its essential core characteristics. Despite the appearance of a common vocabulary, researchers associated with different models, approaches, and domains of scientific explanation often do not share a common set of assumptions and definitions about the essential criteria defining substance use problems. Even when they use the same terminology, they are not necessarily referring to the same phenomena.

For example, many early investigations of "drug abuse" did not reasonably define what drug abuse is. Investigators operationally defined the concept by considering virtually any illicit drug use experience to be drug abuse, and they compared abstainers with all others without differentiating participants' levels and patterns of illegal drug use. Using "any illicit drug use" as the defining criterion for drug abuse obscured critical differences. Not surprisingly, the findings of these studies have proved to have little value in understanding the essential nature of substance use problems. Assessment of individuals' levels and consequences of substance use are now standard considerations in contemporary research, but many other definitional and criteria questions remain.

Standardized formal criteria are widely used for clinical and research diagnostic purposes. There are two major classification systems currently used for the diagnosis of substance use disorders (SUDs): the *Diagnostic and Statistical Manual of Mental Disorders* (4th ed., text rev., or *DSM–IV–TR*; American Psychiatric Association, 2000) and the *International Classification of Diseases and Related Health Problems* (10th ed., or ICD-10; World Health Organization, 2007) systems, both of which have been revised multiple times with future revisions expected. Both systems are similar in their description of two basic categories of SUDs, substance abuse (or harmful use) and substance dependence, which are, for the most part, applied similarly across the range of abusable substances.

The *DSM–IV–TR* states that "the essential feature of Substance Abuse is a maladaptive pattern of substance use manifested by recurrent and significant adverse consequences related to the repeated use of substances" (American Psychiatric Association, 2000, p. 198). According to *DSM–IV–TR*,

> the essential feature of Substance Dependence is a cluster of cognitive, behavioral, and physiological symptoms indicating that the individual continues use of the substance despite significant substance-related problems. There is a pattern of repeated self-administration that usually results in tolerance, withdrawal, and compulsive drug-taking behavior . . . craving. (American Psychiatric Association, 2000, p. 192)

A diagnosis of substance dependence preempts a diagnosis of substance abuse if the individual has ever previously met the criteria for dependence for that class of substances.

For the most part, both the *DSM–IV–TR* and the ICD-10 have defined disorders in terms of polythetic classes, in that each disorder is identified in terms of a set of symptoms with no single symptom usually being either necessary or sufficient to satisfy the diagnostic threshold. The *DSM–IV–TR* category of substance abuse is an exception in that although none of the four qualifying symptoms is necessary to reach diagnosis, any one is sufficient (however, the ICD-10 uses a single criterion for its category of harmful use instead of the multicriteria categorization of *DSM–IV–TR* substance abuse). Although some of the substance use disorder criteria suggest underlying mechanisms (e.g., substance dependence implies some form of neuroadaption and physiological dependence as a primary factor), the *DSM–IV–TR* and ICD-10 are basically nosological rather than explanatory, and they denote disorders in terms of symptom clusters rather than explanatory concepts. Both systems, along with the numerous other clinical and research assessment systems, are very useful in their applications to research and diagnosis. However, their primary purpose is to provide operationalized systems for psychiatric disorder case identification. They were not designed to, nor do they, delineate the essential nature of substance use problems; neither do they encompass the full range of substance use problems (e.g., Sarr, Bucholz, & Phelps, 2000).

To illustrate the need for a fully explicated definition, consider the following questions:

- In terms of describing the primary characteristics defining substance use problems, does it matter which psychophysiologically active substances are used? Are chronic cigarette smoking, high levels of coffee drinking, weekend alcohol binging, daily but low-level use of marijuana, infrequent cocaine abuse, and heroin addiction fundamentally the same phenomenon? Should compulsive overeating be considered a substance abuse problem?

- Is compulsivity the essential defining criterion of substance use problems? If so, should compulsive gambling or other nonsubstance "addictions" be included in the same general category as compulsive substance use?

- Is persistent substance use despite hazard or harm the essential quality of substance use problems, and/or is repeated relapse the definitive characteristic? Are these behaviors the less fundamental but more observable manifestations of a critical underlying physiologically based dependence, a deficiency in self-regulatory function, or some other dysfunction or maladaptive condition? Do the core processes determining substance use problems continue to be active despite extended abstinence; that is, once an individual has become an addict, is he or she an addict forever?

- Is substance abuse on a continuum with substance dependence; that is, is it the same basic condition that is less severe or that has not progressed? How does substance use that has not developed into abuse or dependence relate to those disorders? Are substance use behaviors and problems more usefully characterized dimensionally as points on a continuum or categorically as discrete states of a condition or disorder?

- Are antisocial behaviors or disorders a definitive quality of substance use problems, or, relatedly, is substance abuse one of many alternative manifestations of antisocial characteristics? To what extent is the antisocial component of most SUDs (e.g., using an illegal substance, driving while intoxicated, failing to fulfill major role obligations) an essential characteristic of substance use problems?

- Is psychopathology the core defining determinant of substance use problems, or is substance abuse one of many alternative manifestations of a general underlying psychiatric disorder, a specific psychiatric dysfunction, or perhaps some other central dysfunction?

- Are the ways in which prolonged substance use changes a person the essential quality of substance use problems, and/or are the primary characteristics present before any substance use? Is everyone a potential substance abuser? What would a potential substance abuser be like if external circumstances (such as lack of substance availability) never permitted use?

- Is limited use of psychoactive substances a normal (i.e., nonpathological) behavior or perhaps even, in some cases, adaptive? Is getting intoxicated or high a normal behavior to at least some extent or in some cases? Are substance abuse and substance use problems a harmful extreme of a normal or even adaptive behavior? Is loss of control or the insufficiency of a counterbalancing self-protective mechanism the essential characteristic of substance use problems?

- Do substance abuse and substance dependence share the same underlying essential factors? Is there one basic substance use problem with variations in manifestation (e.g., abuse or addiction), or are there multiple, basically different types?

- Is the essential characteristic of substance use problems the function of a neurobiological mechanism or process? Is the mechanism defective or immature, or is its influence in terms of some other status, role, or interaction?

- With the continued developments in chemistry, pharmacology, and other technologies, will there be new forms of addiction? Will they involve the same neuropsychological processes as substance abuse problems, and will they have the same essential characteristics?

■ Are other central neuropsychological processes fundamentally and specifically involved in the development and course of substance abuse problems? For example, what is the role of memory processes in substance abuse problems?

These questions are just a few examples intended to demonstrate the importance of a comprehensive definition of the essential characteristics of substance use problems. An ideal definition for use by etiological research and theory would go beyond the criteria for case identification, which are likely to focus on sets of observable symptoms rather than on predisposing characteristics and primary underlying mechanisms. The need for such defining and distinguishing characterizations is common across different areas of research. The concept of a phenotype is central in genetics research in which the goal is often to relate a particular genotype—a particular genetic constellation—to a particular phenotype—the observable traits or characteristics of an organism. The quality of such research depends a great deal on the validity of the phenotype description and the extent to which it accurately identifies appropriate instances. Consider the difficulty of effectively researching potential genotypes for substance use problems if the earlier example questions are not resolved by the phenotype as defined by the research.

An expanded version of the phenotype concept has been adopted by the behavioral sciences and is often used to refer to the essential, defining characteristics of a condition. It is useful to include this idea as a requirement for models of the etiology of substance use problems. A theory that purports to describe the origin of a condition should start with a defining description of that condition. However, at this time there is no consensus on even the general parameters of the essential characteristics of substance use problems. Is the cardinal characteristic a premorbid neurobiological condition, a diagnosable psychiatric disorder (i.e., SUD), a range of adverse functional outcomes associated with maladaptive substance use behavior, and so forth? It is important to keep in

mind that a defining description is not necessarily a differential case identification description. Moreover, it is not necessarily the equivalent of nor does it necessarily include an etiological model of the phenomenon. Describing, explaining, and differentiating disorders and their origins may all be related, but they may also refer to significantly different factors, concepts, and information.

Consider that although comets and asteroids are both near-Earth objects, there are significant differences between them. Asteroids are large objects typically composed of rock, iron–nickel metal, and/or carbon compounds. Comets are large objects typically composed of ice, rock, and organic compounds. As the ice in a comet evaporates, it leaves a visible tail that when sighted allows one to distinguish a comet from an asteroid. This information provides both a description of two types of near-Earth objects, including a specification of the differentiating essential characteristic (ice), and a means of making a differential identification, but it provides no account of the origins of the objects and why they might be different. At the very least, an etiological model's definition of substance use problems should specify the intent and limits of the definition and whether it is being proposed as a phenotype.

The phenotype concept has further useful implications for the study of behavior etiology. In genetics, a phenotype is not necessarily assumed to be the direct manifestation of the genotype. The phenotype results from the genotype as it manifests and develops in a particular environment, which points to the importance of approaches that consider Gene × Environment (G × E) interactions. For example, differences in environmental influences and experiences are the reason why even though identical twins have identical DNA, they have similar but not identical fingerprints and people who know them well can usually tell them apart, even as babies. The relationship of the phenotype to the genotype varies with different traits. Eye color, for example, is highly related to specific gene characteristics, whereas other phenotypes, particularly those that are more behavioral in nature, are usually less directly related. The G × E concept applies to behavioral research (Rutter, Moffitt, & Caspi, 2006), including genetic research on substance use problems (e.g., Kendler et al., 2007), and it is reasonable for etiological models of substance use problems to consider how environmental factors affect the development and manifestation of those problems.

There is evidence that onset or initial experience with psychoactive substances as well as nonescalating use is more a function of social factors, whereas escalation to substance use problems, including abuse and dependence, is more a function of biological and psychological processes (Glantz & Pickens, 1992). In addition, the majority of people who engage in the use of psychoactive substances do not develop substance use problems. In this sense, the etiology of substance use is somewhat distinct from the etiology of substance use problems despite the obvious overlap. The discussion of touchstone issues in this chapter focuses primarily on substance use problems, not on psychoactive substance use that does not develop into a problem even if the substance being used has significant abuse liability.

In keeping with the principle of defining the phenomenon being considered, I define *substance use problems,* as the term is used in this chapter. The general core concept of a substance use problem is a maladaptive pattern of behavior in which an individual continues to use a psychoactive substance despite significant negative consequences (harm) or potential harm (hazard). This pattern would include persistent, compulsive use (and typically relapse to use) despite significant adverse consequences, which implies some psychological and/or physiological dependence or severe reliance on the use of the psychoactive substance. This characterization of substance use problems is not intended as a proposed phenotype, a comprehensive explanatory definition, or an etiological model. I present it for the purpose of identifying the phenomenon being considered in this chapter and to focus the discussion by delimiting parameters of the phenomenon. With that goal in mind, the definition is as instructive by what it does not include as by what it does.

Although this concept of substance use problems generally corresponds to *DSM–IV–TR* and ICD-10 substance use disorders, it does not distinguish abuse from dependence, it does not require psychiatric diagnosis as a classification, and it does not include a particular set of symptoms or a case identification algorithm. Moreover, it is not implicitly categorical; it

permits (although it does not require) a dimensional conceptualization; and it therefore readily allows for the inclusion of substance use problems that might be considered subthreshold in a disorder category–based definition. It does not exclude consideration of first substance use or limited use (described by some as "experimental use"; e.g., Petraitis, Flay, & Miller, 1995), but it also does not require explanation of these phenomena. To avoid confusion with the concept of *DSM–IV–TR* and ICD-10 SUDs, the focus of discussion here is on substance use problems including abuse and dependence, shortened to substance abuse–dependence problems (SADPs). I refer to individuals with SADPs as *substance abusers* and to individuals who use psychoactive substances but whose status in regard to SADPs is not being distinguished as *substance users.*

MULTIPLE DETERMINANTS

There is a general consensus that substance use is a complex behavior and that neither substance abuse nor SADPs are caused by a single factor. The G × E approach, including behavior genetics research on SADPs, assumes the importance of individual factors (i.e., a person's genes), manifesting in the context of a range of factors (the environment), and the concept of epigenetics is a reminder that other primary physiological factors also play a role in the manifestation of the phenotype. This perspective is not limited to genetics research. As Rutter (1996) pointed out, even in research on medical conditions, multidimensional causality models are more common than not. In behavioral research, the G × E concept has been expanded to include the range of characteristics of a particular individual as they manifest and develop in the context of a particular environment. The importance of Person × Environment (P × E) interaction models has been described by many researchers (e.g., Cicchetti & Aber, 1998) and has been proposed as necessary to theories of SADP etiology (Glantz, 1992; Loeber, Green, Lahey, Frick, & McBurnett, 2000; Sher, 1994; Tarter & Vanyukov, 1994b; Zucker, 1994). The P × E approach is a well-established perspective in the study of psychopathology etiology. For example, when Meehl (1962, 1990) introduced the concept of vulnerability to schizophrenia, he described it in terms of a diathesis–stress model, that is, endogenous predisposing factors that interact with necessary environmental influences. There is little controversy over whether SADPs are a P × E phenomena, nor is there any question that multiple levels and aspects of the environment are all critical influences. Related to and sometimes referred to as a *biopsychosocial model,* this approach is widely accepted, at least in general terms, and it is a touchstone issue.

However, despite the general acceptance that SADPs are multidetermined, there is no consensus about a central aspect of this touchstone issue. Beyond the question of whether SADPs are multidetermined is the question of the relative importance of particular determinants. Some etiological models have hypothesized that multiple essential factors have a fundamental role in the development of SADPs. For example, developmental psychopathology models have postulated that the etiology of SADPs is a course of individual system-based interactions between endogenous and environmental influences with a developmental emergence of predisposing vulnerability to substance abuse and SADPs, in contrast to the distinct onset of a disorder (e.g., Glantz, 1992; Tarter, 2002; Zucker, 1994). Other models have asserted that although many factors shape the course of SADP development, one is both primary and necessary and the others are more incidental, less fundamental, and not necessary. For example, a single central process model that asserts that SADPs are basically the result of impulse control deficits and sensation seeking might consider that environmental factors significantly influence the details and course of SADPs, but they are secondary in their importance. Such a model might even hypothesize that under varying environmental conditions, the core process will manifest in alternative ways and perhaps even manifest without the involvement of abused substances at all. The touchstone issue of multiple (vs. single) determinants should include some assignment of the primacy of influences.

HETEROGENEITY

There is no question that there is great heterogeneity among substance abusers and great variability in SADPs. For example, substance abusers are quite variable in terms of the substances they use (and the routes of substance administration). This variability is considered to be sufficiently important to make the use of different substances a key factor for differential diagnosis in the *DSM–IV–TR* and ICD-10. In addition, substance abusers vary as to whether they have comorbid psychiatric problems or engage in illegal behavior, whether their substance use involves illegal drugs, whether they are physically dependent on the substances they use, whether they are polysubstance users, and the severity of their SADP and its consequences, as well as being diverse in many other significant ways. The touchstone issue is whether variations in SADPs associated with particular heterogeneities are of sufficient significance in terms of the hypothesized nature of SADPs that they warrant differentiating classifications and, possibly, different etiological and explanatory models. If this is the case and the heterogeneities can reasonably be organized into common, coherent, yet significantly divergent patterns, then this argues that the heterogeneities observed in SADPs are reflections of inherently different subtypes. Whether the heterogeneity of SADPs relates to minor variations of a single primary form of SADP or whether there are multiple significantly different fundamental variations of SADPs is an important touchstone issue.

Whether there is more than one essential type of SADP has been a long-standing question. Even seemingly basic questions, such as whether alcoholism (alcohol abuse–dependence) and drug abuse–dependence are essentially the same disorder, have not been consensually resolved. Lack of a generally accepted phenotype accounts for some of the disparate views on the heterogeneity of SADPs, and so do the self-perpetuating but often unspecified assumptions in research designs and assessment instruments. As Kagan, Snidman, McManis, Woodward, and Hardway (2002) suggested in regard to child temperament, in some cases the nature of self-report data collection and the reifying influence of many assessments can conceal meaningful heterogeneity, effectively combining significantly diverse groups into a single category. They recommended that multiple sources of information, particularly from multiple domains, be used to create the most informative categorizations.

To fully understand SADPs and their etiology, it is necessary to determine which characteristics of SADPs are universal, which are common, which are particular to specific subgroups, and which are idiosyncratic (i.e., variable within a wide range). It is also critical to identify which characteristics are necessary, which are sufficient, which are neither but still have a significant determining influence, and which have strong associations with SADPs but do not seem to have an essential role. Identifying common and distinct patterns of characteristics (i.e., subtypes) of SADPs is a potentially useful approach to better understanding the significance of the various heterogeneous characteristics of SADPs for both heuristic and practical purposes. For example, insufficient consideration of subtypes may be one of the obstacles to identifying a validated phenotype of SADPs or a single empirically supported etiological model (for further discussion, see Basu, Ball, Feinn, Gelernter, & Kranzler, 2004; Glantz & Colliver, 2002; Zucker Fitzgerald, & Moses, 1995).

SUBTYPES

Examinations of heterogeneity and subtypes are a central goal in many areas of psychopathology research, but empirical support has been mixed. Typologies have also been proposed with subtype classifications for both alcohol and drug abusers (e.g., Basu et al., 2004; Cohen, 1984; Penick et al., 1999; Zucker, 1987, 1994). The most widely considered subtype typology for SADPs is a multidimensional classification that distinguishes two main classes of alcoholism on the basis of factors related to onset pattern, premorbid characteristics, severity, psychopathology, family history, chronicity, and antisocial behaviors or disorders. The Type I versus Type II typology was proposed by Cloninger, Bohman, and Sigvardsson (1981); Babor et al. (1992) proposed a similar but more empirically supported Type A versus Type B classification (see also Epstein, Labouvie, McCrady, Jensen, & Hayaki, 2002). The Type I–Type A subtype is generally characterized by later onset, fewer childhood behavior problems, and lower levels of psychopathology. The Type II–Type B subtype is generally characterized by earlier onset, greater chronicity, greater childhood behavior problems,

higher levels of psychopathology, a family history of alcoholism, and more severe associated negative consequences. This typology has also been applied to drug abusers, and numerous studies have investigated the validity of the classification in a range of substance-abusing samples. Although studies have provided support for this binary typology (e.g., Ball, Carroll, Babor, & Rounsaville, 1995; Carpenter, Liu, & Hasin, 2006), some have not (e.g., Bucholz et al., 1996), and others have found partial support (Penick et al., 1999) or support for alternative typologies (e.g., Moss, Chen, & Yi, 2007). Overall, findings have been mixed. Comprehensive research reviews (Babor & Caetano, 2006; Hesselbrock & Hesselbrock, 2006) have concluded that although there is empirical support for the application of subtyping as an approach, there is no conclusive support at this time for any particular typology. Furthermore, although there is some support for a binary system similar to the Type A–B clusters, there is also support for typologies that distinguish four or more homogeneous groups. Considering variables from domains other than or in addition to those used in current typologies, particularly neurological characteristics, may help identify valid and useful subtypes. In some cases, different proposals of etiological models may overlap with proposed different subtypes and may be different perspectives on the same phenomena (e.g., Sher, 1991; Sher, Gotham, & Watson, 2004; Sher, Grekin, & Williams, 2005). It is helpful when proposed models consider both possibilities.

COMMONALITIES

The ways in which addiction behaviors share fundamental characteristics and mechanisms is almost certainly a key concept in understanding SADPs and their etiology (Levison, Gerstein, & Maloff, 1983). Although the possibility of identifying and validating subtypes of SADPs holds some heuristic promise, there is no question that the behavioral and neurological commonalities among SADPs are also compelling and informative. To underestimate the potential importance of the commonalities across SADPs is to risk missing critical information and insights. There is no controversy over whether there are commonalities among substance abusers and across SADPs. Rather, the touchstone issues are unresolved questions about the nature, extent, and implications of these apparently similar core qualities. It is worth noting that a theory's incorporation of concepts of heterogeneity is not incompatible with its also including concepts of core commonalities, even when this involves hypotheses of multiple etiological models. Although not always clearly distinguished in discussions of the issue, consideration of SADP commonalities may focus on similar etiologies, shared essential underlying mechanisms or processes, comparable clinical presentations and manifest behaviors, and/or other common characteristics such as psychopathology or antisocial behaviors and disorders.

An example of the complicated touchstone issue of commonalities is the question of when a hypothesized core commonality is thought to originate or begin its primary influence. Some etiological models have theorized that the main determining factor of substance abuse behaviors, and the common critical influence, is predispositional and operates significantly before the first use of any psychoactive substance. For example, a model that posits that substance abuse develops as one of a cluster of potential conduct disorder–antisocial behavior manifestations suggests that the common factor of antisocial behaviors and disorders precedes and is a causal factor of subsequent substance abuse (e.g., Jessor & Jessor's [1977] problem behavior proneness theory or Robins's [1966] deviance syndrome model). Other models that incorporate hypothesized common causes focus on factors that develop later in the course of SADPs. For example, some neurobiologically oriented models have hypothesized that common neuroplasticities in brain function are responsible for the transition from impulsive to habituated compulsive use of psychoactive substances. Building on the findings that the most abused psychoactive substances activate the mesolimbic dopamine pathway (although through differing acute effects and mechanisms) and findings supporting the supposition that chronic substance use results in chronic pathological functional changes in reward and other brain systems, these models hypothesize that long-term neuropharmacological effects are largely responsible for at least the more chronic and severe forms of SADPs (Kalivas &

O'Brien, 2008; Koob, 2006; Nestler, 2005). From these perspectives, the critical commonality is also a convergence that develops as both a result of and a contributor to chronic psychoactive substance use.

The issues of commonalities are very complex. For example, whether a characteristic is found to be common or not may vary with a variety of factors and dimensions across individuals, subgroups, stages in the course of SADPs, and so forth. *Equifinality* and *multifinality* are two principles of developmental psychopathology that are relevant to this issue. *Equifinality* refers to a convergence and describes the concept that a given endpoint or outcome may be reached from multiple initial conditions and through multiple processes or paths. The related concept of multifinality refers to a divergence and describes the concept that a given initial condition, including ones involving adverse circumstances, may lead to multiple different outcomes, possibly including desirable ones (see Cicchetti & Rogosch, 1996, for a more complete discussion). The perspective encouraged by these principles is the recognition that behavioral conditions are not static, unchanging states with single invariant origins and fixed inevitable outcomes. They are multidetermined dynamic points in complex transactional systems with multiple forms and variations. What is significantly common at one point along a developmental course may not be common at another.

COMMON CO-OCCURRING BEHAVIORS AND CONDITIONS

Not only are there important commonalities among SADPs, but there are similarities and shared characteristics among SADPs and other behaviors and conditions that frequently co-occur with them. Description of these clusters is strongly supported by research, and certain patterns of co-occurrence are sufficiently common and noteworthy that a number of etiological models are based on them. Identification of the two most notable clusters comes from observations that SADPs often co-occur with other problem (antisocial) behaviors and disorders and that they also frequently co-occur with other psychopathologies (Glantz, Weinberg, Miner, & Colliver, 1999). Although there is considerable empirical support for these co-occurrences, the reasons for them are not clear (Kessler, 1995; Willoughby, Chalmers, & Busseri, 2004). Most explanations for these associations hypothesize either a causal influence (i.e., that SADPs cause the co-occurring conditions, that the reverse is true, or that the conditions mutually influence and exacerbate each other) or a third-factor model (i.e., that the clusters are the result of common underlying causes). Several researchers have discussed the complexities of relationships among co-occurring conditions (e.g., Krueger & Markon, 2006; Loeber & Keenan, 1994), and some of the lack of clarity about the relationships of co-occurring behaviors may come in part from incomplete consideration of the range of interrelationships. It is also possible that there is some overlap between the observed clusters and subtypes of behavioral disorders. As etiology theories that emphasize behavior cluster models go beyond descriptions of clusters to include coherent explanatory concepts and empirically demonstrated common liabilities, they increase in heuristic value and credibility (e.g., Kendler, Prescott, Myers, & Neale, 2003; Krueger, Markon, Patrick, Benning, & Kramer, 2007). There is no controversy over whether SADPs often co-occur with other problem behaviors and mental disorders; the touchstone issues are the questions regarding what accounts for these co-occurrences and what their implications are.

COMMON CAUSES

There has been increasing attention to and support for the idea that common causes provide the best explanation for the observed co-occurrences and that this approach may also offer a strong explanatory approach to SADP etiology. There are several different general formulations of common-cause models. For example, a common-cause model may emphasize a common underlying process, such as the neuroadaptive mechanism previously described in this chapter; a psychopathological condition with multiple manifestations, such as an impulse–antisocial behavior disorder; or an intermediary characteristic whose outcome is highly dependent on environmental influences, such as affect dysregulation. It is helpful to consider another concept from genetics research.

The genotype–phenotype association is fairly straightforward when a single gene is associated with a simple (noncomplex) observable trait, such as eye color. However, when the phenotype is complex and when it does not appear to be the direct expression of a single gene or set of genes, then, at least in some cases, it is useful to consider intermediary characteristics, endophenotypes, that fill the gap. This concept is being applied to genetic research on psychiatric disorders (Cannon & Keller, 2006; Gottesman & Gould, 2003; Gottesman & Hanson, 2005). An expanded, less genetically specific version of this concept suggests the general approach of considering not just the primary biological basis of a condition, nor just its observable behavioral manifestations, but also the intermediary characteristics and instrumental processes that are the linkage between them. This approach seems very applicable to etiological models of SADPs. Such intermediary characteristics and mechanisms, or endophenotypes, hold considerable explanatory potential for issues such as the commonalities and co-occurrences that have been discussed. The possibility that multiple different biological substrates or multiple different P × E interactions may lead to the same particular endophenotype would address some questions of how seemingly diverse antecedents and developmental courses could lead to fairly similar SADP outcomes. In addition, in terms of a theoretical framework, the endophenotype concept is readily compatible with a P × E approach, which would potentially account for at least some observed heterogeneities. The concept of endophenotypes may be helpful in accounting for occurrences of both equifinality and multifinality in the course of SADPs.

INTERMEDIARY CONSTRUCTS

On the basis of research findings, a number of characteristics have been proposed as precursors, intermediary factors, underlying common causes, and/or significant predisposing and exacerbating influences. These include deficiencies in executive cognitive function, impulsiveness and behavioral self-regulation problems, negative affect and affect dysregulation, inadequate coping and problem-solving skills, difficult temperament, and novelty–sensation seeking (see Glantz et al., 1999, for a review). Some of the stronger construct proposals are based on assessed precursor or intermediary characteristics that are empirically associated with both premorbid genetic and neurobiological antecedents as well as observable behavioral manifestations.

As a notable example, Tarter, Vanyukov, and colleagues (Tarter, Kirisci, Habeych, Reynolds, & Vanyukov, 2004; Vanyukov et al., 2003) have hypothesized that neurobehavioral disinhibition is a common liability trait for SUDs. It is not just the general idea of neurobehavioral disinhibition that makes this hypothesis noteworthy, however. Other researchers have proposed less heuristically powerful concepts oriented around the idea of affective or behavioral dysregulation. Tarter et al. conceptualized the trait as being a multifactorial predisposing dysfunction associated with diminished inhibitory control, which is the neurobiological substrate underlying risk for a range of behavior disorders, including SUDs. Neurobehavioral disinhibition is a sophisticated construct that integrates concepts and findings from multiple domains of assessment and is conceptualized in terms of a multidetermined P × E developmental framework. It describes an endophenotypic intermediary that is not only a heuristically useful construct but has been shown to be a strong prospective predictor of SUDs in a sample of adolescent boys.

Zucker and Ichiyama (1996) pointed out in their critique of Baumeister and Heatherton's "Self-regulatory theory" theory that a concept can be useful in its recognition of a phenomenon even though it is not adequately comprehensive, explanatory, or substantiated. This is, in fact, an issue for some hypothesized endophenotypes. A proposed endophenotype, a delineated intermediary and/or underlying process construct, can be useful in theory building, hypothesis generation, and even the practical task of case identification. But the validity of the construct is not guaranteed by its having some usefulness. To illustrate, the concept of resilience is widely used to describe well-being, adaptation, and/or effective functioning in circumstances of significant adversity and stress. It is an evocative description used to describe the function of individuals and groups, and it is part of many theoretical frameworks and investigations of protective factors, attempts to ameliorate environmental stressors, and preventive interventions. However, there is no specific trait consistently identified as resilience, nor is there any characteristic that would be likely to convey resilience or even protection in all circumstances. There are no reliable measures of resilience, and it is not necessarily the case that a presumably resilient individual's outcome will consensually be seen as positive. For example, is it a positive resilient outcome to become highly aggressive even if the result is increased personal safety in a violent neighborhood or to become a highly successful drug dealer in a community in which there are few jobs? The weakest formulations of resilience are tautological explanations, which infer the occurrence of resilience from an at-risk group's avoidance of an adverse outcome and then explain the favorable outcome by reference to the group's resilience. For the most part, resilience is a sometimes useful but unanchored single-domain concept, a hypothetical construct without reliable objective criteria or consistent empirical grounding (see Glantz & Sloboda, 1999, for an extended discussion). The endophenotypic constructs proposed as part of some SADP etiology models have limitations similar to those of the concept of resilience. Whether an etiological model includes endophenotype concepts and how they are conceptualized is a touchstone issue.

Hypothesized endophenotypes have greater heuristic value if they are more than just a behavioral attribution and more than just a detailed neurological mechanism. Ideally, they are integrated, multidomain, neurobehavioral constructs that are empirically supported by and commensurate with observed behavior and biological substrates. There may be additional benefit if the endophenotype corresponds with subjective experience. There is not necessarily a distinction between an intermediary factor and an underlying cause, and I use the term *endophenotype* here to designate a concept that is intended to refer to either or both. Etiological models should clarify their use of the term if they incorporate the concept. A theory of an SADP endophenotype would be further enhanced by addressing additional relevant issues.

For example, according to the particular endophenotype hypothesis, do SADPs result from an intermediary or underlying process that is a dysfunctional mechanism in need of repair, an otherwise healthy but immature process, or the insufficiency of a protective or counterbalancing system? Are SADPs the consequence of typically functioning universal endogenous characteristics in particular stressful, adverse, or destabilizing environmental circumstances? Is liability to SADPs associated with natural variations that might be protective or healthy in some circumstances but are hazardous in contemporary environments? The more comprehensively an endophenotype is characterized, the more questions it addresses, and the more domains it is empirically anchored in, the more useful it is likely to be. Well-characterized endophenotypes are likely to be critical components of approaches that significantly advance our understanding of SADP etiology.

Evaluating the usefulness of an endophenotype's characterization highlights the additional issue of multiple levels of micro–macro vantage. Implicit in P × E approaches and biopsychosocial models is the premise that the phenomena of SADPs are influenced by factors from multiple domains including biological, psychological–psychiatric, and social areas. For example, an impulsive adolescent who has older friends who smoke is more likely to try cigarettes and have continued access, which facilitates the establishment of the behavior and the progression to nicotine dependence. This is a description in which influences from several different domains are proposed to interact to create conditions that increase the likelihood that this adolescent will develop a pattern of smoking behavior. This portrayal has a conceptual framework that describes a sort of horizontal integration of constructs from several different contemporaneous endogenous and exogenous domains. Different scientific fields or domains of influence may also provide different viewpoints on a particular event (i.e., characteristic, process, occurrence). For example, a social psychological perspective on an underage drinking incident would probably share some concepts and interpretations with a sociological view, but there would also be significant differences.

However, a particular event can also be considered from multiple vantage points on a micro–macro continuum. Although there may be overlap between these vantage points, there are informational and heuristic implications associated with the differences. There may even be some confusion about the extent to which any two perspectives are focused on the same event or refer to distinct events that may have a causal association with each other. For example, an individual who uses a psychoactive substance will have a substance-induced experience. That experience can be described from the vantage point of the individual's subjective experience and how he or she attributes and labels it, from the vantage point of a real-time brain scan and the acute effects to which it corresponds, and from the vantage point of a neurochemical modeling of brain reward circuitry and how it is activated in the condition of a specific substance exposure. Although the three descriptions depict the same event to at least some extent, unless the issue is directly addressed, the extent and nature of the proposed relationship between the different pictures from the different micro–macro vantage points, the vertical integration, may be unclear. In some cases, it may even be unclear whether the event as delineated in one vantage point description is being proposed as the cause of the event in another vantage point description. Etiological models and descriptions of SADP-related events may intend such an implication, but either way it should be addressed when relevant. Although researchers are cognizant of this concern, proposed etiological models often do not specifically address this issue and do not clarify the relationship of given events depicted from different micro–macro vantage points. Including specific delineations of how etiological factors are related, in terms of both horizontal and vertical integration, would strengthen an SADP etiology model.

VULNERABILITY

The concept of vulnerability denotes increased potential danger of an adverse condition or outcome resulting from some form of dysfunction or insufficiency. It refers to those factors that make a particular individual or group more susceptible because of endogenous predisposing characteristics that may be activated and/or exacerbated by exogenous factors. Vulnerability is typically assumed to vary with time and circumstance as well as with development and experience. Differences in vulnerability are associated not only with differential susceptibility to a condition but also with differences in course, levels of severity, and outcome. Vulnerability is obviously a touchstone issue for models of SADP etiology. Most theories' explication of vulnerability is the central principle of their conceptualization of etiology.

Vulnerability hypotheses also usually address a number of additional questions that are helpful in considering the proposed model. These may include the following:

- What vulnerability factors interact with which external influences to increase or decrease predisposition to substance abuse problems, and how crucial are particular constellations of environmental factors?
- Is vulnerability specific to particular classes of substances, to substance abuse problems in general, to a particular state of increased neurobiological susceptibility, or to a multi-outcome psychiatric dysfunction?
- Is vulnerability a stable and enduring trait, a transient state produced by particular conditions, a consequence of learning and experience, or perhaps an internalizable tendency that is socially propagated?
- Is everyone vulnerable to SADPs?
- How can SADP susceptibility be mitigated, and what are the optimal points, targets, and approaches for reducing vulnerability?
- Is SADP vulnerability an active predisposition in which the individual purposefully engages in substance use behaviors in a goal-seeking manner?
- Is vulnerability a passive predisposition in which the individual is not acting to achieve a goal but is highly sensitive and readily responsive to stimuli that encourage or support substance use behaviors and/or escalation?
- Is vulnerability a latent predisposition that remains dormant unless there are strong and/or repetitive eliciting influences?
- To what extent are the influences and impetus of SADP vulnerability subject to voluntary control or limitation?
- What are necessary, sufficient, and/or strongly influential but fungible factors determining vulnerability?

As these examples show, there are many important touchstone questions that should be addressed by a comprehensive model of SADP etiology, but several of the more conceptually tangled issues are associated with a related construct, the concept of risk.

RISK AND PROTECTIVE FACTORS

Risk addresses questions regarding the relationship between antecedent factors and adverse outcomes. Given the presence of factor X, what is the probability that outcome Y will occur? For example, what is the likelihood that adolescents who have previously been diagnosed as having a conduct disorder will engage in illicit drug use? Kraemer et al. (1997) have discussed how different reports of risk–condition relationships may use a similar terminology but may be referring to significantly different types of associations. They described different meanings underlying risk vocabulary and proposed a standard terminology. Although all of the variations in the Kraemer et al. typology include at least a correlation between factor and outcome, and as such they contribute to prediction of the outcome given the presence of the factor, they vary in the extent to which there is a presumed or demonstrated causal association. Briefly, the major distinction that Kraemer et al. proposed is that for risk–condition relationships in which both correlation and temporal order have been established, a *risk factor* refers only to an antecedent correlated factor, a *marker* refers to an antecedent correlated factor with no presumed causal involvement in the outcome, and a *causal risk factor* refers to an antecedent correlated factor that presumably does causally influence the outcome. A *correlate* refers to a correlated factor, and although each correlate may contribute to prediction of the other, neither of the correlated factors is known to be antecedent or causally determinative of the other.

Despite the cogency and value of the points and proposal made by Kraemer et al. (1997), the distinctions of risk references are often not observed. This is a significant problem for some SADP etiology models. Establishing that there is both an antecedent and a correlational relationship between a factor and an outcome does not necessarily demonstrate a causal relationship even if a mechanism for causal influence can be hypothesized. The antecedent may be a proxy for another influence, there may be an underlying common cause for the factor and outcome (third-variable alternatives), the antecedent may be an earlier form or stage of the outcome, and so forth. For example, adolescents' association with peers with problem behaviors has often been found to precede and be associated with initiation of illicit drug use, and this may be a useful signal for early identification of at-risk adolescents. However, there is not necessarily a significant causal relationship between the peer association and the drug use.

The risk reference distinctions might be more easily and more often applied if the terminology was simpler and more distinctive. It might be helpful to reserve any use of the phrase "risk factors" to include only Kraemer et al.'s (1997) *causal risk factors* and to refer to any other correlated factor as a marker, regardless of whether there is presumed antecedence. This may have the added advantage of not inadvertently implying causality for a variable that is only a proxy for the causal factor. For example, the variable of an individual's sex precedes his or her adolescent behavior. If adolescent boys are found to have an earlier onset of first use of alcohol than are adolescent girls, this might seem to suggest that inherent in the biology that determines that an individual is male is a factor that causes earlier drinking. This may be the case, but it may also be the case that cultural factors determine first drinking age, factors that change over time and might only be recognized with a cultural change and the convergence of male and female typical first drinking age. The relationship between a marker and an outcome is not necessarily constant.

Unless there is evidence to the contrary, it is safest to assume that markers are no more than correlates, not demonstrated causal influences and therefore not risk factors. This is not only a critical issue for precision in SADP etiology models but also in designing effective prevention approaches. Implementing interventions that change risk factors may reduce the occurrence of the associated adverse outcomes. Interventions that change markers are less likely to have such benefits (Glantz et al., 2008). It is also important to remember that there are protective factors, antecedent factors that reduce the likelihood of an adverse outcome. Kraemer, Stice, Kazdin, Offord, and Kupfer (2001) incorporated the concept of protective factors into a more generic concept of risk factors. This is a practical suggestion in some ways, but

it does unintentionally encourage less attention to protective factors that have already been given inadequate weight and consideration. Kraemer et al. also described various types of interactions between risk factors and recommended use of a standard terminology to clarify these issues. Progress in clarifying risk for SADP outcomes will be fostered by research that distinguishes causal factors from indicators, explicates the nature of the association between factors and outcomes, depicts the interactions between influences, and identifies mitigatable factors that would be responsive to intervention. The conceptualization of risk and protective factors in a hypothesized SADP etiology model is a touchstone issue. So are the structural frameworks in which they are proposed.

Many researchers have identified markers and risk factors as a step in developing an etiology theory. This is a practical and powerful empirically based approach to investigating the development and nature of an outcome and to identifying factors that may be effective targets for preventing it (Kazdin, Kraemer, Kessler, Kupfer, & Offord, 1997). Risk factor research can provide a foundation for building more comprehensive integrated models. A wide range of risk factors or markers has been identified for SADPs (Hawkins, Catalano, & Miller, 1992). However, identifying risk factors is not the equivalent of a comprehensive characterization of vulnerability or etiology. Some researchers have not gone beyond proposing risk factors in their conceptualizations of SADP etiology, which are often not distinguished from markers, and their proposals have more limited descriptive and explanatory utility. Vulnerability is not just the degree of accumulation of risk factors; rather, it refers to the overall status of susceptibility, taking into consideration the totality of relevant risk and protective factors and the contexts in which they interact. Etiology is not just a proposition of which risk factors are associated with an outcome; rather, it refers to a comprehensive model of determining influences interacting in context over time, providing a coherent explanatory description of the stages and transitions leading to an outcome. Etiology theories that include the description of observed common patterns of influences and transitions describing the course of a disorder are likely to have greater heuristic value. Descriptions of common courses of SADPs are often characterized in terms of pathways and trajectories.

PATHWAYS

As a description of the course of SADPs, the concept of a pathway focuses on the development of substance use behavior and substance use problems and emphasizes the interactions of critical determinants over time leading to those problems. For example, Wills, Ainette, Mendoza, Gibbons, and Brody (2007; Wills & Dishion, 2004) have proposed a model in which particular childhood temperament characteristics form the substrate of self-control during development, which in the context of certain other influences may lead to substance use in adolescence. Pathway models present conceptually organized findings of risk factors in a dynamic developmental framework describing their course in terms of P × E interactions through intermediary stages and transitions leading to particular outcomes. They are more sophisticated approaches to understanding etiology, and they readily allow for the hypothesis of multiple pathways to SADPs that may more accurately reflect the heterogeneity of SADP etiology (Institute of Medicine Committee on Opportunities in Drug Abuse Research, 1996). Pathway models are inherently developmental psychopathology models that are particularly applicable to the description of SADP etiology (Cicchetti, 1999; Cicchetti & Rogosch, 1999; Glantz, 1992; Glantz & Leshner, 2000; Tarter & Vanyukov, 1994a; Zucker et al., 1995). In fact, most of the touchstone issues being related here to SADP etiology correspond to central concepts of developmental psychopathology approaches.

TRAJECTORIES

The concept of SADP trajectory refers to the course of SADPs described primarily in terms of stages and transitions in a chronological framework rather than in terms of causal influences. Trajectory models provide a useful perspective and draw attention to the importance of age at onset of behaviors, stages and stable periods, transitions and rates of transition, and differences in timing and trajectories associated with different factors and groups (Sher et al., 2004). For

example, numerous studies have reported that early age at onset of the use of a substance is a significant marker if not a risk factor for the development of an SUD (Anthony & Petronis, 1995; Grant & Dawson, 1997; King & Chassin, 2007). Accounting for most trajectory points, transitions, and rates of change is a touchstone issue for an SADP etiology model. Three trajectory-related phenomena may be particularly important for etiology models to address.

PROGRESSIONS

A frequent research finding is that there is a common sequence for individuals' becoming involved with substance use. According to Kandel (1975; Kandel & Yamaguchi, 1999), the *gateway hypothesis* refers to a sequence in which adolescents' involvement with drugs typically begins with alcohol and/or cigarette use, and for those who continue to use additional substances, the next stage is marijuana use, followed by the use of other illicit drugs, such as cocaine or heroin. Research has clearly shown that continuation is not inevitable, and, in fact, the majority of individuals at one stage do not continue to the next. Subsequent research has shown that there is greater variability in the sequence than was originally thought; however, the major unresolved issue is the question of what the nature of the sequence is. It is not clear whether a common sequence is a progression in a developmental sense, that is, whether there is significance in the particular order of substances and what influence, if any, the use of substances earlier in this sequence has on the use of substances later in the sequence (Glantz et al., 1999). There are different possible explanations for findings of a common sequence; for example, the sequence may reflect increasing socially defined deviance associated with the series of substances. However, many explanations do not account for the observation that in some ways, sequences seem to be more than just common orderings. Substance onset sequences appear, at least to some observers, to have characteristics associated with progressions in that use of earlier sequence substances can be construed as causally influencing the likelihood of using later sequence substances.

A phenomenon reported primarily in animal research, cross-sensitization, may account for at least some progression aspects of multiple substance use. *Cross-sensitization* refers to the finding that early exposure to psychoactive substances, particularly in adolescence, increases later sensitivity and/or behavioral responsiveness to other substances in adult animals. Although there is some disagreement on the underlying mechanism of this sensitization (Caprioli, Celentano, Paolone, & Badiani, 2007; Koob & Le Moal, 1997; Robinson & Berridge, 2003; Vezina, 2007), this hypothesis would at least partially account for some of the observed escalation and sequencing of substance use trajectories and would also account for variation and change in the substances in a common sequence.

CONVERGENCE

As previously discussed, there are significant commonalities associated with SADPs, some of which are observable as convergences. For example, many college-age young adults with histories of higher levels of alcohol and drug use curtail their substance use in their mid-20s, around the time that they assume more adult roles and responsibilities. Their substance use behavior then resembles the lower level alcohol and drug use of many of their contemporaries (Bachman et al., 2002). However, there is less agreement about another apparent convergence. It has often been observed that a high percentage of alcohol abusers are tobacco smokers and that although there are many drug users who only use marijuana, most drug abusers are polysubstance users. These convergences are particularly associated with higher quantity or higher frequency users with more severe SADPs. Such seeming convergences may be an artifact of observation or categorization, or they may correspond to a basic characteristic of psychoactive substance use, but it does seem that there is at least some convergence of substance use behavior as SADPs reach more severe levels. There are many possible factors that might contribute to an apparent behavioral convergence, and they may exert their influence in different ways and at different points. Whether or not individuals have predisposing substance class preferences, a number of factors—including a predisposing common liability trait, neuroadaption, cross-sensitization, channeling envi-

ronmental factors, and so forth—might individually or in combination increase convergence to polysubstance use. There have been fewer reports and less consideration of divergences in the course of SADPs. Although this may suggest that divergences are not a common feature of SADPs, at least some divergences are generally recognized.

DESISTENCE

The focus of SADP etiology theories is the onset and course of substance use problems, and the models typically include an account of the differential vulnerability of individuals. In a society with ready availability and prevalent exposure to psychoactive substances, and with at least some substance use experience being common, there are still great differences in individual vulnerability to SADPs. Most SADP models describe the predisposing factors influencing why individuals do or do not follow a course from first use to SADPs, and they typically account for most of the variability in outcomes in terms of variability in premorbid determining characteristics and early trajectory influences. They are ballistic models because they assume that analogous to the flight of a cannonball, most of the variable determinants of the trajectory are primarily active at the beginning of the course and only exceptional mid-course influences can change the largely predetermined outcome. Regardless of the explanatory constructs used (e.g., genetic predispositions, self-regulatory dysfunctions, antisocial traits, neuro-biological mechanisms), many etiology models offer at least a possible account for the course of SADP development and continuation. However, few SADP etiology models provide a well-conceived and tested explanation for the outcomes of those individuals who appear to be on a typical SADP course but who change the course they are on. Apparent change in course is typically attributed to a different original trajectory (e.g., adolescent limited models; Moffitt, 1993; Moffitt, Caspi, Harrington, & Milne, 2002), to a reduced or originally lower level of the primary predisposing factors, or to an extreme change in external influences. Change of course once SADPs are established is typically not well explained. Even models that recognize the phenomenon of desistence do not typically provide a comprehensive explanation of why and how it occurs. Desistence phenomena include the "maturing out" of substance abuse by many young adults, substance abusers with SADPs who stop or control high levels of quantity or frequency of substance use without assistance, and even abusers who overcome SADPs with the aid of treatment. It is one of the tragic puzzles of SADPs that abusers persist in substance use behavior despite significant hazard or harm. Given the powerful causal influences hypothesized in SADP etiology models, it is also something of a mystery when and how abusers curtail their substance use, especially once they have reached the level of severe SADPs. This highlights the most important touchstone issue for any proposed SADP etiology theory, the question of whether the etiology model is useful in developing more effective prevention and treatment interventions.

CONCLUSION

Theories of the etiology of substance abuse–dependence have been developed in diverse ways, including through deductions from observations and empirical findings about substance abusers, through extrapolations from and extensions of specific theories of other behaviors and pathologies (e.g., externalizing behavior disorders, problem behavior proneness), from inferences based on macro (e.g., epidemiological) and micro (e.g., neurological) data, and by implications drawn from general models (e.g., social learning models) and approaches (e.g., developmental psychopathology). However, the ultimate criterion for evaluating all SADP etiology theories is their explanatory effectiveness. How well a theory explains behaviors is determined by the extent of its empirical validation; its consistency with models of other behavioral phenomena; the clarity, coherence, and comprehensiveness of the theory's formulation; the range of issues it satisfactorily addresses; and the practical questions of the theory's utility in predicting the occurrence and variations of SADPs and in providing a basis for the development of effective interventions. Describing the touchstone issues for theories of the etiology of substance abuse–dependence articulates the primary questions and issues that a theory

of SADP etiology must cogently address to maximize its explanatory power and to be valuable as both a heuristic and a utilitarian model. Consideration of the extent to which different SADP etiology theories satisfactorily address these touchstone issues may serve as a useful guide to evaluating and improving the etiological theories.

References

American Psychiatric Association. (2000). *Diagnostic and statistical manual of mental disorders* (4th ed., text rev.). Washington, DC: Author.

Anthony, J. C., & Petronis, K. R. (1995). Early-onset drug use and risk of later drug problems. *Drug & Alcohol Dependence, 40,* 9–15.

Babor, T. F., & Caetano, R. (2006). Subtypes of substance dependence and abuse: Implications for diagnostic classification and empirical research. *Addiction, 101*(Suppl. 1), 104–110.

Babor, T. F., Hofmann, M., DelBoca, F. K., Hesselbrock, V., Meyer, R. E., Dolinsky, Z. S., et al. (1992). Types of alcoholics. I: Evidence for an empirically derived typology based on indicators of vulnerability and severity. *Archives of General Psychiatry, 49,* 599–608.

Bachman, J. G., O'Malley, P. M., Schulenberg, J. E., Johnston, L. D., Bryant, A. L., & Merline, A. C. (2002). *The decline of substance use in young adulthood: Changes in social activities, roles, and beliefs.* Mahwah, NJ: Erlbaum.

Ball, S. A., Carroll, K. M., Babor, T. F., & Rounsaville, B. J. (1995). Subtypes of cocaine abusers: Support for a Type A–Type B distinction. *Journal of Consulting and Clinical Psychology, 63,* 115–124.

Basu, D., Ball, S. A., Feinn, R., Gelernter, J., & Kranzler, H. R. (2004). Typologies of drug dependence: Comparative validity of a multivariate and four univariate models. *Drug and Alcohol Dependence, 73,* 289–300.

Bucholz, K. K., Heath, A. C., Reich, T., Hesselbrock, V. M., Kramer, J. R., Nurnberger, J. I., Jr., et al. (1996). Can we subtype alcoholism? A latent class analysis of data from relatives of alcoholics in a multicenter family study of alcoholism. *Alcoholism: Clinical & Experimental Research, 20,* 1462–1471.

Cannon, T. D., & Keller, M. C. (2006). Endophenotypes in the genetic analyses of mental disorders. *Annual Review of Clinical Psychology, 2,* 267–290.

Caprioli, D., Celentano, M., Paolone, G., & Badiani, A. (2007). Modeling the role of environment in addiction. *Progress in Neuro-Psychopharmacology and Biological Psychiatry, 31,* 1639–1653.

Carpenter, K. M., Liu, X., & Hasin, D. S. (2006). The Type A–Type B classification in a community sample of problem drinkers: Structural and predictive validity. *Addictive Behaviors, 31,* 15–30.

Cicchetti, D. (1999). A developmental psychopathology perspective on drug abuse. In M. D. Glantz & C. R. Hartel (Eds.), *Drug abuse: Origins and interventions* (pp. 97–117). Washington, DC: American Psychological Association.

Cicchetti, D., & Aber, J. L. (1998). Contextualism and developmental psychopathology. *Development and Psychopathology, 10,* 137–141.

Cicchetti, D., & Rogosch, F. A. (1996). Equifinality and multifinality in developmental psychopathology. *Development and Psychopathology, 8,* 597–600.

Cicchetti, D., & Rogosch, F. A. (1999). Psychopathology as risk for adolescent substance use disorders: A developmental psychopathology perspective. *Journal of Clinical Child Psychology, 28,* 355–365.

Cloninger, C. R., Bohman, M., & Sigvardsson, S. (1981). Inheritance of alcohol abuse: Cross-fostering analysis of adopted men. *Archives of General Psychiatry, 38,* 861–868.

Cohen, A. (1984). The "urge to classify" the narcotic addict: A review of psychiatric classification: II. *International Journal of the Addictions, 19,* 335–353.

Epstein, E. E., Labouvie, E., McCrady, B. S., Jensen, N. K., & Hayaki, J. (2002). A multi-site study of alcohol subtypes: Classification and overlap of unidimensional and multi-dimensional typologies. *Addiction, 97,* 1041–1053.

Glantz, M. D. (1992). A developmental psychopathology model of drug abuse vulnerability. In M. D. Glantz & R. W. Pickens (Eds.), *Vulnerability to drug abuse* (pp. 389–418). Washington, DC: American Psychological Association.

Glantz, M. D., Anthony, J. C., Berglund, P. A., Degenhardt, L., Dierker, L., Kalaydjian, A., et al. (2008). Mental disorders as risk factors for later substance dependence: Estimates of optimal prevention and treatment benefits. *Psychological Medicine.* Advance online publication, doi:10.1017/50033291708004510

Glantz, M. D., & Colliver, J. D. (2002). Drug use, drug abuse, and heterogeneity. *Bulletin on Narcotics, 54,* 45–59.

Glantz, M. D., & Leshner, A. I. (2000). Drug abuse and developmental psychopathology. *Development and Psychopathology, 12,* 795–814.

Glantz, M. D., & Pickens, R. W. (1992). Vulnerability to drug abuse: Introduction and overview. In M. D. Glantz & R. W. Pickens (Eds.), *Vulnerability to drug abuse* (pp. 1–14). Washington, DC: American Psychological Association.

Glantz, M. D., & Sloboda, Z. (1999). Analysis and reconceptualization of resilience. In M. D. Glantz & J. L. Johnson (Eds.), *Resilience and development: Positive life adaptations* (pp. 109–126). New York: Kluwer Academic/Plenum Press.

Glantz, M. D., Weinberg, N. Z., Miner, L. L., & Colliver, J. D. (1999). The origins of drug abuse: Mapping the paths. In M. D. Glantz & C. R. Hartel (Eds.), *Drug abuse: Origins and interventions* (pp. 3–45). Washington, DC: American Psychological Association.

Gottesman, I. I., & Gould, T. D. (2003). The endophenotype concept in psychiatry: Etymology and strategic intentions. *American Journal of Psychiatry, 160,* 636–645.

Gottesman, I. I., & Hanson, D. R. (2005). Human development: Biological and genetic processes. *Annual Review of Psychology, 56,* 263–286.

Grant, B. F., & Dawson, D. A. (1997). Age at onset of alcohol use and its association with *DSM-IV* alcohol abuse and dependence: Results from the National Longitudinal Alcohol Epidemiologic Survey. *Journal of Substance Abuse, 9,* 103–10.

Hawkins, J. D., Catalano, R. F., & Miller, J. Y. (1992). Risk and protective factors for alcohol and other drug problems in adolescence and early adulthood: Implications for substance abuse prevention. *Psychological Bulletin, 112,* 64–105.

Hesselbrock, V. M., & Hesselbrock, M. N. (2006). Are there empirically supported and clinically useful subtypes of alcohol dependence? *Addiction, 101*(Suppl. 1), 97–103.

Institute of Medicine Committee on Opportunities in Drug Abuse Research. (1996). *Pathways of addiction: Opportunities in drug abuse research.* Washington, DC: National Academies Press.

Jessor, R., & Jessor, S. (1977). *Problem behavior and psychosocial development: A longitudinal study of youth.* New York: Academic Press.

Kagan, J., Snidman, N., McManis, M., Woodward, S., & Hardway, C. (2002). One measure, one meaning: Multiple measures, clearer meaning. *Development and Psychopathology, 14,* 463–475.

Kalivas, P. W., & O'Brien, C. (2008). Drug addiction as a pathology of staged neuroplasticity. *Neuropsychopharmacology, 33,* 166–180.

Kandel, D. B. (1975, November 28). Stages in adolescent involvement in drug use. *Science, 190,* 912–914.

Kandel, D., & Yamaguchi, K. (1999). Developmental stages of involvement in substance use. In P. Ott, R. Tarter, & R. Ammerman (Eds.), *Sourcebook on substance abuse: Etiology, epidemiology, assessment, and treatment* (pp. 50–74). Boston: Allyn & Bacon.

Kazdin, A. E., Kraemer, H. C., Kessler, R. C., Kupfer, D. J., & Offord, D. R. (1997). Contributions of risk-factor research to developmental psychopathology. *Clinical Psychology Review, 17,* 375–406.

Kendler, K., Jacobson, K., Gardner, C., Gillespie, N., Aggen, S., & Prescott, C. (2007). Creating a social world: A developmental twin study of peer-group deviance. *Archives of General Psychiatry, 64,* 958–965.

Kendler, K. S., Prescott, C. A., Myers, J., & Neale, M. C. (2003). The structure of genetic and environmental risk factors for common psychiatric and substance use disorders in men and women. *Archives of General Psychiatry, 60,* 929–937.

Kessler, R. C. (1995). Epidemiology of psychiatric comorbidity. In M. T. Tsuang, M. Tohen, & G. E. P. Zahner (Eds.), *Textbook in psychiatric epidemiology* (pp. 179–197). New York: Wiley-Liss.

King, K. M, & Chassin, K. (2007). A prospective study of the effects of age of initiation of alcohol and drug use on young adult substance dependence. *Journal of Studies on Alcohol and Drugs, 68,* 256–265.

Koob, G. (2006). The neurobiology of addiction: A neuro-adaptational view relevant for diagnosis. *Addiction, 101*(Suppl. 1), 23–30.

Koob, G. F., & Le Moal, M. (1997, October 3). Drug abuse: Hedonic homeostatic dysregulation. *Science, 278,* 52–58.

Kraemer, H. C., Kazdin, A. E., Offord, D. R., Kessler, R. C., Jensen, P. S., & Kupfer, D. J. (1997). Coming to terms with the terms of risk. *Archives of General Psychiatry, 54,* 337–343.

Kraemer, H. C., Stice, E., Kazdin, A., Offord, D., & Kupfer, D. (2001). How do risk factors work together? Mediators, moderators, and independent, overlapping, and proxy risk factors. *American Journal of Psychiatry, 158,* 848–856.

Krueger, R. F., & Markon, K. E. (2006). Reinterpreting comorbidity: A model-based approach to understanding and classifying psychopathology. *Annual Review of Clinical Psychology, 2,* 111–133.

Krueger, R. F., Markon, K. E., Patrick, C. J., Benning, S. D., & Kramer, M. D. (2007). Linking antisocial behavior, substance use, and personality: An integrative quantitative model of the adult externalizing spectrum. *Journal of Abnormal Psychology, 116,* 645–666.

Levison, P. K., Gerstein, D. R., & Maloff, D. R. (1983). *Commonalities in substance abuse and habitual behavior.* Lexington, MA: Lexington Books.

Loeber, R., Green, S. M., Lahey, B. B., Frick, P. J., & McBurnett, K. (2000). Findings on disruptive behavior disorders from the first decade of the Developmental Trends Study. *Clinical Child and Family Psychology Review, 3,* 37–60.

Loeber, R., & Keenan, K. (1994). Interaction between conduct disorder and its comorbid conditions: Effects of age and gender. *Clinical Psychology Review, 14,* 497–523.

Meehl, P. E. (1962). Schizotaxia, schizotypy, schizophrenia. *American Psychologist, 17,* 827–838.

Meehl, P. E. (1990). Toward an integrated theory of schizotaxia, schizotypy, and schizophrenia. *Journal of Personality Disorders, 4,* 1–99.

Moffit, T. E. (1993). Adolescence-limited and lifecourse-persistent antisocial behavior: A developmental taxonomy. *Psychological Review, 100,* 674–701.

Moffit, T. E., Caspi, A., Harrington, H., & Milne, B. J. (2002). Males on the life-course-persistent and adolescence-limited antisocial pathways: Follow-up at age 26 years. *Development and Psychopathology, 14,* 179–207.

Moss, H. B., Chen, C. M., & Yi, H. (2007). Subtypes of alcohol dependence in a nationally representative sample. *Drug and Alcohol Dependence, 91,* 149–158.

Nestler, E. J. (2005). Is there a common molecular pathway for addiction? *Nature Neuroscience, 8,* 1445–1449.

Penick, E. C., Nickel, E. J., Powell, B. J., Liskow, B. I., Campbell, J., Dale, T. M., et al. (1999). The comparative validity of eleven alcoholism typologies. *Journal of Studies on Alcohol, 60,* 188–202.

Petraitis, J., Flay, B. R., & Miller, T. Q. (1995). Theories of adolescent substance use: Organizing pieces in the puzzle. *Psychological Bulletin, 117,* 67–86.

Robins, L. N. (1966). *Deviant children grow up: A sociological and psychiatric study of sociopathic personality.* Baltimore: Williams & Wilkins.

Robinson, T. E., & Berridge, K. C. (2003). Addiction. *Annual Review of Psychology, 54,* 25–53.

Rutter, M. (1996). Developmental psychopathology: Concepts and prospects. In M. Lenzenseqer & J. Havguard (Eds.), *Frontiers of developmental psychopathology* (pp. 209–237). New York: Oxford University Press.

Rutter, M., Moffitt, T. E., & Caspi, A. (2006). Gene-environment interplay and psychopathology: Multiple varieties but real effects. *Journal of Child Psychology and Psychiatry, 47,* 226–261.

Sarr, M., Bucholz, K. K., & Phelps, D. L. (2000). Using cluster analysis of alcohol use disorders to investigate "diagnostic orphans": Subjects with alcohol dependence symptoms but no diagnosis. *Drug and Alcohol Dependence, 60,* 295–302.

Sher, K. J. (1991). *Children of alcoholics: A critical appraisal of theory and research.* Chicago: University of Chicago Press.

Sher, K. J. (1994). Individual-level risk factors. In R. A. Zucker, G. Boyd, & J. Howard (Eds.), *The development of alcohol problems: Exploring the biopsychosocial matrix of risk* (NIAAA Research Monograph 26, NIH Publication No. 94-3495, pp. 77–108).

Rockville, MD: U.S. Department of Health and Human Services.

Sher, K. J., Gotham, H. J., & Watson, A. L. (2004). Trajectories of dynamic predictors of disorder: Their meanings and implications. *Development and Psychopathology, 16,* 825–856.

Sher, K. J., Grekin, E. R., & Williams, N. A. (2005). The development of alcohol use disorders. *Annual Review of Clinical Psychology, 1,* 493–523.

Tarter, R. E. (2002). Etiology of adolescent substance abuse: A developmental perspective. *American Journal on Addictions, 11,* 171–191.

Tarter, R. E., Kirisci, L., Habeych, M., Reynolds, M., & Vanyukov, M. (2004). Neurobehavior disinhibition in childhood predisposes boys to substance use disorder by young adulthood: Direct and mediated etiologic pathways. *Drug and Alcohol Dependence, 73,* 121–132.

Tarter, R., & Vanyukov, M. (1994a). Alcoholism: A developmental disorder. *Journal of Consulting and Clinical Psychology, 62,* 1096–1107.

Tarter, R. E., & Vanyukov, M. M. (1994b). Stepwise developmental model of alcoholism etiology. In R. A. Zucker, G. Boyd, & J. Howard (Eds.), *The development of alcohol problems: Exploring the biopsychosocial matrix of risk* (NIAAA Research Monograph 26, NIH Publication No. 94-3495, pp 303–330). Rockville, MD: U.S. Department of Health and Human Services.

Vanyukov, M., Tarter, R. E., Kirisci, L., Kirillova, G., Maher, B., & Clark, D. B. (2003). Liability to substance use disorders: 1. Common mechanisms and manifestations. *Neuroscience & Biobehavioral Reviews, 27,* 507–515.

Vezina, P. (2007). Sensitization, drug addiction and psychopathology in animals and humans. *Progress in Neuro-Psychopharmacology and Biological Psychiatry, 31,* 1553–1555.

Willoughby, T., Chalmers, H., & Busseri, M. A. (2004). Where is the syndrome? Examining co-occurrence among multiple problem behaviors in adolescence.

Journal of Consulting and Clinical Psychology, 72, 1022–1037.

Wills, T. A., Ainette, M. G., Mendoza, D., Gibbons, F. X., & Brody, G. H. (2007). Self-control, symptomatology, and substance use precursors: Test of a theoretical model in a community sample of 9-year-old children. *Psychology of Addictive Behaviors, 21,* 205–215.

Wills, T. A., & Dishion, T. J. (2004). Temperament and adolescent substance use: A transactional analysis of emerging self-control. *Journal of Clinical Child and Adolescent Psychology, 33,* 69–81.

World Health Organization. (2007). *International classification of diseases and related health problems* (10th ed.). Geneva, Switzerland: Author.

Zucker, R. A. (1987). The four alcoholisms: A developmental account of the etiologic process. In R. A. Dienstbier & P. C. Rivers (Ed.), *Nebraska Symposium on Motivation: Vol. 34. Alcohol and addictive behaviors* (pp. 27-83). Lincoln: University of Nebraska Press.

Zucker, R. A. (1994). Pathways to alcohol problems and alcoholism: A developmental account of the evidence for multiple alcoholisms and contextual contributions to risk. In R. A. Zucker, G. Boyd, & J. Howard (Eds.), *The development of alcohol problems: Exploring the biopsychosocial matrix of risk* (NIAAA Research Monograph 26, NIH Publication No. 94-3495, pp. 255–289). Rockville, MD: U.S. Department of Health and Human Services.

Zucker, R. A., Fitzgerald, H. E., & Moses, H. D. (1995). Emergence of alcohol problems and the several alcoholisms: A developmental perspective on etiologic theory and life course trajectory. In D. Cicchetti & D. J. Cohen (Eds.), *Developmental psychopathology: Vol. 2. Risk, disorder, and adaptation* (pp. 677–711). New York: Wiley.

Zucker, R. A., & Ichiyama, M. A. (1996). Self-regulation theory: A model of etiology or a route into changing troubled human behavior? *Psychological Inquiry, 7,* 85–89.

PART II

EPIDEMIOLOGY AND THEORY

THE EPIDEMIOLOGY OF SUBSTANCE USE AMONG ADOLESCENTS AND YOUNG ADULTS: A DEVELOPMENTAL PERSPECTIVE

Kenneth W. Griffin

There is a large body of published research on the etiology of substance use, and much of it has focused on young people. The years of adolescence and young adulthood are times of great developmental change involving biological, psychological, interpersonal, occupational, and social role transitions. A broad range of new goals, developmental tasks, and life-span milestones occur during these years, from the biological and physical changes of puberty to the adoption of adult roles such as spouse, partner, or parent. Epidemiologic research has shown that there are dramatic changes in substance use behavior that correspond to these years of developmental change. However, understanding changing patterns of substance use in the context of rapid personal, emotional, and social development is a formidable task for a number of reasons. The etiologic risk and protective factors for substance use among youth are numerous and diverse and include personality characteristics; social influences from family, peers, and community; and genetic and neurobiological factors, to name a few of the many that are addressed as part of this handbook. Furthermore, a large number of developmental pathways and lifestyle choices are available to young people, particularly compared with previous generations. An increasing number of young people delay living independently from parents and postpone marriage and parenthood into later years. Likewise, young adults may delay entering a permanent profession while exploring multiple career options, or they may choose to extend their education beyond college to prepare for a particular career. Thus, the transition to adulthood, or attaining traditional social indicators of adulthood, can sometimes stretch into the late 20s and beyond. Another factor that complicates researchers' understanding of developmental phenomena and substance use is their limited ability to infer causation from observational survey research, even when cohorts of the same youth are followed into adulthood. Even with high-quality data, there are potential problems in interpreting the meaning of significant associations. It may be impossible to distinguish between situations in which new social environments influence substance use behavior (i.e., socialization processes), those in which individuals select particular social environments so they can continue or escalate use (i.e., selection processes), or both. Despite these challenges, it is important to build the knowledge base about the links between development and substance use. Scientific findings can help identify key periods of risk for developing potentially lifelong patterns of substance use and abuse, as well as discrete, specific events and milestones associated with an elevated risk of substance use (e.g., 21st-birthday celebrations, college spring break, divorce). This knowledge can in turn provide researchers, clinicians, and policymakers with insights on ways to improve prevention and treatment efforts.

Preparation of this chapter was supported in part by National Institute on Drug Abuse Grant DA023890.

DEVELOPMENTAL CHANGES IN ADOLESCENCE AND YOUNG ADULTHOOD

Adolescence and young adulthood are marked by changes in many areas of a young person's life. Along with the rapid biological and physical changes of puberty, there are important developments in social, emotional, and cognitive functioning (Keating, 1990; Steinberg & Morris, 2001). Puberty, a hallmark feature of adolescence, is characterized by change in physical appearance, greater hormonal activity, development of secondary sex characteristics, and maturation of areas of the brain responsible for advanced reasoning skills (i.e., the prefrontal cortex). Adolescents develop greater capacities for moral reasoning, perspective taking, and problem solving, and there are important new developmental goals involving identity formation and individuation. Interpersonal changes involve a desire for greater autonomy from parents, an increase in the importance of peers, an emphasis on feelings of sexual attraction, and a heightened awareness of gender roles. Concurrent with puberty, new social roles may emerge in the context of school (e.g., athlete, scholar), employment (e.g., first part-time job outside the home), and social activities such as dating. In young adulthood, social role transitions continue in the contexts of occupation and career, close relationships, living arrangements, and family. On their entry into young adulthood, many people experience a variety of new freedoms, including living independently from parents, along with new responsibilities that come with the adoption of new roles such as college student, full-time employee, spouse, partner, or parent. Throughout the entire period of adolescence and young adulthood, there are new expectations, obligations, and social networks.

CHANGES IN SUBSTANCE USE IN ADOLESCENCE AND YOUNG ADULTHOOD

Patterns of substance use change rapidly during adolescence and young adulthood. Experimentation with substance use often begins during the early years of adolescence, typically in the context of one's peer group with substances that are readily available (e.g., cigarettes, alcohol, inhalants). Prevalence rates often escalate over the course of adolescence, and some youth experiment with new drugs such as marijuana, hallucinogens, cocaine, and the nonmedical use of prescription drugs. Substance use typically reaches a peak during late adolescence and early adulthood, and for most people it begins to decline in the mid- to late 20s, with a more rapid decline occurring in the later years of adulthood.

GOALS OF THE CHAPTER

The goals of this chapter are to review the epidemiology of alcohol, tobacco, marijuana, and other illicit drug use among young people residing in the United States and to review recent research linking patterns of substance use with the developmental transitions and milestones highlighted above. An overarching goal of the chapter is to organize and present findings so they may inform prevention efforts. Therefore, the focus is (a) the general population (subsequent chapters of the handbook address specific racial and ethnic subgroups); (b) substance use rather than abuse because from a population perspective, the risk and protective factors for use are more strongly related to normative developmental changes (whereas factors leading to abuse often include high levels of antisocial behavior or personality disorder, behavioral disinhibition, and affect dysregulation; Glantz, Conway, & Colliver, 2005); and (c) current use (monthly) or recent use (annual) more so than daily or lifetime use. I first describe the epidemiology of substance abuse as a function of age and then summarize recent research examining developmental phenomena and substance use.

EPIDEMIOLOGY OF SUBSTANCE USE ACROSS THE LIFE SPAN

In the United States, there are two major sources of epidemiologic data on substance use among adolescents and adults, and both are highlighted in this chapter. The first is the National Survey on Drug Use and Health (NSDUH), sponsored by the Substance Abuse and Mental Health Services Administration (SAMHSA; 2008b). The second is the Monitoring the Future (MTF) study (Johnston, O'Malley, Bachman, & Schulenberg, 2008a, 2008b), sponsored by the

National Institute on Drug Abuse (NIDA). Each provides slightly different pieces of information, covers unique facets of the U.S. population, and implements a slightly different sampling frame, among other distinctions. These are discussed next with respect to the strengths and limitations of each survey approach.

National Survey on Drug Use and Health

The NSDUH, formerly called the National Household Survey on Drug Use, monitors the nature and extent of substance use among those ages 12 and older in the United States. Initiated in 1971, NSDUH is currently conducted on an annual basis, and its primary objectives are to collect data on the magnitude and patterns of alcohol, tobacco, and illegal substance use and abuse; assess the consequences of substance use and abuse; and identify groups of the population at high risk of substance use and abuse. Each year, NSDUH collects data from about 70,000 participants who are randomly drawn from the civilian, noninstitutionalized population of the United States. In addition to collecting data from households, survey data are obtained from individuals residing in dormitories or shelters and from civilians on military bases, but the study excludes people residing in institutions such as prisons or hospitals. In addition to substance use and problems associated with use, NSDUH collects information on perceptions of risk and drug availability, mental health, criminal behavior, and drug treatment. Since 1991, NSDUH has collected data on the most sensitive behaviors, such as drug use, using audio computer-assisted self-interviewing techniques. Additional methodological improvements to the study were implemented in 2002; however, these changes prevent the comparison of recent data to surveys instituted before 2002. Furthermore, a limitation of NSDUH is that it does not track individuals longitudinally, so it is less informative for drawing conclusions about underlying developmental phenomena occurring over time. Nevertheless, NSDUH is helpful in comparing substance use rates among different age groups at a single point in time; thus, it is best used to characterize a snapshot of substance use in the U.S. population.

In the 2007 NSDUH survey data (SAMHSA, 2008b), 23% of Americans age 12 or older reported binge drinking (defined as five or more drinks on the same occasion) in the past month; 7% reported heavy binge drinking (five or more episodes of binge drinking in the past month); 8% reported current (past month) use of an illicit drug; 6% reported current marijuana use, and 29% reported current cigarette smoking. There were substantial differences in each of these behaviors according to the age category of respondents. Figure 4.1 shows current (past month) prevalence rates for cigarette smoking, binge drinking, and use of any illicit drug among NSDUH respondents in the 2007 survey according to age category, ranging from 12 to 13 through 65-plus years of age. Cigarette smoking and binge drinking in the past month both increase rapidly for age categories from 12 to 13 to 21 to 25, where binge drinking peaks at 46% and cigarette smoking peaks at 39%. Use of these substances follows a similar pattern among those in their late 20s through mid-40s, and then both decrease rapidly for older age categories, although rates of current cigarette smoking remain higher than current binge drinking for all categories after age 45. Rates of past-month illicit drug use also increase rapidly in the teenage years, peaking at 22% among those ages 18 to 20. For older age categories, there is a steady decline in prevalence rates of current illicit drug use. Figure 4.1 demonstrates clearly that beginning with respondents in their 20s, the use of legal substances (cigarette smoking and binge drinking) is much more common than the use of illicit substances, and this difference becomes even more pronounced among older age categories. For example, there are three to four times as many current cigarette smokers and current binge drinkers than current illicit drug users from the late 20s through the late 50s, and this differential doubles after age 60.

Monitoring the Future Study

The MTF study is an ongoing study of substance use among secondary school students, college students, and young adults in the United States (Johnston et al., 2008a, 2008b). The MTF study began in 1975 (it was then named the Youth in Transition Study), and data were initially collected only from 12th graders; the study was then expanded in 1991 to include 8th and 10th graders. Each year, a large nationally representative sample consisting of approximately 50,000 8th-, 10th-, and 12th-grade students completes a

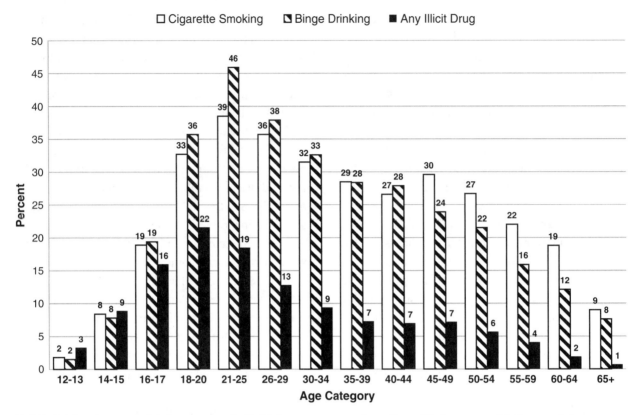

FIGURE 4.1.   Past month substance use in 2007, by age category from 12 to 65-plus years old. Source: Substance Abuse and Mental Health Services Administration (2008b).

self-administered, machine-readable questionnaire in their regular classrooms. In addition to substance use, MTF collects information on attitudes and beliefs about drug use (e.g., perceived harmfulness, personal disapproval, perceived availability of drugs) and perceptions of friends' drug attitudes and behaviors. Since 1976, follow-up questionnaires have been mailed to a sample of each graduating class of high school seniors for a number of years after their initial participation. College students and young adults participating in the follow-up study are mailed surveys every other year until age 30, with additional assessments conducted every 5 subsequent years (e.g., 35, 40, and 45, as of the last data collection). Because the young adult component of the MTF study tracks the same participants over time, it is an excellent resource for understanding historical effects, or changes in population levels of drug use over time reflected across age groups; age effects, or developmental changes in drug use that show up consistently for each cohort when they reach a particular age (e.g.,

reaching legal drinking age); and cohort effects, or patterns of use among all those individuals who are seniors in high school in a given year. A limitation of the MTF young adult data is that they exclude people who do not graduate from high school. However, a NIDA technical review panel concluded that the failure to include dropouts (and absentees) does not substantially affect the estimates of drug use prevalence or incidence (Clayton & Voss, 1982).

Figure 4.2 shows trends over the past several decades in an illicit drug use index (past year use of marijuana, hallucinogens, cocaine, heroin, or nonmedical use of opiates, stimulants, sedatives, or tranquilizers) among several populations assessed in the MTF study. Historical effects of the illicit drug epidemic among high school seniors and college students can be seen in the late 1970s and early 1980s, when more than half of respondents reported illicit drug use in the past year. This represented a peak level of use for both groups over the past 30 years. Prevalence rates decreased steadily through the 1980s

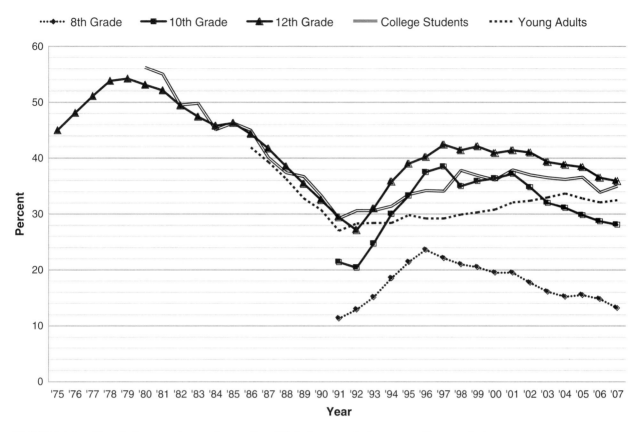

FIGURE 4.2.   Trends in annual prevalence of an illicit drug use index across five populations.
Source: Johnston et al. (2008a, 2008b).

until the early 1990s for high school seniors, college students, and young adults, such that fewer than 1 in 3 participants in these groups reported past-year illicit drug use in 1990. However, soon after the MTF study began collecting data from 8th and 10th graders in the early 1990s, there was a dramatic increase in the illicit drug use index for the next several years, lasting from the early to mid-1990s, particularly among participants in the three secondary school grades. Among college students and young adults, the annual prevalence of use of any illicit drug held relatively stable over this period, as adolescent use rose substantially; among 8th graders, rates doubled over this time period, and rates almost doubled among 10th graders. Some cohort effects can be observed in Figure 4.2, such that the increase first observed among 8th graders from 1991 to 1992 can be seen in subsequent years in the later grades as this cohort got older. In fact, the peak in annual prevalence rates of any illicit drug use was 1996 for 8th graders (24%), 1997 for 10th (39%) and 12th graders (42%), 2001

for college students (38%), and 2004 for young adults (34%). Most recently, on the basis of MTF indicators annual prevalence rates of any illicit drug use have been declining since 2002 across all three grade levels, while holding more or less steady for college students and young adults. In 2007, this rate was 13% for 8th graders, 28% for 10th graders, 36% for 12th graders, 35% for college students, and 33% for young adults (Johnston et al., 2008a, 2008b).

Other Sources of Epidemiological Data

In addition to the NSDUH and MTF studies, several other ongoing national surveys collect substance use data (described in SAMHSA, 2008b, Appendix D). These include the Behavioral Risk Factor Surveillance System and the Youth Risk Behavior Survey, both sponsored by the Centers for Disease Control and Prevention, and the National Health Interview Study, sponsored by the National Center for Health Statistics. By and large, despite slightly different sampling plans across MTF, NSDUH, and each of these supplementary national data sources, prevalence rates for most drugs remain fairly consistent, and each of these surveys can be used independently as a gauge of the severity of the drug use problem in the United States. In addition to these national data sets, there are an increasing number of longitudinal cohort studies that have examined substance use among adolescents and young adults followed over substantial periods of time (Wills, Walker, & Resko, 2005).

ALCOHOL, TOBACCO, AND ILLICIT DRUG USE AMONG ADOLESCENTS AND YOUNG ADULTS

Alcohol, tobacco, and marijuana are the most commonly used substances among adolescents and adults in the United States. Data from NSDUH are shown in Figure 4.3 for current (past month) alcohol, tobacco, and marijuana use, providing an overview of current use among adolescents and young adults by age category starting at age 12 and ending at age 34. Use of

any alcohol rises dramatically from respondents ages 12 to 13 (4%) to those ages 21 to 25 (68%), then gradually falls off but remains above 60% through the last age category shown, ages 30 to 34. Cigarette smoking and marijuana use show a similar pattern of rising and falling across the same age categories; marijuana use increases dramatically from respondents ages 12 to 13 (1%) through ages 18 to 20, where rates peak at 18%, and then gradually decline as well.

Figures 4.4 and 4.5 show a slightly different perspective by combining data from several cohorts of MTF participants tracked over time. As shown in Figure 4.4, the MTF study reveals rates of past-month marijuana use that peak at 19% for 18-year-olds and decrease to 18% for 19- to 20-year-olds, which is comparable to the NSDUH estimate of 19% for 18- to 20-year-olds. After age 20, current marijuana use decreases in both MTF and NSDUH for higher age groups. In MTF data, the peak in past-year marijuana use is clearly visible among 19- to 20-year-olds at 33%, after which rates decrease through the 20s (ending at 18% among 29- to 30-year-olds). As would be

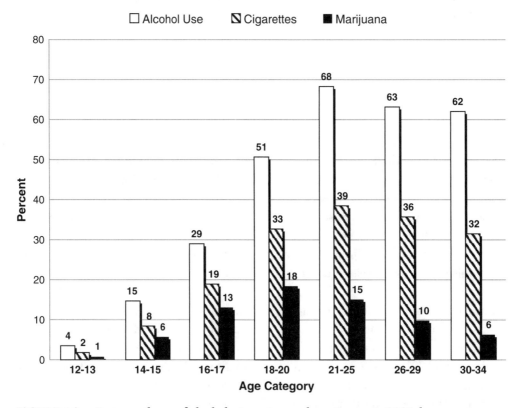

FIGURE 4.3. Past month use of alcohol, cigarettes, and marijuana, in 2007, by age category from 12 to 34 years old. Source: Substance Abuse and Mental Health Services Administration (2008b).

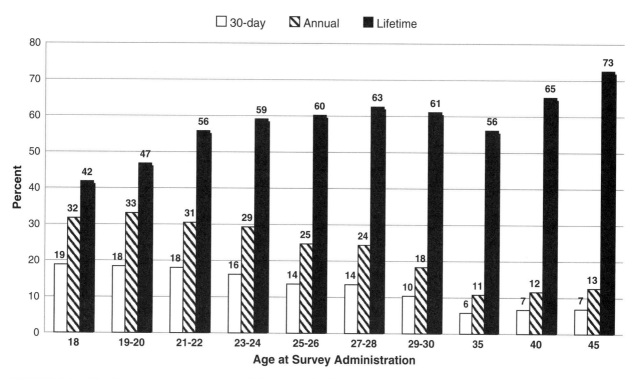

FIGURE 4.4. Marijuana use among young adults, ages 18–45. Source: Johnston et al. (2008a, 2008b).

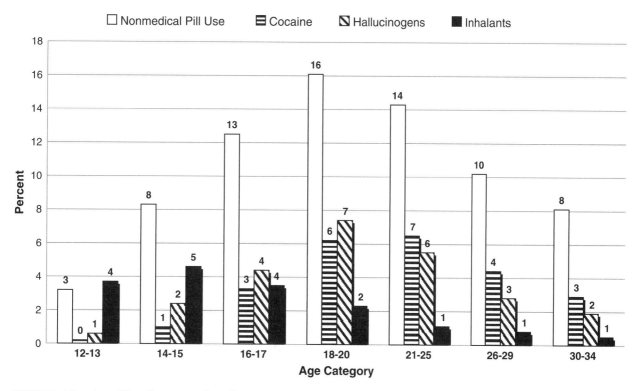

FIGURE 4.5. Any illicit drug use other than marijuana among young adults, ages 18–45.
Source: Johnston et al. (2008a, 2008b).

expected when cohorts of participants are followed over time, rates for lifetime marijuana use generally increase for subsequent age categories in the MTF data. By ages 21 to 22, more than half (56%) of MTF participants report ever having used marijuana. This rate increases to almost 2 in 3 in the mid- to late 20s and to almost 3 in 4 (73%) among 45-year-olds. The latter figure of 73% for lifetime marijuana use among 45-year-olds represents the cohort of individuals who were high school seniors at the height of the drug use epidemic that peaked in the late 1970s and early 1980s. One would therefore expect that lifetime rates for marijuana use among new cohorts of 45-year-olds will decrease in future years.

Marijuana is by far the most commonly used illicit drug among adolescents and adults in the United States. However, there are several other categories of illicit drugs that are prevalent among young people. Figure 4.6 shows annual use of several types of illicit drugs from 2007 NSDUH participants according to age category from 12 to 13 up to 30 to 34 years. Non-medical pill use, defined in the NSDUH as the abuse of prescription psychotherapeutics or prescription stimulants, is the second most prevalent type of illicit drug use after marijuana. In NSDUH, annual rates of nonmedical pill use peak at ages 18 to 20 (16%) and fall steadily throughout the young adult years, with half the prevalence rate (8%) reported by respondents who are ages 30 to 34. At the beginning of adolescence, inhalant use is similar in prevalence among 12- to 13-year olds as nonmedical pill use (4% and 3%, respectively). After peaking among 14- to 15-year-olds at 5%, past-year inhalant use falls dramatically among older age groups, suggesting that the early use of inhalants is because of their easy availability. Annual use rates of hallucinogens and cocaine from NSDUH are shown in Figure 4.6 and are roughly similar to each other across different age groups. There are a few notable differences, however. Hallucinogen use is slightly more common than cocaine use up to ages 18 to 20 (where rates are 7% and 6%, respectively), but hallucinogen use falls behind cocaine in subsequent age groups, beginning with the 21 to 25 age category. Although cocaine is the least prevalent of the four types of illicit drugs shown in Figure 4.6 through ages 16 to 17, cocaine

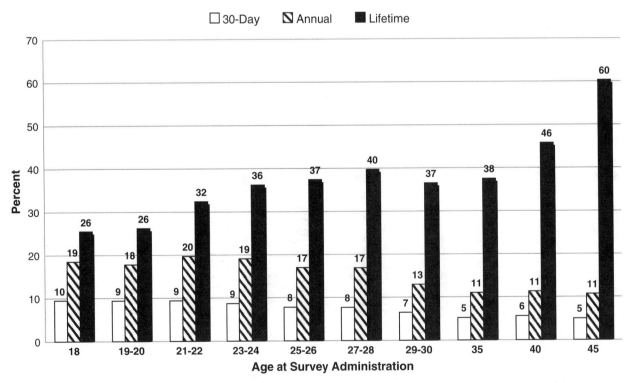

FIGURE 4.6.   Annual use of specific illicit drugs other than marijuana, in 2007, by age category from 12 to 34 years old. Source: Substance Abuse and Mental Health Services Administration (2008b).

use peaks among 21- to 25-year-olds at 7% and is the second most prevalent (after nonmedical pill use) of the four types in older age categories.

A recent NSDUH report showed that misuse of over-the-counter medications is a growing problem among young people (SAMHSA, 2008a). Approximately 5% of people ages 12 to 25 reported ever using an over-the-counter cough and cold medication to get high, and nearly 2% had done so in the past year. The active ingredient in many cough suppressants, dextromethorphan, is found in more than 140 over-the-counter cough and cold medications. Dextromethorphan is generally safe when taken as recommended but can, when taken in large doses, produce hallucinations or dissociative, "out-of-body" experiences similar to those caused by certain hallucinogens (e.g., phencyclidine, ketamine). Among those ages 12 to 17, girls were more likely than boys to have misused over-the-counter cough and cold medications in the past year, but among those ages 18 to 25, men were more likely than women to have misused these medications.

Fortunately, there has been a gradual year-to-year decline in the use of a number of substances, including heroin, cocaine, and amphetamines, among secondary school students over the past several years. Fewer than half (47%) of high school seniors in the 2007 MTF study reported using any illicit drug in their lifetime, down from about 55% in 1999. Figure 4.5 shows prevalence rates of illicit drug use other than marijuana for MTF participants between the ages of 18 and 45. As in Figure 4.4, these data represent average prevalence rates assessed in several cohorts of MTF participants tracked over time. Rates of current use of an illicit drug other than marijuana hover around 9% to 10% for 18- to 20-year-olds and decline with age to slightly more than half of these peak rates, to 5% to 6% among 35-, 40-, and 45-year-olds. Annual rates of illicit drug use other than marijuana decline from a peak of 20% among 21- to 22-year-olds down to 11% of 35-, 40-, and 45-year-olds. Rates for lifetime illicit drug use other than marijuana increase for subsequent age categories in the MTF data from 26% of 18- to 20-year-olds to 60% of 45-year-olds. As in Figure 4.4, the lifetime rate for 45-year-olds represents the cohort of students who were high school seniors at the height of the drug epi-

demic in the United States; thus, these rates should decrease in future cohorts of 45-year-olds.

SUBSTANCE USE CONCEPTUALIZED IN A DEVELOPMENTAL FRAMEWORK

It is clear that no pattern of substance use initiation, escalation, stabilization, and decline can describe the experience of all users. Indeed, at the individual level there is great diversity in patterns of substance use initiation and escalation. However, as shown in the NSDUH, MTF, and other national data sets, there is a clear and consistent pattern of substance use during adolescence and young adulthood that from a population perspective describes the experiences of many people. This general pattern includes initiation of experimental use during early adolescence, a rapid increase in use during adolescence, a peak in consumption during young adulthood, and a more or less gradual decline through the remainder of adulthood. This pattern of use is shaped in part by a series of transitions, goals, and milestones that occur during these years of rapid developmental change. There has been an abundance of research in recent years on the escalation of substance use during adolescence and the characteristic decline in use observed during early adulthood. Next, I review findings on substance use patterns in the context of developmental goals and key normative transitions for different age groups, such as pubertal timing, school transitions, and, later, role transitions in young adulthood (e.g., college student, spouse, parent).

Onset in Early Adolescence

The ongoing developmental processes in early adolescence, such as identity formation, increased autonomy from parents, and increased importance of peer group relations, are typically extended in time and occur over a number of years. In early adolescence, young people begin to strive for self-definition and independence. They increasingly begin to make independent decisions about their own behaviors in a variety of domains including substance use. They make these decisions at a time when they are highly susceptible to societal messages, media portrayals, adult role models, and peer influences that may promote substance use as a way to appear mature, rebellious, or independent. As they explore new roles and negotiate various developmental challenges, some young people will be more successful than others. Those who are less successful in conventional pursuits such as academics and sports may initiate or escalate substance use and other problem behaviors. From the perspective of the adolescent, substance use may help define oneself as rebellious, bond with deviant or like-minded peers, and attract attention from parents and other adults, thus potentially serving a number of important developmental functions. Two discrete transitions that occur in adolescence, pubertal timing and school transitions, have received significant research attention in terms of their relationship to substance use.

Pubertal timing.   Much has been written about the importance of puberty and pubertal timing in adolescent development (e.g., Brooks-Gunn, 1989; Brooks-Gunn & Reiter, 1990). There have been a number of studies examining the relationship between pubertal timing and problem behaviors. Girls typically enter puberty before boys, so much of the research has focused on early-maturing girls. Reaching puberty before one's peers appears to be associated not only with substance use, but with a number of emotional and behavioral problems (Kaltiala-Heino, Marttunen, Rantanen, & Rimpela, 2003), particularly among girls (Graber, Lewinsohn, Seely, & Brooks-Gunn, 1997; Stice, Presnell, & Bearman, 2001). A number of mechanisms linking early pubertal timing and problem behavior have been proposed, including the possibility that early-maturing teenagers (a) experience peer rejection, distress, low self-esteem, or other adjustment problems because their bodies are changing at a time when their peers' are not yet doing so; (b) are monitored less carefully by parents given their more mature physical appearance; and (c) are more likely to seek out (or be sought out by) older peers (and for girls, older boyfriends) who exert pressure to engage in "more adult" behavior like drug use and sexual activity. Several studies on pubertal timing and substance use among girls have shown that early-maturing girls become involved in greater levels of substance use and often escalate at a faster rate than their peers (Dick, Rose, Viken, & Kaprio, 2000; Lanza &

Collins, 2002; Stattin & Magnusson, 1990; Wilson et al., 1994). Although it has been hypothesized that late-maturing boys may be at elevated risk for substance use as a result of heightened emotional distress from being different from their peers, there has not been consistent empirical support for this hypothesis. In fact, studies have found that early-maturing girls and boys report more substance use over time compared with their peers (Costello, Sung, Worthman, & Angold, 2007) and that these effects persist after controlling for psychological distress (Tschann et al., 1994; Wiesner & Ittel, 2002). Additional evidence has suggested that the effects of early maturation on smoking onset and long-term alcohol use are stronger for men than for women (Biehl, Natsuaki, & Ge, 2007; Wiesner & Ittel, 2002). Recent findings have shown that early pubertal maturation was associated with alcohol use among girls and boys who had low parental monitoring (Westling, Andrews, Hampson, & Peterson, 2008). This study also found that for girls, but not for boys, the link between early pubertal timing and substance use was mediated by greater affiliation with deviant peers. In summary, early-maturing boys and girls should be regarded as being at elevated risk for substance use.

School transitions.   The transitions into middle school and, to a lesser extent, high school have been identified as important turning points where young people face new social, personal, and academic challenges (Barone, Aguirre-Deandreis, & Trickett, 1991; Blyth, Simmons, & Carlton-Ford, 1983). During these transitions, many youth appear to experience difficulty adjusting to the change when moving from a smaller, nurturing school environment to a larger, more demanding, and challenging one (Eccles & Midgley, 1991). In addition, in terms of the social "pecking order," students entering a new school environment usually occupy a lower rung on the social influence ladder compared with older youth in higher grades. During school transitions, students report anxieties about navigating or getting lost in the larger school environment, becoming familiar with new policies and procedures, adjusting to the presence of older students and the possibility of being bullied, and feeling increased pressure to perform well academically (Cotterell, 1992; Zeedyk et al., 2003). Research has found that school transitions are often accompanied by decreases in GPAs, modest downturns in school attendance, less involvement in extracurricular activities, declines in school bonding, and increased psychological distress and other psychosocial adjustment problems (Barone et al., 1991; Chung, Elias, & Schneider, 1998; Crockett, Petersen, Graber, Schulenberg, & Ebata, 1989; Isakson & Jarvis, 1999).

Given the linkages between school transitions and negative academic and psychosocial outcomes, one might expect school transitions to be associated with an increase in substance use. Indeed, interventions to prepare elementary school students for the transition to secondary school have been conceptualized as smoking prevention programs (e.g., Côté, Godin, & Gagné, 2006). However, there is remarkably little evidence to support the hypothesis that school transitions increase substance use. In fact, studies have shown that school transitions are not universally as detrimental as they might appear. For example, one study found that the transition to junior high school was associated with an intensification of supportive relationships with school friends and had no negative impact on social relationships (Cantin & Boivin, 2004). Other research has compared the transition from eighth to ninth grades among a group of students who changed schools and a group that did not change schools (Weiss & Bearman, 2007), a specific naturalistic design feature that few similar studies have incorporated. Findings indicated that several academic and nonacademic outcomes (including substance use) got significantly worse but did so equally among both groups. This suggests that certain transitional years of adolescence are associated with decreases in psychosocial adjustment and that this may be independent of school transitions. The study found that for some youth, such as those in socially difficult situations before the transition, a change in schools can in fact be beneficial by providing a fresh start. Taken together, the evidence for a relationship between school transitions and substance use is weak. Like many of the topics reviewed in this chapter, it is difficult to conduct a definitive study on the issue

because direct experimental manipulation (i.e., a randomized, controlled trial) is impractical; thus, we must rely on observational studies that can be compromised by a variety of potential confounds, both measured and unmeasured.

Progression of Drug Use During Adolescence

Among those who initiate substance use during early adolescence, experimentation with alcohol, tobacco, or inhalants may be followed by regular use for a proportion of youth who try these substances. Some will progress from these substances to the use of marijuana and other classes of illicit drugs. Seminal work by Kandel (1975) and others (Hamburg, Kraemer, & Jahnke, 1975) has advanced the notion that there are developmental stages of substance use involvement among adolescents. This work showed that a typical sequencing of substances characterizes how most adolescent substance users progress from experimentation with legal substances (beer or wine, cigarettes, and hard liquor) to regular use of illicit drugs, beginning with marijuana. In one of the first studies examining stages of adolescent drug use, Kandel followed high school students for 6 months and reported that 27% of those who smoked cigarettes and drank alcohol progressed to marijuana use over the course of the study, compared with only 2% who used marijuana without first using cigarettes or alcohol. Similarly, 26% of marijuana users progressed to other classes of illicit drug use compared with only 4% who had only tried legal substances. This general pattern of developmental stages in the progression of adolescent drug use has been demonstrated in many studies over the years (reviewed in Kandel, 2002) and has been referred to as "one of the best replicated findings in the epidemiology of drug use" (Kandel, 2003, p. 482).

Gateway theory of drug use progression. The stage, or "gateway," theory of drug use progression has been of central importance to our understanding of drug use etiology and prevention; it has even been popularized in American culture and invoked in the development of public policy. However, the gateway theory remains controversial because of questions about causality and prognostic utility. If marijuana acts as gateway to the use of cocaine, heroin, and other illicit drugs, the implicit assumption is that marijuana "causes" the use of these other classes of illicit drugs. Researchers continue to interpret their findings through a causal lens. On one hand, Fergusson, Boden, and Horwood (2006) found that regular or heavy cannabis use acts as a gateway to other classes of illicit drug use, that the relationship is strongest during adolescence, and that it weakens with increasing age. In this study, the authors stated that their findings "are consistent with the conclusion that there is a cause and effect association between the use of cannabis and the use or misuse of other illicit drugs" (p. 564). However, they noted that the actual causal mechanisms and the extent to which they are direct or indirect remain unclear. On the other hand, other researchers have found that the drug use sequence predicted by the gateway hypothesis (i.e., use of legal substances followed by marijuana and then other illicit drugs) is highly variable and has poor prognostic utility regarding later drug use disorders (Tarter, Vanyukov, Kirisci, Reynolds, & Clark, 2006). Tarter et al. (2006) concluded that "evidence supporting... the gateway hypothesis was not obtained" (p. 2139).

Clearly, what begins as the experimental use of alcohol and tobacco in social situations during early adolescence can in some cases lead to heavier levels of use including the progression to illicit substance use and abuse, the latter driven by psychological motivations and pharmacological factors (Hartel & Glantz, 1997). It is also true that many individuals discontinue substance use after a short period of experimentation, fail to progress to more involved use, or fail to transition from one drug to another. The typical patterning of drug use progression predicted by the gateway hypothesis can best be understood in terms of probabilities, with an individual's risk of moving to greater involvement with drugs increasing at each step in the developmental progression from alcohol to tobacco, to marijuana, and to other illicit drugs.

Research attempting to identify which adolescents progress in drug use and which risk and protective factors are most relevant to this increase make up much of the research on drug use etiology among adolescents. One discrete developmental milestone that has been linked to increased substance use among adolescents is first employment.

Employment outside the home. In today's society, a majority of high school students work outside the home. Several researchers have examined the extent to which employment among secondary school students is associated with substance use. Although there are likely benefits to part-time work for students, such as learning to handle new responsibilities and gaining valuable work experience, employment may also provide increased opportunities to engage in substance use, such as at after-work social gatherings. Moreover, workplace norms may support use, drugs may be available from older coworkers, and young workers earn sufficient wages that they may choose to spend them on drugs (Arnett, 2004; Wright, Cullen, & Williams, 2002). A number of studies have found higher rates of cigarette use, alcohol use, illicit drug use, and heavy substance use among secondary school students who work outside the home (Paschall, Flewelling, & Russell, 2004; Valois, Dunham, Jackson, & Waller, 1999; Wu, Schlenger, & Galvin, 2003). Recent studies have found that rates of cigarette smoking among employed adolescents are positively correlated with the number of hours worked (Ramchand, Ialongo, & Chilcoat, 2007) and the amount of spending money available (Zhang, Cartmill, & Ferrence, 2008). One study found that work intensity was associated with greater frequency of alcohol use among adolescents, particularly for students younger than age 16 who were not closely monitored by their parents (Longest & Shanahan, 2007). It appears likely that the norms, attitudes, and behaviors regarding substance use among coworkers, as well as factors such as parental monitoring, will be important in determining whether starting a part-time position will adversely affect a student's risk for substance use.

Peak in Late Adolescence and Early Adulthood

The years immediately following high school graduation are often a time of new freedoms such as living independently from parents and attending college.

The period of entering young adulthood may involve relatively few social obligations, particularly among young people who delay marriage and family. To better understand the associations between developmental phenomena and substance use among young adults, it is informative to review the findings from two books published by MTF researchers examining the peak years of use after high school and the decline of drug use in young adulthood (Bachman, Wadsworth, O'Malley, Johnston, & Schulenberg, 1997; Bachman et al., 2002). These books explore whether developmental transitions such as college attendance, full-time employment, living arrangements, current marital or committed relationship status, and current parental status are associated with rates of substance use and abuse. Bachman et al. (1997) summarized the findings in these areas for the MTF young adult follow-up samples, and Bachman et al. (2002) examined the roles of several hypothesized mediators in explaining how transitions may affect substance use. The mediators studied included values, attitudes, and behaviors such as religious views and behavior, perceived risk and disapproval of substance use, friends' drug use, and number of evenings spent out socializing. In the following section, I briefly review findings from the MTF young adult follow-up research along with recent findings in the scientific literature on the association between key developmental transitions and progression to peak levels of substance use.

Substance use among college students, in particular binge drinking and other forms of heavy drinking, has received a great deal of attention from researchers, policymakers, educators, and the public. Findings from the MTF young adult follow-up study and other research have shown that patterns of substance use among those who attend college differ from those who begin to work full time or get married soon after high school graduation (Bachman et al., 1997; Schulenberg & Maggs, 2002). In the MTF data, those who were not planning to attend college engaged in more substance use during their senior year in high school compared with college-bound students, and this was true for the use of cigarettes, alcohol, marijuana, and cocaine. However, in the years after high school graduation, there were additional differences between these two groups,

depending on the specific substance examined. Both cocaine use and cigarette smoking were higher among non–college-bound high school students compared with their college-bound peers, and use of both of these substances remained higher in the years after high school graduation. In fact, smoking increased two to three times as much in the years after high school among nonstudents compared with full-time students. However, although non–college-bound high school seniors engaged in more alcohol and marijuana use than did college-bound seniors, college students caught up in level of marijuana use and surpassed level of alcohol use during the college years relative to nonstudents (Bachman et al., 1997). The MTF data also revealed that being a full-time student living on campus was associated with greater substance use, particularly heavy drinking, because students spent more evenings out with friends and reported a decline in perceived risks and disapproval of substance use (Bachman et al., 2002).

Two issues that have been studied extensively in research on substance use in college students are (a) the extent to which selection versus socialization processes explain the phenomenon of college substance use and (b) the degree to which substance use episodes, particularly heavy drinking, are predictable in time and place over the college years. An interesting research question involves to what degree socialization or selection processes explain the increased substance use among fraternity and sorority members. Although students new to college social environments such as fraternities may be influenced by the drinking behavior, norms, and attitudes of their peers, there appears to be compelling evidence for selection effects as well. A recent analysis of the MTF data examined whether participation in fraternities and sororities was associated with substance use among full-time college students (McCabe et al., 2005). On the basis of an analysis of 10 cohorts of graduating seniors assessed in college, the findings indicated that active members of fraternities and sororities reported higher levels of heavy episodic drinking, annual marijuana use, and current cigarette smoking compared with students who were nonmembers. For fraternity members, rates of annual illicit drug use other than marijuana were higher than rates for nonmembers, but this was not found for sorority members versus nonmembers. McCabe et al. (2005) also found that the higher rates of substance use among students who join fraternities and sororities typically predated their college attendance. This suggests that selection effects are in operation; in other words, entering college students already engaging in high levels of substance use were more likely to become involved in fraternities and sororities compared with entering students with less prior substance use involvement. However, a different line of evidence could support socialization effects. Members of fraternities and sororities reported heavy episodic drinking and marijuana use that increased significantly over the college years compared with nonmembers, although these effects were not found for cigarette use or illicit drug use other than marijuana (McCabe et al., 2005). Other research has found that precollege drinking behaviors and attitudes predict increased alcohol consumption after joining a fraternity (e.g., Capone, Wood, Borsari & Laird, 2007).

In terms of predicting when and where college students engage in substance use, the evidence has strongly suggested that the 1st year of college, in particular the first semester, is a high-risk period for heavy substance use, particularly heavy drinking. For many 1st-year college students, particularly those living away from home, parents, and long-standing friends, an important goal after arriving on campus is to establish new friendships and a social network as part of formulating a new "college identity." Dorm and fraternity or sorority parties present environments in which alcohol and drug use is socially approved and highly prevalent, and 1st-year college students attend these events in a greater proportion than upperclassmen (Harford, Wechsler, & Seibring, 2002). Research on drinking among 1st-year college students has suggested that selection processes play an important role in addition to socialization processes. A review of the literature on 1st-year college drinking found that White students, men, those who drank before college, and those whose parents drink and have positive attitudes about drinking are most likely to engage in heavy drinking in the 1st year of college (Borsari, Murphy & Barnett, 2007). Furthermore, 1st-year heavy drinking can be predicted by precollege variables such as heavy involve-

ment in alcohol and other substances in high school and involvement in a social network in high school in which alcohol consumption is normative and access to alcohol is high (Sher & Rutledge, 2007).

Recent research has demonstrated that drinking does not occur with high frequency for most college students, but when it does occur it tends to be heavy, and it occurs according to predictable patterns. Over the course of the 1st year in college, binge drinking often begins soon after arrival on campus, and throughout the school year half of students who drank in any specific week engaged in heavy episodic drinking; furthermore, the vast majority of drinking was done on Thursday, Friday, and Saturday nights (Del Boca, Darkes, Greenbaum, & Goldman, 2004). First-year college students who go on spring break trips are likely to increase their alcohol consumption and heavy drinking, and this pattern may continue for weeks following the trip (Lee, Maggs, & Rankin, 2006). Students also drink heavily for certain college sporting events such as high-profile college football games and do so at a level comparable to other well-known drinking days such as New Year's Eve and Halloween (Neal & Fromme, 2007b). Research has shown that freshmen often drink beyond the threshold of binge drinking (White, Kraus, & Swartzwelder, 2006) and that as individuals increase their level of intoxication above their average level, they are more likely to engage in unsafe sex, coerced sex as perpetrator or victim, aggressive behavior, and vandalism (Neal & Fromme, 2007a). Other windows of risk for college drinking include orientation or the beginning of the school year, homecoming celebrations, 21st-birthday celebrations, spring break, and graduation; knowledge of these high-risk events can help in developing event-specific prevention activities (Neighbors et al., 2007).

Although the transition to college can involve a significant increase in alcohol and drug use behavior that occurs over a condensed time frame, the escalation of these behaviors does not necessarily persist. In fact, a significant proportion of college students stop drinking heavily during the college years before graduation (Steinman, 2003). For many others, heavy drinking decreases during the years after college. In fact, despite the high-exposure opportunities to drink, college attendance is a protective factor for alcohol use and abuse in the years after college. Longitudinal research has demonstrated that the long-term risk of heavy drinking and alcohol dependence is lower among college graduates relative to high school dropouts and those who do not attend college (Harford, Yi, & Hilton, 2006; Lanza & Collins, 2006).

In summary, college drinking is a widespread phenomenon, not only in the United States but in Europe, South America, and Australia as well (Karam, Kypri, & Salamoun, 2007). Alcohol use appears to represent a rite of passage among college students, and those who drink heavily tend to view alcohol as integral to the student experience and feel entitled to drink irresponsibly (Crawford & Novak, 2006). The evidence also suggests that while in high school, those who later attend college engage in less heavy drinking compared with students who do not later attend college. Once in college, rates of heavy drinking increase among students, particularly in the 1st year when students are establishing new friendships and socializing in alcohol-friendly environments such as fraternities and sororities. Heavy drinking among college students tends to decrease either close to graduation or in the years after graduation. Problem drinking is less prevalent among college graduates compared with those who do not attend college.

Decline in Young Adulthood

Although the new freedoms at the beginning of young adulthood are often associated with increased substance use, the MTF study shows that the new responsibilities that typically occur a bit later are associated with decreased substance use. As young adults begin full-time employment, enter into marriage or committed relationships, or start a family, substance use typically decreases as these responsibilities become central to their lives and identities.

Employment Status. The MTF young adult follow-up study is informative regarding the association between employment status and substance use in the years after high school graduation (Bachman et al., 1997). MTF findings indicate that young adults who work full time after high school tend to have had average rates of substance use while in high school. When they begin full-time work, these individuals are found to increase their

daily smoking but decrease rates of heavy drinking and marijuana use. Participants who became full-time homemakers after high school graduation were found to show decreased alcohol, marijuana, and cocaine use, but most of this effect appeared to be a result of their marital and parental status (Bachman et al., 1997). MTF findings indicated that those who joined the military after high school graduation increased their levels of smoking and alcohol use, but rates of marijuana and cocaine use dropped dramatically on enlisting in the military, likely because of the imposition of drug testing before enlistment and continuing random testing after enlistment. Other findings have indicated that recent unemployment is a predictor of substance use in adulthood (Merline, O'Malley, Schulenberg, Bachman, & Johnston, 2004).

Marriage, Cohabitation, and Divorce Effects. Getting married is a major life event that appears to have pervasive effects on many aspects of young adult life, including drug use behavior. The MTF young adult study (Bachman et al., 1997) found that marriage was associated with a decrease in use of alcohol, cigarettes, marijuana, and cocaine. Of these four substances, the decrease in alcohol use after marriage was limited to women and was not observed in men. Bachman et al. (2002) reported that marriage was associated with a decrease in alcohol and drug use in large part because it ushers in a change in social and recreational activities and attitudes about drugs. Married people reported fewer evenings out for fun and recreation, getting together less often with friends, and rarely going out to bars, nightclubs, and parties compared with those who are not married. MTF findings indicate that married people form stronger negative attitudes about substance use and are more likely to disapprove of drug use and see it as risky. Other researchers have found that entering marriage is associated with decreases in heavy alcohol use (Curran, Muthén, & Harford, 1998; Miller-Tutzauer, Leonard, & Windle, 1991). One study found that the effects of marriage on substance use were limited mostly to binge drinking and marijuana use, but not smoking (Duncan, Wilkerson, & England, 2006). In the MTF study, there were some reductions in substance use associated with getting engaged to be married, perhaps because engagement tends to take people out of the singles scene, but these effects were not as strong as marriage effects (Bachman et al. 2002). In addition, cohabitation with a romantic partner was differentially related to drug use as compared with marriage. Before high school graduation, those who later cohabitated with a romantic partner reported higher levels of substance use than those who later married. Cohabitation likely reflects an embrace of nontraditional ideas and alternative lifestyle choices, and the cohabitation effects observed in MTF were explained by less religious behavior and values, lower perceptions of risk, and less disapproval of substance use among those who choose to live together compared with those who marry or become engaged.

After marriage, the substance use of one spouse can influence the other spouse, although it may depend on the substance. Wives have been found to influence their husband's marijuana use. One study found that new husbands were more likely to stop using marijuana if their wives did not use marijuana and were more likely to start using marijuana if their wives did use it (Leonard & Homish, 2005). Interestingly, the reverse was true for cigarette smoking. Wives were more likely to resume cigarette smoking in the early years of their marriage if their husband smoked, whereas wives' smoking did not predict husband initiation of smoking (Homish & Leonard, 2005). To the extent that people choose partners for marriage who are similar in background, values, and behaviors, an ongoing discrepancy in substance use behavior may suggest a less-than-ideal level of compatibility. When differences in values and behaviors regarding substance use surface after marriage, other facets of the marriage may suffer. In fact, discrepancies in the levels of husbands' and wives' substance use can predict decreased marital satisfaction and divorce (Homish & Leonard, 2007; Homish, Leonard, & Cornelius, 2008), particularly for more serious levels of drug use involvement in one partner (Mudar, Leonard, & Soltysinski, 2001). Controlling for substance use before marriage, marital discord, and religiosity, one study found that alcohol intoxication was an independent predictor of later divorce, although marijuana use was not (Collins, Ellickson,

& Klein, 2007). Although substance use can predict divorce, it is also true that divorce often triggers an increase in substance use. Levels of substance use and abuse tend to be higher among young adults who have been divorced compared with those who remain married (Bachman et al., 1997).

Pregnancy and parenthood effects. Substance use during pregnancy can lead to a number of adverse pregnancy outcomes. Smoking during pregnancy increases the risk of spontaneous abortions, stillbirth, preterm birth, and fetal growth restriction and can contribute to long-term health effects on infants, including neurodevelopmental disorders and cancers (Cnattingius, 2004). Thus, it is not surprising that pregnancy has wide-ranging effects on substance use behavior among women. Smoking prevalence among pregnant women in the United States has decreased dramatically in recent decades. It has been estimated that 40% of pregnant women in the United States smoked in 1967, and this number has crept consistently downward to 12% in 2000. However, much of this decrease is likely a result of lower levels of smoking initiation rather than increased smoking cessation before or during pregnancy (Cnattingius, 2004). In fact, MTF data have shown that the effects of pregnancy on reduced substance use behavior were dramatic for women in terms of alcohol, tobacco, and illicit drugs, but this effect was not observed among their male partners. Parenthood shows a similar effect, although this may be largely explained by marital status.

SUMMARY AND CONCLUSIONS

Substance use and abuse are problems that first begin during the prime years of developmental change in adolescents and young adults. It is important to recognize that from an individual perspective, there is great diversity in substance use patterns and trajectories from early adolescence to young adulthood, and this variation has been the focus of much recent etiologic work on adolescent substance use (e.g., Mayhew, Flay, & Mott, 2000; Oesterle et al., 2004; Schulenberg et al., 2005). However, this chapter focused instead on a population perspective and revealed that the pattern of substance use onset in early adolescence—increase during adolescence, peak in late adolescence and early adulthood, and decrease in young adulthood—is consistently observed for alcohol, cigarette smoking, marijuana use, and most other forms of illicit drug use. From a population perspective, this normative typical course of substance use is well established in national epidemiological data sets. Research has demonstrated that several developmental goals, milestones, and transitions that occur from early adolescence to young adulthood are associated with changes in substance use.

The epidemiologic patterns of substance use, combined with the observed links to age-related tasks and transitions, provide strong evidence that substance use and abuse are developmental phenomena. This in turn has important implications for prevention efforts. Substance use during early adolescence is often a function of identity formation and the relative increase in the importance of peers versus parental influence, both of which are an inherent part of adolescence. To the extent that substance use is a functional response to internal and external cues, prevention programs for early adolescents should be skills focused, helping young people deal with the internal psychological and external social pressures from peers and the media that contribute to substance use experimentation. Compared with early adolescence, high-risk substance use during the transition to young adulthood appears to be more closely linked to specific transitions and discrete milestones such as turning "legal," high school or college graduation celebrations, college spring break, and other major demarcations that are associated with heavy alcohol and drug use. This suggests that new, event-specific prevention strategies at the individual, group, institution, community, and societal levels might be particularly important for addressing peak times of substance use among young adults. Challenges in the future are to learn how the changing transition to young adulthood is associated with substance use and abuse. Today more so than in the past, the years between adolescence and adulthood are extended in time, and there are more opportunities to try on different roles and more lifestyle options and opportunities for self-expression, with young adults transitioning in and out of school, relationships, jobs,

and living arrangements. Thinking about substance use as a developmental phenomenon may help the scientific community to address these and other new prevention challenges in the future.

References

Arnett, J. J. (2004) *Emerging adulthood: The winding road from the late teens through the twenties.* New York: Oxford University Press.

Bachman, J. G., O'Malley, P. M., Schulenberg, J. E., Johnston, L. D., Bryant, A. L., & Merline, A. C. (2002). *The decline of substance use in young adulthood: Changes in social activities, roles, and beliefs.* Mahwah, NJ: Erlbaum.

Bachman, J. G., Wadsworth, K. N., O'Malley, P. M., Johnston, L. D., & Schulenberg, J. E. (1997). *Smoking, drinking, and drug use in young adulthood: The impacts of new freedoms and new responsibilities.* Mahwah, NJ: Erlbaum.

Barone, C., Aguirre-Deandreis, A. I., & Trickett, E. J. (1991). Means-end problem-solving skills, life stress, and social support as mediators of adjustment in the normative transition to high school. *American Journal of Community Psychology, 19,* 207–225.

Biehl, M. C., Natsuaki, M. N., & Ge, X. (2007). The influence of pubertal timing on alcohol use and heavy drinking trajectories. *Journal of Youth and Adolescence, 36,* 153–167.

Blyth, D. A., Simmons, R. G., & Carlton-Ford, S. (1983). The adjustment of early adolescents to school transitions. *Journal of Early Adolescence, 3,* 105–120.

Borsari, B., Murphy, J. G., & Barnett, N. P. (2007). Predictors of alcohol use during the first year of college: Implications for prevention. *Addictive Behaviors, 32,* 2062–2086.

Brooks-Gunn, J. (1989). Pubertal processes and the early adolescent transition. In W. Damon (Ed.), *Child development today and tomorrow* (pp. 155–176). San Francisco: Jossey-Bass.

Brooks-Gunn, J., & Reiter, E. O. (1990). The role of pubertal processes. In G. R. Elliott & S. S. Feldman (Eds.), *At the threshold: The developing adolescent* (pp. 16–53). Cambridge, MA: Harvard University Press.

Cantin, S., & Boivin, M. (2004). Change and stability in children's social network and self-perceptions during transition from elementary to junior high school. *International Journal of Behavioral Development, 28,* 561–570.

Capone, C., Wood, M. D., Borsari, B., & Laird, R. D. (2007). Fraternity and sorority involvement, social influences, and alcohol use among college students: A prospective examination. *Psychology of Addictive Behaviors, 21,* 316–327.

Chung, H. H., Elias, M., & Schneider, K. (1998). Patterns of individual adjustment changes during middle school transition. *Journal of School Psychology, 36*, 83–101.

Clayton, R. R., & Voss, H. L. (1982). *Technical review on drug abuse and dropouts.* Rockville, MD: National Institute on Drug Abuse

Cnattingius, N. (2004). The epidemiology of smoking during pregnancy: Smoking prevalence, maternal characteristics, and pregnancy outcomes. *Nicotine & Tobacco Research, 6*, S125–S140.

Collins, R. L., Ellickson, P. L., & Klein, D. J. (2007). The role of substance use in young adult divorce. *Addiction, 102*, 786–794.

Costello, E. J., Sung, M., Worthman, C., & Angold, A. (2007). Pubertal maturation and the development of alcohol use and abuse. *Drug and Alcohol Dependence, 88*, S50–S59.

Côté, F., Godin, G., & Gagné, C. (2006). Efficiency of an evidence-based intervention to promote and reinforce tobacco abstinence among elementary schoolchildren in a school transition period. *Health Education & Behavior, 33*, 747–759.

Cotterell, J. L. (1992). School size as a factor in adolescents' adjustment to the transition to secondary school. *Journal of Early Adolescence, 12*, 28–45

Crawford, L. A., & Novak, K. B. (2006). Alcohol abuse as a rite of passage: The effect of beliefs about alcohol and the college experience on undergraduates' drinking behaviors. *Journal of Drug Education, 36*, 193–212.

Crockett, L. J., Petersen, A. C., Graber, J. A., Schulenberg, J. E., & Ebata, A. (1989). School transitions and adjustment during early adolescence. *Journal of Early Adolescence, 9*, 181–210.

Curran, P. J., Muthén, B. O., & Harford, T. C. (1998). The influence of changes in marital status on developmental trajectories of alcohol use in young adults. *Journal of Studies on Alcohol, 59*, 647–658.

Del Boca, F. K., Darkes, J., Greenbaum, P. E., & Goldman, M. S. (2004). Up close and personal: Temporal variability in the drinking of individual college students during their first year. *Journal of Consulting and Clinical Psychology, 72*, 155–164.

Dick, D. M., Rose, R. J., Viken, R. J., & Kaprio, J. (2000). Pubertal timing and substance use: Associations between and within families across late adolescence. *Developmental Psychology, 36*, 180–189.

Duncan, G. J., Wilkerson, B., & England, P. (2006). Cleaning up their act: The effects of marriage and cohabitation on licit and illicit drug use. *Demography, 43*, 691–710.

Eccles, J. S., & Midgley, C. (1991). Changes in academic motivation and self-perception during early adolescence. In R. Montemayor, G. R. Adams, & T. P. Gulotta (Eds.), *From childhood to adolescence: A transitional period?* (pp. 134–155). Newbury Park, CA: Sage.

Fergusson, D. M., Boden, J. M., & Horwood, L. J. (2006). Cannabis use and other illicit drug use: Testing the cannabis gateway hypothesis. *Addiction, 101*, 556–569.

Glantz, M. D., Conway, K. P., & Colliver, J. D. (2005). Drug abuse heterogeneity and the search for subtypes. In Z. Sloboda (Ed.), *Epidemiology of drug abuse* (pp. 15–27). New York: Springer.

Graber, J. A., Lewinsohn, P. M., Seely, J., & Brooks-Gunn, J. (1997). Is psychopathology associated with the timing of pubertal development? *Journal of the American Academy of Child & Adolescent Psychiatry, 36*, 1768–1776.

Hamburg, B. A., Kraemer, H. C., & Jahnke, W. (1975). A hierarchy of drug use in adolescence: Behavioral and attitudinal correlates of substantial drug use. *American Journal of Psychiatry, 132*, 1155–1163.

Harford, T. C., Wechsler, H., & Seibring, M. (2002). Attendance and alcohol use at parties and bars in college: A national survey of current drinkers. *Journal of Studies on Alcohol, 63*, 726–728.

Harford, T. C., Yi, H. Y., & Hilton, M. E. (2006). Alcohol abuse and dependence in college and noncollege samples: A ten-year prospective follow-up in a national survey. *Journal of Studies on Alcohol, 67*, 803–809.

Hartel, C. R., & Glantz, M. D. (1997). *Drug abuse: Origins and interventions.* Washington, DC: American Psychological Association.

Homish, G. G., & Leonard, K. E. (2005). Spousal influence on smoking behaviors in a U.S. community sample of newly married couples. *Social Science & Medicine, 61*, 2557–2567.

Homish, G. G., & Leonard, K. E. (2007). The drinking partnership and marital satisfaction: The longitudinal influence of discrepant drinking. *Journal of Consulting and Clinical Psychology, 75*, 43–51.

Homish, G. G., Leonard, K. E., & Cornelius, J. R. (2008). Illicit drug use and marital satisfaction. *Addictive Behaviors, 33*, 279–291.

Isakson, K., & Jarvis, P. (1999). The adjustment of adolescents during the transition into high school: A short-term longitudinal study. *Journal of Youth and Adolescence, 28*, 1–26.

Johnston, L. D., O'Malley, P. M., Bachman, J. G., & Schulenberg, J. E. (2008a). *Monitoring the Future national survey results on drug use, 1975-2007. Volume II: College students and adults ages 19-45* (NIH Publication No. 08-6418B). Bethesda, MD: National Institute on Drug Abuse.

Johnston, L. D., O'Malley, P. M., Bachman, J. G., & Schulenberg, J. E. (2008b). *Monitoring the Future national survey results on drug use, 1975-2007. Volume I: Secondary school students* (NIH Publication

No. 08-6418A). Bethesda, MD: National Institute on Drug Abuse.

Kaltiala-Heino, R., Marttunen, M., Rantanen, P., & Rimpela, M. (2003). Early puberty is associated with mental health problems in middle adolescence. *Social Science & Medicine, 57,* 1055–1064.

Kandel, D. B. (1975, November 28). Stages in adolescent involvement in drug use. *Science, 190,* 912–914.

Kandel, D. B. (2002). Examining the gateway hypothesis: Stages and pathways of drug involvement. In D. B. Kandel (Ed.), *Stages and pathways of drug involvement: Examining the gateway hypothesis* (pp. 3–15). New York: Cambridge University Press.

Kandel, D. B. (2003, January 22). Does marijuana use cause the use of other drugs? *JAMA, 289,* 482–483.

Karam, E., Kypri, K., & Salamoun, M. (2007). Alcohol use among college students: An international perspective. *Current Opinion in Psychiatry, 20,* 213–221.

Keating, D. P. (1990). Adolescent thinking. In S. S. Feldman & G. R. Elliott (Eds.), *At the threshold: The developing adolescent* (pp. 54–89). Cambridge, MA: Harvard University Press.

Lanza, S. T., & Collins, L. M. (2002). Pubertal timing and the onset of substance use in females during early adolescence. *Prevention Science, 3,* 69–82.

Lanza, S. T., & Collins, L. M. (2006). A mixture model of discontinuous development in heavy drinking from ages 18 to 30: The role of college enrollment. *Journal of Studies on Alcohol, 67,* 552–561.

Lee, C. M., Maggs, J. L., & Rankin, L. A. (2006). Spring break trips as a risk factor for heavy alcohol use among first-year college students. *Journal of Studies on Alcohol, 67,* 911–916.

Leonard, K. E., & Homish, G. G. (2005). Changes in marijuana use over the transition into marriage. *Journal of Drug Issues, 35,* 409–429.

Longest, K. C., & Shanahan, M. J. (2007). Adolescent work intensity and substance use: The mediational and moderational roles of parenting. *Journal of Marriage and Family, 69,* 703–720.

Mayhew, K. P., Flay, B. R., & Mott, J. A. (2000). Stages in the development of adolescent smoking. *Drug and Alcohol Dependence, 59,* S61–S81.

McCabe, S. E., Schulenberg, J. E., Johnston, L. D., O'Malley, P. M., Bachman, J. G., & Kloska, D. D. (2005). Selection and socialization effects of fraternities and sororities on US college student substance use: A multi-cohort national longitudinal study. *Addiction, 100,* 512–524.

Merline, A. C., O'Malley, P. M., Schulenberg, J. E., Bachman, J. G., & Johnston, L. D. (2004). Substance use among adults 35 years of age: Prevalence, adulthood predictors, and impact of adolescent substance use. *American Journal of Public Health, 94,* 96–102.

Miller-Tutzauer, C., Leonard, K. E., & Windle, M. (1991). Marriage and alcohol use: A longitudinal study of "maturing out." *Journal of Studies on Alcohol, 52,* 434–440.

Mudar, P., Leonard, K. E., & Soltysinski, K. (2001). Discrepant substance use and marital functioning in newlywed couples. *Journal of Consulting and Clinical Psychology, 69,* 130–134.

Neal, D. J., & Fromme, K. (2007a). Event-level covariation of alcohol intoxication and behavioral risks during the first year of college. *Journal of Consulting and Clinical Psychology, 75,* 294–306.

Neal, D. J., & Fromme, K. (2007b). Hook 'em horns and heavy drinking: Alcohol use and collegiate sports. *Addictive Behaviors, 32,* 2681–2693.

Neighbors, C., Walters, S. T., Lee, C. M., Vader, A. M., Vehige, T., Szigethy, T., & DeJong, W. (2007). Event-specific prevention: Addressing college student drinking during known windows of risk. *Addictive Behaviors, 32,* 2667–2680.

Oesterle, S., Hill, K. G., Hawkins, J. D., Guo, J., Catalano, R. F., & Abbott, R. D. (2004). Adolescent heavy episodic drinking trajectories and health in young adulthood. *Journal of Studies on Alcohol, 65,* 204–212.

Paschall, M. J., Flewelling, R. L., & Russell, T. (2004). Why is work intensity associated with heavy alcohol use among adolescents? *Journal of Adolescent Health, 34,* 79–87.

Ramchand, R., Ialongo, N. S., & Chilcoat, H. D. (2007). The effect of working for pay on adolescent tobacco use. *American Journal of Public Health, 97,* 2056–2062.

Schulenberg, J. E., & Maggs, J. L. (2002). A developmental perspective on alcohol use and heavy drinking during adolescence and the transition to young adulthood. *Journal of Studies on Alcohol, 14*(Suppl.), 54–70.

Schulenberg, J. E., Merline, A. C., Johnston, L. D., O'Malley, P. M., Bachman, J. G., & Laetz, V. B. (2005). Trajectories of marijuana use during the transition to adulthood: The big picture based on national panel data. *Journal of Drug Issues, 35,* 255–279.

Sher, K. J., & Rutledge, P. C. (2007). Heavy drinking across the transition to college: Predicting first-semester heavy drinking from precollege variables. *Addictive Behaviors, 32,* 819–835.

Stattin, H., & Magnusson, D. (1990). *Pubertal maturation in female development: Vol. 2. Paths through life.* Hillsdale, NJ: Erlbaum.

Steinberg, L., & Morris, A. S. (2001). Adolescent development. *Annual Review of Psychology, 52,* 83–110.

Steinman, K. J. (2003). College students' early cessation from episodic heavy drinking: Prevalence and correlates. *Journal of American College Health, 51,* 197–204.

Stice, E., Presnell, K., & Bearman, S. K. (2001). Relation of early menarche to depression, eating disorders, substance abuse, and comorbid psychopathology among adolescent girls. *Developmental Psychology, 37,* 608–619.

Substance Abuse and Mental Health Services Administration. (2008a). *The NSDUH report: Misuse of over-the-counter cough and cold medications among persons aged 12 to 25.* Rockville, MD: Substance Abuse and Mental Health Services Administration, Office of Applied Studies.

Substance Abuse and Mental Health Services Administration. (2008b). *Results from the 2007 National Survey on Drug Use and Health: National findings* (NSDUH Series H-34, DHHS Publication No. SMA 08-4343). Rockville, MD: Substance Abuse and Mental Health Services Administration, Office of Applied Studies.

Tarter, R. E., Vanyukov, M., Kirisci, L., Reynolds, M., & Clark, D. B. (2006). Predictors of marijuana use in adolescents before and after licit drug use: Examination of the gateway hypothesis. *American Journal of Psychiatry, 163,* 2134–2140.

Tschann, J. M., Adler, N. E., Irwin, C. E., Millstein, S. G., Turner, R. A., & Kegeles, S. M. (1994). Initiation of substance use in early adolescence: The roles of pubertal timing and emotional distress. *Health Psychology, 13,* 326–333.

Valois, R. F., Dunham, A.C., Jackson, K. L., & Waller, J. (1999). Association between employment and substance abuse behaviors among public high school adolescents. *Journal of Adolescent Health, 25,* 256–263.

Weiss, C. C., & Bearman, P. S. (2007). Fresh starts: Reinvestigating the effects of the transition to high school on student outcomes. *American Journal of Education, 113,* 395–421.

Westling, E., Andrews, J. A., Hampson, S. E., & Peterson, M. (2008). Pubertal timing and substance use: The effects of gender, parental monitoring and deviant peers. *Journal of Adolescent Health, 42,* 555–563.

White, A. M., Kraus, C. L., & Swartzwelder, H. S. (2006). Many college freshman drink at levels far beyond the binge threshold. *Alcoholism: Clinical and Experimental Research, 30,* 1006–1010.

Wiesner, M., & Ittel, A. (2002). Relations of pubertal timing and depressive symptoms to substance use in early adolescence. *Journal of Early Adolescence, 22,* 5–23.

Wills, T. A., Walker, C., & Resko, J. A. (2005). Longitudinal studies of drug use and abuse. In Z. Sloboda (Ed.), *Epidemiology of drug abuse epidemiology* (pp. 177–192). New York: Springer.

Wilson, D. M., Killen, J. D., Hayward, C., Robinson, T. N., Hammer, L. D., Kraemer, H. C, et al. (1994). Timing and rate of sexual maturation and the onset of cigarette and alcohol use among teenage girls. *Archives of Pediatrics and Adolescent Medicine, 148,* 789–795.

Wright, J. P., Cullen, F. T., & Williams, N. (2002). The embeddedness of adolescent employment and participation in delinquency: A life course perspective. *Western Criminology Review, 4,* 1–19.

Wu, L., Schlenger, W., & Galvin, D. (2003). The relationship between employment and substance use among students aged 12 to 17. *Journal of Adolescent Health, 32,* 5–15.

Zeedyk, M. S., Gallacher, J., Henderson, M., Hope, G., Husband, B., & Lindsay, K. (2003). Negotiating the transition from primary to secondary school: Perceptions of pupils, parents and teachers. *School Psychology International, 24,* 67–79.

Zhang, B., Cartmill, C., & Ferrence, R. (2008). The role of spending money and drinking alcohol in adolescent smoking. *Addiction, 103,* 310–319.

CHAPTER 5

SOCIAL–COGNITIVE MODELS OF DRUG USE ETIOLOGY

Lawrence M. Scheier

This chapter explores several major theories that have been a staple of drug use etiology research. It is divided into three thematic areas. The first section generates a quasi-philosophical argument outlining the basic requirements of theory. Woven into this discussion is a brief exploration of whether drug use etiology theories pass muster and comport with the stated requirements of theory. The second section identifies the historical currents that paved the way for current theoretical models of drug use, emphasizing in particular two highly regarded cognitive models. The chapter then finishes with a discussion of how drug use etiology theories inform current drug prevention themes.

THINKING AND THEORY

The notion of theory is embedded in people's everyday thinking and language. It is not uncommon to hear people say they "have a hunch about something" or that they are mulling over the "reasons something occurs." Theory is at once an expression of cause or a statement about the linkages between events either that people observe on a regular basis or that are not transparent to their mind (senses). Theories are abstractions about events that transpire in the world "out there" and are "basically networks of predictive generalizations" (Godfrey-Smith, 2003, p. 125). They are a point of contact, some have argued, between well-defined concepts and repeated experiments (Adorno, 1992). At a very basic level, theories reflect dependence and can be thought of as an enumeration

of experience, a linguistic confirmation of reality (Popper, 1963). Theories are, however, as with all experience people record in their minds, faulty, tinged with prejudice, reflecting a piece of their own ignorance of how things work. This view is in keeping with that of philosopher Karl Popper (1963), whose critical rationalism suggested that a theory can never be proven, merely falsified. According to Popper, critical rationalism is the method people use to discard or eliminate theories that do not hold explanatory power. They can pare down or whittle away ineffective theories until they are left with the few that work and provide insight into their own behavior.

Consider that even though people know an illusionist on stage at a Las Vegas show is using trickery and sleight of hand, they are still pleasantly amazed at the disappearance of a tiger from its cage or at seeing a person inside a box being ceremoniously cut in half. Only a fool believes the tiger actually disappeared. Theories lead to expressions or statements about relationships and are not equivalent to the relationships themselves. Theories are not based on any authority of knowledge, but rather are built on essential principles and definitions. If we all agreed on experimental techniques and had all the empirical verification we needed, we would not require theoretical explanations because the known would be apparent.

Theories must be built on observation and not mere assertions, and they must be testable, empirically verifiable, and subject to repeated experimentation.

Preparation of this chapter was supported in part by National Institute on Drug Abuse Grant R21 DA015811-01A2.

Theories are not the playthings of ivory-tower-dwelling-academics but rather a means of ordering evidence, a series of rungs on the ladder of knowledge constructed by human minds (Wilson, 1978). Today, given the advances made in statistics and computer innovations, we can easily test theories and gauge their explanatory power in terms of variance accounted for in some designated endpoint. Massive amounts of data can be compiled and analyzed in milliseconds, evaluating the correspondence between sample data and implied population models. However, in truth, a better gauge of a theory rests with determining whether the axioms or principles that form the basis of the theoretical postulates are consistent with observations.

Axioms are the building blocks of theory, and what makes a theory rich and fertile is its ability to explain events or experiences (data) while at the same time achieving parsimony. Axioms are considered initial conditions or postulates; they are the assumptions that are considered true without factual evidence. In general, science moves from axioms to observation through experimentation with logical deductions using rules of reasoning. In statistical theory, the axiom of commutation, for example, is stated as $P-(xy) \geq P-(yx)$. After an axiom is constructed, evidence is gathered to corroborate whether this condition holds true or can be falsified with observational data. In this example, plugging in the numbers 2 for x and 3 for y will always yield an objective truth ($6 = 6$). In addition to axioms, theories have syntax, or the rules for relating theoretical terms. Semantics, however, refers to the means used to relate theoretical terms to data. Take, for instance, the relationship between depression (a hypothetical construct) and drug use. The syntax of this theory is the specified relationship between depression and drug use. If one asserts that depression is a major cause of drug use, then observation should reconcile whether a good portion of drug users report they are depressed and that their depression preceded their drug use (longitudinal data with appropriate statistical controls would help reconcile this argument). Proof of this particular relationship would validate a self-medication theory of drug use (it would not prove it incontrovertibly but merely ascertain this relationship holds true with real data).

INFERENCE FROM THE OUTCOME

Arguably, the words *theory* and *etiology* need to be considered in the same breath. *Webster's Seventh New Collegiate Dictionary* (1967) uses the words *conjecture* and *supposition* to help clarify the meaning of the word *theory*. Inasmuch as etiology is a search for causes, then theory is the conjecture that links the causes in a specified manner, the basic principles or statements of explanatory nature that link processes. The world (reality) is a reflection of people's ideas and scientific notions (this is a form of scientific realism). In the case of drug use, we superimpose what we think causes drug use over consensual observations of behavior. It comes to pass that aided by language, the marriage of ideas with observation results in an inclination to cast behavior in a certain perspective. In other words, drug use is regarded as a deviant form of behavior because of repeated observations that deviant youth use drugs. Here we are working backward from observation of the behavior to the proposition that certain control mechanisms induce behavior. We really do not know whether deviance is what causes drug use, which in fact could be attributed to some third-variable alternative (i.e., spurious causation) such as disenfranchisement, differential association, derogation, or some other cognitively mediated factor (Kaplan, 1995; White, Johnson, & Horwitz, 1986). Once we establish that a majority of youth have used alcohol by the time they reach secondary school, this behavior can no longer be considered deviant but rather as considerably normative on the basis of our own assumptions and observations.

IS THEORY REFUGE FROM DATA?

At the end of the day, either a theory is good or it is not (there is no such thing as bad theory; however, there may be weak theory), and it is verifiable or it can be refuted. The philosophical view called instrumentalism suggests that theories help one deal with experience and that theories cannot be decisively bad, but may not serve people's intuition well (van Fraassen, 1980). At the very least, a theory must be testable but should not be deterministic. In all probability (here I use this statistical term only loosely), a theory will never be proven, and the statistical arguments that support its empirical validity are just that, arguments or pieces of conjecture that help us to approximate the conditions of life that seem to replicate and recur to the point to which we almost expect these events to transpire. In this respect, theories are a sine qua non for making predictions. Again, predictions are no more and no less than confirmations of what people experience in real life. Later, I revisit this notion of anticipation and expectation in terms of behavioral prediction.

All good theories begin with observations of how things occur or are anticipated to occur if they are not directly observable or may be considerably abstract. No matter how theories are dressed up, they are always about something accounting for specific relations as intervening steps. For years, learning theorists argued whether positing something beyond a stimulus–response (S-R) connection was needed to account for behavior. For example, Bolles (1972) suggested that a cognitive model may not need reinforcement as a postulated structural determinant of behavior unless one can show that the construct of reinforcement helps the prediction of behavior. This supposition carried incredible weight with regard to the impetus it provided for learning theorists to move in a considerably more mentalist direction. It does not make a whole lot of difference whether you are a Skinnerian or a firm believer in Tolman as you construct your views of learning theory. It is very important that readers keep sight of the fact that both Skinner and Tolman were talking about the same thing when they discussed learning and cognition; they just went about it in quite different ways. It does not matter that one theorist is happily content with the S-R relationship and requires no intervening mechanism between S and R, whereas the other theorist requires an intervening mechanism as a means of understanding behavior. What matters is that if someone introduces the concept of reinforcement as a cognitive mediator between S and R, and the

accuracy of predictions using this scheme improves, then one's view of learning theory should change accordingly.[1]

One final point to make about theory is that theories should be stated in terms of possible behavior. In other words, one of the most important features of a theory is the explication of the axioms or stated relations. Too many theories include very important measures of influence but do not articulate the precise mechanisms that link one set of behaviors to another. When this occurs, one is left with a kettle full of ideas with no real understanding of what drives influence. In the case of drug use etiology, the goal of all theories should be to explain the nature of experimentation that starts with nonuse and ends with use. The concept of use may be defined in myriad ways, but the mere incorporation or ingestion of a drug is the beginning point from which to understand use (this position would bundle taking puffs of a cigarette and smoking an entire cigarette in the same designated use group). More involved theories that account for protracted or more problematic use are not within the purview of this chapter.

A SISYPHEAN TASK

In many respects, drug use etiology researchers face a Sisyphean task when it comes to developing and explicating theoretical models. Historically speaking, the uphill climb results from a lack of concerted theory development (this point was reviewed in chap. 2, this volume) and few if any attempts to construct detailed axioms specifying conditions of probability

---

[1]Readers are encouraged to familiarize themselves with B. F. Skinner (1950), who questioned whether theories of learning were really necessary. His premise was that theories are statements "about something" often couched in terms substantially different from what was being observed (i.e., neural theories in which synaptic connections cannot be seen). From a purely behavioral standpoint, the connections between S and R are theoretically unimportant (or at least ambiguous) and not essential to explain learning, per se. The theoretical focus in this example would be on manipulation of the S to obtain a designated R. Accordingly, a valid theory of learning would have to be able to explain change (i.e., learning) in terms of the behavior itself, in essence not relying on some other dimension for explanation. The mentalist psychologist steps outside the experimental situation (S-R) by inferring, on the basis of certain postulates, what connects the S with the R, leading to a cognitive theory. Readers will encounter more of this problem in chapter 8 with the introduction of the concept of expectance as a theoretical explanation of what transpires between S and R.

leading to drug use. A good deal of scientific inquiry aims to reduce or summarize instrumentally that which is unknown into the known. It does not take much to realize that germs, genes, and electromagnetic particles like gluons were at one time unknown but theorized to exist. There are innumerable cases in which scientists did not see what they hypothesized but rather theorized relationships in the absence of direct observation. One case in particular, that of British anesthesiologist John Snow, is worth recounting. During a massive outbreak of cholera in 1854, Snow asked his local parish leaders to stave off the epidemic by removing the Broad Street water pump handle (where most town inhabitants collected their drinking water). Snow had theorized that cholera, a vicious gastrointestinal disturbance that led to death, was not caused by a gaseous miasma transported in the atmosphere but rather by white, flocculent particles that existed in the feces-contaminated water. Much later in time, the source of cholera was isolated as the bacterium *Vibrio cholerae*, but all of this was unknown to Snow. Although Snow was unable to see or observe that cholera was a germ, he theorized that the tap water contained some foreign element that was contributing to cholera.

This story provides a nice backdrop to the study of drug use etiology. Other than the actual observation of drug use as an incorporation of a foreign substance, we see very little of the actual mental or psychological experiences (i.e., urges, cravings, triggers, motivations) that promote use. At the very least, these are introspected constructions that are needed to explain behavior and coordinate with reality. They are, as any mathematician would note, representational symbols that help us achieve clarity of understanding. We theorize that they exist and then build models to incorporate their existence. In reality, we may actually be better off, as Popper (1963) suggested, to transit from the known to the unknown. In other words, refinement of the known using tried-and-true measures, creating testable hypotheses, confirming or refuting them, and discarding the false propositions will eventually lead us to the part of the world (our behavior) that we do not know, in this case, the motivations that we hypothesize cause drug use. If we buy into this premise, we can see that drug use

etiology has moved in the reverse direction, from the unknown to the known, and this has limited our understanding of the causes of drug use. One could arguably state that the field is currently characterized by theoretical chaos and that empirical studies have been seriously hogtied by our own propositional misgivings.

THE DATA ARE TAINTED!

Two currents helped push drug use etiology from a field rife with theoretical chaos to a more systematic science, one dealing with the source of drug data and a second focus emphasizing summarization of these data for treatment and prevention. Up until the introduction in the late 1960s of Richard Jessor's problem behavior theory (Jessor, Graves, Hanson, & Jessor, 1968; Jessor & Jessor, 1977), etiology researchers primarily relied on data obtained from clinical studies of drug users and abusers. A significant portion of what was then known about drug abuse was based on data gleaned from private hospitals, psychiatric facilities, and treatment centers. Hastily sketched interviews were used to collect data on a plethora of different types of drugs. The mainstream of users making up the dark underworld of narcotics included housewives addicted to pills, war veterans using heroin, dope-smoking youth, musicians snorting cocaine, and iatrogenic abusers jumpstarted by a naïve medical community. This restricted data collection led to a biased view of drug use based primarily on clinical vignettes emphasizing Freudian psychodynamic concepts (Ball, 1965; Blatt, McDonald, Sugarman, & Wilber, 1984; Hekimian & Gershon, 1968; Wurmser, 1974). This view eventually grew into the deficit model of drug abuse and remains strongly defended even today.

The fact that psychiatrists and others invoked concepts such as self and ego to explain drug abuse left the field in an impoverished state, primarily because of problems inherent with assessing these constructs and the lack of credible and reliable field data reinforcing the involvement of these processes in drug use etiology. Coupled with poor psychometrics and the lack of reliable prediction, society was left with no more than anecdotes and personal stories obtained from drug users.[2] A change in the field of drug use etiology came right about the 1960s and coincided with the political upheaval that marked this epochal period.

The radical social revolution of the 1960s forever changed the political, social, and historical landscape of the United States. The conflict in Vietnam opened the country's doors to an influx of heroin from Southeast Asia as soldiers returned home addicted to smack (Chein, Gerard, Lee, & Rosenfeld, 1964; Musto, 2002). Chapter 2 of this handbook showcases the rich history and precipitating factors that altered the full spectrum of drug use in the United States, including the introduction of psychedelics, marijuana, and illicit pill use. College campuses were hotbeds of social activism, with hippies ("heads" and "freaks") parading the use of marijuana as the new-age drug (Carey, 1968). Ken Kesey (Kesey & Faggen, 1962) and Timothy Leary (1968) became household names to reckon with, and the political world seemed to blow up with student uprisings around the nation. Tom Wolfe (1968) memorialized this era in his classic work *The Electric Kool-Aid Acid Test,* a testament to the mushroom-laden, psychedelic times. The undercurrent of political and moral change riddling the country was captured in Charles Reich's (1970) *The Greening of America,* a book lambasting our political and educational institutions for not teaching self-wisdom as a profitable means to steer our nation in new directions. The radicalism that pervaded the 1960s also introduced a new conceptualization of a drug user as somewhat different from the opium-smoking dope fiends. Drug use was becoming more statistically normative and less a focus of clinical lore (Thomas, Petersen, & Zingraff, 1975). The pervasiveness of drug use influenced researchers to examine the functional role of drug use in adolescence rather than its deviant roots (Akers, 1985; Kaplan, 1995).

Perhaps one of the more precipitous changes in the landscape of drug use etiology came about in the early 1970s when the National Institute on Drug Abuse saw fit to initiate a large epidemiological study invested in tracking drug use trends by our nation's youth, calling the annual survey Youth in Transition (Bachman, O'Malley, & Johnston, 1978; Johnston, 1973). Later this study gained popularity as the National High School Senior Survey (Johnston, O'Malley, & Bachman, 1984), transformed into a much larger epidemiological effort, and eventually took on the moniker Monitoring the Future (MTF), which continues even today (Johnston, O'Malley, Bachman, & Schulenberg, 2007). The MTF study provided a window from which to view trends in drug use among our nation's youth. In addition, expansion of the MTF survey carved out a legitimate base from which to gather information on risk factors associated with drug use (Bachman, Johnston, O'Malley, & Humphrey, 1988). Eventually, the survey was expanded to include 8th- and 10th-grade youth, added a representative sampling of adults through age 45 that were part of the survey as high school students, and included a relatively small follow-up sample that resulted from tracking a cohort of young adults over time (Bachman, Wadsworth, O'Malley, Johnston, & Schulenberg, 1997).

Perhaps the most significant feature of MTF is that the survey provided policymakers with the necessary tools to monitor a social problem of tremendous magnitude and make concerted, empirically based decisions that could guide legislative responses, including allocation of resources for remediation. The survey provided needed information on who uses drugs, when they start, what they use, what precipitates drug use, and what maturational events mark the transition from use to nonuse. Two chapters in this volume, chapters 4 and 30, investigate factors that instigate cessation in greater detail. The extent and nature of the MTF study have incredible ripple effects in congressional hallways. Major initiatives in public health policy, including the tobacco settlement, have their historical roots in MTF. Furthermore, armed with this needed information, theoreticians can now develop more insightful models of drug use, owing to the collection of

---

[2] This state of affairs improved considerably when investigators began to search for linkages between well-defined and reliable classifications of psychopathology and drug (narcotic) use among individuals seeking treatment. The work of Rounsaville, Kosten, Weissman, and Kleber (1986; Rounsaville, Weissman, Wilber, Crits-Christoph, & Kleber, 1982), supported by various institutional studies of addicts in treatment, improved our understanding of the relations of personality and psychological functioning to drug use. This body of evidence eventually improved our diagnostic capabilities and led to refinements in the current architecture for substance abuse disorders (American Psychiatric Association, 1994).

valuable information on prevalence, frequency, and historical trends in drug use.

DEVELOPING INSIGHT INTO THE MIND'S EYE

Sources of data and information on drug use etiology are only one concern, with the other being summarization. *Summarization* is generally taken to mean the manner in which scientists boil down or reduce their data into meaningful packets of information. Summarization often results because scientists want aggregate profiles and the pool of participant data is too large or unwieldy, requiring smoothing and manipulation. In this chapter, summarization has a slightly different meaning, instead referring to the manner in which people go about synthesizing their experiences, putting names to cognitive events inside their head, and reifying these experiences for further scientific exploration. The difference here is that rather than looking at how scientists boil down their data using statistical methods, we are looking at how the mind's eye sifts through social–cognitive information and boils this down into meaningful experiences. In this respect, the chapter uses a slightly different twist, but with the same intention.

One of the more salient and recognized truths about people is that they expect regularity in the world. It is unquestionable that humans spend a great deal of time and cognitive energy anticipating and even predicting how things will come about. In fact, one could argue that people impose regularity on the world and invent laws to account for this regularity. The idea of universal laws as expressions of the need for regularity would stand in direct contrast to someone who says, "The laws are out there and just need to be discovered; they operate all the time." In other words, people's need for precision, prediction, and regularity dictates what laws they will discover, but there are undiscovered laws as well. With regard to behavioral science, we do not base our laws on observation as much as we do on anticipation.

For instance, we anticipate that drug use derives from a few significant relationships that we observe in real life. Because many young people begin smoking cigarettes, for instance, among close friends or as part of an expanded peer group, the field has placed great emphasis on peer influences in cigarette smoking (e.g., Bauman & Fisher, 1986; Duncan, Tildesley, Duncan, & Hops, 1995; Graham, Marks, & Hansen, 1991; Krosnick & Judd, 1982), and a slew of empirical studies have reinforced that perceived peer smoking is usually the most efficient predictor of adolescent self-reported cigarette use (e.g., Hansen et al., 1987; Hu, Flay, Hedeker, Siddiqui, & Day, 1995; W. F. Skinner, Massey, Krohn, & Lauer, 1985; Wills, Resko, Ainette, & Mendoza, 2004). Unfortunately, the precise reasons that motivate cigarette smoking, or for that matter any drug use, are still somewhat outside the purview of our testing procedures. On the basis of sheer intuition, the linkages or dependence seems to point at peers and vicarious learning or some type of modeling effect as prime instigators of early adolescent drug use. Behaviorally speaking, we observe that youth watch their peers using drugs and themselves soon experiment with drugs. It should come as no surprise, then, that we anticipate the connection from peer influences to adolescents' use.

We can quickly see that refutation of peer pressure as a principal force in drug use etiology is made difficult by the very fact that the force of peer pressure is at once internal, perceived by the organism (i.e., "inside the head"). This latter component is termed the *reinforcement effect* and has been the subject of several studies (e.g., Hu et al., 1995). Unfortunately, scientists are limited in their ability to test the premise that peer pressure is the most optimal predictor of drug use. This arises because any attempt to reconcile different pressures or forces must examine perceptions that reside within the organism, which, as already stated, is tainted by false prejudices or self-enhancing hypotheses. Once we make the plunge into the internal subjective experience, the world between the stimulus and response, we are reinforcing the radical (albeit scholarly) nature of social psychological theory (Bem, 1967; Festinger, 1957). The truth is, people are not good perceivers; their thoughts are tainted (by their own overt behavior) and subject to influence (the work of Bem [1967] reinforces the fragility of people's beliefs). This should provide us with some consternation with respect to our own theories because they seem to resonate around the black box.

As this discussion unfolds, we are left holding onto a very simple premise. When people are asked the question, "Do you like bread?" most will generally respond, "I guess so; I eat bread all the time." At face value, then, overt behavior is a simple guide to people's actions, and we do not need any complex intervening mechanisms. As Bem (1967) suggested, the inferences the actor makes about his or her behavior would not be so different from those made by an observer who might also chime in, "He must like bread; he eats it all the time." This type of social psychological ploy reminds us that although we are difficult creatures to understand, there are certain conventions that help us dissect this complexity. More important, although the nature of beliefs and attitudes is very complex, and even though it is hard to measure cognitions, we should not despair. In reality, we do have certain tools that can be used to explain our interior world. In the next section, I review the importance of belief as a central construct in drug use etiology, in particular examining separately the seminal work of Bandura and that of Azjen and Fishbein.

PUTTING THE *I* INTO S-R

Perhaps the most significant theoretical influence in drug use etiology has been Bandura's social learning theory (SLT; Bandura, 1977a, 1977b, 1982, 1986, 1997). The premise of SLT is that mental processes drive people's behavior through a regulated and understandable set of principles. At heart, as with most learning theories at that time, Bandura was concerned with dissecting the construct of motivation (Bandura, 1991). He was very heavily invested in developing a model that explains action (performance) in terms of cognitive anticipation. In fact, Bandura (1997, p. 8) remarked that people are "partial architects of [their] own destiny," engaging in behavior based on their own mental design. People engage in behavior primarily because of self-belief, based on evaluations of their own personal efficacy, which is motivational in its own right.

In the early formulation of SLT, Bandura (1977a, 1977b) was most concerned with differentiating his notions of self-efficacy beliefs from Rotter's (1966) conceptualization of locus of control and also from Tolman's (1932, 1951/1966) concept of expectance. As is shown later in Bandura's conceptualization of human behavior, Rotter's concern with locus of control and causality (internal vs. external) does not adequately describe why people engage in tasks because even if someone believed he or she was responsible for a specific outcome (i.e., internal control), the perception that he or she lacked appropriate skills to effect an outcome (i.e., low self-efficacy) would hinder task engagement. Locus of control may be necessary but not sufficient as a causal explanation of behavior. In the case of youth facing active offers from their peers to use drugs, they may not feel control over the situation, but their conviction they can implement refusal skills can overcome their sense of futility in the situation.

If we travel back in time to the heat of the learning theory debates, a good deal of thinking was arguably concentrated on why the rat runs the maze. A devout follower of Tolman would argue that after some trial and error, the rat expects an outcome that will alter its experience (food or a pellet in the goal box). In effect, the field was concerned with establishing some theoretical notions of how people choose to act (behavioral choice) and what prompts their decision. In his earliest formulations, Bandura (1991) argued that rats do not think or self-reflect about whether they should or can run the maze, but that humans do engage in this cognitive act. In fact, Bandura argued, people are notorious for questioning their performance capability as part of an efficacy evaluation.

According to Bandura (1977a), efficacy is about personal agency and the unification of the person, who, in contrast to Skinner's deterministic S-R view that gave control to the environment, acts on the world. An important distinction from prior learning theory is that people are both the agents of motivation in their behavior and the filter that reviews their own performance. People are in essence thinking about their actions (it would be fair to call Bandura a "mentalist psychologist"), evaluating the outcomes, planning new strategies, and altering those that do not work. There is no inevitability about people's behavior, as deterministic or S-R theories would like one to believe. Rather, people are reflective creatures responsible for their own destinies. As such, the process of reflection is captured by efficacy evaluations in which people consider past performance, contemplate current and future outcomes, and make decisions about a course of action.

It should be clear at this point that Bandura (1977a, 1977b) introduced the concept of cognitive mediation at a time when historically most learning theorists were comfortable with stricter learning explanations that did not require mechanisms responsible for internal thought (Hull, 1930; B. F. Skinner, 1938). Bandura also clarified that there are two types of expectations: one attending to expectations about outcomes (e.g., "If I engage in this behavior, then I should expect this outcome") and a second consisting of an evaluation of one's ability to execute the behavior. Both expectations are conceptualized as beliefs that operate as part of a cognitive motivational enterprise to promote behavioral (task) engagement. The key difference between efficacy and outcome expectancies is that the former is more concerned with evaluation of one's ability to execute the behavior in question (that produces certain outcomes), whereas the latter is more concerned with anticipation of the likely consequences of engaging the behavior.

In short, efficacy is a major determining factor in why some youth will give up on a task, whereas others will persevere, thus creating a compelling reason for why some youth are successful and others fail. Failure (a summation of past performance, or response consequence) has value in that it precedes efficacy ("Am I capable of doing this?"), which in turn prompts whether a youth will engage in a specific task. By its very nature, perceived self-efficacy is persuasive, dictating in which challenges a youth will engage, his or her effort, perseverance in the face of challenges, and level of emotional distress when she or he experiences failures. As one can see, Bandura inserted into the equation of human motivation the notion of rumination owing to the fact that people are reflective creatures. Bandura (1997) suggested that people think about past performance before they engage, validate, or check out their expectations as part of self-referent thinking, and this evaluation process generates behavior. In the case of a youth who does not think he or she is efficacious with respect to a particular behavior, past performance will dictate an emotional response that may include *anxi-*

ety about his or her anticipated poor performance. The dampening effect of anxiety can motivate the youth to avoid the behavior in question. Avoidance, in this respect, is an internal decision to avoid stressful outcomes and has tremendous therapeutic implications. In the case of drug use prevention, low efficacy youth who do not believe they can refuse active drug offers might get anxious and choose to smoke or drink as a means of reducing their anxiety. Although this model shows tinges of self-medication and related social strain theories, readers will get a closer look at different facets of this argument when they read additional chapters in this handbook covering affect, cognitive distortion, and self-regulation. Later, I provide several examples of how the basic science of competence and efficacy is incorporated into prevention (readers will also encounter a great deal more on this subject in Part X of this volume).

Admittedly, this is an overly simplistic view of the construct of efficacy, and Bandura (1986, 1997) provided much greater detail with respect to dimensions of efficacy including magnitude (a quantitative estimation of task difficulty ranging from simple to more difficult), strength (a judgment or estimation of one's ability to perform the task), and generality (whether efficacy expectations generalize to other situations or experiences). Bandura also provided more information regarding the source of efficacy information, positing four sources including (a) past performance that provides a basis for personal mastery; (b) vicarious experience involving observation of people or events that model the behavior in question; (c) verbal persuasion, which involves exhortations to persevere and remain steadfast in effort; and (d) the individual's physiological state, which provides proprioceptive information regarding arousal states and can agitate the individual, impair performance, and interfere with cognitive processing. One can clearly see, however, from this brief overview that Bandura's notion of efficacy is a tremendously rich postulate nestled within a larger social learning model that accounts for human agency.

What has emerged over 50 years of research is that each of the four sources composing efficacy expectations is involved in etiology, and each of the four has been incorporated in some form or another into prevention practices. For instance, stress and anxiety reduction techniques, including visualization, meditation, and progressive relaxation, are all part of a constellation of activities aiming to teach youths to reduce visceral interference that offsets the practice of cognitive skills. Moreover, the notion that people learn from observing others (enactive learning vs. vicarious or observational learning) has been a large part of the argument that youth learn to use drugs from observing or modeling their friends.

What has provided great strength to drug use prevention programs and that has perhaps been misunderstood is that Bandura (1977a, 1986, 1997) was quite specific that efficacy expectations are not a generalized or global personality disposition but rather are expectations about performance in a specific situation. This bodes well for prevention because experts believe that drug-specific efficacy expectations (i.e., refusal skills) can be augmented through training and behavioral rehearsal (i.e., skill acquisition) and further buoyed by external forces (instructional sets in the classroom). Thus, youth who perceive that they are more efficacious are more likely to engage a specific set of skills—in this case, to refuse active drug offers—and benefit from programmed intervention at a critical juncture in their life.

I LIKE BREAD; THEREFORE, I EAT BREAD

The historical emphasis that led to the development of the theory of reasoned action (TRA) grew out of the need to explain the unexpectedly poor relations between attitudes and behavior in prediction models (Ajzen & Fishbein, 1977; Fishbein, 1967; Wicker, 1969). Generally speaking, the tenor of social psychology up to that point was heavily rooted in favor of attitudes being efficient predictors of behavior (see, e.g., Bentler & Speckart, 1979, 1981). The adage "I like bread; therefore, I eat bread" was a dominant force in developing models of human behavior. Doob (1947) came along and suggested that the relationship between attitudes and behavior was not innate, direct, and uncomplicated. In fact, through numerous examples (including the bread example), it came to be accepted that two individuals could hold the same attitude toward something (liking bread) but act differently (one could voraciously eat bread while the other did not consume a

morsel). The attitude–behavior debate prospered with the introduction of a new theoretical perspective (Ajzen & Fishbein, 1970, 1973, 1977; Fishbein, 1967; Fishbein & Ajzen, 1975). It was these two social psychologists, Izek Ajzen and Martin Fishbein, who offered a new spin on the attitude–behavior relationship, showing that the correspondence between attitudes and behavior was overly simplistic and required additional cognitive components to accurately explain behavior.

One of the hallmark features of TRA is that people evaluate a confluence of information in making a decision. The information breaks down into two components: attitudes (specific to the act in question) and beliefs. Beliefs consist of two elements. The first emphasizes normative perceptions of what is considered standard and acceptable behavioral practices. Individuals form norms by gauging their own behavior against significant referent others including their immediate peer or friendship group, significant authorities, community standards, and so forth. A second belief element, *behavioral beliefs,* refers to the expectation of effects, what individuals perceive will happen if they engage in the behavior. Attitudes and beliefs form a cognitive bridge to intentions and serve to motivate behavior. As in other expectancy–value theories, Ajzen and Fishbein (1970, 1977) suggested that attitudes are outgrowths of perceived consequences and subjective evaluation of the value to the person (where value comes from is not clear, but a more detailed description is provided by Allport, 1935). In essence, there is the specter of reinforcement lurking behind TRA, suggesting that people watch, listen, and learn and then evaluate the outcome for themselves. If they anticipate positive reinforcement (belief), this would prompt them to value the act or situation in a similar manner. Here, we are discussing the glue that binds S to R, but in uniquely different terms.

Included in the equation predicting intentions is an estimate of the individual's motivation to comply with normative expectations, usually stemming from an appraisal of the behavior of the immediate reference group (i.e., best friends) irrespective of any demands or based on a specific expectation from the reference group. One way to think about motivation to comply is to consider a situation in which a youth is hanging out with a group of friends who are circulating a marijuana joint. The joint comes full circle to the youth, who has never tried a "blunt" and does not know whether to smoke it or pass. He sees that smoking marijuana is widely accepted by his immediate friends (no other youth in the circle passed) and that smoking marijuana is valued by his peers. In anticipation of some censure, he thinks to himself, "What would happen if I didn't smoke it and just passed it to the person next to me?" In this situation, there is a specific demand that is fueling motivation to comply, but a more general motivation might be considered purely on the basis of the request to hang loose with friends outside of school absent any pressures to smoke. The evaluative component of this model considers whether the youth will smoke (intentions) on the basis of some determination of whether smoking is "cool," whether the youth will lose face in front of his friends if he chooses not to smoke, and so forth.

ROUND 1: BANDURA VERSUS AJZEN AND FISHBEIN

This brief examination of the selected work of Ajzen and Fishbein examined in the preceding section complements Bandura's (1977a, 1997) SLT in several ways. Both theoretical expressions are concerned with cognitive mechanisms that mediate the effects of stimulus on response and could conceivably be called *learning* or *social influence theories*. Both theories are concerned at a very deep level with refining the concept of reinforcement and clarifying the driving forces in behavior (Bandura called this "human agency"). Both theories proffer hypothetical constructions (efficacy, attitudes, and beliefs) in the hope of replacing conjecture with established fact. Whereas a cornerstone feature of Bandura's SLT focuses almost exclusively on self-efficacy expectations as responsible for human agency, Ajzen and Fishbein concentrated more on attitudes and beliefs as independent components that predict behavioral intentions. To be accurate, Ajzen and Fishbein later included a component in their model that represents efficacy (i.e., volitional control), calling the revised model the theory of planned behavior (Ajzen, 1991). The position of this new component was given equal stature as attitudes

and beliefs in the prediction of intentions. Frankly, it is not clear whether Ajzen and Fishbein's more recent thinking evaluates will and control on the same level as Bandura, whose concept of efficacy captures a different facet of mental reflection. Even with this added efficacy component, there is a slightly different focus in TRA, which emphasizes a mediating chain of cognitive events that predicts intentions to execute a behavior (overt response) rather than cognitions in terms of a single evaluation directly predicting behavior.

It may come to pass on the basis of TRA that an individual intends to engage in a certain behavior but for some unforeseen reason cannot. In essence, there are other unspoken motivational states that interfere with completion of the behavior, but they are not specified in TRA. As the progenitor of self-efficacy and social learning theory, Bandura would show disdain for this approach and attribute the unspoken states to perceived self-efficacy, arguing that barriers to execution of behavior are rooted in the individual's perception whether he or she has the proper skills or not. Thus, Bandura adds an important layer to the equation not apparent in TRA. Take, for instance, a girl who is asked out on a date to her senior year high school prom. She knows that she should not drink alcohol; however, during the car ride to the dance, several of the boys drink clandestinely from a bottle of whiskey. Eventually the boys offer the bottle to all the girls in the car, some of whom accept the offer while others refuse. In the months leading up to the prom, the girl attended a drug prevention class that imparted social assertiveness and drug refusal skills to offset negative peer influence situations such as this one. On the basis of his writings, Bandura would depart from Ajzen and Fishbein by suggesting that perceived efficacy is the single motivating factor that dictates whether she will refuse the offers or not. On the basis of TRA, a more rigorous evaluation of the situation would take place, relying on attitudes (subjective appraisal), beliefs (normative and behavioral), and intentions. The totality of these cognitions will dictate whether she intends on taking a sip from the bottle or not. Bandura could not care less about the young girl's expectations of the outcomes, her appraisal of the value of drinking, or her consideration of whether drinking is widely acceptable among her peers. His sole emphasis in the cognitive train leading to behavior is on whether the girl believes that she can efficaciously refuse the active offer (see Graham et al., 1991, for a discussion of the difference between active and passive offers).

There are some internally consistent portions that exist in both SLT and TRA. Both models suggest that external variables can influence the interior components of the model. In SLT, factors such as the persuasiveness of role models, perceived difficulty of the task, and experience with behavior can influence action. In TRA, any number of situational factors can influence attitudes and beliefs, calibrating their effect on behavioral intentions. More important, in TRA all external effects are mediated through intentions and do not influence behavior directly. In addition, both models require proximity or correspondence between the elements of the cognitive chain; in SLT, it is better to have task-specific efficacy predict relevant behaviors, whereas in TRA the intentions should be proximal with respect to action, target, context, and time to the behaviors in question. In essence, both theories incorporate temporal erosion into the causal sequence between cognition and behavior. Last but not least, both theories are concerned with overt behavior and as such attempt to link mental events hidden from view with actions that are clearly observable. In this respect, both theories tap mentalist descriptions of human behavior.

WHAT ELSE IS OUT THERE?

I would be remiss in not including other influential theories in this discussion. Page limitations prevent me from detailing the inner workings of each and every theory pertinent to drug use etiology; however, a few are worth mentioning briefly. One that comes immediately to mind is cognitive dissonance theory (Festinger, 1964). Dissonance is based on the notion that what goes on inside people's heads is best described as a self-evaluation in which they seek to reduce discrepancies between their overt behaviors and what they attribute them to in their minds. Dissonance arises because people parry back and forth in their mind, deciding whether they believe something has value on merit alone or because people tell them it has value. Various experimental paradigms are used in dissonance research to detect whether people are induced to behavior, in essence "changing their cognitions" to achieve behavioral consistency (e.g., forced compliance).

Dissonance research has also included exposure-to-information studies that tease apart whether people make adjustments in their cognitions if the information they receive is discrepant with their self-perception. This type of approach has tremendous implications for the processes underlying normative education (Haines & Spear, 1996; Page, Hammermeister, & Roland, 2002). In normative education, program modules seek to correct youth's misperceptions regarding how many people (or friends) drink alcohol or smoke cigarettes because adolescents are usually far off the mark (overestimating). Part of the problem with this framework is that one kid may say, "All my friends use marijuana" and be correct; all of his or her immediate or close friends do smoke marijuana. The truth is that if one uses MTF data as a gauge, very few kids really smoke (at least not a majority), and a much smaller proportion smoke marijuana. So for individuals whose friends all smoke marijuana, there is a lot of dissonance in the formation of their values and self-perception. These youth experience consistent reinforcement for smoking that is discrepant with the prevailing norms being taught. Programs wanting to implement normative education as a focal prevention modality may have to consider that a broad-brush approach may not net the best results if there are pockets of youth experiencing dissonance on the basis of their own self-perception and observation of overt behaviors.

COMBINATION THEORIES

Some other viewpoints borrow heavily from either SLT or TRA and combine these with other disciplines to explain adolescent drug use. The social stress model of substance abuse incorporates unique facets of SLT, stress-coping models, family systems theory, competence models (skills orientation), and resilience models to account for early stages of drug use (Rhodes & Jason, 1990). Extensive evidence has documented that this approach is useful in accounting for adolescent drug use (e.g., Colder & Chassin, 1993; Dugan, Lloyd, & Lucas, 1999; Sussman et al.,

Lawrence M. Scheier

1993; Wills, 1986). Problematic in this conceptualization is that theorists hypothesize internal resilience factors, like social competence, to offset stressful experiences (in combination with community resources, role models, social networks, and related opportunities). Tension reduction and emotion-focused coping models suffer from the same local problem because they posit that an evaluation of the stressor and a corresponding appraisal of its relative impact on the individual occurs immediately before the decision to drink or use drugs (e.g., Labouvie, 1986a, 1986b). Even if the core feature of a phenomenological emotion-based model is self-regulation and management of positive and negative affective states, one has to ask oneself whether affect is uniquely different from cognition. Ultimately, stress-coping models resemble a more finely tuned version of an efficacy conceptualization in which the final interface (before decisions of engaging behavior) requires an assessment of skill (e.g., "Do I have the proper skills to offset this stressor?"; see also Lazarus & Folkman, 1984, for a more detailed examination of a stress-coping theoretical framework).

The same can be said of peer cluster theory (Oetting & Beauvais, 1986, 1987). Although the theory has received substantial attention along with other social influence and socialization models, there are some concerns as to whether it can be clearly distinguished from TRA or SLT. For instance, Oetting and Beauvais (1987, p. 206) stated, "The single dominant variable in adolescent drug use is the influence provided by the peers with whom an adolescent chooses to associate." They inherently borrowed on the concept of influence, whether this influence is depicted as originating from large social institutions or smaller peer cluster groups. Putting the onus on peers (groups or clusters) still begs the question of how peer influences inform behavior. In peer cluster theory, there is a socialization effect, whereby peer drug use creates favorable norms and a climate in which drugs are positively reinforced (Bauman & Ennett, 1994). According to Oetting and Beauvais, peers "shape attitudes . . . provide the social contexts . . . share ideas and beliefs" (p. 206). Here again, the authors are borrowing terms, like norms (i.e., beliefs), from other theories already adequately cov-

ered (TRA). Conformity disposition theories (Brown, Clasen, & Eicher, 1986; Wills, 1992) might be included as an intermediate step in the cognitive process or for that matter cognitive dissonance, which can account for upward and downward evaluations against relevant standards (peers).

WE ARE ALL THEORISTS AT HEART

People are theoretical creatures, and we regularly use induction and deduction to make cognitive headway in this world. Adolescents are no different, although the overall tenor of their predictions may be more primitive and their outcomes less successful. Consider a situation in which we encounter two youths, one a radical behaviorist and the other more inclined to use dissonance or social learning theory to explain the world. We ask these youths to watch a few of their peers in a laboratory situation in which a confederate will make efforts to induce participants to use drugs (alcohol or cigarettes). Forget about the ethical considerations for a moment and imagine this experiment was feasible without encountering the ire of your institutional review board. The one youth labeled behaviorist is reluctant to really make any predictions because he wants to learn more about the reinforcement history of the participants he is viewing. The other youth, our dissonance and social learning theorist (he can be one, the other, or both), is much more willing to make predictions on the basis of some knowledge of the participants' interior world. In other words, he wants to know who is efficacious and who uses his or her own overt behavior to make judgments or can be induced (persuaded) to make decisions. In this example, we can obtain a better sense of the darkest hour for drug use etiology. Our perspective on drug use etiology will be shaped by our choice of behaviorism or mentalism as a valid theoretical explanation.

One of the more pressing problems facing theory development in the study of drug use etiology is the lack of useful, reliable, and refined outcome measures. Fishbein (1967) reminded us that theorists rarely subject their measures of behavior to the same scrutiny as their predictors, and this may be the sole reason models purporting consistency fail. Behavior is, for the most part, the conditions in which the

104

mental ruminations and cognitive features of most theories "work." At the very least, according to mentalist theories, the behavior in question has to include some component of cognition, given their close alliance. Consider, for instance, that we never really see learning; likewise, we never really see peer influence. Rather, we use specific data points of things we can observe or measure to infer measures of behavior (influence). This need to infer measurement properties has been partly responsible for the explosion of latent variable modeling applications for testing theoretical relations (Bentler, 1978).

The psychometric approach in latent variable modeling uses multiple measures of observed behavior to reduce bias from measurement error. The psychometric model in a confirmatory factor analysis is used to create a statistical abstraction or hypothetical construct (i.e., latent) on the basis of empirical overlap between the measures that share behavioral characteristics. For instance, three moderately correlated observed measures of peer influence (each one tapping a slightly different facet of influence) can be used to posit a hypothetical latent construct of peer influence. In a simple path model, we can use this construct to predict a designated outcome (i.e., drug use). Even though we use multiple measures to designate peer influence and we are able to ascertain that there is conceptual overlap between these measures (even using random parcels to reflect a homogeneous or unidimensional structure), latent variable constructs are still rife with problems. The reason is because, in essence, we have not offered a description of behavior in our theory using a different dimension, but merely inserted a substitute outcome (or predictor) measure that fit the theory. In the case of positing peer influence as a predictor of drug use, we are still very much on the outside (we need to be inside the head): We are not measuring thought processes themselves, just using signposts along the road to guide our journey.

Take the example of peer influence one small step further. To measure this, researchers usually ask youth, "How many of your peers smoke cigarettes?" (i.e., normative beliefs) or "Do you think your best friends would approve if you smoked marijuana?" Youth also frequently encounter questions along the lines of "Do you think it is important for you to smoke to be cool?" (i.e., attitudes toward drugs). In the next step, modeling experts examine the statistical association between youth's beliefs and/or attitudes and their own self-reported drug use ("On average, how much do you smoke?" or "On average, how much do you drink?"). The resulting correlation (or regression coefficient) is an estimate of how much overlap (variance accounted for) exists between beliefs, attitudes, and self-reported drug use. The problem encountered with this approach is that the actual process of learning and the connections between youth's beliefs and attitudes and how they acquire those beliefs and attitudes and actual drug use require a different dimension of understanding (a more mentalist conceptualization located inside the head). Even with latent variable strategies, which provide more reliable assessments, our initial measurements are still one step removed from the actual cause.

Another way of framing this is that we have created an S-R connectionist model of influence and we have no clue what lies between the S and the R. Perhaps, at some atavistic level, we could infer a theory of conformity (e.g., Argyle, 1957; Cialdini & Trost, 1998; Festinger, Schacter, & Back, 1950) and unravel the different pushes and pulls that connect perceptions of friends' use (normative expectations) and actual decisions to use drugs. Even if we made this argument at a single level (avoiding neural substrate arguments), we need to piece together differential association, conformity disposition, cognitive dissonance, peer cluster, persuasive communication, social learning, social contagion, symbolic interaction, subjective expected utility, social comparison, social identity, social strain, TRA, and the health belief model into a unified theoretical framework. This has not happened and is unlikely to occur because of the marriage of many investigators to at most one or two theories that explain youthful drug use.

A second problem that has surfaced in this discussion is that the measure of behavior (self-reported drug use) may have very little to do with attitudes expressed by close friends (or peers) or their beliefs. This is an essential argument made by both Bandura (1977b) and Ajzen and Fishbein (1969; Fishbein, 1967), and one that creates difficult issues for the field of drug use etiology. There may not be a correspondence between perceived friends' attitudes toward drug use and self-reported drug use because of the dissimilarity between the measures (i.e., the lack of correspondence or specificity) and because it is conceivable that youth do not evaluate the importance of their friends' attitudes toward drugs in the decision process prompting their own drug use. In other words, some youth may not care whether their friends favor or disfavor drug use, and this will diminish or undermine any hypothesized attitude–behavior relationship. Furthermore, attitudes toward drug use by friends may not have enough specificity to predict deviant forms of behavior by the adolescent. For example, subjective evaluation of smoking marijuana may not have utility in predicting deviant forms of behavior such as tobacco and alcohol use. If one recalls the profusion of latent variable strategies in today's field, many etiology and prevention scientists model latent constructs of polydrug use or general drug use reflected by multiple indicators of tobacco, alcohol, and marijuana use (Newcomb & Bentler, 1988; Scheier, Botvin, & Griffin, 2001). Again, correspondence is the key operative mechanism and the lack thereof may hamper our understanding of behavior.

IS THEORY USEFUL?

In this chapter, I attempted to address the major components of theory using the critical rationalist perspective (Popper, 1963). This perspective avoids the complications of excessive theorizing; rather, it provides a means to falsify weak or disconfirming theory. Part and parcel of my intention was to elaborate the necessary and sufficient conditions for a good theory (remember, there is no such thing as bad theory) and to frame this activity within the current directions of drug use etiology. I then set out to explore at some length the major postulates of SLT, using this framework to explore the advantages of drug prevention couched in terms of efficacy expectancies for drug refusal and other related program modules. In an effort to create some theoretical balance, I also briefly reviewed the TRA, paying careful attention to the cognitive basis of their model. I also quickly introduced other evaluative and social influence theories

in an effort to show how closely aligned they are with SLT and TRA, creating some theoretical redundancy in the field of drug use etiology. Finally, I engaged in a broad discussion of the utility of theories in general to help us understand drug use etiology, essentially linking etiology and theory as attempts to understand probabilistically how learning and influence occurs.

Learning is a complex and poorly understood phenomenon owing to the fact that we never see learning but rather infer its properties from various dimensions of change. One of the points I have tried to drive home is that the study of drug use etiology is essentially a study encompassing learning and that until we clarify how learning occurs, we are left with poorly defined outcome measures structured to fit existing theories. Little things such as how much youth smoke, how often they smoke, the intensity of their use (i.e., inhalation), under what conditions they smoke, whether they smoke infrequently or steadily, with whom they smoke, and so forth are poorly understood, and our prediction models are not helpful in this regard. We are making some headway in this area with the advent of social network analysis (Ennett et al., 2006), which looks more carefully at cliques and microprocesses of influence. However, for the most part we are essentially not learning from what we observe and are conjuring ideas based on intuition to fill the gaps.

The study of expectancies really helps to illustrate the problems we may encounter from investing in an impoverished theory. The field has witnessed considerable development with regard to expectancy measures, and a substantial literature exists pointing toward expectancies as major determinants of alcohol and drug use (see chap. 8, this volume). The expectancy literature grew out of studies of learning that emphasized clarifying the glue that binds stimulus to response. Expectancies were construed as motivational because expectancy theorists opined that etiology needed inside-the-head explanations, cognitive in nature, that inform us about behavior. According to expectancy theorists, a person consumes alcohol because he or she anticipates outcomes that will be reinforcing (e.g., relaxation, disinhibition, sexual power, magical thinking). This association feature was exemplified by balanced placebo experiments showing that people acted as though they were intoxicated even though they were not consuming alcohol (Marlatt & Rohsenow, 1980; Rohsenow, 1983). Expectancy research eventually matured to the point at which we were able to differentiate positive from negative reinforcement expectancies, explicate factors that influence expectancies, and determine whether changes in expectancies netted change in drinking status.

The problem is that for a theory of expectancies to have heuristic value to the field, it has to state why expectancies have the effect they do and why they predict drug use efficiently when controlling for other major determinants. Lots of people have expectancies for alcohol and do not drink. Hasin and Katz (chap. 13, this volume) eloquently point this out in their defense of genetic environment models: We do not have explanations for why some people react to drug use and others do not. Investigating both intra- and interindividual differences is the focus and perhaps the bane of psychology. To extend this one step further, even though many people have expectancies regarding the reinforcement properties of drugs or alcohol, something acts as a stopgap to prevent one person from using while another person uses too much. This extra step may be motivated reasoning, which is lacking as an explanation in expectancy research. This is what Bandura (1978, p. 237) meant when he discussed "theoretical clarifications of operative mechanisms." As we seek to build bigger and more comprehensive models that can accurately predict behavior, expectancies, as one instantiation of cognition, need to be integrated into these parsimonious expressions. These models should appreciate the impetus provided by expectancies, the cognitive satisfaction that results from acting on expectancies (i.e., efficacy), and the way expectancies fold into other social influences that drive consumption. It is quite plausible that expectancies are only a piece of a larger conformity disposition and that they tie in with other "dimensional" systems, including norms regarding prevalence of drug use and attitudes inferring perceived value of drug use. Although this type of systems approach has been tested by some investigators (e.g., Kuthar, 2002; Scheier & Botvin, 1997), we truly lack a more formal specification of expectancies in light of other major causal determinants. Only when we can seamlessly integrate multiple theories

with their different measurement strategies or combine learning theory with other levels of explanation can we explain why some youth use drugs and others choose differently. Until we can resolve these discrepancies, we are not theoretical enough.

One way to improve our awareness of cause and etiology is to break down the behaviors under scrutiny into smaller units. We can then try to explain these smaller units with existing theory guided by the principles of falsification. Bandura (1991, 1997) suggested using microanalytic procedures, breaking down cognitive events into smaller and smaller measurable units that are in close proximity to the behavior. This approach would enable us to more accurately see what is inside the head with respect to drug use. If drug use is part of a decision tree, then the tree must have branches as well as mental roots. Part of the microanalytic procedure is to recognize that behavior is the best measure of behavior. What would help are more veridical reports provided by youth who are using drugs at the time they use and in the situations that prompt their use. Short of implementing experimental designs that assign youth to drug use and nonuse conditions and that are ethically prohibited, we should conduct more naturalistic studies of youth, use computerized methods that allow private recordings of efficacy judgments (i.e., experience-sampling methods), and develop indirect strategies that dig beneath cognitive recollection and deliberation to layers of mental functioning beneath the radar of consciousness. Eventually, in an even-handed manner, we should be able to build a more complete picture of what behaviors occur under what conditions and for whom.

HOW CAN WE BEST TACKLE PREVENTION?

Finally, into the mix of any discussion of theory and drug use etiology there needs to be included the implications for prevention. It is clear that current prevention is vested in mentalist views of drug use, accentuating a broad swath of cognitive mediators including beliefs, attitudes, expectancies, and motivations (e.g., craving, urges, and triggers) as progenitors of drug use. Decades of research on drug use etiology has naturally supported prevention and helped make headway on refining our knowledge of risk and protection. One would think, with all this information at hand, that we could prevent drug use efficaciously. This, however, is not the case; drug use per se is statistically normative at certain ages, and it takes a long time for many individuals to mature out (see chap. 30, this volume). The relatively small primary prevention effects we obtain can be blamed on poor implementation, poor or unreliable measurement, theoretical failure, or program failure. Another way to account for small program effects is to suggest that we are focused on the wrong measures, and our programs are not developmentally consistent with what we know about adolescence (many youth do not implement the skills we teach, but that does not mean they do not acquire the skills). In many cases, the litmus test we use to gauge programmatic change is a coarse measure of drug use, owing to our inability to measure what goes on inside the head.

The other problem is that we are sometimes using measures of skills to predict behavior change. The incongruity (I noted previously that behavior is the best predictor of behavior) causes a drop in predictive variance that cannot be accounted for. Bandura (1978) was quick to note that efficacy judgments could also serve as a barometer of change (or learning) as opposed to the actual behavior in question. Thus, we should be looking to see whether youth are more efficacious in their skills following exposure to treatment, not whether they move from use to nonuse. In the case of drug use, we are quick to note that endpoints for primary prevention programs usually include 30-day prevalence estimates for cigarettes, measures of daily or weekly alcohol consumption, binge drinking (five or more drinks in one occasion), or ever having used marijuana (see chap. 34, this volume, which examines outcomes for Life Skills Training). I have argued to my colleagues on several occasions that we are often throttled by the very measures we use because in many cases we implement prevention programs in the fifth or sixth grades and the desired endpoints have little variation (and are highly positively skewed) at those young ages. As MTF data confirm, a majority of youth do not use drugs (with the exception of alcohol in the 10th and 12th grades), and this observation is especially compelling for youth younger than 13 (equivalent to the

6th grade). In this respect, we might be better off conditioning ourselves to use measures of perceived efficacy as a gauge of whether a program works and wait for longer term follow-up data to confirm program effects on the behavioral endpoints. Although this may force people to be patient, it is a more logical format for testing change, given that behavior is the best predictor of behavior (Epstein, 1979).

There is another side to this concern that may help paint a clearer picture of how SLT works. Bandura (1997) was quite adamant that congruence between the efficacy judgment and behavior was essential to reify or validate his theory. Reams of evidence have supported that SLT works best when we consider task-specific self-efficacy as a judgment of performance and then link this with behaviors close in proximity and related in kind (A. Bandura, personal communication, July 2005). If we deviate from this position a bit, it is feasible that we can consider using efficacy judgments tethered to one set of skills as predictors of performance in another set of skills. In other words, if youth are really manifesting change (through the process of learning) in their perceived competence or efficacy, then acquisition of these new skills and a change in mental rumination about efficacy should facilitate prediction of behavior for a different but related set of skills that draws on similar reflection of performance. In some previous work along these lines, my colleagues and I were able to show that Life Skills Training supports the cross-over effect for program modules targeting refusal efficacy (task specific) to generalized social competence (Scheier et al., 2001). Refusal of drug offers should be related at some level to assertiveness, initiation, and related skills that involve defense of rights (i.e., returning defective merchandise to the store or asking a friend to return something that has been borrowed). What lurks behind these specific skills, and what should be the focus of our assessment strategy, is the more generalized capacity for social competence that transcends the fixed act. A prudent course of action, then, is to assess whether youth acquire refusal-specific self-efficacy and assess the predictive relations between this task-specific learning and behavioral skills in related domains of social competence. Again, the endpoints are changing, but they are still relative to the overall prime directive of changing the conditions that would lead to drug use.

The overall feeling readers should get at this point is that drug use researchers may have come face to face with a conundrum. At the very outset of this chapter, I established that theory has utility only if it can tell us something about reality. In Bandura's (1977a, 1977b, 1997) quite influential world of social learning, we recognize that our mission is to elaborate a model of human agency that links thought and action. Here may be the difficult question. We want to achieve marked changes in behavior, but the cognitive elements that drive that behavior are somewhat unknown, or at least invisible. The behaviors in question are more visible, or at least more accessible to our measurement tools. We can use biological assays of saliva to assess cotinine or thiocynate content and alcohol breathalyzers to validate the veracity of self-reports, but we cannot do the same with measures of mental activity. Brain measures of cortical electrical activity and functional MRI do not tell us whether a youth is efficacious with respect to refusal skills.

In the world of the youth we study, we are attempting to learn more about their cognitions and how these fuzzy mental constructions fuel actions that we consensually regard as detrimental. If we think about things more carefully, it is, in reality, their thoughts that are detrimental, and the behaviors are just symptomatic of some underlying dysfunction. From a programmatic standpoint, we remain steadfast that behavior change is our focus; however, it is really the underlying cognitions that psychologists would like to change. Accordingly, the argument posed above, that we should consider efficacy judgments as endpoints, may be valid. For the purpose of establishing whether a prevention program is theoretically consistent, we may need to assess immediate effects on drug use. However, long-term studies of drug prevention programs need to establish whether program-related change to efficacy has any enduring effects on related behaviors (e.g., refusal skill efficacy reaches across time to improve overall perceived self-efficacy). In this manner, we can see whether we have made demonstrable and enduring changes in the learning machinery of youth as they venture out into this very complex world.

References

Adorno, T. W. (1992). Why philosophy? In D. Ingram & J. Simon-Ingram (Eds.), *Critical theory: The essential readings* (pp. 20–30). St. Paul, MN: Paragon House.

Ajzen, I. (1991). The theory of planned behavior. *Organizational Behavior and Human Decision Processes, 50,* 179–211.

Ajzen, I., & Fishbein, M. (1969). The prediction of behavioral intentions in a choice situation. *Journal of Experimental Social Psychology, 5,* 400–416.

Ajzen, I., & Fishbein, M. (1970). The prediction of behavior from attitudinal and normative variables. *Journal of Experimental and Social Psychology, 6,* 466–487.

Ajzen, I., & Fishbein, M. (1973). Attitudinal and normative variables as predictors of specific behaviors. *Journal of Personality and Social Psychology, 27,* 41–57.

Ajzen, I., & Fishbein, M. (1977). Attitude–behavior relations: A theoretical analysis and review of empirical research. *Psychological Bulletin, 84,* 888–918.

Argyle, M. (1957). Social pressure in public and private situations. *Journal of Abnormal and Social Psychology, 54,* 172–175.

Akers, R. L. (1985). *Deviant behavior: A social learning approach.* Belmont, CA: Wadsworth.

Allport, G. W. (1935). Attitudes. In C. Murchison (Ed.), *A handbook of social psychology* (pp. 798–844). Worcester, MA: Clark University Press.

American Psychiatric Association. (1994). *Diagnostic and statistical manual of mental disorders* (4th ed.). Washington, DC: Author.

Bachman, J. G., Johnston, L. D., O'Malley, P. M., & Humphrey, R. H. (1988). Explaining the recent decline in marijuana use: Differentiating the effects of perceived risks, disapproval, and general lifestyle factors. *Journal of Health and Social Behavior, 29,* 92–112.

Bachman, J. G., O'Malley, P. M., & Johnston, J. (1978). *Youth in transition. Vol. 6: Adolescence to adulthood: A study of change and stability in the lives of young men.* Ann Arbor, MI: Institute for Social Research.

Bachman, J. G., Wadsworth, K. N., O'Malley, P. M., Johnston, L. D., & Schulenberg, J. E. (1997). *Smoking, drinking and drug use in young adulthood: The impacts of new freedoms and new responsibilities.* Mahwah, NJ: Erlbaum.

Ball, J. C. (1965). Two patterns of narcotic drug addiction in the United States. *Journal of Criminal Law, Criminology and Police Science, 56,* 203–211.

Bandura, A. (1977a). Self-efficacy: Toward a unifying theory of behavior change. *Psychological Review, 84,* 191–215.

Bandura, A. (1977b). *Social learning theory.* Englewood Cliffs, NJ: Prentice-Hall.

Bandura, A. (1978). Reflections on self-efficacy. *Advances in Behavior Research and Therapy, 1,* 237–269.

Bandura, A. (1982). Self-efficacy mechanism in human agency. *American Psychologist, 37,* 122–147.

Bandura, A. (1986). *Social foundations of thought and action: A social cognitive theory.* Englewood Cliffs, NJ: Prentice-Hall.

Bandura, A. (1991). Self-regulation of motivation through anticipatory and self-reactive mechanisms. In R. A. Dienstbier (Ed.), *Nebraska Symposium on Motivation. Vol. 38: Perspectives on motivation* (pp. 69–164). Lincoln: University of Nebraska Press.

Bandura, A. (1997). *Self-efficacy: The exercise of control.* New York: W. H. Freeman.

Bauman, K. E., & Ennett, S. T. (1994). Peer influence on adolescent drug use. *American Psychologist, 49,* 820–822.

Bauman, K. E., & Fisher, L. A. (1986). On the measurement of friend behavior in research on friend influence and selection: Findings from longitudinal studies of adolescent smoking and drinking. *Journal of Youth and Adolescence, 15,* 345–353.

Bem, D. J. (1967). Self-perception: An alternative interpretation of cognitive dissonance phenomena. *Psychological Review, 74,* 183–200.

Bentler, P. M. (1978). The interdependence of theory, methodology, and empirical data: Causal modeling as an approach to construct validation. In D. B. Kandel (Ed.), *Longitudinal research on drug use: Empirical findings and methodological issues* (pp. 267–302). Washington, DC: Hemisphere.

Bentler, P. M., & Speckart, G. (1979). Models of attitude–behavior relations. *Psychological Review, 86,* 452–464.

Bentler, P. M., & Speckart, G. (1981). Attitudes "cause" behaviors: A structural equation analysis. *Journal of Personality and Social Psychology, 40,* 226–238.

Blatt, S. J., McDonald, C., Sugarman, A., & Wilber, C. (1984). Psychodynamic theories of opiate addiction: New directions for research. *Clinical Psychological Review, 4,* 159–189.

Bolles, R.C. (1972). Reinforcement, expectancy, and learning. *Psychological Review, 79,* 394–409.

Brown, B. B., Clasen, D. R., & Eicher, S. A. (1986). Perceptions of peer pressure, peer conformity dispositions, and self-reported behavior among adolescents. *Developmental Psychology, 22,* 521–530.

Carey, J. (1968). *The college drug scene.* Englewood Cliffs, NJ: Prentice-Hall.

Chein, I., Gerard, D. L., Lee, R. S., & Rosenfeld, E. (1964). *The road to H: Narcotics, delinquency, and social policy.* New York: Basic Books.

Cialdini, R. B., & Trost, M. R. (1998). Social influence: Social norms, conformity, and compliance. In D. T. Gilbert, S. T. Fiske, & G. Lindzey (Eds.), *The handbook of social psychology* (151–192). Boston: McGraw-Hill.

Colder, C. R., & Chassin, L. (1993). The stress and negative affect model of adolescent alcohol and the moderating effects of behavioral undercontrol. *Journal of Studies on Alcohol, 54,* 326–333.

Doob, L. W. (1947). The behavior of attitudes. *Psychological Review, 54,* 135–156.

Dugan, S., Lloyd, B., & Lucas, K. (1999). Stress and coping as determinants of adolescent smoking behavior. *Journal of Applied Social Psychology, 29,* 870–888.

Duncan, T., Tildesley, E., Duncan, S., & Hops, H. (1995). The consistency of family and peer influences on the development of substance use in adolescence. *Addictions, 90,* 1647–1660.

Ennett, S. T., Bauman, K. E., Hussong, A. M., Faris, R., Foshee, V. A., DuRant, R., & Cai, L. (2006). The peer context of adolescent substance use: Findings from social network analysis. *Journal of Research on Adolescence, 16,* 159–186.

Epstein, S. (1979) The stability of behavior: I. On predicting most of the people much of the time. *Journal of Personality and Social Psychology, 37,* 1097–1126.

Festinger, L. (1957). *A theory of cognitive dissonance.* Stanford, CA: Stanford University Press.

Festinger, L. (1964). *Conflict, decision, and dissonance.* Stanford, CA: Stanford University Press.

Festinger, L., Schachter, S., & Back, K. (1950). *Social pressures in informal groups.* New York: Harper & Row.

Fishbein, M. (1967). Attitude and prediction of behavior. In M. Fishbein (Ed.), *Readings in attitude theory and measurement* (pp. 477–492). New York: Wiley.

Fishbein, M., & Ajzen, I. (1975). *Belief, attitude, intention, and behavior: An introduction to theory and research.* Reading, MA: Addison-Wesley.

Godfrey-Smith, P. (2003). *Theory and reality: An introduction to the philosophy of science.* Chicago: University of Chicago Press.

Graham, J. W., Marks, G., & Hansen, W. B. (1991). Social influence processes affecting adolescent substance use. *Journal of Applied Psychology, 76,* 291–298.

Haines, M., & Spear, S. F. (1996). Changing the perception of the norm: A strategy to decrease binge drinking among college students. *Journal of American College Health, 45,* 134–140.

Hansen, W. B., Graham, J. W., Sobel, J. L., Shelton, D. R., Flay, B. R., & Johnson, C. A. (1987). The consistency of peer and parent influences on tobacco, alcohol, and marijuana use among young adolescents. *Journal of Behavioral Medicine, 10,* 559–579.

Hekimian, L. J., & Gershon, S. (1968, July 15). Characteristics of drug abusers admitted to a psychiatric hospital. *JAMA, 205*, 125–130.

Hu, F. B., Flay, B. R., Hedeker, D., Siddiqui, O., & Day, L. E. (1995). The influences of friends' and parental smoking on adolescent smoking behavior: The effects of time and prior smoking. *Journal of Applied Social Psychology, 25*, 2018–2047.

Hull, C. L. (1930). Simple trial and error learning: A study in psychological theory. *Psychological Review, 37*, 241–256.

Jessor, R., Graves, T. D., Hanson, R. C., & Jessor, S. (1968). *Society, personality, and deviant behavior: A study of a tri-ethnic community.* New York: Holt, Rinehart & Winston.

Jessor, R., & Jessor, S. L. (1977). *Problem behavior and psychosocial development.* New York: Academic Press.

Johnston, L. D. (1973). *Drugs and American youth.* Ann Arbor, MI: Institute for Social Research.

Johnston, L. D., O'Malley, P. M., & Bachman, J. G. (1984). *Highlights from drugs and American high school students, 1975-1983* (DHHS Publication No. [ADM] 84-1317). Rockville, MD: National Institute on Drug Abuse.

Johnston, L. D., O'Malley, P. M., Bachman, J. G., & Schulenberg, J. E. (2007). *Monitoring the Future national survey results on drug use, 1975-2006. Volume 1: Secondary school students* (NIH Publication No. 07-6205). Bethesda, MD: National Institute on Drug Abuse.

Kaplan, H. B. (Ed.). (1995). *Drugs, crime, and other deviant adaptations.* New York: Plenum Press.

Kesey, K., & Faggen, R. (1962). *One flew over the cuckoos' nest.* New York: Viking Press.

Krosnick, J. A., & Judd, C. M. (1982). Transitions in social influences at adolescence: Who induces cigarette smoking? *Developmental Psychology, 18*, 359–368.

Kuthar, T. L. (2002). Rational decision perspectives on alcohol consumption by youth revising the theory of planned behavior. *Addictive Behaviors, 27*, 35–47.

Labouvie, E. W. (1986a). Alcohol and marijuana use in relation to adolescent stress. *International Journal of the Addictions, 21*, 333–345.

Labouvie, E. W. (1986b). The coping function of adolescent alcohol and drug use. In R. K. Silbereisen, K. Eyferth, & G. Rudinger (Eds.), *Development as action in context: Problem behavior and normal youth development* (pp. 229–240). New York: Springer-Verlag.

Lazarus, R., & Folkman, S. (1984). *Stress, appraisal, and coping.* New York: Springer.

Leary, T. (1968). *The politics of ecstasy.* New York: Putnam.

Marlatt, G. A., & Rohsenow, D. J. (1980). Cognitive processes in alcohol use: Expectancy and the balanced placebo design. In N. K. Mello (Ed.), *Advances in substance abuse: Behavioral and biological research* (pp. 159–199). Greenwich, CT: JAI Press.

Musto, D. F. (Ed.). (2002). *One hundred years of heroin.* Westport, CT: Auburn House.

Newcomb, M. D., & Bentler, P. M. (1988). *Consequences of adolescent drug use: Impact on the lives of young adults.* Newbury Park, CA: Sage.

Oetting, E. R., & Beauvais, F. (1986). Peer cluster theory: Drugs and the adolescent. *Journal of Counseling and Development, 65*, 17–22.

Oetting, E. R., & Beauvais, F. (1987). Peer cluster theory, socialization characteristics, and adolescent drug use: A path analysis. *Journal of Consulting and Clinical Psychology, 34*, 205–213.

Page, R. M., Hammermeister, J., & Roland, M. (2002). Are high school students accurate or clueless in estimating substance abuse among peers? *Adolescence, 37*, 567.

Popper, K. (1963). *Conjectures and refutations: The growth of scientific knowledge.* London: Routledge Classics.

Reich, C. A. (1970). *The greening of America.* New York: Random House.

Rohsenow, D. J. (1983). Drinking habits and expectancies about alcohol's effects for self versus others. *Journal of Consulting and Clinical Psychology, 51*, 536–541.

Rhodes, J. E., & Jason, L. A. (1990). A social stress model of substance use. *Journal of Consulting and Clinical Psychology, 58*, 395–401.

Rotter, J. B. (1966). Generalized experiences for internal versus external control of reinforcement. *Psychological Monographs, 80*, 1014–1053.

Rounsaville, B. J., Kosten, T. R., Weissman, M. M., & Kleber, H. D. (1986). Prognostic significance of psychopathology in treated opiate addicts: A 2.5-year follow-up study. *Archives of General Psychiatry, 43*, 739–745.

Rounsaville, B. J., Weissman, M. M., Wilber, C. H., Crits-Christoph, K., & Kleber, H. (1982). Diagnosis and symptoms of depression in opiate addicts: Course and relationship to treatment outcome. *Archives of General Psychiatry, 39*, 151–156.

Scheier, L. M., & Botvin, G. J. (1997). Expectancies as mediators of the effects of social influences and alcohol knowledge on adolescent alcohol use: A prospective analysis. *Psychology of Addictive Behaviors, 11*, 48–64.

Scheier, L. M., Botvin, G. J., & Griffin, K. W. (2001). Preventive intervention effects on developmental progression in drug use: Structural equation modeling analyses using longitudinal data. *Prevention Science, 2*, 89–110.

Skinner, B. F. (1938). *The behavior of organisms.* New York: Appleton-Century.

Skinner, B. F. (1950). Are theories of learning necessary? *Psychological Review, 57,* 193–216.

Skinner, W. F., Massey, J. L., Krohn, M. D., & Lauer, R. M. (1985). Social influences and constraints on the initiation and cessation of adolescent tobacco use. *Journal of Behavioral Medicine, 8,* 353–376.

Sussman, S., Brannon, B. R., Dent, C. W., Hansen, W. B., Johnson, C. A., & Flay, B. R. (1993). Relations of coping effort, coping strategies, perceived stress, and cigarette smoking among adolescents. *International Journal of the Addictions, 28,* 599–612.

Thomas, C. W., Petersen, D. M., & Zingraff, M. T. (1975). Student drug use: A re-examination of the "hang-loose ethic" hypothesis. *Journal of Health and Social Behavior, 16,* 63–73.

Tolman, E. C. (1932). *Purposive behavior in animals and men.* New York: Century.

Tolman, E. C. (1966). *Behavior and psychological man: Essays in motivation and learning.* Berkeley: University of California Press. (Original work published 1951)

Van Fraassen, B. C. (1980). *The scientific image.* Oxford, England: Oxford University Press.

Webster's seventh new collegiate dictionary. (1967). Springfield, MA: G. & C. Merriam.

White, H. R., Johnson, V., & Horwitz, A. (1986). An application of three deviance theories to adolescent substance use. *International Journal of the Addictions, 21,* 347–366.

Wicker, A. W. (1969) Attitude versus action: The relationship of verbal and overt behavioral responses to attitude objects. *Journal of Social Issues, 25,* 41–78.

Wills, T. A. (1986). Stress and coping in early adolescence: Relationships to substance use in urban school samples. *Health Psychology, 5,* 503–529.

Wills, T. A. (1992). Social comparison and self change. In J. Fisher, J. Chinksy, Y. Klar, & A. Nadler (Eds.), *Self-change: Social-psychological and clinical perspectives* (pp. 231–252). New York: Springer-Verlag.

Wills, T. A., Resko, J. A., Ainette, M. G., & Mendoza, D. (2004). Smoking onset in adolescence: A person-centered analysis with time-varying predictors. *Health Psychology, 23,* 158–167.

Wilson, G. T. (1978). The importance of being theoretical: A commentary on Bandura's "Self-efficacy: Towards a unifying theory of behavioral change." *Advances in Behavior Research and Therapy, 1,* 217–230.

Wolfe, T. (1968). *The electric kool-aid acid test.* New York: Farrar, Strauss, & Giroux.

Wurmser, L. (1974). Psychoanalytic considerations of the etiology of compulsive drug use. *Journal of the American Psychoanalytic Association, 22,* 820–843.

CHAPTER 6

EPIDEMIOLOGY AND ETIOLOGY HAND IN HAND

James C. (Jim) Anthony

It should come as no surprise that epidemiology started out as the science of epidemics. The field's contribution has since expanded to become a more general way of asking questions and seeking evidence about the health of the public. Terris (1985, p. 15) defined epidemiology as "the study of the health of human populations." Epidemiology's main research questions, and the theoretical propositions it seeks to evaluate, can be grouped in relation to five main substantive rubrics, or categories: (a) quantity, (b) location, (c) causes, (d) mechanisms, and (e) prevention and control (Anthony & Van Etten, 1998). This chapter explores each of these rubrics in the context of my long-term involvement in epidemiological studies of drug use, dependence, and associated maladaptive social behaviors. A major goal of the chapter is to show how epidemiology must be appreciated hand in hand with etiology for us to make substantial advances in the prevention and control of diseases and health conditions related to drug use.

For most epidemiologists, the point of departure for epidemiological research is the clinical case, sometimes a patient, who is suffering from a disease, injury, or other health condition that could be located within the *International Classification of Diseases* (10th ed., or ICD-10) of the World Health Organization (2007). Nonetheless, epidemiology's action research agenda works toward the design and evaluation of mass action public health interventions that seek to change the health status of populations (e.g., mass immunization, putting fluoride in the

public water supply, putting niacin and iodine in foodstuffs). For most practicing epidemiologists, the care and management of the health of an individual patient would be incidental to the practice of epidemiology.

For our research group, the condition of primary interest has been drug dependence (see ICD-10 Codes 303.0–304.9). We orient ourselves to a definition of drug dependence as a syndrome ("running together") of clinical features that can be recognized as (a) drug-related disturbances of the mental life (e.g., obsession-like ruminations about or cravings for drug use or drug experiences such as drug seeking, "rolling a joint"), (b) drug-related disturbances of behavior (e.g., compulsion-like repetitive drug taking even when the drug user seeks to exert control and to reduce or stop using), and (c) drug-related neuroadaptational changes (e.g., as manifest in the development of pharmacological tolerance; a withdrawal syndrome characteristic to each drug). The drug compounds of interest include those found in tobacco, alcoholic beverages, and inhalant drugs, as well as internationally regulated drugs that may or may not be illegal (depending on the jurisdiction of interest): cannabis, cocaine, heroin, and hallucinogens.

AN EPIDEMIOLOGIST'S ORIENTATION

Often our epidemiological research on drug dependence, including studies of drug dependence etiology, is organized in relation to a case definition or

Preparation of this chapter was partly supported by National Institute on Drug Abuse Grant K05DA015799.

set of diagnostic criteria from the ICD-10 or from the *Diagnostic and Statistical Manual of Mental Disorders* of the American Psychiatric Association (e.g., the third, third revised, and fourth editions; American Psychiatric Association, 1980, 1987, 1994, respectively). In an assessment session with an individual research participant or with a key informant such as a parent or spouse, standardized items or small groups of items (i.e., "testlets") are used to tap each diagnostic criterion or clinical feature of drug dependence. The assessment sessions originally involved administration of standardized paper-and-pencil questionnaires (e.g., with the participant marking self-ratings on the questionnaire form so that no one else could see the answers) or interviewer-administered question modules as part of a face-to-face or telephone survey interview in a private location. Sometimes the interviewer read out the questions and the participant marked the answers on a concealed questionnaire. In more recent years, the assessment session is one in which the field staff member brings a laptop computer, introduces the research protocol and secures informed consent (or parental consent and child assent), and works through a tutorial on how to put on headphones, read the laptop screen, and use the laptop keyboard to complete a computerized self-assessment. The field staff member can then make ratings (e.g., of the neighborhood or household environment), leaving the participant to complete the computerized self-assessment in privacy, listening to the assessment questions via the headphones while concurrently reading the questions on the laptop display screen. An example of this audiovisually enhanced computer-assisted self-assessment can be found online at http://www.icpsr.umich.edu/SAMHDA/survey-inst/NHSDA_19.pdf. This is the assessment method for drug use and drug dependence used to derive the National Survey on Drug Use and Health (NSDUH) estimates mentioned later in this chapter.

For the most part, our research has been focused on the "extramedical" use of drug compounds and the occurrence of drug dependence once extramedical use has started. The assessment of extramedical drug use involves seeking evidence about experiences such as whether the drug user has taken the drug to get high, for reasons other than those for which it was prescribed, in amounts more than was prescribed, or with greater frequency than was prescribed. In our etiological studies of the mechanisms leading to drug dependence, we have often focused on discrete and generally quite memorable events in the drug user's life that are necessary preconditions in drug dependence etiology, such as (a) the first chance to try cannabis, (b) the first actual use of cannabis, and (c) the first appearance of a clinically recognizable feature of cannabis dependence. The age at first onset of drug dependence is typically specified as an age (or year) of life during which there has been temporal clustering of at least three clinical features of the just-defined drug dependence syndrome (e.g., at least three such features experienced during the year before the date of assessment in an epidemiological field study).

In the domain of drug dependence epidemiology, under the rubric of quantity, epidemiology seeks answers to population-oriented questions of the following form: "Within the population, how many people are becoming drug users and how many drug users are becoming cases of drug dependence?" Under the rubric of location, epidemiology seeks to learn whether the occurrence of drug dependence might differ across subgroups or segments of population experience, in which the subgroups and segments are defined with respect to characteristics of the person (e.g., age, sex), place (e.g., census tract, neighborhood), and time (e.g., season of the year). Evidence under these two rubrics is part of the important "political arithmetic" function of epidemiology.

The epidemiological estimates flowing from quantity and location, now produced year by year, are used to make policy decisions about resource allocations. Throughout the 1st decade of the 21st century, epidemiological estimates of this type from recent NSDUH data have prompted a mobilization of resources in the direction of illegal and other extramedical use of prescription analgesic drugs, much as epidemiological estimates of the 1980s prompted mobilization of resources in the direction of illegal use of cocaine (e.g., see Compton & Volkow, 2006). This shifting and redeployment of resources and realignment of the public health mandate is in direct response to the collection of pertinent epidemiological data.

SEEKING FUNDAMENTAL TRUTHS

A society's interest in and decisions to allocate resources for etiological research on drug use and drug dependence may rise and fall in relation to epidemiologists' capacities to produce credible estimates about a population's drug-taking experiences. If only for this reason, the results from basic descriptive epidemiological research must be of interest to scientists who seek to discover fundamental truths about the causes of drug use and drug dependence and the corresponding methods for prevention and control.

To illustrate, current mobilization of public health resources to counter the tobacco industry's initiatives continues to rely heavily on epidemiology's estimates of tobacco-attributable mortality and morbidity, within the context of the more general World Health Organization Global Burden of Disease initiative. Temporal variation in the Global Burden of Disease projections must now rest to some degree on stabilized effect estimates from etiological inquiries of the past (e.g., the estimated relative risk of developing lung cancer in relation to smoking). Nonetheless, each current projection is much more influenced by each country's age-specific estimates of tobacco-smoking prevalence.

Epidemiology has more to do with etiology under its rubrics of causes, mechanisms, and prevention and control. Looking across these rubrics, the rubric of causes is especially important. In the domain of drug dependence epidemiology, the rubric of causes subsumes research questions about what accounts for some individuals in the population becoming drug dependence cases while others in the population are spared. With respect to most populations of interest, in etiological research it is possible to draw a useful distinction between the causes of incidence as opposed to the causes of cases (Rose, 1985). To conduct proper etiological research on the causes of incidence, it is necessary to step backward in the direction of ecological research on causes and to estimate subgroup variations in the occurrence of a disease (e.g., estimating the risk of developing kidney stones in relation to

calcium content of the public water supply shared by all members of the subgroup; estimating the risk of dental caries in relation to the fluoride content of the water). In contrast, to probe for causes of cases, it is necessary to focus on the suspected determinants of individual-level variation in the risk of becoming a case, and the most traditional approaches in epidemiology are ones that hold constant the causes of incidence (as observed at the population level) to focus estimation on the effects of the causes of cases (as observed at the individual level, net of the population-level influences). As Rose (1985) pointed out, evidence regarding the determinants of variation in the subgroup-level occurrence of disease will often lead directly toward beneficial mass-action public health interventions (e.g., fluoridation of the public water supply to reduce occurrence of dental caries). In contrast, evidence about determinants of variation in the individual-level risk of disease (among individuals) is often used to motivate interventions for high-risk groups—that is, interventions that seek to change risk values for high-risk individuals but that otherwise have nothing to do with the population-averaged risks of developing disease.

THROWING A LIGHT SWITCH IN THE DARK

Epidemiology has been criticized for being a "black-box" branch of the biomedical sciences tree (Susser & Susser, 1996). That is, whereas most biomedical sciences are not satisfied until they have shed light on the causal mechanisms at play, epidemiologists tend to be willing to advocate public health action as soon as they discover "levers" that can make a difference. This tradition in epidemiology dates back at least 160 years ago when London's John Snow had no clue about the nature of the infective agent that was causing cholera epidemics to occur, but his research made clear that future cholera epidemics might be prevented by ensuring a sanitary water supply. The tradition can be taken backward in time by noting Lind's 18th-century experiments with citrus fruits and occurrence of scurvy: On board ocean-going ships, sailors provisioned with citrus fruits were less likely to develop scurvy than

sailors on ships without access to citrus fruits. It is
in this sense that we teach epidemiologists how it is
possible to skate forward toward effective prevention of a disease well before the specific causes or
causal mechanisms that lead toward excess occurrence of the disease are known. The assertion that
the causal mechanisms must be known to be able
to prevent a disease must be rejected as one that
ignores the history of effective public health work
(e.g., see Wynder, 1994).

Indeed, to some extent, epidemiologists are
encouraged to probe black-box enigmas. Within
these black boxes, we turn to directed acyclic graphs,
an analogue to sociology's more formal path diagrams
or structural equations models, used to describe connections between each suspected causal determinant
and (a) excess (or reduced) occurrence of the disease
within a population subgroup or (b) excess (or
reduced) risk of an individual becoming a case of the
disease. This work is subsumed under the rubric of
mechanisms because it pushes us beyond the more
basic question of whether a cause–effect relationship
is present toward the questions about how a cause–
effect relationship surfaces. To the extent that epidemiology participates in research on the natural
history of a disease process, epidemiologists are shed-
ding light on the how question—for example, how to
get from point A in the disease process to point B?
Within the domain of drug dependence epidemiology, we have some evidence that cannabis smokers
are more likely (than nonsmokers) to become cocaine
users, at least in part because they (a) are more likely
than others to be confronted with a chance to try
cocaine and (b) once the chance to try cocaine has
occurred, they are more likely to take the cocaine
(Wagner & Anthony, 2002b).

In sum, epidemiological research on the mechanisms underlying cause–effect relationships is
focused on the question of how a cause–effect relationship happens, not just on the question of
whether it happens. Typically, epidemiological
research on mechanisms requires longitudinal study
designs with at least three separate occasions of
measurement, but there are some exceptions (e.g.,
see Anthony & Van Etten, 1998).

Part X of this handbook is devoted to elucidating
the connections between etiology and prevention.

As many of these chapter authors and others have
argued, the most compelling evidence of cause–
effect relationships in epidemiology can come from
randomized preventive trials to estimate the effects
of suspected beneficial public health maneuvers. For
the most part, epidemiological research under the
rubric of prevention and control seeks to discover or
to estimate the effects of human-crafted interventions to reduce the occurrence of a disease or to
control it by shortening its duration or adverse
impact. What follows in this chapter is a brief
description of epidemiological research issues for
which the evidence, to date, has not provided resolution. As such, this discussion, albeit brief, may
stimulate new research of a more definitive quality
than exists at present.

QUANTITY

Epidemiological population-based estimates of how
many individuals are becoming cases of breast cancer or AIDS are not complicated by interference
from police pressure, although personal privacy
issues are paramount in almost all health research.
The same cannot be said to be true for epidemiological estimates for the population-level occurrence of
illegal drug use. Until there is evidence to the contrary, one must presume that these epidemiological
estimates are influenced, at least in part, by the
prominence of governmental involvement in the
survey initiatives.

Some recent evidence has suggested that this
type of concern is not a mere theoretical issue.
Gruzca, Abbacchi, Przybeck, and Gfroerer (2007)
compared roughly concurrent estimates from the
NSDUH versus estimates from the National Epidemiologic Survey on Alcohol and Related Conditions (NESARC). Whereas the methods of
research should have produced roughly comparable
estimates of illegal drug involvement in the two surveys, there was a systematic pattern of larger illegal
drug involvement estimates from the NSDUH as
compared with the values observed in the concurrent NESARC. The main difference between the two
epidemiological surveys was in the prominence of
governmental involvement. In the NSDUH survey,
the fieldwork is carried out by field staff recruited

and supervised by the Research Triangle Institute, working at a distance from the sponsoring agency within the federal government, the Substance Abuse and Mental Health Services Administration. In the NESARC survey, the fieldwork has been carried out by operatives of the U.S. Census Bureau, who apparently were introduced to the survey respondents as such. There were some other differences in methodological approach, but governmental involvement may prove to have been determinative in that the NSDUH estimates indicate more substantial illegal drug involvement values than did NESARC research conducted at about the same time.

I believe that there is a way to overcome measurement biases of this type. The approach is one that allows each designated epidemiological research participant to remain completely anonymous and deidentified during the process of contributing information for the purposes of epidemiological survey estimation. This approach does not require any change in current processes of sampling, recruitment, and participation to yield NSDUH or NESARC observations. Rather, the approach is one in which the current NSDUH and NESARC research protocols would be improved by asking participants to provide, anonymously, saliva or other biological specimens for bioassay confirmation of what otherwise might not be disclosed during the self-assessments. Johnson and Fendrich (2005) have already developed a model approach that can strengthen NSDUH and NESARC research practices (see chap. 24 of this volume).

LOCATION

My own first experience with politically sensitive epidemiological research involved a question posed during the 1980s crack epidemic by Charles R. (Bob) Schuster, then director of the National Institute on Drug Abuse (NIDA). At that time, I was a part-time NIDA staff fellow detailed to assist the Office of the Director with epidemiology and prevention research. After receiving questions from congressional representatives and staff, Bob came back to me and asked whether there was something about being Black that accounted for crude epidemiological comparisons suggesting that crack cocaine

use was more prevalent among Blacks as compared with Whites. I replied that an overall Black–White comparison might show an excess occurrence of crack cocaine use among Blacks but that this comparison would not merit any causal interpretation. We discussed the situation for awhile and decided that the best comparative study would be one that focused on neighborhoods in which both Blacks and Whites resided; comparisons of Blacks and Whites living in all-Black and all-White neighborhoods were essentially confounded by local area characteristics such as street-level drug availability, police presence, and disorganized characteristics of neighborhoods that might promote illegal drug taking. On face value, Blacks and Whites might consume equal amounts of cocaine once these confounds were controlled, and the prevalence difference would then disappear.

We congratulated ourselves on a prior decision we had made to pull the NIDA National Household Survey on Drug Abuse data sets out of tightly held governmental archives and into the form of public use data, permitting someone to complete a proper analysis of recent epidemiological survey data on this topic. Once basic design issues were sorted out, the next task was to find a talented colleague to undertake the more difficult task of assembling the data and completing the required secondary analyses. Fortunately, our Johns Hopkins School of Hygiene and Public Health colleague Marsha Lillie-Blanton stepped up to the plate.

The resulting scientific report, published in the *Journal of the American Medical Association* (Lillie-Blanton, Anthony, & Schuster, 1993), represents an example of what epidemiology can accomplish in the service of identifying subgroups of the population that might be experiencing an excess burden of a potentially adverse health experience. In this instance, the potentially adverse health experience was the use of crack cocaine, and our working hypothesis was that Blacks might not be more likely than their White neighbors to have become involved in smoking crack.

The epidemiological approach in this context is one that seeks to hold constant the causes of incidence to which Rose (1985) referred and to focus sharply on the causes of cases once local area characteristics are held constant. Most of the time when psychosocial researchers speak of holding local area characteristics constant, they do the hard work of specifying and measuring a comprehensive list of local area characteristics of theoretical importance with respect to the response variable of interest. In part, this approach is based on the fact that psychosocial researchers are often interested in estimating the individual or joint effects of these local area characteristics, and they are sometimes interested in how the several local area characteristics might be linked in causal sequences.

In this particular example of epidemiological research under the rubric of location, our goal was simply to hold constant the local area characteristics to try to sort out whether the crack-smoking experience of Blacks might be different from the crack-smoking experience of Whites living in the same neighborhoods. With this goal in mind, we did not require measurements of the local area characteristics. Instead, we made use of the epidemiological approach of neighborhood matching, such that socially shared local area characteristics are held constant whether they have been prespecified and measured or not. The appropriate statistical model in this context is a special case of the generalized linear model with a logit link function and with an intercept subscripted for each local area under study. Applying this approach to the study of crack cocaine experiences, we believed that we were on safe statistical and conceptual grounds. We had previously used the same approach to investigate causes of cases in a series of epidemiological studies based on different samples, and we had the research approach vetted by anonymous expert peer reviewers in two of epidemiology's premier journals, the *American Journal of Epidemiology* and *Epidemiology* (e.g., Anthony, Tien, & Petronis, 1989; Anthony & Petronis, 1991).

As reported in the *JAMA* article (Lillie-Blanton et al., 1993), we found that crude comparisons (before neighborhood matching) suggested that Blacks were more likely to become crack cocaine users as compared with Whites. However, once we used neighborhood matching to hold constant the socially shared local area characteristics such as local street-level crack availability, there were no Black–White differences in crack-smoking experi-

ence. That is, the original observed Black–White difference became null when we shifted the comparison to Blacks living in the same neighborhoods as Whites.

We do not regard this evidence as compelling with respect to whether there is something about being Black that might increase likelihood of smoking crack, in part because we have not taken into account the experience of Blacks and Whites still living in totally segregated local areas. As such, it is not causal evidence in any compelling sense of that term. Nonetheless, the evidence does raise questions about whether there is anything special associated with being designated racially Black that accounts for the occurrence of crack smoking and points instead toward the issue of location. Looking back on the U.S. cocaine epidemic of the late 20th century and at crude estimates showing a Black excess for smoking crack, it appears that where one resided was more important than one's racial designation.

NEIGHBORHOOD LOCATION MAY PROMOTE DRUG USE

It was during our research on neighborhood-matched crack cocaine smoking that we recognized an opportunity to investigate impoverished neighborhoods as potentially important locations for person-to-person spread of drug involvement, no matter what race or ethnicity a resident might bring to the environment. We were less interested in the public health impact that might result if we were to change an individual's poverty level (e.g., from below to above the federal poverty value) and more interested in the public health impact that might result if neighborhoods were shifted from generally below to generally above those poverty levels. For this reason, we turned to National Household Survey on Drug Abuse data that allowed us to produce population-averaged or marginal model estimates for the occurrence of drug involvement, such as can be derived from the generalized estimating equations (in contrast to subject-specific model estimates for the occurrence of drug involvement, such as can be derived with random effects models). These generalized estimation equations (GEE) approaches represent an elaboration of the general and generalized linear model (GLM) and allow the equations to include covariate terms for each measured individual-level variable (e.g., age, sex, race) and for each measured group-level variable (e.g., neighborhood poverty level).

In addition to estimating associations that link these covariates to a binary response variable of interest (here, drug involvement), these GLM/GEE models provide estimates of the degree to which the binary response is clustered within the groups (here, clustering of drug involvement within neighborhoods). That is, standard survey research analysis approaches treat clustering effects as somewhat of a nuisance that must be extracted in the design effect for the survey analysis (this design effect is also called variance inflation factor). In contrast, our approach is one in which the estimated degree of clustering is modeled as an epidemiological parameter of inherent interest. The interpretation of the clustering parameter is not necessarily causal in that a non-null clustering effect estimate might be a result of differential migration of similar (drug-using) individuals into the same neighborhood because of differential out-migration of non–drug users or some other process (e.g., the contagion hand-to-hand sharing processes mentioned earlier).

This ambiguity of the evidence leads us to group these studies under the rubric of location for epidemiology, not under the rubric of causes, because the evidence cannot be interpreted unambiguously as evidence for or against a causal hypothesis. The rubric of causes can be reserved for evidence that mounts up to the point that a causal inference is warranted, or when any single study's evidence carries an unambiguous definitive quality such that a firm causal inference is warranted. Readers interested in our research on the clustering of drug involvement are referred to Bobashev and Anthony (1998, 2000) and Delva, Bobashev, Gonzalez, Cedeno, and Anthony (2000); research on clustering of cocaine involvement is described elsewhere (Petronis & Anthony, 2000, 2003).

With respect to methodological innovation, epidemiological research under the rubric of location benefits from advances in methods for research under the rubric of causes. For this reason, specific

notes about methodological issues are positioned at the end of the Causes section.

CAUSES

Most epidemiologists possess skeptical, ruminative, and almost obsessive traits that predate graduate education in this discipline. If not, they learn to become skeptical, ruminative, and almost obsessive about the intricacies of making causal inferences. For this reason, it generally takes epidemiologists years, if not decades, of research to draw causal inferences from empirical evidence. Nonetheless, one of the most important sets of research questions for epidemiology includes questions about causes—that is, those answered only through research.

One of the domains of scholarly focus that has interested our research group involves the epidemiological study of education and occupation. Another interrelated domain involves stressors experienced in the workplace (and elsewhere), sometimes so extreme that posttraumatic stress disorder (PTSD) comes into play in response to a traumatic exposure. With respect to workplace environments, we have contributed epidemiological evidence that lends support to the idea that psychosocial stressors at work may be contributing to an increased risk of developing drug dependence syndromes in adult life. This evidence comes not only from cross-sectional survey research, but also from prospective and longitudinal research with careful measurement and control of childhood antecedents that might otherwise be confounding our relative risk estimates (e.g., see Reed, Storr, & Anthony, 2006, for a recent example). Concurrently, we have contributed epidemiological evidence that lends support to the idea that PTSD-qualifying traumatic events, and early PTSD, might be contributing to an increased risk of these syndromes, net of the influence of work stress (e.g., see Reed, Anthony, & Breslau, 2007).

Nonetheless, we would still group this evidence under the rubric of location rather than that of causes. In our view, the evidence can now sustain a claim that the risk of developing drug dependence during adulthood is greater in population subgroups with specific types of psychosocial work environments and in subgroups with specific traumatic or PTSD experiences. It cannot yet sustain a claim that these characteristics are either causes of incidence (operating at the population level) or causes of cases (operating at the individual level).

In addition to these scholarly efforts, our research group has been successful in moving forward toward making a firm causal inference in relation to one and only one suspected determinant of drug involvement—namely, very early rule-breaking behavior in the first years of primary school. As a result of our work with Sheppard Kellam at the Johns Hopkins Prevention Research Center, there is now a mounting body of experimental trial evidence that early interventions intended to reduce rule breaking among boys in primary school (but not among girls) do account for a reduced level of drug involvement in the adolescent years. The early evidence from these epidemiological experiments showed promise with respect to prevention of tobacco smoking and perhaps other drug use in the early adolescent years (e.g., see Furr-Holden, Ialongo, Anthony, Petras, & Kellam, 2004; Kellam & Anthony, 1998; Storr, Ialongo, Kellam, & Anthony, 2002).

Building from a large body of evidence from prior observational studies, including both case control and cohort studies (e.g., see Robins, 1978; Tomas, Vlahov, & Anthony, 1990), these experimental findings from epidemiological field experiments begin to sustain a causal inference that early rule breaking in the primary school years is more than a vulnerability marker or predictor of later drug involvement and drug dependence—at least among boys. It is the experimental evidence that serves to dampen concerns about underlying genetic or other susceptibility traits that might otherwise account for the observational evidence on this suspected causal association—in that randomized assignments to the early interventions should have brought into balance the distributions of these traits. Readers are encouraged to also read chapter 11 of this volume to secure a broad perspective on the importance of genetic liability traits that might influence youthful drug involvement.

MECHANISMS

Epidemiological studies have generally involved cross-sectional data or prospective cohort studies involving no more than two measurement occasions. Some of these measurement occasions have occurred well before the epidemiological study was designed, as in Robins, Gyman, and O'Neal's (1962) classic study of deviant children grown up: In this nonconcurrent prospective study, the early childhood data were recorded in the 1920s, whereas the follow-up measurements were completed in the late 1950s and early 1960s. More often, measurement occasions have occurred after an initial baseline assessment (e.g., see Reed et al., 2007). As such, the research design choices for epidemiological studies have few temporally fine-grained data to offer when the goal is to study dynamic mechanistic relations that are capable of linking one suspected causal antecedent to later responses.

Nonetheless, it is sometimes possible to reconstruct evidence about the natural history or clinical course of a disease by taking a measurement at one or two points in time and by exploiting what can be recollected about the unfolding of events that lead up to disease. When events unfold without the introduction of intervention services (as is often the case in relation to drug dependence in the community), these are studies of natural history (i.e., that which unfolds as a process leading toward and through the disease state, even when there is no more than palliative care). When the unfolding of events includes clinical interventions of presumed efficacy, what we have is a picture of the clinical course, in that the natural history of the condition might have been altered by the efficacious intervention.

Our research group has contributed evidence on the natural history of the drug dependence process from both concurrently conducted prospective studies and cross-sectional observational studies. With respect to the former, one focus has been cannabis dependence, and the epidemiological evidence was consistent with the idea that subjectively felt loss of control over cannabis use and continued cannabis use despite knowledge of harm were the clinical features of cannabis dependence that emerged most rapidly after onset of cannabis use (Rosenberg &

Anthony, 2001). With respect to the cross-sectional observational studies, we have been able to shed new light on the processes that lead from initial drug exposure opportunities toward onset of drug use. In the process, we discovered evidence that a cannabis–cocaine association occurs in part because cannabis users are more likely to experience a chance to try cocaine (as compared with non–cannabis-using alcohol and tobacco users in the community) and in part because those with a history of cannabis smoking are more likely to progress from the first chance to try cocaine to the eventual actual use of cocaine (Wagner & Anthony, 2002b). These estimates are from survival analysis models with time-dependent covariates. In a separate inquiry, we elaborated the survival analysis models to study transitions from first cocaine use to first appearance of a cocaine dependence syndrome. In the process, we found evidence that an estimated 5% to 6% of cocaine users develop a cocaine dependence syndrome within 12 to 24 months after onset of cocaine use, and there appears to be no male–female difference in this level of risk of dependence among users. In contrast, for cannabis and for alcohol, the risk of developing a dependence syndrome in the first 12 to 24 months after onset of use of these drugs is substantially smaller (< 2%), but there is some evidence of a male excess in risk of becoming dependent on these drugs in the first years after onset of their use (Wagner & Anthony, 2002a).

At first blush, estimates of this type appear to have more to do with epidemiology's rubric of quantity and little to do with mechanisms—until one appreciates an analogy with the natural history of human response to infective agents. For example, when we study what accounts for some individuals becoming cases of HIV/AIDS while others are spared, we can trace some of the causal variation back to exposure opportunity and whether individuals live in communities in which they might come into contact with others infected with HIV. We can also trace some of the causal variation back to the actual occurrence of an effective contact with the infective agent for some members of communities in which exposure opportunity is prevalent, whereas other members of those communities never make an effective contact with the agent. Finally, we can

trace some of the causal variation to the rapid or late transition from infection to development of a clinically apparent disease. Each of these steps in the natural history of HIV/AIDS represents a facet of the mechanisms by which HIV/AIDS occurs in human communities. Each facet is a locus for potential intervention that can disrupt the eventual occurrence of HIV/AIDS. By analogy, each of the steps in the drug dependence process is a facet of the mechanisms by which this condition occurs, representing a locus for potential intervention.

On occasion, epidemiology produces longitudinal multiwave evidence about the mechanisms leading to one or another of the just-mentioned steps in the drug dependence process. An example is our research group's work on how levels of parental monitoring and supervision seem to exert a causal influence on levels of affiliation with deviant and drug-using peers, which as it happens are major explanatory variables in relation to the first step mentioned above (i.e., the step of having a chance to try a drug). Lloyd and Anthony (2003) conducted a five-wave longitudinal study with a primary goal of estimating whether changes in level of parental monitoring and supervision during the childhood–adolescence transition might account for changes in level of deviant peer affiliation. The main evidence from that study was consistent with parenting models in which maintenance of parental supervision and monitoring through the transition from childhood to adolescence was beneficial. In covariate-adjusted GLM/GEE models to estimate effects of parenting interventions at the community level, as the parental monitoring dropped over the years, there were subsequent increases in levels of deviant peer affiliation. Except for our research group's decision to focus on population-averaged or marginal estimates of the effects of parenting interventions, the research approach in this study is not too distant from what has been used in social psychological etiological research conducted by others. (Chaps. 19, 20, and 21 of this volume cover different angles of the same question, looking at both parenting and deviant subgroup bonding as precursors to drug use.)

Epidemiological research that falls under the rubric of mechanisms can also address recovery processes, as well as residual comorbidities, disabilities, and impairments that occur secondary to drug taking and drug dependence. In our research group, a focus of inquiry has been a set of hypotheses about the effects of drug use or dependence on psychiatric disturbances. For example, during the just-mentioned cocaine epidemic, there were clinical observations to the effect that cocaine use might precipitate panic attacks in individuals who otherwise would not have developed panic attacks. In an early prospective study on this cocaine–panic hypothesis, we found that risk of developing a panic attack for the first time occurred three times more frequently among cocaine users than among those who had never used (Anthony et al., 1989). In later research, we harnessed a novel epidemiologic case-crossover design to deal with the possibility that this cocaine–panic effect might be an artifact of unmeasured genetic or other underlying susceptibility traits. Control over these traits was accomplished via the choice of the case-crossover design, in which the participant serves as his or her own control (hence, all traits are matched). Even in the case-crossover context, we confirmed the three-fold excess risk for panic attacks observed in the original study (O'Brien, Wu, & Anthony, 2005). Recently, our research group has used the case-crossover design for etiological research on the cannabis–cocaine transition process, and a report on this aspect of the mechanisms of drug involvement is forthcoming.

With respect to methodology, we now face a large number of issues of causal mechanism that cannot be addressed effectively with conventional epidemiological research designs and that require large-sample research if the resulting estimates are to be precise and statistically powerful. Several examples include testing the Koob, Caine, Parsons, Markou, and Weiss (1997) opponent process and negative affect regulation models about the causes of drug dependence; the Kendler et al. (2000) models suggesting that the experience of child sexual abuse is an important determinant of later drug dependence (at least among girls); the work of Bickel, Odum, and Madden (1999) on drug users' development of rapid discounting of the value of delayed outcomes; suggestions from the work of Gentile, Lynch, Linder, and Walsh (2004) on how violent video games might increase aggressive behaviors

and in turn might account for an increased occurrence of drug use and dependence; and finally epigenetic hypotheses about the rapid development of drug dependence once drug use starts, which can only be tested if traditional self-assessment survey methods of epidemiology are yoked with biological assays of specimens from which protein products of gene effects or mRNA residue can be extracted.

Issues of this type have prompted our research group to develop multifaceted research protocols that allow anonymous but trackable epidemiological research participants to provide online self-assessments and linked biological specimens on a daily, weekly, monthly, or quarterly basis—that is, data possessing a quality of fine temporal granularity that reaches for but will never achieve the specificity of data obtained from the laboratory or research clinic. The data-gathering costs for these protocols approach values formerly achieved in postal surveys with mailed questionnaires, but fidelity of participation is maintained via a data-missingness prevention protocol that involves delivery of preincentives and reinforcers following principles outlined by Dillman (2000), among others. New and innovative research methods of this type should help us to advance the understanding of causal mechanisms leading to the first stages of drug involvement (first chance to try, first actual drug use) through the drug dependence processes and their sequelae, with a greater resolving power than has been true of prior epidemiological research, in which the samples have been large and representative of the community, but matters of temporal sequencing and granularity of data have been given short shrift.

PREVENTION AND CONTROL

Contributions of our research group to the epidemiological evidence on prevention and control have already been mentioned under the rubric of causes, and there are whole chapters of this handbook (chaps. 31–34) devoted to the contribution of prevention research to our understanding of etiological research issues. For this reason, this section of the chapter is short.

The only issue to be mentioned involves a line of epidemiological and clinical practice research initiated by others in the health and mental health fields, which can be expanded for application to research on drug use and drug dependence. In specific, our collaborators in Australia (Andrews, 2007; Mackinnon, Griffiths, & Christensen, 2008) have already developed and started to evaluate online interventions that can be harnessed on a mass-action public health scale to influence the individual-level risk of becoming a case and the population-level incidence of caseness. In the prior section, we described a set of online research protocols for observational studies of the mechanisms leading to and beyond drug dependence. In this section, we note that it is possible to nest randomized trials within these observational designs to assess the effects of experimental online interventions and to improve our estimates of the causal effects of variables that are difficult to manipulate (e.g., as in the early rule-breaking construct of the Johns Hopkins Prevention Center's randomized trials; Kellam & Anthony, 1991, 1998).

CONCLUSION

In sum, we are not yet satisfied with epidemiology's contributions to etiological research on drug use or dependence. Via novel methodologies and longitudinal and experimental research designs not previously stressed in epidemiology, we anticipate that our research can shed more light on the causal relationships that are unfolding to influence the occurrence of drug use in human societies and the subsequent adversities that sometime occur after onset of drug use (e.g., drug dependence syndromes, subsequent psychiatric comorbidities). In work along these lines, we hope to lay a more solid foundation for future generations that instills more penetrating and detailed probes linking epidemiological and etiological research.

References

American Psychiatric Association. (1980). *Diagnostic and statistical manual of mental disorders* (3rd ed.). Washington, DC: Author.

American Psychiatric Association. (1987). *Diagnostic and statistical manual of mental disorders* (3rd ed., rev.). Washington, DC: Author.

American Psychiatric Association. (1994). *Diagnostic and statistical manual of mental disorders* (4th ed.). Washington, DC: Author.

Andrews, G. (2007). ClimateGP—Web based patient education. *Australian Family Physician, 36,* 371–372.

Anthony, J. C., & Petronis, K. R. (1991). Suspected risk factors for depression among adults 18–44 years old. *Epidemiology, 2,* 123–132.

Anthony, J. C., Tien, A. Y., & Petronis, K. R. (1989). Epidemiologic evidence on cocaine use and panic attacks. *American Journal of Epidemiology, 129,* 543–549.

Anthony, J. C., & Van Etten, M. L. (1998). Epidemiology and its rubrics. In A. Bellack & M. Hersen (Eds.), *Comprehensive clinical psychology* (pp. 355–390). Oxford, England: Elsevier Science.

Bickel, W. K., Odum, A. L., & Madden, G. J. (1999). Impulsivity and cigarette smoking: Delay discounting in current, never, and ex-smokers. *Psychopharmacology, 146,* 447–454.

Bobashev, G. V., & Anthony, J. C. (1998). Clusters of marijuana use in the United States. *American Journal of Epidemiology, 148,* 1168–1174.

Bobashev, G. V., & Anthony, J. C. (2000). Use of alternating logistic regression in studies of drug-use clustering. *Substance Use & Misuse, 35,* 1051–1073.

Compton, W. M., & Volkow, N. D. (2006). Major increases in opioid analgesic abuse in the United States: Concerns and strategies. *Drug & Alcohol Dependence, 81,* 103–107.

Delva, J., Bobashev, G. V., Gonzalez, G., Cedeno, M., & Anthony, J. C. (2000). Clusters of drug involvement in Panama: Results from Panama's 1996 National Youth Survey. *Drug and Alcohol Dependence, 60,* 251–257.

Dillman, D. A. (2000). The role of behavioral survey methodologists in national statistical agencies. *International Statistical Review, 68,* 200–213.

Furr-Holden, C. D. M., Ialongo, N. S., Anthony, J. C., Petras, H., & Kellam, S. G. (2004). Developmentally inspired drug prevention: Middle school outcomes in a school-based randomized prevention trial. *Drug and Alcohol Dependence, 73,* 149–158.

Gentile, D. A., Lynch, P. J., Linder, J. R., & Walsh, D. A. (2004). The effects of violent video game habits on adolescent hostility, aggressive behaviors, and school performance. *Journal of Adolescence, 27,* 5–22.

Grucza, R. A., Abbacchi, A. M., Przybeck, T. R., & Gfroerer, J. C. (2007). Discrepancies in estimates of prevalence and correlates of substance use and disorders between two national surveys. *Addiction, 102,* 623–629.

Johnson, T., & Fendrich, M. (2005). Modeling sources of self-report bias in a survey of drug use epidemiology. *Annals of Epidemiology, 15,* 381–389.

Kellam, S. G., & Anthony, J. C. (1998). Targeting early antecedents to prevent tobacco smoking: Findings from an epidemiologically based randomized field trial. *American Journal of Public Health, 88,* 1490–1495.

Kellam, S. G., Werthamer-Larsson, L., Dolan, L. J., Brown, C. H., Mayer, L. S., Rebok, G. W., et al. (1991). Developmental epidemiologically based preventive trials: Baseline modeling of early target behaviors and depressive symptoms. *American Journal of Community Psychology, 19,* 563–584.

Kendler, K. S., Bulik, C. M., Silberg, J., Hettema, J. M., Myers, J., & Prescott, C. A. (2000). Childhood sexual abuse and adult psychiatric and substance use disorders in women—An epidemiological and Cotwin control analysis. *Archives of General Psychiatry, 57,* 953–959.

Koob, G. F., Caine, S. B., Parsons, L., Markou, A., & Weiss, F. (1997). Opponent process model and psychostimulant addiction. *Pharmacology Biochemistry and Behavior, 57,* 513–521.

Lillie-Blanton, M., Anthony, J. C., & Schuster, C. R. (1993, February 24). Probing the meaning of racial/ethnic group comparisons in crack cocaine smoking. *JAMA, 269,* 993–997.

Lloyd, J. J., & Anthony, J. C. (2003). Hanging out with the wrong crowd: How much difference can parents make in an urban environment? *Journal of Urban Health, 80,* 383–399.

Mackinnon, A., Griffiths, R. M., & Christensen, H. (2008). Comparative randomised trial of online cognitive–behavioural therapy and an information website for depression: 12-month outcomes. *British Journal of Psychiatry, 192,* 130–134.

O'Brien, M. S., Wu, L. T., & Anthony, J. C. (2005). Cocaine use and the occurrence of panic attacks in the community: A case-crossover approach. *Substance Use & Misuse, 40,* 285–297.

Petronis, K. R., & Anthony, J. C. (2000). Perceived risk of cocaine use and experience with cocaine: Do they cluster within US neighborhoods and cities? *Drug and Alcohol Dependence, 57,* 183–192.

Petronis, K. R., & Anthony, J. C. (2003). A different kind of contextual effect: Geographical clustering of cocaine incidence in the USA. *Journal of Epidemiology and Community Health, 57,* 893–900.

Reed, P. L., Anthony, J. C., & Breslau, N. (2007). Incidence of drug problems in young adults exposed to trauma and posttraumatic stress disorder—Do early life experiences and predispositions matter? *Archives of General Psychiatry, 64,* 1435–1442.

Reed, P. L., Storr, C. L., & Anthony, J. C. (2006). Drug dependence enviromics: Job strain in the work environment and risk of becoming drug-dependent. *American Journal of Epidemiology, 163,* 404–411.

Robins, L. N. (1978). Sturdy childhood predictors of adult antisocial behaviour—Replications from longitudinal studies. *Psychological Medicine, 8,* 611–622.

Robins, L. N., Gyman, H., & O'Neal, P. (1962). The interaction of social class and deviant behavior. *American Sociological Review, 27,* 480–492.

Rose, G. (1985). Sick individuals and sick populations. *International Journal of Epidemiology, 14,* 32–38.

Rosenberg, M. F., & Anthony, J. C. (2001). Early clinical manifestations of cannabis dependence in a community sample. *Drug and Alcohol Dependence, 64,* 123–131.

Storr, C. L., Ialongo, N. S., Kellam, S. G., & Anthony, J. C. (2002). A randomized controlled trial of two primary school intervention strategies to prevent early onset tobacco smoking. *Drug and Alcohol Dependence, 66,* 51–60.

Susser, M., & Susser, E. (1996). Choosing a future for epidemiology. 2: From black box to Chinese boxes and eco-epidemiology. *American Journal of Public Health, 86,* 674–677.

Terris, M. (1985). The changing relationships of epidemiology and society: The Robert Cruikshank lecture. *Journal of Public Health Policy, 6,* 15–36.

Tomas, J. M., Vlahov, D., & Anthony, J. C. (1990). Association between intravenous drug use and early misbehavior. *Drug and Alcohol Dependence, 25,* 79–89.

Wagner, F. A., & Anthony, J. C. (2002a). From first drug use to drug dependence: Developmental periods of risk for dependence upon marijuana, cocaine, and alcohol. *Neuropsychopharmacology, 26,* 479–488.

Wagner, F. A., & Anthony, J. C. (2002b). Into the world of illegal drug use: Exposure opportunity and other mechanisms linking the use of alcohol, tobacco, marijuana, and cocaine. *American Journal of Epidemiology, 155,* 918–925.

World Health Organization. (2007). *International classification of diseases and related health problems* (10th ed.). Geneva, Switzerland: Author.

Wynder, E. L. (1994). Invited commentary: Studies in mechanism and prevention: Striking a proper balance. *American Journal of Epidemiology, 139,* 547–549.

PART III

COGNITIVE AND AFFECTIVE INFLUENCES

TEMPERAMENT, SELF-CONTROL, AND ADOLESCENT SUBSTANCE USE: A TWO-FACTOR MODEL OF ETIOLOGICAL PROCESSES

Thomas A. Wills and Michael G. Ainette

Temperament dimensions are simple behavioral and emotional characteristics that are early appearing, from about 2 to 4 years of age (Angleitner & Ostendorf, 1994; Rothbart & Ahadi, 1994). It has been established that dimensions of temperament measured at early time points predict substance use, and in some cases abuse, years later. One important and pressing question is how this association occurs. This issue is of significant interest to etiological theory but at present is not well understood. In this chapter, we review evidence that demonstrates the significance of these prominent relationships and outline a theoretical approach that may help to understand how this occurs.

Our theoretical approach is rooted in what have been termed *developmental* or *epigenetic* models (Goldsmith, Gottesman, & Lemery, 1997; Rothbart & Ahadi, 1994; Zucker, 1994). The essence of this approach is that temperament dimensions in childhood form a substrate for the development of more complex attributes in adolescence; here, we focus on variables under the rubric of behavioral and emotional self-regulation (Wills, Ainette, Mendoza, Gibbons, & Brody, 2007; Wills & Dishion, 2004). These more complex self-control characteristics influence the extent of the adolescent's exposure to proximal risk or protective factors for substance use, and levels of these risk and protective factors affect the likelihood of substance use initiation and escalation. Following the association between earlier factors and later functioning onward in time, patterns of self-control and substance use in adolescence (including frequency, scope, and motives for use) may set the stage for substance use or abuse at later ages. In the following sections, we consider the theoretical basis for epigenetic models and summarize findings from studies of adolescents that have tested this approach. In the final section, we discuss directions for further research that can be derived from this model.

DEFINITION OF TEMPERAMENT DIMENSIONS

Temperament is defined as behavioral and emotional characteristics that are early appearing, are relatively stable over time, and have some constitutional basis (Buss & Plomin, 1984; Rothbart & Bates, 2006). *Early,* in this case, means they are measurable in the form described here from around 2 to 4 years of age. Measures have been developed that assess temperament characteristics during this period, and longitudinal studies have shown that relative ranking on these attributes has some stability over time even though the morphology and absolute levels of the attributes may change (e.g., Hagekull, 1989; Pedlow, Sanson, Prior, & Oberklaid, 1993). It is important to note that temperament dimensions reflect attributes that are present at some level in all individuals. Although an extreme level of a temperamental

This work was supported by a Research Development Award K02 DA00252 and R01 Grants DA0880, DA12623, and DA021865 from the National Institute on Drug Abuse and by National Cancer Institute Grant R21 CA81646. Collaboration and consultation with Gene Brody, Frederick Gibbons, Meg Gerrard, Mary Rothbart, Ralph Tarter, and Robert Zucker contributed to this work.

characteristic may be defined as pathological (e.g., very high restlessness and physical activity qualifying as attention-deficit/hyperactivity disorder; Barkley, 1997a), measures of temperament dimensions are normally distributed in the population of children and adolescents, and the research we discuss here has for the most part been conducted with general population samples.

Temperament dimensions as measured at early ages are quite simple in form. For example, activity level is how often the individual moves around physically. In this sense, temperament represents the style rather than the content of behavior. Although some researchers have labeled individuals in terms of easy versus difficult temperament, others have focused on the predictive significance of individual dimensions of temperament, and that is the approach we have used in our studies. It should be noted that temperament dimensions may have a constitutional basis, but their expression occurs in transaction with a particular cultural and familial environment that significantly shapes the expression of temperament characteristics (Kochanska, Aksan, & Joy, 2007; Rothbart & Ahadi, 1994; Wills, Sandy, Yaeger, & Shinar, 2001).

Dimensions of Temperament

Although there is some variation in taxonomic systems, research has focused on five to six basic dimensions of temperament (for representative measures, see Capaldi & Rothbart, 1992; Scheier, Casten, & Fullard, 1995; Windle & Lerner, 1986). *Activity level* is the tendency to be physically active. An individual with a high score on this dimension often moves around and feels restless after sitting still for a time (Wills, DuHamel, & Vaccaro, 1995). *Negative emotionality* (also termed *irritability* or *frustration*) is the tendency to be easily and intensely distressed. An individual high on this dimension is readily frustrated or upset and, when this occurs, shows a strong negative emotional reaction (Wills, Windle, & Cleary, 1998). *Rigidity* (also termed *inhibition, fearfulness,* or *harm avoidance*) reflects the tendency to have an inhibitory response to situations. An individual high on rigidity shows hesitation or withdrawal when confronted with a new situation or a novel person, dislikes changes, and

has difficulty in adapting to new situations. These dimensions are typically defined as risk factors, but this designation depends significantly on the outcome; for example, inhibition is a risk factor for depression and anxiety but may be a protective factor for delinquency (Kerr, Tremblay, Pagani, & Vitaro, 1997).

Other dimensions address different aspects of cognitive and emotional characteristics. *Attention* (also termed *persistence* or *task orientation*) reflects the ability to focus attention and concentrate on a task. An individual with a high score on this dimension is able to focus on a task, ignore distracting stimuli, and persist at the task until finished. *Positive emotionality* reflects the tendency to easily and frequently experience positive mood. A person high on this dimension laughs and smiles frequently and shows indications of enjoyment in many situations. A dimension termed *approach* reflects the tendency to move toward new situations. An individual high on this dimension shows an interest in entering new situations or meeting new people. The distinction between social and nonsocial aspects of approach tendency is complex and not well understood at present (Wills et al., 1998; Windle, 1995), and the tendency to enjoy being around people is often defined as a separate dimension termed *sociability* (Buss & Plomin, 1984). It should be noted that these dimensions do not just represent low scores on the attributes described previously. In other words, approach is not just the absence of inhibition, and positive emotionality is statistically distinct from negative emotionality (e.g., Wills, Cleary, Filer, Shinar, Mariani, & Spera, 2001; Wills, Sandy, Shinar, & Yaeger, 1999).

The dimensions of positive emotionality and sociability are typically assumed to be protective factors, but again this may depend on the criterion variable. Sociability has complex effects, and measures indexing extraversion and social popularity are typically correlated with positive affect but may also be related to higher levels of smoking and alcohol use (Wills, Resko, Ainette, & Mendoza, 2004). A striking example of such a relation was noted in a long-term study of a sample of bright, White, middle-class students who were assessed at age 11, using parent and teacher ratings, and then followed up 60 years later. This study included a measure labeled *Cheerfulness,* based on the ratings of "cheerful–optimistic" and "has sense of humor." Results showed that a measure of conscientiousness (analogous to attention and persistence) was inversely related to mortality, but the scale assessing cheerfulness was positively related to mortality, and analyses indicated that people with high cheerfulness scores in childhood were more likely to smoke, drink, and take risks as adults (Friedman et al., 1993, 1995). It remains unclear exactly what was measured in this study, but the results provide a cautionary note about commonsense interpretations concerning outcome implications of temperament dimensions.

A comment is in order about two other dimensions that are sometimes labeled as *temperament.* *Novelty seeking* is a characteristic theoretically linked to alcohol abuse (Cloninger, 1987). It is measured by items indicating a tendency to seek out novel stimuli; a fascination with fun seeking; having a distaste for rules and regulations; liking to spend money; being impulsive, excitable, and prone to exaggeration; and changing interests a lot. Although novelty seeking has been linked to substance use, the complexity of the manifestations reflected in measures of novelty seeking suggests it is a compound attribute that may be a developmental derivative of earlier temperament characteristics. Research with adolescents has in fact shown that novelty seeking is grounded in several different temperament dimensions (Wills et al., 1998). *Sensation seeking* is another dispositional attribute that has been linked to substance use among adolescents. It is defined as seeking out intense stimuli (e.g., loud rock music), being easily bored, liking dangerous and risky activities (e.g., fast driving), and preferring "weird" rather than conventional friends. Although sensation seeking is related to substance use and is suggested as being grounded in biochemical attributes (Zuckerman, 1983), the variety and developmental complexity of the activities encompassed under the rubric of sensation seeking make it difficult to see this as an elementary temperament characteristic, observable from early childhood. It may be that sensation seeking is also a compound syndrome, shaped by several temperament dimensions in concert with parent–child relationships and later

emerging characteristics. In fact, psychometric research has recognized the complexity of the syndrome by adding additional aspects such as impulsiveness and lack of socialization (Zuckerman, 1994).

Predictive Studies of Temperament and Substance Use

Several longitudinal studies have obtained temperament-type measures at early ages and related these to substance use at later ages. Although these studies did not always use the exact same assessments of temperament dimensions as defined above, the similarities are sufficient to draw comparisons.[1] A study with a middle-class sample (Lerner & Vicary, 1984) was based on temperament measures developed by Thomas and Chess (1986) in the New York Longitudinal Study. Here, parent reports about children, obtained at ages 3 to 5, were scored for a composite termed *difficult temperament* (e.g., high activity level, low positive emotionality). In a longitudinal follow-up of the sample, difficult temperament in childhood was related to high-intensity substance use (tobacco, alcohol, and marijuana) as ascertained through direct interviews conducted at ages 16 to 18.

Another study with measures from early childhood was based on a sample of participants recruited from a university nursery school and assessed between the ages of 3 and 4 by trained examiners. Follow-up data obtained at age 14 (Block, Block, & Keyes, 1988) indicated predictive results for marijuana and hard drug use. The future drug users were characterized in early assessments as high on activity and restlessness, negativism and hostility, reactivity to frustration, independence, self-indulgence, and rebelliousness and low on ability to concentrate, dependability and responsibility, ability to delay gratification, cooperativeness and consideration for others, and closeness to others.

An investigation by Pulkkinen and Pitkänen (1994) was based on a sample of Finnish children

---

[1] Similar characteristics have been identified in prodromal studies, which have attempted to link alcohol abuse in adulthood to dispositional measures obtained in late adolescence (see, e.g., Tarter, 1988; Tarter, Alterman, & Edwards, 1985). We do not discuss these in detail because our focus is on prediction from early ages.

who were assessed at ages 8 to 9 through peer reports and teacher ratings of temperament. The sample was followed into young adulthood, and alcohol use status at ages 26 to 27 was determined from self-report and official arrest records. Results indicated that problem drinking was predicted by early ratings of poor concentration ability, high aggressiveness, low "prosociality," and poor school performance (the latter assessed at age 14). In this study, the measure termed *prosociality* was based on items that queried respondents about being reliable, keeping promises, and acting reasonably in problem situations, so this seems more like an index of good self-control than a measure of sociability or extraversion.

A study conducted with a Swedish adoption sample (Cloninger, Sigvardsson, & Bohman, 1988) was based on teacher ratings of children's personality obtained at ages 10 to 11. The investigators used these ratings to construct higher-order scores on the basis of Cloninger's (1987) theoretical system. Results showed that constructed scores for novelty seeking, harm avoidance, and reward dependence predicted alcohol abuse as assessed through direct interview at age 27. Mâsse and Tremblay (1997) studied a sample of lower socioeconomic status participants initially assessed through teacher ratings at ages 5 to 6 and later scored for constructs from Cloninger's system. Data from interviews conducted at ages 11 to 15 showed that a particular profile on early measures (high novelty seeking and low harm avoidance) predicted cigarette smoking, drunkenness, and illicit drug use in mid-adolescence.

Finally, a longitudinal study with a community sample in New Zealand (Caspi, Moffitt, Newman, & Silva, 1996) originally obtained temperament-type measures through examinations conducted at age 3 by trained assessors. A profile score for *undercontrol* was developed post hoc on the basis of examiner ratings of being active, irritable, and impersistent. A second profile, termed "inhibition," was defined on the basis of examiner ratings of being fearful, uncommunicative, and easily upset. Follow-up interviews conducted at age 21 showed a significant relation of undercontrol to substance use disorder in young adulthood, and a significant relation was also observed for inhibition. Again, it is unclear exactly what was measured, and the

measure labeled inhibition could be more similar to the temperament dimension of negative emotionality than to standard measures of behavioral inhibition.

In summary, the studies reviewed were conducted in a range of different contexts, and all indicated that early assessments of temperament-like dimensions showed an ability to predict substance use at later ages. The consistency of results, despite variability in samples and methods, establishes temperament dimensions as significant predictive factors for substance use. Although the assessment methods varied considerably, it is apparent that high activity level, negative emotionality, and poor attentional focusing predict greater likelihood of substance use. There is a suggestion that good social relationships may be protective, whereas social withdrawal is a risk factor (Block et al., 1988; Kellam, Brown, & Fleming, 1982), but the wide variety of measures in the studies precludes firm conclusions about this issue.[2] The fact that temperament measures obtained at ages 3 to 5 predict substance use, and even disorder, in late adolescence and young adulthood indicates that it is important to consider how this effect occurs and what the implications are for etiology and prevention.

TEMPERAMENT AS A SUBSTRATE FOR SELF-CONTROL

The evidence just discussed indicates that measures of early characteristics predict substance use at later time points. A theoretical question is immediately posed: Why is this? What characteristics are these studies measuring? How can such simple measures be predictive of a complex behavioral problem with multiple cognitive and social components? This issue is outlined in Figure 7.1, which illustrates the large conceptual gap in understanding the associa-

---

[2] It should be noted that early measures of aggressiveness also predict substance use at later ages (see, e.g., Brook, Whiteman, Cohen, Shapiro, & Balka, 1995; Wills et al., 2005). We have not included this in the review because aggressiveness is not a temperament dimension per se but rather a label for a behavior that may be based in several dimensions of temperament (e.g., high negative emotionality, low sociability). Additional research is needed that links specific temperament dimensions to indices of externalizing and internalizing symptomatology (Frick & Morris, 2004; Wills, Ainette, et al., 2007).

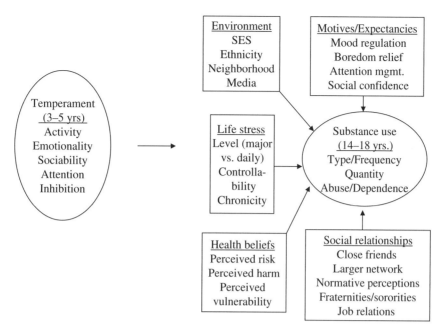

FIGURE 7.1. Conceptual outline of theoretical problem.

tion between simple temperamental attributes and complex behavioral phenomena.

Our approach to answering these questions is based on two propositions. The first proposition is that the studies are, in one way or another, measuring simple temperament characteristics. Although most of the studies were initiated before the development of current temperament inventories, the similarity of their descriptions of what was measured to standard temperament dimensions is striking. The second proposition is that early, simple temperament dimensions underlie the development of a range of complex self-control characteristics. This is the essential concept of epigenetic models (see Cairns, 1979; Rothbart & Ahadi, 1994; Tarter, Moss, & Vanyukov, 1995), suggesting that simple, early attributes form the substrate for development of more complex characteristics. In this case, the temperament dimensions, reflecting style but not content of behavior, are the building blocks on which self-regulation develops, with complex content added through cognitive and social maturation. The development of self-control characteristics begins during the preschool years and is believed to continue throughout adolescence, with prediction demonstrated from 9 to 10 years of age (e.g., Ellis, Rothbart, & Posner, 2004;

Wills, Ainette, et al., 2007; Wills, Gibbons, Gerrard, & Brody, 2000).[3]

We define self-control as two domains of attributes (cf. Carver & Scheier, 2000; Kendall & Williams, 1982; Miller & Brown, 1991). One domain is termed *good self-control* and has been variously termed *constraint* or *planfulness* (Carver, 2005; Rutter et al., 1997). A higher score on this domain reflects being organized, liking to plan things ahead of time, following through on tasks and commitments, paying attention to future consequences of behavior, self-monitoring one's own behavior and progress toward goals, and being able to wait patiently for a desired reward. The other domain is termed *poor control* and is alternatively termed *impulsiveness, disinhibition,* or *undercontrol.* A higher score on this domain reflects doing things without thinking, becoming impatient when having to wait for something, being easily distracted when

[3] As far as we can tell, this is a continuous process, and there is no point at which temperament becomes self-control. There are some characteristics (e.g., focusing attention on a stimulus, inhibiting a proscribed behavior) that could be said to represent self-control at ages 2 to 4 (see, e.g., Kochanska & Knaak, 2003). The distinction is that complex self-control abilities such as planning for long-term goals, using forethought to avoid negative consequences, and applying cognitive strategies for delay of gratification do not exist at early ages because they require cognitive and social maturation. The definition used here for self-control is based on complex abilities that can be measured from ages 8 to 9 and onward.

working on a task, and focusing on immediate rewards rather than long-term outcomes. Although readers accustomed to adult personality research may assume that these domains are ipsative (i.e., a high score on one domain just means a low score on the other), in fact, the two domains are only modestly related in childhood and adolescence, and they have quite different antecedents and consequences (Carver, 2005; Rothbart & Bates, 2006; Wills & Stoolmiller, 2002). Thus, we refer to good self-control (or planfulness) and poor control (or impulsiveness) separately. It is also important to note that scores on these domains are normally distributed in the population of children and adolescents; whereas scores for poor control tend to be shifted a bit lower from their respective mean, both domains have low skewness values (Wills, Ainette, et al., 2007; Wills, Cleary, et al., 2001; Wills, Walker, Mendoza, & Ainette, 2006).

The theoretical reasoning for how temperament influences the development of self-control has been developed from several perspectives (see, e.g., Rothbart, Posner, & Kieras, 2006; Rothbart & Rueda, 2005; Wills, Cleary, Shinar, & Filer, 2002; Wills & Dishion, 2004). The relation between temperament and self-control in general is thought to involve a combination of social and individual processes because development of self-control depends on contributions from socializing agents, first parents and later teachers and peers. A temperament characteristic that promotes good relationships with others (e.g., positive mood) will likely enhance the development of good self-control, whereas a temperament characteristic that causes difficulty for socializing agents (e.g., irritability and fussiness) will probably not contribute to the development of good self-control and will, at worst, retard it. So it is clear that contributions to self-control development come from both temperament characteristics and family environment characteristics (Wills, Cleary, et al., 2001) and, we should note, from the school environment as well (Brody, Dorsey, Forehand, & Armistead, 2002).

Against this background, however, some linkages of temperament to self-control development can be delineated. Attentional focusing has been linked to good self-control because it contributes to problem solving, and the ability to shift attention away from distressing stimuli has been suggested to contribute to development of good emotion regulation (Rothbart & Ahadi, 1994). The ability to focus attention on behaviors and consequences at different time points has also been suggested as an important contributor to self-control (Barkley, 1997b; Wills, Sandy, & Yaeger, 2001). Positive emotionality has been linked to good self-control independent of relationships with parents, suggesting that positive mood contributes to better problem solving because children avoid catastrophic thinking (i.e., constantly thinking about possible negative outcomes) and instead focus on the problem (Wills, Cleary, et al., 2001). From a negative standpoint, high physical activity level is linked to poor self-control, possibly because it presents difficulty in socialization by primary caregivers, but also because restlessness may directly interfere with concentrating on problems and hence retard acquisition of problem-solving strategies in either academic or interpersonal settings. Negative emotionality has also been linked to impulsiveness and poor emotional control. Again, this may involve an individual component, in which quick frustration in problem situations makes it more difficult for children to learn effective strategies for dealing with academic and peer situations, and a social component, in which negative mood leads to difficulties in interaction with peers. The linkages for sociability are less straightforward. In adolescence, sociability is linked with positive mood, which in itself would be conducive to development of good self-control. However, sociability is also linked to strong peer connections, and adolescent peer groups may not always encourage controlled and conventional behavior. This complexity may explain why social dimensions of temperament tend to be positively related to adolescent substance use (Wills et al., 2004).

SELF-CONTROL AND SUBSTANCE USE

Our theoretical approach, then, posits that temperament dimensions are related to the development of self-control. The final part of the approach concerns the relation of self-control to substance use. This connection is supported by several studies conducted during the past 10 years that have shown that self-control is related to substance use. For example, Wills, Vaccaro, and McNamara (1994) used an adaptation of the Kendall–Wilcox Self-Control Rating Schedule (Kendall & Wilcox, 1979) with a sample of 457 middle school students and related this to a composite index for tobacco, alcohol, and marijuana use. Results showed that a group of Kendall–Wilcox items reflecting good self-control (e.g., planning, dependability) were inversely related to substance use, whereas a group of items reflecting poor control (e.g., impatience, distractibility) were positively related to substance use. Relations of self-control to various types of substance use (e.g., tobacco, alcohol, marijuana, methamphetamine, opiates) have now been found in a variety of populations, including middle school students (Wills et al., 1995, 1998), high school students (Audrain-McGovern, Rodriguez, Tercyak, Nenner, & Moss, 2006; Novak & Clayton, 2001; Wills, Sandy, & Shinar, 1999), and college students (Patock-Peckham, Cheong, Balhorn, & Nagoshi, 2001; Simons & Carey, 2002) and in longitudinal and cross-sectional studies (Brody & Ge, 2001; Wills & Stoolmiller, 2002). Relations of self-control measures to substance use behavior have been observed from age 11 (Wills, Cleary, et al., 2001; Wills, Sandy, & Yaeger, 2001), and relations to precursor measures (e.g., intentions and willingness to use tobacco and alcohol) have been observed from ages 9 to 10 (Wills, Ainette, et al., 2007; Wills et al., 2000), hence approaching the developmental period of prior studies with temperament measures (e.g., Pulkkinen & Pitkänen, 1994). In addition to findings of main effects, recent research has shown that good self-control is a buffering agent, reducing the impact of several risk factors (family life events, peer substance use, and adolescent life events) on adolescent substance use (Wills, Ainette, Stoolmiller, Gibbons, & Shinar, 2008).

Relations between self-control and substance use have been demonstrated with a variety of different measures. These include unidimensional measures of generalized self-control (Brody & Flor, 1997; Brody, Stoneman, & Flor, 1996; J. Epstein, Griffin, & Botvin, 2000; Griffin, Botvin, Epstein, Doyle, & Diaz, 2000; Scheier, Botvin, Diaz, & Griffin, 1999)

and specific measures such as impulsivity and affective lability (Simons & Carey, 2002; Simons, Oliver, Gaher, Ebel, & Brummels, 2005). Results have also been found with cognitive assessment paradigms designed to index decision making (Bechara et al., 2001; Grant, Contoreggi, & London, 2000) or delay discounting or delay of gratification (Bickel, Odum, & Madden, 1999; Madden, Petry, Badger, & Bickel, 1997; Petry, Bickel, & Arnett, 1998) and with measures presumed to index the neuropsychological functions underlying self-control ability (Aytaclar, Tarter, Kirisci, & Lu, 1999; Blume, Marlatt, & Schmaling, 2000). In addition to survey research and laboratory assessment studies, relations of self-control to substance use have also been found on a daily basis in experience-sampling studies (Neal & Carey, 2007; Simons, Gaher, Oliver, Bush, & Palmer, 2005). In all these studies, scores on planning or systematic decision making are inversely correlated with substance use, whereas scores on measures such as impulsivity or shortened time perspective are related to higher levels of substance use.[4]

Studies from our laboratory have used a confirmatory approach to testing the structure of self-control measures and have consistently found support for a two-factor model. A latent construct observed for good self-control has a range of indicators. These include scales from the Kendall–Wilcox (1979) inventory for concentration and planfulness, a scale for problem solving from a response-based inventory (Wills, McNamara, Vaccaro, & Hirky, 1996), a measure of future time perspective from the Zimbardo and Boyd (1999) inventory, a measure of delay of gratification (based on work by Shoda, Mischel, & Peake, 1990), and a measure of self-reinforcement (Heiby, 1983). A measure of emotional soothability loads significantly on the good self-control construct but typically at a lower level than the other indicators (see, e.g., Wills, Cleary, et al., 2001). These measures are substantially correlated with each other despite their fairly different

---

[4] Several studies have also shown that self-control has moderating effects, for example, poor control increases the strength of relations between level of substance use and problems associated with use (Neal & Carey, 2007; Simons, Gaher, et al., 2005; Wills, Sandy, & Yaeger, 2002). Our discussion focuses on main effects for self-control to explicate mechanisms, but we should note that moderating effects of self-control are also theoretically important.

content, and in the confirmatory model they all have high loadings on an underlying construct reflecting good self-control.

A second latent construct, termed *poor control,* has high loadings for scales from the Kendall–Wilcox inventory, termed *impatience* and *distractibility,* a scale on angerability (Wills et al., 1996), a measure of impulsiveness (Eysenck & Eysenck, 1978), a scale for present time orientation (Wills, Sandy, & Yaeger, 2001; Zimbardo & Boyd, 1999), and a measure on need to have immediate gratification (Shoda et al., 1990). Again, these indicators are highly correlated with each other (and not substantially correlated with the indicators for good self-control), and in the confirmatory analysis they all have high loadings on a latent construct reflecting poor control. Readers accustomed to adult personality research may assume that good self-control and poor control are unidimensional (i.e., a high score on one necessarily means a low score on the other), but this is not the case. Confirmatory analyses consistently indicate that a one-factor model has poor fit to the data, whereas a two-factor model, with constructs of good self-control and poor control, has good fit (e.g., Wills et al., 1998; Wills & Stoolmiller, 2002). This two-factor measurement model, with the latent constructs inversely but only modestly correlated, has been found across a variety of populations (Wills et al., 2000, 2004; Wills, Ainette et al., 2007; Wills, Cleary, et al., 2001; Wills, Murry, et al., 2007). In every case, the construct for good self-control has been inversely related to measures of tobacco, alcohol, and marijuana use and the construct for poor control has been positively related to substance use. These findings are consistent with personality models that posit two domains variously termed *ego control* and *ego undercontrol, planfulness* and *disinhibition,* or *constraint* and *impulse* (Carver, 2005).

The findings discussed in this section bring together the strands of the previously developed argument. Temperament dimensions are linked to the development of complex self-control characteristics, which in turn are linked to onset or escalation of substance use. To this is added the clarification that the self-control indicators index two domains which we have termed *good self-control* and *poor self-control.* These propositions provide a provisional answer to the theoretical question posed previously by delineating self-control as an intermediate process that links temperament dimensions and substance use outcomes. There is also a theoretical corollary to this argument explaining why early onset of use is particularly prognostic for substance use problems at later ages. This phenomenon has been noted for some time in drug abuse epidemiology (Anthony & Petronis, 1995; Breslau, Fenn, & Peterson, 1993; Hawkins et al., 1997; Robins & Przybeck, 1985) but has not been explained in terms of first principles. The present approach suggests that early onset is related to temperamental characteristics that presage poor control at later ages, and observations of such an effect suggest that this provides the theoretical link to liability for substance abuse (Wills, Cleary, et al., 2001; Wills, Sandy, & Yaeger, 2001). This conceptual approach is outlined in Figure 7.2, which depicts how temperamental attributes are related to intermediate processes that are more proximal to substance use.

SELF-CONTROL AFFECTS EXPOSURE TO PROXIMAL FACTORS

Noting that self-control measures are related to substance use does not necessarily clarify how this part of the process occurs—namely, is self-control directly related to substance use, or does it actually operate through one or more intermediate factors?

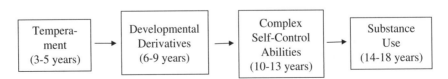

FIGURE 7.2.   Schematic of processes intervening between temperament and substance use.

Our recent research program has focused on clarifying this issue.

Several studies have been conducted to test the ramifications of this question. The general research design involves obtaining measures of temperament and measures of self-control along with measures of variables generally recognized as proximal factors for substance use (Hawkins, Catalano, & Miller, 1992; Petraitis, Flay, & Miller, 1995) and then testing these variables together in a single structural model. This has now been done in several studies, with self-control measured through latent constructs for good self-control and poor control, as discussed previously. Measures of proximal factors have included academic and peer competence, major negative life events and recent events, affiliation with peer substance users, and motives for substance use (Wills et al., 2004; Wills, Cleary, et al., 2001; Wills, Sandy, & Shinar, 1999). The results have been quite consistent, showing that self-control affects exposure to proximal factors but does not generally have direct effects on substance use. Here

we summarize these findings in a generic model (Figure 7.3), which synthesizes relations among variables on the basis of several studies' results. This figure depicts how temperament dimensions are related to self-control constructs as developmental derivatives, and self-control constructs are then related to proximal risk and protective factors for substance use. We should note that the analyses in these studies included covariates, variables that are correlated with temperament and also with adolescent substance use; these include parental behavior and relationship (e.g., parental warmth and support, parental substance use), and demographic variables (e.g., gender, socioeconomic status). Such covariates were part of the analyses, so the observed effects for temperament are independent of these variables, but the covariates are excluded from the figure for graphical simplicity.

In the complete model, temperament dimensions are strongly related to self-control constructs. Dimensions such as task orientation and positive emotionality (Temperament A in the figure) are

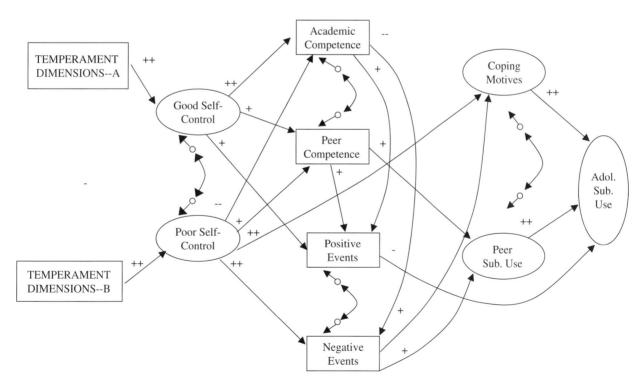

FIGURE 7.3.   Generic model for relation between self-control, proximal factors, and adolescent substance use. Ovals represent entities usually measured as latent constructs, rectangles indicate entities usually analyzed as manifest variables. +, ++ indicate expected (moderate, strong) positive relations. -, — indicate expected (moderate, strong) inverse relations.

positively related to good self-control, and dimensions such as activity level and negative emotionality (Temperament B in the figure) are strongly related to poor control. Temperament dimensions generally do not have direct paths to proximal factors. Rather, temperament dimensions are related to self-control constructs, with good self-control being related to greater academic competence and occurrence of more positive life events, and these combined effects represent the pathways from temperament to outcomes. In contrast, poor control is related to more negative life events, more deviant peer affiliations (e.g., hanging out with peers who smoke and drink), and more coping motives for substance use (e.g., smoking or drinking to reduce tension). These proximal factors are strongly related to adolescent substance use, particularly for peer affiliations and coping motives. Academic competence and negative life events themselves tend to have indirect effects on substance use by tending to either deter or promote affiliation with deviant peers. These combined effects are the pathways from risk-promoting temperament dimensions to adolescents' substance use. Self-control constructs typically do not have direct effects on substance use outcomes; their effects are mediated ones. Thus, the role of self-control in the etiology process is through affecting exposure to proximal factors.

Study Example

An example that illustrates this proposed sequence is a study that was conducted with a multiethnic sample of 1,810 public school students who were all sixth graders at baseline. The study included measures for six dimensions of temperament and measures of tobacco, alcohol, and marijuana use (Wills, Cleary, et al., 2001). The participants completed a baseline questionnaire in sixth grade, and the sample was resurveyed at yearly intervals. We emphasize this study because it had a large sample and a reasonable set of temperament measures, and relations between constructs were demonstrated in longitudinal and cross-sectional analyses. This study used two latent constructs for self-control, based on confirmatory factor analyses. The construct for good self-control had indicators of dependability, planning, and problem solving, and the construct for

poor control had indicators of impatience, distractibility, impulsiveness, and angerability. Results showed that the temperament dimensions of task attentional orientation and positive emotionality were strongly related to good self-control (sociability was more weakly related). Physical activity level and negative emotionality were strongly related to poor control, and activity level also had an inverse path to good self-control.[5]

Results regarding proximal factors showed that good self-control was related to higher academic competence, whereas poor control was related to more negative life events and more affiliation with substance-using peers. In this study, most of the effect of self-control on adolescents' substance use was indirect, mediated through competence, life events, and peer affiliations, but there was also a direct effect from good self-control to (less) substance use. However, in studies with older middle and high school students, no direct effects from self-control to substance use were found (Wills et al., 1999, 2004, 2006), so the direct effect in this study seems to be a consequence of the participants' younger age.

A theoretical alternative was addressed by including measures of tolerance for deviance (Jessor & Jessor, 1977) and risk-taking tendency (Eysenck & Eysenck, 1978). These variables also had pathways to adolescent substance use, but these pathways were independent of those found for self-control, and these variables had relatively small effects compared with those for the self-control constructs. Thus, the results indicated that poor control is not simply a proxy for deviance proneness.

Processes in Relation to Proximal Factors

Although the processes that link self-control with proximal factors have yet to be explicated in detail, likely avenues have been outlined. Good self-control is based on systematic decision making, thoughtful planning, and considering alternatives before acting in problem situations. In this sense, it represents a reasoned approach to situations (Gibbons, Gerrard, & Lane, 2003) and should thus be related to out-

---

[5] Note that we took care to exclude items from the self-control measures that might overlap with items in the temperament measures. Hence, these results are not attributable to item overlap.

comes in which a rational approach and delay of gratification are important. A linkage to academic competence appears straightforward in that people with a high score on good self-control will focus attention on presentations in school, do their homework before turning to leisure activities, use a systematic approach to studying material and monitoring progress toward goals, and keep track of important dates and deadlines for completing assignments (Duckworth & Seligman, 2005; Zimmerman, 2000). However, the intellectual aspect may not be the only important one because emotional factors have also been found to be related to academic competence (Wills et al., 2006). Emotional control may be relevant to establishing good relationships with teachers and helping to keep attention appropriately focused in testing situations, as well as being a useful resource in interpersonal conflict situations. People who use forethought and planning may also be inclined to affiliate with peers who are well controlled and value academic achievement (Scarr & McCartney, 1983; Steinberg, Dornbusch, & Brown, 1992).

Poor control, in contrast, represents a reactive path (Gibbons et al., 2003) based on heuristics and automatic processing, immediate responding to situational pressures, and failure to consider long-term consequences of behavior (Gibbons, Gerrard, Reimer, & Pomery, 2006). Recalling that the two domains of self-control are not highly correlated (Carver, 2005), several avenues have been suggested for the relation of poor control to risk-promoting proximal factors. People who act without thinking are probably more likely to provoke negative life events in the classroom (e.g., talking back to teachers), and a focus on the present can make problem situations more troublesome if people act without thinking about the future consequences of their behavior. Distractibility can interfere with problem solving and academic tasks, and a high level of impatience can annoy other people and turn mild problem situations into worse ones. An element of irritability and poor emotional control also seems likely to cause conflict in peer situations, leading to rejection by more agreeable and mainstream peers and consequent drift into groups of rejected (and deviant) peers. Thus, the individual-level variable of

poor control can exert negative influences on outcomes through both social and nonsocial processes.

SUMMARY AND DISCUSSION

At the beginning of the chapter, we posed the question of how temperament is related to substance use. This presentation has provided a theoretical approach to the question in terms of an indirect effects model: Early temperament dimensions are related to the development of complex self-control characteristics, and these characteristics then affect exposure to proximal risk and protective factors for substance use. This mediation model provides a theoretical answer to the question of how early measures of temperament characteristics can predict substance use over considerable periods of time. In an epigenetic process, simple temperament attributes provide a foundation on which complex self-control characteristics are overlaid, and levels of self-control characteristics affect the risk and protective factors that youth experience in adolescence. There will be some stability to the system because the temperament dimensions shape (within limits and in interaction with family and environmental characteristics) the pattern of planfulness and impulsiveness that helps to channel development through adolescence and shape the nature of outcomes in young adulthood (and possibly farther; Friedman et al., 1993).

This is theoretically an indirect effects model because temperament dimensions do not have direct effects on substance use outcomes, and generally neither do self-control characteristics. Rather, temperament and self-control influence substance use or nonuse through their effects on intermediate processes. People trained to think of behavioral science as a search for direct causative models (i.e., A leads to B) may have some difficulty with models that depend on intermediate processes. However, a quick perusal of a few biological journals shows that models involving complex pathways, signaling systems, and second messengers are the foundation of much current research in biochemistry and pharmacology.

We see the temperament and self-control model as particularly useful for studying adolescent substance use, but note some possible generalizations of this approach. There is reason to believe that similar processes may operate to produce a high level of sexual risk behavior, and several studies (e.g., Rothspan & Read, 1996; Wills, Murry, et al., 2007) have shown this to be a plausible avenue of investigation. In addition, the implication of decision making and regulation of motivation in diet and exercise choices has suggested that self-control concepts may be useful in this area, and recent research has in fact shown self-control measures related to dietary and exercise outcomes (Anderson, Wojcik, Winett, & Williams, 2006; Henson, Carey, Carey, & Maisto, 2006; Wills, Isasi, Mendoza, & Ainette, 2007). Finally, from the standpoint of genetic research it has been clear for some time that there is a substantial genetic contribution to adult personality traits (Bouchard, 1994; Plomin, Owen, & McGuffin, 1994), but the field of behavior genetics has had difficulty finding replicable predictive effects for complex attributes such as novelty seeking (e.g., Kruger, Siegfried, & Ebstein, 2002) or, going the other way, showing replicable relations of specific genetic variants to complex psychiatric syndromes (e.g., Craddock, Owen, & O'Donovan, 2006). Although progress in this area may depend in part on methodological advances, we believe that an epigenetic approach based on temperament dimensions could help provide useful organizing concepts for this area by outlining pathways from early constitutional factors to later outcomes.

Although research has provided considerable support for the utility of the self-control model, several theoretical issues in this area remain to be addressed. As previously noted, there is little understanding at a detailed psychological level of how self-control characteristics influence variables such as academic competence or negative life events or how they influence cognitive factors such as perceived risk from substance use or other problem behaviors (Gerrard, Gibbons, & Gano, 2003). Research is needed to shed light on these questions, using either general population surveys or daily experience sampling designs. Similarly, research may consider how good self-control or poor control act as moderators so as to decrease (or increase) the effect of other variables on the likelihood of substance abuse and dependence (Neal & Carey, 2007; Simons & Carey,

2006; Wills, Sandy, & Yaeger, 2002). In the following section, we pose a few other questions that we think need to be studied or clarified.

Behavioral or Emotional Control

It has been suggested for some time that substance abuse arises from deficits in emotional regulation (e.g., Khantzian, 1990), but research on self-control and substance use, including that described in this chapter, has largely focused on behavioral self-regulation. We addressed this question in a study that tested several defined measures of emotion regulation (sadness control, anger control, and affective lability) in relation to indices of adolescent substance use (Wills et al., 2006). The results showed that various measures of emotional self-regulation, like measures of behavioral control, fit a latent construct model. Findings showed that the constructs for emotional control were, if anything, stronger predictors of substance use than were measures of behavioral control, for which significant unique effects were also observed. So the ability to regulate emotions such as sadness and anger, and to dampen lability of affective states, is highly relevant for the etiology of substance use and abuse (cf. Simons & Carey, 2002, 2006).

The question raised in the above study was where the ability to regulate emotions comes from. There is a fair body of theory in this area (e.g., Cole, Michel, & Teti, 1994; Kopp, 1989) but little empirical data bearing on adolescents and substance use. We have found that behavioral and emotional control are substantially correlated, implying that common factors influence development of both domains (Wills et al., 2006). But whether these reside in the domain of attentional processes, inhibitory processes, socialization effects, or some combination of these is not well understood at present. Clarification of this issue could help in understanding the role of emotion regulation in the etiology of substance abuse.

Where Does the Cognitive Content Come From?

We noted at the outset that early temperament dimensions are simple characteristics that represent the style, not the content, of behavior. But adolescent substance use occurs among individuals who have elaborated systems of beliefs and attitudes; articulated views about the self and the world; feelings of competence and efficacy; complex networks of social relationships with peers, parents, and siblings; and expectancies about what tobacco, alcohol, and other drugs might do for them. The obvious question for a temperament model is "Where does this cognitive content come from?" To say that it comes from cognitive and social maturation is true in some sense but does not get you very far theoretically without propositions about what maturation involves and how temperament shapes maturation. Complex cognitive content must come in some way from observation and modeling (Bandura, 1977), but this does not necessarily indicate how observations of others become integrated into coherent systems of beliefs about the self and attitudes toward the world and how these translate into social relationships and expectancies favorable or unfavorable toward substance use, a process that may be well under way by ages 10 to 11 (Wills, Ainette, et al., 2007; Wills & Cleary, 1999; Wills et al., 2000).

A complete answer to this question is beyond the scope of this chapter and might in principle require a team of cognitive, developmental, and social psychologists to address. One approach we can suggest is that temperament acts in part to shape beliefs and attitudes through the choice of friends. There is evidence that children create their own social niches by spending time with peers with whom they feel most comfortable (Scarr, 1992). Temperament and self-control attributes may help to shape these choices because young people are attracted to friends whose characteristics are similar to their own (e.g., impulsive youth select impulsive friends). As observations of peer interactions in adolescence have shown, deviant peers serve to instruct and inform each other about antisocial behavior and may help to provide justifications and expectations for substance use and aggressive behavior (Dishion, Capaldi, Spracklen, & Li, 1995; Dishion, Nelson, Winter, & Bullock, 2004). Research may explicate this question by studying how temperament characteristics at early ages, and self-control characteristics at later ages, shape the structure of social networks and the types of peers whom children identify as friends (Valente, Gallaher, & Mouttapa, 2004; Wills & Ainette, in press).

A different kind of mechanism could derive from temperament characteristics that lead to peer rejection and exclusion from mainstream peer groups, either through academic failure or because of poor social skills (Coie, Terry, Lenox, Lochman, & Hyman, 1995; Dodge et al., 2003). Rejection by mainstream peers will certainly help to shape one's view of the world, and spending time hanging out with deviant peers could help to elaborate and crystallize these views. Beyond these kinds of indirect social mechanisms, further studies may investigate how temperament characteristics act directly on cognitive or emotional processes to shape the development of beliefs and attitudes.

Poor Control or High Reward Sensitivity?

Because the action of most drugs involves reward pathways (Koob & LeMoal, 1997) there is a question about the fundamental process in the relation between poor control and drug use. It has been suggested that people characterized as impulsive are simply more sensitive to the rewarding effects of drugs and that the empirical relation between impulsivity and drug use is, in some sense, an epiphenomenon. In this view, reward sensitivity rather than self-control could be the important process. This is an important question for research on self-control and substance use. The theoretical positions in this area are complicated, however. For one thing, it is not obvious why people with greater reward sensitivity would be likely to experience more negative life events and affiliate with deviant peers. Moreover, there is a theoretical position arguing that people who engage in drug use do so because they are less likely to experience reward and hence must supplement whatever intrinsic reinforcement they do gain from life with rewards obtained from drugs. This theoretical position has been termed *reward deficiency syndrome* and is itself credible on the basis of some clinical and neurological data (see Blum & Braverman, 2000; Uhl & Volkow, 2001; Volkow, Fowler, & Wang, 2002).

This argument has also been examined from a psychometric standpoint because there are measures available designed to index reward sensitivity. In general, this research has not supported the position that impulsivity is just a proxy for reward orientation because measures of reward sensitivity factor separately from standard measures of impulsiveness and novelty seeking (Dawe, Gullo, & Loxton, 2004; Dawe & Loxton, 2004). From the standpoint of personality theory, the concept of approach derived from Gray's theory (Gray & McNaughton, 2000) has not mapped well onto measures of impulse and constraint (Carver, 2005). This is still an open area, and although one would not want to discourage research into the possibility that drug abusers are more sensitive to the effects of drugs, various lines of evidence have indicated that this position by itself does not give a good account of the sociobehavioral processes that are known predictors of substance abuse.

A Dual-Process Approach?

The approach to conceptualizing self-control that we have outlined here has a notable linkage to current work in cognitive social psychology. Such models posit that behavior may be guided by two information-processing systems: a rational system that involves conscious awareness of decisions and intentions, with systematic but slower decision making, and a more rapid automatic system that is based on heuristics and image-based processing and may operate at least partly outside of conscious awareness. Although research in this area has largely focused on classic problems in attitudes and impression formation (Chaiken & Trope, 1999), the implications of a dual-process theoretical approach have recently been extended to questions in addictive behaviors (Gibbons et al., 2003; Wiers & Stacy, 2004).

The concept that there are two domains of self-control, one more planful and one more impulsive, is quite consistent with the dual-process approach. Indeed, Carver (2005) has noted two-factor concepts in several models of personality, including Block and Block's (1980) classic model of ego control and undercontrol; the rational and experiential systems of personality functioning posited by S. Epstein (1990); and the hot and cold models of decision making outlined by Metcalfe and Mischel (1999). The findings reported here on two statistically distinct domains of self-control provide empirical support for the dual-system theory discussed by Carver because the two domains are only modestly correlated and each clearly exists at some

level within the same individual, rather than characterizing two different types of people. The application of a dual-process approach to adolescent problem behavior by Gibbons et al. (2003) has focused on issues of willingness versus intention for substance use, but the ramifications of this approach for self-control research are evident for other issues, in particular the suggestion that individuals who are high on poor control rely more on automatic processing in problematic situations (Carver, 2005; Gibbons et al., 2006). Cognitive social psychology may help to clarify ways in which adolescents use information so as to exert control (vs. relinquishing responsibility) when they have a problem (Gerrard et al., 2003; Reyna & Farley, 2006).

Implications for Prevention

Because self-control affects exposure to several proximal factors, each of which is an important predictor of substance use, modifying self-control through individual or group interventions could have preventive effects, potentially across a range of situations. Primary prevention programs targeted at proximal factors (e.g., peer substance use) have demonstrated significant effects on reducing adolescent tobacco and alcohol use (see, e.g., Skara & Sussman, 2003; Tobler et al., 2000), and some prevention programs have included material on decision making and personal competence (Botvin, 2000; Botvin & Griffin, 2001). However, the prospect of increasing the impact or maintenance of program effects by augmenting prevention programs with theory-based components aimed at enhancing decision-making processes, time orientation, delay of gratification strategies, and emotional self-control skills is an idea that deserves consideration.

An approach to prevention based on self-control constructs and proximal factors represents a transdisciplinary perspective (Sussman et al., 2004; Wills & Dishion, 2004). Methods for enhancing self-control skills have been outlined in several places from the perspectives of experimental psychology (Logue, 1995), clinical psychology (Kendall & Braswell, 1993), and cognitive neuroscience (Posner & Rothbart, 2006), and some precedents are available from clinical programs conducted with adults (Miller, Leckman, Delaney, & Tinkcom, 1993;

Walters, 2000). The goal is to design skills-training approaches that are feasible in school- or community-based settings and to combine approaches in a way that best complements other program components targeted at families, peers, and environments (Sussman & Wills, 2000). Translating etiological findings into prevention designs is a good use of etiological research and can also help to inform further theoretical development in this area, following from Lewin's suggestion that the most practical thing is a good theory (Brody et al., 2005; Gerrard et al., 2006).

References

Anderson, E. S., Wojcik, J. R., Winett, R. A., & Williams, D. M. (2006). Social-cognitive determinants of physical activity among participants in a church-based health promotion study. *Health Psychology, 25,* 510–520.

Angleitner, A., & Ostendorf, F. (1994). Temperament and the Big Five factors of personality. In C. Halverson, G. Kohnstamm, & R. Martin (Eds.), *The developing structure of temperament and personality from infancy to adulthood* (pp. 69–90). Hillsdale, NJ: Erlbaum.

Anthony, J. C., & Petronis, K. R. (1995). Early-onset drug use and risk of later drug problems. *Drug and Alcohol Dependence, 40,* 9–15.

Audrain-McGovern, J., Rodriguez, D., Tercyak, K. P., Nenner, G., & Moss, H. B. (2006). The impact of self-control indices on peer smoking and adolescent smoking progression. *Journal of Pediatric Psychology, 21,* 139–151.

Aytaclar, S., Tarter, R. E., Kirisci, L., & Lu, S. (1999). Association between hyperactivity and executive cognitive functioning in childhood and substance use in early adolescence. *Journal of the American Academy of Child & Adolescent Psychiatry, 38,* 172–178.

Bandura, A. (1977). *Social learning theory.* Englewood Cliffs, NJ: Prentice-Hall.

Barkley, R. A. (1997a). *ADHD and the nature of self-control.* New York: Guilford Press.

Barkley, R. A. (1997b). Behavioral inhibition, sustained attention, and executive functions: Constructing a unifying theory of ADHD. *Psychological Bulletin, 121,* 65–94.

Bechara, A., Dolan, S., Denburg, N., Hindes, A., Anderson, S. W., & Nathan, P. E. (2001). Decision-making deficits, linked to the ventromedial prefrontal cortex, revealed in alcohol and stimulant abusers. *Neuropsychologia, 39,* 376–389.

Bickel, W. K., Odum, A. L., & Madden, G. J. (1999). Impulsivity and cigarette smoking: Delay discounting in smokers and ex-smokers. *Psychopharmacology, 146,* 447–454.

Biemiller, A., Shany, M., Inglis, A., & Meichenbaum, D. (1998). Factors influencing children's acquisition and demonstration of self-regulation on academic tasks. In D. H. Schunk & B. J. Zimmerman (Eds.), *Self-regulated learning* (pp. 203–224). New York: Guilford Press.

Block, J. H., & Block, J. (1980). The role of ego-control and ego-resiliency in the organization of behavior. In W. A. Collins (Ed.), *Minnesota symposium on child psychology* (Vol. 13, pp. 39–101). Hillsdale, NJ: Erlbaum.

Block, J., Block, J., & Keyes, S. (1988). Foretelling drug use in adolescence: Early personality and environmental precursors. *Child Development, 59,* 336–355.

Blum, K., & Braverman, E. R. (2000). Reward deficiency syndrome: A biogenetic model for the diagnosis and treatment of impulsive, addictive and compulsive behaviors. *Journal of Psychoactive Drugs, 32*(Suppl. 1), 1–112.

Blume, A. W., Marlatt, G. A., & Schmaling, K. B. (2000). Executive cognitive function and heavy drinking among college students. *Psychology of Addictive Behaviors, 14,* 299–302.

Botvin, G. J. (2000). Preventing drug use in schools: Social and competence enhancement approaches targeting individual-level etiologic factors. *Addictive Behaviors, 25,* 887–897.

Botvin, G. J., & Griffin, K. (2001). Life Skills Training: Theory, methods, and effectiveness of a prevention approach. In E. Wagner & H. Waldron (Eds.), *Innovations in adolescent substance use interventions* (pp. 31–50). Amsterdam: Pergamon Press.

Bouchard, T. J. (1994, June 17). Genes, environment, and personality. *Science, 264,* 1700–1701.

Breslau, N., Fenn, N., & Peterson, E. L. (1993). Early smoking initiation and nicotine dependence in a cohort of young adults. *Drug and Alcohol Dependence, 33,* 129–137.

Brody, G. H., Dorsey, S., Forehand, R., & Armistead, L. (2002). Unique contributions of parenting and classroom processes to the adjustment of African American children living in single-parent families. *Child Development, 73,* 274–286.

Brody, G. H., & Flor, D. L. (1997). Maternal psychological functioning, family processes, and child adjustment in rural, single-parent, African American families. *Developmental Psychology, 33,* 1000–1011.

Brody, G. H., & Ge, X. (2001). Linking parenting and self-regulation to psychological functioning and alcohol use in early adolescence. *Journal of Family Psychology, 15,* 82–94.

Brody, G. H., Murry, V. M., McNair, L., Chen, Y.-F., Gibbons, F. X., Gerrard, M., & Wills, T. A. (2005). Linking changes in parenting to youth self-control: The Strong African American Families program. *Journal of Research on Adolescence, 15,* 47–69.

Brody, G. H., Stoneman, Z., & Flor, D. (1996). Parental religiosity, family processes and youth competence in rural, two-parent African American families. *Developmental Psychology, 32,* 696–706.

Brook, J. S., Whiteman, M., Cohen, P., Shapiro, J., & Balka, E. (1995). Longitudinally predicting late adolescent and young adult drug use: Childhood and adolescent precursors. *Journal of the American Academy of Child & Adolescent Psychiatry, 34,* 1230–1238.

Buss, A., & Plomin, R. (1984). *Temperament: Early-developing personality traits.* Hillsdale, NJ: Erlbaum.

Cairns, R. B. (1979). *Social development: The origins and plasticity of social interchanges.* San Francisco: Freeman.

Capaldi, D. M., & Rothbart, M. K. (1992). Development and validation of an early adolescent temperament measure. *Journal of Early Adolescence, 12,* 153–173.

Carver, C. E. (2005). Impulse and constraint: Perspectives from personality psychology. *Personality and Social Psychology Review, 9,* 312–333.

Carver, C. S., & Scheier, M. F. (2000). On the structure of behavioral self-regulation. In M. Boekaerts, P. R. Pintrich, & M. Zeidner (Eds.), *Handbook of self-regulation* (pp. 41–84). San Diego, CA: Academic Press.

Caspi, A., Moffitt, T., Newman, D., & Silva, P. (1996). Behavioral observations at age 3 years predict adult psychiatric disorders. *Archives of General Psychiatry, 53,* 1033–1039.

Chaiken, S., & Trope, Y. (1999). *Dual-process theories in social psychology.* New York: Guilford Press.

Cloninger, C. R. (1987, April 24). Neurogenetic adaptive mechanisms in alcoholism. *Science, 236,* 410–416.

Cloninger, C. R., Sigvardsson, S., & Bohman, M. (1988). Childhood personality predicts alcohol abuse in young adults. *Alcoholism: Clinical and Experimental Research, 12,* 494–505.

Cole, P. M., Michel, M. K., & Teti, L. O. (1994). The development of emotion regulation and dysregulation: A clinical perspective. *Monographs of the Society for Research in Child Development, 59,* 73–100.

Coie, J. D., Terry, R., Lenox, K., Lochman, J., & Hyman, C. (1995). Childhood peer rejection and aggression as predictors of stable patterns of adolescent disorder. *Development and Psychopathology, 7,* 695–713.

Craddock, N., Owen, M. J., & O'Donovan, M. C. (2006). The catechol-O-methyl transferase (COMT) gene as a candidate for psychiatric phenotypes: Evidence and lessons. *Molecular Psychiatry 11,* 446–458.

Dawe, S., Gullo, M. J., & Loxton, N. J. (2004). Reward drive and rash impulsiveness as dimensions of impulsivity: Implications for substance misuse. *Addictive Behaviors, 29,* 1389–1405.

Dawe, S., & Loxton, M. J. (2004). The role of impulsivity in the development of substance use and eating disorders. *Neuroscience and Biobehavioral Reviews, 28,* 343–351.

Dishion, T. J., Capaldi, D., Spracklen, K. M., & Li, F. (1995). Peer ecology of male adolescent drug use. *Development and Psychopathology, 7,* 803–824.

Dishion, T. J., Nelson, S., Winter, C., & Bullock, B. (2004). Adolescent friendship as a dynamic system: Entropy and deviance in the development and course of male antisocial behavior. *Journal of Abnormal Child Psychology, 32,* 651–663.

Dodge, K. A., Lansford, J. E., Burks, V. S., Bates, J. E., Pettit, G. S., Fontaine, R., & Price, J. M. (2003). Peer rejection and social information-processing factors in the development of aggressive behavior problems in children. *Child Development, 74,* 374–393.

Duckworth, A. L., & Seligman, M. E. P. (2005). Self-discipline outdoes IQ in predicting academic performance of adolescents. *Psychological Science, 66,* 939–944.

Ellis, L. K., Rothbart, M. K., & Posner, M. I. (2004). Individual differences in executive attention predict self-regulation and adolescent psychosocial behaviors. In R. E. Dahl & L. P. Spear (Eds.), *Adolescent brain development: Vulnerabilities and opportunities* (pp. 337–340). New York: New York Academy of Sciences.

Epstein, J., Griffin, J. W., & Botvin, G. J. (2000). A model of smoking among inner-city adolescents: The role of personal competence and perceived social benefits of smoking. *Preventive Medicine, 31,* 107–114.

Epstein, S. (1990). Cognitive-experiential self-theory. In L. Pervin (Ed.), *Handbook of personality theory and research* (pp. 165–192). New York: Guilford Press.

Eysenck, S. B. G., & Eysenck, H. J. (1978). Impulsiveness and venturesomeness: A dimensional system for personality description. *Psychological Reports, 43,* 1247–1255.

Frick, P. J., & Morris, A. S. (2004). Temperament and developmental pathways to conduct problems. *Journal of Clinical Child and Adolescent Psychology, 33,* 54–68.

Friedman, H. S., Tucker, J. S., Schwartz, J. E., Tomlinson-Keasey, C., Martin, L. R., Wingard, D. L., & Criqui, M. H. (1995). Psychosocial and behavioral predictors of longevity. *American Psychologist, 50,* 69–78.

Friedman, H. S., Tucker, J. S., Tomlinson-Keasey, C., Schwartz, J. E., Wingard, D. L., & Criqui, M. H. (1993). Does childhood personality predict longevity? *Journal of Personality and Social Psychology, 65,* 176–185.

Gerrard, M., Gibbons, F. X., Brody, G. H., Murry, V. M., Cleveland, M. J., & Wills, T. A. (2006). A theory-based dual-focus alcohol intervention for preadolescents. *Psychology of Addictive Behaviors, 20,* 185–195.

Gerrard, M., Gibbons, F. X., & Gano, M. (2003). Adolescents' risk perceptions and behavioral willingness: Implications for intervention. In D. Romer (Ed.), *Reducing adolescent risk: Toward an integrated approach* (pp. 75–81). Newbury Park, CA: Sage.

Gibbons, F. X., Gerrard, M., & Lane, D. J. (2003). A social reaction model of adolescent health risk. In J. M. Suls & K. A. Wallston (Eds.), *Social psychological foundations of health and illness* (pp. 107–136). Oxford, England: Blackwell.

Gibbons, F. X., Gerrard, M., Reimer, R. A., & Pomery, E. A. (2006). Unintentional behavior: A subrational approach to health risk. In D. T. D. de Ridder & J. B. F. de Wit (Eds.), *Self-regulation in health behavior* (pp. 45–70). New York: Wiley.

Goldsmith, H. H., Gottesman, I. I., & Lemery, K. S. (1997). Epigenetic approaches to developmental psychopathology. *Development and Psychopathology, 9,* 365–387.

Grant, S., Contoreggi, C., & London, E. D. (2000). Drug abusers show impaired performance on a laboratory test of decision making. *Neuropsychologia, 38,* 1180–1187.

Gray, J. A., & McNaughton, N. (2000). *The neuropsychology of anxiety* (2nd ed.). Oxford, England: Oxford University Press.

Griffin, K. W., Botvin, G. J., Epstein, J. A., Doyle, M. M., & Diaz, T. (2000). Psychosocial and behavioral factors in early adolescence as predictors of heavy drinking among high school students. *Journal of Studies on Alcohol, 61,* 603–606.

Hagekull, B. (1989). Longitudinal stability of temperament within a behavioral style framework. In G. A. Kohnstamm, J. E. Bates, & M. K. Rothbart (Eds.), *Temperament in childhood* (pp. 283–297). New York: Wiley.

Hawkins, J. D., Catalano, R. F., & Miller, J. Y. (1992). Risk and protective factors for drug problems in adolescence and early adulthood. *Psychological Bulletin, 112,* 64–105.

Hawkins, J. D., Graham, J. W., Maguin, E., Abbott, R., Hill, K. G., & Catalano, R. F. (1997). Exploring the effects of age of alcohol use initiation and psychosocial risk factors on subsequent alcohol misuse. *Journal of Studies on Alcohol, 58,* 28–290.

Heiby, E. M. (1983). Assessment of frequency of self-reinforcement. *Journal of Personality and Social Psychology, 44,* 1304–1307.

Henson, J. M., Carey, M. P., Carey, K. B., & Maisto, S. A. (2006). Association of health behaviors and time perspective in adults. *Journal of Behavioral Medicine, 29,* 127–137.

Jessor, R., & Jessor, S. (1977). *Problem behavior and psychosocial development.* New York: Academic Press.

Kellam, S. G., Brown, C. H., & Fleming, J. P. (1982). Social adaptation to first grade and teenage drug, alcohol and cigarette use. *Journal of School Health, 52,* 301–306.

Kendall, P. C., & Braswell, L. (1993). *Cognitive–behavioral therapy for impulsive children* (2nd ed.). New York: Guilford Press.

Kendall, P. C., & Wilcox, L. E. (1979). Self-control in children: Development of a rating scale. *Journal of Consulting and Clinical Psychology, 47,* 1020–1029.

Kendall, P. C., & Williams, C. L. (1982). Assessing the cognitive and behavioral components of children's self-management. In P. Karoly & F. H. Kanfer (Eds.), *Self-management and behavior change* (pp. 240–284). New York: Pergamon Press.

Kerr, M., Tremblay, R. E., Pagani, L., & Vitaro, F. (1997). Boys' behavioral inhibition and the risk of later delinquency. *Archives of General Psychiatry, 54,* 809–816.

Khantzian, E. J. (1990). Self-regulation and self-medication factors in alcoholism and the addictions. In M. Galanter (Ed.), *Recent developments in alcoholism* (Vol. 8, pp. 255–271). New York: Plenum Press.

Kochanska, G., Aksan, N., & Joy, M. (2007). Children's fearfulness as a moderator of parenting in early socialization. *Developmental Psychology, 43,* 222–237.

Kochanska, G., & Knaak, A. (2003). Effortful control as a characteristic of young children. *Journal of Personality, 71,* 1087–1112.

Koob, G. F., & Le Moal, M. (1997, October 3). Drug abuse: Hedonic homeostatic dysregulation. *Science, 278,* 52–58.

Kopp, C. B. (1989). Regulation of distress and negative emotions: A developmental view. *Developmental Psychology, 25,* 343–354.

Kruger, A. N., Siegfried, Z., & Ebstein, R. P. (2002). A meta-analysis of the association between DRD4 polymorphism and novelty seeking. *Molecular Psychiatry, 7,* 712–717.

Lerner, J. V., & Vicary, J. R. (1984). Difficult temperament and drug use. *Journal of Drug Education, 14,* 1–8.

Logue, A. W. (1995). *Self-control: Waiting until tomorrow for what you want today.* Englewood Cliffs, NJ: Prentice Hall.

Madden, G. J., Petry, N. M., Badger, G. J., & Bickel, W. K. (1997). Impulsive and self-control choices in opioid-dependent patients and control participants. *Experimental and Clinical Psychopharmacology, 5,* 256–262.

Mâsse, L. C., & Tremblay, R. E. (1997). Behavior of boys in kindergarten and the onset of substance use during adolescence. *Archives of General Psychiatry, 54,* 62–68.

Metcalfe, J., & Mischel, W. (1999). A hot/cool-system analysis of delay of gratification: dynamics of willpower. *Psychological Review, 106,* 3–19.

Miller, W. R., & Brown, J. M. (1991). Self-regulation as a conceptual basis for the prevention of addictive behaviours. In N. Heather, W. R. Miller, & J. Greeley (Eds.), *Self-control and the addictive behaviours* (pp. 3–79). Sydney, Australia: Maxwell Macmillan.

Miller, W. R., Leckman, A. L., Delaney, H. D., & Tinkcom, M. (1993). Long-term follow-up of self-control training for problem drinkers. *Journal of Studies on Alcohol, 53,* 249–261.

Neal, D. J., & Carey, K. B. (2007). Association between intoxication and alcohol-related problems: An event-level analysis. *Psychology of Addictive Behaviors, 21,* 194–204.

Novak, S. P., & Clayton, R. R. (2001). Influence of school environment and self-regulation on transitions between stages of cigarette smoking. *Health Psychology, 20,* 196–207.

Patock-Peckham, J. A., Cheong, J.-W., Balhorn, M. E., & Nagoshi, C. T. (2001). A model of parenting styles, self-regulation, perceived drinking control, and alcohol use and problems. *Alcoholism: Experimental and Clinical Research, 25,* 1284–1292.

Pedlow, R., Sanson, A., Prior, M., & Oberklaid, F. (1993). Stability of maternally reported temperament from infancy to 8 years. *Developmental Psychology, 29,* 998–1007.

Petraitis, J., Flay, B. R., & Miller, T. Q. (1995). Reviewing theories of adolescent substance use: Organizing pieces in the puzzle. *Psychological Bulletin, 117,* 67–86.

Petry, N. M., Bickel, W. K., & Arnett, M. (1998). Shortened time horizons and insensitivity to future consequences in opioid-dependent individuals. *Addiction, 93,* 729–738.

Plomin, R., Owen, M. J., & McGuffin, P. (1994, June 17). The genetic basis of complex human behaviors. *Science, 264,* 1733–1739.

Posner, M. I., & Rothbart, M. K. (2006). *Educating the human brain.* Washington, DC: American Psychological Association.

Pulkkinen, L., & Pitkänen, T. (1994). A prospective study of the precursors to problem drinking in young adulthood. *Journal of Studies on Alcohol, 55,* 578–587.

Reyna, V. F., & Farley, F. (2006). Risk and rationality in adolescent decision making. *Psychological Science in the Public Interest, 7,* 1–44.

Robins, L. N., & Przybeck, T. R. (1985). Age of onset of drug use as a factor in drug and other disorders. In

C. L. Jones & R. J. Battjes (Eds.), *Etiology of drug abuse* (pp. 178–192). Rockville, MD: National Institute on Drug Abuse.

Rothbart, M. K., & Ahadi, S. A. (1994). Temperament and the development of personality. *Journal of Abnormal Psychology, 103,* 55–66.

Rothbart, M. K., & Bates, J. E. (2006). Temperament. In N. Eisenberg, W. Damon, & R. J. Lerner (Eds.), *Handbook of child psychology: Vol. 3, Social, emotional, and personality development* (6th ed., pp. 99–166). Hoboken, NJ: Wiley.

Rothbart, M. K., Posner, M. I., & Kieras, J. (2006). Temperament, attention, and the development of self-regulation. In K. McCartney & D. Phillips (Eds.), *Blackwell handbook of child development* (pp. 338–357). Malden, MA: Blackwell.

Rothbart, M. K., & Rueda, M. R. (2005). The development of effortful control. In U. Mayr, E. Awh, & S. Keele (Eds.), *Developing individuality in the human brain: A tribute to Michael I. Posner* (pp. 156–188). Washington, DC: American Psychological Association.

Rothspan, S., & Read, S. J. (1996). Present versus future time perspective and HIV risk among heterosexual college students. *Health Psychology, 15,* 131–134.

Rutter, M., Dunn, J., Plomin, R., Simonoff, E., Pickles, A., Maughan, B., et al. (1997). Integrating nature and nurture: Implications of person–environment correlations and interactions for developmental psychopathology. *Development and Psychopathology, 9,* 335–364.

Scarr, S. (1992). Developmental theories for the 1990s. *Child Development, 63,* 1–19.

Scarr, S., & McCartney, K. (1983). How people make their own environments: A theory of genotype → environment effects. *Child Development, 54,* 424–435.

Scheier, L. F., Botvin, G. J., Diaz, T., & Griffin, K. W. (1999). Social skills, personal competence, and drug refusal efficacy as predictors of adolescent alcohol use. *Journal of Drug Education, 29,* 251–278.

Scheier, L. F., Casten, R. J., & Fullard, W. (1995). Latent-variable confirmatory analyses of the Adolescent Temperament Questionnaire. *Journal of Adolescent Research, 10,* 246–277.

Shoda, Y., Mischel, W., & Peake, P. K. (1990). Predicting adolescent cognitive and self-regulatory competencies from preschool delay of gratification. *Developmental Psychology, 26,* 978–986.

Simons, J. S., & Carey, K. B. (2002). Risk and vulnerability for marijuana use problems: The role of affect dysregulation. *Psychology of Addictive Behaviors, 16,* 72–75.

Simons, J. S., & Carey, K. B. (2006). An affective and cognitive model of marijuana and alcohol problems. *Addictive Behaviors, 31,* 1578–1592.

Simons, J. S., Gaher, R. M., Oliver, M. N. I., Bush, J. A., & Palmer, M. A. (2005). An experience sampling study of associations between affect and alcohol use and problems among college students. *Journal of Studies on Alcohol, 66,* 459–469.

Simons, J. S., Oliver, M. N., Gaher, R. M., Ebel, G., & Brummels, P. (2005). Methamphetamine and alcohol abuse and dependence symptoms: Associations with affect lability and impulsivity in a rural treatment population. *Addictive Behaviors, 30,* 1370–1381.

Skara, S., & Sussman, S. (2003). A review of 25 long-term adolescent tobacco and other drug use prevention program evaluations. *Preventive Medicine, 37,* 451–474.

Steinberg, L., Dornbusch, S. M., & Brown, B. B. (1992). Ethnic differences in adolescent achievement: An ecological perspective. *American Psychologist, 47,* 723–729.

Sussman, S., Earlywine, M., Wills, T. A., Cody, C., Biglan, A., Dent, C., & Newcomb, M. D. (2004). The motivation, skills, and decision-making model of drug abuse prevention. *Substance Use and Misuse, 39,* 1971–2016.

Sussman, S., & Wills, T. A. (2000). Rationale for program development methods. In S. Sussman (Ed.), *Handbook of program development for health behavior research and practice* (pp. 3–30). Thousand Oaks, CA: Sage.

Tarter, R. E. (1988). Are there inherited behavioral traits that predispose to substance abuse? *Journal of Consulting and Clinical Psychology, 56,* 189–196.

Tarter, R. E., Alterman, A., & Edwards, K. (1985). Vulnerability to alcoholism in men: A behavior-genetic perspective. *Journal of Studies on Alcohol, 46,* 329–356.

Tarter, R. E., Moss, H. B., & Vanyukov, M. M. (1995). Behavior genetic perspective of alcoholism etiology. In H. Begleiter & B. Kissin (Eds.), *Alcohol and alcoholism* (Vol. 1, pp. 294–326). New York: Oxford University Press.

Thomas, A., & Chess, S. (1986). The New York Longitudinal Study: From infancy to early adult life. In R. Plomin & J. Dunn (Eds.), *The study of temperament* (pp. 39–52). Hillsdale, NJ: Erlbaum.

Tobler, N. S., Roona, M. R., Ochshorn, P., Marshall, D. G., Streke, A. V., & Stackpole, K. M. (2000). School-based adolescent drug prevention programs: 1998 meta-analysis. *Journal of Primary Prevention, 20,* 275–336.

Uhl, G. R., & Volkow, N. (2001). Perspectives on reward circuitry, neurobiology, genetics, and pathology: Dopamine and addiction. *Molecular Psychiatry, 6*(Supp. 1), S1–S8.

Valente, T. W., Gallaher, P., & Mouttapa, M. (2004). Using social networks to understand and prevent cig-

arette smoking and alcohol use. *Substance Use & Misuse, 39,* 1685–1712.

Volkow, N., Fowler, J., & Wang, G.-J. (2002). Role of dopamine in drug reinforcement and addiction in humans: Results from imaging studies. *Behavioral Pharmacology, 13,* 355–366.

Walters, G. D. (2000). Behavioral self-control training for problem drinkers. A meta-analysis of controlled studies. *Behavior Therapy, 31,* 135–149.

Wiers, R. W., & Stacy, A. W. (2004). Implicit cognition and addiction. *Current Directions in Psychological Science, 15,* 292–296.

Wills, T. A., & Ainette, M. G. (in press). Social networks and social support. In A. Baum, T. Revenson, & J. Singer (Eds.), *Handbook of health psychology* (2nd ed.). New York: Taylor & Francis.

Wills, T. A., Ainette, M. G., Mendoza, D., Gibbons, F. X., & Brody, G. H. (2007). Self-control, symptomatology, and substance use precursors: Test of a theoretical model in a community sample of 9-year-old children. *Psychology of Addictive Behaviors, 21,* 205–215.

Wills, T. A., Ainette, M. G., Stoolmiller, M., Gibbons, F. X., & Shinar, O. (2008). Good self-control as a buffering agent for adolescent substance use: An investigation in early adolescence with time-varying covariates. *Psychology of Addictive Behaviors, 22,* 459–471.

Wills, T. A., & Cleary, S. D. (1999). Peer and adolescent substance use among 6th–9th graders: Latent growth analyses. *Health Psychology, 18,* 453–463.

Wills, T. A., Cleary, S. D., Filer, M., Shinar, O., Mariani, J., & Spera, K. (2001). Temperament related to early-onset substance use: Test of a developmental model. *Prevention Science, 2,* 145–163.

Wills, T. A., Cleary, S. D., Shinar, O., & Filer, M. (2002). Temperament dimensions and health behavior. In L. L. Hayman, M. M. Mahon, & J. R. Turner (Eds.), *Health and behavior in childhood and adolescence* (pp. 3–36). New York: Springer.

Wills, T. A., & Dishion, T. J. (2004). Temperament and adolescent substance use: A transactional analysis of emerging self-control. *Journal of Clinical Child and Adolescent Psychology, 33,* 69–81.

Wills, T. A., DuHamel, K., & Vaccaro, D. (1995). Activity and mood temperament as predictors of adolescent substance use: Test of a self-regulation mediational model. *Journal of Personality and Social Psychology, 68,* 901–916.

Wills, T. A., Gibbons, F. X., Gerrard, M., & Brody, G. (2000). Protection and vulnerability processes for early onset of substance use: A test among African American children. *Health Psychology, 19,* 253–263.

Wills, T. A., Isasi, C. R., Mendoza, D., & Ainette, M. A. (2007). Self-control constructs are related to measures of dietary intake and physical activity in adolescents. *Journal of Adolescent Health, 41,* 551–558.

Wills, T. A., McNamara, G., Vaccaro, D., & Hirky, A. E. (1996). Escalated substance use: A longitudinal grouping analysis from early to middle adolescence. *Journal of Abnormal Psychology, 105,* 166–180.

Wills, T. A., Murry, V. M., Brody, G. H., Gibbons, F. X., Gerrard, M., Walker, C., & Ainette, M. G. (2007). Ethnic pride and self-control related to protective and risk factors: The Strong African American Families Program. *Health Psychology, 26,* 51–59.

Wills, T. A., Resko, J., Ainette, M., & Mendoza, D. (2004). The role of parent and peer support in adolescent substance use: A test of mediated effects. *Psychology of Addictive Behaviors, 18,* 122–134.

Wills, T. A., Sandy, J. M., & Shinar, O. (1999). Cloninger's constructs related to substance use level and problems in late adolescence: A mediational model based on self-control and coping motives. *Experimental and Clinical Psychopharmacology, 7,* 122–134.

Wills, T. A., Sandy, J. M., Shinar, O., & Yaeger, A. (1999). Contributions of positive and negative affect to adolescent substance use: Test of a bidimensional model in a longitudinal study. *Psychology of Addictive Behaviors, 13,* 327–338.

Wills, T. A., Sandy, J. M., & Yaeger, A. (2001). Time perspective and early-onset substance use. *Psychology of Addictive Behaviors, 15,* 118–125.

Wills, T. A., Sandy, J. M., & Yaeger, A. (2002). Moderators of the relation between substance use level and problems: Test of a self-regulation model in middle adolescence. *Journal of Abnormal Psychology, 111,* 3–21.

Wills, T. A., Sandy, J. M., Yaeger, A., & Shinar, O. (2001). Family risk factors and adolescent substance use: Moderation effects for temperament dimensions. *Developmental Psychology, 37,* 283–297.

Wills, T. A., & Stoolmiller, M. (2002). The role of self-control in early escalation of substance use. *Journal of Consulting and Clinical Psychology, 70,* 986–997.

Wills, T. A., Vaccaro, D., & McNamara, G. (1994). Novelty seeking, risk taking, and related constructs as predictors of adolescent substance use. *Journal of Substance Abuse, 6,* 1–20.

Wills, T. A., Walker, C., Mendoza, D., & Ainette, M. G. (2006). Behavioral and emotional self-control: Relations to substance use in samples of middle- and high-school students. *Psychology of Addictive Behaviors, 20,* 265–278.

Wills, T. A., Walker, C., & Resko, J. A. (2005). Longitudinal studies of drug use and abuse. In Z. Sloboda (Ed.), *Epidemiology of drug abuse* (pp. 177–192). New York: Springer.

Wills, T. A., Windle, M., & Cleary, S. D. (1998). Temperament and novelty-seeking in adolescent substance use. *Journal of Personality and Social Psychology, 74,* 387–406.

Windle, M. (1995). The approach–withdrawal concept: Associations with salient constructs in contemporary theories of personality development. In K. Hood, G. Greenberg, & E. Tobach (Eds.), *Concepts of approach–withdrawal* (pp. 329–370). New York: Garland.

Windle, M., & Lerner, R. M. (1986). Dimensions of temperamental individuality: The Revised Dimensions of Temperament Survey. *Journal of Adolescent Research, 1,* 213–229.

Zimbardo, P. G., & Boyd, J. N. (1999). Time perspective: A valid, reliable individual-differences metric. *Journal of Personality and Social Psychology, 77,* 1271–1288.

Zimmerman, B. J. (2000). Attaining self-regulation: A social cognitive perspective. In M. Boekaerts, P.R. Pintrich, & M. Zeidner (Eds.), *Handbook of self-regulation* (pp. 13–39). San Diego, CA: Academic Press.

Zucker, R. A. (1994). Pathways to alcohol problems: A developmental account. In R. A. Zucker, G. M. Boyd, & J. Howard (Eds.), *The development of alcohol problems* (pp. 255–289). Rockville, MD: National Institute on Alcohol Abuse and Alcoholism.

Zuckerman, M. (Ed.). (1983). *Biological bases of sensation seeking, impulsivity, and anxiety.* Hillsdale, NJ: Erlbaum.

Zuckerman, M. (1994). Impulsive unsocialized sensation seeking. In J. E. Bates & T. D. Wachs (Eds.), *Temperament: Individual differences at the interface of biology and behavior* (pp. 219–255). Washington, DC: American Psychological Association.

CHAPTER 8

EXPLICIT OUTCOME EXPECTANCIES AND SUBSTANCE USE: CURRENT RESEARCH AND FUTURE DIRECTIONS

Amee B. Patel and Kim Fromme

People only see what they are prepared
to see.

—*Ralph Waldo Emerson*

Emerson's words resonate loudly in the field of substance use etiology. His remark could easily be construed to read that people see what they *expect* to see. Imagine Jim, an adolescent who has never used any sort of psychoactive substance. He has *seen* substances used by others on television and among his friends. Jim has *heard* of even more schoolmates who have used other substances. He has also been *taught* about drug use through a drug prevention program that started in elementary school. Even though Jim has never used substances, he has expectations about who uses them, how popular drugs are, and how they are going to affect him.

As many chapters in this book reveal, substance use is a complex phenomenon owing to its affective, biological, cognitive, genetic, psychological, and social determinants. Without a doubt, cognitive determinants have received the greatest amount of interest, with a substantial focus on outcome expectancies as they relate to alcohol and drug use initiation.

In this chapter, we provide an overview of the research on expectancies and discuss motives and perceived norms as other cognitive correlates of substance use. Our intention is to illustrate the similarities and differences between these cognitive factors in an effort to provide a more complete picture of substance use. With this information in hand, and supported by information from other chapters in this handbook, we also suggest new directions for research.

EXPECTANCY THEORY

The concept of outcome expectancies is founded in Tolman's (1932) work on animal and human behavior. Tolman defined *expectation* as "an imm[i]nent cognitive determinant aroused by actually presented stimuli" (p. 444) and further described expectations as perceptual or memorial (i.e., founded in memory). Although Tolman's work on the conceptualization of outcome expectancies was quite preliminary, additional experimental work that followed made clear that expectation functions as some perceived or remembered cognitive representation of the stimulus, such that the stimulus has subjective value to the individual. In the context of existing learning theories, Tolman's notion of expectancy provided a contrast to the traditional stimulus–response (S-R) theory, which used the idea of reinforcement to explain how a stimulus elicits a response. For example, a thirsty (stimulus) rat will perform specific behaviors (response) that have been linked to receiving water (reinforcement). If those behaviors are not linked to the receipt of water, the rat will not enact those behaviors. Missing from this framework, however, is the expectation that the specific behaviors lead to the appearance of water, the perception or memory of which guides the initiation of the behaviors.

Extrapolating from Tolman's work and the cognitive elements missing from S-R theory, Meehl and MacCorquodale (1951) differentiated expectancy theory from the traditional S-R framework by describing a situation in which the outcome of the response influences the association between the stimulus and the response. Simply put, when presented with a stimulus (e.g., being offered a drug), the response (e.g., using the drug) depends on the outcome associated with the choice (e.g., feeling good). Subsequently, MacCorquodale and Meehl (1953) outlined a more formal definition of expectancy theory, based on cognitive models linking stimulus and response. An important postulate of their model suggests that expectancies can strengthen behavior through inference.

Bolles (1972) expanded on the notion of inference in his description of expectancy theory as quite different from traditional S-R theories in that it did not rely on the individual having learned the association between the stimulus and response prior to conducting the behavior. As described by Bolles, expectancy theory differs from reinforcement-driven S-R theory by stipulating that behavior occurs not because of the stimulus, but because of the predictive association between the stimulus and the response; in other words, behavior occurs because of the *expectation* or anticipation of a response. Bolles defined expectancy as "information about a new order of things in the environment [which] is processed and stored for subsequent use by the animal" (p. 402), such that the animal "expects" a particular outcome in a particular situation. This can be represented by the S-S* unit, where S is a specific event or cue that predicts the outcome or consequence (S*). Bolles provided four postulates to encapsulate his model of expectancy. The fourth, of particular interest to expectancy theorists, states that expectancy is a belief about the association between either an environmental stimulus or the individual's own behavior and the occurrence of specific contingent outcomes. In other words, expectancies are beliefs that "glue" behavior and consequence together.[1]

Subsequently, Rotter (1954) further refined the concept of expectancy in the development of his own motivational theory of behavior. Rotter identified expectancy as one of four components that generate behavior. He speculated that an individual's willingness to engage in a specific behavior depends on the subjective value of the outcome associated with that behavior. Rotter further added that behavior can be determined by the probability that the expected outcome will occur. For example, a very desirable outcome (as determined by the individual) that has only a 1% chance of occurring would be less likely to predict behavior than a less desirable outcome that has a 75% chance of occurring. Thus, having expectancies about the outcome of a specific behavior is not enough; the outcome has to be valuable to the individual as well.

Cox and Klinger (1988) conceptualized expectancies within a framework of incentive motivation building from the basic notion that cognitive processes determine behavior. Incentive motivation refers to "an organism's motivation to pursue incentives: positive incentives to which it is attracted and negative incentives by which it is repelled" (p. 169). Unlike previous theories of expectancy, Cox and Klinger's framework incorporated affect, such that incentives were identified by their capacity to elicit a change in emotion. The desire for affective change and the expectation about the capacity for an incentive to elicit a specific change in emotion formulated the basis for the initiation of behavior. Thus, expectancies were thought to collaborate with drives, rather than to act alone, to induce behavioral activation. In the next section, we explore how expectancy theory has been specifically applied to substance use and eventually return to Cox and Klinger's model and its connection to alcohol use.

APPLICATION OF EXPECTANCY THEORY TO SUBSTANCE USE

Expectancy theory was applied to substance use almost 4 decades ago, after MacAndrew and Edgerton (1969) asserted that alcohol's effect on inhibition was not a pharmacological product but instead a socially learned consequence of drinking. Disinhibition is not caused by alcohol itself, but by the belief that alcohol consumption leads to a lack of inhibition. In time, the assertion of a cognitively mediated chain of events led

---

[1]The use of the word *belief* to describe expectancy has been debated in the literature on learning theory and attitude theory. Although in some cases expectancies are too automatic to be termed beliefs, explicit expectancies (the focus of this chapter) are studied as beliefs that are conscious and can be acknowledged by the individual. For this reason, we use *belief* to describe expectancy (see also Leigh, 1987).

to the creation of the balanced placebo design to study alcohol effects. The design, first used with alcohol by Marlatt and Rohsenow (1980), disaggregates alcohol expectancy set from alcohol's pharmacological effects. The 2 (actual beverage: alcohol vs. no alcohol) × 2 (expected beverage: alcohol vs. no alcohol) balanced placebo design creates four conditions whereby participants are (a) instructed they will receive alcohol and actually do, (b) told that they will receive alcohol but do not (some other innocuous liquid similar in consistency and clarity is provided), (c) told that they will not receive alcohol but actually do, or (d) told they will not receive alcohol and do not. If the expected effects of alcohol drive behavior, then those who expect alcohol, regardless of the actual beverage they receive, would behave more extremely.

Findings from research with the balanced placebo design demonstrated that both pharmacological and expectancy effects influence behavior (for reviews, see Hull & Bond, 1986; Marlatt & Rohsenow, 1980). Overall, alcohol itself plays a larger role in eliciting behavioral change; however, when separated into social and nonsocial behaviors, expectancies are more powerful predictors of changes in social behaviors (e.g., aggression, sexual arousal, helpfulness) than pharmacology alone. The balanced placebo studies therefore provide strong support for the study of expectancies as separate and valid predictors of substance use (e.g., Laberg & Löberg, 1989).

Motivational Model of Alcohol Use

Continuing in their efforts to disaggregate pharmacological and expected effects of alcohol use, Cox and Klinger (1988) identified two mechanisms through which incentive motivation predicted alcohol use. The first was a direct pathway—the chemical effects of alcohol elicit certain affective changes. The second was indirect and focused on how alcohol consumption might influence the attainment of other goals and the affective changes associated with them. For example, a student might be worried about an upcoming exam and choose to drink alcohol because she believes it will relieve her stress. She may be just as likely, however, to choose not to drink alcohol because she thinks it will interfere with her ability to study and therefore cause greater anxiety. The former choice illustrates a belief that drinking reduces ten-

sion, whereas the latter outlines a belief that alcohol use leads to an inability to concentrate and study. In both cases, expectancies are a major component in the student's decision about whether or not to drink.

Although it is in many ways similar to the traditional conceptualizations of expectancy, Cox and Klinger's (1988) model incorporates the decision to use a substance, adding a layer between expectancy and behavioral initiation. A desire to change affect in a positive direction by increasing positive affect or decreasing negative affect would lead to the decision to drink, whereas drinking would not occur if it would lead to decreased positive affect or increased negative affect. Furthermore, expectancy alone is considered to be insufficient to explain behavior; having an expectation about the outcome of a behavior fails to consider whether the outcome is desired at that moment on the basis of internal (i.e., personality) and external (i.e., environmental) cues. Thus, this model conceptualizes expectancies as general beliefs regarding the outcome of substance use, but not as the final pathway toward behavior.

ASSESSMENT OF EXPLICIT EXPECTANCIES

Findings from studies using the balanced placebo design spawned an interest in measuring people's expectancies about the effects of drinking alcohol. Because expectancy set (i.e., told alcohol but received placebo) significantly influences social behaviors such as aggression, loss-of-control drinking, and sexual behaviors, investigators soon surmised that underlying expectations about the effects of drinking alcohol drove these behaviors. In addition, experimental studies using the balanced placebo design tested only one behavior at a time, whereas a valid self-report measure of outcome expectancies might allow researchers to examine a wider array of expectancies among diverse drinking populations. This eventually led to the conceptualization and development of the Alcohol Expectancy Questionnaire (AEQ; Brown, Goldman, Inn, & Anderson, 1980).

Tracing the history of the AEQ provides additional insight into how researchers conceptualize expectancy as a learned behavior. To generate a pool of alcohol expectancies, high school and college students, military veterans from a local Veterans Affairs Medical Center, and patients in treatment for alcohol use disorders were asked to report "all of their positive experiences while drinking" (Brown et al., 1980, p. 421). Their answers were converted into the initial set of items for the AEQ, and data summarization techniques were used to yield the final measure of 90 items. Respondents were asked to agree or disagree with whether "a couple or a few drinks of alcohol" would produce each effect listed (Brown et al., 1980, p. 421). Factor analyses revealed six latent factors: (a) Global Positive Changes, (b) Sexual Enhancement, (c) Physical and Social Pleasure, (d) Increased Social Assertiveness, (e) Relaxation and Tension Reduction, and (f) Arousal and Aggression, with the Global Positive Changes factor accounting for 67% of the variance in the items (Brown, Christiansen, & Goldman, 1987). Subsequent analyses showed that the factors were also moderately correlated (Goldman, Brown, Christiansen, & Smith, 1991).

More extensive analyses of the relations between the six expectancy factor scores and indices of alcohol use revealed that less exposure to alcohol and lighter drinking practices were associated with more general positive expectancies, whereas longer exposure and heavier drinking were associated with expectations for enhanced sexual experiences, greater arousal, and aggression. In addition, women were more likely to endorse positive social expectancies, whereas men were more likely to endorse expectancies related to arousal and aggressive behavior.

Without question, development of the AEQ stimulated a tremendous amount of research on self-reported outcome expectancies. Notwithstanding, many in the research community believe the measure falls short of providing a comprehensive assessment of alcohol expectancies. The limited scope of experiences (positive only), quantity of alcohol referenced (a couple or a few drinks), and the fact that responses are based on "personal opinion, belief, and/or experience" (Brown et al., 1980, p. 421) may curtail what we can learn about a wide range of drinking patterns.

In addition to the fact that the AEQ assesses only positive expectancies (Fromme, Kivlahan, & Marlatt, 1986), the measure has been further criticized for inclusion of items unrelated to alcohol effects, the failure to account for subjective evaluations of alcohol's effects, the dichotomous response format, and significant moderate correlations among the six expectancy factors (Leigh, 1989). Critics have suggested that dichotomous measures do not allow for adequate variability in responses, and correlations among factors raise questions about the conceptual independence of the different expectancies.

In response to criticisms of correlated expectancy factors, Goldman (1999; Goldman, Del Boca, & Darkes, 1999) developed a cognitive neural model of expectancies. According to this conceptualization, expectancies are defined as "dynamic information templates stored in the nervous system that are processed to produce behavioral output" (Goldman, 1999, p. 43). These information templates, or nodes, represent learned experiences and are connected through conditioned associations along a cognitive chain. As one node, representing an expectancy belief, is activated, others that share associations along the chain are also activated. Thus, correlations among observed expectancies occur because beliefs about alcohol are cognitively linked, making it impossible for a single expectancy to be activated in isolation.

Not entirely satisfied by a neural network explanation, researchers responded to Leigh's (1989) criticisms through the creation of additional expectancy scales. The typical expectancy questionnaire contains approximately 75 items, which are typically derived from structured interviews, focus groups, existing questionnaires, or the investigators' own biases about relevant item content (Jones, Corbin, & Fromme, 2001b). Exploratory factor analysis has been the dominant means of ascertaining the dimensionality of expectancy content. Whereas most scales share a foundation in outcome expectancy theory and assess the individual's beliefs about the effects of the substance, different instructional sets, response formats, and factor structures raise methodological concerns and create an element of conceptual confusion. The most prevalent expectancy scales for a wide array of substances are summarized in Table 8.1.

Contemporary explicit expectancy measures can be exemplified by the Comprehensive Effects of Alcohol scale (CEOA; Fromme, Stroot, & Kaplan,

TABLE 8.1

Substance-Related Expectancy Measures

Expectancy Measures	Author(s) and Publication Year
Alcohol-Related Assessments	
Alcohol Effects Questionnaire (AEQ)	Rohsenow, 1983
Alcohol Expectancy Questionnaire (AEQ)	Brown, Goldman, Inn, & Anderson, 1980
Alcohol Expectancy Questionnaire – Adolescent (AEQ-A)	Christiansen, Goldman, & Inn, 1982
Comprehensive Effects of Alcohol (CEOA)	Fromme, Stroot, & Kaplan, 1993
Drinking Expectancy Questionnaire (DEQ)	Young & Knight, 1989
Negative Alcohol Expectancy Questionnaire (NAEQ)	Jones & McMahon, 1994
Tobacco-Related Assessments	
Adolescent Smoking Consequences Questionnaire (ASCQ)	Lewis-Esquerre, Rodrigue, & Kahler, 2005
Positive and Negative Outcome Expectations of Smoking	Dalton, Sargent, Beach, Bernhardt, & Stevens, 1999
Smoking Consequences Questionnaire (SCQ)	Brandon & Baker, 1991
Smoking Consequences Questionnaire — Adult (SCQ-A)	Copeland, Brandon, & Quinn, 1995
Smoking Expectancies Scale for Adolescents (SESA)	Hine, Honan, Marks, & Brettschneider 2007
Cannabis-Related Assessments	
Comprehensive Effects of Marijuana (CEOM)	Vangsness, Bry, & LaBouvie, 2005
Marijuana Effect Expectancy Questionnaire (MEEQ)	Schafer & Brown, 1991
Cocaine-Related Assessments	
Cocaine Effect Expectancy Questionnaire (CEEQ)	Schafer & Brown, 1991
Cocaine Expectancy Questionnaire (CEQ)	Jaffe & Kilbey, 1994

1993), which assesses both positive and negative expectancies. Positive expectancy factors include (a) Sociability, (b) Tension Reduction, (c) Liquid Courage, and (d) Sexuality. Negative expectancy factors are (a) Cognitive and Behavioral Impairment, (b) Risk and Aggression, and (c) Self-Perception. The CEOA demonstrates strong reliability, stability, and construct validity with both adolescents and adults (Fromme & D'Amico, 2000; Fromme et al., 1993). In addition to incorporating a wider range of expectancy items that tap more dimensions than the AEQ, the CEOA also includes subjective evaluations of the desirability of each effect. This follows Rotter's (1954) conceptualization of the importance of the desirability of the outcome, given an equal likelihood of obtaining the outcome. Findings to date have been mixed about the utility of subjective evaluations. Some studies have supported their use, suggesting that evaluations add incremental variance to the effect of expectancies (e.g., Fromme & D'Amico, 2000). Other studies have found that the

addition of subjective evaluations yields little beyond expected effects (e.g., Copeland, Brandon, & Quinn, 1995).

The assessment of both positive and negative expectancies in the CEOA addresses one of the most important clinical and theoretical issues surrounding explicit expectancy assessment (e.g., Jones & McMahon, 1992, 1994; Stacy, Widaman, & Marlatt, 1990). From a motivational perspective, anticipated positive and negative consequences of drinking should influence decisions to drink (Cox & Klinger; 1990); thus the measurement of both types of expectancy is necessary to identify their individual contributions. Nonetheless, for theoretical and practical reasons, the vast majority of expectancy research in the 1980s focused on positive expectancies. This was based on the notion that the immediate short-term positive consequences had a greater effect on behavior than the delayed negative consequences (Rohsenow, 1983) and because most expectancy researchers were using the AEQ.

ASSOCIATION BETWEEN EXPLICIT EXPECTANCIES AND SUBSTANCE USE

The role of expectancies in shaping substance use is well documented (e.g., Aarons, Brown, Stice, & Coe, 2001; Brandon & Baker, 1991; Fromme & D'Amico, 2000; Goldman, Del Boca, & Darkes, 1999), and the findings for the effects of outcome expectancies are largely consistent and robust (for review, see Jones et al., 2001b). Research has also shown that expectancies exist before direct experience with alcohol (Dunn & Goldman, 1996), thereby providing support for social learning as a main conduit for expectancy development.

Alcohol Outcome Expectancies

A consistent link between expectancies and alcohol use has been demonstrated over the past 3 decades (e.g., Fromme et al., 1993; Morawska & Oei, 2005; Southwick, Steele, Marlatt, & Lindell, 1981), with a meta-analytic review finding that expectancies account for 12% of the variance in alcohol consumption (McCarthy & Smith, 1996). Expectancies are related to different aspects of alcohol use, including frequency of drinking (e.g., Fromme et al., 1993), quantity of alcohol consumed (e.g., Fromme & D'Amico, 2000), binge drinking or heavy episodic alcohol use (e.g., Morawska & Oei, 2005), proximity to alcohol use (e.g., Wall, Hinson, & McKee, 1998), and alcohol-related consequences (e.g., Blume, Lostutter, Schmaling, & Marlatt, 2003). Expectancies are, however, typically found to be more strongly associated with quantity than with frequency of drinking (e.g., Fromme & D'Amico, 2000).

Positive and negative expectancies. Studies relating positive and negative expectancies to drinking behavior have yielded mixed findings (see Fromme et al., 1993; Jones et al., 2001b, for reviews). Demonstrating the complexity of this literature, Collins, Lapp, Emmons, and Isaac (1990) found that positive and negative expectancies form separate factors but that only positive expectancies are related to drinker status. When studied individually, both positive and negative expectancies influence alcohol use. When evaluated simultaneously, however, only positive expectancies are significantly associated with alcohol use (Fromme et al., 1993). Negative expectancies are also correlated with greater alcohol consequences (Mann, Chassin, & Sher, 1987), but they are relatively lower in heavier drinkers (Leigh, 1987). Lee, Greeley, and Oei (1999) found that positive expectancies serve to explain early drinking, whereas negative expectancies relate to decreased drinking (see also McMahon & Jones, 1993, and McNally & Palfai, 2001, for discussion about the utility of negative expectancies in readiness to reduce alcohol use).

On the basis of studies of the general population, Stacy et al. (1990) suggested that positive expectancies may affect concurrent and situation-specific drinking decisions through their association with cues available in the immediate setting. Accordingly, negative expectancies can be hypothesized to play a greater role in future decisions to drink on the basis of increased individual and vicarious experiences. In a series of studies, Jones and McMahon (e.g., 1992, 1994) showed that negative expectancies provided the motivation for problem drinkers to reduce or stop drinking. More recent studies have also confirmed that including negative expectancies is necessary in explaining substance use (e.g., Hasking & Oei, 2007; Zamboanga, 2006).

Expectancies by age and drinker status. The formation of expectancies begins sometime in childhood, long before actual consumption (e.g., Dunn & Goldman, 1996). For example, preschool children can already make olfactory discriminations among alcoholic and nonalcoholic beverages (Noll, Zucker, & Greenberg, 1990), suggesting that even lacking experience, they begin to learn about alcohol at a very early age. By first grade, children associate negative effects with drinking alcohol, although by seventh grade, these associations are already becoming more positive (Johnson & Johnson, 1995). Schell, Martino, Ellickson, Collins, and McCaffrey (2005) reported that older students (ninth graders) viewed alcohol's effects more positively compared with younger students (fourth graders). Even lacking drinking experience, adolescents spontaneously acknowledge both negative and positive effects of drinking (Christiansen, Goldman, & Inn, 1982). Children appear to learn about the effects of alcohol vicariously by observing the alcohol use of significant others, such as parents, and through portrayals in the media. With increased drinking experience, however, adolescents' expectancies become more clearly defined, with high-frequency drinkers developing specific expectations of enhanced sex, power, and tension reduction (Christiansen et al., 1982). It therefore seems clear that both vicarious processes and actual drinking experience make important contributions to the formation of outcome expectancies in children and adolescents.

Adolescents' alcohol expectancies about social behavior and improved cognitive and motor functioning account for roughly 25% of the variance in their alcohol use, with expectancies about social behavior also predicting changes from non–problem drinking to problem drinking (Christiansen, Smith, Roehling, & Goldman, 1989). Positive expectancies are also associated with greater alcohol use among college students (e.g., Fromme et al., 1993), with heavy drinkers, on one hand, endorsing more positive expectancies. Lighter drinkers, on the other hand, endorse associations between drinking and decreased physical well-being (Orford, Krishnan, Balaam, Everitt, & Van Der Graaf, 2004). In general, heavier drinkers endorse more positive expectancies than do light drinkers, including tension reduction, sexual enhancement, and sociability (Southwick et al., 1981), and people with alcoholism endorse more positive expectancies than do college students (Brown, Goldman & Christiansen, 1985) and problem and non–problem drinkers (Connors, O'Farrell, Cutter, & Thompson, 1986).

Findings from longitudinal studies have reinforced that positive expectancies predict onset of drinking, increased alcohol use, and transitions into hazardous alcohol use over time (e.g., Smith & Goldman, 1994). Most of this work was done with adolescents and young adults to understand the role of expectancies in the onset and development of drinking behaviors (e.g., Stacy, Newcomb, & Bentler, 1991). Among adolescents, social expectancies predict increased alcohol use a year later (Christiansen et al., 1989). The same sample was used to show that after controlling for baseline drinking, expectancies during the 2nd year in turn predicted drinking over

the following year (Smith, Goldman, Greenbaum, & Christiansen, 1995). Studies using lagged designs have further supported that changes in expectancies predict later changes in drinking (e.g., Sher, Wood, Wood, & Raskin, 1996; Wiers, van de Luitgaarden, van den Wildenberg, & Smulders, 2005).

Indirect expectancy influences. Beyond direct associations with alcohol use, expectancies are also studied as part of a larger system of predictors for alcohol use. Several studies have examined expectancies as moderators of different influences on alcohol use; some examples include peer norms (Callas, Flynn, & Worden, 2004; Rimal & Real, 2005), perceived peer pressure (Wood, Read, Palfai, & Stevenson, 2001), intentions to use (Dodge & Jaccard, 2007), and psychological distress (Cable & Sacker, 2007). Using peer norms as an example of expectancy moderation, Rimal and Real (2005) found that expectancies enhance the strength of norms, such that individuals who believe that their peers drink often and heavily (positive norm) and that drinking leads to rewards (positive expectancy) drink more than individuals with positive norms only. In contrast, Callas et al. (2004) found that those who believed that the prevalent attitude supported abstinence, but who held positive expectancies, were more likely to drink. In both cases, positive expectancies interact with norms to predict increases in alcohol use; however, the individual associations are quite different.

Expectancies have also been found to mediate the associations between certain putative risk factors and alcohol use (Sher, Walitzer, Wood, & Brent, 1991; Stacy et al., 1991). Returning to the example of peer norms, this means that expectancies, rather than changing the nature of the influence of norms on drinking, explain how norms influence drinking. Thus, through mediation, expectancies become causally linked to alcohol use. A more direct test of causality evaluates whether changes in expectancies mediate changes in alcohol. Testing this link has yielded mixed findings, however, and contributed to an ongoing debate about whether expectancies causally relate to drinking behavior (e.g., Del Boca & Darkes, 2001; Jones, Corbin, & Fromme, 2001a).

Priming studies have shown that manipulating expectancies yields changes in drinking (Roehrich & Goldman, 1995), but the effects are short lived and therefore questionable in terms of overall clinical significance (Jones et al., 2001b). The most compelling tests of whether changes in expectancies lead to changes in drinking involve expectancy challenge procedures (Goldman, Darkes, & Del Boca, 1999). In expectancy challenges, small groups of participants are told that they may or may not be drinking beverages that contain alcohol (in fact, none contain alcohol) and are subsequently asked to pick out the group members who consumed alcohol (Darkes & Goldman, 1993, 1998). Participants' difficulty in deciding who consumed alcohol is discussed within the context of placebo effects and alcohol expectancies, and self-reported drinking behavior is measured at a later date. Studies using expectancy challenge have shown reductions in alcohol use 6 weeks later (Darkes & Goldman, 1993, 1998); however, these findings have not been replicated independently (e.g., Corbin, McNair, & Carter, 1998; Maddock, Wood, Davidoff, Colby, & Monti, 1999).

Tobacco Outcome Expectancies

Although most of the research on expectancies focuses on alcohol, there has been increasing interest in whether expectancies for other drugs are similar in content and function. Most of this work concerns tobacco use (primarily in the form of cigarette smoking). Smoking outcome expectancies are conceptually similar to alcohol expectancies in that they are beliefs about the presumed effects of the behavior, highlight both positive and negative expectancies, and incorporate the role of subjective evaluations in examining how expectancies function.

A major departure between alcohol and tobacco expectancies is the perceived effects. For example, tobacco, unlike alcohol, is rarely associated with sexual enhancement or liquid courage. Tobacco expectancies focus on tension reduction, health risks, sensory pleasure, and social and physical outcomes (e.g., Brandon, Juliano, & Copeland, 1999). A gold standard in measuring smoking-related expectancies is the Smoking Consequences Questionnaire (Brandon & Baker, 1991). This 50-item questionnaire was developed with a collegiate sample and requests participants to rate the desirability and likelihood of several tobacco expectancy items. The scale consists of four factors: (a) Negative Consequences, (b) Positive Reinforcement/Sensory Satisfaction, (c) Negative Reinforcement/Negative Affect Reduction, and (d) Appetite/Weight Control.

Several studies have supported the association between smoking outcome expectancies and tobacco use (e.g., Copeland et al., 1995; Wetter et al., 1994). Among heavy-smoking adults, Wetter et al. (1994) reported that Smoking Consequences Questionnaire scores are associated with expected negative mood and stress during quitting. Copeland et al. (1995) reported that Smoking Consequences Questionnaire scores are associated with duration of smoking experience and a modified version of the Fagerström Tolerance Questionnaire of nicotine dependence. Palfai (2002) reported that the number of cigarettes that an individual smokes per day influences positive smoking expectancies, and Copeland et al. reported that positive expectancies are more accessible and influential among regular smokers. As well, sensory satisfaction expectancies and coping motives predict more smoking among college students following a short period of abstinence (Brandon, Wetter, & Baker, 1996).

In a study with adolescents 15 to 18 years of age, Kassel et al. (2007) reported that smoking cigarettes containing no nicotine leads to decreased negative affect, suggesting that negative reinforcement expectancies may play a role in smoking initiation and early maintenance before physiological addiction. Earlier work by Kassel and Yates (2002) supported that correcting misperceptions that cigarettes reduce stress may aid in smoking cessation. Among younger adolescents (fifth through eighth grade), positive expectancies strongly mediate the influence of smoking in the media on one's own smoking (Tickle, Hull, Sargent, Dalton, & Heatherton, 2006). A replication of this study using longitudinal data with adolescents who had never smoked suggested that expectancies contribute to smoking initiation. In addition, expectancies are stronger among adolescents who increased smoking during a period of 18 months than for adolescents who did not experience changes in smoking behavior (Wahl, Turner, Mermelstein, & Flay, 2005).

Marijuana Outcome Expectancies

The expectancy literature now includes the Marijuana Effect Expectancy Questionnaire (MEEQ; Schafer & Brown, 1991). Normed using a community sample, the MEEQ is a dichotomous measure (i.e., true–false) that is quite similar to the AEQ. Exploratory and confirmatory factor analyses with a collegiate sample resulted in a 48-item assessment with six expectancy factors: (a) Cognitive and Behavioral Impairment, (b) Relaxation and Tension Reduction, (c) Social and Sexual Facilitation, (d) Perceptual and Cognitive Enhancement, (e) Global Negative Effects, and (f) Craving and Physical Effects. Interestingly, both the AEQ for alcohol and the MEEQ for marijuana contain expectancy items tapping social and sexual facilitation and tension reduction. Despite the different overall effects for alcohol (retardation of motor skills and cognitive functioning, whereas marijuana is psychoactive and increases certain sensory experiences), both drugs appear to share some physiological effects. In addition, the AEQ and MEEQ share a behavioral impairment factor (Southwick et al., 1981).

Subsequent to the development of the MEEQ, additional studies have found that marijuana users endorsed positive expectancies, whereas nonusers endorsed negative expectancies (Galen & Henderson, 1999; Linkovich-Kyle & Dunn, 2001). Weaker negative expectancies are linked to greater marijuana use (e.g., Vangsness, Bry, & LaBouvie, 2005). Aarons et al. (2001) showed that expectancies play a key role in the initiation and maintenance of marijuana use. In their study, adolescent marijuana users held stronger beliefs that marijuana promotes tension reduction and social facilitation compared with youth who were not regular users. Marijuana users also held weaker beliefs about the negative effects of marijuana. The cross-sectional findings for both positive and negative expectancies were replicated using 2-year longitudinal data.

Cocaine Outcome Expectancies

Schafer and Brown (1991) developed the Cocaine Effect Expectancy Questionnaire (CEEQ) using similar psychometric procedures as for the MEEQ. The CEEQ is multifactorial, consisting of expectancy factors tapping (a) Global Positive Effects, (b) Global Negative Effects, (c) Generalized Arousal, (d) Anxiety, and (e) Relaxation and Tension Reduction. Similar to other expectancy measures, the CEEQ can distinguish use patterns on the basis of the endorsed positive and negative expectancies. Current users endorse positive items, whereas past or current nonusers endorse negative expectancies. Interestingly, Galen and Henderson (1999) reported that frequent cocaine users hold fewer positive expectancies compared with infrequent and nonusers. Expectations for arousal are strongest among infrequent users, whereas relaxation expectancies are more robust among nonusers. Jaffe and Kilbey (1994) compared the expectancies of cocaine abusers, infrequent cocaine users, and nonusers. They found that abusers reported expectations of anxiety, depression, decreased sexual performance, and tension reduction. Infrequent users reported that cocaine leads to increased sexual performance, aggression, and euphoria, whereas nonusers believed that cocaine induces euphoria but also provides a gateway to other drug use.

In a recent study, Lundahl and Lukas (2007) administered cocaine to hospitalized cocaine users to better understand the association between expectancy and the subjective experience of cocaine use. As opposed to most other studies, which have asked users to endorse expectancies on the basis of what they would experience "if they were using," Lundahl and Lukas observed whether expectancies "came true" during actual cocaine use. Of the four CEEQ scales associated with individuals' subjective response to the cocaine challenge (Global Positive Effects, Global Negative Effects, Anxiety, and Tension Reduction), Global Negative Effect expectancies were more strongly linked to a positive subjective response during cocaine use.

MOTIVES

Motives to use substances, different from expectancies, are conceptualized as part of the motivational framework for substance use. To assess drinking motives, Cooper (1994; Cooper, Russell, Skinner, & Windle, 1992) developed the Drinking Motives Questionnaire. The Drinking Motives Questionnaire contains two activating affective beliefs outlined by Cox and Klinger (1988) and four factors assessing internal and external rewards. The latter factors include Enhancement (internal reward, increased positive affect), Social (external reward, increased positive affect), Coping (internal reward, decreased negative affect), and Conformity (external reward, decreased negative affect). In one study, Cooper (1994) reported that motives explained between 14% and 20% of the variance in alcohol consumption over a 6-month period, with enhancement motives representing the most optimal predictor of the four internal and external motive factors.

Several studies have evaluated drinking motives as predictors of alcohol use (for a review, see Kuntsche, Knibbe, Gmel, & Engels, 2005). For the most part, heavier drinkers are more likely to endorse coping motives (Cooper, Agocha, & Sheldon, 2000) and enhancement motives (Carey, 1993), whereas moderate or lighter drinkers are more likely to report they drink for social motives (e.g., Kassel, Jackson, & Unrod, 2000). Others have reported that coping motives are related to increased alcohol problems (e.g., Simons, Correia, & Carey, 2000).

Similarities and Differences Between Expectancies and Motives

There is a strong case that expectancies and motives overlap conceptually, although some have argued that there is a clear temporal relationship (see Ham & Hope, 2003, for a review). Thus, one can say that the expectation of a drug's effect precedes the motivation to use it to achieve that effect. Baer (2002, p. 45) referred to motives as "primary psychological effects" that are experienced with substance use, whereas expectancies are conceptualized as "specific beliefs about the behavioral, emotional, and cognitive effects" of substance use. This distinction suggests that motives may function in the capacity of need fulfillment and expectancies as beliefs about how those needs can be met.

The same literature has also suggested that expectancies and motives apparently share a common foundation. Cooper's (1994) model of drinking motives, which is similar to the multidimensional framework proposed by Goldman, Del Boca, and Darkes (1999), consists of multiple dimensions involving outcome and affect. Thus, many of the items in Cooper's assessment of drink-

ing motives are quite similar to those in various expectancy measures. A key difference, however, is that expectancy measures focus on a belief about the effect of a substance (e.g., "After a few drinks, I will feel . . . "), whereas drinking motive items focus on reasons for drinking (e.g., "I drink in order to feel . . . "). This semantic difference points toward a large conceptual difference; one can hold several expectancies about the effects of drinking, but one drinks for specific reasons. In other words, not every belief about drinking leads to the onset of alcohol use.

In addition to Cooper's (1994) drinking motives assessment, Cronin (1997) outlined three primary drinking motives including social camaraderie, mood enhancement, and tension reduction. These motives map closely onto expectancy concepts (e.g., Brown et al., 1980; Fromme et al., 1993). For example, an individual can use substances because he or she believes the substance will reduce stress (i.e., tension reduction expectancy) and because he or she needs to reduce stress (i.e., coping motivation). In contrast, if an individual is not feeling tense or in need of stress reduction, the belief that using a drug will reduce tension should not lead to substance use.

In reviewing the subtle differences between motives and expectancies, it is clearly possible that they reflect two sides of the same coin. This picture emerges from Cox and Klinger's (2004) refinements to their earlier motivational model. They wrote, "Expectancies are people's beliefs about what will happen if they (or other people) drink alcohol, whereas motives are the value placed on the particular effects they want to achieve, which motivate them to drink" (p. 124). In this case, value is hypothesized to mean the desirability of the effect. In essence, an individual must ask him- or herself how valuable the goal is before determining whether he or she will pursue it. If expectancy provides a template for how this goal can be achieved, then the expectancy will be associated with behavior initiation. According to this approach, drinking motives are hypothesized to be the most proximal predictor of alcohol use, providing a pathway for expectancies and other distal factors to exert their influence on consumption.

PERCEIVED NORMS

Although a great deal has been said so far about expectancy and motives, there is another side of the "motivational coin" that needs to be considered. Over the past 2 decades, normative influence has gained tremendous support as a key factor in substance use. Social norms theory is adapted from the classic psychological constructs of false consensus (Ross, Greene, & House, 1977) and pluralistic ignorance (Darley & Latané, 1968). Several chapters in this handbook make mention of these concepts and integrate them into different views of drug use etiology, again reinforcing their theoretical and predictive importance. Briefly, pluralistic ignorance suggests that many people will share a belief despite the inaccurate nature of the belief. In other words, people would much rather strive for a consensus even though there is very little evidence to support their belief. Sher, Wolf, and Martinez (chap. 12, this volume) discuss pluralistic ignorance in terms of the widely held belief that excessive drinking is okay even though there are tremendous negative effects associated with binge drinking (including, in some cases, death). Studies of collegiate drinking have been quite useful in illustrating the concept of normative beliefs and pluralistic ignorance (Perkins & Berkowitz, 1986). Students consistently overestimate peer drinking and permissiveness (e.g., Borsari & Carey, 2001; Haines & Spears, 1996; Larimer & Cronce, 2002). These overestimations are thought to subsequently increase the individual's likelihood of participating in alcohol or drug use by proving the false but widely believed sense that drinking is normal and acceptable behavior (Gomberg, Schneider, & DeJong, 2001).

Two types of social norms exist: injunctive and descriptive norms (Cialdini, Reno, & Kallgren, 1990). Descriptive, or behavioral, norms describe an individual's perception of typical or popular behavior and function by providing information about which behaviors are popular and result in greater social acceptance. Injunctive, or attitudinal, norms describe the perceptions of others' approval or disapproval of specific behaviors. As individuals become aware of societal or peer attitudes and values about a behavior, they may change their own behavior to gain social

approval (or avoid social disapproval). In research on substance use, injunctive norms describe the perceptions of others' approval of substance use and the prescribed rules about drug use for a specific social group, and descriptive norms encompass the perception of the quantity and frequency of peer substance consumption (Borsari & Carey, 2001). Given the previous discussion about expectancies and their motivational role, it is clear that both expectancies and norms are important pieces of the puzzle in alcohol and drug use etiology.

Differences and Similarities Between Expectancies and Norms

Development of expectancies and norms.   The formation of expectancies and norms occurs through similar modalities. Both are subjective heuristics used by an individual to promote organization and recall of information. In social settings, observation of others' behavior increases the likelihood of an individual's engaging in the same behavior. Within the conceptualization of vicarious learning, individuals believe that replication of others' behavior leads to social acceptance and other rewards similar to those obtained by the imitated person. Developmentally, modeling of substance use begins early in an individual's life. Drinking or substance use by parents and other family members, portrayals of drugs in the media, and later exposure through peers can provide observational models long before the individual decides to engage in substance use. Among pre- and young adolescents, peer modeling influences for alcohol use are concurrently related to individual alcohol use, whereas parental modeling is a more efficient predictor of future drinking (Ary, Tildesley, Hops, & Andrews, 1993).

Caudill and Marlatt (1975) demonstrated that among young adults and college students, situation-specific modeling can alter an individual's alcohol use within an experimental setting. In fact, these studies showed that individuals will attempt to match the rates of the model's alcohol consumption in social settings to obtain in-group status and share the perceived enjoyment. Modeling may contribute to the development and maintenance of cognitive determinants (e.g., expectations about future occurrences of the behavior) and then link these with indirect social influence (e.g., normative perceptions of drinking).

In addition to vicarious learning processes, expectancies and norms may also originate from explicit statements derived from others. A young woman can be told that using cocaine is cool, everyone is trying it, and it will make her feel sexy. The same teen further perceives that she will be more popular and better liked by her immediate peers if she uses cocaine. Given the social and physical expectancies and both descriptive and injunctive norms contained in her friends' statements, the young woman may choose to use cocaine. Thus, individuals can regulate peer behavior by providing a context for developing expectancies. Once a behavior is consistently built into the fabric of a peer or reference group, extinction of such behavior is difficult.

Expectancies and norms as perceptual beliefs.

Despite the strength of the influences of norms and expectancies, both are subjective phenomena structured as self-reported beliefs. It is the presence rather than the veracity of these beliefs that apparently drives behavior. Someone may, for example, use marijuana because of outcome expectancies (e.g., "It helps me feel more relaxed") or perceived norms (e.g., "My friends think it's the right thing to do"), regardless of whether any of these beliefs are true. Until an individual gains firsthand experience with drug use, his or her expectations and normative beliefs are influenced solely by perceptions based on other people's drug use. With experience, however, the individual can confirm, repudiate, or even create new expectancies. Experience can also be used to verify social norms by gauging others' responses when a substance is used. This reinforces the dynamic nature of expectancies and norms, which can change with exposure to substance use. It also seems likely that expectancies and norms, with sufficient experience, become less malleable over time. There is evidence that expectancies become crystallized with age (e.g., Dunn & Goldman, 1996; Rather & Goldman, 1994), but research on the expectancies and norms among older adults is limited.

Differences between expectancies and norms.

Numerous studies have examined either expectancies or norms as influences on alcohol and drug use etiology (e.g., Kuther & Timoshin, 2003; Scheier & Botvin, 1997). Much less, however, is known about how these influences predict drug use when modeled simultaneously. The previously cited study by Scheier and Botvin (1997) showed that the effect of injunctive norms was mediated entirely through expectancies, whereas descriptive norms had both a direct and a mediated effect on alcohol use. Other studies have suggested a different picture. For instance, Wall et al. (1998) found that injunctive norms were a strong and consistent predictor of intentions to use alcohol among both men and women, whereas social facilitation expectancies had a smaller unique effect predicting intentions for women. After controlling for intentions to use alcohol, assertiveness expectancies (for women) and sexual enhancement expectancies (for men) were associated with excessive alcohol consumption. Kuther and Timoshin (2003) reported that norms are more efficient predictors of consumption than positive and negative expectancies. Mixed findings about the relative influence of norms and expectancies highlight the need to study both predictors simultaneously, as well as to evaluate their association with each other (e.g., mediation, moderation).

EFFORTS TO COMBINE EXPECTANCIES, MOTIVES, AND NORMS

In the past, expectancies, motives, and norms were studied as independent constructs and were rarely evaluated together. From a theoretical point of view, Cox and Klinger's (1988) motivational model suggests a cognitive chain including norms influencing expectancies, which in turn influence motives and then predict substance use. There are few explicit tests of this model, however, and most have been partial tests of the cognitive chain. Nagoshi, Nakata, Sasano, and Wood (1994) reported that motives explained alcohol use, controlling for expectancies. Cronin (1997), however, found that expectancies no longer explained variance in drinking once motives were statistically controlled. Motives mediate the association between expectancies and substance use, suggesting that future research incorporate more distal factors, such as social influence and situation-specific cues.

To test broader expectancy models, Read, Wood, Kahler, Maddock, and Palfai (2003) examined perceived peer drinking environment, expectancies, personality traits, and motives as predictors of alcohol use in a sample of college students. The model posits expectancies, social influence, and trait impulsive sensation seeking as distal factors that influence substance use via motives. Results suggest that motives partially mediate the effects of norms and expectancies on consumption but that other direct paths remained intact with substantially large effects owing to their distinct predictive value to drinking behavior.

Social influence is often overlooked in models evaluating expectancies and motives. Catanzaro and Laurent (2004), for example, showed that expectancies for mood regulation influence alcohol use via coping motives but did not evaluate social norms. In a recent study examining coping motives as a mediator of the influence of tension reduction expectancies on alcohol use, Kuntsche, Knibbe, Engels, and Gmel (2007) showed that expectancies influence substance use via motives. Again, social influence was not included as a more distal factor.

In another recent study evaluating the relative contribution of social norms, drinking motives, and alcohol-related expectancies to drinking behavior and consequences, norms were the strongest predictor of alcohol use among college students. In contrast, expectancies and motives were less strongly associated with alcohol use but demonstrated greater effects on alcohol problems (Neighbors, Lee, Lewis, Fossos, & Larimer, 2007). Although this study measured all three cognitive constructs, a limitation was the absence of any clear theoretical model to help explain the obtained statistical relations.

DIRECTIONS FOR FUTURE RESEARCH

Expectancies, motives, and social norms are strong correlates and predictors of the initiation and maintenance of substance use, yet they are rarely combined in empirical studies to provide a more comprehensive evaluation of factors contributing to substance use.

This was a mainstay of the motivational model proposed by Cox and Klinger (1988, 1990, 2004). The sum of these efforts was to integrate more cognitive elements and provide a firm springboard for further research. The lack of a clear and consistent body of research attesting to either moderation or mediation also suggests that pursuing new avenues of research would be profitable.

Conceptually, expectancies, motives, and norms share many similarities in their developmental origins, and this perhaps fuels their common association with substance use. Current research efforts have isolated their relative contribution to drug use etiology; however, the general consensus is that substance use is an extremely complicated behavior influenced by many genetic, biological, psychosocial, cognitive, and environmental variables. The use of theoretical frameworks to combine related cognitive factors and further guide the study of substance use is the next step in extending our knowledge of substance use etiology. Newer multivariate statistical methods and techniques to deal with nested data also improve our ability to test integrated models. These techniques were almost impossible a decade ago, but the fact remains that the effects of expectancies, motives, and norms have been prevailing regardless of our ability to tease them apart. Examining these cognitive determinants in a combined, theoretical framework may provide new insights into both the etiology and the treatment of substance use.

References

Aarons, G. A., Brown, S. A., Stice, E., & Coe, M. T. (2001). Psychometric evaluation of the Marijuana and Stimulant Effect Expectancy Questionnaires for adolescents. *Addictive Behaviors, 26,* 219–236.

Ary, D. V., Tildesley, E., Hops, H., & Andrews, J. (1993). The influence of parent, sibling, and peer modeling and attitudes on adolescent use of alcohol. *International Journal of the Addictions, 28,* 853–880.

Baer, J. S. (2002). Student factors: Understanding individual variation in college drinking. *Journal of Studies on Alcohol, 14*(Suppl.), 40–53.

Blume, A. W., Lostutter, T. W., Schmaling, K. B., & Marlatt, G. A. (2003). Beliefs about drinking behavior predict drinking consequences. *Journal of Psychoactive Drugs, 35,* 395–399.

Bolles, R. C. (1972). Reinforcement, expectancy, and learning. *Psychological Review, 79,* 394–409.

Borsari, B., & Carey, K. B. (2001). Peer influences on college drinking: A review of the research. *Journal of Substance Abuse, 13,* 391–424.

Brandon, T. H., & Baker, T. (1991). The Smoking Consequences Questionnaire: The subjective expected utility of smoking in college students. *Psychological Assessment, 3,* 484–491.

Brandon, T. H., Juliano, L. M., & Copeland, A. L. (1999). Expectancies for tobacco smoking. In I. Kirsch (Ed.), *How expectancies shape experience* (pp. 263–299). Washington, DC: American Psychological Association.

Brandon, T. H., Wetter, D. W., & Baker, T. B. (1996). Affect, expectancies, urges, and smoking: Do they conform to models of drug motivation and relapse? *Experimental and Clinical Psychopharmacology, 4,* 29–36.

Brown, S. A., Christiansen, B. A., & Goldman, M. S. (1987). The Alcohol Expectancy Questionnaire: An instrument for the assessment of adolescent and adult alcohol expectancies. *Journal of Studies on Alcohol, 48,* 483–491.

Brown, S. A., Goldman, M. S., & Christiansen, B. A. (1985). Do alcohol expectancies mediate drinking patterns of adults? *Journal of Consulting and Clinical Psychology, 53,* 512–519.

Brown, S. A., Goldman, M. S., Inn, A., & Anderson, L. R. (1980). Expectations of reinforcement from alcohol: Their domain and relation to drinking patterns. *Journal of Consulting and Clinical Psychology, 48,* 419–426.

Cable, N., & Sacker, A. (2007). The role of adolescent social disinhibition expectancies in moderating the relationship between psychological distress and alcohol use and misuse. *Addictive Behaviors, 32,* 282–295.

Callas, P. W., Flynn, B. S., & Worden, J. K. (2004). Potentially modifiable psychosocial factors associated with alcohol use during early adolescence. *Addictive Behaviors, 29,* 1503–1515.

Carey, K. B. (1993). Situational determinants of heavy drinking among college students. *Journal of Counseling Psychology, 40,* 217–220.

Catanzaro, S. J., & Laurent, J. (2004). Perceived family support, negative mood regulation expectancies, coping, and adolescent alcohol use: Evidence of mediation and moderation effects. *Addictive Behaviors, 29,* 1779–1797.

Caudill, B. D., & Marlatt, G. A. (1975). Modeling influences in social drinking: An experimental analogue. *Journal of Consulting and Clinical Psychology, 43,* 405–415.

Christiansen, B. A., Goldman, M. S., & Inn, A. (1982). The development of alcohol-related expectancies in adolescents: Separating pharmacological from social learning influences. *Journal of Consulting and Clinical Psychology, 50,* 336–344.

Christiansen, B. A., Smith, G. T., Roehling, P. V., & Goldman, M. S. (1989). Using alcohol expectancies to predict adolescent drinking behavior after one year. *Journal of Consulting and Clinical Psychology, 57,* 93–99.

Cialdini, R. B., Reno, R. R., & Kallgren, C. A. (1990). A focus theory of normative conduct: Recycling the concept of norms to reduce littering in public places. *Journal of Personality and Social Psychology, 58,* 1015–1026.

Collins, R. L., Lapp, W. M., Emmons, K. M., & Isaac, L. M. (1990). Endorsement and strength of alcohol expectancies. *Journal of Studies on Alcohol, 51,* 336–342.

Connors, G. J., O'Farrell, T. J., Cutter, H. S., & Thompson, D. L. (1986). Alcohol expectancies among male alcoholics, problem drinkers, and non-problem drinkers. *Alcoholism: Clinical and Experimental Research, 10,* 667–671.

Cooper, M. L. (1994). Motivations for alcohol use among adolescents: Development and validation of a four-factor model. *Psychological Assessment, 6,* 117–128.

Cooper, M. L., Agocha, V. B., & Sheldon, M. S. (2000). A motivational perspective on risky behaviors: The role of personality and affect regulatory processes. *Journal of Personality, 68,* 1059–1088.

Cooper, M. L., Russell, M., Skinner, J. B., & Windle, M. (1992). Development and validation of a three-dimensional measure of drinking motives. *Psychological Assessment, 4,* 123–132.

Copeland, A. L., Brandon, T. H., & Quinn, E. P. (1995). The Smoking Consequences Questionnaire—Adult: Measurement of smoking outcome expectancies of experienced smokers. *Psychological Assessment, 7,* 484–494.

Corbin, W. R., McNair, L. D., & Carter, J. A. (1998, June). *The effects of an explicit alcohol expectancy challenge on drinking behavior.* Paper presented at the annual meeting of the Research Society on Alcoholism, Hilton Head, SC.

Cox, W. M., & Klinger, E. (1988). A motivational model of alcohol use. *Journal of Abnormal Psychology, 97,* 168–180.

Cox, W. M., & Klinger, E. (1990). Incentive motivation, affective change, and alcohol use: A model. In W. M. Cox (Ed.), *Why people drink: Parameters of alcohol as a reinforcer* (pp. 291–314). New York: Gardner Press.

Cox, W. M., & Klinger, E. (2004). A motivational model of alcohol use: Determinants of use and change. In W. M. Cox & E. Klinger (Eds.), *Handbook of motivational counseling: Concepts, approaches, and assessment* (pp. 121–138). New York: Wiley.

Cronin, C. (1997). Reasons for drinking versus outcome expectancies in the prediction of college student drinking. *Substance Use and Misuse, 32,* 1287–1311.

Dalton, M. A., Sargent, J. D., Beach, M. L., Bernhardt, A. M., & Stevens, M. (1999). Positive and negative outcome expectations of smoking: Implications for prevention. *Preventative Medicine, 29,* 460–465.

Darkes, J., & Goldman, M. S. (1993). Expectancy challenge and drinking reduction: Experimental evidence for a meditational process. *Journal of Consulting and Clinical Psychology, 61,* 344–353.

Darkes, J., & Goldman, M. S. (1998). Expectancy challenge and drinking reduction: Process and structure in the alcohol expectancy network. *Experimental and Clinical Psychopharmacology, 6,* 64–76.

Darley, J. M., & Latané, B. (1968). Bystander intervention in emergencies: Diffusion of responsibility. *Journal of Personality and Social Psychology, 8,* 377–383.

Del Boca, F. K., & Darkes, J. (2001). Is the glass half full or half empty? An evaluation of the status of expectancies as causal agents. *Addiction, 96,* 1671–1673.

Dodge, T., & Jaccard, J. J. (2007). Negative beliefs as a moderator of the intention–behavior relationship: Decisions to use performance-enhancing substances. *Journal of Applied Social Psychology, 37,* 43–59

Dunn, M. E., & Goldman, M. S. (1996). Empirical modeling of an alcohol expectancy memory network in elementary-school children as a function of grade and risk status. *Experimental and Clinical Psychopharmacology, 4,* 209–217.

Fromme, K., & D'Amico, E. J. (2000). Measuring adolescent alcohol outcome expectancies. *Psychology of Addictive Behaviors, 14,* 206–212.

Fromme, K., Kivlahan, D. R., & Marlatt, G. A. (1986). Alcohol expectancies, risk identification, and secondary prevention with problem drinkers. *Advances in Behaviour Research & Therapy, 8,* 237–251.

Fromme, K., Stroot, E. A., & Kaplan, D. (1993). Comprehensive effects of alcohol: Development and psychometric assessment of a new expectancy questionnaire. *Psychological Assessment, 5,* 19–26.

Galen, L. W., & Henderson, M. J. (1999). Validation of cocaine and marijuana effect expectancies in a treatment setting. *Addictive Behaviors, 24,* 719–724.

Goldman, M. S. (1999). Expectancy operation: Cognitive-neural models and architectures. In I. Kirsch (Ed.), *How expectancies shape experience* (pp. 41–63). Washington, DC: American Psychological Association.

Goldman, M. S., Brown, S. A., Christiansen, B. A., & Smith, G. T. (1991). Alcoholism and memory: Broadening the scope of alcohol-expectancy research. *Psychological Bulletin, 110,* 137–146.

Goldman, M. S., Darkes, J., & Del Boca, F. K. (1999). Expectancy mediation of biopsychosocial risk for alcohol use and alcoholism. In I. Kirsch (Ed.), *How expectancies shape experience* (pp. 233–262). Washington, DC: American Psychological Association.

Goldman, M. S., Del Boca, F. K., & Darkes, J. (1999). Alcohol expectancy theory: The application of cognitive neuroscience. In H. Blane & K. Leonard (Eds.), *Psychological theories of drinking and alcoholism* (2nd ed., pp. 203–246). New York: Guilford Press.

Gomberg, L., Schneider, S. K., & DeJong, W. (2001). Evaluation of a social norms marketing campaign to reduce high-risk drinking at the University of Mississippi. *American Journal of Drug and Alcohol Abuse, 27,* 375–389.

Haines, M. P., & Spears, A. F. (1996). Changing the perception of the norm: A strategy to decrease binge drinking among college students. *Journal of American College Health, 45,* 134–140.

Ham, L. S., & Hope, D. A. (2003). College students and problematic drinking: A review of the literature. *Clinical Psychology Review, 23,* 719–759.

Hasking, P. A., & Oei, T. P. S. (2007). Alcohol expectancies, self-efficacy and coping in an alcohol-dependent sample. *Addictive Behaviors, 32,* 99–113.

Hine, D. W., Honan, C., Marks, A. D., & Brettschneider, K. (2007). Development and validation of the Smoking Expectancy Scale for Adolescents. *Psychological Assessment, 19,* 347–355.

Hull, J. G., & Bond, C. F. (1986). Social and behavioral consequences of alcohol consumption and expectancy: A meta-analysis. *Psychological Bulletin, 99,* 347–360.

Jaffe, A. J., & Kilbey, M. M. (1994). The Cocaine Expectancy Questionnaire (CEQ): Construction and predictive utility. *Psychological Assessment, 6,* 18–26.

Johnson, H. L., & Johnson, P. B. (1995). Children's alcohol-related cognitions: Positive versus negative alcohol effects. *Journal of Alcohol and Drug Education, 40,* 1–12.

Jones, B. T., Corbin, W. R., & Fromme, K. (2001a). Half full or half empty, the glass still does not satisfactorily quench the thirst for knowledge on alcohol expectancies as a mechanism of change. *Addiction, 96,* 1672–1674.

Jones, B. T., Corbin, W. R., & Fromme, K. (2001b). A review of expectancy theory and alcohol consumption. *Addiction, 96,* 57–72.

Jones, B. T., & McMahon, J. (1992). Negative and positive expectancies in lone and group problem drinkers. *British Journal of Addiction, 87,* 929–930.

Jones, B. T., & McMahon, J. (1994). Negative and positive alcohol expectancies and predictors of abstinence after discharge from a residential treatment program:

A one-month and three-month follow-up study in men. *Journal of Studies on Alcohol, 55,* 543–548.

Kassel, J. D., Evatt, D. P., Greenstein, J. E., Wardle, M. C., Yates, M. C., & Veilleux, J. C. (2007). The acute effects of nicotine on positive and negative affect in adolescent smokers. *Journal of Abnormal Psychology, 116,* 543–553.

Kassel, J. D., Jackson, S. I., & Unrod, M. (2000). Generalized expectancies for negative mood regulation and problem drinking among college students. *Journal of Studies on Alcohol, 61,* 332–340.

Kassel, J. D., & Yates, M. (2002). Is there a role for assessment in smoking cessation treatment? *Behaviour Research and Therapy, 40,* 1457–1470.

Kuntsche, E., Knibbe, R., Engels, R., & Gmel, G. (2007). Drinking motives as mediators of the link between alcohol expectancies and alcohol use among adolescents. *Journal of Studies on Alcohol and Drugs, 68,* 76–85.

Kuntsche, E., Knibbe, R., Gmel, G., & Engels, R. (2005). Why do young people drink? A review of drinking motives. *Clinical Psychology Review, 25,* 841–861.

Kuther, T. L., & Timoshin, A. (2003). A comparison of social cognitive and psychosocial predictors of alcohol use by college students. *Journal of College Student Development, 44,* 143–154.

Laberg, J. C., & Löberg, T. (1989). Expectancy and tolerance: A study of acute alcohol intoxication using the balanced placebo design. *Journal of Studies on Alcohol, 50,* 448–455.

Larimer, M. E., & Cronce, J. M. (2002). Identification, prevention, and treatment: A review of individual-focused strategies to reduce problematic alcohol consumption by college students. *Journal of Studies on Alcohol, 14*(Suppl.), 148–163.

Lee, N. K., Greeley, J., & Oei, T. P. S. (1999). The relationship of positive and negative alcohol expectancies to patterns of consumption of alcohol in social drinkers. *Addictive Behaviors, 24,* 359–369.

Leigh, B. C. (1987). Beliefs about the effects of alcohol on self and others. *Journal of Studies on Alcohol, 48,* 467–475.

Leigh, B. C. (1989). In search of the seven dwarves: Issues of measurement and meaning in alcohol expectancy research. *Psychological Bulletin, 105,* 361–373.

Lewis-Esquerre, J. M., Rodrigue, J. R., & Kahler, C. W. (2005). Development and validation of an adolescent Smoking Consequences Questionnaire. *Nicotine & Tobacco Research, 7,* 81–90.

Linkovich-Kyle, T. L., & Dunn, M. E. (2001). Consumption-related differences in the organization and activation of marijuana expectancies in memory. *Experimental and Clinical Psychopharmacology, 9,* 334–342.

Lundahl, L. H., & Lukas, S. E. (2007). Negative cocaine effect expectancies are associated with subjective response to cocaine challenge in recreational cocaine users. *Addictive Behaviors, 32,* 1262–1271.

MacAndrew, C., & Edgerton, R. B. (1969). *Drunken comportment: A social explanation.* Oxford, England: Aldine.

MacCorquodale, K. M., & Meehl, P. E. (1953). Preliminary suggestions as to a formalization of expectancy theory. *Psychological Review, 60,* 55–63.

Maddock, J. E., Wood, M. D., Davidoff, S. M., Colby, S. M., & Monti, P. M. (1999, June). *Alcohol expectancy challenge and alcohol use: Examination of a controlled trial.* Paper presented at the annual meeting of the Research Society on Alcoholism, Santa Barbara, CA.

Mann, L. M., Chassin, L., & Sher, K. J. (1987). Alcohol expectancies and the risk for alcoholism. *Journal of Consulting and Clinical Psychology, 55,* 411–417.

Marlatt, G. A., & Rohsenow, D. J. (1980). Cognitive processes in alcohol use: Expectancy and the balanced placebo design. In N. K. Mello (Ed.), *Advances in substance abuse: Behavioral and biological research* (pp. 159–199). Greenwich, CT: JAI Press.

McCarthy, D. M., & Smith, G. T. (1996, June). *Meta-analysis of alcohol expectancy.* Paper presented at the annual meeting of the Research Society on Alcoholism, Washington, DC.

McMahon, J., & Jones, B. T. (1993). Negative expectancy in motivation. *Addiction Research, 1,* 145–155.

McNally, A. M., & Palfai, T. P. (2001). Negative emotional expectancies and readiness to change among college student binge drinkers. *Addictive Behaviors, 26,* 721–734.

Meehl, P. E., & MacCorquodale, K. M. (1951). Some methodological comments concerning expectancy theory. *Psychological Review, 58,* 230–233.

Morawska, A., & Oei, T. P. (2005). Binge drinking in university students: A test of the cognitive model. *Addictive Behaviors, 30,* 203–218.

Nagoshi, C. T., Nakata, T., Sasano, K., & Wood, M. D. (1994). Alcohol norms, expectancies, and reasons for drinking and alcohol use in a U.S. versus a Japanese college sample. *Alcoholism: Clinical and Experimental Research, 18,* 671–678.

Neighbors, C., Lee, C. M., Lewis, M. A., Fossos, N., & Larimer, M. E. (2007). Are social norms the best predictor of outcomes among heavy drinking college students? *Journal of Studies on Alcohol and Drugs, 68,* 556–565.

Noll, R. B., Zucker, R. A., & Greenberg, G. S. (1990). Identification of alcohol by smell among preschoolers: Evidence for early socialization about drugs occurring in the home. *Child Development, 61,* 1520–1527.

Orford, J., Krishnan, M., Balaam, M., Everitt, M., & Van Der Graaf, K. (2004). University student drinking: The role of motivational and social factors. *Drugs: Education, Prevention & Policy, 11*, 407–421.

Palfai, T. P. (2002). Positive outcome expectancies and smoking behavior: The role of expectancy accessibility. *Cognitive Therapy and Research, 26*, 317–333.

Perkins, H. W., & Berkowitz, A. D. (1986). Perceiving the community norms of alcohol use among students: Some research implication for campus alcohol education programming. *International Journal of the Addictions, 21*, 961–976.

Rather, B. C., & Goldman, M. S. (1994). Drinking-related differences in the memory organization of alcohol expectancies. *Experimental and Clinical Psychopharmacology, 2*, 167–183.

Read, J. P., Wood, M. D., Kahler, C. W., Maddock, J. E., & Palfai, T. (2003). Examining the role of drinking motives in college student alcohol use and problems. *Psychology of Addictive Behavior, 17*, 13–23.

Rimal, R. N., & Real, K. (2005). How behaviors are influenced by perceived norms: A test of the theory of normative social behavior. *Communication Research, 32*, 389–414.

Roehrich, L., & Goldman, M. S. (1995). Implicit priming of alcohol expectancy memory processes and subsequent drinking behavior. *Experimental and Clinical Psychopharmacology, 3*, 402–410.

Rohsenow, D. J. (1983). Drinking habits and expectancies about alcohol's effects for self versus others. *Journal of Consulting and Clinical Psychology, 51*, 536–541.

Ross, L., Greene, D., & House, P. (1977). The false consensus effect: An egocentric bias in social perception and attribution processes. *Journal of Experimental Social Psychology, 13*, 279–301.

Rotter, J. B. (1954). *Social learning and clinical psychology*. Englewood Cliffs, NJ: Prentice-Hall.

Schafer, J., & Brown, S. A. (1991). Marijuana and cocaine effect expectancies and drug use patterns. *Journal of Consulting and Clinical Psychology, 59*, 558–565.

Scheier, L. M., & Botvin, G. J. (1997). Expectancies as mediators of the effects of social influences and alcohol knowledge on adolescent alcohol use: A prospective analysis. *Psychology of Addictive Behaviors, 11*, 48–64.

Schell, T. L., Martino, S. C., Ellickson, P. L., Collins, R. L., & McCaffrey, D. (2005). Measuring developmental changes in alcohol expectancies. *Psychology of Addictive Behaviors, 19*, 217–220.

Sher, K. J., Walitzer, K. S., Wood, P. A., & Brent, E. E. (1991). Characteristics of children of alcoholics: Putative risk factors, substance use and abuse, and psychopathology. *Journal of Abnormal Psychology, 100*, 427–448.

Sher, K. J., Wood, M. D., Wood, P. K., & Raskin, G. (1996). Alcohol outcome expectancies and alcohol use: A latent variable cross-lagged panel study. *Journal of Abnormal Psychology, 105*, 561–574.

Simons, J., Correia, C. J., & Carey, K. B. (2000). A comparison of motives for marijuana and alcohol use among experienced users. *Addictive Behaviors, 25*, 153–160.

Smith, G. T., & Goldman, M. S. (1994). Alcohol expectancy theory and the identification of high-risk adolescents. *Journal of Research on Adolescence, 4*, 229–248.

Smith, G. T., Goldman, M. S., Greenbaum, P. E., & Christiansen, B. A. (1995). Expectancy for social facilitation from drinking: The divergent paths of high-expectancy and low-expectancy adolescents. *Journal of Abnormal Psychology, 104*, 32–40.

Southwick, L. L., Steele, C. M., Marlatt, G. A., & Lindell, M. K. (1981). Alcohol-related expectancies: Defined by phase of intoxication and drinking experience. *Journal of Consulting and Clinical Psychology, 49*, 713–721.

Stacy, A. W., Newcomb, M. D., & Bentler, P. M. (1991). Cognitive motivation and problem drug use: A nine-year longitudinal study. *Journal of Abnormal Psychology, 100*, 502–515.

Stacy, A. W., Widaman, K. F., & Marlatt, G. A. (1990). Expectancy models of alcohol use. *Journal of Personality and Social Psychology, 58*, 918–928.

Tickle, J. J., Hull, J. G., Sargent, J. D., Dalton, M. A., & Heatherton, T. F. (2006). A structural equation model of social influences and exposure to media smoking on adolescent smoking. *Basic and Applied Social Psychology, 28*, 117–129.

Tolman, E. G. (1932). *Purposive behavior in animals and man*. New York: Appleton-Century-Crofts.

Vangsness, L., Bry, B. H., & LaBouvie, E. W. (2005). Impulsivity, negative expectancies, and marijuana use: A test of the acquired preparedness model. *Addictive Behaviors, 30*, 1071–1076.

Wahl, S. K., Turner, L. R., Mermelstein, R. J., & Flay, B. R. (2005). Adolescents' smoking expectancies: Psychometric properties and prediction of behavior change. *Nicotine and Tobacco Research, 7*, 613–623.

Wall, A. M., Hinson, R. E., & McKee, S. A. (1998). Alcohol outcome expectancies, attitudes toward drinking and the theory of planned behavior. *Journal of Studies on Alcohol, 59*, 409–419.

Wetter, D. W., Smith, S. S., Kenford, S. L., Jorenby, D. E., Fiore, M. C., Hurt, R. D., et al. (1994). Smoking outcome expectancies: Factor structure, predictive validity, and discriminant validity. *Journal of Abnormal Psychology, 103*, 801–811.

Wiers, R. W., van de Luitgaarden, J., van den Wildenberg, E., & Smulders, F. T. Y. (2005). Challenging implicit and explicit alcohol-related cognitions in young heavy drinkers. *Addiction, 100,* 806–819.

Wood, M. D., Read, J. P., Palfai, T. P., & Stevenson, J. F. (2001). Social influence processes and college student drinking: The mediational role of alcohol outcome expectancies. *Journal of Studies on Alcohol, 62,* 32–43.

Young, R. M., & Knight, R. G. (1989). The Drinking Expectancy Questionnaire: A revised measure of alcohol related beliefs. *Journal of Psychopathology and Behavioral Assessment, 11,* 99–112.

Zamboanga, B. L. (2006). From the eyes of the beholder: Alcohol expectancies and valuations as predictors of hazardous drinking behaviors among female college students. *American Journal of Drug and Alcohol Abuse, 32,* 599–605.

CHAPTER 9

ASSOCIATIVE MEMORY IN APPETITIVE BEHAVIOR: FRAMEWORK AND RELEVANCE TO EPIDEMIOLOGY AND PREVENTION

Alan W. Stacy, Susan L. Ames, Reinout W. Wiers, and Marvin D. Krank

Theories and measures of associative memory and allied approaches in implicit cognition and automatic processes have increasingly been applied to appetitive and health behaviors during the past 10 years (Wiers & Stacy, 2006b). These theories and assessment strategies have major implications for understanding and preventing drug use and other harmful appetitive habits—an inherently paradoxical set of behaviors. Many people use alcohol, tobacco, or other drugs; eat unhealthy foods; fail to engage in physical activity; or engage in risky sex even though the negative consequences of these actions (or inactions) are well known and pervasive.

The framework in this chapter focuses on several unifying principles, established across multiple basic research disciplines, that can explain the enigma of obviously risky or unhealthful behavior. This approach is dramatically different from traditional theories of health behavior and requires an entirely different domain of concepts, hypotheses, measures, and assumptions compared with widely accepted models applied in prevention science and epidemiologic work on drug abuse and other health behaviors. Yet, the approach is buttressed by extensive basic research from multiple independent lines of evidence across diverse levels of analysis (neural to behavioral) and multiple disciplines. In contrast, most traditional

cognitive or affective approaches to health behavior have relied almost entirely on self-reflective constructs, psychometric analysis of single methods of inquiry, and little or no allied support from truly independent lines of evidence in humans or animals.

This chapter provides an overview of some of the central characteristics of the associative memory framework in health behavior. It gives a selective view of a general set of approaches that a growing number of investigators now share, provides some examples specific to our approach to this framework, and compares the framework with variables that are traditionally studied in health behavior. The chapter is not meant as a review of the now sizable number of studies supporting this set of approaches; reviews of related literatures are already available (see chapters in Wiers & Stacy, 2006a). Rather, the chapter is meant to provide a general overview of an important emerging literature and supply the means to contrast and compare more traditional approaches, better known in behavioral epidemiology and prevention science. Most approaches to this framework focus on at least several, and sometimes all, of the following characteristics and issues:

- nonoptimal decision processes;
- spontaneous memory and affective processes that arise without deliberate effort or forewarning,

This research was supported by a research grant (DA023368) and international supplement (to DA16094) from the National Institute on Drug Abuse. The content is solely the responsibility of the authors and does not necessarily represent the official views of the National Institute on Drug Abuse or the National Institutes of Health.

This chapter is dedicated to the memories of Anne Marie Wall and Lorand Szalay. Anne-Marie was a wonderful friend to all of us and a pioneer in research applying context to cognition and addiction. Lorand Szalay was a pioneer in the effort to apply concepts and methods of association to culture, health behavior, and prevention. These stellar scholars and friends are sorely missed.

usually result from repeated experiences, and are difficult to modify or regulate through controlled processes;

- connections or associations among neural elements, which can be modeled across either elementary or more general units of memory (e.g., nodes);

- dynamic, fluid cognitive, affective, and underlying neural processes that result in activated states or patterns that fluctuate markedly, but quite systematically, under different conditions and settings;

- behavior influenced by a quite limited, "biased" subset of all possible elements or patterns reflecting previous learning and memory;

- cue and context sensitivity of memories, behaviors, motivations, plans, and performance of new learning;

- temporal chaining and transition of activated states or patterns; and

- effects of multiple brain systems and their interactions.

Although these items are the primary foci of this chapter, this type of approach can feature additional qualities beyond the scope of this chapter (e.g., Schneider & Chein, 2003). Some of the predominant areas providing research supporting this class of framework include associative and semantic memory, implicit cognition, implicit memory, automatic processing, connectionism or neural networks, and cognitive neuroscience. Typical assessments focus on ways to measure associations or connections in memory among elements, whether defined as cues, contexts, behaviors, outcomes, concepts, plans, alternatives, nodes, or more primitive elements (e.g., neural populations). Measurement strategies focus on assessing connections indirectly, without directly asking about them. The most compelling measures have received support from multiple lines of independent evidence that demonstrate that the assessed connections are not a product of mere self-reflection, questionnaire processes, or single-method psychometric analysis. The framework shares allegiances with a variety of related work, for example, (a) work on social cognition emphasizing implicit or automatic processes (e.g., Bargh & Ferguson, 2000) and connections modeled in various ways (e.g., Smith &

DeCoster, 1998); (b) basic memory research revealing the power of association parameters (e.g., Steyvers & Tenenbaum, 2005); (c) recent work underscoring the setting or cue-specific associative nature of habit (Wood & Neal, 2007); (d) expectancy approaches that focus on predictive relationships in memory, context, associations, or automatic processes (Krank & Wall, 2006; cf. Goldman, 2002); (e) multiple-system approaches to decision theory (e.g., Kahneman, 2003), automatic and controlled processes (Schneider & Chen, 2003), and affective decision making (Bechara, Noel, & Crone, 2006), as well as allied work in cognitive neuroscience documenting multiple brain systems involved in implicit processes (e.g., Yeates & Enrile, 2005); and (f) neurobiological approaches that address cue salience, neural systems of reward, attention, and memory (e.g., Robinson & Berridge, 2003; White, 1996).

EMPHASIS AND CHARACTERISTICS OF FRAMEWORK

Nonoptimal or Irrational Decision

If an individual's actions put him or her (and others) at considerable risk of addiction and a host of social and health problems, despite ample availability of knowledge of risks, is it likely that the risky action is governed by an entirely rational process? Many approaches to health behavior (e.g., social learning, reasoned action, health beliefs, classical decision theory) assume that behavior involves a rational, or at least deliberate, decision process. In these approaches, decisions may be nonoptimal, but this is because of incorrect beliefs, insufficient knowledge, or failure to appropriately value or weigh consequences within an essentially rational model. Such theories have been studied for many years and have been improved by refinements over time. Although such theories sometimes do help explain risk behavior, this chapter advocates increased focus on more automatic, less reasoned, understudied processes that may lead to more parsimonious explanations and create substantial advances in the understanding of health behavior and intervention effects. In this approach, people engage in risky behavior in large part because of a process that operates independently from long-term optimization, awareness, deliberation, or explicit decision making. Several lines of evidence outlined below suggest that this class of process should receive major attention in research on drug use as well as on other addictions and health behaviors.

Spontaneous Processes, Understudied in Many Health Behaviors

Basic research on decision, cognition, and affect.   One of the most influential approaches addressing spontaneous processes was advanced by Daniel Kahneman (2003), winner of a Nobel Prize for his well-documented decision theory. In his framework, the automatic system is the "default" system for human decisions governing risky judgments. The system is autonomous, associative, and parallel and often involves emotion. Kahneman borrowed significantly from earlier research demonstrating fundamental phenomena in cognition, memory, affect, and judgment. Other approaches from basic research on memory, affect, and social cognition provide allied evidence for the power of spontaneous processes, whether classified as automatic, implicit, or unconscious (see Stacy & Wiers, 2006). Kahneman's (2003) framework also supports effects of a reasoning system, which is less spontaneous, more reflective, serial, and rule governed. Despite the widespread support from basic research examining spontaneous cognitive processes (or mixed models that incorporate these approaches into dual-process theories), research on this topic has rarely been applied to adolescent behavior, prevention, and epidemiologic inquiry.

Addiction Research on Spontaneous Processes

Theorizing about automatic processes in addiction has been available for some time (e.g., Tiffany, 1990), but systematic research only recently gained substantial momentum with the growing application of assessment strategies derived from basic research on affect, memory, and decision (Wiers & Stacy, 2006b). There are now a number of well-researched assessment strategies of implicit or automatic processes in addiction, showing predictive utility in a range of populations and for several different drugs of abuse (for reviews, see chapters in Wiers & Stacy, 2006a). These assessments include well-researched measures

such as implicit memory, the implicit association test, semantic priming, affective priming, and other paradigms. Many of these measures assess the strength of associations among behaviors, affective outcomes, and/or cues. Prospective studies have confirmed important predictive effects of spontaneous cognitions and associative memory on certain addictive behaviors, notably alcohol and marijuana use (Kelly, Masterman, & Marlatt, 2005; Krank, Wall, Stewart, Wiers, & Goldman, 2005; Stacy, 1997; Thush & Wiers, 2007). Several different theoretical approaches relevant to addictive behavior at different levels of analysis (neural to cognitive–affective to behavioral) converge on the importance of implicit or automatic processes (for overviews, see Stacy & Wiers, 2006; Wiers & Stacy, 2006b). These approaches are just as relevant to "hot" (emotionally linked) or "cold" (non-emotional) cognition and can be used to study a wide range of applicable topics such as etiologic models and mediation of program effects.

Connection and associations.   Another organizing principle in this framework involves associations (or connections). Although it is not uncommon in some circles to hear that the concept of association essentially died out with the "cognitive revolution," the cognitive revolution's attack focused only on a subset of the extreme views from early 20th-century learning theory (Hintzman, 1993; cf. Wood & Neal, 2007). Despite little attention paid in prevention science and further neglect in epidemiologic approaches to health behavior, the concept of association is alive and well in contemporary research in cognitive science, learning, and neuroscience. The concept of association pervades much basic research from neural to behavioral levels and explains many diverse findings in humans and animals. Associations in memory predict spontaneously activated memories in many different major paradigms in cognitive science (e.g., for a review, see Stacy, Ames, & Grenard, 2006) and are among the best predictors of the several health behaviors studied with associative memory paradigms to date. Associative memory theories extend to all relationships in memory and their activation, not just a small subset of relationships involving reward or anticipated outcomes (Stacy & Wiers, 2006). Thus, associations in memory are also relevant to anything learned in prevention, regardless of whether the new learning involves skills, knowledge, facts, alternatives, norms, beliefs, expectancies, attitudes, images, motivations, or other concepts.

There are many ways in which associations in memory influence behavior. As just one example, people with stronger associations in memory between a behavior and potential triggers or cues experience more frequent, and stronger, activation of the behavior in memory. In accord with research on automatic processes in social cognition, stronger activation in memory channels cognitive and affective processes and biases behavioral decisions toward the associated behavior (e.g., Bargh & Ferguson, 2000; Todorov & Bargh, 2002). Although this bias is predictive of behavior (and may act as the default in accord with Kahneman, 2003), it does not imply an inevitable effect on behavior—other processes may intervene before the behavior ensues (see Dual-Process Approaches Relevant to Health section). Cognitive channeling or bias may occur in response to a wide variety of activated memories, including activated concepts, images, behaviors, outcomes, and so on. Examples relevant to prevention have previously been outlined (Stacy, Ames, & Knowlton, 2004).

Activated, influential associations need not be restricted to classical definitions of expectancy (Bolles, 1972). Sometimes, they may also be at odds with conscious, expressed beliefs, knowledge, or cognitions about outcomes (e.g., Yin & Knowlton, 2006). Associations supported by habit systems (e.g., Wood & Neal, 2007; Yin & Knowlton, 2006) appear to operate independently from certain implicit conceptual associations that nonetheless bias processing and from deliberately retrieved episodic memories. Different types of associative memories can act in concert, or in opposition, depending on the prevailing cues, processing requirements, neural deficits (e.g., from brain injury, amnesia, Parkinson's disease, or Alzheimer's disease), and other modulators outlined later in this chapter. Despite good evidence for different neural systems supporting behavior-relevant memories (e.g., Yin & Knowlton, 2006), the several implicit or automatic systems implicated in spontaneous associative memories share most of the characteristics outlined earlier as well as the fundamental

quality of plasticity, that is, neurally supported learning that occurs from experience (e.g., Angrilli, Zorzi, Tagliabue, Stegagno, & Umiltà, 2001). Differences in associations arise from divergent experiences (Stacy, Leigh, & Weingardt, 1994) and from some individual differences (e.g., neural modulation) in the encoding of these experiences.

Associations or connections in memory can be described in terms of diverse architectures and computational models, while still retaining the basic ideas inherent in associative memory. We previously outlined both parallel and distinct propositions across spreading activation, neural network, and multiple-trace theories pertaining to addiction (Stacy & Wiers, 2006). These theories and many others that provide architectures for connections (e.g., Schneider & Chein, 2003; Smith & DeCoster, 1998) can represent associations in memory, semantic relationships, and, in many cases, higher order concepts such as schemas or prototypes. In some instances, the resulting models of association can also help unify some of the discrete findings in neuroscience, whether focusing on neural plasticity and new learning (e.g., Angrilli et al., 2001), activation of previously learned connections (e.g., Phillips, Stuber, Heien, Wightman, & Carelli, 2003), or activation of certain areas of the brain in response to appetitive cues (e.g., for food [Gottfried, O'Doherty, & Dolan, 2003], drugs [Boileau et al., 2007; Volkow et al., 2006], or sex [Balfour, Yu, & Coolen, 2004]). Models that represent connections in memory provide a very different way to explain an array of findings in health behavior with unifying principles instead of recourse to a long laundry list of variables that may not be theoretically integrated.

Cue and Context Effects

As we introduced in the preceding section on associations, cue and context effects are quite influential in a variety of research areas that study associative processes relevant to health behavior (Krank & Wall, 2006). Cue and context effects are ubiquitous in basic behavioral and cognitive research and have received increasing attention in neuroscience. Context and cues are the setting for current thoughts and actions and profoundly influence memory retrieval and should thereby affect cognitive transitions and behavioral chaining. Such contextual retrieval effects are embedded in a number of theories of memory (e.g., Hintzman, 1986; Nelson, Goodmon, & Ceo, 2007). Context effects on memory are often spontaneous, automatic, and implicit (Nelson et al., 2007). From this perspective, the question is not whether but which contexts and cues are relevant to retrieval processes for implicit associations.

Context effects occur across a broad domain in basic memory research. The types of context shown to influence memory retrieval include environmental (Smith & Vela, 2001), social (Von Hecker, 2004), mood (Bower & Forgas, 2001), drug state (Weingartner, Putnam, George, & Ragan, 1995), and cognitive processing (Roediger, 2000) conditions. Each of these conditions has implications for health behaviors. Health behaviors often occur in unique physical settings and social occasions, emotional or mood states, or unique drug states or with a specific cognitive set or expectations. With respect to substance use, these various domains of context both influence substance use behavior and modify substance use associations, including explicit outcome expectancies, implicit ambiguous word associates for substance use, and implicit outcome behavior associates (e.g., Krank & Wall, 2006).

Cuing and context effects are often studied in animal research examining the incentive effects of various environmental cues associated with positive reinforcement. Animal studies have the advantage of controlling learning histories and can thus ascribe differences in performance to changes in experience rather than to uncontrolled individual differences from other sources. Recent studies have looked at the effects of associations between environmental cues and positively reinforcing drug effects and have demonstrated that drug-associated cues can reinstate drug-taking and drug-seeking responses during extinction and increase the rate of drug taking and drug seeking during self-administration (e.g., Krank, O'Neill, Squarey, & Jacob, 2008).

Evidence from animal models has also suggested that drug-associated cues can activate incentive salience in a manner that controls both attention and action. Localized drug-associated cues can induce sign-tracking responses, which are signal-directed orientation and locomotion toward a visual spatial cue associated with positive reinforcement, in this instance drug effects. Normally, this signal-directed response enhances reinforced behavior by increasing proximity to the location of the reinforcer; directional responses to cues signaling the availability of drugs are likely to lead to situations in which the drugs are more available and self-administration is more likely. This role is similar to that postulated for attentional bias (Field & Eastwood, 2005), suggesting that signal-directed incentive effects may provide an animal model for attentional bias. The independent and reflexive power of these attentional effects can be shown under conditions in which goal- and signal-directed incentive effects are pitted against each other. When the signal is placed away from the goal location, signal-directed incentive effects can be strong enough to produce paradoxical and seemingly irrational reductions in goal-directed behaviors by drawing behavior away from the source of reinforcement (Krank et al., 2008). Such counterproductive responses make sense when viewed as implicitly activated incentive reactions.

Human cue reactivity studies have tested the impact of naturalistic cues and often assume the differential learning histories by comparing heavy and light users. These studies have also been consistent with implicit incentive salience effects. Neuroimaging studies have suggested that drug cues activate preparatory neural and cognitive responses. Several important neural systems are activated by cues associated with substance use (e.g., Tapert et al., 2003). Cue-dependent brain activation occurs in a variety of areas. For example, imaging studies involving drug-related cue exposure have shown the hippocampus and dorsolateral frontal cortex to be involved in explicit memories, the amygdala to be associated with emotional stimuli, the anterior cingulate cortex to be associated with attentional functions, and the ventral striatum to be associated with cue-elicited craving (for review, see Franken, Zijlstra, Booij, & van den Brink, 2006). Activation in the mesocorticolimbic areas involved in incentive motivation is more pronounced in more frequent and problematic users and is associated with craving. These observations suggest that the cue- or context-elicited activation of neural systems in experienced users may be preparatory to automatic responding and thus contribute to relapse in high-risk situations.

The powerful neurological and behavioral effects of context and cues on choice should be considered in interventions designed to either increase positive health behaviors or decrease negative ones. The retrieval functions of context limit the availability of options for our thoughts and actions. Context determines which of many health behaviors are considered. From this perspective, intervention programs ought to (a) focus on creating stronger associations with healthy behavioral alternatives and (b) pay attention to the cognitive relevance of the interventions to the situations (cues and contexts) in which important choices between healthy and unhealthy activities are made (Krank & Goldstein, 2006). Such efforts would take advantage of the widespread research in diverse areas of basic research on humans and animals supporting the importance of cue and context effects.

Transitions in Activated States

Another related organizing principle is cognitive "transition." In associative and connectionist theories of memory and cognition (e.g., Queller & Smith, 2002), one cognitive or affective state (e.g., promoting either a risky or a preventive behavior) does not come out of a vacuum but depends on the preceding pattern of activation in memory and on the perception of associated cues. Such models can explain behavior chains and apparent functional relations between behaviors (e.g., from one drug to another), as well as the dynamic, fluid nature of cognitive processes, rarely studied in health behavior. For example, certain drugs of abuse (e.g., a gateway drug and a more illicit drug) may become highly associated in memory even among individuals who have not yet used one of the drugs. This can occur through repetitive experiences in settings in which multiple drugs are available or just discussed among peers. Once such an association is established, a cue associated with one drug can activate memories for other drugs. In the absence of countervailing influences, cognitive channeling resulting from increased activation in memory predisposes an individual to using a drug even though it has not been tried before. Associative memory theories and methods provide ways to study these dynamic processes linking one drug to another in memory, unlikely to be uncovered using typical health behavior questionnaires assuming traitlike or nonrelational cognitions. Understanding cognitive linkages and transitions may prove fundamental to understanding why one risky behavior is often linked to another; the absence of such linkages may help explain why some individuals do not transition to more devastating forms of drug abuse.

Detailed evaluation of models of these processes in adolescents could help address a number of more traditional research questions important for progress in understanding the development of risky behavior and its prevention. Some unanswered problems these models can readily address include mediation and perpetuation or escalation of unhealthy habits, drug progression (or cross-drug influences), and individual differences in protection regarding escalation or risky transitions.

Effects of Multiple Brain Systems in Automatic Associative Memories

Spontaneous processes and biological substrates in appetitive behavior. Research in neuroscience has suggested that behaviors that share certain biological substrates may be particularly susceptible to linkages that precede and predict drug use progression as well as some other risk behaviors, such as risky sex. Virtually all drugs of abuse involve common neural systems (i.e., dopaminergic pathways), even though some underlying processes differ at the synaptic and molecular levels (e.g., Baler & Volkow, 2006; Koob, 2002). Some drugs such as cocaine and methamphetamine directly increase dopamine brain levels by facilitating dopamine release and inhibiting its reuptake, whereas alcohol and marijuana indirectly activate dopamine systems by stimulating neurons that modulate the release of dopamine through effects on other receptors (e.g., GABA receptors for alcohol and cannabinoid receptors for marijuana; Baler & Volkow, 2006; Koob, 2002). Amphetamines and cocaine vary in their effects on other neural systems (e.g., Koob, 2002). However, it is the mesocorticolimbic dopamine pathways that are consistently implicated as being important in producing the rewarding effects of amphetamines, cocaine, marijuana, alcohol, and other drugs (Koob, 2002).

Naturally rewarding behaviors, such as sexual activity and eating palatable foods (e.g., chocolate), similarly activate dopamine circuitry implicated in motivation and reward (e.g., Esch & Stefano, 2004; Volkow & Wise, 2005). The reinforcing value of food has been shown with the use of positron emission tomography to be associated with increased dopamine in the dorsal striatum in humans (Small, Jones-Gotman, & Daghar, 2003), whereas in animals consumption of palatable foods has been shown to be associated with dopamine release in the nucleus accumbens (e.g., Hernandez & Hoebel, 1988) and the prefrontal cortex (Hernandez & Hoebel, 1990). Likewise, sexual activity has been shown to facilitate dopamine activity in the nucleus accumbens, inducing positive affective experiences (e.g., Melis & Argiolas, 1995). Although common mesolimbic dopamine pathways are implicated, dopamine projections to the forebrain and other neural circuitry (e.g., endogenous opioid and endocannibinoid systems), as well as certain hormones (e.g., leptin, implicated in feeding behavior), are likely to modulate the rewarding effects of appetitive behaviors (Volkow & Wise, 2005). Nevertheless, rewarding appetitive behaviors (including ingesting drugs of abuse, sexual activity, feeding behavior, and drinking) are mediated by similar mesolimbic neural systems (e.g., Melis & Argiolas, 1995), regardless of some differences across behaviors.

Dopaminergic activity in the nucleus accumbens and some anatomically connected structures reinforces the repetition of behaviors and supports the encoding and processing of proximal stimuli associated with the rewarding experience (e.g., Everitt & Robbins, 2005). Neutral stimuli associated with the appetitive behavior come to represent and cue the behavior. In addition, cues associated with reward are able to elicit "wanting" of the reward (Robinson & Berridge, 2003). As cue–behavior–outcome associations are strengthened, patterns of associations signal and drive behavior without the necessary involvement of reflective processes (e.g., White, 1996). Cues can then trigger spontaneous or implicit patterns of activation in memory that can be described in various neural network or connectionist models (e.g., Queller & Smith, 2002). In these models, the results of neural connections do not simply reflect traditional conditioning phenomena but also reflect other automatic aspects of learning and memory that involve multiple

sources not necessarily requiring the presence or pairing of an unconditioned stimulus. For example, concept-to-concept linkages in memory can be fundamental for cognitive biases and transitions, as argued earlier. Linkages have also been shown between drug-induced neural sensitization and the facilitation of use of a different drug (e.g., the use of some gateway drugs facilitates the use of cocaine in animals; for a review, see Schenk, 2002). Overall, research on the biology of drug use and other appetitive behaviors has shown that these actions are highly sensitive to predictive cues and previous learning episodes, which become encoded into patterns of association. In humans, many types of associations can be assessed with tests of implicit processes (for many examples, see Wiers & Stacy, 2006a).

Pattern matching, implicit conceptual associations, and habit associations. In one of the major neurobiological models of drug use and reward processing, Schultz (1998) provided evidence suggesting that cortical association areas are implicated in the initial processing of predictive cues and in triggering broadcasts of matched patterns to other neural regions implicated in habit, motivation, and drug use (e.g., striatum and midbrain). Cortical association areas are also strongly implicated in conceptual priming or implicit conceptual memory (e.g., Gabrieli, 1998), which is involved in at least some types of pattern matching and the processing of many types of associations. As a general class, implicit conceptual memory has been dissociated from other forms of memory and cognition in a variety of neuropsychological studies, consistent with multiple systems views of memory (e.g., Levy, Stark, & Squire, 2004).

Although many types of implicit conceptual associations appear to be supported by cortical association areas, certain types of associations involving behavior may depend on the basal ganglia (Yin & Knowlton, 2006). These include (a) associations between situational cues and responses (analogous to stimulus–response relationships associated with the dorsolateral striatum) and (b) associations between outcomes and actions (analogous to action–outcome relations associated with the dorsomedial striatum). Associations between cues and affective outcomes (analogous to stimulus–outcome, or S-S*, relations associated with the basolateral amygdala and other regions; Yin & Knowlton, 2006) are also important to consider. Beyond the scope of this chapter, these associations and regions are involved in more complex circuits that can be differentiated (dissociated) with neuroscientific methods.

Tests of implicit conceptual memory involving associations among appetitive behaviors (drug use, sex), cues, and outcomes have been found to predict risky behavior in diverse populations (for a review of drug research, see Ames, Franken, & Coronges, 2006; for risky sexual behavior, see Stacy, Ames, Ullman, Zogg, & Leigh, 2006). Using methods established in basic memory research (Stacy, Ames, & Grenard, 2006), these indirect tests assess whether content promoting risky behavior is spontaneously generated in response to potential social, physical, situational, or affective triggers of the behavior. The target behavior is not mentioned in the assessment, minimizing the effects of self-reflective inferences, explicit recollection, and a host of self-reflective confounders. Any alternative (e.g., healthy) memories have a full chance of competing with a risky response in the assessment. Thus, this is one of the few approaches capable of assessing truly relative memory and cognition, which are rarely addressed in health behavior research but are well acknowledged in basic research and other applications such as advertising research (e.g., Stewart, 1989).

DUAL-PROCESS APPROACHES RELEVANT TO HEALTH

Dual-process theories have gained substantial momentum in basic research, probably because of consistent findings that span diverse disciplines and research areas. Fundamental distinctions in processes or systems have been well documented in decision theory (Kahneman, 2003), memory and cognitive science (Schneider & Chein, 2003), basic social cognition (e.g., Bargh & Ferguson, 2000), and neuroscience (e.g., Bechara et al., 2006). However, incorporation of distinctions from basic research on learning and memory has been rare in epidemiologic studies and research on adolescent drug use and virtually absent from some areas of adolescent appetitive behavior (e.g., stimulant use, diet) and most areas of

prevention science. Below, we highlight several of the many different ways in which dual-process models are relevant to health behavior.

Additive Models

A simple (additive) dual-process model derived from basic research posits that spontaneous processes (e.g., implicit associations) and more reflective (executive, explicit, controlled, or self-reported) processes show some independent predictive effects. Predictive main effects of spontaneous processes are supported in the previous sections, and predictive effects of many different reflective processes are supported by a variety of studies and reviews (e.g., Fals-Stewart & Bates, 2003; Hawkins, Catalano, & Miller, 1992; Petraitis, Flay, & Miller, 1995; Scheier, Botvin, Diaz, & Griffin, 1999). Reflective processes of major focus in our version of the associative memory framework are specific executive functions that receive support from neural to behavioral levels of analysis; these processes serve as potential effect modifiers in a synergistic model shown below. Although useful evaluations of additive dual-process models provide new comparisons of important constructs not normally studied and also demonstrate precisely which constructs and measures have greater predictive utility (e.g., Palfai & Wood, 2001; Stacy, 1997), more complex models show how dual processes are integrated in ways seldom acknowledged in health behavior or prevention research.

Synergistic Model and Neurologically Plausible Differences in Specific Executive Functioning

A synergistic (interaction) model is suggested by recent neuroscience approaches to dual-process models, which often focus on the functioning of different neural systems. Some neural systems support reflective (or very specific executive) processing relevant to protection from poor choices and decision (e.g., Bechara et al., 2006). Extensive research has delineated the likely neural basis of each of these functions, psychometric approaches have confirmed good measurement, and other multiple lines of evidence (from behavioral to neural) have shown that these functions are not figments of a single method of inquiry.

Protection resulting from reflective processing can moderate the effects of spontaneous associations. Although associations fostering risky behavior are often spontaneously activated in response to various cues, these activated associations are not always translated into behavior. Protective functions are expected to modify the behavioral manifestations of activated spontaneous associations.

Figure 9.1 depicts a general dual-process framework suggesting how some neural functions dampen or block the effects of spontaneously activated associations on drug use. The neural functions essentially provide a better capability to effectively think through (regulate or inhibit) a behavior before acting, even when associations in memory are activated that foster a risky behavior. To evaluate this process, it is beneficial to apply some of the best-researched specific functions supported by multiple divergent lines of evidence. These functions (a) have a strong neural basis and are associated with distinct neural systems supported by basic research, (b) demonstrate predictive validity, (c) are assessed through tests of functioning rather than self-reported reflections of behavior, and (d) are more specific than the very general executive functions (Royall et al., 2002) and are therefore more likely candidates for amelioration and compensatory strategies that require a specific focus. Specific functions addressed as examples include working memory (e.g., Kane & Engle, 2000), ability to inhibit responses (Logan, Schachar, & Tannock, 1997; Riggs, Greenberg, Kusché, & Pentz, 2006), and affective decision-making capability involving risky choice (Bechara et al., 2006). Independent lines of evidence have supported the validity of specific tests assessing these functions

(e.g., Brand, Labudda, & Markowitsch, 2006), and assessments of these variables and/or associative memory have been effective in laptop studies in controlled group settings in the field with youth diverse in risk, age, ethnicity, and national residence (e.g., Ames et al., 2007; Grenard et al., 2008; Johnson et al., 2008; Thush et al., 2008; Xiao et al., 2008).

The specific form of the dual-process interaction is shown in Figure 9.2. Several specific functions may make automatically activated associations less powerful in their effects on behavior—essentially putting brakes on spontaneous associations, reducing their "free reign" on behavior or their status as the default (cf. Kahneman, 2003). First, good working memory ability helps individuals keep competing considerations "online" (e.g., Kane & Engle, 2000), even when faced with other demands on cognitive resources (e.g., carrying on a conversation, considering peer's opinions). Without good working memory, multiple considerations are not as likely to be kept active or in mind for any decisions, explicit memory retrieval is less effective (e.g., Kane & Engle, 2000), and therefore a smaller subset of learned effects (only the most spontaneously activated ones) is available to influence behavior. Second, good inhibitory functioning reflects the ability to actively stop a behavior or thought after it has been triggered (e.g., Logan et al., 1997). Inhibitory functions are another important, specific aspect of higher order executive functioning (Winstanley, Eagle, & Robbins, 2006). Finally, high functioning of affective decision making involving risky choice allows the individual to more optimally weigh short-term gains against long-term

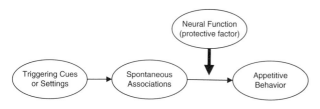

FIGURE 9.1. Conceptual model of buffering effects of neural functions. (Strong associations in memory are spontaneously activated by triggering cues or contexts, but specific neural functions may dampen or block the influence of these associations on carrying out a risky behavior.)

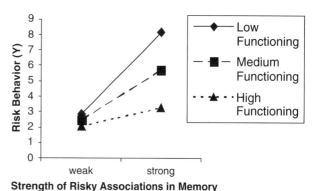

FIGURE 9.2. Dual processes: Neural functioning moderates effects of spontaneous associative memories.

losses (Bechara et al., 2006). Spontaneous pro-drug associations for a risky behavior known to have a short-term benefit (getting high) but long-term negative consequences for health should have less impact in those scoring high in this function. Thus, working memory, inhibitory function, and decision functions may show the buffer (protective) interaction pattern in Figure 9.2. Moreover, a main effect for spontaneous processes is expected, consistent with the additive models already introduced and the consistent support in drug use behaviors; some main effects of neural functions may also occur (e.g., Johnson et al., 2008; Xiao et al., 2008). The dual-process synergistic effects and main effects could be especially important for explaining why some youth intensify risky appetitive habits and others are relatively protected. Some adolescents may keep multiple considerations in mind rather than just the most salient ones (better working memory), adequately weigh the affective considerations (better affective decision making), or be able to stop a triggered thought or action (inhibitory ability). For each functional moderator, the free reign of spontaneously activated harmful associations promoting risky behavior is likely to be dampened as neural functioning increases. Harmful behavior may then become far less likely. It should also be substantially reduced if spontaneous pro-drug associations are weak, requiring less of a need for countervailing influences or protection.

This general form of a dual-process interaction (e.g., Figure 9.2) has already been supported in several diverse areas (social behavior [Payne, 2005], dietary behavior [Hofmann, Rauch, & Gawronski, 2007], problem solving [De Neys, 2006]) and in several studies on two addictive behaviors (alcohol [Finn & Hall, 2004; Thush et al., 2008] and alcohol and tobacco [Grenard et al., 2008]). Thus, dual-process findings across research topics reveal an important degree of generality for this interaction that needs to be evaluated with other behaviors. The only moderator of associative memory effects studied to date in drug use research is working memory (Grenard et al., 2008; Thush et al., 2008), and other moderators of these effects in the current framework (e.g., inhibitory and affective decision functions) remain to be investigated.

If dual-process interaction effects continue to receive support in research on risky appetitive behaviors, then addressing the underlying dual processes could be quite useful to interventions in primary and secondary prevention. A focus on specific functions found to be distinct across neural and psychometric levels of analysis provides much more guidance than findings about very general functioning (e.g., in broad executive abilities). Furthermore, a focus on spontaneous processes (and effects that can be modulated by specific functions) emphasizes the dynamic, cue-dependent nature of memory and cognition, not previously addressed in drug prevention interventions (Stacy et al., 2004). Overall, a focus on spontaneous associations, specific neural functions, and their interaction in dual-process models has much potential for increasing our understanding of risky behaviors in youth and adults.

RELEVANCE TO MORE TRADITIONAL CONCEPTS AND APPROACHES

Self-Reflective Approaches to Attitudes, Beliefs, Expectancies, Proscriptive Norms, and Intentions

For several decades, much of the epidemiologic inquiry into the origins of adolescent drug abuse and other risky behaviors has addressed variables such as attitudes, beliefs, knowledge, norms, and similar constructs. Most assessments of these variables have obtained self-reflections, for example, asking directly about one's attitude or intentions toward a behavior. There are strong and weaker forms of hypotheses from this approach relevant to many of these traditional predictors. The strong form suggests that the self-reflective measures and derived constructs used in most traditional approaches can be explained by a straightforward application of Occam's razor. People may not have an attitude, a belief, an expectancy, a norm, or a self-reported trait (as traditionally defined), but they can readily answer questions about these variables if the assessment directly mentions the behavior or something very similar to it. The variable essentially prompts memory for previous behavior, and the respondent answers in accord with that memory—a simpler explanation than postulates of additional variables. The variable may include other content such as a word implying positive evaluations, negative outcomes, or other meanings, but the central focus of the variable is on a particular behavior. Although this and similar explanations of correlations between self-reflective variables and behavior have been available for some time (e.g., Bem, 1967; Feldman & Lynch, 1988; Schwarz, 1999), it is surprising how seldom simple alternative explanations of correlations in health behavior are addressed. Application of rudimentary psychometrics to traditional measures does little to assuage this concern because such tests are rarely accompanied by even minimal tests of discriminant validity with behavior. The strong form of this alternative hypothesis suggests that direct questions cuing the behavior one is trying to predict will foster self-reflections of that behavior more than they measure anything else; this alternative explanation of predictive effects is rarely, if ever, ruled out. Yet such self-reflections prompting memory for the target behavior are often taken as valid readouts of underlying processes involving content (e.g., beliefs or other cognitions) beyond the behavior.

At least two different forms of hypotheses can be suggested that are weaker in terms of negating self-reflective variables. The first suggests that self-reflective and implicit processes may show independent levels of prediction, consistent with the few studies that have examined both together in appetitive behavior (e.g., Ames et al., 2007; Palfai & Wood, 2001; Stacy, 1997; Thush et al., 2008). A second, weaker form of hypothesis is that self-reflective measures may spawn the operation of an availability heuristic (Tversky & Kahneman, 1973), in which an automatic process activates an association in memory (e.g., between the behavior and the other content of the item), and the stronger the association is, the more its elements will be accessible in memory to bias judgments on a questionnaire item (cf. Kahneman, 2003). An illustration may help make this more concrete. A teenager may have a set of strong associations in memory among positive affect (having fun or feeling good), best friends, and alcohol use, developed on the basis of previous exposures at weekend parties. When prompted with a question about subjective norms and alcohol, or between positive affect and alcohol, adolescents

with stronger associations within this set of associations will respond with stronger norms for drinking or beliefs and attitudes for positive effects from alcohol.

Theories consistent with the associative memory framework inherently consider the context of processing or the "input" to memory systems, as well as connections between the features of that input and the elements of memory (for examples, see Stacy & Wiers, 2006). Entirely different sets of connections can be triggered by different circumstances, and there is no need to postulate unified, context-free attitudes or beliefs. Consider a drug addict responding to questions from a therapist in a clinic. When the therapist asks about the individual's overall attitude toward drugs or whether he or she still likes the drug, this input to memory systems likely prompts a very different set of connections in memory than when the question is asked in a situation in which the drug is normally used. It would not be surprising if the connections that are activated when the individual attends a clinic foster statements about the negative consequences of drugs because these are often what lead to clinical intervention. When one is focused on the bad things, it is natural to indicate an overall disliking of the drug, and at this time, the overall disliking may reflect a quite honest prevailing feeling and tendency. However, when drug cues and facilitative social cues foster memories for appetitive experiences, overall liking may appear to be much different. In this framework, indirect assessments that re-create drug settings, cues, or affective states are more likely to reveal cognitive and affective responses that normally occur in the drug use situation. Quite different computational models of connections in memory, such as multiple-trace or neural network approaches, can easily model this type of dynamic, input-specific but systematic effect that is not captured by traditional theories of attitude, health beliefs, or adolescent health behavior.

Social Influence in Prevention
Many drug prevention programs targeting youth rely on social influence concepts, which may include normative education, social resistance training, or other cognitive–behavioral strategies (e.g., Botvin, Griffin, Diaz, & Ifill-Williams, 2001; Ellickson,

Tucker, Klein, & Saner, 1993; Hansen, Johnson, Flay, Graham, & Sobel, 1988; MacKinnon et al., 1991; Sussman et al., 1993). Despite some misgivings (e.g., Peterson, Kealey, Mann, Marek, & Sarason, 2000), many programs containing social influence components have shown important effects (for reviews, see Sussman, Hansen, Flay, & Botvin, 2001; Tobler et al., 2000).

The associative memory framework suggests an alternative explanation of previous social influence findings. This explanation does not posit a variable that is confounded with experimental condition (a threat to internal validity) but rather focuses on a confounder within the operational definition of the treatment (a threat to the construct validity of cause and effect and the mechanism of change; Cook & Campbell, 1979). Many social influence programs encourage processing of peer situations and implement other strategies, whether focusing on correcting misperceptions as part of normative education, teaching resistance skills, or providing information about the consequences of drug use. To the extent that program content is processed in terms of the characteristics of peer situations, then the associative memory framework assumes that associations in memory may be encoded and strengthened between the features of social situations and program content. To the extent that a program creates interest and enthusiasm, it may even motivate processing outside of the classroom—providing additional opportunities for strengthening associations between program elements (e.g., peer situations and other content). In this perspective, the most effective programs are expected to encourage processing in ways that increase the association between potential cues or risky situations and information or skills learned in the program. In this way, program content may become spontaneously activated when the risky behavior is most likely to occur.

Figure 9.3 illustrates some of the features of situations or types of cues that may trigger memories for program content (for more details, see Stacy et al., 2004). These features are the inputs to memory systems when the program is most relevant (e.g., during risky situations). We assume that something from the program must be spontaneously activated (Processing Phase 1 in Figure 9.3) in response to this input, as the first link to further program-related preventive processing. Otherwise, one must assume an unsupported "tape recorder" model of memory, in which participants consciously "push the button" to deliberately retrieve previously learned program-relevant information whenever it might be needed. Although some deliberate recollection and controlled processing could occur, we think that it is most likely to occur during Phase 2—after something learned from the program is first spontaneously activated. Traditional social influence programs may

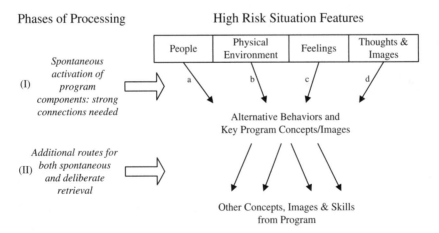

FIGURE 9.3. Likely cues and associations relevant to appetitive behavior, alternative behaviors, and prevention effects. From "Neurologically Plausible Distinctions in Cognition Relevant to Drug Use Etiology and Prevention," by A. W. Stacy, S. L. Ames, and B. J. Knowlton, 2004, *Substance Use & Misuse, 39,* p. 1598. Copyright 2004 by Taylor & Francis. Adapted with permission.

strengthen associations at least between people (peers) and program components (Path a, Figure 9.3). Some programs may also foster associations between additional features of situations and program content, for example, Path b, when certain risky features of the physical environment are encountered; Path c, when hazardous affective states (e.g., negative feelings) are prominent; or Path d, when facilitative thoughts or images cross one's mind. Other potential triggers, likely to occur soon before behavior ensues, are certainly possible and should be considered.

Overall, the associative memory framework argues that the key ingredients and mediators of prevention programs may involve strength of connections between program content and the cues that normally precede or accompany risky or unhealthy behavior. This focus is compatible with several sets of fundamental results mentioned earlier: (a) converging evidence for the importance of connection parameters across a wide range of methods in research on associative memory; (b) studies revealing strong effects of cues on appetitive behaviors and the importance of transitions to automatic processes; and (c) the plausibility of neural plasticity in connections that influence behavior. This focus provides another example of a dramatically different way to conceptualize and understand appetitive behaviors and their intervention through the associative memory framework. Although this view is presently not well represented in prevention science and epidemiologic inquiry, it is quite compatible with contemporary models of learning, memory, and neural bases not usually considered in these areas. It is hard to imagine how prevention effects could occur through educational interventions if not through the retention and access or activation of new information, concepts, behaviors, or skills—that is, through memory processes.

Although to date the study of prevention and associative memory or implicit processes has been extremely rare, research has been initiated. First, research has examined whether current preventive interventions have effects on these processes. For example, Wiers, Van de Luitgaarden, Van den Wildenberg, and Smulders (2005) found that an expectancy challenge preventive intervention was

successful in changing explicit alcohol-related expectancies but had hardly any effect on automatic memory associations. More research needs to be done to see which intervention components do, or do not, affect these associations. Second, new techniques have been developed that try to directly interfere with automatic appetitive processes that normally influence risky behavior (see Schoenmakers, Wiers, Jones, Bruce, & Jansen, 2007; Wiers et al., 2006). Other potential avenues include (a) addressing the motivation to regulate appetitive impulses (e.g., through motivational interventions; Grenard et al., 2007); (b) training the ability to self-regulate (cf. Klingberg et al., 2005); or (c) a variety of strategies that link appetitive cues and contexts to preventive cognitions, alternative behaviors, or other program elements (Krank & Goldstein, 2006; Stacy et al., 2004). We should also mention that a few prevention approaches already address some apparently spontaneous processes with good success (e.g., Gerrard et al., 2006; Gibbons, Gerrard, Lane, Mahler, & Kulik, 2005; see also chap. 18 of this volume).

Cultural and Environmental Differences

In the associative memory framework, both culture and environment place constraints on associative memories. Culture determines a diverse pattern of associations established over an extended period of exposure across the life span. Indeed, the groundbreaking work of Szalay and his colleagues (Diaz-Guerrero & Szalay, 1991; Szalay & Maday, 1983) has clearly shown that culture is an excellent predictor of a variety of different associations in memory. The physical environment delimits the range of physical cues that can possibly be linked to memory. Both culture and the physical environment influence the types of cues that can become salient, or well connected, in memory, as well as the different alternative behaviors that can possibly be linked to triggering cues. Connections between the possible input (set of cues) and possible alternatives in memory also varies (Paths a through d in Figure 9.3), depending on the nature of exposures in a cultural and physical context. Without going into further details, suffice it to say that associative memory approaches offer interesting and potentially fundamental ways to understand cultural and environmental effects on a wide range of behaviors. Diverse, multiple-method support across neural, cognitive, affective, and behavioral levels of analysis for association concepts in humans and animals suggests that an attempt toward a more unified, integrative approach across normally isolated variables in health behavior is plausible and worthy of increased attention.

SUMMARY

Most theorizing on appetitive behaviors based on epidemiological and psychosocial approaches has relied predominantly on frameworks that can be classified under the rubric of "explicit cognition." Explicit cognition concepts focus on traditionally conceptualized and assessed concepts such as attitudes, beliefs, expectancies, self-reported norms or motivations, and other self-reflections of one's opinions, feelings, perceptions, or behaviors. These approaches have dominated theorizing and reviews in adolescent health behavior, in which traditional survey research has been by far the predominant method. Indeed, major reviews of theories of adolescent drug use (e.g., Hawkins et al., 1992; Petraitis et al., 1995) have been almost entirely restricted to research on predictors that likely measure explicit cognition or self-reflection. This may be a product of a limited number of subdisciplines among researchers studying adolescent health behavior, the perceived constraints of survey design, lack of interest in "translation" from basic researchers, historical precedents, or other factors. Although research on explicit cognition and self-reflection has been valuable, this Zeitgeist only tells part of the story. A number of theories and well-validated findings from basic research disciplines have only rarely been applied to adolescent health behavior but offer dramatically different ways to understand and prevent or treat health-compromising behaviors.

This chapter has provided a general overview of a set of approaches applied from basic research. These approaches share certain critical features, particularly involving connection or association parameters, and spontaneous processes. We have argued that this framework, although not completely unitary, is nonetheless of heuristic value in describing approaches that have dramatically different assump-

tions, methods, and lines of evidence than prevailing approaches in epidemiologic research on health behavior, prevention, and public health. Yet these approaches are quite applicable not only to basic research, but also to applied research, as revealed in field studies documented elsewhere (for many examples, see Wiers & Stacy, 2006a). Although theories applicable to this framework differ substantially in their details, they still retain fundamental commonalities of relevance to health behavior theory, prevention, and cessation. The goal was to point out and describe what we see as some of the most distinctive and powerful commonalities of this framework, which is quite applicable to research areas in which it has not been emphasized or considered. We especially look forward to new, more powerful interventions that are likely to be derived in the future from theories consistent with this framework.

References

Ames, S. L., Franken, I. H. A., & Coronges, K. (2006). Implicit cognition and drugs of abuse. In R. W. Wiers & A. W. Stacy (Eds.), *Handbook of implicit cognition and addiction* (pp. 363–378). Thousand Oaks, CA: Sage.

Ames, S. L, Grenard, J. L., Thush, C., Sussman, S., Wiers, R. W., & Stacy, A.W. (2007). Comparison of indirect assessments of association as predictors of marijuana use among at-risk adolescents. *Experimental and Clinical Psychopharmacology, 15,* 204–218.

Angrilli, A., Zorzi, M., Tagliabue, M., Stegagno, L., & Umiltà, C. (2001). Cortical plasticity of spatial stimulus-response associations: Electrophysiological and behavioral evidence. *NeuroReport, 12,* 973–977.

Baler, R. D., & Volkow, N. D. (2006). Drug addiction: The neurobiology of disrupted self-control. *Trends in Molecular Medicine, 12,* 559–566.

Balfour, M. E., Yu, L., & Coolen, L. M. (2004). Sexual behavior and sex-associated environmental cues activate the mesolimbic system in male rats. *Neuropsychopharmacology, 29,* 718–730.

Bargh, J. A., & Ferguson, M. J. (2000). Beyond behaviorism: On the automaticity of higher mental processes. *Psychological Bulletin, 126,* 925–945.

Bechara, A., Noel, X., & Crone, E. A. (2006). Loss of willpower: Abnormal neural mechanisms of impulse control and decision-making in addiction. In R. W. Wiers & A. W. Stacy (Eds.), *Handbook of implicit cognition and addiction* (pp. 215–232). Thousand Oaks, CA: Sage.

Bem, D. J. (1967). Self-perception: An alternative interpretation of cognitive dissonance phenomena. *Psychological Review, 74*, 183–200.

Boileau, I., Dagher, A., Leyton, M., Welfeld, K., Booij, L., Diksic, M., & Benkelfat, C. (2007). Conditioned dopamine release in humans: A positron emission tomography [11C] raclopride study with amphetamine. *Journal of Neuroscience, 27*, 3998–4003.

Bolles, R. (1972). Reinforcement, expectancy, and learning. *Psychological Review, 79*, 394–409.

Botvin, G. J., Griffin, K. W., Diaz, T., & Ifill-Williams, M. (2001). Preventing binge drinking during early adolescence: One- and two- year follow-up of a school-based preventive intervention. *Psychology of Addictive Behaviors, 15*, 360–365.

Bower, G. H., & Forgas, J. P. (2001). Mood and social memory. In J. P. Forgas (Ed.), *Handbook of affect and social cognition* (pp. 95–120). Mahwah, NJ: Erlbaum.

Brand, M., Labudda, K., & Markowitsch, H. J. (2006). Neuropsychological correlates of decision-making in ambiguous and risky situations. *Neural Networks, 19*, 1266–1276.

Cook, T. D., & Campbell, D. T. (1979). *Quasi-experimentation: Design & analysis issues for field settings.* Boston: Houghton Mifflin.

De Neys, W. (2006). Dual processing in reasoning: Two systems but one reasoner. *Psychological Science, 17*, 428–433.

Diaz-Guerrero, R., & Szalay, L. B. (1991). *Understanding Mexicans and Americans: Cultural perspectives in conflict.* New York: Plenum Press.

Ellickson, P. L., Tucker, J. S., Klein, D. J., & Saner, H. (1993). Changing adolescent propensities to use drugs: Results from Project ALERT. *Health Education and Behavior, 20*, 227–242.

Esch, T., & Stefano, G. B. (2004). The neurobiology of pleasure, reward processes, addiction and their health implications. *Neuroendocrinology Letters, 25*, 235–251.

Everitt, B. J., & Robbins, T. W. (2005). Neural systems of reinforcement for drug addiction: From actions to habits to compulsion. *Nature Neuroscience, 8*, 1481–1489.

Fals-Stewart, W., & Bates, M. E. (2003). The neuropsychological test performance of drug-abusing patients: An examination of latent cognitive abilities and associated risk factors. *Experimental and Clinical Psychopharmacology, 11*, 34–45.

Feldman, J. M., & Lynch, J. G. (1988). Self-generated validity and other effects of measurement on belief, attitude, intention, and behavior. *Journal of Applied Psychology, 73*, 421–435.

Field, M., & Eastwood, B. (2005). Experimental manipulation of attentional bias increases the motivation to drink alcohol. *Psychopharmacology, 183*, 350–357.

Finn, P. R., & Hall, J. (2004). Cognitive ability and risk for alcoholism: Short-term memory capacity and intelligence moderate personality risk for alcohol problems. *Journal of Abnormal Psychology, 113*, 569–581.

Franken, I. H. A., Zijlstra, C., Booij, J., & van den Brink, W. (2006). Imaging the addicted brain: Reward, craving and cognitive processes. In R.W. Wiers & A.W. Stacy (Eds.), *Handbook of implicit cognition and addiction* (pp. 185–199). Thousand Oaks, CA: Sage.

Gabrieli, J. D. E. (1998). Cognitive neuroscience of human memory. *Annual Review of Psychology, 49*, 87–115.

Gerrard, M., Gibbons, F. X., Brody, G. H., Murry, V. M., Cleveland, M. J., & Wills, T. A. (2006). A theory-based dual-focus alcohol intervention for preadolescents: The Strong African American Families Program. *Psychology of Addictive Behaviors, 20*, 185–195.

Gibbons, F. X., Gerrard, M., Lane, D. J., Mahler, H. I. M., & Kulik, J. A. (2005). Using UV photography to reduce use of tanning booths: A test of cognitive mediation. *Health Psychology, 24*, 358–363.

Goldman, M. S. (2002). Expectancy and risk for alcoholism: The unfortunate exploitation of a fundamental characteristic of neurobehavioral adaptation. *Alcoholism: Clinical & Experimental Research, 26*, 737–746.

Gottfried, J. A., O'Doherty, J., & Dolan, R. J. (2003, August 22). Value in human amygdala and orbitofrontal cortex. *Science, 301*, 1104–1107.

Grenard, J. L., Ames, S. L., Wiers, R., Thush, C., Stacy, A.W., & Sussman, S. (2007). Brief intervention for substance use among at-risk adolescents: A pilot study. *Journal of Adolescent Health 40*, 188–191.

Grenard, J. L., Ames, S. L., Wiers, R., Thush, C., Sussman, S., & Stacy, A.W. (2008). Working memory capacity moderates the predictive effects of drug-related associations on substance use. *Psychology of Addictive Behaviors, 22*, 426–432.

Hansen, W. B., Johnson, C. A., Flay, B. R., Graham, J. W., & Sobel, J. L. (1988). Affective and social influences approaches to the prevention of multiple substance abuse among seventh grade students: Results from Project SMART. *Preventive Medicine, 17*, 135–154.

Hawkins, J. D., Catalano, R. F., & Miller, J. Y. (1992). Risk and protective factors for alcohol and other drug problems in adolescence and early adulthood: Implications for substance abuse prevention. *Psychological Bulletin, 112*, 64–105.

Hernandez, L., & Hoebel, B. G. (1988). Feeding and hypothalamic stimulation increase dopamine turnover in the accumbens. *Physiology & Behavior, 44*, 599–606.

Hernandez, L., & Hoebel, B. G. (1990). Feeding can enhance dopamine turnover in the prefrontal cortex. *Brain Research Bulletin, 25*, 975–979.

Hintzman, D. L. (1986). "Schema abstraction" in a multiple-trace memory model. *Psychological Review, 93,* 411–428.

Hintzman, D. L. (1993). Twenty-five years of learning and memory: Was the cognitive revolution a mistake? In D. E. Meyer & S. Kornblum (Eds.), *Attention and performance 14: Synergies in experimental psychology, artificial intelligence, and cognitive neuroscience* (pp. 359–391). Cambridge, MA: MIT Press.

Hofmann, W., Rauch, W., & Gawronski, B. (2007). And deplete us not into temptation: Automatic attitudes, dietary restraint, and self-regulatory resources as determinants of eating behavior. *Journal of Experimental Social Psychology, 43,* 497–504.

Johnson, C. A., Xiao, L., Palmer, P., Sun, P., Wang, Q., Wei, Y., et al. (2008). Affective decision-making deficits, linked to a dysfunctional ventromedial prefrontal cortex, revealed in 10th grade Chinese adolescent binge drinkers. *Neuropsychologia, 46,* 714–726.

Kahneman, D. (2003). A perspective on judgment and choice: Mapping bounded rationality. *American Psychologist, 58,* 697–720.

Kane, M. J., & Engle, R. W. (2000). Working-memory capacity, proactive interference, and divided attention: Limits on long-term memory retrieval. *Journal of Experimental Psychology: Learning, Memory, and Cognition, 26,* 336–358.

Kelly, A. B., Masterman, P. W., & Marlatt, G. A. (2005). Alcohol-related associative strength and drinking behaviours: Concurrent and prospective relationships. *Drug and Alcohol Review, 24,* 1–10.

Klingberg, T., Fernell, E., Olesen, P., Johnson, M., Gustafsson, P., Dahlström, K., et al. (2005). Computerized training of working memory in children with ADHD: A randomized clinical trial. *Journal of the Academy of Child & Adolescent Psychiatry, 44,* 177–186.

Koob, G. F. (2002). Neurobiology of drug addiction. In D. B. Kandel (Ed.), *Stages and pathways of drug involvement: Examining the gateway hypothesis* (pp. 337–361). New York: Cambridge University Press.

Krank, M. D., & Goldstein, A. L. (2006). Adolescent changes in implicit cognitions and prevention of substance abuse. In R. W. Wiers & A. W. Stacy (Eds.), *Handbook of implicit cognition and addiction* (pp. 439–453). Thousand Oaks, CA: Sage.

Krank, M. D., O'Neill, S., Squarey, K., & Jacob, J. (2008). Goal- and signal-directed incentive: Conditioned approach, seeking, and consumption established with unsweetened alcohol in rats. *Psychopharmacology, 196,* 397–405.

Krank, M. D., & Wall, A.-M. (2006). Context and retrieval effects on implicit cognition for substance use. In R. W. Wiers & A. W. Stacy (Eds.), *Handbook of implicit cognition and addiction* (pp. 281–292). Thousand Oaks, CA: Sage.

Krank, M. D., Wall, A.-M., Stewart, S. H., Wiers, R. W., & Goldman, M. S. (2005). Context effects on alcohol cognitions. *Alcoholism: Clinical and Experimental Research, 29,* 196–206.

Levy, D. A., Stark, C. E. L., & Squire, L. R. (2004). Intact conceptual priming in the absence of declarative memory. *Psychological Science, 15,* 680–686.

Logan, G. D., Schachar, R. J., & Tannock, R. (1997). Impulsivity and inhibitory control. *Psychological Science, 8,* 60–64.

MacKinnon, D. P., Johnson, C. A., Pentz, M. A., Dwyer, J. H., Hansen, W. B., Flay, B. R., & Wang, E. Y. (1991). Mediating mechanisms in a school-based drug prevention program: First-year effects of the Midwestern Prevention Project. *Health Psychology, 10,* 164–172.

Melis, M. R., & Argiolas, A. (1995). Dopamine and sexual behavior. *Neuroscience and Biobehavioral Reviews, 19,* 19–38.

Nelson, D. L., Goodmon, L. B., & Ceo, D. (2007). How does delayed testing reduce effects of implicit memory: Context infusion or cuing with context? *Memory & Cognition, 35,* 1014–1023.

Palfai, T. P., & Wood, M. D. (2001). Positive alcohol expectancies and drinking behavior: The influence of expectancy strength and memory accessibility. *Psychology of Addictive Behaviors, 15,* 60–67.

Payne, B. K. (2005). Conceptualizing control in social cognition: How executive functioning modulates the expression of automatic stereotyping. *Journal of Personality and Social Psychology, 89,* 488–503.

Peterson, A. V., Kealey, K. A., Mann, S. L., Marek, P. M., & Sarason, I. G. (2000). Hutchinson Smoking Prevention Project: Long-term randomized trial in school-based tobacco use prevention—Results on smoking. *Journal of the National Cancer Institute, 92,* 1979–1991.

Petraitis, J., Flay, B. R., & Miller, T. Q. (1995). Reviewing theories of adolescent substance use: Organizing pieces in the puzzle. *Psychological Bulletin, 117,* 67–86.

Phillips, P. E., Stuber, G. D., Heien, M. L., Wightman, R. M., & Carelli, R. M. (2003, April 10). Subsecond dopamine release promotes cocaine seeking. *Nature, 422,* 614–618.

Queller, S., & Smith, E. R. (2002). Subtyping versus bookkeeping in stereotype learning and change: Connectionist simulations and empirical findings. *Journal of Personality and Social Psychology, 82,* 300–313.

Riggs, N. R., Greenberg, M. T., Kusché, C. A., & Pentz, M. A. (2006). The mediational role of neurocognition in the behavioral outcomes of a social-emotional prevention program in elementary school students:

Effects of the Paths curriculum. *Prevention Science, 7,* 91–102.

Robinson, T. E., & Berridge, K. C. (2003). Addiction. *Annual Review of Psychology, 54,* 25–53.

Roediger, H. L., III. (2000). Why retrieval is the key process in understanding human memory. In E. Tulving (Ed.), *Memory, consciousness, and the brain: The Tallinn conference* (pp. 52–75). New York: Psychology Press.

Royall, D. R., Lauterbach, E. C., Cummings, J. L., Reeve, A., Rummans, T. A., Kaufer, D. I., et al. (2002). Executive control function: A review of its promise and challenges for clinical research: A report from the committee on research of the American Neuropsychiatric Association. *Journal of Neuropsychology and Clinical Neuroscience, 14,* 377–405.

Scheier, L. M., Botvin, G. J., Diaz, T., & Griffin, K. W. (1999). Social skills, competence, and drug refusal efficacy as predictors of adolescent alcohol use. *Journal of Drug Education, 29,* 251–278.

Schenk, S. (2002). Sensitization as a process underlying the progression of drug use via gateway drugs. In D. B. Kandel (Ed.), *Stages and pathways of drug involvement: Examining the gateway hypothesis* (pp. 318–336). New York: Cambridge University Press.

Schneider, W., & Chein, J. M. (2003). Controlled & automatic processing: Behavior, theory, and biological mechanisms. *Cognitive Science: A Multidisciplinary Journal, 27,* 525–559.

Schoenmakers, T., Wiers, R. W., Jones, B. T., Bruce, G., & Jansen, A. T. M. (2007). Attentional retraining decreases attentional bias in heavy drinkers without generalization. *Addiction, 102,* 399–405.

Schultz, W. (1998). Predictive reward signal of dopamine neurons. *Journal of Neurophysiology, 80,* 1–27.

Schwarz, N. (1999). Self-reports: How the questions shape the answers. *American Psychologist, 54,* 93–105.

Small, D. M., Jones-Gotman, M., & Dagher, A. (2003). Feeding-induced dopamine release in dorsal striatum correlates with meal pleasantness ratings in healthy human volunteers. *NeuroImage, 19,* 1709–1715.

Smith, E. R., & DeCoster, J. (1998). Knowledge acquisition, accessibility, and use in person perception and stereotyping: Simulation with a recurrent connectionist network. *Journal of Personality and Social Psychology, 74,* 21–35.

Smith, S. M., & Vela, E. (2001). Environmental context-dependent memory: A review and meta-analysis. *Psychonomic Bulletin & Review, 8,* 203–220.

Stacy, A. W. (1997). Memory activation and expectancy as prospective predictors of alcohol and marijuana use. *Journal of Abnormal Psychology, 106,* 61–73.

Stacy, A. W., Ames, S. L., & Grenard, J. (2006). Word association tests of associative memory and implicit processes: Theoretical and assessment issues. In R. W. Wiers & A. W. Stacy (Eds.), *Handbook of implicit cognition and addiction* (pp. 75–90). Thousand Oaks, CA: Sage.

Stacy, A. W., Ames, S. L., & Knowlton, B. J. (2004). Neurologically plausible distinctions in cognition relevant to drug use etiology and prevention. *Substance Use & Misuse, 39,* 1571–1623.

Stacy, A. W., Ames, S. L., Ullman, J. B., Zogg, J. B., & Leigh, B. C. (2006). Spontaneous cognition and HIV risk behavior. *Psychology of Addictive Behaviors, 20,* 196–206.

Stacy, A. W., Leigh, B. C., & Weingardt, K. R. (1994). Memory accessibility and association of alcohol use and its positive outcomes. *Experimental and Clinical Psychopharmacology, 2,* 269–282.

Stacy, A. W., & Wiers, R. W. (2006). An implicit cognition, associative memory framework for addiction. In M. Munafo & I. P. Albery (Eds.), *Cognition and addiction* (pp. 31–71). London: Oxford University Press.

Stewart, D. W. (1989). Measures, methods, and models in advertising research. *Journal of Advertising Research, 29,* 54–60.

Steyvers, M., & Tenenbaum, J. B. (2005). The large-scale structure of semantic networks: Statistical analyses and a model of semantic growth. *Cognitive Science: A Multidisciplinary Journal, 29,* 41–78.

Sussman, S., Dent, C. W., Stacy, A. W., Sun, P., Craig, S., Simon, T. R., et al. (1993). Project towards no tobacco use: 1-year behavior outcomes. *American Journal of Public Health, 83,* 1245–1250.

Sussman, S., Hansen, W. B., Flay, B. R., & Botvin, G. J. (2001). Correspondence re: Hutchinson Smoking Prevention Project: Long-term randomized trial in school-based tobacco use prevention—Results on smoking. *Journal of the National Cancer Institute, 93,* 1267.

Szalay, L. B., & Maday, B. C. (1983). Implicit culture and psychocultural distance. *American Anthropologist, 85,* 110–118.

Tapert, S. F., Cheung, E. H., Brown, G. G., Frank, L. R., Paulus, M. P., Schweinsburg, A. D., et al. (2003). Neural response to alcohol stimuli in adolescents with alcohol use disorder. *Archives of General Psychiatry, 60,* 727–735.

Thush, C., & Wiers, R. W. (2007). Explicit and implicit alcohol-related cognitions and the prediction of future drinking in adolescents. *Addictive Behaviors, 32,* 1367–1383.

Thush, C., Wiers, R. W., Ames, S. L., Grenard, J. L., Sussman, S., & Stacy, A. W. (2008). The interactions between implicit and explicit cognition and working memory capacity in the prediction of alcohol use in at-risk adolescents. *Drug and Alcohol Dependence, 94,* 116–124.

Tiffany, S. T. (1990). A cognitive model of drug urges and drug-use behavior: Role of automatic and nonautomatic processes. *Psychological Review, 97,* 147–168.

Tobler, N. S., Roona, M. R., Ochshorn, P., Marshall, D. G., Streke, A. V., & Stackpole, K. M. (2000). School-based adolescent drug prevention programs: 1998 meta-analysis. *Journal of Primary Prevention, 20,* 275–336.

Todorov, A., & Bargh, J. A. (2002). Automatic sources of aggression. *Aggression & Violent Behavior, 7,* 53–68.

Tversky, A., & Kahneman, D. (1973). Availability: A heuristic for judging frequency and probability. *Cognitive Psychology, 5,* 207–232.

Volkow, N. D., Wang, G. J., Telang, F., Fowler, J. S., Logan, J., Childress, A. R., et al. (2006). Cocaine cues and dopamine in dorsal striatum: Mechanism of craving in cocaine addiction. *Journal of Neuroscience, 26,* 6583–6588.

Volkow, N. D., & Wise, R. A. (2005). How can drug addiction help us understand obesity? *Nature Neuroscience, 8,* 555–560.

Von Hecker, U. (2004). Disambiguating a mental model: Influence of social context. *Psychological Record, 54,* 27–43.

Weingartner, H. J., Putnam, F., George, D. T., & Ragan, P. (1995). Drug state-dependent autobiographical knowledge. *Experimental and Clinical Psychopharmacology, 3,* 304–307.

White, N. M. (1996). Addictive drugs as reinforcers: Multiple partial actions on memory systems. *Addiction, 91,* 921–949.

Wiers, R. W., Cox, W. M., Field, M., Fadardi, J. S., Palfai, T. P., Schoenmakers, T., & Stacy, A. W. (2006). The search for new ways to change implicit alcohol-related cognitions in heavy drinkers. *Alcoholism, Clinical and Experimental Research, 30,* 320–331.

Wiers, R. W., & Stacy, A. W. (Eds.). (2006a). *Handbook of implicit cognition and addiction.* Thousand Oaks, CA: Sage.

Wiers, R. W., & Stacy, A. W. (2006b). Implicit cognition and addiction. *Current Directions in Psychological Science, 15,* 292–296.

Wiers, R. W., Van de Luitgaarden, J., Van den Wildenberg, E., & Smulders, F. T. Y. (2005). Challenging implicit and explicit alcohol-related cognitions in young heavy drinkers. *Addiction, 100,* 806–819.

Winstanley, C. A., Eagle, D. M., & Robbins, T. W. (2006). Behavioral models of impulsivity in relation to ADHD: Translation between clinical and preclinical studies. *Clinical Psychology Review, 26,* 379–395.

Wood, W., & Neal, D. T. (2007). A new look at habits and the habit–goal interface. *Psychological Review, 114,* 843–863.

Xiao, L., Bechara, A., Cen, S., Grenard, J. L., Stacy, A. W., Gallaher, P., et al. (2008). Affective decision-making deficits, linked to a dysfunctional ventromedial prefrontal cortex, revealed in 10th grade Chinese adolescent smokers. *Nicotine & Tobacco Research, 10,* 1085–1097.

Yeates, K. O., & Enrile, B. G. (2005). Implicit and explicit memory in children with congenital and acquired brain disorder. *Neuropsychology, 19,* 618–628.

Yin, H. H., & Knowlton, B. J. (2006). Addiction and learning in the brain. In R. W. Wiers & A. W. Stacy (Eds.), *Handbook of implicit cognition and addiction* (pp. 167–184). Thousand Oaks, CA: Sage.

CHAPTER 10

AFFECTIVE INFLUENCES IN DRUG USE ETIOLOGY

Jon D. Kassel, Andrea M. Hussong, Margaret C. Wardle, Jennifer C. Veilleux,
Adrienne Heinz, Justin E. Greenstein, and Daniel P. Evatt

The notion that drug use is linked to emotion, or affect, has taken on the status of near universal truth. Virtually everyone, on the basis of their own experience or beliefs derived from cultural norms (e.g., MacAndrew & Edgerton, 1969; Peele, 1985), views the use of drugs as both being shaped by, and subsequently influencing, the way an individual feels. Interestingly, within the scope of etiological models of drug use and abuse, the role of affect has historically received relatively short shrift. Emphasis has typically been placed instead on the seemingly profound influence of peer and familial factors in promoting said use. Indeed, there is ample evidence to support such claims (see chaps. 19, 20, and 21, this volume). At the same time, however, even when acknowledging the important roles played by peer and family pressure, there is growing reason to believe that affective influences may play a more pronounced role in the etiology of drug use and abuse than previously thought. Indeed, Panksepp, Nocjar, Burgdorf, Panskepp, and Huber (2004, p. 93) posed the following interesting question: "Would individuals exhibit addictive behaviors if there were no affective payoffs?" and then went on to answer, "We suspect an answer of 'No' for both humans and other species."

As much of the content of this handbook enumerates, it is important to remember that the pathways to drug use and abuse are, no doubt, complex (Kassel, Weinstein, Skitch, Veilleux, & Mermelstein, 2005). However, of the numerous genetic, societal, intrapersonal, and interpersonal factors believed to heighten vulnerability both to drug use initiation and subsequent development of dependence, the role played by various forms of psychopathology and concomitant emotional distress appears particularly critical. That is, and as discussed in more detail shortly, numerous studies have reliably revealed higher rates of drug use among selected populations of individuals with mental illness, particularly psychological disorders epitomized by emotional distress (e.g., depression, anxiety). It is ultimately these correlational observations—individuals who experience affective distress are at increased risk of using and abusing drugs—that really form the foundation of the assertion that affect and drug use are inextricably linked.

As we have argued elsewhere in some detail (Kassel & Hankin, 2006; Kassel, Stroud, & Paronis, 2003), it is important to remember that the association between affect and drug use is perhaps more complex than it may first seem (see Figure 10.1). Indeed, a thorough understanding of the relations between affect and drug abuse requires asking, at the very least, the following distinct, but frequently blurred questions:

1. Do various manifestations of positive and/or negative affect actually promote drug use? More specifically, are there valid and reliable associations between affect and (a) drug use status (drug user vs. nonuser) and (b) actual cuing (prompting) of drug use? Also, even if it were established that affect is linked to drug self-

Preparation of this chapter was supported in part by National Cancer Institute Grant 1PO1CA98262 and National Institute on Alcohol Abuse and Alcoholism Grant 5RO1AA12240-04 to Jon D. Kassel and National Institute on Drug Abuse Grant DA15398 to Andrea M. Hussong.

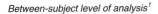

Between-subject level of analysis[1]

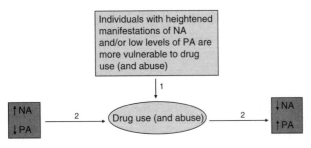

Within-subject level of analysis[2] ------------------------------------->

FIGURE 10.1.   Subject-level analysis. Between-subjects designs (cross-sectional or correlational) are well suited to answer the question of whether differences among groups of people heighten vulnerability to drug use (downward arrow labeled 1). However, questions of whether affect genuinely cues drug use and whether drug use influences affect (arrows labeled 2) are best addressed via within-subject designs and analyses. NA = negative affect; PA = positive affect.

administration (at either or both of these levels of analysis), this does not necessarily mean that drug use inevitably influences, or modifies, affect. Hence, this frequently ignored distinction leads to another, very different, question.

2. Does drug use genuinely influence affect? Although the self-reports of drug users themselves are certainly an important source of data with respect to answering this question, the extent to which experimental and/or controlled field studies reveal drug effects on emotion must also be considered.

Simply put, then, whereas the question of whether various manifestations of affect (and affective distress) differentiate drug users from nonusers necessarily requires a between-subjects level of analysis, the other questions posed above ultimately call for within-subjects, or perhaps mixed-model, analyses.[1] That being said, we believe that these distinct levels of analysis are often confounded, leading to potentially confusing or just plain erroneous conclusions (e.g., "If depressed individuals are more likely to be[come] smokers, then smoking must [inevitably]

be cued by depressive symptoms and smoking must [inevitably] relieve such symptoms").

Keeping these issues in mind, our primary goal in this chapter is to review the literature to determine whether affect does, indeed, play a consequential role in the development of drug use. Toward this end, we adopt the following approach, replete with caveats and qualifications. In fact, we believe that part of the difficulties plaguing this particular area of empirical inquiry is that extant conceptual approaches have been too simplistic, frequently overlooking the inherent complexities in mapping linkages between affect and drug use. We begin with a brief overview of the epidemiology of drug use initiation, followed by a discussion of the manner in which highly relevant constructs like affect, emotion, mood, and arousal have been operationalized and why acknowledgment of these conceptual issues is critical to the study of drug–affect relationships.

Next, we provide a brief overview of why the developmental period of adolescence in and of itself predisposes some individuals to affective lability, which in turn may heighten vulnerability to drug use. We then discuss several theoretical models pertinent to understanding affective influences in the etiology of drug use and subsequently consider various methodological approaches to the study of drug–affect associations. We next assess the extent to which affect (particularly manifestations of negative affect) is associated with drug use. These studies typically take the form of either cross-sectional or longitudinal epidemiological investigations examined primarily with adolescent and young adult samples (because this is most typically the time of life when drug initiation begins). Although few studies of drug use initiation actually allow for within-person analyses addressing whether affect cues the self-administration of drugs, several studies that at least tangentially bear on this important issue are reviewed. We then tackle the question of whether drug use influences or modifies affective response. Inherent to this discussion is the identification of contextual variables (both within and outside the individual) that may moderate any observed drug–affect relationships. Finally, we conclude with considerations and recommendations for future research in this area of clinical inquiry.

---

[1] At the level of within-subjects analyses, one might pose the following question: For a given person, is his or her drug use cued by negative affect? A mixed-model approach affords one the opportunity to also ask, Is there a subset of individuals whose drug use is cued by negative affect (vs. one of those whose use is not cued by negative affect)?

THE NATURE OF THE BEAST: EPIDEMIOLOGY OF ADOLESCENT DRUG USE

Whereas a thorough review of the epidemiology of adolescent drug use is covered elsewhere in this volume (see chap. 4), we provide some brief points on this matter here. Perhaps most important, research has indicated that most people first try drugs as adolescents (Compton, Thomas, Conway, & Colliver, 2005). The Monitoring the Future Survey, using a nationally representative sample of 8th- to 12th-grade students, found that almost half (47%) of Americans have tried cigarettes by the time they graduate from high school, and current smoking rates of 12th graders (22%) rival national adult statistics (Johnston, O'Malley, Bachman, & Schulenberg, 2007). Alcohol use rates are even higher; 73% of 12th graders have tried alcohol, and 45% reported use in the month before survey completion (Johnston et al., 2007). More than a quarter (27%) of youth have used an illicit drug other than marijuana, with marijuana being the most popular illicit drug, with prevalence rates of 31.5% among high school students. Of even greater concern, many adolescents begin using drugs or alcohol before high school; 19.5% of eighth graders reported having been drunk sometime in their lives. More important, earlier age at first use has been associated with greater drug use problems in adulthood (Hu, Davies, & Kandel, 2006; Reboussin & Anthony, 2006; Simkin, 2002).

Rates of abuse and dependence follow a distinct developmental trajectory, such that drug use disorders are more common among 18- to 29-year-olds as compared with older adults (Compton et al., 2005; Compton, Thomas, Stinson, & Grant, 2007). Recent advances in statistical methodologies have allowed researchers to determine that this trend likely reflects a developmental phenomenon and not a cohort effect (Sher, Grekin, & Williams, 2005), suggesting that among young adults with drug problems, many will cease problematic usage with increased maturity. However, Hasin, Stinson, Ogburn, and Grant (2007) noted that there may be a shift in trends for alcohol abuse and dependence because many individuals currently belonging to the "Generation X" age bracket (30–44) manifest higher rates of lifetime alcohol abuse compared with those in other age ranges.

In sum, then, the problem is clear: Drug use, in all of its various manifestations, is a highly prevalent disorder that proves costly both to those affected and to society at large. Moreover, the vast majority of individuals who go on to become drug dependent begin taking drugs as adolescents. As such, understanding the etiological pathways of drug use and abuse becomes imperative.

CONCEPTUAL BASIS OF AFFECT

Before embarking further on an examination of affective influences on drug use, we first consider how the construct of affect has come under scientific scrutiny. Although there is by no means anything approaching universal consensus, most would agree that the primary defining characteristic of affect is a valenced positive or negative feeling, possessing some degree of hedonic tone (Ortony & Turner, 1990; Russell, 2003). Affect is evaluative, signaling something about either the properties of an eliciting stimulus or the individual's internal resources (Larsen, 2000; Morris, 2000). Furthermore, affect has frequently been used as a blanket term encompassing the more specific phenomena of moods and emotions (Clore & Ortony, 2000; Forgas, 1995). Moods are typically seen as less intense, longer lasting affective states that are not directed at a particular object or prompted by a particular conscious event (Forgas, 1995; Russell, 2003). Moods may exist below consciousness, although they can also be consciously perceived (Morris, 2000). In contrast, emotions are usually defined as discrete, short-lived affective events prompted by particular causes and associated with specific cognitions and "action tendencies" or motivated behavior (Ekman, 1999; Forgas, 1995; Russell, 2003).

We believe that acknowledging and understanding these distinctions between mood and emotion are critical to formulating (and testing) theories of affect and drug use. For example, Baker, Piper, McCarthy, Majeskie, and Fiore's (2004) reformulation of the negative reinforcement model of drug addiction draws a distinction between the processes that maintain drug use at low levels of negative affect, before negative affect is consciously perceived (e.g., during a negative mood), and the processes engaged by high levels of negative affect (e.g., during the experience of a negative emotion). Establishing whether a given affective experience is, in fact, a diffuse mood or an object-directed emotion would thus be important for understanding which of these processes are actively motivating drug-seeking behavior.

There are several distinct ways that theories of affective experiences can be organized. Broadly speaking, the theoretical models consist of three types: (a) dimensional models of emotional experience, which attempt to reduce affective experiences to a parsimonious set of broad dimensions (Russell, 2003; Tellegen, Watson, & Clark, 1999; Watson, Wiese, Vaidya, & Tellegen, 1999); (b) basic emotions models, which posit specific and categorical emotion constructs such as anger, fear, and disgust (instead of broad dimensions) and additionally conceive of emotions as evolutionarily and biologically based (Ekman, 1992, 1999; Izard, 1992; Panksepp, 2005); and (c) appraisal theories, in which the final common pathway for elicitation of affect is cognition (Scherer, Dan, & Flykt, 2006; Smith & Ellsworth, 1985; Smith & Lazarus, 1993). Although many researchers in the field of drug use have treated affect in a relatively atheoretical manner (see Stritzke, Lang, & Patrick, 1996, for a critique of this tendency in the alcohol literature), we, along with other researchers (Baker et al., 2004; Kassel et al., 2003; Panksepp, Knutson, & Burgdorf, 2002; Stritzke et al., 1996) believe careful consideration of these theoretical stances on affect is crucial to obtain productive research examining drug use–affect links.

Dimensional theories generally share the view that two affective dimensions create a circumplex within which all affective experiences can be located. Dimensions are derived from factor analyses of ratings of emotional stimuli and are presumed to reflect the actions of underlying neural substrates (Lang, Bradley, & Cuthbert, 1992). However, there are at least two different views with respect to the properties of these dimensions. Specifically, the valence–arousal model posits dimensions of valence (positive vs. negative feelings) and arousal (excitement vs. calm) and predicts that the experience of pleasant and unpleasant emotional states is necessarily bipolar (Feldman Barrett & Russell, 1998; Green, Salovey, & Truax, 1999). In contrast, the positive affect (PA)–negative affect (NA) model proposes dimensions of PA and

NA and contends that pleasant and unpleasant affective states are independent (Watson & Clark, 1997; Watson et al., 1999). The differences between these models may prove critical to drug use researchers. If the valence–arousal model is the adopted stance, there is no need to distinguish conceptually, or in measurement, between low PA (anhedonia) and high NA (distress) in measurements of withdrawal or affect prompting drug taking. However, several models of drug use have suggested that systems of PA and NA may play independent and separable roles in addiction (Ichitani & Iwasaki, 1986; Panksepp et al., 2002). For example, one model proposes that opiate effects may involve the removal of NA, leading to feelings of calmness and security and a resultant withdrawal syndrome involving high emotional distress. Psychostimulants, however, are believed to result in an increase in PA, with apathy and anhedonia being prominent features of withdrawal. Such observations are in contrast with theories positing that all addictive substances provoke a common syndrome of negative affect during withdrawal (Baker et al., 2004), a theoretical stance congruent with the valence–arousal conception.

Moving beyond the broad affective distinctions offered by the dimensional models, basic emotions models propose many more discrete emotional states. According to this view, discrete emotions arise from separate brain systems that have evolved to quickly recruit and organize physiology and behavior in response to evolutionarily significant challenges (Ekman, 1999; Panksepp, 2005). This position is significant to drug use researchers because it has long been theorized that drugs "hijack" evolutionarily significant emotional brain systems (Panksepp et al., 2002; Robinson & Berridge, 2003). Basic emotions theory suggests that drugs may have effects on many distinct systems, including substrates governing anger or disgust, an intriguing possibility that has not been thoroughly explored in drug use research. Furthermore, discrete negative emotions such as anger have been shown to yield different effects on judgments of risk than do other negative emotions such as anxiety (Lerner & Keltner, 2000, 2001). It is entirely possible that these differential influences on risk taking may also be found in risky decisions to use substances. Research on NA and drug use that does not take these distinctions into account runs the risk of inappropriately averaging across very different response biases.

Finally, the appraisal model of emotions focuses on cognitive elicitors of emotion. In appraisal theories, the subjective meaning assigned to an event, or appraisal, elicits and differentiates emotions. According to the tenets of this theory, then, the subjective meaning assigned to an event, or the appraisal of such an event, can vary along several dimensions, such as goal conduciveness, certainty, and novelty of the event, with each emotion elicited by its own distinct pattern of appraisals (Smith & Ellsworth, 1985). This organizing framework may also be important to drug use research because some drugs may influence emotion through effects on the appraisal process (Sayette, 1993). Whereas some drugs, such as opiates, appear to act directly on primary emotional valence systems, alcohol appears to operate, at least in part, by disrupting the cognitive ability of the individual to appraise threatening events (Sayette, Martin, Perrott, Wertz, & Hufford, 2001).

All of these different viewpoints acknowledged, it is impossible to recommend to researchers one right way to think about and measure affect in the context of drug use. However, keeping these different theoretical stances in mind while at the same time considering the literature on drug abuse provokes interesting and important questions and provides new avenues for future research. As such, we believe that more deference needs to be given to theoretical frameworks of affect and emotion by those exploring such issues within the realm of drug abuse research.

WHY DO MOST INDIVIDUALS BEGIN USING DRUGS AS ADOLESCENTS?

Simply put, adolescence is a time of life typified by heightened risk of emotional and behavioral problems. In concert with this observation, adolescence is, for many, a period marked by multiple transitional events and developmental challenges (Cicchetti & Rogosch, 2002). Hence, given the tremendous biological, cognitive, emotional, and social changes that occur during adolescence, it is not particularly surprising that of those individuals who have used drugs, most initiated their use during this particular developmental period.

Burgeoning evidence from diverse areas of research inquiry (e.g., neuropsychology, brain imaging, animal work) has reliably shown that adolescence is a time of neurodevelopmental plasticity and change (Steinberg et al., 2004). Indeed, such changes in the structure and function of the brain during this period likely affect behavior and psychological functioning in numerous and profound ways (Spear, 2002). Evidence has suggested that transformations include alterations in the mesocorticolimbic dopaminergic systems, which have been implicated in modulating the reinforcing properties of drugs and alcohol. In addition, maturation of the prefrontal cortex and the amygdala occurs in adolescence, and these brain regions are involved in goal-directed behaviors, emotional processing, and emotional reactivity (Spear, 2002). Specific to the prefrontal cortex, research with nonhuman primates has indicated that glutamate (an excitatory neurotransmitter) and gamma-aminobutyric acid (an inhibitory neurotransmitter) activity is reduced in the prefrontal cortex during adolescence, although dopaminergic activity increases (Lewis, 1997).

Hence, during adolescence, development takes place in brain regions and systems responsible for regulating critical aspects of behavior, emotion, and cognition, as well as perceptions of risk and reward (Steinberg et al., 2004). Such neurobiological reorganization renders adolescence a unique period of vulnerability to extreme emotional lability, and as such, the propensity to use and misuse drugs is increased (Steinberg et al., 2004). Correspondingly, research has suggested that sensation- and novelty-seeking behavior is highest during adolescence (Zuckerman, 1994). Indeed, these temperament risk factors have been shown to predict cigarette and alcohol use in adolescence (Crawford, Pentz, Chou, Li, & Dwyer, 2003; see chap. 7 of this volume for additional discussion of temperament and drug use).

Pubertal timing has been linked to both emotional distress and drug use initiation. In light of the fact that this particular life transitory phase is marked by dramatic physical, hormonal, and maturational changes, perhaps this observation brings with it a certain amount of intuitive appeal. Although the specific etiological processes linking pubertal change and adolescent drug use are unclear, the timing of this stage relative to same-age peers may negatively influence the completion of developmental tasks in adolescence (e.g., developing one's identity, autonomy from parents, and forging romantic relationships; Dawes et al., 2000). The inability to complete these stage-salient tasks in turn increases susceptibility for high-risk behaviors, including sexual promiscuity and drug use and abuse (Cicchetti & Rogosch, 2002).

In addition to the biological and cognitive changes that accompany adolescence, emotional lability represents another phenomenological hallmark experienced by most young people. Although adolescence is no longer characterized as a period of inevitable and universal storm and stress (Hall, 1904), mood disruptions are nonetheless considered a central feature of teenage development (Arnett, 1999). A considerable body of research has demonstrated that dysphoria and emotional instability rise with entry into adolescence (Garber, Keiley, & Martin, 2002; Larson, Moneta, Richards, & Wilson, 2002), with one third to one half of adolescents reporting feelings of depressed mood (Compas, Hinden, & Gerhardt, 1995). Moreover, adolescence is associated with more frequent NA relative to middle and later adulthood (Carstensen, Pasupathi, Mayr, & Nesselroade, 2000). These well-established increases in negative emotion constitute a major risk factor for adolescent drug use. Feelings of distress in adolescence, particularly those emphasizing negative mood, have been linked with, and shown to prospectively predict, cigarette and alcohol use in both cross-sectional and longitudinal studies (e.g., Brown, Lewinsohn, Seeley, & Wagner, 1996; Chassin, Pillow, Curran, Molina, & Barrera, 1993; Colder & Chassin, 1997).

In sum, given the substantial changes occurring across biological and psychological domains of development, adolescence emerges as a period of unique risk for drug use and misuse. However, these factors do not operate in isolation. Rather, it is the complex interactions of these factors, in addition to simultaneous contextual changes, that heighten vulnerability to maladaptive drug use trajectories. To better understand the theoretical underpinnings that may govern affect–drug use etiology relationships, we next review several influential theoretical models of drug use etiology, all of which view affect as a critical factor in promoting drug use and misuse.

THEORETICAL FRAMEWORKS OF AFFECT AND DRUG ABUSE

Numerous theoretical models have been proposed to explain the relationship between drug abuse and affect. Indeed, most of these conceptualizations assert that the affective payoffs of drugs with abuse liability represent the primary motivating force governing drug use and progression to dependence. Perhaps the most influential of these models (e.g., stress coping [Wills & Shiffman, 1985], self-medication [Khantzian, 1997], tension reduction [Conger, 1956]) are all steeped in the belief that individuals who take drugs do so primarily as a means of regulating affect or escaping aversive affective states.

Earlier models of addiction argued that the central motivating factor underlying drug use is the alleviation of negative affect (negative reinforcement). For instance, Wikler's (1980; Jellinek, 1960) influential withdrawal–relief model posits that addicted individuals use drugs to escape or avoid aversive withdrawal symptoms. This model also notes that using drugs to escape withdrawal symptoms increases the likelihood that the addicted individual will engage in drug use in the future, thus perpetuating a cycle of negative reinforcement and dependence liability. Of course, one limiting factor of Wikler's model and others that identify withdrawal relief as the central motivating force in drug use is that such a stance cannot readily explain use that occurs early in the developmental sequence (e.g., adolescence), that is, before the onset of dependence and withdrawal.

Other early models of addiction also focused on the relationship between negative reinforcement and drug abuse. According to Solomon's (1977; Solomon & Corbit, 1974) opponent-process model, drug administration inevitably elicits an affective response, known as the "a-process," typically experienced as pleasurable by the user. However, this a-process necessarily activates a negative, opponent (in terms of affective valence) "b-process" in the individual, the belief being that this b-process restores the person to a state of homeostasis that had been disrupted by the initial a-process. The resulting affective end state experienced by the individual varies as a function of the difference in magnitude between these two opponent processes. When the pleasurable a-process is larger in magnitude than the b-process, the resulting affective state is experienced as positive ("A-state"). By contrast, if the b-process is greater in magnitude than the a-process, the affective outcome will be unpleasant. More important, after repeated drug use, the b-process is believed to grow in strength and magnitude, such that its onset is earlier and its duration longer. This evolving process thereby results in a less pleasurable A-state and the emergence of tolerance. Eventually, the b-process becomes greater in magnitude than the a-process, and the user experiences an unpleasant "B-state" typically associated with withdrawal symptoms. Only through abstinence can the user restore the b-process back to its original level, and when this occurs, the individual has escaped the throes of addiction. It is important to note that the opponent-process model does go some way toward explaining drug use that occurs relatively early in the individual's life. As such, this approach offers one intriguing explanation for drug use–affect relationships in the context of etiological processes.

In addition to the opponent-process model, a variety of classical conditioning models examining the relationship between negative reinforcement and drug abuse have been proposed. According to Siegel's (1983) model of compensatory response, the direct effect of a drug on the individual serves as the unconditioned stimulus (UCS), whereas the individual's homeostatic regulatory system's attempt to defend itself against the drug's effect and maintain homeostasis is the unconditioned response (UCR). Through repeated drug administration, a stimulus that is often paired with the UCS becomes a conditioned stimulus (CS) and serves as an early warning signal to the homeostatic regulatory system that a UCS is imminent. The regulatory system then prepares itself by eliciting a defensive conditioned response (CR). Through repeated drug administration episodes, the link between the UCS and the CS becomes stronger and, eventually, the CS can elicit a CR in the absence of the UCS. This CR may then influence the individual's homeostatic state resulting in the onset of withdrawal symptoms, craving, and likely future drug use (in order to alleviate the aversive withdrawal syndrome).

Recently, Baker et al. (2004) attempted to clarify how negative reinforcement influences drug use by proposing a reformulated model of negative rein-

forcement in the context of addiction. According to their affective model of drug motivation, negative affect is viewed as the motivational core of the withdrawal syndrome. Thus, the model proposes that over time, the addicted individual becomes sensitive to internal cues that signal NA through repeated withdrawal–drug use cycles. When drug levels begin to fall in the addicted individual's body, the individual begins to experience low levels of NA. However, the detection of these NA cues occurs outside of the individual's conscious awareness. This preconscious detection of NA cues biases response options toward increasing the likelihood that previously reinforced responses will be performed (i.e., drug use). As such, for the addicted individual who has access to drugs, the motivational processing leading up to drug use occurs without awareness and serves to escape or avoid the NA caused by falling levels of the drug. If an individual does not have access to drugs or experiences a significant stressor, NA increases, and may do so to a point whereby the individual becomes aware of its presence, resulting in biased information processing. More specifically, the increased NA may influence "hot" information processing, biasing behavioral responses toward those that have previously decreased NA (i.e., drug use) and away from alternative responses that are not as effective (at least in the short term) at diminishing NA. The increased NA may also influence "cold" information processing by decreasing the influence of declarative (objective and rational) knowledge and controlled cognitive processing, rendering the individual more likely to engage in drug use. Although Baker et al.'s model clearly argues for the importance of negative reinforcement processes in governing drug use, it still lends itself to understanding drug use–affect relationships in the context of drug use etiology.

Many researchers have espoused theoretical stances identifying negative reinforcement as a primary motivating factor governing drug use. Nonetheless, critics of these models have emerged. As noted earlier, some have argued that individuals often use drugs for reasons other than withdrawal relief. Moreover, it has been suggested that because withdrawal symptoms emerge only after extensive drug self-administration, other processes must account for drug use in its earlier developmental stages (e.g., Falk, Schuster, Bigelow, & Woods, 1982). As such, others have asserted that drug use may, in fact, increase PA and produce positive reinforcing effects (e.g., de Wit & Phan, 2010; Stewart, de Wit, & Eikelboom, 1984). Some addiction scientists have also argued that withdrawal states are not as effective in producing drug-seeking behavior relative to the positive reinforcement induced by most drugs. In support of this contention, findings from animal research have revealed that a small priming dose of a previously self-administered drug can serve as a potent cue in eliciting reinstatement of drug-seeking behavior (Stewart & Wise, 1992), a phenomenon that cannot likely be explained by negative reinforcement mechanisms. Moreover, this priming dose was more effective at reinstating drug-seeking behavior than naltrexone, an opioid antagonist that can reliably induce precipitated withdrawal symptoms in heroin-dependent individuals. Such findings have strongly suggested that positive reinforcement may, indeed, serve as a powerful motivating force underlying drug use. This could be particularly true for adolescent users or those in the early phase of their drug use trajectory. Critics of negative reinforcement models have also observed that relapse often occurs when withdrawal symptoms should long since have abated (e.g., Stewart et al., 1984). Last, it has been argued that many, perhaps even most, individuals who use (or abuse) drugs report euphoria as the primary reason for their drug use (McAuliffe, 1982; McAuliffe, Rohman, Feldman, & Launer, 1985).

Taken together, then, there is compelling evidence to support both negative and positive reinforcement models of drug use and dependence. In an attempt to partially reconcile these seemingly contradictory views, Robinson and Berridge (1993, 2003) proposed an influential alternative to viewing the unfolding process of addiction. Their incentive sensitization theory posits that addictive drugs alter brain systems responsible for incentive salience, or motivational significance. This process is believed to result in various neural systems becoming hypersensitive or sensitized to drug effects and to stimuli previously associated with these effects. Hence, this process of classical conditioning results in excessive activation of the incentive-salience processes, or "wanting," in the presence of drugs or drug-related stimuli.

Moreover, these sensitized neural systems involved in the excessive incentive salience are distinct from the neural mechanisms responsible for determining the pleasurable effects of the drugs, or the extent to which drugs are experienced as liked. As a result, the ensuing subjective effects of drugs, or the "liking," are viewed as independent of the reinforcing effects, or the "wanting" of drugs. In addition, separate neural mechanisms are posited to be involved in the liking and wanting aspects of drug effects. One interesting implication of this model is that drug use may not be expected to inevitably result in "feeling better" at all, through either negative or positive reinforcement processes.

To summarize, theoretical models positing a strong motivational relationship between affect and drug use have endured for many years. The tenets of these models emphasize the importance of NA, PA, and incentive salience, among other affective factors, in promoting and maintaining drug use. Whereas some aspects of these various conceptualizations might be viewed as competitive, we believe there is in fact room for overlap among the models, such that all of them may be "right," at least in part. Next, we touch on several methodological considerations and issues relevant to both theory building and testing and to the actual study of drug–affect relationships.

METHODOLOGICAL CONSIDERATIONS

Examination of the dynamic relationship between drug use and affect requires attention to several complex and multifaceted methodological issues. Such issues include temporal relevance to the research question of interest and appropriateness of the conclusions that can be drawn from the data. Careful design consideration and methodological rigor is therefore critical to generating an accurate depiction of the influence of drug use on affectivity and, conversely, the impact of affect on drug use. Indeed, investigators have taken a variety of methodological approaches toward elucidating the enigmatic relations between drug use and affective response. Such studies fall under the umbrella of four distinct types of research methodologies, including (a) cross-sectional or correlation designs, (b) controlled laboratory studies, (c) longitudinal designs, and (d) daily process or ecological momentary assessment (EMA). The wide variety of available methodological approaches, however, may be partly responsible for conflicting results within the extant literature. Equivocal conclusions therefore warrant closer evaluation of the selected time frame surrounding the phenomenon of interest and of other factors such as variation in operational definitions of NA (e.g., issues of affect specificity) and drug use behavior (e.g., puff volume, frequency and quantity of use).

First, an explicit distinction between approaches to capturing within- and between-subjects effects is warranted. Most of the evidence that links stress and NA with cigarette smoking, for example, has been generated at a between-subjects level of analysis (Kassel et al., 2003). Between-subjects designs typically approach examination of the influence of drug use on affect in one of two ways. On one hand, researchers may be interested in differences in affect or prevalence of mood disorders between individuals who use drugs and those who do not. Other approaches may aspire to capture differences in affect change scores between users and nonusers following, for example, mood manipulation or acute drug administration. On the other hand, evidence in support of affect regulation and self-medication models, discussed earlier in the chapter, is most commonly generated by studies of within-subject differences regarding change in affect following drug use (at least in adult samples). Such studies typically assess change in NA (caused by a naturalistic incidence or planned mood induction) directly following drug administration; in some cases, researchers opt to examine these effects over the course of time. Inclusion of both within- and between-subjects components in studies of drug use and emotional response is therefore attractive because it maximizes the amount of information that can be captured.

Correlation or Cross-Sectional Studies

Studies that assess motivational correlates of drug use offer important information regarding potential antecedents and consequences of drug use. Unfortunately, reliance on retrospective recall weakens the reliability of reported relationships. Furthermore, causation cannot be inferred in correlation studies of drug use and affect. Although correlation

data are clearly important and warrant further inspection, careful laboratory studies and field investigations that capture the underlying mechanisms governing the influence of drugs on affect are required to infer causation (Kassel et al., 2003). Cross-sectional designs, although more adept at capturing influences of potential third variables, are inherently limited in that valid conclusions cannot be drawn regarding the extent to which drug use may actually precede or even cause elevations or decreases in NA.

Controlled Laboratory Studies

Controlled laboratory studies allow for examination of the relationship between affect and drug use in a manner that minimizes the influence of confounding factors. That is, given a carefully controlled physical environment, change in affect should primarily be related to the use of, or an expectation for, a drug. The ability to determine proximal effects of psychoactive drugs on affect allows researchers to determine how or whether a drug influences emotional response. This particular methodology is ideal for capturing the short-lived effects of acute drug administration on many levels (e.g., psychophysiologically, biologically, subjectively). Conversely, the extent to which affect influences drug use behavior (e.g., craving, self-administration of a drug) can also be carefully assessed. One important limitation of controlled laboratory studies, however, is the potential for compromised ecological (external) validity. Laboratory settings may feel contrived and unnatural to the participant such that the artificiality of the setting may not generalize to real-world contexts.

Longitudinal Designs

The temporal relationship between affect and drug use is perhaps of greatest interest in understanding drug use etiology. Simply put, how does drug use influence affect, and in turn, how does affect influence subsequent drug use? Longitudinal designs are particularly well suited to capturing how the effects of drug use on affective response may change over time at the level of the individual. Such differences may influence or even predict trajectories of drug use patterns. Furthermore, the directionality of the relationship between drug use and affect holds potentially significant implications. A thorough understanding of the sequence in which these dynamic components play off each other is critical for the purposes of developing prevention initiatives and effective interventions. Longitudinal studies are needed for such purposes because they allow researchers to draw meaningful conclusions regarding the temporal precedence of affect and drug use. At the same time, it is important to note that establishing temporal precedence with longitudinal studies is still challenging because they often study a process that is already in place, such that directionality can no longer truly be established.

Despite numerous strengths, longitudinal designs still possess inherent limitations. In some cases, longitudinal analyses may draw on data from as few as two or three time points to make inferences about the effect of drug use on affect. Such an approach may be problematic because not only is affect considered a dynamic construct that fluctuates at the level of days or even moments, it may also be influenced by any number of contextual factors. For example, multivariate models often fail to detect the relationships between drug use and affect identified at the univariate level of analysis (Kassel et al., 2003). One possible explanation is that specific components of NA (e.g., anxiety, depression) often covary to the extent that issues of collinearity mask the variance explained by affect. It is more likely, however, that contextual factors moderate and/or mediate the relationship between affect and drug use. Randomized intervention trials, although still compromised in terms of ecological validity, represent one available approach to capturing the prospective effects observed in longitudinal studies with limited interference from an unmeasured third variable (Burton, Stice, Bearman, & Rohde, 2007).

Daily Process Designs

Daily process studies, a relatively new addition to the assessment armamentarium, offer a potent methodology for examining the relationship between drug use and affect. Most commonly implemented through the use of paper-and-pencil diaries or handheld palmtop computers, ecological momentary assessment (EMA) requires participants to report frequently on their environment, activities, and feelings (Shiffman & Stone, 1998). Both event-contingent sampling (e.g., craving or actual drug use) and random sampling (e.g., randomly generated prompts)

are used to gather information on the who, what, how, why, and where of drug use. Analyses drawing on such rich data sets ultimately allow investigators to discern antecedents and consequences of drug use behavior (Paty, Kassel, & Shiffman, 1992). In addition to addressing between- and within-subject questions, EMA also moves these observations out of the laboratory and into the field, thus maximizing ecological validity.

Experience-sampling methodology does, however, also possess its own notable limitations. Not only is it expensive to implement, but it also requires constant vigilance on the part of investigators with regard to participant burden and potential measurement reactivity. Reactivity may interfere with or contaminate primary measures of interest (e.g., affect), although there is emerging evidence suggesting such reactivity is negligible (Shiffman & Stone, 1998).

In sum, methodological issues present daunting challenges for those interested in assessing affective influence on drug use and abuse. Clearly, cross-sectional (between-subjects) design and analyses have been used most often. As noted earlier, however, it is critical to resist the temptation to make causal inferences from such data. Laboratory studies and well-designed field studies (e.g., EMA) do lend themselves to within-subject analyses that hold the potential to reveal mechanisms governing drug–affect relationships. Yet each of these respective approaches also comes with inherent strengths and limitations. As such, researchers should ideally strive toward use of multimethod approaches in the effort to shed light on the processes governing the complex relationships between drug use and affect.

DOES AFFECT INFLUENCE DRUG USE?

One reliable and critical observation is that drug use disorders often co-occur in the context of other psychological problems, with higher comorbidity rates for drug use and externalizing disorders (i.e., antisocial personality disorder) relative to internalizing disorders such as mood and anxiety problems (Compton et al., 2007; Kessler, 2004). Nonetheless, overlap between internalizing disorders and drug use is not inconsequential; rates of depression and anxiety are significantly higher in drug users compared with national samples (e.g., Lasser et al., 2000).

Although a relationship between drug use and emotional disorders has clearly been established, researchers have thus far been unable to clearly identify the causal ordering of events: Are mental disorders, particularly depression and anxiety, risk factors for drug problems, or do drug problems cause later emotional problems?

Although the average age of onset of mental disorders is generally earlier than the typical age of onset for drug abuse (Kessler, 2004), epidemiological studies of successive comorbidity have yielded mixed results. Some studies have identified drug use as a precursor to later emotional or behavioral problems, with results indicating that drug use predicts the onset of mood disorders (Brook, Brook, Zhang, Loken, & Whiteman, 2002; van Laar, van Dorsselaer, Monshouwer, & de Graaf, 2007) and anxiety disorders (Kandel et al., 1997). However, more effort has focused on the opposite temporal relationship, that mental disorders predate, and purportedly predispose one to, drug problems. Kessler (2004) reviewed several longitudinal studies and found that in general, anxiety and depression predicted later drug use disorders, with marked variability observed in the predictive power of various disorders. For example, one study found that tobacco smoking predicted incidence of generalized anxiety disorder (GAD), dysthymia, and alcohol abuse among adults (Cuijpers, Smit, ten Have, & de Graaf, 2007). However, the same study found that participants with GAD and drug abuse were more likely to initiate smoking, leaving the temporal relationship unclear or suggesting a bidirectional relationship. Although PA has generally received short shrift in the field of drug use, Wills, Sandy, Shinar, and Yaeger (1999) found that low levels of PA were prospectively associated with high levels of adolescent drug use. Furthermore, Colder and Chassin (1997) similarly found that low PA was associated with adolescent alcohol use, but this relation was only true for adolescents characterized by high levels of impulsivity.

The scenario is further complicated (or conversely, perhaps clarified) by considering the impact of moderating factors. For example, a number of studies have found that the relationship between depression–anxiety and drug use–abuse is stronger for girls than for boys (Federman, Costello, Angold, Farmer, &

Erkanli, 1997; Patton et al., 1998), that mental disorders predict alcohol use for American Indian youth but not White youth (Federman et al., 1997), and that depression and anxiety do not predict amphetamine use (Degenhardt, Coffey, Carlin, Moran, & Patton, 2007). In the tobacco supplement to the National Comorbidity Survey, Breslau, Novak, and Kessler (2004) found that a variety of active but not remitted mental disorders predicted progression from experimentation to daily smoking and from daily smoking to dependence.

With respect to the specific influence of stress on drug use initiation, numerous studies have found associations between various indices of psychological stress and cigarette smoking uptake. Childhood abuse and household dysfunction (Felitti et al., 1998), adverse childhood experiences (Anda et al., 1999), parental divorce (Patton et al., 1998), negative life events (Koval & Pederson, 1999), acute and chronic stressors (Koval, Pederson, Mills, McGrady, & Carvajal, 2000), and perceived stress (Dugan, Lloyd, & Lucas, 1999) have been found to increase the risk of smoking initiation. Byrne and Mazanov (1999) reported that the impact of different types of stressors on smoking uptake varied by gender, such that overall relationships were generally stronger for girls, particularly with respect to family-related stress and smoking. More important, affective distress and negative life events also appear to predict transition from experimental to regular smoking (Hirschman, Leventhal, & Glynn, 1984; Orlando, Ellickson, & Jinnett, 2001).

Clearly, the field has yet to reach consensus on the "typical" temporal relationship between mental disorders and drug use disorders, if a typical relationship even exists. Methodological differences may account for some of the variability because many epidemiological studies have failed to control for risk factors common to both drug use and mental disorders and for the comorbidities among mental disorders (Kessler, 2004). Moreover, the qualitative nature of the developmental period itself (e.g., adolescence vs. adulthood) may serve to moderate the relationship between manifestations of affect and drug use. More recent epidemiological studies have begun to differentiate drug use and dependence because there is reason to believe that dependence is associated with greater disability than is abuse (Compton et al, 2007). Moreover, several recent studies using the National Epidemiologic Survey on Alcohol and Related Conditions from 2001 to 2002 have examined comorbidities among drug use and mental disorders after controlling for other psychiatric comorbidities and sociodemographic factors (Compton et al., 2007; Hasin et al., 2007). Results have suggested that although drug abuse was initially associated with a variety of mood, anxiety, and personality disorders, after controlling for psychiatric comorbidity, the only associations observed were between drug abuse and other drug problems and antisocial personality disorder. Drug dependence, however, was still associated with GAD, all mood disorders except bipolar II, and antisocial personality disorder (Compton et al., 2007). Similarly, after controlling for psychiatric comorbidities, alcohol abuse was related only to other drug use disorders, whereas alcohol dependence was also associated with bipolar disorders. Lifetime dependence was still associated with the full range of mood and anxiety disorders (Hasin et al., 2007). These promising new results suggest that future epidemiologic studies hold the potential to disentangle the antecedents and consequences of drug use and will, it is hoped, delineate the temporal relationship between mental disorders and drug problems.

In sum, burgeoning evidence points to robust associations between various manifestations of emotional distress and drug use. At the same time, many questions remain unanswered regarding the mechanisms underlying such relationships. As already briefly noted, moderator variables (e.g., sex), different psychological disorders (e.g., GAD vs. depression), and different drugs (e.g., tobacco smoking vs. alcohol use) all bear on the nature of these relationships. As such, more research is clearly needed to more carefully unpack and understand drug–affect associations. Moreover, we must resist the temptation to draw premature causal interpretations in the absence of data that truly support such conclusions.

DOES AFFECT GENUINELY PROMPT DRUG USE IN THE MOMENT?

To review what has been discussed so far, in order to truly discern whether a given affective state cues drug use at the level of an individual, one would need to draw on controlled laboratory studies (in which the participant is given the opportunity to self-administer a drug) or some type of controlled field study (e.g., EMA) in which affect and drug use can be assessed in real time in the individual's natural environment. Simply put, there is a dearth of research using either approach with adolescents. Nonetheless, several studies have yielded findings that are relevant to this important area of research inquiry.

Mermelstein and colleagues (Mermelstein, Flay, Hedeker, & Shiffman, 2003; Mermelstein, Hedeker, Flay, & Shiffman, 2003; Turner, Mermelstein, & Flay, 2004) have been one of the few research groups to use EMA in the study of adolescent drug use, specifically cigarette smoking. On the basis of assessment of young, very light smokers, their findings suggested that adolescents who remained cigarette experimenters (e.g., never progressed to daily smoking) reported feeling significantly less PA and heightened NA before smoking episodes compared with randomly sampled nonsmoking episodes. Interestingly, among those adolescents who did progress to heavier smoking, affective states preceding smoking episodes were comparable to those observed before nonsmoking episodes. Indeed, there was a tendency for the smoking episodes of these adolescents to be preceded by elevated PA. Similarly, EMA daily process studies of adolescents have also shown stronger daily covariation of negative mood and alcohol use among adolescents who also reported elevated rates of depressive symptoms, lower rates of conduct problems, and less effective socialization about emotion from their parents (Hersh & Hussong, 2007; Hussong, Feagans Gould, & Hersh, 2008).

One interesting study examined the role of affective variability rather than mean levels of affect per se as a predictor of subsequent smoking behavior over time (Weinstein, Mermelstein, Shiffman, & Flay, 2008). Using EMA methods, high levels of negative mood variability at baseline significantly differentiated adolescents who escalated in their smoking behavior over time from those who never progressed beyond low levels of experimentation during the course of the 12-month study. Also of note, mixed-effects regression models revealed that adolescents who escalated in their smoking experienced a reduction in mood variability as smoking increased, whereas mood variability levels were more stable among those with consistently high or low levels of cigarette use. These intriguing findings therefore suggest that high negative mood variability may be a risk factor for future smoking escalation, and mood-stabilizing effects may reinforce and maintain daily cigarette use among youth.

Finally, research on drug expectancies (as assessed via self-report questionnaires) has also suggested that affect is often viewed as a salient precipitant of drug use (see chap. 8 of this volume for an in-depth discussion of expectancy theory and research). Indeed, a burgeoning literature has indicated that adolescents hold the expectation that affect prompts drug use (e.g., "I smoke when feeling stressed or angry") and that a host of diverse drugs of abuse are perceived to assuage NA (e.g., alcohol [Newcomb, Chou, Bentler, & Huba, 1988], cigarettes [Lewis-Esquerre, Rodrigue, & Kahler, 2005], marijuana [Newcomb et al., 1988]). Furthermore, both short-term (Newcomb et al., 1988) and long-term (Stacy, Newcomb, & Bentler, 1991) longitudinal studies of alcohol use have suggested that many individuals possess expectancies that alcohol will facilitate NA regulation and that this belief actually predicts subsequent increased drinking frequencies (at 1-year and 9-year follow-ups, respectively). Investigations of the effects of expectancies on smoking (Wetter et al., 2004) and marijuana (Newcomb et al., 1988) use among adolescents have also found that affect regulation expectancies predict increased use and adverse outcomes.

DOES DRUG USE INFLUENCE AFFECT?

Although more research has historically focused on the influence of affect on drug use, accumulating studies of adolescents and young adults have also indicated that drugs of abuse (including alcohol and nicotine) have an impact on affect. Most of these studies use cross-sectional or longitudinal multimonth or multiyear designs to assess this effect. For example, longitudinal studies controlling for preexisting risk factors have reported a greater risk for anxiety disorders at age 22 for youth who smoked more than a pack of cigarettes a day at age 16 (Johnson et al., 2000) and greater depression in adolescents following

heavier alcohol use (Halfors, Waller, Bauer, Ford, & Halpern, 2005).

Notably, Trim, Meehan, King, and Chassin (2006) examined the impact of adolescent drug use on young adult internalizing symptoms. Recognizing the large risk matrix often associated with adolescent drug use, these authors tested whether drug use was simply a marker of a broader spectrum of risk factors affecting subsequent internalizing or whether a more direct relation between the two was plausible. Several factors may account for a direct long-term relation between drug use behaviors and subsequent internalizing symptoms, including the interference of drug use in the development of healthy competencies (e.g., coping, self-regulation) necessary for subsequent adjustment, the ensnaring effect of secondary stressors resulting from drug use (e.g., long-term health, educational, occupational, or legal problems), and the detrimental effects of drinking (and other drugs) on adolescent brain development (a period of heightened activation for hormonal and neuroendocrine changes). Trim et al. (2006) found that adolescents more involved in drug use at age 13 reported higher levels of internalizing symptoms in young adulthood (ages 18–22), even after controlling for shared risk factors associated with both adolescent internalizing symptoms and drug use. Moreover, these effects were maintained after controlling for young adult drug use. Thus, early drug use influenced young adult internalizing symptoms beyond its ability to serve as a marker for other risk factors or of continuity in drug use into young adulthood.

The long-term developmental processes linking drug use and affect suggested by these findings likely occur in tandem with the more short-term regulatory processes that are the focus of EMA and other daily assessment studies. For example, Henker, Whalen, Jamner, and Delfino (2002) used an EMA paradigm to show that aggregated indices of daily negative mood were associated with greater tobacco use. Specifically, moderately and highly anxious teenagers reported stronger urges to smoke and more frequent instances of smoking than did teenagers low in daily reported anxiety. Although these daily associations reflect cross-sectional associations, the short-term prospective association of drinking with negative mood was also evident in a sample of adolescents assessed the summer before high school. In this study, adolescents with more conduct problems reported greater negative mood on days after drinking in a 21-day experience-sampling protocol as compared with adolescents reporting fewer conduct problems (Hussong et al., 2008). Although still relatively novel, such studies indicate that daily assessment data have much to offer the study of drug use–affect relations in adolescents.

More is known about the short-term impact of drug use on affect in college students and adults. For example, Hussong, Hicks, Levy, and Curran (2001) examined the impact of drinking on four types of negative emotion (i.e., fear, sadness, guilt, hostility) as a function of when in the week drinking occurred (i.e., the weekend vs. weekday) and the drinker's sex. They showed that college students who participated in a 28-day experience-sampling study were more likely to report guilt during the week if they drank more heavily the weekend before. Weekend drinking was also more likely to increase weekday hostility in students whose best friendship was less intimate and supportive, whereas both weekend and weekday drinking increased risk for subsequent sadness in students with less supportive friendships. No effects were found for the impact of drinking on subsequent fear. Effects of smoking on subsequent negative mood were also reported in an experience-sampling study of adults ages 18 to 42 that showed that smoking was followed by decreased anger in men and women and by decreased sadness in men (Delfino, Jamner, & Whalen, 2001).

The accumulating findings from experience-sampling methodology studies thus support prospective effects of drug use on affect within a natural context. However, by manipulating drug use involvement through prevention programs, intervention studies provide a more stringent test of the effect of drug use on affect. Initial findings from the Parenting in the Drug Free Years prevention program for families have provided some support for an effect of drug use on affective functioning (Mason et al., 2007). Specifically, parents of children ages 8 to 14 participated in a multimedia skills training program administered in five 2-hr sessions. These sessions focused on strengthening parenting skills and parent–child interaction skills. The intervention showed an indirect effect on depressive symptoms over time through its impact on reducing the typically noted increases in polydrug use over adolescence. Compared with families from control schools assigned using a random block design, experimentally treated youth showed slower increases in polydrug use over time, which in turn predicted reduced growth in depression symptoms from the time of program completion to 12th grade.

Whereas there is little research in the way of controlled laboratory studies of drug–affect associations in adolescents (for obvious ethical and legal reasons), Kassel et al. (2007) recently tested the acute effects of nicotine on PA and NA in a group of 15- to 18-year-olds. A matched group of nonsmokers served as a comparison group. Findings revealed that whereas adolescents who smoked a cigarette experienced reductions in both PA and NA, the observed reductions in NA were moderated by nicotine content of the cigarette (high yield vs. denicotinized), level of nicotine dependence, level of baseline craving, and smoking expectancies pertinent to NA regulation. Nonsmokers experienced no change in affect over the 10-minute assessment period, and no interaction effects were observed for PA. Hence, these findings conformed to a negative reinforcement model of nicotine effects and strongly suggest that even among young, light smokers, nicotine dependence and resultant withdrawal symptomatology may serve as motivating factors governing smoking behavior. More important (and harkening back to our earlier discussion of the importance of understanding the theoretical base of affective constructs), Kassel et al. noted that PA, as measured by the Positive and Negative Affect Schedule (Watson, Clark, & Tellegen, 1988) contains only high-activation (arousing) items with positive valence (Watson et al., 1988). Therefore, the reduction in PA observed in this study among those who smoked either cigarette may, in fact, have reflected an increase in low-arousal aspects of PA (e.g., relaxation, calm). Such an interpretation would certainly be consistent with a wealth of self-report data suggesting that adolescent smokers find smoking relaxing (Dozois, Farrow, & Miser, 1995; McNeill, Jarvis, & West, 1987).

Other laboratory-based studies of adult samples have identified potentially important pharmacological effects of alcohol and other drugs on affect (for a review, see Sher & Grekin, 2006) and salient moderators of the relation between alcohol or drug use and affect. Notably, gender differences may qualify this relationship. Several studies of young adults have shown a stronger cross-sectional association between stress–negative mood and drinking in men than in women (Cooper, Russell, Skinner, Frone, & Mudar, 1992). In addition, drinking appears to increase risk for subsequent negative mood more strongly in men than in women (Hussong et al., 2001). Additional moderating factors identified in studies of adults and college students include dose, expectancies about the pharmacological effects of alcohol, the use of multiple drugs together, and individual differences resulting from such influences as metabolic and pharmacodynamic factors, family history and genetic variation, personality traits, and cognitive functioning (Sher & Grekin, 2006).

As MacAndrew and Edgerton (1969) pointed out a long time ago, social context matters. For example, in an experience-sampling study of heavy and social drinking adults, Armeli et al. (2003) found more consistent effects of alcohol on reducing negative mood and increasing positive mood when drinking occurred with others than when drinking occurred alone. Moreover, the stress response–dampening effects of alcohol (or the extent to which alcohol serves to reduce the negative affect related to the anticipation of stressors) were only evident for drinking that occurred in the presence of others. In contrast, drinking alone actually predicted increases in nervousness on days when negative daily events were greater. These findings are consistent with the larger literature that has generally shown solitary as opposed to group drinking in adults promotes sedation and dysphoria (Sher & Grekin, 2006).

Expanding the contexts relevant to drinking–affect relations, Hussong et al. (2001) found a moderating effect of friendship quality. Specifically, college students in friendships that were less supportive and intimate reported greater hostility and sadness following drinking than did students in more supportive and intimate friendships. These findings suggest that young adults with access to social supports may have other coping resources on which to draw that decrease the risk

for negative affect subsequent to drinking. The extent to which these findings regarding social context and other moderating influences on drinking–affect relations extend to adolescents, however, is unclear.

One moderating factor that has emerged in studies of adolescents is impulsivity and other markers of behavioral disinhibition. However, pertinent findings differ as a function of study design. For example, cross-sectional analyses have shown impulsivity to strengthen the positive association between depression and alcohol use in mid-adolescence (Hussong & Chassin, 1994; Whalen, Jamner, Henker, & Delfino, 2001). More methodologically rigorous longitudinal surveys and experience-sampling studies have suggested that negative affect is a stronger predictor of alcohol use among youth with fewer conduct or inhibitory control problems (Hussong et al., 2008; Pardini, Lochman, & Wells, 2004). These findings have particular import for identifying those individuals vulnerable to the negative effects of drug use on affective functioning.

In addition to suggesting potentially salient moderators, preliminary findings have suggested specificity in the forms of affect most readily influenced by alcohol, tobacco, and other drug use. As noted earlier, in an experience-sampling study of adults, Armeli et al. (2003) found that drinking served to reduce self-reported anger (when drinking with others) and nervousness (when drinking both alone or with others) but not sadness. A similar pattern of findings emerged in an experience-sampling study of college students (Hussong et al., 2001). These findings suggest a temporal ordering in the types of NA that precede versus follow from alcohol use. However, the potentially different contributions of alcohol, tobacco, and other drug use to varying types of NA remain understudied.

There is also evidence for genetic vulnerability to the development of drug use disorders that corresponds to the question of whether and/or how drug use influences affective response. One mechanism that has been proposed is a genetic predisposition toward behavioral disinhibition and emotional dysregulation (Tarter, Kirisci, Habeych, Reynolds, & Vanyukov, 2004). Findings have supported this as a potential mechanism underlying genetic vulnerability to the development of drug use problems (McGue,

Iacono, Legrand, & Elkins, 2001; Mustanski, Viken, Kaprio, & Rose, 2003). More important, it has also been proposed that individuals who possess genetic vulnerability to the development of drug use disorders may differ from others in their sensitivity to the pharmacological effects of drug usage (e.g., Pomerleau, Collins, Shiffman, & Pomerleau, 1993; Schuckit, Li, Cloninger, & Dietrich, 1985). Hence, an implication of this idea is that there may be individuals who are more innately sensitive to the affect-inducing or affect-assuaging (e.g., anxiolytic) effects of drugs.

Individuals who are genetically predisposed to drug use problems also appear to manifest altered autonomic activity in response to stressors and differ from non–genetically predisposed individuals in their sensitivity to the acute effects of drug use (for a review, see Newlin & Thomson, 1997). Some studies have suggested that children and adolescents from families with a history of drug misuse demonstrate hyperactivity following a stressor (Harden & Pihl, 1995), whereas other studies have indicated that these children and adolescents demonstrate autonomic hyporeactivity following a stressor (Taylor, Carlson, Iacono, Lykken, & McGue, 1999). One consistent and compelling finding is that alcohol consumption has a greater stress-dampening effect in individuals with a family history of drug use disorders relative to individuals without a similar history (Levenson, Oyama, & Meek, 1987; Zimmerman et al., 2004). That is, genetically predisposed individuals' ingestion of alcohol reduces their autonomic stress response following an aversive stimulus to a greater degree than is observed in non–genetically predisposed individuals. Genetically predisposed people may be more sensitive to the pharmacologically reinforcing qualities of drug use and therefore be more inclined to use these drugs heavily relative to non–genetically predisposed people (Newlin & Thomson, 1997). Consistent with this hypothesis, there is evidence that individuals with a family history of drug use problems are also more sensitive to the stimulating properties of alcohol consumption than are individuals without a similar history (Conrod, Peterson, Pihl, & Mankowski, 1997; Erblich, Earleywine, Erblich, & Bovbjerg, 2003).

Finally, interesting work is emerging implicating the period of development itself as a potential moderating variable of drug use–affect relationships. For instance, Varlinskaya and Spear (2006) found that older adolescent female rats evidenced greater sensitivity to the anxiolytic benefits of alcohol as compared with males and younger adolescent females. Correspondingly, research has suggested that behavioral responsivity to nicotine may change from adolescence to adulthood (Faraday, Elliott, & Grunberg, 2001). More specifically, adolescent male rats were more sensitive than adults or adolescent females to nicotine's activity-enhancing effects. Physiological sensitivities to drugs like alcohol and nicotine, then, appear to vary as a function of sex and developmental maturity in important ways, suggesting that these factors warrant further empirical scrutiny in human studies of drug–affect relationships.

In sum, research regarding the nature of drug effects on affective responses is still in its earliest stages. The best prospective studies have pointed to meaningful and reliable associations between various indices of affective distress and subsequent drug use. At the same time, much more work is clearly needed to better understand the precise nature of these observed relationships.

FINAL THOUGHTS

Our primary intention in this chapter was to provide an overview of issues pertinent to understanding the admittedly complex question of whether, and/or how, affect influences the etiology of drug use. Toward this end, we emphasized a number of what we believe are particularly important conceptual and methodological considerations. First, clarification of precisely what is meant by *affect* is viewed as imperative to researchers aspiring to address drug use–affect relationships. Hence, distinctions between emotion, mood, and more traitlike manifestations of affect (e.g., neuroticism) must be clearly specified a priori.

Correspondingly, acknowledging the theoretical framework of affect in which the research is steeped is also critical. Simply put, atheoretical attempts at delineating drug use–affect associations are likely to result in misguided, and potentially confusing or misleading, outcomes. Indeed, it is also conceivable that some drugs exert differential effects on specific dimensions (or categories) of affect, but not on others.

In this respect, little research has systematically set out to examine the specificity of a given drug's effects on affect. As such, we would strongly encourage researchers to do just that: to assess, steeped in a particular model of affect (e.g., dimensional PA–NA model vs. a basic emotions model), the influence of a given drug on a variety of affective outcomes.

Conversely, clarifying one's definition of affect also profoundly influences questions of how and whether affect genuinely influences drug use, at both between- and within-person levels of analysis. For example, whereas some manifestations of anxiety (GAD) appear to promote alcohol use in adolescents, other variants of the same class of disorder (separation anxiety) may actually prove prophylactic (Kaplow, Curran, Angold, & Costello, 2001). Moreover, a number of well-designed prospective investigations have found that whereas anxiety disorders do not reliably predict the onset of cigarette smoking during adolescence (e.g., Costello, Erkanli, Federman, & Angold, 1999; Dierker, Avenevoli, Merikangas, Flaherty, & Stolar, 2001; Johnson et al., 2000) or adulthood (Johnson et al., 2000), they do predict the onset of nicotine dependence, even among teenagers (Dierker et al., 2001; Johnson et al., 2000). Such findings point to the importance of differentiating among stages of drug use when considering the role played by affect (see Kassel et al., 2003).

Second, as noted throughout this chapter, we believe it is important to recognize the difference between between- and within-person approaches to the study of drug–affect relationships. Too often, causal inferences are derived from cross-sectional or correlation-based data sets that simply do not lend themselves to such conclusions. Hence, the approach we took in examining this subject was to acknowledge and differentiate several distinct questions, the first of which is whether affect influences drug use. This can be asked in the context of a between-persons approach such that what we are really interested in assessing is the extent to which affect precedes, and perhaps predisposes one to, the initiation of drug use (hence, differentiating drug users from nonusers). The evidence in this regard, although certainly not overwhelming, appears to offer a qualified "yes," such that at least for some drugs (e.g., cigarette smoking), some manifestations of affective distress do increase the likelihood of initiation.

The second question that arises under the rubric of "Does affect influence drug use?" is whether, at a within-person level of analysis, affect cues or prompts drug use at a given moment in time. Given the ethical and legal constraints associated with adolescent drug administration, few studies have actually attempted to answer this question. Nonetheless, some intriguing studies have offered data that bear on this important issue. For example, it was observed that cigarette smoking (nicotine use) appears to decrease both NA and PA in adolescent smokers (Kassel et al., 2007). Moreover, this same study also suggested that even among young, relatively light smokers, nicotine dependence may emerge at low levels and, as such, serve to motivate smoking. Again, acknowledging that research of this kind (i.e., drug administration studies) is difficult to conduct with adolescents, we would nevertheless still encourage investigators to meet these obstacles head on because behavioral pharmacology studies have much to offer by way of elucidating actual drug effects early on in the developmental process of drug use and abuse. By doing so, the field can then shed light on the affective mechanisms subserving drug use etiology.

Third, whereas this chapter focused predominantly on studies of alcohol and nicotine—simply because these drugs have received far more empirical scrutiny than have other, illicit drugs of abuse—the question ultimately arises as to whether effects observed with one drug are applicable to other drugs. Implicit assumptions made by many researchers (including us) seem to convey that what holds for one drug likely holds for others. And, of course, in the end this may prove to simply not be true. As such, drug-specific research is encouraged to determine the similarities and differences among drugs of abuse and the respective role played by affective influences in each. Indeed, we strongly encourage more collaborative effort and cross-talk among those in different drug "camps" because such conversations hold great potential to reveal both commonalities and differences in etiological processes across diverse drugs of abuse.

Fourth, we observed that methodological differences may ultimately account for some of the contrasting findings on drug use–affect relationships. Thus, findings that support an association between drug use and some affective variable at the cross-sectional level of analysis, but fail to replicate within the context of a longitudinal design, speak to this issue. Correspondingly, and as noted throughout this chapter, there are numerous potential moderator variables that may also play critical roles in drug–affect associations. Acknowledgment and identification of such moderators may ultimately help to clarify what have otherwise been difficult-to-reconcile findings.

In the end, it can be argued that the relationship between drug use and affective precipitants and responses are important solely because drug users tell us they are important. Indeed, as we observed at this chapter's outset, the affective payoffs afforded by drugs may be the prepotent motivating factor for drug use. However, the charge of delineating the precise nature of this affective payoff, the behavioral and neurophysiological processes that subserve it, and the conditions under which it is experienced is a critically important charge that presents daunting challenges to researchers—particularly in the context of better understanding affective influences in the etiology of drug use. Hence, as is often the case in the realm of behavioral research, whereas the questions may appear simple—Does affect influence drug use? and Does drug use influence affect?—the answers are not. Only through thoughtful and theoretically guided research and sound methodologies can we begin to unravel the processes governing this most complex and destructive of behaviors.

References

Anda, R. F., Croft, J. B., Felitti, V. J., Nordenberg, D., Giles, W. H., Williamson, D. F., & Giovino, G. A. (1999, November 3). Adverse childhood experiences and smoking during adolescence and adulthood. *JAMA, 282,* 1652–1658.

Armeli, S., Tennen, H., Todd, M., Carney, M. A., Mohr, C., Affleck, G., & Hromi, A. (2003). A daily process examination of the stress-response dampening effects of alcohol consumption. *Psychology of Addictive Behaviors, 17,* 260–276.

Arnett, J. J. (1999). Adolescent storm and stress, reconsidered. *American Psychologist, 54,* 317–326.

Baker, T. B., Piper, M. E., McCarthy, D. E., Majeskie, M. R., & Fiore, M. C. (2004). Addiction motivation reformulated: An affective processing model of negative reinforcement. *Psychological Review, 111,* 33–51.

Breslau, N., Novak, S. P., & Kessler, R. C. (2004). Psychiatric disorders and stages of smoking. *Biological Psychiatry, 55,* 69–76.

Brook, D. W., Brook, J. S., Zhang, C., Cohen, P., & Whiteman, M. (2002). Drug use and the risk of major depressive disorder, alcohol dependence, and substance use disorders. *Archives of General Psychiatry, 59,* 1039–1044.

Brown, R. A., Lewinsohn, P. M., Seeley, J. R., & Wagner, E. F. (1996). Cigarette smoking, major depression, and other psychiatric disorders among adolescents. *Journal of the American Academy of Child & Adolescent Psychiatry, 35,* 1602–1610.

Burton, E., Stice, E., Bearman, S. K., & Rohde, P. (2007). Experimental test of the affect-regulation theory of bulimic symptoms and substance use: A randomized trial. *International Journal of Eating Disorders, 40,* 27–36.

Byrne, D. G., & Mazanov, J. (1999). Sources of adolescent stress, smoking, and the use of other drugs. *Stress Medicine, 15,* 215–227.

Carstensen, L., Pasupathi, M., Mayr, U., & Nesselroade, J. (2000). Emotional experience in everyday life across the adult life span. *Journal of Personality and Social Psychology, 79,* 644–655.

Chassin, L., Pillow, D. R., Curran, P. J., Molina, B. S. G., & Barrera, M., Jr. (1993). Relation of parental alcoholism to early adolescent substance use: A test of three mediating mechanisms. *Journal of Abnormal Psychology, 102,* 3–19.

Cicchetti, D., & Rogosch, F. A. (2002). A developmental psychopathology perspective on adolescence. *Journal of Consulting and Clinical Psychology, 70,* 6–20.

Clore, G. L., & Ortony, A. (2000). Cognition in emotion: Always, sometimes, or never? In R. D. Lane & L. Nadal (Eds.), *Cognitive neuroscience of emotion* (pp. 24–61). New York: Oxford University Press.

Colder, C. R., & Chassin, L. (1997). Affectivity and impulsivity: Temperament risk for adolescent alcohol involvement. *Psychology of Addictive Behaviors, 11,* 83–97.

Compas, B. E., Hinden, B. R., & Gerhardt, C. A. (1995). Adolescent development: Pathways and processes of risk and resilience. *Annual Review of Psychology, 46,* 265–293.

Compton, W. M., Thomas, Y. F., Conway, K. P., & Colliver, J. D. (2005). Developments in the epidemiology of drug use and drug use disorders. *American Journal of Psychiatry, 162,* 1494–1502.

Compton, W. M., Thomas, Y. F., Stinson, F. S., & Grant, B. F. (2007). Prevalence, correlates, disability, and comorbidity of *DSM-IV* drug abuse and dependence in the United States. *Archives of General Psychiatry, 64,* 566–578.

Conger, J. J. (1956). Alcoholism: Theory, problem and challenge. II. Reinforcement theory and the dynamics of alcoholism. *Quarterly Journal of Studies on Alcohol, 13,* 260–276.

Conrod, P. J., Peterson, J. B., Pihl, R. O., & Mankowski, S. (1997). Biphasic effects of alcohol on heart rate are influenced by alcoholic family history and rate of alcohol ingestion. *Alcoholism: Clinical and Experimental Research, 21,* 140–149.

Cooper, M. L., Russell, M., Skinner, J. B., Frone, M. R., & Mudar, P. (1992). Stress and alcohol use: Moderating effects of gender, coping and alcohol expectancies. *Journal of Abnormal Psychology, 101,* 139–152.

Costello, E. J., Erkanli, A., Federman, E., & Angold, A. (1999). Development of psychiatric comorbidity with substance abuse in adolescents: Effects of timing and sex. *Journal of Clinical Child Psychology, 28,* 298–311.

Cuipers, P., Smit, F., ten Have, M., & de Graaf, R. (2007). Smoking is associated with first-ever incidence of mental disorders: A prospective population-based study. *Addiction, 102,* 1303–1309.

Crawford, A. M., Pentz, M. A., Chou, C., Li, C., & Dwyer, J. H. (2003). Parallel developmental trajectories of sensation-seeking and regular substance use in adolescents. *Psychology of Addictive Behaviors, 17,* 179–192.

Dawes, M. A., Antelman, S. M., Vanyukov, M. M., Giancola, P., Tarter, R. E., Susman, E. J., et al. (2000). Developmental sources of variation in liability to adolescent substance use disorders. *Drug and Alcohol Dependence, 61,* 3–14.

Degenhardt, L., Coffey, C., Carlin, J. B., Moran, P., & Patton, G. C. (2007). Who are the new amphetamine users? A 10-year prospective study of young Australians. *Addiction, 102,* 1269–1279.

Delfino, R. J., Jamner, L. D., & Whalen, C. K. (2001). Temporal analysis of the relationship of smoking behavior and urges to mood states in men versus women. *Nicotine and Tobacco Research, 3,* 235–248.

de Wit, H., & Phan, L. (2010). Positive reinforcement theories of drug use. In J. D. Kassel (Ed.), *Substance abuse and emotion* (43–60). Washington, DC: American Psychological Association.

Dierker, L. C., Avenevoli, S., Merikangas, K. R., Flaherty, B. P., & Stolar, M. (2001). Association between psychiatric disorders and the progression of tobacco use behaviors. *Journal of the American Academy of Child & Adolescent Psychiatry, 40,* 1159–1167.

Dozois, D. N., Farrow, J. A., & Miser, A. (1995). Smoking patterns and cessation motivations during adolescence. *International Journal of the Addictions, 30,* 1485–1498.

Dugan, S., Lloyd, B., & Lucas, K. (1999). Stress and coping as determinants of adolescent smoking behavior. *Journal of Applied Social Psychology, 29,* 870–888.

Ekman, P. (1992). An argument for basic emotions. *Cognition & Emotion, 6,* 169–200.

Ekman, P. (1999). Basic emotions. In T. Dalgleish & M. J. Power (Eds.), *Handbook of cognition and emotion* (pp. 45–60). New York: Wiley.

Erblich, J., Earleywine, M., Erblich, B., & Bovbjerg, D. H. (2003). Biphasic stimulant and sedative effects of ethanol: Are children of alcoholics really different? *Addictive Behaviors, 28,* 1129–1139.

Falk, J. L., Schuster, C. R., Bigelow, G. E., & Woods, J. H. (1982). Progress and needs in the experimental analysis of drug and alcohol dependence. *American Psychologist, 37,* 1124–1127.

Faraday, M. M., Elliott, B. M., & Grunberg, N. E. (2001). Adult vs. adolescent rats differ in biobehavioral responses to chronic nicotine administration. *Pharmacology Biochemistry and Behavior, 70,* 475–489.

Federman, E. B., Costello, E. J., Angold, A., Farmer, E. M. Z., & Erkanli, A. (1997). Development of substance use and psychiatric comorbidity in an epidemiologic study of white and American Indian young adolescents: The Great Smoky Mountains Study. *Drug and Alcohol Dependence, 44,* 69–78.

Feldman Barrett, L., & Russell, J. A. (1998). Independence and bipolarity in the structure of current affect. *Journal of Personality and Social Psychology, 74,* 967–984.

Felitti, V. J., Anda, R. F., Nordenberg, D., Williamson, D. F., Spitz, A. M., Edwards, V., et al. (1998). Relationship of childhood abuse and household dysfunction to many of the leading causes of death in adults: The Adverse Childhood Experiences (ACE) Study. *American Journal of Preventive Medicine, 14,* 245–258.

Forgas, J. P. (1995). Mood and judgment: The affect infusion model (AIM). *Psychological Bulletin, 117,* 39–66.

Garber, J., Keiley, M. K., & Martin, N. C. (2002). Developmental trajectories of adolescents' depressive symptoms: Predictors of change. *Journal of Consulting and Clinical Psychology, 70,* 79–95.

Green, D. P., Salovey, P., & Truax, K. M. (1999). Static, dynamic, and causative bipolarity of affect. *Journal of Personality and Social Psychology, 76,* 856–867.

Hall, G. S. (1904). *Adolescence: Its psychology and its relation to physiology, anthropology, sociology, sex, crime, religion, and education.* Englewood Cliffs, NJ: Prentice Hall.

Hallfors, D. D., Waller, M. W., Bauer, D., Ford, C. A., & Halpern, C. T. (2005). Which comes first in adolescence—Sex and drugs or depression? *American Journal of Preventive Medicine, 29,* 163–170.

Harden, P. W., & Pihl, R. O. (1995). Cognitive function, cardiovascular reactivity, and behavior in boys at high risk for alcoholism. *Journal of Abnormal Psychology, 104*, 94–103.

Hasin, D. S., Stinson, F. S., Ogburn, E., & Grant, B. F. (2007). Prevalence, correlates, disability, and co-morbidity of *DSM-IV* alcohol abuse and dependence in the United States. *Archives of General Psychiatry, 64*, 830–842.

Henker, B., Whalen, C. K., Jamner, L. D., & Delfino, R. J. (2002). Anxiety, affect, and activity in teenagers: Monitoring daily life with electronic diaries. *Journal of the Academy of Child & Adolescent Psychiatry, 41*, 660–670.

Hersh, M. A., & Hussong, A. M. (2007, April). *The influence of parental emotion socialization on adolescent self-medication.* Poster presented at the biennial meeting of the Society for Research in Child Development, Boston.

Hu, M. C., Davies, M., & Kandel, D. B. (2006). Epidemiology and correlates of daily smoking and nicotine dependence among young adults in the United States. *American Journal of Public Health, 96*, 299–308.

Hirschman, R. S., Leventhal, H., & Glynn, K. (1984). The development of smoking behavior: Conceptualization and supportive cross-sectional survey data. *Journal of Applied Social Psychology, 14*, 184–206.

Hussong, A. M., & Chassin, L. A. (1994). The stress-negative affect model of adolescent alcohol use: Disaggregating negative affect. *Journal of Studies on Alcohol, 55*, 707–718.

Hussong, A. M., Feagans Gould, L., & Hersh, M. A. (2008). Conduct problems moderate self-medication and mood-related drinking consequences in adolescents. *Journal of Studies on Alcohol and Drugs, 69*, 296–307.

Hussong, A. M., Hicks, R. E., Levy, S. A., & Curran, P. J. (2001). Specifying the relations between affect and heavy alcohol use among young adults. *Journal of Abnormal Psychology, 110*, 449–461.

Ichitani, Y., & Iwasaki, T. (1986). Approach and escape responses to mesencephalic central gray stimulation in rats: Effects of morphine and naloxone. *Behavioural Brain Research, 22*, 63–73.

Izard, C. E. (1992). Basic emotions, relations among emotions, and emotion–cognition relations. *Psychological Review, 99*, 561–565.

Jellinek, E. M. (1960). *The disease concept of alcoholism.* New Brunswick, NJ: Hillhouse Press.

Johnson, J. G., Cohen, P., Pine, D., Klein, D., Kasen, S., & Brook, J. (2000, November 8). Association between cigarette smoking and anxiety disorders during adolescence and early adulthood. *JAMA, 284*, 2348–2351.

Johnston, L. D., O'Malley, P. M., Bachman, J. G., & Schulenberg, J. E. (2007). *Monitoring the Future national results on adolescent drug use: Overview of key findings, 2006* (NIH Pub. No. 07-6202). Bethesda, MD: National Institute on Drug Abuse.

Kandel, D. B., Johnson, J. G., Bird, H. R., Canino, G., Goodman, S. H., Lahey, B. B., et al. (1997). Psychiatric disorders associated with substance use among children and adolescents: Findings from the methods for the epidemiology of child and adolescent mental disorders (MECA) study. *Journal of Abnormal Child Psychology, 25*, 121–132.

Kaplow, J. B., Curran, P. J., Angold, A., & Costello, E. J. (2001). The prospective relation between dimensions of anxiety and the initiation of adolescent alcohol use. *Journal of Clinical Child Psychology, 30*, 316–326.

Kassel, J. D., Evatt, D. P., Greenstein, J. E., Wardle, M. C., Yates, M. C., & Veilleux, J. C. (2007). The acute effects of nicotine on positive and negative affect in adolescent smokers. *Journal of Abnormal Psychology, 116*, 543–553.

Kassel, J. D., & Hankin, B. L. (2006). Smoking and depression. In A. Steptoe (Ed.), *Depression and physical illness* (pp. 321–346). Cambridge, England: Cambridge University Press.

Kassel, J. D., Stroud, L. R., & Paronis, C. A. (2003). Smoking, stress, and negative affect: Correlation, causation, and context across stages of smoking. *Psychological Bulletin, 129*, 270–304.

Kassel, J. D., Weinstein, S., Skitch, S. A., Veilleux, J., & Mermelstein, R. (2005). The development of substance abuse in adolescence. In B. L. Hankin & J. R. Abela (Eds.), *Development of psychopathology: A vulnerability–stress perspective* (pp. 355–384). Thousand Oaks, CA: Sage.

Kessler, R.C. (2004). The epidemiology of dual diagnosis. *Biological Psychiatry, 56*, 730–737.

Khantzian, E. J. (1997). The self-medication hypothesis of substance use disorders: A reconsideration and recent applications. *Harvard Review of Psychiatry, 4*, 231–244.

Koval, J. J., & Pederson, L. J. (1999). Stress-coping and other psychosocial risk factors: A model for smoking in grade 6 students. *Addictive Behaviors, 24*, 207–218.

Koval, J. J., Pederson, L. L., Mills, C. A., McGrady, G. A., & Carvajal, S. C. (2000). Models of the relationship of stress, depression, and other psychosocial factors to smoking behavior: A comparison of a cohort of students in grades 6 and 8. *Preventive Medicine, 30*, 463–477.

Lang, P. J., Bradley, M. M., & Cuthbert, B. N. (1992). A motivational analysis of emotion: Reflex–cortex connections. *Psychological Science, 3*, 44–49.

Larsen, R. J. (2000). Toward a science of mood regulation. *Psychological Inquiry, 11,* 129–141.

Larson, R. W., Moneta, G., Richards, M. H., & Wilson, S. (2002). Continuity, stability and change in daily emotional experience across adolescence. *Child Development, 73,* 1151–1165.

Lasser, K., Boyd, J. W., Woolhandler, S., Himmelstein, D. U., McCormick, D., & Bor, D. H. (2000, November 22). Smoking and mental illness: A population-based prevalence study. *JAMA, 284,* 2606–2610.

Lerner, J. S., & Keltner, D. (2000). Beyond valence: Toward a model of emotion-specific influences on judgement and choice. *Cognition & Emotion, 14,* 473–493.

Lerner, J. S., & Keltner, D. (2001). Fear, anger, and risk. *Journal of Personality and Social Psychology, 81,* 146–159.

Levenson, R. W., Oyama, O. N., & Meek, P. S. (1987). Greater reinforcement from alcohol for those at risk: Parental risk, personality risk, and gender. *Journal of Abnormal Psychology, 96,* 242–253.

Lewis, D. A. (1997). Development of the prefrontal cortex during adolescence: Insights into vulnerable neural circuits in schizophrenia. *Neuropsychopharmacology, 16,* 385–398.

Lewis-Esquerre, J. M., Rodrigue, J. R., & Kahler, C. W. (2005). Development and validation of an adolescent smoking consequences questionnaire. *Nicotine & Tobacco Research, 7,* 81–90.

MacAndrew, C., & Edgerton, B. (1969). *Drunken comportment: A social explanation.* Chicago: Aldine.

McAuliffe, W. E. (1982). A test of Wikler's theory of relapse: The frequency of relapse due to conditioned withdrawal sickness. *International Journal of the Addictions, 17,* 19–33.

McAuliffe, W. E., Rohman, M., Feldman, B., & Launer, E. K. (1985). The role of euphoric effects in the opiate addictions of heroin addicts, medical patients, and impaired health professionals. *Journal of Drug Issues, 15,* 203–224.

Mason, W. A., Kosterman, R., Hawkins, J. D., Haggerty, K. P., Spoth, R. L., & Redmond, C. (2007). Influence of a family-focused substance use preventive intervention on growth in adolescent depressive symptoms. *Journal of Research on Adolescence, 17,* 541–546.

McGue, M., Iacono, W. G., Legrand, L. N., & Elkins, I. (2001). Origins and consequences of age at first drink: II. Familial risk and heritability. *Alcoholism: Clinical & Experimental Research, 25,* 1166–1173.

McNeill, A. D., Jarvis, M., & West, R. (1987). Subjective effects of cigarette smoking in adolescents. *Psychopharmacology, 92,* 115–117.

Mermelstein, R., Flay, B., Hedeker, D., & Shiffman, S. (2003, March). *Adolescent tobacco use: Trajectories and mood.* Paper presented at the annual meeting of the Society for Behavioral Medicine, Salt Lake City, UT.

Mermelstein, R., Hedeker, D., Flay, B., & Shiffman, S. (2003, February). *Do changes in mood following smoking predict longitudinal changes in adolescent smoking patterns?* Paper presented at the annual meeting of the Society for Research on Nicotine and Tobacco, New Orleans, LA.

Morris, W. N. (2000). Some thoughts about mood and its regulation. *Psychological Inquiry, 11,* 200–202.

Mustanski, B. S., Viken, R. J., Kaprio, J., & Rose, R. J. (2003). Genetic influences on the association between personality risk factors and alcohol use and abuse. *Journal of Abnormal Psychology, 112,* 282–289.

Newcomb, M. D., Chou, C., Bentler, P. M., & Huba, G. J. (1988). Cognitive motivations for drug use among adolescents: Longitudinal tests of gender differences and predictors of change in drug use. *Journal of Counseling Psychology, 35,* 426–438.

Newlin, D. B., & Thomson, J. B. (1997). Alcohol challenge with sons of alcoholics: A critical review and analysis. In A. G. Marlatt & G. R. VandenBos (Eds.), *Addictive behaviors: Readings on etiology, prevention, and treatment* (pp. 534–578). Washington, DC: American Psychological Association.

Orlando, M., Ellickson, P. L., & Jinnett, K. (2001). The temporal relationship between emotional distress and cigarette smoking during adolescence and young adulthood. *Journal of Consulting and Clinical Psychology, 69,* 959–970.

Ortony, A., & Turner, T. J. (1990). What's basic about basic emotions? *Psychological Review, 97,* 315–331.

Panksepp, J. (2005). Affective consciousness: Core emotional feelings in animals and humans. *Consciousness and Cognition: An International Journal, 14,* 30–80.

Panksepp, J., Knutson, B., & Burgdorf, J. (2002). The role of brain emotional systems in addictions: A neuro-evolutionary perspective and new "self-report" animal model. *Addiction, 97,* 459–469.

Panksepp, J., Nocjar, C., Burgdorf, J., Panksepp, J. B., & Huber, R. (2004). The role of emotional systems in addiction: A neuroethological perspective. In R. A. Bevins & M. T. Bardo (Eds.), *Nebraska Symposium on Motivation: Vol. 50. Motivation factors in the etiology of drug abuse* (pp. 85–126). Lincoln: University of Nebraska.

Pardini, D., Lochman, J., & Wells, K. (2004). Negative emotions and alcohol use initiation in high-risk boys: The moderating effect of good inhibitory control. *Journal of Abnormal Child Psychology, 32,* 505–518.

Patton, G. C., Carlin, J. B., Coffey, C., Wolfe, R., Hibbert, M., & Bowes, G. (1998). Depression, anxiety, and smoking initiation: A prospective study over 3 years. *American Journal of Public Health, 88,* 1518–1522.

Paty, J., Kassel, J., & Shiffman, S. (1992). The importance of assessing base rates for clinical studies: An example of stimulus control of smoking. In M. deVries (Ed.), *The experience of psychopathology: Investigating mental disorders in their natural settings* (pp. 347–352). New York: Cambridge University Press.

Peele, S. (1985). *The meaning of addiction.* Lexington, MA: Lexington Books.

Pomerleau, O. F., Collins, A. C., Shiffman, S., & Pomerleau, C. S. (1993). Why some people smoke and others do not: New perspectives. *Journal of Consulting and Clinical Psychology, 61,* 723–731.

Reboussin, B. A., & Anthony, J. C. (2006). Is there epidemiological evidence to support the idea that a cocaine dependence syndrome emerges soon after onset of cocaine use? *Neuropsychopharmacology, 31,* 2055–2064.

Robinson, T. E., & Berridge, K. C. (1993). The neural basis of drug craving: An incentive-sensitization theory of addiction. *Brain Research Reviews, 18,* 247–291.

Robinson, T. E., & Berridge, K. C. (2003). Addiction. *Annual Review of Psychology, 54,* 10.1–10.29.

Russell, J. A. (2003). Core affect and the psychological construction of emotion. *Psychological Review, 110,* 145–172.

Sayette, M. A. (1993). An appraisal-disruption model of alcohol's effects on stress responses in social drinkers. *Psychological Bulletin, 114,* 459–476.

Sayette, M. A., Martin, C. S., Perrott, M. A., Wertz, J. M., & Hufford, M. R. (2001). A test of the appraisal-disruption model of alcohol and stress. *Journal of Studies on Alcohol, 62,* 247–256.

Scherer, K. R., Dan, E. S., & Flykt, A. (2006). What determines a feeling's position in affective space? A case for appraisal. *Cognition & Emotion, 20,* 92–113.

Schuckit, M. A., Li, T. K., Cloninger, C. R., & Dietrich, R. A. (1985). Genetics of alcoholism. *Alcoholism: Clinical and Experimental Research, 9,* 475–492.

Sher, K. J., & Grekin, E. R. (2006). Alcohol and affect regulation. In J. J. Gross (Ed.), *Handbook of emotion regulation* (pp. 560–580). New York: Guilford Press.

Sher, K. J., Grekin, E. R., & Williams, N. A. (2005). The development of alcohol use disorders. *Annual Review of Clinical Psychology, 1,* 493–523.

Shiffman, S., & Stone, A. A. (1998). Ecological momentary assessment: A new tool for behavioral medicine research. In D. S. Krantz & A. Baum (Eds.), *Technology and methods in behavioral medicine* (pp. 117–131). Mahwah, NJ: Erlbaum.

Siegel, S. (1983). Classical conditioning, drug tolerance, and drug dependence. In R. G. Smart, F. B. Glaser, Y. Israel, H. Kalant, R. E. Popham, & W. Schmidt (Eds.), *Research advances in alcohol and drug problems* (Vol. 7, pp. 202–246). New York: Plenum.

Simkin, D. R. (2002). Adolescent substance use disorders and comorbidity. *Pediatric Clinics of North America, 49,* 463–477.

Smith, C. A., & Ellsworth, P. C. (1985). Patterns of cognitive appraisal in emotion. *Journal of Personality and Social Psychology, 48,* 813–838.

Smith, C. A., & Lazarus, R. S. (1993). Appraisal components, core relational themes, and the emotions. *Cognition & Emotion, 7,* 233–269.

Solomon, R. L. (1977). An opponent-process theory of acquired motivation: The affective dynamics of addiction. In J. D. Maser & M. E. P. Seligman (Eds.), *Psychopathology: Experimental models* (pp. 66–103). San Francisco: W. H. Freeman.

Solomon, R. L., & Corbit, J. D. (1974). An opponent-process theory of motivation: I. Temporal dynamics of affect. *Psychological Review, 81,* 119–145.

Spear, L. P. (2002). Alcohol's effects on adolescents. *Alcohol Research & Health, 26,* 287–291.

Stacy, A. W., Newcomb, M. D., & Bentler, P. M. (1991). Cognitive motivation and drug use: A 9-year longitudinal study. *Journal of Abnormal Psychology, 100,* 502–515.

Steinberg, L., Dahl, R., Keating, D., Kupfer, D., Masten, A., & Pine, D. (2004). The study of developmental psychopathology in adolescence: Integrating affective neuroscience with the study of context. In D. Cicchetti (Ed.), *Handbook of developmental psychopathology* (pp. 2–46). New York: Wiley.

Stewart, J., de Wit, H., & Eikelboom, R. (1984). Role of unconditioned and conditioned drug effects in the self-administration of opiates and stimulants. *Psychological Review, 91,* 251–268.

Stewart, J., & Wise, R. A. (1992). Reinstatement of heroin self-administration habits: Morphine prompts and naltrexone discourages renewed responding after extinction. *Psychopharmacology, 108,* 79–84.

Stritzke, W. G., Lang, A. R., & Patrick, C. J. (1996). Beyond stress and arousal: A reconceptualization of alcohol–emotion relations with reference to psychophysiological methods. *Psychological Bulletin, 120,* 376–395.

Tarter, R. E., Kirisci, L., Habeych, M., Reynolds, M., & Vanyukov, M. (2004). Neurobehavior disinhibition in childhood predisposes boys to substance use disorder by young adulthood: Direct and mediated etiologic pathways. *Drug and Alcohol Dependence, 73,* 121–132.

Taylor, J., Carlson, S. R., Iacono, W. G., Lykken, D. T., & McGue, M. (1999). Individual differences in electrodermal responsivity to predictable aversive stimuli and substance dependence. *Psychophysiology, 36,* 193–198.

Tellegen, A., Watson, D., & Clark, L. A. (1999). On the dimensional and hierarchical structure of affect. *Psychological Science, 10,* 297–303.

Trim, R. S., Meehan, B. T., King, K. M., & Chassin, L. (2006). The relation between adolescent substance use and young adult internalizing symptoms: Findings from a high-risk longitudinal study. *Psychology of Addictive Behaviors, 21,* 97–107.

Turner, L., Mermelstein, R., & Flay, B. (2004). Individual and contextual influences on adolescent smoking. *Annals of the New York Academy of Sciences, 1021,* 175–197.

van Laar, M., van Dorsselaer, S., Monshouwer, K., & de Graaf, R. (2007). Does cannabis use predict the first incidence of mood and anxiety disorders in the adult population? *Addiction, 102,* 1251–1260.

Varlinskaya, E. I., & Spear, L. P. (2006). Differences in the social consequences of ethanol emerge during the course of adolescence in rats: Social facilitation, social inhibition, and anxiolysis. *Developmental Psychobiology, 48,* 146–161.

Watson, D., & Clark, L. A. (1997). Measurement and mismeasurement of mood: Recurrent and emergent issues. *Journal of Personality Assessment, 68,* 267–296.

Watson, D., Clark, L. A., & Tellegen, A. (1988). Development and validation of brief measures of positive and negative affect: The PANAS scales. *Journal of Personality and Social Psychology, 54,* 1063–1070.

Watson, D., Wiese, D., Vaidya, J., & Tellegen, A. (1999). The two general activation systems of affect: Structural findings, evolutionary considerations, and psychobiological evidence. *Journal of Personality and Social Psychology, 76,* 820–838.

Weinstein, S. M., Mermelstein, R., Shiffman, S., & Flay, B. (2008). Mood variability and cigarette smoking escalation among adolescents. *Psychology of Addictive Behaviors, 22,* 504–513.

Wetter, D. W., Kenford, S. L., Welsch, S. K., Smith, S. S, Fouladi, R. T., Fiore, M. C., & Baker, T. B. (2004). Prevalence and predictors of transitions in smoking behavior among college students. *Health Psychology, 23,* 168–177.

Whalen, C. K., Jamner, L. D., Henker, B., & Delfino, R. J. (2001). Smoking and moods in adolescents with depressive and aggressive dispositions: Evidence from surveys with electronic diaries. *Health Psychology, 20,* 99–111.

Wikler, A. (1980). *Opioid dependence: Mechanisms and treatment.* New York: Plenum.

Wills, T. A., Sandy, J. M., Shinar, O., & Yaeger, A. (1999). Contributions of positive and negative affect to adolescent substance use: Test of a bidimensional model in a longitudinal study. *Psychology of Addictive Behaviors, 13,* 327–338.

Wills, T. A., & Shiffman, S. (1985). Coping and substance use: A conceptual framework. In S. Shiffman & T. A. Wills (Eds.), *Coping and substance use* (pp. 3–24). New York: Academic Press.

Zimmerman, U., Spring, K., Kunz-Ebrecht, S. R., Uhr, M., Wittchen, H. U., & Holsboer, F. (2004). Effect of ethanol on hypothalamic-pituitary-adrenal system response to psychosocial stress in sons of alcohol-dependent fathers. *Neuropsychopharmacology, 29,* 1156–1165.

Zuckerman, M. (1994). *Behavioral expressions and biosocial bases of sensation seeking.* New York: Cambridge University Press.

PART IV

USE, ABUSE, AND LIABILITY

CHAPTER 11

NEURODEVELOPMENTAL LIABILITY FOR ADOLESCENT SUBSTANCE USE DISORDERS

Dawn L. Thatcher and Duncan B. Clark

This chapter presents a neurodevelopmental conceptualization of liability for substance use disorders (SUDs). The *Oxford English Dictionary* has defined *liability* as "apt or likely to do something" (Simpson & Weiner, 1989). In this context, we focus on research that has advanced our understanding of adolescents likely to grapple with clinically significant SUDs.

Traditionally, individuals liable to develop SUDs have been identified by family SUD history. By young adulthood, individuals at risk of SUDs have typically experienced substance-related problems (Thatcher & Clark, 2006). Because the effects of SUDs are difficult to distinguish from risk characteristics, the search for predictive, observable manifestations of risk must focus on childhood and early adolescence (Clark & Winters, 2002). Among individuals with positive family histories of SUD, furthermore, substantial variability in SUD outcomes has been observed. Attempts to characterize and understand the reasons for this variability, along with the insight that the effects of SUDs may obscure such attempts, have led to a substantial body of research examining the characteristics of children from these families (Tarter, Vanyukov, Giancola, Dawes, Blackson, Mezzich, et al., 1999).

The identification of individual characteristics in childhood and adolescence that predict SUDs has provided insights into the nature of SUD liability. As shown through observations of children of parents with alcoholism and children of parents with other SUDs, at-risk children have been observed to manifest specific mental disorders, including conduct disorder, attention-deficit/hyperactivity disorder, and disorders involving negative affect. The persistent manifestations of these psychopathological characteristics from childhood into adulthood have led to the conceptualization of these disorders as personality traits. Furthermore, the clustering of these disorders has suggested that these characteristics may make up a unitary dimension. Affective, behavioral, and cognitive difficulties during childhood and early adolescence have been found to coalesce into a dimension that may provide an important organizing concept for advancing our understanding of SUD liability. This dimension has been labeled *psychological dysregulation* (Clark & Winters, 2002), linking this conceptual framework to the neurodevelopmental literature.

The abilities involved in regulating the behavior and emotions that develop in adolescence may originate in structural brain changes, including the organization of connections among brain areas. Deficits or delays in the organization of these connections may result from heritable or environmental mechanisms. In any case, recent advances in neurophysiology and neuroimaging have made it possible to characterize previously unknown aspects of adolescent brain development. Neurodevelopmental endophenotypes relevant for understanding psychological dysregulation include the P300 neurophysiological response, white matter organization, and neural responses to

Preparation of this chapter was supported in part by National Institute on Drug Abuse Grant K01-DA-018698 and National Institute on Alcohol Abuse and Alcoholism Grants R21-AA-16272, K02-AA-00291, and R21-AA-017312.

laboratory tasks involving reward contingencies (Clark, Thatcher, & Tapert, 2008). Brain structures—including the prefrontal cortex, hippocampus, amygdala, and other components of the limbic system—are actively developing throughout adolescence and young adulthood (Chambers, Taylor, & Potenza, 2003; Spear, 2000). Deficits in these systems may represent critical risk factors for and presage the development of SUDs during adolescence (Clark, Thatcher, & Tapert, 2008). Advances in neuroimaging and genetics have thus provided valuable research tools for understanding vulnerabilities related to deficits in adolescent brain maturation.

Although heritable factors and neurodevelopmental vulnerabilities account for a substantial proportion of variance in SUDs, substance-related problems necessarily involve facilitative environmental conditions. Such environmental factors, including drug-taking opportunities, may particularly influence at-risk adolescents. In this chapter, we describe a conceptualization of SUD liability that incorporates observations on SUD heritability, psychological dysregulation, and neuroimaging research on the characteristics of at-risk children and adolescents and adults with SUDs. These three dimensions of liability are likely to exert their effects interactively in the context of a facilitative environment.

HERITABLE RISKS

Family history of a given disorder has traditionally been treated as a proxy measure for genetic vulnerability; this approach has value and even complements research on the human genome as regards SUDs. SUDs are thought to be transmitted from parent to child through genetic and environmental pathways and their interactions (Falconer, 1965; Hill, Shen, Lowers, & Locke, 2000; Sartor, Lynskey, Bucholz, et al., 2007). For example, children of parents with alcoholism are significantly more likely to develop alcohol use disorders than are children of parents without psychiatric disorders (Chassin, Pitts, & Frost, 2002; Schuckit & Smith, 1996; Sher, Walitzer, Wood, & Brent, 1991). More important, children of parents with SUDs also show features predictive of adolescent SUDs and tend to exhibit earlier alcohol and other substance initiation and involvement (Clark, Parker,

& Lynch, 1999). A large longitudinal study demonstrated that parent alcoholism significantly predicted SUD diagnoses in young adulthood (Chassin, Pitts, DeLucia, & Todd, 1999) after controlling for other parental psychopathology. In a sample including both high- and low-risk children, Tarter, Kirisci, Habeych, et al. (2004; Tarter, Kirisici, Reynolds, & Mezzich, 2004) reported parental SUD to be directly predictive of adolescent SUD. Despite this compelling research, it remains the case that only a proportion of individuals with a positive family history of SUDs eventually develop these disorders themselves. This has led to the necessary investigation of what is inherited in the context of apparently "heritable risks."

Clark, Cornelius, Kirisci, and Tarter (2005) demonstrated a "general liability typology" based on the variables of parental SUD, psychological dysregulation, and early tobacco and alcohol use in children before any significant substance use. Individuals in higher risk categories were more likely to exhibit any drug use and to be diagnosed with any drug-related disorder, regardless of the effects of specific substances or of modeling of specific drug-taking behavior. This study lends credence to the idea that when heritable risks influence SUDs, the primary factor that is inherited is not metabolic or even necessarily biological, but it is also not simply behavioral (modeling drug-taking behavior). Rather, it can be conceptualized as a general liability for childhood phenotype, common across all substances and present before the onset of any drug use.

Genomewide searches for possible genes reflecting vulnerability to the development of SUDs are ongoing (e.g., Hill et al., 2004; Stallings et al., 2005). Some of these genes may be common to SUDs and to associated antisocial disorders (Malone, Taylor, Marmorstein, McGue, & Iacono, 2004). Although the identification of relevant genes is of importance, it is also critical to consider the role of Gene × Environment interactions. In a classic adoption study, Cadoret, Yates, Troughton, Woodworth, and Stewart (1995) demonstrated both genetic and environmental factors associated with adolescent SUDs. A direct pathway from biological parent SUD to adolescent SUD was identified, as was an indirect pathway from biological parent antisocial personality disorder to child conduct problems and eventual antisocial personality disorder and SUD. Environmental factors in the adoptive family, including psychiatric conditions, predicted adolescent antisocial behavior in the adoptee, but not SUD.

In a Gene × Environment study of adolescent alcohol use and dependence, both the presence of the 5-HTTLPR s-allele and child maltreatment were found to be important predictors of early adolescent alcohol use (Kaufman et al., 2007). A significant Gene × Environment interaction was also observed. This interaction was not observed when the MAO-A gene was investigated (Young et al., 2006), although child maltreatment was replicated as a predictor of adolescent SUDs.

Studies of heritable risks for adolescent SUDs underscore the importance of continuing to search for relevant genes and genetic polymorphisms that play a role in the development of disorders, increasing our understanding of what the inherited phenotype actually is, and placing genetic findings in the appropriate environmental contexts. The Clark et al. (2005) study showed that common liabilities for substance use and related disorders can be established without regard to drug type, suggesting that these liabilities are not dependent on particular metabolic or any other unique aspect of that drug, but rather on the more behavioral aspects of psychological dysregulation.

PSYCHOLOGICAL DYSREGULATION AS PREDICTIVE PHENOTYPE

Adolescent SUDs are most often predicted by conduct problems, attention difficulties, and irritability during childhood (Chassin et al., 1999; Clark et al., 1997, 2005; Tapert & Schweinsburg, 2002). Children exhibiting these behaviors might be diagnosed with certain psychiatric disorders, including conduct disorder, attention-deficit/hyperactivity disorder, or major depressive disorder. For example, childhood conduct disorder is one of the most salient predictors of adolescent SUD (Bukstein, 2000; Clark, Bukstein, & Cornelius, 2002; Sartor, Lynskey, Heath, Jacob, & True, 2007). Empirical and theoretical evidence has suggested that these disorders overlap in a clinically significant way. For example, symptoms of alcohol dependence, conduct disorder, and major depressive disorder clustered together in a configural frequency

analysis (Clark, De Bellis, Lynch, Cornelius, & Martin, 2003). Similarly, two significantly correlated factors were identified in a similar analysis using continuous variables (Martin, Romig, & Kirisci, 2000). A Behavioral Undercontrol factor included conduct disorder symptoms, aggression, and decreased constraint, and a Negative Emotionality factor included depressive symptoms, anxiety, and distress reactivity. Recent theories have implicated these and other similar dimensions, which transcend diagnostic categorical structures in the common liability for adolescent SUDs (Tarter, Vanyukov, Giancola, Dawes, Blackson, Mezzich, & Clark, 1999).

Psychological dysregulation is a construct that encompasses the symptoms and dimensional psychopathological features that predict adolescent SUDs (Clark & Winters, 2002). Psychological regulation is purported to include cognitive, behavioral, and affective components. Behavioral regulation, one aspect of psychological regulation, is more generally defined as the ability to regulate behavior in the face of environmental challenges (Dawes et al., 2000) and involves the ability to modulate responses to optimize opportunities for reward in the environment. The cognitive component of psychological dysregulation includes executive cognitive functions (ECFs), higher order cognitive functions such as planning, organization, and cognitive inhibition that moderate emotional reactions and facilitate behavioral control. The efficiency of psychological dysregulation often depends on affective components. Hence, the components of psychological regulation are theoretically intertwined, and recent empirical studies have supported these hypothesized interrelationships.

Deficits or delays in the acquisition of any or all of the components may result in deficiencies in psychological dysregulation more generally. Psychological regulation skills continue to improve throughout childhood and adolescence. Therefore, developmental stage is an important consideration in determining the adequacy of psychological regulation in an individual.

An ongoing longitudinal study of children at high risk for the development of SUDs (Tarter et al., 2003) has operationally defined the construct of psychological dysregulation with a latent trait termed *neurobehavioral disinhibition* (ND). The ND latent trait was derived using a comprehensive measurement protocol and both conventional factor analytic and item response theory methods. Indicators of ECF, behavioral undercontrol, and affective dysregulation were used in this approach. ND has been shown to be a stable trait from late childhood through the adolescent developmental period (Mezzich, Tarter, et al., 2007; Tarter et al., 2003).

A series of recent studies have demonstrated that the ND construct, which is reflective of psychological dysregulation, discriminates boys with and without parental SUD and predicts early-onset adolescent SUDs (Chapman, Tarter, Kirisci, & Cornelius, 2007; Clark et al., 2005; Habeych, Charles, Sclabassi, Kirisci, & Tarter, 2005; Habeych, Sclabassi, Charles, Kirisci, & Tarter, 2005; Mezzich, Tarter, Kirisci, et al., 2007; Tarter et al., 2003) and related problems, including adolescent suicidality (Tarter, Kirisci, Reynolds, & Mezzich, 2004). With respect to the prediction of adolescent SUD, Tarter et al. (2003) found the odds ratio for ND (6.83) was more than twice that for frequency of substance use (3.19). Tarter, Kirisci, Habeych, et al. (2004) identified ND as the mediator of the direct relationship between parental SUD and adolescent SUD. A series of recent articles from the same ongoing study have identified a variety of possible mediators of these associations, including cognitive distortions regarding substance use (Kirisci, Tarter, Vanyukov, Reynolds, & Habeych, 2004), social maladjustment (Kirisci, Vanyukov, & Tarter, 2005), and approval of antisociality (Kirisci, Tarter, Mezzich, & Vanyukov, 2007).

Some evidence from ongoing studies suggests that ECF is of particular relevance in the development of adolescent SUDs (Giancola & Tarter, 1999; Nigg et al., 2006). Tapert, Baratta, Abrantes, and Brown (2002), in a study of 66 high-risk adolescents, found that both ECF and attention scores predicted substance use and SUDs 8 years later, after controlling for parental SUD, baseline adolescent substance use, and conduct disorder. Nigg et al. (2006) found similar prospective relations using response inhibition as the predictor of adolescent alcohol and substance use and after controlling for other relevant factors such as parental SUD, adolescent conduct symptoms, and IQ.

NEUROBIOLOGICAL ENDOPHENOTYPES

Adolescence has been described as the "critical period for addiction vulnerability" (Chambers et al., 2003, p. 1042), owing to the continuing development of the prefrontal cortex and associated cortical and subcortical monoaminergic systems. Chambers et al. (2003) concluded that the same neurocircuitry that allows for the transition to adult roles is also associated with increased vulnerability to addictive properties of drugs of abuse. Functional manifestations of psychological dysregulation—including ECF, behavioral control, and emotional regulation—have hypothesized substrates in the frontal cortex and frontal–subcortical connections. It is well established that these abilities improve substantially during the adolescent developmental period (Levin et al., 1991; Welsh, Pennington, & Groisser, 1991) in parallel with the ongoing biological development of the prefrontal cortex. For example, improvement of ECF skills during adolescence is thought to be related to the coincident development of frontal cortex (Happaney, Zelazo, & Stuss, 2004; Spear, 2000). Conversely, adolescents with behavioral problems related to psychological dysregulation have been found to also have frontal abnormalities (Rubia et al., 2000), especially decreased P300 amplitude (Habeych, Charles, et al., 2005; Habeych, Sclabassi, et al., 2005). Difficulties in the skills related to psychological regulation could thus be reflective of developmental delays or deficits in the neurobiological systems underlying these skills.

Endophenotypes are phenomena that are measurable but not directly observed and are correlated with both heritable factors and behavioral outcomes (Gottesman & Gould, 2003). Endophenotypes can thus be understood theoretically as mediators of the relationship between genotype and behavioral phenotypes or outcomes such as psychological dysregulation.

Reduced P300 Amplitude

Reduced P300 amplitude is one of the original phenomena conceived as an endophenotype in psychiatric research involving adolescent SUDs. Children at high risk for the development of SUDs, as defined by the presence of parental SUDs, show distinct patterns of P300 amplitude, including significantly lower amplitude during childhood and a smaller rate of change during adolescence (Hill et al., 2000). This finding seems to be particularly relevant for boys (Hill & Shen, 2002). Iacono, Malone, and McGue (2003) found that reduced P300 amplitude was associated with paternal psychiatric disorders and SUDs during young adulthood. P300 amplitude has been shown to directly predict SUDs at age 19 (Habeych, Charles, et al., 2005), but it was not a significant mediator between parental SUDs and adolescent ND (Habeych, Sclabassi, et al., 2005). The availability of modern neuroimaging techniques has led to the investigation of many other endophenotypes related to adolescent SUDs, including white matter development and neural responses to tasks involving varying reward contingencies.

White Matter Development

The advent of the diffusion tensor imaging (DTI) modality has facilitated the study of white matter development in normally developing and clinical populations. DTI measures the directionality of water molecules in the brain by applying a series of magnetic gradients in a minimum of six nonorthogonal directions, which results in maps of the brain indicating level of anisotropy, or directionality of water molecules in a given brain voxel or region. Hence, DTI is able to capitalize on the diffusive properties of water molecules in the brain and results in quantifiable indicators of white matter development. The most commonly studied indicators are fractional anisotropy (FA), apparent diffusion coefficient, mean diffusivity, and radial diffusivity.

FA, which measures water movement parallel to axons and is an indicator of directional coherence, is by far the most frequently reported index resulting from DTI. It is not clear why this is the case, considering that indices such as radial diffusivity, which measures water movement perpendicular to axons, may actually prove to be more relevant for certain research questions involving myelination of white matter tracts, for example.

Studies using DTI in normally developing populations have indicated that white matter organization, operationally defined by FA, continues to increase from early childhood through young adulthood (Barnea-Goraly et al., 2005). This increase is observed throughout the entire cortex, including the frontal, temporal, parietal, and occipital areas (Schneider, Il'yasov, Hennig, & Martin, 2004). The frontal cortex is of particular relevance because a large number of major structural changes are occurring in this region throughout adolescence. For example, gray matter pruning occurs in the prefrontal cortex during adolescence, resulting in an overall decrease in gray matter volume during this period (Gogtay et al., 2004; Lenroot & Giedd, 2006; Sowell, Thompson, Tessner, & Toga, 2001; Sowell et al., 2004). Conversely, white matter volumes increase during the adolescent developmental period, particularly in the prefrontal cortex (Ashtari et al., 2007; Barnea-Goraly et al., 2005; Lenroot & Giedd, 2006).

The corpus callosum, one of structures most thoroughly studied using DTI techniques, also exhibits increased white matter organization from childhood through adolescence and decreased organization associated with aging in late adulthood (McLaughlin et al., 2007). Conversely, Schneiderman et al. (2007) also demonstrated decreases in a number of cortical association structures such as the interior capsule posterior limb and superior longitudinal fasciculus, but decreases with age were not observed in the corpus callosum. Although there is some inconsistency among current developmental studies of white matter organization, there is agreement that white matter organization is a highly dynamic phenomenon throughout childhood and adolescence, and possibly into adulthood as well.

The relationship of white matter organization to various aspects of cognitive functioning has been the focus of several recent studies. Schmithorst, Wilke, Dardzinski, and Holland (2005) studied 47 normally developing children ages 5 to 18. FA was significantly positively associated with age within this sample, and FA in frontal and occipital–parietal association regions was significantly associated with full-scale IQ scores after controlling for age and gender. Mabbot, Noseworthy, Bouffet, Laughlin, and Rockel (2006), in a sample of 17 children and adolescents, found right frontal and parietal FA to be related to information-processing speed. Both FA and speed were found to increase from childhood to adolescence. Finally, FA in the frontal cortex was significantly correlated with two well-known measures of executive cognitive functioning, the Trail Making Test and the Stroop Color–Word Test, in a sample of children with prenatal cocaine exposure and controls (Warner et al., 2006).

Studies of children and adolescents at risk for the development of alcohol- and substance-related disorders provide insights into the possibility that deficits in white matter development could precede and predict adolescent SUDs as well as be caused by them. It could be that white matter structure and organization and related brain functions might affect the development of psychological regulation. Adolescents with disruptive behavior disorders exhibited lower FA in the frontal brain regions. Because alcohol use disorders (AUDs) and SUDs were not assessed in this study, these data have limited value in contributing to the model, although they serve as impetus for future research in this area.

Prenatal alcohol and other substance exposure is a recognized risk factor for adolescent alcohol- and substance-related disorders. For example, Day, Goldschmidt, and Thomas (2006) recently showed in a sample of 583 prospectively assessed mother–child pairs that prenatal marijuana exposure predicted adolescent marijuana use in the offspring at 14 years old, after controlling for salient factors such as family SUD and current alcohol and drug use. Studies of white matter development in children and adolescents with documented prenatal substance exposure have demonstrated deficits in white matter development in these children in brain areas important to the development of psychological regulation. For example, lower FA has been observed in several regions of the corpus callosum in individuals with fetal alcohol syndrome (Ma et al., 2005) and subclinical fetal alcohol spectrum disorders (Wozniak et al., 2006). In a study of 28 children with prenatal cocaine exposure and 25 children without exposure, white matter abnormalities were noted in left frontal callosal and right frontal projection fiber tracts (Warner et al., 2006).

White matter deficiencies in individuals with prenatal substance exposures may represent a risk for the development of psychological dysregulation and eventual SUDs. The study of individuals with AUDs or other SUDs with respect to these variables is also of importance, in that among individuals at risk who then begin consuming alcohol and other substances heavily, there are likely to be many interactive effects of psychological dysregulation and substance use, culminating in even poorer outcomes.

Among adults, AUD is associated with white matter loss as measured by conventional computed tomography (Carlen, Wortzman, Holgate, Wilkinson, & Rankin, 1978; Carlen et al., 1986), structural magnetic resonance imaging (MRI) (Agartz et al., 2003), and histology of postmortem specimens (Krill, Halliday, Svoboda, & Cartwright, 1997). There is growing evidence that these losses may be reversible. For example, Shear, Jernigan, and Butters (1994) demonstrated that increases in white matter volume and decreases in cerebrospinal fluid volume were related to abstinence from alcohol.

Adolescents with AUDs have been found to have smaller hippocampi (DeBellis et al., 2000) and prefrontal white matter volume (DeBellis et al., 2005). DeBellis et al. (2005) compared 14 adolescents diagnosed with AUDs and 28 control adolescents on a variety of brain regions including prefrontal cortex and cerebellum. The groups did not differ on gray matter volume; however, compared with controls, adolescents with AUDs exhibited significantly smaller prefrontal white matter volumes.

Findings with respect to brain correlates of marijuana and cocaine use are mixed. Smaller overall white matter volumes were found in adolescents with heavy marijuana use (Medina, Nagel, Park, McQueeny, & Tapert, 2007). Conversely, DeLisi et al. (2006) found no association between marijuana use and white matter volumes. A variety of methodological factors could have accounted for these discrepant findings. Overall, these and related findings indicate the need for future research examining neuroanatomical substrates of SUDs, particularly with adolescents. Although the study of volume differences between groups is informative and useful, it may be more relevant to our understanding of the relations between alcohol and other substance use and neurodevelopment to target the application of DTI and other modern neuroimaging techniques to the study of brain development.

Relatively few studies have focused on the application of DTI techniques to AUDs and other SUDs. In a study of 15 men with AUDs and 31 controls, white matter organization in the corpus callosum and centrum semiovale was found to be lower in men with AUDs (Pfefferbaum & Sullivan, 2000). White matter organization measures were significantly and positively associated with performance on tests of working memory and attention. The use of DTI techniques allows for a microstructural investigation of white matter development in the brain. In a similar study, 12 women with AUDs and 18 controls were studied. Although gross white matter volumes did not differ between groups, women with AUDs exhibited lower FA values compared with controls. In a preliminary study, Tapert and Schweinsburg (2005) reported a trend toward white matter organization deficits in the corpus callosum of eight adolescents with AUDs compared with eight control adolescents.

The apparent effect of alcohol on brain white matter organization prompts the question of mechanism. The mechanism for this relationship remains unclear, in large part because of the diffuse nature of changes. One possibility is that excessive intracellular and extracellular fluid may result from disrupted cellular structures, accounting for lowered FA (Pfefferbaum & Sullivan, 2005). In contrast, effects of alcohol on brain white matter organization may result from changes in gene expression. In some respects, postmortem studies allow for the study of this phenomenon. In a postmortem study of adults with AUDs and controls, RNA extracted from the superior frontal cortex of adults with AUDs revealed downregulation of myelin-generating genes in this region (Lewohl et al., 2000), a negative feedback mechanism thought to decrease the region's sensitivity to alcohol. The search for mechanisms to explain the deficits in white matter organization both in children and adolescents at risk for the development of alcohol- and substance-related disorders and in those who already have these disorders remains an area of very active study.

Limbic System Development

The limbic system is a critical brain structure with respect to memory formation and affect processing and regulation. The hippocampus, amygdala, and other limbic system structures appear to be vulnerable to alcohol-related damage. Relative to controls, adults with AUDs exhibited smaller hippocampus volumes

(Sullivan, Marsh, Mathalon, Lim, & Pfefferbaum, 1995). Because the limbic system is one of the brain systems rapidly developing during adolescence, excessive alcohol use during this period might be especially detrimental to this brain area and to the frontal cortex. The frontal cortex is understood to mediate cognitive control mechanisms including risk taking.

DeBellis et al. (2000) compared hippocampus volumes of 12 adolescents with AUDs and 24 control adolescents, using a region-of-interest methodology. Hippocampus volumes in AUD adolescents were found to be significantly smaller bilaterally than in controls. Smaller hippocampus volume across hemispheres and across groups was associated with longer duration of alcohol use and lower age of onset of alcohol use, after controlling for age at assessment and overall brain volume. Groups did not differ, however, on gray matter volumes. This study indicates that the hippocampus may be particularly vulnerable to the effects of alcohol during adolescence.

Many of the participants in the DeBellis et al. (2000) study had significant use of other substances in addition to alcohol, so the specific effects of alcohol could not be determined. These preliminary findings were replicated in a sample of adolescents with AUD and no other substance use or psychiatric disorder except conduct disorder (Nagel, Schweinberg, Phan, & Tapert, 2005). Compared with controls similar on demographic variables, smaller left hippocampus volumes were noted in adolescents with AUDs. Smaller volumes were associated with greater severity of AUD symptoms. Similar findings were obtained even after excluding individuals with conduct disorder.

Besides alcohol involvement, hippocampus differences have also been found in adolescents with marijuana use disorders. Medina et al. (2007) compared 16 adolescents with heavy marijuana use with 16 control adolescents. Adolescents with marijuana use exhibited smaller white matter volumes and more depressive symptoms relative to controls. The interaction between marijuana use and white matter volume significantly predicted depressive symptoms. The authors interpreted the results of this study in terms of the possible disruption of important connections between areas of the brain involved in mood regulation among adolescents with heavy substance involvement.

The results of studies on hippocampus volume must be considered preliminary because the literature contains conflicting findings. For example, Barros-Loscertales et al. (2006) investigated hippocampus volumes in three groups: 16 adolescents with alcohol use, 26 adolescents with alcohol and marijuana use, and 21 control adolescents. Only the alcohol use group was found to have smaller left hippocampus volumes relative to the other two groups. Behavioral inhibition measures were also correlated with both hippocampus and amygdala gray matter volume. Variations in methodologies across these studies limit the confidence with which systematic conclusions can be drawn.

The amygdala is another limbic system structure that appears to be particularly relevant in understanding liability for SUDs and neurodevelopmental effects of substances. Theories have held that the amygdala is an important structure in reward processing and is therefore likely to be an important component in substance use causes and consequences over time (Koob, 1999). Among high-risk adolescents and adults with SUDs, amygdala volumes have been found to be smaller than among controls (Hill et al., 2001; Makris et al., 2004). Although Makris et al. (2004) found smaller amygdala volumes among adults with SUDs relative to controls, correlations between these volumes and level of substance use were not significant. Deficits in amygdala structure and/or function may therefore be more likely to precede and predict substance involvement and related problems. Moreover, although volumetric and white matter structure studies using MRI and DTI methodology have provided important insights into predisposing characteristics and consequences of alcohol and other substance involvement, the investigation of brain function through examination of neural circuits involved in reward processing, decision making, and other key cognitive functions is likely to provide new information about liability to adolescent SUDs not evident through investigation of structural components.

The neurocircuitry involved in motivation, reward processing, and decision making has been hypothesized to be of critical importance in understanding liability to SUDs and neurodevelopmental effects of substances (Chambers et al., 2003; McClure, York, &

Montague, 2004; Verdejo-Garcia, Perez-Garcia, & Bechara, 2006). Prefrontal cortex, amygdala, and nucleus accumbens, and the connections between these structures, appear to form the neurocircuitry involved in reward processing and incentive dependence. Reactivity to emotional stimuli appears to be mediated particularly by networks involving the amygdala (Hariri, Drabant, & Weinberger, 2006; Schwartz et al., 2003). Because these systems are actively developing during adolescence, they are likely to be of particular importance in understanding liability for SUDs.

Skills pertaining to reward and decision-making processes are undergoing active formation and refinement during the adolescent developmental period in concert with continuing development of relevant brain structures and circuitry. This has been demonstrated in studies of cognitive functioning and brain function through functional MRI in adolescents (Bjork, Smith, Danube, & Hommer et al., 2007; Galvan, Hare, Voss, Glover, & Casesy, 2007). Levels of impulsivity have been shown to progressively decline throughout late childhood and adolescence; this decline has been hypothesized to be partially accounted for by continuing neural development of the prefrontal cortex (Casey, Galvan, & Hare, 2005). During tasks involving response inhibition, activation of prefrontal cortex has been found to be positively correlated with age. That is, adolescents recruit prefrontal cortex during response inhibition tasks to a greater degree than do children; this change seems to occur during the same developmental period during which the ability to suppress automatic, prepotent behaviors increases (Luna, Garver, Urban, Lazar, & Sweeney, 2004; Luna & Sweeney, 2004). Impulse control, the ability to suppress an automatic, salient response in favor of a more adaptive response, is a key feature of psychological regulation. These abilities are thought to develop during adolescence as a result of increased functional connectivity among relevant structures and to be mediated by ongoing myelination (see also chap. 9, this volume, which discusses implicit memory and automatic processes as precursors to drug use among youth).

Functional MRI studies allow for the measurement of activation in response to particular tasks performed in the MRI scanner and are a window into the functional connectivity of brain structures involved in psychological dysregulation and adolescent SUD liability. Functional MRI studies could be combined with DTI to construct a comprehensive model of the relations among substance use, brain structure, and brain function. Among adults with alcohol dependence, completing a verbal working memory task was found to be associated with increased activation in left frontal and right cerebellar regions, although the groups exhibited similar performance on the task. Adolescents with features of psychological dysregulation and adults with alcohol dependence exhibit deficits in tasks requiring behavioral inhibition (Bjork, Hommer, Grant, & Danube, 2004; Bjork, Knutson, et al. 2004; Dougherty et al., 2003; Schweinsburg et al., 2004).

In a study of brain activation in adolescents with substance use and associated conduct problems, Banich et al. (2007) compared 12 adolescents with conduct problems such as disruptive behaviors during school and substance use histories and 12 controls on functional MRI activation during the Stroop task. During the Stroop task, participants are presented with stimuli with two competing features. For example, the participant might see the word *red* printed in green ink. Participants are asked to respond to the less salient feature; in the example above the participant would need to respond "green" rather than "red." The Stroop task is generally regarded to be a classic task of response inhibition because an individual is asked to inhibit the automatic response in favor of the less salient one. Adolescents with substance use and conduct problems performed equally as well on the task as control adolescents; however, a more extensive set of brain structures was recruited in performing the task.

Even more specific results with respect to neural activation were obtained by Tapert et al. (2007). In this study, adolescents with heavy marijuana use, compared with control adolescents, exhibited higher levels of activation in prefrontal cortex during tasks requiring behavioral inhibition. In both studies, adolescents with SUDs appeared to require greater effort and recruitment of neural resources to complete the laboratory tasks. Understanding of the neurodevelopmental precursors for adolescent SUDs may require further study of similar response inhibi-

tion and other tasks thought to be mediated by limbic system structures.

NEURAL STRUCTURES MEDIATING RISKY BEHAVIORS

Engagement in risky behaviors has been extensively studied as both a precursor to and a correlate of adolescent substance involvement. Although a component of impulsivity and related prefrontal cortex recruitment is very likely to be associated with risky behaviors, cognitive evaluation of consequences, both positive and negative, is also involved in these complex behaviors. Anticipation of negative consequences is, on one hand, associated with increased inhibition of the behavior among adults (Fromme, Katz, & Rivet, 1997) and adolescents (Galvan et al., 2007). On the other hand, adolescents who hold positive expectancies with respect to alcohol use tend to exhibit less inhibitory processing (Anderson, Schweinsburg, Paulus, Brown, & Tapert, 2005). The ability to anticipate negative consequences of behaviors emerges during the adolescent developmental period, and there is variation in this ability among individuals throughout adolescence and adulthood. The transition from focusing on short-term positive outcomes to possibly long-term negative outcomes could account for the dramatic decrease in engagement in risky behaviors from adolescence to adulthood.

Adolescents who tend to focus on immediate rewards versus long-term consequences—a phenomenon that is mediated by prefrontal, limbic system, and related structures—may be at increased liability for the development of SUDs. For example, Wulfert, Block, Santa Ana, Rodriguez, and Colsman (2002) demonstrated that students who chose a lesser immediate monetary reward rather than a greater delayed (by 1 week) monetary reward were more likely to have early substance involvement including cigarettes, marijuana, and alcohol. They were also more likely to have behavioral problems at school. The preference to focus on lesser immediate rewards has been conceptualized as incentive dependence (Clark et al., 2008). The dimension of incentive dependence is distinct from reward dependence (Cloninger, Sigvardsson, & Bohman, 1988) in that it emphasizes cognitive aspects of reward processing rather than processing of social reinforcement.

The nucleus accumbens appears to be an important structure in the mediation of incentive dependence. Adolescents at risk of SUDs by virtue of deficits in psychological dysregulation are likely to exhibit high levels of incentive dependence, perhaps because of deficits or delays in neurocircuitry involved in motivation (Bjork, Knutson, et al., 2004). Bjork, Knutson, et al. found that compared with adults, adolescents exhibited lower nucleus accumbens activation during the anticipation of reward. Because motivation is a critical component of the ability to delay gratification, adolescents with psychological dysregulation may pursue immediate positive rewards, such as drug effects, over more delayed rewards because of deficits or delays in the development of motivation-related neurocircuitry. Related to this idea is the phenomenon of excessive discounting of delayed rewards seen in adults with SUDs (Bjork, Hommer, et al., 2004; Petry & Casarella, 1999; Vuchinich & Simpson, 1999). Because of the cross-sectional nature of most studies of this phenomenon, it is unclear whether this phenomenon is a predictor or a consequence of substance involvement and related problems.

The neural circuits involved in reward processing and decision making are continuing to mature during adolescence. Adolescents with psychological dysregulation are more likely to show strong preference for immediate rewards over delayed gratification and to engage in risky behaviors with little regard for possible negative consequences because the neural circuitry involved in motivation is underdeveloped. A complete understanding of psychological dysregulation during adolescence and its role in the liability for adolescent SUDs will require the integration of concepts of behavioral inhibition, incentive dependence, decision making, and the associated neural circuitry. These tendencies are likely to be present before initiation of substance involvement, thus serving as a precursor for adolescent SUDs. However, continuing alcohol and drug use is likely to desensitize systems involved in reward processing and other functions, leading to an interactive interdependence between dysfunctional neural circuitry and ongoing neurotoxicity resulting from substance use.

ENVIRONMENTAL CONTEXT

Although neurodevelopmental characteristics stemming from heritable factors form the basis for liability for adolescent SUDs, certain environmental contingencies, especially availability of substances of abuse, are necessary for the emergence of the behavioral syndrome leading to SUDs. Environmental influences contribute to the liability for adolescent SUDs and form the context for the development and expression of phenotypes including psychological dysregulation. Child maltreatment and other traumatic events as well as parental supervision and monitoring have been found to contribute significantly to the development of adolescent SUDs.

Adolescents with SUDs report more physical and sexual abuse compared with control adolescents (Clark et al., 1997; Sartor, Lynskey, Bucholz, et al., 2007). Although these studies were cross-sectional, longitudinal studies have demonstrated similar relations. In a Gene × Environment study of 76 maltreated children and 51 matched control children, those who had experienced maltreatment were seven times more likely to report early alcohol use at age 12. The genetic results indicated that an interaction between presence of the s-allele of the 5-HTTLPR polymorphism and history of maltreatment was associated with risk of alcohol use (Sartor, Lynskey, Bucholz, et al., 2007).

Low levels of parental involvement (i.e., monitoring, support, communication) have been found to be associated with adolescent SUDs (DiClemente et al., 2001; Griffin, Botvin, Scheier, Diaz, & Miller, 2000; Pilgrim, Schulenberg, O'Malley, Bachman, & Johnston, 2006). In a longitudinal design, adolescents recruited from the community who had not previously reported SUDs and who reported low levels of perceived parental supervision, monitoring, and communication were more likely to subsequently develop an AUD. The previously discussed effects of parental SUDs on adolescent SUDs may be partially mediated by parental behaviors such as monitoring and supervision (Barnes, Reifman, Farrell, & Dintcheff, 2000). Other studies have reported both genetic and environmental factors as a mechanism of parental influences on adolescent SUDs (Ellis, Zucker, & Fitzgerald, 1997; Jacob & Johnson, 1997). Parental influences and other environmental factors are most likely to affect development of adolescent SUDs through interactions with neurodevelopmental factors such as psychological dysregulation.

CONCLUSIONS

In this chapter, we presented a conceptual framework for understanding SUD liability, with a particular focus on adolescents. Our conceptualization suggests that psychological dysregulation represents a latent dimension with developmentally specific manifestations, including childhood mental disorders such as conduct disorder, adolescent SUDs, and adulthood personality disorders such as borderline personality disorder and chronic SUDs (Thatcher et al., 2005). We contend that the neurobiological underpinnings of psychological dysregulation are manifested as heritable neurodevelopmental endophenotypes. Although this neurodevelopmental theory is still speculative, it has become testable through advances in neuroimaging techniques.

A great deal of work remains to test and refine this conceptualization. The relevant neuroimaging studies supporting these ideas have typically been unreplicated studies with small samples and cross-sectional designs. These concerns and others make interpretation of this literature problematic (Clark et al., 2008). Large, prospective studies with comprehensive measurement initiated by late childhood will be needed to determine the extent to which neurodevelopmental immaturity leads to SUDs. Because such studies are not likely to be completed for another decade, the field must proceed with less than definitive information on these topics.

With that caveat, the advancement of capacities in psychological regulation likely has a neurodevelopmental basis. Psychological dysregulation, conceptualized as a persistent characteristic with developmentally specific manifestations, may provide an organizing framework for considering the importance of neurodevelopmental changes in the context of predictive childhood phenotypes. Integrative studies considering the results of neuroimaging examinations, genetic sequencing, and diachronic behavioral characterizations will likely yield insights into the relationship between variations in adolescent brain development and SUD liability. The results of such studies are not needed, however, to continue the advance of preventive interventions.

The available research has demonstrated that childhood manifestations of psychological dysregulation—including conduct problems, deficits in executive functioning, and irritability—have definitively been shown to predict accelerated alcohol and other drug use during adolescence and the onset of SUDs (Clark, Cornelius, Wood, & Vanyukov, 2004). With limited resources available for research on prevention programs, children who exhibit psychological dysregulation are a reasonable focus for the development of preventive interventions. For example, the effective treatment of childhood disruptive behavior disorders might decelerate alcohol and other drug involvement in adolescence.

This work also has implications for SUD treatment. Adolescents in treatment for SUDs typically show disruptive behavior disorders and increased irritability compared with adolescents without SUDs. These adolescents often do not respond optimally to treatment programs focusing primarily on abstinence from alcohol and other drugs. Multimodal programs including interventions to improve psychological regulation skills may improve responses to substance-focused treatments. If the conceptual model described in the chapter proves to be valid, effective prevention and treatment programs will need to take into consideration the limited capabilities implied by immature adolescent neurodevelopment and will need to improve adolescents' regulatory skills in addition to focusing on substance involvement.

References

Agartz, I., Brag, S., Franck, J., Hammarberg, A., Okugawa, G., Svinhufvud, K., et al. (2003). MR volumetry during acute alcohol withdrawal and abstinence: A descriptive study. *Alcohol & Alcoholism, 38,* 71–78.

Anderson, K. G., Schweinsburg, A., Paulus, M. P., Brown, S. A., & Tapert, S. F. (2005). Examining personality and alcohol expectancies using functional magnetic resonance imaging (fMRI) with adolescents. *Journal of Studies on Alcohol, 66,* 323–331.

Ashtari, M., Cervellione, K. L., Hasan, K. M., Wu, J., McIlree, C., Kester, H., et al. (2007). White matter development during late adolescence in healthy males: A cross-sectional diffusion tensor imaging study. *NeuroImage, 35,* 501–510.

Banich, M. T., Crowley, T. J., Thompson, L. L., Jacobson, B. L., Liu, X., Raymond, K. M., et al. (2007). Brain activation during the Stroop task in adolescents with severe substance and conduct problems: A pilot study. *Drug and Alcohol Dependence, 90,* 175–182.

Barnea-Goraly, N., Menon, V., Eckert, M., Tamm, L., Bammer, R., Karchemskiy, A., et al. (2005). White matter development during childhood and adolescence: A cross-sectional diffusion tensor imaging study. *Cerebral Cortex, 15,* 1848–1854.

Barnes, G. M., Reifman, A. S., Farrell, M. P., & Dintcheff, B. A. (2000). The effects of parenting on the development of adolescent alcohol misuse: A six-wave latent growth model. *Journal of Marriage and the Family, 62,* 175–186.

Barros-Loscertales, A., Meseguer, V., Sanjuan, A., Belloch, V., Parcet, M. A., Torrubia, R., et al. (2006). Behavioral inhibition system activity is associated with increased amygdala and hippocampal gray matter volume: A voxel-based morphometry study. *NeuroImage, 33,* 1011–1015.

Bjork, J. M., Hommer, D. W., Grant, S. T., & Danube, C. (2004). Impulsivity in abstinent alcohol-dependent patients: Relation to control subjects and type 1-/type 2-like traits. *Alcohol, 34,* 133–150.

Bjork, J. M., Knutson, B., Fong, G. W., Caggiano, D. M., Bennet, S. M., & Hommer, D. W. (2004). Incentive-elicited brain activation in adolescents: Similarities and differences from young adults. *Journal of Neuroscience 24,* 1793–1802.

Bjork, J. M., Smith, A. R., Danube, C. L., & Hommer, D. W. (2007). Developmental differences in posterior mesofrontal cortex recruitment by risky rewards. *Journal of Neuroscience. 27,* 4839–4849.

Bukstein, O. G. (2000). Disruptive behavior disorders and substance use disorders in adolescents. *Journal of Psychoactive Drugs, 32,* 67–79.

Cadoret, R. J., Yates, W. R., Troughton, E., Woodworth, G., & Stewart, M. A. (1995). Adoption study demonstrating two genetic pathways to drug abuse. *Archives of General Psychiatry, 52,* 42–52.

Carlen, P. L., Penn, R. D., Fornazzari, L., Bennett, J., Wilkinson, D. A., & Wortzman, G. (1986). Computerized tomographic scan assessment of alcoholic brain damage and its potential reversibility. *Alcoholism: Clinical & Experimental Research, 10,* 226–232.

Carlen, P. L., Wortzman, G., Holgate, R. C., Wilkinson, D. A., & Rankin, J. C. (1978, June 2). Reversible cerebral atrophy in recently abstinent chronic alcoholics measured by computed tomography scans. *Science, 200,* 1076–1078.

Casey, B. J., Galvan, A., & Hare, T. (2005) Changes in cerebral functional organization during cognitive development. *Current Opinions in Neurobiology, 15,* 239–244.

Chambers, R. A., Taylor, J. R., & Potenza, M. N. (2003). Developmental neurocircuitry of motivation in adolescence: A critical period of addiction vulnerability. *American Journal of Psychiatry, 160,* 1041–1052.

Chapman, K., Tarter, R. E., Kirisci, L., & Cornelius, M. D. (2007). Childhood neurobehavior disinhibition amplifies the risk of substance use disorder: Interaction of parental history and prenatal alcohol exposure. *Journal of Developmental and Behavioral Pediatrics, 28,* 219–224.

Chassin, L., Pitts, S. C., DeLucia, C., & Todd, M. (1999). A longitudinal study of children of alcoholics: Predicting young adult substance use disorders, anxiety, and depression. *Journal of Abnormal Psychiatry, 108,* 106–119.

Chassin, L., Pitts, S. C., & Prost, J. (2002). Binge drinking trajectories from adolescence to emerging adulthood in a high-risk sample: Predictors and substance abuse outcomes. *Journal of Consulting and Clinical Psychology, 70,* 67–78.

Clark, D. B., Bukstein, O., & Cornelius, J. (2002). Alcohol use disorders in adolescents: Epidemiology, diagnosis, psychosocial interventions, and pharmacological treatment. *Paediatric Drugs, 4,* 493–502.

Clark, D. B., Cornelius, J., Wood, D. S., & Vanyukov, M. (2004). Psychopathology risk transmission in children of parents with substance use disorders. *American Journal of Psychiatry, 161,* 685–691.

Clark, D. B., Cornelius, J. R., Kirisci, L., & Tarter, R. E. (2005). Childhood risk categories for adolescent substance involvement: A general liability typology. *Drug and Alcohol Dependence, 77,* 13–21.

Clark, D. B., De Bellis, M. D., Lynch, K. G., Cornelius, J. R., & Martin, C. S. (2003). Physical and sexual abuse, depression and alcohol use disorders in adolescents: Onsets and outcomes. *Drug and Alcohol Dependence, 69,* 51–60.

Clark, D. B., Feske, U., Masia, C. L., Spaulding, S. A., Brown, C., Mammen, O., et al. (1997). Systematic assessment of social phobia in clinical practice. *Depression and Anxiety, 6,* 47–61.

Clark, D. B., Parker, A. M., & Lynch, K. G. (1999). Psychopathology and substance-related problems during early adolescence: A survival analysis. *Journal of Clinical and Child Psychology, 28,* 333–341.

Clark, D. B., Thatcher, D. L., & Tapert, S. (2008). Alcohol, psychological dysregulation and adolescent brain development. *Alcoholism: Clinical and Experimental Research, 32,* 375–385.

Clark, D. B., & Winters, K. C. (2002). Measuring risks and outcomes in substance use disorders prevention research. *Journal of Consulting and Clinical Psychology, 70,* 1207–1223.

Cloninger C. R., Sigvardsson, S., & Bohman, M. (1988). Childhood personality predicts alcohol abuse in young adults. *Alcoholism: Clinical & Experimental Research, 12,* 494–505.

Dawes, M. A., Antelman, S. M., Vanyukov, M. M., Giancola, P., Tarter, R. E., Susman, E. J., et al. (2000). Developmental sources of variation in liability to adolescent substance use disorders. *Drug and Alcohol Dependence, 61,* 3–14.

Day, N. L., Goldschmidt, L., & Thomas, C. A. (2006). Prenatal marijuana exposure contributes to the prediction of marijuana use at age 14. *Addiction, 101,* 1313–1322.

De Bellis, M. D., Clark, D. B., Beers, S. R., Soloff, P. H., Boring, A. M., Hall, J., et al. (2000). Hippocampal volume in adolescent-onset alcohol use disorders. *American Journal of Psychiatry, 157,* 737–744.

De Bellis, M. D., Narasimhan, A., Thatcher, D. L., Keshavan, M. S., Soloff, P., & Clark, D. B. (2005). Prefrontal cortex, thalamus, and cerebellar volumes in adolescents and young adults with adolescent-onset alcohol use disorders and comorbid mental disorders. *Alcoholism: Clinical and Experimental Research, 29,* 1590–1600.

Delisi, L. E., Bertisch, H. C., Szulc, K. U., Majcher, M., Brown, K., Bappal, A., et al. (2006). A preliminary DTI study showing no brain structural change associated with adolescent cannabis use. *Harm Reduction Journal, 3,* 17.

DiClemente, R. J., Wingood, G. M., Crosby, R., Sionean, C., Cobb, B. K., Harrington, K., et al. (2001). Parental monitoring: Association with adolescents' risk behaviors. *Pediatrics, 107,* 1363–1368.

Dougherty, D. M., Bjork, J. M., Harper, A. R., Marsh, D. M., Moeller, F. G., Mathias, C. W., & Swann, A. C. (2003). Behavioral impulsivity paradigms: A comparison in hospitalized adolescents with disruptive behavior disorders. *Journal of Child Psychology and Psychiatry, 44,* 1145–1157.

Ellis, D. A., Zucker, R. A., & Fitzgerald, H. E. (1997). The role of family influences in development and risk. *Alcohol Health & Research World, 21,* 218–226.

Falconer, D. S. (1965). The inheritance of liability to certain diseases, estimated from the incidence among relatives. *Annals of Human Genetics, 29,* 51–76.

Fromme, K., Katz, E. C., & Rivet, K. (1997). Outcome expectancies and risk-taking behavior. *Cognitive Therapy and Research, 21,* 421–442.

Galvan, A., Hare, T., Voss, H., Glover, G., & Casey, B. J. (2007). Risk-taking and the adolescent brain: Who is at risk? *Developmental Science, 10,* 8–14.

Giancola, P. R., & Tarter, R. E. (1999). Executive cognitive functioning and risk for substance abuse. *Psychological Science, 10,* 203–205.

Gogtay, N., Giedd, J. N., Lusk, L., Hayashi, K. M., Greenstein, D., Vaituzis, A. C., et al. (2004). Dynamic mapping of human cortical development during childhood through early adulthood. *Proceedings of the National Academy of Sciences of the United States of America, 101,* 8174–8179.

Gottesman, I. I. & Gould, T. D. (2003). The endophenotype concept in psychiatry: Etymology and strategic intentions. *American Journal of Psychiatry, 160,* 636–645.

Griffin, K. W., Botvin, G. J., Scheier, L. M., Diaz, T., & Miller, N. L. (2000). Parenting practices as predictors of substance use, delinquency, and aggression among urban minority youth: Moderating effects of family structure and gender. *Psychology of Addictive Behaviors, 14,* 174–184.

Habeych, M. E., Charles, P. J., Sclabassi, R. J., Kirisci, L., & Tarter, R. E. (2005). Direct and mediated associations between P300 amplitude in childhood and substance use disorders outcome in young adulthood. *Biological Psychiatry, 57,* 76–82.

Habeych, M. E., Sclabassi, R. J., Charles, P. J., Kirisci, L., & Tarter, R. E. (2005). Association among parental substance use disorder, p300 amplitude, and neurobehavioral disinhibition in preteen boys at high risk for substance use disorder. *Psychology of Addictive Behaviors, 19,* 123–130.

Happaney, K., Zelazo, P. D., & Stuss, D. T. (2004). Development of orbitofrontal function: Current themes and future directions. *Brain and Cognition, 55,* 1–10.

Hariri, A. R., Drabant, E. M., & Weinberger, D. R. (2006). Imaging genetics: Perspectives from studies of genetically driven variation in serotonin function and corticolimbic affective processing. *Biological Psychiatry 59,* 888–897.

Hill, S. Y., De Bellis, M. D., Keshavan, M. S., Lowers, L., Shen, S., Hall, J., et al. (2001). Right amygdala volume in adolescent and young adult offspring from families at high risk for developing alcoholism. *Biological Psychiatry, 49,* 894–905.

Hill, S. Y., & Shen, S. (2002). Neurodevelopmental patterns of visual P3b in association with familial risk for alcohol dependence and childhood diagnosis. *Biological Psychiatry, 51,* 621–631.

Hill, S. Y., Shen, S., Lowers, L., & Locke, J. (2000). Factors predicting the onset of adolescent drinking in families at high risk for developing alcoholism. *Biological Psychiatry, 48,* 265–275.

Hill, S. Y., Shen, S., Zezza, N., Hoffman, E. K., Perlin, M., & Allan, W. (2004). A genome wide search for alcoholism susceptibility genes. *American Journal of*

Medical Genetics Part B—Neuropsychiatric Genetics, 128B, 102–113.

Iacono, W. G., Malone, S. M., & McGue, M. (2003). Substance use disorders, externalizing psychopathology, and P300 event-related potential amplitude. *International Journal of Psychophysiology, 48,* 147–178.

Jacob, T., & Johnson, S. (1997). Parenting influences on the development of alcohol abuse and dependence. *Alcohol Health & Research World, 21,* 204–209.

Kaufman, J., Yang, B. Z., Douglas-Palumberi, H., Crouse-Artus, M., Lipschitz, D., Krystal, J. H., et al. (2007). Genetic and environmental predictors of early alcohol use. *Biological Psychiatry, 61,* 1228–1234.

Kirisci, L., Tarter, R., Mezzich, A., & Vanyukov, M. (2007). Developmental trajectory classes in substance use disorder etiology. *Psychology of Addictive Behaviors, 21,* 287–296.

Kirisci, L., Tarter, R. E., Vanyukov, M., Reynolds, M., & Habeych, M. (2004). Relation between cognitive distortions and neurobehavior disinhibition on the development of substance use during adolescence and substance use disorder by young adulthood: A prospective study. *Drug and Alcohol Dependence, 76,* 125–133.

Kirisci, L., Vanyukov, M., & Tarter, R. (2005). Detection of youth at high risk for substance use disorders: A longitudinal study. *Psychology of Addictive Behaviors, 19,* 243–252.

Koob, G. F. (1999). The role of the striatopallidal and extended amygdala systems in drug addiction. *Annals of the New York Academy of Sciences, 877,* 445–460.

Krill, J. J., Halliday, G. M., Svoboda, M. D., & Cartwright, H. (1997). The cerebral cortex is damaged in chronic alcoholics. *Neuroscience, 79,* 983–998.

Lenroot, R. K., & Giedd, J. N. (2006). Brain development in children and adolescents: Insights from anatomical magnetic resonance imaging. *Neuroscience & Biobehavioral Reviews, 30,* 718–729.

Levin, H. S., Culhane, K. A., Hartman, J., Evankovich, K., Mattson, A. J., Harward, H., et al. (1991). Developmental changes in performance on tests of purported frontal lobe functioning. *Developmental Neuropsychopathology 7,* 377–395.

Lewohl, J. M., Wang, L., Miles, M. F., Zhang, L., Dodd, P. R., & Harris, R. A. (2000). Gene expression in human alcoholism: Microarray analysis of frontal cortex. *Alcoholism: Clinical & Experimental Research, 24,* 1873–1882.

Luna, B., Garver, K. E., Urban, T. A., Lazar, N. A., & Sweeney, J. A. (2004). Maturation of cognitive processes from late childhood to adulthood. *Child Development, 75,* 1357–1372.

Luna, B., & Sweeney, J. A. (2004). The emergence of collaboration brain function: fMRI studies of the development of response inhibition. *Annals of the New York Academy of Sciences, 1021,* 296–309.

Ma, X. Y., Coles, C. D., Lynch, M. E., LaConte, S. M., Zurkiya, O., Wang, D. L., et al. (2005). Evaluation of corpus callosum anisotropy in young adults with fetal alcohol syndrome according to diffusion tensor imaging. *Alcoholism: Clinical & Experimental Research, 29,* 1214–1222.

Mabbott, D. J., Noseworthy, M., Bouffet, E., Laughlin, S., & Rockel, C. (2006). White matter growth as a mechanism of cognitive development in children. *NeuroImage, 33,* 936–946.

Makris, N., Gasic, G. P., Seidman, L. J., Goldstein, J. M., Gastfriend, D. R., Elman, I., et al. (2004). Decreased absolute amygdala volume in cocaine addicts. *Neuron, 44,* 728–740.

Malone, S. M., Taylor, J., Marmorstein, N. R., McGue, M., & Iacono, W. G. (2004). Genetic and environmental influences on antisocial behavior and alcohol dependence from adolescence to early adulthood. *Development and Psychopathology, 16,* 943–966.

Martin, C. S., Romig, C. J., & Kirisci, L. (2000). *DSM–IV* learning disorders in 10- to 12-year-old boys with and without a parental history of substance use disorders. *Prevention Science, 1,* 107–113.

McClure, S. M., York, M. K., & Montague, P. R. (2004). The neural substrates of reward processing in humans: The modern role of fMRI. *Neuroscientist, 10,* 260–268.

McLaughlin, N. C., Paul, R. H., Grieve, S. M., Williams, L. M., Laidlaw, D., DiCarlo, M., et al. (2007). Diffusion tensor imaging of the corpus collosum: A cross-sectional study across the lifespan. *International Journal of Neuroscience, 25,* 215–221.

Medina, K. L., Nagel, B. J., Park, A., McQueeny, T., & Tapert, S. F. (2007). Depressive symptoms in adolescents: Associations with white matter volume and marijuana use. *Journal of Child Psychology and Psychiatry, 48,* 592–600.

Mezzich, A. C., Tarter, R. E., Feske, U., Kirisci, L., McNamee, R. L., & Day, B.-S. (2007). Assessment of risk for substance use disorder consequent to consumption of illegal drugs: Psychometric validation of the neurobehavior disinhibition trait. *Psychology of Addictive Behaviors, 21,* 508–515.

Mezzich, A. C., Tarter, R. E., Kirisci, L., Feske, U., Day, B.-S., & Gao, Z. (2007). Reciprocal influence of parent discipline and child's behavior on risk for substance use disorder: A nine-year prospective study. *American Journal of Drug and Alcohol Abuse, 33,* 851–867.

Nagel, B. J., Schweinsburg, A. D., Phan, V., & Tapert, S. F. (2005). Reduced hippocampal volume among adolescents with alcohol use disorders without psychiatric comorbidity. *Psychiatry Research, 139,* 181–190.

Nigg, J. T., Wong, M. M., Martel, M. M., Jester, J. M., Puttler, L. I., Glass, J. M., et al. (2006). Poor response inhibition as a predictor of problem drinking and illicit drug use in adolescents at risk for alcoholism and other substance use disorders. *Journal of the American Academy of Child & Adolescent Psychiatry, 45,* 468–475.

Petry, N. M., & Casarella, T. (1999). Excessive discounting of delayed rewards in substance abusers with gambling problems. *Drug and Alcohol Dependence, 56,* 25–32.

Pfefferbaum, A., & Sullivan, E. V. (2005). Disruption of brain white matter microstructure by excessive intracellular and extracellular fluid in alcoholism: Evidence from diffusion tensor imaging. *Neuropsychopharmacology, 30,* 423–432.

Pfefferbaum, A., & Sullivan, E. V. (2002). Microstructural but not macrostructural disruption of white matter in women with chronic alcoholism. *NeuroImage, 15,* 708–718.

Pfefferbaum, A., Sullivan, E. V., Hedehus, M., Adalsteinsson, E., Lim, K. O., & Moseley, M. (2000). In vivo detection and functional correlates of white matter microstructural disruption in chronic alcoholism. *Alcoholism: Clinical & Experimental Research, 24,* 1214–1221.

Pilgrim, C. C., Schulenberg, J. E., O'Malley, P. M., Bachman, J. G., & Johnston, L. D. (2006). Mediators and moderators of parental involvement on substance use: A national study of adolescents. *Prevention Science, 7,* 75–89.

Rubia, K., Overmeyer, S., Taylor, E., Brammer, M., Williams, S. C., Simmons, A., et al. (2000). Functional frontalisation with age: Mapping neurodevelopmental trajectories with fMRI. *Neuroscience & Biobehavioral Reviews, 24,* 13–19.

Sartor, C. E., Lynskey, M. T., Bucholz, K. K., McCutcheon, V. V., Nelson, E. C., Waldron, M., et al. (2007). Childhood sexual abuse and the course of alcohol dependence development: Findings from a female twin sample. *Drug and Alcohol Dependence, 89,* 139–144.

Sartor, C. E., Lynskey, M. T., Heath, A. C., Jacob, T., & True, W. (2007). The role of childhood risk factors in initiation of alcohol use and progression to alcohol dependence. *Addiction, 102,* 216–225.

Schmithorst, V. J., Wilke, M., Dardzinski, B. J., & Holland, S. K. (2005). Cognitive functions correlate with white matter architecture in a normal pediatric population: A diffusion tensor MRI study. *Human Brain Mapping, 26,* 139–147.

Schneider, J. F., Il'yasov, K. A., Hennig, J., & Martin, E. (2004). Fast quantitative diffusion-tensor imaging of cerebral white matter from the neonatal period to adolescence. *Neuroradiology 46,* 258–266.

Schneiderman, J. S., Buchsbaum, M. S., Haznedar, M. M., Hazlett, E. A., Brickman, A. M., Shihabuddin, L., et al. (2007). Diffusion tensor anisotropy in adolescents and adults. *Neuropsychobiology, 55,* 96–111.

Schuckit, M. A., & Smith, T. L. (1996). An 8-year follow-up of 450 sons of alcoholic and control subjects. *Archives of General Psychiatry, 53,* 202–210.

Schwartz, C. E., Wright, C. I., Shin, L. M., Kagan, J., Whalen, P. J., McMullin, K. G., et al. (2003). Differential amygdalar response to novel versus newly familiar neutral faces: A functional MRI probe developed for studying inhibited temperament. *Biological Psychiatry, 53,* 854–862.

Schweinsburg, A. D., Paulus, M. P., Barlett, V. C., Killeen, L. A., Caldwell, L. C., Pulido, C., et al. (2004). An FMRI study of response inhibition in youths with a family history of alcoholism. *Annals of the New York Academy of Sciences, 1021,* 391–394.

Shear, P. K., Jernigan, T. L., & Butters, N. (1994). Volumetric magnetic resonance imaging quantification of longitudinal brain changes in abstinent alcoholics. *Alcoholism: Clinical and Experimental Research, 18,* 172–176. (Erratum appears in *Alcoholism: Clinical and Experimental Research, 18,* 766)

Sher, K. J., Walitzer, K. S., Wood, P. K., & Brent, E. E. (1991). Characteristics of children of alcoholics: Putative risk factors, substance use and abuse, and psychopathology. *Journal of Abnormal Psychology, 100,* 427–448.

Simpson, J., & Weiner, E. (1989). *Oxford English dictionary* (2nd ed.). Oxford, England: Oxford University Press.

Sowell, E. R., Thompson, P. M., Leonard, C. M., Welcome, S. E., Kan, E., & Toga, A. W. (2004). Longitudinal mapping of cortical thickness and brain growth in normal children. *Journal of Neuroscience, 24,* 8223–8231.

Sowell, E. R., Thompson, P. M., Tessner, K. D., & Toga, A. W. (2001). Mapping continued brain growth and gray matter density reduction in dorsal frontal cortex: Inverse relationships during postadolescent brain maturation. *Journal of Neuroscience, 21,* 8819–8829.

Spear, L. P. (2000). The adolescent brain and age-related behavioral manifestations. *Neuroscience & Biobehavioral Reviews, 24,* 417–463.

Stallings, M. C., Corley, R. P., Dennehey, B., Hewitt, J. K., Krauter, K. S., Lessem, J. M., et al. (2005). A genome-wide search for quantitative trait loci that influence antisocial drug dependence in adolescence. *Archives of General Psychiatry, 62,* 1042–1051.

Sullivan, E. V., Marsh, L., Mathalon, D. H., Lim, K. O., & Pfefferbaum, A. (1995). Anterior hippocampal volume deficits in nonamnesic, aging chronic alcoholics. *Alcoholism: Clinical & Experimental Research, 19,* 110–122.

Tapert, S. F., Baratta, M. V., Abrantes, A. M., & Brown, S. A. (2002). Attention dysfunction predicts substance involvement in community youths. *Journal of the American Academy of Child & Adolescent Psychiatry, 41,* 680–686.

Tapert, S. F., & Schweinsburg, A. D. (2005). The human adolescent brain and alcohol use disorders. *Recent Developments in Alcoholism, 17,* 177–197.

Tapert, S. F., Schweinsburg, A. D., Drummond, S. P. A., Paulus, M. P., Brown, S. A., Yang, T. T., & Frank, L. R. (2007). Functional MRI of inhibitory processing in abstinent adolescent marijuana uses. *Psychopharmacology, 194,* 173–183.

Tarter, R. E., Kirisci, L., Habeych, M., Reynolds, M., & Vanyukov, M. (2004). Neurobehavior disinhibition in childhood predisposes boys to substance use disorder by young adulthood: Direct and mediated etiologic pathways. *Drug and Alcohol Dependence, 73,* 121–132.

Tarter, R. E., Kirisci, L., Mezzich, A., Cornelius, J. R., Pajer, K., Vanyukov, M., et al. (2003). Neurobehavioral disinhibition in childhood predicts early age at onset of substance use disorder. *American Journal of Psychiatry, 160,* 1078–1085.

Tarter, R. E., Kirisci, L., Reynolds, M., & Mezzich, A. (2004). Neurobehavior disinhibition in childhood predicts suicide potential and substance use disorder by young adulthood. *Drug and Alcohol Dependence, 76*(Suppl.), S45–S52.

Tarter, R., Vanyukov, M., Giancola, P., Dawes, M., Blackson, T., Mezzich, A., et al. (1999). Etiology of early age onset substance use disorder: A maturational perspective. *Development and Psychopathology, 11,* 657–683.

Tarter, R., Vanyukov, M., Giancola, P., Dawes, M., Blackson, T., Mezzich, A., & Clark, D. B. (1999). Epigenetic model of substance use disorder etiology. *Development and Psychopathology, 11,* 657–683.

Thatcher, D. L., & Clark, D. B. (2006). Adolescent alcohol abuse and dependence: Development, diagnosis, treatment and outcomes. *Current Psychiatry Reviews, 2,* 159–177.

Verdejo-Garcia, A., Perez-Garcia, M., & Bechara, A. (2006). Emotion, decision-making and substance dependence: A somatic-marker model of addiction. *Neuropharmacology 4,* 17–31.

Vuchinich, R. E., & Simpson, C. A. (1999) Hyperbolic temporal discounting in social drinkers and problem drinkers. *Experimental and Clinical Psychopharmacology, 6,* 292–305.

Warner, T. D., Behnke, M., Eyler, F. D., Padgett, K., Leonard, C., Hou, W., et al. (2006). Diffusion tensor imaging of frontal white matter and executive functioning in cocaine-exposed children. *Pediatrics, 118,* 2014–2024.

Welsh, M. C., Pennington, B. F., & Groisser, D. B. (1991). A normative-developmental study of executive function: A window of prefrontal function in children. *Developmental Neuropsychology, 7,* 131–149.

Wozniak, J. R., Mueller, B. A., Chang, P. N., Muetzel, R. L., Caros, L., & Lim, K. O. (2006). Diffusion tensor imaging in children with fetal alcohol spectrum disorders. *Alcoholism: Clinical & Experimental Research, 30,* 1799–1806.

Wulfert, E., Block, J. A., Santa Ana, E., Rodriguez, M. L., & Colsman, M. (2002). Delay of gratification: Impulsive choices and problem behaviors in early and late adolescence. *Journal of Personality, 70,* 533–552.

Young, S. E., Smolen, A., Hewitt, J. K., Haberstick, B. C., Stallings, M. C., Corley, R. P., et al. (2006). Interaction between MAO-A genotype and maltreatment in the risk for conduct disorder: Failure to confirm in adolescent patients. *American Journal of Psychiatry, 163,* 1019–1025.

HOW CAN ETIOLOGICAL RESEARCH INFORM THE DISTINCTION BETWEEN NORMAL DRINKING AND DISORDERED DRINKING?

Kenneth J. Sher, Scott T. Wolf, and Julia A. Martinez

In this chapter, we take on the charge assigned to us by the editor, namely to describe how research on etiology can inform the distinction between normal use and abuse. This basic question is an important one for those interested in trying to establish criteria sets and diagnostic thresholds for distinguishing normal from abnormal use and, from a practical perspective, for developing assessment strategies that can help individual drinkers and treatment professionals decide when drinking behavior might require either concerted efforts at self-change or formal treatment. Additionally, if there is some fundamental, dynamic process that indexes the transition from normal use to more pathological use, this process can become the target of treatment efforts. An important corollary of this is that monitoring this process over the course of treatment and follow-up can reveal how well treatment is progressing and how vulnerable the recovering drinker is to relapse.

Although we believe the general question we address is an important one from a nosological perspective, from a public health perspective it is a narrow one and, arguably, overcomplicated. For example, if we were only interested in identifying individuals whose drinking behavior is likely to cause harm because of either acute intoxication or chronic consumption, the goal is much simpler. Specifically, all we would need to do is identify levels of consumption associated with acute harm (e.g., unintentional injury) or chronic medical complications (e.g., hypertension and liver disease; see Dawson, 2000), an approach promoted by the publication of recommended drinking limits in the *Dietary Guidelines for Americans 2005* (U.S. Department of Agriculture, 2005). From a clinical standpoint, it could be argued that any drinking that is hazardous (i.e., puts one at risk of adverse consequences) or directly leads to consequences (e.g., health, vocational, family, legal, or social problems) is deserving of attention. However, we view our current task not as the simple one of identifying safe consumption levels or enumerating the kinds of problems that are of potential concern to drinkers and treatment providers but as the more theoretical one of defining when drinking becomes disordered as opposed to merely unwise or dangerous.

However, before discussing this topic further, we first slightly change the terminology, eschewing the term *abuse* for the more defensible one of *disordered drinking,* which roughly corresponds to the notion of alcohol dependence as defined in later editions of the *Diagnostic and Statistical Manual of Mental Disorders* (*DSM*)—specifically the third revised edition (*DSM–III–R*) and the fourth edition (*DSM–IV*)—of the American Psychiatric Association (APA; 1987, 1994, 2000).

THE PROBLEM WITH THE TERM *ABUSE* AND A BRIEF HISTORY OF RELATED CONCEPTS

Although the problems of intoxication and chronic drunkenness have been recognized since antiquity, formal recognition by the medical establishment of a clinical syndrome labeled *alcoholism* (associated with a history of excessive consumption and problems) dates to Magnus Huss, a 19th-century Swedish psychiatrist (Keller & Doria, 1991). The term *alcoholism* or its close synonyms has been conceptualized as virtually any use of alcohol that negatively affects the drinker or society (Jellinek, 1960), as a syndrome of problem drinking (International Classification of Diseases, eighth revision; World Health Organization [WHO], 1967), as a personality disorder (first edition of the *DSM*; APA, 1951), or as a disease marked by signs of physiological adaptation (e.g., tolerance or withdrawal) or loss of control over drinking (Feighner, 1972; National Council on Alcoholism, 1972).

The concept of abuse was introduced as a distinct disorder in *DSM–III* (APA, 1980) and contrasted with dependence, with *abuse* defined as a pattern of maladaptive alcohol use characterized by negative social, legal, or occupational consequences and *dependence* (equivalent to the earlier term, alcoholism) reserved for patterns of maladaptive use characterized by physical dependence (i.e., tolerance or withdrawal). Early operational definitions of alcohol dependence such as the *DSM–III* (APA, 1980), National Council on Alcoholism (1972), and WHO (Edwards, Arif, & Hodgson, 1981) criteria for alcohol dependence required evidence of physiological dependence, indicated by tolerance and/or withdrawal. This narrow conceptualization of dependence was challenged by Edwards and Gross (1976), who proposed a broader spectrum construct, the alcohol dependence syndrome. In alcohol dependence syndrome, physiological signs and symptoms of dependence were indicators but not necessary criteria for the diagnosis of dependence. Edwards and Gross reshaped the concept of dependence, rooted in neuroadaptation and indicated by tolerance and withdrawal, into a broader one that, roughly stated, corresponded to a varied set of signs and symptoms that reflected the importance of alcohol in the day-to-day life of the drinker. These signs and symptoms include what Edwards (1982, 1986; Edwards & Gross, 1976) described as "a narrowing of the drinking repertoire" (Edwards & Gross, 1976, p. 1058), centrality of drinking in the person's life relative to other life tasks and responsibilities, tolerance and

withdrawal, "awareness of the compulsion to drink" (Edwards & Gross, 1976, p. 1060), and rapid reinstatement of dependence symptoms after a period of abstinence. This expanded construct of dependence was influential in later revisions of the *DSM,* and tolerance and/or withdrawal symptoms were no longer required for the diagnosis of substance dependence in *DSM–III–R* (APA, 1987) and *DSM–IV* (APA, 1994).

Edwards (1986) distinguished the construct of the alcohol dependence syndrome from alcohol-related consequences (or disabilities) and negative life events that directly the result from alcohol consumption. These consequences include social problems (e.g., physical or verbal aggression, marital difficulties, loss of important social relationships), legal problems (e.g., arrests for driving while intoxicated, public inebriation), vocational problems (e.g., termination from employment, failure to achieve career goals), and medical problems (e.g., physical injury, liver disease, central nervous system disease). Within this framework, both dependence and consequences are clearly graded phenomena. The abuse–dependence distinction in the current *DSM–IV* roughly corresponds to Edwards and Gross's (1976) distinction between dependence and consequences (disabilities), with the major differences being the dimensional (Edwards & Gross, 1976) versus categorical (*DSM*) approach to classification, and that, in *DSM,* the diagnosis of dependence supersedes a diagnosis of abuse as opposed to both being graded phenomena that covary.

Although the distinction between dependence symptomatology and consequences is conceptually compelling, the empirical basis for this definition is uncertain. Although factor analysis of alcohol symptom scales in clinical samples of those with alcoholism tend to suggest a multidimensional structure, with at least one factor representing dependence (e.g., Skinner, 1981; Svanum, 1986), this same analytic approach using population-based samples paints a less clear-cut picture. More specifically, mixed abuse and dependence indicators can be well represented by a single factor (e.g., Hasin, Muthén, Wisnicki, & Grant, 1994). When evidence for more than one factor is found, the item content of the factors are not consistent with the *DSM* criteria sets (e.g., Muthén, Grant, & Hasin, 1993) for separate abuse and dependence symptoms. Moreover, when multiple dimensions are empirically identified, correlations among the factors appear to be exceptionally high, calling into question the value of a multidimensional approach (e.g., Allen, Fertig, Towle, & Altshuler, 1994; Hasin et al., 1994; Saxon, Kivlahan, Doyle, & Donovan, 2007). Additionally, analyses using item response theory (Hambleton, Swaminathan, & Rogers, 1991), an analysis technique that treats symptoms as differentially sensitive indicators of a single latent trait, have tended to clearly challenge implicit notions that abuse is a milder condition than dependence. That is, some criteria of dependence (e.g., tolerance, impaired control) are relatively common (and, therefore, statistically less severe), and some criteria of abuse (especially legal difficulties) are rare (and therefore more severe; Kahler & Strong, 2006; Saha, Stinson, & Grant, 2007). Further problems with the abuse–dependence distinction within *DSM–IV* are that the current system leaves undiagnosed someone who has one or two dependence symptoms but no abuse symptoms (i.e., diagnostic orphans; Pollock & Martin, 1999). Moreover, the majority of individuals who meet criteria for abuse do so because of hazardous use (e.g., driving while intoxicated; Dawson, Grant, Stinson, & Chou, 2004; Hasin, Paykin, Endicott, & Grant, 1999; Schuckit et al., 2005) that, although a clear public health problem, may reflect a general incautious approach to a variety of day-to-day risk and not reflect a pathology specific to alcohol.

The above-noted problems with the concept of alcohol abuse (and substance abuse more generally) should not distract us from our general goal, which is to understand how etiological research can inform precisely where to draw the line between normal use and use that is disordered or pathological in some sense. For the rest of this chapter, we use the term *disordered* to refer to drinking associated with underlying psychological and physical changes that occur as a function of regular or chronic alcohol use and that tend to promote further drinking.

This working definition, although somewhat general, is not meant to encompass all clinically relevant drinking conditions. For example, various types of drunken excess such as alcohol-related

aggression, high-risk or injudicious sexual behavior, and drinking to gross intoxication may be associated with disordered drinking but can clearly occur in individuals who are not regular drinkers. For example, in his description of psychopathic individuals, Cleckley (1982) noted that they often show "fantastic and uninviting behavior with alcohol *and sometimes without* [italics added]" (p. 204). That is, for many behaviors associated with alcohol intoxication, alcohol consumption may be an important facilitator or cofactor but is not necessarily the primary causal factor. It is for this reason that the concept of pathological intoxication and alcohol idiosyncratic reaction, described in early versions of the *DSM* and referring to small doses of alcohol causing grossly disinhibited behavior, was viewed as controversial and was rejected for inclusion in *DSM–IV* (Schuckit, 1994).

Additionally, and perhaps less obviously, we can argue that someone who evidences an ostensibly normal drinking pattern (e.g., a person whose drinking never exceeds one or two standard drinks per day) may still be an abnormal drinker if drinking in such a controlled way requires a high degree of self-control. Such a drinking pattern may not put an individual at risk of most alcohol consequences, but it does suggest that there is something abnormal about the person's desire for alcohol. As an analogy, we would not consider a person with snake phobia who is willing to hold a python to be fearless if he or she experienced severe emotional distress and high autonomic arousal when holding it or contemplating holding it (although we might consider him or her courageous; Rachman, 1989). The manifestation of addictive behaviors reflects the joint operations of impelling and restraining tendencies (Orford, 2001), and consequently, the absence of excess does not necessarily imply the absence of impelling tendencies. Although much research on alcohol use disorders (AUDs) has focused on the critical role of self-regulation (Hull & Slone, 2004; Muraven & Baumeister, 2000; Sayette, 2004), self-regulation of drinking is important only insofar as there are impelling forces that must be regulated. The net result of these arguments is that although drinking in excess may represent something abnormal about the drinker's relation to alcohol and moderate drinking may represent a normal relation between the drinker and alcohol, similar manifest drinking patterns can reflect different underlying dynamics.

ETIOLOGY RESEARCH: WHAT ASPECTS ARE RELEVANT TO UNDERSTANDING DIAGNOSTIC DISTINCTIONS?

In human research, much existing etiology research represents the search for risk factors that presage the development of AUDs. Many of the risk factors that have been identified, such as sex, family history, childhood externalizing disorders, personality, and ethnic heritage (Grant, 1994, 1997; Schuckit & Smith, 2000; Sher, 1991), although extremely important for identifying vulnerability, are not very helpful by themselves for informing the question of when drinking becomes disordered. By definition, most of these static risk factors are proxies for enduring processes or traits that typically precede the onset of drinking and are therefore not probative with respect to identifying a dynamic change in drinking. Certainly, such risk factors can be related to risk processes that are the operative mechanisms that lead to disordered drinking, but they are not the processes themselves. Moreover, one would not want to assert that someone who simply has a risk factor for AUDs (e.g., a biological father who is an alcoholic) is disordered simply because he or she drinks and has a risk factor. A drinker (perhaps even a former alcoholic, a topic we address later in this chapter) can drink and show no obvious or even subtle signs of being disordered. It is for this reason that it is dynamic, etiological processes (and not risk factors that are merely etiologically relevant) that require our attention.

HOW DO WE KNOW THAT DRINK IS AFFECTING THE DRINKER AND WHEN IS IT A PROBLEM?

There are a number of ways in which regular alcohol use appears to affect the drinker. For example, the individual can become more (i.e., sensitization) or less sensitive (i.e., tolerance) to the reinforcing or punishing effects of alcohol over time. The individual may start to think differently about alcohol as a drug, that is, view its effects as being particularly

reinforcing or punishing (i.e., expectancies). The motivation behind a drug's use might change in some way (e.g., the motive, say, for mood regulation may intensify or there may be a change in the number and kinds of motivations that goad drinking). With chronic use, one's baseline level of mood can change, and alcohol may be relied on to improve or maintain mood. In addition, the individual may begin to view both drinking in general and his or her own drinking in particular differently.

In thinking about changes that occur in the drinker as a function of increasing drinking, we need to distinguish changes that may be normal from those that are disordered. As Sartor, Lynskey, Heath, Jacob, and True (2007) showed in their analysis of risk of alcohol dependence, (a) some risk factors increase the likelihood of becoming a regular drinker and therefore increase the likelihood of dependence by increasing the group of individuals (i.e., drinkers) who are potentially vulnerable to progression (e.g., male gender, attention-deficit/hyperactivity disorder, family history of alcohol dependence); (b) some risk factors increase the likelihood of a drinker's progressing to dependence but are unrelated to one's becoming a drinker in the first place (e.g., nicotine and marijuana use, generalized anxiety disorder); and (c) some risk factors may operate at both levels, increasing the likelihood of drinking in the first place and then increasing the likelihood that drinkers will develop dependence (e.g., conduct disorder). These types of findings suggest that certain changes (especially those that are relevant to both normal drinking and dependent drinking) may indicate a general process that spans normal and disordered drinking (e.g., tolerance), whereas other processes may be more specific to disordered drinking (e.g., an alteration in tonic mood states, withdrawal). Both general processes and specific processes may be important for understanding the transition to disordered drinking, but general processes suggest a quantitative change (e.g., a light drinker may show mild tolerance, and an alcohol-dependent individual may show severe tolerance) and imply some (possibly arbitrary) threshold associated with the transition to disordered drinking, whereas specific processes (in the sense used here) suggest a qualitative change associated with the appearance of a new process (e.g., withdrawal relief begins to become a drinking motive).

BASIC LEARNING AND NEUROBIOLOGICAL PERSPECTIVES ON HOW INDIVIDUALS ADAPT TO REGULAR DRINKING

Given this chapter's focus on the centrality of dynamic processes associated with drinking, it is therefore helpful to consider a range of theoretical perspectives proposed by researchers to explain how pharmacological experiences with substances change responses to these substances and the motivations to use them. In discussing these perspectives, our goal is not to provide a critical evaluation of the relevant theories; it is probably safe to say that each has significant support in some contexts but that not all explicit tests of the theories have been successful in demonstrating robust effects with alcohol or have been adequately tested with respect to alcohol. However, each perspective provides theoretically informed, plausible accounts of what is occurring "under the hood" of the drinker as his or her drinking progresses and can guide research on the distinction between normal and disordered use.

Opponent Processes and Conditioned Compensatory Responses

Perhaps one of the earliest observable changes related to drinking behavior is tolerance, the tendency to manifest less of a response to a given dose of alcohol as a function of drinking experience. Acquired changes in response to repeated exposure to a psychological or physical challenge appear to be general phenomena and are well described by opponent-process theory (Solomon & Corbit, 1974). According to this theory, a positive (or negative) hedonic state (or A-State) elicits a countervailing negative (or positive) hedonic state (or B-State) that serves to counteract the initial state as part of a natural homeostatic mechanism. Over time, the B-state is thought to strengthen, thereby reducing the reaction to the drug (i.e., the opponent B-state reduces the initial A-state). In this way, tolerance is thought to develop. It should be noted that there is nothing in Solomon and Corbit's (1971) account to suggest that tolerance acquisition, at least to a mild degree, is neces-

sarily disordered. Adaptation to homeostatic challenges as described by opponent-process theory is an important function, and opponent processes appear to occur across a wide range of phenomena and levels of biological organization (Solomon, 1980). Additionally, we know from survey data that tolerance is common in regular drinkers (Grant et al., 2007) and from psychometric studies of drinking symptomatology that tolerance is a low-threshold symptom (Grant et al., 2007; Kahler & Strong, 2006) and appears to develop early in drinking careers (O'Neill & Sher, 2000). Thus, although we know that tolerance is common in disordered drinking and develops as a function of drinking experience, tolerance development per se does not clearly distinguish normal from disordered drinking (although, in its extreme form, it is probably a reasonable indicator of disordered drinking). Although tolerance development is typically viewed as a form of neuroadaptation, a considerable body of research has highlighted the role of conditioning processes (Siegel, Baptista, Kim, McDonald, & Weise-Kelly, 2000), in which opponent processes can be viewed as conditioned responses elicited by conditioned stimuli accompanying the consumption of alcohol (e.g., drinking context; the olfactory and gustatory cues associated with a given beverage; even the initial, proprioceptive effects of alcohol). The concept of conditioned alcohol effects is important to consider because it implies that with sufficient drinking experience, cues (conditioned stimuli) associated with alcohol can come to elicit a variety of responses from the drinker. Thus, both the clinician and the researcher might be able to probe the individual drinker's degree of adaptation to alcohol by exposing him or her to alcohol-related cues and measuring relevant responses. Consequently, in seeking to identify dynamic, drinking-related processes that might inform the distinction between normal and disordered drinking, various types of cue exposure might be useful in assessing potentially pathogenic processes.

Allostasis

The opponent-process theory of motivation and the theory of conditioned, compensatory drug effects provide plausible accounts of the adaptive processes that result in altered responses to alcohol as a function of drinking experience. However, by themselves these accounts do not provide an insight into how drug exposure alters the drinker when he or she is not drinking or motivates subsequent drinking. Koob and LeMoal (2001) have extended opponent-process theory to account for changes in homeostatic set point, or *allostasis*. That is, over time, there is a change in the natural homeostatic set point so that the B-state no longer balances the evoking A-state and actually serves to overshoot the initial homeostatic set point. This type of "allostatic derangement" is thought to characterize chronic dependence, and this deviation from the (original) natural set point to the allostatic set point is believed to represent significant adaptive cost to the individual (increased negative affectivity, impaired self-regulation) and lead to a spiraling escalation of drinking. That is, according to this model, chronic alcohol consumption dynamically resets homeostatic mechanisms, altering the individual's tonic, hedonic set point. From this perspective and from related conditioning models (e.g., Siegel et al., 2000), withdrawal phenomena can be viewed as opponent processes acting in the absence of reward and involving the same underlying brain systems. It is for this reason that resumption of alcohol intake (initiating a new A-state) counteracts withdrawal symptoms, which can be viewed as reflecting allostatic processes. The allostatic model suggests that prolonged alcohol use can induce changes in the drinker that can have widespread effects (altering hedonic tone), persist for some extended period of time, and motivate further drinking. Being able to track allostatic changes may, therefore, is one approach to distinguishing one's position on a continuum from normal to disordered consumption.

Incentive Sensitization

Although opponent-process–based theories and the theory of allostasis provide useful perspectives on what types of changes we might hope to observe in the transition from normal to disordered drinking, they do not necessarily provide an account of why individuals might choose to seek out a particular substance. Robinson and Berridge's (1993, 2003) incentive sensitization theory of addiction offers an alternative and, potentially, complementary perspective on alcohol-related adaptations of the brain. These authors propose that through a process of classical conditioning, cues associated with psychoactive drug use acquire incentive reward properties, or *incentive salience*. The role of drug cues is thought to initiate excessive incentive motivation for drugs, which in turn causes compulsive drug seeking, drug taking, and relapse. As Robinson and Berridge (2003) articulated, "Incentive salience attribution is hypothesized to transform the neural representations of otherwise neutral stimuli into salient incentives, able to 'grab' attention and makes [*sic*] them attractive and wanted" (p. 42). The central tenet of their theory is that the use of substances (including, presumably, alcohol) hypersensitizes neural circuits associated with the effects of the substances to cues associated with the drug. This, in turn, causes a pathological "wanting" rather than a simple "liking" of the drug. *Wanting* can be thought of as a sensitized arousal, whereas *liking* can be thought of as an attitude. These reactions to alcohol-related cues (which lead to drug wanting) are thought to be mediated by alcohol-induced changes in the neural networks in the prefrontal cortex associated with emotional regulation, inhibition, decision making, and judgment, an idea that is gaining support through experimental and neuroimaging studies (Noël et al., 2007; Wrase et al., 2007). An important implication of this perspective is that explicit attitudes and outcome expectations (e.g., Goldman, Brown, & Christiansen, 1987) surrounding alcohol (and indexing likes or dislikes) might not be as relevant for charting the transitions from normal to disordered use if wanting and liking are not tightly coupled, and they do not appear to be. For example, in a series of three studies, Hobbs, Remington, and Glautier (2005) found little evidence for a relation between these two constructs. That is, an alcohol priming dose increased wanting but not liking of alcohol. Furthermore, reducing liking did not affect wanting levels. These results support an incentive-sensitization model such that liking and wanting appear to occur on the basis of distinct and separate neural substrates. It seems quite reasonable to speculate that the development of wanting perhaps represents a key motivational process in the transition from normal to disordered use and that when users experience persistent and/or high levels of wanting alcohol, their drinking has progressed.

Summary

Regular alcohol use induces changes in the brain that affect the magnitude of responses to alcohol consumption and alcohol-related motivation. Specifically, allostatic changes in hedonic tone (i.e., affect) may motivate further drinking via negative reinforcement, especially if associated with impaired self-regulation and the development of incentive sensitization. We can think of these neurobiological adaptations as akin to wiring the brain to become more "alcohol-centric," where alcohol becomes important for regulating negative affective states (see Sher & Grekin, 2007) and becomes a particularly salient reinforcement that may come to hijack other natural reinforcers in the environment (Volkow & Fowler, 2000).

THE CONCEPT OF CRAVING AND EMERGENCE OF DRINKING-RELATED MOTIVATION

Craving has historically been considered a cardinal symptom of alcoholism (Jellinek, 1960). Although widely considered an index of pathological drinking patterns (Kahler, Epstein, & McCrady, 1995; Singleton & Gorelick, 1998), it is not considered a symptom of alcohol dependence in *DSM–IV* criteria. Perhaps because craving is not specifically given the status of a *DSM* diagnostic criterion, there is a lack of consensus on and considerable debate over its definition (Tiffany, Carter, & Singleton, 2000). In the simplest sense, craving describes the urge or desire for alcohol (Singleton & Gorelick, 1998). However, such a definition does not necessarily differentiate between wanting alcohol and liking it (Robinson & Berridge, 1993).

Furthermore, craving appears to be highly situational and variable in its manifestations. For example, alcohol craving may serve similar functions to those of obsessive–compulsive disorder in the sense that there is a high level of preoccupation that is difficult to dismiss (Modell, Glaser, Cyr, & Mountz, 1992), with a notable difference being that the

obsessive thoughts characteristic of obsessive–compulsive disorder are often unwanted and are not necessarily associated with anticipated reinforcement (Anton, 2000). Furthermore, situational cues—such as the presence and smell of alcohol (Cooney, Gillespie, Baker, & Kaplan, 1987; Litt, Cooney, Kadden, & Gaupp, 1990), advertisements for alcohol or visual cues of alcohol (Cassisi, Delehant, Tsoutsouris, & Levin, 1998; Chiang, Schuetz, & Soyka, 2002), and auditory cues, such as the sound of a beer can being opened (Heinze, Wölfling, & Grüsser, 2007)—have been found to elicit craving in individuals ranging from those characterized as social drinkers to those having alcohol dependence. Of note, negative mood states, guilt, and irritability were correlates of craving for individuals with alcohol dependence in these studies (Chiang et al., 2002; Cooney, Litt, Morse, Bauer, & Gaupp, 1987), perhaps indicative of the proposed link between allostasis and alcohol seeking proposed by Koob and LeMoal (2001).

Researchers and clinicians have approached the assessment of craving in numerous ways, including self-report, autonomic and central nervous system responding (including electrophysiological and functioning neuroimaging) to a range of stimuli associated with alcohol or drinking (Cassisi et al., 1998; Heinze et al. 2007), and full-scale multi-dimensional craving questionnaires (Tiffany et al., 2000), as well as single questions and assessments and animal studies of alcohol self-administration following experimental manipulations, such as limiting availability to alcohol (Sayette et al., 2000; Spanagel, 2000).

We believe the concept of craving is important in distinguishing normal from disordered use of alcohol because the phenomenon patently represents the importance that alcohol has taken on in the life of the drinker. That is, to crave or want alcohol is prima facie evidence of alcohol's having a high degree of incentive value to the individual. Although theories such as those of Koob and LeMoal (2001) and Robinson and Berridge (1993, 2003) provide plausible accounts for the origins of craving, other theoretical accounts have been proposed as well.

Of the many theories regarding craving, the elaborated intrusion theory of desire is a complex cognitive model that posits, at the simplest level, that individuals experience craving through their own cognitive elaboration of the visual, olfactory, and auditory components of alcohol (Kavanagh, Andrade, & May, 2005; May, Andrade, Panabokke, & Kavanagh, 2004). This theory may account for findings related to increased attention to alcohol stimuli in heavy- versus light-drinking adolescents (Field, Christiansen, Cole, & Goudie, 2007). This theory also connects individual's craving for alcohol with people's comparatively highly practiced, elaborative, appetitive, and somatovisceral craving for such substances as food and non-alcoholic beverages (May et al., 2004). Support for this perspective comes from findings showing increased serum leptin levels (a peptide that is implicated in appetite regulation) in people with alcoholism who had higher levels of craving for alcohol (Hillemacher et al., 2007). Furthermore, there has historically been an association between the preference for sweets and heavy drinking, which is thought to have an appetitive mechanism in individuals (Kampov-Polevoy, Garbutt, & Janowsky, 1999).

Of particular relevance to this discussion is the cognitive processing model of craving that posits that there are automatic and nonautomatic processes involved in craving and, ultimately, whether an individual eventually drinks alcohol (Tiffany, 1990). Namely, alcohol-seeking actions become automated with time; that is, they become more rapid, it becomes more easy to initiate them without intention, they are difficult to inhibit once begun, and they become effortless and do not require conscious awareness. Craving, per se, is not necessarily an automatic response but rather arises when these automatic processes to seek alcohol are somehow thwarted or blocked by obstacles in the environment (e.g., the unavailability of alcohol, drinking-incompatible contexts) or personal decisions to refrain from drinking. From this perspective, craving is a manifestation of a core motivational process and is not a direct proxy for the underlying process of disordered alcohol use. Rather, craving results from an interaction between the automated process of alcohol consumption and the environment (i.e., whether and how obstacles in the environment thwart automatic processes) or the self (i.e., whether and how one's wishes to restrict alcohol use thwart automatic

processes; e.g., see Tiffany & Conklin, 2000). Thus, Tiffany and Conklin's (2000) cognitive approach suggests that we might be able to more directly tap into the underlying pathological process by studying the extent to which alcohol itself or alcohol-related cues (both in the environment and within the individual) activate automatic processes associated with alcohol seeking.

IMPLICIT COGNITION, MOTIVATION, AND AUTOMATICITY: RELEVANCE FOR DISTINGUISHING REGULAR USE FROM DISORDERED USE

We have argued that an important consideration in distinguishing normal from disordered use is the extent to which alcohol changes the brain in such a way as to make alcohol motivationally important and alcohol seeking more of an automatic process. Although at first blush craving might appear to represent such a motivationally relevant and automatic process, under accounts such as Tiffany and Conklin's (2000), craving is related to core processes but is not isomorphic with them. Rather, craving is posited to represent an interaction between automated alcohol-seeking processes and external and internal obstacles to these being executed. It would therefore be desirable to develop approaches to study these automatic processes more directly.

Implicit cognitive processing potentially represents such an approach (for a brief review of implicit cognition in addiction, see Ames, Franken, & Coronges, 2006; also see chap. 9 of this volume). *Implicit cognitions* refer to thoughts that bypass conscious deliberation, require no effort, and occur relatively automatically (Bargh, 1994; Bargh & Ferguson, 2000; Wegner & Bargh, 1998). Within cognitive dual-process theories (for a review, see Smith & DeCoster, 2000), a continuum is assumed in which automatic cognitions are contrasted with those that are deliberate, controlled, conscious, and effortful.

One approach to assessing how alcohol-centric the brain has become is to measure the extent to which alcohol is automatically associated with a range of ambiguous stimuli. For example, Stacy (1995) measured implicit alcohol-related associations by presenting participants with ambiguously alcohol-related cue words (e.g., *draft, pitcher, tap*) or objects (e.g., a six-pack without labels) mixed with alcohol-unrelated cues and then asking them to list the first word that entered their minds. Alcohol-related associations are considered strong when a participant consistently associates ambiguous cues with alcohol-related concepts. In an even more indirect method, the modified alcohol Stroop test has been used to measure the salience of alcohol in drinkers (for a review of the use of the Stroop test in addictions research, see Cox, Fadardi, & Pothos, 2006). In the modified Stroop test, participants are presented with words displayed in various colors and are asked to classify the words by their color as quickly as possible. Words unrelated to alcohol are presented along with words related to alcohol, and response latencies are measured. According to the underlying theoretical rationale, the Stroop effect occurs when an individual harbors extensive mental associations with alcohol-related words and thus finds it harder to ignore the word meaning of alcohol-related words compared with alcohol-irrelevant words. In essence, the alcohol-related words grab more attention than the alcohol-irrelevant words. As a result, response latencies for identifying the color of alcohol-related words will be longer than those for alcohol-irrelevant words. Similarly, the Implicit Association Test (Greenwald, Nosek, & Banaji, 2003) is thought to measure implicit attitudes, and versions measuring implicit attitudes toward alcohol have been developed (e.g., Palfai & Ostafin, 2003; Wiers, van Woerden, Smulders, & de Jong, 2002). As an example, a participant might be asked to classify various words or pictures associated with alcoholic beverages, soft drinks, "good" concepts, and "bad" concepts. At certain times, the participant is asked to indicate whether words presented are in the alcohol–good category (e.g., *beer, kindness*) or the nonalcohol–bad category (e.g., *cola, death*). These categories are then switched, such that the participant is asked to classify words in the alcohol–bad category and the nonalcohol–good category. Ostensibly, if the participant associates *alcohol* and *good*, he or she will find it more mentally taxing to sort bad concepts into the same category as alcohol. As a result, the response latencies for these trial blocks should be longer than for those in which the participant

classifies good things into the same category as alcohol. Although the assessment of cognitive processing is necessarily indirect, the recognition of automatic cognitions can provide insight into the distinction between simple alcohol use and AUDs and associated cravings, as well the progression from normative alcohol use to nonnormative, disordered drinking.

When people are exposed to stimuli previously associated with alcohol use, these associations are thought to produce automatic alcohol-related cognitions that have motivational properties. Because alcohol-related cognitions make alcohol salient, we can hypothesize that subsequent alcohol use is much more likely when these conditions are primed. Presumably, if one is exposed to a variety of stimuli and a variety of contexts when using alcohol, these additional associations will increase the likelihood that one will drink in these situations. That is, regardless of whether these cognitive processes reach awareness, automatic alcohol-related thoughts ostensibly increase the salience of alcohol, thereby making it more likely that actual alcohol use will result in relevant contexts. With repeated activation of alcohol-related thoughts, the associative strength of a formerly ambiguous cue becomes fused with alcohol-related concepts. These strengthened associations may be the means by which alcohol-related cues can grab one's attention, as they are proposed to do in the incentive-sensitization model (Robinson & Berridge, 2003). It is easy to see how this explanation describes the progression from normative alcohol use to more disordered drinking. With repeated and frequent alcohol use in a variety of contexts, the number of alcohol-related associations could become so extensive that alcohol cues become ubiquitous and the salience of alcohol is consistently heightened, thereby priming the individual for drinking at many times and in multiple contexts. (This is not to say that drinking will necessarily occur in primed contexts, only that the individual is more likely to have attention devoted to drinking-related cues and activities.)

Determining whether alcohol-related implicit cognitions can lead to disordered drinking should involve evidence that these types of thoughts are related to alcohol use. Several studies have shown that implicit cognitions about alcohol predict recent alcohol use (e.g., Benthin et al., 1995; Stacy, 1995), even after controlling for a series of variables related to alcohol use, such as parental alcohol use, level of acculturation, and gender. These findings suggest that memory associations can trigger alcohol-related thoughts following exposure to ambiguous alcohol-related stimuli and that this increased alcohol salience can motivate alcohol use (space precludes detailed discussion of this topic, which is covered in depth in chap. 9, this volume).

Alcohol-related implicit memories are related to problematic drinking, and the strength of these associations decreases with effective treatment. Cognitive differences in alcohol-related implicit associations in people with AUD diagnoses compared with those without suggest that the stronger associations found among dependent drinkers may be useful in diagnosing AUDs (Hill & Paynter, 1992). These results have also been noted in heavy social drinkers (Cox, Yeates, & Regan, 1999), and changes in the strength of implicit associations predict the success of inpatient alcohol treatment (Cox, Hogan, Kristian, & Race, 2002; Szalay, Carroll, & Tims, 1993). Thus, the development of automatic alcohol-related cognitions appears to track severity of drinking problems and may provide an important endophenotype for what we usually think of as disordered drinking.

IMPAIRED CONTROL: RELEVANCE FOR DISTINGUISHING REGULAR USE FROM DISORDERED USE

Loss of control, defined as drinking in larger amounts or for a longer period of time than intended, is arguably the most florid manifestation of severely pathological alcohol use. It is emphasized as a core symptom of alcohol dependence by both clinicians and researchers and listed as a diagnostic criterion for alcohol dependence in the *DSM* (Alcoholics Anonymous, 2001; APA, 2000; Jellinek, 1960; Randall et al., 1999). Despite the widespread recognition of loss of control as a sign of pathological drinking, it has not consistently been operationalized (Kahler et al., 1995) either in humans (Heather, Booth, & Luce, 1998) or in animal models of consumption (Spanagel, 2000).

A number of correlates of impaired control have been identified, including low self-efficacy with regard to limiting alcohol intake (Fiorentine & Hillhouse, 2001; Lee, Oei, & Greeley, 1999), attentional biases toward alcohol (Townshend & Duka, 2007), individual differences in reactions to alcohol (Poulos, Parker, & Lê, 1998), and expectancies concerning the likelihood of losing control (Marlatt, Demming, & Reid, 1973). Several of these correlates most likely reflect individual differences that may be largely preexisting (e.g., alcohol sensitivity, outcome expectancies), and it is therefore unclear how loss of control might be a useful indicator of the transition from normal to disordered use.

Moreover, impaired control may manifest itself quite early in individuals' drinking careers. Langenbucher and Chung (1995) found that impaired control (defined as drinking larger amounts or for longer periods of time than expected) was the earliest occurring diagnostic criterion for problematic drinking for AUDs. In addition to occurring early, item response theory analyses reveal that impaired control is a low-threshold indicator of a latent trait of AUD (and is very similar in its psychometric properties to an item assessing drinking heavily once per week; Saha et al., 2007). That is, as one progresses on a latent trait of disordered drinking, impaired control is, on average, the most likely *DSM* AUD symptom to manifest itself. On the basis of these dual findings of early appearance and low threshold, reports of impaired control can represent a useful symptom in identifying those individuals for whom drinking has become disordered. However, it is an imperfect indicator, and not all individuals who show other symptoms of disordered drinking will necessarily have impaired control. In addition, although some theories posit that loss of control is a consequence of chronic alcohol effects on prefrontal cortex and associated executive cognitive functions engaged in self-control (e.g., Lyvers, 2000), theories of acute alcohol effects on social behavior (e.g., "alcohol myopia," the tendency of alcohol to narrow one's focus of attention to the most salient stimuli in the near environment to the exclusion of less salient, inhibitory stimuli; see Josephs & Steele, 1990) have provided a theoretical basis for positing that loss-of-control drinking can occur very early on in a person's drinking career, even in the absence of an alcoholcentric brain. Consequently, it should not be too surprising to find that impaired control, as it has been operationally defined up to the present (see Heather, Tebbutt, Mattick, & Zamir, 1993), is not clearly related to drinking history and can arise at any temporal stage in a person's drinking career (Leeman, Fenton, & Volpicelli, 2006).

Operationally defining *loss of control* or *impaired control* as drinking in larger amounts or longer than intended presupposes that an individual is attempting to restrict his or her drinking. Therefore, individuals who desire to drink to excess but have no desire to control their drinking in the first place cannot (by definition) experience this symptom. In Kenneth J. Sher's experience, the drinking survey items that college students have the most difficulty understanding are those related to impaired control, probably because the concept of controlling one's drinking is alien to many of them. However, late adolescence and young adulthood are the life stages associated with the highest levels of AUDs in our society (Grant, 1997; Grant et al., 2004). Although the symptom profiles of older adolescents and young adults with alcohol dependence are generally comparable to those of similarly diagnosed older adults, there are a few differences. Most notably, younger individuals (those ages 18–29) with alcohol dependence were significantly more likely to report spending much time drinking or recovering from drinking (e.g., spending a lot of time being sick or getting over bad effects of drinking) compared with alcohol-dependent individuals older than 30. In contrast, these younger alcohol-dependent individuals were less likely to have the desire to attempt or made unsuccessful attempts to reduce or stop drinking (e.g., wanted to stop more than once; Littlefield & Sher, 2008). This pattern of findings suggests that many younger disordered drinkers drink to excess (as indicated by spending a lot of time drinking or recovering from drinking) but do not necessarily see these extremes as a problem (they are less likely to try to stop or reduce drinking). Thus, although loss of control is an important phenomenon and can be a sensitive indicator of disordered drinking for many individuals, it presupposes a desire to control drink-

ing and therefore can fail to detect unconstrained, excessive consumption.

COGNITIVE DISTORTIONS: UNREALISTIC APPRAISALS OF ONE'S OWN DRINKING

Up until this point, we have focused our discussion on the motivational importance that alcohol comes to serve in the drinker's life and the extent to which an individual shows impaired control over the amount of alcohol consumed. Both of these ideas have been central topics in alcohol studies for many years and are consistent with traditional notions of alcohol dependence. However, clinical lore has long posited that lack of insight into the problematic nature of one's drinking (e.g., denial) is a common, notable symptom that is frequently observed in alcoholism (Sher & Epler, 2004). Although the current status of denial as a useful clinical concept is questionable (Sher & Epler, 2004), there can be little doubt that the failure to realistically appraise one's drinking as abnormal or problematic when it comes to take on special importance in one's life represents a potentially important consideration in designating a person's drinking as disordered.

Thus, we propose that cognitive distortions about one's drinking can serve as an indicator (although probably not a universal one) of disordered drinking. By *cognitive distortions*, we mean errors in thinking or faulty rationales for drinking behavior that possibly lead to or maintain increasingly deviant drinking practices. Given the great ambivalence many societies have about the acceptability of alcohol (Heath, 1995) due to its complex mix of prized and dangerous effects (Thakker, 1998), one's own drinking pattern would appear to be difficult for many to accurately appraise. Indeed, one increasingly accepted, evidence-based treatment for alcohol dependence, motivational enhancement therapy (Miller, Zweben, DiClemente, & Rychtarik, 1995), accepts lack of awareness as a common feature of the disorder and attempts to foster more realistic appraisals of drinking as a primary therapeutic goal.

Cognitive theorists have long asserted that errors in thinking can contribute to increases in behavioral and emotional psychopathology in general (Beck, 1995). The literature on explicit alcohol outcome expectancies (Goldman et al., 1987) has clearly documented that many individuals hold unrealistic beliefs about the effects of alcohol (e.g., alcohol enhances cognitive and psychomotor performance; Brown, Goldman, Inn, & Anderson, 1980), and such beliefs are associated with disordered drinking (Sher, Gotham, & Watson, 2004). For the present purposes, we consider a few types of distortions relevant to how one judges one's own drinking with respect to societal and local norms.

Most relevant to the question of evaluating the normative nature of one's own drinking is the concept of drinking norms. The theory of reasoned action (Ajzen & Fishbein, 1980) and the related theory of planned behavior (Ajzen, 1991) propose that descriptive norms (perceptions regarding the normative quality of the behavior) are powerful predictors of behavior. Both the theory of reasoned action and the theory of planned behavior have been applied to explain a wide range of behaviors (Madden, Ellen, & Ajzen, 1992; Sheppard, Hartwick, & Warshaw, 1988), and an immense body of literature has documented the robustness of drinking norms as a strong predictor of both the onset of drinking and the intensity of drinking among drinkers (Laflin, Moore-Hirschl, Weis, & Hayes, 1994; Marcoux & Shope, 1997). Largely because of the robustness of this association, many campus- and community-based prevention programs are based on the assumption that altering these perceived norms will lead to reduced consumption (Mattern & Neighbors, 2004; Werch et al., 2000), although the ultimate effectiveness of existing approaches is controversial at this time (e.g., Wechsler et al., 2003).

Although some sizable proportion of variance in perceived norms is based on accurate perceptions of drinking in the environment, much of the variance is the result of inaccurate perception. With respect to drinking, at least two sources of distortion have been identified. The first, *pluralistic ignorance,* refers to widely held but inaccurate beliefs (Prentice & Miller, 1993). It is widely believed among college students that their peers view heavy drinking positively, even though most view it negatively (Bourgeois & Bowen, 2001; Hines, Saris, & Throckmorton-Belzer, 2002), and this phenomenon appears to be especially prevalent among male college students (Suls & Green,

2003). What happens when a person mistakenly believes that his or her attitude is at odds with a relevant reference group? If one chooses to decrease the discrepancy, one can (a) change the attitude to make it closer to the perceived norm, (b) attempt to change the norm so it is closer to the attitude, or (c) decrease the importance of the reference group altogether (Prentice & Miller, 1993). Because it is easier and less costly, the simplest route to reducing the discrepancy is to change one's attitude to match the perceived norm, and evidence suggests that this is the most likely route as well (Prentice & Miller, 1993). Consistent with this perspective is the finding that the magnitude of college students' overestimations of peer consumption is associated with the actual amount of alcohol they themselves consume (Perkins, Haines, & Rice, 2005). Although pluralistic ignorance represents a potentially important distortion that can lead to drinking excess, the unrealistic perceived norm is pluralistic (i.e., not idiosyncratic to the drinker and not necessarily motivated by the drinker's own drinking history) and, therefore, may not be particularly helpful in distinguishing normal from disordered use.

Another social-cognitive process, false consensus (Ross, Greene, & House, 1977), may be more helpful in identifying a transition from normal to disordered use. *False consensus* refers to individuals' tendency to see others as more similar to themselves than they are in reality and is, in a sense, a type of projection. For example, skiers are more likely than nonskiers to estimate that a higher proportion of the population skis, and heavy drinkers are more likely to see heavy drinking as more normative, and thus less socially deviant, than it is in reality (Suls, Wan, & Sanders, 1988). According to Ross et al. (1977), false consensus can arise through several mechanisms including selective exposure to similar people, salience of one's own beliefs relative to other sources of information, information-processing biases that lead people to assume that others in similar situations will behave as they do, and motivation to maintain the normative compatibility of one's own behavior by distorting the behavior of others to conform to one's personal norm (see Whitley, 1998). The relevance of false consensus to disordered drinking was noted by Wolfson (2000), who argued that both selective exposure and self-justifying motivation will serve to keep the excessive drinker from viewing his or her drinking as aberrant (and therefore as an area of concern).

The motivational component of false consensus can be viewed as a type of self-serving bias that serves to maintain a positive image of the self by distorting the established norms of others. Other self-protective, cognitive biases may also be relevant here. For example, the theory of motivated reasoning hypothesizes that individuals will predictably arrive at conclusions that they wish to arrive at, often through a biased search of memory or available evidence (Kunda, 1990). For example, to maintain the illusion of being a normal drinker, a person worried about his or her problematic drinking can selectively search memorable instances in which drinking did not occur or was socially accepted and rewarded, thereby concluding the absence of a drinking problem when one might actually exist. This selective memory search can allow for the directed (rather than accurate) conclusion that one does not have a drinking problem, while using real events to reach the conclusion. This gives the distinct impression of objectivity and rationality, which becomes a highly persuasive point both to oneself and also to others (Kunda, 1990), fueling the plausibility of the cognitive distortion. These ideas are supported by findings that combinations of cognitive distortions, real or perceived alcohol availability, and opportunities to use alcohol predict subsequent alcohol craving and use (Wertz & Sayette, 2001).

A long career of chronic, excessive consumption can lead to neurologic defects that directly impair the ability to evaluate the significance of one's own drinking, and premorbid neurological deficits might also impair the ability to accurately appraise one's drinking pattern (for a review of this literature, see Sher & Epler, 2004). Thus, not all cognitive distortions should necessarily be viewed as self-serving biases and, depending on the underlying cause, can emerge in the early, middle, or late stages of a disordered drinking career.

Additionally, cognitive distortions that serve to maintain deviant drinking practices may relate to a number of underlying mechanisms, such as implicit cognitions, motivations, sensitivity to the effects of alcohol, and emotional state (Wiers et al., 2007); consequently, understanding the determinants of specific cognitive distortions is not straightforward. Nevertheless, we view cognitive distortions with respect to one's own drinking as evidence for disordered drinking. However, its absence does not suggest absence of disorder; there is no reason to speculate that heavily alcohol-involved individuals are incapable of realistically appraising their drinking. However, when present, it is important clinically because it provides an obstacle in helping the disordered drinker to recognize the nature of his or her problem.

IS DRINKING NECESSARY TO BE A DISORDERED DRINKER? THE QUESTION OF PERSISTENCE OF ALCOHOL-SEEKING MOTIVATION

The widespread lay belief that an alcoholic forever remains so (Alcoholics Anonymous, 2001) indicates that even in abstinence, individuals with previous disordered drinking may continue to differ from others without alcohol problems. This may especially be seen as the case when individuals are coerced into abstinence for medical or legal reasons; that is, they must nonvoluntarily abstain from alcohol (Kelly et al., 2006; Watson, Brown, Tilleskjor, Jacobs, & Pucel, 1988). Risk of relapse, although highly time dependent (with most relapse occurring in the first 3 months of abstinence) can persist for many years (Walitzer & Dearing, 2006), and the sleep quality of abstinent alcoholics has been found to be poorer and more fragmented even after 2 years of abstinence (Drummond, Gillin, Smith, & DeModena, 1998). Cognitive approaches to relapse focus on abstinent alcoholics' appraisal of environments and situations, their sense of efficacy with regard to tempting situations, and their overall resources for coping in a highly alcohol-laden and tempting world (Cooney et al., 1997; Miller, Westerberg, Harris, & Tonigan, 1996). The threat of relapse hangs over the head of many former disordered drinkers like the sword of Damocles (Marlatt, 1996).

Learning and Reinstatement

As discussed earlier regarding opponent-process theory, allostasis, and incentive motivation, one of the primary reasons that abstinent alcoholics may be differentiated from individuals with no past history of alcohol problems is that they have, in effect, been exposed to an extensive learning history concerning alcohol. Animal studies are fundamental to showing that such a conditioning paradigm indeed plays a role in later relapse, a phenomenon known as reinstatement (Shaham, Shalev, Lu, de Wit, & Stewart, 2003). In such experiments, animals learn to self-administer large doses of alcohol, and then this behavior is gradually extinguished. Later, animals are exposed to experimental stimuli including other drugs, such as nicotine (Lê, Wang, Harding, Juzytsch, & Shaham, 2003); discrete cues, such as the presence of the odor of alcohol (Maccioni et al., 2007); and situational contexts or environments associated with previous alcohol consumption (Zironi, Burattini, Aicardi, & Janak, 2006), and reinstatement of previously extinguished behaviors is frequently observed (for a discussion of the validity of these models for alcoholic relapse, see Epstein, Preston, Stewart, & Shaham, 2006). These findings point to the persistence of alcohol-related learning (or memory) and beyond periods of active alcohol consumption.

Controlled Drinking in Former Alcoholics

There is probably no more contentious issue anywhere in alcohol studies than the question of whether individuals with a history of severe alcohol dependence can learn to become controlled or social drinkers (e.g., Marlatt, 1983; Sobell & Sobell, 1978, 1995). There can be little doubt that some individuals with a history of severe dependence can, for extended periods of time, drink in a way that appears normal (e.g., Edwards et al., 1981; Finney & Moos, 1991; Polich, Armor, & Braiker, 1981). Moreover, the large epidemiological literature on the prevalence of AUDs across the life course clearly indicates that many, if not most, individuals who meet criteria for alcohol dependence at one stage of their life are likely to become nondependent drinkers (e.g., Grant, 1997; Grant et al., 2004). Equally as important, prospective studies have indicated that although alcohol dependence is typically stable in middle adulthood, it tends to regress rather than progress at this stage of life among drinkers in the general population (Jackson, O'Neill, & Sher, 2006). What is currently

unclear is what factors distinguish individuals who have been disordered drinkers yet can adopt drinking styles that are not disordered from those in whom reversion to severe drinking patterns is likely to result if regular drinking is attempted.

LIMITATIONS OF OUR APPROACH

As we alluded to earlier, the approach adopted for our current analysis is a somewhat parochial one, focusing on how alcohol changes the neurobiology of the drinker's brain to motivate further drinking. By cutting to the chase of what we see as a central mechanism underlying pathological alcohol seeking, we sidestepped many important etiological processes that can contribute to this end state. For example, use of alcohol as an emotion regulation strategy because of preexisting psychiatric illness, psychological stress, or allostatic changes induced by alcohol could be proposed as a form of disordered use (see Sher & Grekin, 2007). We also barely touched on the important literature on dispositional and social factors that lead to both initiation and progression of drinking problems (see Sher, Grekin, & Williams, 2005, for a broad overview of these topics), again focusing on what we believe are central processes related to alcohol-induced changes in the brain that make the brain more alcohol-centric. As noted at the outset, the manifestation of addictive behaviors represents the joint effects of approach and restraint, and the other side of the coin with respect to the processes we have just discussed is self-regulation, which not only constrains impulse but is also affected by it (Muraven & Baumeister, 2000). Clearly, there are many divergent conceptual approaches one can take in applying etiological research to understanding the progression from normal to disordered drinking.

Also missing from our analysis is a more fine-grained, stagelike approach to drinking progression, articulated by clinical theorists like Jellinek (1952) but not yet receiving much empirical support. Researchers are beginning to study progression across multiple milestones (Stallings, Hewitt, Beresford, Heath, & Eaves, 1999), and the item response theory analyses of alcohol symptomatology and sequences of symptom onset discussed earlier suggest that it is possible that different processes are associated with different stages of disorder. However, at present, existing prospective data that could inform this issue are inadequate, and the probabilistic nature of the order in which milestones of alcohol progression are reached presents important methodological challenges.

Because we were interested in trying to identify processes that are emergent in the transition from normal to disordered use, we did not consider the importance of withdrawal as a defining symptom, largely because it is both a severe and an uncommon symptom (Saha et al., 2007). However, there is arguably no better validated symptom of dependence than withdrawal, leading some to even argue that it can be considered pathognomic (i.e., necessary and sufficient) to a clinically important alcohol phenotype (Langenbucher et al., 2000).

Finally, we sidestepped the entire question of diversity. There might be important differences in the manifestation of drinking symptomatology across groups defined by gender, ethnicity, and culture. By focusing on what we believe is a core neurobiological process, we believe that this limitation is less critical than if we were examining specific alcohol-related consequences or drinking patterns, but it would be hubristic to dismiss this as a limitation entirely.

SUMMARY

There are many ways in which alcohol consumption can represent a problem to the individual and society, and determining the threshold at which consumption becomes a concern can be viewed from a number of perspectives. In a culture that strictly forbids any alcohol consumption, homeopathic doses of alcohol can in and of themselves be viewed as a problem to the individual, but it does not necessarily represent a disorder in the sense that there is an alcohol-related dysfunction that is motivating the problem. Even flagrant drunken excess that leads to severe consequences for the drinker (e.g., motor vehicle crashes, sexual indiscretions) and may warrant clinical attention does not necessarily indicate that there is something about the drinker that is abnormal beyond poor judgment (which could manifest itself multiple ways, some of them alcohol independent).

Using etiological research to inform nosology is not as straightforward as it might appear because most etiological research focuses on risk factors for the development of disordered drinking, not the dynamic changes that occur as a function of drinking and that motivate further drinking. However, it is clear that with regular alcohol consumption (that might be motivated by any of a variety of reasons; Cooper, Frone, Russell, & Mudar, 1995), alcohol can begin to take on increasing motivational significance for the person as a stimulus in its own right as a result of allostatic changes that motivate further drinking. In such ways, the brains of drinkers can become more alcoholcentric so that the drinker becomes increasingly motivated to use alcohol. Most traditional symptoms of alcohol dependence (e.g., impaired control, craving) are markers for this process but are highly fallible because they are multiply determined. For example, impaired control presupposes a desire for control, and craving implies that alcohol seeking is thwarted to some degree. Directly assessing alcohol salience through implicit cognitive measures might represent one way to overcome obstacles associated with traditional clinical approaches. Progression of disordered drinking does not necessarily bring with it awareness of the disorder, presenting barriers to problem recognition and clinical challenges. The extent to which an alcohol-centric brain normalizes over periods of abstinence or moderate drinking is difficult to assess, but it is clear from preclinical research that there is nontrivial durability to the adaptive brain changes that occur during the development of disordered drinking, placing formerly disordered drinkers at risk of relapse.

References
Ajzen, I. (1991). The theory of planned behavior. *Organizational Behavior and Human Decision Processes, 50,* 179–211.

Ajzen, I., & Fishbein, M. (1980). *Understanding attitudes and predicting social behavior.* Englewood Cliffs, NJ: Prentice-Hall.

Alcoholics Anonymous. (2001). *Alcoholics anonymous.* New York: Alcoholics Anonymous World Services.

Allen, J. P., Fertig, J. B., Towle, L. H., & Altshuler, V. B. (1994). Psychometric analyses of the Alcohol Dependence Scale among United States and Russian clinical samples. *International Journal of the Addictions, 29,* 71–87.

American Psychiatric Association. (1951). *Diagnostic and statistical manual of mental disorders* (1st ed.). Washington, DC: Author.

American Psychiatric Association. (1980). *Diagnostic and statistical manual of mental disorders* (3rd ed.). Washington, DC: Author.

American Psychiatric Association. (1987). *Diagnostic and statistical manual of mental disorders* (3rd ed., rev.). Washington, DC: Author.

American Psychiatric Association. (1994). *Diagnostic and statistical manual of mental disorders* (4th ed.). Washington, DC: Author.

American Psychiatric Association. (2000). *Diagnostic and statistical manual of mental disorders* (4th ed., text rev.). Washington, DC: Author.

Ames, S. L., Franken, I. H. A., & Coronges, K. (2006). Implicit cognition and drugs of abuse. In R. W. Wiers & A. W. Stacy (Eds.), *Handbook of implicit cognition and addiction* (pp. 363–378). Thousand Oaks, CA: Sage.

Anton, R. F. (2000). Obsessive-compulsive aspects of craving: Development of the Obsessive Compulsive Drinking Scale. *Addiction, 95*(Suppl. 2), S211–S217.

Bargh, J. A. (1994). The Four Horsemen of automaticity: Awareness, efficiency, intention, and control in social cognition. In R. S. Wyer Jr. & T. K. Srull (Eds.), *Handbook of social cognition* (2nd ed., pp. 1–40). Hillsdale, NJ: Erlbaum.

Bargh, J. A., & Ferguson, M. L. (2000). Beyond behaviorism: On the automaticity of higher mental processes. *Psychological Bulletin, 126,* 925–945.

Beck, J. S. (1995). *Cognitive therapy: Basics and beyond.* New York: Guilford Press.

Benthin, A., Slovic, P., Moran, P., Severson, H., Mertz, C. K., & Gerrard, M. (1995). Adolescent health-threatening and health-enhancing behaviors: A study of word association and imagery. *Journal of Adolescent Health, 17,* 143–152.

Bourgeois, M. J., & Bowen, A. (2001). Self-organization of alcohol-related attitudes and beliefs in a campus housing complex: An initial investigation. *Health Psychology, 20,* 434–437.

Brown, S. A., Goldman, M. S., Inn, A., & Anderson, L. R. (1980). Expectations of reinforcement from alcohol: Their domain and relation to drinking patterns. *Journal of Consulting and Clinical Psychology, 48,* 419–426.

Cassisi, J. E., Delehant, M., Tsoutsoris, J. S., & Levin, J. (1998). Psychophysiological reactivity to alcohol advertising in light and moderate social drinkers. *Addictive Behaviors, 23,* 267–274.

Chiang, S. W., Schuetz, C. G., & Soyka, M. (2002). Effects of irritability on craving before and after cue exposure in abstinent alcoholic inpatients: Experimental data on subjective response and heart rate. *Neuropsychobiology, 46,* 150–160.

Cleckley, H. M. (1982). *The mask of sanity* (6th ed.). New York: Plume.

Cooney, N. L., Gillespie, R. A., Baker, L. H., & Kaplan, R. F. (1987). Cognitive changes after alcohol cue exposure. *Journal of Consulting and Clinical Psychology, 55,* 150–155.

Cooney, N. L., Litt, M. D., Morse, P. A., Bauer, L. O., & Gaupp, L. (1997). Alcohol cue-reactivity, negative mood reactivity, and relapse in treated alcoholic men. *Journal of Abnormal Psychology, 106,* 243–250.

Cooper, M., Frone, M. R., Russell, M., & Mudar, P. (1995). Drinking to regulate positive and negative emotions: A motivational model of alcohol use. *Journal of Personality and Social Psychology, 69,* 990–1005.

Cox, W. M., Fadardi, J. S., & Pothos E. M. (2006). The addiction-Stroop test: Theoretical considerations and procedural recommendations. *Psychological Bulletin, 132,* 443–476.

Cox, W. M., Hogan, L. M., Kristian, M. R., & Race, J. H. (2002). Alcohol attentional bias as a predictor of alcohol abusers' treatment outcomes. *Drug and Alcohol Dependence, 68,* 237–243.

Cox, W. M., Yeates, G. N., & Regan, C. M. (1999). Effects of alcohol cues on cognitive processing in heavy and light drinkers. *Drug and Alcohol Dependence, 55,* 85–89.

Dawson, D. A. (2000). Alternative measures and models of hazardous consumption. *Journal of Substance Abuse, 12,* 79–91.

Dawson, D. A., Grant, B. F., Stinson, F. S., & Chou, P. S. (2004). Another look at heavy episodic drinking and alcohol use disorders among college and noncollege youth. *Journal of Studies on Alcohol, 65,* 477–488.

Drummond, S. P. A., Gillin, J. C., Smith, T. L., & DeModena, A. (1998). The sleep of abstinent pure primary alcoholic patients: Natural course and relationship to relapse. *Alcoholism: Clinical & Experimental Research, 22,* 1796–1802.

Edwards, G. (1982). *The treatment of drinking problems: A guide for the helping professions.* New York: McGraw-Hill.

Edwards, G. (1986). The alcohol dependence syndrome: A concept as stimulus to enquiry. *British Journal of Addiction, 81,* 171–183.

Edwards, G., Arif, A., & Hodgson, R. (1981). Nomenclature and classification of drug- and alcohol-related problems: A WHO memorandum. *Bulletin of the World Health Organization, 59,* 225–242.

Edwards, G., & Gross, M. (1976). Alcohol dependence: Provisional description of a clinical syndrome. *British Medical Journal, 1,* 1058–1061.

Epstein, D. H., Preston, K. L., Stewart, J., & Shaham, Y. (2006). Toward a model of drug relapse: An assessment of the validity of the reinstatement procedure. *Psychopharmacology, 189*, 1–16.

Feighner, J. P., Robins, E., Guze, S. B., Woodruff, R. A., Winokur, G., & Muñoz, R. (1972). Diagnostic criteria for use in psychiatric research. *Archives of General Psychiatry, 26*, 57–63.

Field, M., Christiansen, P., Cole, J., & Goudie, A. (2007). Delay discounting and the alcohol Stroop in heavy drinking adolescents. *Addiction, 102*, 579–586.

Finney, J. W., & Moos, R. H. (1991). The long-term course of treated alcoholism: I. Mortality, relapse and remission rates and comparisons with community controls. *Journal of Studies on Alcohol, 52*, 44–54.

Fiorentine, R., & Hillhouse, M. P. (2001). The addicted-self model: An explanation of "natural" recovery? *Journal of Drug Issues, 31*, 395–424.

Goldman, M. S., Brown, S. A., & Christiansen, B. A. (1987). Expectancy theory: Thinking about drinking. In H. T. Blane & K. E. Leonard (Eds.), *Psychological theories of drinking and alcoholism* (pp. 181–226). New York: Guilford Press.

Grant, B. F. (1994). Alcohol consumption, alcohol abuse and alcohol dependence: The United States as an example. *Addiction, 89*, 1357–1365.

Grant, B. F. (1997). Prevalence and correlates of alcohol use and *DSM-IV* alcohol dependence in the United States: Results of the National Longitudinal Epidemiologic Survey. *Journal of Studies on Alcohol, 58*, 464–473.

Grant, B. F, Dawson, D. A, Stinson, F. S., Chou, S. P., Dufour, M. C., & Pickering, R. P. (2004). The 12-month prevalence and trends in *DSM-IV* alcohol abuse and dependence: United States, 1991-1992 and 2001-2002. *Drug and Alcohol Dependence, 74*, 223–234.

Grant, B. F., Harford, T. C., Muthén, B. O., Hsiao-Ye, Y., Hasin, D. S., & Stinson, F. S. (2007). *DSM-IV* alcohol dependence and abuse: Further evidence of validity in the general population. *Drug and Alcohol Dependence, 86*, 154–166.

Greenwald, A. G., Nosek, B. A., & Banaji, M. R. (2003). Understanding and using the implicit association test: I. An improved scoring algorithm. *Journal of Personality and Social Psychology, 85*, 197–216.

Hambleton, R. K., Swaminathan, H., & Rogers, H. J. (1991). *Fundamentals of item response theory.* Newbury Park, CA: Sage.

Hasin, D. S., Muthén, B., Wisnicki, K. S., & Grant, B. (1994). Validity of the bi-axial dependence concept: A test in the US general population. *Addiction, 89*, 573–579.

Hasin, D. S., Paykin, A., Endicott, J., & Grant, B. (1999). The validity of *DSM-IV* alcohol abuse: Drunk drivers versus all others. *Journal of Studies on Alcohol, 60*, 746–755.

Heath, D. B. (Ed.). (1995). *International handbook on alcohol and culture.* Westport, CT: Greenwood Press.

Heather, N. Tebbutt, J. S., Mattick, R. P., & Zamir, R. (1993). Development of a scale for measuring impaired control over alcohol consumption: A preliminary report. *Journal of Studies on Alcohol, 54*, 700–709.

Heather, N., Booth, P., & Luce, A. (1998). Impaired Control Scale: Cross-validation and relationships with treatment outcome. *Addiction, 93*, 761–771.

Heinze, M., Wölfling, K., & Grüsser, S. M. (2007). Cue-induced auditory evoked potentials in alcoholism. *Clinical Neurophysiology, 118*, 856–862.

Hill, A. B., & Paynter, S. (1992). Alcohol dependence and semantic priming of alcohol related words. *Personality and Individual Differences, 13*, 745–750.

Hillemacher, T., Bleich, S., Frieling, H., Schanze, A., Wilhelm, J., Sperling, W., et al. (2007). Evidence of an association of leptin serum levels and craving in alcohol dependence. *Psychoneuroendocrinology, 32*, 87–90.

Hines, D., Saris, R. N., & Throckmorton-Belzer, L. (2002). Pluralistic ignorance and health risk behaviors: Do college students misperceive social approval for risky behaviors on campus and in media? *Journal of Applied Social Psychology, 32*, 2621–2640.

Hobbs, M., Remington, B., & Glautier, S. (2005). Dissociation of wanting and liking for alcohol in humans: A test of the incentive-sensitization theory. *Psychopharmacology, 178*, 493–499.

Hull, J. G., & Slone, L. B. (2004). Self-regulatory failure and alcohol use. In R. F. Baumeister & K. D. Vohs (Eds.), *Handbook of self-regulation: Research, theory, and applications* (pp. 466–491). New York: Guilford Press.

Jackson, K. M., O'Neill, S., & Sher, K. J. (2006). Characterizing alcohol dependence: Transitions during young and middle adulthood. *Experimental and Clinical Psychopharmacology, 14*, 228–244.

Jellinek, E. M. (1952). Phases of alcohol addiction. *Quarterly Journal of Studies on Alcohol, 13*, 673–684.

Jellinek, E. M. (1960). *The disease concept of alcoholism.* New Haven, CT: Hillhouse.

Josephs, R. A., & Steele, C. M. (1990). The two faces of alcohol myopia: Attentional mediation of psychological stress. *Journal of Abnormal Psychology, 99*, 115–126.

Kahler, C. W., Epstein, E. E., & McCrady, B. S. (1995). Loss of control and inability to abstain: The measurement of and the relationship between two constructs in male alcoholics. *Addiction, 90*, 1025–1036.

241

Kahler, C. W., & Strong, D. R. (2006). A Rasch model analysis of *DSM-IV* alcohol abuse and dependence items in the National Epidemiological Survey on Alcohol and Related Conditions. *Alcoholism: Clinical and Experimental Research, 30,* 1165–1175.

Kampov-Polevoy, A. B., Garbutt, J.C., & Janowsky, D. S. (1999). Association between preference for sweets and excessive alcohol intake: A review of animal and human studies. *Alcohol and Alcoholism, 34,* 386–395.

Kavanagh, D.J., Andrade, J., & May, J. (2005). Imagery relish and exquisite torture: The elaborated intrusion theory of desire. *Psychological Review, 112,* 446–467.

Keller, M., & Doria, J. (1991). On defining alcoholism. *Alcohol Health & Research World, 15,* 253–259.

Kelly, M., Chick, J., Gribble, R., Gleeson, M., Holton, M., Winstanley, J., et al. (2006). Predictors of relapse to harmful alcohol after orthotopic liver transplantation. *Alcohol & Alcoholism, 41,* 278–283.

Koob, G. F., & LeMoal, M. (2001). Drug addiction, dysregulation of reward and allostasis. *Neuro-psychopharmacology, 24,* 97–127.

Kunda, Z. (1990). The case for motivated reasoning. *Psychological Bulletin, 108,* 480–498.

Laflin, M. T., Moore-Hirschl, S., Weis, D. L., & Hayes, B. E. (1994). Use of the theory of reasoned action to predict drug and alcohol use. *International Journal of Addictions, 29,* 927–940.

Langenbucher, J. W., & Chung, T. (1995). Onset and staging of *DSM–IV* alcohol dependence using mean age and survival–hazard methods. *Journal of Abnormal Psychology, 104,* 346–354.

Langenbucher, J., Martin, C. S., Labouvie, E., Sanjuan, P. M., Bayly, L., & Pollock, N. K. (2000). Toward the *DSM–V*: The withdrawal-gate model versus the *DSM–IV* in the diagnosis of alcohol abuse and dependence. *Journal of Consulting and Clinical Psychology, 88,* 799–809.

Lê, A. D., Wang, A., Harding, S., Juzytsch, W., & Shaham, Y. (2003). Nicotine increases alcohol self-administration and reinstates alcohol seeking in rats. *Psychopharmacology, 168,* 216–221.

Lee, N. K., Oei, T. P., & Greeley, J. D. (1999). The interaction of alcohol expectancies and drinking refusal self-efficacy in high and low risk drinkers. *Addiction Research, 7,* 91–102.

Leeman, R. F., Fenton, M., & Volpicelli, J. R. (2006). Impaired control and undergraduate problem drinking. *Alcohol & Alcoholism, 42,* 42–48.

Litt, M. D., Cooney, N. L., Kadden, R. M., & Gaupp, L. (1990). Reactivity to alcohol cues and induced moods in alcoholics. *Addictive Behaviors, 15,* 137–146.

Littlefield, A.K., & Sher, K.J. (2008). *Alcohol use disorders in young adulthood.* Unpublished manuscript, University of Missouri, Columbia.

Lyvers, M. (2000). "Loss of control" in alcoholism and drug addiction: A neuroscientific interpretation. *Experimental and Clinical Psychopharmacology, 8,* 225–249.

Maccioni, P., Orrú, A., Korkosz, A., Gessa, G. L., Carai, M. A. M., Colombo, G., et al. (2007). Cue-induced reinstatement of ethanol seeking in Sardinian alcohol-preferring rats. *Alcohol, 41,* 31–39.

Madden, T. J., Ellen, P. S., & Ajzen, I. (1992). A comparison of the theory of planned behavior and the theory of reasoned action. *Personality and Social Psychology Bulletin, 18,* 3–9.

Marcoux, B. C., & Shope, J. T. (1997). Application of the theory of planned behavior to adolescent use and misuse of alcohol. *Health Education Research, 12,* 323–331.

Marlatt, G. A. (1983). The controlled-drinking controversy: A commentary. *American Psychologist, 38,* 1097–1110.

Marlatt, G. A. (1996). Models of relapse and relapse prevention: A commentary. *Experimental and Clinical Psychopharmacology, 4,* 55–60.

Marlatt, G. A., Demming, B., & Reid, J. B. (1973). Loss of control drinking in alcoholics: An experimental analogue. *Journal of Abnormal Psychology, 81,* 233–241.

Mattern, J. L., & Neighbors, C. (2004). Social norms campaigns: Examining the relationship between changes in perceived norms and changes in drinking levels. *Journal of Studies on Alcohol, 65,* 489–493.

May, J., Andrade, J., Panabokke, N., & Kavanagh, D. (2004). Images of desire: Cognitive models of craving. *Memory, 12,* 447–461.

Miller, W. R., Westerberg, V. S., Harris, R. J., & Tonigan, J. S. (1996). What predicts relapse? Prospective testing of antecedent models. *Addiction, 91*(Suppl.), S155–S171.

Miller, W. R., Zweben, A., DiClemente, C. C., & Rychtarik, R. G. (1995). *Motivational enhancement therapy manual: A clinical research guide for therapists treating individuals with alcohol abuse and dependence.* Rockville, MD: U.S. Department of Health and Human Services.

Modell, J. G., Glaser, F. B., Cyr, L., & Mountz, J. M. (1992). Obsessive and compulsive characteristics of craving for alcohol in alcohol abuse and dependence. *Alcoholism: Clinical and Experimental Research, 16,* 272–274.

Muraven, M., & Baumeister, R. F. (2000). Self-regulation and depletion of limited resources: Does self-control resemble a muscle? *Psychological Bulletin, 126,* 247–259.

Muthén, B. O., Grant, B., & Hasin, D. (1993). The dimensionality of alcohol abuse and dependence: Factor analysis of *DSM-III-R* and proposed *DSM-IV* criteria in the 1988 National Health Interview Survey. *Addiction, 88,* 1079–1090.

National Council on Alcoholism. (1972). Criteria for the diagnosis of alcoholism. *American Journal of Psychiatry, 129,* 127–135.

Noël , X., Van der Linden, M., d'Acremont, M., Bechara, A., Dan, B., Hanak, C., & Verbanck, P. (2007). Alcohol cues increase cognitive impulsivity in individuals with alcoholism. *Psychopharmacology, 192,* 291–298.

O'Neill, S., & Sher, K. J. (2000). Physiological alcohol dependence symptoms in early adulthood: A longitudinal perspective. *Experimental and Clinical Psychopharmacology, 8,* 493–508.

Orford, J. (2001). *Excessive appetites: A psychological view of addictions* (2nd ed.). Chichester, England: Wiley.

Palfai, T. P., & Ostafin, B. D. (2003). Alcohol-related motivational schema among hazardous drinkers: Assessing implicit response tendencies using the modified-IAT. *Behaviour Research and Therapy, 49,* 1149–1162.

Perkins, H. W., Haines, M. P., & Rice, R. (2005). Misperceiving the college drinking norm and related problems: A nationwide study of exposure to prevention information, perceived norms and student alcohol misuse. *Journal of Studies on Alcohol, 66,* 470–478.

Polich, J. M., Armor, D. J., & Braiker, H. B. (1981). *The course of alcoholism: Four years after treatment.* Santa Monica, CA: Rand.

Pollock, N. K., & Martin, C. S. (1999). Diagnostic orphans: Adolescents with alcohol symptoms who do not qualify for *DSM-IV* abuse or dependence diagnoses. *American Journal of Psychiatry, 156,* 897–901.

Poulos, C. X., Parker, J. L., & Lê, D. A. (1998). Increased impulsivity after injected alcohol predicts later alcohol consumption in rats: Evidence for "loss-of-control drinking" and marked individual differences. *Behavioral Neuroscience, 112,* 1247–1257.

Prentice, D. A., & Miller, D. T. (1993). Pluralistic ignorance and alcohol use on campus: Some consequences of misperceiving the social norm. *Journal of Personality and Social Psychology, 64,* 243–256.

Rachman, S. J. (1989). *Fear and courage* (2nd ed.). San Francisco: Freeman.

Randall, C. L., Roberts, J. S., Del Boca, F. K., Carroll, K. M., Connors, G. J., & Mattson, M. E. (1999). Telescoping of landmark events associated with drinking: A gender comparison. *Journal of Studies on Alcohol, 60,* 252–260.

Robinson, T. E., & Berridge, K. C. (1993). The neural basis of drug craving: An incentive-sensitization theory of addiction. *Brain Research Reviews, 18,* 247–291.

Robinson, T. E., & Berridge, K. C. (2003). Addiction. *Annual Review of Psychology, 54,* 25–53.

Ross, L., Greene, D., & House, P. (1977). The false consensus effect: An egocentric bias in social perception and attribution processes. *Journal of Experimental Social Psychology, 13,* 279–301.

Saha, T. D., Stinson, F. S., & Grant, B. F. (2007). The role of alcohol consumption in future classifications of alcohol use disorders. *Drug and Alcohol Dependence, 89,* 82–92.

Sartor, C. E., Lynskey, M. T., Heath, A. C., Jacob, T., & True, W. (2007). The role of childhood risk factors in initiation of alcohol use and progression to alcohol dependence. *Addiction, 102,* 216–225.

Saxon, A. J., Kivlahan, D. R., Doyle, S., & Donovan, D. M. (2007). Further validation of the alcohol dependence scale as an index of severity. *Journal of Studies on Alcohol and Drugs, 68,* 149–156.

Sayette, M. A. (2004). Self-regulatory failure and addiction. In R.F. Baumeister & K. D. Vohs (Eds.), *Handbook of self-regulation* (pp. 447–465). New York: Guilford Press.

Sayette, M. A., Shiffman, S., Tiffany, S. T., Niaura, R. S., Martin, C. S., & Shadel, W. G. (2000). The measurement of drug craving. *Addiction, 95*(Suppl. 2), S189–S210.

Schuckit, M. A. (1994). Substance-related disorders. In *DSM-IV sourcebook* (Vol. 1, pp. 5–19). Washington, DC: American Psychiatric Association.

Schuckit, M. A., & Smith, T. L. (2000). The relationships of a family history of alcohol dependence, a low level of response to alcohol and six domains of life functioning to the development of alcohol use disorders. *Journal of Studies on Alcohol, 61,* 827–835.

Schuckit, M. A., Smith, T. L., Danko, G. P., Kramer, J., Godinez, J., Bucholz, K. K., et al. (2005). Prospective evaluation of the four *DSM-IV* criteria for alcohol abuse in a large population. *American Journal of Psychiatry, 162,* 350–360.

Shaham, Y., Shalev, U., Lu, L., de Wit, H., & Stewart, J. (2003). The reinstatement model of drug relapse: History, methodology and major findings. *Psychopharmacology, 168,* 3–20.

Sheppard, B. H., Hartwick, J., & Warshaw, P.R. (1988). The theory of reasoned action: A meta-analysis of past research with recommendations for modifications and future research. *Journal of Consumer Research, 15,* 325–343.

Sher, K. J. (1991). *Children of alcoholics: A critical appraisal of theory and research.* Chicago: University of Chicago Press.

Sher, K. J., & Epler, A. J. (2004). Alcoholic denial: Self-awareness and beyond. In B. D. Beitman & J. Nair (Eds.), *Self-awareness deficits in psychiatric patients: Neurobiology, assessment and treatment* (pp. 184–212). New York: W. W. Norton.

Sher, K. J., Gotham, H. J., & Watson, A. (2004). Trajectories of dynamic predictors of disorder: Their meanings and implications. *Development and Psychopathology, 16,* 825–856.

Sher, K. J., & Grekin, E. R. (2007). Alcohol and affect regulation. In J. Gross (Ed.), *Handbook of emotion regulation* (pp. 560–580). New York: Guilford Press.

Sher, K. J., Grekin, E. R., & Williams, N. (2005). The development of alcohol problems. *Annual Review of Clinical Psychology, 1,* 493–523.

Siegel, S., Baptista, M. A., Kim, J. A., McDonald, R. V., & Weise-Kelly, L. (2000). Pavlovian psychopharmacology: The associative basis of tolerance. *Experimental and Clinical Psychopharmacology, 8,* 276–293.

Singleton, E. G., & Gorelick, D. A. (1998). Mechanisms of alcohol craving and their clinical implications. In M. Galanter (Ed.), *Recent developments in alcoholism: The consequences of alcoholism: Medical, neuropsychiatric, economic, cross-cultural* (Vol. 14, pp. 177–195). New York: Plenum Press.

Skinner, H. A. (1981). Primary syndromes of alcohol abuse: Their measurement and correlates. *British Journal of Addiction, 76,* 63–76.

Smith, E. R., & DeCoster, J. (2000). Dual process models in social and cognitive psychology: Conceptual integration and links to underlying memory systems. *Personality and Social Psychology Review, 4,* 108–131.

Sobell, M. B., & Sobell, L. C. (1978). *Behavioral treatment of alcohol problems: Individualized therapy and controlled drinking.* New York: Plenum Press.

Sobell, M. B., & Sobell, L. C. (1995). Controlled drinking after 25 years: How important was the great debate? *Addiction, 90,* 1149–1153.

Solomon, R. L. (1980). The opponent-process theory of acquired motivation: The costs of pleasure and the benefits of pain. *American Psychologist, 35,* 691–712.

Solomon, R. L., & Corbit, J. D. (1974). An opponent-process theory of motivation: I. Temporal dynamics of affect. *Psychological Review, 81,* 119–145.

Spanagel, R. (2000). Recent animal models of alcoholism. *Alcohol Research & Health, 24,* 124–131.

Stacy, A. W. (1995). Memory association and ambiguous cues in models of alcohol and marijuana use. *Experimental and Clinical Psychopharmacology, 3,* 183–194.

Stallings, M. C., Hewitt, J. K., Beresford, T., Heath, A. C., & Eaves, L. J. (1999). A twin study of drinking and smoking onset and latencies from first use to regular use. *Behavior Genetics, 29,* 409–421.

Suls, J., & Green, P. (2003). Pluralistic ignorance and college student perceptions of gender-specific alcohol norms. *Health Psychology, 22,* 479–486.

Suls, J., Wan, C. K., & Sanders, G. S. (1988). False consensus and false uniqueness in estimating the prevalence of health-protective behaviors. *Journal of Applied Social Psychology, 8,* 66–79.

Svanum, S. (1986). Alcohol-related problems and dependence: An elaboration and integration. *International Journal of the Addictions, 21,* 539–558.

Szalay, L. B., Carroll, J. F., & Tims, F. (1993). Rediscovering free associations for use in psychotherapy. *Psychotherapy, 30,* 344–356.

Thakker, K. D. (1998). An overview of health risks and benefits of alcohol consumption. *Alcoholism: Clinical & Experimental Research, 22*(Suppl. 7), 285S–298S.

Tiffany, S. T. (1990). A cognitive model of drug urges and drug use behavior: Role of automatic and nonautomatic processes. *Psychological Review, 97,* 147–168.

Tiffany, S. T., Carter, B. L., & Singleton, E. G. (2000). Challenges in the manipulation, assessment and interpretation of craving relevant variables. *Addiction, 95*(Suppl. 2), S177–S187.

Tiffany, S. T., & Conklin, C. A. (2000). A cognitive processing model of alcohol craving and compulsive alcohol use. *Addiction, 95*(Suppl. 2), S145–S153.

Townshend, J. M., & Duka, T. (2007). Avoidance of alcohol-related stimuli in alcohol-dependent inpatients. *Alcoholism: Clinical & Experimental Research, 31,* 1349–1357.

U.S. Department of Agriculture & U.S. Department of Health and Human Services. (2005). *Dietary guidelines for Americans, 2005* (6th ed.). Washington, DC: U.S. Government Printing Office.

Volkow, N. D., & Fowler, J. S. (2000). Addiction, a disease compulsion and drive: Involvement of the orbitofrontal cortex. *Cerebral Cortex, 10,* 318–325.

Walitzer, K. S., & Dearing, R. L. (2006). Gender differences in alcohol and substance use relapse. *Clinical Psychology Review, 26,* 128–148.

Watson, C. G., Brown, K., Tilleskjor, C., Jacobs, L., & Pucel, J. (1988). The comparative recidivism rates of voluntary- and coerced-admission male alcoholics. *Journal of Clinical Psychology, 44,* 573–581.

Wechsler, H., Nelson, T. F., Lee, J. E., Seibring, M., Lewis, C., & Keeling, R. P. (2003). Perception and reality: A national evaluation of social norms marketing interventions to reduce college students' heavy alcohol use. *Journal of Studies on Alcohol, 64,* 484–494.

Wegner, D. M., & Bargh, J. A. (1998). Control and automaticity in social life. In D. Gilbert, S. T. Fiske, & G. Lindzey (Eds.), *Handbook of social psychology* (4th ed., Vol. 1, pp. 446–496). New York: McGraw-Hill.

Werch, C. E., Pappas, D. M., Carlson, J. M., DiClemente, C. C., Chally, P. S., & Sinder, J. A. (2000). Results of a social norm intervention to prevent binge drinking among first-year residential college students. *Journal of American College Health, 49,* 85–92.

Wertz, J. M., & Sayette, M. A. (2001). A review of the effects of perceived drug use opportunity on self-reported urge. *Experimental and Clinical Psychopharmacology, 9,* 3–13.

Whitley, B. E. (1998). Factors associated with cheating among college students: A review. *Research in Higher Education, 39,* 235–274.

Wiers, R. W., Bartholow, B. D., van den Wildenberg, E., Thush, C., Engels, R., Sher, K.J., et al. (2007). Automatic and controlled processes and the development of addictive behaviors in adolescents: A review and a model. *Pharmacology Biochemistry and Behavior, 86,* 263–283.

Wiers, R. W., van Woerden, N., Smulders, F. T. Y., & de Jong, P. J. (2002). Implicit and explicit alcohol-related cognitions in heavy and light drinkers. *Journal of Abnormal Psychology, 111,* 648–658.

Wolfson, S. (2000). Students' estimates of the prevalence of drug use: Evidence for a false consensus effect. *Psychology of Addictive Behaviors, 14,* 295–298.

World Health Organization. (1967). *Manual of the international statistical classification of diseases, injuries, and causes of death* (8th rev.). Geneva, Switzerland: Author.

Wrase, J., Schlagenhauf, F., Kienast, T., Wustenberg, T., Bermpohl, F., Kahnt, T., et al. (2007). Dysfunction of reward processing correlates with alcohol craving in detoxified alcoholics. *NeuroImage, 35,* 787–794.

Zironi, I., Burratini, C., Aicardi, G., & Janak, P. H. (2006). Context is a trigger for relapse to alcohol. *Behavioral Brain Research, 167,* 150–155.

CHAPTER 13

GENETIC AND ENVIRONMENTAL FACTORS IN SUBSTANCE USE, ABUSE, AND DEPENDENCE

Deborah S. Hasin and Hila Katz

Substance use disorders (SUDs) have a complex etiology consisting of environmental and genetic factors; these range from macro to micro and from external to internal. In this chapter, we address these levels both independently and as they possibly interact. We begin with macro–external factors such as substance availability and pricing, after which we review intermediate-level factors such as social influences and move steadily toward micro–internal levels, including personality variables and genetics. We conclude by discussing the Gene × Environment interaction. This area is important in understanding the etiology of SUDs because individuals clearly differ in their responses to different environmental influences. Incorporating information about biological inheritance in the form of genotypes may greatly clarify our understanding of the influences of environmental factors and who is particularly vulnerable to (or resilient against) them. As we constructed this chapter, we were aware that other portions of this book would attend to a wide array of risk and protective factors related to drug use etiology. This is an especially rich part of this handbook owing to its breadth of coverage and strong theoretical impetus. In this respect, readers are encouraged to seek out these chapters as deeper reservoirs of information. However, the brief synthesis we provide of these diverse areas is essential to building our case as we explore person, environment, and genetic determinants of drug abuse.

Dependence is the main outcome of interest in this chapter; we review findings on substance use as a necessary but not sufficient condition for the development of dependence. The substance dependence criteria in the *Diagnostic and Statistical Manual of Mental Disorders* (4th ed., or *DSM–IV*; American Psychiatric Association, 1994) are based on alcohol dependence syndrome (Edwards & Gross, 1976), which was extended to drugs in 1981 (World Health Organization [WHO], 1981). A biaxial concept of SUDs resulted in the distinction between abuse criteria (e.g., social, legal, or role problems or hazardous use) and dependence criteria (tolerance, withdrawal, multiple indicators of impaired control); dependence formed one axis, a mix of psychological and physiological processes that lead to an increasing lack of control over substance use in the face of negative consequences, and the consequences of heavy use (e.g., hazardous use and social, medical, and legal problems) formed a different axis of substance problems (Edwards, 1986).

Of the two disorders, we focus on dependence because of its centrality in SUD research and its psychometric properties. Both *DSM–IV* and International Statistical Classification of Diseases (10th revision; WHO, 2003) dependence diagnoses show good to excellent reliability across instruments and samples (B. F. Grant, Harford, Dawson, Chou, & Pickering, 1995; Hasin, Grant, et al., 1997; Hasin, Li, McCloud, & Endicott, 1996;

Preparation of this chapter was supported in part by National Institute on Alcohol Abuse and Alcoholism Grant K05-AA-014223.

Ustun et al., 1997), with few exceptions (e.g. hallucinogens). Dependence validity is also good, as shown in multimethod comparisons (Hasin, Grant, et al., 1997; Pull et al., 1997; Rounsaville, Bryant, Babor, Kranzler, & Kadden, 1993), longitudinal studies (B. F. Grant, Stinson, & Harford, 2001; Hasin, Grant, & Endicott, 1990; Hasin, Van Rossem, McCloud, & Endicott, 1997a, 1997b; Schuckit et al., 2001), and studies using more sophisticated latent variable analyses (Blanco, Harford, Nunes, Grant, & Hasin, 2007; Harford & Muthén, 2001; Muthén, Grant, & Hasin, 1993) and construct validation analyses (Hasin, Hatzenbuehler, Smith, & Grant, 2003; Hasin & Paykin, 1999).

In contrast to what we know about use, the diagnosis of *DSM–IV* substance abuse presents a different case; it does not necessarily lead to dependence (B. F. Grant et al, 2001; Hasin et al., 1990; Hasin, Van Rossem, et al., 1997a, 1997b; Schuckit et al., 2001), and abuse symptoms do not manifest in all cases of dependence (Hasin & Grant, 2004; Hasin, Hatzenbuehler, Smith, & Grant, 2005). Latent variable analyses of *DSM–IV* alcohol use disorder (AUD) criteria (Harford & Muthén, 2001; Muthén et al., 1993) have indicated two distinct yet correlated factors corresponding to alcohol abuse and dependence, although other analyses have suggested that abuse and dependence criteria lie intermixed on an underlying continuum of severity (Saha, Chou, & Grant, 2006; Saha, Stinson, & Grant, 2007). Findings for cannabis and cocaine (Blanco et al., 2007) have also suggested two highly correlated factors. Interestingly, a recent study of Ecstasy use in a general community sample showed a more variegated pattern of symptom reporting, leading to a broader diagnostic classification scheme (Scheier, Ben-Abdallah, Inciardi, Copeland, & Cottler, 2008). In the general population, *DSM–IV* alcohol abuse is diagnosed mostly on the basis of one criterion, driving while intoxicated (Hasin, Paykin, Endicott, & Grant, 1999). Abuse may thus depend on one's access to a car, whereas dependence is a heritable and complex condition, decidedly more familial than is abuse (Hasin & Paykin, 1999; Hasin, Van Rossem, et al., 1997b).

EPIDEMIOLOGY OF SUBSTANCE USE DISORDERS

The most comprehensive epidemiologic U.S. data come from the National Epidemiologic Survey on Alcohol and Related Conditions (NESARC), a survey of 43,093 respondents ages 18 and older conducted in 2001 and 2002 (B. F. Grant et al., 2003, 2004). Its sample included noninstitutionalized individuals and netted an 81% response rate. The diagnostic interview, designed for nonclinicians, was the Alcohol Use Disorder and Associated Disabilities Interview Schedule—*DSM–IV* version (B. F. Grant et al., 2003), a structured interview with high validity and reliability for SUDs (B. F. Grant et al., 1995; Hasin et al., 1996; Ustun et al., 1997).

In the NESARC, prevalence of current (past 12 months) alcohol abuse and dependence is 4.7% and 3.8%, respectively (Hasin, Stinson, Ogburn, & Grant, 2007), and prevalence of current drug abuse and dependence is 1.4% and 0.6%, respectively (Compton, Thomas, Stinson, & Grant, 2007). Current SUDs are more prevalent in men than in women, and prevalence decreases with age. However, gender differences in the prevalence of AUDs, frequency of binge drinking, and lifetime largest number of drinks appear to be decreasing in younger birth cohorts (Keyes, Grant, & Hasin, 2008). SUD prevalence rose between 1992 and 2002 (Compton, Grant, Colliver, Glantz, & Stinson, 2004; B. F. Grant et al., 2004), largely because of increases in abuse rather than in dependence.

MACRO-LEVEL FACTORS IN SUBSTANCE USE DISORDER ETIOLOGY

Substances can be used only if they are available in the environment. An entire section of this handbook (Part VIII) deals extensively with environmental effects on drug use, and readers are encouraged to find greater depth of information in those chapters. It is clear that in Western societies, conflicting forces influence availability and, by extension, substance consumption. Alcohol and drug sellers seek to increase consumption, even as various public health, grassroots, moral and religious groups, and governmental agencies strive to reduce availability and consumption. Social attitudes toward substance use can also influence drug and alcohol behaviors and availability.

Efforts to Reduce Alcohol and Drug Consumption and Availability

Pricing. A key determinant of state variation in alcohol prices is alcohol taxation, a government intervention (chap. 26, this volume, provides a more complete overview of pricing effects on consumption and environmental stopgaps to lower consumption). State-level alcohol prices are inversely related to per capita consumption or adverse drinking consequences (Chaloupka, Grossman, & Saffer, 2002). Reducing the tax on spirits has been followed by increased per capita alcohol consumption (Heeb, Gmel, Zurbrugg, Kuo, & Rehm, 2003) outside of the United States, although price increases for only one type of beverage may cause consumers to switch to a different drink (Gruenewald, Ponicki, Holder, & Romelsjo, 2006). Government measures such as beer taxes and restrictions on the location of cigarette machines deter adolescent drinking and smoking (Bishai, Mercer, & Tapales, 2005).

State distribution policies. U.S. alcohol consumption and sales patterns are influenced by whether states exert control through the operation of state alcoholic beverage sales or whether they exert less control by licensing alcohol outlets (Wagenaar & Holder, 1991). Notably, "dry" areas in which alcohol is not sold or regulated stringently have lower rates of alcohol-related accidents, detoxification admissions, driving-under-the-influence (DUI) arrests, and cirrhosis mortality than "wet" areas (Room, 2004; Wilson, Niva, & Nicholson, 1993).

Alcohol laws. Alcohol legislation also affects consumption, as seen in the example of the 18th Amendment to the U.S. Constitution, which outlawed alcohol production, transport, and sale from 1920 to 1933. By 1935, per capita alcohol consumption was very low, showing that the amendment had fulfilled its purpose; however, drinking levels rose steadily afterward (Herd, 1992; Lender & Martin, 1982), once the law was repealed

because of its widespread unpopularity. In the former Soviet Union, an area of high per capita alcohol consumption (WHO, 1999), the government attempted to restrict drinking in the mid-1980s; although the policies did reduce consumption, they were so unpopular and unacceptable to the public that they contributed to the collapse of the Soviet government (Shkolnikov & Nemtsov, 1997).

Several measures have decreased hazardous use and alcohol-related traffic deaths, including stricter DUI laws (Asbridge, Mann, Flam-Zalcman, & Stoduto, 2004; Maghsoodloo, Brown, & Greathouse, 1988; Voas, Tippetts, & Fell, 2003), enforcing underage drinking laws (Fell, Fisher, Voas, Blackman, & Tippetts, 2007), lowering the legal blood alcohol concentration level (Wagenaar, Maldonado-Molina, Ma, Tobler, & Komro, 2007), and preconviction drivers' license suspensions (Wagenaar & Maldonado-Molina, 2007).

Drug laws. Studies on government efforts to crack down on drug use by reducing availability have been inconsistent (Day et al., 2003; Weatherburn, Jones, Freeman, & Makkai, 2003; Weatherburn & Lind, 1997; Wood et al., 2003). Reducing the supply of specific drugs may lead to unintended consequences, such as increases in the supply and availability of other drugs (Topp, Day, & Degenhardt, 2003).

Outlet density. Areas with higher alcohol outlet density have higher drinking levels and rates of alcohol-related problems, including hospital admissions and crash fatalities (Cohen, Mason, & Scribner, 2002; Gruenewald, Ponicki, & Holder, 1993; Tatlow, Clapp, & Hohman, 2000). Multilevel analysis controlling for individual-level factors has indicated that outlet density is associated with higher mean group rates of alcohol consumption and drinking norms scores and with driving and drinking (Gruenewald, Treno, & Johnson, 2002; Scribner, Cohen, & Fisher, 2000).

Grassroots groups. In 1980, the nonprofit group Mothers Against Drunk Driving was founded after a repeat-offense drunk driver killed a teenage girl. Developed into a national organization, Mothers Against Drunk Driving has influenced state laws on driving under the influence of alcohol, such as enforcing maximum blood alcohol concentration laws and raising the legal drinking age from 18 to 21 (Russell, Voas, Dejong, & Chaloupka, 1995). Likewise, "Rate the State," a media campaign grading states on DUI countermeasures, pressured legislators to increase the strictness of these laws, which are effective in reducing alcohol-impaired driving (e.g., Voas, Tippetts, & Fell, 2000).

Efforts to Increase Alcohol and Drug Consumption and Availability

Through product development and marketing, alcohol companies aim to increase sales and consumption (Centers for Disease Control and Prevention, 2003). These companies have extensive resources to study consumer preferences and market their products (Garfield, Chung, & Rathouz, 2003). In contrast, resources are limited for definitive public health studies.

Marketing that targets adolescents is a primary focus of public health concerns (Casswell, 2004) because early onset of drinking is associated with an increased risk of AUDs (B. F. Grant et al., 2001; J. D. Grant et al., 2006). Research has demonstrated associations between exposure to advertisements in late childhood and early adolescence and subsequent drinking initiation, frequency, and positive attitudes toward alcohol (Ellickson, Collins, Hambarsoomians, & McCaffrey, 2005; Grube & Wallack, 1994; Wyllie, Zhang, & Casswell, 1998). Tobacco advertisements and marketing practices strongly influence smoking behaviors (Pierce, 2007); tobacco control programs can offset these negative effects by cracking down on the sale of cigarettes to minors and regulating tobacco advertisements (Pierce, 2007).

INTERMEDIATE-LEVEL FACTORS IN SUBSTANCE USE DISORDER ETIOLOGY

Intermediate-level factors are those between the large-scale macro-level factors and the micro-level factors. Although the designation of factors at the boundaries of these levels could be done differently, we present them here in this manner to ease organization of discussion.

Religiosity

Religiosity has been referred to as a highly important environmental factor that affects the risk for substance use and dependence (Kendler, Gardner, & Prescott, 1997). An inverse relationship, replicated across cultures, exists between religiosity and drinking (e.g., Aharonovich, Hasin, Rahav, Meydan, & Neumark, 2001; Perkins, 1987). Longitudinal studies with adolescents and college and professional students have demonstrated that religiosity protects against later heavy alcohol use (Barnes, Farrell, & Banerjee, 1994; Igra & Moos, 1979; Margulies, Kessler, & Kandel, 1977; Moore, Mead, & Pearson, 1990). Within twin pairs, religiosity is strongly correlated because of shared environmental effects (Kendler et al., 1997; Kirk et al., 1999; Truett et al., 1994), and in twins studied longitudinally (Kendler et al., 1997), religiosity predicted later drinking more than drinking predicted religiosity. Furthermore, the difference found in drinking heritability between religious and nonreligious twins is an example of a Gene × Environment interaction (Koopmans, Slutske, van Baal, & Boomsma, 1999). Religiosity, which past studies have indicated is largely environmental, protects against drug disorders as well (e.g., C. Y. Chen, Dormitzer, Bejarano, & Anthony, 2004; Miller, Davies, & Greenwald, 2000).

Parental and Peer Influences

Parenting practices. This volume also includes a section dealing specifically with peer and parental influences, particularly chapters 19 through 21. As these three chapters specifically elaborate, parenting style either confers protective benefits or functions as a risk factor for adolescent substance use. The risk of associating with substance-using peers increases with poor parental monitoring and supervision (Clark, Thatcher, & Maisto, 2005; Hawkins, Catalano, & Miller, 1992); a permissive parenting style in the same-gender parent is associated with greater impulsiveness and poorer alcohol-related control processes (Patock-Peckham & Morgan-Lopez, 2006). Harsh, inconsistent parenting predicts earlier onset of alcohol use, as well as conduct problems and poor self-regulation (Kumpfer & Bluth, 2004; Repetti, Taylor, & Seeman, 2002).

In contrast, warm, authoritative parenting styles protect adolescents from alcohol problems (Patock-Peckham, Cheong, Balhorn, & Nagoshi, 2001), and adequate parental monitoring protects against the risk of adolescent drug use (Yanovitzky, 2005).

Peers. Peer associations predict adolescent substance use and related problems (Fergusson, Lynskey, & Horwood, 1995; Kandel, 1973; Kokkevi et al., 2007; Walden, McGue, Iacono, Burt, & Elkins, 2004); for example, peer attitudes toward cannabis are strongly correlated with cannabis initiation in young women (Agrawal, Lynskey, Bucholz, Madden, & Heath, 2007). Two explanatory models include socialization and selection (Kandel, 1985). According to peer selection theory, children displaying deviant behavior in childhood will choose deviant friendships in adolescence (Fergusson, Woodward, & Horwood, 1999), leading to initiation of drug use and possibly transition to harder drugs. Traits such as sensation seeking and impulsivity may influence both peer selection and substance use (Donohew et al., 1999). In contrast, socialization theory posits that adolescents are influenced by their peers (Deater-Deckard, 2001) through offers of drugs, both active and passive modeling of substance use behaviors, exposure to certain social norms, and the development of expectancies and attitudes favorable to substance use (Borsari & Carey, 2001; Clapper, Martin, & Clifford, 1994; Fergusson, Swain-Campbell, & Horwood, 2002). Simons-Morton and Chen (2006) reported that both socialization and selection influences were evident in a large sample of middle school students. Peer relations, however, do not always constitute a risk factor. For example, among U.S. ethnic and immigrant groups with low rates of substance use, adolescents with ethnically homogeneous peers face less pressure to use substances (Brook et al., 1998; Brook, Balka, Brook, Win, & Gursen, 1998). There is also a growing body of evidence that siblings can also influence substance use (Bullock, Bank, & Burraston, 2002; Kokkevi et al., 2007).

External Stressors

In many cases, SUDs are preceded and accompanied by conduct problems and disruptive behavior (Elkins, McGue, & Iacono, 2007; Kuperman et al., 2001) that have a shared genetic vulnerability with drug disorders (Kendler, Jacobson, Prescott, & Neale, 2003). Discerning a causal direction between stress and disease onset is difficult because these conduct problems as disruptive behaviors may provoke negative reactions from the environment and thus be a result of psychopathology rather than a cause of it. Causal direction is clearer in animal studies and in human studies of early stressors that precede the onset of SUDs and related disorders.

Animal models. The timing and application of stress can be manipulated in animal studies. Along with exposure to physical stressors (Goeders & Guerin, 1994; Piazza, Deminiere, le Moal, & Simon, 1990; Shaham & Stewart, 1994) and social stressors (Kabbaj et al., 2001; Maccari et al., 1991; Tidey & Miczek, 1997), exposure to early stressful conditions also leads to an increase in substance use among animals. For example, rats isolated neonatally are at greater risk of developing stimulant self-administration behaviors (Kosten, Miserebdino, & Kehoe, 2000; Lynch, Mangini, & Taylor, 2005); they also manifest higher dopamine levels in response to cocaine than handled rats, thus linking early stress to later increased cocaine reward (Brake, Zhang, Diorio, Meaney, & Gratton, 2004; Kosten, Zhang, & Kehoe, 2003). Rearing stressors predict ethanol-seeking behavior in primates (Barr, Schwandt, Newman, & Higley, 2004), and isolated rearing leads to greater ingestion of morphine (Marks-Kaufman & Lewis, 1984).

Early stressors and drug use: humans. Early stressors including parental loss and physical, sexual, and emotional abuse are associated with later substance use and SUDs (Dube et al., 2003; Hope, Power, & Rodgers, 1998; Hyman et al., 2008; Kendler et al., 1996; Kessler, Davis, & Kendler, 1997). Most studies have failed to control for parental substance abuse, which is associated with poor parenting and might confound these relations (Locke & Newcomb, 2004).

However, twin studies have shown that childhood sexual abuse is a risk factor for SUDs (Kendler et al., 2000; Nelson et al., 2002).

Terrorism. Problematic substance use and SUDs increase after exposure to terrorism. In urban Israeli adolescents, proximity to terrorist attacks predicted higher levels of subsequent cannabis use (Schiff, Zweig, Benbenishty, & Hasin, 2007) and alcohol consumption (Schiff et al., 2006, 2007), controlling for depressive and posttraumatic stress symptoms. After the terrorist attacks of September 11, 2001, residents of Manhattan showed a sustained increase in alcohol, cigarette, and cannabis use (Vlahov et al., 2004); alcohol consumption was increased among high school students (Wu et al., 2006); and proximity to the attack and past alcohol dependence predicted high levels of drinking following 9/11 among New Jersey adults (Hasin, Keyes, Hatzenbuehler, Aharonovich, & Alderson, 2007).

MICRO-LEVEL FACTORS IN SUBSTANCE USE DISORDER ETIOLOGY

Micro-level factors are those that occur on a personal or biological level. Here, we include psychological factors, personality traits, subjective reactions to substances, and genetic factors.

Psychological Factors

Alcohol expectancies and drinking motives. Positive alcohol expectancies constitute an important risk factor for the development of alcohol dependence (e.g., Shen, Locke-Wellman, & Hill, 2001; see also chap. 8 of this volume). These are expectations that alcohol will have a positive effect when consumed. A twin study found that expectancies are largely environmental rather than genetic (Slutske et al., 2002) and may stem from interactions with parents and peers. Drinking motives are also important risk factors for AUDs. For example, among individuals with a family history of alcoholism, those drinking for social facilitation or to reduce negative affect have shown a greater risk of developing alcohol dependence (Beseler, Aharonovich, Keyes, & Hasin, 2008).

Personality traits. Traits associated with AUDs include novelty seeking (Cloninger, Sigvardsson, Przybeck, & Svrakic, 1995) and sensation seeking (Martin et al., 2002; Zuckerman & Kuhlman, 2000). Personality traits less consistently related to drug use are neuroticism–negative emotionality (e.g., Zimmerman et al., 2003), disinhibition–impulsivity (e.g., McGue, Slutske, Taylor, & Iacono, 1997), and Cluster B personality disorder symptoms (Tragesser, Sher, Trull, & Park, 2007). Drug use disorders display similar relations to these traits (Conway, Swendsen, Rounsaville, & Merikangas, 2002; McGue, Slutske, & Iacono, 1999).

Subjective Reactions

Individuals with a low level of response to alcohol drink more to feel the effects of alcohol. Level of response is linked to an increased risk of AUDs (Schuckit, Smith, & Kalmijn, 2004), with several chromosomal regions as possible candidates for influencing level of response (Wilhelmsen et al., 2003). Research has also shown that level of response varies depending on ethnicity. A high level of response is found among Jews (Schuckit et al., 2004), a group with low levels of AUDs (Hasin et al., 2002b; Levav, Kohn, Golding, & Weissman, 1997). People with low levels of response are found among groups at high risk of AUDs, including Native Americans and Koreans (Ehlers, Garcia-Andrade, Wall, Cloutier, & Phillips, 1999; Wall et al., 1999). Level of response predicts onset of alcohol dependence in young adult men (Schuckit & Smith, 1996) and is also predictive of drinking frequency and quantity (Schuckit, Smith, Pierson, Danko, & Beltran, 2006).

Positive subjective reactions to alcohol include the stimulating effect identified in moderate to heavy drinkers (Holdstock, King, & DeWit, 2000) and those with untreated alcoholism (Thomas, Drobes, Voronin, & Anton, 2004) in response to drinking. Negative reactions include flushing, in which drinking produces unpleasant physical sensations (Higuchi, Matsushita, Murayama, Takagi, & Hayashida, 1995; W. J. Chen, Chen, Yu, & Cheng, 1998); moderate flushing protects against alcohol dependence, whereas severe flushing might prevent an individual from drinking at all. Subjective responses to marijuana, which are moderately heritable, also differ between individuals (Lyons et al., 1997).

Genetics

Family and twin studies of substance dependence. SUDs have a strong familial component (Bierut et al., 1998; Cotton, 1979; Nurnberger et al., 2004). Heritability estimates of alcohol dependence typically range from 50% to 60% (Dick & Bierut, 2006; Heath, 1995; Rhee et al., 2003; Tsuang, Bar, Harley, & Lyons, 2001), and although heritability estimates for illicit drugs have shown greater variability, they have a range similar to that for alcohol (Kendler et al., 2003; Lynskey et al., 2002; Tsuang et al., 2001).

Some twin studies have shown a high level of shared genetic variance across substances (Karkowski, Prescott, & Kendler, 2000; Kendler et al., 2003; Tsuang et al., 2001; Young, Rhee, Stallings, Corley, & Hewitt, 2006). Other studies, however, have indicated that genetic influences are not interchangeable between different classes of drugs (Bierut et al., 1998; Kendler, Myers, & Prescott, 2007; Tsuang et al., 1998).

Genetic linkage studies of alcohol and drug dependence. The purpose of linkage studies, which are conducted with families or sibling pairs, is to identify chromosomal regions likely to contain genes linked to specific disorders or traits. The Collaborative Study on the Genetics of Alcoholism (COGA; Reich et al., 1998) has generated linkage results on several alcohol-related phenotypes, including alcohol use, dependence, comorbidity, and brain electrophysiological measures (Porjesz et al., 2002). These phenotypes showed linkage to regions on chromosomes 1, 2, 4, 7, 8, 10, 15, and 16 (Agrawal et al., 2008; Corbett et al., 2005; Dick et al., 2004; Foroud et al., 1998, 2000). Non-COGA studies also suggest linkage at chromosomes 6, 12, 14, and 17 (Hill et al., 2004) and a region in chromosome 4 (Prescott et al., 2006) near a cluster of alcohol dehydrogenase (ADH) genes, which encode enzymes involved in alcohol metabolism. In drug dependence linkage studies, cannabis dependence criteria have shown linkage to regions on chro-

mosome 14, and dependence criteria for any illicit drug have been linked to chromosomes 10 and 13 in the COGA sample (Agrawal et al., 2008); combined alcohol and drug dependence have demonstrated linkage to areas on chromosomes 2, 10, and 13 (Agrawal et al., 2008), which provides evidence for a shared genetic basis for alcohol and drug dependence. In a substance abuse treatment sample of 324 sibling pairs ages 12 to 25, cannabis dependence criteria demonstrated linkage to areas on chromosomes 3 and 9 (Hopfer et al., 2007). Evidence from a sample of 393 families studied by investigators at Yale University and the University of Connecticut (Yale–UConn) has suggested linkage of opioid dependence to an area of chromosome 17 among a subset of heavy users (Gelernter, Panhuysen, et al., 2006), with additional linkage between opioid dependence and chromosome 2 in African American participants.

Genes Affecting Substance Metabolism. Alcohol metabolism takes place mainly in the liver through a two-step process involving the enzymes ADH and aldehyde dehydrogenase (ALDH; Edenberg, 2000; Li, 2000). After ADH converts the alcohol to acetaldehyde, a toxic substance, ALDH quickly converts the acetaldehyde to acetate and transports it out of the liver. Polymorphisms in ADH and ALDH genes affect the efficiency of alcohol metabolism by encoding isozymes with different activity levels, which affect an individual's risk for heavy drinking and AUDs. Alleles contributing to an inefficient alcohol metabolism process (e.g., ALDH2*2, ADH1B*2) are therefore protective. These allele types are prevalent in Asian groups (C. C. Chen et al., 1999; Goedde et al., 1992). Among Jews in the United States and Israel, there is also a high prevalence of the protective form of ADH1B, which predicts lower drinking levels (Carr et al., 2002; Hasin et al., 2002b; Neumark, Friedlander, Thomasson, & Li, 1998) and fewer alcohol dependence symptoms (Hasin et al., 2002a).

Other ADH variants are also associated with alcohol dependence. Numerous ADH4 single nucleotide polymorphisms (SNPs) are strongly associated with alcohol dependence in both COGA and Yale–UConn samples (Edenberg et al., 2006; Luo et al., 2005, 2006). Furthermore, SNPs in the ADH variants ADH1A and ADH1B (Edenberg et al., 2006; Luo et al., 2006), as well as ADH5 and ADH7 (Luo et al., 2006), are also significantly related to alcohol dependence and warrant further investigation.

Interestingly, ADH4 variants have also shown associations with drug dependence. Yale–UConn samples have suggested that the ADH4 variation is related to cocaine and opioid dependence, even without comorbid alcohol dependence (Luo et al., 2005, 2006). Although ADH genes are thought to influence alcohol dependence through their effect on alcohol metabolic enzymes, the results for drug dependence without comorbid alcohol dependence suggest the role of other mechanisms, such as the possible involvement of ADH enzymes in the signaling pathways of serotonin, dopamine, and norepinephrine (Luo et al., 2006) or the heightened sensitivity of brain reward systems to other addictive drugs following early exposure to high levels of alcohol.

Genes involved in neurotransmitter systems. Genetic vulnerability to SUDs may also arise from variations of genes that affect the functioning of the nervous system.

GABA receptor genes. Alcohol enhances the activity of gamma-aminobutyric acid (GABA), the brain's major inhibitory neurotransmitter; GABA(A) receptors mediate several important effects of alcohol, such as tolerance, sedation, anxiolysis, impairment of motor coordination, and electroencephalograph in the beta band (Davies, 2003). Several studies with human and animal samples have suggested that GABA receptor genes affect the risk for alcohol dependence (Grobin, Matthews, Devaud, & Morrow, 1998; Korpi & Lurz, 1989). GABRA2 receptor genes on chromosome 4 have shown a strong relationship to alcohol dependence and brain wave oscillations in the beta frequency range (Edenberg et al., 2004), an endophenotype related to alcohol dependence (Porjesz et al., 2002). The GABRA2 relationship to alcohol dependence was identified in the Yale–UConn and COGA studies (Covault, Gelernter, Hesselbrock, Nellissery, & Kranzler, 2004; Edenberg et al., 2004) and replicated in

Russian (Lappalainen et al., 2005) and German samples (Fehr et al., 2006; Soyka et al., 2007). Furthermore, a study of Project MATCH patients showed that individuals homozygous for the low-risk GABRA2 allele drink less after treatment (Bauer et al., 2007), a finding with implications for the relationship between genotype and behavioral treatment.

One complication with GABRA2 findings concerns whether the genetic variation in GABRA2 is related to alcohol dependence, drug dependence, or a combined phenotype. COGA findings have suggested that GABRA2 predicts comorbid alcohol and drug dependence but not alcohol dependence alone (Agrawal et al., 2006), but the Yale–UConn studies have suggested that GABRA2 is related more strongly to alcohol dependence alone (Covault et al., 2004). Future studies conducted in different settings and with different samples are needed to clarify these issues.

DRD2, ANKK1, TTC12, and NCAM1. The D2 dopamine receptor gene, *DRD2*, encodes a G-protein-coupled receptor located on postsynaptic dopaminergic neurons that play a central role in reward. The relationship of *DRD2* to alcohol dependence, particularly *DRD2* Taq1A, has been inconsistent and controversial (Dick & Bierut, 2006; Gelernter, Goldman, & Risch, 1993). Recently, the correct location of Taq1A was discovered to be 10 kilobase (kb) downstream from *DRD2* in a neighboring gene, ankyrin repeat and kinase domain containing 1 (*ANKK1*; Neville, Johnstone, & Walton, 2004).

DRD2, ANKK1, TTC12, NCAM1, and nicotine dependence. In a family linkage study of nicotine dependence, Yale–UConn investigators noted suggestive linkage in an area containing four genes within a 542-kb area on chromosome 11 that included *DRD2*, *ANKK1* (where Taq1A is found), tetratricopeptide repeat domain 12 (*TTC12*), and neural cell adhesion molecule 1 (*NCAM1*; Gelernter et al., 2007). Using family-based association and haplotype analysis to study 43 SNPs spanning the *DRD2–ANKK1–TTC12–NCAM1* region of chromosome 11 and nicotine dependence (Gelernter, Yu, et al., 2006), multiple SNPs at *TTC12* and *ANKK1* and a haplotype spanning

TTC12 and *ANKK1* were strongly associated with nicotine dependence, with weaker evidence for associations of the flanking *DRD2* and *NCAM1* markers.

DRD2, ANKK1, TTC12, NCAM1, *and alcohol dependence.* These relationships were explored in two Yale–UConn samples that were independent of the samples used in the nicotine analyses (Yang et al., 2007). These included a family-based sample and a case-control sample. These showed that a haplotype in exon 3 of *TTC12* was strongly related to alcohol dependence. Haplotypes in *NCAM1* also affected risk in the family study, and haplotypes in *ANKK1* affected risk in the case-control study. These findings indicate that genes in this region have a complex, interrelated effect on substance dependence risk that remains to be explained, particularly at *TTC12*, whose biological function is not yet clear.

COGA data were used to investigate SNPs across *DRD2* and *ANKK1* (Dick et al., 2007). These data showed that associations were most strongly concentrated in SNPs in the 5′ block of *ANKK1*. This study did not query SNPs in *TTC12* or *NCAM1*, so it could not fully address the issues raised in the Yale–UConn studies.

None of these studies showed that the former *DRD2* Taq1A (rs1800497 in *ANKK1*) was associated with alcohol or nicotine dependence. However, rs1800497 is in linkage disequilibrium with markers that were implicated in the risk for these disorders (Gelernter, Yu, et al., 2006; Yang et al., 2007). This linkage disequilibrium is likely to explain the early positive results for Taq1A and subsequent inconsistencies. Furthermore, rs1800497 is in linkage disequilibrium with other markers in *DRD2*, so some functional risk-influencing markers may still be found in *DRD2*. Thus, although *DRD2* Taq1A controversies appear resolved, the region of chromosome 11 spanned by *NCAM1* to *DRD2* is promising for further investigation of alcohol and related phenotypes.

CHRM2. Cholinergic receptors mediate acetylcholine response, which gives rise to intracellular and intranuclear events that could directly or indirectly (via dopaminergic or adrenergic effects, or cognition) underlie effects of substances,

thereby contributing to alcohol and drug dependence (Luo et al., 2007). The cholinergic receptors include muscarinic cholinergic receptors (CHRM) that belong to a family of G-protein-coupled receptors that activate pathways important for modulating neuronal excitability, synaptic plasticity, and feedback of acetylcholine release (Volpicelli & Levey, 2004). *CHRM2* is involved in many brain functions, including attention, learning, memory, and cognition.

COGA data showed linkage of the *CHRM2* region of chromosome 7 (Foroud et al., 2000; Reich et al., 1998) to major depression (Nurnberger et al., 2001) and to P3, an event-related potential associated with psychiatric disorders including alcohol and drug dependence (Jones et al., 2004, 2006). In COGA, a number of SNPs across *CHRM2* were associated with alcohol dependence, major depression, or a combined phenotype (Wang et al., 2004). The most common haplotype protected against alcohol dependence and major depression and their co-occurrence, and other haplotypes conferred vulnerability for each of these phenotypes. In the Yale–UConn studies, additional fine mapping provided support for this region (Luo et al., 2005); this Yale–UConn study showed strongest effects for alcohol dependence (minimum $p = .003$), weaker effects for drug dependence (minimum $p = .011$), and only suggestive or modest effects for major depression ($.011 > p > .085$).

The Yale–UConn studies also demonstrated that SNPs in *CHRM2,* including those linked to SUDs, were related to neuroticism and agreeableness, traits associated with SUDs (Luo et al., 2007). In COGA data (Dick et al., 2007), *CHRM2* SNP variants were linked to alcohol plus drug dependence but not to alcohol dependence alone. Dick et al. (2007) interpreted this as showing that *CHRM2* variation is associated with a more severe phenotype, which combines alcohol and drug dependence. In an additional COGA study (Dick et al., 2008), indicators of alcohol and drug dependence, antisocial personality, conduct disorder, and novelty seeking and sensation seeking were used to create a general externalizing factor that was tested for association with *CHRM2* SNPs. One SNP was related to alcohol dependence, one to drug dependence, and two each (nonoverlapping) to novelty seeking and sensation seeking. The general externalizing factor was significantly related to a larger number (six) of *CHRM2* SNPs than were any of its components, interpreted by the authors as suggesting that *CHRM2* variation affects an element shared between externalizing disorders. Of note, the single *CHRM2* SNP related to alcohol dependence in this analysis was not significantly related to the general externalizing factor.

COGA and the Yale–UConn studies have been consistent in showing a relationship between *CHRM2* SNP variants and alcohol dependence. However, whether these SNPs are related to purely alcohol dependence or drug dependence or to traits underlying both substance disorders is not yet clear. Further studies are needed to address these issues.

Serotonin-related genes. Serotonin plays a role in mood regulation, sleep, aggression, and appetite, and serotonin levels are related to impulsive behavior (Reist, Mazzanti, Vu, Fujimoto, & Goldman, 2004) and to major depressive disorder (Fehr et al., 2000), both common among individuals with SUDs. A relatively low rate of serotonin turnover has been observed in alcoholism (Olsson et al., 2005), and activity of the central serotonin system has been shown to modulate alcohol consumption.

The serotonin transporter protein (5-HTT) regulates serotonergic activity by controlling the extracellular concentration of serotonin (5-HT; Fabre et al., 2000). Initially, the gene encoding the 5-HTT protein was examined as a candidate gene for alcohol dependence risk; however, the polymorphism in question, 5-HTT–linked promoter region (5-HTTLPR), showed mixed results when examined as a direct influence on alcohol dependence (Feinn, Nellissery, & Kranzler, 2005). In the Discussion section, however, we discuss studies of the interaction of 5-HTTLPR and stress with substance-related outcomes.

Mu-opioid receptor gene. The primary action site for opioids is the mu-opioid receptor gene (*OPRM1*) on chromosome 6, which mediates the reinforcing effects of opioids and indirectly moderates the effects of other psychoactive substances. Studies with mice have provided evidence that the mu-opioid receptor gene affects opioid dependence (Alexander, Heydt, Ferraro, Vogel, &

Berrettini, 1996; Berrettini, Ferraro, Alexander, Buchberg, & Vogel, 1994) and sensitivity to cocaine (Hummel, Ansonoff, Pintar, & Unterwald, 2004). Human studies have produced both positive findings (Hoehe et al., 2000; Luo, Kranzler, Zhao, & Gelernter, 2003; Oslin et al., 2003) and negative ones (Crowley et al,. 2003; Franke et al., 2001; Xuei et al., 2007).

Discussion

Genetic studies require informative, accurate phenotypes. Although the reliability and validity of *DSM–IV* dependence has been found to be consistently good to excellent, recent research has suggested that transforming dependence into a quantitative trait would yield a more informative phenotype (Hasin, Liu, Alderson, & Grant, 2006; Helzer, Bucholz & Gossop, 2007); other findings have provided evidence that both dependence and abuse criteria fall in an intermixed order on a single underlying continuum of severity (Hasin & Beseler, in press; Saha et al., 2006, 2007). Studies with dependence-only quantitative traits have shown positive results (Dick et al., 2008; Hasin et al., 2002b), but additional studies of this kind as well as studies using combined dependence and abuse criteria as a quantitative phenotype are needed. As discussed previously, some research has already been undertaken on phenotypes involving combinations of alcohol and drug dependence, or one or both of these disorders and psychiatric comorbidity; regularly addressing potential inconsistencies between studies because of comorbidity in the sample should help provide better interpretation of study findings in general.

Gene × Environment Interaction

Gene × Environment interaction is an exciting area of research that has taken major steps forward in the past 5 years with the rapid developments in the field of genetics (Caspi & Moffitt, 2006; Rutter, Moffitt, & Caspi, 2006). Gene × Environment interaction studies are needed because not everyone exposed to a given environmental influence responds in the same way, and not everyone with a particular risk genotype develops a disorder. Studying how the relationship between a genotype and a disorder is altered by exposure to an environmental influence or how the relationship between an environmental influence and a disorder is modified by genotype is the nature of the Gene × Environment interaction study. Relatively few such studies have been conducted up till now. However, an elegant example of such a study is that of Caspi et al. (2003), who showed that among individuals with the "s" allele of 5-HTTLPR, the chances that stressful life events would lead to major depressive disorder were greatly elevated. These findings have been replicated by others and have paved the way for additional studies of this type.

Few studies have directly investigated whether environmental events and conditions modify the relationship between specific genotypes and substance phenotypes. Recently, two Yale–UConn studies addressed 5-HTTLPR interactions with stress and alcohol. The "s" allele of 5-HTTLPR interacted with current stressors in predicting heavy drinking and drug use among college students (Covault et al., 2007) and with childhood maltreatment in predicting early drinking among low-income children and early adolescents (Kaufman et al., 2007). An important question to explore is whether the relationship among stress, 5-HTTLPR, and drinking phenotypes is further modified by genetic variants associated with an elevated risk of alcohol dependence (e.g., ADH4, GABRA2). In an Israeli sample, age cohort modified the effects of ADH1B*2 (Spivak et al., 2007). Lifetime maximum drinking was low among older respondents, regardless of genotype, whose early adolescence (the main period of risk for early drinking onset) took place in the absence of much alcohol advertising and a culture without much interest in alcohol. Younger Israeli respondents have been exposed to much more alcohol advertising and changing social norms regarding drinking during early adolescence. Among these youth, those with at least one copy of the protective allele of ADH1B also drank less. However, individuals homozygous for the nonprotective form of ADH1B exceeded the National Institute on Alcoholism and Alcohol Abuse safe drinking guidelines.

Other environmental factors reviewed here could also affect the outcome of genetic studies and will need to be investigated in future genetic studies

of SUDs. For example, relatives of substance-dependent probands may show high levels of religiosity, which may protect them from their genetic vulnerability to and risk of developing dependence. Inconsistent results may arise if there are variations in the proportion of relatives with high religiosity between family and sibling pair studies. Researching various environmental factors would likely incur little additional cost but would require the adjustment of investigative instruments and analytic procedures.

CONCLUSION

Studying Gene × Environment interaction is crucial for the detection and prevention of SUDs. Greater accuracy and knowledge in this area may facilitate the early identification of individuals at risk of using substances in excess; these individuals may then be provided with additional supervision, early education, or support. In addition, improved knowledge may also help identify individuals who have been exposed to certain stressors and who also have a specific genetic vulnerability to SUDs; this would help at-risk individuals benefit from early intervention. A better understanding of the interaction of environmental and genetic effects will also foster new research on the biological mechanisms of risk-enhancing or protective environmental events and conditions. Although the research to date has identified a number of factors influencing the risk for SUDs, particularly dependence, researchers from different disciplines will need to work together to address multilevel factors conjointly to clarify the influence of these factors on the development and persistence of SUDs.

References

Agrawal, A., Edenberg, H. J., Foroud, T., Bierut, L. J., Dunn, G., Hinrichs, A. L., et al. (2006). Association of GABRA2 with drug dependence in the Collaborative Study on the Genetics of Alcoholism sample. *Behavioral Genetics, 36,* 640–650.

Agrawal, A., Hinrichs, A. L., Dunn, G., Bertelsen, S., Dick, D. M., Saccone, S. F., et al. (2008). Linkage scan for quantitative traits identifies new regions of interest for substance dependence in the Collaborative Study on the Genetics of Alcoholism (COGA) sample. *Drug and Alcohol Dependence, 93,* 12–20.

Agrawal, A., Lynskey, M. T., Bucholz, K. K., Madden, P. A., & Heath, A. C. (2007). Correlates of cannabis initiation in a longitudinal sample of young women: The importance of peer influences. *Preventive Medicine, 45,* 31–34.

Aharonovich, E., Hasin, D., Rahav, G., Meydan, J., & Neumark, Y. (2001). Differences in drinking patterns among Ashkenazic and Sephardic Israeli adults. *Journal of Studies on Alcohol, 62,* 301–305.

Alexander, R. C., Heydt, D., Ferraro, T. N., Vogel, W., & Berrettini, W. H. (1996). Further evidence for a quantitative trait locus on murine chromosome 10 controlling for morphine preference in inbred mice. *Psychiatric Genetics, 6,* 29–31.

American Psychiatric Association. (1994). *Diagnostic and statistical manual of mental disorders* (4th ed.). Washington, DC: Author.

Asbridge, M., Mann, R. E., Flam-Zalcman, R., & Stoduto, G. (2004). The criminalization of impaired driving in Canada: Assessing the deterrent impact of Canada's first per se law. *Journal of Studies on Alcohol, 65,* 450–459.

Barnes, G. M., Farrell, M. P., & Banerjee, S. (1994). Family influences on alcohol abuse and other problem behaviors among Black and White adolescents in a general population sample. *Journal of Research on Adolescence, 4,* 183–201.

Barr, C. S., Schwandt, M. L., Newman, T. K., & Higley, J. D. (2004). The use of adolescent nonhuman primates to model human alcohol intake: Neurobiological, genetic, and psychological variables. *Annals of the New York Academy of Sciences, 1021,* 221–233.

Bauer, L. O., Covault, J., Harel, O., Das, S., Anton, R., & Kranzler, H. R. (2007). Variation in genes encoding GABA-A subunits predicts drinking behavior in Project MATCH. *Alcoholism: Clinical & Experimental Research, 31,* 1780–1787.

Berrettini, W. H., Ferraro, T. N., Alexander, R. C., Buchberg, A. M., & Vogel, W. H. (1994). Quantitative trait loci mapping of three loci controlling morphine preference using inbred mouse strains. *Nature Genetics, 7,* 54–58.

Beseler, C. L., Aharonovich, E. A., Keyes, K. M., & Hasin, D. S. (2008). Adult transition from at-risk drinking to alcohol dependence: The relationship of family history and drinking motives. *Alcoholism: Clinical & Experimental Research, 32,* 607–616.

Bierut, L. J., Dinwiddie, S. H., Begleiter, H., Crowe, R. R., Hesselbrock, V., Nurnberger, J. I., et al. (1998). Familial transmission of substance dependence: Alcohol, marijuana, cocaine, and habitual smoking: A report from the Collaborative Study on the Genetics of Alcoholism. *Archives of General Psychiatry, 55,* 982–988.

Bishai, D. M., Mercer, D., & Tapales, A. (2005). Can government policies help adolescents avoid risky behavior? *Preventive Medicine, 40,* 197–202.

Blanco, C., Harford, T. C., Nunes, E., Grant, B., & Hasin, D. (2007). The latent structure of marijuana and cocaine use disorders: Results from the National Longitudinal Alcohol Epidemiologic Survey (NLAES). *Drug and Alcohol Dependence, 91,* 91–96.

Borsari, B., & Carey, K. B. (2001). Peer influences on college drinking: A review of the research. *Journal of Substance Abuse, 13,* 391–424.

Brake, W. G., Zhang, T. Y., Diorio, J., Meaney, M. J., & Gratton, A. (2004). Influence of early postnatal rearing conditions on mesocorticolimbic dopamine and behavioral responses to psychostimulants and stressors in adult rats. *European Journal of Neuroscience, 19,* 1863–1874.

Brook, J. S., Balka, E. B., Brook, D. W., Win, P. T., & Gursen, M. D. (1998). Drug use among African Americans: Ethnic identity as a protective factor. *Psychological Reports, 83,* 1427–1446.

Brook, J. S., Brook, D. W., De La Rosa, M., Duque, L. F., Rodriguez, E., Montoya, I. D., et al. (1998). Pathways to marijuana use among adolescents: Cultural/ ecological, family, peer, and personality influences. *Journal of the American Academy of Child & Adolescent Psychiatry, 37,* 759–766.

Bullock, B. M., Bank, L., & Burraston, B. (2002). Adult sibling expressed emotion and fellow sibling deviance: A new piece of the family process puzzle. *Journal of Family Psychology, 16,* 307–317.

Carr, L. G., Foroud, T., Stewart, T., Castellucio, P., Edenberg, H. J., & Li, T. K. (2002). Influence of ADH1B polymorphism on alcohol use and its subjective effects in a Jewish population. *American Journal of Medical Genetics, 112,* 138–143.

Caspi, A., & Moffitt, T. E. (2006). Gene–environment interactions in psychiatry: Joining forces with neuroscience. *Nature Reviews Neuroscience, 7,* 583–90.

Caspi, A., Sugden, K., Moffitt, T. E., Taylor, A., Craig, I. W., Harrington, H., et al. (2003, July 18). Influence of life stress on depression: moderation by a polymorphism in the 5-HTT gene. *Science, 301,* 386–389.

Casswell, S. (2004). Alcohol brands in young peoples' everyday lives: New developments in marketing. *Alcohol and Alcoholism, 39,* 471–476.

Centers for Disease Control and Prevention. (2003, April 11). Point-of-purchase alcohol marketing and promotion by store type—United States, 2000–2001. *Morbidity and Mortality Weekly Reports, 52,* 310–313.

Chaloupka, F. J., Grossman, M., & Saffer, H. (2002). The effects of price on alcohol consumption and alcohol-related problems. *Alcohol Research & Health, 26,* 22–34.

Chen, C. C., Lu, R. B., Chen, Y. C., Wang, M. F., Chang, Y.C., Li, T. K., et al. (1999). Interaction between the functional polymorphisms of the alcohol-metabolism genes in protection against alcoholism. *American Journal of Human Genetics, 65,* 795–807.

Chen, C. Y., Dormitzer, C. M., Bejarano, J., & Anthony, J. C. (2004). Religiosity and the earliest stages of adolescent drug involvement in seven countries of Latin America. *American Journal of Epidemiology, 159,* 1180–1188.

Chen, W. J., Chen, C. C., Yu, J. M., & Cheng, A. T. (1998). Self-reported flushing genotypes of ALDH2, ADH2, and ADH3, among Taiwanese Han. *Alcoholism: Clinical Experimental Research, 22,* 1048–1052.

Clapper, R. L., Martin, C. S., & Clifford, P. R. (1994). Personality, social environment, and past behavior as predictors of late adolescent alcohol use. *Journal of Substance Abuse, 6,* 305–313.

Clark, D. B., Thatcher, D. L., & Maisto, S. A. (2005). Supervisory neglect and adolescent alcohol use disorders: Effects on AUD onset and treatment outcomes. *Addictive Behaviors, 30,* 1737–1750.

Cloninger, C. R., Sigvardsson, S., Przybeck, T. R., & Svrakic, D. M. (1995). Personality antecedents of alcoholism in a national area probability sample. *European Archives of Psychiatry and Clinical Neuroscience, 245,* 239–244.

Cohen, D. A., Mason, K., & Scribner, R. (2002). The population consumption model, alcohol control practices, and alcohol-related traffic fatalities. *Preventive Medicine, 34,* 187–197.

Compton, W. M., Grant, B. F., Colliver, J. D., Glantz, M. D., & Stinson, F. S. (2004, May 5). Prevalence of marijuana use disorders in the United States: 1991–1992 and 2001–2002. *JAMA, 291,* 2114–2121.

Compton, W. M., Thomas, Y. F., Stinson, F. S., & Grant, B. F. (2007). Prevalence, correlates, disability, and comorbidity of *DSM-IV* drug abuse and dependence: Results from the National Epidemiologic Survey on Alcohol and Related Disorders. *Archives of General Psychiatry, 64,* 566–576.

Conway, K. P., Swendsen, J. D., Rounsaville, B. J., & Merikangas, K. R. (2002). Personality, drug of choice, and comorbid psychopathology among substance abusers. *Drug and Alcohol Dependence, 65,* 225–234.

Corbett, J., Saccone, N. L., Foroud, T., Goate, A., Edenberg, H., Nurnberger, J., et al. (2005). A sex-adjusted and age-adjusted genome screen for nested alcohol dependence diagnoses. *Psychiatric Genetics, 15,* 25–30.

Cotton, N. S. (1979). The familial incidence of alcoholism: A review. *Journal of Studies on Alcohol, 40,* 89–116.

Covault, J., Gelernter, J., Hesselbrock, V., Nellisery, M., & Kranzler, H. R. (2004). Allelic and haplotypic association of GABRA2 with alcohol dependence. *American Journal of Medical Genetics Part B: Neuropsychiatric Genetics, 129B,* 104–109.

Covault, J., Tennen, H., Armeli, S., Conner, T. S., Herman, A. I., Cillessen, A. H., et al. (2007). Interactive effects of the serotonin transporter 5-HTTLPR polymorphism and stressful life events on college student drinking and drug use. *Biological Psychiatry, 61,* 609–616.

Crowley, J. J., Oslin, D. W., Patkar, A. A., Gottheil, E., DeMaria, P. A., O'Brien C. P., et al. (2003). A genetic association study of the mu opioid receptor and severe opioid dependence. *Psychiatric Genetics, 13,* 169–173.

Davies, M. (2003). The role of GABAA receptors in mediating the effects of alcohol in the central nervous system. *Journal of Psychiatry and Neuroscience, 28,* 263–274.

Day, C., Topp, L., Rouen, D., Darke, S., Hall, W., & Dolan, K. (2003). Decreased heroin availability in Sydney in early 2001. *Addiction, 98,* 93–95.

Deater-Deckard, K. (2001). Annotation: Recent research examining the role of peer relationships in the development of psychopathology. *Journal of Child Psychology and Psychiatry, 42,* 565–579.

Dick, D. M., Agrawal, A., Wang, J. C., Hinrichs, A., Bertelsen, S., Bucholz, K. K., et al. (2007). Alcohol dependence with comorbid drug dependence: Genetic and phenotypic associations suggest a more severe form of the disorder with stronger genetic contribution to risk. *Addiction, 102,* 1131–1139.

Dick, D. M., Aliev, F., Wang, J. C., Grucza, R. A., Schuckit, M. A., Kuperman, S., et al. (2008). Using dimensional models of externalizing psychopathology to aid in gene identification. *Archives of General Psychiatry, 65,* 310–318.

Dick, D. M., & Bierut, L. J. (2006). The genetics of alcohol dependence. *Current Psychiatry Reports, 8,* 151–157.

Dick, D. M., Edenberg, H. J., Xuei, X., Goate, A., Kuperman, S., Schuckit, M., et al. (2004). Association of GABRG3 with alcohol dependence. *Alcoholism: Clinical & Experimental Research, 28,* 4–9.

Donohew, R. L., Hoyle, R. H., Clayton, R. R., Skinner, W. F., Colon, S. E., & Rice, R. E. (1999). Sensation seeking and drug use by adolescents and their friends: models for marijuana and alcohol. *Journal of Studies on Alcohol, 60,* 622–631.

Dube, S. R., Felitti, V. J., Dong, M., Chapman, D. P., Giles, W. H., & Anda, R.F. (2003). Childhood abuse, neglect, and household dysfunction and the risk of illicit drug use: The adverse childhood experiences study. *Pediatrics, 111,* 564–572.

Edenberg, H. J. (2000). Regulation of the mammalian alcohol dehydrogenase genes. *Progress in Nucleic Acid Research and Molecular Biology, 64,* 295–341.

Edenberg, H. J., Dick, D. M., Xuei, X., Tian, H., Almasy, L., Bauer, L. O., et al. (2004). Variations in GABRA2, encoding the α2 subunit of the GABA$_A$ receptor, are associated with alcohol dependence and with brain oscillations. *American Journal of Human Genetics, 74,* 705–714.

Edenberg, H. J., Xuei, X., Chen, H. J., Tian, H., Wetherill, L. F., Dick, D. M., et al. (2006). Association of alcohol dehydrogenase genes with alcohol dependence: A comprehensive analysis. *Human Molecular Genetics, 15,* 1539–1549.

Edwards, G. (1986). The alcohol dependence syndrome: A concept as stimulus to enquiry. *British Journal of Addictions, 81,* 171–183.

Edwards, G., & Gross, M. M. (1976). Alcohol dependence: Provisional description of a clinical syndrome. *British Medical Journal, 1,* 1058–1061.

Ehlers, C. L., Garcia-Andrade, C., Wall, T. L., Cloutier, D., & Phillips, E. (1999). Electroencephalographic responses to alcohol challenge in Native American Mission Indians. *Biological Psychiatry, 45,* 776–787.

Elkins, I. J., McGue, M., & Iacono, W. G. (2007). Prospective effects of attention-deficit/hyperactivity disorder, conduct disorder, and sex on adolescent substance use and abuse. *Archives of General Psychiatry, 64,* 1145–1152.

Ellickson, P. L., Collins, R. L., Hambarsoomians, K., & McCaffrey, D. F. (2005). Does alcohol advertising promote adolescent drinking? Results from a longitudinal assessment. *Addiction, 100,* 235–246.

Fabre, V., Beaufour, C., Evrard, A., Rioux, A., Hanoun, N., Lesch, K. P., et al. (2000). Altered expression and functions of serotonin 5-HT1A and 5-HT1B receptors in knock-out mice lacking the 5-HT transporter. *European Journal of Neuroscience, 12,* 2299–2310.

Fehr, C., Grintschuk, N., Szegedi, A., Angehelescu, I., Klawe, C., Singer, P., et al. (2000). The HTR1B 861G>C receptor polymorphism among patients suffering from alcoholism, major depression, anxiety disorders and narcolepsy. *Psychiatry Research, 97,* 1–10.

Fehr, C., Sander, T., Tadic, A., Lenzen, K. P., Anghelescu, I., Klawe, C., et al. (2006). Confirmation of association of the GABRA2 gene with alcohol dependence by subtype-specific analysis. *Psychiatry and Genetics, 16,* 9–17.

Feinn, R., Nellissery, M., & Kranzler, H. R. (2005). Meta-analysis of the association of a functional serotonin transporter promoter polymorphism with alcohol dependence. *American Journal of Medical Genetics Part B: Neuropsychiatric Genetics, 133B,* 79–84.

Fell, J. C., Fisher, D. A., Voas, R. B., Blackman, K., & Tippetts, A.S. (2007). The relationship of 16 underage drinking laws to reductions in underage drinking drivers in fatal crashes in the United States. *Annual Proceedings of the Association for the Advancement of Automotive Medicine, 51,* 537–557.

Fergusson, D. M., Lynskey, M. T., & Horwood, L. J. (1995). The role of peer affiliations, social, family and individual factors in continuities in cigarette smoking between childhood and adolescence. *Addiction, 90,* 647–659.

Fergusson, D. M., Swain-Campbell, N. R., & Horwood, L. (2002). Deviant peer affiliations, crime and substance abuse: A fixed effects regression analysis. *Journal of Abnormal and Child Psychology, 30,* 419–430.

Fergusson, D. M., Woodward, L. J., & Horwood L. J. (1999). Childhood peer relationship problems and young people's involvement with deviant peers in adolescence. *Journal of Abnormal & Child Psychology, 27,* 357–369.

Foroud, T., Bucholz, K. K., Edenberg, H. J., Goate, A., Neuman, R. J., Porjesz, B., et al. (1998). Linkage of an alcoholism-related severity phenotype to chromosome 16. *Alcoholism: Clinical & Experimental Research, 22,* 2035–2042.

Foroud, T., Edenberg, H. J., Goate, A., Rice, J., Flury, L., Koller, D. L., et al. (2000). Alcoholism susceptibility loci: Confirmation studies in a replicate sample and further mapping. *Alcoholism: Clinical & Experimental Research, 24,* 933–945.

Franke, P., Wang, T., Nothem, M. M., Knapp, M., Neidt, H., Albrecht, S., et al. (2001). Nonreplication of association between mu-opioid-receptor gene (OPRM1) A118G polymorphism and substance dependence. *American Journal of Medical Genetics Part B: Neuropsychiatric Genetics, 105B,* 114–119.

Garfield, C. F., Chung, P. J., & Rathouz, P. J. (2003, May 14). Alcohol advertising in magazines and adolescent readership. *JAMA, 289,* 2424–2429.

Gelernter, J., Goldman, D., & Risch, N. (1993, April 7). The A1 allele at the D2 dopamine receptor gene and alcoholism: A reappraisal. *JAMA, 269,* 1673–1677.

Gelernter, J., Panhuysen, C., Weiss, R., Brady, K., Poling, J., Krauthammer, M., et al. (2007). Genomewide linkage scan for nicotine dependence: Identification of a chromosome 5 risk locus. *Biological Psychiatry, 61,* 119–126.

Gelernter, J., Panhuysen, C., Wilcox, M., Hesselbrock, V., Rounsaville, B., Poling, J., et al. (2006). Genomewide linkage scan for opioid dependence and related traits. *American Journal of Human Genetics, 78,* 759–769.

Gelernter, J., Yu, Y., Weiss, R., Brady, K., Panhuysen, C., Yang, B. Z., et al. (2006). Haplotype spanning TTC12 and ANKK1, flanked by the DRD2 and NCAM1 loci, is strongly associated to nicotine dependence in two distinct American populations. *Human Molecular Genetics, 15,* 3498–3507.

Goedde, H. W., Agarwal, D. P., Fritze, G., Meier-Tackmann, D., Singh, S., Beckmann, G., et al. (1992). Distribution of ADH2 and ALDH2 genotypes in different populations. *Human Genetics, 88,* 344–346.

Goeders, N. E., & Guerin, G. F. (1994). Non-contingent electric footshock facilitates the acquisition of intravenous cocaine self-administration in rats. *Psychopharmacology, 114,* 63–70.

Grant, B. F., Dawson, D. A., Stinson, F. S., Chou, P. S., Kay, W., & Pickering, R. (2003). The Alcohol Use Disorder and Associated Disabilities Interview Schedule–IV (AUDADIS-IV): Reliability of alcohol consumption, tobacco use, family history of depression and psychiatric diagnostic modules in a general population sample. *Drug and Alcohol Dependence, 71,* 7–16.

Grant, B. F., Dawson, D. A., Stinson, F. S., Chou, S. P., Dufour, M. C., & Pickering, R. P. (2004). The 12-month prevalence and trends in *DSM-IV* alcohol abuse and dependence: United States, 1991–1992 and 2001–2002. *Drug and Alcohol Dependence, 74,* 223–234.

Grant, B. F., Harford, T. C., Dawson, D. A., Chou, P. S., & Pickering, R.P. (1995). The Alcohol Use Disorder and Associated Disabilities Interview Schedule (AUDADIS): Reliability of alcohol and drug modules in a general population sample. *Drug and Alcohol Dependence, 39,* 37–44.

Grant, B. F., Stinson, F. S., & Harford, T. C. (2001). The 5-year course of alcohol abuse among young adults. *Journal of Substance Abuse, 13,* 229–238.

Grant, J. D., Scherrer, J. F., Lynskey, M. T., Lyons, M. J., Eisen, S. A., Tsuang, M. T., et al. (2006). Adolescent alcohol use is a risk factor for adult alcohol and drug dependence: Evidence from a twin design. *Psychological Medicine, 36,* 109–118.

Grobin, A. C., Matthews, D. B., Devaud, L. L., & Morrow, A. L. (1998). The role of GABAA receptors in the acute and chronic effects of ethanol. *Psychopharmacology (Berl), 139,* 2–19.

Grube, J. W., & Wallack, L. (1994). Television beer advertising and drinking knowledge, beliefs, and intentions among schoolchildren. *American Journal of Public Health, 84,* 254–259.

Gruenewald, P. J., Ponicki, W. R., & Holder, H. D. (1993). The relationship of outlet densities to alcohol consumption: A time series cross-sectional analysis. *Alcoholism: Clinical & Experimental Research, 17,* 38–47.

Gruenewald, P. J., Ponicki, W. R., Holder, H. D., & Romelsjo, A. (2006). Alcohol prices, beverage quality, and the demand for alcohol: Quality substitutions and price elasticities. *Alcoholism: Clinical & Experimental Research, 30,* 96–105.

Gruenewald, P. J., Treno, A. J., & Johnson, F. (2002). Outlets, drinking and driving: A multilevel analysis of availability. *Journal of Studies on Alcohol, 63,* 460–468.

Harford, T. C., & Muthén, B. O. (2001). The dimensionality of alcohol abuse and dependence: A multivariate analysis of *DSM-IV* symptom items in the National Longitudinal Survey of Youth. *Journal of Studies on Alcohol, 62,* 150–157.

Hasin, D., Aharonovich, E., Liu, X., Mamman, Z., Matseoane, K., Carr, L., et al. (2002a). Alcohol and ADH2 in Israel: Ashkenazi Sephardics and recent Russian immigrants. *American Journal of Psychiatry, 159,* 1432–1434.

Hasin, D., Aharonovich, E., Liu, X., Mamman, Z., Matseoane, K., Carr, L. G., et al. (2002b). Alcohol dependence symptoms and alcohol dehydrogenase 2 polymorphism: Israeli Ashkenazis, Sephardics, and recent Russian immigrants. *Alcoholism: Clinical & Experimental Research, 26,* 1315–1321.

Hasin, D., & Beseler, C. (in press). Dimensionality of lifetime alcohol abuse, dependence, and binge drinking. *Drug and Alcohol Dependence.*

Hasin, D. S., & Grant, B. F. (2004). The co-occurrence of *DSM-IV* alcohol abuse in *DSM-IV* alcohol dependence: Results of the National Epidemiologic Survey on Alcohol and Related Conditions on heterogeneity that differ by population subgroup. *Archives of General Psychiatry, 61,* 891–896.

Hasin, D., Grant, B. F., Cottler, L., Blaine, J., Towle, L., Ustun, B., et al. (1997). Nosological comparisons of alcohol and drug diagnoses: A multisite, multi-instrument international study. *Drug and Alcohol Dependence, 47,* 217–226.

Hasin, D. S., Grant, B., & Endicott, J. (1990). The natural history of alcohol abuse: Implications for definitions of alcohol use disorders. *American Journal of Psychiatry, 147,* 1537–1541.

Hasin, D. S., Hatzenbuehler, M., Smith, S., & Grant, B. F. (2005). Co-occurring *DSM-IV* drug abuse in *DSM-IV* drug dependence: Results from the National Epidemiologic Survey on Alcohol and Related Conditions. *Drug and Alcohol Dependence, 80,* 117–123.

Hasin, D. S., Keyes, K. M., Hatzenbuehler, M. L., Aharonovich, E. A., & Alderson, D. (2007). Alcohol consumption and posttraumatic stress after exposure to terrorism: Effects of proximity, loss, and psychiatric history. *American Journal of Public Health, 97,* 2268–2275.

Hasin, D., Li, Q., McCloud, S., & Endicott, J. (1996). Agreement between *DSM-III, DSM-III-R, DSM-IV* and ICD-10 alcohol diagnoses in US community-sample heavy drinkers. *Addiction, 91,* 1517–1527.

Hasin, D. S., Liu, X., Alderson, D., & Grant, B. F. (2006). *DSM-IV* alcohol dependence: A categorical or dimensional phenotype? *Psychological Medicine, 36,* 1695–1705.

Hasin, D., & Paykin, A. (1999). Alcohol dependence and abuse diagnoses: Concurrent validity in a nationally representative sample. *Alcoholism: Clinical & Experimental Research, 23,* 144–150.

Hasin, D., Paykin, A., Endicott, J., & Grant, B. (1999). The validity of *DSM-IV* alcohol abuse: Drunk drivers versus all others. *Journal of Studies on Alcohol, 60,* 746–755.

Hasin, D. S., Schuckit, M. A., Martin, C. S., Grant, B. F., Bucholz, K. K., & Helzer, J. E. (2003). The validity of *DSM-IV* alcohol dependence: What do we know and what do we need to know? *Alcoholism: Clinical & Experimental Research, 27,* 244–252.

Hasin, D. S., Stinson, F. S., Ogburn, E., & Grant, B. F. (2007). Prevalence, correlates, disability, and comorbidity of *DSM-IV* alcohol abuse and dependence in the United States: Results from the National Epidemiologic Survey on Alcohol and Related Conditions. *Archives of General Psychiatry, 64,* 830–842.

Hasin, D., Van Rossem, R., McCloud, S., & Endicott, J. (1997a). Alcohol dependence and abuse diagnoses: Validity in community sample heavy drinkers. *Alcoholism: Clinical & Experimental Research, 21,* 213–219.

Hasin, D. S., Van Rossem, R., McCloud, S., & Endicott, J. (1997b). Differentiating *DSM-IV* alcohol dependence and abuse by course: Community heavy drinkers. *Journal of Substance Abuse, 9,* 127–135.

Hawkins, J., Catalano, R. F., & Miller, J. Y. (1992). Risk and protective factors for alcohol and other drug problems in adolescence and early adulthood: Implications for substance abuse prevention. *Psychological Bulletin, 112,* 64–105.

Heath, A. C. (1995). Genetic influences on alcoholism risk: A review of adoption and twin studies. *Alcohol Health and Research World, 19,* 166–171.

Heeb, J., Gmel, G., Zurbrugg, C., Kuo, M., & Rehm, J. (2003). Changes in alcohol consumption following a reduction in the price of spirits. *Addiction, 98,* 1433–1446.

Helzer, J. E., Bucholz, K. K., & Gossop, M. (2007). A dimensional option for the diagnosis of substance dependence in DSM-V. *International Journal of Methods and Psychiatric Research, 16*(Suppl. 1), S24–S33.

Herd, D. (1992). Ideology, history and changing models of liver cirrhosis epidemiology. *British Journal of Addictions, 87,* 1113–1126.

Higuchi, S., Matsushita, S., Murayama, M., Takagi, S., & Hayashida, M. (1995). Alcohol and aldehyde dehydrogenase polymorphisms and the risk for alcoholism. *American Journal of Psychiatry, 152,* 1219–1221.

Hill, S. Y., Shen, S., Zezza, N., Hoffman, E. K., Perlin, M., & Allan, W. (2004). A genome wide search for alcoholism susceptibility genes. *American Journal of Medical Genetics Part B: Neuropsychiatric Genetics, 128,* 102–113.

Hoehe, M. R., Kopke, K., Wendel, B., Rohde, K., Flachmeier, C., Kidd, K. K., et al. (2000). Sequence variability and candidate gene analysis in complex disease: Association of mu opioid receptor gene variation with substance dependence. *Human Molecular Genetics, 9,* 2895–2908.

Holdstock, L., King, A. C., & DeWit, H. (2000). Subjective and objective responses to ethanol in moderate/heavy and light social drinkers. *Alcoholism: Clinical & Experimental Research, 24,* 789–794.

Hope, S., Power, C., & Rodgers, B. (1998). The relationship between parental separation in childhood and problem drinking in adulthood. *Addiction, 93,* 505–514.

Hopfer, C. J., Lessem, J. M., Hartman, C. A., Stallings, M. C., Cherny, S. S., Corley, R. P., et al. (2007). A genome-wide scan for loci influencing adolescent cannabis dependence symptoms: Evidence for linkage on chromosomes 3 and 9. *Drug and Alcohol Dependence, 89,* 34–41.

Hummel, M., Ansonoff, M. A., Pintar, J. E., & Unterwald, E. M. (2004). Genetic and pharmacological manipulation of mu opioid receptors in mice reveals a differential effect on behavioral sensitization to cocaine. *Neuroscience, 125,* 211–220.

Hyman, S. M., Paliwal, P., Chaplin, T. M., Mazure, C. M., Rounsaville, B. J., & Sinha, R. (2008). Severity of childhood trauma is predictive of cocaine relapse outcomes in women but not men. *Drug and Alcohol Dependence, 92,* 208–216.

Igra, A., & Moos, R. H. (1979). Alcohol use among college students: Some competing hypotheses. *Journal of Youth and Adolescence, 8,* 393–405.

Jones, K. A., Porjesz, B., Almasy, L., Bierut, L., Dick, D., Goate, A., et al. (2006). A cholinergic receptor gene (CHRM2) affects event-related oscillations. *Behavioral Genetics, 36,* 627–639.

Jones, K. A., Porjesz, B., Almasy, L., Bierut, L., Goate, A., Wang, J. C., et al. (2004). Linkage and linkage disequilibrium of evoked EEG oscillations with CHRM2 receptor gene polymorphisms: Implications for human brain dynamics and cognition. *International Journal of Psychophysiology, 53,* 75–90.

Kabbaj, M., Norton, C. S., Kollack-Walker, S., Watson, S. J., Robinson, T. E., & Akil, H. (2001). Social defeat alters the acquisition of cocaine self-administration in rats: Role of individual differences in cocaine-taking behavior. *Psychopharmacology, 158,* 382–387.

Kandel, D. (1973, September 14). Adolescent marihuana use: The role of parents and peers. *Science, 181,* 1067–1070.

Kandel, D. B. (1985). On processes of peer influences in adolescent drug use: A developmental perspective. *Advances in Alcohol and Substance Abuse, 4,* 139–163.

Karkowski, L. M., Prescott, C. A., & Kendler, K. S. (2000). Multivariate assessment of factors influencing illicit substance use in twins from female–female pairs. *American Journal of Medical Genetics Part B: Neuropsychiatric Genetics, 96B,* 665–670.

Kaufman, J., Yang, B. Z., Douglas-Palumberi, H., Crouse-Artus, M., Lipschitz, D., Krystal, J. H., et al. (2007). Genetic and environmental predictors of early alcohol use. *Biological Psychiatry, 61,* 1228–1234.

Kendler, K. S., Bulik, C. M., Silberg, J., Hettema, J. M., Myers, J., & Prescott, C. A. (2000). Childhood sexual abuse and adult psychiatric and substance use disorders in women: An epidemiological and cotwin control analysis. *Archives of General Psychiatry, 57,* 953–959.

Kendler, K. S., Gardner, C. O., & Prescott, C. A. (1997). Religion, psychopathology, and substance use and abuse: A multimeasure, genetic-epidemiologic study. *American Journal of Psychiatry, 154,* 322–329.

Kendler, K. S., Jacobson, K. C., Prescott, C. A., & Neale, M. C. (2003). Specificity of genetic and environmental risk factors for use and abuse/dependence of cannabis, cocaine, hallucinogens, sedatives, stimulants, and opiates in male twins. *American Journal of Psychiatry, 160,* 687–695.

Kendler, K. S., Myers, J., & Prescott, C. A. (2007). Specificity of genetic and environmental risk factors for symptoms of cannabis, cocaine, alcohol, caffeine, and nicotine dependence. *Archives of General Psychiatry, 64,* 1313–1320.

Kendler, K. S., Neale, M. C., Prescott, C. A., Kessler, R. C., Heath, A. C., Corey, L. A., et al. (1996). Childhood parental loss and alcoholism in women: A causal analysis using a twin-family design. *Psychological Medicine, 26,* 79–95.

Kessler, R. C., Davis, C. G., & Kendler, K. S. (1997). Childhood adversity and adult psychiatric disorder in the US National Comorbidity Survey. *Psychological Medicine, 27,* 1101–1119.

Keyes, K. M., Grant, B. F., & Hasin, D. S. (2008). Evidence for a closing gender gap in alcohol use, abuse, and dependence in the United States population. *Drug and Alcohol Dependence, 93,* 21–29.

Kirk, K. M., Maes, H. H., Neale, M. C., Heath, A. C., Martin, N. G., & Eaves, L. J. (1999). Frequency of church attendance in Australia and the United States:

Models of family resemblance. *Twin Research, 2,* 99–107.

Kokkevi, A. E., Arapaki, A. A., Richardson, C., Florescu, S., Kuzman, M., & Stergar, E. (2007). Further investigation of psychological and environmental correlates of substance use in adolescence in six European countries. *Drug and Alcohol Dependence, 88,* 308–312.

Koopmans, J. R., Slutske, W. S., van Baal, G. C., & Boomsma, D. I. (1999). The influence of religion on alcohol use initiation: Evidence for Genotype × Environment interaction. *Behavioral Genetics, 29,* 445–453.

Korpi, E. R., & Lurz, F. W. (1989). GABAA receptor-mediated chloride flux in brain homogenates from rat lines with differing innate alcohol sensitivities. *Neuroscience, 32,* 387–392.

Kosten, T. A., Miserebdino, M. J. D., & Kehoe, P. (2000). Enhanced acquisition of cocaine self-administration in adult rats with neonatal isolation stress experience. *Brain Research, 875,* 44–50.

Kosten, T. A., Zhang, X. Y., & Kehoe, P. (2003). Chronic neonatal isolation stress enhances cocaine-induced increases in ventral striatal dopamine levels in rat pups. *Brain Research: Developments in Brain Research, 141,* 109–116.

Kumpfer, K. L., & Bluth, B. (2004). Parent/child transactional processes predictive of resilience or vulnerability to "substance use disorders." *Substance Use & Misuse, 39,* 671–698.

Kuperman, S., Schlosser, S. S., Kramer, J. R., Bucholz, K., Hesselbrock, V., Reich, T., et al. (2001). Developmental sequence from disruptive behavior diagnosis to adolescent alcohol dependence. *American Journal of Psychiatry, 158,* 2022–2026.

Lappalainen, J., Krupitsky, E., Remizov, M., Pchelina, S., Taraskina, A., Zvartau, E., et al. (2005). Association between alcoholism and gamma-amino butyric acid alpha2 receptor subtype in a Russian population. *Alcoholism: Clinical & Experimental Research, 29,* 493–498.

Lender, M. E., & Martin, J. K. (1982). *Drinking in America: A history.* New York: Free Press.

Levav, I., Kohn, R., Golding, J. M., & Weissman, M. M. (1997). Vulnerability of Jews to affective disorders. *American Journal of Psychiatry, 154,* 941–947.

Li, T. K. (2000). Pharmacogenetics of responses to alcohol and genes that influence alcohol drinking. *Journal of Studies on Alcohol, 61,* 5–12.

Locke, T. F., & Newcomb, M. D. (2004). Child maltreatment, parent alcohol and drug-related problems, polydrug problems, and parenting practices: A test of gender differences and four theoretical perspectives. *Journal of Family Psychology, 18,* 120–134.

Luo, X., Kranzler, H. R., Zhao, H., & Gelernter, J. (2003). Haplotypes at the OPRM1 locus are associated with susceptibility to substance dependence in European-Americans. *American Journal of Genetics Part B: Neuropsychiatric Genetics, 120B,* 97–108.

Luo, X., Kranzler, H. R., Zuo, L., Wang, S., Schork, N. J., & Gelernter, J. (2006). Diplotype trend regression analysis of the ADH gene cluster and the ALDH2 gene: Multiple significant associations with alcohol dependence. *American Journal of Human Genetics, 78,* 973–987.

Luo, X., Kranzler, H., Zuo, L., Yang, B., Lappalainen, J., & Gelernter, J. (2005). ADH4 gene variation is associated with alcohol and drug dependence: Results from family controlled and population-structured association studies. *Pharmacogenetics and Genomics, 15,* 755–768.

Luo, X., Kranzler, H. R., Zuo, L., Zhang, H., Wang, S., & Gelernter, J. (2007). CHRM2 variation predisposes to personality traits of agreeableness and conscientiousness. *Human Molecular Genetics, 16,* 1557–1568.

Lynch, W. J., Mangini, L. D., & Taylor, J. R. (2005). Neonatal isolation stress potentiates cocaine seeking behavior in adult male and female rats. *Neuropsychopharmacology, 30,* 322–329.

Lynskey, M. T., Heath, A. C., Nelson, E. C., Bucholz, K. K., Madden, P. A., Slutske, W.S., et al. (2002). Genetic and environmental contributions to cannabis dependence in a national young adult twin sample. *Psychological Medicine, 32,* 195–207.

Lyons, M. J., Toomey, R., Meyer, J. M., Green, A. I., Eisen, S. A., Goldberg, J., et al. (1997). How do genes influence marijuana use? The role of subjective effects. *Addiction, 92,* 409–417.

Maccari, S., Piazza, P. V., Deminiere, J. M., Lemaire, V., Mormede, P., Simon, H., et al. (1991). Life events-induced decrease of corticosteroid type I receptors is associated with reduced corticosterone feedback and enhanced vulnerability to amphetamine self-administration. *Brain Research, 547,* 7–12.

Maghsoodloo, S., Brown, D. B., & Greathouse, P. A. (1988). Impact of the revision of DUI legislation in Alabama. *American Journal of Drug and Alcohol Abuse, 14,* 97–108.

Margulies, R. Z., Kessler, R. C., & Kandel, D. B. (1977). A longitudinal study of onset of drinking among high-school students. *Journal of Studies on Alcohol, 38,* 897–912.

Marks-Kaufman, R., & Lewis, J. L. (1984). Early housing experience modifies morphine self-administration and physical dependence in adult rats. *Addictive Behaviors, 9,* 235–243.

Martin, C. A., Kelly, T. H., Rayens, M. K., Brogli, B. R., Brenzel, A., Smith, W. J., et al. (2002). Sensation seeking, puberty, and nicotine, alcohol, and mari-

juana use in adolescence. *Journal of the American Academy of Child & Adolescent Psychiatry, 41,* 1495–1502.

McGue, M., Slutske, W., & Iacono, W. G. (1999). Personality and substance use disorders: II. Alcoholism versus drug use disorders. *Journal of Consulting and Clinical Psychology, 67,* 394–404.

McGue, M., Slutske, W., Taylor, J., & Iacono, W. G. (1997). Personality and substance use disorders: Effects of gender and alcoholism subtype. *Alcoholism: Clinical & Experimental Research, 21,* 513–520.

Miller, L., Davies, M., & Greenwald, S. (2000). Religiosity and substance use and abuse among adolescents in the National Comorbidity Survey. *Journal of the American Academy of Child & Adolescent Psychiatry, 39,* 1190–1197.

Moore, R. D., Mead, L., & Pearson, T. A. (1990). Youthful precursors of alcohol abuse in physicians. *American Journal of Medicine, 88,* 332–336.

Muthén, B. O., Grant, B., & Hasin, D. (1993). The dimensionality of alcohol abuse and dependence: Factor analysis of *DSM-III-R* and proposed *DSM-IV* criteria in the 1988 National Health Interview Survey. *Addiction, 88,* 1079–1090.

Nelson, E. C., Heath, A. C., Madden, P. A., Bucholz, K. K., Madden, P. A., Statham, D. J., et al. (2002). Association between self-reported childhood sexual abuse and adverse psychosocial outcomes: Results from a twin study. *Archives of General Psychiatry, 59,* 139–145.

Neumark, Y. D., Friedlander, Y., Thomasson, H. R., & Li, T. K. (1998). Association of the ADH2*2 allele with reduced ethanol consumption in Jewish men in Israel: A pilot study. *Journal of Studies on Alcohol, 59,* 133–139.

Neville, M. J., Johnstone, E. C., & Walton, R. T. (2004). Identification and characterization of ANKK1: A novel kinase gene closely linked to DRD2 on chromosome band 11q23.1. *Human Mutation, 23,* 540–545.

Nurnberger, J. I., Foroud, T., Flury, L., Su, J., Meyer, E. T., Hu, K., et al. (2001). Evidence for a locus on chromosome 1 that influences vulnerability to alcoholism and affective disorder. *American Journal of Psychiatry, 158,* 718–724.

Nurnberger, J. I., Wiegand, R., Bucholz, K., O'Connor, S., Meyer, E. T., Reich, T., et al. (2004). A family study of alcohol dependence: Coaggregation of multiple disorders in relatives of alcohol-dependent probands. *Archives of General Psychiatry, 61,* 1246–1256.

Olsson, C. A., Byrnes, G. B., Lotfi-Miri, M., Collins, V., Williamson, R., Patton, C., et al. (2005). Association between 5-HTTLPR genotypes and persisting patterns of anxiety and alcohol use: Results from a

10-year longitudinal study of adolescent mental health. *Molecular Psychiatry, 10,* 868–876.

Oslin, D. W., Berrettini, W., Kranzler, H. R., Pettinati, H., Gelernter, J., Volpicelli, J. R., et al. (2003). A functional polymorphism of the mu-opioid receptor gene is associated with naltrexone response in alcohol-dependent patients. *Neuropsychopharmacology, 28,* 1546–1552.

Patock-Peckham, J. A., Cheong, J., Balhorn, M. E., & Nagoshi, C. T. (2001). A social learning perspective: A model of parenting styles, self-regulation, perceived drinking control, and alcohol use and problems. *Alcoholism: Clinical & Experimental Research, 25,* 1284–1292.

Patock-Peckham, J. A., & Morgan-Lopez, A. A. (2006). College drinking behaviors: Mediational links between parenting styles, impulse control, and alcohol-related outcomes. *Psychology of Addictive Behaviors, 20,* 117–125.

Perkins, H.W. (1987). Parental religion and alcohol use problems as intergenerational predictors of problem drinking among college youth. *Journal of the Scientific Study of Religion, 26,* 340–357.

Piazza, P. V., Deminiere, J. M., le Moal, M., & Simon, H. (1990). Stress- and pharmacologically-induced behavioral sensitization increases vulnerability to acquisition of amphetamine self-administration. *Brain Research, 514,* 22–26.

Pierce, J. P. (2007). Tobacco industry marketing, population-based tobacco control, and smoking behavior. *American Journal of Preventive Medicine, 33,* S327–S334.

Porjesz, B., Begleiter, H., Wang, K., Almasy, L., Chorlian, D. B., Stimus, A. T., et al. (2002). Linkage and linkage disequilibrium mapping of ERP and EEG phenotypes. *Biological Psychology, 61,* 229–248.

Prescott, C. A., Sullivan, P. F., Kuo, P. H., Webb, B. T., Vittum, J., Patterson, D. G., et al. (2006). Genomewide linkage study in the Irish affected sib pair study of alcohol dependence: Evidence for a susceptibility region for symptoms of alcohol dependence on chromosome 4. *Molecular Psychiatry, 11,* 603–611.

Pull, C. B., Saunders, J. B., Mavreas, V., Cottler, L. B., Grant, B. F., Hasin, D., et al. (1997). Concordance between ICD-10 alcohol and drug use disorder criteria and diagnoses as measured by the AUDADIS-ADR, CIDI and SCAN: Results of a cross-national study. *Drug and Alcohol Dependence, 47,* 207–216.

Reich, T., Edenberg, H. J., Goate, A., Williams, J. T., Rice, J. P., Van Eerdewegh, P., et al. (1998). Genome-wide search for genes affecting the risk for alcohol dependence. *American Journal of Medical Genetics, 81,* 207–215.

Reist, C., Mazzanti, C., Vu, R., Fujimoto, K., & Goldman, D. (2004). Inter-relationships of intermediate phenotypes for serotonin function, impulsivity, and a 5-HT2A candidate allele: His452Tyr. *Molecular Psychiatry, 9,* 871–878.

Repetti, R. L., Taylor, S. E., & Seeman, T. E. (2002). Risky families: Family social environments and the mental and physical health of offspring. *Psychological Bulletin, 128,* 330–366.

Rhee, S. H., Hewitt, J. K., Young, S. E., Corley, R. P., Crowley, T. J., & Stallings, M. C. (2003). Genetic and environmental influences on substance initiation, use, and problem use in adolescents. *Archives of General Psychiatry, 60,* 1256–1264.

Room, R. (2004). Effects of alcohol controls: Nordic research traditions. *Drug and Alcohol Review, 23,* 43–53.

Rounsaville, B. J., Bryant, K., Babor, T. F., Kranzler, H., & Kadden, R. (1993). Cross system agreement for substance use disorders: DSM-III-R, DSM-IV, and ICD-10. *Addiction, 88,* 337–348.

Russell, A., Voas, R. B., Dejong, W., & Chaloupka, M. (1995). MADD rates the states: A media advocacy event to advance the agenda against alcohol-impaired driving. *Public Health Reports, 110,* 240–245.

Rutter, M., Moffitt, T. E., & Caspi, A. (2006). Gene–environment interplay and psychopathology: Multiple varieties but real effects. *Journal of Child Psychology and Psychiatry, and Allied Disciplines, 47,* 226–61.

Saha, T. D., Chou, S. P., & Grant, B. F. (2006). Toward an alcohol use disorder continuum using item response theory: Results from the National Epidemiologic Survey on Alcohol and Related Conditions. *Psychological Medicine, 36,* 931–941.

Saha, T. D., Stinson, F. S., & Grant, B. F. (2007). The role of alcohol consumption in future classifications of alcohol use disorders. *Drug and Alcohol Dependence, 89,* 82–92.

Scheier, L. M., Ben-Abdallah, A., Inciardi, J. A., Copeland, J., & Cottler, L. B. (2008). Tri-city study of Ecstasy problems: A latent class analysis. *Drug and Alcohol Dependence, 98,* 249–264.

Schiff, M., Benbenishty, R., McKay, M., Devoe, E., Liu, X., & Hasin, D. (2006). Exposure to terrorism and Israeli youths' psychological distress and alcohol use: An exploratory study. *American Journal of Addictions, 15,* 220–226.

Schiff, M., Zweig, H. H., Benbenishty, R., & Hasin, D. S. (2007). Exposure to terrorism and Israeli youths' cigarette, alcohol, and cannabis use. *American Journal of Public Health, 97,* 1852–1858.

Schuckit, M. A., & Smith, T. L. (1996). An 8-year follow-up of 450 sons of alcoholic and control subjects. *Archives of General Psychiatry, 53,* 202–210.

Schuckit, M. A., Smith, T. L., Danko, G. P., Bucholz, K. K., Reich, T., & Bierut, L. (2001). Five-year clinical course associated with DSM-IV alcohol abuse or dependence in a large group of men and women. *American Journal of Psychiatry, 158,* 1084–1090.

Schuckit, M. A., Smith, T. L., & Kalmijn, J. (2004). The search for genes contributing to the low level of response to alcohol: Patterns of findings across studies. *Alcoholism: Clinical & Experimental Research, 28,* 1449–1458.

Schuckit, M. A., Smith, T., Pierson, J., Danko, G., & Beltran, I. A. (2006). Relationships among the level of response to alcohol and the number of alcoholic relatives in predicting alcohol-related outcomes. *Alcoholism: Clinical & Experimental Research, 30,* 1308–1314.

Scribner, R. H., Cohen, D. A., & Fisher, W. (2000). Evidence of a structural effect for outlet density: A multilevel analysis. *Alcoholism: Clinical & Experimental Research, 24,* 188–195.

Shaham, Y., & Stewart, J. (1994). Exposure to mild stress enhances the reinforcing efficacy of intravenous heroin self-administration in rats. *Psychopharmacology, 114,* 523–527.

Shen, S., Locke-Wellman, J., & Hill, S. Y. (2001). Adolescent alcohol expectancies in offspring from families at high risk for developing alcoholism. *Journal of Studies on Alcohol, 62,* 763–772.

Shkolnikov, V., & Nemtsov, A. (1997). The anti-alcohol campaign and variations in Russian mortality. In J. Bobadilla, C. Costello, & F. Mitchell (Eds.), *Premature death in the new independent states* (pp. 239–261). Washington, DC: National Academies Press.

Simons-Morton, B., & Chen, R. S. (2006). Over time relationships between early adolescent and peer substance use. *Addictive Behaviors, 31,* 1211–1223.

Slutske, W. S., Cronk, N. J., Sher, K. J., Madden, P. A., Bucholz, K. K., & Heath, A. C. (2002). Genes, environment, and individual differences in alcohol expectancies among female adolescents and young adults. *Psychology of Addictive Behaviors, 16,* 308–317.

Soyka, M., Preuss, U. W., Hesselbrock, V., Zill, P., Koller, G., & Bondy, B. (2007). GABA-A2 receptor subunit gene (GABRA2) polymorphisms and risk for alcohol dependence. *Journal of Psychiatric Research, 42,* 184–191.

Spivak, B., Frisch, A., Maman, Z., Aharonovich, E., Alderson, D., Carr, L. G., et al. (2007). Effect of ADH1B genotype on alcohol consumption in young Israeli Jews. *Alcoholism: Clinical & Experimental Research, 31,* 1297–1301.

Tatlow, J. R., Clapp, J. D., & Hohman, M. M. (2000). The relationship between the geographic density of alcohol outlets and alcohol-related admissions in San Diego County. *Journal of Community Health, 25,* 79–88.

Thomas, S. E., Drobes, D. J., Voronin, K., & Anton, R. F. (2004). Following alcohol consumption, nontreatment-seeking alcoholics report greater stimulation but similar sedation compared with social drinkers. *Journal of Studies on Alcohol, 65,* 330–335.

Tidey, J. W., & Miczek, K. A. (1997). Acquisition of cocaine self-administration after social stress: Role of accumbens dopamine. *Psychopharmacology, 130,* 203–212.

Topp, L., Day, C., & Degenhardt, L. (2003). Changes in patterns of drug injection concurrent with a sustained reduction in the availability of heroin in Australia. *Drug and Alcohol Dependence, 70,* 275–286.

Tragesser, S. L., Sher, K. J., Trull, T. J., & Park, A. (2007). Personality disorder symptoms, drinking motives, and alcohol use and consequences: Cross-sectional and prospective mediation. *Experimental and Clinical Psychopharmacology, 15,* 282–292.

Truett, K. R., Eaves, L. J., Walters, E. E., Heath, A. C., Hewitt, J. K., Meyer, J. M., et al. (1994). A model system for analysis of family resemblance in extended kinships of twins. *Behavioral Genetics, 24,* 35–49.

Tsuang, M. T., Bar, J. L., Harley, R. M., & Lyons, M. J. (2001). The Harvard Twin Study of Substance Abuse: What we have learned. *Harvard Review of Psychiatry, 9,* 267–279.

Tsuang, M. T., Lyons, M. J., Meyer, J. M., Doyle, T., Eisen, S. A., Goldberg, J., et al. (1998). Co-occurrence of abuse of different drugs in men: The role of drug-specific and shared vulnerabilities. *Archives of General Psychiatry, 55,* 967–972.

Ustun, B., Compton, W., Mager, D., Babor, T., Baijewu, O., Chatterji, S., et al. (1997). WHO Study on the reliability and validity of the alcohol and drug use disorder instruments: Overview of methods and results. *Drug and Alcohol Dependence, 47,* 161–169.

Vlahov, D., Galea, S., Ahern, J., Resnick, H., Boscarino, J. A., Gold, J., et al. (2004). Consumption of cigarettes, alcohol, and marijuana among New York City residents six months after the September 11 terrorist attacks. *American Journal of Drug and Alcohol Abuse, 30,* 385–407.

Voas, R. B., Tippetts, A. S., & Fell, J. (2000). The relationship of alcohol safety laws to drinking drivers in fatal crashes. *Accident Analysis and Prevention, 32,* 483–492.

Voas, R. B., Tippetts, A. S., & Fell, J. C. (2003). Assessing the effectiveness of minimum legal drinking age and zero tolerance laws in the United States. *Accident Analysis and Prevention, 35,* 579–587.

Volpicelli, L. A., & Levey, A. I. (2004). Muscarinic acetylcholine receptor subtypes in cerebral cortex and hippocampus. *Progress in Brain Research, 145,* 59–66.

Wagenaar, A. C., & Holder, H. D. (1991). A change from public to private sale of wine: Results from natural experiments in Iowa and West Virginia. *Journal of Studies in Alcohol, 52,* 162–173.

Wagenaar, A. C., & Maldonado-Molina, M. M. (2007). Effects of drivers' license suspension policies on alcohol-related crash involvement: Long term follow-up in forty-six states. *Alcoholism: Clinical & Experimental Research, 31,* 1399–1406.

Wagenaar, A. C., Maldonado-Molina, M. M., Ma, L., Tobler, A. L., & Komro, K. A. (2007). Effects of legal BAC limits on fatal crash involvement: Analyses of 28 states from 1976 through 2002. *Journal of Safety Research, 38,* 493–499.

Walden, B., McGue, M., Iacono, W. G., Burt, S. A., & Elkins, I. (2004). Identifying shared environmental contributions to early substance use: The respective roles of peers and parents. *Journal of Abnormal Psychology, 113,* 440–450.

Wall, T. L., Johnson, M. L., Horn, S. M., Carr, L. G., Smith, T. L., & Schuckit, M. A. (1999). Evaluation of the Self-Rating of the Effects of Alcohol form in Asian Americans with aldehyde dehydrogenase polymorphisms. *Journal of Studies on Alcohol, 60,* 784–789.

Wang, J. C., Hinrichs, A. L., Stock, H., Budde, J., Allen, R., Bertelsen, S., et al. (2004). Evidence of common and specific genetic effects: Association of the muscarinic acetylcholine receptor M2 (CHRM2) gene with alcohol dependence and major depressive syndrome. *Human Molecular Genetics, 13,* 1903–1911.

Weatherburn, D., Jones, C., Freeman, K., & Makkai, T. (2003). Supply control and harm reduction: Lessons from the Australian heroin "drought." *Addiction, 98,* 83–91.

Weatherburn, D., & Lind, B. (1997). The impact of law enforcement activity on a heroin market. *Addiction, 92,* 557–569.

Wilhelmsen, K. C., Schuckit, M., Smith, T. L., Lee, J. V., Segall, S. K., Feiler, H. S., et al. (2003). The search for genes related to a low-level response to alcohol determined by alcohol challenges. *Alcoholism: Clinical & Experimental Research, 27,* 1041–1047.

Wilson, R. W., Niva, G., & Nicholson, T. (1993). Prohibition revisited: County alcohol control consequences. *Journal of the Kentucky Medical Association, 91,* 9–12.

Wood, E., Tyndall, M. W., Spittal, P. M., Li, K., Anis, A. H., Hogg, R. S., et al. (2003). Impact of supply-side policies for control of illicit drugs in the face of the AIDS and overdose epidemics: Investigation of a massive heroin seizure. *Canadian Medical Association Journal, 168,* 165–169.

World Health Organization. (1981). Nomenclature and classification of drug- and alcohol-related problems: WHO memorandum. *Bulletin of the World Health Organization, 99,* 225–242.

World Health Organization. (1999). *Global status report on alcohol.* Geneva, Switzerland: Author.

World Health Organization. (2003). *International statistical classification of diseases and related health problems* (10th rev.). Geneva, Switzerland: Author.

Wu, P., Duarte, C. S., Mandell, D. J., Fan, B., Liu, X., Fuller, C. J., et al. (2006). Exposure to the World Trade Center attack and the use of cigarettes and alcohol among New York City public high-school students. *American Journal of Public Health, 96,* 804–807.

Wyllie, A., Zhang, J. F., & Casswell, S. (1998). Responses to televised alcohol advertisements associated with drinking behaviour of 10–17-year-olds. *Addiction, 93,* 361–371.

Xuei, X., Flury-Wetherill, L., Bierut, L., Dick, D., Nurnberger, J., Foroud, T., et al. (2007). The opioid system in alcohol and drug dependence: Family-based association study. *American Journal of Medical Genetics Part B: Neuropsychiatric Genetics, 144,* 877–884.

Yang, B. Z., Kranzler, H. R., Zhao, H., Gruen, J. R., Luo, X., & Gelernter, J. (2007). Association of haplotypic variants in DRD2, ANKK1, TTC12 and NCAM1 to alcohol dependence in independent case-control and family samples. *Molecular Genetics, 16,* 2844–2853.

Yanovitzky, I. (2005). Sensation seeking and adolescent drug use: The mediating role of association with deviant peers and pro-drug discussions. *Health Communications, 17,* 67–89.

Young, S. E., Rhee, S. H., Stallings, M. C., Corley, R. P., & Hewitt, J. K. (2006). Genetic and environmental vulnerabilities underlying adolescent substance use and problem use: General or specific? *Behavioral Genetics, 36,* 603–615.

Zimmerman, P., Wittchen, H., Hofler, M., Pfister, H., Kessler, R. C., & Lieb, R. (2003). Primary anxiety disorders and the development of subsequent alcohol use disorders: A 4-year community study of adolescents and young adults. *Psychological Medicine, 33,* 1211–1222.

Zuckerman, M., & Kuhlman, D. (2000). Personality and risk-taking: Common biosocial factors. *Journal of Personality, 68,* 999–1029.

CHAPTER 14

AGE AT DRINKING ONSET AND ALCOHOL USE DISORDERS: ALCOHOL DEPENDENCE AND ABUSE

Ralph W. Hingson, Timothy Heeren, and Michael R. Winter

Starting to drink at an early age has been linked to the development of alcohol dependence (Grant & Dawson, 1997; Hingson, Heeren, & Winter, 2006a; Hingson, Heeren, & Winter, 2006b). A potential association with alcohol use has not been as extensively explored. This chapter (a) describes the prevalence and characteristics of alcohol dependence and abuse in the noninstitutionalized population in the United States, (b) examines the association between the age at which people start to drink (not counting tastes or sips) and the prevalence and severity of alcohol dependence and abuse, and (c) assesses whether potential associations between age at drinking onset and alcohol dependence and abuse significantly differ. These analyses provide insight into whether alcohol dependence and abuse are distinct diagnostic entities and help inform alcohol problem prevention efforts by exploring whether preventing early drinking onset should be a priority. Analyses use the National Epidemiological Study of Alcohol Related Conditions (NESARC), the U.S. national survey of more than 43,000 adults ages 18 and older collected in 2001–2002.

Mortality statistics have shown that more than 75,000 deaths annually in the United States are attributable to alcohol, and alcohol is the third leading contributor to death in the country. Of alcohol-attributable deaths, 40,000 result from injuries, both unintentional (e.g., motor vehicle, falls, drownings, burns, poisonings) and intentional (homicide or suicide), and the balance is attributable to chronic diseases such as liver cirrhosis, other liver disease, cancer, heart disease, and so forth (Midanik et al., 2004).

In its fourth edition of the *Diagnostic and Statistic Manual of Mental Disorders (DSM–IV)*, the American Psychiatric Association (1994) identified two major alcohol use disorders, alcohol dependence and alcohol abuse. Alcohol dependence and abuse have been linked to higher levels of alcohol consumption than are found among people without alcohol use disorders and with enhanced risk of future alcohol-related difficulties (Schuckit et al., 2005). The *DSM–IV* diagnostic criteria for dependence include the following:

- tolerance;
- withdrawal syndrome or drinking to relieve or avoid withdrawal symptoms;
- drinking larger amounts for a longer period of time than intended;
- persistent desire or unsuccessful attempts to cut down on drinking;
- spending a great deal of time obtaining alcohol, drinking, or recovering from the effects of drinking;
- giving up important social, occupational, or recreational activities in favor of drinking; and
- continued drinking despite physical or psychological problems caused by drinking.

A diagnosis of dependence requires that in any given year a person must meet at least three of the seven criteria. In the 2001–2002 NESARC, the most recent national survey examining the prevalence of alcohol

This research was supported in part by National Institute on Alcohol Abuse and Alcoholism Grant P60-AA013759 awarded to the Youth Center Alcohol Prevention Center, School of Public Health, Boston University.

dependence in individuals, 12% of respondents reported that they had experienced alcohol dependence at least once in their life, and 4% had done so during the year of the survey (Grant, Dawson, et al., 2004).

Alcohol abuse was introduced as a separate alcohol use disorder to indicate repetitive problems linked to alcohol when the difficulties did not include withdrawal or tolerance (Schuckit et al., 2005). A person can be diagnosed with abuse if he or she meets any one of the following four criteria associated with alcohol use: "Recurrent drinking resulting in failure to meet major role obligations at work, school, or home"; "recurrent alcohol use in hazardous situations"; "recurrent legal problems associated with alcohol"; and "continued drinking despite recurrent social or interpersonal problems linked to alcohol" (Shuckit et al., 2005. p. 350). Comparison of the National Longitudinal Alcohol Epidemiology Survey (NLAES; N = 42,682, response rate, 90%) in 1991–1992 with the NESARC in 2001–2002 indicates that the past 12-month prevalence of alcohol abuse increased from 3% in NLAES to 4.7% in NESARC, the latter representing 9.7 million adults (Grant, Dawson, et al., 2004).

As defined in *DSM–IV*, alcohol abuse appears to be a relatively independent diagnosis from dependence, with fewer than 10% of those who experience abuse developing dependence. Test–retest reliability is lower for abuse than for dependence, and one study indicated that 70% of those with dependence will have continued problems over time, compared with 30% of those with abuse (Schuckit, Danko, Smith, & Buckman, 2002). Although alcohol abuse is generally considered to be a less severe alcohol disorder than dependence because alcohol abuse has a one-symptom threshold for diagnosis, some of the alcohol-related problems covered by abuse criteria (e.g., legal problems associated with alcohol) may be more severe than those covered by dependence criteria (Chung, Martin, & Winters, 2005).

There has been some debate about whether alcohol abuse and dependence are separate phenomena or different manifestations of the same underlying disorder (e.g., Harford & Muthén, 2001; Hasin, Grant, & Endicott, 1990; Muthén, Grant, & Hasin, 1993; Saha, Chou, & Grant, 2006). Langenbucher and

Chung (1995) and Nelson, Little, Health, and Kessler (1996) reported that alcohol abuse precedes alcohol dependence in time. Ridenour, Cottler, Compton, Spitznagel, and Cunningham-Williams (2003) also reported that there is a progression from alcohol abuse to dependence.

However, in the NESARC survey, 29% experienced alcohol abuse at some point, compared with 13% who experienced dependence. Of people who ever experienced alcohol abuse, 62% never experienced dependence. NESARC data show that 13% of the respondents experienced alcohol dependence, 85% of whom had experienced both alcohol dependence and alcohol abuse. Of those who had experienced both alcohol abuse and dependence, 45% first experienced abuse with dependence during the same year. Eighteen percent experienced dependence at least 1 year before abuse, and 36% experienced abuse at least 1 year before dependence. Thus, NESARC data do not provide compelling support for abuse being prodromal to dependence.

An item response theory analysis examining each dependence and abuse criterion and its relation to a continuum of alcohol use disorder severity found that abuse and dependence criteria did not form distinct separate disorders (Saha et al., 2006) but rather were intermixed in their relation to an alcohol use disorder severity continuum. A comparison of persons who met each abuse and dependence criterion in the past year also revealed no consistent ordering by abuse or dependence. People meeting some abuse criteria drank more than did those meeting some of the dependence criteria, although people meeting other abuse criteria drank less (data available on request). However, analyses of the NESARC data revealed that a greater percentage of those meeting past-year dependence criteria than meeting past-year abuse criteria engaged in binge drinking daily or near daily (19% vs. 6%). The National Institute on Alcohol Abuse and Alcoholism (NIAAA) has defined binge drinking as males consuming five or more and females consuming four or more drinks in a 2-hr period (NIAAA, 2004–2005). In the NESARC study, a greater percentage of past-year alcohol-dependent persons than past-year alcohol abusers exceeded NIAAA's safe drinking guidelines (66% vs. 36%).

AGE AT DRINKING ONSET, DEPENDENCE, AND ABUSE

The Centers for Disease Control and Prevention's 2003 Youth Risk Behavior Survey of high school students nationwide revealed that 28% drank alcohol other than a few sips before age 13 (Grunbaum et al., 2004). By age 17, these students were seven times more likely than those who waited until age 17 for their first drink to consume five or more drinks six or more times per month. For the average person, binge drinking on an empty stomach produces blood alcohol levels of 0.08% or higher, the legal level of intoxication in every state. Thus, those who begin drinking before age 13 are much more likely, even in high school, to frequently drink to intoxication. Compared with other students, the approximately 1 million frequent heavy drinkers more often exhibit behaviors that pose risk to themselves and others, such as riding with drinking drivers, driving after drinking, never wearing safety belts, carrying guns and other weapons, becoming injured in suicide attempts, having unplanned and unprotected sex, having sex after drinking, making someone pregnant or becoming pregnant, and using tobacco, marijuana, and other illicit drugs (Hingson & Kenkel, 2004).

Starting to drink at an early age is also associated with alcohol dependence and related problems during adolescence and adulthood. According to analyses of the NLAES, among those who began drinking before age 14, 45% developed dependence at some point in their lives, compared with 10% of those who waited until they were 21 or older to start drinking (Grant & Dawson, 1997). These relations have been found to persist after controlling statistically for family history of alcoholism, sex, race or ethnicity, history of cigarette and drug use, education, and marital status (Hingson, Heeren, Jamanka, & Howland, 2000; Hingson, Heeren, Zakocs, Winter, & Wechsler, 2003). More recent research has indicated that not only are those who start drinking at earlier ages more likely to experience alcohol dependence, but they are also more likely to develop dependence within 10 years of drinking onset or before age 25. Nearly half of adults ever classifiable as alcohol dependent met the criteria before age 22, and two thirds did so before age 25 (Hingson et al., 2006b). Furthermore, those classifiable as alcohol dependent at a young age were, in turn, more likely to experience dependence during the survey year (when the mean respondent age was 44), as well as chronic relapsing and dependence characterized by more episodes and longer episodes, and were more likely to meet more diagnostic criteria for dependence (Hingson et al., 2006a).

Early drinking onset has also been linked among both adolescents and adults to unintentional injuries (Hingson et al., 2000), motor vehicle crashes (Hingson, Heeren, Levenson, Jamanka, & Voas, 2002), physical fights (Hingson, Heeren, & Zakocs, 2001), unplanned and unprotected sex after drinking (Hingson, Heeren, Winter, & Wechsler, 2003), nicotine dependence, illicit substance use and dependence, antisocial personality, conduct disorder, and academic underachievement (McGue, Iacono, Legrand, & Elkins, 2001).

Presumably, although never tested, if alcohol dependence and abuse are not distinct diagnostic conditions but rather different manifestations of an underlying spectrum of disorder, then their associations with early drinking onset should be similar. In this chapter, we explore whether early drinking onset is associated with a greater likelihood of developing (a) alcohol dependence, (b) alcohol abuse, (c) dependence and abuse more rapidly, (d) dependence and abuse before age 25, and (e) chronic relapsing alcohol dependence and abuse that is characterized by multiple and longer episodes and meeting more of the diagnostic criteria for dependence and abuse. We also assess the relative strengths of the potential associations between age at drinking onset and these parallel outcomes of alcohol dependence and abuse.

HISTORICAL BACKGROUND AND STUDY METHOD

During 2001 and 2002, the NIAAA conducted the NESARC. Under contract, the NIAAA supervised the U.S. Census Bureau in conducting face-to-face interviews with a multistage probability sample of 43,093 adults ages 18 and older (response rate = 81%). The research protocol, including informed consent procedures, received full ethical review and approval from the U.S. Census Bureau and the Office of Management and Budget. The survey methods, quality control procedures, and test–retest reliability tests have been detailed by Grant, Dawson, et al. (2004).

DIAGNOSTIC ASSESSMENT OF ALCOHOL DEPENDENCE AND ABUSE IN NESARC

The NESARC used the NIAAA Alcohol Use Disorder and Associated Disabilities Interview Schedule—*DSM–IV* Version (AUDADIS-IV), a state-of-the-art, structured, diagnostic interview designed for use by nonclinician lay interviewers. Computer algorithms were designed to produce diagnoses of abuse and dependence consistent with the final *DSM–IV* criteria. Numerous national and international psychometric studies have documented good to excellent reliability and validity of the AUDADIS-IV measures of alcohol abuse and dependence, including clinical reappraisals conducted by psychiatrists in clinical and general population samples (Grant et al., 2003; Stinson et al., 2006).

Diagnosis of 12-month alcohol dependence required that respondents satisfy three of the seven criteria for dependence in the past year or during any year before the past year. Diagnosis of dependence before the past year also required clustering, as specified in *DSM–IV*, of at least three dependence criteria in any 1 year of the respondent's life. Lifetime diagnosis included all respondents who were dependent in the past year or before the past year. Alcohol dependence withdrawal criteria required at least two positive symptoms of withdrawal as defined by *DSM–IV* alcohol withdrawal diagnosis. *DSM–IV* alcohol abuse was manifested by meeting one or more of the abuse symptoms cited earlier during the past year or any single year before the past year (not by concurrently meeting *DSM–IV* alcohol dependence criteria in the same year).

Duration criteria associated with diagnosis of either alcohol abuse or dependence in NESARC defines the repetitiveness with which the diagnostic criteria must occur to be positive. Duration criteria were provided operational definitions by means of qualifiers such as *recurrent, often,* and *persistent* and were embedded directly in the symptom questions. The following alcohol dependence and abuse classifications were examined: lifetime dependence or abuse,

dependence or abuse within 10 years of drinking onset, and dependence or abuse before age 25.

To determine the number of episodes experienced, people who met dependence criteria were asked,

> In your entire life how many separate periods like this did you have when some of these experiences were happening around the same time? By separate periods, I mean times that were separated by at least one year when you did not have any of the experiences you mentioned with alcohol at all or you stopped drinking entirely.

Duration of longest dependence was ascertained by asking diagnosed people the longest period they had when some of these experiences were happening around the same time. Parallel procedures were used to determine number of abuse episodes and duration of longest abuse. People with lifetime and past-year dependence were stratified into those who met six to seven versus three to five diagnostic criteria. Those with lifetime and past-year abuse were stratified into those who met one versus two or more abuse criteria.

POTENTIAL AND INDEPENDENT PREDICTORS OF ALCOHOL DEPENDENCE AND ABUSE

Respondents were asked the age at which they first started drinking (not counting tastes or sips), which was categorized (a) as younger than 14 years, (b) for each year separately from 14 through 20 years old, and (c) as 21 years or older (the minimum legal drinking age in the United States). Family history of alcohol problems was positive if first-degree relatives (i.e., a mother, father, sister, brother, son, daughter) had an alcohol problem. Antisocial behavior was positive if respondents reported three or more antisocial behaviors before age 15, and depression was based on meeting *DSM–IV* criteria before age 14. The *DSM–IV* criteria for dysthymia and generalized anxiety were also examined. Test–retest reliability of AUDADIS-IV measures for depression, dysthymia, and antisocial behaviors were good (κs = 0.65, 0.58, and 0.67, respectively; mean κ = 0.64; Grant, Dawson, et al., 2004; Grant, Stinson, et al., 2004).

Respondents were asked whether they had ever and in the past year used one of following 10 types of drugs: sedatives, tranquilizers, painkillers, stimulants, marijuana, cocaine, hallucinogens, inhalants, heroin, and other medicines. People who had ever smoked 100 cigarettes were considered cigarette users.

DATA ANALYSIS

The NESARC incorporated a multistage probability sample of the noninstitutionalized adult population of the United States. The sample was stratified by individual housing units and group quarters, including military personnel living off base and people residing in nontransient hotels and motels, boarding houses, and rooming houses. Blacks, Hispanics, and those between the ages of 18 and 24 were oversampled. Because of this complex survey sampling design, statistical analyses must account for both the differential sampling weights and the correlation structure resulting from the sampling design. The SUDAAN Version 8.1 statistical software program was used to account for the complexity (*Software for Survey Data Analysis,* 2002). This program accounts for sampling weights and correlation structure in estimating population parameters (such as population means or percentages), in calculating standard errors of population parameters (by using first-order Taylor series approximations to adjust standard errors for the sample correlation structure), and in testing hypotheses.

To be consistent with previous NLAES age-at-drinking-onset analyses, analyses of this study focused only on respondents who drank 12 or more drinks in a year of their life. Analyses of alcohol dependence outcomes focused on respondents who drank 12 or more drinks in at least one year of their lives, and analyses of alcohol abuse outcomes focused on respondents who drank 12 or more drinks in at least 1 year of their lives and never simultaneously met alcohol dependence criteria. In the NESARC, a person who simultaneously met alcohol dependence and abuse criteria was classified as alcohol dependent.

The goals of our analyses are (a) to describe the prevalence and the characteristics of alcohol dependence and alcohol abuse in the U.S. noninstitutionalized population, (b) to examine the association between age at drinking onset and the prevalence and

severity of alcohol dependence and abuse, and (c) to assess whether potential associations between age at drinking onset and alcohol dependence versus alcohol abuse significantly differ. To achieve our first goal, we describe the prevalence and characteristics of alcohol dependence and abuse through estimated percentages, accounting for sampling design. We tested bivariate associations between demographic characteristics, alcohol-related risk factors, and the prevalence and characteristics of alcohol dependence and abuse through chi-square analyses.

When exploring our second goal (examination of the association between age at drinking onset and the prevalence and severity of alcohol dependence and abuse), we recognized that outcomes of ever developing alcohol dependence or abuse are time-to-event outcomes and are appropriately analyzed through statistical methods for survival data. Because of the cross-sectional nature of the NESARC sample, older respondents had longer follow-up and therefore a greater opportunity to develop dependence. Statistical methods for the analysis of survival data (Kaplan-Meier survival curves and Cox proportional hazards models) appropriately account for this differential follow-up by treating respondents who have not developed dependence or abuse as censored at their age of interview. We described the unadjusted incidence of alcohol dependence and abuse, by age and by time since drinking onset, through Kaplan-Meier survival curves. We analyzed associations between age at drinking onset and the incidence of alcohol dependence or abuse, controlling for demographic characteristics and other factors known to be related to age at drinking onset (e.g., expression of antisocial behaviors before age 15, major depression before age 14, family history of alcohol dependence) through Cox proportional hazards regression models and described them through hazard ratios and their 95% confidence intervals. These hazard ratios describe the increased (or decreased) risk of dependence or abuse for those with drinking onset before age 14 and at each age from 14 through 20 relative to those with drinking onset at age 21 or older (the reference group). We also used Cox proportional hazards models to examine associations between age at drinking onset and developing dependence or abuse within 10 years of drinking onset or by age 25.

The prevalence of past-year dependence or abuse is not a time-to-event outcome, and associations between age at drinking onset and past-year dependence or abuse, controlling for demographic characteristics and alcohol-related risk factors, were analyzed through logistic regression models and described through odds ratios (ORs) and their 95% confidence intervals. These ORs describe the increase (or decrease) in the odds of past-year dependence or abuse for those with drinking onset before age 14 and at each age from 14 through 20 relative to those with drinking onset at age 21 or older. We also used logistic regression to examine associations between age at drinking onset and experiencing two or more episodes of dependence or abuse. Among the subsamples of respondents who were ever alcohol dependent or alcohol abusers, we used logistic regression to examine associations between age at drinking onset and severity-related outcomes of (a) having an episode last more than 1 year or (b) meeting more diagnostic criteria (six or seven criteria vs. three to five criteria for dependence, two or more criteria vs. one criterion for abuse).

To achieve our third goal of formally testing for differences in the associations between age at drinking onset and alcohol dependence and abuse, for outcomes analyzed through logistic regression we used generalized estimating equation logistic regression models for repeated measures data. This approach appropriately treats alcohol dependence and abuse as two outcomes measured on the same sample of respondents and allows control for the covariates described above. Differences in the age-at-onset ratios for those with dependence versus abuse were modeled through cross-product interaction terms for age at onset and type of substance use disorder.

RESULTS

Prevalence and Severity of Alcohol Dependence and Abuse

On the basis of the total NESARC sample, 66% of the adult population qualified as current or former drinkers. Of interest, 12.5% of the sample met alcohol dependence criteria at some point during their lives, representing more than 26 million Americans. Eight percent met the dependence criteria before age 25,

representing more than 16 million people. During the survey year, 3.8% of the sample, representing 7.9 million people, met alcohol dependence criteria, which was one third of lifetime dependents. Three percent of the sample reported two or more episodes.

At some point in their lives, 18% met alcohol abuse criteria without ever being alcohol dependent. Similar proportions of people ever alcohol dependent or ever alcohol abusers met the criteria before age 25, had multiple periods in which they met these criteria, and met respective criteria during the year of the survey. Among those who were ever alcohol dependent, two thirds met dependence criteria before the age of 25. Similarly, just under three fourths who met abuse criteria did so before age 25. Just under one third of people ever alcohol dependent during their lives met dependence criteria during the year of the survey. Similarly, just under one third of those who were ever alcohol abusers were abusing during the year of the survey. One in four who met alcohol dependence criteria did so at least twice during their lives. Just more than one in four who were ever alcohol abusers were abusers at least twice during their lives.

Associations Between Age at Drinking Onset and Alcohol Dependence and Abuse

Separate analyses revealed that early age at drinking onset was associated with a greater likelihood of ever experiencing alcohol dependence and alcohol abuse, meeting dependence and abuse criteria within 10 years of drinking onset, and meeting dependence and abuse criteria before age 25. Early drinking onset was also associated with experiencing past-year dependence and abuse and experiencing two or more episodes of dependence and abuse (see Table 14.1). In general, the association between early age at drinking onset and the various alcohol dependence outcomes was slightly but not significantly stronger than the relation between early age at drinking onset and the various alcohol abuse outcomes.

Among persons ever alcohol dependent or abusers of alcohol, those who began drinking at younger ages were more likely to experience periods of alcohol dependence and abuse that exceeded 2 years or more and to meet multiple criteria for diagnosis of alcohol dependence and alcohol abuse. In general, the strength of association was similar between early age

TABLE 14.1

Association Between Age at Drinking Onset and Alcohol Dependence and Alcohol Abuse

Age started drinking	Alcohol dependence						Alcohol abuse					
	Ever drank (N = 26,829)	Ever dependent	Within 10 years	Before age 25	Past year	2+ episodes	Ever drank (not dependent, N = 21,674)	Ever abuse	Within 10 years	Before age 25	Past year	2+ episodes
<14	1,380	47%	27%	33%	13%	15%	854	54%	34%	40%	8%	16%
14	956	45	28	31	12	11	589	60	49	49	10	15
15	1,516	38	26	27	10	9	1,036	58	46	46	8	17
16	2,925	32	21	22	10	8	2,102	55	45	43	12	15
17	2,761	28	19	19	8	7	2,124	53	41	38	10	12
18	5,834	15	10	10	4	3	4,756	41	30	27	7	9
19	2,063	17	11	10	4	5	1,747	34	27	23	6	8
20	1,978	11	6	6	3	3	1,783	25	20	14	4	5
21+	7,416	9	2	4	2	2	6,683	18	13	7	4	3

	Ever alcohol dependent			Ever alcohol abuse				
	Duration of longest episode		Number of criteria met	Duration of longest episode		Number of criteria met		
Age at drinking onset	13–24 months	25+ months	6–7 criteria	13–24 months	25+ months	2 criteria	3 criteria	4 criteria
<14	17%	41%	54%	13%	39%	26%	15%	5%
14	11	38	50	13	34	27	13	4
15	13	34	41	13	33	23	11	3
16	12	33	30	14	28	22	9	1
17	12	28	30	14	24	20	7	2
18	12	31	23	12	27	18	5	1
19	15	31	33	10	25	18	2	1
20	6	26	24	10	27	16	4	1
21+	12	27	24	7	24	15	4	0

TABLE 14.2

Among Those Ever Alcohol Dependent and Alcohol Abusers and According to Age at Drinking Onset, Duration of Longest Episodes of Alcohol Dependence and Alcohol Abuse and Number of Dependence and Abuse Criteria Met

at drinking onset and these parallel dependence and abuse criteria (see Table 14.2).

Multivariate Analyses of the Association Between Age at Drinking Onset and Alcohol Dependence and Abuse

We calculated separate sets of Kaplan-Meier curves describing the unadjusted incidence of alcohol dependence (see Figure 14.1a) and alcohol abuse (see Figure 14.1b) criteria according to age at drinking onset. The curves for alcohol abuse and dependence according to age at drinking onset are remarkably similar. Most of the onset of dependence and abuse occurred within 10 years of drinking onset. In general, the earlier the age at drinking onset, the greater the proportion of people who developed alcohol dependence and alcohol abuse. There was one partial exception to this finding. Unlike alcohol dependence, where the likelihood of ever meeting dependence criteria increases each year, people who began drinking at ages 14 and 15 were actually more likely to experience alcohol abuse than those who began drinking before age 14. People who started drinking before age 16 were more likely to experience alcohol abuse than those who began drinking at older ages. Similarly,

people who started drinking before age 16 were more likely than those who started drinking later to develop alcohol dependence.

Separate sets of hazards ratios examining the associations between age at drinking onset and (a) ever developing alcohol dependence and (b) ever developing alcohol abuse revealed quite similar patterns of association when the following covariates were statistically controlled: age, gender, race or ethnicity, education, marital status, past or current smoking, past or current drug use, family history of alcoholism, childhood antisocial behavior, and childhood depression (see Figure 14.2). ORs between early age at drinking onset and alcohol abuse were not significantly different but were slightly higher and parallel to those for alcohol dependence at each age at drinking onset.

The associations between age at drinking onset and the development of alcohol dependence and alcohol abuse within 10 years of drinking onset and before age 25 (see Figures 14.3 and 14.4) were also quite similar. Relative to persons who started drinking at age 21 or older, those who started drinking before age 21 were more likely to develop alcohol abuse and dependence within 10 years of drinking

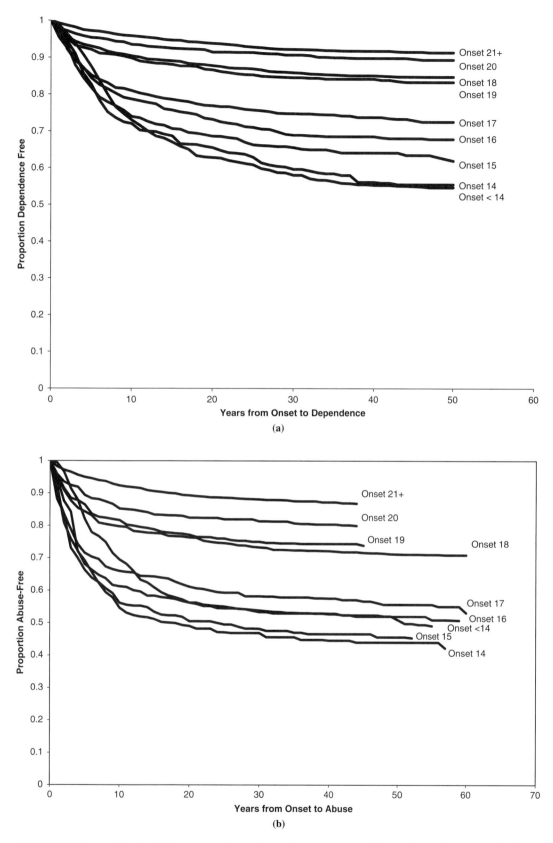

FIGURE 14.1.   A: Kaplan-Meier curves describing the proportion of dependence-free individuals by age at drinking onset. B: Kaplan-Meier curves describing the proportion of abuse-free individuals by age at drinking onset.

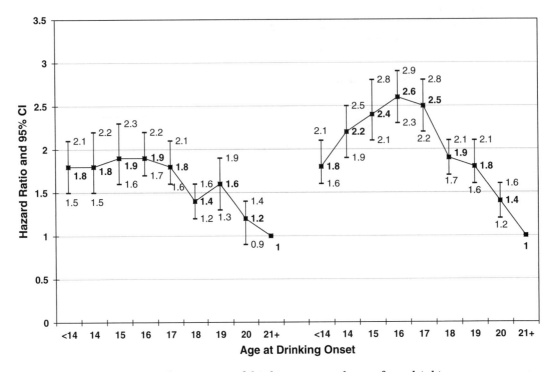

FIGURE 14.2. Association between age of drinking onset and years from drinking onset to onset of developing alcohol dependence (left) and association between age of drinking onset and years from drinking onset to onset of developing alcohol abuse (right). CI = confidence interval.

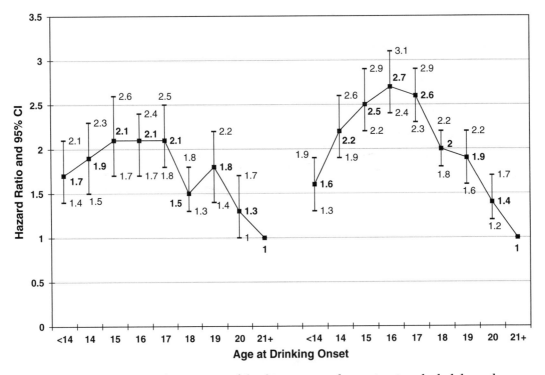

FIGURE 14.3. Association between age of drinking onset and experiencing alcohol dependence within 10 years of drinking onset (left) and association between age of drinking onset and experiencing alcohol abuse within 10 years of drinking onset (right). CI = confidence interval.

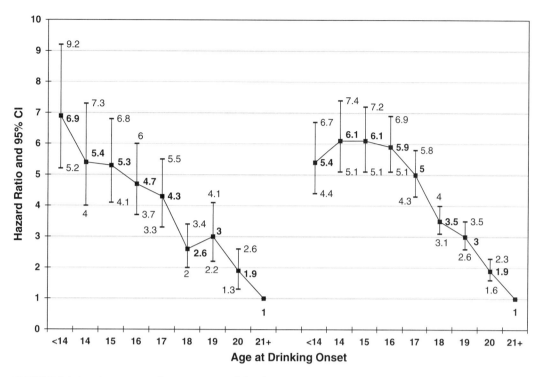

FIGURE 14.4.   Association between age of drinking onset and development of alcohol dependence before age 25 (left) and association between age of drinking onset and development of alcohol abuse before age 25 (right). CI = confidence interval.

onset and before age 25. Earlier age at drinking onset was also associated with a greater likelihood of experiencing alcohol abuse or dependence during the year of the survey (see Figure 14.5), when the average respondent age was 44. Relations were significant for all onset age groups, except for ages 19 and 20 for past-year alcohol dependence and age 20 for alcohol abuse.

Among people who were ever alcohol dependent or who ever experienced alcohol abuse, the younger the age at which respondents began to drink the greater their likelihood of (a) experiencing two or more episodes of alcohol dependence or alcohol abuse (see Figure 14.6), (b) experiencing episodes of alcohol dependence and alcohol abuse that exceeded 1 year of duration (see Figure 14.7), and (c) meeting six to seven criteria for alcohol dependence or two or more alcohol abuse criteria (see Figure 14.8).

Finally, generalized estimating equation logistic regression models showed no significant differences in the ORs describing age at onset associations with dependence and abuse for the number of criteria met (see Figure 14.8, global test of interaction $p = .123$) or

for dependence episodes of at least 1 year (see Figure 14.7, global test of interaction $p = .321$). There was a significant difference in ORs describing the association between age at onset and past-year dependence and abuse (see Figure 14.5, global test of interaction $p = .015$). Examination of individual interaction terms revealed that onset before age 14 has a stronger association with dependence than with abuse (OR = 1.9 vs. OR = 1.3, $p = .004$), as does onset at age 15 (OR = 1.7 vs. OR = 1.3, $p = .040$); other ORs did not significantly differ. For the outcome of two or more dependence episodes (see Figure 14.6), the OR for onset age of 18 versus 21 or older was significantly lower for dependence than for abuse (global test of interaction $p = .001$, OR = 1.2 vs. 2.1, $p = .001$); other ORs did not significantly differ.

REVIEW OF FINDINGS

Prior research with the NESARC data set (Hingson et al., 2006a, 2006b) has found that the younger respondents were when they began drinking, the greater their likelihood of experiencing lifetime

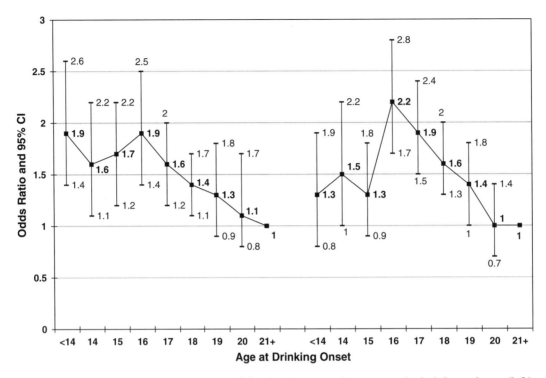

FIGURE 14.5. Association between age of drinking onset and past-year alcohol dependence (left) and association between age of drinking onset and past-year alcohol abuse (right). CI = confidence interval.

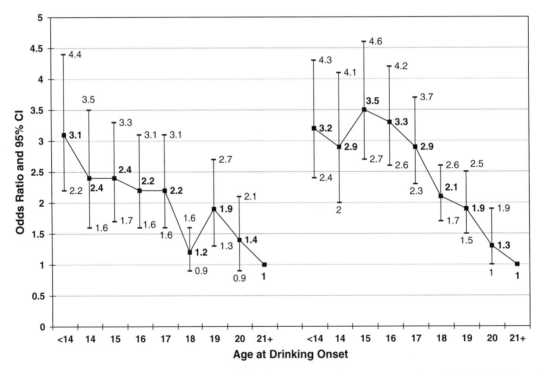

FIGURE 14.6. Association between age of drinking onset and two or more episodes of alcohol dependence (left) and association between age of drinking onset and two or more episodes of alcohol abuse (right). CI = confidence interval.

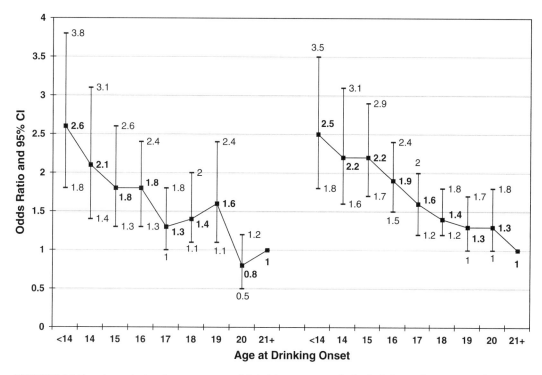

FIGURE 14.7.   Association between age of drinking onset and alcohol dependence episodes exceeding 1 year (left) and association between age of drinking onset and alcohol abuse episodes exceeding 1 year (right). CI = confidence interval.

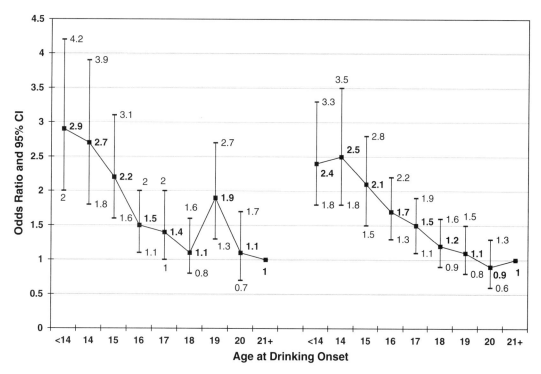

FIGURE 14.8.   Association between age at drinking onset and meeting six to seven criteria of alcohol dependence (left) and association between age at drinking onset and meeting three to five criteria of alcohol abuse (right). CI = confidence interval.

alcohol dependence (after analytically controlling for family history of alcoholism and numerous behavioral and personality characteristics related to age at drinking onset). Separate analyses of the data controlling for the same set of demographic variables and variables associated with early drinking onset revealed that early age at drinking onset was associated with the development of both alcohol dependence and abuse at some point in a respondent's life. Also, early drinking onset was associated with more rapid development of both alcohol dependence and abuse, thus resulting in dependence and abuse being more likely to be diagnosable before age 25. Furthermore, among those ever alcohol dependent or abusers, the earlier respondents began to drink, the greater the likelihood that they would experience chronic relapsing dependence and chronic relapsing abuse characterized by longer episodes, more episodes, past-year diagnosis of abuse and dependence, and meeting more of the diagnostic criteria for alcohol abuse and dependence.

The pattern, strength, and direction of associations between early age at drinking onset and development of the various alcohol dependence outcomes and the various alcohol abuse outcomes examined in this study were very similar. The one exception was that very early age at drinking onset (before age 16) was more strongly related to past-year dependence than to past-year abuse. Overall, our analyses yielded little evidence that alcohol abuse and dependence are sharply different alcohol use disorders, even though a smaller proportion of those who abuse alcohol than those dependent on alcohol engage in daily binge drinking. That these similarities were observed when exactly the same sample was being examined strengthens the observation that age at drinking onset increases risk of alcohol dependence and abuse as well as chronic relapsing alcohol dependence and abuse.

In this study, early age at drinking onset related to alcohol dependence and abuse in a couple of notable ways. First, early age at drinking onset heightened the risk of developing both alcohol dependence and abuse at an early age. As mentioned earlier, nearly half (47%) of respondents who ever experienced alcohol dependence did so before age 21, and two thirds did so before the age of 25.

Similarly, of those who ever met alcohol abuse criteria, 54% did so before age 21, and 76% did so before they reached age 25. Second, people who first met alcohol dependence and those who met alcohol abuse criteria at an early age were less likely to have sought alcohol treatment. Of those first alcohol dependent before age 21, 22% ever sought treatment, compared with 35% who were first dependent after age 30. Six percent who were first abusing alcohol before age 21 ever sought treatment, compared with 15% who were first abusing after age 30.

METHODOLOGICAL CONSIDERATIONS AND FUTURE RESEARCH QUESTIONS

Several issues should be considered in interpreting the results of this study. First, the results are based on cross-sectional surveys, which required recall many years earlier by some respondents to pinpoint the age at which they first began consuming alcohol, experiencing at some level childhood depression, having incidents of antisocial behavior, and having symptoms of alcohol dependence and abuse. Of note, our analysis indicated that the age at drinking onset and alcohol dependence and abuse relations were strongest among participants younger than age 34, for whom the recall period was shortest. Despite this survey's excellent response rates and the statistical adjustments for respondent age and numerous personal and behavioral characteristics, longitudinal studies that begin during childhood and follow adolescents into adult life would be preferable. With data spread out over time on the same individual, researchers can prospectively test the potential relations between age at drinking onset and alcohol dependence and abuse and clarify those mechanisms at work that exacerbate risk. A 12-year follow-up study of the National Longitudinal Study of Youth found earlier age at drinking onset to be prospectively associated with alcohol abuse and dependence (Grant, Stinson, & Harford, 2001), as did another analysis of a community sample followed longitudinally from ages 12 to 30, which showed the strongest association among those who began drinking outside the home (Warner & White, 2003).

Second, social desirability bias may result in the underreporting of alcohol use and associated problems, prompting underdiagnosis of alcohol dependence and abuse. Nevertheless, people willing to report heavy drinking may be more willing to report adverse drinking consequences. Also, people who are alcohol dependent or alcohol abusers may be more likely to remember when they started drinking because of consequences suffered later in life, thereby generating stronger relations between age at drinking onset and development of alcohol dependence and abuse.

Third, and to be consistent with earlier drinking onset research, our analysis focused on drinkers as defined by the NLAES, that is, respondents who drank 12 or more drinks in at least 1 year of their life. We repeated our analysis with the larger set of NESARC participants who reported ever having one or more drinks ($N = 38,827$, response rate $= 81\%$) and observed the same patterns and relationships (data available on request).

Fourth, although extensive research has established reliability of lifetime and past-year alcohol abuse and dependence criteria (based on *DSM–IV* criteria using AUDADIS-IV), the reliability of numbers and duration of episodes of alcohol dependence and abuse has not received the same attention. Therefore, the potential relations between age at drinking onset and the numbers and duration of these episodes require more cautious interpretation.

Fifth, potential spurious or confounding variables not considered may have been responsible for the observed relations. Genetic factors, disinhibiting behavior patterns, and other psychopathology may relate to both early drinking onset and the development of both alcohol dependence and alcohol abuse. Children who experience overt physical, sexual, or psychological abuse or whose parents exhibited psychopathology may start to drink at younger ages and drink larger amounts to cope with posttraumatic stress disorders.

Sixth, although this analysis controlled for family history of alcoholism, many children born to nonalcoholic parents may nonetheless be raised in environments that allow youth access to alcohol. Also, some adolescents may have peers who engage in heavy drinking and drug use, which may contribute to earlier and heavier drinking, thereby fostering alcohol dependence and abuse.

Seventh, Moss, Chen, and Yi (2007) recently identified five subtypes of alcohol dependence. Whether earlier age at drinking onset independently predicts each of these subtypes and whether the strength of the associations differs also warrant future exploration.

CLINICAL AND PUBLIC HEALTH IMPLICATIONS

These considerations notwithstanding, the results of the analysis reported here reinforce the need to implement screening and counseling of adolescent patients regarding drinking and alcohol dependence and abuse. Because pediatric medical care providers considerably underdiagnose alcohol use, abuse, and dependence among patients ages 14 to 18, structured screening devices have been recommended to more accurately identify those conditions (Wilson, Sherritt, Gates, & Knight, 2004). However, according to Kulig and the Committee on Substance Abuse of the American Academy of Pediatrics (2005), adolescent substance use disorders may be the most commonly missed pediatric diagnosis. These authors cited multiple barriers to physician involvement in prevention screening and management of substance abuse, such as (a) time constraints associated with high patient volume, (b) inadequate reimbursement related to the time and effort required to address substance abuse disorders with patients and their families, (c) physician fear of labeling patients and their families, (d) inadequate training in substance abuse and addiction, (e) lack of dissemination to physicians of research supporting positive treatment outcomes and the negative effects of failure to intervene early in substance abuse, and (f) lack of information about how to access referral and treatment resources.

Recent clinical trial reviews have indicated that screening and motivational counseling interventions can result in decreases in drinking and alcohol-related consequences among adolescents and college students (O'Leary-Tevyaw & Monti, 2004; Larimer & Cronce, 2002, 2007). Raising the drinking age to 21 also reduced drinking, alcohol-related traffic deaths, and deaths from other unintentional injuries among people under 21 (Shults et al., 2001; Wagenaar & Toomey, 2002). A national analysis found the law further reduced drinking among those between 21 and 24 years of age (O'Malley & Wagenaar, 1991; Wagenaar & Toomey, 2002). Comprehensive community interventions (Hingson et al., 1996; Holder et al., 2000; Weitzman, Nelson, Lee, & Wechsler, 2004; Wagenaar, Erickson, Harwood, & O'Malley, 2006; Treno, Gruenewald, Lee, & Remer, 2007) and heightened enforcement of the maximum legal drinking age (Wagenaar et al., 2000) can further reduce drinking and alcohol-related problems among adolescents and young adults. The results of this study and previous studies on age at drinking onset and the development of alcohol dependence and/or abuse clearly underscore the pressing need for pediatric health care providers and others concerned about the consequences of underage drinking to expand these initiatives. The similarities between the associations of early age at drinking onset and the development of alcohol dependence and alcohol abuse suggest that prevention of early drinking onset is an important objective regardless of whether alcohol dependence and abuse are separate diagnostic entities or part of an alcohol use disorder continuum.

References

American Psychiatric Association (1994). *Diagnostic and statistical manual of mental disorder* (4th ed.). Washington, DC: American Psychiatric Association.

Chung, T., Martin, C. S., & Winters, K. C. (2005). Diagnosis, course, and assessment of alcohol abuse and dependence in adolescents. *Recent Developments in Alcoholism, 17,* 5–27.

Grant, B., & Dawson, D. (1997). Age at onset of alcohol use and its association with *DSM–IV* alcohol abuse and dependence: Results from the National Longitudinal Alcohol Epidemiological Survey. *Journal of Substance Abuse, 9,* 103–110.

Grant, B., Dawson, D., Stinson, F., Chou, S., Dufour, M., & Pickering, R. (2004). The 12-month prevalence and trends in *DSM–IV* alcohol abuse and dependence, 1991-1992 and 2001-2002. *Drug and Alcohol Dependence, 74,* 223–234.

Grant, B., Dawson, D., Stinson, F., Chou, S., Kay, W., & Pickering, R. (2003). The Alcohol Use Disorder and Associated Disabilities Interview Schedule-IV (AUDADIS-IV): Reliability of alcohol consumption, tobacco use, family history of depression and psychiatric diagnostic modules in a general population sample. *Drug and Alcohol Dependence, 71,* 7–16.

Grant, B., Stinson, F., Dawson, D., Chou, S., Dufour, M., Compton, W., et al. (2004). Prevalence and co-occurrence of substance use disorders and independent mood and anxiety disorders: Results from the National Epidemiologic Survey on Alcohol and Related Conditions. *Archives of General Psychiatry, 61,* 807–816.

Grant, B., Stinson, F., & Harford, T. (2001). Age at onset of alcohol use and *DSM–IV* alcohol abuse and dependence: A 12-year follow-up. *Journal of Substance Abuse, 13,* 493–504.

Grunbaum, J., Kann, L., Kinchen, S., Ross, J., Hawkins, J., Lowry, R., et al. (2004). Youth Risk Behavior Surveillance—United States, 2003. *Morbidity and Mortality Weekly Report: Surveillance Summaries, 53,* 1–96.

Harford, T. C., & Muthén, B. O. (2001). The dimensionality of alcohol abuse and dependence: A multivariate analysis of *DSM–IV* symptom items in the National Longitudinal Survey of Youth. *Journal of Studies on Alcohol, 62,* 150–157.

Hasin, D. S., Grant, B., & Endicott, J. (1990). The natural history of alcohol abuse: Implications for definitions of alcohol disorders. *American Journal of Psychiatry, 147,* 1537–1541.

Hingson, R., Heeren, T., Jamanka, A., & Howland, J. (2000, September 27). Age of drinking onset and unintentional injury involvement after drinking. *JAMA, 284,* 1524–1533.

Hingson, R., Heeren, T., Levenson, S., Jamanka, A., & Voas, R. (2002). Age of drinking onset, driving after drinking, and involvement in alcohol related motor-vehicle crashes. *Accident Analysis and Prevention, 34,* 85–92.

Hingson, R., Heeren, T., & Winter, M. (2006a). Age of alcohol-dependence onset: Associations with severity of dependence. *Pediatrics, 118,* e755–e763.

Hingson, R., Heeren, T., & Winter, M. (2006b). Age of drinking onset and alcohol dependence—Age of onset, duration and severity. *Journal of Pediatrics and Adolescent Medicine, 17,* 739–746.

Hingson, R., Heeren, T., Winter, M., & Wechsler, H. (2003). Early age of first drunkenness as a factor in college students' unplanned and unprotected sex due to drinking. *Pediatrics, 111,* 34–41.

Hingson, R., Heeren, T., & Zakocs, R. (2001). Age of drinking onset and involvement in physical fights after drinking. *Pediatrics, 108,* 872–877.

Hingson, R., Heeren, T., Zakocs, R., Winter, M., & Wechsler, H. (2003). Age of first intoxication, heavy drinking, driving after drinking and risk of unintentional injury among U.S. college students. *Journal of Studies on Alcohol, 64,* 23–31.

Hingson, R., & Kenkel, D. (2004). Social, health, and economic consequences of underage drinking. In

Reducing underage drinking: A collective responsibility, Background papers [CD-ROM]. Washington, DC: National Academies Press.

Hingson, R., McGovern, T., Howland, J., Heeren, T., Winter, M., & Zakocs, R. (1996). Reducing alcohol-impaired driving in Massachusetts: The Saving Lives Program. *American Journal of Public Health, 86,* 791–797.

Holder, H., Gruenewald, P. J., Ponicki, W. R., Treno, A. J., Grube, J. W., Saltz, R. F., et al. (2000, November 8). Effects of community-based interventions on high risk driving and alcohol related injuries. *JAMA, 284,* 2341–2347.

Kulig, J. W., & the Committee on Substance Abuse. (2005). Tobacco, alcohol, and other drugs: The role of the pediatrician in prevention, identification, and management of substance abuse. *Pediatrics, 115,* 816–821.

Langenbucher, J. W., & Chung, T. (1995). Onset and staging of *DSM–IV* alcohol dependence using mean age and survival hazard methods. *Journal of Abnormal Psychology, 104,* 346–354.

Larimer, M., & Cronce, J. (2002). Identification, prevention and treatment: A review of individual focused strategies to reduce problematic alcohol consumption by college students. *Journal of Studies on Alcohol, 14*(Suppl.), 148–163.

Larimer, M., & Cronce, J. (2007). Identification, prevention, and treatment revisited: Individual-focused college drinking prevention strategies, 1999–2006. *Addictive Behaviors, 32,* 2439–2468.

McGue, M., Iacono, W., Legrand, N., & Elkins, I. (2001). Origins and consequences of age at first drink. II: Familial risk and heritability. *Alcoholism: Clinical & Experimental Research, 25,* 1166–1173.

Midanik, L., Chaloupka, F., Saitz, R., Toomey, T. L., Fellows, J. L., Dufour, M., et al. (2004). Alcohol-attributable deaths and years of potential life lost—United States, 2001. *Morbidity and Mortality Weekly Report, 53,* 866–870.

Moss, H., Chen, C. M., & Yi, H. (2007). Subtypes of alcohol dependence in a nationally representative sample. *Drug and Alcohol Dependence, 91,* 149–158.

Muthén, B. O., Grant, B., & Hasin, D. (1993). The dimensionality of alcohol abuse and dependence: Factor analysis of *DSM–III–R* and proposed *DSM–IV* criteria in the 1988 National Health Interview Survey. *Addiction, 88,* 1079–1090.

National Institute of Alcohol Abuse and Alcoholism. (2004–2005). Alcohol and development in youth: A multidisciplinary overview. *Alcohol Research and Health, 28,* 105–176.

Nelson, C. B., Little, R. J., Health, A. C., & Kessler, R. C. (1996). Patterns of *DSM–III–R* alcohol dependence symptom progression in a general population survey. *Psychological Medicine, 26,* 449–460.

O'Leary-Tevyaw, T., & Monti, P. (2004). Motivational environment and other brief interventions for adolescent substance abuse: Foundations, applications and evaluations. *Addiction, 99*(Suppl. 2), 63–75.

O'Malley, P. M., & Wagenaar, A. C. (1991). Effects of minimum drinking age laws on alcohol use, related behaviors, and traffic crash involvement among American youth: 1976–1987. *Journal of Studies on Alcohol, 52,* 478–491.

Ridenour, T., Cottler, L. B., Compton, W. M., Spitznagel, E. L., & Cunningham-Williams, R. M. (2003). Is there a progression from abuse disorders to dependence disorders? *Addiction, 98,* 635–644.

Saha, T., Chou, S. P., & Grant, B. (2006). Toward an alcohol use disorder continuum using item response theory: Results from the National Epidemiological Study of Alcohol Related Conditions. *Psychological Medicine, 36,* 931–941.

Schuckit, M. A., Danko, G. P., Smith, T. L., & Buckman, K. R. (2002). The five year predictive validity of each of the seven *DSM–IV* items for alcohol dependence among alcoholics. *Alcoholism: Clinical & Experimental Research, 26,* 980–987.

Schuckit, M. A., Smith, T. L., Danko, G. P., Kramer, J., Godinez, J., Bucholz, K. K., et al. (2005). Prospective evaluation of four *DSM–IV* criteria for alcohol abuse in a large population. *American Journal of Psychiatry, 162,* 350–360.

Shults, R. A., Elder, R. W., Sleet, D. A., Nichols, J. L., Alao, M. O., Carande-Kulis, V. G., et al. (2001). Reviews of evidence regarding interventions to reduce alcohol impaired driving. *American Journal of Preventive Medicine, 21,* 66–88.

Software for Survey Data Analysis (SUDAAN; Version 8.1) [Computer software]. (2002). Research Triangle Park, NC: Research Triangle Institute.

Stinson, F. S., Grant, B. F., Dawson, D. A., Ruan, W. J., Huang, B., & Saha, T. (2006). Comorbidity between *DSM–IV* alcohol and specific drug use disorders in the United States: Results from the National Epidemiologic Survey on Alcohol and Related Conditions. *Alcohol Research and Health, 29,* 94–106.

Treno, A. J., Gruenewald, P. J., Lee, J. T., & Remer, L. G. (2007). The Sacramento Neighborhood Alcohol Prevention Project: Outcomes from a community prevention trial. *Journal of Studies on Alcohol and Drugs, 68,* 197–207.

Wagenaar, A. C., Erickson, D. J., Harwood, E. M., & O'Malley, P. M. (2006). Effects of state coalitions to reduce underage drinking: A national evaluation. *American Journal of Preventive Medicine, 31,* 307–315.

Wagenaar, A. C., Murray, D. M., Gehan, J. P., Wolfson, M., Forster, J. L., Toomey, T. L., et al. (2000). Communities mobilizing for change on alcohol: Outcomes from a randomized community trial. *Journal of Studies on Alcohol, 61,* 85–94.

Wagenaar, A. C., & Toomey, T. L. (2002). Effects of minimum drinking age laws: Review and analysis of the literature from 1960 to 2000. *Journal of Studies on Alcohol, 14*(Suppl.), 206–225.

Warner, L. A., & White, H. R. (2003). Longitudinal effects of age at onset and first drinking solutions on problem drinking. *Substance Use and Misuse, 38,* 1983–2003.

Weitzman, E. R., Nelson, T. F., Lee, H., & Wechsler, H. (2004). Reducing drinking and related harms in college: Evaluation of the "A Matter of Degree" program. *American Journal of Preventive Medicine, 27,* 187–196.

Wilson, C., Sherritt, L., Gates, E., & Knight, J. R. (2004). Are clinical impressions of adolescent substance use accurate? *Pediatrics, 114,* e526–e540.

PART V

RACE, ETHNICITY, AND CULTURE

AN EXPLORATION OF ETHNICITY AND RACE IN THE ETIOLOGY OF SUBSTANCE USE: A HEALTH DISPARITIES APPROACH

Flavio F. Marsiglia and Scott J. Smith

Substance use is a universal phenomenon affecting people from all ethnic and racial backgrounds. Researchers and practitioners tend to follow the premise that race and ethnicity may have some explanatory power in accounting for differences in substance use prevalence across communities. It is not clear, however, how the constructs of race and ethnicity are related to drug use etiology or how they affect the consumption of drugs. There is more certainty that the intersection of cultural norms, socioeconomic status, gender, and age is somehow related to the etiology of substance use among ethnic and racial groups. The precise relations between ethnicity, the construct of ethnic identity, and substance use remain uncertain despite efforts by researchers to incorporate these concepts into their explanatory models (Marsiglia, Kulis, & Hecht, 2001; Phinney, 1996).

There is some consensus that membership and identification with racial or ethnic groups in unique social and historical settings can be a source of resiliency and protection, although researchers also recognize their role in stimulating vulnerability (Hawkins, Catalano, & Miller, 1992). The social context and the stressors and protections that social environments provide are key components of the etiology of substance use in ethnic and racial minority communities.

From a health disparities perspective, identifying differences in the etiology of substance use and their consequences among ethnic and racial groups is a complex but necessary exercise. Identifying what protects ethnic minorities or what makes them more

vulnerable to drug use has important implications not only in terms of prevalence rates but also in terms of the impact that drug use may have on their overall health status.

Health disparities are those diseases, disorders, and conditions that disproportionately affect individuals who are members of racial and ethnic minority groups and certain other groups, such as the poor (National Institutes of Health, 2006). To identify such disparities, researchers need to rely on predetermined ethnic and racial labels that are applied to individuals and groups. These distinctions are tools that help identify differences in drug use prevalence between groups. The limited consensus regarding the precise means of constructing racial or ethnic categories, their various naming conventions, and how individuals identify or are designated as part of these groups is certainly challenging. This murkiness is troublesome to researchers and policymakers, leading perhaps to overgeneralizations and stereotypes when attempting to establish the etiology of substance use in ethnic minority communities.

In many respects, paper-and-pencil surveys and even computer-assisted interviews may compel individuals to choose a prescribed identity, that is, a racial or ethnic label, but individuals would much rather identify themselves in a specific context. Compounding this, attempts at identification can vary from context to context. Thus, although it is helpful to the field in general to note substance use trends among various racial or ethnic groups, large variations may occur with successive administrations of the survey because of the dynamic nature of cultural identity. It is clear that racial and ethnic identity is a multidimensional concept, and as such, one cannot reduce it to a few key characteristics (Phinney, 1990). Although as this précis makes clear, definitive conclusions and assertions about ethnic and racial epidemiological data are not possible, in this chapter we still aim to provide an overview of drug use etiology among the major ethnic and racial groups. We also explore some of the protective and risk factors and processes related to possible differences in substance use trends across groups.

CLARIFYING VIEWS OF RACE AND ETHNICITY AND DRUG USE

In describing how race and ethnicity possibly relate to certain risks and protections, we adhere to an ecological health disparities perspective. This approach enables us to integrate ethnic culture as an important factor and minimize possible overgeneralizations arising from the racial–genetic models, attributing racial and ethnic disparities in substance use to population differences in the distribution of genetic variants. For the most part, models incorporating powerful genetic effects lack explanatory power, especially when social factors are considered (Dressler, Oths, & Gravlee, 2005). The socioeconomic model provides a more helpful perspective by attributing disparities to differences in socioeconomic status (SES) between ethnic groups and is a better model for studying the epidemiology of drug use (ter Bogt, Schmid, Gabhainn, Fotiou, & Vollebergh, 2006). The latter framework provides important evidence for the strong association between SES and health status, but the consistency of this approach is questionable. For instance, the SES approach cannot account for many exceptions to the rule because some members of low-SES groups maintain relatively high levels of well-being and experience low rates of substance use despite limited economic resources.

The theory of fundamental causes of disease complements the SES model. It accounts for improvements in the health status of communities while examining the existing vast SES and ethnic and racial disparities in mortality associated with certain diseases such as substance use (Phelan & Link, 2005). The perspective inherent in the theory

of fundamental causes is useful not only for explaining substance use etiology but also for explaining differences in drug use rates across racial and ethnic groups. Although research on mortality trends has demonstrated consistency over time with the fundamental cause explanation, little research exists regarding the protective factors buffering some ethnic minority communities against substance use. Following a fundamental-causes-of-disease perspective, the exploration of drug use etiology among ethnic and racial minorities focuses on how cultural processes operate as protective and risk factors to mitigate the effects of substance use.

CULTURALLY SPECIFIC RISK AND PROTECTIVE FACTORS

It has been reported that adolescents from most ethnic and racial minority populations have lower rates of substance abuse than their White peers (Bachman, Johnston, & O'Malley, 2007). African American youth show substantially lower rates of overall use than do Whites, and Latino youth show rates of drug use between those of these two other groups. African American youth are known to use substances less frequently than their White peers but experience more problems from substance use, notably more criminal justice involvement (Paradies, 2006). Prevalence rates alone do not appear to tell the complete story because issues of access to treatment and overall health status vary greatly from group to group.

In addition to differences between the main ethnic and racial groups in the United States, there are regional variations in the prevalence of substance use by racial groups (e.g., Flannery, Vazsonyi, Torquati, & Fridrich, 1994). Prevalence rates for crack and Ecstasy (cheaper drugs) tend to be higher among ethnic minority groups, and Latino youth show the highest use rates when compared with other ethnic groups (Bachman et al., 2007). However, specific developmental, historical, or cultural events may affect one racial group more than another and thus bias reported statistics. For instance, a higher school dropout rate by Hispanic youth may lead to an underestimatation of substance use rates among Latinos because the school is often the first source of identification of a problem, for example, in-school surveys (U.S. Department of Education, 2007). Youth experiencing school failure—that is, poor academic performance and truancy—who are at higher risk for substance use tend not to be represented among school-based survey respondents (Bachman et al., 2007).

Some groups may be susceptible to substance use because of economic, environmental, or cultural factors that underlie racial health disparity. For example, American Indian youth report an inhalant use rate higher than that of other major ethnic groups. They also report higher rates of lifetime alcohol use and marijuana abuse compared with other ethnic groups (Herring, 1994). American Indian youth report significantly higher lifetime marijuana and cocaine use than non-American Indian youth, whereas non-American Indian youth report substantially higher rates of tobacco use (Plunkett & Mitchell, 2000). Many factors and conditions affecting American Indian youth may be part of the fundamental causes related to these noted differences, and our models must become sensitive to what causes these disparities in consumption.

Epidemiological studies have made an important contribution to developing an evolving understanding of substance use for different ethnic and racial groups. However, those data do not directly address the processes of resiliency or risk that may be responsible for those differences. In other words, racial and ethnic groups may differ in certain mean levels of risk or resilience, but the causal factors responsible for these differences may transcend race and ethnicity and touch on general societal concerns, including health disparities. There is also a danger of exaggerating the prevalence of use or arriving at the erroneous conclusion that for some ethnic minority communities, substance abuse does not reflect a health disparity. These and related concerns support the need to complement existing epidemiological data with information about the health and social impact that substance use has on ethnic minority communities. When these types of studies have been conducted and the consequences of substance use and abuse more clearly identified, negative health impacts have been found to be more damaging to the well-being of ethnic minorities than to those of Whites.

Some of the reasons for health disparities in substance use are related to barriers to treatment encountered by ethnic minorities, the harsher penal sentencing they receive, the cheaper and more harmful types of drugs they consume (e.g., powder cocaine vs. crack cocaine), and the higher social stressors ethnic minority populations experience (Beauvais & Oetting, 2002). In this respect alone, preventing the onset of substance use among ethnic minority populations can have important favorable effects on the overall well-being of its members and of society in general. Reducing and preventing health disparities may positively influence the economic viability of whole communities (Substance Abuse and Mental Health Services Administration, 2004).

There are also important developmental concerns related to race and ethnicity and drug use etiology. Some of the recognized disparities in substance use encountered in early adolescence are indicative of multiple risk behaviors ultimately contributing to greater health disparities later in life. Substance use during childhood and adolescence has been shown to increase the risk of sexual activity at an early age, multiple sexual partners, unprotected sex, unplanned pregnancies, and abortions (French & Dishion, 2003). Early substance use is also linked to various mental disorders across different ethnic groups, particularly depression, anxiety, disruptive disorders, mood disorders, suicide ideation, and behavior (Hallfors, Waller, Bauer, Ford, & Halpern, 2005). The implementation of efficacious and culturally competent prevention interventions can have not only a positive impact on the prevention of substance abuse among ethnic minorities but also can translate into an overall improved physical and mental health status.

Within-group (race or ethnicity) differences can obscure discrete protective and risk factors responsible for different patterns of substance use. For example, length of residency in the United States seems to make a difference among Mexican and Mexican American youth. Those reporting longer residency report higher substance use prevalence than do more recent Mexican national immigrants residing in the same neighborhoods and attending the same schools (Marsiglia, Kulis, Wagstaff, Elek, & Dran, 2005). These types of findings appear to confirm previous studies suggesting that the transition away from a strong identification with culture of origin can lead to an increase in the substance use rates of ethnic minority youth (De La Rosa, Khalsa, & Rouse, 1990).

In summary, epidemiological data are helpful to better understand and serve the needs of different ethnic and racial groups. From an ecological health disparities perspective, however, those data need to be treated with caution to avoid stereotypes and oversimplifications. This type of knowledge is particularly useful when it leads to improving access to effective prevention and treatment interventions for members of ethnic and racial minorities. Prevalence differences between ethnic and racial groups become more useful when they are grounded in the social, cultural, and economic context of the communities under study. A better understanding of the context in which those differences emerge includes the identification of the key ecological factors that protect or make communities more vulnerable to substance use. Such findings in turn lead to the design and testing of interventions aimed at reducing health disparities.

ECOLOGICAL FACTORS

As this handbook shows, a host of risk and protective factors influence drug use, and there is no easy way to group them under a single meaningful rubric. The various nomenclatures for grouping them tend to include personal, behavioral, interpersonal, and environmental dimensions (Bachman et al., 2002). The following summary of commonly identified protective and risks factors organized by ecosystem levels is offered as a means to advance the exploration of the etiology of substance use among ethnic and racial minority communities:

- Community-level protective factors: social cohesion, shared norms, caring adults, and shared ethnic and cultural identity (pride). Risk factors include social disorganization, low neighborhood attachment, and easy access to alcohol, tobacco, and other drugs.
- Family-level protective factors: effective and horizontal parent–child communication, clear rules,

consistent consequences, religiosity and spirituality, and sharing cross-generational experiences in fun activities. Risk factors include poor communication, lack of parental monitoring, lack of or inconsistent rules and expectations, and family history of addiction.

- School protective factors: positive school climate, welcoming and caring environment, clear rules and expectations, and academic excellence. Risk factors include diffuse academic standards and support, lack of discipline, chaotic environment, and unclear drug policies.
- Individual and peer protective factors: high academic achievement, participation in extracurricular activities, problem-solving and critical thinking skills, adult role models, and antidrug norms. Risk factors include antisocial behaviors, sensation seeking, susceptibility to peer influences, prodrug norms, low school achievement, age of initiation, and intraindividual biological susceptibility (Botvin et al., 2000; Center for Substance Abuse Research, 2006; Kumpfer & Adler, 2003).

An important question to be addressed is how these risk and protective factors manifest themselves within ethnic and racial minority communities. An initial consideration is that protective factors in more traditional cultures seem to fall naturally mostly within collective dimensions such as community and family. However, distinctions between single risk or resiliency factors on the basis of their respective categorical assignment are artificial because most cultural processes cut across ecosystemic levels. For example, it is not helpful to treat a cultural process such as acculturation only as a cultural factor given that the process of acculturation affects the individual, family, peers, school, and community. Likewise, assigning poverty and social anomie to economic or structural indicators is not meaningful given that acculturation influences monetary gain because many recent immigrants tend to be less educated and encounter language barriers that limit financial opportunity. To advance the ecological health disparities position in our exploration of the intersection of race and ethnicity and drug use etiology, we depart from the more conventional nomenclature of protective and risk factors and instead review cultural processes that may produce protective and risk factors at one or more ecosystem levels in the context of specific ethnic and racial minority groups.

CULTURAL TRANSITIONS AND SUBSTANCE ABUSE

We argue that most commonly it is not culture itself that leads to risk behaviors but instead that cultural transitions and related dislocations can become the source of risk. The United States' strong history of immigration (voluntary and forced) contributes to the establishment of variations in substance use across ethnic and racial groups. The process of migration is usually perceived as a source of hope and social and economic advancement; however, it can also dislocate families from their traditional support networks, creating increased family stress (Menjivar, 2000). Migration potentially erodes some protective aspects of culture, and individuals may experience acculturation stress. Both phenomena are associated with increased vulnerability to drug use, especially among adolescents (Beauvais, 1998).

The process of shifting cultural identity from culture of origin to culture of residence is called *acculturation*. Acculturation occurs as a result of contact between two cultures, and it can lead to a rapid erosion of the protective effects associated with the culture of origin. Immigrants experience changes in values, acquire new behaviors, learn new ways of expression, join new social networks, and develop linguistic idioms reflecting a new sense of self-concept.

Acculturation in substance use research focuses on protective social and personal factors potentially stemming from continued attachment to the culture of origin. Perhaps the greatest downside to acculturation is the weakening of protective forces arising from lateral transmission of values and systemic influences with more assimilated and acculturated peers. Declining parental and family influence and increasing acculturation-related stress exemplify this process. Acculturation processes have been linked to higher levels of substance use and to lowered educational aspirations for some immigrants and U.S.-born Latino youth (De La Rosa, 2002).

Asian Americans experience acculturation in uniquely intense fashion because it is postulated that first-generation Asian immigrants tend to place a high value on community and interdependence, whereas their children, who are immersed in the dominant culture, come to value independence as defined by mainstream culture (Hahm, Lahiff, & Guterman, 2003). This transition can result in increased family conflict, potentially eroding the protective benefits of the family and increasing stress in the adolescent, possibly increasing the likelihood for substance use.

American Indians have had a historically different acculturation experience—one of forced assimilation through various elements of European conquest including missionary movements and boarding schools and policies of extermination and assimilation (Garrett & Pichette, 2000). Thus, acculturation takes on a patina slightly different from that of Latinos, for example, and conveys different meaning. Acculturation for American Indians residing on a reservation is different than for those living off the reservation. Most important, identifying as an American Indian is more difficult off the reservation, creating increased stress for urban American Indians around the experience of living in two worlds.

On the basis of the above review of selected ethnic groups, it is perhaps best to approach measures of acculturation from a multidimensional perspective because there are many layers of acculturation (Weigers & Sherraden, 2001). Developmental concerns suggest the implementation of a twofold approach to measuring acculturation among youth given the different milestones faced by children compared with adolescents. In younger children, issues pertaining to identity crystallization are not of paramount importance; however, on reaching the threshold of adolescence, these developmental milestones surface, necessitating attention to acculturation in the context of identity formation (Serrano & Anderson, 2003). In the absence of developmentally appropriate measures assessing acculturation, generation status and language use continue to be the most commonly used measures. Although preferred language has been criticized as an oversimplified measure of acculturation, it has been demonstrated to be a good proxy for more sophisticated and multidimensional measures, accounting for up to 65% of the variance in acculturation status (Samaniego & Gonzales, 1999). Moreover, language use measures have proven useful in alerting researchers to the existence of acculturative stress and its effects on substance use (Cuellar, Arnold, & Maldonado, 1995). Complex studies positing mediation in research predicting Latino adolescents' substance use have effectively used measures of linguistic acculturation based on preferred language use (Epstein, Doyle, & Botvin, 2003). These studies have often concluded that bilingualism—a reflection of biculturalism—offers the most protection against drug use (Marsiglia et al., 2005).

LANGUAGE AND ACCULTURATION

Language is a key vehicle for communication of culture. Purposive language provides a vehicle for youth to communicate with their parents, creating a conduit for value transmission and opportunities for protection. Communication between parents and youth is a key reason for lower drug use rates among adolescents (Kim, Zane, & Hong, 2002). Parents can use language and communication as a prevention tool, inquiring about activities in which their child engages.

Investigations of the relations between race and ethnicity and substance use continue to examine the role of preferred language use (which language is spoken in the home). A household survey of alcohol use including several groups of Latino youth—Cuban, Mexican American, Puerto Rican, South American, and Central American—showed little difference in alcohol use among the national origin groups, but large and consistent differences across all groups by language use (Nielsen & Ford, 2001). Respondents who stated they preferred using the English language were more likely to drink alcohol. A separate study of Latino youth in New York City showed that students using Spanish at home reported significantly less marijuana use than students who spoke English with their parents, and bilingual youth were found to be at greater risk of alcohol use than Spanish

monolingual youth (Epstein, Botvin, & Díaz, 2001).

Relative to their immigrant parents, ethnic youth commonly learn English more quickly and maintain less of their language of origin (Xiong, Eliason, Detzner, & Cleveland, 2005). This faster acquisition results in a language gap in the home that can be stressful and lead youth to feel disenfranchised from their home. The resulting linguistic acculturation gap can undermine parent–child closeness and parents' ability to monitor their children regarding drug use behaviors (Birman, Persky, Basu, & Pulley, 2004). As ethnic minority youth learn English, they may be more aware of their minority status and perceive more ethnic discrimination. Again, internalization of ethnic stereotypes and prejudices can set the stage for coping through substance use (Vega & Gil, 1998).

It is apparent that the protective effects of family can be eroded by language gaps between parents and their children, out-group experiences, and acculturative stress. It is clear that language and acculturation are closely intertwined but conceptually reflect unique facets of a complex cultural transition process. Both language and acculturation predict drug use, but do so differently among different racial and ethnic groups and subgroups.

In addition, language as metaphor—the essence of linguistic symbolism—provides additional insight into the role of race and ethnicity in drug use etiology. For American Indian youth in particular, metaphor may hold the key to understanding the relationship between language and acculturation (Smircich, 1985). The role of storytelling and oral tradition, and even how these cultural groups construct their understanding of the natural world, come together with the American Indian metaphor. The richness of metaphors and their cultural importance requires someone who tells the story and someone who listens. The storyteller helps illuminate special features of culture. Most of American Indian storytellers reside on the reservations or within Indian communities. Most American Indian youth and their families now live in cities and thus have less access to the transmission of important cultural values and their protective effects against alcohol and drug use.

OTHER FAMILY-LEVEL PROTECTIONS AND RISKS

Although African Americans are not frequently included in acculturation studies, some researchers have identified important protective effects of ethnic identity that affect the mental health of African American youth (Goodstein & Ponterotto, 1997). The erosion of Black cultural values has been identified as being associated with increased substance use (Nobles, Goddard, Cavil, & George, 1987). Two of these Afrocentric values, religiosity and strong family and kinship ties, have been empirically linked to increased protective benefits (Brook & Pahl, 2005).

There are two sides to family-based research in studies of drug use among adolescents of diverse ethnic and racial backgrounds. One side examines family factors that are related to adolescent resilience (Howard, 1996) and includes family strength (cohesiveness) and familial prohibitions against substance use. The other side shows how family-based factors can engender susceptibility (see chap. 19, this volume). Much of the latter focus emphasizes adolescent perception of family drug use, actual family drug use, family discord, family separation, lack of family guidance, father absence, low family bonding, low parental investment or involvement, parental conflict, poor parent–adolescent communications, and low parental monitoring (Friedman & Glassman, 2000). Predictably, the risk-engendering role of the family in early-stage substance use varies among ethnic groups (Vega & Gil, 1998).

A major feature of family protection among ethnic minority communities is labeled *familism,* which reflects emotional attachment to parents. The attachments youth have to their family provide the support, guidance, and supervision that create barriers to substance use. In the case of Latino families, stripping away the *respeto* that originates from familism can be disruptive and limit protective influences that arise from communication, monitoring, and transmission of values (McQueen, Getz, & Bray, 2003). Latino families tend to have a strong sense of family pride and family closeness, their children hold respect for parents, and the culture is defined by mutual obligation, trust, and cohesion

(Chandler, Tsai, & Wharton, 1999). Traditional Mexican norms such as parental monitoring and involvement with children and the tendency of married couples to settle close to parents and other family members provide children with more attention by a greater number of caring adults and situate children in more cohesive communities (Denner, Kirby, & Coyle, 2001).

The traditional listing of protective and risk factors within ecosystems does not comfortably fit Latino cultures. Relative to European American parents, Latino parents tend to use an authoritarian style of parenting, characterized by stricter discipline. However, as Latino parents acculturate, their parenting practices may change. Mothers of more acculturated Mexican American adolescents have been found to use inconsistent discipline and monitor their children less, with the result of higher levels of delinquency among youth (Samaniego & Gonzalez, 1999). It stands to reason that when parental monitoring is weaker and permissiveness is high, adolescent drug use will likely increase. Moreover, acculturation, assimilation, and cultural change are significant concerns among immigrant and racial and ethnic populations, wherein the loss of traditional cultural practices and family supports may compromise the resilience exhibited by some less acculturated populations (Martinez, Eddy, & DeGarmo, 2003). The stress created by identity confusion creates a situation ripe for substance use.

The concept of familism has also been applied to African American families (Brook & Pahl, 2005). In this context, familism refers to the value placed on the extended family, not the personal benefit of the individual; thus, altruism becomes the critical element in familism within the African American community. Among African American youth, reliance on kinship networks and value placed on community can be strong protective factors against substance abuse. The traditions developing from the historical experience of slavery have created extended kinship relationships providing a wide buffer of influence and protection (Brook & Pahl, 2005).

Within the Asian American community, family also operates in a protective fashion. Research with Asian American families has found that family support is negatively correlated with substance use

(Kim et al., 2002). In other words, this research has indicated that the higher the quality of the relationship between Asian American adolescents and their parents, the lower their vulnerability to peer pressure. There is some evidence suggesting that Asian families may function at times in a way conducive to increased substance use. Asian families tend to operate on a shame and honor system, and the desire to keep shame from the family leads to concealing problems, including limiting access to counseling resources (Nemoto, Huang, & Aoki, 1999). This honor code is potentially advantageous in terms of drug use because Asian families may view substance use as a taboo and source of shame to the family. Conflicts between generations tend to emerge when native-born Asian Americans become highly acculturated into the dominant culture and separate themselves from the traditional values espoused by their family and community. By adopting dominant culture values, Asian American youth also risk losing the protective benefits of their culture of origin against drug use.

Like other ethnic minority groups, American Indians are a diverse population, with 535 tribes inhabiting the United States, each with a distinct culture. Language usage, level of acculturation, tribal affiliation, place of residence, educational levels, SES, the knowledge and observance of traditional practices, and religious affiliation are some of the major factors that differentiate individuals and communities (Edwards & Edwards, 1984). Despite their heterogeneity, American Indians share certain core values such a strong connection to family and community. Throughout each individual's life span, community members gather as a family, clan, tribe, or nation to celebrate, provide support, and participate in rituals. Many of these religious and sociocultural activities are similar across tribal and clan lines. Some of the common values include the centrality of the extended family, strong allegiance to the group, sharing, and respect for each individual regardless of age (Dykeman, Nelson, & Appleton, 1995).

The prevalence of substance use among some American Indian youth has been associated with higher rates of substance abuse by their families ("Alcohol and Drug Services Study (ADSS) Cost Study," 1996). Families within an American Indian context are often defined by a complex web of relationships entailing connections that exist on the basis of blood relations, clan, tribe, and formal and informal adoption (Waller, Okamoto, Miles, & Hurdle, 2003). In many indigenous languages, for example, there are no terms for extended family (e.g., for niece or nephew). Rather, members of the extended family are perceived in the same way as the dominant culture views members of the immediate family (Cross, 1986). Despite these familial distinctions, ties to family are much stronger than extrafamilial ties. In fact, a person's social network may consist almost entirely of family relations (Austin, 1993). For people living in urban or rural areas away from reservation communities, social networks likely include more nonfamily individuals than blood family relations. The distinction between family and peers that is often used by the substance use literature is not as applicable to American Indians and can lead to misunderstanding and stereotypes. American Indian family networks combine both nuclear family and extended family and peer influences and as such can be at the same time protective and a source of risk for substance use.

The concept of family for ethnic minority communities has a less clear set of boundaries than in majority culture. Because of its flexibility and dynamic nature, approaching family in a rigid manner can lead to misunderstandings and stereotypes. Family processes that were protective against drug use at one point can very quickly become weaker or in turn become risk factors. There is a need to infuse the term *family* with the meaning that emerges from culture and the social and cultural processes experienced by communities. Other social actors such as organized religion can be sources of support to families as their members navigate a complex process of dislocation and change.

RELIGION AND SPIRITUALITY

Arguably, religion is a protective factor for substance use across all racial and ethnic communities (Adlaf & Smart, 1985), but as with family, its effect is not unidirectional or static. Religion serves to provide secondary supervision and reinforcement of conventional, law-abiding, community-centered values, decreasing the likelihood of substance use. In addition, religious communities are often able to meet the psychosocial needs of individuals, creating less impetus for substance use. When people feel down, experience despair, or need instrumental support, the religious community can provide assistance. The centerpiece of most religions is outreach to those who are downtrodden and the message of a higher power as an earthly fixture in this life. Thus, religion is protective because it creates hope and offers needed support counteracting the factors driving drug use.

Latino culture is inextricably linked to Catholicism, with an estimated 70% of Hispanics in the United States identifying as Roman Catholic (Perl, Greely, & Gray, 2005). The value placed on gender roles, temperance, and adherence to laws is strongly rooted in Catholicism and can be a protective factor for adolescents. Potentially, the trust and support that Latino families have in the church can become a risk factor because parental monitoring may decrease around church activities as a result of the implicit trust in the church as an extension of the family (Dishion & McMahon, 1998).

For African Americans, church attendance is related to lower substance use. Religious participation provides protection because it offsets any felt experience of racial discrimination (see chap. 28, this volume). The church also provides a message of moderation or abstinence from substances, as well as a general message of intolerance of deviance.

Approximately 80% of Asian Americans claim a religious affiliation (Le, 2007). However, given their lower rates of substance abuse, very little is known about the specific influence religion exerts as a protective factor. The indigenous traditions of Confucianism and Buddhism teach moderation and encourage meditation, and both practices possess efficacious roots in substance abuse prevention by lowering stress and increasing a sense of personal agency (Carter, 1999).

Religion for American Indians is focused on the spiritual and on balance, an understanding of life in a holistic manner (Lowery, 1998). In this way, spiritual values lead community members to find balance and harmony, and there is a recognition that substance use interferes with this balance. Because of

colonialism, many American Indian families have lost connection with their traditional spiritual beliefs and have incorporated European conceptions of good and evil, which may lead to value confusion and cultural disorientation.

Organized religion appears to be an important source of support to ethnic minority families and is commonly identified as having a protective effect against drug use. Again, because of cultural transitions and dislocations, the effects of organized religion need to be examined carefully in the historical, cultural, and social contexts of diverse communities.

SCHOOL-LEVEL PROTECTIONS AND RISKS

Most people will be quick to agree that schools provide a protective environment conducive to learning and the formation of beneficial social ties. In truth, the school domain does generally include protective factors against substance use including academic achievement, educational aspirations, and educational commitment (Simons-Morton et al., 1999; Vazsonyi & Flannery, 1997). However, there is another, less-understood side to schools that considers the effects of racial and ethnic composition on students' substance use (Kumar, O'Malley, Johnston, Schulenberg, & Bachman, 2002). For example, the incidence of inhalant use by African American and Latino students was found to be twice as high as in predominately White (non-Hispanic) schools, and Latino youth were more likely to be smokers when they attended predominately White schools (Cook, Ungemack, & Mark, 2001). These findings support the notion that an ethnic mismatch can be disadvantageous, at least for some groups. However, research findings have shown that among all students, regardless of ethnicity, alcohol use was higher in schools that were predominately White, and cigarette use was higher in ethnically heterogeneous schools. These results suggest that school ethnic composition may influence a youth's outcomes independent of his or her ethnic concordance with the numerical majority.

There is some conceptual guidance for theorizing about the effect of school ethnic composition (Kumar et al., 2002). One theoretical explanation based on the contagion model suggests that higher proportions of drug-using students aggregated in a school provide more opportunities for drug use (Ennett, Flewelling, Lindrooth, & Norton, 1997; see also chap. 23, this volume). In a slightly different twist on this early sociological model, the aggregation model suggests that students within schools develop similar habits through the diffusion of prevailing norms (Kennedy, 1995). This is the argument behind "intact social clusters" and the notion that students within a school are more like each other than students from different schools. Once some students in a school start using substances, others will rapidly follow. Different researchers have proposed that schools that were more pro-substance use at the aggregate (school mean) level had higher levels of lifetime alcohol, lifetime cigarette, and current cigarette use. Because youth substance use patterns vary by ethnicity (Wallace et al., 2003), the substance use patterns of one ethnic group may be contagious to other ethnic groups in a school. The reverse appears to be true as well; when an ethnic group or subgroup is characterized by low use within a school, its members can influence students from other groups and subgroups toward no use when they reach a certain level of representation within the school population (Kulis, Marsiglia, Nieri, Sicotte, & Hohmann-Marriott, 2004).

Classmates tend to be categorized as part of the broader peer context and are able to influence each others' behavior. School-level disapproval of daily cigarette use, heavy drinking, and marijuana use have been associated with lower probabilities of students' use of these substances. In addition, an antidrug school environment was found to protect even those students who themselves approved of daily cigarette use. We know that youth friendships often form along ethnic lines (Tatum, 1997), yet these results suggest that youth's substance use may be influenced by other peers at school, especially if those peers have substance use norms that predominate.

Schools are very important environments in the lives of all young people and can be a source of protection or risk. The ethnic composition of the school appears to influence the drug norms and behaviors of minority youth in unique ways. Strong representation of recent immigrant youth groups connected to more traditional antidrug norms appears to have

important protective effects on all students, regardless of their ethnicity.

CULTURAL PROCESSES AND COMMUNITY CHARACTERISTICS

Certain regions of the United States have higher populations of different racial and ethnic groups. For example, in the southwestern United States, Latino adolescents, representing one quarter of the population (U.S. Census Bureau, 2004), report more substance offers and actual use compared with non-Hispanic White students (Marsiglia et al., 2005). In addition to understanding geographic variability by region of the country, another important context to consider is the effect of substance use in urban versus rural settings. Mexican American youth who cross the border tend to settle in Arizona, Nevada, and southern California, where there are historical and well-established social and economic binational networks. Drug use trends in these parts of the country reflect competing forces, including acculturation, geographic and racial distributions of the population, and SES factors (Plunkett & Mitchell, 2000).

Regional variations in lifetime substance use are apparent when one looks more closely at areas heavily populated by American Indian youth. For example, when controlling for geographic region, American Indian youth drug use rates are significantly higher than those of other racial groups on only three of seven substances: alcohol, marijuana, and cocaine (Plunkett & Mitchell, 2000). Other use patterns, however, appear more in line with national prevalence rates. A different study showed that inhalant use is less prevalent among American Indian youth residing in urban locations compared with those residing on reservations (Howard, Walker, Walker, Cottler, & Compton, 1999). A high percentage of American Indian tribal youth reside on reservations in the southwestern United States, perhaps contributing to some of the regional variation.

The experience of American Indian urban youth is often seen through the lens of a relocation or movement away from the reservation. This relocation means they are stripped of certain protections provided by the reservation. More than half of the American Indian population lives off reservation in urban environments (Burhansstipanov, 2000). Moreover, on the basis of patterns of migration out of reservations, tribal youth tend to move out for educational opportunities during a crucial time when their ethnic identity is not solidified, further straining contact with their culture of origin. Certain social stressors, specifically discrimination, are experienced by Indian youth at a greater level off the reservation, possibly contributing to increased substance use (Moran & Reaman, 2002). In urban environments, youth's networks become intertribal and can be exposed to a Pan-Indian cultural identity that can be equally protective but in a different and less studied manner.

African American youth residing in urban environments face certain hardships, including a high incidence of one-parent households (Brewer, 1988), the strong influence of peers, and the high exposure to substances (Wallace & Muroff, 2002). African American youth seem to be very vulnerable to substance use during the transition from middle school to high school (Sullivan & Farrell, 1999), and this may parallel their immersion in identity issues, acquisition of Afrocentric values, and transition from elementary or junior high feeder schools to larger, more racially heterogeneous high schools. In these environments, the positive influence of extended kinships, organized religion, and well-functioning schools are key to support the protective effects of family in a challenging neighborhood environment.

Asian adolescents encounter problems similar to those of other racial minority youth when they reside in an urban environment—increased exposure, increased access, and earlier initiation. Their intergroup diversity by national origin tends to explain some prevalence rate differences between subgroups of Asian American youth. In addition, compared with foreign-born youth, U.S.-born Asian American adolescents—very much like U.S.-born Latino youth—are more likely to engage in drug risk behaviors. Family and residential characteristics associated with immigrant status such as living in inner-city resource-poor neighborhoods partly explain these behaviors (Hussey et al., 2007).

Living in a rural or urban environment and the type of neighborhood within cities appear to be important variables to consider as we examine the etiology of drug use in ethnic minority communities. The choices of where to live are conditioned by many other variables, and in the case of recent immigrants, we encounter the paradox of place of residence as a context in which the protective effects of culture of origin can rapidly be eroded. However, ethnic enclaves can provide the supports and monitoring necessary to nurture antidrug norms and behaviors. It appears that social organization matters.

DISCUSSION

A common theme emerging from the examination of different ecosystems and social contexts is that many assets and protective factors are present in ethnic cultures and communities, but they can rapidly become weaker or disappear. There is a great opportunity presented here to identify those protective factors and intervene to support them and maintain them as community assets. As data continue to be gathered about prevalence rates, more attention needs to be placed on those who are not using substances and the conditions and processes that enable their nonuse. Prevention interventions that recognize existing community-based protective factors appear to have the best chances of attaining effectiveness.

Researchers have long recognized that the most successful substance use prevention programs reflect in their content and format aspects of the adolescent's culture and learning style (Castro, Proescholdbell, Abeita, & Rodriguez, 1999). At the most general level, this means integrating youth culture into prevention curriculums. However, there is a slight difference between integrating culture to make the program culturally sensitive and incorporating culture in the manner in which the program is delivered. This difference, between adaptation of content and the style in which the content is delivered, can be elusive (see chap. 34, this volume). Ideally, a program that includes both cultural specificity in content and delivery should work better with racial and ethnic youth. However, we live in a globalized age of universal or generic programs in which the preferred delivery method is primary prevention to the masses.

Although the importance of culturally appropriate messages in prevention is increasingly acknowledged, tests of the effectiveness of such messages among minority youth are limited. An early study by Dorr (1982) examining the effectiveness of television ads, for example, suggested that minority youth were more likely to endorse messages that reflected their own culture. More recent studies have demonstrated how youth and their parents respond more positively to drug prevention messages in the media that appear culturally specific (Teinowitz, 2001). One way in which a drug prevention program might be effective with ethnic minority populations is by slowing the erosion of traditional cultural norms regarding the family and drug involvement. Through a process called additive acculturation, culturally grounded and multicultural interventions can help children and youth deal with acculturation issues by encouraging successful integration into the new culture without losing the identity-enhancing and protective aspects of the old culture (Gibson, 1995). Despite American Indian adolescents' relatively high rates of alcohol and drug use, which have long been noted in the literature (French & Hornbuckle, 1980), prevention and intervention resources available to these communities are negligible (Inouye, 1993). Considerable effort has been made to delineate the scope of the problem (Brady, 1995) and to develop strategies for prevention and intervention (Schinke et al., 1988).

Professionals, community leaders, and policymakers seem to agree that community drug problems threaten the social welfare of entire communities. This recognition is also reinforced in the scientific literature in which concern arises over how to develop successful drug use prevention programs for ethnic minority youth (e.g., Potthoff et al., 1998). In addition, much remains to be learned from the experiences of large numbers of adolescents who do not use drugs. Of four patterns of drug use found to characterize most American youth—abstaining, using predominantly alcohol, using predominantly alcohol and marijuana, and using multiple substances—abstinence represents the largest group (Mitchell & Plunkett, 2000).

Programs that are culturally grounded effortlessly bring prevention messages to youth, who recognize them as being about them and applicable to their own lives. As we continue documenting differences in prevalence among ethnic and racial groups, it is

important to maintain an ongoing effort to revisit the nomenclature we use. Because ethnicity and race are socially constructed phenomena, there needs to be a constant dialogue with the community being studied to allow research participants to name themselves. Only then can the prevalence rates and the contexts in which they emerge be approached with confidence.

References

Adlaf, E. M., & Smart, R. G. (1985). Drug use and religious affiliation, feelings, and behavior. *British Journal of Addiction, 80,* 163–171.

Alcohol and Drug Services Study (ADSS) cost study. (2004, June 18). *The DASIS Report.* Retrieved August 14, 2007, from http://www.drugabusestatistics. samhsa.gov/2k4/costs/costs.pdf

Austin, R. (1993). Freedom, responsibility and duty: ADR and the Navajo peacemaker court. *Judges Journal, 32,* 8–11, 47–48.

Bachman J. G., Johnston L. D., & O'Malley P. M. (2007). *Monitoring the Future: A continuing study of the lifestyles and values of youth, 1976* (Report No. ICPSR07927-v4). Ann Arbor, MI: Inter-University Consortium for Political and Social Research.

Bachman, J. G., O'Malley, P. M., Schulenberg, J. E., Johnston, L. D., Bryant, A. L., & Merline, A. C. (2002). *The decline of substance use in young adulthood: Changes in social activities, roles, and beliefs.* Mahwah, NJ: Erlbaum.

Beauvais, F. (1998). Cultural identification and substance use in North America—Annotated bibliography. *Substance Use and Misuse, 33,* 1315–1336.

Beauvais, F., & Oetting, E. R. (2002). Variances in the etiology of drug use among ethnic groups of adolescents. *2002 US Department of Health and Human Services Public Health Reports Public Health Reports, 117,* s8–s14.

Birman, D., Persky, I., Basu, A., & Pulley, E. (2004, March). *Acculturation and acculturation gaps in families: Former Soviet and Vietnamese refugee parents and adolescents in the U.S.* Paper presented at the annual meeting of the Society for Research on Adolescence, Baltimore, MD.

Botvin, G. J., Griffin, K. W., Diaz, T., Scheier, L. M., Williams, C., & Epstein, J. A. (2000). Preventing illicit drug use in adolescents: Long-term follow up data from a randomized control trial of a school population. *Addictive Behaviors, 25,* 769–774.

Brady, M. (1995). Culture in treatment, culture as treatment: A critical appraisal of developments in addictions programs for indigenous North Americans and Australians. *Social Science & Medicine, 41,* 1487–1498.

Brewer, R. M. (1988). Black women in poverty: Some comments on female-headed families. *Signs, 13,* 331–339.

Brook, J. S., & Pahl, K. (2005). The protective role of ethnic and racial identity and aspects of an Africentric orientation against drug use among African American young adults. *Journal of Genetic Psychology, 166,* 329–345.

Burhansstipanov, L. (2000). Urban Native American health issues. *Cancer, 88,* 1207–1213.

Carter, T. M. (1999). The effects of spiritual practices on recovery from substance abuse. *Journal of Psychiatric & Mental Health Nursing, 5,* 409.

Castro, F. G., Proescholdbell, R. J., Abeita, L., & Rodriguez, D. (1999). Ethnic and cultural minority groups. In B. S. McCrady & E. E. Epstein (Eds.), *Addictions: A comprehensive guidebook* (pp. 499–526). New York: Oxford University Press.

Center for Substance Abuse Research. (2006, June 5). Dramatic increase in national treatment admissions for methamphetamine coincides with increase in criminal justice referrals. *CESAR Fax, 15* (22).

Chandler, C. R., Tsai, Y., & Wharton, R. (1999). Twenty years after: Replicating a study of Anglo- and Mexican-American cultural values—Tradition and change. *Social Science Journals, 36,* 353–367.

Cook, M. J., Ungemack, J. A., & Mark, H. (2001, October). *Patterns of recent alcohol, tobacco, and other drug use among 7th–10th grade Caucasian, African-American, and Hispanic students attending racially homogeneous and heterogeneous school districts.* Paper presented at the 129th annual meeting of the American Public Health Association, Atlanta, GA.

Cross, T. L. (1986). Drawing on cultural tradition in Indian child welfare. *Social Casework, 67,* 283–289.

Cuéllar, I., Arnold, B., & Maldonado, R. (1995). Acculturation Rating Scale for Mexican Americans–II: A revision of the original ARSMA scale. *Hispanic Journal of Behavioral Sciences, 17,* 275–304.

De La Rosa, M. (2002). Acculturation and Latino adolescents' substance use: A research agenda for the future. *Substance Use and Misuse, 37,* 429–456.

De La Rosa, M., Khalsa, J. H., & Rouse, B. A. (1990). Hispanics and illicit drug use: A review of recent findings. *International Journal of Addictions, 26,* 665–691.

Denner, J., Kirby, D., & Coyle, K. (2001). The protective role of social capital and cultural norms in Latino communities: A study of adolescent births. *Hispanic Journal of Behavioral Sciences, 23,* 3–21.

Dishion, T. J., & McMahon, R. J. (1998). Parental monitoring and the prevention of child and adolescent problem behavior: A conceptual and empirical formulation. *Clinical Child & Family Psychology Review, 1,* 61–75.

Dorr, A. (1982). Television and the socialization of the minority child. In G. I. Mitchell-Kernan & C. Mitchell-Kernan (Eds.), *Television and the socialization of the minority child* (pp. 15–36). New York: Academic Press.

Dressler, W. W., Oths, K. S., & Gravlee, C. C. (2005). Race and ethnicity in public health research: Models to explain health disparities. *Annual Review of Anthropology, 34,* 231–252.

Dykeman, C., Nelson, R., & Appleton, V. (1995). Building strong working alliances with American Indian families. *Social Work in Education, 17,* 148–158.

Edwards, D., & Edwards, M. (1984). Group work practice with American Indians. *Social Work With Groups, 7,* 7–19.

Ennett, S. T., Flewelling, R. L., Lindroth, R. C., & Norton, E. C. (1997). School and neighborhood characteristics associated with school rates of alcohol, cigarette, and marijuana use. *Journal of Health and Social Behavior, 38,* 55–71.

Epstein, J. A., Botvin, G. J., & Diaz, T. (2001). Linguistic acculturation associated with higher marijuana and polydrug use among Hispanic adolescents. *Substance Use and Misuse, 6,* 477–499.

Epstein, J. A., Doyle, M., & Botvin, G. J. (2003). A mediational model of the relationship between linguistic acculturation and polydrug use among Hispanic adolescents. *Psychological Reports, 93,* 859–866.

Flannery, D., Vazsonyi, A., Torquati, J., & Fridrich, A. (1994). Ethnic and gender differences in risk for early adolescent substance use. *Journal of Youth and Adolescence, 23,* 195–213.

French, D. C., & Dishion, T. J. (2003). Predictors of early initiation of sexual intercourse among high-risk adolescents. *Journal of Early Adolescence, 23,* 295–315.

French, L., & Hornbuckle, J. (1980). Alcoholism among Native Americans: An analysis. *Social Work, 25,* 275–280.

Friedman, A., & Glassman, K. (2000). Family risk factors versus peer risk factors for drug abuse: A longitudinal study of African American urban community sample. *Journal of Substance Abuse Treatment, 18,* 267–275.

Garrett, M. T., & Pichette, E. F. (2000). Red as an apple: Native American acculturation and counseling with or without reservation. *Journal of Counseling & Development, 78,* 3–13.

Gibson, M. A. (1995). Additive acculturation as a strategy for school improvement. In R. G. Rumbaut & W. A. Cornelius (Eds.), *California's immigrant children: Theory, research and implications for educational policy* (pp. 77–105). San Diego: Center for U.S.-Mexican Studies, University of California.

Goodstein, R., & Ponterotto, J. G. (1997). Racial and ethnic identity: Their relationship and their contribution to self-esteem. *Journal of Black Psychology, 23,* 275–292.

Guthrie, B. J., & Low, L. K. (2000). A substance use prevention framework: Considering the social context for African American girls. *Public Health Nursing, 17,* 363–373.

Hahm, H. C., Lahiff, M., & Guterman, N. B. (2003). Acculturation and parental attachment in Asian-American adolescents' alcohol use. *Journal of Adolescent Health, 33,* 119–129.

Hallfors, D. D., Waller, M. W., Bauer, D., Ford, C. A., & Halpern, C. T. (2005). Which comes first in adolescence-sex and drugs or depression? [Abstract]. *American Journal of Preventive Medicine, 29,* 163–170.

Hawkins, J. D., Catalano, R. F., & Miller, J. Y. (1992). Risk and protective factors for alcohol and other drug problems in adolescence and early adulthood: Implications for substance abuse prevention. *Psychological Bulletin, 112,* 64–105.

Herring, R. D. (1994). Substance use among Native American Indian youth: A selected review of causality. *Journal of Counseling and Development, 72,* 578–584.

Howard, D. (1996). Searching for resilience among African American youth exposed to community violence: Theoretical issues. *Journal of Adolescent Health, 18,* 254–262.

Howard, M. O., Walker, R. D., Walker, P. S., Cottler, L. B., & Compton, W. M. (1999). Inhalant use among urban American Indian youth. *Addiction, 94,* 83–95.

Hussey, J. M., Hallfors, D. D., Waller, M. W., Iritani, B. J., Halpern, C. T., & Bauer, D. J. (2007). Sexual behavior and drug use among Asian and Latino adolescents: Association with immigrant status. *Journal of Immigrant and Minority Health, 9,* 84–94.

Inouye, D. K. (1993). Our future is in jeopardy: The mental health of Native American adolescents. *Journal of Health Care for the Poor and Underserved, 4,* 6–8.

Kennedy, E. (1995). Contextual effects on academic norms among elementary school students. *Educational Research Quarterly, 18,* 5–13.

Kim, I. J., Zane, N. W. S., & Hong, S. (2002). Protective factors against substance use among Asian American youth: A test of the peer cluster theory. *Journal of Community Psychology, 300,* 565–584.

Kulis, S., Marsiglia, F. F., Nieri, T., Sicotte, D., & Hohmann-Marriott, B. (2004). Majority rules? The effects of school ethnic composition on substance use by Mexican heritage adolescents. *Sociological Focus, 37,* 373–393.

Kumar, R., O'Malley, P. M., Johnston, L. D., Schulenberg, J. E., & Bachman, J. G. (2002). Effects of school-level norms on student substance use. *Prevention Science, 3,* 105–124.

Kumpfer, K. L., & Adler, S. (2003). Dissemination of research-based family interventions for the prevention of substance abuse. In Z. Sloboda & W. J. Bukoski (Eds.), *Handbook of drug abuse prevention: Theory, science, and practice* (pp. 75–100). New York: Kluwer Academic/Plenum.

Le, C. N. (2007). Religion, spirituality, and faith. *Asian-Nation: The Landscape of Asian America.* Retrieved October 10, 2007, from http://www.asian-nation.org/religion.shtml

Lowery, C. T. (1998). American Indian perspectives on addiction and recovery. *Health & Social Work, 23,* 127–135.

Marsiglia, F. F., Kulis, S., & Hecht, M. L. (2001). Ethnic labels and ethnic identity as predictors of drug use and drug exposure among middle school students in the Southwest. *Journal of Research on Adolescence, 11,* 21–48.

Marsiglia, F. F., Kulis, S., Wagstaff, D. A., Elek, E., & Dran, D. (2005). Acculturation status and substance use prevention with Mexican and Mexican-American youth. *Journal of Social Work Practice in the Additions, 5,* 85–111.

Martinez, C. R., Jr., Eddy, J. M., & DeGarmo, D. S. (2003). Preventing substance use among Latino youth. In W. J. Bukoski & Z. Sloboda (Eds.), *Handbook of drug abuse prevention: Theory, science, and practice* (pp. 365–380). New York: Kluwer Academic/Plenum.

McQueen, A., Getz, G., & Bray, J. H. (2003). Acculturation, substance use, and deviant behavior: Examining separation and family conflict as mediators. *Child Development, 74,* 1737–1750.

Menjivar, C. (2000). *Fragmented ties: Salvadoran immigrant networks in America.* Berkeley: University of California Press.

Mitchell, C. M., & Plunkett, M. (2000). The latent structure of substance use among American Indian adolescents: An example using categorical variables. *American Journal of Community Psychology, 28,* 105–125.

Moran, J. R., & Reaman, J. A. (2002). Critical issues for substance abuse prevention targeting American Indian youth. *Journal of Primary Prevention, 22,* 201–233.

National Institutes of Health. (2006). *Fact sheet: Health disparities.* Retrieved August 30, 2007, from http://www.nih.gov/about/researchresultsforthepublic/HealthDisparities.pdf

Nemoto, T., Huang, K., & Aoki, B. (1999). Strategies for accessing and retaining Asian drug users in research studies. In M. R. De Las Rosa, B. Segal, & R. Lopez (Eds.), *Conducting drug abuse research with minority populations: Advances and research* (pp. 151–165). New York: Haworth Press.

Nielsen, A., & Ford, J. A. (2001). Drinking patterns among Hispanic adolescents: Results from a national household survey. *Journal of Studies on Alcohol, 62,* 448–456.

Nobles, W. W., Goddard, L., Cavil, W. E., & George, P. Y. (1987). *In the culture of drugs in the Black community.* Oakland, CA: Black Family Institute.

Paradies, Y. (2006). A systematic review of empirical research on self-reported racism and health. *International Journal of Epidemiology, 35,* 888–901.

Perl, P., Greely, J. Z., & Gray, M. M. (2005). *How many Hispanics are Catholic? A review of survey data and methodology.* Washington, DC: Center for Applied Research in the Apostolate, Georgetown University. Retrieved October 25, 2007, from http://cara.georgetown.edu/Hispanic%20Catholics.pdf

Phelan, J. C., & Link, B. G. (2005). Controlling disease and creating disparities: A fundamental cause perspective. *Journals of Gerontology: Psychological Sciences and Social Sciences, 60B,* S27–S33.

Phinney, J. S. (1990). Ethnic identity in adolescents and adults: Review of research. *Psychological Bulletin, 108,* 499–514.

Phinney, J. S. (1996). Understanding ethnic diversity: The role of ethnic identity. *American Behavioral Scientist, 40,* 143–152.

Plunkett, M., & Mitchell, C. M. (2000). Substance use rates among American Indian adolescents: Regional comparisons with monitoring the future high school seniors. *Journal of Drug Issues, 30,* 575–591.

Potthoff, S. J., Bearinger, L. H., Skay, C. L., Cassutto, N., Blum, R. W., & Resnick, M. D. (1998). Dimensions of risk behaviors among American Indian youth. *Archives of Pediatrics and Adolescent Medicine, 152,* 157–163.

Samaniego, R. Y., & Gonzales, N. A. (1999). Multiple mediators of the effects of acculturation status on delinquency for Mexican American adolescents. *American Journal of Community Psychology, 27* (2), 189–210.

Schinke, S., Orlandi, M., Botvin, G., Gilchrist, L., Trimble, J., & Locklear, V. (1988). Preventing substance abuse among American Indian adolescents: A bicultural competence skills approach. *Journal of Counseling Psychology, 35,* 87–90.

Serrano, E., & Anderson, J. (2003). Assessment of a refined short acculturation scale for Latino preteens in rural Colorado. *Hispanic Journal of Behavioral Sciences, 25,* 240–253.

Simons-Morton, B. G. (2004). The protective effect of parental expectations against early adolescent smoking initiation. *Health Education Research, 29,* 561–569.

Simons-Morton, B., Haynie, D. L., Crump, A. D., Saylor, K. E., Eitel, P., & Yu, K. (1999). Expectancies and other psychosocial factors associated with alcohol use among early adolescent boys and girls. *Addictive Behavior, 24,* 229–238.

Smircich, L. (1985). Is the concept of culture a paradigm for understanding organizations and ourselves? In P. J. Frost, L. F. Moore, M. R. Louis, C. C. Lundberg, & J. Martin (Eds.), *Organizational culture* (pp. 55–72). Newbury Park, CA: Sage.

Sullivan, T. N., & Farrell, A. D. (1999). Identification and impact of risk and protective factors for drug use among urban African American adolescents. *Journal of Clinical Child Psychology, 28,* 122–136.

Tatum, B. D. (1997). *"Why are all the Black kids sitting together in the cafeteria?" and other conversations about race.* New York: Basic Books.

Teinowitz, I. (2001). Anti-drug messages should send ethnic adults distinct culture cues. *Advertising Age, 72,* 14.

ter Bogt, T., Schmid, H., Gabhainn, S. N., Fotiou, A., & Vollebergh, W. (2006). Economic and cultural correlates of cannabis use among mid-adolescents in 31 countries. *Addiction, 101,* 241–251.

U.S. Census Bureau News. (2004, March 18). *More diversity, slower growth* [Press release]. Retrieved August 9, 2007, from http://www.census.gov/Press-Release/www/releases/archives/population/001720.html

U.S. Department of Education. (2007). *The condition of education 2007: Indicator 23.* Retrieved February 7, 2008, from http://nces.ed.gov/pubs2007/2007064_TOC.pdf

Vazsonyi, A. T., & Flannery, D. J. (1997). Early adolescent delinquent behaviors: Associations with family and school domains. *Journal of Early Adolescence, 17,* 271–293.

Vega, W., & Gil, A. G. (1998). Different worlds. In W. Vega & A. Gil (Eds.). *Drug use and ethnicity in early adolescence* (pp. 1–12). New York: Plenum Press.

Wallace, J. M., Bachman, J. G., O'Malley, P. M., Schulenberg, J. E., Cooper, S. M., & Johnston, L. D. (2003). Gender and ethnic differences in smoking, drinking and illicit drug use among American 8th, 10th and 12th grade students, 1976–2000. *Addiction, 98,* 225–234.

Wallace, J. M., & Muroff, J. R. (2002). Preventing substance abuse among African American children and youth: Race differences in risk factor exposure and vulnerability. *Journal of Primary Prevention, 22,* 235–261.

Waller, M. A., Okamoto, S. K., Miles, B. W., & Hurdle, D. E. (2003). Resiliency factors related to substance use/resistance: Perceptions of native adolescents of the southwest. *Journal of Sociology & Social Welfare, 30,* 79–94.

Weigers, M., & Sherraden, M. (2001). A critical examination of acculturation: The impact of health behaviors, social support, and economic resources on birth weight among women of Mexican descent. *International Migration Review, 35,* 804–839.

Xiong, Z. B., Eliason, P. A., Detzner, D. F., & Cleveland, M. J. (2005). Southeast Asian immigrants' perceptions of good adolescents and good parents. *Journal of Psychology, 139,* 159–175.

CHAPTER 16

CULTURAL FACTORS IN DRUG USE ETIOLOGY: CONCEPTS, METHODS, AND RECENT FINDINGS

Felipe González Castro and Tanya Nieri

This chapter examines the role of culture and related cultural factors, such as ethnic and racial identity, in drug use etiology and the prevention of drug use and abuse. Although this is no simple task given the diffuse nature of this literature, we focus on several important facets including definitions of key constructs, conceptualization of the problem, patterns of drug use for different racial and cultural groups, and finally research design and methodological considerations. The synthesis of this focus is designed to improve the knowledge base regarding the role of cultural factors as determinants of drug use etiology and to inform the design of future culturally sensitive drug use prevention research.

DIVERSIFICATION OF ETHNIC IDENTITY IN CONTEMPORARY AMERICAN SOCIETY

Growing Complexity of Ethnic Identity

In the United States during this 1st decade of the 21st century, the construct of ethnic identity has become more complex and diversified. Historically, a rich intellectual and historical tradition has informed the current understanding of ethnicity in general and ethnic identity in particular. In the United States, one consequence of the 1960s Civil Rights Movement and the elimination of institutionalized racial segregation and reduction of overt racial discrimination was an increase in racially mixed marriages in the 1970s and thereafter (McGoldrick & Giordano, 1996), producing children of mixed racial and ethnic backgrounds. Today, children within the same family can differ considerably in skin color and other aspects of their physical appearance. Mixed-heritage children face complex

issues and choices regarding their personal and ethnic identification. These choices and conflicts reflect the complex racial, ethnic, religious, and cultural heritages passed down from their parents. It is of tremendous interest how an adolescent child with an African American father and Latina mother or a Native American father and Chinese mother identifies him- or herself. These differences are compounded when the parents come from different religious backgrounds. Additional complexity stems from the ways in which skin color and other physical attributes influence a child's identity-related choice of friends, clothes, music, and favorite pastimes. A means to examine the importance of ethnic identity in the lives of ethnic minority youth is to examine drug prevalence rates among these different groups to determine whether any observed differences are attributed to cultural factors.

Dynamic Changes in Drug Use Rates by Gender and Ethnicity

Within this growing complexity, ethnic patterns in drug use exhibited by adolescents today also depart significantly from those of their parents. Data from the 2005 Youth Risk Behavior Survey has suggested growing patterns of risk observed for Latino[1] adolescents,

[1] The Latino population of the United States numbered 42.68 million as of July 1, 2005, constituting 14.43% of the U.S. population, thus making Latinos the largest racial and ethnic population of the United States (U.S. Census Bureau, 2006). We use the generic terms *Latinos* and *Hispanics* interchangeably, based on the dual usage that occurs within the contemporary literature. Unless specified, *Latinos* refer to people living in the United States, primarily Mexican Americans, Chicanos or Chicanas who live in the southwestern United States, Puerto Ricans (both from the island of Puerto Rico and from the mainland United States), and Cubans, as well as other Latinos who include Colombians, Guatemalans, Nicaraguans, and other immigrants and naturalized persons from Central America and South America.

patterns not observed in this manner 2 and 3 decades ago. Table 16.1 presents rates of risk behaviors by gender and ethnicity. A careful inspection of this table reveals some interesting patterns. First, with regard to negative emotions, specifically depression and suicide, clear gender differences emerge. Adolescent girls exhibit higher rates of reported mood problems, including feeling sad and hopeless, having seriously considered suicide, and actually having attempted suicide (Centers for Disease Control, 2006). Moreover, what existed as a clear gender differential in drug prevalence rates during the 1970s has now essentially disappeared, with more parity observed between adolescent boys and girls in rates of alcohol and cigarette use. The one exception involves higher rates of episodic heavy drinking among male adolescents (see Table 16.1).

Examining ethnic differences, relative to European American and Latino youth, African American adolescent boys and girls exhibit lower rates of current cigarette use, lifetime alcohol use,

current alcohol use, and episodic heavy drinking. Relative to other groups, African American adolescent girls exhibit the lowest rates in lifetime use of cocaine, heroin, methamphetamine, and Ecstasy. By contrast, relative to the other gender–ethnic groups, Latino adolescent boys exhibit the highest rates of lifetime use of cigarettes, alcohol, cocaine, heroin, methamphetamine, and Ecstasy (see Table 16.1). These results suggest that within the span of a single generation, a new cohort of Latino youth is exhibiting higher rates of certain risk behaviors, relative to their peers. However, the factors contributing to these outcomes remain unclear and require further empirical scrutiny.

Other epidemiological sources have corroborated these emerging high levels of risk for some ethnic minority youth. For instance, on the basis of the Monitoring the Future study, Johnston, O'Malley, Bachman, and Schulenberg (2005) reported that Latino eighth graders, in comparison with African American and European American youth, now exhibit

TABLE 16.1

Risk Behaviors among Youth—2005

	Gender		EuroAmerican		African American		Latino	
Risk behavior	M	F	M	F	M	F	M	F
Depression & Suicide								
* Felt Sad and Hopeless	20.4	36.7	18.4	33.4	19.5	36.9	26.0	46.7
* Seriously Considered Suicide	12.0	21.8	12.4	21.5	7.0	17.1	11.9	24.2
* Attempted Suicide	6.0	10.8	5.2	9.3	5.2	9.8	7.8	14.9
Cigarettes & Alcohol								
* Lifetime Cigarette Use	55.9	52.7	54.9	53.2	56.3	53.2	62.1	52.0
* Current Cigarette Use	22.9	23.0	24.9	27.0	14.0	11.9	24.8	19.2
* Lifetime Alcohol Use	73.9	74.8	75.0	75.7	66.5	71.4	79.9	79.0
* Current Alcohol Use	43.8	42.8	47.0	45.9	29.6	32.5	48.9	44.8
* Episodic Heavy Drinking	27.5	23.5	31.8	28.1	11.9	10.4	28.7	21.9
Illegal Drugs Lifetime								
* Lifetime Marijuana Use	40.9	35.9	40.0	36.0	43.8	37.8	47.7	37.5
* Lifetime Cocaine Use	8.4	6.8	7.8	7.7	3.4	1.2	14.9	9.4
* Lifetime Heroin Use	3.3	1.4	2.7	1.6	2.5	0.5	6.0	1.2
* Lifetime Methamphetamine Use	6.3	6.0	6.1	6.9	2.7	0.8	9.9	7.7
* Lifetime Ecstasy Use	7.2	5.3	6.2	5.3	5.3	2.5	12.5	6.5

Note. Rates are in percentages. Data from Centers for Disease Control (2006).

the highest rates of nearly all classes of drugs used. Again, this reinforces the noted shift from the 1970s when nonminority White (European American) youth exhibited the highest rates of use for most drugs (Booth, Castro, & Anglin, 1990). Increasingly apparent, however, is that gender and ethnicity alone do not fully explain these observed differences (Trimble, 1995). Certain cultural factors may contribute to these differing rates of substance use, thus highlighting the importance of examining the effects of culture generally and of several cultural factors specifically.

CULTURE AND CULTURAL FACTORS: WHY ARE THEY IMPORTANT?

Concepts of Culture

Culture is a rich, complex, and multifaceted construct that embodies the diversity of worldviews (i.e., *Weltanschauung*) and lifeways that is observed within and across populations, subpopulations, and ethnic groups (Baldwin & Lindsley, 1994). Thus, culture is not a single variable but rather consists of a complex multifactorial entity whose effects can be described by deconstructing it into several core elements of culture that can be represented by specific cultural factors or variables (Castro & Hernández-Alarcón, 2002). Culture is created by ethnic group members who interpret and give meaning to their experiences in creating a system of worldviews that form the basis of their ethnic culture (Dana, 1998; D. C. Locke, 1998). Furthermore, from generation to generation, elders pass down to their children their ethnic worldviews—cultural beliefs, values, expectations, and norms. This cyclical process occurring across generations creates an ethnic group's core beliefs, values, norms, and other lifeways, which collectively characterize that group's cultural heritage (Dana, 1998). *Cultural heritage* thus includes historical accounts about ancestors, their achievements, and their sacred or revered customs and traditions. *Culture,* therefore, represents a system of information and communications, a sharing of symbols and accounts that convey deep meaning to members of that ethnic group. Often, the deepest facets of a culture are captured best through folk art, music, and drama. Psychologically, a

group's cultural heritage and identity also confer a sense of "peoplehood" and unity, which operate as the foundation of ethnicity itself (McGoldrick & Giordano, 1996).

Traditionalism and Modernism

Although culture is dynamic and evolves across time, it does not change haphazardly. Across time for a specific group or society, an abiding tension exists between cultural construction that favors new and innovative practices (i.e., modernism) versus efforts to retain past traditions and/or recapture dwindling customs and practices (i.e., traditionalism; Ramirez, 1999). Conflicts may emerge from this tension between traditionalism and modernism as individuals, families, communities, and nations disagree among themselves about the best approach for their collective survival and the correct way to live life (Trimble, 2003). Within many groups, the need persists to honor and retain ancient cultural, religious and other beliefs, values, customs, traditions, and rituals, thus favoring traditionalism. Conversely, changing environments and times dictate that groups must respond to these changing environmental conditions, thus prompting the need to adopt new practices and/or to adapt existing practices, in accord with meeting these new challenges, thus favoring modernism.

Traditionalism involves a dedication and adherence to conservative "old world" familial life norms and values. This often involves an acceptance of old-fashioned lifeways, which have survived across generations because of their utility for promoting group survival and maintaining the cultural group's sense of peoplehood (Castro & Coe, 2007; McGoldrick & Giordano, 1996). For immigrants, traditionalism involves adherence to old-time norms and values from the migrant's native country (Castro & Coe, 2007; Castro & Gutierres, 1997; Ramirez, 1999). Traditionalism often involves strict adherence to restrictive cultural beliefs, behaviors, and norms and may involve actively resisting change and modernization, as well as the uncritical acceptance of prescribed gender roles and expectations (Castro & Coe, 2007; Cuadrado & Lieberman, 1998). Traditional gender roles and expectations are most often observed within agrarian societies that endorse collectivistic forms of family and social relations, as contrasted with individualistic and more permissive gender roles and expectations that are observed within modern Westernized societies (Castro & Garfinkle, 2003; Costa, Terracciano, & McCrae, 2001; Schwartz, Montgomery, & Briones, 2006). Conservative traditional family norms are often proscriptive, can be rigid or inflexible, and often impose constraints on behavior. This restrictiveness may also confer protection against antisocial behavior, including early tobacco, alcohol, and drug use, if a youth obeys these conservative traditional norms (A. G. Gil, Wagner & Vega, 2000).

Specific conservative cultural norms observed within Latino cultures, such as *familism,* a strong collectivistic family orientation, may exert protective effects by emphasizing youth social responsibility to the family (see also chap. 15, this volume). In this regard, strong family ties tend to discourage antisocial behaviors such as alcohol, tobacco, and other drug use (A. G. Gil et al., 2000). Castro and Hernández-Alarcón (2002) observed that Latino youth from families reporting more permissive and nontraditional family values as well as high ethnic pride exhibited higher levels of lifetime alcohol use relative to Latino youth from traditional families who also espoused high ethnic pride. That is, Latino youth expressing high pride who also lived in traditional families exhibited the lowest rates of alcohol use. Thus, among Latino youth, ethnic pride may exert protective effects against alcohol, although only within the context of living within traditional family systems.

Cultural Factors

Castro and Hernández-Alarcón (2002) summarized several cultural variables or factors that influence the lives of Latino and other racial or ethnic minority populations in the United States and may relate to drug use and other risk behaviors. Table 16.2 lists these variables. In this chapter, we briefly examine several of these cultural factors, including acculturation, biculturalism, cultural flex, enculturation, ethnic affirmation, ethnic identity, ethnic pride, familism, *machismo, marianismo,* modernism, *respeto,* and traditionalism. Given that culture changes constantly, cultural factors should be conceptualized and operationally defined as complex factors that are also evolving and thus can change from one generation to another, and for the

individual even from one developmental stage to another. For example, individuals born into one ethnic group may change their identification and affiliation with this group over time, and these changes are often context dependent (Ramirez, 1998). Some cultural variables, such as *machismo* and *marianismo,* may be more prevalent or more salient among Latinos relative to the mainstream European American population. *Machismo* refers to hypermasculine gender role norms and expectations that emphasize male dominance and privilege (Mirande, 1997; Neff, 2001). The stereotypical negative traits that define machismo are observed among certain Latino male adolescents and adults, although the expression of these traits varies by individual and social context (Torres, Solberg, & Carlstrom, 2002). Positive traits of machismo, such as the expression of loyalty to family and obligation to protect one's family have also been described (Casas, Wagenheim, Banchero, & Mendoza-Romero, 1994). Negative aspects of machismo, such as aggressiveness, have been linked to greater substance use among youth, whereas positive aspects of machismo have been linked with less use (Kulis, Marsiglia, & Hurdle, 2003). *Marianismo* refers to feminine gender-role norms and expectations that emphasize self-sacrifice and a dedication to family and the household (Kulis, Marsiglia, Lingard, Nieri, & Nagoshi, 2008). Both positive and negative aspects of *marianismo* (R. M. Gil & Vazquez, 1996), such as nurturance and submissiveness, have been linked to lower risks of substance use (Kulis et al., 2003).

Several recent studies have explored the influence of cultural factors as risk or protective factors for drug use among Latino youth (Castro, Garfinkle, et al., 2006; Kulis, Marsiglia, Sicotte, & Nieri, 2007; Marsiglia, Kulis, Hecht, & Sills, 2004). These studies only crack the surface of this important issue, and additional studies are needed to clarify the potential risk-inducing or protective influences of specific cultural factors.

CLASSIC PARADIGM FOR UNDERSTANDING DRUG USE ETIOLOGY

More than a decade ago, Hawkins, Catalano, and Miller (1992) outlined a paradigm for understanding drug use etiology, suggesting that the causes of drug

TABLE 16.2

Cultural Variables

Cultural variable	Description
Acculturation	Extent of belief and behavior that conforms to the mainstream U.S. American way of life
Afrocentricity	Cultural orientation and pride toward being African American
Biculturalism	A well developed capacity to function effectively within two distinct cultures based on the acquisition of the norms, values and behavioral routines of the dominant culture as well as those of one's own ethnic or cultural group
Cultural Flex	Capacity to function effectively and to "shuttle" adaptively between two cultures
Enculturation	An orientation toward a learning about one's ethnic culture
Ethnic Affirmation and Belonging	An expression of personal identification as a member of an ethnic minority group
Ethnic Identity	Personal identification with one's ethnic cultural group or group of origin
Ethnic Pride	The expression of a positive attitude, a sense of belonging, and gratification from belonging to one's ethnic, cultural, or national group
Familism	Strong family orientation, involvement, and loyalty
Field independence	A "self-oriented" preference or style in ways of thinking and in ways of approaching work and tasks
Field sensitivity	An "others-oriented" preference or style in ways of thinking and ways of relating to others
Individualism–Collectivism	Cognitive and behavioral orientations involving a tendency to prefer an individualistic, self-oriented style, or to prefer a group-oriented collectivistic style
Machismo	A traditional Latino gender role orientation that believes in male dominance as a proper or acceptable form of male identity and conduct
Marianismo	A traditional Latino female role orientation that accepts motherly nurturance, and the demure and pure identity of a virgin (Virgin Mary) as a proper form of female identity and conduct
Modernism	An emphasis on innovation and accepting change and modern beliefs and behaviors as being better and preferred ways to live one's life
Personalismo	Preference for personalized attention and courtesy in relating to others
Respeto	Emphasis on respect and attention to issues of social position in interpersonal relations, as for example, respect for elders.
Simpatia	A deferential posture toward family members and other efforts to maintain harmony in family and in interpersonal relations. Traits of agreeableness, respect, and politeness are core aspects of *simpatia*
Spirituality	A belief in a higher source of strength and well-being, and a related appreciation for natural and beneficial aspects of the world
Tiu lien (Loss of Face)	Among Asian Americans, especially among those who are more traditional, "loss of face" involves the shame of improper behavior or a failing to live up to social obligations. Engaging in proper conduct helps to "save face" and avoid this loss of face
Traditionalism	A preference for maintaining and adhering to established and often conservative beliefs and behaviors. These customs and traditions are seen as appropriate and proper ways to live life

Note. Adapted from "Integrating cultural variables into drug abuse prevention and treatment with racial/ethnic minorities," by F. G. Castro and E. Hernandez-Alarcon, 2002, *Journal of Drug Issues, 32,* pp. 783–810. Copyright 2002 by the *Journal of Drug Issues.* Adapted with permission.

use were best understood using a risk and protective factor framework. From this perspective, drug use emerges when risks mount in the presence of insufficient protections to offset these risks. A core issue for racial and ethnic minority populations is whether risk factors identified for European American youth operate as risk factors in the same manner and to the same extent within various racial and ethnic minority populations. Thus, whereas epidemiologic data have indicated that living in a single-parent family operates as a risk factor for alcohol, tobacco, and illegal drug use among European American adolescents, the question arises of whether the same conditions of risk operate equally for adolescents from racial and ethnic minority families, and if so, are the risk factors equally potent? For example, recent research conducted at the neighborhood level shows that the presence of single-mother families may protect some youth from substance use in geographic areas in which Latinos, particularly immigrant Latinos, may live in high proportions; this finding runs counter to prior research showing that among nonminority youth this same characteristic operates to increase risk for youth substance use (Kulis et al., 2007). Related questions also emerge about protective factors identified for European American youth as applied to racial minority youth and whether these factors are exhaustive. Ethnic identity, for example, which some research has suggested may protect against substance use among minority youth (Scheier, Botvin, Diaz, & Ifill-Williams, 1997), may differ in its respective salience by ethnicity (Marsiglia et al., 2004). Similarly, although self-management skills may protect against substance use among White suburban youth, they have been found to be less protective among urban minority youth (Griffin, Botvin, & Scheier, 2006).

EXPANDING EXTANT MODELS

Although characterization of racial minority youth in the United States needs to include diverse peoples, minority youth share a common thread—having an ascribed minority status and a related non-White, nonmainstream ethnic or racial identity (Viruell-Fuentes, 2007). The U.S. Census (2008) now estimates that 26% of the American population is of minority origin. Depending on their stage of ethnic identity development, minority youth may or may not acknowledge their racial or ethnic minority heritage. Nonetheless, many minority youth may still encounter unfavorable racial experiences including discrimination, pejorative stereotypes, and related stressors (Dana, 1998; see also chap. 18, this volume). Given the growing presence of these minority youth and their exposure to conditions that promote drug use, it is important to develop a better understanding of drug use etiology among this population. Toward this end, the existing risk and protective factors paradigm and its derived models should be expanded to include cultural factors (Castro & Hernández-Alarcón, 2002). Furthermore, because some of these cultural factors may exert important risk or protective effects in minority populations (Cuellar, Arnold, & Gonzalez, 1995), they are worthy of being incorporated into existing prevention and treatment theory. Doing so may increase the cultural relevance of research and enhance the efficacy of interventions offered to racial and ethnic minority populations.

ACCULTURATION AND CULTURAL PROCESS

Immigration, Acculturation, and Cultural Development

Acculturation. Acculturation is a worldwide phenomenon that occurs when individuals, families, and/or populations migrate from one sociocultural environment to another, usually in quest of better living conditions and opportunities (Rudmin, 2003). This process is initiated in part by a search for upward socioeconomic mobility, and thus the process of acculturation covaries with financial, educational, and other opportunities. *Acculturative change* occurs not only in cases of cross-national migration but also in cases of migration within a nation's geographic boundaries, such as migration from rural to urban environments (Castro & Gutierres, 1997; Portes & Rumbaut, 1996).

Cultural integration into a new society involves the acquisition of *cultural competencies* that are prevalent and sanctioned favorably by the new society. These cultural competencies include (a) new knowledge about local and regional laws and social customs; (b) new skills, including occupational and language skills; (c) new networks of neighbors, acquaintances, friends, and other sources of social support; and (d) new values, norms, and behaviors (Berry, 2003). In the United States, acculturation involves the acquisition of American cultural norms, values, behaviors, and skills (Trimble, 2003). For immigrant children, the acquisition of cultural competencies typically occurs as a natural part of their development, but because it raises challenges beyond those experienced in the process of typical adolescent development, it can be stressful (Castro, Boyer, & Balcazar, 2000). For immigrant adults, especially elders, the acquisition of these new competencies may be complicated by competition with preexisting competencies from their native culture and may therefore involve stress and frustration.

At the macro level, acculturation also occurs in populations and may exhibit regional variations. For example, on the basis of their extensive U.S.–Mexico cross-border activities, "borderlanders," people living in Mexico along the U.S.–Mexico border, may be more Americanized relative to southern Mexicans who live far from the border (Martinez, 1994). The observation that entities, like whole populations, can acculturate prompts the question, "How are the origin culture and the new culture defined?" Cultural facets experienced by the immigrant will exhibit unique local community features, in addition to regional and nationwide patterns. The facets of both the native and the new host culture will exhibit stable features but will also present changing features. At the population level, a culture of origin will exhibit changes with the egress of people to the new culture, and the new culture will also change with the entrance of people from other cultures. This dynamic flux of old into new, and new back into old, creates a cultural bridge that reveals itself across populations and temporal periods. It also fosters the development of local subcultures, communities, or regions, for example, being "Texans" or "from the Midwest." Furthermore, identification with local subcultures may be stronger than with the more distal mainstream or cultures of origin.

Acculturative change. Early conceptions of acculturation posited that acculturation was a linear, unidirectional process involving the loss of a person's origin culture as he or she adopts the ways of the new host culture. Along the lines of the melting pot notion of integration (Berry, 2003), the term *assimilation* rather than *acculturation* has been used, referring to the complete loss (unintended or desired) of a distinct ethnic identity on blending into the new culture. In early acculturation research within psychology, the concept of acculturation was measured as a unidimensional continuum (Cuellar, Harris, & Jasso, 1980), implying this loss of the original cultural identity with increasing levels of acculturation toward mainstream American culture. Many investigators have written about the process of acculturation, although few studies have truly examined or modeled acculturation as a process of acculturative change across time.

It is now accepted that acculturation is not a zero-sum process, given that the acquisition of elements of a new culture does not automatically involve the loss of the origin culture (Rogler, 1994; Rogler, Cortes, & Malgady, 1991). Consequently, acculturation is now conceptualized as a two-factor, bidimensional, and orthogonal process: (a) acculturation to a new ethnic or minority culture and (b) enculturation to the origin culture (Cuellar, Arnold, & Maldonado, 1995; Marin & Gamboa, 1996). According to this orthogonal acculturation model (Oetting & Beauvais, 1991), variations in cultural identification can develop, including a bicultural–bilingual identity in which an individual exhibits strong identification with two cultures (Berry, 1994; Cuellar et al., 1995; Marin & Gamboa, 1996). Despite strong conceptual and other support for the orthogonal model (Ryder, Alden, & Paulhus, 2000), assessment strategies have fallen short and population-level studies have provided mixed psychometric support for the complete orthogonality (independence) of contrasting cultural factors. For example, in one multiethnic dataset, American orientation and Latino orientation were positively correlated ($r = .50$; Castro, Garfinkle, et al., 2006), suggesting a significant amount of construct overlap and unidimensionality between both factors. Berry (1997) has proposed one of the most often cited versions of this orthogonal model. His model involves two factors that allow four possible acculturation experiences: (a) *marginalization* (low affiliation with both cultures), (b) *separation* (high origin culture affiliation, low new culture affiliation), (c) *assimilation* (high new culture affiliation, low origin culture affiliation), and (d) *integration* (high affiliation with both cultures). Within this framework, acculturation is not a process toward a single ideal outcome; rather, it reflects a person's (or group's) particular pattern of orientation toward two distinct cultures. Implicit in this conceptualization is that acculturation is not linear or dimensional but rather categorical. An abiding and unresolved issue involves the specific elements of each culture that constitute "core cultural features" toward which an individual, family, or population will orient and attempt to acquire.

Acculturation and context.   There is now a considerable recognition of context as a determinant of acculturation because it influences the range of acculturation and its form. A bilingual child may speak English with friends at school, yet converse exclusively in Spanish at home with his or her family. Similarly, an adult may identify as American at work, but as *un puro Mexicano* among family and friends. Such context-specific expressions of acculturative identity and behaviors represent forms of "cultural flex," an expression of bicultural capabilities (Ramirez, 1999) and may differentially influence the process of acculturative change (Berry, 1994). Furthermore, social constraints, such as racial or ethnic discrimination, and pressure toward forced assimilation, a form of psychological colonialization, may thus facilitate certain kinds of acculturation while discouraging others (Ramirez, 1998).

Community-level factors.   Prior research has identified several ways in which the structural characteristics of a community, such as the concentration of poverty and racial segregation, may contribute to substance use at the individual level. The community most likely shapes a normative environment or creates a climate conducive to drug use (for a review, see Kulis et al., 2007). The crack cocaine epidemic of the 1980s, which disproportionately affected poor Black communities, exemplifies how changing community environments and events can shape drug use

norms. For example, the concentration of certain ethnic groups into ethnic enclaves may relate to substance use. East Los Angeles, an area heavily concentrated with Mexican and Mexican American families, was influenced in the late 1940s by the introduction of heroin into existing Mexican-origin gangs. This event created heroin-using subcliques and converted many Mexican American youth into *tecatos* (dedicated heroin users) and *pintos* (prison inmates), while also producing multigenerational *cholo* families (drug-using, gang-involved families; Moore, 1990). Years later, the heroin epidemic that hit the Boyle Heights *barrio* section of East Los Angeles in the 1980s expanded this historical community context. Drug-trafficking patterns from Mexico and South America introduced black tar heroin into this community, which now included concentrations of Latinos from Central and South America. Eventually, a grassroots movement based in recovery took over, and the same close-knit community that introduced heroin fought off the scourge of addiction with treatment and interdiction. This example also illustrates that a community can foster resilience by providing crucial social support and resources through closer knit kin networks of families and neighbors who share similar cultural values (Portes, 1997; Zhou, 1997). Conversely, ethnic enclaves can foster risk by isolating individuals from a wider set of social and economic resources and opportunities that exist in the mainstream society, thus creating patterns of segmented assimilation (Portes & Zhou, 1993).

Because acculturation also occurs at the group level (Berry, 1997), community-level acculturation may operate in ways similar to that at the individual level, with higher rates of substance use found in communities that exhibit higher levels of acculturation. Furthermore, a sociopolitical context that communicates hostility toward certain ethnic or cultural groups, such as immigrants or ethnic minorities, may foment a communitywide "oppositional culture" (Ogbu, 1995). In response to such hostility, marginalized groups may develop a counteroppositional culture that rejects mainstream society's values and goals (e.g., sobriety) and recognizes an alternative subculture that can include gang activity, drug trafficking, and sanctioning illegal drug use and other antisocial behaviors (Moore, 1990). The influence of this sociopolitical context may extend beyond the present and exert lasting effects on community members into the future by producing a ripple effect that occurs across several generations. Research on American Indian communities, for example, has documented the relationship between historical trauma and substance use (Walters, Simoni, & Evans-Campbell, 2002).

Acculturation stress.   Acculturation stress can arise from social and economic deprivation that results from the migrant experience, cultural conflicts within individuals and families, and experiences of racism (Clark, Anderson, Clark, & Williams, 1999), discrimination (Walker, 2007), and colonization (Ramirez, 1998). This stress arises when minority youth are judged as inferior by certain mainstream groups or institutions, receiving messages that communicate that "you aren't good enough for us." For immigrant families, acculturation-related conflicts between parents and children may emerge when youth acculturate faster than their parents. Typically, youth learn the new cultural skills, cultural norms, and behaviors more quickly, thus changing in relation to their relatively more traditional and less acculturated Latino parents. This cultural imbalance between parents and youth may then introduce conflict, communication barriers, and alienation between parent and child and can permeate the entire family system. This parent–child "acculturation gap" may also introduce a communications gap based in part on parent–child disagreements regarding appropriate behavior. These conflicts may lead to a loss of parental control over the adolescent's behavior (Valez & Ungemack, 1995) and other conditions that facilitate adolescent drug use and delinquency as the child strives for independence and creates emotional distance from his or her parents (A. G. Gil et al., 2000; Valez & Ungemack, 1995). The consequences of acculturation and its stressors can extend beyond the individual. Stress resulting from this acculturation process may compromise family values, attitudes, and familistic behaviors that serve to promote healthy outcomes (A. G. Gil et al., 2000). Acculturative change toward the majority culture may also erode traditional protective factors, including strong religious values, extended family

and kin networks, and a strong sense of spirituality, thus increasing the prevalence of various health-compromising disorders, such as suicide among African American youth (Walker, 2007).

Culture change and drug use.   In general terms, higher acculturation toward mainstream American culture has been associated with poorer health outcomes. Among U.S. immigrants, longer residence in the United States, later generation status, and higher resulting acculturation levels have been associated with negative effects on mental health (Alderete, Vega, Kolody, & Aguilar-Gaxiola, 2000; Gonzales, Knight, Morgan-Lopez, Saenz, & Sirolli, 2002; U.S. Department of Health and Human Services, 2001), suggesting the potential benefits of preserving strong ties to one's traditional cultural roots and developing a strong ethnic identification. However, the mechanisms involving this indicated "protective immigrant paradox" (Markides & Coreil, 1986; Palloni & Morenoff, 2001) remain unclear. One hypothesized mechanism is family traditionalism, which involves the presence of intimate but restrictive family bonds, but with high levels of social support (Lara, Gamboa, Kahramanian, Morales, & Hayes Bautista, 2005; Walker, 2007).

The effects of cultural change on drug use have been recognized, although new and integrative research approaches are needed to address the complexities of cultural change, risk and protective behaviors, and newer patterns of drug use as observed within various minority populations (Warner et al., 2006). Acculturative change toward mainstream American culture has been associated with increased risks of drug use (Vega, Alderete, Kolody, & Aguilar-Gaxiola, 1998) and with more frequent use, greater quantities of use, and higher rates of lifetime use of hard drugs among adolescents (A. G. Gil et al., 2000; J. S. Brook, Whiteman, Balka, Win, & Gursen, 1998; Feliz-Ortiz & Newcomb, 1999; Perez & Padilla, 1980; Vega, Gil, & Zimmerman, 1993). Similarly, Ebin et al. (2001) found that higher levels of acculturation were associated with an increased likelihood of substance use and sexual activities. By contrast, among adults, relative to U.S.-born Mexican Americans and non-Latino White Americans, low-acculturated immigrant Mexican farm workers have exhibited low rates of drug abuse, substance dependence, and mental disorders (Alderate et al., 2000). Similarly, foreign-born Latinos have been observed to be significantly less likely to engage in these problem behaviors relative to those born in the United States (Alderete et al., 2000).

There are several proposed explanations for the link between culture, cultural change, and substance use. The exposure to a comparatively more permissive cultural environment that permits greater freedom of choice, including the choice to experiment with drug use, offers one explanation. The contrast between permissive (liberal–modernistic) versus restrictive (conservative–traditional) cultural environments and the pressure of decoding their ambient messages may create conditions that prompt drug use. In the case of children and youth, linguistic acculturation has been associated with a developmentally driven expansion of their social networks that puts them at greater risk for encountering pro-drug peers and opportunities to use substances (Escobar, 1998). The same process can also distance youth from the protective effects of family and their culture of origin (Duncan, Duncan, Biglan, & Ary, 1998; Flannery, Williams, & Vazsonyi, 1999).

Changes in family dynamics serve as another explanation for cultural conflict and risks for drug use. Family conflicts between parents and children, as indicated by differential acculturation between parent and child, have been associated with chronic disease risk behaviors and behavioral problems, such as substance use (Elder, Broyles, Brennan, Zuniga de Nuncio, & Nader, 2005; Valez & Ungemack, 1995), and a maladaptive stress-coping response involving substance use (A. G. Gil et al., 2000). In addition, prior research has shown that the quality of the parent–adolescent relationship exerts a direct effect on discouraging youth substance use (D. W. Brook, Brook, Rubenstone, Zhang, & Gerochi, 2006; Fagin, Brook, Rubenstone, & Zhang, 2005). However, youth from minority homes may be ill equipped to cope with parent–child conflicts and may feel torn between competing cultural solutions (White vs. minority). In response to these conflicts and frustrations, the options minority youth choose may include drug use or hanging out with nonminority and deviant youth. In

this regard, acculturation stress resulting from cultural conflicts or discrimination may introduce an additional link between cultural change and substance use. Drug use can be an escapist means of reducing discrimination-related stress (Castro, Brook, Brook, & Rubenstone, 2006; Felix-Ortiz & Newcomb, 1995; Martin, Tuch, & Roman, 2003; Nieri, Kulis, & Marsiglia, 2007; Vega et al, 1993). The challenges of adapting to a new environment, the internalization of negative stereotypes, and the loss of traditional support systems constitute risk conditions that in combination may create acute acculturative stress and operate as contextual factors for other life stressors, which in synergy may prompt dysfunctional antisocial behaviors and risk-taking behaviors, including drug use (Elder et al., 2005; Marsiglia et al., 2004).

These findings highlight the importance of families as a focal point for the origination of cultural change–related substance use problems, but also for the prevention of these problems by implementing culturally sensitive prevention interventions (Prado et al., 2007). Families must develop an awareness and understanding of these stress-inducing cultural conflicts and gain the requisite knowledge and skills to make adaptive decisions regarding parent–child and other family conflicts that occur as a consequence of these acculturation-related stressors. For this reason, some believe that successful drug prevention programs with minority populations must be family oriented (Gfroerer & De La Rosa, 1993). The role of the family and, in particular, the influence of parental messages and familial norms constitute fertile areas for continued research (McQueen, Gertz, & Bray, 2003).

Need for enhanced acculturation research. Given the complexity present today in conceptualizing and measuring acculturation, some scholars have argued that further research on acculturation should be eschewed (Hunt, Schneider, & Comer, 2004). Yet, migration, sociocultural mobility, and acculturative change are pervasive phenomena that introduce challenges that require adaptation among migrating populations and that influence ethnic identity development. Furthermore, the association of acculturation with health, well-being, and ethnic minority identity development has been examined in many studies, although a greater understanding of the underlying mechanisms is still needed. Instead of avoiding the analysis of acculturative processes because of extant problems in conceptualization and measurement, the field should develop theory-driven and systems-oriented models that describe a place for acculturation (Viruell-Fuentes, 2007) within a drug use etiology framework. In addition, the field should conduct more in-depth analyses of acculturative processes, using innovative yet rigorous approaches, to better understand identity development in its total temporal and systemic context. With these two approaches, more scientific evidence can be obtained that clarifies the challenges involved in the adaptive acculturation of minority populations in ways that avoid or discourage high-risk behaviors, including the use and abuse of illegal drugs (Castro, 2007).

Ethnic Identity Development

Ethnic identity is a form of self-concept and refers to the extent to which a person identifies with his or her ethnic heritage and group. Erikson's (1968) theory of identity development postulates that identity formation involves a process of exploration and commitment. Thus, ethnic identity development consists of an exploration phase of learning about one's ethnic group, followed by an achievement phase in which the person commits to his or her ethnicity. Considerable theorizing about ethnic identity is tied to Tajfel and Turner's (1986) social identity theory, which focuses on the sense of belonging to a group and the attitudes and feelings that emerge from that sense of group membership. Group identity, of which ethnic identity is one type, may thus shape self-concept and serve as a source of self-esteem including ethnic pride. To determine the person's stage of ethnic identification, the person's ethnicity must first be identified, although as noted previously, this is becoming increasingly more difficult in today's society given an increasing diffusion of ethnicity.

Phinney (1990, 1993) proposed a model of ethnic identity development with three stages: (a) unexamined ethnic identity, (b) ethnic identity search, and (c) ethnic identity achievement. In Stage 1, the adolescent accepts without question the values and atti-

tudes communicated by the dominant mainstream culture, including negative views of his or her own ethnic group (e.g., Black prejudice). In addition, a minority youth may regard him- or herself as being White or as belonging to the mainstream culture and lack awareness and interest in the distinctive nature of his or her ethnicity. In Stage 2, a youth becomes aware of his or her ethnic identity, sometimes in response to a shocking personal or social ethnicity-related event. A youth may feel angry because not all values espoused by the dominant culture group are complementary or beneficial to racial and ethnic minorities. In Stage 3, a minority youth develops a clear and confident sense of his or her ethnicity. The individual thus resolves uncertainties, accepts and internalizes his or her own ethnic identity, and often expresses ethnic pride (Phinney, 1993). Transitions from stage to stage are regarded as occurring naturally during adolescence, although major life course changes, such as immigration, can disrupt or modify this natural process. Moreover, youth may develop multiple ethnic identities, including identification with one's own ethnic group(s), the mainstream group, and in some instances with a pan-ethnic group, such as Asian Americans (Chung, Kim, & Abreu, 2004).

Identity formation is a fundamental life challenge for every human being, a developmental task that involves fundamental questions that shape the person's unique personal identity. Major questions revolve around who you are, what you believe in, and where you are going in life. Accordingly, people with low self-worth, unclear value orientations, and undefined or ambiguous life goals may experience a vague sense of identity and identity confusion along with related feelings of emptiness, worthlessness, and aimlessness. As noted previously, during this developmental process, ethnic minority youth often face particular challenges involving competing and conflicting cultural values, especially when transitioning from one cultural environment to another (Berry, 2005).

Ethnic identification may be measured in terms of attitudes, behaviors, and cultural preferences. For example, identification has been measured in terms of (a) attitudes regarding appropriate behavior, (b) involvement with ethnic peers, (c) participation in cultural traditions, and (d) pride in one's ethnic heritage.

Schwartz et al. (2006) conceptualized identity as a complex construct consisting of several components, including (a) personal identity (personal goals, values, and beliefs), (b) social identity (group identification and affiliation), and (c) cultural identity, which is a subset of social identity. *Cultural identity* refers to solidarity and connectedness with one's cultural or ethnic group. Schwartz et al.'s model is rooted in social cognition and the representation of group-level symbolism as linked to the individual's overarching identity. According to Schwartz et al., personal identity anchors the person. This anchoring is especially important for immigrant and ethnic minority youth because they may struggle during the transition from their home cultural environment to a new cultural environment (Berry, 2005). For these youth, the development of a stable personal, social, and cultural identity, culminating in identity integration, appears essential for effective coping with cultural conflicts because this anchoring may afford these youth a stable frame of reference and the capacity to resolve cultural conflicts in a satisfying manner. In this regard, a stable and integrated bilingual–bicultural identity may well be characterized by the capacity for resolving such dialectical cultural conflicts, for example those involving individualism versus collectivism or traditionalism versus modernism (Ramirez, 1998).

Achieved Ethnic Identity, Ethnic Pride, and Resilience

Identity development in the presence of discrimination. Ethnic minority youth who are anchored with a well-defined ethnic identity schema (Alvarez & Helms, 2001) and who express pride in their ethnic identity may benefit from the cultural strengths afforded by this identification despite exposure to stressful, adverse experiences. For many minority youth, the development of a mature and adaptive ethnic identity constitutes a major life challenge (Schwartz et al., 2006). Healthy adjustment may well involve negotiating difficult life challenges, such as discrimination, in forms not often faced by majority White adolescents (Schwartz et al., 2006). Among dominant majority culture adolescents,

healthy adjustment typically involves (a) stable emotional adjustment, (b) skills for planning and self-control, and (c) harmonious attachments to parents, school, and peers. Healthy adjustment among minority youth may also include (a) recognition or acknowledgment of their cultural heritage; (b) development of a mature (achieved) ethnic identity (Phinney, 1990); (c) bicultural skills in negotiating demands in two cultures (*cultural flex;* Ramirez, 1999); (d) interest and involvement in one's local community (Ramirez, 1998); and (e) the development of leadership interests and skills (Castro et al., 2000; Esthier & Deaux, 1994). This process includes adaptive coping with discrimination, such as when racial minority youth are regarded by others as culturally different and inferior to the majority culture's in-group (Kulis et al., 2003, Walker, 2007).

Bicultural identity development. Despite the consequences of social experiences that discourage identification as an ethnic minority youth, acknowledgment of one's own ethnic heritage can be beneficial, particularly when it co-occurs with an acknowledgment of one's acquired ethnic heritage—that is, affiliation with the mainstream or majority culture. A dual-cultural identity, or bicultural competence, has been associated with positive youth development (La Fromboise, Coleman, & Gerton, 1993). Biculturally competent youth can exhibit cultural flex, that is, the ability to shuttle or transition between majority and minority cultures (La Fromboise et al., 1993; Ramirez, 1999). This is illustrated by the case of bicultural youth who are capable of "language brokering"—that is, translating for parents or others from English to Spanish and vice versa (Weisskirch, 2005). Children who act as language brokers appear to have a positive sense of ethnic identity and may thrive under conditions of dual-culture exposures. This bicultural orientation, which includes positive skills and attitudes toward both cultures, may foster positive emotions and a positive self-concept (Tugade & Frederickson, 2004), which may in general foster a sense of social and cultural competence (Izard, 2002).

Multiracial identity development. People with mixed racial and ethnic heritages face many choices (risks or opportunities) about how they will identify themselves and with which groups of friends they will relate. These choices may be fraught with conflict and insecurity while also offering opportunities for adaptive personal growth (Root, 1996). Ridicule and rejection from other people can lead to self-doubts and resentment over being different. Some mixed-heritage people will exhibit self-hate, wishing that they were born different, with different skin color, hair, or other more desirable personal features that would make them physically or psychologically different from what they are. Some parents have raised their mixed-heritage children in accord with mainstream (i.e., Westernized) ways and avoid teaching ethnic lifeways (i.e., language, traditions, customs, religion) to protect their child from discrimination. An unfortunate consequence of this strategy, however, is that some mixed-heritage youth later complain about missing elements of their identity. Some youth may then actively seek to reconnect with their lost heritage. Despite potential psychological distress and conflict, youth with a mixed racial identity may develop adaptive ways of coping (Berry, 2005). Resolving conflicts may lead to the development of a unique, complex, yet integrated identity, one that reflects personal growth and a full appreciation for the richness of their multiracial–ethnic heritage. In this regard, a pressing question is, "What aspects of this complex ethnic identity operate as protective factors for youth, fortifying their capacity to avoid negative developmental outcomes or to rise above them?"

Ethnic pride and resilience. Ethnic "identity maturation" has been associated with sound psychological adjustment. In relation to this, ethnic pride, which is synonymous with collective self-esteem (Alvarez & Helms, 2001) or group esteem, reflects a person's positive feelings about belonging to his or her native racial or ethnic group. Adolescents who belong to a minority cultural group can recognize their ethnic identity, and can express a positive self-appraisal. Despite their minority status, they may demonstrate resilience, personal agency, self-confidence, and personal resources that aid in actively avoiding negative outcomes such as substance use (Klohnen, 1996; Masten, 2001). Although some research

examining ethnic pride as a source of resilience in the face of substance use risk has been conducted (e.g., with American Indian youth; Kulis, Napoli, & Marsiglia, 2002), much more is needed.

CULTURALLY SENSITIVE METHODS FOR RESEARCH ON DRUG USE ETIOLOGY AND PREVENTION

Culturally Sensitive Research Design Strategies

Enhanced theory for acculturation and cultural identity research. As other chapters in this handbook highlight, the field of drug use etiology is undergoing considerable change. New conceptual models are being tested with more advanced statistical techniques, giving us hope that we can pare away extraneous information to obtain new and generalizable scientific knowledge. Coupled with these advances, more attention is being paid to individuals within their various contexts, whether cultural, environmental, or biogenetic. As this chapter sets forth, to meet this challenge and benefit from this new information, the field also needs a new generation of systems-oriented theories and models that include cultural variables. Such theories will permit the study of resilience and adaptive forms of acculturation (Berry, 2005; Portes & Rumbaut, 1996) and recognize the complexity and dynamic nature that characterizes cultural variables (Berry, 2005; Cabassa, 2003; see Table 16.2). Understanding this complexity calls for the use of rigorous, integrative mixed-methods (qualitative and quantitative) approaches (Carey, 1993; Castro & Coe, 2007; Smith-Hoerter, Stasiewicz, & Bradizza, 2004; Tashakkori & Teddlie, 2003). Such approaches can reveal case-related processes that offer insights and in-depth illustrations of complex acculturative processes (Caetano & Clark, 2003; Hanson, Creswell, Clark, Petska, & Creswell, 2005; Lara et al., 2005; Viruell-Fuentes, 2007). Research designs and prevention programs should incorporate the most potent and empirically validated protective factors such as perceptions of harm and social disapproval (Bachman et al., 2002), life skills, and refusal self-efficacy (Wynn,

Schulenberg, Maggs, & Zucker, 2000). These models can then be augmented with measures that lend cultural sensitivity and ideally increase the variation accounted for in select endpoints.

The design of culturally relevant research should ideally include contributions from members of the local cultural community to ensure community-informed approaches, culturally relevant definitions of cultural variables, and culturally sound interpretations of study results (Dickens & Watkins, 1999; Gosin, Dustman, Drapeau, & Harthun, 2003; Minkler, Blackwell, Thompson, & Tamir, 2003). Because culture is dynamic, cultural variables may require periodic checks and psychometric refinement to maintain ecological relevance across time (Harris & Firestone, 1998; Page, 2005).

Testing systems models with multivariate methods. New forms of culturally sensitive research should test multivariate and systemic models using advanced multivariate data analytic procedures. The biopsychosocial model is one systems approach for conceptualizing the multiple influences on risk behaviors. A variant of the biopsychosocial model, the ecodevelopmental model, incorporates temporal developmental effects (Pantin, Schwartz, Sullivan, Prado, & Szapocznik, 2004; Szapocznik & Coatsworth, 1999). The ecodevelopmental model as applied to youth consists of a hierarchy of systems involving four domains: (a) the *macrosystems,* broad social and philosophical ideals such as culture and values; (b) the *exosystems,* factors not directly affecting the adolescent but that exert indirect influences on the youth such as social supports that are available to the youth's parents; (c) *mesosystems,* factors that directly affect the youth such as parental monitoring of the youth's involvement with peers; and (d) *microsystems,* contexts in which the youth participates directly, such as family, school, and peers (Pantin et al., 2004).

These broad multilevel models offer useful descriptions of potential mechanisms of effect, although poorly defined constructs may hamper their usefulness for scientifically testing hypothesized relations and identifying mechanisms of effect. Current refinements include a schematic model that more explicitly defines the effects of ethnicity and related concepts (e.g., minority status, culture, iden-

tity) on specific health outcomes (survival, quality of life; Meyerowitz, Richardson, Hudson, & Leedham, 1998). Another schematic model posits influences of stressful social stimuli, perceptions, coping responses, and the effects of racism on various health outcomes (Clark et al., 1999). Recently, T. F. Locke, Newcomb, and Goodyear (2005) tested a multiple systemic factor model to examine the determinants of HIV risk behaviors using structural equation modeling. The resulting model showed that traditional gender roles, defined by a strong value of respect, male toughness, and negative attitudes toward femininity, were associated with two risk behaviors: more frequent sexual intercourse with less condom use.

Using structural equation modeling techniques, Trimble (1995) examined the effects of gender, American Indian identity, youth alcohol associations, and peer and family alcohol associations as predictors of alcohol involvement in a sample of American Indian youth residing either on rural reservations or in urban environments. Significant predictors included peer alcohol associations (affiliating with peers who use alcohol) and poor academic performance. Several studies have supported the limited prediction of alcohol or substance use from ethnicity or ethnic pride. These results differ to some extent from those of studies with Latino youth that have reported some buffering or protective effects of ethnic identity on youth drug use (J. S. Brook et al., 1998). Similarly, the effects of cultural traditionalism and social responsibility have been observed as predictors of family bonding, which may then operate as a protective factor against youth substance use (Castro, Garfinkle, et al., 2006).

Also using a structural equations model, Wills et al. (2007) examined parenting practices (mesosystems factors) and youth factors (microsystems factors) as predictors of youth substance use among African American adolescents. This study showed that parental endorsement of cultural pride (racial socialization) preceded ethnic pride (positive ethnic esteem), which preceded low substance use willingness and high substance resistance efficacy, both of which mediated the path to youth substance use. These results show that ethnic pride may mediate effective parenting on substance use and precede avoidance attitudes toward substance use, all operating as a system of influences that contributes to low rates of youth substance use (cigarette smoking and alcohol use). Thus, among minority youth, ethnic pride can operate as a protective factor, albeit when examined within the systemic context of several other factors that operate in synergy as precursors of low rates of alcohol and cigarette use (J. S. Brook et al., 1998).

So what constitutes core "American culture"? Another challenge in the study of acculturative change involves the need to more accurately and operationally define the core elements of "American culture." Whereas a distinct set of American ideals and core patterns of American beliefs and behaviors appears to exist, paradoxically, no one single American culture exists, given broad variations in American culture by geographic region, urbanicity, subpopulation, and so forth. As scholars examine models of cultural orientation toward a "core culture" (e.g., American culture), they must also recognize the extensive diversity existing within a culture and specify the core cultural components that serve as targets of motivational efforts to acquire them as a part of the process of acculturation.

Retrospective–prospective studies of cultural change. A challenge in the study of acculturation and other cultural variables involves the need for prospectively designed longitudinal studies that examine actual cultural change across time. For example, this can involve differential changes in various components of acculturation such as (a) English language acquisition and proficiency; (b) increases in close European American (Anglo-Saxon) friends; (c) the adoption of core American (Anglo-Saxon) cultural values such as freedom, individualism, achievement orientation, capitalism and entrepreneurship, work efficiency, future time orientations, and so forth (D. C. Locke, 1998); (d) changes toward adopting normative American cultural behaviors such as consumerism; and (e) changes in certain health-related behaviors such as dieting and engaging in aerobic exercise.

Longitudinal studies of acculturation change are ideally conducted across time to examine changes in acculturation toward mainstream American cultural

elements, as well as related changes in cultural and ethnic identity, in gender roles, and in cultural beliefs and behaviors, because these changes are associated with various health outcomes. However, ideal studies of this type would require following a cohort prospectively for 2 to 4 decades, which would be expensive and perhaps prohibitive. By contrast, acculturative change might be modeled more economically using a dual retrospective–prospective study design. Such a study might include baseline assessments that retrospectively evaluate acculturation status and other cultural variables as they have occurred during specific childhood milestones, while also following a cohort of individuals prospectively for a decade or 2. Such a study could then examine multiple trajectories of acculturative change using latent growth models (Bollen & Curran, 2006) and could also use latent class analyses (Lubke & Muthén, 2005) to detect specific within-sample subgroups on the basis of their similarity on specific cultural variables or on trajectories of acculturative change.

These are just a few emerging theoretical, measurement, research design, and data analytic approaches to be considered in the design of future research that is sensitive to the cultural factors described here. Dialogue about ways to address the complex issues involved in the study of cultural factors will help address current challenges in the design of a new generation of culturally sensitive drug prevention research with Latino and other ethnic minority populations.

References

Alderete, E., Vega, W. A., Kolody, B., & Aguilar-Gaxiola, S. (2000). Lifetime prevalence of and risk factors for psychiatric disorders among Mexican migrant farmworkers in California. *American Journal of Public Health, 90,* 608–614.

Alvarez, A. N., & Helms, J. E. (2001). Radical identity and reflected appraisals as influences on Asian Americans' racial adjustment. *Cultural Diversity and Ethnic Minority Psychology, 7,* 217–231.

Bachman, J. G., O'Malley, P. M., Schulenberg, J. E., Johnson, L. D., Bryant, A. L., & Merline, A. C. (2002). *The decline of substance use in young adulthood.* Mahwah, NJ: Erlbaum.

Baldwin, J. R., & Lindsley, S. L. (1994). *Conceptualizations of culture.* Tempe: Arizona State University.

Berry, J. W. (1994). Acculturative stress. In W. Lonner & R. Malpass, (Eds.), *Psychology and culture* (pp. 211–215). Boston: Allyn & Bacon.

Berry, J. W. (1997). Immigration, acculturation, and adaptation. *Applied Psychology: An International Review, 46,* 5–68.

Berry, J. W. (2003). Conceptual approaches to acculturation. In K. M. Chun, P. B. Organista, & G. Marin (Eds.), *Acculturation: Advances in theory, measurement, and applied research* (pp. 17–37). Washington, DC: American Psychological Association.

Berry, J. W. (2005). Acculturation: Living successfully in two cultures. *International Journal of Intercultural Relations, 29,* 697–712.

Bollen, K. A., & Curran, P. J. (2006). *Latent curve models: A structural equation perspective.* Hoboken, NJ: Wiley.

Booth, M. W., Castro, F. G., & Anglin, D. M. (1990). What do we know about Hispanic substance abuse? A review of the literature. In J. W. Moore & R. Glick (Eds.), *Drugs in Hispanic communities* (pp. 21–43). New Brunswick, NJ: Rutgers University Press.

Brook, D. W., Brook, J. S., Rubenstone, E., Zhang, C., & Gerochi, C. (2006). Cigarette smoking in the adolescent children of drug-abusing fathers. *Pediatrics, 117,* 1339–1347.

Brook, J. S., Whiteman, M., Balka, E. B., Win, P. T., & Gursen, M. D. (1998). Drug use among Puerto Ricans: Ethnic identity as a protective factor. *Hispanic Journal of Behavioral Sciences, 20,* 241–254.

Cabassa, L. J. (2003). Measuring acculturation: Where we are and where we need to go. *Hispanic Journal of Behavioral Sciences, 25,* 127–146.

Caetano, R., & Clark, C. L. (2003). Acculturation, alcohol consumption, smoking, and drug use among Latinos. In K. M. Chun, P. B. Organista, & G. Marin (Eds.), *Acculturation: Advances in theory, measurement, and applied research* (pp. 223–239). Washington, DC: American Psychological Association.

Carey, J. W. (1993). Linking qualitative and quantitative methods: Integrating cultural factors into public health. *Qualitative Health Research, 3,* 298–318.

Casas, J. M., Wagenheim, B. R., Banchero, R., & Mendoza-Romero, J. (1994). Hispanic masculinity: Myth or psychological schema meriting clinical consideration. *Hispanic Journal of Behavioral Sciences, 16,* 315–331.

Castro, F. G. (2007). Is acculturation really detrimental to health? *American Journal of Public Health, 97,* 1162.

Castro, F. G., Boyer, G. R., & Balcazar, H. G. (2000). Healthy adjustment in Mexican American and other Latino adolescents. In R. Montemayor, G. R. Adams, & T. P. Gullotta (Eds.), *Adolescent diversity in ethnic, economic and cultural contexts* (pp 141–178). Thousand Oaks, CA: Sage.

Castro, F. G., Brook, J. S., Brook, D. W., & Rubenstone, E. (2006). Paternal, perceived maternal, and youth risk factors as predictors of youth stage of substance use: A longitudinal study. *Journal of Addictive Diseases, 25,* 65–75.

Castro, F. G., & Coe, K. (2007). Traditions and alcohol use: A mixed-methods analysis. *Cultural Diversity and Ethnic Minority Psychology, 13,* 269–284.

Castro, F. G., & Garfinkle, J. (2003). Critical issues in the development of culturally relevant substance abuse treatments for specific minority groups. *Alcoholism: Clinical and Experimental Research, 27,* 1–8.

Castro, F. G., Garfinkle, J., Naranjo, D., Rollins, M., Brook, J. S., & Brook, D. (2006). Cultural traditions as protective factors among Latino children of illicit drug users. *Substance Use and Misuse, 42,* 621–642.

Castro, F. G., & Gutierres, S. (1997). Drug and alcohol use among rural Mexican Americans. In E. R. Robertson, Z. Sloboda, G. M. Boyd, L. Beatty, & N. J. Kozel (Eds.), *Rural substance abuse: State of knowledge and issues* (NIDA Research Monograph No. 168, pp. 499–533). Rockville, MD: National Institute on Drug Abuse.

Castro, F. G., & Hernández-Alarcón, E. (2002). Integrating cultural variables into drug abuse prevention and treatment with racial/ethnic minorities. *Journal of Drug Issues, 32,* 783–810.

Centers for Disease Control. Youth Risk Behavior Surveillance—United States 2005. (2006, June 9). Youth Risk Behavior Surveillance—United States 2005. *Morbidity and Mortality Weekly Report, 55,* 1–108.

Chung, R. H. G., Kim, B. S. K., & Abreu, J. M. (2004). Asian American Multidimensional Acculturation Scale: Development, factor analysis, reliability and validity. *Cultural Diversity and Ethnic Minority Psychology, 10,* 66–80.

Clark, R., Anderson, N. D., Clark, V. R., & Williams, D. R. (1999). Racism as a stressor for African Americans. *American Psychologist, 54,* 805–816.

Costa, P. T., Terracciano, A., & McCrae, R. R. (2001). Gender differences in personality traits across cultures: Robust and surprising findings. *Journal of Personality and Social Psychology, 81,* 322–331.

Cuadrado, M., & Lieberman, L. (1998). Traditionalism in the prevention of substance misuse among Puerto Ricans. *Substance Use and Misuse, 33,* 2737–2755.

Cuellar, I., Arnold, B., & Gonzalez, G. (1995). Cognitive referents of acculturation: Assessment of cultural constructs in Mexican Americans. *Journal of Community Psychology, 23,* 339–356.

Cuellar, I., Arnold, B., & Maldonado, R. (1995). Acculturation Rating Scale for Mexican-Americans II: A revision of the original ARMSA scale. *Hispanic Journal of Behavioral Sciences, 17,* 275–304.

Cuellar, I., Harris, L. C., & Jasso, R. (1980). An acculturation rating scale for Mexican American normal and clinical populations. *Hispanic Journal of Behavioral Sciences, 2,* 199–217.

Dana, R. H. (1998). *Multicultural assessment perspectives for professional psychology.* Boston: Allyn & Bacon.

Dickens, L., & Watkins, K. (1999) Action research: Rethinking Lewin. *Management Learning, 30,* 127–140.

Duncan, S. C., Duncan, T. E., Biglan, A., & Ary, D. (1998). Contributions of the social context to the development of adolescent substance use: A multivariate latent growth modeling approach. *Drug and Alcohol Dependence, 50,* 57–71.

DuRant, R. H., Altman D., Wolfson M., Barkin S., Kreiter S., & Krowchuk, D. (2000). Exposure to violence and victimization, depression, substance use, and the use of violence by young adolescents. *Journal of Pediatrics, 137,* 707–713.

Ebin, V. J., Sneed, C. D., Morisky, D. E., Rotheram-Borus, M. J., Magnusson, A. M., & Malotte, C. K. (2001). Acculturation and interrelationship between problem and health-promoting behaviors among Latino adolescents. *Journal of Adolescent Health, 28,* 62–72.

Elder, J. P., Broyles, S. L., Brennan, J. J., Zuniga de Nuncio, M. L., & Nader, P. R. (2005). Acculturation, parent-child acculturation differential, and chronic disease risk factors in a Mexican-American population. *Journal of Immigrant Health, 7,* 1–9.

Erikson, E. (1968). *Identity: Youth and crisis.* New York: Norton.

Escobar, J. I. (1998). Immigration and mental health: Why are immigrants better off? *Archives of General Psychiatry, 55,* 781–782.

Esthier, K. A., & Deaux, K. (1994). Negotiating social identity when contexts change: Maintaining identification and responding to threat. *Journal of Personality and Social Psychology, 67,* 243–251.

Fagin, P., Brook, J. S., Rubenstone, E., & Zhang, C. (2005). Parental occupation, education, and smoking as predictors of offspring tobacco use in adulthood: A longitudinal study. *Addictive Behaviors, 30,* 517–529.

Felix-Ortiz, M., & Newcomb, M. D. (1995). Cultural identity and drug use among Latino adolescents. In G. Botvin, S. Schinke, & M. Orlandi (Eds.), *Drug abuse prevention with multi-ethnic youth* (pp. 147–165), Newbury Park: Sage.

Felix-Ortiz, M., & Newcomb, M. D. (1999). Vulnerability for drug use among Latino adolescents. *Journal of Community Psychology, 27,* 257–280.

Flannery, D. J., Williams, L. L., & Vazsonyi, A. T. (1999). Who are they with and what are they doing? Delinquent behavior, substance use, and early adolescents' after-school time. *American Journal of Orthopsychiatry, 69,* 247–253.

Gfroerer, J., & De La Rosa, M. (1993). Protective and risk factors associated with drug use among Latino youth. *Journal of Addictive Disorders, 12,* 87–107.

Gil, A. G., Wagner, E. F., & Vega, W. A. (2000). Acculturation, familism, and alcohol use among Latino adolescent males: Longitudinal relations. *Journal of Community Psychology, 28,* 443–458.

Gil, R. M., & Vazquez, C. I. (1996). *The Maria paradox: How Latinas can merge old world traditions with new world self-esteem.* New York: G. P. Putnam.

Gonzales, N., Knight, G. P., Morgan-Lopez, A. A., Saenz, D., & Sirolli, A. (2002). Acculturation and the mental health of Latino youths: An integration and critique of the literature. In J. M. Contreras, K. A. Kerns, & A. M. Neal-Barnett (Eds.), *Latino children and families in the United States: Current research and future directions* (pp. 45–74). Westport, CT: Praeger.

Gosin, M. N., Dustman, P. A., Drapeau, A. E., & Harthun, M. L. (2003). Participatory action research: Creating an effective prevention curriculum for adolescents in the Southwest. *Health Education Research: Theory and Practice, 18,* 363–379.

Griffin, K. W., Botvin, G. J., & Scheier, L. M. (2006). Racial/ethnic differences in the protective effects of self-management skills on adolescent substance use. *Substance Abuse, 27*(1–2), 47–52.

Hanson, W. E., Creswell, J. W., Clark, V. L. P., Petska, K. S., & Creswell, J. D. (2005). Mixed methods research designs in counseling psychology. *Journal of Counseling Psychology, 52,* 224–235.

Harris, R., & Firestone, J. (1998). Changes in predictors of gender role ideologies among women: A multivariate analysis. *Sex Roles, 38,* 239–252.

Hawkins, J. D., Catalano, R. F., & Miller, J. Y. (1992). Risk and protective factors for alcohol and other drug problems in adolescence and early adulthood: Implications for substance abuse prevention. *Psychological Bulletin, 112,* 64–105.

Hunt, L. M., Schneider, S., & Comer, B. (2004). Should "acculturation" be a variable in health research? A critical review of research on US Latinos. *Social Science & Medicine, 59,* 973–986.

Izard, C. E. (2002). Translating emotion theory and research into preventive interventions. *Psychological Bulletin, 128,* 796–824.

Johnston, L. D., O'Malley, P. M., Bachman, J. G., & Schulenberg, J. E. (2005). *Monitoring the future national results on adolescent drug use: Overview of key findings 2004* (NIH Publication No. 05-5726). Bethesda, MD: National Institute on Drug Abuse.

Klohnen, E. C. (1996). Conceptual analysis and measurement of the construct of ego-resiliency. *Journal of Personality and Social Psychology, 70,* 1067–1079.

Kulis, S., Marsiglia, F. F., & Hurdle, D. (2003). Gender identity, ethnicity, acculturation and drug use: Exploring differences among adolescents in the Southwest. *Journal of Community Psychology, 31*, 1–22.

Kulis, S., Marsiglia, F. F., Lingard, E. C., Nieri, T., & Nagoshi, J. (2008). Gender identity and substance use among students in two high schools in Monterrey, Mexico. *Drug and Alcohol Dependence, 95*, 258–268.

Kulis, S., Marsiglia, F. F., Sicotte, D. M., & Nieri, T. (2007). Neighborhood effects on youth substance use in a southwestern city. *Sociological Perspectives, 50*, 273–301.

Kulis, S., Napoli, M., & Marsiglia, F. F. (2002). Ethnic pride, biculturalism, and drug use norms of urban American Indian adolescents. *Social Work Research, 26*, 101–112.

La Fromboise, T., Coleman, H. L. K., & Gerton, J. (1993). Psychological impact of biculturalism: Evidence and theory. *Psychological Bulletin, 114*, 395–412.

Lara, M., Gamboa, C., Kahramanian, M. I., Morales, L. S., & Hayes Bautista, D. E. (2005). Acculturation and Latino health in the United States: A review of the literature and its sociopolitical context. *Annual Review of Public Health, 26*, 367–397.

Locke, D. C. (1998). *Increasing multicultural understanding* (2nd ed.). Thousand Oaks, CA: Sage.

Locke, T. F., Newcomb, M. D., & Goodyear, R. K. (2005). Childhood experiences and psychosocial influences on risky sexual behavior, condom use, and HIV attitudes–behaviors among Latino males. *Psychology of Men and Masculinity, 6*, 25–38.

Lubke, G. H., & Muthén, B. (2005). Investigating population heterogeneity with factor mixture models. *Psychological Methods, 10*, 21–39.

Marin, G., & Gamboa, R. J. (1996). A new measurement of acculturation for Latinos: The Bidimensional Acculturation Scale for Latinos (BAS). *Hispanic Journal of Behavioral Sciences, 18*, 297–316.

Markides, K. S., & Coreil, J. (1986). The health of Hispanics in the southwestern United States: An epidemiologic paradox. *Public Health Reports, 101*, 253–265.

Marsiglia, F. F., Kulis, S., Hecht, M. L., & Sills, S. (2004). Ethnicity and ethnic identity as predictors of drug norms and drug use among preadolescents in the US Southwest. *Substance Use and Misuse, 39*, 1061–1094.

Martin, J. K., Tuch, S. A., & Roman, P. M. (2003). Problem drinking patterns among African Americans: The impacts of reports of discrimination, perceptions of prejudice, and "risky" coping strategies. *Journal of Health and Social Behavior, 44*, 408–425.

Martinez, O. J. (1994). *Border people: Life and society in the U.S.-Mexico borderlands.* Tucson: University of Arizona Press.

Masten, A. S. (2001). Ordinary people: Resilience process in development. *American Psychologist, 56*, 227–238.

McGoldrick, M., & Giordano, J. (1996). Overview: Ethnicity and family therapy. In M. McGoldrick, J. Giordano, & J. K. Pearce (Eds.), *Ethnicity and family therapy* (2nd ed., pp. 1–27). New York: Guilford Press.

McQueen, A., Getz, G., & Bray, J. H. (2003). Acculturation, substance use, and deviant behavior: Examining separation and family conflict as mediators. *Child Development, 74*, 1737–1750.

Meyerowitz, B. E., Richardson, J., Hudson, S., & Leedham, B. (1998). Ethnicity and cancer outcomes: Behavioral and psychosocial considerations. *Psychological Bulletin, 123*, 47–70.

Minkler, M., Blackwell, A. G., Thompson, M., & Tamir, H. (2003). Community-based participatory research: Implications for public health funding. *American Journal of Public Health, 93*, 1210–13.

Mirande, A. (1997). *Hombres y machos: Masculinity and Latino culture.* Boulder, CO: Westview Press.

Moore, J. (1990). Mexican-American women addicts: The influence of family background. In R. Glick & J. Moore (Eds.), *Drugs in Hispanic communities.* New Brunswick, NJ: Rutgers University Press.

Neff, J. A. (2001). A confirmatory factor analysis of a measure of "machismo" among Anglo, African American, and Mexican American male drinkers. *Hispanic Journal of Behavioral Sciences, 23*, 171–88

Nieri, T., Kulis, S., & Marsiglia, F. F. (2007, May). *Acculturation stress or perceived ethnic discrimination? Assessing their relative influences on substance use among Latino elementary students.* Poster session presented at the annual meeting of the Society for Prevention Research, Washington, DC.

Oetting, E. R., & Beauvais, F. (1991). Orthogonal cultural identification theory: The cultural identification of minority adolescents. *International Journal of the Addictions, 25*, 655–685.

Ogbu, J. U. (1995). Cultural problems in minority education: Their interpretations and consequences—Part One: Theoretical background. *Urban Review, 27*, 189–205.

Page, J. B. (2005). The concept of culture: A core issue in health disparities. *Journal of Urban Health, 82*, iii35–iii43.

Palloni, A., & Morenoff, J. D. (2001). Interpreting the paradoxical in the Latino paradox: Demographic and epidemiological approaches. *Annals of the New York Academy of Sciences, 954*, 140–174.

Pantin, H., Schwartz, S. J., Sullivan, S., Prado, G., & Szapocznik, J. (2004). Ecodevelopmental HIV prevention program for Hispanic adolescents. *American Journal of Orthopsychiatry, 74*, 545–588.

Perez, R., & Padilla, A. (1980). Correlates and changes over time in drug and alcohol use within a barrio population. *American Journal of Community Psychology, 8,* 621–636.

Phinney, J. (1990). Ethnic identity in adolescents and adults: Review and research. *Psychological Bulletin, 108,* 499–514.

Phinney, J. S. (1993). A three-stage model of ethnic identity development in adolescence. In M. E. Bernal & G. P. Knight (Eds.), *Ethnic identity: Formation and transmission among Hispanics and other minorities* (pp. 61–79). Albany: State University of New York Press.

Portes, A. (1997). Immigration theory for a new century: Some problems and opportunities. *International Migration Review, 31,* 799–825.

Portes, A., & Rumbaut, R. G. (1996). *Immigrant America: A portrait* (2nd ed.). Berkeley: University of California Press.

Portes, A., & Zhou, M. (1993). The new second generation: Segmented assimilation and its variants. *Annals of the American Academy of Political and Social Science, 530,* 74–96.

Prado, G., Pantin, H., Briones, E., Schwartz, S. J., Feaster, D., Huang, S., et al. (2007). A randomized controlled trial of a parent–child intervention in preventing substance use and HIV risk behaviors in Hispanic adolescents. *Journal of Consulting and Clinical Psychology, 75,* 914–926.

Ramirez, M. (1998). *Multicultural/multiracial psychology: Mestizo perspectives in personality and mental health.* Northvale, NJ: Jason Anderson.

Ramirez, M. (1999). *Multicultural psychotherapy: An approach to individual and cultural differences* (2nd ed.). Boston: Allyn & Bacon.

Rogler, L. H. (1994). International migrations: A framework for directing research. *American Psychologist, 49,* 701–708.

Rogler, L. H., Cortes, D. E., & Malgady, R. G. (1991). Acculturation and mental health status among Latinos. *American Psychologist, 46,* 585–597.

Root, M. (1996). *The multiracial experience: Racial borders as the new frontier.* Thousand Oaks, CA: Sage.

Rudmin, F. W. (2003). Critical history of the acculturation psychology of assimilation, separation, integration, and marginalization. *Review of General Psychology, 7,* 3–37.

Ryder, A. G., Alden, L. E., & Paulhus, D. L. (2000). Is acculturation unidimensional or bidimensional? A head-to-head comparison in the prediction of personality, self-identity, and adjustment. *Journal of Personality and Social Psychology, 79,* 49–65.

Scheier, L. M., Botvin, G. J., Diaz, T., & Ifill-Williams, M. (1997). Ethnic identity as a moderator of psychosocial risk and adolescent alcohol and marijuana use: Concurrent and longitudinal analyses. *Journal of Child and Adolescent Substance Abuse, 6,* 21–47.

Schwartz, S. J., Montgomery, M. J., & Briones, E. (2006). The role of identity in acculturation among immigrant people: Theoretical propositions, empirical questions, and applied recommendations. *Human Development, 49,* 1–30.

Smith-Hoerter, K., Stasiewicz, P. R., & Bradizza, C. M. (2004). Subjective reactions to alcohol cue exposure: A qualitative analysis of patients' self-reports. *Psychology of Addictive Behaviors, 18,* 402–406.

Szapocznik, J., & Coatsworth, J. D. (1999). An ecodevelopmental framework for organizing the influences of drug abuse: A developmental model of risk and protection. In M. Glanz & C. Hartel (Eds.), *Drug abuse: Origins & interventions* (pp. 331–366). Washington, DC: American Psychological Association.

Tajfel, H., & Turner, J. (1986). The social identity theory of intergroup behavior. In S. Worchel & W. Austin (Eds.), *Psychology of intergroup relations* (pp. 7–24). Chicago: Nelson-Hall.

Tashakkori, A., & Teddlie, C. (2003). *Handbook of mixed methods in social & behavioral research.* Thousand Oaks, CA: Sage.

Torres, J. B., Solberg, S. H., & Carlstrom, A. H. (2002). The myth of sameness among Latino men and their machismo. *American Journal of Orthopsychiatry, 72,* 163–181.

Trimble, J. E. (1995). Toward an understanding of ethnicity and ethnic identity, and their relationship with drug use research. In G. J. Botvin, S. Schinke, & M. A. Orlandi (Eds.), *Drug abuse prevention with multiethnic youth* (pp. 3–27). Thousand Oaks, CA: Sage.

Trimble, J. E. (2003). Introduction: Social change and acculturation. In K. M. Chun, P. B. Organista, & G. Marin (Eds.), *Acculturation: Advances in theory, measurement, and applied research* (pp. 3–13). Washington, DC: American Psychological Association.

Tugade, M. M., & Frederickson, B. L. (2004). Resilient individuals use positive emotions to bounce back from negative emotional experiences. *Journal of Personality and Social Psychology, 86,* 320–333.

U.S. Census Bureau. (2006). *Table 4. Annual estimates of the population by age and sex of Hispanic or Latino origin for the United States: April 1, 2000 to July 1, 2005* (NC-EST 2005-04-HISP). Retrieved November 19, 2008, from http://www.census.gov/popest/national/asrh/NC-EST2005/NC-EST2005-04-HISP.xls

U.S. Census Bureau. (2008). *2006 American Community Survey.* Retrieved January 13, 2008, from http://factfinder.census.gov/servlet/DTTable?_bm=y&-geo_id=01000US&-ds_name=ACS_2006_EST_G00_&-mt_name=ACS_2006_EST_G2000_B02001

U.S. Department of Health and Human Services. (2001). *Mental health: Culture, race, and ethnicity. A supplement to mental health: A report of the Surgeon General.* Rockville, MD: Author.

Valez, C. N., & Ungemack, J. A. (1995). Psychosocial correlates of drug use among Puerto Rican youth: Generational status differences. *Social Science & Medicine, 40,* 91–103.

Vega, W. A., Alderete, E., Kolody, B., & Aguilar-Gaxiola, S. (1998). Illicit drug use among Mexicans and Mexican Americans in California: The effects of gender and acculturation. *Addiction, 93,* 1839–1850.

Vega, W. A., Gil, A. G., & Zimmerman, R. S. (1993). Patterns of drug use among Cuban-American, African-American and White, non-Latino boys. *American Journal of Public Health, 83,* 257–259.

Viruell-Fuentes, E. A. (2007). Beyond acculturation: Immigration, discrimination, and health research among Mexicans in the United States. *Social Science & Medicine, 65,* 1524–1535.

Walker, R. L. (2007). Acculturation and assimilation stress as indicators of suicide risk among African Americans. *American Journal of Orthopsychiatry, 77,* 386–391.

Walters, K. L., Simoni, J. M., & Evans-Campbell, T. (2002). Substance use among American Indians and Alaska Natives: Incorporating culture in an "indigenist" stress-coping paradigm. *Public Health Reports, 117*(Suppl. 1), S104–S117.

Warner, L. A., Valdez, A., Vega, W. A., de la Rosa, M., Turner, R. J., & Canino, G. (2006). Latino drug abuse in an evolving cultural context: An agenda for research. *Drug and Alcohol Dependence, 84*(Suppl. 1), S8–S16.

Weisskirch, R. S. (2005). The relationship of language brokering to ethnic identity for Latino early adolescents. *Hispanic Journal of Behavioral Sciences, 27,* 286–299.

Wills, T. A., Murry, V. M., Brody, G. H., Gibbons, F. X., Gerrard, M., Walker, C., & Ainette, M. G. (2007). Ethnic pride and self-control related to protective and risk factors: Test of the theoretical model for the Strong African American Families Program. *Health Psychology, 26,* 50–59.

Wynn, S. R., Schulenberg, J., Maggs, J. L. & Zucker, R. A. (2000). Preventing alcohol misuse: The impact of refusal skills and norms. *Psychology of Addictive Behaviors, 14,* 36–47.

Zhou, M. (1997). Growing up American: The challenge confronting immigrant children and children of immigrants. *Annual Review of Sociology, 23,* 63–95.

CHAPTER 17

DRUG ABUSE RESEARCH: ADDRESSING THE NEEDS OF RACIAL AND ETHNIC MINORITY POPULATIONS

Lula A. Beatty

There is little overall difference by race or ethnicity in the prevalence rate of drug use in the United States (Substance Abuse and Mental Health Services Administration, 2002); however, there are a number of notable differences between groups in drug use patterns, preferences, risk factors, and reported drug consequences (National Institute on Drug Abuse, 2003). These differences in experience and consequences have had a tremendous deleterious impact on racial and ethnic minority individuals and communities. To create appropriate and acceptable interventions, educational programs, and viable policies, research must be specific to the realities and circumstances of each racial and ethnic minority group. The purpose of this chapter is to address four questions:

1. Why is it necessary to conduct drug abuse research specific to racial and ethnic minority populations?
2. What are the major obstacles to conducting drug abuse research with racial and ethnic minority populations?
3. How has the National Institute on Drug Abuse (NIDA) encouraged research on drug abuse in racial and ethnic minority populations? and
4. What are continuing research needs related to drug abuse and addiction in racial and ethnic minority populations?

In addressing these four pressing issues, I use the past experiences of NIDA and the National Institutes of Health (NIH) to illustrate certain points. NIH is the federal agency charged with the development of scientific medical research that will improve the health of the nation. NIDA, an institute within NIH, focuses on the problem of drug abuse and addiction and provides the majority of the country's support for research on the health-related aspects of drug abuse and addiction.

NECESSITY OF DRUG ABUSE RESEARCH FOR RACIAL AND ETHNIC MINORITY POPULATIONS

Federal Initiatives

Even as the nation's overall health has improved, disparities in health by race and ethnicity have long been acknowledged in this country. In 1985, the *Report of the Secretary's Task Force on Black and Minority Health* was released (U.S. Department of Health and Human Services, 1985). The report, developed under the leadership of the deputy director of NIH at the time, documented significant differences in the burden of morbidity and mortality experienced by Blacks and other racial and ethnic minority groups.

The Task Force on Black and Minority Health developed the concept of excess deaths, a novel statistical technique, to illustrate the deaths that would not have occurred if the minority population of the same age and sex as the White population had the same death rate as the White population. Approximately 60,000 excess deaths were reported. Nearly 80% of these were found to be related to six

The opinions expressed herein are the personal views of the author and do not necessarily reflect those of the National Institute on Drug Abuse or the National Institutes of Health (and are not endorsed thereby).

causes, specifically, cancer, cardiovascular disease and stroke, chemical dependency related to cirrhosis of the liver, diabetes, homicides and accidents, and infant mortality. The task force recommended that these health conditions become national priorities. Subsequently, an agenda was proposed for the country to address health disparities primarily through concerted efforts to improve health care and education.

Not all racial and ethnic minority groups were equally affected by each of these diseases. Moreover, gender and age contributed to the difference in excess deaths within different racial and ethnic groups. For example, cardiovascular diseases accounted for 24% of excess mortality among Black men and for 41% among Black women. Homicides accounted for 60% of excess mortality among Hispanics who were younger than 65, and unintentional injuries accounted for 44% of excess deaths among male, and 30% among female, Native Americans. Cirrhosis of the liver associated with excessive use of alcohol accounted for 13% of excess mortality among Native American men and 22% among Native American women under age 70 (Centers for Disease Control, 1986). Valid data on all of the major racial and ethnic groups were not always available, owing to insufficient epidemiological data collection methods in racial and ethnic minority communities.

In the late 1990s, based on reports of and concerns about disparities in health experienced by racial and ethnic minority groups, the U.S. Congress requested that the Institute of Medicine conduct a study to assess differences in the kind and quality of health care received by U.S. racial and ethnic minorities and nonminorities. Following an extensive review, the IOM released its findings in a book titled *Unequal Treatment: Confronting Racial and Ethnic Disparities in Health Care* (Smedley, Stith, & Nelson, 2003), which clearly indicated consistent evidence of racial and ethnic disparities in disease and health care. The IOM findings and other political activities eventually led Congress in 2000 to pass the Minority Health and Health Disparities Research and Education Act of 2000 to address "the significant disparity in the overall rate of disease incidence, prevalence, morbidity, mortality or survival rates." The act required federal agencies with health-related mandates to develop strategies

to reduce or eliminate health disparities. As part of its commitment to this goal, each NIH institute, including NIDA, had to develop a strategic plan to eliminate health disparities. Each plan had to address research, research capability and infrastructure, dissemination, and outreach.

The diseases and health concerns highlighted by NIH in its health disparities strategic plan of 2002–2006 (National Institutes of Health, n.d.) still reinforce striking disparities in the same designated areas and a few others not highlighted in the 1985 *Report of the Secretary's Task Force on Black and Minority Health* (U.S. Department of Health and Human Services, 1985): shorter life expectancy and higher rates of cardiovascular disease, cancer, infant mortality, birth defects, asthma, diabetes, stroke, sexually transmitted diseases, and mental illness.

Each of these major federal plans for action acknowledges the persistence of the differences in the experience of illness, death, and health care that can easily be attributable to race or ethnicity. What may be more perplexing is their degree of persistence given the long-term recognition and awareness of these differences and previous efforts to address them. Challenges encountered in reaching these overall goals include the difficulty of accounting for the complex interactions of individual, economic, social, and political factors and the adequacy of data sources (Murray et al., 2006) and the intricacies of classifying race and ethnicity in public health research (Mays, Ponce, Washington, & Cochran, 2004).

Drug Abuse and Health

NIDA (n.d.) states in its health disparities plan that

> based on the epidemiologic data, racial/ethnic minority populations are consistently and greatly overrepresented in the United States as (1) groups who suffer disproportionately from the consequences of drug use and addiction, or (2) groups for whom we have little good scientific data about their drug use but for whom there are disturbing prevention, therapeutic, and service concerns.

The plan notes, as examples, the great increase in HIV and other medical consequences of drug use among African Americans from the mid-1980s to the present (e.g., African Americans make up about 12% of the U.S. population but more than half of the new HIV/AIDS cases), the limited epidemiologic data available for Asian Americans (even as some local data and the reports of clinicians and service providers working in those communities suggest that drug use and addiction is a hidden and growing problem), and the lack of knowledge specific to groups of different ethnicity or country of origin within the broader racial and ethnic classification of Asian American/Pacific Islander.

Although drug abuse and addiction were not emphasized in the 1985 Secretary's Report or the 2000 IOM report on health disparities, drug use is related to six of the nine actual causes of death cited by Mokdad, Marks, Stroup, and Geberding (2004): licit drug use (tobacco and alcohol) and illicit drug use and behaviors often associated with drug use (sexual behavior, firearms, and motor vehicle accidents). The relatively few overall differences in the incidence and prevalence of drug use and abuse by race or ethnicity may be one reason why drug use and addiction were not emphasized in these reports. That is, there may be differences by racial and ethnic minority groups in factors such as age of initiation of use, drugs most commonly used, and progression to problem use; however, overall lifetime use of drugs is about the same for all racial and ethnic groups. Research has revealed, however, that there are important disparities in consequences or outcomes of drug use that have a differential impact on the health and well-being of racial and ethnic minority groups. For example, Barnes and Welte (1986) found that even though White youth reported higher drinking rates, Black and Hispanic youth experienced more social problems as a result of drinking than did White youth. Drug use and related behaviors have led to much higher rates of HIV and criminal justice involvement in African Americans (Beatty, Jones, & Doctor, 2005). Minority youth whose drug use patterns are similar to those of Whites are more likely to be arrested and treated more severely by the juvenile justice system (Belenko, Sprott, & Petersen, 2004). Some have also suggested that the War on Drugs has disproportionately affected the health and well-being of minority communities by using sanctions or penal-

ties that exacerbate problems in gaining access to health and housing benefits (Drug Policy Research Center, 2001).

Inclusion in Research Studies

A long-standing premise of scientific research is that all groups of concern be adequately included in research studies. The need for such broad inclusion is even more pronounced in public health research and in countries in which there is great diversity in population groups and great disparities and inequities in health and other social indicators of well-being directly associated with membership in racial and ethnic minority populations. In 1994, the NIH issued formal guidelines requiring investigators to address the appropriate inclusion of women and minorities in research involving human participants (Corbie-Smith, Miller, & Ransohoff, 2004). Implementing this policy has proven to be difficult particularly for minority populations for a number of reasons, including investigator access to participants, effectiveness of recruitment efforts, and participant willingness to participate in research (Corbie-Smith et al., 2001; Miranda, Nakamura, & Bernal, 2003; Wendler et al., 2006). In 2001, the NIH reissued the guidelines to clarify their purpose and provide additional guidance on reporting analyses of sex–gender and race–ethnicity. Despite implementation difficulties, the need for inclusion of racial minorities (and women and children as underrepresented groups) has not been seriously disputed. For drug use studies, in which prevention and treatment efforts are to some degree dependent on drug use patterns and drug preferences, it is even more critical to understand the epidemiology and etiology of drug abuse for each racial and ethnic group.

OBSTACLES TO CONDUCTING DRUG ABUSE RESEARCH IN RACIAL AND ETHNIC MINORITY COMMUNITIES

A number of long-standing issues have made conducting research on minority populations difficult. The Council of National Psychological Associations for the Advancement of Ethnic Minority Interests (2000) identified conceptual, methodological, and interpretational considerations and an inattention to historical and sociocultural realities as barriers to research with racial and ethnic minority population groups. These barriers were specified for each population group. For example, Asian American/Pacific Islander concerns included their underrepresentation in research, the lack of recognition that they are arguably the most diverse racial and ethnic group in the United States, the lack of standardized measures, and difficulty in obtaining representative samples. American Indian concerns included the exclusion of American Indians in the development of the research, the intent of the research, attending to acculturation and biculturalism, and geographical representation.

NIDA established working groups of scholars and researchers expert in drug abuse research to provide advice and recommendations on drug abuse research needs for the African American/Black, Asian American/Pacific Islander, Hispanic, and Native American/Alaska Native racial and ethnic minority populations. The groups are convened periodically by NIDA to discuss drug abuse and addiction concerns of the groups they represent, identify research and training needs, and make recommendations to NIDA. They all expressed some common research needs and concerns that paralleled the assessment of the Council of National Psychological Associations for the Advancement of Ethnic Minority Interests. These needs include having or gaining access to racial and ethnic minority people as research participants; mistrust of research and researchers by minority populations; use of inappropriate measures or measures not validated for use with the population; insufficient sample sizes that limit statistical power; language and translation barriers; the exclusion of culture in theories or models and other factors and variables germane to the experiences of specific racial and ethnic groups; and assumptions of universality.

They all agreed that research needs to include members from the respective groups in research studies and, more important, that inclusion alone is not adequate to provide a good knowledge base for responsive and effective prevention and interventions. Research needs to focus on the specific factors that influence drug use and addiction in each of the racial and ethnic minority groups. For example,

members of the National Hispanic Science Network on Drug Abuse (Hispanic work group) discussed research needs and opportunities in Hispanic populations in a special issue of *Drug and Alcohol Dependence* (Amaro & Iguchi, 2006). Topics discussed included addressing the cultural context of drug abuse, biological research, HIV transmission, treatment and services, and research dissemination. The African American Researchers and Scholars Group identified HIV prevention and criminal justice consequences of drug use as high research priorities. The Native American/Alaska Native and Asian American/Pacific Islander groups have both noted the low number of studies that include participants from their populations and the need for much better epidemiologic studies that emphasize factors relevant to their respective racial groups.

Another common concern is the need to recognize the diversity of people captured within each of the major racial and ethnic categories and to design studies, recruit participants, and conduct analyses using these smaller population or cultural groups. Lumping people into the same large racial and ethnic group category may cloud or hide important findings pertinent to their drug use. So, for example, there may be significant differences in drug use patterns, responsiveness to prevention, and treatment interventions between Mexicans and Cubans, although both are regarded as Hispanic. Similarly, not distinguishing among the hundreds of tribes or nations of Native Americans/Alaska Natives may affect the validity of findings when applied to any one community group. Other discussions on similar issues are available (e.g., Amaro & Iguichi, 2003; De La Rosa & Adrados, 1993).

Drug abuse research in minority communities has been especially affected by the following issues.

Conceptual and Theoretical Models

Over the past 30 years, research has been successful in developing drug abuse prevention and intervention programs (NIDA, 2004). An overriding characteristic of successful programs is that they have strong conceptual or theoretical underpinnings. NIDA's prevention and treatment guides (NIDA, 1999, 2004) and the Substance Abuse and Mental Health Services

Administration's (SAMHSA's; n.d.) listing of evidence-based best practice models are all based on research with strong conceptual models. The extent to which these models specifically included testing for cultural appropriateness varies; however, NIDA and SAMHSA have both affirmed the need for research and programs to be culturally appropriate and adapted to meet the needs of each racial and ethnic group.

Research has shown that culturally specific or adapted interventions enhance effectiveness with racial and ethnic populations. A meta-analysis of 76 outcome studies of mental health therapies found that mental health therapies culturally adapted for specific racial and ethnic client groups were more effective (Griner & Smith, 2006). A cultural enhancement of a NIDA standard intervention led to success in getting African Americans and Puerto Ricans into drug treatment, although the cultural enhancement showed no other greater benefits than the standard intervention (Dushay, Singer, Weeks, Rohena, & Gruber, 2001). Cultural adaptations of generic risky behavior prevention programs have been reported to increase retention (Kumpfer, Alvarada, Smith, & Bellamy, 2002), involvement and retention (Aktan, 1999), and participant satisfaction (Chipungu, Hermann, & Sambrano, 2000).

Culture has been defined as the "innumerable aspects of life . . . that encompass the behaviors, beliefs, and attitudes that are characteristic of a particular society or population" (Ember & Ember, 1977, p. 23). It is a construct that has proven elusive to the rigors of scientific research (see chap. 16 of this volume). Wilson and Miller (2003) conducted a review of articles published between 1985 and 2001 to discover how culture was defined or measured in studies that claimed culture as a component of HIV interventions. They found that the overwhelming majority of the studies did not define culture. When it was defined, it was found to be synonymous with membership in a racial or ethnic group category. Accepting membership in an racial or ethnic group as a sufficient measure of culture leads to "ethnic gloss," or the "overgeneralization or simplistic categorical label used to refer to ethnocultural groups such as American Indians, Asian Americans, Hispanics, and African Americans and nationalistic or indigenous groups where unique cultural and ethnic differences found among group members are ignored" (Trimble & Dickson, 2005, p. 412).

This gap in our understanding of the role of culture derives primarily from the absence of a concerted research agenda that tests either etiology or prevention with racial minority groups. The universality of a theory must be tested; it cannot be assumed. Examples of theories with demonstrated effectiveness in prevention include Bandura's (1977, 1986) social learning and self-efficacy model (Bandura, 1977, 1986), which informed the Life Skills Training model (Botvin, Baker, Dusenbury, Tortu, & Botvin, 1990); problem behavior theory (Jessor & Jessor, 1977); the theory of reasoned action (Fishbein & Middlestadt, 1989); and the transtheoretical model of behavior change (Prochaska, DiClemente, & Norcross, 1992). These theories can sometimes be combined with other conceptual frameworks to account for the cultural experiences of racial and ethnic groups. For example, Belgrave (2002) developed Project Naja, a risky behavior prevention program for African American girls. The program used a standard intervention model based on Life Skills Training and other theories. Afrocentric cultural enhancements were added, including African music, dress, and dance; use of traditional rituals; and exposure to Afrocentric values. In a related vein, Native American researchers have emphasized the role of historical trauma in understanding addiction in American Indians (Evans-Campbell & Walters, 2006).

In addition to focusing on individual-level risk and protective factors, the field recognizes the need to extend theory beyond the individual and family to focus on understanding structural intervention approaches (Cohen, Scribner, & Farley, 2000; Smedley & Syme, 2001) and the complex interaction of biological and environmental factors (Volkow, Fowler, & Wang, 2003).

Inclusion and Geographic Distribution

As previously indicated, the NIH established guidelines to increase the participation of racial and ethnic minority populations in federally sponsored research. The participation rates of racial and ethnic minority populations in drug abuse research vary from group to group. On the basis of NIDA and NIH data on the reported race and ethnicity of research participants, it appears that African American and Hispanic populations are more likely to be represented in NIDA-sponsored research and drug abuse research in general. There are fewer NIDA-sponsored studies of Asian Americans/Pacific Islanders and Native Americans/Alaska Natives.

No group in all of its diversity, however, is well represented in research, including drug abuse research. Differences within each racial and ethnic group have been masked by focusing on the larger group membership category. This is more likely to be seen when a White sample is used as a comparison group. There is great diversity of clinical significance within the different racial and ethnic groups that can be lost if attention is not paid to the full range of contextual factors contributing to drug use (Szapocznik, Prado, Burlew, Williams, & Santisteban, 2007). African Americans also vary in their ethnic and cultural diversity. Collapsing individuals from Africa, the Caribbean, and other countries under the African American/Black category may obscure important differences. One study (Broman, Neighbors, Delva, Torres & Jackson, 2008) found that overall rates of substance use disorders among African Americans and Caribbean Blacks were not significantly different; however, there were differences by gender, age, place of residence, and time in the United States. For example, prevalence rates among African Americans exceeded that of Caribbean Blacks in women and those who were divorced. African Americans in the South had lower rates than African Americans living in other places.

Asian Americans may not often be the focus of addiction research because they are perceived as being a "model" group. Their low reported prevalence rates of drug use (with the exception of cigarettes and other chew substances) often skew distributions and prohibit analyses using this racial category. Members of NIDA's expert work group have argued that epidemiologic data are needed to ascertain the true rates of use within this population group by specific nationality and to include sufficient numbers so that separate analyses can be done.

Native Americans/Alaska Natives present other special challenges regarding their inclusion in research, for example, gaining tribal approval and remote locations of communities. There is a great need for drug abuse–related research with Native Americans/Alaska Natives because data have indicated, for example, an increasingly high rate of methamphetamine use among some Native Americans (National Congress of American Indians, 2007).

Drug abuse research often focuses on school-age children, urban and suburban youth, and economically poorer communities. High drop-out rates may lower the number of racial and ethnic minority youth, especially those who are Hispanic, participating in school-based studies or may not reach those at most risk within the populations (Amaro & Cortes, 2003). This means that the youth most in need of prevention and those most at risk for school failure are not available for further study. More studies are needed on rural and frontier groups, which would include people living on reservations (Robertson, Sloboda, Boyd, Beatty, & Kozel, 1997). Rural populations are extremely hard to reach, given the physical barriers, distance from home to school, lack of transportation, and concerns with anonymity. Because socioeconomic status is a significant predictor of disease and health outcomes, it is important to be able to examine its influence on drug use and addiction. Socioeconomic status is seldom controlled in drug abuse research with any population group, minority or nonminority. The research community has begun to pay closer attention to gender issues in drug abuse research, but there is still a need for more attention to the concerns of girls and women from racial and ethnic minority populations (Scott, Gilliam, & Braxton, 2005).

Racial and ethnic minority populations are generally not randomly distributed in the United States. Housing for racial minorities is still segregated into distinct, separate neighborhoods. In this respect, the recruitment of racial and ethnic minorities into research studies may need different strategies to maintain sampling and statistical requirements. Researchers at the University of Michigan have developed unique strategies to include a nationally representative sample of diverse African Americans in their studies (Jackson, Neighbors, Nesse, Trierweller, & Torres, 2004).

Mistrust and Stigma

A common concern across groups is mistrust of research and stigma attached to drug abuse in particular. African Americans and Native Americans have historically expressed concerns about research, especially government-based research. The Tuskegee syphilis study, which withheld medical treatment from Black men, is often used as an example to illustrate African American mistrust (Jones, 1981; White, 2005). Native Americans have cited the numerous broken treaties and abuse at boarding schools as examples of reasons to not trust government-sponsored work. Racial and ethnic minorities are concerned about how research will be conducted, interpreted, presented, and used and the limited participation of community members involved in the research process (Council of National Psychological Associations for the Advancement of Ethnic Minority Interests, 2000; Washington, 2006).

Drug addiction is a stigmatized disease that is associated with poorer health outcomes (Ahern, Stuber, & Galea, 2007). The stigma associated with drug abuse and HIV influences the degree to which individuals will seek treatment and participate in research and programs. In African American populations, for example, the stigma associated with HIV and perceived rejection by family, friends, employers, and so forth has hindered prevention efforts. In smaller communities in which confidentiality may be assured but anonymity is difficult to guarantee (and many racial and ethnic minority individuals dwell in smaller, more intimate neighborhoods and communities), the perceived risk of participation may be great. Social norms around such concerns as the appropriateness of revealing personal and family information (common in certain Asian communities) and the morality of drug use and homosexuality can affect research participation, especially epidemiologic, prevention, and services research.

Measures and Instruments

There is a need to have measures that are appropriate and valid for the participant groups. This ranges from instruments that have been properly translated into the language of the participants to instruments with demonstrated reliability and validity for the group under study. Measures that do not behave similarly for the different racial and ethnic groups will not be sensitive to group-based change or detect subtle differences in performance. The performance of measures may vary between cultural or racial groups, leading to erroneous conclusions about underlying psychological causation or, conversely, benefits from interventions (Hui & Triandis, 1985). The potential for "differential item bias" is a major reason for establishing measurement equivalence between racial groups before engaging in intervention-based studies (Drasgow & Kanfer, 1985; Knight & Hill, 1998).

Review

NIDA's expert work group members have expressed concerns with the scientific review process. They believe that a good scholarly and egalitarian review is necessary, but also that review committees need a better understanding of cultural issues and to know more about research concerns that can affect investigations with racial and ethnic minority populations. These concerns include knowledge of cultural factors appropriate to the group, validity of the measures and instruments, appropriateness of the design and statistical analyses, and overall value of the research proposed. Another related issue is the lack of scientific consensus on the proper conduct of health disparity research. Adler (2006) provided an overview of some of the major challenges in addressing health disparities research, including lack of consensus on definitions of health disparities and minority group membership, and adequacy of conceptual approaches—challenges that can affect consensus in review.

Researchers

Researchers who are conducting studies on racial and ethnic minority issues need to be well informed about the population and properly trained in health disparity research. The nonarticulation of cultural hypotheses and poor representation of variables in research that goes beyond racial and ethnicity membership (Wilson & Miller, 2003) may reflect this lack of awareness and lack of scientific consensus on how to best conduct research with these populations.

Minimum knowledge should include basic facts about the group's history and experience in this country, familiarity with the strengths and weaknesses of extant research, and the merit and limitations of proposed research designs and measures.

There is also a need for greater participation of researchers from each of the racial and ethnic groups. The inclusion of racial minority investigators may add legitimacy to the research, strengthen ties to the community, and bring an awareness and greater knowledge of the history and status of the community. Researchers from the community may hold longer term interests and ties to the community. This is not only helpful in conducting the research but also may provide a conduit for dissemination of findings back to the community.

NIDA'S EFFORTS TO IMPROVE KNOWLEDGE ON DRUG ABUSE IN RACIAL AND ETHNIC MINORITY POPULATIONS

Over the past few decades, NIDA has implemented a number of initiatives, programs, and practices to address the needs identified above and to provide encouragement and support for increased drug abuse research in racial and ethnic minority populations. Examples of some of these efforts are presented.

Funding

In addition to its ongoing funding mechanisms, NIDA has offered funding opportunities specific to racial and ethnic minority health disparities research through the release of administrative supplements and funding opportunity announcements (program announcements). The funding outlets were specifically aimed at increasing the emphasis on racial and ethnic minority concerns and the inclusion of racial and ethnic minority populations in drug abuse research. There have been four such NIDA-wide funding opportunities since 2001.

In 2001, NIDA released a health disparities funding opportunity (Health Disparities: Drug Use and Its Adverse Behavioral, Social, Medical, and Mental Health Consequences). The purpose of this program was to stimulate epidemiological, prevention, treatment, and services research that

addresses issues relating to the differential drug use patterns and/or their associated behaviors and social, medical, and mental health consequences within and across racial and ethnic minority populations. Nine grants were awarded. In 2002, an administrative supplements program for health disparities research was released to allow current grantees to recruit additional study participants or expand analyses of existing cohorts that already have sufficient representation from various racial and ethnic populations to assess patterns of drug use, effects, and potential adverse behavioral, social, and health consequences or differential treatment outcomes within and across racial and ethnic groups. A total of 28 awards were made under this specific funding announcement. In 2005, six administrative supplements were provided for research on the intersection of drug use and criminal justice consequences in the African American population. In 2005, two funding opportunities were released to stimulate research on drug use, HIV, criminal justice involvement, and African Americans. They were titled Drug Abuse as a Cause, Correlate, or Consequence of Criminal Justice Related Health Disparities Among African Americans and Health Disparities in HIV/AIDS: Focus on African Americans. In 2007, seven administrative supplements were provided to support research on Asian American/Pacific Islander and Native American/Alaska Native populations.

All of the programs increased the inclusion of racial and ethnic minority populations in drug abuse, especially for Native Americans and Asian Americans. Furthermore, some of the funding mechanisms increased studies in research areas of special need and interest such as criminal justice and HIV in African Americans. Moreover, the research supported included a wide range of theoretical and conceptual frameworks and measures. Many of the studies used designs and analyses that compared groups by race or ethnicity, but some did allow for more within-group analyses. These studies are expected to contribute to the scientific knowledge base with findings that speak directly to drug abuse in racial and ethnic minority populations rather than being hidden as minor analyses as part of other research foci.

Researcher Development Programs

Research training is a major component of the funding portfolio at NIDA, as it is for all of NIH. NIDA has several long-term programs that focus specifically on preparing scholars from underrepresented minority populations for drug abuse research. These specialized training programs include the Diversity Supplement Program (an NIH-wide program formerly called the Minority Supplement Program), the Summer Research With NIDA program, the Seminar Series, and the Diversity—Promoting Institutions Drug Abuse Research Program (DIDARP), which for many was the Minority Institutions Drug Abuse Research Program (MIDARP). The Diversity Supplement Program gives support to current grantees to provide research experiences and mentoring to students and faculty from minority or health disparity populations who are underrepresented in biomedical research. Asian Americans are not underrepresented in biomedical research. NIDA, however, recognizes them as underrepresented in certain areas of clinical drug abuse research and has provided them support in these areas of underrepresentation. Support is provided at five different career stages (high school students, undergraduate students, graduate students, postdoctoral fellows, and faculty). NIDA requires that every applicant provide a mentoring plan in addition to the research plan, and applicants at the postdoctoral and investigator levels must include their plans for the development of a research application. Timelines are required.

Since 1994, NIDA has supported 489 people from racial and ethnic minority populations in the Diversity Supplement Program. The majority of the participants were women (67%), and most participants were at the predoctoral level (50%) of support, followed by the investigator/faculty (20%) and postdoctoral (20%) levels of support. Participants were more likely to be African American/Black (56%) or Hispanic (31%). Asian Americans made up approximately 5% of the program participants, as did Pacific Islanders. Native Americans were least likely to participate in the program (3%), although their rate of participation exceeded their approximately 1.5% representation in the U.S. population (Ogunwole, 2002).

Data access prohibitions and other restrictions limit the extent to which evaluations can be conducted of the NIH minority training programs (Committee for the Assessment of NIH Minority Research Training Programs, 2005). NIDA was able to explore the involvement of 72 diversity supplement recipients in the NIH research process for the years 1995 and 2000. Of the 72 recipients identified, 27 (37.5%) submitted applications to NIH for funding consideration. Of those submitting applications, 12 (44%) received a grant, and of that number, 8 (30%) had published (as identified through a PubMed search). These results indicate that the program demonstrates some success in encouraging independent research careers.

The Summer Research With NIDA program was started in 1997 as a pilot, offshoot program of the Diversity Supplement Program. It was created to bring high school and undergraduate students into the research career pipeline by assisting investigators with some of the added responsibilities–for example, recruitment, selection, and mentoring–encountered in working with younger, less experienced students. Selected students work with grantees for 6 to 10 weeks during the summer. Most grantees receive one student; however, support has been given to investigators to establish miniprograms that include an array of individual and group experiences. Since 1997, the summer program has supported 586 students. The majority of student participants were female (72%). About 65% were African American/Black, 17% were Hispanic, 13% were Asian American/Pacific Islander, and 5% were Native American. Most participants were enrolled in minority institutions or universities that are not research intensive. Common student experiences included working in laboratories, taking courses and attending seminars, and working on literature reviews. It has become a popular program with students and grantees as well, as indicated by their interest in serving as placement sites.

The Seminar Series was created in the mid-1980s. It provides intensive technical assistance to scholars and faculty members who are ready and in a position to apply for independent research awards. They participate in sessions that address scientific areas of interest, research development skills, and the grant review process. They also receive mentoring from NIDA staff and extramural scientists. An expectation of the program is that participants submit a grant proposal. A number of participants have secured support for drug abuse research from NIDA or other governmental and nongovernmental funding sources.

The DIDARP is a research capacity development grant program designed to increase the participation of colleges and universities with diversity goals and a little sponsored drug abuse research. Each DIDARP must have student, faculty, and institutional development components. Typically, NIDA supports about five to seven DIDARP programs annually. Progress reports indicate success across a range of indicators, including students entering graduate school with the intention of pursuing research, publications by graduate students and faculty, grants obtained by faculty, and additional research on minority health disparities issues.

A recent book (Scheier & Dewey, 2007) provides a comprehensive listing of all NIH grant, fellowship, and minority-focused funding mechanisms. The book compiles information about various training opportunities and international and minority supplements and addresses the internal workings of grants, along with how grants can attend to race as a focal concern (one chapter articulates specific aims from a grant that addressed ethnic-specific risk mechanisms).

The success of these and similar programs is vital to the NIH mission. NIDA's informal assessments and experience of its programs suggest that the programs have led to the increased participation of racial and ethnic minority scholars in applying for and receiving NIH grants and, on a larger scale, becoming involved in drug abuse research or other drug abuse–related activities outside of NIH. It is particularly striking that researchers participating in these programs usually pursue research relevant to racial and ethnic minority populations even when such interest is not required for program participation.

Initiatives in Response to Specific Needs

NIDA has undertaken initiatives in response to an urgent need identified though epidemiologic data or concerns identified by experts or key informants. In response to the great disparity in the prevalence of drug-related HIV/AIDS and criminalization on the African American/Black community, NIDA's director established an African American Initiative in 2004. The purpose of the initiative was to develop strategies

to increase the involvement of NIDA in this area. Activities developed as a part of this initiative included a scientific meeting held with presentations from NIDA-supported and other scholars who are expert in this area, a special issue of the *Journal of Health Care for the Poor and Underserved* (Beatty et al., 2005) devoted to the subject matter, and the development of two funding opportunity announcements. Moreover, NIDA staff and members of the NIDA African American Scholars and Researchers expert work group made presentations at professional meetings to increase awareness of the issue and held meetings for researchers, students, and health and human service professionals.

A concern with the underrepresentation of Native Americans as drug abuse researchers and as research participants and the reportedly high rates of methamphetamine and other substances in Native American/Alaska Native population led to NIDA staff developing strategies to understand and encourage research development for these communities. Collaboration with the Indian Health Service has been one approach taken. NIDA supports drug abuse–related research under the Native American Research Centers for Health sponsored by the Indian Health Service. In addition, NIDA staff have organized meetings focusing on Native American issues (e.g., methamphetamine use by Native Americans) and participated in workshops and conferences sponsored by Indian Health Service and Native American organizations.

Scientific Meetings

Scientific meetings are frequently held to fully explore the significance of the issue being addressed and to discuss the need and elements of a research agenda. In addition to the scientific meetings identified earlier that were part of specific initiatives, NIDA has sponsored, for example, two health disparities conferences in 2000 and 2005. In 2006, a meeting on Drug Use Trajectories Among African Americans brought together researchers from a variety of disciplines to consider the basis for the consistent finding of divergent trajectories in drug use between African Americans and their White counterparts. In addition, NIDA has provided financial support and staff participation to other groups holding meetings on racial and ethnic minority issues. For example, the National Hispanic Science Network holds an annual conference on issues germane to Hispanic/Latino populations and an annual research training workshop for students and researchers interested in research in that population.

Impact on the Field

NIDA efforts have contributed to increased and better quality research and publications on racial and ethnic minority health disparities. Some examples follow.

Life Skills Training is a cognitive–behavioral, skills-based, middle school drug abuse prevention program. Life Skills Training, developed by Gilbert J. Botvin, has had proven success with primarily White, suburban, middle-class youth (Botvin, Baker, Dusenbury, Botvin, & Diaz, 1995; Botvin, Baker, Dusenbury, et al., 1990; Botvin, Baker, Filazzola, & Botvin, 1990). In the early years of the program, its success with racial and ethnic minority youth was not known. Notwithstanding the success of this or any other program, the structural axioms that form the theoretical foundation of these programs must be particularized or made to operationally fit unique or special populations. In addition, measures that were psychometrically refined with White, middle-class youth must be tested for their appropriateness with racial minority youth. This was an important argument made when Botvin and colleagues responded to a NIDA funding opportunity to establish minority prevention centers and received support to establish the Multiethnic Drug Abuse Prevention Research Center. The purposes of the center were to determine the applicability and cultural appropriateness of the Life Skills Training program for racial and ethnic minority youth and to examine whether any special features of the program required modification to achieve broader application with inner-city, minority youth. Over time, an accumulation of studies reinforced the finding that the Life Skills Training program is highly efficacious with various racial and ethnic minority groups (Botvin et al., 1989; Botvin, Dusenbury, Baker, James-Ortiz, & Kerner, 1989; Botvin et al., 1992; Botvin, Epstein, Baker, Diaz, & Williams, 1997; Botvin, Griffin, Diaz, & Ifill-Williams, 2001; Botvin, Schinke, Epstein, & Diaz, 1994; Botvin, Schinke, Epstein, Diaz, & Botvin, 1995).

Current research studies appear to reflect a greater diversity of research participants, variables, and conceptual models that address more fully the role of race and culture. There also seems to be greater awareness of the issues on the part of researchers, with more publications emphasizing the role of race, ethnicity, and culture in drug abuse. Wong, a NIDA grantee and member of the NIDA Asian American/ Pacific Islander work group, has with his colleagues and students explored substance use and HIV awareness among Asian Americans and Pacific Islanders (So & Wong, 2006; Wong, Campsmith, Nakamura, Crepaz, & Begley, 2004). NIDA's October 28, 2005, issue of *News Scan* focused on health disparities research supported by NIDA. Research highlighted included work on gang membership; length of incarceration related to injection drug abuse among jailed Puerto Rican drug injectors; drugs as a factor in Hispanic teen suicide; drug abuse and HIV preventive interventions for Hispanic adolescents; smoking cessation in African Americans, Whites, and Hispanics; and preventing drug use in rural African Americans.

A special issue of the *Journal of Ethnicity in Substance Abuse*, "21st Century Research on Drugs and Ethnicity: Studies Supported by the National Institute on Drug Abuse" (Myers, 2007), featured the work of several NIDA investigators. This was not a NIDA-sponsored special issue but one that evolved when the editor noted that the papers accepted came from NIDA-supported research. The nine articles in the issue investigate treatment readiness; response of Native American clients to treatment methods for alcohol dependence; race, ethnicity, and gender differences among college students; acculturation; drug use among dually diagnosed Hispanic youth; field experiences in cultural adaptations; and the effect of neighborhood context on the drug use of American Indian youth. Native Americans were the focus of two of the articles and Hispanics were included in seven.

There are more researchers involved in health disparities research from underrepresented and majority populations and serving as mentors.

CONTINUING NEEDS

Although there has been significant progress in drug abuse research with racial and ethnic minority populations at NIDA and in the field in general, much work remains. Some major areas of need are as follows:

- better conceptualization and clearer operational definitions of culture;

- fuller representation of diversity within racial and ethnic population groups, including diversity by gender, age, socioeconomic status, national origin, and other factors determined to be critical to the population of interest;

- innovative research designs and statistical analyses to accommodate the scattered and nonrandom distribution of racial and ethnic minority groups in this country and the small sample sizes of certain groups;

- more studies that explore factors beyond individual characteristics and behaviors such as structural, environmental, and policy aspects of drug abuse;

- more studies that explore the interaction of the individual, family, genetic, structural, and other factors known to contribute to drug abuse;

- more dissemination and translational work on how to prepare health professionals and communities to accept and use proven prevention and treatment strategies; and

- ways to improve scientific reviews, perhaps through training of reviewers or the development of research resource guides for potential reviewers, and the exploration of the establishment of minimal expectations or standards regarding acceptable variations in models, methods, and analyses.

More researchers are needed who can develop a continued ongoing platform of studies involving racial minorities as participants and as investigators. Researchers of all races and ethnicities need to be skilled in conducting health disparities research. Faculty, graduate training programs, universities, and professional associations, among others, should provide training. Native American, Alaska Native, and Native Hawaiian and other Pacific Islander researchers are severely underrepresented in drug abuse research and should be encouraged to become involved.

More research is needed on translating research into practice for prevention and treatment. Better dissemination strategies should be developed.

Publishing in scientific journals is important, but more attention has to be paid to reaching a broader audience.

References

Adler, N. E. (2006). Overview of health disparities [Appendix D]. In G. E. Thomson, F. Mitchell, & M. Williams (Eds.), *Examining the health disparities research plan of the National Institutes of Health: Unfinished business* (pp. 121–174). Washington, DC: National Academies Press.

Ahern, J., Stuber, J., & Galea, S. (2007). Stigma, discrimination and the health of illicit drug users. *Drug and Alcohol Dependence, 88,* 188–196.

Aktan, G. (1999). A cultural consistency evaluation of a substance abuse prevention program with inner city African-American families. *Journal of Primary Prevention, 19,* 227–239.

Amaro, H., & Cortes, D. E. (Eds.). (2003). *National strategic plan on Hispanic drug abuse research: From the molecule to the community.* Boston: National Hispanic Science Network on Drug Abuse, Northeastern University Institute on Urban Health Research.

Amaro, H., & Iguichi, M. Y. (Eds.). (2006). Scientific opportunities in Hispanic drug abuse research [Special issue]. *Drug and Alcohol Dependence, 84*(Suppl. 1).

Bandura, A. (1977). *Social learning theory.* Englewood Cliffs, NJ: Prentice Hall.

Bandura, A. (1986). *Social foundations of thought and action: A social cognitive theory.* Englewood Cliffs, NJ: Prentice Hall.

Barnes, G. M., & Welte, J. W. (1986). Patterns and predictors of alcohol use among 7–12th grade students in New York state. *Journal of Studies on Alcohol, 47,* 53–62.

Beatty, L. A., Jones, D., & Doctor, L. (2005). Introduction. *Journal of Health Care for the Poor and Underserved, 16*(Suppl. B), 1–5.

Belenko, S., Sprott, J. B., & Petersen, C. (2004). Drug and alcohol involvement among minority and female juvenile offenders: Treatment and policy issues. *Criminal Justice Policy Review, 15,* 3–36.

Belgrave, F. Z. (2002). Relational theory and cultural enhancement interventions for African American adolescent girls. *Public Health Reports, 117*(Suppl. 1), S76–S81.

Botvin, G. J., Baker, E., Dusenbury, L., Botvin, E. M., & Diaz, T. (1995, April 12). Long-term follow-up results of a randomized drug abuse prevention trial in a White middle-class population. *JAMA, 273,* 1106–1112.

Botvin, G. J., Baker, E., Dusenbury, L., Tortu, S., & Botvin, E. M. (1990). Preventing adolescent drug abuse through a multimodal cognitive behavioral approach: Results of a 3-year study. *Journal of Consulting and Clinical Psychology 58,* 437–446.

Botvin, G. J., Baker, E., Filazzola, A., & Botvin, E. M. (1990). A cognitive-behavioral approach to substance abuse prevention: A one-year follow-up. *Addictive Behaviors 15,* 47–63.

Botvin, G. J., Batson, H., Witts-Vitale, S., Bess, V., Baker, E., & Dusenbury, L. (1989). A psychosocial approach to smoking prevention for urban black youth. *Public Health Reports, 104,* 573–582.

Botvin, G. J., Dusenbury, L., Baker, E., James-Ortiz, S., Botvin, E. M., & Kerner, J. (1992). Smoking prevention among urban minority youth: Assessing effects on outcome and mediating variables. *Health Psychology, 11,* 290–299.

Botvin, G. J., Dusenbury, L., Baker, E., James-Ortiz, S., & Kerner, J. (1989). A skills training approach to smoking prevention among Hispanic youth. *Journal of Behavioral Medicine, 12,* 279–296.

Botvin, G. J., Epstein, J. A., Baker, E., Diaz, T., & Williams, M. I. (1997). School-based drug abuse prevention with inner-city minority youth. *Journal of Child & Adolescent Substance Abuse, 6,* 5–19.

Botvin, G. J., Griffin, K. W., Diaz, T., & Ifill-Williams, M. (2001). Drug abuse prevention among minority adolescents: One-year follow-up of a school-based preventive intervention. *Prevention Science 2,* 1–13.

Botvin, G. J., Schinke, S. P., Epstein, J. A., & Diaz, T. (1994). Effectiveness of culturally focused and generic skills training approaches to alcohol and drug abuse prevention among minority youths. *Psychology of Addictive Behaviors, 8,* 116–127.

Botvin, G. J., Schinke, S. P., Epstein, J. A., Diaz, T., & Botvin, E. M. (1995). Effectiveness of culturally focused and generic skills training approaches to alcohol and drug abuse prevention among minority adolescents: Two-year follow-up results. *Psychology of Addictive Behaviors, 9,* 183–194.

Broman, D. L., Neighbors, H. W., Delva, J., Torres, M., & Jackson, J. S. (2008). Prevalence of substance use disorders among African Americans and Caribbean Blacks in the national survey of American life. *American Journal of Public Health, 98,* 1107–1114.

Centers for Disease Control. (1986). Perspectives in disease prevention and health promotion: Report of the secretary's task force on Black and minority health. *Morbidity and Mortality Weekly Report, 35,* 109–112.

Chipungu, S., Hermann, J., & Sambrano, S. (2000). Prevention programming for African American youth: A review of strategies in CSAP's national cross-site evaluation of high-risk youth programs. *Journal of Black Psychology, 26,* 360–385.

Cohen, D. A., Scribner, R. A., & Farley, T. A. (2000). A structural model of health behavior: A pragmatic approach to explain and influence health behaviors at the population level. *Preventive Medicine, 30,* 146–154.

Committee for the Assessment of NIH Minority Research Training Programs. (2005). *Assessment of NIH Minority Research and Training Programs: Phase 3.* Washington, DC: National Academies Press.

Corbie-Smith, G., Miller, W. C., & Ransohoff, D. F. (2004). Interpretations of "appropriate" minority inclusion in clinical research. *American Journal of Medicine, 116,* 249–252.

Council of National Psychological Associations for the Advancement of Ethnic Minority Interests. (2000). *Guidelines for research in ethnic minority communities.* Washington, DC: American Psychological Association.

De La Rosa, M. R., & Adrados, J.-L. R. (1993). *Drug abuse among minority youth: Advances in research and methodology* (NIDA Research Monograph 130). Rockville, MD: U.S. Department of Health and Human Services, National Institutes of Health, National Institute on Drug Abuse.

Drasgow, F., & Kanfer, R. (1985). Equivalence of psychological measurement in heterogeneous populations. *Journal of Applied Psychology, 70,* 662–680.

Drug Policy Research Center. (2001, June). *How the war on drugs influences the health and well-being of minority communities* [Newsletter]. Santa Monica, CA: Rand Drug Policy Research Center.

Dushay, R. A., Singer, M., Weeks, M. R., Rohena, L., & Gruber, R. (2001). Lowering HIV risk among ethnic minority drug users: Comparing a culturally targeted intervention to a standard intervention. *American Journal of Drug and Alcohol Abuse, 27,* 501–524.

Ember, C. R., & Ember, M. (1977). *Cultural anthropology.* Englewood Cliffs, NJ: Prentice-Hall.

Evans-Campbell, T., & Walters, K. L. (2006). Indigenist practice competencies in child welfare practice: A decolonization framework to address family violence, substance abuse, and historical trauma among First Nations peoples. In R. Fong, R. McRoy, & C. Ortiz Hendricks (Eds.), *Intersecting child welfare, substance abuse, and family violence: Culturally competent approaches* (pp. 266–290). Washington, DC: CSWE Press.

Fishbein, M., & Middlestadt, S. E. (1989). Using the theory of reasoned action as a framework for understanding and changing AIDS related behaviors. In V. M. Mays, G. W. Albee, & S. F. Schneider (Eds.), *Primary prevention of AIDS: Psychological approaches* (pp. 93–110). Newbury Park, CA: Sage.

Griffin, K. W., Scheier, L. M., Botvin, G. J., & Diaz, T. (2000). Ethnic and gender differences in psychosocial risk, protection, and adolescent alcohol use. *Prevention Science, 1,* 199–212.

Griner, D., & Smith, T. B. (2006). Culturally adapted mental health interventions: A meta-analytic review. *Psychotherapy: Theory, Research, Practice, Training, 43*, 531–548.

Hui, C. H., & Triandis, H. C. (1985). Measurement in cross-cultural psychology: A review and comparison of strategies. *Journal of Cross-Cultural Psychology, 16*, 131–152.

Jackson, J. S., Neighbors, H. W., Nesse, R. M., Trierweiler, S. G., & Torres, M. (2004). Methodological innovations in the national survey of American life. *International Journal of Methods in Psychiatric Research, 13*, 289–298.

Jessor, R., & Jessor, S. L. (1977). *Problem behavior and psychosocial development: A longitudinal study of youth.* New York: Academic Press.

Jones, J. (1981). *Bad blood: The Tuskegee syphilis experiment: A tragedy of race and medicine.* New York: Free Press.

Knight, G. P., & Hill, N. E. (1998). Measurement equivalence in research involving minority adolescents. In V. V. McLoyd & L. Steinberg (Eds.), *Studying minority adolescents: Conceptual, methodological, and theoretical issues* (pp. 183–210). Mahwah, NJ: Erlbaum.

Kumpfer, K., Alvarado, R., Smith, P., & Bellamy, N. (2002). Cultural sensitivity and adaptation in family-based prevention interventions. *Prevention Science, 3*, 241–246.

Mays, V. M., Ponce, N. A., Washington, D. L., & Cochran, S. D. (2003). Classification of race and ethnicity: Implications for public health. *Annual Review of Public Health, 24*, 83–110.

Minority Health and Health Disparities Research and Education Act of 2000, Pub. L. No. 106-525, 114 Stat. 2495 (2000).

Miranda, J., Nakamura, R., & Bernal, G. (2003). Including ethnic minorities in mental health intervention research: A practical approach to a long-standing problem. *Culture, Medicine and Psychiatry, 27*, 467–486.

Mokdad, A. H., Marks, J. S., Stroup, D. F., & Gerberding, J. L. (2004, March 10). Actual causes of death in the United States, 2000. *JAMA, 291*, 1238–1245.

Murray, C. J. L., Kulkarni, S. C., Michaud, C., Tomijima, N., Bulzacchelli, M. T., Iandiorio, T. J., & Ezzati, M. (2006). Eight Americas: Investigating mortality disparities across races, counties, and race–counties in the United States. *PloS Medicine, 3*, 1513–1524.

Myers, P. L. (Ed.). (2007). 21st century research on drugs and ethnicity: Studies supported by the National Institute on Drug Abuse [Special issue]. *Journal of Ethnicity in Substance Abuse, 6*(2).

National Congress of American Indians. (2007). *Methamphetamines in Indian country: An American problem uniquely affecting Indian country.* Retrieved on January 26, 2008, from http://ncai.org/ncai/Meth/Meth_in_Indian_Country_Fact_Sheet.pdf

National Institute on Drug Abuse. (1999). *Principles of drug addiction treatment: A research-based guide* (NIH Publication No. 99-4180). Rockville, MD: National Institutes of Health.

National Institute on Drug Abuse. (2003). *Drug use among racial/ethnic minorities* (NIH Publication No. 03-3888). Bethesda, MD: U.S. Department of Health and Human Services, National Institutes of Health, National Institute on Drug Abuse.

National Institute on Drug Abuse. (2004). *Preventing drug use among children and adolescents: A research-based guide for parents, educators, and community leaders* (2nd ed., NIH Publication No. 04-4212[A]). Rockville, MD: National Institutes of Health.

National Institute on Drug Abuse. (2005). *News scan: Health disparities research.* Bethesda, MD: National Institutes of Health, National Institute on Drug Abuse.

National Institute on Drug Abuse (n.d.). *Strategic plan on reducing health disparities.* Retrieved January 23, 2008, from http://www.drugabuse.gov/strategicplan/healthstratplan.html

National Institutes of Health. (2001). *NIH policy on reporting race and ethnicity data: Subjects in clinical research.* Bethesda, MD: U.S. Department of Health and Human Services. Retrieved January 23, 2008, from http://grants1.nih.gov/grants/guide/notice-files/NOT-OD-01-053.html

National Institutes of Health. (n.d.). *Strategic plan.* Retrieved January 23, 2008, from http://ncmhd.nih.gov/our_programs/strategic/index.asp

Ogunwole, S. U. (2002). *The American Indian and Alaska Native Population: 2000* [Census 2000 Brief]. Washington, DC: U.S. Department of Commerce, Economics and Statistics Administration, U.S. Census Bureau. Retrieved January 28, 2008, from http://factfinder.census.gov/jsp/saff/SAFFInfo.jsp?_pageId=tp9_race_ethnicity

Prochaska, J. O., DiClemente, C. C., & Norcross, J. C. (1992). In search of how people change: Applications to addictive behaviors. *American Psychologist, 47*, 1102–1114.

Robertson, E. B., Sloboda, Z., Boyd, G. M., Beatty, L., & Kozel, N. J. (Eds.). (1997). *Rural substance abuse: State of knowledge and issues* (NIDA Research Monograph 168). Rockville, MD: U.S. Department of Health and Human Services, National Institutes of Health.

Scheier, L. M., & Dewey, W. L. (Eds.). (2007). *The complete writing guide to NIH behavioral science grants.* New York: Oxford University Press.

Scott, K. D., Gilliam, A., & Braxton, K. (2005). Culturally competent HIV prevention strategies for women of color in the United States. *Health Care for Women International, 26,* 17–45.

Smedley, B. C., & Syme, S. L. (2001). Promoting health: Intervention strategies from social and behavioral research. *American Journal of Health Promotion, 15,* 149–166.

Smedley, B. C., Stith, A. Y., & Nelson, A. R. (Eds.). (2003). *Unequal treatment: Confronting racial and ethnic disparities in health care.* Washington, DC: National Academies Press.

So, D. W., & Wong, F. Y. (2006). Alcohol, drugs, and substance use among Asian-American college students. *Journal of Psychoactive Drugs, 38,* 35–42.

Substance Abuse and Mental Health Services Administration. (2002). *Results from the 2001 national household survey on drug abuse: Volume I. Summary of national findings* (DHHS Publication No. [SMA] 02-3758). Rockville, MD: Substance Abuse and Mental Health Services Administration, Office of Applied Studies.

Substance Abuse and Mental Health Services Administration. (n.d.). *SAMHSA's national registry of evidence-based programs and practices.* Retrieved January 28, 2008, from http://www.nrepp.samhsa.gov

Szapocznik, J., Prado, G., Burlew, A. K., Williams, R. A., & Santisteban, D. A. (2007). Drug abuse in African American and Hispanic adolescents: Culture, development, and behavior. *Annual Review of Clinical Psychology, 3,* 77–105.

Trimble, J. E., & Dickson, R. (2005). Ethnic gloss. In C. B. Fisher & R. M. Lerner (Eds.), *Encyclopedia of applied developmental science* (Vol. 1, pp. 412–415). Thousand Oaks, CA: Sage.

U.S. Department of Health and Human Services. (1985). *Report of the secretary's task force on Black and minority health.* Washington, DC: U.S. Government Printing Office.

Volkow, N. D., Fowler, J. S., & Wang, F. (2003) The addicted human brain: Insights from imaging studies. *Journal of Clinical Investigation, 111,* 1444–1451.

Washington, H. A. (2006). *Medical apartheid: The dark history of medical experimentation on Black Americans from colonial times to the present.* New York: Harlem Moon.

Wendler, D., Kington, R., Madans, J., Van Wye, G., Christ-Schmidt, H., Pratt, L. A., et al. (2006). Are racial and ethnic minorities less willing to participate in health research? *PLOS Medicine, 3,* 201–210. Retrieved January 23, 2008, from http://medicine.plosjournals.org/perlserv/?request=get-document&doi=10.1371/journal.pmed.0030019&ct=1

White, R. M. (2005). Misinformation and misbeliefs in the Tuskegee study of untreated syphilis fuel mistrust in the healthcare system. *Journal of the National Medical Association, 97,* 1566–1573.

Wilson, B. D. M., & Miller, R. L. (2003). Examining strategies for culturally grounded HIV prevention: A review. *AIDS Education and Prevention, 15,* 184–202.

Wong, F. Y., Campsmith, M. L., Nakamura, G. V., Crepaz, N., & Begley, E. (2004). HIV testing and awareness of care-related services among a group of HIV-positive Asian Americans and Pacific Islanders in the United States: Findings from a supplemental HIV/AIDS surveillance project. *AIDS Education and Prevention, 16,* 440–447.

CHAPTER 18

RACIAL DISCRIMINATION AND SUBSTANCE ABUSE: RISK AND PROTECTIVE FACTORS IN AFRICAN AMERICAN ADOLESCENTS

Frederick X. Gibbons, Elizabeth A. Pomery, and Meg Gerrard

One of the more interesting paradoxes in the adolescent substance use literature has to do with rates of drug use by minority versus White youth. Minority adolescents, especially Black adolescents, start using substances later than White youth, and they tend to use them less frequently (White, Nagin, Replogle, & Stouthame-Loeber, 2004), in spite of the fact that they are more likely than White adolescents to be raised in low–socioeconomic status (SES) environments that are high in risk factors (i.e., more substance availability; Ardelt & Eccles, 2001) and they encounter more sources of stress (i.e., financial, social, and physical risk), all of which are associated with increased substance use (Lambert, Brown, Phillips, & Ialongo, 2005). Black adolescents are also exposed to another source of stress that many have suggested is associated with increased drug use: perceived racial discrimination. In this chapter, we focus on the link between discrimination and substance use in African American adolescents and young adults.

We begin this chapter with a brief review of the literature on trajectories of substance use among African American adolescents, including some discussion of factors thought to increase and decrease risk for use. We then broaden our perspective to include a discussion of our own work in this area, beginning with a description of the theoretical model that we have been using in this research, the prototype–willingness (prototype) model (Gibbons, Gerrard, & Lane, 2003). Our work includes several studies showing prospective relations between perceived racial discrimination and substance use (alcohol and drugs) in African American adolescents and their parents. We follow this with a more detailed discussion of a preventive intervention that we have been working on that is based partly on the prototype model; that intervention has been shown to effectively delay onset of alcohol consumption in African American adolescents. We conclude with suggestions for future work in the area. Our focus throughout the chapter is on substance use in African American adolescents; this has been the primary population included in our own research. However, we review studies with other minority groups as well.

TRAJECTORIES OF USE AMONG AFRICAN AMERICANS

Adolescence

A number of explanations for the later onset of substance use among African American youth have been proposed, most of which fall into one or more of three categories: *spiritual, familial,* and *cultural.* Some have speculated, for example, that because Black adolescents are more religious than White adolescents (Chatters, Taylor, & Lincoln, 1999) and religion is negatively associated with substance use (Wills, Gibbons, Gerrard, Murry, & Brody, 2003), religiosity protects Black youth (more than other youths) from substance use (Wallace & Bachman, 1991). Recent studies have questioned this explanation, however, suggesting that religiosity is protective

Preparation of this chapter was supported in part by National Institute on Drug Abuse Grant DA018871 and National Institute of Mental Health Grant MH062668.

for all adolescents, not just African Americans (Brown, Parks, Zimmerman, & Phillips, 2001). A more common explanation for racial differences in use involves family ties and parenting. This argument posits that Black families tend to be more closely knit than other families, and as a result, Black parents have more influence over their children (Clark, Scarisbrick-Hauser, Gautam, & Wirk, 1999). Catalano et al. (1992), for example, found evidence that attachment to parents and parental monitoring were stronger protective factors against substance use for Black children than for White children (cf. Wallace & Muroff, 2002). Once again, some recent research has questioned the role that differences in parenting style or effectiveness play in explaining racial differences in use (see Nowlin & Colder, 2007), but family factors remain a popular explanation for reduced rates of use among adolescents, especially Black adolescents.

The third category of protective factors (cultural) involves racial or ethnic identity (EI). Black youth who identify more with their race and have Afrocentric values also tend to have more negative attitudes toward drugs, and they appear to be better able to resist or delay drug use initiation (Corneille & Belgrave, 2007; Pugh & Bry, 2007). Holley, Kulis, Marsiglia, and Keith (2006) showed that EI was stronger among minority groups and that EI, in turn, was associated with more negative attitudes toward substances and less reported use; thus, EI mediated the negative relation between minority group status and substance use. A similar negative relation between EI and use has also been found among Native Americans (Kulis, Napoli, & Marsiglia, 2002). Along the same lines, a survey conducted by Marsiglia, Kulis, and Hecht (2001) found that Black, Mexican American, and mixed-ethnicity adolescents with a strong sense of EI reported less drug exposure and use, whereas ethnically proud White students reported more drug use and more exposure to drugs. Scheier, Botvin, Diaz, and Ifill-Williams (1997) reported that EI buffered minority adolescents against social influence risk for marijuana use—that is, a belief that marijuana was available and relatively common among friends, peers, and adults. Finally, Orozco and Lukas (2000) found that the best predictor of risk of drug use among Black males was identi-

fication and socialization with someone of a different ethnic group. In sum, of the three putative reasons for delayed onset of use among African American adolescents, the cultural factor (Black pride, EI) has received the most empirical support.

Adulthood

There is evidence, however, that certain protective factors among minority adolescents do not carry over into adulthood. For most individuals, emerging adulthood—the transition period between late adolescence and adulthood (roughly ages 18 to 24; see Arnett & Tanner, 2006)—is a period during which substance use habits shift from erratic and/or episodic to more stable, or adultlike. Notably, the dramatic acceleration of heavy or binge drinking and drug use that occurs around age 18 or 19 peaks in the early 20s and then starts to decline. This "maturing-out" process is typical, but several studies have shown that it is less evident among African Americans (Mudar, Kearns, & Leonard, 2002; Schulenberg, O'Malley, Bachman, & Johnston, 2005). In fact, some surveys have suggested that substance use may actually be greater among African American adults than among adults of other racial and ethnic groups. The 2002 National Survey on Drug Use and Health (Substance Abuse and Mental Health Services Administration, 2003) indicated that among adults between 18 and 32 years of age, African Americans' drug use was significantly higher than that of European Americans and exceeded national averages for both rural and urban dwellers (Reardon & Buka, 2002; see also Substance Abuse and Mental Health Services Administration, 2005; the same is true for smoking, see Gardiner, 2001). This disordinal interaction pattern in trajectories of substance use from adolescence to adulthood has been referred to as a "racial crossover effect" (Kandel, Johnston, Bird, & Canino, 1997; Wallace & Bachman, 1991).

Exploration of the Racial Crossover Effect

Racial disparities have also been detected for the problems that accompany substance use (Gil, Wagner, & Tubman, 2004; Mudar et al., 2002). Although fewer Black (than White) adolescents use drugs, those who do appear to be at higher risk of developing abuse in emerging adulthood (Gil et al.,

2004). Problems associated with heavy drug use, such as arrests and clinic admissions, are higher among Black adults (Dawkins & Williams, 1997; Substance Abuse and Mental Health Services Administration, 2003). Undoubtedly, that is partly a reflection of discrimination in the criminal justice system (Iguchi, Bell, Ramchand, & Fain, 2005), as well as of reduced access to substance use treatment among African Americans (Carroll et al., 2007). However, drug-related mortality is also higher among Blacks (Drucker, 1999; National Institute on Alcohol Abuse and Alcoholism, 2003). African Americans experience more negative consequences per ounce of drug consumed than do other racial and ethnic groups (Ensminger, Joon, & Fothergill, 2002). The same appears to be true with regard to problems per ounce of alcohol (Johnston, O'Malley, Bachman, & Schulenberg, 2005). Precisely when the crossover occurs is not yet clear, but data suggest it may begin in emerging adulthood, when adolescents leave the home (Brown, Flory, Lynam, Leukefeld, & Clayton, 2004; Trinidad, Gilpin, Lee, & Pierce, 2004). Several reasons as to why this increase in substance use and related problems occurs among Black adults have been proposed; they are reviewed briefly next.

Families and peers in emerging adulthood. One factor that may contribute to increasing trajectories of substance use among some African American young adults has to do with the changing impact of the family. As African American adolescents enter emerging adulthood, developmental changes occur in the processes that deterred substance use when they were younger (Simons, Chen, Stewart, & Brody, 2003). Parental monitoring diminishes, and other factors outside the home become more influential. In fact, most young adults, regardless of their racial or ethnic group, spend more time with peers and romantic partners when they leave home. As a result, some Black adolescents end up exchanging some of the protection conferred by their family environment when they were younger for (elevated) risk factors outside the family, including risk associated with their nonfamilial relationships.

Relationships and gender. Having a romantic partner who is using substances increases the likelihood of use (Cavacuit, 2004), more so for people of lower

SES (Moden, van Lenthe, Graaf, & Kraaykamp, 2003) and for women (Gaughan, 2006). Marriage usually results in a decline in substance use for men (Flora & Chassin, 2005); however, that appears to be less true among African American men (Curran, Muthén, & Harford, 1998). For example, Mudar et al. (2002) found that alcohol problems increased in the first 2 years of marriage for the Black men in their sample. They suggested that marital happiness and perceptions of marital roles may be partly responsible (cf. Arnett, 2007). More generally, African Americans tend to marry later than European Americans (average age = 29 vs. 26), have higher divorce rates (as high as 70%), and are more likely to cohabitate (Arnett, 2007), all of which are factors that have been associated with more substance use (Schulenberg & Maggs, 2002).

Opportunity. When they leave school, many rural African Americans have no jobs; only 12% attend college (Boatright & Bachtel, 2003). Many young Black adults in rural and small city areas are confronted with impoverished environments that provide minimal resources and diminishing community (social) support. The same appears to be true in larger cities, where Blacks face more economic and social stressors (Gil et al., 2004). Unemployment rates among Black adults are 2.5 times those of other racial and ethnic groups (Kaiser Family Foundation, 2006), and unemployment is associated with more substance use in emerging adulthood (Schulenberg & Maggs, 2002). Even if African Americans find employment, job turnover rates are relatively high during this period for them because the combined effects of poor preparation for employment and disadvantageous hiring practices make the transition to the workforce difficult (Holz & Tienda, 1998). Prison also effectively limits the opportunities of many young Black men. Twenty percent of Black men (vs. 3% of White men) spend some time in prison between the ages of 20 and 34 (Pettit & Western, 2004). Incarcerated individuals are at higher risk of mental health and substance abuse problems and HIV infection, before and after prison (Hochstetler, Murphy, & Simons, 2004). In short, of the three contributing factors—changing role of family, relationship instability, and limited opportunity—the last one appears to explain more of the variance in substance use: Frustration resulting from limited opportunities will undoubtedly lead to more use. However, there is a more fundamental issue that African Americans and other minorities face that may underlie the problem of limited opportunity, and that is racial discrimination.

The impact of psychosocial factors, such as racial discrimination, on the mental and physical health of African Americans has been the focus of our research in the Family and Community Health Study (FACHS). With colleagues, we have been examining the impact of these factors on the health behavior of Black families living in Iowa and Georgia, including health-promoting (e.g., nutrition, exercise) and health-impairing behaviors, such as substance use. Before describing that research, we provide an outline of the theoretical model that we have developed and applied to the study of adolescent health behavior in FACHS and other studies.

THE PROTOTYPE–WILLINGNESS (PROTOTYPE) MODEL

Dual Processing

Two paths. The prototype model is a modified dual-processing model of health behavior (Gerrard et al., 2008; Gibbons et al., 2003, 2006). It has been applied mostly to adolescent health risk behavior—for example, substance use—but it has been used to examine and predict other types of health behavior as well, including health-promoting actions, such as condom use, UV (sun) protection, and exercise. The basic assumption underlying the model is that there are two types of information processing involved in health decision making: heuristic and analytic (see Chaiken & Trope, 1999, for a discussion of dual-processing models). These two processing modes are reflected in two pathways to health behavior. The reasoned path comes directly from expectancy-value theories, such as the theory of reasoned action (Fishbein & Ajzen, 1975), which are the most popular attitude–behavior theories in health psychology. This path involves analytic processing, which is more systematic and deliberative, and it includes some forethought or planning about the behavior. There are two distal antecedents in the reasoned path: attitudes toward the behavior (e.g., assump-

tions about outcomes associated with the behavior) and perceptions of norms—whether others approve of and engage in the behavior. The proximal antecedent to behavior in this path is behavioral intention (BI), which is defined as plans to carry out specific actions or attain certain goal states (Ajzen, 1996). These plans are the result of some deliberation about the behavior and its possible outcomes. BI is the only proximal antecedent to behavior in the expectancy-value perspective.

Willingness. The second pathway to behavior in the prototype model is the social reaction path. This path involves heuristic processing, which is characterized by much less forethought and deliberation about the behavior and especially about its attendant outcomes. In the heuristic processing mode, affect has more influence, as do images and, of course, heuristics.[1] This path includes a second proximal antecedent to behavior, termed *behavioral willingness* (BW). BW is defined as an openness to risk opportunity—what a person would be willing to do under different risk-conducive circumstances. It captures the unintentional or unplanned component of behavior, which is especially characteristic of health risk behavior (e.g., substance use). Whereas BI questions typically include assessments of plans, for example "Do you plan on smoking in the future?" willingness questions are worded in the subjunctive: "Suppose you were at a party and there were some drugs there; how willing would you be to . . . ?" BI and BW are correlated (correlations range from the .20s to the .60s, depending on age and type of behavior), but they differ in several ways (see Gibbons et al., 2003, for a discussion). The most important difference is that BI involves more reasoning and planning (hence the term *reasoned action*), whereas BW is more reactive. Some college students, for example, plan ahead of time to binge drink on the weekend or to seek a casual sexual encounter; for others, such events are fortuitous. This latter group is willing to take risks

---

[1] Examples of heuristics in the social reaction path would include "risk is cool," "there is safety in numbers," and "it won't happen to me." This last example is a form of what Weinstein (1984) termed *optimistic bias,* the idea that one can get away with risky behaviors that might cause problems for others. Optimistic bias is an important element in the social reaction path because it is associated with BW (Gibbons, Gerrard, Ouellette, & Burzette, 1998).

but is not actively seeking them. Those who are intending to engage in risk have given some thought to the risks involved but are not deterred by them; those who are willing, but not intending, to engage tend to avoid such thoughts (Gerrard et al., 2002, 2008).

Prototypes. The second (new) element in the social reaction path (and in the prototype model) is the construct of risk prototypes. These are the images that individuals have of the type of person who engages in a particular behavior—the "typical smoker" or "druggie," for example. They are not so much visual images as impressions—what is this type of person like? Research has shown that these images affect decision making and that their influence is mediated by BW (Gibbons et al., 2006). Generally, the images tend to be negative, and so their impact is more often inhibitory than facilitative. Overall, the more favorable (or less negative) the image, the more willing the adolescent is to engage in the behavior. Thus, an adolescent with a (relatively) favorable image of drug users will be more willing to partake when given the opportunity, even though she or he had (or has) no specific plans to use drugs.

Predicting Substance Use

Generally speaking, the expectancy-value approach (termed the *consequentialist* perspective because of its focus on cognitive deliberations about the behavior and its possible outcomes; see Loewenstein, Weber, Hsee, & Welch, 2001) has been very effective at predicting health-promoting (i.e., reasoned) behaviors. It has been less successful when applied to health-risk actions, such as unprotected sex, drunk driving, or illegal drug use—behaviors that would not generally be considered reasoned or rational (Reyna & Farley, 2006; Webb & Sheeran, 2006). It has also been less effective at predicting the behavior of adolescents (Albarracin, Johnson, Fishbein, & Muellerleile, 2001), especially when the behavior involves risk, in part because adolescents' actions tend to be less reasoned and more reactive. In particular, the evidence has suggested that for adolescents, most risky behaviors (a) have a significant affective component (Boyer, 2006; Wiers et al., 2007); (b) are socially determined (they seldom use drugs or drink alone, e.g.; Ouellette,

Gerrard, Gibbons, & Reis-Bergan, 1999); and (c) are more reactive than planned (Reyna & Farley, 2006; Webb & Sheeran, 2006). That is one reason why BW is a better predictor than BI for behaviors such as substance use, up to approximately age 16 or 17 (Pomery, Gibbons, Reis-Bergan, & Gerrard, 2008). At that point, the behavior is likely to become at least intentional if not planned, and so BW then "gives way" to BI or behavioral expectation[2] or, in some cases, previous behavior or habits (e.g., smoking). Because of its inclusion of heuristic processing and its dual-processing focus, we believe the prototype model is especially useful in examining the role of discrimination as a predictor of substance use and also affect as a mediator of that relation. We have been using the prototype model to study adolescent health behavior in FACHS.

THE FAMILY AND COMMUNITY HEALTH STUDY

FACHS is a panel study of African American families. The first wave (Time 1, or T1) sample size was 897 families, half of whom live in Iowa and half in Georgia. Each family included an adolescent (age 10 or 11 at T1) and a primary caregiver (parent), who in most cases was the child's mother. Some of the families also had an older sibling and/or secondary caregiver participate in the study when they were available (total $N > 2,500$). Four waves of data collection have been completed over 9 years; there will be two additional waves, which will allow the research group to follow the adolescents through age 24 or 25. Discrimination has been assessed at all four waves using a modified version of the Schedule of Racist Events (Landrine & Klonoff, 1996). The scale was originally intended for adults, so the modifications included simplifying the language and replacing items about discrimination in the workplace with items about discrimination in the community. The

---

[2] Most studies assessing health risk behavior have used a combination of behavioral intention and behavioral expectation items (Armitage & Connor, 2001). Behavioral expectation items are typically worded "How likely is it that you will . . . ?" or "Do you think that you will . . . ?" (Warshaw & Davis, 1985). These measures are often more predictive than straight BI measures for behaviors that are risky or socially undesirable, such as adolescent health risk behavior (Parker, Manstead, Stradling, Reason, & Baxter, 1992).

scale has proven both valid and reliable over the first four waves.

Studies coming out of the FACHS project have consistently demonstrated the major impact that discrimination has had on the adolescents and their parents. At T1, 90% of the adolescents reported some experience with discrimination, although for most that experience was minimal. Regarding the mental health consequences of those experiences, Brody, Chen, et al. (2006) tested multiple-group latent growth models and found that the adolescents' reports of early discrimination (at T1) were strongly associated with their early reports of depression and conduct problems (e.g., vandalism, physical assault, lying). In addition, reports of both discrimination and conduct problems increased over time (depression did not), and the slope of the discrimination growth factor was also positively associated with the slopes of both depression and conduct problems. In addition, a cross-lag analysis showed that the discrimination → conduct problem lag was significantly stronger than the reverse lag, suggesting that the behavior problems were more a reaction to perceived discrimination than a cause of it.

Another FACHS study examined the relation between discrimination and externalizing behavior among boys in the first two waves (Simons et al., 2006). Results indicated that discrimination had an impact on affect and cognition (attitudes) as well as behavior. More specifically, discrimination predicted an increase in anger and violent delinquency and an increase in what was labeled *hostile view of relationships* or *aggressive cynicism* (e.g., "Sometimes you need to threaten people to get them to treat you fairly"). More important, the impact of discrimination on violent delinquency was mediated by its effects on anger. On the positive side, although these negative effects were pronounced, they appeared to be countered by effective parenting, which was operationally defined as reasoning with the child and providing warmth, support, and consistent discipline that was not harsh. This parenting style significantly reduced the negative impact of discrimination on anger and hostile attitude in one study (Simons et al., 2006) and on depression and conduct problems in another (Brody, Chen, et al., 2006). Our research has exam-

ined the effects of discrimination on substance use in FACHS and other studies.

DISCRIMINATION AND SUBSTANCE USE

Health Effects of Discrimination

Without a doubt, experiencing racial discrimination is stressful. Numerous studies have documented associations (correlations) between perceived discrimination and various kinds of distress in Black adults and children, including depression (Kessler, Mickelson, & Williams, 1999; Simons et al., 2002) and other types of negative affect, such as frustration, anxiety, guilt, and general distress (Gee, Ryan, Laflamme, & Holt, 2006). Within the past 8 to 10 years, several studies have emerged indicating that discrimination also has an impact on physical health. This relation has been shown to be both direct and indirect. In the former category, both laboratory (experimental) and correlational studies have shown that perceived discrimination is associated with increased blood pressure (Richman, Bennett, Pek, Siegler, & Williams, 2007), which is a precursor to cardiovascular disease. Discrimination also has an indirect impact on physical health through its (direct) relation with health-compromising behaviors, such as substance use.

An association between perceived discrimination and health-impairing behavior has now been documented in a series of correlational studies. For example, African Americans who report higher levels of discrimination are more likely to report that they smoke cigarettes (Bennett, Wolin, Robinson, Fowler, & Edwards, 2005; Landrine, Klonoff, Corral, Fernandez, & Roesch, 2006). Landrine and Klonoff (2000) suggested that this relation may be a reflection of an effort to use tobacco as a means of coping with the stress produced by racial discrimination (cf. Guthrie, Young, Williams, Boyd, & Kintner, 2002), although they did not have any coping measures in their study. Similar relations have been found among African Americans for alcohol (Gil et al., 2004). Kwate, Valdimarsdottir, Guevarra, and Bovbjerg (2003) found that reports of discrimination over the past year were correlated with number of cigarettes smoked and drinks consumed. They also found that reports of discrimination were associated with twice the odds of problem drinking. To a lesser extent, discrimination has also been linked with drug use (Gil et al., 2004). In a study by Borrell et al. (2006), for example, African Americans who reported more experiences with discrimination (e.g., in school, in getting medical care, from the police) also reported more lifetime marijuana and cocaine use. Resnicow, Braithwaite, Selassie, and Smith (1999) found positive relations between self-reported drug use and perceptions of racism in one study and anti-White attitudes in a second study (see also Williams & Neighbors, 2001). Although most of these studies used cross-sectional designs, the pattern of correlations in them has been consistent: Discrimination is directly and indirectly associated with both mental and physical health problems. This is why a number of social scientists have suggested that racial discrimination is a central, perhaps the primary, reason for the significant disparity that exists in the United States between Blacks and Whites in terms of physical health (Krieger, 2000; Mays, Cochran, & Barnes, 2007; Williams, Neighbors, & Jackson, 2003).

Main Effects of Discrimination

Conduct disorder.   Following up on these two previous studies showing a strong relation between discrimination and externalizing behavior (Brody, Chen, et al., 2006; Simons et al., 2006), we examined the impact of early experiences with both discrimination and behavior problems (conduct disorder, or CD) on drug use. We did this using structural equation modeling (SEM) with data from the first three waves of FACHS (Gibbons, Yeh, et al., 2007). The SEM included a number of control measures related to use (e.g., parental use and distress, SES, friends' use). At T1, fewer than 3% of the adolescents reported substance use, but the figure rose to 20% by T2 and reached 41% by T3. Marijuana was clearly the preferred drug (20% reported use at T3). At T1, 4.3% of the adolescents reported three or more CD symptoms (i.e., behavioral problems), which is the minimum for a diagnosis of CD; at T2, the figure was up to 7%. CD and discrimination were correlated at T1 (p < .001), and both predicted drug use at T3 (5 years later; both ps < .05).

One statistic best illustrates the discrimination effect: Among those in the top quarter of the distribution on self-reported discrimination at T1, 24%

reported they were using drugs at T3; this was twice the rate reported by those in the bottom three fourths of the distribution. Moreover, the combination of discrimination and CD problems was particularly important, although, fortunately, the combination was rare. There were 14 adolescents who were high in self-reported discrimination distribution at T1 and had a (diagnosable) CD problem; 8 of the 14 were using drugs at T3, and the amount of their use was more than six times that of the rest of the sample. It is also worth noting that the cross-lag analyses conducted over multiple waves of data suggested, once again, that the influence of discrimination on problem behavior (CD and drug use) was stronger then the reverse relation. Although both kinds of problem behavior may increase the likelihood of eliciting negative reactions from others, some of which may reflect discrimination, it does not appear to be the case that the relation between problematic behavior and discrimination is primarily attributable to the behavior leading to more discrimination. Instead, the reverse pattern appears to be the case.

A similar link between perceived discrimination and substance use was found with the parents of the FACHS adolescents (Gibbons, Gerrard, Cleveland, Wills, & Brody, 2004). First, the zero-order correlation between discrimination and substance use (defined here as drug use and alcohol-related problems) was stronger than the relations between use and any other measure of risk, including a number of stressors that have been shown to be reliable predictors of substance use: relationship problems, financial strain, pessimism, neighborhood risk, low SES, social support, religiosity, and perceived control. More important, T1 discrimination predicted change in parents' use over the 2-year period, taking into account the high stability of drug use over time and the strong correlation between use and discrimination that existed at T1 and also controlling for the various stressors mentioned above. This is the first study that we are aware of to show a prospective relation between discrimination and substance use. A similar prospective relation was found among the adolescents. As mentioned earlier, there was very little substance use reported by the adolescents at T1 (age 10.5), but about 30% of them indicated some willingness (BW) to try alcohol or drugs if presented with the opportunity (although in most cases, the willingness was minimal). Discrimination was correlated with reports of willingness. In addition, T1 discrimination predicted BW, and substance use at T2, 2 years later ($p < .001$).

Trajectories. To further examine the relation over time between discrimination and drug use, we conducted latent growth curve analyses on the first four waves of adolescent FACHS data (Gibbons, Gerrard, Wills, Weng, & Kingsbury, 2008). We controlled for the T1 measures of adolescents' level of risk taking and the level of risk in their neighborhood (e.g., crime, gang activity, drug selling), both of which were positively related to the intercepts of use and discrimination. Parental substance use was related to the intercept, but not the slope, of their child's use, whereas SES was (positively) related to the slope, but not to the intercept. We believe the latter reflects a tendency for Black adolescents who live in higher SES neighborhoods to have increasing contact with White adolescents, who are using drugs more, and that, as suggested above, leads to more use (Chen & Killeya-Jones, 2006; Johnston, O'Malley, & Bachman, 2003). Reports of both discrimination and use increased over time. More important, however, the slope of substance use was related to both the intercept and the slope of discrimination (both $ps \le .003$), providing further evidence of the impact that early experience with discrimination and the cumulative effect of discrimination over time were having on these adolescents.

Mediation of the Discrimination → Use Relation: Cognitive and Behavioral Factors

Cognition. Gibbons et al. (2004) was the first of several studies we have conducted in the FACHS that have examined factors that mediate the prospective relation between discrimination and substance use. These factors fall into three categories: cognitive, affective, and behavioral. First, in the cognitive category, using the prototype model as a theoretical basis (and SEM as the analysis technique), we found that perceived discrimination was associated with more favorable images (prototypes) of adolescents who use substances, and favorable images lead to more BW

and more use (Gibbons et al., 2003). Consistent with this, adolescents who reported more discrimination were also more likely to say that their friends were using. This latter relation was also prospective: T1 discrimination was correlated with reports of friends' use ($p \le .001$), but it also predicted a change (increase) in affiliation with users ($p \le .05$).

Behavior. The discrimination → hostile behavior relation mentioned earlier was extended in a recent study to include substance use at T3 (Gibbons, Etcheverry, et al., 2008). Among the adolescents, the pattern that emerged was as anticipated: T1 discrimination led to more CD symptoms at T2. These behavior problems, in turn, were related to both T2 BW and T3 substance use (which was assessed 3 years later; all $ps \le .001$). The indirect paths from discrimination through anger to use, and also through T2 CD and T2 BW to use, were significant (all $ps \le .003$). The pattern was similar among the parents, even though the measures were somewhat different. For them, we had a measure of hostility, or antisocial personality—an adult version of CD—that included behaviors such as physical violence, stealing, and harming others. At T1, parents' discrimination was correlated with this measure of hostile behavior, and then discrimination predicted an increase in hostility at T2. The latter increase then predicted an increase in use (alcohol problems and drug use) 3 years later ($p \le .001$), again, in spite of the very high stability of use over the 5-year span from T1 to T3 ($\beta = 0.74$, $p \le .001$). As expected, the indirect path from T1 discrimination through hostility to T3 use was significant ($p = .002$).

Mediation of the Discrimination → Substance Use Relation: Affect

Given the accumulation of evidence documenting a correlation between reports of discrimination and distress, it made sense to look for comparable evidence of negative affect (NA) as a mediator of the discrimination → use relation. We found some preliminary evidence to that effect in the Gibbons et al. (2004) study. For both the parents and the adolescents at T1 and T2, NA, which consisted of measures of depression and anxiety, mediated the discrimination → drug use relation. In addition, two aspects of these relations are worth noting. First, although the stability in reports of NA was very high for the parents and reasonable for the adolescents, for both of them, T1 discrimination predicted the measure of T2 NA in addition to T1. Thus, those who had experienced more discrimination at T1 reported more NA at that time, and they also reported a significant increase in NA over the next 2 years.

The other, unexpected effect was a cross-lagged relation between discrimination and NA for the two members of the family. Discrimination experienced by the adolescents was correlated with parental distress, controlling for the effect of parents' own discrimination on their distress. The same set of relations worked in the opposite direction: Parents' reports of discrimination were related to their child's distress, controlling for the impact of the child's own discrimination on that distress. As a result of these relations, parents' discrimination had a significant indirect effect on their child's substance use: parent discrimination → child NA → child BW → child use ($p \leq .01$). Although we do not know the exact underlying nature of these relations, it seems likely that observing a family member experiencing prejudicial treatment from others is very stressful by itself. More important, this is another example of the significant negative impact that racial discrimination can have on African Americans and their families.

Anger as a Mediator

Why anger? We view the issue of affect mediation as important, and so we have conducted several studies on the topic with FACHS adolescents that have added T3 reports of substance use and have included lab-based experimental methods. On the basis of the results of previous studies (some related to discrimination and some not), we have focused on anger as a primary affective response linking discrimination with use. For example, in one of our previous studies (Simons et al., 2006), we found that among Black boys, discrimination was prospectively related to violent delinquency more than it was to depression and that anger, rather than depression or anxiety, mediated the effect of discrimination on their violent behavior. In a two-wave study, Curry and Youngblade (2006) found a direct relation between anger and risky

behavior, including alcohol and drug use; however, the relation between depression and risk was mediated by other factors (e.g., lower levels of perceived risk). Finally, in the FACHS study on discrimination and affect (Gibbons, Etcheverry, et al., 2008), when we included the measure of hostility in the SEM with the parents, the indirect path from discrimination to use through depression and anxiety (reported in Gibbons et al., 2004) was replaced by the new indirect path through hostility.

Besides these studies examining discrimination effects directly, there is also some indirect support for the anger → substance use link in the affect–risk behavior literature. For example, evidence based on correlational studies suggests that risk taking is related to anger, whereas risk avoidance is related to fear (Lerner & Keltner, 2001) and to anxiety and sadness (Raghunathan & Phan, 1999). Similarly, there is also evidence that anger (more than sadness) prompts heuristic processing (Bodenhausen, Sheppard, & Kramer, 1994), which is associated with riskier behavior (Gerrard et al., 2008). On the basis of this research, we conducted another study that directly addressed the issue of type of affect as a mediator of discrimination effects on use.

Anger versus depression and anxiety. Our measure of anger in this more recent study of FACHS adolescents (Gibbons, Etcheverry, et al., 2008) included four self-descriptive items (e.g., "gets mad," "loses temper"), which we entered into the SEM along with a measure of negative affect (depression and anxiety). As expected, there was a strong relation between T1 discrimination and both T1 anger and T1 negative affect ($ps \leq .001$). Anger and negative affect were, of course, also correlated ($r = .42$, $p \leq .001$). However, only anger and not negative affect—neither depression nor anxiety—predicted use (alcohol and drugs—again, mostly marijuana) 5 years later ($p \leq .01$). The model also included both behavioral intentions and BW at T2. As is usually the case, the two constructs were highly correlated, but when both were included in the model, only willingness predicted use 3 years later ($p \leq .001$). Also as expected, there was a path from T1 anger to T2 BW ($p \leq .05$), and the indirect paths from T1 discrimination to use were significant in one case, discrimination → anger → use ($p \leq .002$), and marginal in the other, discrimination → anger → BW → use ($p = .06$). These indirect paths were in line with our hypotheses, which came from the prototype model: Because of the significant affect involvement, discrimination should predict substance use via the social reaction path, which involves heuristic processing and willingness more than intention. More generally, these analyses were consistent with the assumption that it is anger and hostility triggered by discrimination that eventually leads to use. To provide a more convincing demonstration, however, experimental studies are needed.

Manipulating discrimination. We brought a subsample of the FACHS participants ($n = 116$) into the lab and exposed them to an experimental manipulation that asked them to imagine a stressful work-related scenario that either did or did not include racial discrimination (Gibbons, Etcheverry, et al., 2008, Study 2). After envisioning the scenario, they were presented with a list of 15 negative mood adjectives (4 for each of the three focal mood states: anxiety, depression, and anger) and asked to indicate whether they would experience each one of them in that kind of situation. Later, they reported their BW to use drugs. Results from this experimental study were in line with those from the survey (correlational) study. First, envisioning the discrimination scenario resulted in significantly higher reports in all three of the mood states, but the biggest differences between the discrimination and nondiscrimination conditions were in reports of anger—there was much more of it in the discrimination condition. Second, envisioning discrimination also led to more BW to use drugs. Third, anger led to more BW to use—especially among those who reported prior use of drugs. A Prior Use × Anger interaction ($p \leq .004$) reflected the fact that the most BW was reported by users who were most angered by the scenario. Finally, and most important, the relation between discrimination and (increased) drug BW was fully mediated by the impact that manipulated discrimination had on anger: discrimination → anger → BW. In contrast, neither depression nor anxiety mediated this relation. This convergence of results across the two studies, which involved the same participants but were separated by 2 years and included two different research methods (correlational vs. experimental), adds credence to our belief that it is externalizing behavior and anger, more so than internalizing responses, that link discrimination with heavier substance use.

What Moderates the Discrimination → Substance Use Relation: Coping

There has been considerable speculation as to what the underlying reason is for the oft-found correlation between discrimination and substance use. A common hypothesis is that drugs and alcohol may be used as a means of coping with the distress produced by discrimination (Landrine & Klonoff, 2000). This is a difficult relation to examine experimentally; however, a correlational study by Martin, Tuch, and Roman (2003) found that endorsement of "escapism" (e.g., using alcohol to relax) mediated the statistical relation between reports of discrimination and drinking. To further explore this question in the laboratory study, we included a two-item measure of substance use as a form of coping (i.e., when under stress "I drink alcohol or take drugs, in order to think about it less [feel better]") and then used this measure as a moderator of the reactions to the discrimination scenario. Regressing BW on reports of prior use, condition (i.e., the discrimination manipulation), coping, and the Coping × Condition interaction produced main effects of use, coping, and condition (all $ps \leq .02$), all in the expected directions.

The anticipated Coping × Condition interaction was also significant ($p = .01$), with the expected pattern of results: Discrimination led to higher reports of BW only among those who indicated that they used drugs or alcohol as a means of coping with stress. Coping did not moderate the effect of discrimination on reports of anger—regardless of coping style, participants were angered by the scenario; coping only moderated the impact of the discrimination on BW to use drugs. The fact that previous use was controlled in the analysis (so that it was not just drug use that predicted the outcomes, but use as coping) adds support to the contention that the elevated substance use that is associated with discriminatory experiences may reflect an effort to cope with the anger the experiences have generated. However, given the importance of the issue and the fact that we used only a two-item scale, additional empirical attention seems warranted.

Conclusion. Overall, the results suggest two possible mechanisms or pathways by which discrimination can lead to drug use. One is more planful or instrumental: It involves using substances in an effort to deal with the stress brought on by the discrimination. The other is more reactive: Anger activates a heuristic processing mode that includes less consideration of negative consequences, lower levels of perceived risk (Lerner & Keltner, 2000; Trumbo, 2002), and also more willingness (but not necessarily more intention) to use when the opportunity affords itself.

Buffering

Parenting. We also examined factors that previous research suggested might protect adolescents from drug use or, more specifically, protect them from use in response to discriminatory experiences. As mentioned earlier, in a previous study (Simons et al., 2006) we found that supportive parenting buffered the effect of discrimination on anger in the FACHS boys. We found the same result (on anger) with the full sample (male and female) in Study 1 reported by Gibbons, Etcheverry, et al. (2008). We also found the same buffering pattern for the discrimination → T2 BW relation, and the interaction was significant ($p \le .003$). The pattern was there for the discrimination → T3 use relation as well, although it was marginal ($p = .06$). Thus, supportive parenting early on reduced the effect of discriminatory experiences on anger, as well as BW to use substances and its effect on actual use, which was measured 5 years after assessing parenting measures. These were three separate regression analyses (anger, BW, and use), so the protective influence of parenting occurred for all three criteria, not just anger (which then affected BW and use). Finally, although there was some evidence that supportive parenting buffered against the impact of discrimination on both negative affect (anxiety and depression) and conduct disorder, the interaction terms were not significant (both $ps > .11$). In short, anger appears to be the functional affective response linking discrimination with use.

Ethnic identity. There is evidence that EI generally buffers Black adolescents against substance use. As mentioned earlier, high-EI adolescents tend to have more negative attitudes toward drugs than do low-EI adolescents (Corneille & Belgrave, 2007), and they tend to use less (Pugh & Bry, 2007). Moreover, EI has been shown to enhance the protective effect of factors such as high levels of perceived drug risk and low peer use and to buffer against risk factors such as rebelliousness, watching violent TV, and receiving drug offers from peers (Brook, Balka, Brook, Win, & Gursen, 1998; Brook & Pahl, 2005). This may be one reason why preventive interventions that include elements of EI and/or Black pride have been shown to be effective (Brody, Murry, et al., 2006; Wills et al., 2007; see discussion below).

Ethnic identity and racial integration. Although Black adolescents generally tend to use substances less than their White counterparts, this difference is less pronounced in mostly White neighborhoods (Chen & Killeya-Jones, 2006), which, as we pointed out at the beginning of the chapter, presents a paradox of sorts. Substances are generally more accessible in high-risk environments in which Black adolescents are more likely to live. However, presumably because White adolescents use substances more than do Black adolescents, Black adolescents growing up in more integrated environments are exposed to more substances and are more likely to use (Johnston et al., 2003). Surprisingly, there has been little research on the question of how integration affects trajectories of use among Black adolescents, even though levels of integration are higher now than they have been in almost a century (Iceland, 2004). In Stock, Gibbons, Gerrard, Houlihan, and Simons (2007), we looked at EI as a protective factor among FACHS adolescents growing up in more versus less integrated environments. We used a variation of Phinney's (1992) EI measure that focused on what might be considered Black pride (e.g., "You have a lot of pride in your ethnic group. . . ." "You feel good about your ethnic background. . . ."). The hypothesis was that EI would be more of a buffer against substance vulnerability among Black adolescents living in mostly White neighborhoods (the mean percentage Black population in the segregated neighborhoods was 71%; in the mostly White neighborhoods, it was 22%). Once again, we used FACHS adolescents and combined survey and correlation-based methods with experimental methods.

In Study 1, which used survey methods, we found, as expected, that reports of substance availability were higher among adolescents living in mostly White neighborhoods despite less overall risk reported in those neighborhoods (e.g., less crime, gang activity, and open selling of drugs). Also as expected, EI buffered against this elevated substance risk. Multigroup SEM showed that EI, which was measured at T1, had a strong negative relation with T3 use for the integrated adolescents, but very little effect for those living in mostly Black neighborhoods ($p = .001$ vs. $p > .30$, respectively). The negative relation between EI and use observed among the racially integrated adolescents was mediated by several factors, including the positive effect of EI on their academic orientation and the negative impact of EI on their tendency to affiliate with others who were using drugs and on their willingness to use drugs. All of these salutary EI effects were significantly stronger in the neighborhoods that were mostly White.

Discrimination and ethnic identity. A follow-up experimental study involved analyses of different data collected from the same subsample of 116 FACHS adolescents who participated in Study 2 of Gibbons, Etcheverry, et al. (2008). The study was intended to examine why EI was protective in the integrated neighborhoods and, correspondingly, why absence of EI was a risk factor. Consistent with previous research, the assumption was that EI was protective with respect to substance use because it buffered the adolescents in the integrated environments against the harmful effects of discrimination. The first step, then, was to determine the level of reported discrimination in the different environments. As expected, reports of discrimination were significantly higher among those participants living in the integrated environments (cf. Kessler et al., 1999).

The second step was to look at reactions to manipulated discrimination in the laboratory setting. The primary analysis for this study examined EI as a buffer against substance vulnerability (drug BW). As mentioned earlier, reports of drug BW were higher in the discrimination condition, much more so among those who indicated they had used substances before. In addition, the anticipated four-way interaction (Condition × Previous Use × Integration × EI) indicated that among drug users in the discrimination condition, by far the most BW was reported by those from integrated communities who were low in EI.[3] Simple slope analyses of BW among just the users revealed that among the integrated adolescents, the slope for discrimination was significant only for those with low levels of EI ($\beta = -0.59$, $p \le .01$). In contrast, willingness to use substances was not significantly associated with condition among nonusers or among users who had high levels of EI. In short, EI was most protective for those adolescents in the discrimination condition who were at high risk, that is, those who had used drugs before and lived in mostly White neighborhoods.

To supplement the BW measure, later in the session we included a projective measure of substance use, which asked participants to imagine being at a party with some friends and then state what kinds of activities were going on at the party. These open-ended responses were then coded in terms of frequency of mentioning risk behavior, including drug and alcohol use. Forty-three percent mentioned some use by themselves and/or others at the party, most of it either alcohol or marijuana use. These reports of substance use were modestly correlated with the drug BW measure that came earlier in the session ($r = .28$, $p \le .01$), indicating that the two measures were not redundant. The four-way interaction emerged again ($p \le .001$), and it followed the same pattern as before. The most frequent spontaneous mention of substance use came from the same group: low EI users in the discrimination condition who lived in integrated environments.

Conclusion

There has never really been any debate in the literature as to whether experiencing discrimination is stressful, but until fairly recently there was not a lot of evidence to suggest that these experiences affect

---

[3] The sample size of 116 is small for a four-factor analysis. Because the study was conducted in Iowa, the majority of the sample ($n = 81$) lived in mostly White neighborhoods. This subsample was the focus of the study; the pattern of responses among them was consistent with the hypotheses and the effects were robust, in spite of the small sample size.

physical health. That evidence now exists, but for the most part, it is still not clear how these effects occur. A review of the literature suggests that internalizing reactions to discrimination are associated with health problems such as cardiovascular disease, whereas externalizing reactions are associated with health behavior problems such as substance use. This link between discrimination and use has been shown to be mediated by affect, behavior, and cognition. In the latter category, research has shown that Black adolescents who report experiencing more discrimination also have more prorisk cognitions, including more favorable prototypes of users. This reflects what appears to be a concurrent behavioral tendency toward affiliating with others who are using. Perceived discrimination is also associated with an increase in hostile and antisocial behavior in adults and CD in children, all of which are reliable predictors of drug and alcohol use. Consistent with this behavioral link, our studies have shown that anger, depression, and anxiety are all elevated by discrimination, but anger is the key ingredient that connects aversive discriminatory experiences with substance use. Preliminary evidence has also pointed to coping as at least one motivator behind the behavior. On the positive side, there is reason to believe that supportive parenting and ethnic identity, especially among Black adolescents living in mostly White environments, can buffer or protect adolescents against the effects of discrimination. Finally, our correlation-based and experimental studies both suggest that, in general, the prototype model can be effectively applied to the study of discrimination and, in particular, that discrimination affects substance use through the social reaction pathway that includes affect and heuristic processing.

INTERVENTIONS AND INTERVENTION IMPLICATIONS

The FACHS project and the prototype model have both been instrumental in the development of a preventive intervention with African American adolescents in Georgia. The Strong African American Families (SAAF) program is a dual-focus, family-centered intervention that has been shown to be very effective at delaying onset and escalation of drinking

over time (Brody, Murry, et al., 2006). SAAF draws on Brody and Murry's work with African American families demonstrating the protective aspects of regulated and protective home environments (e.g., parental monitoring, communication about expectations regarding alcohol, parental support; Brody, Kim, Murry, & Brown, 2004), and it draws from the prototype model as it has been applied in FACHS.

An assumption in the prototype model is that social influence (e.g., from peers, media) affects health behavior via the social reaction path, including prototypes and BW as mediators. Parents, however, are more likely to influence their children via the reasoned path; this influence occurs in two ways. First, simply observing consistent use or nonuse by the parent(s) over time will induce some thought about the behavior and its consequences in the child, and contemplation is part of analytic processing and is therefore related to intentions. Second, to the extent that parents discuss substance use and other risky behaviors with their child, that discussion is likely to be oriented toward reasoning, that is, encouraging the child to think about the type of risky situations she or he is likely to encounter and perhaps planning a course of action ahead of time (e.g., leaving, thinking of alternative activities). In short, parents' actions are intentionally and/or unintentionally likely to encourage some forethought in their children about the behavior. Analyses conducted with three waves of FACHS have provided some empirical support for this assumption. Figure 18.1 presents results from part of a SEM (Gibbons, Gerrard, et al., 2008). As can be seen, there are paths from social influence (friends' use) and prototypes to BW, but not to BI, whereas the opposite is true for parents' use and the parenting measure, which included communication, monitoring, and warmth.

Both the reasoned and the reactive pathways from the prototype model are targeted in the SAAF intervention. The parent component focuses on communication (e.g., setting clear expectations about alcohol; monitoring the child, including being involved in his or her life) and on getting the child to think ahead about his or her actions. The child component has four elements: (a) taking advantage of ethnic pride, for example, by educating the adolescents about the fact that Black adolescents typically engage in less

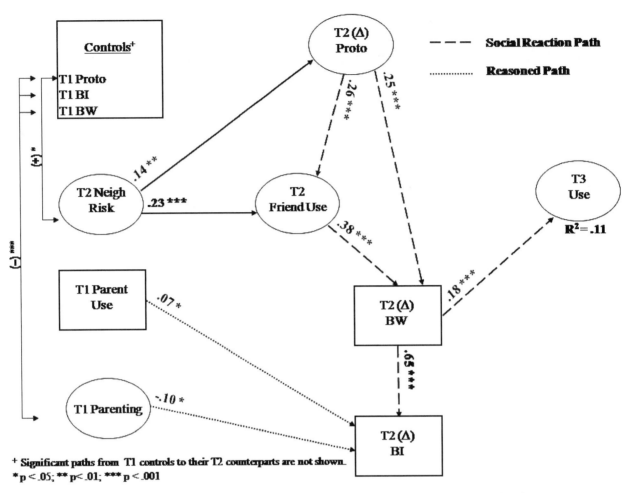

FIGURE 18.1. Parents' influence on behavioral intention (BI) versus behavioral willingness (BW). T1 = Time (Wave) 1; T2 = Time 2; Proto = prototype; Neigh Risk = neighborhood risk. +Significant paths from T1 controls to their T2 counterparts are not shown. *$p < .05$. **$p < .01$. ***$p < .001$. From *Early and Cumulative Effects of Perceived Discrimination on African American Adolescents' Substance Use: A Latent Growth Curve Analysis*, by F. X. Gibbons, M. Gerrard, T. A. Wills, C.-Y. Weng, and J. Kingsbury, J., 2008.

substance use; (b) regarding prototypes, informing the child, via a social norm approach (cf. Donaldson et al., 1996), that other children, especially African American children, have negative images of adolescents who drink (Gerrard et al., 2002); (c) reinforcing those negative images that the child has of precocious drinkers; and (d) conveying the distinction between BW and BI. On this latter dimension, unlike many resistance efficacy-based approaches, SAAF acknowledges children's curiosity about the behavior (curiosity is part of willingness) and does not suggest to the children that their drinking or other forms of risky behavior are the result of pressure from others coupled with an inability by the child to resist that pressure.

The dual-path combination contained in the intervention has proven effective. For example, in one SAAF study ($N = 281$; mean age at pretest = 11.2 and at follow-up = 13.3), there was a significant increase in drinking overall during the 24 months after the intervention—typical of this age range—but there was significantly less of an increase in the intervention condition (Gerrard et al., 2006). Moreover, as can be seen in Figure 18.2, the two pathways of influence did emerge in the model. The intervention produced a positive change in reports of effective parenting (provided by the parents) that, in turn, was related to less intention to use. There was also a positive effect on the children's alcohol prototypes—that is, less of an increase in image favorability, which is typical of this

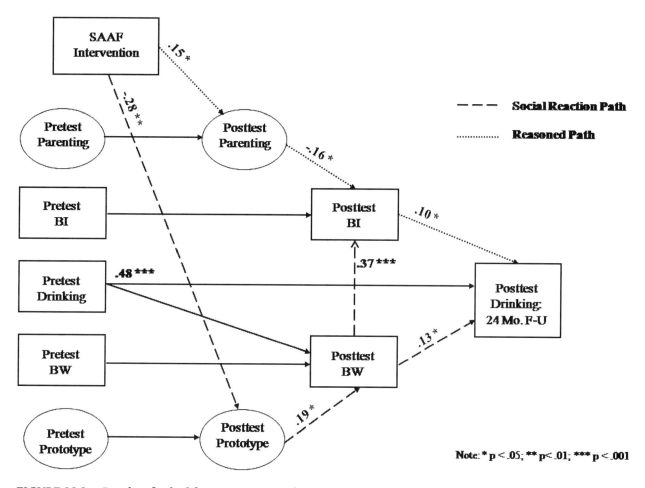

FIGURE 18.2.   Results of a dual-focus intervention from Strong African American Families (SAAF). BI = behavioral intentions; BW = behavioral willingness; F-U = follow-up. *p < .05. **p < .01. ***p < .001. From "A Theory-Based Dual-Focus Alcohol Intervention for Preadolescents: The Strong African American Families Program," by M. Gerrard, F. X. Gibbons, G. H. Brody, V. M. Murry, M. J. Cleveland, and T. A. Wills, 2006, *Psychology of Addictive Behaviors, 20*, p. 192. Copyright 2006 by the American Psychological Association. Adapted with permission.

age range (Andrews, Hampson, Barckley, Gerrard, & Gibbons, 2008; Gerrard et al., 2005). The analyses also indicated that the social reaction pathway to use, through prototypes and BW, was significant, whereas the reasoned path through parenting and intentions was marginal. Nonetheless, the model specifying both paths fit significantly better than did either single-path model; that is, constraining either the reasoned or the social reaction path to zero resulted in a significant decline in model fit compared with the dual-path model (for both $\Delta\chi^2$s, $ps \leq .005$).

In this sense, these results are promising because they attest to the efficacy of a theory-based intervention and they provide several recommendations for future intervention efforts. One consideration is that a prime time for these types of interventions is early

adolescence, when children are curious about the behavior and likely to report some willingness to drink or use drugs, but before their BW has developed into intentions to use. A second consideration is that both heuristic and analytic processing can be addressed in an intervention; when this is done in an efficacious manner, the chances of altering or delaying the targeted behavior will increase. Finally, there is reason to believe that interventions and preventive interventions for Black adolescents may be able to use information about actual prevalence of African American adolescents' substance use habits—which are lower than those of adolescents from other racial and ethnic groups—as part of a general Black pride strategy (cf. Brook & Pahl, 2005).

FUTURE DIRECTIONS

In many respects, the various lines of research discussed here raise more questions than they answer, which suggests that there is still a lot of work to be done. Several topics strike us as more central, based on what we and other investigative teams have done. First, we have only started to examine the racial cross-over effect in terms of drug use and abuse. With additional waves of FACHS (at least through age 24), we hope to get a better sense of when and why the crossover occurs, with an eye toward examining the cumulative effects that years of discrimination have on health in general and on substance use in particular. It will also be important to look at factors in the health care system (e.g., accessibility of treatment; Carroll et al., 2007) and the justice system (e.g., profiling of African Americans with regard to drug crimes; Taxman, Byrne, & Pattavina, 2005) that might contribute to this problem. We have an idea of what factors can reduce the relation between perceived discrimination and substance use among African American adolescents and young adults (e.g., ethnic identity, supportive parenting), but we still do not know a lot about what promotes this specific relation. Using substances as a means of coping appears to be one possibility, but our two-item coping measure (Gibbons, Etcheverry, et al., 2008) is only suggestive. Our assumption that coping style may be a factor in distinguishing users and nonusers and that internalizing responses (such as depression) lead to cardiovascular problems, whereas externalizing reactions (anger and hostility) increase risk for drug use, seems worthy of further investigation. We would suggest that these issues can best be addressed using a combination of survey and laboratory (experimental) studies.

One caveat worth noting is that all of our work so far has been done with African Americans. There is some evidence to suggest that African Americans experience more discrimination than other racial minorities (Darden, 2001) and that it has more of an impact on them (Gee et al., 2006). That could mean that the effect of discrimination on use is greater for African Americans and/or that the process involved is different for other minorities. If so, this would perhaps suggest a different approach in terms of

intervention and preventive intervention strategies that might effectively buffer discrimination effects. For that matter, a very basic question is what does a racial or ethnic pride component add to interventions, such as SAAF, and would additional elements that focus on racial socialization help prepare and protect African American children from the risks of the discrimination they are likely to face? Finally, most measures of racial discrimination focus on personal, day-to-day experiences; such is the case with the Schedule of Racist Events (Landrine & Klonoff, 1996) that we have used in our research. However, it is clear that discriminatory messages are conveyed in a variety of ways through many different sources. A prime example would be the media. Messages from movies and TV may affect implicit racial attitudes more than explicit attitudes among both Black and White adolescents. The ways in which stereotyping and prejudice are conveyed in the media and how these portrayals relate to substance use may prove fruitful as an area of future research (Gibbons, Pomery, et al., 2007).

CONCLUSION

African American adolescents use substances less than adolescents of other racial and ethnic groups even though they are at much higher risk of use because of contextual factors (e.g., crime, substance availability) and also because of the increased stress that comes from these high-risk environments and from their experiences with racial discrimination. Those experiences do have an impact on their substance use and may eventually contribute to the increase in abuse problems that some African Americans experience as adults—the racial crossover effect. Our research has provided evidence of a prospective link between discrimination and use in Black adolescents and their parents. We have also found that this link is mediated by distress, especially anger, and that it may be a reflection of a coping process. At the same time, there is also evidence that supportive parenting and strong ethnic identity can buffer Black adolescents against the negative effects of discrimination, particularly in mostly White neighborhoods, where reports of discrimination and substance availability are higher. Finally, there is some evidence in our research and that of others of the utility of a dual-processing perspective, exemplified in the prototype model, in examining the effects of discrimination on behavior, and perhaps in countering those effects with theory-based interventions.

References

Ajzen, I. (1996). The social psychology of decision making. In E. T. Higgins & A. W. Kruglanski (Eds.), *Social psychology: Handbook of basic principles* (pp. 297–328). New York: Guilford Press.

Albarracín, D., Johnson, B. T., Fishbein, M., & Muellerleile, P. A. (2001). Theories of reasoned action and planned behavior as models of condom use: A meta-analysis. *Psychological Bulletin, 127,* 142–161.

Andrews, J. A., Hampson, S. E., Barckley, M., Gerrard, M., & Gibbons, F. X. (2008). The effect of early cognitions on cigarette and alcohol use in adolescence. *Psychology of Addictive Behaviors, 28,* 96–106.

Ardelt, M., & Eccles, J. S. (2001). Effects of mothers' parental efficacy beliefs and promotive parenting strategies on inner-city youth. *Journal of Family Issues, 22,* 944–972.

Armitage, C. J., & Connor, M. (2001). Efficacy of the theory of planned behavior: A meta-analytic review. *British Journal of Social Psychology, 40,* 471–499.

Arnett, J. J. (2007). *African American emerging adults.* Manuscript submitted for publication.

Arnett, J. J., & Tanner, J. L. (Eds.). (2006). *Emerging adults in America: Coming of age in the 21st century.* Washington, DC: American Psychological Association.

Bennett, G. G., Wolin, K. Y., Robinson, E. L., Fowler, S., & Edwards, C. L. (2005). Perceived racial/ethnic harassment and tobacco use among African American young adults. *American Journal of Public Health, 95,* 238–240.

Boatright, S. R., & Bachtel, D. C. (2003). *The Georgia county guide* (22nd ed.). Athens, GA: University of Georgia Cooperative Extension Service.

Bodenhausen, G. V., Sheppard, L. A., & Kramer, G. P. (1994). Negative affect and social judgment: The differential impact of anger and sadness. *European Journal of Social Psychology, 24,* 45–62.

Borrell, L. N., Kiefe, C. I., Williams, D. R., Diez-Roux, A. V., & Gordon-Larsen, P. (2006). Self-reported health, perceived racial discrimination, and skin color in African Americans in the CARDIA study. *Social Science & Medicine, 63,* 1415–1427.

Boyer, T. W. (2006). The development of risk-taking: A multi-perspective review. *Developmental Review, 26,* 291–345.

Brody, G. H., Chen, Y., Murry, V., Ge, X., Gibbons, F. X., Gerrard, M., & Cutrona, C. (2006). Perceived discrimination and the adjustment of African American youths: A five-year longitudinal analysis with contextual moderation effects. *Child Development, 77,* 1170–1189.

Brody, G. H., Kim, S., Murry, V. M., & Brown, A. C. (2004). Protective longitudinal paths linking child competence to behavioral problems among African American siblings. *Child Development, 75,* 455–467.

Brody, G. H., Murry, V. M., Kogan, S. M., Gerrard, M., Gibbons, F. X., Molgaard, V., et al. (2006). The Strong African American Families Program: A cluster-randomized prevention trial of long-term effects and a mediational model. *Journal of Consulting and Clinical Psychology, 74,* 356–366.

Brook, J. S., Balka, E., Brook, D. W., Win, P., & Gursen, M. D. (1998). Drug use among African Americans: Ethnic identity as a protective factor. *Psychological Reports, 83,* 1427–1446.

Brook, J. S., & Pahl, K. (2005). The protective role of ethnic and racial identity and aspects of an Africentric orientation against drug use among African American young adults. *Journal of Genetic Psychology, 166,* 329–345.

Brown, T. L., Flory, K., Lynam, D. R., Leukefeld, C., & Clayton, R. R. (2004). Comparing the developmental trajectories of marijuana use of African American and Caucasian adolescents: Patterns, antecedents, and consequences. *Experimental and Clinical Psychopharmacology, 12,* 47–56.

Brown, T. L., Parks, G. S., Zimmerman, R. S., & Phillips, C. M. (2001). The role of religion in predicting adolescent alcohol use and problem drinking. *Journal of Studies on Alcohol, 62,* 696–705.

Carroll, K. M., Rosa, C., Brown, L. S., Jr., Daw, R., Magruder, K. M., & Beatty, L. (2007). Addressing ethnic disparities in drug abuse treatment in the clinical trial networks. *Drug and Alcohol Dependence, 90,* 101–106.

Catalano, R. F., Morrison, D. M., Wells, E. A., Gillmore, M. R., Iritani, B., & Hawkins, J. D. (1992). Ethnic differences in family factors related to early drug initiation. *Journal of Studies on Alcohol, 53,* 208–217.

Cavacuit, C. A. (2004). You, me . . . and drugs–A love triangle: Important considerations when both members of a couple are abusing substances. *Substance Use and Misuse, 39,* 645–656.

Chaiken, S., & Trope, Y. (1999). *Dual-process theories in social psychology.* New York: Guilford Press.

Chatters, L. M., Taylor, R. J., & Lincoln, K. D. (1999). African American religious participation: A multi-sample comparison. *Journal for the Scientific Study of Religion, 38,* 132–145.

Chen, K. W., & Killeya-Jones, L. A. (2006). Understanding differences in marijuana use among urban Black and suburban White high school students from two U.S. community samples. *Journal of Ethnicity Substance Abuse, 5,* 51–73.

Clark, P. I., Scarisbrick-Hauser, A., Gautam, S. P., & Wirk, S. J. (1999). Anti-tobacco socialization in homes of African American and Caucasian parents, and smoking and nonsmoking parents. *Journal of Adolescent Health, 24,* 329–339.

Corneille, M. A., & Belgrave, F. Z. (2007). Ethnic identity, neighborhood risk, and adolescent drug and sex attitudes and refusal efficacy: The urban African American girls' experience. *Journal of Drug Education, 37,* 177–190.

Curran, P. J., Muthén, B. O., & Harford, T. C. (1998). The influence of changes in marital status on developmental trajectories of alcohol use in young adults. *Journal of Studies on Alcohol, 59,* 647–658.

Curry, L. A., & Youngblade, L. M. (2006). Negative affect, risk perception, and adolescent risk behavior. *Journal of Applied Developmental Psychology, 27,* 468–485.

Darden, J. T. (2001). Blacks and other racial minorities: The significance of color in inequality. In E. Cashmore & J. Jennings (Eds.), *Racism: Essential readings* (pp. 237–246). London: Sage.

Dawkins, M. P., & Williams, M. M. (1997). Substance abuse in rural African-American populations. In E. B. Robertson, Z. Sloboda, G. M. Boyd, L. Beatty, & N. J. Kozel (Eds.), *Rural substance abuse: State of knowledge and issues* (National Institute on Drug Abuse Research Monograph No. 168, pp. 484–498). Rockville, MD: Author.

Donaldson, S. I., Sussman, S., MacKinnon, D. P., Severson, H. H., Glynn, T., Murray, D. M., et al. (1996). Drug abuse prevention programming: Do we know what content works? *American Behavioral Scientist, 39,* 868–883.

Drucker, E. (1999). Drug prohibition and public health: 25 years of evidence. *Public Health Reports, 114,* 14–29.

Ensminger, M. E., Joon, H. S., & Fothergill, K. E. (2002). Childhood and adolescent antecedents of substance use in adulthood. *Addiction, 97,* 833–844.

Fishbein, M., & Ajzen, I. (1975). *Belief, attitude, intention, and behavior: An introduction to theory and research.* Reading, MA: Addison-Wesley.

Flora, D. B., & Chassin, L. (2005). Changes in drug use during young adulthood: The effects of parent alcoholism and transition into marriage. *Psychology of Addictive Behaviors, 19,* 352–362.

Gardiner, P. S. (2001). African American teen cigarette smoking: A review. In *Changing adolescent smoking prevalence: Where it is and why* (pp. 213–225).

Bethesda, MD: U.S. Department of Health and Human Services.

Gaughan, M. (2006). The gender structure of adolescent peer influence on drinking. *Journal of Health and Social Behavior, 47,* 47–61.

Gee, G. C., Ryan, A., Laflamme, D. J., & Holt, J. (2006). Self reported discrimination and mental health status among African descendants, Mexican American, and other Latinos in the New Hampshire REACH 2010 Initiative: The added dimension of immigration. *American Journal of Public Health, 96,* 1821–1828.

Gerrard, M., Gibbons, F. X., Brody, G. H., Murry, V. M., Cleveland, M. J., & Wills, T. A. (2006). A theory-based dual-focus alcohol intervention for preadolescents: The Strong African American Families Program. *Psychology of Addictive Behaviors, 20,* 185–195.

Gerrard, M., Gibbons, F. X., Houlihan, A. E., Stock, M. L., & Pomery, E. A. (2008). A dual-process approach to health risk decision making: The prototype willingness model. *Developmental Review, 28,* 29–61.

Gerrard, M., Gibbons, F. X., Reis-Bergan, M., Trudeau, L., Vande Lune, L., & Buunk, B. P. (2002). Inhibitory effects of drinker and non-drinker prototypes on adolescent alcohol consumption: *Health Psychology, 21,* 601–609.

Gerrard, M., Gibbons, F. X., Stock, M. L., Vande Lune, L. S., & Cleveland, M. J. (2005). Images of smokers and willingness to smoke among African American pre-adolescents: An application of the prototype/willingness model of adolescent health risk behavior to smoking initiation. *Journal of Pediatric Psychology, 30,* 305–318.

Gibbons, F. X., Etcheverry, P. E., Stock, M. G., Gerrard, M., O'Hara, R., & Simons, R. L. (2008). *Exploring the discrimination to substance use link in young African Americans: What mediates, what moderates?* Manuscript submitted for publication.

Gibbons, F. X., Gerrard, M., Brody, G. H., Roberts, M., Wills, T. A., & Murry, V. (2008). *Support for a dual-focus, dual-process approach to adolescent substance use interventions: Lessons from FACHS and SAAF.* Manuscript in preparation.

Gibbons, F. X., Gerrard, M., Cleveland, M. J., Wills, T. A., & Brody, G. H. (2004). Perceived discrimination and substance use in African American parents and their children: A panel study. *Journal of Personality and Social Psychology, 86,* 517–529.

Gibbons, F. X., Gerrard, M., & Lane, D. J. (2003). A social-reaction model of adolescent health risk. In J. M. Suls & K. A. Wallston (Eds.), *Social psychological foundations of health and illness* (pp. 107–136). Oxford, England: Blackwell.

Gibbons, F. X., Gerrard, M., Ouellette, J. A., & Burzette, R. (1998). Cognitive antecedents to adolescent health risk: Discriminating between behavioral intention and behavioral willingness. *Psychology and Health, 13,* 319–339.

Gibbons, F. X., Gerrard, M., Reimer, R. A., & Pomery, E. A. (2006). Unintentional behavior: A subrational approach to health risk. In D. T. M. de Ridder & J. B. F. de Wit (Eds.), *Self-regulation in health behavior* (pp. 45–70). Chichester, England: Wiley.

Gibbons, F. X., Gerrard, M., Wills, T. A., Weng, C.-Y., & Kingsbury, J. (2008). *Early and cumulative effects of perceived discrimination on African American adolescents' substance use: A latent growth curve analysis.* Manuscript in preparation.

Gibbons, F. X., Pomery, E. A., Gerrard, M., Sarget, J. D., Yeh, H.-C., Wills, T. A., et al. (2007). *Media as social influence: Individual differences in the effects of media on adolescent alcohol cognitions and consumption.* Manuscript submitted for publication.

Gibbons, F. X., Yeh, H., Gerrard, M., Cleveland, M. J., Cutrona, C., Simons, R. L., & Brody, G. H. (2007). Early experience with discrimination and conduct disorder as predictors of subsequent drug use: A critical period analysis. *Drug and Alcohol Dependence, 88,* S27–S37.

Gil, A. G., Wagner, E. F., & Tubman, J. (2004). Associations between early adolescent substance use and subsequent young-adult substance use disorders and psychiatric disorders among a multiethnic male sample in south Florida. *American Journal of Public Health, 94,* 1603–1609.

Guthrie, B. J., Young, A. M., Williams, D. R., Boyd, C. J., & Kintner, E. K. (2002). African American girls' smoking habits and day-to-day experiences with racial discrimination. *Nursing Research, 51,* 183–190.

Hochstetler, A., Murphy, D. S., & Simons, R. L. (2004). Damaged goods: Exploring predictors of distress in prison inmates. *Crime & Delinquency, 50,* 436–457.

Holley, L. C., Kulis, S., Marsiglia, F. F., & Keith, V. M. (2006). Ethnicity versus ethnic identity: What predicts substance use norms and behaviors? *Journal of Social Work Practice in the Addictions, 6,* 53–79.

Holz, V. J., & Tienda, M. (1998). Education and employment in a diverse society: Generating inequality through the school to work transition. In N. D. S. Tolnay (Ed.), *American diversity: A demographic challenge for the twenty-first century* (pp. 249–281). Albany, New York: SUNY Press.

Iceland, J. (2004). Beyond black and white: Metropolitan residential segregation in multi-ethnic America. *Social Science Research, 33,* 248–271.

Iguchi, M. Y., Bell, J., Ramchand, R. N., & Fain, T. (2005). How criminal system racial disparities may translate into health disparities. *Journal of Health Care for the Poor and Underserved, 16,* 48–56.

Johnston, L. D., O'Malley, P. M., & Bachman, J. G. (2003). *Monitoring the Future national survey results on drug use, 1975–2002. Vol. 1: Secondary school students* (NIH Publication No. 03-5375). Bethesda, MD: National Institute on Drug Abuse.

Johnston, L. D., O'Malley, P. M., Bachman, J. G., & Schulenberg, J. E. (2005). *Monitoring the Future national survey results on drug use, 1975–2004. Vol. 1: Secondary school students* (NIH Publication No. 05-5727). Bethesda, MD: National Institute on Drug Abuse.

Kaiser Family Foundation. (2006). *Race, ethnicity & health care: Young African American men in the United States* (Publication No. 7541). Washington, DC: Author.

Kandel, D. B., Johnston, J. G., Bird, H. R., & Canino, G. (1997). Psychiatric disorders associated with substance use among children and adolescents: Findings from the methods for the epidemiology of child and adolescent mental disorders (MECA) study. *Journal of Abnormal Child Psychology, 25,* 121–132.

Kessler, R. C., Mickelson, K. D., & Williams, D. R. (1999). The prevalence, distribution, and mental health correlates of perceived discrimination in the United States. *Journal of Health and Social Behavior, 40,* 208–230.

Krieger, N. (2000). Refiguring "race": Epidemiology, racialized biology, and biological expressions of race relations. *International Journal of Health Services, 30,* 211–216.

Kulis, S., Napoli, M., & Marsiglia, F. (2002). The effects of ethnic pride and biculturalism on the drug use norms of urban American Indian adolescents in the Southwest. *Social Work Research, 26,* 101–112.

Kwate, N. O. A., Valdimarsdottir, H. B., Guevarra, J. S., & Bovbjerg, D. H. (2003). Experiences of racist events are associated with negative health consequences for African American women. *Journal of the National Medical Association, 95,* 450–460.

Lambert, S. F., Brown, T. L., Phillips, C. M., & Ialongo, N. (2005). The relationship between perceptions of neighborhood characteristics and substance use among urban African American adolescents. *American Journal of Community Psychology, 34,* 205–218.

Landrine, H., & Klonoff, E. A. (1996). The schedule of racist events: A measure of racial discrimination and a study of its negative physical and mental health consequences. *Journal of Black Psychology, 22,* 144–168.

Landrine, H., & Klonoff, E. (2000). Racial discrimination and cigarette smoking among Blacks: Findings from two studies. *Ethnicity & Disease, 10,* 195–202.

Landrine, H., Klonoff, E. A., Corral, I., Fernandez, S., & Roesch, S. (2006). Conceptualizing and measuring ethnic discrimination in health research. *Journal of Behavioral Medicine, 29,* 79–94.

Lerner, J. S., & Keltner, D. (2000). Beyond valence: Toward a model of emotion-specific influences on judgment and choice. *Cognition & Emotion, 14,* 473–493.

Lerner, J. S., & Keltner, D. (2001). Fear, anger, and risk. *Journal of Personality and Social Psychology, 81,* 146–159.

Loewenstein, G. F., Weber, E. U., Hsee, C. K., & Welch, N. (2001). Risk as feelings. *Psychological Bulletin, 127,* 267–286.

Marsiglia, F. F., Kulis, S., & Hecht, M. L. (2001). Ethnic labels and ethnic identity as predictors of drug use among middle school students in the southwest. *Journal of Research on Adolescence, 11,* 21–48.

Martin, J. K., Tuch, S. A., & Roman, P. M. (2003). Problem drinking patterns among African Americans: The impacts of reports of discrimination, perceptions of prejudice, and "risky" coping strategies. *Journal of Health and Social Behavior, 44,* 408–425.

Mays, V. M., Cochran, S. D., & Barnes, N. W. (2007). Race, race-based discrimination, and health outcomes among African Americans. *Annual Review of Psychology, 58,* 201–225.

Moden, C. W. S., van Lenthe, F., Graaf, N. D. D., & Kraaykamp, G. (2003). Partner's and own education: Does who you live with matter for self-assessed health, smoking, and excessive alcohol consumption? *Social Science & Medicine, 57,* 1902–1912.

Mudar, P., Kearns, J. N., & Leonard, K. E. (2002). The transition to marriage and changes in alcohol involvement among Black couples and White couples. *Journal of Studies on Alcohol, 63,* 568–576.

National Institute on Alcohol Abuse and Alcoholism. (2003). *Underage drinking: A major public health challenge (Alcohol Alert 59)*. Rockville, MD: Author.

Nowlin, P. R., & Colder, C. R. (2007). The role of ethnicity and neighborhood poverty on the relationship between parenting and adolescent cigarette use. *Nicotine & Tobacco Research, 9,* 545–556.

Orozco, S., & Lukas, S. (2000). Gender differences in acculturation and aggression as predictors of drug use in minorities. *Drug and Alcohol Dependence, 59,* 156–176.

Ouellette, J. A., Gerrard, M., Gibbons, F. X., & Reis-Bergan, M. (1999). Parents, peers, and prototypes: Antecedents of adolescent alcohol expectancies, alcohol consumption, and alcohol-related life problems. *Psychology of Addictive Behaviors, 13,* 183–197.

Parker, D., Manstead, A. S. R., Stradling, S. G., Reason, J. T., & Baxter, J. S. (1992). Intention to commit driving violation: An application of the theory of planned behavior. *Journal of Applied Psychology, 77,* 94–101.

Pettit, B., & Western, B. (2004). Mass imprisonment and the life course: Race and class inequality in U.S. incarceration. *American Sociological Review, 69,* 151–169.

Phinney, J. S. (1992). The multigroup Ethnic Identity Measure: A new scale for use with diverse groups. *Journal of Adolescent Research, 7,* 156–176.

Pomery, E. A., Gibbons, F. X., Reis-Bergan, M., & Gerrard, M. (2008). *From willingness to intention: Experience moderates the shift from reactive to reasoned behavior.* Manuscript in preparation.

Pugh, L. A., & Bry, B. H. (2007). The protective effects of ethnic identity for alcohol and marijuana use among Black young adults. *Cultural Diversity and Ethnic Minority Psychology, 13,* 187–193.

Raghunathan, R., & Pham, M. T. (1999). All negative moods are not equal: Motivational influences of anxiety and sadness on decision making. *Organizational Behavior & Human Decision Processes, 79,* 56–77.

Reardon, S. F., & Buka, S. L. (2002). Differences in onset and persistence of substance abuse and dependence among Whites, Blacks, and Hispanics. *Public Health Reports, 117,* S51–S59.

Resnicow, K., Soler, R. E., Braithwaite, R. L., Selassie, M. B., & Smith, M. (1999). Development of a racial and ethnic identity scale for African American adolescents: The Survey of Black Life. *Journal of Black Psychology, 25,* 171–188.

Reyna, V. F., & Farley, F. (2006). Risk and rationality in adolescent decision making: Implications for theory, practice, and public policy. *Psychological Science in the Public Interest, 7,* 1–44.

Richman, L. S., Bennett, G. G., Pek, J., Siegler, I., & Williams, R. B., Jr. (2007). Discrimination, dispositions, and cardiovascular responses to stress. *Health Psychology, 26,* 675–683.

Scheier, L. M., Botvin, G. J., Diaz, T., & Ifill-Williams, M. (1997). Ethnic identity as a moderator of psychosocial risk and adolescent alcohol and marijuana use: Concurrent and longitudinal analyses. *Journal of Child and Adolescent Substance Abuse, 6,* 21–47.

Schulenberg, J. E., & Maggs, J. L. (2002). A developmental perspective on alcohol use and heavy drinking during adolescence and the transition to young adulthood. *Journal of Studies on Alcohol, 114,* 54–70.

Schulenberg, J., O'Malley, P. M., Bachman, J. G., & Johnston, L. D. (2005). Early adult transitions and their relation to well-being and substance use. In R. A. Settersten, F. F. Furstenberg Jr., & R. G. Rumbaut (Eds.), *On the frontier of adulthood: Theory, research, and public policy* (pp. 417–453). Chicago: University of Chicago Press.

Simons, R. L., Chen, Y., Stewart, E., & Brody, G. (2003). Incidents of discrimination and risk for delinquency: A longitudinal test of strain theory with an African American sample. *Justice Quarterly, 20,* 827–854.

Simons, R. L., Dummund, H., Stewart, E., Brody, G. H., Gibbons, F. X., & Cutrona, C. (2006). Supportive parenting moderates the effect of discrimination upon anger: Hostile view of relationships, and violence among African American boys. *Journal of Health and Social Behavior, 47,* 373–389.

Simons, R. L., Murry, V., McLoyd, V., Lin, K.-H., Cutrona, C. E., & Conger, R. D. (2002). Discrimination, crime, ethnic identity, and parenting as correlates of depressive symptoms among African American children: A multilevel analysis. *Development & Psychopathology, 14,* 371–393.

Stock, M. L, Gibbons, F. X., Gerrard, M., Houlihan, A. E., & Simons, R. L. (2007). *Ethnic identification, integration, and substance use vulnerability among African American adolescents.* Manuscript submitted for publication.

Substance Abuse and Mental Health Services Administration. (2003). *Results from the 2002 National Survey on Drug Use and Health: National findings* (Office of Applied Studies, NHSDA Series H-22, DHHS Publication No. SMA 03-3836). Rockville, MD: Author.

Substance Abuse and Mental Health Services Administration. (2005). *National household survey on drug abuse, 2000 and 2001.* Rockville, MD: Author.

Taxman, F., Byrne, J. M., & Pattavina, A. (2005). Racial disparity and the legitimacy of the criminal justice system: Exploring consequences for deterrence. *Journal for Health Care for the Poor and Underserved, 16,* 57–77.

Trinidad, D. R., Gilpin, E., Lee, L., & Pierce, J. P. (2004). Has there been a delay in the age of regular smoking onset among African Americans? *Annals of Behavioral Medicine, 28,* 152–157.

Trumbo, C. W. (2002). Information processing and risk perception: An adaptation of the heuristic-systematic model. *Journal of Communication, 52,* 367–382.

Wallace, J. M., & Bachman, J. G. (1991). Explaining racial/ethnic differences in adolescent drug use: The impact of background and lifestyle. *Social Problems, 38,* 333–357.

Wallace, J. M., & Muroff, J. R. (2002). Preventing substance abuse among African American children and youth: Race differences in risk factor exposure and vulnerability. *Journal of Primary Prevention, 22,* 235–261.

Warshaw, P. R., & Davis, F. O. (1985). Disentangling behavior intention and behavioral expectation. *Journal of Experimental Social Psychology, 21,* 213–228.

Webb, T. L., & Sheeran, P. (2006). Does changing behavioral intentions engender behavior change? A meta-analysis of the experimental evidence. *Psychological Bulletin, 132,* 249–268.

Weinstein, N. D. (1984). Why it won't happen to me: Perceptions of risk factors and illness susceptibility. *Health Psychology, 3,* 431–457.

White, H. R., Nagin, D., Replogle, E., & Stouthamer-Loeber, M. (2004). Racial differences in trajectories of cigarette use. *Drug and Alcohol Dependence, 76,* 219–227.

Wiers, R. W., Bartholow, B. D., van den Wildenberg, E., Thush, C., Engels, R. C. M. E., Sher, K. J., et al. (2007). Automatic and controlled process and the development of addictive behaviors in adolescents: A review and a model. *Pharmacology Biochemistry and Behavior, 86,* 263–283.

Williams, D. R., & Neighbors, H. (2001). Racism, discrimination, and hypertension: Evidence and needed research. *Ethnicity and Disease, 11,* 800–816.

Williams, D. R., Neighbors, H. W., & Jackson, J. S. (2003). Racial/ethnic discrimination and health: Findings from community studies. *American Journal of Public Health, 93,* 200–208.

Wills, T. A., Gibbons, F. X., Gerrard, M., Murry, V. M., & Brody, G. H. (2003). Family communication and religiosity related to substance use and sexual behavior in early adolescence: A test for pathways through self-control and prototype perceptions. *Psychology of Addictive Behavior, 17,* 312–323.

Wills, T. A., Murry, V. M., Brody, G. H., Gibbons, F. X., Gerrard, M., Walker, C., & Ainette, M. G. (2007). Ethnic pride and self-control related to protective and risk factors: Test of the theoretical model for the strong African American families program. *Health Psychology, 26,* 50–59.

PART VI

PEER AND FAMILY INFLUENCES

CHAPTER 19

FAMILY PROCESSES IN DRUG USE ETIOLOGY

Wendy Kliewer

Jamilla[1] is a 13-year-old African American girl living in Richmond, Virginia, a relatively small metropolitan city boasting a southern hospitality. Richmond is primarily known for its thriving legal, financial, and banking communities; however, there is a segment of underserved poor minorities that populate sections of Richmond. Jamilla resides with her mother and older brother in a public housing community. Jamilla's mother works long hours and as a result does not get to spend as much time as she would like raising and caring for her children. The long hours translate into less parental supervision, which has led to greater self-reliance on the part of her children. They often prepare their own meals, do household chores, and tend to their own personal needs. Although Jamilla's mother works full time, she reports major financial problems in the past year, including a household relocation that was quite stressful.

The housing community in which they recently resided is rife with violence and drug use. During the past year, Jamilla experienced significant stress when she was caught in the gunfire between two adults and shot in the face. The men were arguing over a drug deal that had gone bad, a frequent event in this housing community. It took several months for Jamilla to recover from the facial wounds, and the hospital expenses and costs of medical treatment added significantly to her mother's financial stress. Despite the seemingly insurmountable problems and the hard life before them, Jamilla has a close

relationship with her mother and a strong personal faith in God. Although Jamilla's parents never married, she also reports a close relationship with her father, who lives nearby. In response to the shooting, Jamilla's mother relocated the family to another housing community in the city. A year later, Jamilla reports few psychological aftereffects of the violence and is coping well.

In contrast, Gregory is a 15-year-old African American boy who also resides in Richmond. Gregory lives with his mother, who is divorced; three brothers and sisters; the young infant of his older sister; and another female adult. His mother has had some college education but is currently unemployed. The household income is somewhere between $201 and $300 per week, which has created significant stress for the family, including the inability to consistently pay utility bills. Gregory's family environment would best be described as chaotic. On numerous occasions, the police have responded to domestic disputes at the house stemming partly from his mother's alcohol abuse problem. Gregory's father is in and out of his children's lives, disappearing for months at a time. During the past year, Gregory has reported feeling suicidal and threatened to blow up his high school, which resulted in a suspension but no follow-up counseling from the school. He also reported being the target of a school gang shooting. His main social support appears to be his 21-year-old girlfriend. Gregory's mother is unable to deal with his stress, given her own alcohol involvement, and the household and personal problems seem to mount to the point of despair.

---

[1] Names have been changed to conceal identities.

FAMILIAL INFLUENCE ON ADOLESCENT DRUG USE

These two case studies from my ongoing research illustrate the powerful ways in which parents and families can mitigate or exacerbate adolescent risk for using and abusing drugs and alcohol. The central purpose of this chapter is to describe parent and family factors that are linked to drug use in adolescents. A number of authors have suggested that the family is one of the single most important factors in understanding adolescent drug use because of the myriad risk and protective factors that may be directly influenced by the family (Branstetter, Masse, & Greene, 2007; Hawkins, Catalano, & Miller, 1992; Kandel, 1996; M. A. Miller, Alberts, Hecht, Trost, & Krizek, 2000). Given the primacy of the family unit in development, many scholars believe that parents are the most underused resource in preventing youth drug abuse (Califano, 2000; Office of National Drug Control Policy, 1997).

The conceptual model used to frame this chapter is based on a socialization model of adolescent drug use (see Figure 19.1). The model recognizes that socialization agents other than parents and family members, including peers and neighborhood residents, have an influence on adolescent drug use. The model also recognizes that unique features of the situation, biology and temperament, and local or national culture play a role in shaping adolescent behaviors that lead to drug use or affect drug use directly. Thus, parents and family members are important influences on adolescent drug use, but clearly other influences should be considered when attempting to understand why adolescents use or abstain from using drugs and alcohol.

The perspective shaped in this chapter differs from other family influence models (e.g., family interactional theory [Brook, Brook, & Pahl, 2006], social control theory [Elliott, Huizinga, & Ageton, 1985], social development theory [Hawkins & Weis, 1985]) because it considers three distinct pathways through which parents and families affect adolescent behavior: coaching (messages parents relay to their children), modeling (parents' own behavior), and family context (features of the family environment that either support or inhibit behavior). Figure 19.1 shows the different pathways for

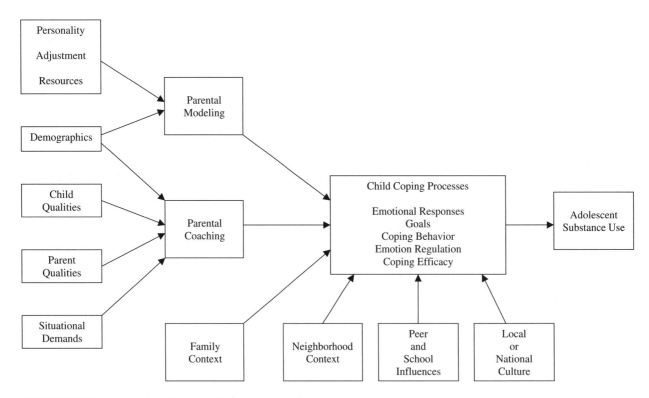

FIGURE 19.1.   A socialization model of adolescent drug use.

the family influence model. As depicted, parental coaching is influenced by demographics (e.g., parent gender, socioeconomic status, age), qualities of the parent (e.g., personality, adjustment, resources, values), qualities of the child (e.g., age, gender, temperament and personality, adjustment, history of coping), and situational demands (e.g., controllability, novelty). Parental modeling is informed by demographics and parent personality, adjustment, values, and resources. Thus, the messages parents convey to their children—overt or subtle, intended or unintended—are multiply determined. Family context represents the broad backdrop against which parental coaching and modeling occur. As architects of the home environment, parents establish rules and set the emotional tone for family interactions. Collectively, parental coaching, modeling, and family context affect child coping processes.

The family influence model posits that coping processes are closely situated to the development of drug use behaviors (some would consider this a proximal variable). In this respect, and as part of my research team's efforts to organize family-based variables that influence drug use into a coherent system, we believe that the final stage in the process leading to drug use emphasizes personal coping skills. These skills are the endpoint in a long learning process that includes how youth manage stress and the way in which they respond to the implicit and explicit messages conveyed by their parents regarding how to manage stress. Taken together, these stress-related processes influence the extent to which youth will engage in drug use. Thus, this model considers a host of family factors that are related to coping processes (e.g., emotional responses, appraisals, coping behavior, coping efficacy), which in turn affect adolescent drug use.

In the following sections, I highlight the existing literature linking parental coaching, modeling, and family context to adolescent drug use and feather in with this material other studies linking coping processes with drug use. Because of its centrality to the socialization model, I begin by describing coping processes and reviewing the literature linking adolescent coping processes to drug use.

COPING PROCESSES AND ADOLESCENT DRUG USE

Lazarus and Folkman (1984) conceptualized coping processes as emotional, cognitive, and behavioral responses to stressors. The response mechanisms are multifaceted, including (a) appraisal, in which an individual evaluates the potential harm or benefit of a situation as well as his or her resources to manage the situation; (b) coping, in which an individual consciously engages in cognitive and/or behavioral efforts to manage situations appraised as stressful; and (c) efficacy evaluations, in which an individual assesses the extent to which coping behaviors that were enacted had the intended effect. The concept of emotion regulation overlaps substantially with coping but includes nonvolitional and sometimes unconscious responses to stressors. There is extensive evidence that coping processes matter for adolescents: A substantial number of studies have shown that the responses adolescents make to manage stressors predict their well-being (Compas, Connor-Smith, Saltzman, Thomsen, & Wadsworth, 2001; Wolchik & Sandler, 1997). Although there are some exceptions, in general, adolescents who engage with the stressor and use approach-oriented strategies (e.g., planning, problem solving, meaning making) or religious coping enjoy better physical and mental well-being than adolescents who disengage from the stressor and use avoidance strategies (e.g., wishing the problem did not exist, refusing to think about the situation, avoiding reminders of the situation). A number of specific studies have linked coping behavior prospectively with drug use in adolescence (see Wills & Filer, 1996, and Wills & Hirky, 1996, for reviews).

As researchers come to understand the basic psychological ingredients that constitute coping, it is imperative that they link these processes with real-life experiences of youth. In particular, the family context has a lot to do with how adolescents choose their coping resources and apply these skills in different situations. It is clear from the outset that coping within the family serves as a platform for additional social encounters available in school, with peers, or in other social situations that place demands on youth. In this respect, *learning about* the value of coping embedded within the family milieu should be quite informative in learning why some youth engage in deviant behaviors like drug use and others do not. The next section explores the role of coping as seen from a family interaction perspective, looking at the three major modalities of parental influence and how they relate to drug use.

PARENTAL COACHING AND ADOLESCENT DRUG USE

Parental coaching refers to messages parents verbally, explicitly relay to their children. In the context of drug use, this can refer to messages regarding attitudes toward drug use and actual drug use. *Coaching* also refers to messages related to coping processes that are associated with drug use. For example, parents may encourage avoidant coping, which is associated with greater drug use (Wills, Sandy, & Yeager, 2002), or appraisals or coping strategies that encourage adolescents to actively deal with their stressors, which are associated with less drug use (Wills, 1986). Thus, through coaching, parents can encourage specific attitudes regarding drug use in their children, as well as specific ways of handling stress that are more or less strongly associated with drug use. As shown in Figure 19.1 and noted earlier, the coaching messages parents relay to their children do not occur in a vacuum. What parents convey to their children is driven partly by the behavior of the child, partly by the parents' own values and experiences, and partly by the demands of the situation. In dealing with parent coaching, I also note the lack of extensive research on actual parental communication strategies and how they influence drug attitudes or drug use (Ennett, Bauman, Foshee, Pemberton, & Hicks, 2001; Miller-Day, 2002).

Effective parent–child communication is a key component of parental investment in the child, and this continues through adolescence and even beyond. Parent–child communication is one of the four protective processes identified by the Center for Substance Abuse Prevention Predictor Variable Initiative as a target of interventions (Szapocznik, Tolan, Smabrano, & Schwartz, 2007). Furthermore, as evidence of its importance, the National Institute on Drug Abuse Web site (http://www.nida.nih.gov)

has a section for parents on how to communicate effectively with their children. These tips include "Be a good listener," "Give clear no-use messages about drugs and alcohol," "Help your child deal with peer pressure to use drugs," and "Maintain an open and honest dialogue with your child." The Web site also stresses the important role parents play in helping and guiding children in making healthy decisions. A body of evidence accumulated from both national and regional drug abuse surveys shows that adolescents perceive parents as credible sources of information about drugs and that youth talk more with their parents about drugs than with any other resource. For example, in a relatively large nationwide survey of 7th–12th graders, youth were asked about drug use, family sanctions for use, and communication about drugs (Kelly, Comello, & Hunn, 2002). Slightly more than a quarter (27%) of the youth indicated they would ask their mother if they had a question about alcohol or drugs; the mother was the most frequently identified person when youth were asked to identify all of the people who had talked to them about alcohol and drugs. Notably, fewer than 15% of adolescents reported having conversations with their parents in the past year about the dangers of drugs. Most parent–child conversations on this topic occurred when the youth was between 10 and 12 years old.

This is one of several studies that illustrate the potential benefits of parent–adolescent communication. As much as the study underscores the importance of parents as an effective barrier to drug use, it also highlights the large percentages of youth who are not communicating with parents about drug use. Interestingly, research on adolescents' and parents' conceptions of parental authority found that nearly all adolescents and parents in the study affirmed parents' legitimate authority to regulate, and adolescents' obligations to comply with, rules concerning smoking cigarettes, drinking wine or beer, doing illicit drugs, or having sex (Smetana, 2000). For the most part, adolescents expect parents to establish and enforce rules regarding drug use. However, the same literature does not fully explore the nature of these conversations, the reasons they are protective, or the depth of communication when parents and adolescents do talk about drug use.

To my knowledge, only a handful of studies have explored the quality of parent–child communication as a protective factor in drug use etiology. In a series of studies, Miller-Day (2002; see also Miller-Day & Dodd, 2004) interviewed African American and Caucasian adolescents (ages 11–17), asking questions about conversations they had with their parents about drug use. The authors addressed which family members adolescents preferred conversing with on these topics and whether parent–adolescent communication regarding drugs influenced drug refusal. Fewer than half of the adolescents reported talking to parents about alcohol, tobacco, or other drugs. Moreover, the likelihood of talking with parents did not differ across ethnicity. Mothers were the preferred conversational partner for important topics, with more than two thirds of the sample reporting that they preferred to talk with mothers versus other family members. Using proportional analyses, Miller-Day (2002) reported that adolescents who discussed drug use more frequently with their parents were also more likely to report that they more often rejected drug offers from their friends.

Miller-Day and Dodd (2004) extended the abovementioned study in an investigation that used narrative content analysis. A group of college freshman and their parents participated in an online study in which each dyadic pair independently related personal stories recounting times when they had a conversation (between the parent or guardian and adolescent) regarding alcohol, tobacco, or other drug use. Narrative content analyses involved reading the transcribed responses from these talks line by line, comparing data across responses, labeling concepts as they developed, and clustering similar themes into larger categories. The content analyses included three major themes: framing drugs and drug use as a problem, using evidence to substantiate claims, and providing proscriptive (what children should not do or believe) and prescriptive (what children should do or believe) information. Consistent with previous findings, mothers initiated conversations with their children about drugs, and more mothers than fathers talked to their children about drugs. Interestingly, most parent–adolescent conversations occurred at home or in the car. Talks

were both proactive (before an event perceived as risky might occur) and reactive (after an event occurred). They occurred out of concerns for the health and safety of the adolescent or out of sheer necessity. Miller-Day and Dodd identified different patterns of communication regarding drugs on the basis of two dimensions: targeted conversations versus ongoing talks and direct versus indirect communication. For example, if a parent had an intentional conversation with their adolescent in which they made specific statements about expectations regarding drugs or drug use, this was then classified as a direct, targeted conversation. If a parent and an adolescent were watching TV and the parent made a specific comment that conveyed his or her disapproval of drug use, this exemplified direct, ongoing communication. If a parent hinted at his or her disapproval regarding drug use or made nonspecific statements about doing drugs, this was considered indirect, targeted communication. If a parent, by virtue of house rules, conveyed conservative drug use norms, it was classified as indirect, ongoing communication. Almost all (97%) of the dyads agreed about the particular conversational approaches used by the parent. Indirect messages—which were implied or nonverbal communications regarding rules, behaviors, attitudes, or expectations regarding drug use—were more common than direct verbal messages.

The approach of asking parents or youth to recollect conversations is one of several tactics to find out more about communication as a barrier to drug use. Other means include observing parent–child dyads in vivo to study the quality of their communication. For example, Caughlin and Malis (2004) audiotaped parent–child dyads while they engaged in conversations about alcohol and drug use. They also obtained self-reports and independent ratings of patterns of demand and withdrawal. These ratings captured the pattern of one person nagging or criticizing while the other person avoids the topic; interestingly, demanding conversation was positively associated with alcohol and drug use for both adolescents and parents.

Negative communication patterns like the ones identified by Caughlin and Malis (2004) are key targets of change in interventions to prevent or reduce adolescent drug use. One intervention that uses this strategy is *Familias Unidas,* a family-centered preventive intervention for Hispanic immigrant adolescents (Pantin et al., 2007). Key components of the *Familias Unidas* intervention involve improving family environment and positive parenting practices, including instilling more effective parent–adolescent communication about drug use. Using role-plays with other parents acting as adolescents, parents discuss their own views and attitudes toward drug use and abuse and practice discussing drug use in the context as though they were talking with their own adolescent. The intervention has undergone several revisions to improve content on the basis of qualitative interviews with intervention participants and has subsequently been implemented and tested with a new group of participants. Although efficacy data for the revised intervention were not available, qualitative analysis indicated that the initial intervention was effective in fostering communication and promoting investment in Hispanic families (Pantin et al., 2007).

Emotional Tone and Content

One glaring problem that affects what is known about parent–child communication is that few etiology studies have emphasized the content of communication. Likewise, intervention-based studies that seek to alter parent–child communication also neglect to measure the quality of the communication and rather focus primarily on quantity (frequency). Absent from these studies is a focus on the specific messages parents relay to their children, the emotional tone with which the messages are delivered, and the context with which they are delivered. Understanding the specific messages parents convey to their children is important because the message (and the messenger) matters (Ennett et al., 2001; Miller-Day, 2008). For instance, not all parent–adolescent communication is associated with drug use. Miller-Day (2008) quantified this in a recent set of studies focused on the kinds of strategies parents use to deter adolescent drug use and the impact of those strategies on actual adolescent drug use in the past month. In the first study, Miller-Day used qualitative methods with a college-age sample to identify the strategies parents convey to adolescents regarding their expectations about alcohol and other drug use. The most com-

monly identified strategies included using their own judgment, hinting, declaring a no-tolerance rule, providing information about drug use, threatening punishment, rewarding the adolescent for nonuse, and simply not addressing the issue. In a second related study, college freshmen responded to questions about parental strategies gleaned from the first study, along with questions probing their 30-day recent alcohol, tobacco, and marijuana use. Only the parental strategy invoking a no-tolerance rule was associated with lower use of tobacco, alcohol, and marijuana.

Parental disapproval also figured prominently in a large longitudinal study that assessed specific parental messages about tobacco and alcohol use and their relation to the initiation of smoking or drinking (Ennett et al., 2001). The parent–adolescent dyads were controls from a family-based adolescent drug use prevention program. Ennett et al. (2001) found that parent–adolescent communication surrounding drug use focused on rules, consequences, and media portrayals. Controlling for demographic and parenting characteristics, logistic regression models provided little support for significant associations between overt communication style and youth tobacco and alcohol use over time. However, parental reports of their disapproval of tobacco and alcohol use were associated with a lower probability of escalation of drinking 1 year after baseline. Parental disapproval of use was positively associated with parent–child communication about rules and media, illustrating the role that parental values play in coaching. These results also indicate the complexity of the phenomenon. In some studies, parental attitudes predict adolescent drug use more strongly than messages per se; however, as in the Ennett et al. study, the way in which a message was delivered was not captured in the data analysis. Thus, information about the messages youth received from their parents is incomplete.

As the model presented in this chapter suggests and as illustrated in Ennett et al. (2001), parental values and attitudes toward drug use affect the nature of conversations parents have with their adolescents on this topic and subsequently influence adolescent attitudes and behavior. Reinforcing this finding, Nash, McQueen, and Bray (2005) used structural equation modeling with three waves of data from a study of high school students to evaluate a model testing relations between parental attitudes toward alcohol use, youth alcohol use, and alcohol-related problems. Overall, the model indicated that parents' disapproval of alcohol use was associated with less alcohol use and fewer alcohol-related problems. Youth with parents reporting high disapproval were also less involved with peers who used alcohol and displayed greater confidence in avoiding alcohol use. This finding builds on previous research highlighting the importance of effectively communicating parental expectations and values to adolescents. Other studies with somewhat younger populations have shown that effective parental communication that clearly articulates expectations to avoid risky behaviors, including drug use, is associated with greater avoidance of risk taking (Nelson, Patience, & MacDonald, 1999).

Findings similar to those in studies of adolescent alcohol use have also been observed in those of adolescent tobacco use. Castrucci and Gerlach (2005) conducted a cross-sectional survey with a large sample of high school students from across the United States who reported having smoked tobacco in the previous month. They queried youth about their thoughts regarding quitting smoking, and if they had thought about quitting, they were asked when and how many times they had tried to quit. Adolescents also reported on their parents' views regarding smoking. Adolescents who reported that their parents did not want them to smoke were significantly more likely to report thinking seriously about quitting, even if their parents were smokers.

In sum, there is evidence that parental values around drug use, typically defined as disapproval, influence adolescent drug use. However, the mechanisms that account for this association—likely coaching and modeling—have typically not been studied simultaneously. More research is needed to understand how parental values are played out in parent–adolescent discourse about drugs and the conditions under which parental disapproval of drug use is most likely to predict less adolescent drug use. It is also clear from some empirical studies (e.g., Nelson et al., 1999) that there are instances in which parental values and parental communication specifically address-

ing drugs do not get transmitted to adolescents. This disconnect may result from several factors, including lack of clarity on the part of the parent, mixed messages from parents because of inconsistency between parental messages and parental behavior, or unwillingness of an adolescent to listen. Clearly, more research is needed to understand the conditions under which parental messages regarding drug use are understood and embraced by adolescents and the conditions under which parental messages are associated with lower levels of drug use or less risky use.

Parent Coaching and Coping Processes

The work reviewed above concerns parental communication and adolescent drug use. Much of the work at our center has emphasized specific coping messages parents use with their children and whether these strategies influence adolescent coping and adjustment (Kliewer et al., 2006; Kliewer, Fearnow, & Miller, 1996). Although most of this work has not explicitly examined parent communication style and youth drug use, I believe it is conceptually relevant because of the potential links between coping and emotion regulation and drug use. For example, in a study of families with fourth- and fifth-grade children, Kliewer et al. (1996) reported that active and supportive coping among youth—which are associated with less drug use in other studies—were positively associated with parental suggestions to think about the situation positively and to take steps to address the problem. Furthermore, mothers who both coached and modeled avoidance coping had children who reported higher levels of avoidance coping relative to other groups. This is important because drug use may represent a form of avoidance coping.

Kliewer et al. (2006) used a parent–child discussion task to identify the coping suggestions parents made, using a sample of African American families and their 9- to 13-year-old children. Parent and child viewed an affect-arousing video clip together and then talked about the situation they viewed and similar situations that might occur in their own neighborhood. Coping suggestions to the child were coded on the basis of the work of Sandler and colleagues (P. A. Miller, Kliewer, Hepworth, & Sandler, 1994; Sandler, Tien, & West, 1994). The resulting six factors included active suggestions, resignation, emotional support seeking, proactive coping, cognitive decision making, and aggressive actions.

Regression analyses revealed that coaching suggestions from a caregiver were uniquely associated with child reports of coping. For example, active coping suggestions by the maternal caregiver were positively associated with child reports of problem-focused coping. Furthermore, problem-focused coping by the child was the coping behavior most strongly associated with reductions in negative and increases in positive child- and caregiver-rated adjustment 6 months later. Additional analyses revealed that caregivers' suggestions to cope actively were associated with boys' reports of lifetime alcohol use. Boys who reported lifetime alcohol use at 6 months after the initial interview were half as likely as boys who reported no lifetime alcohol use to receive active coping suggestions from their caregivers (Kliewer, 2007).

Jamilla and Gregory, our case studies, illustrate very different experiences with regard to parental coaching. Jamilla enjoys open communication with her mother, and they frequently discuss how Jamilla could respond to situations at school or in her neighborhood that involve drugs and violence. Jamilla's mother has made it very clear that she disapproves of drug use, citing the negative consequences that result from involvement with drugs or alcohol. In contrast, communication between Gregory and his mother is virtually nonexistent.

Summary of the Coaching Pathway

In sum, parents convey messages to their children regarding alcohol, tobacco, and other drug use; this action represents an important pathway through which parents influence their offspring's behavior. Most family-focused interventions focus on parent–child communication as a central mechanism of change designed to reduce adolescent drug use. Despite the importance of this pathway, only a handful of studies, many from the persuasive communication literature, have attempted to document the nature of parent–adolescent communication regarding drug use and the contributions of these communication patterns to initiation or escalation of drug use in adolescence. Even fewer studies have exam-

ined overt parental communication that is linked to coping processes that are in turn associated with drug use. The dearth of research in this area has left the field with incomplete knowledge of how parent–adolescent communication regarding drug use may differ across socioeconomic status, developmental stage, or gender of the adolescent or parent. All of these important questions have tremendous implications for how interventions are conceptualized, designed, and implemented.

In our work in this area, my research team and I are using both qualitative and quantitative methods to understand the nature of parent–adolescent communication, aspects of the situation (e.g., frequency, controllability, stressfulness), and qualities of the parent and adolescent that are associated with particular messages regarding drug use. We are also examining coping messages from parents, some of which are strongly associated with drug use, and factors that influence these messages.

PARENTAL MODELING AND ADOLESCENT DRUG USE

In contrast to parental coaching, there is more direct evidence that parental modeling—that is, parental use of alcohol, tobacco, or other drugs—is associated with increased risk of adolescent drug use. It is quite clear from numerous studies using a variety of samples, methods, and research designs that parents' drug use increases the odds that their children will use (Bransetter et al., 2007). This is true for tobacco use (e.g., Chassin, Presson, Todd, Rose, & Sherman, 1998; Flay et al., 1994), alcohol use (e.g., Chassin, Curran, Hussong, & Colder, 1996; Chassin, Pillow, Curran, Molina, & Barrera, 1993), marijuana use (e.g., Duncan, Duncan, Hops, & Stoolmiller, 1995; Kliewer & Murrelle, 2007; Peterson, Hawkins, Abbott, & Catalano, 1995), and hard drug use (Kilpatrick et al., 2000). Notably, most of these associations were present after accounting for demographics and in many cases controlling statistically for peer influence.

By and large, many of these studies draw heavily from the theoretical strengths of social learning theory (SLT; Bandura, 1977, 1986, 1992). The basic premise behind SLT (see chap. 5, this volume, for a more complete discussion of the conceptual model underlying SLT) is that youth can observe their parents vicariously (from a distance) and also directly model the behaviors in question with an expectation that the same outcome will occur to them. Thus, if a parent smokes a cigarette and somehow exemplifies that this behavior is relaxing, the connection made in the mind of the youth observing this practice is "I can smoke and be relaxed as well." The same holds for alcohol; parents often drink alcohol as a form of social facilitation (drinking wine at dinner with friends or beers at parties with friends). According to SLT, the child observing these behaviors makes a connection between performance of the behavior and the expected outcome (i.e., relaxation). A direct analogy to youth is that if they observe a close friend smoke cigarettes and they come to appreciate that this behavior is perceived by their immediate social crowd as cool, this association will endure to the point that they may initiate to smoking for the sheer purpose of obtaining similar social approval.

The basic premise of SLT suggests that parents who use drugs, particularly parents who abuse drugs, would be more likely than parents who do not to have adolescents who use alcohol, tobacco, or other drugs. On the basis of the brief discussion of SLT above, a more interesting question concerns the mechanisms through which parental modeling influences adolescent drug use. Of the several mechanisms mentioned, the ones receiving the most attention today are possible heritability (see chaps. 11 and 13, this volume, for a more complete discussion of genetic liability), disrupted family mechanisms and poor parenting skills encouraging deviant peer selection by the children, and poor regulation of affect in the adolescent (mimicking poor coping skills of the parents), leading to drug use as a form of emotional coping.

Chassin et al. (1993) examined three potential pathways through which parental alcoholism could influence adolescent drug use. Their study involved a subset of two-parent families drawn from a larger longitudinal study examining the effects of parental alcoholism on family functioning. Possible pathways to adolescent drug use tested included parental alcohol use's overall effect to (a) disrupt parenting skills and influence parental monitoring, (b) offset or inhibit stress and negative affect regulation by the

adolescent, and (c) modulate adolescent personality and temperament, specifically emotionality and sociability. Consistent with prior research (e.g., Dishion, Patterson, & Reid, 1988), Chassin et al. theorized that these paths would lead directly to adolescent drug use, but would also operate through association with drug-using peers. Thus, for example, if parents did not effectively monitor their children, know about their whereabouts, or provide supervision, this would allow youth to associate with deviant and drug-abusing peers. Results of multivariate analyses revealed strong support for the parenting pathway and stress and the negative affect regulation pathway and mixed support for the personality–temperament pathway. There is additional evidence that some of these pathways also explain linkages between parent and adolescent smoking (Chassin et al., 1998). Specifically, in a longitudinal multigenerational study, Chassin et al. (1998) found that maternal smoking was associated with less consistent discipline, which was related to the adolescent's peers' smoking and the adolescent's own smoking behavior.

In the case of Gregory, one of the adolescents in the case studies, his mother directly modeled alcohol misuse, but she also was clearly not available emotionally as a parent and was not monitoring his behavior. In contrast, although Jamilla was exposed to neighborhood models of drug use, her mother did not abuse drugs or alcohol. Furthermore, Jamilla's mother closely monitored her activities and relationships with peers.

Kandel, Hu, Griesler, and Schaffran (2007; Kandel & Wu, 1995) have also reported findings supporting the strong influence of parental modeling on adolescent smoking and nicotine dependence. Kandel and Wu (1995) reported that maternal smoking was more strongly associated with smoking in daughters versus sons, indicating that parental identification may be a moderator of linkages between parental modeling and adolescent tobacco use. Parental influence on adolescent smoking persisted even after accounting for peer influence.

Parent Modeling and Coping Processes

It is easy to surmise that communication between parent and child is the foundation for the transmission of values and attitudes related to a wide range of behaviors including drug use. Relations over time in the home can support inculcation of values related to academic performance, athletic activities, friendships, and other important developmental milestones (i.e., dating for teenagers). Some studies have supported the hypothesis that transmission of liberal values and prodrug attitudes from parents can induce drug use in children (e.g., Hansen, Malotte, Collins, & Fielding, 1987).

Parental drug use can interfere with the normative transitions of a youth whose parents are remiss in communicating important positive messages to their children. If parents use or abuse drugs, they can send the message that drug use is an effective means of dealing with stress. When stressful situations arise for youth, they lack important models and effective coping skills to reduce stress or deliberate about positive alternatives. Studies that have documented links between parent and adolescent coping are relevant to this point. There are strong associations between adult use of active and approach-oriented coping strategies and lower levels of drug use (Carver, 2007) and, conversely, positive associations between avoidant coping and drug use. Thus, adults who model active coping for their adolescents may be communicating the appropriateness of dealing with stressors directly versus strategies that encourage avoidance. Our own work on socialization of coping with community violence found that maternal caregivers who reported using avoidant coping to manage stress had adolescents who were rated as using more avoidant coping strategies in response to a discussion task on how to manage violence (Kliewer, Adams Parrish, et al., 2006). Maternal caregivers who were more emotionally competent (Gottman, Katz, & Hooven, 1997) had adolescents with higher levels of emotional understanding and self-regulation (Cunningham, Kliewer, & Gardner, 2009).

Summary of the Modeling Pathway

In summary, parental modeling of alcohol, tobacco, and other drug use is an important pathway through which parents influence adolescent drug use. Although there is a large literature examining linkages between parent and adolescent drug use,

there is less information regarding how parental modeling of coping processes (e.g., appraisal, coping behavior, and efficacy evaluation) is related to adolescent coping processes and drug use, making this an area ripe for further inquiry. In addition, our work also leads us to believe that efficacious, family-focused, adolescent drug abuse prevention programs concentrate extensively on family management and communication skills but pay relatively less attention to parents' own emotion regulation and coping skills. Helping parents to regulate their affect and adaptively cope may assist them in managing their adolescents more effectively and may provide adolescents with better models of stress management.

FAMILY CONTEXT AND ADOLESCENT DRUG USE

Of the three pathways described in the socialization model of adolescent drug use presented here, the focus on family context has been by far the most heavily researched and most informative to the field of drug use etiology. The study of context and parenting and family influences on drug use and drug use disorders is a cornerstone piece needed for both theory development and refinement of preventive and treatment interventions (e.g., Chassin & Handley, 2006). The concept of family context is a broad catchall that includes family structure (Farrell & White, 1998); parent mental health (Brook, Brook, Whiteman, Gordon, & Cohen, 1990); quality of the parent–adolescent relationship, including support, warmth, affection, child centeredness, and mutual attachment (Brook et al., 1990; Brook, Whiteman, Finch, & Cohen, 1998; Brook et al., 2001; Farrell & White, 1998; Marshall & Chassin, 2000; Sullivan, Kung, & Farrell, 2004; Wills, Sandy, Yeager, & Shinar, 2001); family management, including monitoring, rule and boundary setting, and discipline strategies (Baumrind, 1991; Bogenschneider, Wu, Raffaelli, & Tsay, 1998; Brody et al., 2004, 2006; Brook et al., 1990; Chilcoat & Anthony, 1996; Hawkins et al., 1992; Kliewer, Murrelle, et al., 2006; Kosterman, Hawkins, Guo, Catalano, & Abbott, 2000; Sullivan et al., 2004); and general family climate, including cohesion, conflict, and emotional expression (Brook, Brook, de la Rosa, Whiteman, &

Montoya, 1999; Kliewer & Murrelle, 2007; Spoth, Guyll, Chao, & Molgaard, 2003; Spoth, Redmond, & Shin, 2001; Spoth, Redmond, Shin, & Azevedo, 2004; Spoth, Shin, Guyll, Redmond, & Azevedo, 2006; Vakalahi, 2002). Evidence supporting family context effects on drug use comes primarily from observational, naturalistic, and survey-based studies and experimental studies using planned interventions. Additional evidence has shown that family context moderates relations between risk and drug use, conditioning risk reflecting peer influences. There is also evidence that family context affects coping processes that are associated with adolescent drug use (Dusek & Danko, 1994; Kliewer, Adams Parrish, et al., 2006; Sieffge-Krenke, 1995; Skinner & Wellborn, 1994; Timko & Moos, 1996; Wolchik & Sandler, 1997; Zimmer-Gembeck & Locke, 2007).

Taken as a whole, evidence suggests that a warm, affectionate relationship between parents and their adolescent can delay the initiation and likelihood of drug use and drug use disorders (Brook et al., 1998; Brook, Brook, de la Rosa, Whiteman, & Montoya, 1999). One reason mutual attachment between parent and child is important is that it increases the likelihood that adolescents will identify with their parents and adopt their parents' values and behaviors. In essence, the dimension of family context strengthens the coaching and modeling paths leading to adolescent drug use or nonuse. Jamilla, one of the case studies at the beginning of the chapter, is a good example of this point. Although the weight of evidence has suggested that a strong parent–adolescent attachment is associated with less adolescent drug use, there are some exceptions to this finding. For instance, van der Vorst, Engels, Meeus, and Dekovic (2006) found that a strong parent–adolescent attachment was associated with less alcohol use cross-sectionally; however, this did not persist over time, and parent–adolescent attachment did not prevent adolescents from drinking.

Other aspects of the parent–adolescent relationship, highlighting chiefly perceived instrumental and emotional support, predict drug use in a range of samples including urban (Farrell & White, 1998) and rural (Sullivan et al., 2004) youth. Sullivan et al. (2004) found that parental support was associated with delayed initiation of drug use in rural 6th graders

followed over a single school year. Farrell and White (1998) found that lack of support in the mother–adolescent relationship exacerbated associations between peer pressure and drug use in urban 10th graders. Baumrind's (1991) seminal work on parenting style suggested that authoritative parenting, characterized by high levels of responsiveness coupled with stringent demands (which includes direct confrontation, monitoring, and a pattern of firm, consistent discipline with high maturity demands), was associated with less problematic drug use when adolescents were 15. Cross-cultural studies reinforcing these parenting styles exist outside the United States (Steinberg, 2001). In a cross-cultural study of adolescents living in Panama and Costa Rica, Kliewer, Murrelle, et al. (2006) found that parental monitoring was associated with lower risk of drunkenness, tobacco use, number of illicit drugs used, and problems with drugs and alcohol. Furthermore, parental monitoring interacted with exposure to witnessed violence to reduce risk for number of illicit drugs used and problems with drugs and alcohol.

In addition to family management style, family climate, specifically assessed by cohesion, low levels of conflict, and emotional expression, also has robust associations with adolescent drug use. For example, in a study of Central American youth, Kliewer and Murrelle (2007) found that negative family interactions (low cohesion, high conflict, poor communication) were uniquely associated with increased risk for tobacco use, other drug use, and problems with alcohol. Brook et al. (1999) found similar results in a South American sample of adolescents and their families. The poor family climate to which our case study Gregory is exposed enhances his risk for substance use problems.

Findings From Intervention Studies

Some of the strongest evidence for the effects of family management strategies and family climate on adolescent drug use, however, comes from intervention studies designed to modify or alter dimensions of family life. Most family-focused interventions designed to reduce adolescent drug use place a great deal of emphasis on family management and attempt to alter the emotional tone in the home (Branstetter et al., 2007). For example, the Coping Power program

(Lochman, Wells, & Murray, 2007) is an intervention that attempts to change parental inconsistency and targets additional social and cognitive factors that affect risk for youth delinquency and drug use. In an earlier evaluation study using high-risk boys and their families, Lochman and Wells (2002) found that compared with controls, intervention families were more consistent in their parenting and this in turn was associated with positive changes in adolescent behavior. Santisteban et al. (2003) conducted a family-based study with high-risk youth from Hispanic immigrant families. Participating youth with either behavior problems or drug use were assigned to either brief strategic family therapy or a control group treatment. Family cohesion, rated by adolescents and outside observers, improved as a result of participating in the brief strategic family therapy intervention. This improvement in cohesion was linked to reductions in adolescent marijuana use.

Brody et al. (2004, 2006) targeted a different set of parenting behaviors in evaluating the effects of the Strong African American Families program, a preventive intervention tested with rural African American families with 11-year-old children living in Georgia. Unlike the Coping Power program and brief strategic family therapy, a community sample was used to evaluate this intervention. An underlying tenet of the Strong African American Families program is that changing specific aspects of parenting (involvement and vigilance, racial socialization, communication about sex, and expectations for alcohol use) will boost protection (increase negative attitudes about early alcohol use and sexual activity, negative images of drinking youth, resistance efficacy, goal-directed future orientation, and acceptance of parental influence). Program efficacy analyses revealed that the intervention improved the targeted parenting behaviors, and changes in these behaviors were associated with increases in protective factors.

Structural Components of the Family

Several researchers have highlighted the effect of structural components of the family, including father absence, on adolescent drug use. For example, Farrell and White (1998) found that the relation between peer pressure and drug use for 10th-grade

youth was stronger in families without fathers or stepfathers. Mandara and Murray (2006) also found increased risk for drug use in father-absent homes, but only among boys. It is important that these effects remained intact even after accounting for socioeconomic status, neighborhood crime, parental monitoring, and peer drug use. Breivik and Olweus (2006) found that in postdivorce families, adolescents living with fathers (without another adult in the home) had exceptionally high levels of drug use relative to those living in other family structures. In contrast to the above findings, Brook et al. (1990; Brook, Whiteman, Balka, Win, & Gursen, 1997) have shown that protective characteristics of the father (e.g., his bond with the adolescent) enhance other protective factors in predicting drug use. These and related studies highlight the important role of fathers, although specific mechanisms supporting their protective role remain obscure (McMahon & Rounsaville, 2002).

One reason parent–adolescent affection, family management, and family emotional climate, as well as family structure, might predict adolescent drug use is because these dimensions of family life capitalize on adolescents' identity formation, fueling their need for relatedness, competence, and autonomy (Skinner & Wellborn, 1994). Social relations in an independent framework are a hallmark feature of adolescent development. As such, threats to relationships can result in isolation, and threats to competence (social and academic) provide a framework for escapism (e.g., Skinner, Edge, Altman, & Sherwood, 2003). It is not difficult to see how an adolescent who does not feel supported at home, or whose family life is chaotic and unpredictable, might turn to tobacco, alcohol, or other drugs as a way of coping.

Family Context and Coping Processes

In addition to the vast literature directly linking aspects of family context to adolescent drug use, there is a smaller literature that has documented ways in which family context is associated with adolescent coping behaviors. The ways in which adolescents cope with stress can increase or decrease their risk of drug use. In general, adolescents who tend to use active, approach-oriented coping are less likely to engage in drug use, particularly problematic use. In contrast, adolescents who tend to avoid confronting their stressors are more likely to engage in drug use and misuse (Wills, Vaccaro, & Benson, 1995). Family context is relevant because parents create the emotional tone of the home and establish household norms. Patterns of family interaction either support or inhibit the development of adaptive coping strategies (Kliewer et al., 1996; Kliewer, Adams Parrish, et al., 2006). In a recent test of linkages between family context and adolescent coping, Zimmer-Gembeck and Locke (2007) examined relationships with family members and teachers and coping behaviors in a sample of youth living in Australia. They found that adolescents with more positive family relationships used more active coping with problems at home and at school. Other studies have reinforced the family context coping assertion using a wide range of samples, different measures, outcomes, and testing various family context hypotheses. For instance, Timko and Moos (1996) reported moderate associations between family cohesion, low conflict, and communication and active coping strategies. Additionally, Dusek and Danko (1994) reported that authoritative parenting was associated with greater problem-focused coping in a sample of high school students. Kliewer, Adams Parrish, et al. (2006) examined family relations and coping skills in a sample of African American low-income families. In their study, observer-rated caregiver–adolescent interaction quality and adolescent reports of felt acceptance were associated with problem-focused and proactive coping.

My current work applies a stress and coping framework to understanding associations between family context (monitoring, family climate, parent–adolescent relationship quality) and both adolescent coping and adolescent initiation and escalation of drug use. My research team is using a two-cohort, longitudinal design with a predominantly low-income, African American sample. In addition to examining direct associations between family context and adolescent coping and drug use, we hope to examine how coaching, modeling, and family context interact to predict these outcomes.

Summary of the Family Context Pathway

To summarize, family context, which includes the quality of the parent–adolescent relationship, family management, and family emotional climate, as well as aspects of family structure, is an important pathway through which parents influence adolescent drug use. As with the data on parental modeling, although there is a large literature on linkages between family environment and adolescent drug use, there is less specific information on the mechanisms through which family climate is associated with drug use in adolescence. Furthermore, more information is needed regarding links between family climate, adolescent coping processes, and drug use. This knowledge will advance our theories about the role of families in adolescent drug use and drug use disorders and will also help us refine our interventions.

SUMMARY

In this chapter, I described a socialization model of adolescent drug use and presented evidence for three pathways by which parents and families influence adolescent drug use: coaching, modeling, and context. Despite the enormous body of literature on family factors associated with adolescent drug use, several research questions remain to be explored, including the mechanisms through which these pathways operate and how they interact. Although peers gain prominence during adolescence, families remain important and are an underused resource in preventing youth drug abuse (Califano, 2000).

References

Bandura, A. (1977). *Social learning theory.* Oxford, England: Prentice-Hall.

Bandura, A. (1986). *Social foundations of thought and action: A social cognitive theory.* Englewood Cliffs, NJ: Prentice-Hall.

Bandura, A. (1992). *Social cognitive theory.* In R. Vasta (Ed.), *Six theories of child development: Revised formulations and current issues* (pp. 1–60). London: Jessica Kingsley.

Baumrind, D. (1991). The influence of parenting style on adolescent competence and substance use. *Journal of Early Adolescence, 11,* 56–95.

Bogenschneider, K., Wu, M., Raffaelli, M., & Tsay, J. C. (1998). Parent influences on adolescent peer orientation and substance use: The interface of parenting practices and values. *Child Development, 69,* 1672–1688.

Bransetter, S. A., Masse, J., & Greene, L. (2007). Parent training for parents of adolescents with substance use and delinquent behavior problems. In J. M. Briesmeister & C. F. Schaefer (Eds.), *Handbook of parent training. Helping parents prevent and solve behavior problems* (3rd ed., pp. 467–509). Hoboken, NJ: Wiley.

Breivik, K., & Olweus, D. (2006). Adolescents' adjustment in four post-divorce family structures: Single mother, stepfather, joint physical custody, and single father families. *Journal of Divorce and Remarriage, 44,* 99–124.

Brody, G. H., Murry, V. M., Gerrard, M., Gibbons, F. X., McNair, L., Brown, A. C., et al. (2006). The Strong African American Families Program: Prevention of youth's high-risk behavior and a test of a model of change. *Journal of Family Psychology, 20,* 1–11.

Brody, G. H., Murry, V. M., Gerrard, M., Gibbons, F. X., Molgaard, V., McNair, L., et al. (2004). The Strong African American Families Program: Translating research into prevention programming. *Child Development, 75,* 900–917.

Brook, J. S., Brook, D. W., de la Rosa, M., Whiteman, M., Johnson, E., & Montoya, I. (2001). Adolescent illegal drug use: The impact of personality, family, and environmental factors. *Journal of Behavioral Medicine, 24,* 183–203.

Brook, J. S., Brook, D. W., de la Rosa, M., Whiteman, M., & Montoya, I. D. (1999). The role of parents in protecting Colombian adolescents from delinquency and marijuana use. *Archives of Pediatrics and Adolescent Medicine, 153,* 457–464.

Brook, J. S., Brook, D. W., & Pahl, K. (2006). The developmental context for adolescent substance abuse intervention. In H. A. Liddle & C. L. Rowe (Eds.), *Adolescent substance abuse: Research and clinical advances* (pp. 25–51). New York: Cambridge University Press.

Brook, J. S., Brook, D. W., Whiteman, M., Gordon, A. S., & Cohen, P. (1990). The psychosocial etiology of adolescent drug use and abuse. *Genetic, Social and General Psychology Monographs, 116,* 111–267.

Brook, J. S., Whiteman, M., Balka, E. B., Win, P. T., & Gursen, M. D. (1997). African American and Puerto Rican drug use: A longitudinal study. *Journal of the American Academy of Child & Adolescent Psychiatry, 36,* 1260–1268.

Brook, J. S., Whiteman, M., Finch, S., & Cohen, P. (1998). Mutual attachment, personality, and drug use: Pathways from childhood to young adulthood. *Genetic, Social and General Psychology Monographs, 124,* 492–510.

Califano, J. A. (2000). Winning the war on drugs: It's all in the family. *America, 182,* 6–8.

Carver, C. S. (2007). Stress, coping, and health. In H. S. Friedman & R. Cohen (Eds.), *Foundations of health psychology* (pp. 117–144). New York: Oxford University Press.

Castrucci, B. C., & Gerlach, K. K. (2005). The association between adolescent smokers' desire and intention to quit smoking and their views of parents' attitudes and opinions about smoking. *Maternal and Child Health Journal, 9,* 377–384.

Caughlin, J. P., & Malis, R. S. (2004). Demand/withdrawal communication between parents and adolescents: Connections with self-esteem and substance use. *Journal of Social and Personal Relationships, 21,* 125–148.

Compas, B. E., Connor-Smith, J. K., Saltzman, H., Thomsen, A. H., & Wadsworth, M. E. (2001). Coping with stress during childhood and adolescence: Problems, progress, and potential in theory and research. *Psychological Bulletin, 127,* 87–127.

Chassin, L., Curran, P. J., Hussong, A. M., & Colder, C. R. (1996). The relation of parent alcoholism to adolescent substance use: A longitudinal follow-up study. *Journal of Abnormal Psychology, 105,* 70–80.

Chassin, L., & Handley, E. D. (2006). Parents and families as contexts for the development of substance use and substance use disorders. *Psychology of Addictive Behaviors, 20,* 135–137.

Chassin, L., Pillow, D. R., Curran, P. J., Molina, B. S., & Barrera, M. (1993). Relation of parental alcoholism to early adolescent substance use: A test of three mediating mechanisms. *Journal of Abnormal Psychology, 102,* 3–19.

Chassin, L., Presson, C. C., Todd, M., Rose, J. S., & Sherman, S. J. (1998). Maternal socialization of adolescent smoking: The intergenerational transmission of parenting and smoking. *Developmental Psychology, 34,* 1189–1201.

Chilcoat, A. A., & Anthony, J. C. (1996). Impact of parent monitoring on initiation of drug use through late childhood. *Journal of the American Academy of Child & Adolescent Psychiatry, 35,* 91–100.

Cunningham, J. N., Kliewer, W., & Garner, P. (2009). Emotion socialization, child emotion understanding and regulation, and adjustment in urban African American families: Differential associations across child gender. *Development and Psychopathology, 21,* 261–283.

Dishion, T. J., Patterson, G. R., & Reid, J. R. (1988). Parent and peer factors associated with drug sampling activity in early adolescence: Implications for treatment. In E. R. Rahdert & J. Grabowski (Eds.), *Adolescent drug abuse: Analyses of treatment research* (DHHS Publication No. ADM88-1523, pp. 69–83). Washington, DC: U.S. Government Printing Office.

Duncan, T. E., Duncan, S. C., Hops, H., & Stoolmiller, M. (1995). An analysis of the relationship between parent and adolescent marijuana use via generalized estimating equation methodology. *Multivariate Behavioral Research, 30,* 317–339.

Dusek, J. B., & Danko, M. (1994). Adolescent coping styles and perceptions of parental child rearing. *Journal of Adolescent Research, 9,* 412–426.

Elliott, D. S., Huizinga, D., & Ageton, S. (1985). *Explaining delinquency and drug use.* Beverly Hills, CA: Sage.

Ennett, S. T., Bauman, K. E., Foshee, V. A., Pemberton, M., & Hicks, K. A. (2001). Parent-child communication about adolescent tobacco and alcohol use: What do parents say and does it affect youth behavior? *Journal of Marriage and the Family, 63,* 48–62.

Farrell, A. D., & White, K. S. (1998). Peer influences and drug use among urban adolescents: Family structure and parent–adolescent relationship as protective factors. *Journal of Consulting and Clinical Psychology, 66,* 248–258.

Flay, B. R., Hu, F. B., Siddiqui, Q., Day, L. E., Hedeker, D., Petraitis, J., et al. (1994). Differential influence of parental smoking and friends' smoking on adolescent initiation and escalation of smoking. *Journal of Health and Social Behavior, 35,* 248–265.

Gottman, J. M., Katz, L. F., & Hooven, C. (1997). *Meta-emotion: How families communicate emotionally.* Mahwah, NJ: Erlbaum.

Hansen, W. B., Malotte, C. K., Collins, L., & Fielding, J. E. (1987). Dimensions and psychosocial correlates of adolescent alcohol use. *Journal of Alcohol and Drug Education, 32,* 19–31.

Hawkins, J. D., Catalano, R. F., & Miller, J. Y. (1992). Risk and protective factors for alcohol and other drug problems in adolescence and early adulthood: Implications for substance abuse prevention. *Psychological Bulletin, 112,* 64–105.

Hawkins, J. D., & Weis, J. G. (1985). The social development model: An integrated approach to delinquency prevention. *Journal of Primary Prevention, 6,* 73–97.

Kandel, D. B. (1996). The parental and peer contexts of adolescent deviance: An algebra of interpersonal influences. *Journal of Drug Issues, 26,* 289–315.

Kandel, D. B., Hu, M., Griesler, P. C., & Schaffran, C. (2007). On the development of nicotine dependence in adolescence. *Drug and Alcohol Dependence, 91,* 26–39.

Kandel, D. B., & Wu, P. (1995). The contributions of mothers and fathers to the intergenerational transmission of cigarette smoking in adolescence. *Journal of Research on Adolescence, 5,* 225–252.

Kelly, K. J., Comello, M. L., & Hunn, L. C. (2002). Parent-child communication, perceived sanctions against drug use, and youth drug involvement. *Adolescence, 37,* 775–787.

Kilpatrick, D. G., Acierno, R., Saunders, B., Resnick, H. S., Best, C. L., & Schnurr, P. P. (2000). Risk factors for adolescent substance abuse and dependence: Data from a national sample. *Journal of Consulting and Clinical Psychology, 68,* 19–30.

Kliewer, W. (2007). *Parental coping suggestions and adolescent alcohol use in a low-income, urban sample.* Manuscript in preparation.

Kliewer, W., Adams Parrish, K., Taylor, K. W., Jackson, K., Walker, J. M., & Shivy, V. A. (2006). Socialization of coping with community violence: Influences of caregiver coaching, modeling, and family context. *Child Development, 77,* 605–623.

Kliewer, W., Fearnow, M. D., & Miller, P. A. (1996). Coping socialization in middle childhood: Tests of maternal and paternal influences. *Child Development, 67,* 2339–2354.

Kliewer, W., & Murrelle, L. (2007). Risk and protective factors for adolescent substance use: Findings from a study in selected Central American countries. *Journal of Adolescent Health, 40,* 448–455.

Kliewer, W., Murrelle, L., Prom, E., Ramirez, M., Obando, P., & Sandi, L. (2006). Violence exposure and drug use in Central American youth: Family cohesion and parental monitoring as protective factors. *Journal of Research on Adolescence, 16,* 455–478.

Kosterman, R., Hawkins, J. D., Guo, J., Catalano, R. F., & Abbott, R. D. (2000). The dynamics of alcohol and marijuana initiation: Patterns of predictors of first use in adolescence. *American Journal of Public Health, 90,* 360–366.

Lazarus, R. S., & Folkman, S. (1984). *Stress, appraisal, and coping.* New York: Springer.

Lochman, J. E., & Wells, K. C. (2002). Contextual social-cognitive mediators and child outcome: A test of the theoretical model in the Coping Power Program. *Development and Psychopathology, 14,* 945–967.

Lochman, J. E., Wells, K. C., & Murray, M. (2007). The Coping Power Program: Preventive intervention at the middle school transition. In P. Tolan, J. Szapocznik, & S. Sambrano (Eds.), *Preventing youth substance abuse. Science-based programs for children and adolescents* (pp. 185–210). Washington, DC: American Psychological Association.

Mandara, J., & Murray, C. B. (2006). Father's absence and African American adolescent drug use. *Journal of Divorce and Remarriage, 46,* 1–12.

Marshall, M. P., & Chassin, L. (2000). Peer influence on adolescent alcohol use: The moderating role of parental support and discipline. *Applied Developmental Science, 4,* 80–88.

McMahon, T. J., & Rounsaville, B. J. (2002). Substance abuse and fathering: Adding poppa to the research agenda. *Addiction, 97,* 1109–1115.

Miller, M. A., Alberts, J. K., Hecht, M. L., Trost, M. R., & Krizek, R. L. (2000). *Adolescent relationships and drug use.* Mahwah, NJ: Erlbaum.

Miller, P. A., Kliewer, W., Hepworth, J. T., & Sandler, I. N. (1994). Maternal socialization of children's post-divorce coping: Development of a measurement model. *Journal of Applied Developmental Psychology, 15,* 457–487.

Miller-Day, M. (2002). Parent-adolescent communication about alcohol, tobacco, and other drug use. *Journal of Adolescent Research, 17,* 604–616.

Miller-Day, M. (2008). Talking to youth about drugs: What do late adolescents say about parental suggestions? *Family Relations, 57,* 1–12.

Miller-Day, M., & Dodd, A. H. (2004). Toward a descriptive model of parent-offspring communication about alcohol and other drugs. *Journal of Social and Personal Relationships, 21,* 69–91.

Nash, S. G., McQueen, A., & Bray, J. H. (2005). Pathways to adolescent alcohol use: Family environment, peer influence, and parental expectations. *Journal of Adolescent Health, 37,* 19–28.

Nelson, B. V., Patience, T. H., & MacDonald, D. C. (1999). Adolescent risk behavior and the influence of parents and education. *Journal of the American Board of Family Practitioners, 12,* 436–443.

Office of National Drug Control Policy. (1997). *National youth anti-drug media campaign: Communication strategy statement.* Washington, DC: Office of National Drug Control Policy.

Pantin, H., Schwartz, S. J., Coatsworth, J. D., Sullivan, S., Briones, E., & Szapocznik, J. (2007). Familias Unidas: A systemic, parent-centered approach to preventing problem behavior in Hispanic adolescents. In P. Tolan, J. Szapocznik, & S. Sambrano (Eds.), *Preventing youth substance abuse: Science-based programs for children and adolescents* (pp. 211–238). Washington, DC: American Psychological Association.

Peterson, P. L., Hawkins, J. D., Abbott, R. D., & Catalano, R. F. (1995). Disentangling the effects of parental drinking, family management, and parental alcohol norms on current drinking by Black and White adolescents. In G. M. Boyd, J. Howard, & R. A. Zucker (Eds.), *Alcohol problems among adolescents: Current directions in prevention research* (pp. 33–57). Hillsdale, NJ: Erlbaum.

Sandler, I. N., Tien, J., & West, S. G. (1994). Coping, stress, and psychological symptoms of children of divorce: A cross-sectional and longitudinal study. *Child Development, 65,* 1744–1763.

Santisteban, D. A., Coatsworth, D. J., Perez-Vidal, A., Kurtines, W. M., Schwartz, S. J., LaPerriere, A., et al. (2003). Efficacy of brief strategic family therapy in modifying Hispanic adolescent behavior problems and substance use. *Journal of Family Psychology, 17,* 121–133.

Sieffge-Krenke, I. (1995). *Stress, coping, and relationships in adolescence.* Mahwah, NJ: Erlbaum.

Skinner, E. A., Edge, K., Altman, J., & Sherwood, H. (2003). Searching for the structure of coping: A review and critique of category systems for classifying ways of coping. *Psychological Bulletin, 129,* 216–269.

Skinner, E. A., & Wellborn, J. G. (1994). Coping during childhood and adolescence: A motivational perspective. In D. L. Featherman, R. M. Lerner, & M. Perlmutter (Eds.), *Life-span development and behavior* (Vol. 12, pp. 91–133). Hillsdale, NJ: Erlbaum.

Smetana, J. G. (2000). Middle-class African American adolescents' and parents' conceptions of parental authority and parenting practices: A longitudinal investigation. *Child Development, 71,* 1672–1686.

Spoth, R., Guyll, M., Chao, W., & Molgaard, V. (2003). Exploratory study of a preventive intervention with general population African American families. *Journal of Early Adolescence, 23,* 435–468.

Spoth, R., Redmond, C., & Shin, C. (2001). Randomized trial of brief family interventions for general populations: Adolescent substance use outcomes 4 years following baseline. *Journal of Consulting and Clinical Psychology, 69,* 627–642.

Spoth, R., Redmond, C., Shin, C., & Azevedo, K. (2004). Brief family intervention effects on adolescent substance initiation: School-level growth curve analyses 6 years following baseline. *Journal of Consulting and Clinical Psychology, 72,* 535–542.

Spoth, R., Shin, C., Guyll, M., Redmond, C., & Azevedo, K. (2006). Universality of effects: An examination of the comparability of long-term family intervention effects on substance use across risk-related subgroups. *Prevention Science, 7,* 209–224.

Steinberg, L. (2001). We know some things: Parent-adolescent relationships in retrospect and prospect. *Journal of Research on Adolescence, 11,* 1–19.

Sullivan, T. N., Kung, E. M., & Farrell, A. D. (2004). Relation between witnessing violence and drug use initiation among rural adolescents: Parental monitoring and family support as protective factors. *Journal of Clinical Child and Adolescent Psychology, 33,* 488–498.

Szapocznik, J., Tolan, P., Smabrano, S., & Schwartz, S. J. (2007). Preventing youth substance abuse: An overview. In P. Tolan, J. Szapocznik, & S. Sambrano (Eds.), *Preventing youth substance abuse: Science-based programs for children and adolescents* (pp. 3–17). Washington, DC: American Psychological Association.

Timko, C., & Moos, R. H. (1996). The mutual influence of family support and youth adaptation. In G. R. Pierce, B. R. Sarason, & I. G. Sarason (Eds.), *Handbook of social support and the family* (pp. 289–310). New York: Plenum Press.

Vakalahi, H. F. (2002). Family-based predictors of adolescent substance use. *Journal of Child and Adolescent Substance Abuse, 11,* 1–15.

van der Vorst, H., Engels, R. C. M. E., Meeus, W., & Dekovic, M. (2006). Parental attachment, parental control, and early development of alcohol use: A longitudinal study. *Psychology of Addictive Behaviors, 20,* 107–116.

Wills, T. A. (1986). Stress and coping in early adolescence: Relationships to substance use in urban school samples. *Health Psychology, 5,* 503–529.

Wills, T. A., & Filer, M. (1996). Stress-coping model of adolescent substance use. In T. H. Ollendick & R. J. Pinz (Eds.), *Advances in clinical child psychology* (Vol. 18, pp. 91–132). New York: Plenum Press.

Wills, T. A., & Hirky, A. E. (1996). Coping and substance abuse. In M. Zeidner & N. S. Endler (Eds.), *Handbook of coping: Theory, research, and applications* (pp. 279–302). New York: Wiley.

Wills, T. A., Sandy, J. M., & Yeager, A. M. (2002). Moderators of the relation between substance use level and problems: Test of a self-regulation model in middle adolescence. *Journal of Abnormal Psychology, 111,* 3–21.

Wills, T. A., Sandy, J. M., Yeager, A. M., & Shinar, O. (2001). Family risk factors and adolescent substance use: Moderation effects for temperament dimensions. *Developmental Psychology, 37,* 283–297.

Wills, T. A., Vaccaro, D., & Benson, G. (1995). Coping and competence in adolescent alcohol and drug use. In J. L. Wallander & L. Siegel (Eds.), *Adolescent health problems: Behavioral perspectives* (pp. 160–178). New York: Guilford Press.

Wolchik, S. A., & Sandler, I. N. (Eds.). (1997). *Handbook of children's coping: Linking theory and intervention.* New York: Plenum.

Zimmer-Gembeck, M. J., & Locke, E. M. (2007). The socialization of adolescent coping behaviours: Relationships with families and teachers. *Journal of Adolescence, 30,* 1–16.

CHAPTER 20

PEER INFLUENCES ON SUBSTANCE USE DURING ADOLESCENCE AND EMERGING ADULTHOOD

Robert J. Pandina, Valerie L. Johnson, and Helene Raskin White

Research has consistently found that peer influences are a robust predictor of substance use in adolescence and emerging adulthood (Walden, McGue, & Iacono, 2004; White & Jackson, 2004–2005). The complex question of whether peers exert influence over the individual or youth select their peers on the basis of their own behaviors has been an issue of interest and debate among substance use researchers for the past several decades. Although it has generally been conceded that influences are bidirectional, the relative magnitude of selection and socialization effects and the manner in which they moderate or mediate use behaviors remain at issue. Questions also remain as to whether peer influence may differ as a function of the types of substances (e.g., alcohol, cigarettes, marijuana, cocaine, steroids; see, e.g., Maxwell, 2002), developmental stage of substance use (e.g., initiation, habit formation, and maintenance), and the transitions between use stages (Pandina, 2002; Pandina & Johnson, 1999). The association between individual and peer substance use has been attributed to socialization, selection, and social norms (Borsari & Carey, 2001). The issues of directionality of peer influences and differential influences in different use stages have potentially major implications for the design, implementation, and evaluation of prevention and intervention programs.

This chapter reviews several of the prominent psychosocial theoretical models used to explain adolescent and young adult substance use behaviors vis-à-vis peer group interactions. We also examine the selection versus socialization debate regarding peer influence on the development of adolescent and young adult behaviors and provide an overview of the tenets of recent social norms programming efforts. Finally, we end with a review of several leading secondary and college-level school-based prevention programs and a discussion of the complexity of both peer dynamics and the nature and extent of prevention programs that can spring from the knowledge of such dynamics. This chapter and chapter 21 together provide a comprehensive discussion of peer group interactions in the development of use behaviors among youth. In this chapter, our focus is primarily on developmental transitions and the importance of peer norms. Chapter 21 focuses on describing direct, mediated, and moderated effects of peer groups on the development of substance use behaviors.

THEORETICAL MODELS EXPLICATING PEER INFLUENCES

Peer influence can work directly through explicit offers and indirectly via modeling and perception of peer norms. In this chapter, we focus on peer influences during the periods of adolescence through emerging adulthood. Numerous theoretical frameworks have been used to explain the processes by which social relationships affect a person's substance use (Kobus, 2003). Such perspectives include, but are not limited to, social learning theory (Akers, 1985), peer cluster theory (Oetting, Spooner, Beauvais, &

Preparation of this chapter was supported in part by National Institute on Drug Abuse Grant DA 17552.

Banning, 1991), primary socialization theory (Oetting & Donnermeyer, 1998), and integrated theories, such as the social development model (Catalano, Kosterman, Hawkins, Newcomb, & Abbott, 1996).

Associational theories date back more than 60 years to Sutherland's (1947) differential association theory and were first developed to explain delinquency among youth. Sutherland maintained that criminal behavior is learned in interaction with other people, primarily in proximal groups. The theory proposes that individuals become deviant if there are stronger definitions (norms) favorable to violation of the law over definitions unfavorable to violation within their proximal group. Groups (including peers) provide individuals with patterns, motives, and definitions of norms either favorable or unfavorable to engaging in a given behavior.

Differential association theory was reformulated by Burgess and Akers (1966) to provide a more behaviorally oriented specification of the learning process. Their reformulation combined the principles of differential association theory with Bandura's (1977) more general social learning theory and was termed *differential association–reinforcement theory*. Bandura's social learning theory suggests that social reinforcers are salient determinants of human behavior (White, Bates, & Johnson, 1990). When the reactions of others are perceived as approving or consisting of withdrawal of disapproval, these reinforcements will increase the likelihood that the behavior will be repeated. In contrast, if the reactions of others are perceived as disapproving, these reactions will decrease the probability that the behavior will persist. The belief that consequences of behavior determine whether new behaviors will be acquired and existing behaviors will be modified is central to most learning perspectives. Social learning theory also emphasizes that perceptions and observations of others will influence learning. Finally, social learning theory stresses the reciprocal interaction among the person, environment, and behavior (for applications of Bandura's social learning theory to drinking among adolescents and emerging adults, see Borsari & Carey, 2003; White, Bates, & Johnson, 1991).

Burgess and Akers's (1966) reformalization emphasized that deviant behavior is learned, like all behavior, according to the principles of conditioning and that behavior is a function of reinforcements. What is at times difficult to understand or explain are the factors that sustain various deviant behaviors in light of the fact that engaging in such behaviors often results in serious negative consequences (e.g., arrest, overdose, and interpersonal conflict, among many). It is important to view such behaviors within the context of other broadly conceived environmental factors. Particularly salient is the notion of peer support and association with particular peer subcultures as a secondary gain related to behaviors that may have punishing attributes.

Akers (1985), some 20 years after first describing differential association–reinforcement theory, reformulated his model and postulated that behavior is learned in groups, which are the greatest source of reinforcement for the individual and provide the context in which learning takes place. According to this perspective, social behavior is acquired both through direct conditioning and through imitation of others' behavior. Behavior is strengthened through reinforcement and weakened by punishment. People learn definitions of behavior as good or bad in interaction with significant groups. One important referent is the peer group. Akers included four core concepts within his model: imitation, differential associations, definitions (e.g., drug use norms), and differential reinforcement. His perspective suggests a process whereby differential associations provide the environment in which exposure to definitions, imitation of models, and reinforcement takes place. Definitions, in interaction with modeling and anticipated reinforcement, produce initial substance use behavior. After the initiation of use, definitions and consequences (reinforcement or punishment) become more important for the continuation of the behavior.

A noteworthy variant on differential association theory is peer-cluster theory (Oetting et al., 1991). This theory postulates that among adolescents, drug use takes place in peer clusters (small cohesive groups) that reinforce use. Peers initiate individuals into drug use, provide drugs, model drug use behavior, and shape drug use attitudes. According to this theory, exposure to these groups, in large part, depends on social factors that make adolescents vulnerable to drug use, which may include family cohesion and sanctions, religious identification, and school adjustment. Such formulations take into account the reinforcing value of peer acceptance and peer group identity as secondary gains that may sustain use behaviors above and beyond the potential primary reinforcing value of use and the consequent state of intoxication. Thus, use becomes embedded in a complex peer cultural matrix. Such formulations help explain why use behaviors may be resistant to elimination when interventions focus principally on use behavior at the individual level.

Primary socialization theory (Oetting & Donnermeyer, 1998), a more refined version of peer-cluster theory, maintains that deviant behavior is a learned social behavior and that norms for these use behaviors are largely developed in the context of the interactions with three sources: the family, school, and peer clusters. According to this perspective, peer clusters can communicate either prosocial or deviant norms, but are commonly the main source of deviant behavior. Primary socialization theory distinguishes between various forms of peer influence, including peers in the general environment, peer lifestyle groups, and peer clusters. Peer clusters consist of best friend dyads, small groups of close friends, or couples, and it is believed that this is where the forming and sustaining of norms predominately occurs. Primary socialization theory posits that weak or unhealthy bonds with the family or school will increase the chances that the adolescent will bond with a deviant peer cluster. The theory further postulates that an individual's personal characteristics may not directly relate to drug use but can affect the interaction between the adolescent and the socialization sources. For example, primary socialization theory would propose that if high self-esteem is derived from academic success, it is likely to be negatively correlated with drug use. Conversely, if self-esteem is derived from peer acceptance (and those peers support deviant norms), then self-esteem may be positively associated with drug use (Lopez et al., 2001).

Oetting and Donnermeyer (1998) argued that there are strong selection factors in the formation of peer clusters. For example, similarity of attitudes, interests, and abilities strongly influences the selection of friends. Interestingly, many influences on selection are peripheral to the individual and, for that matter, to any potential peer cluster, including

location in and characteristics of a specific neighborhood or school classroom. Even the structure of a school system may influence peer clustering. For example, structural differences in school districts that are organized as kindergarten through eighth grade versus kindergarten through fifth grade plus middle school appear to lead to significant differential outcomes for putative peer group–influenced behaviors (Bierman et al., 2007). Moreover, these influences persist over time. Hence, factors that may be relatively hidden from the individual or the peer cluster may affect the development, course, and persistence of behaviors putatively transmitted via peer mechanisms and processes.

R. E. Johnson, Marcos, and Bahr (1987) suggested that the associational influence of peers is not a result of peers influencing an adolescent's view of the behavior (as good or bad or right or wrong) but rather a result of associations with peers in situations that place immediate pressure on an adolescent to go along with the crowd and fear of rejection if he or she refuses. The theories of Oetting et al. (1991; Oetting & Donnermeyer, 1998) and R. E. Johnson et al. (1987) relate to the social nature of drug use among adolescents (i.e., adolescents usually take drugs when they are with their friends rather than when they are alone) and are, therefore, most relevant for deviant behaviors that surface in a group context. Hence, these theories emphasize the importance of secondary gains in the transmission and maintenance of use behavior.

The social development model is an integrated theory that purports to explain the development of both prosocial and antisocial behavior over the life course (Catalano & Hawkins, 1996; Hawkins & Weis, 1985). This formulation combines elements of differential association, social learning, and social control perspectives. The social development model assumes that individuals learn types or classes of behaviors and that socialization follows the same processes of social learning whether it produces positive or problem behaviors. Recognizing that many individuals experience both positive and negative influences, the social development model hypothesizes that an individual's behavior will be shaped by the amount of association with various types of individuals and by the level of involvement in prosocial and antisocial activities. Interaction with pro-alcohol peers and involvement in prosocial activities are postulated to lead to social bonding and the internalization of the attitudes and beliefs of the groups with whom these bonds are formed. In addition, the social development model stresses that bonds and behaviors formed during a prior developmental period will have a lasting influence even as social environments change. The social development model has been shown to predict various styles of both positive and problematic behavior in childhood and adolescence (Catalano et al., 2005; Lonczak et al., 2001). This integrated theory supports Sutherland's (1947) conception regarding the importance of frequency, duration, priority, and intensity for determining engagement in antisocial or prosocial activities (see also Warr, 1993).[1]

All of these socialization and social learning perspectives suggest that individuals learn substance use behaviors in interaction with significant others who model or reinforce such behavior. Before adulthood, the principal significant others who have influence on substance use are parents and peers. In this chapter, we concentrate on the influence of peers. Other chapters in this volume focus on the influence of parents.

PEER INFLUENCES IN ADOLESCENCE

The importance of peer influences on substance use during adolescence has been studied widely over the past several decades (Crosnoe, Muller, & Frank, 2004). More recent research findings have demonstrated that social learning variables (including attitudes, norms, and approval of use) have an effect on frequency of both alcohol use and alcohol abuse for adolescents (Preston & Goodfellow, 2006) and that the unique groups of best friendships, peer cliques, and social crowds differentially predict adolescent substance use (Hussong, 2002).

Research findings have suggested that peer pressures to try alcohol or cigarettes, although sometimes coercive, are usually normative. That is, many times adolescents feel the need to use alcohol or drugs if others around them do, perhaps as a way to access the secondary gains associated with peer group membership. The decision to try cigarettes, for example, has been tied to an adolescent's efforts to avoid exclusion by peers and gain their approval (Kobus, 2003). The role of peer pressure as a component of drug offers appears to decline substantially as the adolescent ages, and the decision to experiment with drugs increasingly becomes a matter of personal choice (McIntosh, MacDonald, & McKeganey, 2006). McIntosh et al. (2006) argued that the normative definition regarding drug use changes from that of a risk-taking behavior to one of drug use as a recreational activity. Although it has been shown that the similarity of drinking habits within friendship dyads in early and middle adolescence is significant, the impact of friends' drinking on the individual's use over time has been found to be limited (Jaccard, Blanton, & Dodge, 2005; Poelen, Engels, Van Der Vorst, Scholte, & Vermulst, 2007). In addition, the influence of deviant peers may serve as a mediating factor between intrapersonal risk factors (e.g., sensation-seeking propensity) and substance use (Yanovitzy, 2005). Engels and Ter Bogt (2001) found that substance use was related to some positive aspects of peer relations. That is, adolescents who used alcohol and other drugs were found to be strongly attached to their friends, gained more social support from them, and were more socially competent in their friendships.

These and related observations highlight the theoretical importance of considering the differential impact of peers on use behaviors at various development stages. For example, distinctions should be made about the influence of peers at the time of initiation, when use behavior is relatively novel and serves, in part, as an entrance requirement to a group, versus the maintenance stage, when behavior becomes more related to an individual's identity. From a practical perspective, in planning interventions it is important to consider the implications of the functional utility of use behaviors at various use stages. Programs aimed at preventing initiation may have limited impact if, for example, they do not take into account the manner in which peer clusters come to adopt use behavior as a salient identity

[1] Parts of this section were adapted from "You Can Choose Your Friends, but Do They Choose Your Crime? Implications of Differential Association Theories for Crime Prevention Policy," by D. Gorman and H. R. White, 1995, in H. Barlow (Ed.), *Criminology and public policy: Putting theory to work* (pp. 131–155). Copyright 1995 by D. Gorman and H. R. White. Adapted with permission.

marker. Equally as important is the manner in which this marker of behavioral desirability is signaled and transmitted to potential group members. Likewise, if an intervention is aimed at eliminating or limiting use in an individual or a peer cluster, where use behavior is well established, programs aimed at use initiation would be expected to have limited potential. These issues have obvious implications for evaluators attempting to determine the impact of planned interventions accurately.

PEER INFLUENCES IN EMERGING ADULTHOOD

Studies of emerging adults have demonstrated that peers are among the strongest influences on substance use regardless of whether one is measuring perceptions of peers' use or actual reports by peers (Andrews, Tildesley, Hops, & Li, 2002; Baer, 2002; Jackson, Sher, & Park, 2006; Perkins, 2002; White & Jackson, 2004–2005). Emerging adulthood is the stage in the life cycle between adolescence and young adulthood (Arnett, 2000). It begins following high school and ends with the adoption of adult roles such as marriage, parenthood, and career. Emerging adulthood generally covers the age period of 18–25, although in some cases it may extend to the late 20s and early 30s. The construct of the "emerging adult" has proven to be important and informative, partly in recognition of the fact that in the past several decades a relatively larger proportion of individuals (both male and female) than in the past may delay the assumption of adult roles and responsibilities. This is especially important inasmuch as large increases in substance use occur during the period of emerging adulthood (Bachman, Wadsworth, O'Malley, Johnston, & Schulenberg, 1997). Emerging adulthood represents a time when most youth initiate new roles, develop new friendship networks, and gain independence from their families of origin (Arnett, 2000; Schulenberg & Maggs, 2002). During this stage of the life cycle, individuals are not mired in the constraints associated with certain major adult roles (e.g., marriage, parenthood, providing familial support), which are often associated with a decrease in substance use (Labouvie, 1996).

Several researchers have attributed the changes in substance use during this time frame to certain aspects of the college environment, although several studies have indicated that increases also occur for emerging adults who do not attend college (White, Labouvie, & Papadaratsakis, 2005; White et al., 2006). The college environment provides a safe haven for experimentation with substance use, perhaps because during the transition to college, individuals experience changes in normative expectations and increased opportunities to drink and use drugs. To some extent, the safe haven notion may be more the outgrowth of expectations and perceptions than reality, given that serious consequences of drinking and drug taking (e.g., overdoses, crime, violence including sexual assaults) on college campuses have been consistently documented (Engs, Diebold, & Hansen, 1996; Hingson, Heeren, Winter, & Wechsler, 2005; Presley, Meilman, & Cashin, 1996; Wechsler et al., 2002). Peer norms and modeling may be especially important in a college setting, in which individuals are isolated from contact with other groups, including family members. Such isolation may be particularly significant for new students who are exposed to novel situations when making the transition to the college (Perkins, 2002; Read, Wood, & Capone, 2005). Moreover, there appears to be rather universal expectations that experiential learning in college includes at least some level of experimentation with high-risk use situations. There may also be a perception that college authorities (e.g., student life personnel, campus police) are, or perhaps should be, more tolerant of behavioral excesses occurring on the college campus. Thus, the college environment provides strong social influences for alcohol and drug consumption, which include modeling and socialization (peer use), alcohol-related opportunities, and reinforcement (encouragement or pressure to use; Read et al., 2005).

Particular living situations during emerging adulthood affect drinking and drug use. Studies have consistently found that college students living with their parents drink to a lesser extent than college students who live on or off campus (Harford, Wechsler, & Muthén, 2002; White et al., 2006). In some college residential settings (e.g., fraternity houses), alcohol use is more common, and there may be greater modeling of drinking, encouragement to drink, and availability of alcohol. Besides residence, other social settings (e.g., parties, bars) have been found to affect drinking patterns among college students, and attendance at these functions differs by residence and gender (Demers et al., 2002; Harford, Wechsler, & Seibring, 2002). Preexisting differences among students may account for differences in selected place of residence, in the types of schools chosen (Baer, 1994; Harford & Muthén, 2001; Harford, Wechsler, & Muthén, 2002), and in exposure to pro-alcohol influences in college (Pandina, 2002).

SELECTION VERSUS SOCIALIZATION

In the process of socialization, attitudes and behaviors are transmitted and reciprocally reinforced between and among peer group members. Social norms emerge from diffused attitudes and behaviors that are significant to the peer group. Individuals become aware of social rewards (i.e., secondary gains) for adhering to the group norms, including concepts such as popularity and social rejection. Over time, this collective pressure toward uniformity has an effect on a youth's behavior. The more time peer group members spend together, the more similar their attitudes and behaviors become and the more likely that certain indicators (e.g., excessive drinking) begin to define group status (including, for example, such labels as "druggies," "alkies," "jocks," and "nerds"). In the process of selection, individuals choose peers who display attitudes, norms, and behaviors similar to their own.

Although research has established that peers influence one another's substance use, it is just as likely that adolescents select friends whose behaviors seem attractive as it is that the behavior is learned from the peer group. Sieving, Perry, and Williams (2000) found that similarity in drinking behavior among adolescent friends may be more related to processes of peer influence than to processes of peer selection. Fite, Colder, and O'Connor (2006) examined selection and socialization processes in the pathways from internalizing and externalizing behavior problems to substance use and found that delinquent peer affiliations were associated with increases in externalizing behaviors (including substance use). Their results

support a socialization model whereby the probable mechanisms of imitation and reinforcement act to increase individual behaviors such as drinking. For the most part, however, the research has suggested that the relationship between an individual's substance use and his or her peers' use is reciprocal (White, Fleming, Kim, Catalano, & McMorris, 2008). That is, association with substance-using peers is just as much a consequence of use as a cause of it. Adolescents originally select friends who are like themselves in terms of shared behaviors and attitudes. Friends continue to influence one another as a result of continued associations and reciprocal reinforcement of behaviors that define, or at least characterize, relationships.

Leibsohn (1994) found that entering college freshman sought out new friends with whom to drink and use drugs and whose use patterns were similar to those of their friends from high school. Furthermore, when a youth's peers used alcohol, the individual experienced pressure to also use (Leibsohn, 1994). Read et al. (2005) found a reciprocal relationship between social influence variables (including peer alcohol use and related attitudes and alcohol offers) and alcohol use over three periods in time from summer prematriculation to the spring of sophomore year. Prematriculation social modeling and alcohol offers predicted alcohol use in the sophomore year, and prematriculation alcohol use predicted sophomore year alcohol offers and social modeling.

In a study of emerging adults both attending and not attending college, White et al. (2008) found that both socialization and selection processes influence drinking during the transition to emerging adulthood. Greater drinking in high school predicted involvement 6 months later with peers who drank heavily and reinforced heavy drinking, thus supporting a selection process. In addition, emerging adults with friends who were heavier drinkers post–high school were more likely to increase their drinking from high school to a year later, supporting socialization processes. White et al.'s findings extended prior research by showing that these selection and socialization processes were also important for emerging adults who did not attend college.

Some studies have suggested that selection and socialization effects may vary for young men and women. Female college students tend to be influenced by the college environment and high-risk drinking environments (Harford, Wechsler, & Muthén, 2002; Lo & Globetti, 1995; Slutske et al., 2004), whereas male college students tend to demonstrate stronger selection effects into heavy drinking environments (e.g., the Greek fraternity system; Lo & Globetti, 1995; McCabe et al., 2005). White et al. (2008) found few gender differences in the selection and socialization process among emerging adults. However, among youth who did not go to college but who moved away from their parents, young men reported greater pro-alcohol peer involvement than did young women. This latter finding may support the contention that men establish friendship networks around drinking behaviors at bars or other locales (football games) and use alcohol as a social lubricant.

In sum, research examining peer influences on substance use has been conducted extensively, using a variety of models and measures. Positive associations between the two constructs have led many researchers to conclude that youth exert considerable influence on their friends' behavior. However, some researchers have claimed that such conclusions may be oversimplified (Bauman & Ennett, 1996). It is true that many, if not most, of the published studies of adolescent and emerging adult peer influence simply ask participants how many friends have engaged in a behavior and then correlate this measure with the participants' behavior. Critics have observed that the relationship between one's own behavior and one's reports of friends' behavior should not be taken as indisputable confirmation of peer influence. For example, some studies have found that adolescents may be mistaken in reporting the level of their friends' behaviors (Donohew, Clayton, Skinner, & Colon, 1999; Kandel, 1996). Bauman and Ennett (1996), in particular, suggested that the statistical correspondence between adolescent and peer measures may reflect response artifacts resulting from study participants' projection of behaviors. In addition, the interplay of a variety of peer influences might be confounded with selection effects (Bauman & Ennett, 1996). For example, individuals choose their friends and peer groups on the basis of a set of shared norms. These values and norms can be related

to behaviors in their own right. The individual predisposed to use substances might engage in this behavior regardless of the peer group membership. Kandel (1996, p. 289) suggested that the role of peers has been greatly inflated and the influence of parents has been underestimated because of "reliance on cross-sectional designs, reliance on perceptual reports of friends' behaviors, which reflect projection and attribution, failure to take into account parent's contributions to peer selection, and failure to consider genetic contributions to observed parental effects."

It has been proposed that selection effects may be addressed by using longitudinal designs to document concomitant changes in behavior over time between peers and the target individual (Ennett & Bauman, 1996). In addition, further clarification of the peer socialization and selection processes as contributors to the explanation of substance use requires that researchers pay closer attention to design concerns, measurement issues, and unspecified third-variable alternatives that may influence statistical relations. Although there is overwhelming evidence that adolescents' risk behaviors are associated with the behaviors of their close friends, it is not evident that such associations are pure reflections of peer influence. As suggested, the relationships may be a sign of measurement artifacts, peer group selection, or the operation of parallel or co-occurring events. Other research has suggested, however, that perceptions (i.e., projection and attribution) of peer use are important regardless of actual peer use (Perkins, 2002). We next examine the role of peer norms as they influence substance use in light of the socialization and selection models already discussed.

PEER NORMS RESEARCH

Research on peer norms has focused predominantly on college populations, although some of this research has also been applied in a more limited fashion to high school students (Perkins & Craig, 2003). The reason why social norms programming has not been applied in high schools to the same extent as in college populations is in part because of the challenges of recommending norms of moderate use where abstinence is the openly acceptable standard for underage students. In a study of 7th to

12th graders, Olds and Thombs (2001) found that at all grade levels, peer norms correlated significantly with participant use. Perkins and Craig (2003) studied 28 middle and high schools selected from a nationally representative pool. Their data documented the pervasive nature of misperception of use among peers across grades, various school characteristics, and substances. These researchers found misperceptions among students regarding same-grade peers as well as older peers. Studies have consistently found large differences between what college students believe to be their peer norms and the actual reported prevalence rates (Perkins, 2002). For the most part, both high school and college students tend to overestimate the degree to which their peers drink and use drugs. In college populations, even among groups such as fraternities, whose drinking actually exceeds that of non-Greek college peers, youth overestimate drinking among their own subgroups (Larimer et al., 2001).

Perceived drinking norms of peers are one of the strongest correlates of drinking, with many college students perceiving both permissive attitudes toward drinking and actual consumption rates to be much greater than they actually are (Baer, Stacy, & Larimer, 1991; Borsari & Carey, 2001, 2003; Perkins, 2002). This finding appears to be robust regardless of the specific reference group (e.g., best friend, close friends, typical students; Borsari & Carey, 2003). For example, Perkins and Berkowitz (1986) found that although three fourths of the undergraduate students at one college believed that students should never drink to intoxication or that intoxication was permitted under certain conditions, almost two thirds of these same students thought that intoxication that did not interfere with responsibilities was acceptable. Findings such as this have been replicated across U.S. college campuses. Similar misperceptions have been found for drug use as well (Perkins, 2002). In addition, such misperceptions have been found among emerging adults not attending college.

As a possible refinement to this literature, Borsari and Carey (2003) distinguished between descriptive norms and injunctive norms. Descriptive norms are the perception of others' drinking behavior (how much and how often). Injunctive norms are perceived approval of drinking. The former are based

primarily on observation, whereas the latter are based on inference. Using meta-analysis, Borsari and Carey found greater self–other discrepancies for injunctive as opposed to descriptive norms and greater self–other discrepancies for women as compared with men. In addition, discrepancies increased as the reference group became more distal (e.g., moved from close friends to typical students).

Because normative misperceptions appear firmly established in the minds of most youth, they may place pressure on youth to conform to erroneously perceived peer expectations by drinking in a manner that meets these expectations. These misperceptions have other negative consequences as well because they discourage students who drink less from publicly expressing opposition to heavy drinking and intervening with peers who misuse alcohol (Perkins, 2002). Finally, these misperceptions become self-fulfilling prophecies, leading to more drinking and, thus, exaggerating perceptions through self-affirmation. Hence, the excessive drinkers are bolstered by these misperceptions and believe that their drinking is acceptable according to peer norms.

Lewis and Neighbors (2004) found that same-sex norms were more strongly associated with problematic drinking than were gender-nonspecific norms. They also found that same-sex norms were stronger predictors of alcohol consumption for women than for men. These findings suggest that socially proximal comparisons groups are more relevant and have greater influence than distal comparison groups (Lewis & Neighbors, 2004, p. 334). Conversely, Martens, Dams-O'Connor, Duffy-Paiement, and Gibson (2006) found that male athletes were more influenced by their same-sex athlete peer norms than by nonathlete peer norms, whereas female athletes were more influenced by their same-sex nonathlete peer norms than by athlete peer norms.

IMPLICATIONS FOR INTERVENTIONS

The observation that youth who use substances tend to have friends who also use has led to the development of peer group programs designed to both enhance protective factors and reduce risk factors for problem behavior. Peer group prevention programs are usually based on the view that values and behaviors are acquired through association with peers. That is, these programs are based on the assumption that if affiliating with substance-using role models encourages the development of substance use, then sufficient exposure to positive role models may diminish the appeal of deviant friends and hence foster more conventional social ties and behaviors.

Peer-Led Programs With Adolescents

In the late 1980s and early 1990s, the social influence perspective dominated the development of drug use prevention programs for youth. These programs fit into one of two basic types, one of which was focused chiefly on resistance skills training and one of which integrated broader personal and social skills training through the inclusion of more affective components such as stress reduction, self-esteem enhancement, and decision making (Gorman & White, 1995, p. 140; Hansen, 1992). Essential to both types of programs was the notion that initiation into drug use results principally from the adverse influence of negative peers (and pressure from the media). Thus, adolescents were taught the skills required to identify and resist these pressures.

Over the past few decades, many prevention programs that attempt to reduce the rate of initiation into drug use have been developed. The delivery of many of these programs involved peer leaders and traditional adult educators. The concept of peer-led drug abuse prevention has been studied for more than 25 years. The shortcomings of the first attempts at peer-led prevention programming included high levels of teacher facilitator attrition, primarily because of lack of training or compensation. Most of the programs were not integrated into a curriculum; therefore, time limitations hindered the extent to which leadership skills were fostered, and there was limited flexibility and adaptability as to the content of the program. Last, students who were most at risk for substance abuse often did not benefit from the program because of their high absenteeism and their low motivation to participate in any activities associated with the school.

Cuijpers (2002) conducted a meta-analysis of a dozen peer-led and adult-led school-based drug prevention programs and concluded that these programs' effectiveness is determined by several factors, includ-

ing content, number of regular and booster sessions, and who leads the implementation. Similarly, Tobler et al. (2000), in a meta-analysis of school-based prevention programs, found that interactive programs reported better outcomes than did noninteractive programs. Programs that involve youth directly in the implementation may not only enhance skills transmission but may also change the social climate of the school, as suggested by DeJong and Langford's (2002) research, which showed that peer-led programs helped to change students' social norms.

There has recently been an outcropping of peer-led initiatives for addressing a wide variety of health-risk behaviors, most of which have not been subjected to intense scientific scrutiny. However, several programs using peers as facilitators in addressing substance use have been deemed model programs by national experts and have shown that the use of peers for delivering positive messages about substance use can be promising. Next, we briefly review a few of these programs to illustrate the way in which they incorporate the etiology literature regarding peer socialization and selection mechanisms.

Project ALERT was a school-based, prevention program for middle or junior high school students that focused on substance use. It was based on the social influence model and was designed to instruct youth in the skills they need to resist social influences and to build norms against use. The implementation approach involved high school students as leaders in the delivery of the middle school program. Lessons involved small-group activities, role-playing, and rehearsal of new skills to encourage students' participation. Two major evaluations of this program involved more than 85 schools and found substance use–related positive results (Ellickson, Bell, & McGuigan, 1993; Ghosh-Dastidar, Longshore, Ellickson, & McCaffrey, 2004).

Project Northland was a multilevel intervention model focused on alcohol use and involved students, peers, parents, and the community. The program was typically provided to middle school students on a weekly basis. The peer-led curriculum focused on resistance skills and normative expectations regarding teenage alcohol use and was implemented using discussions, games, problem-solving tasks, and role-plays. Among young adolescents, peer influence was shown to have a statistically significant effect on the tendency to use alcohol. Important mediators of the program's effect on alcohol use included peer influence to use, including normative estimates, functional meanings of alcohol use, and attitudes and behaviors associated with alcohol and drug use. Overall, the results suggested that some of Project Northland's effectiveness on a student's decision whether to use was because of its impact on peer influences (Komro et al., 2001).

Valente et al. (2007) tracked the outcomes of two cohorts of students involved in the Project Towards No Drug Abuse prevention program. This program attempts to enhance both prosocial norms and those norms opposed to the use of substances. A health educator led one group, and the other group was led by peer leaders. The sessions provided the chance for exchanges among participants focusing on motivation factors (i.e., students' attitudes, beliefs, and expectations regarding drug use), skills (social, self-control, and coping), and decision making. The evaluation found that when surveyed a year later, the peer-led group exhibited lower rates of substance use than the teacher-led group. Although the researchers found that peer-led interactive substance prevention programs can enhance peer influences, they were quick to point out that among students who are close to other peers who support drug use, such an interactive program may have deleterious effects. (For additional discussions on the issues surrounding peer clustering of high-risk youth, see, e.g., Dishion, McCord, & Poulin, 1999; Weiss et al., 2005.)

More recently, a peer-led program (Peer Group Connection) has been implemented as an integrated, school-based program for urban minority youth transitioning into high school (V. L. Johnson, Holt, Bry, & Powell, 2008). The design of this pilot project was quasi-experimental in nature, with one freshman physical education class assigned to receive the intervention and one to receive no program (i.e., treatment as usual). The peer leaders were upper class students (half boys and half girls), chosen on the basis of various leadership qualities and to mirror the racial and ethnic background of the 1st-year students. During one class period a week for the entire school year, two-person teams

of peer leaders met with approximately 12–15 1st-year students per group. The weekly topics included team building, stress and anger management, risk assessment, conflicts in relationships, normative beliefs about drug and alcohol use, refusal skills, decision making, and communication skills. Significant program effects were found in terms of increased ability to make friends and resist peer pressure to participate in negative behaviors. In addition, when baseline academic risk status was controlled, there were decreases in tolerance of friends' use of substances and self-reported acts of school misconduct.

Peer-Led Programs With College Students

Brief interventions for college students have also used peer counselors. Those studies that have evaluated peer counselors using randomized control designs have found that peers are effective intervention providers. Fromme and Corbin (2004) compared undergraduate peer leaders with graduate student leaders in providing a skills training program to both mandated and volunteer high-risk students. Although participants rated graduate students as superior presenters, the results indicated no outcome differences between the two groups. Larimer et al. (2001) evaluated the efficacy of a brief motivational intervention for fraternity members using both peers (trained undergraduates) and professionals (trained psychology graduate students) to administer the intervention. They found that students who received their intervention from peers rather than professionals reported significantly greater reductions in peak blood alcohol concentration. Tevyaw, Borsari, Colby, and Monti (2007) incorporated peers into a brief motivational intervention for mandated college students. Specifically, in one condition mandated students brought a peer to their intervention session and in the other condition the student received an individualized brief motivational intervention. At the 1-month follow-up, there were reductions in drinking for both groups, but effect sizes indicated that those students who participated with a peer showed greater reductions than those in the individualized intervention. Peer drinking, however, did not predict outcomes.

IMPLICATIONS FOR SOCIAL NORM INTERVENTIONS

The social norms approach, which refers to the modification of misperceptions of peer norms, should be distinguished from public health approaches that attempt to actually change social norms. The literature on social norms and youthful substance use has been reviewed at length by Perkins (2002). Studies of middle or high school students have found that perceiving the peer group norm as more permissive or tolerant than it really is can facilitate early onset or increased use (e.g., Haines, Barker, & Rice, 2003; Perkins & Craig, 2003). At the college level, there is extensive research suggesting that the majority of college students overestimate the alcohol use of their peers (Borsari & Carey, 2003; Perkins, 2002).

Social norms interventions are based on the notion that by receiving information about actual norms, students will reevaluate their own drinking and change it. Later in this volume (chap. 32), Sussman goes to great lengths to describe how cognitive misperceptions, fallacies, and erroneous perceptions can induce alcohol and drug use. He also describes in great detail the components of prevention programs that seek to correct these misperceptions as part of their focal intervention strategies. In a sense, these programs attempt to capitalize on the idea that shaping perceptions of a peer environment will be expressed as direct influences on the behavior of individuals operating in that particular peer environment. A basic premise is that individuals not only misperceive norms within the peer environment by overestimating actual drinking behavior but by overestimating the tolerance of harmful and risky drinking practices as well. Misperceptions may be attributed to inappropriate expectations about the nature of the environment (e.g., the college campus as a protective haven for excessive behavior), selective observations of excessive consumption (e.g., night-time partiers in the dorms), or overgeneralization of the extent of use opportunities (e.g., parties in homes where parents are absent, tailgating, fraternity parties). Misperceptions tend to increase as social distance from the model of behavior increases, but peer groups who are closer are more influential in shaping behavior. This leads to the question of whether closer, more selectively

defined peer norms or more distal environmental clusters (i.e., school or campus) should be addressed in designing an intervention.

Several social norms intervention studies focusing on middle and high school students have demonstrated success in changing misperceptions and preventing initiation of use or decreasing use (Haines et al., 2003; Hansen & Graham, 1991). Kumar, O'Malley, Johnston, Schulenberg, and Bachman (2002) studied the relationship between schoolwide norms of drug use disapproval and drug use by students. They found that in general, school-level disapproval lowered the probability of student use of drugs, controlling for individual intolerance of use. The benefit of school-level disapproval was more salient among middle school students than among high school students and was primarily protective against cigarette and marijuana use rather than alcohol use. These results highlight the importance of both less proximal peer norms and the salience of grade and individual drug differences (Kumar et al., 2002). Ott and Doyle (2005) conducted a study to determine whether misconceptions of alcohol and other drug use among high school students could be corrected with a peer-to-peer interactive social norms approach based on their small group norms challenging model. They found a significant decrease in misperceptions from pretest to posttest.

Personal Feedback Interventions

One type of brief intervention that has been particularly effective with college students is brief personal feedback interventions (PFIs). PFIs assume that receiving information about one's drinking pattern in relation to one's peers and personal risk factors will motivate the individual to change, develop a strategy for change, and implement change (Miller, Toscova, Miller, & Sanchez, 2000). PFIs are designed, therefore, to heighten the student's awareness of personal patterns of use, peer norms, risks related to use, and the experience of negative consequences under certain drinking conditions. A key component of PFIs is the comparison between one's drinking behavior and peer norms. Because as previously discussed, students tend to overestimate the acceptability of heavy drinking by peers and the amount that other students may drink, individualized feedback to counteract these misperceptions is hypothesized to reduce harmful drinking. It is expected that personalized feedback will have a greater impact than universal presentations of norms because the feedback is more salient to the individual (Neighbors, Larimer, & Lewis, 2004).

Many PFIs for college students have been modeled on the Brief Alcohol Screening and Intervention for College Students (BASICS) model, which was designed as a model brief motivational intervention for alcohol prevention among college students (Dimeff, Baer, Kivlahan, & Marlatt, 1999). The BASICS program combines Miller and Rollnick's (2002) concept of motivational enhancement with cognitive–behavioral skills training (Baer et al., 1992) within a harm reduction perspective (Marlatt, Baer, & Larimer, 1995). The primary goal is to move the student to reduce risky behaviors and avoid the harmful effects of drinking rather than to focus on a specific drinking goal, such as abstinence (Dimeff et al., 1999, p. 5). The BASICS program is conducted in two sessions. In the first session, assessments of drinking are made, and information is presented about alcohol use, such as the effects of varying blood alcohol concentrations. In the second session, the student is given feedback about his or her drinking in relation to other students, and then strategies to reduce risk are discussed. The feedback sheet contains information on a student's drinking pattern relative to other college students, peak blood alcohol concentration, alcohol-related problems, and personal risk factors (e.g., dependence symptoms and family history of alcoholism; see Dimeff et al., 1999; Murphy et al., 2001). Overall, the evaluations of PFIs for high-risk college students have been quite promising, at least on a short-term basis, regardless of whether they have been delivered in person, by mail, or by computer (Walters & Neighbors, 2005; White, 2006).

One problem with most of the prior evaluations of PFIs is that it is difficult, if not impossible, to determine what component of the intervention is having an effect because PFIs generally have many different components (e.g., normative feedback, blood alcohol content effects, strategies for harm reduction). Neighbors et al. (2004) evaluated the efficacy of a personal computer-delivered PFI, which included only information about the amount the student drank;

the student's perceptions about other students' drinking; and other students' actual drinking. Heavy drinkers completed a baseline assessment and were randomly assigned to receive a PFI delivered immediately by computer and then printed out or to a no-treatment control group. The results indicated that there were significant reductions in drinking behavior for the intervention group relative to the control group at both the 3- and 6-month follow-ups with moderate effect sizes. In addition, at both follow-ups there were significant differences in perception of peer norms with relatively large effect sizes. The reduction in drinking was mediated by the reduction in perceptions of peer use (see also Borsari & Carey, 2000). Later research by this team found that although normative feedback worked for both male and female college students, gender-specific norms were more important for women than for men (Lewis & Neighbors, 2007). This approach has been demonstrated to be effective in reducing, although not in eliminating, use behavior even among identified groups (e.g., fraternities) whose group (as well as individual) use behaviors significantly exceed general peer norms and who have been demonstrated to have a higher degree of tolerance of risky practices (Larimer, Cronce, Lee, & Kilmer, 2004–2005). Although most PFIs have focused primarily on alcohol use, they have been shown to reduce the prevalence of cigarette smoking and marijuana use (White et al., 2006). The results of these types of interventions, although important in and of themselves, can be viewed as "experimental etiological" exercises serving to affirm the nature and importance of peer group influences even when behaviors have become initiated and have become part of the drinking repertoire of individuals or groups.

Social Norms Marketing Campaigns

In addition to individualized feedback regarding norms, there have also been attempts to provide norms using more broad-brush approaches. Social marketing campaigns are based on the idea that communication to students of factual information about peer norms in terms of what students are actually doing and thinking can reduce consumption. Such information has been provided through campus newspaper ads and articles, campus poster campaigns, flyers, school radio programs, and other mass communication methods (Neighbors et al., 2004; Perkins, 2002). Disseminating such information can reduce students' misperceptions, which should reduce drinking behavior. However, because the feedback is relatively impersonal compared with PFIs, these interventions are limited. In addition, there is no way to guarantee that the students observe and process the information, thus limiting the ability to measure precise dosage effects and obtain accurate information regarding fidelity of implementation (Neighbors et al., 2004).

In fact, there has been considerable debate regarding the efficacy of these types of campaigns. According to Perkins (2002), those campaigns that intensively and persistently communicate accurate norms have demonstrated significant reductions in heavy episodic drinking. Haines and Spear (1996) conducted a 5-year study to compare changes in perceptions of use and self-reported drinking behavior among college students following the delivery of two different prevention modalities. One was a traditional campaign focused on educational presentations, and the other focused on addressing the issue of misperceptions of campus alcohol use. Haines and Spear found that the second method produced a significant drop in the proportions of students who believed that binge drinking was the norm. DeJong et al. (2006) obtained similar positive outcomes over a 3-year period using an 18-site randomized trial of a social marketing campaign that delivered school-specific, data-driven messages through a mix of campus media settings. However, Werch et al. (2000) introduced a social norm intervention for binge drinking among 1st-year college students and could not detect any program effects on alcohol use risk measures. They concluded that a program consisting of only print material and telephone contacts with no personal interaction has limited promise for changing behaviors.

CONCLUSIONS

Social interaction is a fundamental defining characteristic of the human condition. From an evolutionary perspective, the ability of individuals to function collectively has arguably high survival value for the species. Group interactions and dynamic processes, both formal and informal, are central to social intercourse and structure. Such interactions are functionally important to effectively and efficiently accomplish group goals (e.g., hunting game, gathering food, constructing bridges, building governments) that potentially and actually enhance the individual's chances of survival. Moreover, the collective experiences of individuals functioning in groups serve to foster culture and transmit knowledge and beliefs (formal and informal) regarding the nature and shared defining characteristics of the referent group. In addition, group interactions provide the context and opportunities to acquire (i.e., "learn" and "adopt") a wide array of behaviors. Hence, it stands to reason that learning to function as individuals immersed in clusters of peers as we traverse the life course is an important, necessary, and perhaps unavoidable developmental task presenting difficult challenges.

It also stands to reason that the dynamics that drive peer association and group processes are highly complex. The manner in which peer groups are formed, defined, and maintained; the emergence of leaders and trendsetters; and the challenges faced by individuals and the group as a whole are some of the factors that play key roles in shaping peer-based learning. Peer dynamics are fluid inasmuch as the boundaries of the peer group are often loosely defined and maintained. In addition, the context and structure of the environments (e.g., neighborhoods, schools, regions of the country) where peer groups are formed and function sometimes shape the peer experience in ways that are not directly observable by the individual or the peer cluster. Factors such as age, gender, race or ethnicity, and developmental stage of the individual (e.g., early, middle, or late adolescence and emerging adulthood) likely all have an impact on the emergence, relative strength, and sustainability of peer influence. Consideration must be given to potent moderators and mediators that function at the individual level (e.g., state and trait personality characteristics) and that may affect peer group selection or increase susceptibility to peer norms. Extrapeer influences cannot be ignored either. Larger and more distal sociocultural norms (e.g., tolerance of drinking, intolerance of drunk driving or cigarette smoking, acceptability of some forms of therapeutic drug use, punishment of illicit drug use) and competing pressures from other potent influences (e.g., parents, non-peer role models, the media) probably also affect peer dynamics.

The nature and value of behaviors such as alcohol or drug use play an equally important, if not always central, role in determining the level of influence exerted through peer dynamics. In theory, it might be expected that behaviors acquired through peer mechanisms, however characterized, would have high positive survival value. Furthermore, natural selection should not favor behaviors that are negative (e.g., excessive alcohol and drugs, gratuitous violence) either for the individual or for the group. Hence, such behaviors would not, in theory, be carried forward via this potent group processes. However, in a complex heterogeneous society, the reality is that many potentially undesirable behaviors appear to persist and are transmitted within the context of peer functioning not only among adolescents and emerging adults but also among presumably emerged adults. The desirability and attraction of such negative behaviors (or at least those viewed by adults as negative or destructive behaviors when applied to youth) are sustained by factors derived from multiple levels of analysis and transmitted via powerful social vehicles.

Messages about the utility and function of alcohol drinking have long been embedded in the culture of many countries including the United States. These messages are carried via role models in the emerged adult society (including parents, social icons, and media transmitters), providing ample opportunity for youth to observe their anticipated future as drinkers. Myths and practices of the youth culture also serve as models. That is, youth in earlier developmental cohorts (e.g., middle adolescence) have ready access to images (real and perceived) of drinking in older cohorts (e.g., late adolescents and emerging adults) that serve to prime and anticipate their own behavior. Such role models are embellished and sustained by overt advertisements and covert media portrayals depicting the desirability and acceptability of use. Often the portrayals have high symbolic value that reinforces the secondary gains associated with status as a drinker.

Perhaps far more interesting is the more subtle transmission of messages about drug use that currently affect youth. Except for underground media, little in the way of formal advertising has taken place. By and large, use of illicit drugs (e.g., marijuana, cocaine, amphetamines, heroin, and hallucinogens) was relatively limited to circumscribed subpopulations before the 1960s. In the 1960s, the United States experienced an unprecedented explosion of drug use among a broad cross-section of previously unexposed American youth. Although there has been a decline from the high-water levels of the late 1970s and early 1980s, use of a wide variety of illicit drugs continues to the present. It appears that the trends established in the 1960s persist even in the face of major drug prevention campaign efforts that are mandated in today's environment.

Although it is unclear as to what factors sustain current levels of drug use, it is clear that many adolescents and emerging adults continue to be exposed to, initiate, and use a variety of drugs. How the message about the desirability and attractiveness of drugs is transmitted remains a subject of study that, arguably, has not been fully explored or explained. Several factors are obviously at play. It is tempting to postulate that the peer culture maintains a central position as a transmitting vehicle; intuitively, this hypothesis seems very sensible. It also appears that the general youth-oriented culture (e.g., media representations, music) has incorporated the myths and reality of the 1960s drug culture and projected it forward to the present day. Of course, the fact that drugs continue to be widely available no doubt plays a key role. Here again we need to consider the interplay between supply and demand dynamics. What is more difficult to calculate is the impact of the meteoric rise of therapeutic prescription medications developed and targeted to ameliorate serious disorders including anxiety and depression. Adjunct to the introduction of these medications are the intense media campaigns aimed at informing potential users about the availability and desirability of these medications. Whatever the factors that sustain the messages about use, it seems clear that peer group transmission dynamics are major significant vectors influencing and initiating youthful drug use.

In sum, it is clear that peer groups, however conceived or characterized, constitute a powerful, ecologically valid, relevant, and opportunistic medium for the transmission of messages and models for alcohol and drug use behaviors. It is also clear that attempts to study peer influences present a clear challenge to researchers given the myriad factors that moderate and mediate such influences. Moreover, the peer culture provides many important opportunities to shape important behaviors, including use of alcohol and other drugs. Continuing to understand peer dynamics and learning to apply these dynamics to intervention strategies is the next great challenge for scientists.

References

Akers, R. L. (1985). *Deviant behavior: A social learning approach*. Belmont, CA: Wadsworth.

Andrews, J. A., Tildesley, E., Hops, H., & Li, F. (2002). The influence of peers on young adult substance use. *Health Psychology, 21,* 349–357.

Arnett, J. J. (2000). Emerging adulthood: A theory of development from the late teens through the twenties. *American Psychologist, 55,* 469–480.

Baer, J. S. (1994). Effects of college residence on perceived norms for alcohol consumption: An examination of the first year in college. *Psychology of Addictive Behaviors, 8,* 43–50.

Baer, J. S. (2002). Student factors: Understanding individual variation in college drinking. *Journal of Studies on Alcohol, 14*(Suppl.), 40–53.

Baer, J. S., Marlatt, G. A., Kivlahan, D. R., Fromme, K., Larimer, M. E., & Williams, E. (1992). An experimental test of three methods of alcohol risk reduction with young adults. *Journal of Consulting and Clinical Psychology, 64,* 974–979.

Baer, J. S., Stacy, A., & Larimer, M. (1991). Biases in the perception of drinking norms among college students. *Journal of Studies on Alcohol, 52,* 580–586.

Bachman, J. G., Wadsworth, K. N., O'Malley, P. M., Johnston, L. D., & Schulenberg, J. E. (1997). *Smoking, drinking, and drug use in young adulthood: The impacts of new freedoms and new responsibilities.* Mahwah, NJ: Erlbaum.

Bandura, A. (1977). *Social learning theory*. Englewood Cliffs, NJ: Prentice-Hall.

Bauman, K. E., & Ennett, S. T. (1996). On the importance of peer influence for adolescent drug use: Commonly neglected considerations. *Addiction, 91,* 185–198.

Bierman, K. L., Coie, J. D., Dodge, K. A., Foster, E. M., Greenberg, M. T., Lochman, J. E., et al. (2007). Fast track randomized controlled trial to prevent externalizing psychiatric disorders: Findings from grades 3 to 9. *Journal of the American Academy of Child & Adolescent Psychiatry, 46,* 1250–1262.

Borsari, B., & Carey, K. B. (2000). Effects of a brief motivational intervention with college student drinkers. *Journal of Consulting and Clinical Psychology, 68,* 728–733.

Borsari, B., & Carey, K. B. (2001). Peer influences on college drinking: A review of the research. *Journal of Substance Abuse, 13,* 391–424.

Borsari, B., & Carey, K. B. (2003). Descriptive and injunctive norms in college drinking: A meta-analytic integration. *Journal of Studies on Alcohol, 34,* 331–341.

Borsari, B., & Carey, K. B. (2006). How the quality of peer relationships influences college alcohol use. *Drug and Alcohol Review, 25,* 361–370.

Burgess, R. L., & Akers, R. L. (1966). A differential-association-reinforcement theory of criminal behavior. *Social Problems, 14,* 128–147.

Catalano, R. F., & Hawkins, J. D. (1996). The social development model: A theory of antisocial behavior. In J. D. Hawkins (Ed.), *Delinquency and crime: Current theories* (pp. 149–197). New York: Cambridge University Press.

Catalano, R. F., Kosterman, R., Hawkins, J. D., Newcomb, M. D., & Abbott, R. D. (1996). Modeling the etiology of adolescent alcohol use: A test of the social development model. *Journal of Drug Issues, 26,* 429–455.

Catalano, R. F., Park, J., Harachi, T. W., Haggerty, K. P., Abbott, R. D., & Hawkins, J. D. (2005). Mediating the effects of poverty, gender, individual characteristics, and external constraints on antisocial behavior: A test of the social development model and implications for developmental life-course theory. In D. P. Farrington (Ed.), *Advances in criminological theory: Vol. 14. Integrated developmental and life-course theories of offending* (pp. 93–123). New Brunswick, NJ: Transaction.

Crosnoe, R., Muller, C., & Frank, K. (2004). Peer context and the consequences of adolescent drinking. *Social Problems, 51,* 288–304.

Cuijpers, K. (2002). Effective ingredients of school based prevention programs: A systematic review. *Addictive Behaviors, 27,* 1009–1023.

DeJong, W., & Langford, L. M. (2002). A typology for campus-based alcohol prevention: Moving toward environmental management strategies. *Journal of Studies on Alcohol, 14*(Suppl.), 140–147.

DeJong, W., Schneider, S. K., Towvim, L. G., Murphy, M. J., Doerr, E. E., Simonsen, N. R., et al. (2006). A multisite randomized trial of social norms marketing campaigns to reduce college student drinking. *Journal of Studies on Alcohol, 67,* 868–879.

Demers, A., Kairouz, S., Adlaf, E. M., Gliksman, L., Newton-Taylor, B., & Marchand, A. (2002). Multilevel analysis of situational drinking among Canadian undergraduates. *Social Science & Medicine, 55,* 415–424.

Dimeff, L. A., Baer, J. S., Kivlahan, D. R., & Marlatt, G. A. (1999). *Brief alcohol screening and intervention for college students: A harm reduction approach.* New York: Guilford Press.

Dishion, T. J., McCord, J., & Poulin, F. (1999). When interventions harm: Peer groups and problem behavior. *American Psychologist, 54,* 755–764.

Donohew, L., Clayton, R. R., Skinner, W. F., & Colon, S. (1999). Peer networks and sensation seeking: Some implications for primary socialization theory. *Substance Use & Misuse, 34,* 1013–1023.

Ellickson, P. L., Bell, R. M., & McGuigan, K. (1993). Preventing adolescent drug use: Long-term results of a junior high school program. *American Journal of Public Health, 83,* 856–861.

Engels, R., & Ter Bogt, T. (2001). Influences of risk behaviors on the quality of peer relations in adolescence. *Journal of Youth and Adolescence, 30,* 675–695.

Engs, R. C., Diebold, B. A., & Hansen, D. J. (1996). The drinking patterns and problems of a national sample of college students, 1994. *Journal of Studies on Alcohol, 41,* 13–33.

Ennett, S. T., & Bauman, K. E. (1996). Adolescent social networks: School, demographic and longitudinal considerations. *Journal of Adolescent Research, 11,* 194–215.

Fite, P. J., Colder, C. R., & O'Connor, R. M. (2006). Childhood behavior problems and peer selection and socialization: Risk for adolescent alcohol use. *Addictive Behaviors, 31,* 1454–1459.

Fromme, K., & Corbin, W. (2004). Prevention of heavy drinking and associated negative consequences among mandated and voluntary college students. *Journal of Consulting and Clinical Psychology, 72,* 1038–1049.

Ghosh-Dastidar, B., Longshore, D. L., Ellickson, P. L., & McCaffrey, D. F. (2004). Modifying pro-drug risk factors in adolescents: Results from Project ALERT. *Health Education & Behavior, 31,* 318–334.

Gorman, D., & White, H. R. (1995). You can choose your friends, but do they choose your crime? Implications of differential association theories for crime prevention policy. In H. Barlow (Ed.), *Criminology and public policy: Putting theory to work* (pp. 131–155). Boulder, CO: Westview Press.

Haines, M. P., Barker, G. P., & Rice, G. P. (2003). Using social norms to reduce alcohol and tobacco use in two midwestern high schools. In H. W. Perkins (Ed.), *A social norms approach to preventing school and college age substance abuse: A handbook for educators, counselors and clinicians* (pp. 235–244). San Francisco: Jossey-Bass.

Haines, M. P., & Spear, S. F. (1996). Changing the perception of the norm: A strategy to decrease binge drinking among college students. *Journal of American College Health, 45,* 134–140.

Hansen, W. B. (1992). School-based substance abuse prevention: A review of the state of the art in curriculum, 1980–1990. *Health Education Research: Theory and Practice, 7,* 403–430.

Hansen, W. B., & Graham, J. W. (1991). Preventing alcohol, marijuana, and cigarette use among adolescents: Peer pressure resistance training versus establishing conservative norms. *Preventive Medicine, 20,* 414–430.

Harford, T. C., & Muthén, B. O. (2001). Alcohol use among college students: The effects of prior problem behaviors and change of residence. *Journal of Studies on Alcohol, 62,* 306–312.

Harford, T. C., Wechsler, H., & Muthén, B. O. (2002). The impact of current residence and high school drinking on alcohol problems among college students. *Journal of Studies on Alcohol, 63,* 271–279.

Harford, T. C., Wechsler, H., & Seibring, M. (2002). Attendance and alcohol use at parties and bars in college: A national survey of current drinkers. *Journal of Studies on Alcohol, 63,* 726–733.

Hawkins, J. D., & Weis, J. G. (1985). The social development model: An integrated approach to delinquency prevention. *Journal of Primary Prevention, 6,* 73–97.

Hingson, R., Heeren, T., Winter, M., & Wechsler, H. (2005). Magnitude of alcohol-related mortality and morbidity among U.S. college students ages 18–24: Changes from 1998 to 2001. *Annual Review of Public Health, 26,* 259–279.

Hussong, A. (2002). Differentiating peer contexts and risk for adolescent substance use. *Journal of Youth and Adolescence, 31,* 207–220.

Jaccard, J., Blanton, H., & Dodge, T. (2005). Peer influences on risk behavior: An analysis of the effects of a close friend. *Developmental Psychology, 41,* 133–147.

Jackson, K. M., Sher, K. J., & Park, A. (2006). Drinking among college students: Consumption and consequences. In M. Galanter (Ed.), *Alcohol problems in adolescents and young adults: Epidemiology, neurobiology, prevention, and treatment* (pp. 85–117). New York: Springer Science.

Johnson, R. E., Marcos, A. C., & Bahr, S. J. (1987). The role of peers in the complex etiology of adolescent drug use. *Criminology, 25,* 323–339.

Johnson, V. L., Holt, L. J., Bry, B. H., & Powell, S. (2008). Effects of an integrated preventative intervention on urban youth transiting into high school. *Journal of Applied School Psychology, 24,* 225–246.

Kandel, D. B. (1996). The parental and peer contexts of adolescent deviance: An algebra of interpersonal influences. *Journal of Drug Issues, 26,* 289–315.

Kobus, K. (2003). Peers and adolescent smoking. *Addiction, 98,* 37–55.

Komro, K. A., Perry, C. L., Williams, C. L., Stigler, M. H., Farbakhsh, K., & Veblen-Mortenson, S. (2001). How did Project Northland reduce alcohol use among young adolescents? Analysis of mediating variables. *Health Education Research, 16,* 59–70.

Kumar, R., O'Malley, P. M., Johnston, L. D., Schulenberg, J. E., & Bachman, J. G. (2002). Effects of school level norms on student substance use. *Prevention Science, 3,* 105–124.

Labouvie, E. W. (1996). Maturing out of substance use: Selection and self-correction. *Journal of Drug Issues, 26,* 457–476.

Larimer, M. E., Cronce, J. M., Lee, C. M., & Kilmer, J. R. (2004–2005). Brief intervention in college settings. *Alcohol Research & Health, 28,* 94–104.

Larimer, M. E., Turner, A. P., Anderson, B. K., Fader, J. S., Kilmer, J. R., Palmer, R. S., et al. (2001). Evaluating a brief alcohol intervention with fraternities. *Journal of Studies on Alcohol, 62,* 370–380.

Leibsohn, J. (1994). The relationship between drug and alcohol use and peer group associations of college freshmen as they transition from high school. *Journal of Drug Education, 24,* 177–192.

Lewis, M. A., & Neighbors, C. (2004). Gender-specific misperceptions of college student drinking norms. *Psychology of Addictive Behaviors, 18,* 334–339.

Lewis, M. A., & Neighbors, C. (2007). Optimizing personalized normative feedback: The use of gender-specific referents. *Journal of Studies on Alcohol and Drugs, 68,* 228–237.

Lo, C. C., & Globetti, G. (1995). The facilitating and enhancing roles Greek associations play in college drinking. *International Journal of the Addictions, 30,* 1311–1322.

Lonczak, H. S., Huang, B., Catalano, R. F., Hawkins, J. D., Hill, K. G., Abbott, R. D., et al. (2001). The social predictors of adolescent alcohol misuse: A test of the social development model. *Journal of Studies on Alcohol, 62,* 179–189.

Lopez, J. S., Martinez, J. M., Martin, A., Martin, J. M., Martin, M. J., & Scandroglio, B. (2001). An exploratory multivariate approach to drug consumption patterns in young people based on primary socialization theory. *Substance Use & Misuse, 36,* 1611–1649.

Marlatt, G. A., Baer, J. S., & Larimer, M. E. (1995). Preventing alcohol abuse in college students: A harm-reduction approach. In G. M. Boyd, J. Howard, & R. A. Zucker (Eds.), *Alcohol problems among adolescents: Current directions in prevention research* (pp. 147–172). Hillsdale, NJ: Erlbaum.

Martens, M. P., Dams-O'Connor, K., Duffy-Paiement, C., & Gibson, J. T. (2006). Perceived alcohol use among friends and alcohol consumption among college athletes. *Psychology of Addictive Behaviors, 20,* 178–84.

Maxwell, K. A. (2002). Friends: The role of peer influence across adolescent risk behaviors. *Journal of Youth and Adolescence, 31,* 267–277.

McCabe, S. E., Schulenberg, J. E., Johnston, L. D., O'Malley, P. M., Bachman, J. G., & Kloska, D. D. (2005). Selection and socialization effects of fraternities and sororities on US college student substance use: A multi-cohort national longitudinal study. *Addiction, 100,* 512–524.

McIntosh, J., MacDonald, F., & McKeganey, N. (2006). Why do children experiment with illegal drugs? The declining role of peer pressure with increasing age. *Addiction Research and Theory, 14,* 275–287.

Miller, W. R., & Rollnick, S. (2002). *Motivational interviewing: Preparing people to change addictive behavior* (2nd edition). New York: Guilford Press.

Miller, W. R., Toscova, R. T., Miller, J. H., & Sanchez, V. (2000). A theory based motivational approach for reducing alcohol/drug problems in college. *Health Education and Behavior, 27,* 744–759.

Murphy, J. G., Duchnick, J. J., Vuchinich, R. E., Davison, J. W., Karg, R. S., Olson, A. M., et al. (2001). Relative efficacy of a brief motivational intervention for college student drinkers. *Psychology of Addictive Behaviors, 15,* 373–379.

Neighbors, C., Larimer, M. E., & Lewis, M. A. (2004). Targeting misperceptions of descriptive drinking norms: Efficacy of a computer-delivered personalized normative feedback intervention. *Journal of Consulting and Clinical Psychology, 72,* 434–447.

Oetting, E. R., & Donnermeyer, J. F. (1998). Primary socialization theory: The etiology of drug use and deviance I. *Substance Use & Misuse, 33,* 995–1026.

Oetting, E. R., Spooner, S., Beauvais, F., & Banning J. (1991). Prevention, peer clusters, and the paths to drug abuse. In L. Donohew, H. E. Sypher, & W. J. Bukoski (Eds.), *Persuasive communication and drug abuse prevention.* Hillsdale, NJ: Erlbaum.

Olds, R. S., & Thombs, D. L. (2001). The relationship of adolescent perceptions of peer norms and parent involvement to cigarette and alcohol use. *Journal of School Health, 71,* 223–228.

Ott, C. H., & Doyle, L. H. (2005). An evaluation of the small group norms challenging model: Changing substance use misperceptions in five urban high schools. *High School Journal, Feb/Mar,* 45–55.

Pandina, R. J. (2002). Drinking in college: One professor's personal history (or, look where you're leaping). *Journal of Studies on Alcohol, 63,* 133–135.

Pandina, R. J., & Johnson, V. (1999). Why do people use, abuse and become dependent on drugs? Progress toward a heuristic model. In M. Glantz & C. R. Hartel (Eds.), *Drug abuse: Origins and preventions* (pp. 119–148). Washington, DC: American Psychological Association.

Perkins, H. W. (2002). Social norms and the prevention of alcohol misuse in collegiate contexts. *Journal of Studies on Alcohol, 14*(Suppl.), 164–172.

Perkins, H. W., & Berkowitz, A. D. (1986). Perceiving the community norms of alcohol use among students: Some research implications for campus alcohol education programming. *International Journal of the Addictions, 21,* 961–976.

Perkins, H. W., & Craig, D. W. (2003). The imaginary lives of peers: Patterns of substance use and misperceptions of norms among secondary school students. In H. W. Perkins (Ed.), *A social norms approach to preventing school and college age substance abuse: A handbook for educators, counselors and clinicians* (pp. 209–223). San Francisco: Jossey-Bass.

Poelen, E., Engels, R., Van Der Vorst, H., Scholte, R., & Vermulst, A. (2007). Best friends and alcohol consumption in adolescence: A within family analysis. *Drug and Alcohol Dependence, 88,* 163–173.

Presley, C. A., Meilman, P. W., & Cashin, J. R. (1996). *Alcohol and drugs on American campuses: Use, consequences, and perceptions of the campus environment* (Vol. 4, 1992–1994). Carbondale: CORE Institute, Southern Illinois University.

Preston, P., & Goodfellow, M. (2006). Cohort comparisons: Social learning explanations for alcohol use among adolescents and older adults. *Addictive Behaviors, 31,* 2268–2283.

Read, J. P., Wood, M. D., & Capone, C. (2005). A prospective investigation of relations between social influences and alcohol involvement during the transition into college. *Journal of Studies on Alcohol, 66,* 23–34.

Schulenberg, J. E., & Maggs, J. L. (2002). A developmental perspective on alcohol use and heavy drinking during adolescence and the transition to young adulthood. *Journal of Studies on Alcohol, 14,* 54–70.

Sieving, R. E., Perry, C., & Williams, C. L. (2000). Do friendships change behaviors or do behaviors change friendships? Examining paths of influence in young adolescents' alcohol use. *Journal of Adolescent Health, 26,* 27–35.

Slutske, W. S., Hunt-Carter, E. E., Nabors-Oberg, R. E., Sher, K. J., Bucholz, K. K., Madden, P. A., et al. (2004). Do college students drink more than their non-college-attending peers? Evidence from a population-based longitudinal female twin study. *Journal of Abnormal Psychology, 113,* 530–540.

Sutherland, E. H. (1947). *Principles of criminology.* Philadelphia: Lippincott.

Tevyaw, T. O., Borsari, B., Colby, S. M., & Monti, P. M. (2007). Peer enhancement of a brief motivational intervention with mandated college students. *Psychology of Addictive Behaviors, 21,* 114–119.

Tobler, N. S., Roona, M. R., Ochshorn, P., Marshall, A. V., Streke, A. V., & Stackpole, K. M. (2000). School based adolescent drug prevention programs: 1998 meta-analysis. *Journal of Primary Prevention, 20,* 275–336.

Valente, T. W., Ritt-Olson, A., Stacy, A., Unger, J. B., Okamoto, J., & Sussman, S. (2007). Peer acceleration: Effects of a social network tailored substance abuse prevention program among high-risk adolescents. *Addiction, 102,* 1804–1815.

Walden, B., McGue, M., & Iacono, W. G. (2004). Identifying shared environmental contributions to early substance use: The respective roles of peers and parents. *Journal of Abnormal Psychology, 113,* 440–450.

Walters, S. T., & Neighbors, C. (2005). Feedback interventions for college alcohol misuse: What, why and for whom? *Addictive Behaviors, 30,* 1168–1182.

Warr, M. (1993). Age, peers, and delinquency. *Criminology, 31,* 17–40.

Wechsler, H., Lee, J., Kuo, M., Seibring, M., Nelson, T., & Lee, H. (2002). Trends in college binge drinking during a period of increased prevention efforts: Findings from 4 Harvard School of Public Health College Alcohol Study surveys: 1993–2001. *Journal of American College Health, 50,* 203–217.

Weiss, B., Caron, A., Ball, S., Tapp, J., Johnson, M., & Weisz, J. R. (2005). Iatrogenic effects of group treatment for antisocial youths. *Journal of Consulting and Clinical Psychology, 73,* 1036–1044.

Werch, C. C., Pappas, D. M., Carlson, J. M., DiClemente, C. C., Chally, P. S. & Sinder, J. A. (2000). Results of a social norm intervention to prevent binge drinking among first year residential college students. *Journal of American College Health, 49,* 85–92.

White, H. R. (2006). Reduction of alcohol-related harm on United States college campuses: The use of personal feedback interventions. *International Journal of Drug Policy, 17,* 310–319.

White, H. R., Bates, M. E., & Johnson, V. (1990). Social reinforcement and alcohol consumption. In W. M. Cox (Ed.), *Why people drink people drink: Parameters of alcohol as a reinforcer* (pp. 233–261). New York: Gardner Press.

White, H. R., Bates, M. E., & Johnson, V. (1991). Learning to drink: Familial, peer, and media influences. In D. Pittman & H. R. White (Eds.), *Society, culture, and drinking patterns reexamined* (pp. 177–197). New Brunswick, NJ: Rutgers Center of Alcohol Studies.

White, H. R., Fleming, C. B., Kim, M. J., Catalano, R. F. & McMorris, B. J. (2008). Identifying two potential mechanisms for changes in alcohol use among college-attending and non-college-attending emerging adults. *Developmental Psychology, 44,* 1625–1639.

White, H. R., & Jackson, K. (2004–2005). Social and psychological influences on emerging adult drinking behavior. *Alcohol Research & Health, 28,* 182–190.

White, H. R., Labouvie, E. W., & Papadaratsakis, V. (2005). Changes in substance use during the transition to adulthood: A comparison of college students and their noncollege age peers. *Journal of Drug Issues, 35,* 281–306.

White, H. R., McMorris, B. J., Catalano, R. F., Fleming, C. B., Haggerty, K. P., & Abbott, R. D. (2006). Increases in alcohol and marijuana use during the transition out of high school into emerging adulthood: The effects of leaving home, going to college, and high school protective factors. *Journal of Studies on Alcohol, 67,* 810–822.

Yanovitzky, I. (2005). Sensation seeking and adolescent drug use: The mediating role of association with deviant peers and pro-drug discussions. *Health Communications, 17,* 67–89.

CHAPTER 21

THE INFLUENCE OF PEERS
ON SUBSTANCE USE

Judy A. Andrews and Hyman Hops

Peers are considered a primary influence on the behavior of youth, and their importance appears to remain in effect from childhood through emerging adulthood. Numerous studies have provided support for the importance of peers in the development of substance use and abuse (Andrews, Tildesley, Hops, & Li, 2002; Ary, Duncan, Duncan, & Hops, 1999; Bauman & Ennett, 1994; Curran, Stice, & Chassin, 1997; Dishion, Capaldi, Spracklen, & Li, 1995; Hawkins, Catalano, & Miller, 1992; Huba, Wingard, & Bentler, 1980; Kandel & Davies, 1991). We view peer influence as consisting of various facets, including peers' behaviors and attitudes, youth's perceptions of these behaviors and attitudes, and youth's relationships with their peers. Peer relationships can occur in groups, ranging from an intimate dyad to a large social network.

Several studies have compared the influence of parents on substance use with that of peers across the developmental period spanning the years from childhood to emerging adulthood and have, in general, found that the influence of peers on substance use increases developmentally, whereas the influence of parents wanes considerably over time. In an early study, Krosnick and Judd (1982) showed that parent and peers provided smoking models that equally influenced the smoking behavior of preadolescents, but the effect of peer models increased across adolescence and the effect of parent models decreased. Similarly, T. E. Duncan, Tildesley, Duncan, and Hops (1995) found that although both

parents' and peers' use predicted initial use, only changes in peer encouragement predicted changes in adolescent substance use over time. In addition, modes of influence between parents and peers may vary. For example, Biddle, Bank, and Marlin (1980) showed that parents influence adolescent drinking through norms, whereas peers influence adolescent drinking through behavior. Overall, however, peers were more influential than were parents. The differential influence of peers over that of parents may in part be a result of the increasing amount of time youth spend with peers. Nevertheless, the influence of the family can remain salient even during the transition to emerging adulthood. For example, Wood, Read, Mitchell, and Brand (2004) showed that parental influences (nurturing and monitoring) in high school attenuated the influences of peers on substance use after the child went to college.

The contribution of peers to the development of substance use cannot be examined in isolation as a direct effect but must be examined as part of a broader contextual framework, including neighborhoods and families. Furthermore, consistent with the tenets of developmental contextualism (Lerner, 1991), the development of substance use is considered a function of the interaction of genetic, biological, cognitive, and personality systems as well as the environmental contextual system, including peers and family.

Hence, in this chapter not only do we review the direct effects of peers on youth substance use, but

Preparation of this chapter was supported in part by National Institute of Drug Abuse Grant DA10767. We gratefully acknowledge the assistance of Christine Lorenz in manuscript preparation.

we also examine mediators that are involved in the process and variables that may moderate the direct effects of peers. In addition, we review the moderating effect of peers on biological influences and genetics and end with a summary of implications, including a discussion of the role of these processes in the design of interventions.

PEER USE: SOCIALIZATION AND SELECTION

Similarity in substance use between peers has been consistently shown in the adolescent literature (Curran, Stice, & Chassin, 1997; Ennett & Bauman, 1994; Gaughan, 2006; Henry, Slater, & Oetting, 2005; Hops & Davis, 1998, Urberg, Degirmencioglu, & Pilgrim, 1997) and emerging adult literature (Andrews et al., 2002). For example, Dinges and Oetting (1993) found that almost all of the friends of marijuana users also used marijuana, compared with only half of the friends of nonusers. Similarity in substance use between peers has typically been attributed to two processes: socialization, wherein the peer group influences the substance use behavior of the adolescent or young adult; and selection, wherein the adolescent or young adult associates with peers who are similar to them in their substance use behavior or whom they would like to emulate. The socialization process involves encouragement through normative behavior processes, whereas selection more involves "choosing" friends who endorse and even promote drug use behaviors (Kandel, 1986).

Adolescence

In the adolescent literature, results from longitudinal studies have shown the effects of both socialization (Bailey & Hubbard, 1991; Curran, Stice, & Chassin, 1997; Ennett & Bauman, 1994; Henry et al., 2005; Pilgrim, Luo, Urberg, & Fang, 1999; Schulenberg et al., 1999; Simons-Morton & Chen, 2006; Urberg et al., 1997; Wills & Cleary, 1999) and, less frequently, selection (Curran, Stice, & Chassin, 1997; Ennett & Bauman, 1994; Fisher & Bauman, 1988; Wang, Eddy, & Fitzhugh, 2000). In support of socialization, Bricker et al. (2006) showed that in childhood having a close friend who smoked predicted trying smoking, the transition from trying to monthly

smoking, and the transition from monthly to daily smoking. Likewise, Simons-Morton and Chen (2006) and Sieving, Perry, and Williams (2000) showed that peer drinking predicted subsequent drinking by the adolescent across middle school. Conversely, Wang et al. (2000) demonstrated that both male and female smoking adolescents with nonsmoking best friends tended to have best friends who smoked 4 years later. Moreover, there is evidence that selection and socialization may occur at the same time (Curran, Stice, & Chassin, 1997). Modeling growth across 3 years, Curren et al. (1997) showed that initial friends' substance use predicted change in adolescent use and initial adolescent substance use predicted change in friends' use. Parent socialization may also influence selection. Engels, Vitaro, Den-Exter-Blockard, de-Kemp, and Scholte (2004) showed that adolescents with smoking parents were more likely to affiliate with smoking friends in subsequent years.

Emerging and Young Adulthood

Research investigating similarity in substance use between emerging and young adult peers has been less common and has primarily been limited to marital partners or college students. Emerging adulthood has recently been conceptualized as a distinct developmental period, spanning the ages of 18 to 25 (Arnett, 2005), with young adulthood spanning the ages of 26 to 30. Studies of young marital partners have demonstrated similarity between spouses in their alcohol and drug dependence (McLeod, 1995); socialization of problem drinking, but only for women (Windle, 1997); and selection of a mate on the basis of the mate's illegal drug use (Yamaguchi & Kandel, 1997) and problem drinking (Windle, 1997). Leonard and Mudar (2004) showed that a newlywed husband's drinking before marriage influenced his wife's drinking after marriage, and the wife's drinking in the 1st year of marriage influenced her husband's alcohol use a year later.

Several studies have investigated the influence of peers among college students (e.g., Read, Wood, & Capone, 2005; Yanovitzky, 2006; Yanovitzky, Stewart, & Lederman, 2006), showing a strong influence of perceived substance use of close friends. Alcohol use by close friends before college prospectively predicted problem drinking 3 years later, while at college (Read et al., 2005). To our knowledge, the only studies investigating the influence of peers, beyond that of the mate or partner, on substance use among emerging and young adults in general were those conducted by Labouvie (1996), Andrews et al. (2002), and Leonard and colleagues (Leonard, Kearns, & Mudar, 2000; Leonard & Mudar, 2004). Labouvie, using data from Rutgers University's Health and Human Development Study, found that perception of peers' drinking was related to change in the young adult's drinking, providing support for the process of socialization. Andrews et al. made a similar point using data from young adults and their same- and opposite-sex best friends or mates collected independently in the Oregon Research Institute's Smoking in the Family Study (Hops, Andrews, Duncan, Duncan, & Tildesley, 2000). These authors showed that earlier peer use predicted change in the young adult's substance use, including cigarette use, binge drinking, and problem use. Results were generally consistent across genders and for both same- and opposite-sex peers. Leonard and Mudar (2003), however, found evidence for peer selection in their Adult Development Study examining the transition into marriage. Both spouses were more likely to affiliate with drinking peers following marriage, predicted only by the husband's premarital drinking.

This brief review shows that results from both cross-sectional and longitudinal studies support socialization and selection processes as major influences in drug use etiology spanning the period from adolescence into young adulthood. The findings reinforce the importance of peer influences whether using measures of perceived friends' use or friends' reports of their own use.

AFFILIATION WITH DEVIANT PEERS

In problem behavior theory (Jessor & Jessor, 1977), substance use is considered part of an underlying problem behavior syndrome, along with antisocial behavior and conduct disorders. Several studies have provided empirical support for this conceptualization (e.g., Ary et al., 1999; Donovan & Jessor, 1985; Tildesley, Hops, Ary, & Andrews, 1995).

Although not all peers who use substances are deviant (i.e., engage in externalizing behaviors, such as delinquency, aggression, and substance use), according to problem behavior theory deviant peers tend to use more substances. Many longitudinal studies have shown a relation between affiliation with deviant peers and subsequent substance use (e.g., Barrera, Biglan, Ary, & Li, 2001; Dishion et al., 1995; Fergusson, Swain-Campbell, & Horwood, 2002; Westling, Andrews, Hampson, & Peterson, 2008). Fergusson et al. (2002), using data from the Dunedin sample, showed that affiliation with deviant peers was associated with alcohol and cannabis abuse and nicotine dependence from ages 14 to 21. Interestingly, the predictions were strongest for children in the younger compared with the older age groups. In a related vein, Li, Barrera, Hops, Fisher, and Harmer (2002) showed that association with deviant peers was more strongly related to substance use among those with low initial levels of use. Thus, both studies provided support for a stronger effect of deviant peers at earlier stages of use.

Poor social skills, peer victimization, and rejection are related to affiliation with deviant peers (Hawkins et al., 1992; Patterson et al., 1992) and subsequently to substance use. Dishion (1990) hypothesized that those who cannot get along with their more conventional peers are likely to seek out deviant peers and be vulnerable to their influence. In one study, Rusby, Forrester, Biglan, and Metzler (2005) showed that the effect of experiencing frequent peer harassment in middle school on concurrent cigarette and alcohol use in high school was mediated through affiliation with deviant peers. Quite possibly, the acceptance by a deviant group of peers replaces more conventional bonds and mitigates any feelings of disenfranchisement or dysphoria that might accompany rejection. Difficulty with peer relations can have much longer effects, as shown by Hops, Davis, and Lewin (1999), who found that peer problems in elementary school predicted more multiple drug use in high school.

According to social interaction theory (e.g., Cairns, Perrin, & Cairns, 1985; Dishion, 1990; Patterson, Reid, & Dishion, 1992), conflict in the home combined with poor parental discipline and inadequate monitoring encourages youth to bond with deviant peers. A range of antisocial behaviors, including substance use, are acquired and maintained through these affiliations. Ineffectual parents appear to reinforce problem behavior at home, increasing its frequency and intensity. This drives youth to associate with other deviant and drug-abusing peers with similar conflicting family histories and deficits in coping skills (Patterson, Dishion, & Yoerger, 2000). This family-based coercion model has received support in several longitudinal studies (Ary et al., 1999; Barrera et al., 2001). Ary et al. (1999) found a prospective relation between family conflict and association with deviant peers 1 year later, followed by problem behaviors, including substance use, 2 years later. However, of equal importance is the finding that association with conventional and prosocial peers lessens the likelihood of engaging in or increasing drug use and other deviant behaviors (Bukowski & Adams, 2005; Catalano, Berglund, Ryan, Lonczak, & Hawkins, 2003).

These and related studies have shown that association with deviant peers increases the probability of acquiring or maintaining drug use habits, especially when adolescents are young or at the initial stages of substance use (Li et al., 2002). Dishion (1990) suggested that these processes are stronger among youth at heightened risk of deviant behavior. In contrast, Schulenberg et al. (1999) reported that selection of deviant peers for non–drug-related purposes was predictive of subsequent alcohol use. Thus, both socialization and selection provide useful conceptual frameworks to explain the association between affiliation with deviant peers and substance use.

PERCEPTIONS OF PEER USE

With many notable exceptions (Andrews et al., 2002; Ennett & Bauman, 1994; Fisher & Bauman, 1988; Gaughan, 2006; Jaccard, Blanton, & Dodge, 2005; Kandel, 1985; Pilgrim et al., 1999; Urberg et al., 1997; Yamaguchi & Kandel, 1997), the majority of studies examining peer influence have relied on adolescents' or young adults' perceptions of their peers' substance use rather than on peers' self-report. Although studies based on youth's perceptions have been informative, the validity of the perception of peers' behavior as a measure of actual peer use is open to question. The

similarity between peers shown in these studies could be partially attributable to beliefs about their friends' behavior rather than to the peers' substance use per se. Adolescents consistently overestimate the similarity between their own patterns of drug use and those of their friends (Fisher & Bauman, 1988; Neighbors, Dillard, Lewis, Bergstrom, & Neil, 2006; Urberg, Cheng, & Shyu, 1991). This over- or underestimation of others' substance use depending on their own use has been termed the *false consensus effect* (Marks & Miller, 1987; Ross, Greene, & House, 1977). Marks, Graham, and Hansen (1992) demonstrated two possible mechanisms that could underlie the false consensus effect. They showed that not only social projection (i.e., adolescents' own alcohol use predicted prevalence estimates 1 year later) but also social conformity (i.e., prevalence estimates predicted change in alcohol use 1 year later) can account for behavioral similarity.

Despite the lack of concordance between perceived friends' use and friends' actual use, the perception of peers' use nonetheless has a large effect on adolescent use. Bauman and Fisher (1986) showed that adolescents' perceptions of their three best friends' use was a stronger correlate of the adolescents' substance use behavior than was the friends' report of their own use and concluded that adolescents' beliefs about their friends' behavior is more important to both socialization and selection than how friends actually behave.

The concept of perceived norms (the general perception of peers' substance use) is a central part of several health behavior theories (e.g., Ajzen and Fishbein's theories of reasoned action and planned behavior; Ajzen, 1988, 1991; Ajzen & Fishbein, 1973, 1980) and Gibbons and Gerrard's prototype–willingness model (Gibbons & Gerrard, 1995; see chap. 18 of this volume). Normative beliefs, or subjective norms, as they are sometimes called, predict intentions to use substances as well as actual substance use throughout development. Hampson, Andrews, and Barckley (2007; Hampson, Andrews, Barckley, & Severson, 2006) showed that an increase in perceived norms regarding peers' use of tobacco and alcohol during the elementary school years (from the 4th through the 8th grade) predicted the development of intentions to smoke and use alcohol, respectively, across this same period. Andrews, Hampson, Barckley, Gerrard, and Gibbons (2008) demonstrated that perceived norms as early as 2nd grade and increases in these norms throughout the elementary years predicted the extent of tobacco and alcohol use in the 10th grade. Several other studies (Neighbors et al., 2006; Yanovitzky, 2006; Yanovitzky et al., 2006) found that perceived norms of peer drinking, despite being overestimated, predicted subsequent frequency and quantity of alcohol use among college students.

SOCIAL IMAGES OF SUBSTANCE USERS

A variety of other cognitions can influence the substance use of the adolescent. A key concept in the prototype–willingness model of Gibbons and Gerrard (1995; see chap. 18) is that of prototypes or social images of the typical individual who engages in a behavior. If adolescents attribute positive images to peers who use substances, they may well think that others will attribute positive images to them if they use substances, leading to an increase in willingness and subsequent use. In a recent study, Andrews, Hampson, Barckley, et al. (2008) showed that 2nd through 5th graders' image of kids who use alcohol and tobacco and the increase in the favorability of these social images over the next 4 years predicted the quantity of both alcohol and tobacco use, respectively, in 8th through 11th grade.

Perceptions about other characteristics of peers can also predict subsequent substance use. Andrews, Hampson, and Barckley (2008) showed that adolescents' perceptions about peers' social images of smokers subsequently influenced their own social images (i.e., prototypes) and that these perceptions were stronger predictors of subsequent cigarette use than were the adolescents' own prototypes. Similarly, Donohew et al. (1999) found that adolescents tend to pick friends who are similar to themselves in terms of sensation seeking and that the perception of peers' sensation seeking predicted the adolescents' subsequent use of both alcohol and marijuana 2 years later.

OTHER SOURCES OF PEER INFLUENCE

Direct Offers and Encouragement

Peer socialization has been conceptualized as both active and passive (Graham, Marks, & Hansen, 1991;

Read et al., 2005). *Passive influence* is defined as direct modeling of peers' behavior and normative influence (e.g., the influence of the group as a whole). *Active influence* is defined as the effect of direct offers or encouragement to use. Graham et al. (1991) emphasized the need to separate these two processes conceptually to further the understanding of peer influences. Much of the research we reviewed earlier falls under the rubric of passive influence. However, as shown here, active influence is also of importance. The frequency of direct offers was related to marijuana use in adolescence (Ellickson, Tucker, Klein, & Saner, 2004) and heavy episodic drinking among college students, particularly for those with more parental permissiveness for drinking (Wood et al., 2004). Peer encouragement, defined by the number of a participant's five closest friends who encourage him or her to use a substance, also plays a role in predicting drug use. Longitudinal studies have shown that peer encouragement has been related to an increase in alcohol use across both early (S. C. Duncan, Duncan, & Stryker, 2006) and late adolescence (Li, Duncan, & Hops, 2001). Moreover, peer encouragement may be as important as family cohesion in predicting use in early adolescence but more important than family cohesion in predicting changes in substance use from early to late adolescence (T. E. Duncan, Duncan, & Hops, 1994; T. E. Duncan et al., 1995).

Sociometric Status

Sociometric analyses (Coie, Dodge, & Coppotelli, 1982; Hops & Lewin, 1984) have been used to classify students depending on number of positive and negative nominations received and given. Although there are variations in sociometric methodology (e.g., Asher & Dodge, 1986), in general, students are asked to nominate a fixed number of children (usually three) whom they most (positive nomination) and least (negative nomination) like to play with. The context can be the classroom, an entire grade level, or a larger social grouping. Using standard scores of nominations within groups, individuals can be classified as popular (more positive than negative), rejected (more negative than positive), controversial (both positive and negative), and average. Friendships may also be defined by a child's choices of others or by reciprocal choices. Furthermore, individuals may be classified as part of a group (friendships consist of several individuals), a dyad (a single reciprocal friend), or an isolate (receives no nominations). The effects of sociometric status appear to be dependent on the substance studied. Pearson et al. (2006) reported that smoking was higher among isolates and dyads compared with those who were members of a group. Similarly, Aloise-Young and Kaeppner (2005) found that rejected and controversial youth, who received few positive peer nominations, smoked more cigarettes during their lifetime than did other youth.

In contrast, Pearson et al. (2006) showed that alcohol use, more normative than cigarette use, was higher among those who received many nominations and those who nominated several friends. Hops et al. (1999) reported similar findings. In a direct observation study of students in elementary school playgrounds, they found that higher levels of reciprocated positive behavior predicted alcohol use in high school. Thus, alcohol appears to be used by more social, well-liked individuals, whereas less normative cigarette use appears to be more prevalent among those with few friends. In another longitudinal study, Vitaro, Pedersen, and Brendgen (2007) showed that it was not deviance by peers but rather peers' rejection that mediated the link between early disruptiveness and later substance use. Disruptive children who are well accepted by peers (similar to controversial children) may be at risk for substance use because they have sufficient skills to be part of a peer network through which substances become available.

Although alcohol and cigarettes appear to be used by more and less popular adolescents, respectively, there is some evidence that the perceived norms within the school context moderate the effect of sociometric class membership. Turner, West, Gordon, Young, and Sweeting (2006) showed that smokers in schools in which smoking was normative tended to be popular or belonged to groups, whereas smokers in schools in which tobacco use was less normative tended to be dyads and isolates.

Alcohol use by less popular individuals, those with lower sociometric status, may be influenced by the alcohol use of "wannabe" friends with higher

status. Bot, Engels, Knibbe, and Meeus (2005) found that wannabe best friends (i.e., unreciprocated friendships; the participant nominated a friend who did not reciprocate) were more likely to influence the alcohol use of the participant if the friend was rated as more popular. They concluded that adolescents may alter or calibrate their behavior on the basis of a selection of friends they emulate in an effort to encourage reciprocity and improve their standing or popularity. These results are consistent with the prototype–willingness model (Gibbons & Gerrard 1995), showing that perceived popularity of peers who use substances is an important influence on adolescent substance use.

Taken together, these studies suggest that in schools and communities in which smoking is not normative, smoking may be considered a deviant behavior ascribed more to isolates and other rejected children or youth. In contrast, more normative alcohol consumption is more likely to occur in group social situations and among more popular, socially skilled individuals.

Peer Group Networks

Both selection and socialization are processes involved in the influences of peer group networks on adolescent substance use. Selection occurs when individuals decide to be part of a group to whom they attribute certain characteristics that they perceive they have or desire to have in common with members of that group. At the same time, peer groups or crowds can exert a socializing influence on their members (Brown & Klute, 2003) by providing them with certain behavioral standards and opportunities to engage in the behavior. Although Huba et al. (1980) showed that deviant peer culture did not predict an increase in substance use among early adolescents, more recent studies have found that the norms of the adolescent's self-identified peer group can affect their substance use. Furthermore, the extent of identification can moderate the effect of the group's perceived substance use norms. Schofield, Pattison, Hill, and Borland (2002, 2003) showed that the perceived norms of the group or crowd influenced individual substance use and that this relationship was stronger for those who more strongly identified with their peer group.

In an extensive review, Sussman, Pokhrel, Ashmore, and Brown (2007) showed that the deviant group (i.e., rejected, druggies, punks), as compared with the academics (i.e., nerds, brains) and athletes (i.e., jocks), were those most likely to use substances. However, several studies showed that alcohol use was more prevalent among popular youth characterized as elites (Dolcini & Adler, 1994; Tolone & Tieman, 1990) and athletes (Barber, Eccles, & Stone, 2001; Miller et al., 2003). High school group affiliation is also related to substance use post–high school. For example, Sussman, Unger, and Dent (2004) found that students who were more likely to identify with high-risk peer groups in high school reported greater involvement in drug use in emerging adulthood. Taken together, these studies show that the perceived norms and extent of self-identification within the group influence the individual's behavior through both selection and socialization.

EFFECTS OF DEMOGRAPHIC VARIABLES ON PEER INFLUENCE

Gender
Investigations of gender differences on the effects of peer use on adolescent substance use have provided mixed results; however, most have shown that girls are more easily directly influenced by their peers as compared with boys (Berndt & Keefe, 1995; Brooks, Stuewig, & LeCroy, 1998; Kung & Farrell, 2001). For example, substance use is more likely to occur in a peer context among girls compared with boys (Emler, Reicher, & Ross, 1997). Gender may also moderate the peer influence processes. In a cross-sectional study of more than 10,000 9th- to 11th-grade students, Leatherdale et al. (2006) showed that whereas beliefs about the prevalence of smoking among older peers influenced girls' smoking, for boys the effect of these beliefs was moderated by whether their five closest friends smoked. Such results may reflect gender differences in cross-gender associations in high school when girls tend to have older boys as romantic partners.

Studies of gender differences in peer influences conducted with emerging and young adults have primarily been based on marital couples and also produce mixed findings. A significant effect of only wives' use on husbands' subsequent use was found for marijuana (Leonard & Homish, 2005; Yamaguchi & Kandel, 1997) but the opposite effect, husbands' use on wives, was found for problem drinking (Windle, 1997).

Race and Ethnicity
Studies assessing the effects of race and ethnicity on the influence of peers are rare. However, there is some evidence that the effects of peers on substance use are stronger for European Americans than for other racial and ethnic groups, particularly for smoking. Unger et al. (2001) demonstrated that best friend's smoking and perceived norms were stronger influences of 30-day prevalence of smoking for European Americans than for Asian Americans, Pacific Islanders, Hispanics, or African Americans. Similarly, Robinson et al. (2006) showed that peer modeling was a more important predictor of onset of smoking for European American than for African American adolescents, and Pilgrim et al. (1999) found that close friends' use had a moderate influence on adolescent use for both Chinese and European American adolescents, but less so for African American adolescents. However, Barrera et al. (2001) showed that the influence of affiliation with deviant peers on overall substance use was similar across Native American, Hispanic, and European American adolescents. Ethnic and racial differences in peer influences may in part be governed by greater cohesion within the family and greater parental monitoring, which are more frequently encountered in Hispanic (Barerra & Reese, 1993; Parke, 2004) and African American (Catalano et al., 1992) families than in European American families. In general, African Americans and youth of newly emigrated, less acculturated Hispanics tend to drink less than other cultural groups. As Hispanic youth become more acculturated and less constrained by family influence, drinking rates tend to increase and become more similar to that of the larger peer group in which they reside.

Urban Versus Rural Area
Researchers investigating the effects of community have suggested that the effect of peer influence on substance use is stronger for urban than for rural

youth (Rose, Dick, Viken, Pulkkinen, & Kaprio, 2001; Wilson & Donnermeyer, 2006). Rose et al. (2001), in a study of Finnish twins from ages 16 to 18, found that drinking habits were a greater function of the environment among those in rural as compared with urban areas, despite the influence of a large genetic component. They postulated that this Gene × Environment interaction was primarily a result of both the lower availability of alcohol and the fewer people who drank in rural than in urban regions.

PEER INFLUENCE AS A MEDIATOR

Peer influence has often been conceptualized as a mediator or intervening mechanism linking major risk domains including personality, contextual influences, and biological variables with youth substance use. We briefly review the evidence for peer influence as a mediator, paying particular attention to the dominant risk and protective factors that have emerged in the literature.

Personality and Temperament

Several studies have shown that the effects of early temperament and personality variables, including self-control, sensation seeking, sociability, and hostility, on substance use or intentions to use are indirectly mediated through peer influence. Individuals may be selecting peers with similar personality characteristics (i.e., homophilic selection), who in turn may reinforce and sustain their behavioral propensities. Wills, Sandy, and Yaeger (2000) proposed and supported a model wherein good self-control may act as a deterrent to affiliation with deviant peers and subsequently to substance use (see chap. 7 of this volume). These theorists have also proposed that propensity to take risks has the opposite effect, increasing affiliation with substance-using peers. Several studies in the adolescent and emerging adult literature have supported this model. Using data from the Oregon Youth Substance Use Project, Hampson, Andrews, and Barckley (2008), showed that sensation seeking in the 4th and 5th grades influenced marijuana use in 10th and 11th grades and, through affiliation with deviant peers, in 8th through 10th grades. Similar findings were noted

among college students, among whom sensation seeking mediated both the association with alcohol-using peers and perceived norms on subsequent alcohol use (Yanovitzky, 2006).

Personality factors, relatively stable across childhood (Hampson, Andrews, Barckley, & Peterson, 2007), are predictive of peer influences later in childhood or in adolescence. Chassin, Flora, and King (2004) found that children from alcoholic families who were more impulsive and low in agreeableness were more likely to become involved with deviant peers and at risk for substance dependence. Using latent growth modeling, Hampson et al. (2006) found that early sociability in the 1st through 5th grades was related to higher initial intentions and more rapid growth in reported intentions to use alcohol across 4 years and that these effects were mediated by perceived norms. In contrast, Hampson et al. (2007) showed that children who were more hostile, rather than sociable, had higher initial levels of intentions and a greater increase in intentions to smoke cigarettes when older. The effect of hostility on cigarette use was mediated by both perceived norms and the child's social images of cigarette users. Thus, youths' personality not only influenced with whom they chose to affiliate, which could be conceptualized as a selection mechanism, but also their perceptions of friends' use and their images of substance users, both clearly representing socialization.

The Environment

Peer influence may mediate the effects of the family, the neighborhood, and the school context on substance use. Studies have suggested that poor parenting practices and parental drinking behavior and norms affect the substance use of the adolescent through peer use, affiliation with deviant peers, social images, and other variables. For example, the effect of parental use and norms on the adolescent's alcohol use was mediated by the teen's social images of alcohol users such that adolescents whose parents use more alcohol and who had higher subjective norms were more likely to have more positive social images (Spijkerman, van den Eijnden, Overbeek, & Engels, 2006). These positive social images, in turn, influenced their alcohol use. Furthermore, the effect of parents' disapproval of alcohol use on their adolescent's use was mediated by lack of use and low approval of use by peers (Nash, McQueen, & Bray, 2005). Thus, children who had parents who were more likely to disapprove had peers who were less likely to use substances and did not approve of their use. These variables, in turn, influenced the adolescent's use. Ary et al. (1999) showed that high level of parent–child conflict and less parent–child involvement were related to greater affiliation with deviant peers and subsequent increased levels of drug use.

The adolescents' neighborhood and school also represent important contextual influences (S. C. Duncan, Duncan, & Strycker, 2002; see also chap. 22 of this volume). Living in low–socioeconomic status neighborhoods was related to the extent of peer drinking, which, in turn, mediated the effect of neighborhood on alcohol use (Chuang, Ennett, Bauman, & Foshee, 2005). Thus, adolescents who live in low–socioeconomic status neighborhoods associate with peers who drink more often, which in turn leads adolescents to drink more themselves. Cleveland and Wiebe (2003) showed not only that the prevalence of use within the school influenced the adolescent's use but also that similarity in substance use between friends was higher in schools with higher prevalence of use of both tobacco and alcohol. It is likely that within schools characterized by high levels of substance use, there exists more support and reinforcement for use, which increases the similarity among peers (see also chap. 23 of this volume).

Other Psychosocial Influences

Peer influences have been shown to mediate the effect of other psychosocial variables on substance use. For example, the relation of depressive symptoms to smoking was completely mediated by friends' approval of substance use (Ritt-Olson et al., 2005). Thus, depressed individuals who used substances did so only if their friends approved of their use. Furthermore, Lillehoj, Trudeau, and Spoth (2005) showed that low academic achievement predicted an increase in perceived norms, which in turn predicted substance use. Perhaps those who were less academically inclined increased their perception of norms because of the substance use among their immediate peer group, which consisted of low achievers.

MODERATORS OF PEER INFLUENCE

A number of variables have been identified as moderators of the effect of peer influence on substance use, changing the relation by amplifying or attenuating the effect. Identification of these moderator variables is essential for informing the development of prevention and intervention methods (Kazdin, 2007). In this next section, we briefly review the evidence for variables that moderate the effect of peer influences on early-stage drug use.

Parental Influences

Various forms of parenting behavior, family relations, and family structure influence whether children affiliate with deviant or drug-using peers as well as their susceptibility to such influences. Parke and O'Neil (1999) differentiated between parenting practices, such as monitoring or supervision, and parenting style, such as authoritative versus authoritarian parenting, the former characterized by being both demanding and responsive or supportive, the latter by being demanding and directive. Both of these constructs have received support in the literature in terms of their moderating effect on adolescents' association with members of a peer group and peers' subsequent influence on their own drug use (e.g., Steinberg, Mounts, Lamborn, & Dornbusch, 1991). For example, Dorius, Bahr, Hoffman, and Harmon (2004) found that adolescents' perception of the risk of being caught by their parents while using drugs, which may be considered a variant of monitoring, attenuated the relation between peer and adolescent drug use. That is, high levels of a measure of perceived risk of being caught significantly lowered the effect of high drug-using peers on the drug use of the focal adolescent. Mounts (2002) found that the combination of monitoring and perceived risk was inversely related to peers' drug use, but only when parents used an authoritative style as compared with being authoritarian, indulgent, or uninvolved. Furthermore, although friends' use predicted adolescents' use over time, the effect was greatest for those with authoritarian parents.

Several studies have suggested that perceived closeness to parents and parental support are protective by attenuating the influence of drug-abusing peers on the substance use of the adolescent. In the absence of perceived parental support, peers have an especially marked effect on substance use (Wills & Cleary, 1996), whereas the presence of parental support lessened the influence of smoking friends on the adolescent's smoking (Barrera & Li, 1996). Similarly, Dorius et al. (2004) found that the relation between peer and adolescent drug use was moderated by perceived closeness to the father, in addition to the risk of being caught by parents. However, the protective effects of a positive, nurturing, and warm relationship with parents may depend on the parents' use. Andrews, Hops, and Duncan (1997), guided by social learning theory (Bandura, 1977), found that teen modeling of parent substance use behavior depended on the quality of the parent–adolescent relationship. They found that if a parent used a substance, a good relationship created a greater likelihood of the adolescent's also using the substance. Thus, a good parent–adolescent relation alone may be insufficient as a buffer to protect against substance use. It is more likely that specific communication of antidrug attitudes and healthy alternatives is required as an effective deterrent.

Studies have repeatedly shown that two-parent families are associated with lower drug use as compared with single-parent or blended families (e.g., Hops, Duncan, Duncan, & Stoolmiller, 1996; Hops, Tildesley, Lichtenstein, Ary, & Sherman, 1990). Living with two parents appears to be protective and create barriers to drug use. However, the traditional household may not always work as a protective factor. Eitle (2005) showed that the influence of family structure moderated the effect of exposure to peers who use substances, such that adolescents in traditional families, compared with those in blended two-parent families, are more likely to use substances when they associate with drug-using peers. Eitle hypothesized that the unexpected difference may be the result of greater stability and less mobility in the traditional family, leading to more stable friendships and consequently to greater peer influence. Clearly, further research is required to test these and related peer influence hypotheses.

Together, these studies suggest that parental influence plays an important role throughout development, although the context and form of influence vary at different stages. Ineffective monitoring and child management with younger children has been shown to be predictive of entry into deviant peer associations. During mid- to late adolescence and emerging adulthood, as peer activities increase and family influences become subordinate, family conflict (Hops et al., 1990), disruption (Conger, Ge, Elder, Lorenz, & Simons, 1994), or disengagement could lead to overinvolvement with substance-using friends. As Zucker (1989) noted, different etiologies may predict substance use during high-risk periods, such as adolescence and emerging adulthood, when considerable social, emotional, physical, and cognitive change takes place. Disagreeable and unsupportive relations with parents at the same time as adolescents are striving for independence may influence their selection of drug-using friends.

Personality

Curran, White, and Hansell (1997, 2000) proposed that substance use is the result of the interaction between the personality and social systems, that is, reminiscent of the problem behavior theory Person × Environment interaction. As such, childhood temperament and personality traits can serve as protective factors for subsequent substance use (Tarter, 1988). Several studies have shown a moderating effect of personality on the effects of peer substance use on adolescent use (e.g., Slater, 2003; Stacy, Newcomb, & Bentler, 1992). Slater (2003) showed that sensation seeking exacerbates the effect of peer influence on marijuana and cigarette use. Specifically, teens high in sensation seeking smoked more marijuana and cigarettes than did those low in sensation seeking if they perceived their friends were users. High sensation seekers were also more likely to use marijuana if they received encouragement and offers from their peers to use drugs. Thus, sensation seeking as a personality feature appears to exacerbate deviant peer influences.

Social Competence

In general, social competence has been viewed as a protective factor, protecting youth from engaging in problem behaviors, including substance use (Pandina et al., 1990; Scheier & Botvin, 1999, 1998). One aspect of social competence shown to moderate the effect of peers is refusal assertiveness. Recently,

Epstein, Zhou, Bang, and Botvin (2007) reported that the level of refusal skills moderated the perceived relationship between perceived social benefits of drinking and current drinking. Higher levels of refusal skills lowered the relationship between perceived benefits and current use.

However, our own studies have demonstrated that social competence is not always protective, particularly in the case of normative substances, such as alcohol (Hampson et al., 2006; Hops et al., 1999). Perrine and Aloise-Young (2004) further substantiated this finding by demonstrating that youth high in self-monitoring, defined as the ability to adjust to social situations, were more readily influenced by alcohol norms than youth low in self-monitoring. Thus, this research suggests that together, sociability and social competence are potential risk factors for the use of normative substances such as alcohol.

IMPLICATIONS FOR PREVENTION AND INTERVENTION

Ideally, prevention and intervention programs are guided by the knowledge of the processes or mechanisms related to the etiology of substance use. In this chapter, we focused on one primary path to substance use, via peer influence. Thus, a focus of prevention–intervention programs has been and should be malleable factors that predict peer influence, factors that moderate the effect of peer influence on substance use, and the direct effect of peers on substance use and abuse. As our brief review also articulates, understanding these processes can only be ascertained within a developmental framework.

Our review suggests that the design of prevention–intervention programs that focus on changing affiliation with substance-using peers should take into account the stage of substance use and the age of the child. For example, Andrews, Gordon, Hampson, and Christiansen (2007) are developing a primary tobacco prevention program that focuses on changing young children's social images of smokers and children's subjective norms regarding the number of their peers who smoke (decreasing overestimation bias) to change children's intentions and willingness to smoke. Furthermore, interventions must also target those youth who are not necessarily deviant, and

hence most susceptible to peer influences. For example, Hops et al. (1999) found that high school students' use of alcohol, a normative substance (Johnston, O'Malley, Bachman, & Schulenberg, 2006), was predicted by more conventional behaviors in elementary school. Similarly, Hampson et al. (2006) showed that the more sociable children were in elementary school, the more they intended to use alcohol when in elementary and middle school, an effect mediated by their perceived norms. Because alcohol use is considered normative, to prevent the onset of more deviant drug use behaviors these adolescents may benefit most from universal prevention and intervention strategies that include family interventions specifically addressing alcohol, tobacco, and other drug use (Dishion & Andrews, 1995). The overall goal of these strategies is to change adolescent alcohol norms and to inform parents about the normative aspects of adolescent behavior, including the potential for normative experimentation.

A number of prevention and intervention procedures have been developed to enhance social development and improve peer relations with the goal of preventing and/or reducing drug use behaviors among adolescents. Such programs are based on previous work that has shown a relationship between various levels of social competence—for example, refusal skills—and subsequent drug use or peer influence (e.g., Pandina et al., 1990). However, in the 1980s and 1990s, considerable controversy arose regarding the primary purpose of prevention programs. The traditional perspective focused on the prevention of problem behaviors such as drug use via the elimination or reduction of those mediating risk behaviors such as deviant peer associations. At the same time, a second focus emphasized programs that focused on positive youth development (for a review, see Catalano et al., 2003). Today's efforts realize that both components are necessary. For example, the Life Skills Training approach (Botvin, Baker, Dusenbury, Botvin, & Diaz, 1995; Botvin, Malgady, Griffin, Scheier, & Epstein, 1998) attempts to improve the social competence of adolescents by improving their refusal and decision-making skills to withstand the potential deviant peer influences in the environment. All such programs bear the imprint of cognitive–behavioral therapy components that have relied primarily on classical, operant, and social learning theories to understand behavior. Within this framework, substance use is viewed as behavior that is learned in the context of social interactions (e.g., observing parents, siblings, peers, or other models in the media) and established as a result of environmental contingencies. This has led to the development of effective group and individual cognitive–behavioral therapy procedures for use with substance-abusing adolescents (see Waldron, Slesnick, Brody, Turner, & Peterson, 2001; Waldron & Kaminer, 2004; Waldron & Turner, in press) who have reached a level of abuse or dependence that has impaired their functioning. Cognitive–behavioral therapy procedures rely heavily on skills training to improve decision making and refusal skills as part and parcel of their focus.

Peer contagion, as one form of negative peer influence on behaviors and attitudes with considerable face validity, has become a popular construct since its introduction by Dishion and Patterson in the early 1990s. Early studies by Dishion (1990) found that among young adolescents at risk of drug use and other problematic behaviors, deviant talk conducted as part of group settings was positively reinforced with peer laughter and other positive behaviors. Furthermore, adolescents placed in group-focused treatments did worse than youth in a family-based treatment setting. These studies led to the concept of deviancy training (Dishion, McCord, & Poulin, 1999; Patterson et. al., 2000). However, the quick acceptance of this concept by researchers and policymakers alike has generated a series of studies examining its validity. In general, several investigators have suggested that the construct or concept has limited generalizability with weak effect sizes (Lipsey, 2006; Weiss, Caron, Ball, Tapp, Johnson, & Weisz, 2005). Furthermore, a number of recent studies have shown that peer contagion does not hold in all cases and its impact appears to be limited to specific situations with younger teens who are more vulnerable to the influences of deviant peers.

In a review of the literature, Weiss et al. (2005) concluded that the evidence for peer contagion effects for antisocial youth in treatment settings is very weak, and neither deviancy training nor iatro-genic effects were supported in a series of meta-analyses they conducted. They suggested that the evidence is stronger for youth in natural settings than for those participating in a group treatment. Similarly, Lipsey (2006), in a meta-analysis of community-based delinquency interventions, did not find large effects when comparing group and individual treatment programs but found this to be more likely in prevention programs, presumably with high-risk teens.

Dodge, Dishion, and Lansford (2006) focused on this concept in more detail and especially addressed the implications for prevention and treatment. Moreover, Dodge et al. acknowledged that the concept of peer contagion may not apply to all individuals. Other variables that need to be considered include level of maturity and severity of deviance. For example, evidence from Waldron and Kaminer (2004) suggested that group interventions with adolescents with a documented substance abuse disorder are effective and do not result in peer contagion. It is likely that deviant peer influences operate more strongly on those adolescents who are only marginally deviant. Youth who are firmly well adjusted may be able to resist deviant peer influences, and youth with very severe levels of deviance may be beyond the influence of others. Consequently, clinicians and policymakers need to consider a host of variables derived from the etiological literature regarding peer influences before determining which intervention procedures are best for which individuals.

References

Ajzen, I. (1988). *Attitudes, personality and behavior.* New York: Open University Press.

Ajzen, I. (1991). The theory of planned behavior. *Organizational Behavior and Human Decision Processes, 50,* 179–211.

Ajzen, I., & Fishbein, M. (1973). Attitudinal and normative variables as predictors of specific behavior. *Journal of Personality and Social Psychology, 27,* 41–57.

Ajzen, I., & Fishbein, M. (1980). *Understanding attitudes and predicting social behavior.* Englewood Cliffs, NJ: Prentice-Hall.

Aloise-Young, P. A., & Kaeppner, C. J. (2005). Sociometric status as a predictor of onset and progression in adolescent cigarette smoking. *Nicotine and Tobacco Research, 7,* 199–206.

Andrews, J. A., Gordon, J., Hampson, S. E., & Christiansen, S. (2007). *Development of a school-based tobacco prevention: A focus on mediating mechanisms and component evaluation.* Unpublished manuscript.

Andrews, J. A., Hampson, S. E., & Barckley, M. (2008). The effect of subjective normative social images of smokers on children's intentions to smoke. *Nicotine and Tobacco Research, 10,* 589–597.

Andrews, J. A., Hampson, S. E., Barckley, M., Gerrard, M., & Gibbons, F. X. (2008). The effect of early cognitions on cigarette and alcohol use during adolescence. *Psychology of Addictive Behaviors, 22,* 96–106.

Andrews, J. A., Hops, H., & Duncan, S. C. (1997). Adolescent modeling of parent substance use: The moderating effect of the relationship with the parent. *Journal of Family Psychology, 11,* 259–270.

Andrews, J. A., Tildesley, E., Hops, H., & Li, F. (2002). The influence of peers on young adult substance use. *Health Psychology, 21,* 349–357.

Arnett, J. J. (2006). Emerging adulthood: Understanding the new way of coming of age. In J. J. Arnett & J. T. Tanner (Eds.), *Emerging adults in America* (pp. 3–19). Washington, DC: American Psychological Association.

Ary, D. V., Duncan, T. E., Biglan, A., Metzler, C. W., Noell, J. W., & Smolkowski, K. (1999). Development of adolescent problem behavior. *Journal of Abnormal Child Psychology, 27,* 141–150.

Ary, D. V., Duncan, T. E., Duncan, S. C., & Hops, H. (1999). Adolescent problem behavior: The influence of parents and peers. *Behaviour Research and Therapy, 37,* 217–230.

Asher, S. R., & Dodge, K. A. (1986). Identifying children who are rejected by their peers. *Developmental Psychology, 22,* 444–449.

Bailey, S. L., & Hubbard, R. L. (1991). Developmental changes in peer factors and the influence on marijuana initiation among secondary school students. *Journal of Youth and Adolescence, 20,* 339–360.

Bandura, A. (1977). *Social learning theory.* Englewood Cliffs, NJ: Prentice-Hall.

Barber, B. L., Eccles, J. S., & Stone, M. R. (2001). Whatever happened to the jock, the brain, and the princess? Young adult pathways linked to adolescent activity involvement and social identity. *Journal of Adolescent Research, 16,* 429–455.

Barrera, M., Jr., Biglan, A., Ary, D., & Li, F. (2001). Modeling parental and peer influences on problem behavior of American Indian, Hispanic, and non-Hispanic Caucasian youth. *Journal of Early Adolescence, 21,* 133–156.

Barrera, M., Jr., & Li, S. A. (1996). The relation of family support to adolescents' psychological distress and problem behaviors. In G. R. Pierce, I. Sarason, &

B. Sarason (Eds.), *The handbook of social support and family relationships* (pp. 313–343). New York: Plenum.

Barrera, M., Jr., & Reese, F. (1993). Natural support systems and Hispanic substance abuse. In T. D. Watts, R. S. Mayers, & B. L. Kail (Eds.), *Hispanic substance abuse* (pp. 115–130). Springfield, IL: Charles C Thomas.

Bauman, K. E., & Ennett, S. T. (1994). Peer influence on adolescent drug use. *American Psychologist, 49,* 820–822.

Bauman, K. E., & Fisher, L. A. (1986). On the measurement of friend behavior in research on friend influence and selection: Findings from longitudinal studies of adolescent smoking and drinking. *Journal of Youth and Adolescence, 15,* 345–353.

Berndt, T. J., & Keefe, K. (1995). Friends' influence on adolescents' adjustment to school. *Child Development, 66,* 1312–1329.

Biddle, B. J., Bank, B. J., & Marlin, M. M. (1980). Social determinants of adolescent drinking: What they think, what they do and what I think and do. *Journal of Studies on Alcohol, 41,* 215–241.

Bot, S. M., Engels, R. C. M. E., Knibbe, R. A., & Meeus, W. (2005). Friend's drinking behaviour and adolescent alcohol consumption: The moderating role of friendship characteristics. *Addictive Behaviors, 30,* 929–947.

Botvin, G. J., Baker, E., Dusenbury, L., Botvin, E. M., & Diaz, T. (1995, April 12). Long-term follow-up results of a randomized drug abuse prevention trial in a White middle-class population. *JAMA, 273,* 1106–1112.

Botvin, G. J., Malgady, R. G., Griffin, K. W., Scheier, L. M., & Epstein, J. A. (1998). Alcohol and marijuana use among rural youth: Interaction of social and interpersonal influences. *Addictive Behaviors, 23,* 379–387.

Bricker, J. B., Peterson, A. V., Andersen, M., Rajan, K. B., Leroux, B. G., & Sarason, I. G. (2006). Childhood friends who smoke: Do they influence adolescents to make smoking transitions? *Addictive Behaviors, 31,* 889–900.

Brooks, A., Stuewig, J., & LeCroy, C. W. (1998). A family based model of Hispanic adolescent substance use. *Journal of Drug Education, 28,* 65–86.

Brown, B. B., & Klute, C. (2003). Friendships, cliques, and crowds. In G. R. Adams & M. D. Berzonsky (Eds.), *Blackwell handbook of adolescence* (pp. 330–348). Oxford, England: Blackwell.

Bukowski, W. M., & Adams, R. (2005). Peer relationships and psychopathology: Markers, moderators, mediators, mechanisms, and meanings. *Journal of Clinical Child and Adolescent Psychology, 34,* 3–10.

Cairns, R. B., Perrin, J. E., & Cairns, B. D. (1985). Social structure and social cognition in early adolescence: Affiliative patterns. *Journal of Early Adolescence, 5,* 339–355.

Catalano, R. F., Berglund, M. L., Ryan, J. A. M., Lonczak, H. S., & Hawkins, J. D. (2003). Positive youth development in the United States: Research findings on evaluations of positive youth development programs. *Prevention & Treatment, 5,* Article 15.

Catalano, R. F., Morrison, D. M., Wells, E. A., Gillmore, M. R., Iritani, B., & Hawkins, J. D. (1992). Ethnic differences in family factors related to early drug initiation. *Journal of Studies on Alcohol, 53,* 208–217.

Chassin, L., Flora, D. B., & King, K. M. (2004). Trajectories of alcohol and drug use and dependence from adolescence to adulthood: The effects of familial alcoholism and personality. *Journal of Abnormal Psychology, 4,* 483–498.

Chuang, Y. C., Ennett, S. T., Bauman, K. E., & Foshee, V. A. (2005). Neighborhood influences on adolescent cigarette and alcohol use: Mediating effects through parent and peer behaviors. *Journal of Health and Social Behavior, 46,* 187–204.

Cleveland, H. H., & Wiebe, R. P. (2003). The moderation of adolescent-to-peer similarity in tobacco and alcohol use by school levels of substance use. *Child Development, 74,* 279–291.

Coie, J. D., Dodge, K. A., & Coppotelli, H. (1982). Dimensions and types of social status: A cross-age perspective. *Developmental Psychology, 18,* 557–570.

Conger, R., Ge, X., Elder, G. H., Lorenz, F. O., & Simons, R. L. (1994). Economic stress, coercive family process, and developmental problems of adolescents. *Child Development, 5,* 541–561.

Curran, G. M., White, H. R., & Hansell, S. (1997). Predicting problem drinking: A test of an interactive social learning model. *Alcoholism: Clinical and Experimental Research, 21,* 1379–1390.

Curran, G. M., White, H. R., & Hansell, S. (2000). Personality, environment, and problem drug use. *Journal of Drug Issues, 30,* 375–405.

Curran, P. J., Stice, E., & Chassin, L. (1997). The relation between adolescent alcohol use and peer alcohol use: A longitudinal random coefficients model. *Journal of Consulting and Clinical Psychology, 65,* 130–140.

Dinges, M. M., & Oetting, E. R. (1993). Similarity in drug use patterns between adolescents and their friends. *Adolescence, 28,* 253–266.

Dishion, T. J. (1990). The peer context of troublesome child and adolescent behavior. In P. E. Leone (Ed.), *Understanding troubled and troubling youth* (pp. 128–153). Beverly Hills, CA: Sage.

Dishion, T. J., & Andrews, D. W. (1995). Preventing escalation in problem behaviors with high-risk young adolescents: Immediate and 1-year outcomes. *Journal of Consulting and Clinical Psychology, 63,* 538–548.

Dishion, T. J., Capaldi, D., Spracklen, K. M., & Li, F. (1995). Peer ecology of male adolescent drug use. *Development and Psychopathology, 7,* 803–824.

Dishion, T. J., Dodge, K. A., & Lansford, J. E. (2006). Findings and recommendations: A blueprint to minimize deviant peer influence in youth interventions and programs. In K. A. Dodge, T. J. Dishion, & J. E. Lansford (Eds.), *Deviant peer influences in programs for youth* (pp. 366–394). New York: Guilford Press.

Dishion, T. J., McCord, J., & Poulin, F. (1999). When interventions harm: Peer groups and problem behavior. *American Psychologist, 54,* 755–764.

Dodge, K. A., Dishion, T. J., & Lansford, J. E. (Eds.). (2006). *Deviant peer influences in programs for youth.* New York: Guilford Press.

Dolcini, M. M., & Adler, N. E. (1994). Perceived competencies, peer group affiliation, and risk behavior among early adolescents. *Health Psychology, 13,* 496–506.

Donohew, R. L., Hoyle, R. H., Clayton, R. R., Skinner, W. F., Colon, S. E., & Rice, R. E. (1999). Sensation seeking and drug use by adolescents and their friends: Models for marijuana and alcohol. *Journal of Studies on Alcohol, 60,* 622–631.

Donovan, J. E., & Jessor, R. (1985). Structure of problem behavior in adolescence and young adulthood. *Journal of Consulting and Clinical Psychology, 53,* 890–904.

Dorius, C. J., Bahr, S. J., Hoffmann, J. P., & Harmon, E. L. (2004). Parenting practices as moderators of the relationship between peers and adolescent marijuana use. *Journal of Marriage and Family, 66,* 163–178.

Duncan, S. C., Duncan, T. E., & Strycker, L. A. (2002). A multilevel analysis of neighborhood context and youth alcohol and drug problems. *Prevention Science, 3,* 125–133.

Duncan, S. C., Duncan, T. E., & Strycker, L. A. (2006). Alcohol use from ages 9–16: A cohort-sequential latent growth model. *Drug and Alcohol Dependence, 81,* 71–81.

Duncan, T. E., Duncan, S. C., & Hops, H. (1994). The effect of family cohesiveness and peer encouragement on the development of adolescent alcohol use: A cohort-sequential approach to the analysis of longitudinal data. *Journal of Studies on Alcohol, 55,* 588–599.

Duncan, T. E., Tildesley, E., Duncan, S. C., & Hops, H. (1995). The consistency of family and peer influences on the development of substance use in adolescence. *Addiction, 90,* 1647–1660.

Eitle, D. (2005). The moderating effects of peer substance use on the family structure-adolescent substance use association: Quantity versus quality of parenting. *Addictive Behaviors, 30,* 963–980.

Ellickson, P. L., Tucker, J. S., Klein, D. J., & Saner, H. (2004). Antecedents and outcomes of marijuana use initiation during adolescence. *Preventive Medicine, 39,* 976–984.

Emler, N., Reicher, S., & Ross, A. (1997). The social context of delinquent conduct. *Journal of Child Psychology and Psychiatry, 28,* 99–109.

Engels, R. C. M. E., Vitaro, F., Den-Exter-Blokland, E., de-Kemp, R., & Scholte, R. H. J. (2004). Influence and selection processes in friendships and adolescent smoking behavior: The role of parental smoking. *Journal of Adolescence, 27,* 531–544.

Ennett, S. T., & Bauman, K. E. (1994). The contributions of influence and selection to adolescent peer group homogeneity: The case of adolescent cigarette smoking. *Journal of Personality and Social Psychology, 67,* 653–663.

Epstein, J. A., Zhou, X. K., Bang, H., & Botvin, G. J. (2007). Do competence skills moderate the impact of social influences to drink and perceived social benefits of drinking on alcohol use among inner-city adolescents? *Prevention Science, 8,* 65–73.

Fergusson, D. M., Swain-Campbell, N. R., & Horwood, J. J. (2002). Deviant peer affiliations, crime and substance use: A fixed effects regression analysis. *Journal of Abnormal Child Psychology, 30,* 419–430.

Fisher, L. A., & Bauman, K. E. (1988). Influence and selection in the friend-adolescent relationship: Findings from studies of adolescent smoking and drinking. *Journal of Applied Social Psychology, 18,* 289–314.

Gaughan, M. (2006). The gender structure of adolescent peer influence on drinking. *Journal of Health and Social Behavior, 47,* 47–61.

Gibbons, F. X., & Gerrard, M. (1995). Predicting young adults' health-risk behavior. *Journal of Personality and Social Psychology, 69,* 505–517.

Graham, J. W., Marks, G., & Hansen, W. B. (1991). Social influence processes affecting adolescent substance use. *Journal of Applied Psychology, 76,* 291–298.

Hampson, S. E., Andrews, J. A., & Barckley, M. (2008). Childhood predictors of adolescent marijuana use: Early sensation seeking, deviant peer affiliation, and social images. *Addictive Behaviors, 33,* 1140–1147.

Hampson, S. E., Andrews, J. A., & Barckley, M. (2007). Predictors of development of elementary-school children's intentions to smoke cigarettes: Hostility, prototypes, and subjective norms. *Nicotine and Tobacco Research, 9,* 751–760.

Hampson, S. E., Andrews, J. A., Barckley, M., & Peterson, M. (2007). Trait stability and continuity in childhood: Relating sociability and hostility to the five-factor model of personality. *Journal of Research in Personality, 41,* 507–523.

Hampson, S. E., Andrews, J. A., Barckley, M., & Severson, H. H. (2006). Personality predictors of the development of elementary-school children's intentions to drink alcohol: The mediating effects of attitudes and subjective norms. *Psychology of Addictive Behaviors, 20,* 288–297.

Hawkins, J. D., Catalano, R. F., & Miller, J. Y. (1992). Risk and protective factors for alcohol and other drug problems in adolescence and early adulthood: Implications for substance abuse prevention. *Psychological Bulletin, 112,* 64–105.

Heath, A. C., Bucholz, K. K., Madden, P. A. F., Dinwiddie, S. H., Slutske, W. S., Bierut, L. J., et al. (1997). Genetic and environmental contributions to alcohol dependence risk in a national twin sample: Consistency of findings in women and men. *Psychological Medicine, 27,* 1381–1391.

Henry, K. L., Slater, M. D., & Oetting, E. R. (2005). Alcohol use in early adolescence: The effect of changes in risk-taking, perceived harm, and friends' alcohol use. *Journal of Studies on Alcohol, 66,* 275–283.

Hops, H., Andrews, J. A., Duncan, S. C., Duncan, T. E., & Tildesley, E. (2000). Adolescent drug use development: A social interactional and contextual perspective. In A. J. Sameroff, M. Lewis, & S. M. Miller (Eds.), *Handbook of developmental psychopathology* (2nd ed., pp. 589–605). New York: Kluwer Academic/Plenum.

Hops, H., & Davis, B. (1998, November). *Longitudinal and developmental perspective on drug use development: Family and peer influences.* Paper presented at the National Institute on Alcohol Abuse and Alcoholism Workshop on Research on Treatment for Adolescent Alcohol Problems: Methodological Issues, Bethesda, MD.

Hops, H., Davis, B., & Lewin, L. (1999). The development of alcohol and other substance use: A gender study of family and peer context. *Journal of Studies on Alcohol, 13*(Suppl.), 22–31.

Hops, H., Duncan, T. E., Duncan, S. C., & Stoolmiller, M. (1996). Parent substance use as a predictor of adolescent use: A six-year lagged analysis. *Annals of Behavioral Medicine, 18,* 157–164.

Hops, H., & Lewin, L. (1984). Peer sociometric forms. In T. H. Ollendick & M. Hersen (Eds.), *Child behavioral assessment: Principles and procedures* (pp. 124–147). New York: Pergamon Press.

Hops, H., Tildesley, E., Lichtenstein, E., Ary, D. V., & Sherman, L. (1990). Parent-adolescent problem-solving interactions and drug use. *American Journal of Drug and Alcohol Abuse, 16,* 239–258.

Huba, G. J., Wingard, J. A., & Bentler, P. M. (1980). Longitudinal analysis of the role of peer support, adult models, and peer subcultures in beginning adolescent substance use: An application of setwise canonical correlation methods. *Multivariate Behavioral Research, 15,* 259–279.

Jaccard, J., Blanton, H., & Dodge, T. (2005). Peer influences on risk behavior: An analysis of the effects of a close friend. *Developmental Psychology, 41,* 135–137.

Jessor, R., & Jessor, S. L. (1977). *Problem behavior and psychosocial development: A longitudinal study of youth.* New York: Academic Press.

Johnston, L. D., O'Malley, P. M., Bachman, J. G., & Schulenberg, J. E. (2006). *Monitoring the Future national survey results on drug use, 1975–2005. Volume I: Secondary school students* (NIH Publication No. 06-5883). Bethesda, MD: National Institute on Drug Abuse.

Kandel, D. B. (1985). On processes of peer influences in adolescent drug use: A developmental perspective. *Advances in Alcohol and Substance Abuse, 4,* 139–163.

Kandel, D. B. (1986). Processes of peer influences in adolescence. In R. K. Silbereisen, K. Eyferth, & G. Rudinger (Eds.), *Development as action in context: Problem behavior and normal youth development* (pp. 203–228) New York: Springer-Verlag.

Kandel, D. B., & Davies, M. (1991). Friendship networks, intimacy and illicit drug use in young adulthood: A comparison of two competing theories. *Criminology, 29,* 601–629.

Kazdin, A. E. (2007). Mediators and mechanisms of change in psychotherapy research. *Annual Review of Clinical Psychology, 3,* 1–27.

Krosnick, J. A., & Judd, C. M. (1982). Transitions in social influence at adolescence: Who induces cigarette smoking? *Developmental Psychology, 13,* 359–368.

Kung, E. M., & Farrell, A. D. (2001). The role of parents and peers in early adolescent substance use: An examination of mediating and moderating effects. *Journal of Child and Family Studies, 9,* 509–528.

Labouvie, E. (1996). Maturing out of substance use: Selection and self correction. *Journal of Drug Issues, 26,* 457–476.

Leatherdale, S. T., Manske, S., & Kroeker, C. (2006). Sex differences in how older students influence younger student smoking behavior. *Addictive Behaviors, 31,* 1308–1318.

Leonard, K. E., & Homish, G. G. (2005). Changes in marijuana use over the transition into marriage. *Journal of Drug Issues, 35,* 409–430.

Leonard, K. E., Kearns, J., & Mudar, P. (2000). Peer networks among heavy, regular and infrequent drinkers prior to marriage. *Journal of Studies on Alcohol, 61,* 669–673.

Leonard, K. E., & Mudar, P. (2003). Peer and partner drinking and the transition to marriage: A longitudi-

nal examination of selections and influence processes. *Psychology of Addictive Behaviors, 17,* 115–125.

Leonard, K. E., & Mudar, P. (2004). Husbands' influence on wives' drinking: Testing a relationship motivation model in the early years of marriage. *Psychology of Addictive Behaviors, 18,* 340–349.

Lerner, R. M. (1991). Changing organism–context relations as the basic process of development: A developmental contextual perspective. *Developmental Psychology, 27,* 27–32.

Li, F., Barrera, M., Jr., Hops, H., Fisher, J., & Harmer, P. (2002). The longitudinal influence of peers on the development of alcohol use in late adolescence: A growth mixture analysis. *Journal of Behavioral Medicine, 25,* 293–315.

Li, F., Duncan, E., & Hops, H. (2001). Examining developmental trajectories in adolescent alcohol use using piecewise growth mixture modeling analysis. *Journal of Studies on Alcohol, 62,* 199–210.

Lillehoj, C. J., Trudeau, L., & Spoth, R. (2005). The longitudinal modeling of adolescent normative beliefs and substance initiation. *Journal of Alcohol and Drug Education, 49,* 7–41.

Lipsey, M. W. (2006). The effects of community-based group treatment for delinquency: A meta-analytic search for cross-study generalizations. In J. E. Lansford, K. A. Dodge, & T. J. Dishion (Eds.), *Deviant peer influences in programs for youth: Problems and solutions.* (pp. 162–184). New York: Guilford Press.

Marks, G., Graham, J. W., & Hansen, W. B. (1992). Social projection and social conformity in adolescent alcohol use: A longitudinal analysis. *Personality and Social Psychology Bulletin, 18,* 96–101.

Marks, G., & Miller, N. (1987). Ten years of research on the false-consensus effect: An empirical and theoretical review. *Psychological Bulletin, 102,* 72–90.

McLeod, J. D. (1995). Social and psychological bases of homogamy for common psychiatric disorders. *Journal of Marriage and the Family, 57,* 201–214.

Miller, K. E., Hoffman, J. H., Barnes, G. M., Farrell, M. P., Sabo, D., & Melnick, M. J. (2003). Jocks, gender, race, and adolescent problem drinking. *Journal of Drug Education, 33,* 445–462.

Mounts, N. S. (2002). Parental management of adolescent peer relationships in context: The role of parenting style. *Journal of Family Psychology, 16,* 58–69.

Nash, J. H., McQueen, A., & Bray, J. H. (2005). Pathways to adolescent alcohol use: Family environment, peer influence, and parental expectations. *Journal of Adolescent Health, 37,* 19–28.

Neighbors, C., Dillard, A. J., Lewis, M. A., Bergstrom, R. L., & Neil, T. A. (2006). Normative misperceptions and temporal precedence of perceived norms and drinking. *Journal of Studies on Alcohol, 67,* 290–299.

Pandina, R. J., Labouvie, E. W., Johnson, V., & White, H. R. (1990). The relationship between alcohol and marijuana use and competence in adolescence. *Journal of Health and Social Policy, 1,* 89–108.

Parke, R. D. (2004). Development in the family. *Annual Review of Psychology, 55,* 365–399.

Parke, R. D., & O'Neil, R. (1999). Social relationships across contexts: Family-peer linkages. In W. A. Collins & B. Laursen (Eds.), *Relationships as developmental contexts. Vol. 30: Minnesota Symposium on Child Psychology* (pp. 211–39). Hillsdale, NJ: Erlbaum.

Patterson, G. R., Dishion, T. J., & Yoerger, K. L. (2000). Adolescent growth in new forms of problem behavior: Macro- and micro-peer dynamics. *Prevention Science, 1,* 3–13.

Patterson, G. R., Reid, J. B., & Dishion, T. J. (1992). *A social interactional approach: IV. Antisocial boys.* Eugene, OR: Castalia.

Pearson, M., Sweeting, H., West, P., Young, R., Gordon, J., & Turner, K. (2006). Adolescent substance use in different social and peer contexts: A social network analysis. *Drugs: Education, Prevention and Policy, 13,* 519–536.

Perrine, N. E., & Aloise-Young, P. A. (2004). The role of self-monitoring in adolescents' susceptibility to passive peer pressure. *Personality and Individual Differences, 37,* 1701–1716.

Pilgrim, C., Luo, Q., Urberg, K. A., & Fang, X. (1999). Influence of peers, parents, and individual characteristics on adolescent drug use in two cultures. *Merrill-Palmer Quarterly, 45,* 85–107.

Read, J. P., Wood, M. D., & Capone, C. (2005). A prospective investigation of relations between social influences and alcohol involvement during the transition into college. *Journal of Studies on Alcohol, 66,* 23–34.

Ritt-Olson, A., Unger, J., Valente, T., Nezami, E., Chou, C.-P., Trinidad, D., et al. (2005). Exploring peers as a mediator of the association between depression and smoking in young adolescents. *Substance Use & Misuse, 40,* 77–98.

Robinson, L. A., Murray, D. M., Alfano, C. M., Zbikowski, S. M., Blitstein, J. L., & Klesges, R. C. (2006). Ethnic differences in predictors of adolescent smoking onset and escalation: A longitudinal study from 7th to 12th grade. *Nicotine and Tobacco Research, 8,* 297–307.

Rose, R. J., Dick, D. M., Viken, R. J., Pulkkinen, L., & Kaprio, J. (2001). Drinking or abstaining at age 14? A genetic epidemiological study. *Alcoholism: Clinical and Experimental Research, 25,* 1594–1604.

Ross, L., Greene, D., & House, P. (1977). The false consensus phenomenon: An attributional bias in self-perception and social psychological processes. *Journal of Experimental Social Psychology, 13,* 279–301.

Rusby, J. C., Forrester, K. K., Biglan, A., & Metzler, C. W. (2005). Relationships between peer harassment and adolescent problem behaviors. *Journal of Early Adolescence, 25,* 453–477.

Scheier, L. M., & Botvin, G. J. (1998). Relations of social skills, personal competence, and adolescent alcohol use: A developmental exploratory study. *Journal of Early Adolescence, 18,* 77–114.

Scheier, L. M., & Botvin, G. J. (1999). Social skills, competence, and drug refusal efficacy as predictors of adolescent alcohol use. *Journal of Drug Education, 29,* 253–280.

Schofield, P. E., Pattison, P. E., Hill, D. J., & Borland, R. (2002). The influence of group identification on the adoption of peer group smoking norms. *Psychology and Health, 16,* 1–16.

Schofield, P. E., Pattison, P. E., Hill, D. J., & Borland, R. (2003). Youth culture and smoking: Integrating social group processes and individual cognitive processes in a model of health-related behaviors. *Journal of Health Psychology, 8,* 291–306.

Schulenberg, J., Maggs, J. L., Dielman, T. E., Leech, S. L., Kloska, D. D., Shope, J. T., & Laetz, V. B. (1999). On peer influences to get drunk: A panel study of young adolescents. *Merrill Palmer Quarterly, 45,* 108–142.

Sieving, R. E., Perry, C. L., & Williams, C. L. (2000). Do friendships change behaviors, or do behaviors change friendships? Examining paths of influence in young adolescents' alcohol use. *Journal of Adolescent Health, 26,* 27–35.

Simons-Morton, B., & Chen, R. S. (2006). Over time relationships between early adolescent and peer substance use. *Addictive Behaviors, 31,* 1211–1223.

Slater, M. D. (2003). Sensation-seeking as a moderator of the effects of peer influences, consistency with personal aspirations, and perceived harm on marijuana and cigarette use among younger adolescents. *Substance Use & Misuse, 38,* 865–880.

Spijkerman, R., van den Eijnden, R. J. J. M., Overbeek, G., & Engels, R. C. M. E. (2006). The impact of peer and parental norms and behavior on adolescent drinking: The role of drinker prototypes. *Psychology and Health, 22,* 7–29.

Stacy, A. W., Newcomb, M. D., & Bentler, P. M. (1992). Interactive and higher-order effects of social influences on drug use. *Journal of Health and Social Behavior, 33,* 226–241.

Steinberg, L., Mounts, N., Lamborn, S., & Dornbusch, S. (1991). Authoritative parenting and adolescent adjustment across various ecological niches. *Journal of Research on Adolescence, 1,* 19–36.

Sussman, S., Pokhrel, P., Ashmore, R. D., & Brown, B. B. (2007). Adolescent peer group identification and characteristics: A review of the literature. *Addictive Behaviors, 32,* 1602–1627.

Sussman, S., Unger, J. B., & Dent, C. W. (2004). Peer group self-identification among alternative high school youth: A predictor of their psychosocial functioning five years later. *International Journal of Clinical and Health Psychology, 4,* 9–25.

Tarter, R. E. (1988). Are there inherited behavioral traits that predispose to substance abuse? *Journal of Consulting and Clinical Psychology, 56,* 189–196.

Tildesley, E., Hops, H., Ary, D., & Andrews, J. A. (1995). A multitrait-multimethod model of adolescent deviance, drug use, academic, and sexual behaviors. *Journal of Psychopathology and Behavioral Assessment, 17,* 185–215.

Tolone, W. L., & Tieman, C. R. (1990). Drugs, delinquency and "nerds": Are loners deviant? *Journal of Drug Education, 20,* 153–162.

Turner, K., West, P., Gordon, J., Young, R., & Sweeting, H. (2006). Could the peer group explain school differences in pupil smoking rates? An exploratory study. *Social Science & Medicine, 62,* 2513–2525.

Unger, J. B., Rohrbach, L. A., Cruz, T. B., Baezconde-Garbanati, L., Howard, K. A., Palmer, P. H., & Johnson, C. A. (2001). Ethnic variation in peer influences on adolescent smoking. *Nicotine and Tobacco Research, 3,* 167–176.

Urberg, K. A., Cheng, C. H., & Shyu, S. J. (1991). Grade changes in peer influence on adolescent cigarette smoking: A comparison of two measures. *Addictive Behaviors, 16,* 21–28.

Urberg, K. A., Degirmencioglu, S. M., & Pilgrim, C. (1997). Close friend and group influence on adolescent cigarette smoking and alcohol use. *Developmental Psychology, 33,* 834–844.

Vitaro, F., Pedersen, S., & Brendgen, M. (2007). Children's disruptiveness, peer rejection, friends' deviancy, and delinquent behaviors: A process-oriented approach. *Development and Psychopathology, 19,* 433–453.

Waldron, H. B., & Kaminer, Y. (2004). On the learning curve: Cognitive-behavioral therapies for adolescent substance abuse. *Addiction, 99,* 93–105.

Waldron, H. B., Slesnick, N., Brody, J. L., Turner, C. W., & Peterson, T. R. (2001). Treatment outcomes for adolescent substance abuse at 4- and 7-month assessments. *Journal of Consulting and Clinical Psychology, 69,* 802–813.

Waldron, H. B., & Turner, C. W. (2008). Psychosocial treatments for adolescent substance abuse: A review and meta-analyses. *Journal of Clinical Child and Adolescent Psychology, 37,* 238–261.

Wang, M. Q., Eddy, J. M., & Fitzhugh, E. C. (2000). Smoking acquisition: Peer influence and self-selection. *Psychological Reports, 86,* 1241–1246.

Weiss, B., Caron, A., Ball, S., Tapp, J., Johnson, M., & Weisz, J. R. (2005). Iatrogenic effects of group treatment for antisocial youths. *Journal of Consulting and Clinical Psychology, 73,* 1036–1044.

Westling, E., Andrews, J. A., Hampson, S. E., & Peterson, M. (2008). Pubertal timing and substance use: The effects of gender, parental monitoring and deviant peers. *Journal of Adolescent Health, 42,* 555–563.

Wills, T. A., & Cleary, S. D. (1996). How are social support effects mediated? A test with parental support and adolescent substance use. *Journal of Personality and Social Psychology, 71,* 937–952.

Wills, T. A., & Cleary, S. D. (1999). Peer and adolescent substance use among 6th–9th graders: Latent growth analyses of influence versus selection mechanisms. *Health Psychology, 18,* 453–463.

Wills, T. A., Sandy, J. M., & Yaeger, A. (2000). Temperament and adolescent substance use: An epigenetic approach to risk and protection. *Journal of Personality, 68,* 1127–1152.

Wilson, J. M., & Donnermeyer, J. F. (2006). Urbanity, rurality, and adolescent substance use. *Criminal Justice Review, 31,* 337–356.

Windle, M. (1997). Mate similarity, heavy substance use, and family history of problem drinking among young adult women. *Journal of Studies on Alcohol, 58,* 573–580.

Wood, M. D., Read, J. P., Mitchell, R. E., & Brand, N. H. (2004). Do parents still matter? Parent and peer influences on alcohol involvement among recent high school graduates. *Psychology of Addictive Behaviors, 18,* 19–30.

Yamaguchi, K., & Kandel, D. B. (1997). The influence of spouses' behavior and marital dissolution on marijuana use: Causation or selection. *Journal of Marriage and the Family, 59,* 22–36.

Yanovitzky, I. (2006). Sensation seeking and alcohol use by college students: Examining multiple pathways of effects. *Journal of Health Communication, 11,* 269–280.

Yanovitzky, I., Stewart, L. P., & Lederman, L. C. (2006). Social distance, perceived drinking by peers, and alcohol use by college students. *Health Communication, 19,* 1–10.

Zucker, R. A. (1989). Is risk for alcoholism predictable? A probabilistic approach to a developmental problem. *Drugs and Society, 3,* 69–93.

PART VII

ENVIRONMENTAL INFLUENCES (SCHOOL, NEIGHBORHOOD, CENSUS)

CHAPTER 22

NEIGHBORHOOD INFLUENCES ON SUBSTANCE USE ETIOLOGY: IS WHERE YOU LIVE IMPORTANT?

Margo Gardner, R. Gabriela Barajas, and Jeanne Brooks-Gunn

Conventional wisdom suggests that neighborhood residence has important implications for individual health and development generally and for substance use specifically. This position is consistent with prominent ecological theories of human development (Bronfenbrenner, 1977), which suggest that context plays a critical role in shaping individual outcomes. Decades of research support this assertion and indicate that family, peer, and educational contexts do, indeed, make important contributions to human development. Research on distal contextual influences like neighborhoods has been slower to gain prominence, however. Consequently, relatively fewer studies have investigated the relations between neighborhood residence and substance use outcomes. The paucity of research on neighborhoods and substance use may stem, in part, from concerns about selection bias. Because families choose the neighborhoods in which they live, it is difficult to disentangle the influence of neighborhoods from the influence of the individual-level characteristics that lead people to select residence in particular neighborhoods (Fauth & Brooks-Gunn, 2008). Nevertheless, recent studies designed to minimize this type of selection bias have suggested that neighborhoods likely do influence behavioral and mental health (e.g., Fauth, Leventhal, & Brooks-Gunn, 2007; Kling, Leibman, & Katz, 2007; Leventhal & Brooks-Gunn, 2003).

Despite a relative dearth of empirical research, sociological and criminological theory provide a strong foundation for exploring neighborhood influences on residents' behavioral and mental health.

Much of this theory focuses on the implications of living in poor neighborhoods. For instance, social disorganization theory (Shaw & McKay, 1969)—an extremely influential theory that examines relations between neighborhoods and crime—suggests that neighborhood-level characteristics like low socioeconomic status (SES), ethnic heterogeneity, and residential mobility disrupt social organization and lead to crime and delinquency. Newer theories, which seek to explain relations between neighborhood residence and a variety of individual-level outcomes (see Jencks & Mayer, 1990, and Leventhal & Brooks-Gunn, 2000, for reviews), build on the underlying assumption of social disorganization theory—namely, that structural features of neighborhoods (e.g., SES, ethnic diversity, and mobility) influence individuals' behavior through their impact on neighborhood-level social processes.

Little is known about the social processes that link neighborhood structure and substance use outcomes. Relevant extant research is limited in scope and has focused primarily on the direct, unmediated influence of neighborhood SES. As discussed in this chapter, findings on the influence of neighborhoods are mixed. Some studies have suggested that residents in lower SES neighborhoods are at greater risk of substance use and substance use problems than are residents in higher SES neighborhoods (Boardman, Finch, Ellison, Williams, & Jackson, 2001; Carpiano, 2007; Chaix, Merlo, Subramanian, Lynch, & Chauvin, 2005; Datta et al., 2006; Finch, Kolody, & Vega, 1999; Kleinschmidt, Hills, & Elliott, 1995; Saxe et al., 2001;

Preparation of this chapter was supported in part by National Institute of Child Health and Human Development Grant R01 HD049796.

Steptoe & Feldman, 2001; Stimpson, Ju, Raji, & Eschbach, 2007). Other studies have indicated that the opposite is true (Chuang, Ennett, Bauman, & Foshee, 2005; Fauth, Leventhal, & Brooks-Gunn, 2007; Galea, Ahern, Tracy, Rudenstine, & Vlahov, 2007; Galea, Ahern, Tracy, & Vlahov, 2007; Pollack, Cubbin, Ahn, & Winkleby, 2005).

Borrowing heavily from the theoretical traditions just described (Jencks & Mayer, 1990; Leventhal & Brooks-Gunn, 2000; Shaw & McKay, 1969), we provide a framework for understanding how neighborhood-level processes might explain these mixed findings. Our review is divided into three parts. First, we discuss different approaches to measuring the influence of neighborhood residence. Second, we review the empirical literature describing links between neighborhood SES—the most frequently researched dimension of neighborhood structure—and substance use outcomes among adolescents and adults. Finally, we discuss the processes through which neighborhood SES might influence adolescent and adult substance use outcomes.

METHODS OF STUDYING NEIGHBORHOODS

Some neighborhood research designs are more likely to yield accurate parameter estimates than are others. Thus, it is necessary to provide a context for weighting the discrepant findings that emerge from studies using different methods. We borrow extensively from prior reviews (Fauth & Brooks-Gunn, 2008; Leventhal & Brooks-Gunn, 2000) and discuss four designs used in neighborhood research: (a) individual-level designs, (b) nested designs, (c) experimental and quasi-experimental designs (relocation projects), and (d) natural experiments (exogenous shocks).

Individual-Level Designs
Data sets obtained from individual-level survey research are often used in studies that examine neighborhood influences on individual-level outcomes (see Brooks-Gunn, Duncan, & Aber, 1997, and Leventhal & Brooks-Gunn, 2000, for discussion and examples). These individual-level data sets may contain cross-sectional or longitudinal data, and data on neighborhood characteristics may come either from

participants' reports of neighborhood conditions and processes or from appended census data that are matched to participants' geocoded addresses. Longitudinal studies with appended census data may yield more accurate estimates of neighborhood effects than do cross-sectional studies or studies that rely entirely on participants' reports of neighborhood conditions. Unlike cross-sectional data, longitudinal data allow researchers to control for prior outcomes and to determine whether neighborhood residence is associated with changes in outcomes over time. This is one way to reduce the likelihood that findings may be entirely attributed to selection bias. Additionally, when compared with studies that rely exclusively on participants' reports of neighborhood conditions, studies that append census measures of neighborhood conditions are less likely to capitalize on common source variance (i.e., inflated correlations between neighborhood- and individual-level measures completed by the same source).

Longitudinal individual-level studies with appended census measures are, however, also unlikely to yield entirely accurate estimates of neighborhood effects. This is because most individual-level data sets were not intended to be used in neighborhood research. To the extent that individual-level studies inadvertently sample multiple participants within neighborhoods, assumptions of independent observations are violated and parameter estimates from traditional individual-level regression analyses are likely to be biased. Multilevel regression analysis—which can accommodate individuals nested within neighborhoods—is also problematic under these circumstances because individual-level sampling strategies often result in very small samples of individuals within neighborhood units. Fauth and Brooks-Gunn (2008) pointed out that very small within-neighborhood samples may make it impossible to parcel out the amount of variance that exists between, versus within, neighborhoods, and within-neighborhood samples of fewer than 20 people may not yield reliable measures of some neighborhood-level constructs (Raudenbush & Sampson, 1999).

Nested Designs
Given the problems with individual-level studies described here, neighborhood researchers have

turned to designs that nest individual-level studies within neighborhood-level studies. These designs yield data that are well suited to multilevel analyses. The Project on Human Development in Chicago Neighborhoods (PHDCN; Earls & Buka, 1997; Sampson, 1997; Sampson, Raudenbush, & Earls, 1997) is perhaps the best-known study in this category. The PHDCN was designed to examine child and adolescent development in the context of neighborhoods. Data on individual-level health and development were collected as part of the PHDCN Longitudinal Cohort Study. Using a multistage sampling process, seven cohorts of children and adolescents (ages 0, 3, 6, 9, 12, 15, and 18 years) were recruited from 80 Chicago neighborhood clusters (NCs; aggregates of two to three census tracts each) between 1995 and 1996. These NCs were selected from a larger sample of 343 NCs that were stratified by ethnic composition (seven categories) and SES (i.e., high, medium, and low). Nearly equal numbers of NCs were selected from the resulting 21 strata, yielding a representative sample of 80 NCs.[1] More than 6,000 children and adolescents were recruited from these 80 NCs during the first wave of data collection. Investigators conducted follow-up assessments approximately 2 and 4 years later.

PHDCN investigators also conducted two separate neighborhood-level studies in 1995—a community survey and a systematic social observations study. The community survey was administered to an independent sample of 8,782 adults residing in Chicago's 343 NCs (20 to 50 adults per NC). Respondents rated their neighborhood on dimensions such as disorder, violence and victimization, cohesion, informal social control, danger, and the availability of resources (Sampson, 1997; Sampson et al., 1997). The systematic social observations study (Sampson & Raudenbush, 1999) was conducted within the 80 focal PHDCN NCs. Trained observers drove at slow speeds down every street within these NCs and recorded observations (manually and via video recorder) of social exchanges and physical conditions for each block face (one side of the street on one city block).

Although the PHDCN and other nested studies (e.g., the Los Angeles Family and Neighborhood Study; see Sastry, Pebley, & Zonta, 2002) are examples of rigorously designed research, they are not without methodological problems. First, neighborhood-level data can be aggregated at different levels (e.g., block groups, census tract, zip codes). Evidence has suggested that altering the size of the neighborhood unit can have marked implications for the magnitude and statistical significance of parameter estimates (Brooks-Gunn, Duncan, Klebanov, & Sealand, 1993; Hipp, 2007). Moreover, recent findings have indicated that the ideal unit of aggregation may be different for different outcome variables (Hipp, 2007). Definitions of neighborhood units must therefore be grounded in theory. Theoretically inappropriate decisions about neighborhood boundaries may result in misleading conclusions about neighborhood influences on individual-level outcomes. Second, the structure of nested, longitudinal data sets changes over time as families relocate to new neighborhoods. When many families in a study relocate, some neighborhoods may ultimately contain too few individuals to obtain accurate estimates of neighborhood effects. Finally, as is true of all survey research, estimates from nested studies are unavoidably influenced by selection bias. Only experimental designs using random assignment can fully address the issue of selection bias.

Experimental or Quasi-Experimental Designs (Relocation Projects)

Neighborhood relocation projects typically involve moving residents of very low-SES neighborhoods to higher SES neighborhoods through the distribution of housing vouchers. Some relocation projects are true experiments that use random assignment; others are quasi-experimental studies that assign residents partly on the basis of housing availability. Relocation projects are complex, expensive, and rare, but some believe that they represent the best existing solution to the problem of selection bias. Here we review three of the best-known neighborhood relocation projects: Gautreaux, Moving to Opportunity (MTO), and Yonkers.

[1] Three strata were empty—predominantly European American neighborhoods of low SES, predominantly Hispanic neighborhoods of high SES, and mixed African American and Latino neighborhoods of high SES. Thus, the final sample of neighborhood clusters did not include neighborhoods in these strata.

The Gautreaux project—one of the first neighborhood relocation projects in the United States—resulted from a 1966 lawsuit filed against the Chicago Housing Authority and the U.S. Department of Housing and Urban Development (Keels, Duncan, DeLuca, Mendenhall, & Rosenbaum, 2005). The suit alleged that the Chicago Housing Authority had "located its buildings and assigned tenants on a racially segregated basis" with approval and funding from the Department of Housing and Urban Development (Rubinowitz & Rosenbaum, 2000, p. 1). The U.S. Supreme Court ruled in favor of the plaintiffs, and the Gautreaux project ensued. Between 1976 and 1998, more than 7,000 low-income African American residents in Chicago public housing (or those on waiting lists for public housing) moved into new apartments within the city or the surrounding suburban areas using federal Section 8 housing vouchers made available through the Gautreaux project (Leventhal & Brooks-Gunn, 2000; Keels et al., 2005). Follow-up studies have since compared the outcomes of those who moved to new urban neighborhoods with those who moved to higher SES suburban neighborhoods (e.g., Popkin, Rosenbaum, & Meaden, 1993; Rosenbaum, 1995). There is some dispute, however, about whether assignment to city versus suburban neighborhoods was truly random (Oreopoulos, 2003). Thus, it is not clear whether and to what extent findings from the Gautreaux project are tainted by selection bias.

Bolstered by some of the successes of Gautreax, the Department of Housing and Urban Development sponsored the MTO project in five U.S. cities—Baltimore, Boston, Chicago, Los Angeles, and New York City (see Feins & Shroder, 2005, for a review of the methodology). Families eligible for MTO included those who (a) had at least one child under the age of 18 and (b) lived in public housing in neighborhoods in which at least 40% of the population lived below the poverty line. Approximately one quarter of eligible families applied, yielding a sample of 4,608 families. These families were randomly assigned to one of three conditions in 1997: (a) an experimental group who received mobility counseling and time-limited (90 days) rental assistance vouchers to move to census tracts in which fewer than 10% of residents lived below the poverty line; (b) a Section 8

voucher group who received time-limited vouchers to move anywhere in the city (no mobility counseling); and (c) a control group who did not receive vouchers (Feins & Shroder, 2005).

Although MTO used random assignment, participants in experimental and Section 8 groups ultimately chose whether to use the vouchers. Slightly more than 47% of experimental families used the vouchers to move to new neighborhoods, and only 42% of experimental families moved to neighborhoods with fewer than 10% poor residents (Feins & Shroder, 2005). A greater percentage of Section 8 families used vouchers to move (61.7%), but only 6.5% moved to neighborhoods with fewer than 10% poor residents (Feins & Shroder, 2005). Studies have shown that a number of individual-level characteristics predicted voucher use in the experimental and Section 8 groups (Feins & Shroder, 2005). Analyses that control for these characteristics may reduce the influence of selection bias, but statistical controls cannot account for unmeasured characteristics associated with voucher use. Thus, attempts to compare the treatment and control groups must consider the possibility that individual-level characteristics are at least partly responsible for observed neighborhood effects.

Finally, the Yonkers project, like the Gautreaux project, resulted from a court ruling against segregation in public housing. In 1985, city officials in Yonkers, New York, were charged with intentionally clustering poor African American and Hispanic families in the southwest quarter of town (Briggs, Darden, & Aidala, 1999). In response to the ruling, the city of Yonkers constructed 200 townhouses scattered throughout the city's largely White, middle-class neighborhoods (Briggs et al., 1999). One thousand eligible families living in public housing or on the waiting list for public housing (see Fauth, Leventhal, & Brooks-Gunn, 2005, for list of eligibility criteria) participated in a lottery for residence in the new, publicly owned townhouses. Just fewer than 95% (N = 189) of the 200 families selected through the lottery moved to the scattered-site housing between 1992 and 1994 (Briggs et al., 1999; Fauth Leventhal, & Brooks-Gunn, 2007). Because the Yonkers project was not originally undertaken for research purposes, none of the families who participated in the lottery were assigned to a nonmover control group. Consequently, researchers have since identified a quasi-control group of 366 demographically comparable nonmover families. All of these families would have been eligible for the lottery, and some of them actually participated in the lottery (Fauth et al., 2005; Fauth, Leventhal, & Brooks-Gunn 2007). Because the control group was designated post hoc, studies that use the Yonkers data must be considered quasi-experimental rather than truly experimental.

Although neighborhood relocation projects like Gautreaux, MTO, and Yonkers represent some of the best existing solutions to selection bias, readers must keep several limitations in mind. First, these projects do not entirely eliminate selection bias. Even when assignment to mover and nonmover conditions is entirely random, families make choices about whether to accept housing vouchers. Second, because families in mover conditions must first take the initiative to sign up for relocation projects and then decide whether to use a voucher, samples of movers are often very small. This can undermine external validity and diminish statistical power. Finally, the effects of neighborhood residence and moving are inevitably confounded. Recent findings have suggested that moving in the context of a neighborhood relocation project stresses family systems (Leventhal & Brooks-Gunn, 2005) and disrupts ties to supportive networks and institutions (Clampet-Lundquist, 2007). Thus, adverse effects associated with moving to a higher SES neighborhood may stem more from the stress of moving than from residence in a higher SES neighborhood.

Natural Experiments (Exogenous Shocks)

Natural experiments occur when residents in some neighborhoods are exposed to an exogenous shock while residents in other neighborhoods remain unaffected (see Fauth & Brooks-Gunn, 2008, for additional discussion). Such shocks may include environmental policies that increase or decrease exposure to toxic substances or laws that ban, restrict, or permit the sale of specific products (e.g., firearms, alcohol, tobacco). Studies that examine the impact of exogenous shocks typically compare pre- and postshock scores on individual-level outcomes. For instance, researchers recently investigated the

consequences of new laws permitting the Saturday retail sale of alcohol in six counties in Sweden (changes were later extended to the entire country; Norstrom & Skog, 2005). In the counties affected by the new law, researchers found marked increases in the sales of beer, wine, and liquor and increases in drunk driving offenses (likely because of simultaneous increases in police interdiction), but they did not find increases in alcohol-related assault (Norstrom & Skog, 2005). Although this study examined the impact of changes instituted at the county rather than at the neighborhood level, it nicely illustrates the impact of geographically limited exogenous shocks on individual-level behavior. It is, however, important to keep in mind that studies of exogenous shocks are not intended to examine the impact of neighborhood residence per se; rather, they are intended to examine the impact of policies and practices that affect residents in given neighborhoods or geographic regions (see chap. 26, this volume, for a thorough description of how policy changes may affect behavior).

Conclusions Regarding the Measurement of Neighborhoods

Although there are methodological limitations associated with each of the above-described research designs, our review suggests that experimental and nested designs, when compared with individual-level designs, are more likely to yield accurate estimates of neighborhood effects. The following review of the literature on neighborhood structure and substance use outcomes therefore emphasizes findings from studies that use experimental or nested designs. A relative dearth of such studies, however, necessitates that we also review findings from studies that use individual-level data sets with appended census-based measures of neighborhood structure.

ASSOCIATIONS BETWEEN NEIGHBORHOOD STRUCTURE AND SUBSTANCE USE OUTCOMES

In keeping with the tenets of social disorganization theory, neighborhood structure is most often defined according to scores on three dimensions: SES (neighborhood-level measures of income, occupational status, and/or educational attainment), racial and ethnic composition (measures of ethnic heterogeneity and immigrant concentration), and residential stability (measures of residence over an extended period of time; Elliott et al., 1996; Hipp, 2007; Sampson et al., 1997). Because very little is known about the relations between substance use and the latter two of these three dimensions, the following review focuses exclusively on the influence of neighborhood SES. We examine evidence on the associations between neighborhood SES and adolescent and adult substance use outcomes in each of the following four categories: tobacco, alcohol, illegal drugs, and general substance use (e.g., composite measures of cigarette, alcohol, and/or illegal drug use outcomes). Where possible, we include studies that examine both substance use (i.e., whether and/or to what extent individuals use substances) and substance use disorders (i.e., clinical diagnoses of abuse or dependence). In keeping with the limited scope of the extant research, however, most of the reviewed studies focus on substance use. Unless otherwise indicated, all of the reviewed studies control for the influence of individual-level SES (as indexed by variables like income or educational attainment), which is often highly correlated with neighborhood-level SES. Finally, we note that this section is intended to be descriptive; we reserve discussion of potential explanatory mechanisms for the final section of the chapter.

Neighborhood SES and Tobacco Use Outcomes

In the following paragraphs, we first review research on the association between neighborhood SES and adolescents' tobacco use and then review research on the link between neighborhood SES and adults' tobacco use.

Studies of adolescents. Surprisingly, findings from at least one experimental study have suggested that there is a positive association between neighborhood SES and cigarette smoking. Recent analyses of 2002 MTO follow-up data revealed that boys in the experimental group (i.e., those who moved to less poor neighborhoods) were more likely to endorse recent cigarette smoking than boys in the control group (i.e.,

the nonmovers; Kling et al., 2007). Assignment to the experimental group did not, however, have an impact on girls' cigarette use (Kling et al., 2007).

Multilevel analyses suggest null or inverse associations between neighborhood SES and adolescent tobacco use. For instance, analyses of PHDCN data did not find significant relations between the percentage of census-tract residents living below the poverty line and adolescent and young adult (ages 11 to 23) reports of recent cigarette smoking (Novak, Reardon, Raudenbush, & Buka, 2006). However, a large-scale study of White and Mexican American seventh graders residing in Phoenix, Arizona ($N = 3,721$), found that the percentage of neighborhood (i.e., school catchment area) residents living in poverty was positively associated with youth's self-reports of recent cigarette smoking (Kulis, Marsiglia, Sicotte, & Nieri, 2007). This finding was only observed in a subset of highly acculturated Mexican American youth, however.

Nonmultilevel analyses also provide an unclear picture of the association between neighborhood SES and adolescents' tobacco use. First, in a study of more than 4,000 11- to 12-year-old London youth, individual-level analyses revealed positive associations between a census-based indicator of neighborhood deprivation (measured at the level of enumeration districts containing roughly 500 residents) and the odds of cigarette smoking (Wardle et al., 2003). The measure of neighborhood-level deprivation used in this study, however, assessed both socioeconomic conditions (i.e., indicated by rates of car ownership, unemployment, and overcrowding) and residential stability (i.e., indexed by housing tenure). It is unclear whether a more narrowly defined measure of neighborhood SES would have yielded similar results. The only other relevant nonmultilevel study that we identified—which used a straightforward measure of neighborhood SES in a sample of roughly 1,000 American youth—found that low SES at the census-tract level (i.e., indexed by the percentage of residents earning less than $12,500 per year, jobless men, and residents living under the poverty line) was indirectly associated with less adolescent tobacco use mediated through greater parental monitoring (Chuang et al., 2005). Neither of these studies controlled for the associations between individual-level

SES and tobacco use, however. Findings like these must therefore be interpreted cautiously.

Studies of adults. Findings on the direction of the association between neighborhood SES and adult cigarette smoking are relatively consistent. With the exception of one study that reported null findings (Galea, Ahern, Tracy, Rudenstine, & Vlahov, 2007; Galea, Ahern, Tracy, & Vlahov, 2007), evidence from a host of multilevel analyses has indicated that adults in neighborhoods of lower, versus higher, SES are at greater risk of cigarette smoking. Analysis of data from the Los Angeles Family and Neighborhood Study with approximately 2,500 participants from 65 census tracts revealed a positive association between neighborhood disadvantage at the census tract level (i.e., a composite of income inequality, mean family income, percentage of foreign-born residents, percentage of female-headed households, and percentage of residents living below the poverty line) and adults' daily smoking (Carpiano, 2007). Although the measure of neighborhood disadvantage used in this study blurred the constructs of SES and ethnic composition, data from at least two other studies have corroborated these findings. Multilevel analyses of data from the national Black Women's Health Study ($N \approx 42,000$) revealed that the odds of past-year cigarette smoking were higher in census tracts in which more than 10%, versus fewer than 5%, of residents lived below the poverty level (Datta et al., 2006). Multilevel analyses of data from nearly 8,000 London area adults also found that the odds of smoking were significantly higher in census wards (i.e., units of approximately 6,000 residents each; Martuzzi, Grundy, & Elliott, 1998) in the highest, versus lowest, quintile of economic deprivation (as indexed by census measures of male unemployment, overcrowding, low social class, and lack of automobile access; Kleinschmidt et al., 1995).

Findings from nonmultilevel analyses have also suggested that residence in low-SES neighborhoods is a risk factor for adult cigarette use. Bivariate analyses of data from a sample of 658 London area adults revealed an inverse association between a census-based indicator of neighborhood SES measured at the postal sector level (i.e., units of roughly 2,600 households) and rates of current cigarette smoking

(Steptoe & Feldman, 2001). This is consistent with evidence from multivariate models that control for individual-level SES. For instance, examination of data from the Third National Health and Nutrition Examination Survey (1988–1994; $N \approx 20,000$) found a positive association between neighborhood deprivation (i.e., a composite of 11 census indicators related to educational attainment, occupational status, income, living conditions, and cost of living) and positive serum cotinine tests (i.e., evidence of nicotine in blood samples) among 17- to 90-year-olds (Stimpson et al., 2007).[2] Analyses of data from the 1992 California Perinatal Substance Exposure Study also revealed a positive association between neighborhood poverty (as indexed by census data on the percentage of residents in postal zip codes receiving public assistance) and the odds of tobacco use among nearly 13,000 pregnant women (Finch et al., 1999).

Neighborhood SES and Alcohol Use Outcomes

In this section, we review research on the relations between neighborhood SES and alcohol use separately for adolescents and adults.

Studies of adolescents. The extant literature on neighborhood SES and alcohol use includes one experimental study, one study using multilevel analyses, and one study using nonmultilevel analyses. Findings from these studies are mixed with the experimental and multilevel studies indicating null findings. Analyses of 2002 MTO follow-up data failed to identify significant differences in recent alcohol use between youth in the experimental (i.e., those who moved to less poor neighborhoods) and nonmover control groups (Kling et al., 2007). Similarly, the above-mentioned study of Phoenix, Arizona, seventh graders found no relation between neighborhood poverty and youth's self-reports of recent alcohol consumption (Kulis et al., 2007). However, nonmultilevel structural equation models used by Chuang et al. (2005) revealed a significant, indirect

---

[2] This sample included individuals as young as 17 years of age. Because adolescents and children under the age of 17 were excluded from the analyses, we have included this study in our review of neighborhood SES and adult substance use.

association between a census-tract–level measure of low neighborhood SES and greater adolescent alcohol use (mediated by greater peer alcohol use). Interestingly, these same models also revealed an indirect relation between low neighborhood SES and less adolescent alcohol use (via greater parental monitoring) and an indirect relation between high neighborhood SES and greater adolescent alcohol use (via greater parental alcohol use; Chuang et al., 2005). Although such nonmultilevel models must be interpreted cautiously, these findings suggest that (a) residence in low-SES neighborhoods may be associated with factors that both increase and decrease the risk for adolescent alcohol use and (b) residence in high-SES neighborhoods may be associated with factors that increase the risk for adolescent alcohol use.

Studies of adults. In keeping with studies of adolescents, findings on the relations between neighborhood SES and adult alcohol use are mixed. The Los Angeles Family and Neighborhood Study failed to find significant associations between neighborhood socioeconomic disadvantage and adults' binge drinking (Carpiano, 2007). However, findings from other multilevel analyses have generally suggested that adults in higher SES neighborhoods are more likely to use alcohol than are adults in lower SES neighborhoods. For instance, analysis of data from 59 New York City community districts (i.e., aggregates of multiple census tracts) suggests that neighborhood-level educational attainment and income are both positively associated with the odds and frequency of alcohol use (Galea, Ahern, Tracy, Rudenstine, & Vlahov, 2007; Galea, Ahern, Tracy, & Vlahov, 2007). Additionally, Pollack et al. (2005) recently used multilevel models to analyze data from the Stanford Heart Disease Prevention Program ($N \approx 8,000$) and found that deprivation at the tract or block group level (defined by the percentage of residents living in crowded housing units, unemployed persons, tenant-occupied housing units, and occupied housing units without a vehicle available) was inversely related to the odds of heavy alcohol consumption.

Findings from nonmultilevel analyses provide a completely different picture. Although bivariate and multivariate analyses in two studies revealed null associations between neighborhood SES and adult

alcohol use (Finch et al., 1999; Steptoe & Feldman, 2001), analyses of data from the Third National Health and Nutrition Examination Survey found that very low SES at the census-tract level was associated with excessive alcohol use (Stimpson et al., 2007).

Neighborhood SES and Illegal Drug Use Outcomes

In the following paragraphs, we review research on the associations between neighborhood SES and illegal drug use, first for adolescents and then for adults.

Studies of adolescents. Few studies have examined the link between neighborhood SES and adolescents' illegal drug use, and the limited extant findings are mixed. First, in a follow-up study of MTO families, Kling et al. (2007) found that girls, but not boys, in the experimental group (i.e., those who moved to less poor neighborhoods) were less likely to endorse recent marijuana use than were girls in the nonmover control group. Second, recent analyses of PHDCN data revealed significant neighborhood-level variation in adolescents' perceptions of the risks of using hard drugs (i.e., cocaine, crack, heroin, inhalants, and steroids; Novak, Reardon, & Buka, 2002). Unfortunately, these analyses did not address the question of whether neighborhood-level SES explained any of the neighborhood-level variation in perceptions, nor did the authors examine adolescents' actual use of illegal drugs as an outcome. Finally, the previously described study of Phoenix, Arizona, youth (Kulis et al., 2007) failed to identify a significant relation between neighborhood poverty and adolescents' self-reports of recent marijuana use (Kulis et al., 2007).

Studies of adults. Findings on the relations between neighborhood SES and adults' illegal drug use are also somewhat mixed. Multilevel analyses of a previously described New York City data set revealed positive relations between neighborhood-level measures of income and educational attainment and the odds of marijuana use (Galea, Ahern, Tracy, Rudenstine, & Vlahov, 2007; Galea, Ahern, Tracy, & Vlahov, 2007). However, studies that model the use of other illegal drugs—either alone or in combination with marijuana use—have consistently found that adults in lower, versus higher, SES neighborhoods are at greater risk of use. First, Williams and Latkin (2007) used data from a study of 1,305 adults participating in an HIV intervention and found that residence in higher poverty block groups was positively associated with the odds of using heroin, cocaine, and/or crack. Second, using data from a national phone survey of 42,650 older adolescents and adults (ages 16–44 years), Saxe et al. (2001) found that neighborhood poverty at the census-tract level (i.e., a composite of adult unemployment, high school dropouts, female-headed households, individuals receiving public assistance, and number below poverty lines) was associated positively with illicit drug use and dependence (marijuana, cocaine, amphetamines, barbiturates, inhalants, LSD, or heroin). These findings must be interpreted cautiously, however; Saxe et al. (2001) did not control for individual-level SES.

Results from nonmultilevel analyses have also suggested that residence in low-SES neighborhoods may be a risk factor for adults' illegal drug use. For example, individual-level analyses of data from the 1995 Detroit Area Study ($N = 1,101$ adults) showed that residence in lower, versus higher, SES neighborhoods (i.e., census tracts characterized by a greater percentage of residents living below the poverty line, female-headed households, unemployed men, and families on public assistance) was associated with greater odds of past-year drug use (i.e., use of sedatives, tranquilizers, amphetamines, inhalants, marijuana, cocaine, crack, or heroin; Boardman et al., 2001). Additionally, analyses of data from the previously described California Perinatal Substance Exposure Study revealed a positive relation between neighborhood poverty (indexed by the percentage of residents in postal zip codes receiving public assistance) and the odds of using marijuana, opiates, and amphetamines (but not cocaine; Finch et al., 1999).

Neighborhood SES and General Substance Use Outcomes

Researchers occasionally construct measures that assess the use of substances in one or more of the above three categories (e.g., a dichotomous measure of tobacco, alcohol, or drug use; a measure of the average frequency of tobacco, alcohol, and drug use). In the following paragraphs, we review research on the relations between neighborhood SES and these general measures of substance use, first for adolescents and then for adults.

Studies of adolescents. We identified two such studies of neighborhood SES and adolescent substance use. One study using Yonkers data found that 15- to 18-year-olds who moved to higher SES neighborhoods reported more substance use (on a measure of tobacco, alcohol, and marijuana use) 7 years after moving than did those who remained in low-SES neighborhoods (Fauth, Leventhal, & Brooks-Gunn, 2007). However, an individual-level study of just over 100 urban 9th and 10th graders failed to identify a significant association between conditions at the block group level (i.e., a composite of five census-based indicators: male joblessness, welfare receipt, high school dropout rates, vacant housing, home ownership) and scores on a composite measure of alcohol and tobacco use (Allison et al., 1999). The measure of neighborhood conditions used in this study combined neighborhood SES and residential stability, however. Thus, it is difficult to draw definitive conclusions about the link between neighborhood SES and adolescents' combined cigarette and alcohol use.

Studies of adults. Although outcome measures that combine different categories of substances are less commonly used in studies of adults (vs. adolescents), we did identify one such study. Using a sample of more than 65,000 adults (ages 40–59) in the city of Malmo, Sweden, researchers examined the association between neighborhood SES and substance abuse (defined by the occurrence of alcohol- or drug-related behavioral or mental health problems). Multilevel geospatial models—which account for both the nonindependence of observations within neighborhoods and the nonindependence of observations in spatially contiguous neighborhoods—identified a positive association between neighborhood poverty and the odds of substance abuse (Chaix et al., 2005). Specifically, investigators found that the odds of substance abuse were higher among adults in the lowest two quartiles of neighborhood income than among adults in the highest quartile of neighborhood income.

Conclusions on Neighborhood SES and Substance Use Outcomes

The relations between neighborhood SES and substance use are complex, particularly among adolescents. There is insufficient evidence to draw conclusions about the relations between neighborhood SES and adolescents' illegal drug use. More attention has been paid to the relations between neighborhood SES and adolescents' tobacco and alcohol use, but the findings are mixed. Studies have supported both inverse and positive associations between neighborhood SES and adolescents' tobacco and alcohol use. Methodological differences between studies may be partly responsible for these discrepancies. It is also plausible that the mixed findings point toward a curvilinear relation between neighborhood SES and tobacco and alcohol use. In other words, adolescents who live in very low- and relatively high-SES neighborhoods may be at higher risk for alcohol and tobacco use than those who live in neighborhoods of more moderate SES. The above-reviewed findings hint at this trend, but researchers have not, to our knowledge, explicitly investigated this possibility.

Our review presents a clearer picture of the relations between neighborhood SES and adult substance use outcomes. Although studies have identified both inverse and positive associations between neighborhood SES and adults' alcohol use and abuse, the weight of evidence from multilevel (vs. nonmultilevel) analyses suggests that alcohol use and abuse is more common in higher than in lower SES neighborhoods. Research examining tobacco and illegal drug use suggests an opposite trend. That is, findings from most analyses suggest that residence in lower, versus higher, SES neighborhoods places adults at greater risk for the use of these substances.

MECHANISMS OF NEIGHBORHOOD INFLUENCE

A three-part framework articulated by Leventhal and Brooks-Gunn (2000) suggests that neighborhood structure influences individual-level outcomes through (a) institutional resources—the quantity, quality, and accessibility of supportive resources in the neighborhood; (b) relationships—the quality of within-family relationships (i.e., intrafamilial rela-

tionships) and the quantity and quality of relationships between residents (i.e., interfamilial relationships); and (c) collective efficacy—the extent to which informal mechanisms are present to monitor residents' behavior and protect against threats to residents' well-being. In the following section, we discuss the possibility that these three constructs mediate the associations between neighborhood SES and adolescent and adult substance use outcomes. Although these constructs are typically used to explain the adverse consequences of residence in low-SES neighborhoods, we highlight findings that suggest that in some cases, they might also explain the adverse outcomes observed among residents in higher SES neighborhoods.

Institutional Resources

Institutional resources refer to supportive community resources like child care centers, schools, youth organizations, community organizations, medical facilities, and employers (Leventhal & Brooks-Gunn, 2000). The quantity, quality, and accessibility of these resources vary as a function of neighborhood SES, and differences in access to high-quality institutional resources may have important implications for individual-level outcomes. We focus on three categories of institutional resources that have demonstrated associations with substance use—schools, youth organizations, and employment opportunities. The relevance of these specific institutional resources depends to some extent on an individual's developmental stage. Accordingly, although our discussion of schools and youth organizations focuses on adolescents, our discussion of employment opportunities extends to adults as well. We discuss the extent to which each resource may explain substance use risks in low- and/or high-SES neighborhoods.

Schools. Schools are thought to influence adolescents' substance use through one or both of two paths. First, school failure is a risk factor for substance use (Chassin et al., 2004), and schools that do not encourage achievement may thus increase adolescents' risks for substance use. Second, evidence has suggested that school-level norms regarding substance use may influence individual-level substance use (Kumar, O'Malley, Johnston, Schulenberg, &

Bachman, 2002). There is little empirical evidence on the extent to which specific neighborhood characteristics promote such school-level risks for substance use (see chap. 23 of this volume for a much more detailed review of this material). The assumption is often that schools in lower SES neighborhoods are more likely to promote substance use than are schools in higher SES neighborhoods. This line of reasoning is perhaps partly true. Schools attended by poor children are often of lower quality than schools attended by higher income children; low-quality schools are a risk factor for school failure (Rouse & Barrow, 2006), and school failure, in turn, is a risk factor for substance use (Chassin et al., 2004). Some have speculated, however, that intense achievement pressures in high-SES schools may also promote substance use (Luthar, 2003). Accordingly, evidence from at least one study has suggested that alcohol use is more prevalent in schools located in high-SES communities (i.e., as indexed by characteristics like lower residential mobility and lower population density) than in schools located in lower SES communities (Ennett, Flewelling, & Lindroth, 1997). Thus, certain characteristics of schools in low- and high-SES neighborhoods may increase adolescents' vulnerability to substance use.

Youth organizations. Youth organizations are another set of institutional resources with demonstrated links to adolescent substance use. With the exception of team sports (see Feldman & Matjasko, 2005, for a review), evidence has suggested that participation in organized activities (e.g., extracurricular activities, religious youth groups, afterschool programs) during adolescence protects against substance use (Darling, 2005; Elder, Leaver-Dunn, Wang, Nagy, & Green, 2000; Fauth, Roth, & Brooks-Gunn, 2007; Tebes et al., 2007). The benefits of participation are contingent on the quality of youth activities, however. A study of Swedish youth centers found that youth who attended centers with little structure or adult supervision were more likely to participate in juvenile offending than were youth who did not attend these centers (Mahoney, Stattin, & Magnusson, 2001). Although this study did not examine substance use, these findings highlight the fact that low-quality activities may increase adolescents' risks for problem

behavior. Differences in the quantity and quality of available youth activities may thus partly explain the observed relations between low neighborhood SES and adolescent substance use. More research is needed, but at least one study has suggested that lower SES neighborhoods offer fewer organized youth activities than higher SES neighborhoods (Littell & Wynn, 1989). Additionally, although we know of no research on the relations between neighborhood SES and the quality of youth activities, it is conceivable that programs in low-SES neighborhoods face funding shortages that lead to high youth-to-adult ratios and thus to less supervision and formal structure.

Employment opportunities. Findings from studies with large, socioeconomically diverse samples have suggested that employment during adolescence, particularly when intensive, increases risks for substance use (e.g., Bachman & Schulenberg, 1993; Mihalic & Elliott, 1997; Steinberg & Dornbusch, 1991; Steinberg, Fegley, & Dornbusch, 1993). The adverse consequences of adolescent employment have been attributed to premature affluence (i.e., access to excessive disposable income; Bachman, 1983) and work-related stressors (e.g., task meaninglessness, poor environmental conditions, autocratic supervision; Greenberger, Steinberg, & Vaux, 1981). Leventhal and Brooks-Gunn (2000), however, highlighted findings suggesting that employment may have positive consequences for lower income youth. The shortcomings of the adolescent work environment may pale in comparison to the risks that lower income youth face during idle time in their neighborhoods. Lerman (2000) pointed out, however, that adolescent job opportunities may be limited in low-SES neighborhoods. Thus, although myriad job opportunities may increase substance use risks among adolescents in high-SES neighborhoods, an insufficient supply of jobs may increase substance use risks among adolescents in low-SES neighborhoods.

Employment also has important implications for adult substance use. Unemployment and related stressors are frequently cited risk factors for substance use (e.g., Atkinson, Montoya, Whitsett, Bell, & Nagy, 2003; Boardman et al., 2001; Peirce, Frone, Russell, & Cooper, 1996). Recent analyses of data from the Monitoring the Future study found that at age 35, the odds of cigarette smoking, marijuana use, and prescription drug misuse were 45%, 49%, and 52% higher, respectively, among those who reported recent unemployment than among those who reported continuous employment (Merline, O'Malley, Schulenberg, Bachman, & Johnston, 2004). Although relations between unemployment and substance use are likely bidirectional, evidence of limited employment opportunities in low-SES neighborhoods may partly explain the elevated rates of substance use among adults who live in these neighborhoods (Squires & Kubrin, 2005). However, with some exceptions (e.g., Cooper, Russell, & Frone, 1990), evidence has suggested that very demanding jobs also increase adults' risks for substance use (Albertsen, Borg, & Oldenburg, 2006; Harris & Fennell, 1988). To the extent that demanding jobs are concentrated at the lower and higher ends of the socioeconomic spectrum, job-related stress may thus partly explain the observed risks for tobacco, alcohol, and illegal drug use and abuse among adults in low-SES neighborhoods and likewise explain the risks for alcohol use and abuse among adults in higher SES neighborhoods.

Relationships

Interpersonal relationships refer to (a) intrafamilial relationships, or the quality of the relationships between individuals within families, and (b) interfamilial relationships, or the quantity and quality of relationships between residents and families (i.e., as indexed by measures of social support). In the following paragraphs, we consider the possibility that neighborhood-level differences in intra- and interpersonal relationships partly explain the patterns of adolescent and adult substance use outcomes observed in higher and lower SES neighborhoods.

Intrafamilial relationships. Intrafamilial relationships play an important role in adolescent substance use. For instance, findings from the Seattle Social Development Project ($N \approx 800$ families) have indicated that throughout adolescence, the odds of initiating illicit drug use are greater for youth from higher conflict families than for youth from lower conflict families (Guo, Hill, Hawkins, Catalano, & Abbott, 2002). Parenting practices have also been linked to adolescents' substance use. Studies have

consistently found that parenting characterized by high levels of both warmth–involvement and monitoring–supervision protects against substance use (e.g., Adamczyk-Robinette, Fletcher, & Wright, 2002; Cleveland, Gibbons, Gerrard, Pomery, & Brody, 2005; Lamborn, Mounts, Steinberg, & Dornbusch, 1991). Evidence has further suggested that parental monitoring, relative to other parenting dimensions, may play a particularly important role in preventing adolescent substance use (Barnes, Hoffman, Welte, Farrell, & Dintcheff, 2006).

Although the extant literature says little about whether intrafamilial processes mediate the relations between neighborhood SES and adolescent substance use, several studies have documented relations between neighborhood SES and intrafamilial processes. Evidence has suggested that parents who live in relatively poorer or more dangerous neighborhoods demonstrate less warmth and more harsh control than parents living in safer, more affluent neighborhoods (e.g., Chung & Steinberg, 2006; Earls, McGuire, & Shay, 1994; Klebanov, Brooks-Gunn, & Duncan, 1994). At least one study has also suggested that neighborhood poverty is positively associated with family stress and conflict (Paschall & Hubbard, 1998). This evidence is consistent with models of economic hardship and family stress, which suggest that poverty-related stressors lead to conflict and compromised parenting (Conger et al., 1993; Conger, Ge, Elder, Lorenz, & Simons, 1994; McLoyd, 1990). These findings may thus partly explain the risks for substance use observed among adolescents in low-SES neighborhoods.

Adolescents from higher SES neighborhoods may also confront intrafamilial risks for substance use. Some evidence has suggested that parents in higher SES neighborhoods may monitor their children less closely than parents in lower SES neighborhoods (Briggs, 1997; Chuang et al., 2005). Lax monitoring in higher SES neighborhoods has been attributed to the perception that these communities pose few risks to youth's safety (see Leventhal & Brooks-Gunn, 2000, for discussion). Not all studies have found neighborhood differences in parental monitoring, however (e.g., Browning, Leventhal, & Brooks-Gunn, 2005; Leventhal & Brooks-Gunn, 2005). Moreover, even if parents in higher SES neighborhoods monitor their children less closely than do parents in lower SES neighborhoods, lax monitoring may be less dangerous for adolescents in higher SES neighborhoods. More research is needed to determine whether lax monitoring is equally predictive of substance use in higher and lower SES neighborhoods.

Intrafamilial relationships—particularly when characterized by conflict—also have important implications for adult substance use. Studies of both clinical and nonclinical populations have suggested that intimate partner violence is associated with elevated risks for substance use among women (Carbone-Lopez, Kruttschnitt, & MacMillan, 2006; El-Bassel et al., 2003; El-Bassel, Gilbert, Wu, Go, & Hill, 2005; Martino, Collins, & Ellickson, 2005; Salomon, Bassuk, & Huntington, 2002). Findings from recent longitudinal studies of married adults have also suggested that marital distress and marital dissatisfaction are positively associated with the odds of receiving a substance use disorder diagnosis (Whisman, 2007; Whisman, Uebelacker, & Bruce, 2006). Perhaps because of the stressors associated with living in poverty, researchers have documented higher rates of intimate partner conflict in lower, versus higher, SES neighborhoods (Benson, Fox, DeMaris, & Van Wyk, 2003; Cunradi, Caetano, Clark, & Schafer, 2000). Thus, intimate partner conflict may mediate relations between neighborhood poverty and adult substance use.

Interfamilial relationships. The support of extended family and nonfamily members has been linked to substance use among both adolescents and adults. With some exceptions (e.g., Peirce et al., 1996), studies have generally found that adults with greater, versus lesser, access to supportive social networks are less likely to have substance use problems (Schuckit & Smith, 2000) and are more likely to respond favorably to substance use treatment (Groh, Jason, Davis, Olson, & Ferrari, 2007). Although one study has suggested that social support from same-age peers increases adolescents' risks for substance use (Averna & Hesselbrock, 2001), the implications of social support for adolescents are similarly favorable overall. To the extent that parents' access to social support leads to better parenting (Green, Furrer, & McAllister, 2007; McLoyd, 1990), adolescents with socially supported parents may be at less

risk of substance use. Evidence has also suggested that access to supportive nonfamilial adults during adolescence is inversely associated with substance use (Zimmerman, Bingenheimer, & Notaro, 2002).

To our knowledge, no one has explicitly considered the extent to which social support mediates associations between neighborhood SES and adolescents' and adults' substance use. Moreover, findings on the direction of the relation between SES and social support are mixed. A review of individual- and neighborhood-level research has suggested that low-SES families often have less access to supportive social networks than do higher SES families (Evans, 2004). However, analyses of data from the Infant Health and Development Project failed to find a significant association between neighborhood poverty (as defined by the percentage of families living on less than $10,000 per year) and mothers' access to social support, but did find a significant inverse association between neighborhood affluence (as defined by the percentage of families living on more than $75,000 per year) and mothers' reports of social support (Klebanov et al., 1994). Taken together, these findings suggest that low- and high-SES neighborhoods may be characterized by low social support. Low social support in low-SES neighborhoods has been attributed to poverty-related stressors that diminish residents' abilities to provide support (Cattell, 2001), and low social support in high-SES neighborhoods has been attributed to a reliance on market-based services (e.g., fee-based child care or care provided in the home) instead of help from neighbors (Luthar, 2003). Low social support may thus play a role in the risks for substance use observed among adolescents and adults in low- and high-SES neighborhoods.

Collective Efficacy (and Disorder)

Neighborhood research on substance use often focuses on the implications of two kinds of neighborhood disorder—physical disorder (i.e., signs of property decay like abandoned cars and building graffiti) and social disorder (i.e., displays of deviance like drug trafficking, loitering, fighting; Sampson & Raudenbush, 1999). Although much of this research is not multilevel and must therefore be interpreted cautiously, studies have consistently identified positive associations between measures of disorder and adolescents' and adults' substance use (Choi, Harachi, & Catalano, 2006; Jang & Johnson, 2001; Lambert, Brown, Phillips, & Ialongo, 2004; Latkin, Curry, Hua, & Davey, 2007; Latkin, Williams, Wang, & Curry, 2005; Scheier, Botvin, & Miller, 1999; Scheier, Miller, Ifill-Williams, & Botvin, 2001; Wilson, Syme, Boyce, Battistich, & Selvin, 2005). Widespread access to tobacco and alcohol sales outlets—which might be considered an indicator of disorder—has also been identified as a neighborhood-level risk factor for adolescents' and adults' substance use (Novak et al., 2006; Scribner, Cohen, & Fisher, 2000). Not surprisingly, evidence has suggested that neighborhood SES is inversely associated with general measures of disorder (Sampson & Raudenbush, 1999) and with tobacco and alcohol outlet density (Novak et al., 2006; Pollack et al., 2005). Neighborhood disorder may thus partly explain the risks for substance use in low-SES neighborhoods.

There is, however, some debate about whether neighborhood disorder has causal implications for deviance in general and substance use in particular. Extrapolating from the "broken windows" theory (Wilson & Kelling, 1982)—which seeks to explain relations between neighborhood disorder and crime—one might argue that disorder cues potential substance users and abusers to the weakness of neighborhood norms and thus encourages substance use and abuse. Several compelling theories also suggest that greater access to alcohol outlets has a causal impact on alcohol consumption and related problems (see Gruenwald, 2007, and Scribner et al., 2000, for discussion). Evidence from the PHDCN, however, has suggested that disorder does not cause deviant behavior; rather, disorder and deviant behavior are both by-products of low collective efficacy (Sampson & Raudenbush, 1999), or a lack of "mutual trust (i.e., social cohesion) and the willingness to intervene for the common good (i.e., informal social control)" (Sampson et al., 1997, p. 919). Although it is possible that disorder plays a causal role in shaping individual-level substance use outcomes (particularly insofar as it is associated with opportunities to purchase substances), these findings highlight the fact that low collective efficacy at the neighborhood level likely precedes disorder.

To our knowledge, no one has explicitly investigated the possibility that collective efficacy mediates associations between neighborhood SES and substance use outcomes, and there is little conclusive evidence on the association between collective efficacy and substance use.[3] Somewhat greater attention has been devoted to investigating the link between neighborhood SES and collective efficacy. Findings from the PHDCN have suggested that high scores on neighborhood poverty predict low scores on collective efficacy (Sampson et al., 1997). Conversely, some researchers have speculated that very affluent neighborhoods may also be characterized by low collective efficacy (Luthar, 2003). This is based on the observation that affluent neighborhoods—particularly in suburban areas—are often structured with an emphasis on privacy (i.e., houses with gates, sprawling lawns, and long driveways) rather than an emphasis on cohesion (Luthar, 2003). The emphasis on privacy may prevent neighbors from intervening when personal problems like substance abuse are detected. Although findings from the PHDCN do not support a link between neighborhood affluence and low collective efficacy (Sampson, Morenoff, & Earls, 1999), it is important to point out that the PHDCN sample did not include the kinds of affluent suburban neighborhoods hypothesized to inhibit the development of collective efficacy. Consequently, the hypothesized link between neighborhood affluence and low collective efficacy deserves further investigation in other data sets. Such research is needed to determine whether low collective efficacy could potentially explain the risks for substance use observed in low- and high-SES neighborhoods.

Conclusions on Neighborhood Mechanisms and Directions for Future Research

This review suggests that adolescents and adults in both low- and high-SES neighborhoods are at risk for

---

[3] We identified only one study examining the relation between collective efficacy and substance use. This study failed to identify significant associations between college students' substance use and retrospective perceptions of collective efficacy in students' home neighborhoods (Brady, 2006). It is not surprising that collective efficacy in a neighborhood in which students previously resided did not protect against substance use in an entirely different context. Because this chapter focuses on the relations between current neighborhood residence and substance use, we excluded this study from our review.

substance use and/or substance use disorders. Using Leventhal and Brooks-Gunn's (2000) three-part framework as guide, we have developed a number of testable explanations for these findings: (a) The risks for adolescent substance use in low-SES neighborhoods are partly explained by low-performing schools, few high-quality youth organizations, limited job opportunities, family conflict, low parental warmth, low social support, neighborhood disorder, and low collective efficacy; (b) the risks for adolescent substance use in high-SES neighborhoods are partly explained by achievement pressures, a large supply of low-quality job opportunities, lax parental monitoring, low social support, and low collective efficacy; (c) the risks for adult substance use in low-SES neighborhoods are partly explained by limited job opportunities, job-related stressors, intimate partner conflict, low social support, neighborhood disorder, and low collective efficacy; and (d) the risks for adult substance use in high-SES neighborhoods are partly explained by job-related stressors, low social support, and low collective efficacy. We urge researchers to investigate these largely untested pathways using appropriate multilevel sampling and analytic techniques. Given tentative evidence that the influence of neighborhood residence varies as a function of gender (e.g., Browning et al., 2005) and ethnicity (e.g., Kulis et al., 2007), we also encourage investigators to consider the possibility that these mechanisms operate differently in different demographic groups.

References

Adamczyk-Robinette, S. L., Fletcher, A. C., & Wright, K. (2002). Understanding the authoritative parenting–early adolescent tobacco use link: The mediating role of peer tobacco use. *Journal of Youth and Adolescence, 31,* 311–318.

Albertsen, K., Borg, V., & Oldenburg, B. (2006). A systematic review of the impact of work environment on smoking cessation, relapse and amount smoked. *Preventive Medicine, 43,* 291–305.

Allison, K. W., Crawford, I., Leone, P. E., Trickett, E., Perez-Febles, A., Burton, L. M., et al. (1999). Adolescent substance use: Preliminary examinations of school and neighborhood context. *American Journal of Community Psychology, 27,* 111–141.

Atkinson, J. S., Montoya, I. D., Whitsett, D. D., Bell, D. C., & Nagy, C. W. (2003). The relationship

among psychological distress, employment, and drug use over time in a sample of female welfare recipients. *Journal of Community Psychology, 13,* 223–234.

Averna, S., & Hesselbrock, V. (2001). The relationship of perceived social support to substance use in offspring of alcoholics. *Addictive Behaviors, 26,* 363–374.

Bachman, J. G. (1983). Premature affluence: Do high school students earn too much? *Economic Outlook USA, 10,* 64–71.

Bachman, J. G., & Schulenberg, J. (1993). How part-time work intensity relates to drug use, problem behavior, time use, and satisfaction among high school seniors: Are these consequences or merely correlates? *Developmental Psychology, 29,* 220–235.

Barnes, G. M., Hoffman, J. H., Welte, J. W., Farrell, M. P., & Dintcheff, B. A. (2006). Effects of parental monitoring and peer deviance on substance use and delinquency. *Journal of Marriage and Family, 68,* 1084–1104.

Benson, M. L., Fox, G. L., DeMaris, A., & Van Wyk, J. (2003). Neighborhood disadvantage, individual economic distress and violence against women in intimate relationships. *Journal of Quantitative Criminology, 19,* 207–235.

Boardman, J. D., Finch, B. K., Ellison, C. G., Williams, D. R., & Jackson, J. S. (2001). Neighborhood disadvantage, stress, and drug use among adults. *Journal of Health and Social Behavior, 42,* 151–165.

Brady, S. S. (2006). Lifetime community violence exposure and health risk behavior among young adults in college. *Journal of Adolescent Health, 39,* 610–613.

Briggs, X. D. (1997). Moving up versus moving out: Neighborhood effects in housing mobility programs. *Housing Policy Debate, 8,* 195–234.

Briggs, X. D., Darden, J. T., & Aidala, A. (1999). In the wake of desegregation: Early impacts of scattered-site public housing on neighborhoods in Yonkers, New York. *Journal of the American Planning Association, 65,* 27–49.

Bronfenbrenner, U. (1977). Toward an experimental ecology of human development. *American Psychologist, 32,* 513–531.

Brooks-Gunn, J., Duncan, G., & Aber, J. L. (Eds.). (1997). *Neighborhood Poverty I: Context and consequences for children.* New York: Russell Sage Foundation.

Brooks-Gunn, J., Duncan, G. J., Klebanov, P. K., & Sealand, N. (1993). Do neighborhoods influence child and adolescent development? *American Journal of Sociology, 99,* 353–395.

Browning, C. R., Leventhal, T., & Brooks-Gunn, J. (2005). Sexual initiation in early adolescence: The nexus of parental control and community control. *American Sociological Review, 70,* 758–778.

Carbone-Lopez, K., Kruttschnitt, C., & MacMillan, R. (2006). Patterns of intimate partner violence and their associations with physical health, psychological distress, and substance use. *Public Health Reports, 121,* 382–392.

Carpiano, R. M. (2007). Neighborhood social capital and adult health: An empirical test of a Bourdieu-based model. *Health and Place, 13,* 639–655.

Cattell, V. (2001). Poor people, poor places, and poor health: The mediating role of social networks and social capital. *Social Science & Medicine, 52,* 1501–1516.

Chaix, B., Merlo, J., Subramanian, S. V., Lynch, J., & Chauvin, P. (2005). Comparison of a spatial perspective with the multilevel analytical approach in neighborhood studies: The case of mental and behavioral disorders due to psychoactive substance use in Malmo, Sweden, 2001. *American Journal of Epidemiology, 162,* 171–182.

Chassin, L., Hussong, A., Barrera, M., Molina, B. S. G., Trim, R., & Ritter, J. (2004). Adolescent substance use. In R. M. Lerner & L. Steinberg (Eds.), *Handbook of adolescent psychology* (2nd ed., pp. 665–696). Hoboken, NJ: Wiley.

Choi, Y., Harachi, T., & Catalano, R. (2006). Neighborhoods, family, and substance use: Comparisons of the relations across racial and ethnic groups. *Social Service Review, 80,* 675–704.

Chuang, Y., Ennett, S. T., Bauman, K. E., & Foshee, V. A. (2005). Neighborhood influences on adolescent cigarette and alcohol use: Mediating effects through parent and peer behaviors. *Journal of Health and Social Behavior, 46,* 187–204.

Chung, H. L., & Steinberg, L. (2006). Relations between neighborhood factors, parenting behaviors, peer deviance, and delinquency among serious juvenile offenders. *Developmental Psychology, 42,* 319–331.

Clampet-Lundquist, S. (2007). No more 'Bois Ball: The effect of relocation from public housing on adolescents. *Journal of Adolescent Research, 22,* 298–323.

Cleveland, M. J., Gibbons, F. X., Gerrard, M., Pomery, E. A., & Brody, G. H. (2005). The impact of parenting on risk cognitions and risk behavior: A study of mediation and moderation in a panel of African American adolescents. *Child Development, 76,* 900–916.

Conger, R. D., Conger, K. J., Elder, G. H., Lorenz, F. O., Simons, R. L., & Whitbeck, L. B. (1993). Family economic stress and adjustment of early adolescent girls. *Developmental Psychology, 29,* 206–219.

Conger, R. D., Ge, X., Elder, G. H., Lorenz, F. O., & Simons, R. L. (1994). Economic stress, coercive family process, and developmental problems of adolescents. *Child Development, 65,* 541–561.

Cooper, M. L., Russell, M., & Frone, M. R. (1990). Work stress and alcohol effects: A test of stress-induced drinking. *Journal of Health and Social Behavior, 31,* 260–276.

Cunradi, C. B., Caetano, R., Clark, C., & Schafer, J. (2000). Neighborhood poverty as a predictor of intimate partner violence among White, Black, and Hispanic couples in the United States: A multilevel analysis. *Annals of Epidemiology, 10,* 297–308.

Darling, N. (2005). Participation in extracurricular activities and adolescent adjustment: Cross-sectional and longitudinal findings. *Journal of Youth and Adolescence, 34,* 493–505.

Datta, G. D., Subramanian, S. V., Colditz, G. A., Kawachi, I., Palmer, J. R., & Rosenberg, L. (2006). Individual, neighborhood, and state-level predictors of smoking among U.S. Black women: A multilevel analysis. *Social Science & Medicine, 63,* 1034–1044.

Earls, F., & Buka, S. L. (1997). *Project on Human Development in Chicago Neighborhoods: Technical report.* Rockville, MD: National Institute of Justice.

Earls, F., McGuire, J., & Shay, S. (1994). Evaluating a community intervention to reduce the risk of child abuse: Methodological strategies in conducting neighborhood surveys. *Child Abuse and Neglect, 18,* 473–485.

El-Bassel, N., Gilbert, L., Witte, S., Wu, E., Gaeta, T., Schilling, R., et al. (2003). Intimate partner violence and substance abuse among minority women receiving care from an inner-city emergency department. *Women's Health Issues, 13,* 16–22.

El-Bassel, N., Gilbert, L., Wu, E., Go, H., & Hill, J. (2005). Relationship between drug abuse and intimate partner violence: A longitudinal study among women receiving methadone. *American Journal of Public Health, 95,* 465–470.

Elder, C., Leaver-Dunn, D., Wang, M. Q., Nagy, S., & Green, L. (2000). Organized group activity as a protective factor against adolescent substance use. *American Journal of Health Behavior, 24,* 108–113.

Elliott, D., Wilson, W. J., Huizinga, D., Sampson, R. J., Elliott, A., & Rankin, B. (1996). The effects of neighborhood disadvantage on adolescent development. *Journal of Research in Crime and Delinquency, 33,* 389–426.

Ennett, S. T., Flewelling, R. L., & Lindroth, R. C. (1997). Social and neighborhood characteristics associated with school rates of alcohol, cigarettes, and marijuana use. *Journal of Health Social Behavior, 38,* 55–71.

Evans, G. W. (2004). The environment of childhood poverty. *American Psychologist, 59,* 77–92.

Fauth, R. C., & Brooks-Gunn, J. (2008). Are some neighborhoods better for child health than others? In R. F. Schoeni, J. S. House, G. A. Kaplan, & H. Pollack (Eds.), *Making Americans healthier: Social and eco-*

nomic policy as health policy (pp. 334–376). New York: Russell Sage Foundation.

Fauth, R. C., Leventhal, T., & Brooks-Gunn, J. (2005). Early impacts of moving from poor to middle-class neighborhoods on low-income youth. *Applied Developmental Psychology, 26,* 415–439.

Fauth, R. C., Leventhal, T., & Brooks-Gunn, J. (2007). Welcome to the neighborhood? Long-term impacts of moving to low-poverty neighborhoods on poor children's and adolescents' outcomes. *Journal of Research on Adolescence, 17,* 249–284.

Fauth, R. C., Roth, J. L., & Brooks-Gunn, J. (2007). Does the neighborhood context alter the link between youth's after school time activities and developmental outcomes? A multilevel analysis. *Developmental Psychology, 43,* 760–777.

Feins, J. D., & Shroder, M. D. (2005). Moving to opportunity: The demonstration's design and its effects on mobility. *Urban Studies, 42,* 1275–1299.

Feldman, A. F., & Matjasko, J. L. (2005). The role of school-based extracurricular activities in adolescent development: A comprehensive review and future directions. *Review of Educational Research, 75,* 159–210.

Finch, B. K., Kolody, B., & Vega, W. A. (1999). Contextual effects of perinatal substance exposure and Black and White women in California. Social *Perspectives, 42,* 141–156.

Galea, S., Ahern, J., Tracy, M., Rudenstine, S., & Vlahov, D. (2007). Education inequality and use of cigarettes, alcohol, and marijuana. *Drug and Alcohol Dependence, 90*(Suppl. 1), S4–S15.

Galea, S., Ahern, J., Tracy, S., & Vlahov, D. (2007). Neighborhood income and income distribution and the use of cigarettes, alcohol, and marijuana. *American Journal of Preventive Medicine, 32*(6, Suppl.), S195–S202.

Green, B. L., Furrer, C., & McAllister, C. (2007). How do relationships support parenting? Effects of attachment style and social support on parenting behavior in an at-risk population. *American Journal of Community Psychology, 40,* 96–108.

Greenberger, E., Steinberg, L., & Vaux, A. (1981). Adolescents who work: Health and behavioral consequences of job stress. *Developmental Psychology, 17,* 691–703.

Groh, D. R., Jason, L. A., Davis, M. I., Olson, B. D., & Ferrari, J. R. (2007). Friends, family, and alcohol abuse: An examination of general and alcohol-specific social support. *American Journal on Addictions, 16,* 49–55.

Gruenwald, P. J. (2007). The spatial ecology of alcohol problems: Niche theory and assortative drinking. *Addiction, 102,* 870–878.

Guo, J., Hill, K. G., Hawkins, D., Catalano, R. F., & Abbott, R. D. (2002). A developmental analysis of sociodemographic, family, and peer effects on adolescent illicit drug initiation. *Journal of the American Academy of Child & Adolescent Psychiatry, 41,* 838–845.

Harris, M. M., & Fennell, M. L. (1988). A multivariate model of job stress and alcohol consumption. *Sociological Quarterly, 29,* 391–406.

Hipp, J. R. (2007). Block, tract, and levels of aggregation: Neighborhood structure and crime and disorder as a case in point. *American Sociological Review, 72,* 659–680.

Jang, S. J., & Johnson, B. (2001). Neighborhood disorder, individual religiosity, and adolescent use of illicit drugs: A test of multilevel hypotheses. *Criminology, 39,* 109–143.

Jencks, C., & Mayer, S. E. (1990). The social consequences of growing up in a poor neighborhood. In L. E. Lynn Jr. & M. G. H. McGeary (Eds.), *Inner-city poverty in the United States* (pp. 111–186). Washington, DC: National Academy Press.

Keels, M., Duncan, G. J., DeLuca, S., Mendenhall, R., & Rosenbaum, J. (2005). Fifteen years later: Can residential mobility programs provide a long-term escape from neighborhood segregation, crime, and poverty? *Demography, 42,* 51–73.

Klebanov, P. K., Brooks-Gunn, J., & Duncan, G. J. (1994). Does neighborhood and family poverty affect mothers' parenting, mental health, and social support? *Journal of Marriage and the Family, 56,* 441–455.

Kleinschmidt, I., Hills, M., & Elliott, P. (1995). Smoking behaviour can be predicted by neighbourhood deprivation measures. *Journal of Epidemiology and Community Health, 49*(Suppl. 2), S72–S77.

Kling, J. R., Leibman, J. B., & Katz, L. F. (2007). Experimental analysis of neighborhood effects. *Econometrica, 75,* 83–119.

Kulis, S., Marsiglia, F. F., Sicotte, D., & Nieri, T. (2007). Neighborhood effects on youth substance use in a southwestern city. *Sociological Perspectives, 50,* 273–301.

Kumar, R., O'Malley, P. M., Johnston, L. D., Schulenberg, J. E., & Bachman, J. G. (2002). Effect of school-level norms on student substance use. *Prevention Science, 3,* 105–124.

Lambert, S. F., Brown, T. L., Phillips, C. M., & Ialongo, N. S. (2004). The relationship between perceptions of neighborhood characteristics and substance use among urban African American adolescents. *American Journal of Community Psychology, 34,* 205–218.

Lamborn, S. D., Mounts, N. S., Steinberg, L., & Dornbusch, S. M. (1991). Patterns of competence and adjustment among adolescents from authoritative, authoritarian, indulgent, and neglectful families. *Child Development, 62,* 1049–1065.

Latkin, C. A., Curry, A. D., Hua, W., & Davey, M. (2007). Direct and indirect associations of neighborhood disorder with drug use and high-risk sexual partners. *American Journal of Preventive Medicine, 32*(6, Suppl.), S234–S241.

Latkin, C. A., Williams, C. T., Wang, J., & Curry, A. D. (2005). Neighborhood social disorder as a determinant of drug injection behaviors: A structural equation modeling approach. *Health Psychology, 24,* 96–100.

Lerman, R. I. (2000). *Are teens in low-income and welfare families working too much?* (Series B, No. B-25). Washington, DC: Urban Institute.

Leventhal, T., & Brooks-Gunn, J. (2000). The neighborhoods they live in: The effects of neighborhood residence on child and adolescent outcomes. *Psychological Bulletin, 26,* 309–337.

Leventhal, T., & Brooks-Gunn, J. (2003). Moving to opportunity: An experimental study of neighborhood effects on mental health. *American Journal of Public Health, 93,* 1576–1582.

Leventhal, T., & Brooks-Gunn, J. (2005). Neighborhood and gender effects on family processes: Results from the Moving to Opportunity program. *Family Relations, 54,* 633–643.

Littell, J., & Wynn, J. (1989). *The availability and use of community resources for young adolescents in an inner-city and a suburban community.* Chicago: Chapin Hall Center for Children at the University of Chicago.

Luthar, S. S. (2003). The culture of affluence: Psychological costs of material wealth. *Child Development, 74,* 1581–1593.

Mahoney, J. L., Stattin, H., & Magnusson, D. (2001). Youth recreation centre participation and criminal offending: A 20-year longitudinal study of Swedish boys. *International Journal of Behavioral Development, 25,* 509–520.

Martino, S. C., Collins, R. L., & Ellickson, P. L. (2005). Cross-lagged relationships between substance use and intimate partner violence among a sample of young adult women. *Journal of Studies on Alcohol, 66,* 139–148.

Martuzzi, M., Grundy, C., & Elliott, P. (1998). Perinatal mortality in an English health region: Geographical distribution and association with socio-economic factors. *Paediatric and Perinatal Epidemiology, 12,* 263–276.

McLoyd, V. (1990). The impact of economic hardship on Black families and children: Psychological distress, parenting, and socioemotional development. *Child Development, 61,* 311–346.

Merline, A. C., O'Malley, P. M., Schulenberg, J. E., Bachman, J. G., & Johnston, L. D. (2004). Substance use among adults 35 years of age: Prevalence, adulthood predictors, and impact of adolescent substance use. *American Journal of Public Health, 94,* 96–102.

Mihalic, S. W., & Elliott, D. (1997). Short- and long-term consequences of adolescent work. *Youth and Society, 28,* 464–498.

Norstrom, T., & Skog, O. (2005). Saturday opening of alcohol retail shops in Sweden: An experiment in two phases. *Addiction, 100,* 767–776.

Novak, S. P., Reardon, S. F., & Buka, S. L. (2002). How beliefs about substance use differ by socio-demographic characteristics, individual experiences, and neighborhood environments among urban adolescents. *Journal of Drug Education, 32,* 319–342.

Novak, S. P., Reardon, S. F., Raudenbush, S. W., & Buka, S. L. (2006). Retail tobacco outlet density and youth cigarette smoking: A propensity-modeling approach. *American Journal of Public Health, 96,* 670–676.

Oreopoulos, P. (2003). The long-run consequences of living in a poor neighborhood. *Quarterly Journal of Economics, 118,* 1533–1575.

Paschall, M. J., & Hubbard, M. L. (1998). Effects of neighborhood and family stressors on African American male adolescents' self-worth and propensity for violent behavior. *Journal of Consulting and Clinical Psychology, 66,* 825–831.

Peirce, R. S., Frone, M. R., Russell, M., & Cooper, M. L. (1996). Financial stress, social support, and alcohol involvement: A longitudinal test of the buffering hypothesis in a general population survey. *Health Psychology, 15,* 38–47.

Pollack, C. E., Cubbin, C., Ahn, D., & Winkleby, M. (2005). Neighbourhood deprivation and alcohol consumption: Does the availability of alcohol play a role? *International Journal of Epidemiology, 34,* 772–780.

Popkin, S. J., Rosenbaum, J. E., & Meaden, P. M. (1993). Labor market experiences of low-income Black women in middle-class suburbs: Evidence from a survey of Gautreaux program participants. *Journal of Policy Analysis and Management, 12,* 556–573.

Raudenbush, S. W., & Sampson, R. J. (1999). Ecometrics: Toward a science of assessing ecological settings, with application to the systematic social observation of neighborhoods. *Sociological Methodology, 29,* 1–41.

Rosenbaum, J. E. (1995). Changing the geography of opportunity by expanding residential choice: Lessons from the Gautreaux program. *Housing Policy Debate, 6,* 231–269.

Rouse, C. E., & Barrow, L. (2006). U.S. elementary and secondary schools: Equalizing opportunity or replicating the status quo? *Future of Children, 16,* 99–123.

Rubinowitz, L. S., & Rosenbaum, J. E. (2000). *Crossing the class and color lines: From public housing to White suburbia.* Chicago: University of Chicago Press.

Salomon, A., Bassuk, S. S., & Huntington, N. (2002). The relationship between intimate partner violence and the use of addictive substances in poor and homeless single mothers. *Violence Against Women, 8,* 785–815.

Sampson, R. J. (1997). Collective regulation of adolescent misbehavior: Validation results from eighty Chicago neighborhoods. *Journal of Adolescent Research, 12,* 227–244.

Sampson, R. J., Morenoff, J. D., & Earls, F. (1999). Beyond social capital: Spatial dynamics of collective efficacy for children. *American Sociological Review, 64,* 633–660.

Sampson, R. J., & Raudenbush, S. W. (1999). Systematic social observation of public spaces: A new look at disorder in urban neighborhoods. *American Journal of Sociology, 105,* 603–651.

Sampson, R. J., Raudenbush, S. W., & Earls, F. (1997, August 15). Neighborhoods and violent crime: A multilevel study of collective efficacy. *Science, 277,* 918–924.

Sastry, N., Pebley, A. R., & Zonta, M. (2002). *Neighborhood definitions and the spatial dimensions of daily life in Los Angeles.* Santa Monica, CA: RAND.

Saxe, L., Kadushin, C., Beveridge, A., Livert, D., Tighe, E., Rindskopf, D., et al. (2001). The visibility of illicit drugs: Implications for community-based drug control strategies. *American Journal of Public Health, 91,* 1987–1994.

Scheier, L. M., Botvin, G. J., & Miller, N. L. (1999). Life events, neighborhood stress, psychosocial functioning, and alcohol use among urban minority youth. *Journal of Child and Adolescent Substance Use, 9,* 19–50.

Scheier, L. M., Miller, N. L., Ifill-Williams, M., & Botvin, G. J. (2001). Perceived neighborhood risk as a predictor of drug use among ethnic minority adolescents: Moderating influences of psychosocial functioning. *Journal of Child and Adolescent Substance Abuse, 11,* 67–105.

Schuckit, M. A., & Smith, T. L. (2000). The relationships of a family history of alcohol dependence, a low level of response to alcohol and six domains of life functioning to the development of alcohol use disorders. *Journal of Studies on Alcohol, 61,* 827–835.

Scribner, R. A., Cohen, D. A., & Fisher, W. (2000). Evidence of a structural effect for alcohol outlet density: A multilevel analysis. *Alcoholism: Clinical and Experimental Research, 24,* 188–195.

Shaw, C., & McKay, H. (1969). *Juvenile delinquency and urban areas* (Rev. ed.). Chicago: University of Chicago Press.

Squires, G. D., & Kubrin, C. E. (2005). Privileged places: Race, uneven development and the geography of opportunity in urban America. *Urban Studies, 42,* 47–68.

Steinberg, L., & Dornbusch, S. M. (1991). Negative correlates of part-time employment during adolescence: Replication and elaboration. *Developmental Psychology, 27,* 304–313.

Steinberg, L., Fegley, S., & Dornbusch, S. M. (1993). Negative impact of part-time work on adolescent adjustment: Evidence from a longitudinal study. *Developmental Psychology, 29,* 171–180.

Steptoe, A., & Feldman, P. J. (2001). Neighborhood problems as sources of chronic stress: Development of a measure of neighborhood problems, and associations with socioeconomic status and health. *Annals of Behavioral Medicine, 23,* 177–185.

Stimpson, J., Ju, H., Raji, M. A., & Eschbach, K. (2007). Neighborhood deprivation and health risk behaviors in NHANES III. *American Journal of Health Behavior, 31,* 215–222.

Tebes, J. K., Feinn, R., Vanderploeg, J. J., Chinman, M. J., Shepard, J., Brabham, T., et al. (2007). Impact of a positive youth development program in urban after-school settings on the prevention of adolescent substance use. *Journal of Adolescent Health, 41,* 239–247.

Wardle, J., Jarvis, M. J., Steggles, N., Sutton, S., Williamson, S., Farrimond, H., et al. (2003). Socioeconomic disparities in cancer-risk behaviors in adolescence: Baseline results from the Health and Behaviour in Teenagers Study (HABITS). *Preventive Medicine, 36,* 721–730.

Whisman, M. A. (2007). Marital distress and DSM–IV psychiatric disorders in a population-based national survey. *Journal of Abnormal Psychology, 116,* 638–643.

Whisman, M. A., Uebelacker, L. A., & Bruce, M. L. (2006). Longitudinal association between marital dissatisfaction and alcohol use disorders in a community sample. *Journal of Family Psychology, 20,* 164–167.

Williams, C. T., & Latkin, C. A. (2007). Neighborhood socioeconomic status, personal network attributes, and use of heroin and cocaine. *American Journal of Preventive Medicine, 32*(6, Suppl.), S203–S210.

Wilson, J. Q., & Kelling, G. (1982). The police and neighborhood safety: Broken windows. *Atlantic, 127,* 29–38.

Wilson, N., Syme, S. L., Boyce, W. T., Battistich, V. A., & Selvin, S. (2005). Adolescent alcohol, tobacco, and marijuana use: The influence of neighborhood disorder and hope. *American Journal of Health Promotion, 20,* 11–19.

Zimmerman, M. A., Bingenheimer, J. B., & Notaro, P. C. (2002). Natural mentors and adolescent resiliency: A study of urban youth. *American Journal of Community Psychology, 30,* 221–243.

CHAPTER 23

THE SCHOOL CONTEXT OF ADOLESCENT SUBSTANCE USE

Susan T. Ennett and Susan Haws

The social experience of adolescence as distinct from childhood and young adulthood has been shaped and sustained by public education. Early in U.S. history, schools typically served youth younger than age 14, grouped students of all ages, and were open for only a few months of the year when youth were free from their farming and home activities (Demos & Demos, 1969; Modell & Goodman, 1990). Industrialization, stricter child labor laws that limited youth participation in the workforce, and the emergence of public high schools in the 20th century channeled youth into their own social world at school apart from family and work (Fuller, 1983; Modell & Goodman, 1990). Then and today, with about a third of adolescents' waking hours spent at school in the company of their peers, schools help construct the social world of adolescents.

We examine how schools, both as peer-oriented social systems and as formally organized institutions with adult governance, affect development of adolescent alcohol, tobacco, and other drug use. Although schools have been the primary venue for substance use prevention programs, the school context has typically not been a focus of research concerned with the etiology of adolescent substance use. Yet from the research evaluating school substance use prevention programs, we know that schools differ in the prevalence of student substance use, suggesting that characteristics of schools may account for these differences. From the standpoint of social ecological theories, which are increasingly prevalent in guiding understanding of youth risk

behaviors, part of the explanation for these school differences must reside in characteristics of schools.

We (a) review theories that suggest how schools might influence adolescent substance use; (b) visit the evidence that schools differ appreciably in prevalence of substance use; (c) address methodological challenges to determining whether those prevalence differences are meaningful in an etiologic sense, specifically, the challenges in separating school characteristics that influence substance use from attributes of the students populating schools; (d) describe methodological approaches to identifying school effects on adolescent substance use; and (e) review the empirical evidence supporting school effects on adolescent substance use. We conclude with an assessment of whether schools matter in explaining adolescent drug use.

THEORETICAL PERSPECTIVES

A social ecological perspective is aptly applied to research on the school context of adolescent substance use. An ecological perspective posits effects on substance use of the complex of relations among an adolescent's personal characteristics; the ever-changing immediate social environments in which the adolescent lives, including school; and the larger cultural environment (Bronfenbrenner, 1979; Cook, Herman, Phillips, & Settersten, 2002). Along with the family, peers, and neighborhood, schools are posited as a primary socialization agent that directly influences and conditions adolescent substance use.

We are grateful for the helpful comments of Heathe Luz McNaughton-Reyes.

Despite their centrality, little is known regarding the importance of schools given current theoretical models of drug use. Furthermore, we know little about schools as compared with family and peer groups and even less with respect to the elements of schools that convey the greatest impact on drug use.

Theoretical attention to schools is needed given their primacy as a socialization context and because of their complex nature. Specifically, schools are both a social setting and an institutional setting, characterized on the one hand by social interactions among students and on the other hand by school policies and organizational and management practices involving interactions with teachers and school administrators. The dual social and institutional nature of schools is rarely emphasized in theories of adolescent substance use. In addition, theories of adolescent substance use that include consideration of the school context generally do not highlight the processes through which school- and individual-level attributes jointly influence youth substance use, although some indirect effects of schools through more proximal, individual-level attributes are posited.

We review six theories relevant to how schools influence adolescent substance use, emphasizing theories that include school-level constructs and processes. Social contagion theory (Rowe & Rodgers, 1991) and social network theory (e.g., Knoke & Kuklinski, 1982; Wasserman & Faust, 1994) focus on how the network of relationships among all adolescents in the school can promote or inhibit substance use. The theory of health-promoting schools is concerned almost exclusively with how institutional aspects of schools—the instructional and regulatory climate—influence adolescent substance use (Aveyard, Markham, Lancashire, et al., 2004; Markham & Aveyard, 2003). Elliott's integrated theory of delinquency and drug use (Elliott, Ageton, & Canter, 1979; Elliott, Huizinga, & Ageton, 1985), the social development model (Catalano & Hawkins, 1996; Hawkins & Weis, 1985), and primary socialization theory (Oetting & Donnermeyer, 1998), integrate constructs from social learning and social control theories, such as social modeling and social bonds, in positing effects of both peers and the school setting on adolescent sub-

stance use. Organizational aspects of schools as learning environments are emphasized in these three theories, but the peer group is conceptualized primarily at the more immediate level of close friends rather than at the school level.

Social Contagion Theory

Social contagion theory is based on epidemiologic disease transmission models and posits the spread of adolescent transitional behaviors, such as smoking and drinking, through an interactive adolescent social network (Rowe, Chassin, Presson, & Edwards, 1992; Rowe & Rodgers, 1991). The theory assumes that behaviors will spread on the basis of their attractiveness, or the positive utility that adolescents attach to the behaviors. Substance use spreads from carriers (substance users) to susceptible individuals (nonusers) through social contact, with opportunity for contact between users and nonusers as the key mechanism for the spread. Some individuals are posited to be immune to the contagion process. Nonlinear dynamic mathematical models are applied to examine the fit of the social contagion process to observed transitions in adolescent substance use.

Although the programming and mathematical requirements of fitting contagion models have possibly limited application of the theory, it has conceptual utility. The theory draws attention to the larger social system of peers in the school setting and emphasizes the spread of substance use through the opportunity for social contact and face-to-face interactions. Where substance use is valued, the theory suggests faster spread through more socially involved individuals and slower spread to those more socially isolated. Similarly, the theory suggests that there may be boundaries of contagion, depending on the extent to which subpopulations, such as those defined by race and ethnicity, interact with each other.

Social Network Theory

Social network theory is concerned with the social relationships between individuals in a social system, such as between adolescents in school. The crux of the theory is that the social relationships linking individuals provide channels that facilitate flow of information or other resources, and these relationships form complex patterns that have direct implications for the behavior of individuals (e.g., Knoke & Kuklinski, 1982; Wasserman & Faust, 1994). Social network analysis is the analysis of the ties between individuals, such as friendship ties between adolescents, that can reveal relational patterns. Social network theory and network analytic methods provide a perspective on how to conceptualize and measure adolescent substance use behavior in a relational context.

Although it provides a relational perspective, social network theory is not so much a single theory as a set of relational properties for characterizing social networks. As applied to adolescent substance use, less attention has been focused on properties of the overall school network than on attributes of adolescents within school networks, albeit attributes that can only be defined in reference to the entire set of relationships among students in a school. Two examples of individual-level attributes are an adolescent's social position in the school network as a group member, liaison or bridge between groups, or isolate (e.g., Ennett & Bauman, 1993) and an adolescent's centrality in the network (e.g., Killeya-Jones, Nakajima, & Costanzo, 2007). At the school level, measures could be defined operationally as the proportion of each social position and proportion of substance users in each position, or in terms of the substance use behavior of the most central adolescents in the school. The distribution of social positions should have relevance to the social contagion process. The most central adolescents in the school network, by virtue of having friendship patterns that connect them directly and indirectly with many others in the network, are influential members of the student body and may set standards for substance use behavior followed by other students.

Social network theory also assumes that patterns characterizing the whole network are important for understanding the behavior of the whole population. Two network properties that have received some attention in the adolescent substance use literature are the overall connectedness, or density, of a network and the average social distance between pairs of substance users and nonusers (Ennett et al., 2006). Denser networks are characterized by higher proportions of friendship ties among adolescents and

more closely knit school communities with presumed greater potential for social contagion of substance use and for regulating behavioral norms. In schools with shorter average social distance to a substance user, via friends of friends, opportunity for social contact between a nonuser and a user are greater, thus enhancing the possibility of social contagion of substance use.

Theory of Health-Promoting Schools

Noting the scarcity of investigations into the effects of schools on adolescent substance use and the lack of theoretical justification for the characteristics of schools studied, Aveyard, Markham, Lancashire, et al. (2004; Markham & Aveyard, 2003) proposed a theory of health-promoting schools. The theory is based on the idea that adolescent health is promoted when students function well and that the primary mechanisms through which schools promote student functioning are school organization, curriculum development, and pedagogic practice.

Schools are thought to facilitate two types of learning, termed the *instructional* and the *regulatory* orders. The instructional order is focused on relaying knowledge and skills; the regulatory order is focused on relaying values and concerned with the conduct and character of students. Schools that effectively relay the instructional order are seen as providing appropriate support needed for learning, where support refers to practical assistance, advice, and responsiveness. Schools that effectively relay the regulatory order are hypothesized as providing appropriate control, meaning expectations for behavior and disciplinary practices that result in students learning appropriate forms of behavior, including reasons to avoid drug use.

Schools that provide better quality support and control, termed *authoritative* schools, are posited to have more influence on students than schools with lower quality support and control and thus to be marked by better-than-expected student learning outcomes and social behaviors after accounting for the students' background characteristics. In authoritative schools, students are likely to adopt values and identities that the school explicitly espouses and implicitly embodies. Because all schools hold antisubstance use values, authoritative schools are likely to have lower rates of substance use than schools with poorer quality support and control.

Integrated Theory of Delinquency and Drug Use

Elliott's integrated theory (Elliott et al., 1979, 1985) is one of several theories of adolescent risk behaviors that integrates concepts from social control and social learning theories (Petraitis, Flay, & Miller, 1995). Social learning theory posits that adolescent substance use is learned behavior acquired through social interactions and reinforcement and the resulting ratio of exposure to prosocial versus antisocial definitions for use. Social control theory posits that a tendency toward deviance is universally shared but manifested only when the bond between an individual and society is weakened. The integrated theory proposes that in the face of strain from frustrated needs and wants, inadequate socialization by parents, and social disorganization in primary contexts, adolescents form weak conventional bonds. The breakdown of ties to family, school, and community and feelings of disenfranchisement from friends lead adolescents to form strong bonds with delinquent, substance-using peers, with these bonds leading to substance use.

Elliott's integrated theory (Elliott et al., 1979, 1985) places more emphasis than other integrated theories on social structural and systems variables, particularly neighborhood and school contextual variables (Petraitis et al., 1995). According to the theory, social disorganization is the breakdown of established institutions or the inability of local institutions to control the behavior of their members. Socially disorganized neighborhoods are marked by the absence of effective social or cultural organization that makes it difficult to establish common values and norms, informal support networks, and effective social controls. In a similar fashion, socially disorganized schools are characterized by low levels of monitoring and supervision. Elliott (1994) noted that schools are social systems to be negotiated by students, with school and peer performance demands and developmental tasks to be met. These include expectations for academic success, peer approval, development of interpersonal competencies, and the like. Stress and frustration result when students fail

to meet such expectations, with exacerbated effects in socially disorganized schools.

Social Development Model

The social development model provides a life-span perspective from birth through high school on development of prosocial and antisocial behaviors, such as substance use (Catalano & Hawkins, 1996; Hawkins & Weis, 1985). The theory incorporates concepts from social learning (opportunities, reinforcements, and rewards for prosocial and antisocial behaviors), social control (social bonds to parents, peers, school, and community; belief in the moral order; belief in values consistent with prosocial behavior), and differential association (role for both prosocial and antisocial bonding) theories in positing developmental processes that predict both pro- and antisocial behaviors.

The pathways to pro- and antisocial behaviors emphasize individual-level characteristics such as adolescents' perceptions of opportunities for participation in school activities as distinct from actual opportunities. School-level variables are incorporated in the exogenous construct of external constraint. The clarity, consistency, and immediacy of external constraints, such as rules, policies, and management practices that govern schools and classrooms, are hypothesized to influence an adolescent's perceived reinforcement for pro- and antisocial behavior. A clearly stated substance use policy and consistent monitoring of student behavior and policy enforcement are posited to result in students perceiving negative consequences for behaviors that violate the rules and reinforcement for not engaging in substance use. The same principles of how external constraints operate can be applied to school rules and practices that promote prosocial behaviors. External factors, however, have no direct effects on behavior. All effects of external constraints in schools and other socializing units are hypothesized to be mediated by the developmental pathways to pro- and antisocial behavior.

Perhaps one of the most salient aspects of the social development model to consideration of the school context of adolescent substance use is the theory's use of school phases—preschool, elementary school, middle school, and high school—to mark developmental periods. In so doing, the theory calls attention to the importance of the school experience and transitions, as opposed, for example, to cognitive or moral development, in marking development and the importance of the school as a socialization unit. The pathways in the general model of social development are tailored to each phase of schooling to take account of the changing social environment in schools and the shifting balance of influence among families, schools, and peers.

Primary Socialization Theory

The fundamental premise of primary socialization theory is that normative and deviant behaviors are learned in the context of interactions with three primary socialization sources, namely, family, school, and peers (Oetting & Donnermeyer, 1998). The theory posits that the bonds between an adolescent and his or her family, school, and peers are the channels through which prosocial and deviant norms are communicated and through which behavior is directly monitored, reinforced, and sanctioned. Weak bonds between the adolescent and his or her family or school, as well as weak bonds between the family and school, are hypothesized to increase the likelihood of the adolescent's bonding with a deviant peer cluster and thus of engaging in deviant behaviors. Although the theory hypothesizes that bonds to family and school are typically prosocial, it allows for the possibility of deviant norms in these contexts.

Dysfunctional schools are characterized as those in which deviant behavior is not adequately controlled and other school problems compromise the ability of schools to teach and transmit prosocial norms. On the basis of several empirical studies, Oetting and Donnermayer (1998) cited examples of school problems such as unclear rules, poorly trained teachers, disruptive classrooms, prejudice against minority students, and lack of financial or other resources needed to provide youth with successful learning experiences and rewards for being in school. When the school is not functioning well, students will not form strong bonds to the school and are more likely to seek friendships with deviant peers. In contrast, when the school is functioning well, students form positive ties to school, allowing

the school to communicate positive norms and provide strong sanctions against behaviors.

The peer focus in primary socialization theory emphasizes the activity of peer clusters, consisting of best friend dyads, small groups of close friends, and couples. Although the theory recognizes the broader peer environment at school, it suggests that its effects will be indirect and weak compared with the direct and powerful effects of peer clusters.

Need for Theoretical Integration of Social and Institutional Processes in the School Context

None of the six theories elaborated here provides an explanation for adolescent substance use that explicitly integrates aspects of the school social and institutional environments. Theoretical consideration of how processes in the social and institutional environments interrelate is needed. In this respect, the social network that characterizes a school's peer environment and the school's organizational practices and learning culture are undoubtedly interdependent. When the school environment is disorganized and dysfunctional, and perhaps specifically when clear communication of antisubstance use norms and policies does not exist and consistent enforcement is lacking, it is likely that effects will be evident in the peer network. For example, the peer social network in disorganized school environments may be characterized by low density (connections among students) and higher proportions of isolated groups and individuals, with a resulting lack of consensus around norms for behaviors. The transitions from elementary to middle school and from middle school to high school are certain to cause disruptions in peer social networks, perhaps with accompanying impact on the clarity of peer substance use norms that leaves adolescents particularly vulnerable to substance use engagement.

Similarly, when there is not clear and consistent communication about substance use norms, policies, and enforcement, perhaps youth leaders emerge who represent values other than the traditional antisubstance use values attributed to schools. In contrast, perhaps well-functioning schools promote social competencies among adolescents, including the formation of friendships among students. More

447

cohesive social networks in well-functioning schools may support prosocial norms of behavior, with the social network as an effective enforcer of norms that reflect the policies and practices of teachers and school administrators.

Although integrated theory, the social development model, and primary socialization theory suggest indirect effects of school contextual factors on adolescent substance use through the formation of friendships with deviant peers, additional consideration of the mechanisms of school influences is needed. In particular, social ecological theories focus on the importance of interactions between contextual and individual characteristics. How school characteristics condition effects of other contextual or student attributes is a useful area for theorizing.

VARIABILITY ACROSS SCHOOLS IN SUBSTANCE USE

Both national and local studies of adolescent alcohol, tobacco, and other drug use, as well as studies from other countries, have noted appreciable differences in school prevalence of substance use (e.g., Aveyard, Markham, & Cheng, 2004; Ennett, Flewelling, Lindrooth, & Norton, 1997; Roski et al., 1997). As an example, in a sample of 36 elementary schools, Ennett et al. (1997) reported that school prevalence of lifetime alcohol use of 6th graders ranged from 20% to almost 80%. At the same grade level, prevalence of lifetime cigarette and marijuana use across schools ranged from 0% to 55% and 0% to 28%, respectively.

Other evidence of school variability in substance use comes primarily from trials of school-based smoking and other substance use prevention programs that reported the intraclass correlation coefficient (ICC) for substance use outcome measures (e.g., Murray et al., 1994; Murray & Short, 1997; O'Malley, Johnston, Bachman, Schulenberg, & Kumar, 2006; Scheier, Griffin, Doyle, & Botvin, 2002). The ICC statistic measures the similarity or homogeneity among individuals within a group, such as students in the same school, on some dimension. For a sample of n students nested within j schools, an ICC of .05 can be interpreted as the average correlation in substance use between any two students in the same school. As a measure of school variance in substance use, it can also be interpreted as the proportion of variance in substance use due exclusively to variations between schools. Interpreted this way, an ICC of .05 signifies that 5% of variance in substance use is the result of differences among schools. ICCs can range between 0 and 1; a value of 1 indicates perfect positive correlation of individual behavior within schools, meaning that all students within schools have the same substance use behavior and all of the variance in substance use can be attributed to differences among schools. A value of zero indicates no association within schools, meaning that the behavior of students within schools is not correlated and none of the variance in substance use can be attributed to differences among schools. ICCs for alcohol, tobacco, and marijuana use are consistently found to be significantly different from zero, suggesting within-school similarity of substance use and school-to-school differences in use.

School ICCs for adolescent substance use (including primarily alcohol, cigarettes, and marijuana) have typically ranged from just above zero to around .07, meaning that up to about 7% of the variance in youth substance use is the result of school effects and thus potentially explainable by school characteristics. These estimates were confirmed in the most recent and comprehensive report on substance use differences in U.S. middle and high schools from the Monitoring the Future project's annual surveys of nationally representative samples of 8th-, 10th-, and 12th-grade students (O'Malley et al., 2006). On the basis of reports of use in the past 30 days, the variance between schools in cigarette smoking ranged from approximately 3% to 6%; for alcohol use, from 2% to 7%; and for marijuana use, from 3% to 4%. The higher estimates for alcohol use as compared with those for cigarettes and marijuana are generally consistent with estimates from other studies (Ennett et al., 1997; Scheier et al., 2002).

The reported variations in school prevalence of substance use and consistent findings of small but significant school ICC estimates suggest that students attending the same school resemble each other in substance use. Variance in individual substance use cannot be explained by individual characteristics alone: A significant proportion of variance in substance use is the result of differences between schools. According to theories of school contextual effects, similarity among students in the same school is likely due to the shared peer environment or common school climate. As also suggested by theory (Markham & Aveyard, 2003), however, some of the differences between schools is because of the shared background characteristics of students.

Aveyard, Markham, and Cheng (2004) distinguished between compositional, aggregate, and contextual group effects. *Compositional effects* refer to student-level characteristics (e.g., race and ethnicity, gender), *aggregate effects* represent summary measures of student characteristics (e.g., proportion of minority students), and *contextual effects* are features of schools not reducible to characteristics of the group, such as policies and physical characteristics of schools. Because student selection into schools is not random, with schools often drawing students from the same neighborhoods, students in the same school tend to share similar background characteristics. Because demographic and other individual-level characteristics may be related to both the school attended and adolescent substance use, individual-level characteristics may confound the association between school and substance use. When student compositional characteristics are not accounted for, estimates of the effect of school aggregate and contextual characteristics may be misleading.

Murray and Short (1997) adjusted school ICCs for several tobacco use measures for age, gender, and other individual-level variables (e.g., family structure; mother, father, and sibling smoking). Control for the covariates reduced the total between-school variance by 16% to 24%, making it clear that at least some of the apparent effect of school characteristics on student substance use was because of the differences between schools in the individual characteristics of their student bodies. In a study conducted by Aveyard et al. (2005), several student compositional characteristics were significantly associated with school prevalence of smoking, but controlling for the compositional variables had the reverse effect of increasing the estimate of unexplained between-school variation in smoking. The findings of both studies suggest the importance of unmeasured school variables in explaining school differences in smoking prevalence. As described in the next section, the need to adjust in analysis for the similarity among students within schools and for student characteristics is critical to the estimation of school-level effects on adolescent substance use.

METHODS OF ESTIMATING SCHOOL-LEVEL EFFECTS ON ADOLESCENT SUBSTANCE USE

Three approaches to examining school-level effects on adolescent substance use reflected in the literature are contextual studies, ecological studies, and multilevel studies. In contextual studies, individual adolescents are the unit of analysis, but school-level variables are appended to each adolescent and examined in addition to individual-level attributes. Contextual studies allow investigation of school effects after controlling for individual-level variables, but they do not provide a means to estimate school-to-school variability in designated measures. Additionally, unless special methods are used to account for the clustering of observations within schools, standard errors of estimates will be incorrect, potentially leading to spurious statistically significant associations (Diez Roux, 2003). Before the more recent advent of multilevel studies, studies of school effects often used contextual analysis without correction for dependence among students in the same school (e.g., Allison et al., 1999; McBride et al., 1995).

In ecological studies, schools are the unit of analysis, and associations between school-level measures of substance use, such as the proportion of current users, and contextual and/or aggregate compositional characteristics of schools, are examined (e.g., Ennett et al., 1997; Roski et al., 1997). Ecological studies allow investigation of school characteristics that could explain differences across schools in substance use. However, the joint distribution of individual-level variables within schools is unknown in ecological studies, making it difficult to determine the presence and extent of confounding or moderation of ecological relationships by characteristics of the students (Diez Roux, 2003). Although, as suggested in the previous section, confounding is reduced by including student compositional characteristics, student-level influences that are not controlled can produce spurious relationships or lead to underestimation or overestimation of the strength of ecological relationships (Aveyard, Markham, & Cheng, 2004). In addition to limitations in drawing inferences about ecological relationships, inferences from ecological studies about effects of school characteristics on individual-level substance use are inappropriate. Because in most cases interest rests with explaining variability across individuals in substance use as a function of both individual and school characteristics, ecological studies are not a preferred approach.

Multilevel studies are the method of choice for examining school effects on youth substance use. In multilevel studies, the individual is the unit of analysis, and both individual- and school-level characteristics are simultaneously examined as predictors of individual adolescent substance use. The statistical details of multilevel models, also known as random effects models, random coefficient models, and hierarchical linear models, are beyond the scope of this chapter (see, for example, Kreft & Leeuw, 1998; Raudenbush & Bryk, 2002). The conceptual underpinnings and application to analysis of school-level effects, however, are intuitive.

Multilevel models explicitly recognize and model the hierarchical data structure that describes students nested within school. Two-level models are specified, through equations, in which many Level 1 units (students) are nested within fewer Level 2 units (schools). By extension, three-level models can be specified in which, for example, students are nested within classrooms nested within schools, or in which, for longitudinal data, repeated measures of substance use are nested within students nested within schools. Multilevel models allow variability in substance use at both the individual and the school levels to be examined, and the roles of both individual-level and school-level variables in explaining adolescent substance use and variability across schools in substance use to be investigated. An important feature of multilevel studies is that the correlation in substance use among students within schools (the ICC) is estimated, allowing for valid statistical tests of relationships. In addition, of key importance to investigation of the school context of adolescent substance use, multilevel models allow

the inclusion of control variables at the individual and school levels, the estimation of main effects of individual- and school-level variables, and estimation of cross-level effects. Thus, contextual hypotheses about how school-level characteristics condition relationships between substance use and individual-level characteristics can be examined.

A barrier to use of multilevel models is having a sufficient number of schools in the sample to provide adequate power for analysis and capture sufficient variation in school-level predictors. In addition, although multilevel studies provide valid statistical tests of school-level effects, in a review of the methodological adequacy of studies of school factors implicated in youth smoking, Aveyard, Markham, and Cheng (2004; Aveyard et al., 2005) cautioned that multilevel studies have been subject both to under- and overcontrol of confounders. Studies need to control for individual-level risk factors that could confound relationships between school attributes and smoking, including both demographic and family characteristics such as parental and sibling smoking and measures of the family environment. At the same time, studies should not control for individual characteristics that could be on the causal pathways of school influences, such as school engagement, friend smoking, and psychological variables. Aveyard, Markham, and Cheng (2004; Aveyard et al., 2005) warned that under- and overcontrol of confounding limits conclusions that can be drawn about how schools influence adolescent substance use.

Another caution, with perhaps less severe consequences when ignored, is the potential for school effects to be confounded with uncontrolled higher order effects of communities in which schools are situated (Aveyard et al., 2005; Gottfredson, 2000; Smolkowski, Biglan, Dent, & Seeley, 2006). The demographic composition of schools is primarily determined by characteristics of the community, making compositional indicators for schools and communities largely redundant (Gottfredson, 2000). But to the extent that uncontrolled community characteristics account for school differences in substance use, estimates of school effects will be inflated.

EMPIRICAL EVIDENCE FOR SCHOOL EFFECTS ON ADOLESCENT SUBSTANCE USE

Three main areas of inquiry into school effects on adolescent substance use have been pursued in the literature: (a) school-level peer factors, (b) school climate, and (c) the role of school policies related to substance use. We review the empirical findings from each of these three areas of interest. In addition, we briefly review evidence concerning effects of school structural and compositional characteristics on student drug use.

Because of the methodological advantages described in the previous section, unless otherwise noted, we review only studies that applied multilevel methods or used methods to adjust for clustering of students in schools. Cross-sectional designs are the rule, with exceptions also noted. In almost all studies, the investigators began by investigating school-to-school differences in substance use outcomes. We do not review these findings because whenever examined, significant between-school differences were found, with ICCs consistent in magnitude to those reviewed earlier.

Peer Environment

Research on the school peer environment for adolescent substance use, similar to research on close friends, has focused mainly on peer substance use and secondarily on other indicators of the normative environment, such as extent of peer disapproval or perceived harm in substance use. The difference is the investigation of population prevalence of substance use and schoolwide norms. Although a few studies examined only main effects of school variables, it is noteworthy that most studies examined cross-level interactions between school- and individual-level variables.

Two studies applied social contagion models to describe transitions from substance nonuse to use among students in several schools; both are exceptions to the standard of using multilevel analysis of the school peer environment (Rowe et al., 1992; Rowe & Rodgers, 1991). In the first study, epidemic models fit the data well (Rowe & Rodgers, 1991). In longitudinal samples of youth between the ages of 12 and 17 from schools in North Carolina, Florida,

and Baltimore, Maryland, some adolescents were immune to the epidemic process, whereas susceptible individuals converted from nonuse status for cigarettes or alcohol to use status 1 year later after adequate contact with smokers or drinkers. In the second study, the process of transition among four smoking states—nonsmoker, trier, regular smoker, and ex-smoker—was examined in four successive annual cross-sectional samples of youth in Grades 6 through 11 (Rowe et al., 1992). The social contagion model fit best in predicting the transition from nonsmoker to trier, whereas a noncontagion, constant transition rate process better predicted the transition from trier to regular smoker. The findings suggested that peer interactions are more important in the initial transition from abstinence to experimental smoking than in later transitions to regular smoking.

Findings on the contributions of school-level peer variables have been mixed in recent studies that examined only main effects, depending on both the peer attribute examined and the substance use outcome. Ennett et al. (2006) used several waves of data from a panel of sixth, seventh, and eighth graders in three North Carolina school districts to investigate attributes of school social networks related to adolescent substance use. The study design was motivated by social network theory and required that adolescents identify their friends who were also likely to have participated in data collection. This data collection strategy allowed the investigators to measure peer substance use on the basis of peers' actual reports rather than adolescent perceptions. After controlling only for adolescent demographic characteristics, higher prevalence of recent smoking in the school network predicted adolescent smoking, but higher prevalence of drinking and marijuana use did not predict adolescent alcohol or marijuana use. Other social network findings demonstrated that adolescents in school networks characterized by greater density had significantly lower odds of recent smoking and marijuana use but not of alcohol use. The results suggest a protective effect for some substances of a more tightly knit student body.

Pokorny, Jason, and Schoeny (2004) examined the association between an aggregated, school-level variable of perceived peer tobacco use and individual-level current smoking status, controlling for individual perceived peer use and other individual-level variables (e.g., presence of an adult tobacco user in the home). This study relied on data from a sample of 14 schools containing middle-school grades from randomly selected towns in Illinois. The effect of the school-level variable was not significantly associated with adolescent cigarette smoking after controlling for individual-level variables. Swaim (2003) examined aggregated student reports of perceived harm in using marijuana and perceived availability of marijuana, based on data collected from a national sample of 12th graders in 187 public high schools who completed the American Drug and Alcohol Survey. Perceived school availability of marijuana use was significantly associated with adolescent marijuana use, but the average school perception of harm in using marijuana was not associated with reported marijuana use.

Most studies examining the main effects of school-level variables and cross-level interactions between school- and individual-level variables found significant cross-level interactions. Using data collected from 7th through 12th graders in 80 high schools and their feeder schools for the National Longitudinal Study of Adolescent Health, Cleveland and Wiebe (2003) examined the impact of school-level smoking and drinking on adolescent–peer similarity for smoking and drinking. For both tobacco and alcohol use, after adjusting for sex and race and ethnicity, the effect of peer alcohol and tobacco use on adolescent use of these substances was significantly moderated by school-level substance use. The strength of the relationship increased substantially as school levels of use increased.

In another study using National Longitudinal Study of Adolescent Health data but restricted to a subset of 13 schools, Alexander, Piazza, Mekos, and Valente (2001) found a significant interaction between school prevalence of recent smoking and adolescent popularity. Although the study did not use multilevel methods, the investigators adjusted standard errors for the clustering of students within schools. Using a social network approach, adolescent popularity, an indicator of network centrality, was measured by how often each adolescent was nominated as a friend by others in the school, adjusted for the school size. In schools with low smoking rates, popular students were less likely to smoke, whereas in schools with high smoking rates, popular students were more likely to smoke. The authors concluded that popularity carries a differential risk for smoking depending on the school smoking environment.

Kumar, O'Malley, and Johnston (2005) examined 8th-, 10th-, and 12th-grade school norms for drug use in nationally representative samples of public and private schools from the 1999 Monitoring the Future project. Norms were obtained for heavy smoking, drinking, and marijuana use by aggregating student reports of their disapproval of daily cigarette use, heavy drinking, and marijuana use within each school. The probability of a student's daily smoking, heavy alcohol use, and marijuana use was higher in schools in which aggregated school norms reflected a greater tolerance of use, controlling for the student's own disapproval and student and school demographic characteristics. Of greatest interest, there was a significant cross-level interaction indicating a protective effect for 8th- and 10th-grade students who were not themselves disapproving of daily cigarette use but who attended a school in which the school environment was disapproving of cigarette use.

Kuntsche and Jordan (2006) analyzed data from an international health behavior survey conducted with school-age children (eighth and ninth grades) in 182 schools in Switzerland. Data were also obtained from their teachers to assess school factors associated with students' frequency of drunkenness and cannabis (marijuana) use. The school-level variables assessed teachers' perceptions of the frequency of students coming to school drunk or high. The analysis included the school-level variables, each student's report of his or her friends' drunkenness and marijuana use, and the cross-level interactions between use on school premises and perceived friends' use. Marijuana use on school premises, friends' marijuana use, and the cross-level interaction between these variables were significantly associated with adolescent marijuana use after controlling for student age and gender. The strength of the relationship between the adolescent's and friends' use increased with teachers' reports of increasing frequency of student marijuana use on school premises.

Neither the school-level variable nor the cross-level interaction, however, was significant in the alcohol use model.

In a series of studies, Leatherdale and colleagues demonstrated that the prevalence of smoking among students in higher grades in Ontario, Canada, schools, based on aggregated self-reports, was associated with smoking susceptibility (Leatherdale, McDonald, Cameron, Jolin, & Brown, 2006) and experimental smoking (Leatherdale, Cameron, Brown, & McDonald, 2005) among students in lower grades. In addition, these investigators examined interactions between the school prevalence measures and adolescents' reports of their friends' smoking. For 6th and 7th graders in 57 schools and 9th, 10th, and 11th graders in 29 schools, the strength of the relationship between friends' smoking and an adolescent's susceptibility to smoking or to experimental smoking increased when the adolescent attended a school with a relatively high smoking rate among 8th graders or high school students, respectively. In a third study, these researchers found a significant main effect and cross-level interaction between student smoking on the school periphery (aggregated from student reports) and perceived friends' disapproval of smoking (individual level; Leatherdale, Brown, Cameron, & McDonald, 2005). Adolescents with friends who disapproved of smoking were more likely to be susceptible to smoking if they attended a school with smoking on the periphery; for those with friends who approved of smoking, the school environment did not strengthen the relationship between adolescent and friend smoking.

Results of these studies of the school peer environment suggest that student substance use behavior and norms, whether based on aggregated student reports or on teacher reports, are correlated with adolescent substance use. The findings are more consistent for cigarette smoking than for alcohol or marijuana use, although generalizations are limited because of the small samples of schools in some studies and use of nonprobability samples. Of perhaps greatest interest, all of the studies that examined cross-level interactions found significant conditioning effects of the school environment on individual attributes. Higher school prevalence of substance use or other indicators of greater school tolerance of

use typically exacerbated the risk of substance use for adolescents with friends who use substances.

As Cleveland and Wiebe (2003) suggested, in spite of modest main effects of the school environment, as was the case in all studies reviewed here, the conclusion that the school context is relatively unimportant may be warranted only when interactions between school- and individual-level variables are found to be nonsignificant. When investigators examine only main effects of school variables, they fail to recognize that schools do more than directly influence students. As these researchers demonstrated, the range in variance explained by a commonly measured adolescent attribute (i.e., adolescent–peer similarity in tobacco and alcohol use) was increased by severalfold depending on overall school levels of substance use.

School Climate

A substantial body of evidence demonstrates that individual students who bond well to school are less likely to engage in substance use behaviors (see, e.g., Hawkins, Catalano, & Miller, 1992). An emerging area of research revolves around how school climate, most often conceptualized by indicators of school bonding, operates as a school-level predictor of student substance use.

Battistich and Hom (1997), building on the school bonding construct outlined by Hawkins and Weis (1985), proposed a school-level construct reflecting students' sense of their school as a community, defined as schools characterized by caring and supportive relationships, opportunities to participate in school activities and decision making, and shared norms, goals, and values. School community was measured by a 38-item scale tapping these attributes that was administered to a sample of 1,434 fifth and sixth graders from 24 elementary schools in six U.S. school districts. After controlling for individual (gender, ethnicity, grade) and school (school-level poverty, school size, percentage of students with limited English proficiency, and mean achievement level) background characteristics, both the individual and the school measures of school community were negatively associated with a combined measure of cigarette, alcohol, and marijuana use, as well as with the other problem behaviors examined.

A decade later, Henry and Slater (2007) used data from the pretest of a longitudinal drug prevention study involving more than 4,200 middle school students from 32 middle schools in 16 U.S. communities to examine the contextual effect on alcohol use of school attachment as a schoolwide phenomenon, above and beyond individual student reports of attachment. Referencing both the social development model (Hawkins & Weis, 1985) and Elliott's integrated theory of delinquency and drug use (Elliott et al., 1979), Henry and Slater suggested that antisocial behavior is most likely to occur among adolescents experiencing high levels of individual risk factors in a setting in which students tend not to be attached or bonded to school and antisocial norms are prevalent. School attachment was measured by a scale that assessed the student's perception of school and teachers, sense of fitting into school and being liked by teachers, and self-reported school performance. After adjusting for individual and school demographic variables, both the individual-level measures of school attachment and the contextual measure of school attachment were related significantly and inversely to multiple alcohol-related measures.

Taking a different approach to measuring school climate, Aveyard, Markham, Lancashire, et al. (2004) and Bisset, Markham, and Aveyard (2007) operationally defined the theoretical constructs of authoritative or "value-added" and laissez-faire or "value-denuded" schools. The value-added and value-denuded measures were derived from past 5-year averages of data on school achievement and half-day truancy rates routinely collected for every school in England and Wales. School achievement and truancy rates were conceptualized as indirect indicators of the support and control schools provide to relay the instructional and regulatory orders, which were posited to influence substance use behavior. The investigators calculated a combined measure that adjusted for sociodemographic characteristics of each school and described whether a school had better-than-expected or worse-than-expected values on achievement and truancy averages given its sociodemographic profile. Schools 1 standard deviation or more above the average score were categorized as authoritative schools and schools at least 1 standard deviation below the average were categorized as laissez-faire schools.

In the first study, Aveyard, Markham, Lancashire, et al. (2004) examined the effect of being in an authoritative school on risk of regular cigarette smoking in a sample of 23,282 students in the 7th-, 9th-, and 11th-grades in 166 U.K. secondary schools. After adjusting for student demographic characteristics and the smoking habits of mother, father, and siblings, students in authoritative schools had significantly lower odds of smoking compared with students in average schools, whereas those in laissez-faire schools had significantly higher odds of smoking compared with students in average schools. Using data from the same study, Bisset et al. (2007) demonstrated that students in authoritative schools were at lower risk of early initiation of alcohol use, heavy alcohol use, and illicit drug use.

Results of the school climate studies coalesce to provide support for the idea that some aspect(s) of the school's climate and the bonding that it promotes or inhibits are related in important ways to youth substance use. Although the effect sizes tend to be small, they are consistently significant. As the authors of these investigations pointed out, more theoretically grounded explanations for how school-level bonding or climate affects school-to-school variation in substance use are needed, and identification of the school characteristics that facilitate bonding must be pursued through further empirical study.

Substance Use Policies

Assuming school substance use policies are clearly communicated and judiciously enforced, they set norms and expectations for student behavior and specify the disciplinary measures for policy violations. In some sense, substance use policies are an indicator of school climate in conveying a school's commitment to a drug-free environment. Research on the effects of school policies on adolescent substance use has almost uniformly focused on smoking prevention policies. Because more than 96% of U.S. schools have written policies prohibiting cigarette smoking (Jones, Fisher, Greene, Hertz, & Pritzl, 2007), with equivalent percentages prohibiting alcohol and other drug use on school premises

(Small et al., 2001), simple effects of having a policy cannot be determined in U.S. schools or in countries with similar universal levels of policy adoption. In a sample of secondary schools in Belgium, however, Maes and Lievens (2003) measured several policy variables, including whether the school had a drug policy. Having a drug policy, as measured by school administrator data, did not predict students' self-reported regular smoking or drinking. However, and consistent with the school climate findings reviewed previously, students in schools with rules (the nature of the rules was unspecified) that were clearly formulated and communicated to them were at lower risk of smoking and drinking.

Variability across schools has been demonstrated in policy strength or comprehensiveness (Moore, Roberts, & Tudor-Smith, 2001; Pentz et al., 1989) and school compliance or enforcement (Kumar et al., 2005; Pentz et al., 1989; Pinilla, Gonzalez, Barber, & Santana, 2002; Wakefield et al., 2000). In the earliest U.S. study of school smoking policies, and the only study reviewed here that did not use multilevel methods, Pentz et al. (1989) found lower mean amounts of smoking in middle schools with more rather than less comprehensive policies. Similarly, in a more recent multilevel study conducted in secondary schools in Wales, Moore et al. (2001) reported that school prevalence of daily and weekly smoking was inversely related to policy strength. As well, after adjustment for several individual-level variables, policy strength was significantly negatively associated with daily smoking by students.

In the Moore et al. (2001) study, the investigators found that enforcement of school tobacco policies, as reported by teachers, was associated with lower odds of daily and weekly tobacco use by students. Similarly, students in a sample of secondary schools in Spain had lower odds of daily smoking if they attended schools that complied with their antismoking policies, as reported by school directors, as compared with schools that allowed smoking in prohibited areas (Pinilla et al., 2002). Wakefield et al. (2000) reported analogous findings in a U.S. national sample of high schools and students, but with policy enforcement based on aggregated student reports of how many students obeyed the rules. Students in schools with higher levels of

enforcement of smoking bans were less likely to transition through five phases of smoking, from nonsusceptible nonsmoker to established smoker. Finally, in a recent study using national Monitoring the Future data from 8th-, 10th-, and 12th-grade students, students were at lower risk of daily smoking if they attended a school in which compliance with their school tobacco use policy was strictly monitored (Kumar et al., 2005). Monitoring of student behavior was measured by teacher reports obtained through a linked survey of teachers in participating schools. The investigators also found that high school students, but not middle school students, were at higher risk of smoking if school staff were permitted to smoke, which was the case in almost 20% of the middle and high schools in the sample. In contrast to the message of intolerance conveyed by strict monitoring of student behavior, permitting staff smoking may have sent the message that smoking is okay.

Although enforcement has been demonstrated to have a beneficial effect on student substance use, punitive enforcement appears to be counterproductive. In the Pentz (1989) study, policies that emphasized punishment of and severe consequences for violations did not decrease school smoking prevalence or mean amounts of smoking. As well, in the Kumar et al. (2005) study, the severity of consequences for school tobacco policy infractions, as reported by teachers, was not related to daily cigarette smoking for either middle or high school students. For perhaps the same reason as the perceived punitive nature of the policy, two studies found no or limited evidence that student drug-testing policies were associated with marijuana or other illicit drug use by any students (Yamaguchi, Johnston, & O'Malley, 2003) or student athletes (Goldberg et al., 2007). Even so, approximately 14% of school districts nationwide are estimated to have adopted drug-testing policies in the high school grades (Ringwalt et al., 2008).

School Contextual and Aggregate Compositional Characteristics

Ecological studies have suggested that some of the differences across schools in substance use prevalence may be because of contextual characteristics measuring school structure, such as public versus private schools, or compositional characteristics, such as the socioeconomic status or race and ethnicity of students (both of which could be confounded with each other and school type; O'Malley et al., 2006; Skager & Fisher, 1989). As noted earlier, because ecological studies cannot separate the effects of the compositional characteristics of students from the effects of other unmeasured individual-level characteristics, multilevel studies are required to determine the effects of school contextual, compositional, and aggregate characteristics on youth substance use.

Only two studies focused specifically on whether school aggregate compositional effects explained between-school variation in smoking after controlling for student characteristics, with mixed findings (Johnson & Hoffmann, 2000; Kim & McCarthy, 2006). Most of the studies reviewed earlier, however, included school- and individual-level control variables that allowed examination of some school structural and aggregate variables. The findings suggested that school size (Battistich & Hom, 1997; Henry & Slater, 2007; Johnson & Hoffmann, 2000; Kim & McCarthy, 2006; Kumar, O'Malley, Johnston, Schulenberg, & Bachman, 2002; Maes & Lievens, 2003), school type (Kumar et al., 2002; Maes & Lievens, 2003), and school socioeconomic status (Battistich & Hom, 1997; Henry & Slater, 2007) are not meaningfully associated with adolescent substance use net of individual characteristics.

Johnson and Hoffman (2000) and Maes and Lievens (2003) investigated a few other school structural and compositional characteristics. Neither study found evidence for effects of student–teacher ratio, although the Maes and Lievens study found that higher-than-average teacher workload was associated with higher odds of cigarette smoking but not drinking. Johnson and Hoffman found that cigarette smoking risk increased with the academic competitiveness of the school, especially among girls, after controlling for the adolescent's academic performance and other school- and individual-level variables.

Although school differences in compositional characteristics account for some of the between-school differences in substance use (Aveyard et al., 2005), our review suggests that when individual characteristics are controlled, school structural and aggregated compositional characteristics have relatively little association with youth substance use. The small body of studies and limited examination of cross-level interactions, however, suggest the need for additional investigation of how school structural characteristics directly influence youth substance use and condition effects of other variables.

CONCLUSION: DO SCHOOLS MATTER IN EXPLAINING ADOLESCENT SUBSTANCE USE?

Because of the small amount of between-school variance in adolescent substance use relative to the very large amount of variance among individuals within schools, some researchers have concluded that examination of the school context may prove unfruitful to etiology, while affirming the need to adjust analyses for the nesting of students in schools (Smolkowski et al., 2006; Swaim, 2003). The present review of theory and empirical findings suggests that schools do matter in the development of adolescent substance use. Both social and institutional aspects of schools directly influence adolescent substance use net of student characteristics and, more important, significantly interact with adolescent attributes related to substance use. Nevertheless, this favorable conclusion about school effects is tempered by recognition of the complexity of the school environment and the observation that explanatory theories for how schools matter are weakly supported; most studies of school effects have not been guided by theory, and few studies have adequately met the methodological challenges inherent to investigation of contextual effects on individual behavior.

As noted earlier, none of the six theories reviewed integrated aspects of both school social and school institutional environments or highlighted how school and adolescent characteristics might interact in influencing substance use. Although the social ecological perspective has particular utility in identifying schools as a primary socialization context and emphasizes interrelationships among social contexts and personal characteristics, it lacks specificity in the attributes or processes of interest. Theoretical attention to the relations among social and institutional aspects of schools and student characteristics is needed, as is attention to how relationships between contexts, such as school and family, influence youth substance use.

Although multilevel methods have increasingly been used in school effects research, most of the studies adjusted for relatively few student-level factors, leaving open the possibility of confounding of effect estimates. Additionally, some studies adjusted for factors that should not be controlled because they were proxies for school influence, perhaps leading to underestimation of the contribution of school variables to adolescent substance use (Aveyard et al., 2005). A further and substantial limitation is that almost all studies were cross-sectional, thus limiting interpretation of causal relationships between school variables and substance use. Aveyard, Markham, and Cheng (2004; Aveyard et al., 2005) suggested that longitudinal studies that control for baseline substance use are more effective at controlling confounders than are cross-sectional studies because of the many unknown risk factors associated with baseline substance use that are implicitly controlled. Longitudinal studies of school effects are warranted, as is more careful attention to the control variables included in analysis.

With these caveats in mind, the present review suggests that the social environment constructed by adolescents and the institutional climate created by teachers and administrators mutually transact to foster adolescent substance use. Students are at lower risk of substance use when they are in schools characterized by lower prevalence of use and norms that are not favorable to use. Also, they are less likely to be substance users if the school climate is characterized by providing both support and control and by consistently enforcing substance use policies. The school climate is likely of key importance in shaping the social environment, but whether the social environment conforms to the institutional environment remains to be investigated in studies that integrate an array of school and adolescent variables.

References

Alexander, C., Piazza, M., Mekos, D., & Valente, T. (2001). Peers, schools, and adolescent cigarette smoking. *Journal of Adolescent Health, 29,* 22–30.

Allison, K. W., Crawford, I., Leone, P. E., Trickett, E., Perez-Febles, A., Burton, L. M., et al. (1999). Adolescent substance use: Preliminary examinations of school and neighborhood context. *American Journal of Community Psychology, 27,* 111–141.

Aveyard, P., Markham, W. A., & Cheng, K. K. (2004). A methodological and substantive review of the evidence that schools cause pupils to smoke. *Social Science & Medicine, 58,* 2253–2265.

Aveyard, P., Markham, W. A., Lancashire, E., Almond, J., Griffiths, R., & Cheng, K. K. (2005). Is inter-school variation in smoking uptake and cessation due to differences in pupil composition? A cohort study. *Health and Place, 11,* 55–65.

Aveyard, P., Markham, W. A., Lancashire, E., Bullock, A., Macarthur, C., Cheng, K. K., et al. (2004). The influence of school culture on smoking among pupils. *Social Science & Medicine, 58,* 1767–1780.

Battistich, V., & Hom, A. (1997). The relationship between students' sense of their school as a community and their involvement in problem behaviors. *American Journal of Public Health, 87,* 1997–2001.

Bisset, S., Markham, W. A., & Aveyard, P. (2007). School culture as an influencing factor on youth substance use. *Journal of Epidemiology and Community Health, 61,* 485–490.

Bronfenbrenner, U. (Ed.). (1979). *The ecology of human development.* Cambridge, MA: Harvard University Press.

Catalano, R. F., & Hawkins, J. D. (1996). The social development model: A theory of antisocial behavior. In J. D. Hawkins (Ed.), *Delinquency and crime* (pp. 149–197). Cambridge, England: Cambridge University Press.

Cleveland, H. H., & Wiebe, R. P. (2003). The moderation of adolescent-to-peer similarity in tobacco and alcohol use by school levels of substance use. *Child Development, 74,* 279–291.

Cook, T. D., Herman, M. R., Phillips, M., & Settersten, R. A., Jr. (2002). Some ways in which neighborhoods, nuclear families, friendship groups, and schools jointly affect changes in early adolescent development. *Child Development, 73,* 1283–1309.

Demos, J., & Demos, V. (1969). Adolescence in historical perspective. *Journal of Marriage and the Family, 31,* 632–638.

Diez Roux, A. V. (2003). The examination of neighborhood effects on health: Conceptual and methodological issues related to the presence of multiple levels of organization. In L. F. Kawachi (Ed.), *Neighborhoods and health* (pp. 45–64). Oxford, England: Oxford University Press.

Elliott, D. S. (1994). *Youth violence: An overview.* Boulder: Center for the Study and Prevention of Violence, Institute for Behavioral Sciences, University of Colorado, Boulder.

Elliott, D. S., Ageton, S. S., & Canter, R. J. (1979). An integrated theoretical perspective on delinquent behavior. *Journal of Research on Crime and Delinquency, 16,* 13–27.

Elliott, D. S., Huizinga, D., & Ageton, S. S. (Eds.). (1985). *Explaining delinquency and drug use.* Beverly Hills, CA: Sage.

Ennett, S. T., & Bauman, K. E. (1993). Peer group structure and adolescent cigarette smoking: A social network analysis. *Journal of Health and Social Behavior, 34,* 226–236.

Ennett, S. E., Bauman, K. E., Hussong, A., Faris, R., Foshee, V., DuRant, R., et al. (2006). The peer context of adolescent substance use: Findings from social network analysis. *Journal of Research on Adolescence, 16,* 159–186.

Ennett, S. T., Flewelling, R. L., Lindrooth, R. C., & Norton, E. C. (1997). School and neighborhood characteristics associated with school rates of alcohol, cigarette, and marijuana use. *Journal of Health and Social Behavior, 38,* 55–71.

Fuller, B. (1983). Youth job structure and school enrollment, 1890–1920. *Sociology of Education, 56,* 145–156.

Goldberg, L., Elliot, D. L., MacKinnon, D. P., Moe, E. L., Kuehl, K. S., Yoon, M., et al. (2007). Outcomes of a prospective trial of student-athlete drug testing: The Student Athlete Testing Using Random Notification (SATURN) study. *Journal of Adolescent Health, 41,* 421–429.

Gottfredson, D. C. (2000). *Schools and delinquency.* Cambridge, England: Cambridge University Press.

Hawkins, J. D., Catalano, R. F., & Miller, J. Y. (1992). Risk and protective factors for alcohol and other drug problems in adolescence and young adulthood: Implications for substance use prevention. *Psychological Bulletin, 111,* 64–105.

Hawkins, J. D., & Weis, J. G. (1985). The social development model: An integrated approach to delinquency prevention. *Journal of Primary Prevention, 6,* 73–97.

Henry, K. L., & Slater, M. D. (2007). The contextual effect of school attachment on young adolescents' alcohol use. *Journal of School Health, 77,* 67–74.

Johnson, R. A., & Hoffmann, J. P. (2000). Adolescent cigarette smoking in U.S. racial/ethnic subgroups: Findings from the National Education Longitudinal Study. *Journal of Health and Social Behavior, 41,* 392–407.

Jones, S. E., Fisher, C. J., Greene, B. Z., Hertz, M. F., & Pritzl, J. (2007). Healthy and safe school environment, Part I: Results from the School Health Policies and Programs Study 2006. *Journal of School Health, 77,* 522–543.

Killeya-Jones, L. A., Nakajima, R., & Costanzo, P. R. (2007). Peer standing and substance use in early-adolescent grade-level networks: A short-term longitudinal study. *Prevention Science, 8,* 11–23.

Kim, J., & McCarthy, W. J. (2006). School-level contextual influences on smoking and drinking among Asian and Pacific Islander adolescents. *Drug and Alcohol Dependence, 84,* 56–68.

Knoke, D., & Kuklinski, J. H. (Eds.). (1982). *Network analysis.* Beverly Hills, CA: Sage.

Kreft, I. G. G., & Leeuw, J. D. (1998). *Introducing multilevel modeling.* London: Sage.

Kumar, R., O'Malley, P. M., & Johnston, L. D. (2005). School tobacco control policies related to students' smoking and attitudes toward smoking: National survey results, 1999–2000. *Health Education & Behavior, 32,* 780–794.

Kumar, R., O'Malley, P. M., Johnston, L. D., Schulenberg, J. E., & Bachman, J. G. (2002). Effects of school-level norms on student substance use. *Prevention Science, 3,* 105–124.

Kuntsche, E., & Jordan, M. D. (2006). Adolescent alcohol and cannabis use in relation to peer and school factors. Results of multilevel analyses. *Drug and Alcohol Dependence, 84,* 167–174.

Leatherdale, S. T., Brown, K. S., Cameron, R., & McDonald, P. W. (2005). Social modeling in the school environment, student characteristics, and smoking susceptibility: A multi-level analysis. *Journal of Adolescent Health, 37,* 330–336.

Leatherdale, S. T., Cameron, R., Brown, K. S., & McDonald, P. W. (2005). Senior smoking at school, student characteristics, and smoking onset among junior students: A multilevel analysis. *Preventive Medicine, 40,* 853–859.

Leatherdale, S. T., McDonald, P. W., Cameron, R., Jolin, M. A., & Brown, K. S. (2006). A multi-level analysis examining how smoking friends, parents, and older students in the school environment are risk factors for susceptibility to smoking among non-smoking elementary school youth. *Prevention Science, 7,* 397–402.

Maes, L., & Lievens, J. (2003). Can the school make a difference? A multilevel analysis of adolescent risk and health behaviour. *Social Science & Medicine, 56,* 517–529.

Markham, W. A., & Aveyard, P. (2003). A new theory of health promoting schools based on human functioning, school organization and pedagogic practice. *Social Science & Medicine, 56,* 1209–1220.

McBride, C. M., Curry, S. J., Cheadle, A., Anderman, C., Wagner, E. H., Diehr, P., et al. (1995). School-level application of a social bonding model to adolescent risk-taking behavior. *Journal of School Health, 65,* 63–68.

Modell, J., & Goodman, M. (1990). Historical perspectives. In S. S. Feldman & G. R. Elliott (Eds.), *At the threshold: The developing adolescent* (pp. 93–122). Cambridge, MA: Harvard University Press.

Moore, L., Roberts, C., & Tudor-Smith, C. (2001). School smoking policies and smoking prevalence among adolescents: Multilevel analysis of cross-sectional data from Wales. *Tobacco Control, 10,* 117–123.

Murray, D. M., Rooney, B. L., Hannan, P. J., Peterson, A. V., Ary, D. V., Biglan, A., et al. (1994). Intraclass correlation among common measures of adolescent smoking: Estimates, correlates, and applications in smoking prevention studies. *American Journal of Epidemiology, 140,* 1038–1050.

Murray, D. M., & Short, B. J. (1997). Intraclass correlation among measures related to tobacco use by adolescents: Estimates, correlates, and applications in intervention studies. *Addictive Behaviors, 22,* 1–12.

Oetting, E. R., & Donnermeyer, J. F. (1998). Primary socialization theory: The etiology of drug use and deviance. *Substance Use & Misuse, 33,* 995–1026.

O'Malley, P. M., Johnston, L. D., Bachman, J. G., Schulenberg, J. E., & Kumar, R. (2006). How substance use differs among American secondary schools. *Prevention Science, 7,* 409–420.

Pentz, M. A., Brannon, B. R., Charlin, V. L., Barrett, E. J., MacKinnon, D. P., & Flay, B. R. (1989). The power of policy: The relationship of smoking policy to adolescent smoking. *American Journal of Public Health, 79,* 857–862.

Petraitis, J., Flay, B. R., & Miller, T. Q. (1995). Reviewing theories of adolescent substance use: Organizing pieces in the puzzle. *Psychological Bulletin, 117,* 67–86.

Pinilla, J., Gonzalez, B., Barber, P., & Santana, Y. (2002). Smoking in young adolescents: An approach with multilevel discrete choice models. *Journal of Epidemiology and Community Health, 56,* 227–232.

Pokorny, S. B., Jason, L. A., & Schoeny, M. E. (2004). Current smoking among young adolescents: Assessing school based contextual norms. *Tobacco Control, 13,* 301–307.

Raudenbush, S. W., & Bryk, A. S. (2002). *Hierarchical linear models applications and data analysis methods.* Thousand Oaks, CA: Sage Publications.

Ringwalt, C. L., Vincus, A. A., Ennett, S. E., Hanley, S., Bowling, J. M., Yacoubian, G. S., et al. (2008). Suspicionless or random drug testing in U.S. public school districts. *American Journal of Public Health, 98,* 826–828.

Roski, J., Perry, C. L., McGovern, P. G., Williams, C. L., Farbaksh, K., & Veblen-Mortenson, S. (1997). School and community influence on adolescent alcohol and drug use. *Health Education Research, 12,* 255–266.

Rowe, D. C., Chassin, L., Presson, C., & Edwards, D. (1992). An epidemic model of adolescent cigarette smoking. *Journal of Applied Social Psychology, 22,* 261–285.

Rowe, D. C., & Rodgers, J. L. (1991). Adolescent smoking and drinking: Are they "epidemics"? *Journal of Studies on Alcohol, 52,* 110–117.

Scheier, L. M., Griffin, K. W., Doyle, M. M., & Botvin, G. J. (2002). Estimates of intragroup dependence for drug use and skill measures in school-based drug abuse prevention trials: An empirical study of three independent samples. *Health Education & Behavior, 29,* 85–103.

Skager, R., & Fisher, D. G. (1989). Substance use among high school students in relation to school characteristics. *Addictive Behaviors, 14,* 129–138.

Small, M. L., Jones, S. E., Barrios, L. C., Crossett, L. S., Dahlberg, L. L., Albuquerque, M. S., et al. (2001). School policy and environment: Results from the School Health Policies and Programs Study 2000. *Journal of School Health, 71,* 325–334.

Smolkowski, K., Biglan, A., Dent, C., & Seeley, J. (2006). The multilevel structure of four adolescent problems. *Prevention Science, 7,* 239–256.

Swaim, R. C. (2003). Individual and school level effects of perceived harm, perceived availability, and community size on marijuana use among 12th-grade students: A random effects model. *Prevention Science, 4,* 89–98.

Wakefield, M. A., Chaloupka, F. J., Kaufman, N. J., Orleans, C. T., Barker, D. C., & Ruel, E. E. (2000). Effect of restrictions on smoking at home, at school, and in public places on teenage smoking: Cross sectional study. *British Medical Journal, 321,* 333–337.

Wasserman, S., & Faust, K. (Eds.). (1994). *Social network analysis: Methods and applications.* New York: Cambridge University Press.

Yamaguchi, R., Johnston, L. D., & O'Malley, P. M. (2003). Relationship between student illicit drug use and school drug-testing policies. *Journal of School Health, 73,* 159–164.

CHAPTER 24

THE ASSOCIATION BETWEEN NEIGHBORHOODS AND ILLICIT DRUG USE AMONG ADULTS: EVIDENCE FROM A CHICAGO HOUSEHOLD SURVEY

Michael Fendrich, Adam M. Lippert, Timothy P. Johnson, and Michael J. Brondino

What role do neighborhoods and neighborhood context have in the etiology of drug abuse? The answer to this question is of critical importance for prevention and intervention research for several reasons. Substance abuse prevention has typically been carried out through programs that are targeted to school-age populations and usually address individual- or family-level risk factors (National Institute on Drug Abuse, 2003). Nevertheless, epidemiological data have clearly shown that although drug use initiation typically occurs in late adolescence, for many progression and experimentation persist through young adulthood (e.g., Johnston, O'Malley, Bachman, & Schulenberg, 2006; Substance Abuse and Mental Health Services Administration, 2007). Programs targeted to young adults need to be informed by knowledge of the extrainstitutional contexts in which their substance initiation and use occurs. Furthermore, if rates of drug abuse vary by neighborhood context or if contextual variables (e.g., poverty, social decay, and crime, to name a few) exert an independent effect on drug abuse in adulthood, substance abuse prevention may need to be reconceptualized in terms of macrolevel policies aimed at improving social conditions giving rise to those detrimental contexts (see chap. 26 of this volume for a more extensive discussion of environmental policies).

The notion that neighborhoods independently influence drug use has a strong theoretical rationale. A stress and coping perspective (e.g., Moos, 2005) considers the impact of stressful life events, such as job loss, disease and mortality, criminal victimization, and discrimination, that proliferate in impoverished neighborhoods (Boardman, Finch, Ellison, Williams, & Jackson, 2001). Residents in relatively deprived, blighted neighborhoods characterized by low levels of social services and many dilapidated or abandoned buildings may be vulnerable to higher levels of chronic stress as a result of their physical surroundings. The effect this can have is that residents may turn to drug use as a means of coping with the elevated stress caused directly by these neighborhood conditions and indirectly by the plethora of stressors proliferating in these contexts. Supporting this notion, there is ample evidence for multiple adverse psychological sequelae resulting from residing in impoverished neighborhoods. Studies have suggested that adults living in impoverished conditions experience diminished self-mastery or perceived efficacy (Sampson, Raudenbush, & Earls, 1997). Children (especially boys) living in such adverse neighborhoods experience elevated adverse psychological symptoms and behavior problems (Aneshensel & Sucoff, 1996; Luthar & Cushing, 1999; Winslow & Shaw, 2007).

Preparation of this chapter was supported by National Institute on Drug Abuse Grants R01DA012425 and R01DA018625. The survey data were collected by the University of Illinois Survey Research Laboratory. We acknowledge support for the data collection effort provided by Christine Orland, project director. We also thank the Chicago Police Department for furnishing the crime data used for this chapter. The contents of this chapter are solely the responsibility of the authors and do not represent the official views of the National Institute on Drug Abuse or the Chicago Police Department.

Higher rates of drug use in deteriorated neighborhoods are also supported by social learning theory (Bandura, 1973; Moos, 2005). The increased visibility of drug use and drug crime noted above may result in increased acceptability of this behavior, creating a prevailing norm. Because illegal substances are more widespread and easier to procure in impoverished neighborhoods, individuals living in those neighborhoods are more likely to use them (Crum, Lillie-Blanton, & Anthony, 1996). Accordingly, impoverished neighborhoods may provide a normative context in which use of illicit substances may be less frowned upon or even regarded favorably (Boardman et al., 2001; Moos, 2005).

With some notable exceptions (e.g., Galea, Ahern, Tracy, & Vlahov, 2007), recent empirical research has generally supported the notion that neighborhood disadvantage and deterioration are positively associated with drug use in adult residents. For instance, in a study evaluating census tracts in New York, Hannon and Cuddy (2006) found that poverty, the prevalence of boarded-up housing, and the rate of home ownership were each independently associated with one extreme indicator of substance abuse problems—drug dependence mortality. An analysis of data from a national evaluation of a community-based substance abuse prevention campaign targeted to high-risk neighborhoods ("Fighting Back") has suggested that aggregate indicators of neighborhood deterioration show a significant but weak (in terms of variance explained) association with individual-level measures of any past-year drug use and/or drug dependence (Saxe et al., 2001). A separate analysis of these same "Fighting Back" data that focused on specific drugs (marijuana, cocaine, barbiturates, and inhalants) found no pattern of consistent associations between use of these substances and aggregate measures of neighborhood disadvantage (Ford & Beveridge, 2006), although there were clearly elevated rates for certain substances. Using the 1995 Detroit Area Study in conjunction with 1990 census-tract data, Boardman et al. (2001) found a positive association between neighborhood disadvantage and individual reports of any past-year drug use that was more pronounced among lower income respondents. Galea, Ahern, and Vlahov (2003) assessed drug use

within New York City zip codes and found that frequency of injection drug use was positively associated with the percentage of low-income households. Finally, Latkin, Curry, Hua, and Davey (2007) found that individual perceptions of neighborhood disorder were positively associated with past 6-month use of injection drugs or crack cocaine, but only among men. These findings parallel earlier work focused on the impact of perceptions of neighborhood risk on the early stages of drug use in inner city minority youth (Scheier, Miller, Ifill-Williams, & Botvin, 2001).

It should be underscored that unlike studies focused on adverse health correlates of neighborhoods—such as rates of sexually transmitted diseases (Cohen et al., 2000, 2003) and violence (Sampson et al., 1997), which rely on official health records or crime statistics to evaluate outcomes—and with few exceptions (i.e., Hannon & Cuddy, 2006), most previous research evaluating the impact of neighborhood context on drug use has relied entirely on self-report drug use measures. An accumulation of data has suggested that drug use is underreported in epidemiological surveys (e.g., Fendrich, Johnson, Wislar, Hubbell, & Spiehler, 2004). There are also data supporting the role of neighborhood context on underreporting, with higher rates of underreporting observed in less integrated neighborhoods (Richardson, Fendrich, & Johnson, 2003). Accordingly, studies comparing rates of self-reported drug use across neighborhood contexts may underestimate differences as a consequence of self-report bias.

Another type of bias in previous research is typically referred to as selection bias (Shadish, Cook, & Campbell, 2002). What may appear to be the effects of deteriorated or dysfunctional neighborhoods in prior research may actually be the result of differences between participants who select themselves into these neighborhoods. Participants with more risk factors for substance use may disproportionately populate certain problematic neighborhoods. This notion, referred to in other contexts as social drift (Baum & Barnes, 1993), was mentioned by Boardman et al. (2001) as an alternative explanation for their findings. Social drift revolves around the notion that certain individuals experiencing problems in living (e.g., mental health problems) may eventually drift toward a particular neighborhood that provides the necessary infrastructure to support alternative, cottage industry employment and facilities for treatment (e.g., halfway houses) and provide community resources for other like-minded souls. These neighborhoods are typically poorer and have higher unemployment, more alcohol retail stores, and less residential stability. Although statistical adjustments in regression analysis are an attempt to correct for some of these biases, such models are inferior to matching strategies that typically characterize well-designed quasi-experiments. Failure to address this type of selection bias would tend to overstate neighborhood context effects (Type I error).

The study presented in this chapter describes an additional investigation of the role of neighborhood context in adult illicit drug use. We overcame one major measurement limitation of prior research by using a measure of substance use that takes into account both self-report and biological test results. By incorporating the results of biological markers in our analysis, we overcame the potential problem of underreporting of recent drug use that may be particularly problematic in urban contexts (Fendrich & Johnson, 2005). We address the possible problem of selection bias by using propensity score matching strategies in our comparisons (see Guo, Barth, & Gibbons, 2006; Jones, D'Agostino, Gondolf, & Heckert, 2004; Oakes & Johnson, 2006).

METHOD

Sample

Data used for this study came from a probability sample of English-speaking adults who resided in the city of Chicago. The survey was conducted from June 2001 to January 2002. Residents between the ages of 18 and 40 were selected randomly to participate in a household drug use survey using a multistage area probability design (Levy & Lemeshow, 1991). At Stage 1, census tracts in Chicago were selected randomly. At Stage 2, one block was selected randomly from within each sampled tract. At Stage 3, every household on the sampled block was screened for eligibility. At Stage 4, an 18- to

40-year-old adult was selected at random from within each eligible household.

Before screening for eligibility, field staff distributed letters to selected households that provided a general introduction to the study. Household informants also received study brochures at first contact that provided additional information. At each contact, households were informed that the study was being conducted by researchers at the University of Illinois at Chicago and that it was being sponsored by the federal government (the National Institute on Drug Abuse). The study was approved by the University of Illinois at Chicago Institutional Review Board (UIC IRB No. 1998-0550). All study participants were asked to provide written consent.

A total of 627 surveys were completed. We used American Association for Public Opinion Research (2000) definitions for response rates (Formula 3) and cooperation rates (Formula 1). According to this definition, the response rate is the number of completed interviews divided by the eligible sample. The cooperation rate is the number of completed interviews divided by the sum of the number of completed interviews and the number of refusals. Note that because those in the eligible sample included potential participants who were never contacted by the interviewers despite repeated attempts, the response rate tends to be lower than the cooperation rate. Accordingly, the overall response and cooperation rates for this study were 40% and 74%, respectively. These rates reflect the challenges of conducting survey interviews in urban environments, where response rates tend to be lower for many reasons (Groves & Couper, 1998). When restricted-access, high-rise apartment buildings are excluded from consideration, the comparable response and cooperation rates were 51% and 75%, respectively.

Using unweighted sample estimates, 42.8% of the sample were between ages 18 and 25, 25.5% were between the ages of 26 and 30, and 31.8% were older than 31 (with a maximum age of 40 years). African Americans were the modal racial and ethnic group, making up 35.6% of all respondents; about one third (33.2%) were White, 22.1% were Hispanic, and 9.2% were classified as other. Approximately 60% of the unweighted sample was female. Characteristics of the full sample are shown in Table 24.1.

Survey Administration

Surveys were administered in each participant's home by trained interviewers from the University of Illinois at Chicago Survey Research Laboratory using audio computer self-interview procedures. Although the vast majority of participants (90%) self-administered the substance use questions, they could also opt to have their questions administered by the interviewer. Quality control activities included recontacting randomly selected respondents to verify interview and specimen collection activities.

Survey participants were asked questions about past-month substance use, following the format used in the 2000 National Household Survey on Drug Abuse (Office of Applied Studies, 2001). For the purposes of this study, we focused on the two measures of drug use for which we had sufficient

TABLE 24.1

Sample Demographics

Variable	*n*	%
Age		
18–25	244	38.92
26–30	164	26.16
31+[a]	219	34.93
Race or ethnicity		
Black	252	40.58
Hispanic	113	18.20
Other	57	9.18
White[a]	199	32.05
Income		
< $30K	281	47.39
≥ $30K[a]	312	52.61
Education		
< High school	109	17.38
High school	137	21.85
Some college	171	27.27
College[a]	210	33.49
Children present		
Yes	332	53.29
No[a]	291	46.71
Past-day's tobacco use		
Yes	195	31.20
No[a]	430	68.80

[a]Reference category

prevalence and biological measures of use: marijuana and cocaine.

Drug-Testing Procedures

Immediately following the drug assessment portion of the survey, participants were asked to consent to participate in hair, oral fluid, and urine drug-testing procedures and were offered either $10 or $20 for each sample provided, depending on random assignment. The strengths and limitations of each of these procedures are articulated clearly by Wolff et al. (1999). Of particular importance from an epidemiological perspective is that although the methods are generally consistent with respect to the types of substances they can detect, they vary with respect to their typical windows of detection, with oral fluid testing having the shortest (most drugs are detectable within 12–24 hours of use) and hair testing having the longest (Cone, 1997; Jehanli, Brannan, Moore, & Spiehler, 2001). Note that consent for the drug testing procedures was not obtained until after the drug survey portion of the study had been completed (for further details about the drug-testing protocol and toxicological analyses, see Fendrich, Johnson, Wislar, & Hubbell, 2003).

Neighborhood-Level Data

We used data drawn from two sources. First, we obtained data from the 2000 U.S. Census (U.S. Census Bureau, 2007). We also obtained arrest and incident-level data from the Chicago police department. The police department records, which were collected at the beat level, were coded to appropriately conform to respective census-tract boundaries. For this study, we used incident-level crime data for index offenses (see below). These data were then merged with our person-level file, yielding a total of 44 unique census tracts, or neighborhoods, as they are considered here.

Measures Used in the Study

Drug use classification. For the purposes of this study, we used a "best estimate" indicator of substance use, combining self-reports of past-month marijuana and cocaine use with results from biological testing. Respondents were treated as positive cases for marijuana or cocaine if they reported any

TABLE 24.2

Drug Use Comparisons by Estimate Type

Drug	Self-reported use			Drug test result			Combined estimate		
	n	% yes	% no	*n*	% yes	% no	*n*	% yes	% no
Cocaine	627	2.23	97.77	566	12.72	87.28	627	11.96	88.04
Marijuana	623	18.62	81.38	568	18.66	81.34	627	23.76	76.24

past-month use or tested positive for marijuana or cocaine on any of the biological testing procedures. Accordingly, if a biological test indicated use but a self-report contradicted that test, an individual would be classified as a user of that substance. Likewise, respondents who reported no such use and who tested negative on all tests were considered to be negative cases for use of that substance. In instances in which data from biological testing were unavailable, self-reports were used exclusively as indicators of substance use. Table 24.2 summarizes the drug classification results for the entire sample, indicating the source of the information across each of the two substance use indicators. For the entire sample, we derived self-reported past-month cocaine use rates of 2.2% and self-reported marijuana past-month marijuana use rates of 18.7%. The drug test rates are based on the people for whom at least one drug test was available.

Neighborhood risk. The focus of this study is on gauging the impact that living in a high-risk neighborhood has on individual substance use. We defined a high-risk neighborhood as a census tract with a high rate of economic deprivation plus a high crime rate. Definitions for these two constructs are given in the following sections.

We operationally defined economic deprivation using five indicators of tract-level poverty and disadvantage derived from data from the 2000 census. These measures were grouped to form a summative measure of neighborhood deprivation that has been used in other studies of neighborhood influences on health outcomes (e.g., Boardman et al., 2001; Cohen et al., 2003; Pearl, Braveman, & Abrams, 2001). The five items that made up our deprivation measure included percentage of female-headed households,

percentage of people age 25 or older with less than a high school diploma, percentage of households receiving public assistance, percentage of households under the poverty line, and percentage of the working-age population who are unemployed. Table 24.3 contains the distribution of these variables for the current sample. Previous studies (e.g., Boardman et al., 2001; Sampson et al., 1997) have shown that these measures are highly interrelated and load on a single factor that approximates neighborhood disadvantage. A principal-axis factor analysis of our tract poverty indicators supported the viability of a single component. The single component explained more than 60% of the variance in the correlation matrix, and all measures except the diploma variable showed relatively high loadings (>.60) on the component (the diploma variable had a .43 loading). Thus, the data supported treating the poverty indicators as a single deprivation scale (Cronbach's α = .85). Accordingly, tracts above the median value of the deprivation measure were operationally defined as high-deprivation tracts.

TABLE 24.3

Item Statistics for Neighborhood Deprivation Scale

Variable	*Mdn*	Min	Max
% female-headed households	18.1	2.1	55.5
% high school dropouts	34.35	0.7	70.6
% households receiving public assistance	6.4	0	30.5
% households under the poverty line	20.4	4.6	64.8
% population unemployed	6.35	0.7	20.5
Summative deprivation scale	18.58	1.88	41.1
Cronbach's α		.851	

Crime data included tract-level incident rates (i.e., incidents per 1,000 persons) for uniform index crimes. We computed a scale of the tract-level crime rates by summing the following measures: sexual assaults, robbery, aggravated assault, aggravated battery, burglary, larceny–theft, motor vehicle theft, arson, and homicide. We took the natural log of this sum to form a tract-level total crime score. The distribution of these variables and for the summed scale for the current sample of tracts is shown in Table 24.4. A principal-axis factor analysis of the incident rate measures supported the viability of a single component. The single component explained more than 80% of the variance in the correlation matrix, and all variables demonstrated very high loadings on this component (all loadings were greater than .75). Thus, the data supported treating the incident rate measures as a single crime scale (Cronbach's $\alpha = .81$). Tracts above the median value on the crime scale were operationally defined as high-crime tracts.

After constructing scales for neighborhood deprivation and crime, we combined the two measures to form a binary variable called neighborhood risk. In doing so, we noted the significant correlation between the crime and deprivation scales ($r = .30$, $p \leq .05$). In addition, we were interested in characterizing neighborhoods as high risk—that is, as showing relatively high rates of both economic deprivation and criminal activity. Tracts above the

median on both the neighborhood deprivation and crime scales were operationally defined as high-risk neighborhoods, whereas all other tracts were treated as non–high risk. Roughly 23% of individuals in the total study sample resided in 13 high-risk tracts.

Propensity Score Matching Procedures

Rosenbaum and Rubin (1983) defined the propensity score for a participant as the conditional probability of receiving a particular treatment given a vector of observed covariates (for a detailed discussion, see D'Agostino, 1998). Propensity matching methods begin with the principle that in many observational studies, selection into a particular treatment condition is biased and, in part, a function of factors that can be used in a regression-type context to estimate the likelihood (i.e., propensity) of selection into such a condition. By estimating propensity scores for all cases with nonmissing data, treated cases can be matched with control cases on the basis of likelihood of treatment, regardless of actual exposure status. This process yields a matched sample not unlike the samples produced in experimental studies using randomized treatment assignments. When estimated correctly, propensity score matching will yield identical conditional distributions for observed covariates across both treated and control conditions, effectively reducing the effect of selection bias on differences in outcomes. Any difference in the outcome of interest between treated and untreated units is then an unbiased estimate of the average treatment effect.

In this study, propensity scores estimating the likelihood of residing in a high-risk neighborhood were estimated using the "pscore" command in STATA (Becker & Ichino, 2002; StataCorp, 2005). This procedure estimates a logistic model predicting the likelihood of treatment given a vector of covariates, stratifies treated and untreated units according to propensity values, and evaluates how well balanced the two treatment groups are by strata. Typically, one selects covariates not on the basis of theoretical grounds but rather with the aim of deriving a set of variables that maximally predicts selection into the quasi-experimental group or treatment group (Oakes & Johnson, 2006). In this case, we wanted to select variables that maximally predicted

TABLE 24.4

Item Statistics for Crime Scale

Variable	*Mdn*	Min	Max
Sexual assault	6.5	2	20
Robbery	64	17	131
Aggravated assault	27	6	73
Aggravated battery	59	7	207
Burglary	115	7	241
Larceny–theft	344	120	1,103
Motor vehicle theft	105.5	54	285
Arson	4.5	0	15
Murder	2	0	13
Log-transformed summative crime scale	5.58	4.13	9.52
Cronbach's α			.815

selection into a high-risk neighborhood. The propensity model in the current study included the following covariates: age, race or ethnicity, education, income, presence of children in the household, and past-day tobacco use (the model was unable to derive estimations using gender).

One problem inherent in propensity matching is the issue of data loss, and at this point, a brief digression is in order to explore the impact of this issue on this study. Data loss in propensity matching is largely an artifact of incomplete matching, which can occur from either missing data or incongruent ranges of propensity scores between treated cases and controls (Parsons, 2001). Procedures used to predict propensity scores depend on complete data for proper estimation of such scores. As in any multivariate model using listwise deletion, cases with missing data on any of the covariates in the propensity model will be excluded from the model, and no propensity scores will be estimated for these cases. In the current study, propensity estimation procedures yielded scores for 139 treated cases out of a total of 149. This data loss is attributable to missing values for several covariates in the model.

Once propensity scores were estimated for our sample, we implemented nearest neighbor matching within a caliper of ± 0.06 using the "psmatch2" command in STATA (Leuven & Sianesi, 2003). Our choice of matching within a caliper of ±0.06 is based on conventions proposed by Rosenbaum and Rubin (1983), who noted optimal matching outcomes when calipers were set equal to one quarter of the standard deviation of the propensity scale.

This procedure successfully matched 80 (54%) of the cases from high-risk neighborhoods (or so-called "treated" cases) with 80 cases from non–high-risk neighborhoods (or so-called "control" cases) out of a possible pool of 443 non–high-risk neighborhood cases with valid propensity scores. Thus, 80 treated cases from 13 high-risk census tracts were successfully matched with 80 control cases from 17 other tracts. Data loss is attributable to another issue affecting matching: incongruent propensity ranges. In our data, the minimum propensity value for treated cases was .022, and the minimum value for control cases was .002. Maximum propensity values for treated and control groups were .87 and .85,

respectively. Control cases with propensity values falling outside the range of treated cases are excluded. Of the remaining control cases, matches are made, and matched controls are removed from the pool and no longer eligible for subsequent matches. This poses a problem for the remaining treated cases, especially those with more extreme values. Once an untreated case is matched and removed from the pool, treated cases must look elsewhere for appropriate matches. Treated cases with extreme propensity values will have more difficulty identifying suitable matches. In our data, many such cases were eliminated. In fact, of the 59 excluded treated cases with valid propensity scores, each case had a propensity value between .55 and .87, scores that fell outside of the range of the excluded control cases with propensity scores. Although this attrition has a toll on sample size, it is a necessary expense because including these extreme cases may bias the estimate of the treatment effect (Rubin & Thomas, 2000).

The overall goal in propensity score matching is to generate comparisons on outcomes across two roughly equivalent groups. We evaluate the difference between proportions across the two propensity score matched groups. The z test in the comparison uses a boot-strapping methodology to construct the standard error for the comparison (Heckman, Ichimura, Smith, & Todd, 1998; Heckman, Ichimura, & Todd, 1997, 1998). Because the goal in propensity score matching is to generate matched pairs or samples that are similar on most critical background variables, a final step in the process involves evaluating the covariate balance between treated and untreated cases before and after matching procedures.

RESULTS

The results of the nearest-neighbor matching procedure pertaining to cocaine and marijuana use are presented in Table 24.5. With respect to cocaine, when drug testing is incorporated in the construction of the use variable—that is, either when the measure is based on the combined best estimate or when the drug test only is used as the criterion, participants in the high-risk neighborhood have significantly higher rates of cocaine use than those in other neighborhoods. Indeed, using the best estimate

TABLE 24.5

Nearest Neighbor Matching Results by Substance and Estimate Type

| Drug and outcome measure | Proportion of use by treatment status | | Difference | Z | Bootstrapped Z |
	High risk	Non–high risk			
Cocaine					
Best estimate (n = 160)	.275	.138	.138	2.17*	2.09*
Drug test only (n = 148)	.284	.135	.149	2.24*	2.17*
Self-report only (n = 160)	.038	.025	.013	0.45	0.44
Marijuana					
Best estimate (n = 160)	.225	.338	−113	−1.59	−1.56
Drug test only (n = 148)	.176	.284	−.108	−1.57	−1.54
Self-report only (n = 160)	.163	.138	.025	-0.44	-0.44

Note. Caliper set at .06, which is equal to one quarter of the standard deviation of the propensity score (see Rosenbaum & Rubin, 1985).
*$p < .05$.

measure of use, high-risk neighborhood residents have more than twice the risk of cocaine use than do non–high-risk residents. In terms of the average effect of treatment on the treated (see Oakes & Johnson, 2006), an absolute difference in proportions of about .14 suggests that if 100 low-risk neighborhood residents were to move into one of the high-risk neighborhoods, there would be 14 new cocaine users in that group.

With respect to marijuana use, postmatching results yielded no significant differences in rates of use by neighborhood status. We note, however, that in contrast to the findings for cocaine, the nonsignificant differences tended to show higher rates for the non–high-risk group. Best-estimate and drug-test-only comparisons for marijuana approached but did not reach statistical significance at the .10 level.

These findings suggest that high-risk neighborhood residency exacerbates cocaine use. This increased risk is only apparent when the outcome measure incorporates drug testing. These findings also suggest that underreporting of recent cocaine use is a more salient problem in high-risk neighborhoods, whereas underreporting of recent marijuana use is more of an issue in non–high-risk neighborhoods. Accordingly, failure to incorporate drug test-

ing into survey protocols may lead to underestimation of the effects of adverse neighborhood conditions on drug use. Using the measure that takes into account all available sources of information on drug use, the so-called "best-estimate measure," it appears that living in neighborhoods characterized by high rates of economic deprivation and crime is associated with an increased risk of cocaine use; living in such neighborhoods has no effect on marijuana use.

As a follow-up to our analyses, we evaluated the success of our propensity score matching procedures by comparing the covariate balance before and after matching adjustments (e.g., Oakes & Johnson, 2006). The results of this post hoc check on our procedures are shown in Table 24.6. Note that the first set of comparisons (unmatched) is based on the larger sample sizes available from the unmatched full comparison on each variable for those living within and outside of high-risk neighborhoods (these comparisons involve 139 participants from the high-risk neighborhoods and 443 participants from the other neighborhoods; individual sample sizes for specific comparisons vary depending on the number of missing values for each variable). The second set of comparisons is based on cases from

TABLE 24.6

Propensity Score Matching and Covariate Balance

Variable and sample	n	M		Standardized difference	% Reduction in |bias|
		High risk	Non–high risk		
Propensity score					
Unmatched	582	.608	.123	156.96	
Matched	160	.510	.484	10.79	93.1
Age					
18–25					
Unmatched	244	.403	.385	3.68	
Matched	56	.325	.375	−10.44	−5.76
26–30					
Unmatched	164	.235	.270	−8.05	
Matched	33	.188	.225	−9.24	−0.15
31+ (referent)					
Unmatched	219	.362	.345	3.55	
Matched	71	.488	.400	17.57	−3.95
Race or ethnicity					
Black[a]					
Unmatched	252	.926	.242	192.68	
Matched	140	.875	.875	0	100.0
Hispanic[a]					
Unmatched	113	.047	.225	−53.78	
Matched	14	.088	.088	0	100.0
Other[a]					
Unmatched	57	.013	.117	−43.15	
Matched	2	.013	.013	0	100.0
White (referent)[a]					
Unmatched	199	.013	.417	−112.85	
Matched	4	.025	.025	0	100.0
Income					
< $30K					
Unmatched	281	.814	.369	101.37	
Matched	111	.700	.688	2.69	97.3
≥ $30K (referent)					
Unmatched	312	.186	.631	−101.37	
Matched	49	.300	.313	−2.69	97.3
Education					
<High school					
Unmatched	109	.369	.113	65.98	
Matched	36	.263	.188	17.90	72.9
High school					
Unmatched	137	.349	.178	39.49	
Matched	51	.300	.338	−8.00	79.8
Some college					
Unmatched	171	.248	.280	−7.26	
Matched	63	.375	.413	−7.64	−0.05
College degree (referent)[a]					
Unmatched	210	.034	.429	−105.90	
Matched	10	.063	.063	0	100
Children present					

(continued)

TABLE 24.6 *(cont.)*

| Variable and sample | *n* | *M* | | Standardized difference | % Reduction in \|bias\| |
		High risk	Non–high risk		
Yes[a]					
Unmatched	332	.777	.457	69.56	
Matched	116	.725	.725	0	100.0
No (referent)[a]					
Unmatched	291	.223	.543	−69.56	
Matched	44	.275	.275	0	100.0
Past-day tobacco use					
Yes					
Unmatched	195	.336	.305	6.62	
Matched	62	.375	.400	−5.10	23.0
No (referent)					
Unmatched	430	.664	.695	−6.62	
Matched	98	.625	.600	5.10	23.0

[a]Exactly matched by design.

the high-risk neighborhoods that were matched with cases from the other neighborhoods. For most of the comparisons, the propensity score matched samples showed a reduction in differences across groups after matching. This is reflected in the trend toward positive numbers for most variables in the percentage bias reduction statistics. In addition, one typically wants to see absolute differences of 10% or less between the matched samples on covariates (Oakes & Johnson, 2006). Although these patterns did not consistently hold across all categories of all variables, we note particularly the failure of matching to improve the balance between the groups with respect to age. Nevertheless, the percentage increase in bias observed for this variable was relatively small (less than 10% for all three of the age categories). In addition, when we reran analyses omitting the age variable in the construction of the propensity score, it had little impact on the substantive findings.

DISCUSSION

Propensity score matching procedures are one method for adjusting for selection bias in quasi-experimental designs. Obviously, it would be impossible (as well as unethical) to randomly assign participants to neighborhoods even though that would be the only way to accurately gauge neighborhood effects. Nevertheless, the procedure provides one means of potentially controlling for selection bias, and this chapter represents an innovative application of this methodology. Note that had propensity score matching not been used, the best estimate comparisons for cocaine would have yielded larger absolute differences across the two neighborhood contexts. The rate of best-estimate cocaine use for the high-risk group was about 28% before and after the implementation of matching. However, the rate of cocaine use in the non–high-risk sample increased from 7% to 14% after the implementation of matching. Thus, failure to account for differences in sample composition could potentially have overstated the impact of neighborhood on best-estimate cocaine use.

Our covariate adjustment procedure suggests that our attempts at bias reduction were successful. Nevertheless, improvements are always possible. A better designed study, with a priori interest in evaluating the impact of neighborhoods, might have conceptualized improved variables to include in the propensity score generating procedure. This improvement or refinement is a laudable goal for future epidemiological studies of drug use.

The classification of neighborhood risk was based on two variables, crime and economic deprivation. We neglected to incorporate more visible indices of neighborhood deterioration, such as boarded-up buildings, in our measure of neighborhood dysfunction. Such indices have figured prominently in health-related research that has explored the viability of "broken windows" theories of community problems (e.g., Cohen et al., 2000, 2003). Future research might consider alternative classification strategies that include such measures. Indeed, it would be worth exploring how alternative conceptualizations of deterioration affect the type of comparisons explored in this chapter.

One potential limitation of these comparisons is the fact that potentially eligible cases were excluded from generating comparisons. This is particularly problematic with respect to the exclusion of 69 high-risk participants from the analysis. To evaluate the potential impact that these excluded cases might have on the study conclusions, we computed logistic regression models comparing matched high-risk cases with unmatched high-risk cases on the best-estimate drug use measures. These analyses indicated no significant differences between the two groups with respect to cocaine use. Comparisons with respect to marijuana use were marginally significant ($p \leq .10$), suggesting a tendency for marijuana users to be underrepresented in the matched high-risk sample. This suggests potential problems with the external validity of comparisons with respect to marijuana use. Nevertheless, the failure to find significance differences between the treatment and control groups in the matched analyses and the small between-group differences observed in the unmatched analyses alleviate these concerns. Because the data with respect to cocaine suggest that the drug-use behavior of the high-risk neighborhood participants who were excluded from the analysis was very similar to those who were included, conclusions about neighborhood effects on cocaine use were unlikely to be biased as a result of our matching strategy.

We limited our comparisons to two illegal substances, marijuana and cocaine. We did this because these substances have a relatively high prevalence in urban settings and because they are easily detected in the biological measures that we used. Although follow-up analyses focusing on other substances (including alcohol) are recommended, we caution that failure to include measures with biological confirmation may be problematic, especially in contexts in which underreporting may be differential across neighborhoods.

Alternative analytic strategies, perhaps using multilevel modeling, can be used to evaluate alternative sources of variation in drug use. Indeed, at least two prior analyses using these strategies suggested that neighborhoods explained less variance in drug use than they did in visible drug problems (Ford & Beverage, 2006; Saxe et al., 2001). Although our propensity score derivation strategy was potentially limited (see above), the multilevel modeling approach is limited in that it fails to adequately account for selection biases. We also raise questions about the use of national data to derive general principles about neighborhood context. These strategies fail to take into account unique and variable urban contexts. Studies focusing on within-city comparisons may yield more meaningful results. This suggests the need for studies replicating our Chicago findings in other urban contexts and regions. As noted below, however, visible drug problems may be an indicator of potential risk that needs to be addressed through community-based prevention strategies.

Our inclusion of hair testing as a criterion measure of drug use could be considered controversial. Some have claimed that the issue of passive exposure (Kidwell & Blank, 1996) and racial bias (Cone & Joseph, 1996) may be particularly problematic for this biological measure. Propensity score matching strategies may ameliorate concerns about the effects of bias because of sample composition. In previous reports (Fendrich, Johnson, Wislar, Sudman, & Spiehler, 1999; Fendrich et al., 2004), we noted that hair testing was not informative regarding possible marijuana use. Our data suggest that hair testing did, however, provide considerable information about possible cocaine use. Although it would be optimal to draw conclusions about drug use from drug testing, if we were limited to drawing inferences about recent environmental exposure to cocaine use (e.g., living in areas in which others are consuming or dealing the substance), our findings still have critical implications. In other words, if our findings should be reinterpreted to mean that those in high-risk neighborhoods are more likely to be exposed to cocaine than those in other contexts, the profound societal implications of our findings persist. Drug exposure creates opportunities for use and shapes social norms. Because exposure may precede and facilitate use, our data underscore the need for effective, broad-based prevention strategies targeted specifically to high-risk neighborhoods.

By definition, the biggest ongoing prevention strategy in high-risk neighborhoods in our study was law enforcement. The seemingly contradictory finding that neighborhoods with the highest rate of cocaine use have more law enforcement activity (i.e., are recorded as having more crime incidents) underscores the notion that law enforcement alone cannot serve as effective drug prevention. Drug offenders can be removed from the streets and incarcerated, but ultimately they must be reintegrated back into the community. If they come back to the same community, in the absence of massive neighborhood improvement, they return to the same drug use environment and facilitating conditions from which they were removed. Consequently, at some point, prevention must also focus on changing the neighborhood environment. We need to consider viable approaches to enhancing the quality of life across neighborhood contexts so we can eliminate disparities in employment opportunities, health care, affordable housing, and the myriad conditions that facilitate criminal behavior, drug use, and recidivism. Prevention in this context may succeed by focusing on broader policy strategies that enhance educational opportunities, health care access, job growth, and the renovation of those pockets of crumbling urban infrastructure that have deteriorated and persisted in recent decades.

References

American Association for Public Opinion Research. (2000). *Standard definitions: Final dispositions of case codes and outcome rates surveys.* Ann Arbor, MI: Author.

Aneshensel, C., & Sucoff, C. A. (1996). The neighborhood context of adolescent mental health. *Journal of Health and Social Behavior, 37,* 293–310.

Bandura, A. (1973). *Aggression: A social learning analysis.* Englewood Cliffs, NJ: Prentice Hall.

Baum, A. S., & Barnes, D. W. (1993). *A nation in denial: The truth about homelessness.* Boulder, CO: Westview Press.

Becker, S., & Ichino, A. (2002). Estimation of average treatment effects based on propensity scores. *Stata Journal, 2,* 358–377.

Boardman, J. D., Finch, B. K., Ellison, C. G., Williams, D. R., & Jackson, J. S. (2001). Neighborhood disadvantage, stress, and drug use among adults. *Journal of Health and Social Behavior, 42,* 151–165.

Cohen, D. A., Mason, K., Bedimo, A., Scribner, R., Basolo, V., & Farley, T. (2003). Neighborhood physical conditions and health. *American Journal of Public Health, 93,* 467–471.

Cohen, D., Spear, S., Scribner, R., Kissinger, P., Mason, K., & Widgen, J. (2000). "Broken windows" and the risk of gonorrhea. *American Journal of Public Health, 90,* 230–236.

Cone, E. J. (1997). New developments in biological measures of drug prevalence. In L. Harrison & A. Hughes (Eds.), *The validity of self-reported drug use: Improving the accuracy of survey estimates* (National Institute on Drug Abuse Research Monograph No. 167, pp. 108–129). Rockville, MD: U.S. Department of Health and Human Services.

Cone, E. J., & Joseph, R., Jr. (1996). The potential for bias in hair testing for drugs of abuse. In P. Kintz (Ed.), *Drug testing in hair* (pp. 69–94). Boca Raton, FL: CRC Press.

Crum, R. M., Lillie-Blanton, M., & Anthony, J. C. (1996). Neighborhood environment and opportunity to use cocaine and drugs in late childhood and early adolescence. *Drug and Alcohol Dependence, 43,* 155–161.

D'Agostino, R. B. (1998). Propensity score methods for bias reduction in the comparison of a treatment to a non-randomized control group. *Statistics in Medicine, 17,* 2265–2281.

Fendrich, M., & Johnson, T. P. (2005). Race/ethnicity differences in the validity of self-reported drug use: Results from a household survey. *Journal of Urban Health, 82*(Suppl. 3), Siii67–Siii81.

Fendrich, M., Johnson, T. P., Wislar, J. S., & Hubbell, A. (2003). Drug test feasibility in a general population household survey. *Drug and Alcohol Dependence, 73,* 237–250.

Fendrich, M., Johnson, T. P., Wislar, J. S., Hubbell, A., & Spiehler, V. (2004). The utility of drug testing in epidemiological research: Results from a general population survey. *Addiction, 99,* 197–208.

Fendrich, M., Johnson, T., Wislar, J., Sudman, S., & Spiehler, V. (1999). The validity of drug use reporting in a high risk community sample: A comparison of cocaine and heroin survey reports with hair tests. *American Journal of Epidemiology, 149,* 955–962.

Ford, J. M., & Beveridge, A. A. (2006). Varieties of substance use and visible drug problems: Individual and neighborhood factors. *Journal of Drug Issues, 22,* 377–392.

Galea, S., Ahern, J., Tracy, M., & Vlahov, D. (2007). Neighborhood income and income distribution and the use of cigarettes, alcohol and marijuana. *American Journal of Preventive Medicine, 32*(Suppl. 6), S195–S202.

Galea, S., Ahern, J., & Vlahov, D. (2003). Contextual determinants of drug use risk behavior: A theoretic framework. *Journal of Urban Health, 80*(Suppl. 3), Siii50–Siii58.

Groves, R. M., & Couper, M. P. (1998). *Nonresponse in household interview surveys.* New York: Wiley.

Guo, S., Barth, R., & Gibbons, C. (2006). Propensity score matching strategies for evaluating substance abuse services for child welfare clients. *Children and Youth Services Review, 28,* 357–383.

Hannon, L., & Cuddy, M. M. (2006). Neighborhood ecology and drug dependence mortality: An analysis of New York City Census Tracts. *American Journal of Drug and Alcohol Abuse, 32,* 453–463.

Heckman, J., Ichimura, H., Smith, J., & Todd, P. (1998). Characterizing selection bias using experimental data. *Econometrica, 66,* 1017–1098.

Heckman, J., Ichimura, H., & Todd, P. (1997). Matching as an econometric evaluation estimator: Evidence from a job training program. *Review of Economic Studies, 64,* 605–654.

Heckman, J., Ichimura, H., & Todd, P. (1998). Matching as an econometric evaluation estimator. *Review of Economic Studies, 65,* 261–294.

Jehanli, A., Brannan, S., Moore, L., & Spiehler, V. (2001). Blind trials of an onsite saliva drug test. *Journal of Forensic Science, 46,* 206–212.

Johnston, L., O'Malley, P., Bachman, J, & Schulenberg, J. E. (2006) *Monitoring the Future national survey results on drug use: 1975–2005. Volume II: College students and adults ages 19–45* (NIH Publication No. 06-5884). Bethesda, MD: National Institute on Drug Abuse.

Jones, A. S., D'Agostino, R. B., Gondolf, E. W., & Heckert, A. (2004). Assessing the effect of batterer program completion on reassault using propensity scores. *Journal of Interpersonal Violence, 19,* 1002–1020.

Kidwell, D. A., & Blank, D. L. (1996). Environmental exposure—The stumbling block of hair testing. In P. Kintz (Ed.), *Drug testing in hair* (pp. 17–68). Boca Raton, FL: CRC Press.

Latkin, C. A., Curry, A. D., Hua, W., & Davey, M. A. (2007). Direct and indirect associations of neighborhood disorder with drug use and high risk sexual partners. *American Journal of Preventive Medicine, 326,* S231–S241.

Leuven, E., & Sianesi, B. (2003). *PSMATCH2: Stata module to perform full Mahalanobis and propensity score matching, common support graphing, and covariate imbalance testing.* Retrieved November 20, 2007, from http://ideas.repec.org/c/boc/bocode/s432001.html

Levy, P. S., & Lemeshow, S. (1991). *Sampling of populations: Methods and applications.* New York: John Wiley & Sons, Inc.

Luthar, S., & Cushing, G. (1999). Neighborhood influences and child development: A prospective study of substance abusers' offspring. *Development and Psychopathology, 11,* 736–784.

Moos, R. H. (2005). Social contexts and substance use. In W. R. Miller & K. M. Carroll (Eds.), *Rethinking substance abuse: What the science shows and what we should do about it* (pp. 182–200). New York: Guilford Press.

National Institute on Drug Abuse. (2003). *Preventing drug use among children and adolescents.* (2nd ed., NIH Publication No. 04-4212[A]). Bethesda, MD: Author.

Oakes, J. M., & Johnson, P. J. (2006). Propensity score matching for social epidemiology. In J. M. Oakes & J. S. Kaufman (Eds.), *Methods in social epidemiology* (pp. 370–392). San Francisco, CA: Jossey-Bass.

Office of Applied Studies. (2001). *Summary of findings from the 2000 National Household Survey on Drug Abuse* (DHHS Publication No. SMA 01-3549, NHSDA Series H-13). Rockville, MD: Substance Abuse and Mental Health Services Administration.

Parsons, L. S. (2001). Reducing bias in a propensity score matched-pair sample using greedy matching techniques. In *Proceedings of the 26th Annual SAS Users Group International Conference* (Paper 214-26). Cary, NC: SAS Institute.

Pearl, M., Braveman, P., & Abrams, B. (2001). The relationship of neighborhood socioeconomic characteristics to birthweight among 5 ethnic groups in California. *American Journal of Public Health, 91,* 1808–1814.

Richardson, J., Fendrich, M., & Johnson, T. J. (2003). Neighborhood effects on drug reporting. *Addiction, 98,* 1705–1711.

Rosenbaum, P. R., & Rubin, D. B. (1983). The central role of the propensity score in observational studies for causal effects. *Biometrika, 70,* 41–55.

Rubin, D., & Thomas, N. (2000). Propensity score matching with additional adjustments for prognostic covariates. *Journal of the American Statistical Association, 95,* 573–585.

Sampson, R. J., Raudenbush, S. W., & Earls, F. (1997, August 15). Neighborhoods and violent crime: A multilevel study of collective efficacy. *Science, 277,* 919–924.

Saxe, L., Kadushin, C., Beveridge, A., Livert, D., Tighe, E., Rindskopf, D., et al. (2001). The visibility of illicit drugs: Implications for community-based drug control strategies. *American Journal of Public Health, 91,* 1987–1994.

Scheier, L. M., Miller, N. L., Ifill-Williams, M., & Botvin, G. J. (2001). Perceived neighborhood risk as a predictor of drug use among ethnic minority adolescents: Moderating influences of psychosocial functioning. *Journal of Child and Adolescent Substance Abuse, 11,* 67–105.

Shadish, W. R., Cook, T. D., & Campbell, D. T. (2002). *Experimental and quasi-experimental designs for generalized causal inference.* Boston: Houghton-Mifflin.

StataCorp. (2005). *Stata statistical software: Release 9.* College Station, TX: Author.

Substance Abuse and Mental Health Services Administration. (2007). *Results from the 2006 National Survey on Drug Use and Health: National findings* (DHHS Publication No. SMA 07-4293, NSDUH Series H-32). Rockville, MD: Author.

U.S. Census Bureau. (2007). *Census 2000, Summary File 2.* Retrieved August 8, 2007, from http://factfinder. census.gov/servlet/DatasetMainPageServlet?_program= DEC&_submenuId=datasets_1&_lang=en

Winslow, E. B., & Shaw, D. S. (2007). Impact of neighborhood disadvantage on overt behavior problems during early childhood. *Aggressive Behavior, 33,* 207–219.

Wolff, K., Farrell, M., Marsden, J., Montiero, M. G., Ali, R., Welch, S., et al. (1999). A review of biological indicators of illicit drug use: Practical considerations and clinical usefulness. *Addiction, 94,* 1279–1298.

CHAPTER 25

YOUTH SUBSTANCE USE
AND THE MEDIA

Leslie B. Snyder and P. Gayle Nadorff

An interesting finding in media research is that people generally assume that whereas others are duped by the media, they themselves are not. This phenomenon, termed the *third-person hypothesis*, is fairly robust (Davison, 1983; Paul, Salwen, & Dupagne, 2006). Yet it begs the question, when do the media really have a negative influence on people? Under what circumstances does research support media critiques in the popular press, such as the campaign by Tipper Gore against objectionable lyrics in popular music, including pro-drug lyrics ("Tipper Gore Widens War on Rock," 1988)? Most of us are media consumers, and as we grew up we absorbed countless beer commercials on television, watched movies and television shows that glamorized drug use and drug dealing, and listened to lyrics waxing rhapsodic about altered mind states without becoming alcoholics, drug users, or dealers. Are we the special ones, protected by education or media smarts? Or have we, too, been influenced in subtle ways by the media we consumed?

This chapter briefly reviews the nature of drug, tobacco, and alcohol content in the media and focuses on the relation between the media and substance use among youth. *Youth* here means children, teens, and emerging adults. Much of the media and drug literature concerns how substances are portrayed in the media, how many messages concern drug use, and the nature of regulations and voluntary guidelines governing their appearance. Although policy and content studies are valuable for understanding the nature of media environments, they do not

address whether the content made a difference in people's ways of thinking or behaving. It is important to directly examine the influence of the media on substance use and abuse by examining what the mass communication literature calls *effects studies*—studies that measure outcomes such as substance use initiation or amount of substance use compared with media exposure or amount of coverage.

In the first sections of this chapter, we explore a number of issues common to the study of media and substance use. In the next sections, we review the literature on the effects of the media on use of tobacco, alcohol, prescription drugs, over-the-counter drugs, and illicit drugs.

GENERALIZATION ISSUES

When thinking about the effects of the substance-related content in the media, it is useful to wonder about the degree of generalization of the effects from the specific stimulus in the media to a broader category. For instance, if a person sees an advertisement for Bud Light beer, does it stimulate the desire for a Bud Light? A more general effect would suggest that the ad stimulates the desire for any Budweiser product. An even more powerful general effect would include stimulating any beer use, including that of Budweiser's competitors. Likewise, one could conceivably extend this argument and suggest that the ad might stimulate consumption of hard liquor, including whisky and other distilled spirits. In its

Preparation of this chapter was supported in part by Centers for Disease Control and Prevention Grant P01 CD000237. We thank Deborah Barrett and Shu Li for their assistance in preparing the manuscript.

broadest context, an ad could stimulate use of an illicit drug like marijuana.

A company sponsoring an advertisement does not benefit from an ad stimulating a vague desire that was fulfilled by a competitor's product; rather, the aim is to enhance and reinforce the image of the particular brand and to promote use of that brand. In this regard, the tobacco and alcohol industries state that their ads are designed to promote brand switching, not to stimulate additional use of alcohol or tobacco. Marketing-oriented studies for alcohol, tobacco, and pharmaceuticals often examine the effectiveness of marketing for particular brands of substances and do not explore the possibility of increased usage of the substance across brands. However, it is possible that ads, movies, and other content for specific products or even substances have more generalized effects, influencing views not just about the brand and parent company but also the product category (e.g., smokeless tobacco or rum), the type of substance (e.g., alcohol or tobacco), and substances in general.

The generalization issue is important when deciding the appropriate level at which to test an effect of exposure to substance-related content in the media. The concern voiced by public health experts is typically at the level of specific types of substances, such as alcohol, tobacco, illicit drugs, or over-the-counter drugs. Sometimes more specificity is warranted because it will inform future interventions aimed at curbing use of a particular substance that is causing a public health concern, such as crystal methamphetamine or chewing tobacco. Occasionally, the public health community is interested in putting pressure on a particular company because of the manner in which the company promotes its brand, in which case data about the brand-specific effects are appreciated. For example, public concern about the Budweiser frogs and Joe Camel ads, which were seen as being particularly enticing to young children, led to the withdrawal of those ads. Most public health research, however, remains concerned with higher levels of generalization.

AFFECTED TARGET GROUP

The impact of the media on substance use may vary greatly by population. Children, teens, young adults,

mentally challenged individuals, and those who abuse substances are often thought to be more vulnerable to media messages about substances. There has also been concern about the impact of prosubstance media on youth substance use in ethnic populations, including Hispanics, African Americans, and Native Americans. Sometimes the concern is driven by evidence of greater use of particular substances among a group, or it may be driven by observations of greater rates of advertising or entertainment messages in the media targeted to the groups. In general, however, we lack research into how different groups use the media and how their media use, in turn, relates to drug use.

TYPES OF EFFECT AND MECHANISMS

The literature encompasses a range of potential media effects on drug use. The behavioral effects of media exposure include seeking information about the substance, requesting assistance in obtaining the substance, initial trial or experimental use, initiation into habitual use, reinforcement, escalation of use to greater amounts, and cessation of use. The media may affect each level or stage of substance use through different mechanisms. Understanding the precise mechanisms through which the media affect substance use may also make it possible to improve interventions.

Many different mechanisms for media effects have been proposed from different theoretical perspectives (Atkin, 2001; Austin, Chen, & Grube, 1006; McGuire, 1981; Slater & Rouner, 2002). For example, exposure to media messages may alter expectancies, attitudes, and beliefs about substances (including beliefs about social norms and risks) that increase the appeal of the substance and lead to more or less use. Media presentations about substance users can create or reinforce stereotypes about users and influence identification with substance users, enabling some people to see themselves as users and thereby increasing trial and initiation and inhibiting cessation. Sometimes media presentations of substance use create or reinforce positive or negative emotional associations (like happiness or disgust) with substance use in the minds of the media consumers that can ultimately affect decisions about use. Messages may also serve an informational function, presenting rational pro- or antisubstance use arguments, acting as a cue to action, or reminding people of their substance use options. Messages may prompt a need for additional information by creating uncertainty or sparking curiosity. Metamessages may be used to try to break the influence of other messages, as in media literacy programs or the Truth Anti-Tobacco Campaign. New social media can provide linkages to geographically dispersed members of drug-using subcultures. Unfortunately, going into these theories and models is beyond the scope of this chapter, and our review focuses on substance use as an outcome rather than on the potential intervening or explanatory factors. It is important, however, to note that more research is needed because the explanatory power of the mechanisms varies tremendously across field studies.

The way media exposure is measured reveals some assumptions about the mechanism of causal effects. Studies often examine media effects in a dose–response fashion, assuming that a greater dose of media will produce a greater effect. However, the quality of media messages matters—people respond more favorably to some ads than to others. A few exposures to a memorable ad (such as the Budweiser frogs or Joe Camel ads) may cause a much more powerful effect than many exposures to forgettable ads. The implication is that effect sizes based purely on quantity probably underestimate the effect of the media on substance-related behaviors. Alternative measures that include audience evaluations of the messages (e.g., receptivity to advertising) may find higher effect sizes than quantity-of-exposure measures. The difficulty with measures incorporating evaluations is in disentangling the audience members' preexisting propensities to respond to messages in a certain way from the fact that they were exposed.

CAUSAL DIRECTION

One of the more persistent concerns in the substance use and media literature is that of the causal direction of influence. Does exposure to substance messages cause substance use? If so, reducing exposure may reduce use. Or do people who use substances use the media differently—deliberately exposing themselves to prosubstance messages or noticing and remember-

ing those messages longer than do people who do not use substances? If this is the case, then self-report measures may not be valid measures of exposure.

There is evidence that the causal direction works both ways. Supporting the view that exposure influences use, studies (reviewed below) have found that media use relates to alcohol and tobacco initiation at a later date and that objective measures of advertising amounts are related to alcohol and tobacco use. At the same time, brain imaging and physiological studies have shown that heavy drinkers process alcohol-related words, pictures, scents, tactile cues, and images differently from those who rarely drink (George et al., 2001; McCusker & Brown, 1995; Monti et al., 1987; Stormark, Laberg, Nordby, & Hugdahl, 2000; Tapert et al., 2003). Thus, the media appear to influence substance use, which in turn alters the way in which the media are used, which over time affects substance use in a spiral of influence (Slater, 2007).

It is notoriously difficult to prove media effects beyond a reasonable doubt. Longitudinal studies, particularly prospective studies, are a good methodological tool to examine initiation of behavior and mechanisms underlying media effects. However, it is sometimes very difficult to disentangle whether the effect of prior media exposure on current substance use is substantively important, given the typically strong relationship between prior and current exposure. Lab experiments lack external validity because of the contrived setting and constrained exposure. Field experiments are expensive, and it is sometimes unethical (in the case of potentially harmful messages) or impossible (in the case of national media) to randomly assign participants to experimental exposure conditions. Trend studies often avoid self-report problems by using more objective measures such as advertising spending and substance sales figures, but they remain fundamentally based on correlation evidence, are usually unable to address both causation and the mechanisms underlying the media–drug use relationship, and are typically generalizable to the total population rather than to youth. The best approach is to look across diverse methods because each one has certain advantages and to explore hybrid approaches such as those combining trend data with self-report information.

TOBACCO USE AND THE MEDIA

The literature on youth tobacco use and the media is the largest and most comprehensive of that for all the substances. Much of the literature has focused on the question of whether advertising, marketing promotions, and smoking depicted in movies contributes to youth smoking initiation. Another large area of research has examined media as an intervention tool promoting smoking prevention and cessation. More research is needed on how the commercial media hinder smoking cessation and how media fare affects second-hand smoke reduction. The picture that emerges from the literature is that there are media effects on tobacco initiation and continued use and that the conclusions are fairly robust across different methodologies.

Tobacco Advertising and Marketing Effects

One of the most important issues in the media and tobacco domain is whether there is an effect of industry advertising and marketing practices on youth tobacco use. On the basis of a presumed influence, tobacco advertising on broadcast media has been restricted since 1971, and print media need to include one of four health warnings embedded in the ads. In 1998, the attorneys general from 46 states agreed to an out-of-court settlement based on a lawsuit filed against a number of the larger tobacco companies. The Master Settlement Agreement (1998), as it was called, contained several concessions by the tobacco giants, including a stipulation against marketing tobacco products to youth, elimination of billboard advertising, restrictions on sponsorships of some sports, and exclusion of animated characters in tobacco advertisements and promotions (i.e., Joe Camel). The 1998 restrictions coincided with a downturn in smoking among teens, reversing a 10-year increasing trend (Johnston, O'Malley, Bachman, & Schulenberg, 2007). Note that tobacco companies have a great deal of latitude when it comes to placing content in movies, television programming, and music.

With the availability of tobacco industry documents, we now have a more complete picture of how media strategies have been a key element of tobacco marketing. (Unfortunately, the same documents are not available for alcohol and pharmaceutical marketing, and researchers must analyze the content of advertising and promotion to deduce industry strategies.) The tobacco industry realized the importance of attracting young smokers and carefully monitored the behaviors of 14- to 17-year-old youth (Perry, 1999). One major campaign for Camel cigarettes used the animated figure of Joe Camel, which had great appeal for children and adolescents and led to an increase in cigarette sales to youth (DiFranza et al., 1991; Pierce et al., 1991). Furthermore, historical analysis has noted that during periods in which industry targeted one gender more than the other, smoking initiation was much greater for the targeted gender, such as the large-scale marketing of so-called women's brands like Virginia Slims in the 1960s (Pierce & Gilpin, 1995).

Media-based marketing is often complemented by a pricing strategy. During periods of time when the tobacco industry ran promotions subsidizing the price of cigarettes (such as by offering discount coupons), initiation rates among 14- to 17-year-olds increased, effectively countering public health efforts to raise prices through taxation (Pierce et al., 2005).

The power of tobacco advertising can also be shown by policy changes that curtail marketing outreach. A systematic review (Quentin, Nuebauer, Leidl, & Konig, 2007) found that reductions in advertising through partial bans (in which some forms of advertising are still allowed) can sometimes achieve short-term population-based reductions in smoking, and complete bans can significantly reduce consumption.

Exposure and content. In recent years, the tobacco industry has shifted away from traditional forms of advertising toward other marketing techniques, including promotions, price strategies, in-store advertising, and physical displays (Pierce, 2007). Promotions include sponsorship of events and promotional items like t-shirts printed with brand names. The amount spent on traditional advertising in 2006 for tobacco—nearly $142 million—was substantially less than that spent on other substances (TNS Media Intelligence, n.d.).

Although tobacco advertisements are prohibited on television, other types of tobacco messages are permitted. During 1999–2003, each month youth watched on average 3.4 public health–sponsored anti-tobacco public service announcements, 3.8 tobacco company–sponsored public service announcements, 2.6 ads for smoking cessation drugs, and 1 corporate advertisement for a tobacco company (Wakefield et al., 2005). Internal industry documents have shown that tobacco-sponsored public service announcements are designed as public relations strategies rather than aimed at reducing or preventing smoking (Landman, Ling, & Glantz, 2002). Indeed, tobacco-sponsored antismoking messages are associated with an increase in intentions to smoke (Farrelly, Healton, Davis, Messeri, & Haviland, 2002). In addition, tobacco product brand names are occasionally visible on television as part of sports sponsorships, within advertisements for other products, and in movie trailers.

Effects of advertising and marketing on youth smoking initiation. The progression from experimentation with tobacco to being an established smoker occurs between ages 12 and 21, and daily smoking begins between ages 16 and 18 (Kandel, Kiros, Schaffran, & Hu, 2004; Pierce, 2007). A recent meta-analysis (Wellman, Sugarman, DiFranza, & Winickoff, 2006) of methodologically diverse studies found that exposure to tobacco marketing and cigarette use in films increased the odds of becoming a smoker (odds ratio = 2.33, 95% confidence interval = 2.03–2.67, $p \leq .001$). Among the 13 prospective, and thus more methodologically rigorous, studies, the effects on smoking initiation were consistently strong and positive for each measure of exposure, including participating in promotions, awareness of advertising, and receptivity to advertising (see Wellman et al., 2006, Table 1 and Figure 2). Similarly, a more recent prospective study found that having a favorite cigarette ad at a young age and using a promotional item while still a nonsmoker predicted smoking initiation 3 to 6 years later (Gilpin, White, Messer, & Pierce, 2007). A recent national study found that higher levels of cigarette advertising inside local retail outlets (such as chain drug stores and convenience stores) were associated with a greater number of youth trying smoking for the first time (Slater, Chaloupka, Wakefield, Johnston, & O'Malley, 2007).

Coming from a different perspective, a marketing analysis concluded that cigarette advertisements create new smokers rather than just promote brand switching (Roberts & Samuelson, 1988).

Effects of tobacco advertising and marketing on use and cessation. Each year, a high proportion of smokers attempt to quit, but most fail within a week, and only 3%–4% of quit attempts last more than a year (Pierce, 2007). It is therefore important to examine the extent to which the media influence continued use of cigarettes and, by implication, the converse, smoking cessation.

The prospective studies included in the Wellman et al. (2006) meta-analysis showed effects for smoking status by awareness of advertising, appreciation of advertising, and receptivity to smoking. Progression of use toward becoming a heavier smoker was predicted by ad exposure and receptivity (Wellman et al., 2006). Recently, in-store tobacco promotions were associated with teens moving closer to becoming established smokers (Slater et al., 2007).

Cigarette packages provide another medium to reach smokers. Warning labels on cigarettes vary by country, and the United States mandates fairly mild messages on cigarette packages. A study of newly introduced strong warnings on packages in Canada—full color, often graphic displays covering more than 50% of the front and back—showed that the warnings had an emotional impact on smokers, and they were more likely to quit or reduce smoking (Hammond, Fong, McDonald, Brown, & Cameron, 2004).

Effects of Tobacco Depicted in Movies

Youth can potentially see massive numbers of movies scenes depicting smoking (Sargent, Tanski, & Gibson, 2007). Although the tobacco industry agreed voluntarily in 1991 and signed the Master Settlement Agreement in 1998 to prohibit paid brand placement in movies, smoking in movies increased rapidly in the 1990s (Charlesworth & Glantz, 2006). The overall rate of smoking depicted in movies is higher than its actual prevalence rate in the United States (Omidvari et al., 2005). Movies portray the glamorous, positive side of tobacco use; downplay the negative consequences; and tend to depict smokers as White, male, and wealthy (Charlesworth & Glantz, 2006; Roberts

& Christenson, 2000). Adolescents with more exposure to smoking in movies tended to be older, male, and African American and knew others who smoked; less often viewed movies with their parents; had higher levels of sensation seeking; and reported poorer school performance (Sargent et al., 2007).

Studies have shown that smoking initiation is related to greater exposure to smoking in movies (Dalton et al., 2003; Sargent et al., 2005). Youth 10 to 14 years old whose parents have rules against watching R-rated films (which have more smoking than G- and PG-rated films) were less likely to initiate smoking (Sargent et al., 2004). In addition, the more young adults viewed smoking in movies, the greater their likelihood of smoking in the past 30 days (Song, Ling, Neilands, & Glantz, 2007).

Smoking depictions in film appear to have an effect through modeling, attaching positive qualities to people who perform the behavior. Nonsmoking girls whose favorite movies stars smoked onscreen had a greater risk of later initiating smoking than those who did not have favorite stars who smoked (Distefan, Pierce, & Gilpin, 2004). Among youth whose parents do not smoke, heavy exposure to smoking in movies raises their risk of smoking initiation to equal that of youth whose parents do smoke (Dalton et al., 2003). Viewing smoking in movies also creates or reinforces positive expectancies about smoking (Pechmann & Shih, 1999).

Tobacco and Other Media Formats

Music.   Media research has not focused on the effects of references to tobacco in music. Only 8% of music videos have shown actual tobacco use (Gruber, Thau, Hill, Fisher, & Grube, 2005), and only 3% of songs lyrics have referenced tobacco, with a preponderance observed in rap and hip-hop (64%; Roberts & Christenson, 2000).

News.   News coverage about tobacco has the potential to support advocacy efforts at the community, state, and national levels. An analysis of elite newspaper coverage leading up to the Master Settlement Agreement suggested that the protobacco themes were consistent and that the antitobacco messages were less compelling (Menashe & Siegel, 1998). How much has changed since 1998 is unclear. We did not find any studies on the effect of news of youth smoking.

ALCOHOL USE AND THE MEDIA

Alcohol differs from tobacco in that within certain parameters, it is socially acceptable and healthy for adults to use. The main public health concerns center around alcohol abuse and underage drinking. In recent years, research has concentrated on the latter, particularly on the effects of alcohol advertising. Very little is known about how the media relate to abusive drinking and cessation, aside from the effect of public health media campaigns.

Alcohol Advertising Effects

Policies.   For the most part, advertising and marketing are self-regulated by an alcohol industry group representing each product category—beer, wine, and spirits. The advertising codes for all three groups prohibit blatant appeals to youth, but compliance with the voluntary codes can be spotty. In recent years, the Federal Trade Commission (FTC) has become more involved in dealing with complaints, and the recent Sober Truth on Preventing Underage Drinking (STOP) Act of 2006 requests that Congress fund reviews of alcohol advertising independent of the alcohol industry. At issue is the tension between protecting vulnerable youth and the First Amendment right to advertise. Alcohol content in movies and music lyrics is not covered by industry codes.

Exposure and content.   Youth are exposed to large amounts of alcohol advertising each year. Spending on beer, wine, and spirits advertising was almost $1.7 billion in 2006, the majority of which was on television (TNS Media Intelligence, n.d.). Although the 1999 FTC recommendation that television advertising of alcohol be limited to shows for which at most 30% of viewers are underage, large numbers of youth watch adult programs—including sports—that contain large amounts of alcohol advertising or product placements. In 2006, alcohol ads appeared during 14 out of 15 television programs with the largest teen audiences ages 12 to 17 (Center on Alcohol Marketing and Youth, 2007a). Alcohol ads use messages of sex appeal and status to sell their products (Austin & Hust, 2005).

One national survey found that youth remembered exposure to 23 ads on average in the past month, and nearly all (93%) of youth 14–19 years old said they felt targeted at least to some degree by alcohol ads (Fleming Milici, 2006). Youth exposure to industry-sponsored messages about drinking responsibly remains low compared with exposure to overall alcohol advertising (Center on Alcohol Marketing and Youth, 2007b). Even if there was greater exposure, the effect of industry-sponsored public service announcements and alcohol ads with embedded responsibility messages is unknown.

Youth initiation.   The findings from longitudinal studies have supported a link between alcohol advertising and marketing and alcohol initiation. Two studies—one national and one in South Dakota—have shown that exposure to advertising at baseline was related to alcohol initiation in the subsequent 2 years (Ellickson, Collins, Hambarsoomians, & McCaffrey, 2005; Snyder & O'Connell, 2008). Alcohol initiation was associated with possession of or willingness to use alcohol promotional items like t-shirts, hats, or pens in two national studies and a study of middle school students in New England (Fisher, Miles, Austin, Camargo, & Colditz, 2007; McClure, Cin, Gibson, & Sargent, 2006; Snyder & O'Connell, 2008).

Youth alcohol use.   The evidence from longitudinal studies has also supported the conclusion that exposure to alcohol advertising is associated with an increase in alcohol consumption among youth both younger and older than the legal drinking age of 21. An early longitudinal study conducted in New Zealand found an association between ad exposure at age 15 and drinking larger quantities of beer at age 18 among boys but not girls (Connolly, Casswell, Zhang, & Silva, 1994). As the same cohort aged, men and women who liked alcohol ads and had favorite brands at age 18 subsequently drank greater quantities of beer at age 21 and in their mid-20s (Casswell, Pledger, & Pratap, 2002; Casswell & Zhang, 1998). More recent studies have found that greater advertising exposure in seventh grade was related to consuming three or more drinks per episode in eighth grade (Stacy, Zogg, Unger, & Dent,

2004) and to greater frequency of drinking in ninth grade (Ellickson et al., 2005).

The first national longitudinal study in the United States found that drinking amounts in the prior month increased by 1% for every alcohol ad youth 15 to 26 years old reported seeing and that youth who lived in markets with more alcohol advertising expenditures drank more, controlling for the total amount of alcohol sales in the market (Snyder, Fleming Milici, Slater, Sun, & Strizhakova, 2006). The latter finding is important because it shows that the relationship between advertising and consumption is not dependent on drinkers noticing and self-reporting greater amounts of exposure. The same results were observed for the subset of the sample under the legal drinking age of 21. In addition, examination of drinking trajectories found that among youth who lived in markets with less advertising, drinking amounts peaked in their early 20s, whereas those residing in markets with more advertising continued to show increases in drinking amounts into their late 20s. Saffer and Dave (2006) also found that alcohol advertising expenditures per market related to youth drinking levels. As with tobacco, population-level studies have shown that advertising bans reduce overall alcohol consumption (Saffer & Dave, 2002), but the effects on youth are unknown.

Problem drinking.   There is some evidence that alcohol advertising may be associated with a greater rate of car crashes (Saffer, 1997), which occur disproportionately among young drivers. However, alcohol advertising does not seem to be related directly to youth alcohol-related aggression, including being told to leave a place, getting into a serious argument, or physical fighting (Casswell & Zhang, 1998).

Alcohol and Music

Exposure.   Among the few studies investigating alcohol messages in music lyrics, rap and hip-hop have received the most attention because they carry the greatest number of references to alcohol as compared with other genres (Gruber et al., 2005; Herd, 2005). For example, one study found that just more than one third of all hip-hop music videos showed alcohol (Gruber et al., 2005). The alcohol-related content of song lyrics boasts about power and sex appeal, glamor and wealth, violence, and use of other drugs (Herd, 2005).

Youth initiation and use. Research examining effects of music on drinking is scant. There is some support for music video exposure leading to alcohol initiation (Robinson, Chen, & Killen, 1998). However, longitudinal studies of the role of music video exposure in continued use have sometimes found a positive relationship (Van den Bulck & Beullens, 2005) and sometimes found no relationship (Robinson et al., 1998). Listening to rap music was associated with a host of negative behaviors among African American girls ages 14 to 18 who were sexually active, including alcohol and drug use, arrest, and acquiring a sexually transmitted disease (Wingood et al., 2003).

On a different note, music volume can affect drinking quantities. Gueguen, Helene, and Jacob (2004) reported that patrons randomly assigned to drink in a bar with higher music sound levels consumed more alcohol than did patrons drinking in a bar with quieter music.

Alcohol, Entertainment Television, Movies, and News

Exposure. Many studies have shown that nearly all movies depict alcohol and that these depictions are usually positive (Everett, Schnuth, & Tribble, 1998; Roberts & Christenson, 2000). Two fifths of teen characters depicted in movies drank alcohol, and there were no long-term consequences of drinking for about two thirds of those who drank (Stern, 2005).

Alcohol has a greater presence than other substances on television entertainment programming and was present in more than two thirds of all television shows in the United States (Roberts & Christenson, 2000). Adult characters drank alcohol for longer periods on screen than they drank nonalcoholic beverages, and drinking was often treated as humorous, routine, and resulting in few negative consequences (Roberts & Christenson, 2000). News stories in television, newspapers, and magazines about violent crimes like murders mention alcohol far less often than estimates of actual prevalence (Slater, Long, and Ford, 2006).

Effects

There is limited evidence regarding the effect of exposure to entertainment content on actual drinking practices, and no studies on the effects of exposure to news about alcohol. One study (Dalton et al., 2006) found that youth whose parents restrict their viewing of R-rated movies—which depict more drinking than G and PG films—were less likely to use alcohol. Another cross-sectional study found that entertainment media exposure, primarily late-night television, was directly associated with teen drinking (Austin, Pinkleton, & Fujioka, 2000). In Belgium, the amount of television viewing at baseline was positively related to the amount of alcohol drunk while going out a year later (Van den Bulck & Beullens, 2005).

PRESCRIPTION DRUGS AND THE MEDIA

Prescription drugs are legal for youth when used as prescribed by a physician. The prescription drug literature has focused largely on adult populations, and research questions typically concern optimizing prescription drug use among patient populations. However, of great concern to public health is a rising trend in nonmedical, or recreational, use of prescription drugs among young people. Nonmedical use can include misuse (using your own prescription outside the instructions of a physician) and abuse (using the drug without a prescription). Nonmedical use of prescription drugs is slightly less frequent than marijuana use, and new users of nonmedical prescription pain relievers outnumber new marijuana users age 12 or older (Colliver, Kroutil, Dai, & Gfroerer, 2006). Given the growing problem with prescription drug abuse and misuse, it is a pity that there has been so little research on the relationship between exposure to entertainment, news, or marketing messages about prescription drugs and nonmedical prescription drug use by youth.

Prescription Drug Advertising and Marketing

Only two countries legally permit the controversial practice of direct-to-consumer advertising of prescription drugs—the United States and New Zealand. Prescription drugs are the most commonly advertised substance in the United States, with more than

$4.1 billion spent in advertising in 2006 (TNS Media Intelligence, n.d.). The total amount of advertising spending has increased dramatically since 1996 when the Food and Drug Administration loosened media regulations to allow marketing directly to consumers (Donohue, Cevasco, & Rosenthal, 2007). Despite a very large advertising budget, it represents a small fraction (15% in 2000) of the total marketing activities used by pharmaceutical companies (Rosenthal, Berndt, Donohue, Frank, & Epstein, 2002). Other marketing strategies include sales representatives meeting face to face with physicians, free samples, advertising in professional journals, sponsorship, or hosting meetings and events. National surveys have found that about 80% of adults have seen a prescription drug ad in the past 12 months (Aiken, Swasy, & Braman, 2004; Murray, Lo, Pollack, Donelan, & Lee, 2004). About half of Web users visited at least one pharmaceutical Web site, especially women and younger adults (Choi & Lee, 2007).

The appeals used in drug ads emphasize control over the medical condition, social approval, and drug effectiveness, innovativeness, and convenience (Frosch, Krueger, Hornik, Cronholm, & Barg, 2007; Wilkes, Bell, & Kravitz, 2000). Research has found that the quality of the drug information in ads is inconsistent, many ads have not complied with Food and Drug Administration and FTC advertising regulations, and the literacy level may be too high for many people (FTC, 2003; Wallace, Rogers, Turner, Keenum, & Weiss, 2006; Wilkes et al., 2000).

Use of prescription drugs. Studies of adults and physicians have provided evidence that prescription drug ads in the mass media lead patients to request and physicians to prescribe the advertised drugs (e.g., Huh & Langteau, 2007; Kravitz et al., 2005; Mintzes et al., 2003; Murray et al., 2004; Weissman et al., 2004). Direct-to-consumer advertising has also seemed to increase the number of new diagnoses of a condition and may improve drug adherence (Donohue, Berndt, Rosenthal, Epstein, & Frank, 2004; 't Jong, Stricker, & Sturkenboom, 2004; Weissman et al., 2003, 2004), but more controlled studies are needed. Remarkably, physicians admit to agreeing to inappropriate prescriptions for patients about 15% of times in which the patient makes a drug request on the basis of an ad (Murray, Lo, Pollack, Donolan, & Lee, 2003).

Presumably, similar drug advertising effects would hold for teens, young adults, and parents, but we found only one study, which showed a moderate correlation between the amount of magazine advertising exposure and the number of medications college students reported taking (Burak, 1999). None of the physician studies have examined prescriptions for young people. For youth, the potential for inappropriate prescriptions is more critical because advertised drugs may not have been tested with younger people when they are first on the market. Ads may also inadvertently lead youth to believe that pharmaceuticals are safe (or safer than illegal drugs), even when used without a prescription. Research should also examine how often youth obtain their drugs through nonmedical sources, including family members and the Internet.

Prescription Drugs and the News and Entertainment Media

Very little research has been done on prescription drugs and the effects of exposure to news about prescription drugs or depictions of prescription drug use in entertainment media. News about breakthroughs and drug scares may be an important source of information.

Prescription Drugs and the Internet

The Internet can be a source of information about drugs, a means to purchase them, and a way to connect with other drug users and people with similar health issues. An estimated 17% of 18- to 27-year-olds searched online for prescription drug information (Fox, 2004). Online discussion groups and postings to Web sites may also inform the medical and public health community about problems with drug use, including abuse (Blenkinsopp, Wilkie, Wang, & Routledge, 2006; Butler et al., 2007).

An increasing number of Web sites sell drugs, but Web site content is often problematic (Lorence & Churchill, 2007). At present, Internet sales seem to be a very small part of the nonmedical drug use market (Fox, 2004; Office of Applied Studies, 2006).

There has been no research as to whether drugs marketed via the Internet to healthy people that purport to enhance sexual, mental, and physical performance or provide psychotropic experiences prompt an increase in use of the drugs or exposure to adulterated or harmful substances or create unreal expectations about sexual relationships. Of unsolicited e-mails in 2002, 10% were for health, particularly diet and sexual enhancement ads, and about half appeared to contain false messages (FTC, 2003). It is possible that young people, if they perceive the drug messages as targeting people like themselves, may be more susceptible to such claims because of their focus on appearance, identity, and sexual issues.

OVER-THE-COUNTER DRUGS

Concern is rising about youth abuse of over-the-counter drugs. New estimates are that 3.1 million people ages 12 to 25 (5.3%) have used an over-the-counter cough and cold medication to get high, and 1.7% used it in the past year (Substance Abuse and Mental Health Services Administration, 2008). Advertising spending for over-the-counter medications is second only to prescription drugs and was more than $2.4 billion in 2006 (TNS Media Intelligence, n.d.; the figure excludes advertising for personal beauty products). In addition, 49% of U.S. adult Internet users said they received spam for an over-the-counter medication (Fox, 2004).

Evidence linking over-the-counter drug advertising and drug use is scant. Although it did not examine the effects on youth, one trend study found that over-the-counter advertising can increase drug sales (Ling, Berndt, & Kyle, 2002). News stories about Reye's syndrome had an effect on parents, decreasing their use of aspirin with their children (Soumerai, Ross-Degnan, & Kahn, 1992). No studies have examined the link between youth drug abuse and over-the-counter drug advertising, news coverage, or entertainment media.

ILLICIT SUBSTANCES

There is a surprising dearth of research on how media messages about illicit drugs affect youth drug use. Most of the research has concerned the content of the entertainment media and news, not the amount of exposure to and effects of that content. There is much more research on anti-illicit drug interventions that involve the media, but the results have been mixed at best.

Although both prodrug and antidrug messages are often present on the same medium, let alone across media, few studies have accounted for the positive or negative direction of messages and may therefore miss an important confound. Studies of the effects of prodrug and antidrug news stories (Stryker, 2003) and prevention messages (Wright & Pemberton, 1999) have supported the contention that the valence of marijuana messages affects youth drug use.

Illicit Drugs on Entertainment and News Media

Drug use on television is often depicted in a negative, although somewhat humorous light, such that the humor may undercut the antidrug messages (Roberts & Christenson, 2000). Analyses of top-grossing movies have shown that up to 20% portrayed illicit drug use (Roberts & Christenson, 2000). These movie portrayals often glamorize drugs and fail to show negative consequences of drug use among users, but there are often other characters who refuse illicit drugs. More than 15% of teen characters cast in top-grossing films from 1999 to 2001 used illicit drugs (Stern, 2005). Teen drug users in films cut across gender and socioeconomic status lines and appeared mostly in R-rated movies (Stern, 2005).

Very little work has been done on the effects of entertainment media on illicit drug use by youth. One of the few studies conducted found that more than a third of 12- to 16-year-olds in Scotland said they had learned a lot about drugs from TV and newspapers but that learning from the media was unrelated to drug use (Hammersley, Ditton, & Main, 1997).

News coverage in general is not supportive of illicit drug use, mostly focusing on the criminal aspect of drugs and drug regulation (Noto, Pinsku, & Mastroianni, 2006; Slater et al., 2006). A study of the effects of news about marijuana found that increases in promarijuana coverage were associated with increasing teen drug use in the United States and that increases in antimarijuana coverage were associated with downturns in adolescent drug use (Stryker, 2003).

Prosubstance Media

A number of groups lobby for policies supporting scientific research, medical use, and religious use of illicit drugs. Other organizations see their role, in part, as presenting balanced information about the risks and benefits of illicit drug use, tips on safe use of a substance, and practical information to facilitate use (Jenks, 1995). The types of media these organizations use include pro–illicit drug Web sites, print materials, fundraising direct mail, product catalogues, promotional items, and alternative news stories. For example, the Web site http://www.marihemp.com featured this "Daily Factoid" at the top of their homepage: "U.S. National Toxicity Program TR-446 Study concluded that THC-9 (primary active ingredient in cannabis) presented virtually no cancer risk; may even reduce cancer risk." The effect of exposure to messages sponsored by prodrug organizations is not known.

Illicit Substances and Music

Despite enduring hit songs like Eric Clapton's famous "Cocaine," only a little attention has been paid to the relationship between exposure to drug-related content in music and drug use. Estimates of the number of music videos that contain references to illicit drugs range from 13% to 20%, with more references in rap and hip-hop than in pop, rock, or rhythm and blues songs (Gruber et al., 2005; Roberts & Christenson, 2000).

Effects of music on illicit drug use. Certain types of music appear to be identified with illicit drug-using cultures in a particular historical period, such as protest rock music in the 1970s, heavy metal in the late 1980s and early 1990s, and hip-hop and rap more recently (Diamond, Bermudez, & Schensul, 2006; Roberts & Christenson, 2000). It may be that troubled youth are attracted to extreme music, and the music in turn may reinforce their depression, anger, and alienation (Roberts & Christenson, 2000; Roe, 1995) and increase the likelihood of illicit drug use. Places or events may also be associated with drug culture, as was found for attendance at live music concerts in France (Peretti-Watel & Lorente, 2004). Prospective studies that can help establish causality are needed.

ANTISUBSTANCE MEDIA CAMPAIGNS

Meta-analyses have shown that media campaigns tend to report small effect sizes, although small effects can translate into substantial behavior change at the population level when the target group is large (Snyder et al., 2004). Youth substance campaigns have even more modest effects than most social marketing campaigns, but the magnitude of effects are in line with those obtained using school-based and other prevention strategies that can be more expensive per capita (Snyder, 2006). Cessation campaign effect sizes have also been quite modest (Snyder et al., 2004).

Media campaigns within state tobacco control programs aim to change social norms about tobacco use, prevent initiation, and promote cessation. Comprehensive control efforts (in which communication efforts were combined with other policies like increased taxes on cigarettes) in California, Massachusetts, and Florida were all associated with downward trends in youth smoking (Hersey et al., 2003). Evaluations of Florida's truth campaign provide the strongest evidence that statewide media campaigns aimed at youth can succeed (Niederdeppe, Farrelly, & Haviland, 2004). The Florida campaign was the first to feature messages attacking the tobacco companies for promoting a dangerous substance in a misleading way. The messages also aimed to make nonsmoking seem cool and rebellious. Unfortunately, the successful Massachusetts and Florida campaigns have lost most of their funding.

Given the preliminary success of the Florida effort, the Master Settlement Agreement provided for a national antismoking campaign that averaged $100 million per year initially. The national campaign followed Florida's lead, also using brand-name "truth" and featuring messages that attacked tobacco and their advertisements. The national Truth Anti-Tobacco Campaign was associated with a decrease in youth smoking (Farrelly, Davis, Haviland, Messeri, & Healton, 2005).

In contrast, meta-analyses have shown that media campaigns against illicit drugs have had very poor success rates (Derzon & Lipsey, 2002). The Office of National Drug Control Policy antidrug campaign—pegged at $1 billion over 5 years and the largest publicly funded media campaign in the United States—had very limited success, although the evaluation was severely handicapped by the lack of a control group (Hornik et al., 2003). It will be important to see whether the new Office of National Drug Control Policy campaigns—the positively focused "Above the Influence" campaign (launched in November 2005) and a prescription drug abuse campaign (begun in 2007)—have greater success.

Alcohol reduction campaigns for youth have historically had slightly higher effect sizes than either tobacco or illicit drug campaigns (Snyder, 2006). Here, too, there are new efforts to watch: In the United States, the STOP Act of 2006 mandated money for a national campaign against youth alcohol consumption. However, only $1 million a year has been allocated for the campaign, and there is no provision for scientific oversight or evaluation.

Youth campaigns against substances have traditionally had less success with at-risk youth (Derzon & Lipsey, 2002), but some campaigns have shown how it is possible to design messages to appeal successfully to high-risk youth, who also tend to be high sensation seekers (Palmgreen, Donohew, Lorch, Hoyle, & Stephenson, 2002). Girls have been on average slightly more responsive to media campaigns than boys (Derzon & Lipsey, 2002).

Antisubstance campaigns that were relatively successful featured high amounts of message repetition, messages for parents, and messages for youth about alternatives to substance use, positive attitudes toward nonuse, consequences of use, and resistance skills (Derzon & Lipsey, 2002). Campaigns relying on electronic channels were more successful than those using only print channels like posters and flyers, and supplementing media channels with outreach approaches like discussion groups or counseling appeared valuable (Derzon & Lipsey, 2002). Across health topics, campaigns that used messages about the enforcement of policies, emphasized information new to the target groups, had better evaluation designs, and had greater reach were relatively more successful than campaigns that did not (Snyder & Hamilton, 2002). Given the amount of prosubstance messages in popular culture, it is probably important to use two-sided messages. Experimental studies have also suggested that anti-

substance messages aimed at youth may be more successful if they focus on young victims who suffer from substance-related problems and the social disapproval norms (e.g., Pechman, Zhao, Goldberg, & Reibling, 2003).

CONCLUSION

Across the many different substances covered in this chapter, media exposure appears to be linked to initiation of substance use. There is also some evidence of the effects of the media on continued and escalating levels of substance use, although the evidence is not as strong as that for initiation. Furthermore, the evidence seems to suggest that visual entertainment formats like prodrug messages in movies and promotional items are at least as strong as advertising in their ability to influence people, and may be stronger. More studies are needed on the effects of the media on over-the-counter drug abuse, illicit substance use, and abuse of prescription drugs and of the effects of entertainment media on substances other than tobacco in movies.

To counter prosubstance messages, several global strategies follow from the analysis of the literature. First, a concerted effort is needed to reduce media exposure through public policies, household rules, and promotion of selective exposure. Second, organizations can strive to improve media content by educating writers and producers about the negative consequences of substance use and difficulties of cessation. Third, the public health community and parents can look for ways to reframe prosubstance messages, as was done in Truth Anti-Tobacco Campaign messages. Fourth, the public health community should recognize that media campaigns are often a cost-effective way to reach a large number of people and that media campaign effectiveness is often on par with other drug prevention programs.

References

Aiken, K. J., Swasy, J. L., & Braman, A. C. (2004). *Patient and physician attitudes and behaviors associated with DTC promotion of prescription drugs—Summary of FDA survey research results.* Washington, DC: U.S. Department of Health and Human Resources, Food and Drug Administration.

Atkin, C. K. (2001). Theory and principles of media health campaigns. In R. E. Rice & C. K. Atkin (Eds.), *Public communication campaigns* (pp. 49–68). Beverly Hills, CA: Sage.

Austin, E. W., Chen, M., & Grube, J. W. (2006). How does alcohol advertising influence underage drinking? The role of desirability, identification and skepticism. *Journal of Adolescent Health, 38,* 376–384.

Austin, E. W., & Hust, S. J. T. (2005). Targeting adolescents? The content and frequency of alcoholic and nonalcoholic beverage ads in magazine and video formats—November 1999–April 2000. *Journal of Health Communication, 10,* 769–785.

Austin, E. W., Pinkleton, B. F., & Fujioka, Y. (2000). The role of interpretation processes and parental discussion in the media's effects on adolescents' use of alcohol. *Pediatrics, 105,* 343–253.

Blenkinsopp, A., Wilkie, P., Wang, M., & Routledge, P. A. (2006). Patient reporting of suspected adverse drug reactions: A review of published literature and international experience. *British Journal of Clinical Pharmacology, 63,* 148–156.

Burak, L. J. (1999). Effects of direct-to-consumer advertising of pharmaceutical products on college students. *Health Marketing Quarterly, 17,* 19–29.

Butler, S. F., Venuti, S. W., Benoit, C., Beaulaurier, R. L., Houle, B., & Katz, N. (2007). Internet surveillance: Content analysis and monitoring of product-specific Internet prescription opioid abuse-related postings. *Clinical Journal of Pain, 23,* 619–628.

Casswell, S., Pledger, M., & Pratap, S. (2002). Trajectories of drinking from 18 to 26 years: Identification and prediction. *Addiction, 97,* 1427–1437.

Casswell, S., & Zhang, J.-F. (1998). Impact of liking for advertising and brand allegiance on drinking and alcohol-related aggression: A longitudinal study. *Addiction, 93,* 1209–1217.

Center on Alcohol Marketing and Youth. (2007a). *CAMY Monitoring Report: Youth exposure to alcohol advertising on television and in national magazines, 2001 to 2006.* Washington, DC: Author.

Center on Alcohol Marketing and Youth. (2007b). *Drowned out: Alcohol industry "responsibility" advertising on television, 2001–2005.* Washington, DC: Author.

Charlesworth, A., & Glantz, S. A. (2006). Tobacco and the movie industry. *Clinics in Occupational and Environmental Medicine, 5,* 73–84.

Choi, S. M., & Lee, W.-N. (2007). Understanding the impact of direct-to-consumer (DTC) pharmaceutical advertising on patient-physician interactions: Adding the web to the mix. *Journal of Advertising, 36,* 137–149.

Colliver, J. D., Kroutil, L. A., Dai, L., & Gfroerer, J. C. (2006). *Misuse of prescription drugs: Data from the 2002, 2003, and 2004 National Surveys on Drug Use and Health* (DHHS Publication No. SMA 06-4192, Analytic Series A-28). Rockville, MD: Substance Abuse and Mental Health Services Administration, Office of Applied Studies.

Connolly, G., Casswell, S., Zhang, J. F., & Silva, P. (1994). Alcohol in the mass media and drinking by adolescents: A longitudinal study. *Addiction, 89,* 1255–1263.

Dalton, M. A., Adachi-Mejia, A. M., Longacre, M. R., Titus-Ernstoff, L. T., Gibson, J. J., Martin, S. K., et al. (2006). Parental rules and monitoring of children's movie viewing associated with children's risk for smoking and drinking. *Pediatrics, 118,* 1932–1942.

Dalton, M. A., Sargent, J. D., Beach, M. L., Titus-Ernstoff, L., Gibson, J. J., Ahrens, M. B., et al. (2003). Effect of viewing smoking in movies on adolescent smoking initiation: A cohort study. *Lancet, 362,* 281–285.

Davison, W. P. (1983). The third-person effect in communication. *Public Opinion Quarterly, 47,* 1–15.

Derzon, J. H., & Lipsey, M. W. (2002). A meta-analysis of the effectiveness of mass-communication for changing substance-use knowledge, attitudes, and behavior. In W. D. Crano & M. Burgoon (Eds.), *Mass media and drug prevention: Classic and contemporary theories and research* (pp. 231–258). Mahwah, NJ: Erlbaum.

Diamond, S., Bermudez, R., & Schensul, J. (2006). What's the rap about ecstasy? Popular music lyrics and drug trends among American youth. *Journal of Adolescent Research, 21,* 269–298.

DiFranza, J. R., Richards, J. W., Paulman, P. M., Wolf-Gillespie, N., Fletcher, C., Jaffee, R. D., et al. (1991, December 11). RJR Nabisco's cartoon camel promotes Camel cigarettes to children. *JAMA, 266,* 3149–3153.

Distefan, J. M., Pierce, J. P., & Gilpin, E. A. (2004). Smoking in movies influences adolescents to start smoking: A longitudinal study. *American Journal of Public Health, 94,* 1–6.

Donohue, J. M., Berndt, E. R., Rosenthal, M., Epstein, A. M., & Frank, R. G. (2004). Effect of pharmaceutical promotion on adherence to the treatment guidelines for depression. *Medical Care, 42,* 1176–1185.

Donohue, J. M., Cevasco, M., & Rosenthal, M. B. (2007). A decade of direct-to-consumer advertising of prescription drugs. *New England Journal of Medicine, 357,* 673–681.

Ellickson, P. L., Collins, R. L., Hambarsoomians, K., & McCaffrey, D. F. (2005). Does alcohol advertising promote adolescent drinking? Results from a longitudinal assessment. *Addiction, 100,* 235–246.

Everett, S. A., Schnuth, R. L., & Tribble, J. L. (1998). Tobacco and alcohol use in top-grossing American films. *Journal of Community Health, 23,* 317–324.

Farrelly, M. C., Davis, K. C., Haviland, M. H., Messeri, P., & Healton, C. G. (2005). Evidence of a dose-response relationship between "truth" antismoking ads and youth smoking prevalence. *American Journal of Public Health, 95,* 425–431.

Farrelly, M. C., Healton, C. G., Davis, K. C., Messeri, P., & Haviland, M. H. (2002). Getting to the truth: Evaluating national tobacco countermarketing campaigns. *American Journal of Public Health, 92,* 901–907.

Federal Trade Commission. (2003, April 30). *False claims in spam: A report by the FTC's Division of Marketing Practices.* Retrieved January 10, 2008, from http://www.ftc.gov/reports/spam/030429spamreport.pdf

Fisher, L. B., Miles, I. W., Austin, S. B., Camargo, C. A., Jr., & Golditz, G. A. (2007). Predictors of initiation of alcohol use among U.S. adolescents: Finding from a prospective cohort study. *Archives of Pediatric and Adolescent Medicine, 161,* 959–966.

Fleming Milici, F. (2006). *Is this ad targeting me? The effects of perceiving oneself as a target of alcohol advertising for people under the legal drinking age.* Unpublished doctoral dissertation, University of Connecticut, Storrs.

Fox, S. (2004). *Prescription drugs online.* Washington, DC: Pew Internet & American Life Project. Retrieved January 10, 2008, from http://pewInternet.org/pdfs/PIP_Prescription_Drugs_Online.pdf

Frosch, D. L., Krueger, P. M., Hornik, R. C., Cronholm, P. F., & Barg, F. K. (2007). Creating demand for prescription drugs: A content analysis of television direct-to-consumer advertising. *Annals of Family Medicine, 5,* 6–13.

George, M. S., Anton, R. F., Bloomer, C., Teneback, C., Drobes, D. J., Lorberbaum, J. P., et al. (2001). Activation of prefrontal cortex and anterior thalamus in alcoholic subjects on exposure to alcohol-specific cues. *Archives of General Psychiatry, 58,* 345–352.

Gilpin, E. A., White, M. M., Messer, K., & Pierce, J. P. (2007). Receptivity to tobacco advertising and promotions among young adolescents as a predictor of established smoking in young adulthood. *American Journal of Public Health, 97,* 1489–1495.

Gruber, E. L., Thau, H. M., Hill, D. L., Fisher, D. A., & Grube, J. W. (2005). Alcohol, tobacco and illicit substances in music videos: A content analysis of prevalence and genre. *Journal of Adolescent Health, 37,* 81–83.

Gueguen, N., Helene, L. G., & Jacob, C. (2004). Sound level of background music and alcohol consumption: An empirical evaluation. *Perceptual & Motor Skills, 99,* 34–38.

Hammersley, D., Ditton, J., & Main, D. (1997). Drug-use and sources of drug information in a 12–16-year-old school sample. *Drugs: Education, Prevention Policy, 3,* 231–241.

Hammond, D., Fong, G. T., McDonald, P. W., Brown, K. S., & Cameron, R. (2004). Graphic Canadian cigarette warning labels and adverse outcomes: Evidence from Canadian smokers. *American Journal of Public Health, 94,* 1442–1445.

Herd, D. (2005). Changes in the prevalence of alcohol use in rap song lyrics, 1979–97. *Addiction, 100,* 1258–1269.

Hersey, J. C., Niederdeppe, J., Evans, W. D., Nonnemaker, J., Blahut, S., Farrelly, M. C., et al. (2003). The effects of state counterindustry media campaigns on beliefs, attitudes, and smoking status among teens and young adults. *Preventive Medicine, 37,* 544–522.

Hornik, R., Maklan, D., Cadell, D., Barmada, C., Jacobsohn, L., Henderson, V. R., et al. (2003). *Evaluation of the National Youth Anti-Drug Media Campaign: 2003 Report of Findings.* Retrieved January 14, 2008, from http://www.drugabuse.gov/PDF/DESPR/1203report.pdf

Huh, J., & Langteau, R. (2007). Presumed influence of direct-to-consumer (DTC) prescription drug advertising on patients. *Journal of Advertising, 36,* 151–172.

Jenks, S. M. (1995). An analysis of risk reduction among organized groups that promote marijuana and psychedelic drugs. *Journal of Drug Issues, 25,* 629–647.

Johnston, L. D., O'Malley, P. M., Bachman, J. G., & Schulenberg, J. E. (2007). *Monitoring the Future national survey results on drug use, 1975–2006. Volume I: Secondary school students* (NIH Publication No. 07-6205). Bethesda, MD: National Institute on Drug Abuse.

Kandel, D. B., Kiros, G. E., Schaffran, C., & Hu, M.-C. (2004). Racial/ethnic differences in cigarette smoking initiation and progression to daily smoking: A multilevel analysis. *American Journal of Public Health, 94,* 128–135.

Kravitz, R. L., Epstein, R. M., Feldman, M. D., Franz, C. E., Azari, R., Wilkes, M. S., et al. (2005, April 27). Influence of patient's requests for direct-to-consumer advertised antidepressants: A randomized controlled trial. *JAMA, 293,* 1995–2002.

Landman, A., Ling, P. M., & Glantz, S. A. (2002). Tobacco industry youth smoking prevention programs: Protecting the industry and hurting tobacco control. *American Journal of Public Health, 92,* 917–930.

Ling, D. C., Berndt, E. R., & Kyle, M. K. (2002). Deregulating direct-to-consumer marketing of prescription drugs: Effects on prescription and over-the-counter product sales. *Journal of Law and Economics, 45,* 691–722.

Lorence, D., & Churchill, R. (2007). A study of the Web as DTC drug marketing agent. *Journal of Medical Systems, 31,* 551–556.

Master Settlement Agreement. (1998). Retrieved December 7, 2008, from http://ag.ca.gov/tobacco/msa.php

McClure, A. C., Cin, S. D., Gibson, J., & Sargent, J. D. (2006). Ownership of alcohol-branded merchandise and initiation of teen drinking. *American Journal of Preventive Medicine, 30,* 277–283.

McCusker, C. G., & Brown, K. (1995). Cue-exposure to alcohol-associated stimuli reduces autonomic reactivity, but not craving and anxiety, in dependent drinkers. *Alcohol and Alcoholism, 30,* 319–327.

McGuire, W. J. (1981). Theoretical foundations of campaigns. In R. E. Rice & W. J. Paisley (Eds.), *Public communication campaigns* (pp. 41–70). Beverly Hills, CA: Sage.

Menashe, C. L., & Siegel, M. (1998). The power of a frame: An analysis of newspaper coverage of tobacco issues—United States, 1985–1996. *Journal of Health Communication, 3,* 307–325.

Monti, P. M., Binkoff, J. A., Abrams, D. B., Zwick, W. R., Nirenberg, T. D., & Liepman, M. R. (1987). Reactivity of alcohols and nonalcoholics to drinking cures. *Journal of Abnormal Psychology, 96,* 122–126.

Mintzes, B., Barer, M. L., Kravitz, R. L., Bassett, K., Lexchin, J., Kazanjian, A., et al. (2003). How does direct-to-consumer advertising (DTCA) affect prescribing? A survey in primary care environments with and without legal DTCA. *Canadian Medical Association Journal, 169,* 405–412.

Monti, P. M., Binkoff, J. A., Abrams, D. B., Zwick, W. R., Nirenberg, T. D., & Liepman, M. R. (1987). Reactivity of alcoholics and nonalcoholics to drinking cures. *Journal of Abnormal Psychology, 96,* 122–126.

Murray, E., Lo, B., Pollack, L., Donelan, K., & Lee, K. (2003). Direct-to-consumer advertising: Physicians' views of its effects on quality of care and the doctor-patient relationship. *Journal of the American Board of Family Practice, 16,* 513–524.

Murray, E., Lo, B., Pollack, L., Donelan, K., & Lee, K. (2004). Direct-to-consumer advertising: Public perceptions and its effects on health behaviors, health care, and the doctor-patient relationship. *Journal of the American Board of Family Practice, 17,* 6–18.

Niederdeppe, J., Farrelly, M. C., & Haviland, M. L. (2004). Confirming "truth": More evidence of a successful tobacco countermarketing campaign in Florida. *American Journal of Public Health, 94,* 255–257.

Noto, A. R., Pinsky, I., & Mastroianni, F. D. (2006). Drugs in the Brazilian print media: An exploratory survey of newspaper and magazine stories in the year 2000. *Substance Use & Misuse, 41,* 1263–1276.

Office of Applied Studies. (2006). *Results from the 2005 National Survey on Drug Use and Health: National findings* (DHHS Publication No. SMA 06-4194, NSDUH Series H-30). Rockville, MD: Substance Abuse and Mental Health Services Administration.

Omidvari, K., Lessnau, K., Kim, J., Mercante, D., Weinacker, A., & Mason, C. (2005). Smoking in contemporary American cinema. *Chest, 128,* 746–754.

Palmgreen, P., Donohew, L., Lorch, E. P., Hoyle, R. H., & Stephenson, M. T. (2001). Television campaigns and adolescent marijuana use: Tests of sensation seeking targeting. *American Journal of Public Health, 91,* 292–296.

Paul, B., Salwen, M. B., & Dupagne, M. (2006). The third person effect: A meta-analysis of the perceptual hypothesis. In R. W. Preiss, B. M. Gayle, N. Burrell, M. Allen, & J. Bryant (Eds.), *Mass media effects research: Advances through meta-analysis* (pp. 81–102). Hillsdale, NJ: Erlbaum.

Pechmann, C., Zhao, G., Goldberg, M. E., & Reibling, E. T. (2003). What to convey in antismoking advertisements for adolescents: The use of protection motivation theory to identify effective message themes. *Journal of Marketing, 67,* 1–18.

Pechmann, C., & Shih, C.-F. (1999). Smoking scenes in movies and antismoking advertisements before movies: Effects on youth. *Journal of Marketing, 63,* 1–13.

Peretti-Watel, P., & Lorente, F. O. (2004). Cannabis use, sport practice and other leisure activities at the end of adolescence. *Drug and Alcohol Dependence, 73,* 251–257.

Perry, C. L. (1999). The tobacco industry and underage youth smoking: Tobacco industry documents from the Minnesota litigation. *Archives of Pediatric and Adolescent Medicine, 153,* 935–941.

Pierce, J. P. (2007). Tobacco industry marketing, population-based tobacco control, and smoking behavior. *American Journal of Preventive Medicine, 33*(Suppl. 6), S327–S334.

Pierce, J. P., Gilmer, T. P., Lee, L., Gilpin, E. A., de Beyer, J., & Messer, K. (2005). Tobacco industry price-subsidizing promotions may overcome the downward pressure of higher prices on initiation of regular smoking. *Health Economics, 14,* 1061–1071.

Pierce, J. P., & Gilpin, E. A. (1995). A historical analysis of tobacco marketing and the uptake of smoking by youth in the United States: 1890–1977. *Health Psychology, 14,* 500–508.

Pierce, J. P., Gilpin, E., Burns, D. M., Whalen, E., Rosbrook, B., Shopland, D., et al. (1991, December 11). Does tobacco advertising target young people to start smoking? Evidence from California. *JAMA, 266,* 3154–3158.

Quentin, W., Nuebauer, S., Leidl, R., & Konig, H.-H. (2007). Advertising bans as a means of tobacco control policy: A systematic literature review of time-series analysis. *International Journal of Public Health, 52,* 295–307.

Roberts, D. F., & Christenson, P. G. (2000). *"Here's looking at you, kid": Alcohol, drugs, and tobacco in entertainment media.* Menlo Park, CA: Kaiser Family Foundation.

Roberts, M. J., & Samuelson, L. (1988). An empirical analysis of dynamic, nonprice competition in an oligopolistic industry. *Rand Journal of Economics, 19,* 200–220.

Robinson, T. N., Chen, H. L., & Killen, J. D. (1998). Television and music video exposure and risk of adolescent alcohol use. *Pediatrics, 102,* e54.

Roe, K. (1995). Adolescents' use of socially disvalued media—Towards a theory of media delinquency. *Journal of Youth and Adolescence, 24,* 617–631.

Rosenthal, M. B., Berndt, E. R., Donohue, J. M., Frank, R. G., & Epstein, A. M. (2002). Promotion of prescription drugs to consumers. *New England Journal of Medicine, 346,* 498–505.

Saffer, H. (1997). Alcohol advertising and motor vehicle fatalities. *Review of Economics and Statistics, 79,* 431–432.

Saffer, H., & Dave, D. (2002). Alcohol consumption and alcohol advertising bans. *Applied Economics, 34,* 1325–1335.

Saffer, H., & Dave, D. (2006). Alcohol advertising and alcohol consumption by adolescents. *Health Economics, 15,* 617–637.

Sargent, J. D., Beach, M. L., Adachi-Mejia, A. M., Gibson, J. J., Titus-Ernoff, L. T., Carusi, C., et al. (2005). Exposure to movie smoking: Its relation to smoking initiation among US adolescents. *Pediatrics, 116,* 1183–1191.

Sargent, J. D., Beach, M. L., Dalton, M. A., Ernstoff, L. T., Gibson, J. J., Tickle, J. J., et al. (2004). Effect of parental R-rated movie restriction on adolescent smoking initiation: A prospective study. *Pediatrics, 114,* 149–156.

Sargent, J. D., Tanski, S. E., & Gibson, J. (2007). Exposure to movie smoking among U.S. adolescents aged 10 to 14 years: A population estimate. *Pediatrics, 119,* e1167–e1176.

Slater, M. D. (2007) Reinforcing spirals: The mutual influence of media selectivity and media effects and their impact on individual behavior and social identity. *Communication Theory, 17,* 281–303.

Slater, M. D., Long, M., & Ford, V. L. (2006). Alcohol, illegal drugs, violent crime, and traffic-related and other unintended injuries in US local and national news. *Journal of Studies on Alcohol, 67,* 904–910.

Slater, S. J., Chaloupka, F. J., Wakefield, M., Johnston, L. D., & O'Malley, P. M. (2007). The impact of retail cigarette marketing practices on youth smoking uptake. *Archives of Pediatric and Adolescent Medicine, 161,* 440–444.

Slater, M. D., & Rouner, D. (2002). Entertainment-education and elaboration likelihood: Understanding the processing of narrative persuasion. *Communication Theory, 12,* 173–191.

Snyder, L. B. (2006). Meta-analyses of mediated health campaigns. In R. W. Preiss, B. M. Gayle, N. Burrell, M. Allen, & J. Bryant (Eds.), *Mass media effects research: Advances through meta-analysis* (pp. 327–344). Hillsdale, NJ: Erlbaum.

Snyder, L. B., Fleming Milici, F., Slater, M., Sun, H., & Strizhakova, Y. (2006). Effects of alcohol advertising exposure on youth drinking. *Archives of Pediatric and Adolescent Medicine, 160,* 18–24.

Snyder, L. B., & Hamilton, M. A. (2002). Meta-analysis of U.S. health campaign effects on behavior: Emphasize enforcement, exposure, and new information, and beware the secular trend. In R. Hornik (Ed.), *Public health communication: Evidence for behavior change* (pp. 357–383). Hillsdale, NJ: Erlbaum.

Snyder, L. B., Hamilton, M. A., Mitchell, E. W., Kiwanuka-Tondo, J., Fleming-Milici, F., & Proctor, D. (2004). A meta-analysis of the effect of mediated health communication campaigns on behavior change in the United States. *Journal of Health Communication, 9*(Suppl. 1), 71–96.

Snyder, L. B., & O'Connell, A. A. (2008). Event history analysis for communication research. In A. Hayes, M. D. Slater, & L. B. Snyder (Eds.), *The Sage sourcebook of advanced data analysis methods for communication research* (pp. 125–158). Thousand Oaks, CA: Sage.

Sober Truth on Preventing Underage Drinking Act of 2006, Pub. L. 109-422, 120 Stat. 2890–2899. (2006).

Song, A. V., Ling, P. M., Neilands, T. B., & Glantz, S. A. (2007). Smoking in movies and increased smoking among young adults. *American Journal of Preventive Medicine, 33,* 396–403.

Soumerai, S. B., Ross-Degnan, D., & Kahn, J. S. (1992). The effects of professional and media warnings about the association between aspirin use in children and Reye's syndrome. *Milbank Quarterly, 70,* 155–182.

Stacy, A. W., Zogg, J. B., Unger, J. B., & Dent, C. W. (2004). Exposure to televised alcohol ads and subsequent adolescent alcohol use. *American Journal of Health Behavior, 28,* 498–509.

Stern, S. R. (2005). Messages from teens on the big screen: Smoking, drinking, and drug use in teen-centered films. *Journal of Health Communication, 10,* 331–346.

Stormark, K. M., Laberg, J. C., Nordby, H., & Hugdahl, K. (2000). Alcoholics' selective attention to alcohol stimuli: Automated processing? *Journal of Studies on Alcohol, 61,* 18–23.

Stryker, J. E. (2003). Media and marijuana: A longitudinal analysis of news media effects on adolescents' marijuana use and related outcomes, 1977–1999. *Journal of Health Communication, 8,* 305–328.

Substance Abuse and Mental Health Services Administration. (2008, January 10). *The NSDUH report: Misuse of over-the-counter cough and cold medications among persons aged 12–25.* Rockville, MD: Substance Abuse and Mental Health Services Administration, Office of Applied Studies. Retrieved on January 10, 2008, from http://oas.samhsa.gov/2k8/cough/cough.pdf

Tapert, S. F., Cheung, E. H., Brown, G. G., Frank, L. R., Paulus, M. P., Schweinsburg, A. D., et al. (2003). Neural response to alcohol stimuli in adolescents with alcohol use disorder. *Archives of General Psychiatry, 60,* 727–35.

Tipper Gore widens war on rock. (1988, January 4). *New York Times.* Retrieved December 7, 2008, from http://query.nytimes.com/gst/fullpage.html?res=940DE6DF173DF937A35752C0A96E948260&sec=&spon=&pagewanted=1

't Jong, G. W., Stricker, B. H. C., & Sturkenboom, M. C. J. M. (2004). Marketing in the lay media and prescriptions of terbinafine in primary care: Dutch cohort study. *British Medical Journal, 328,* 931.

TNS Media Intelligence. (n.d.). *Strategy* [Data file]. Retrieved January 14, 2008, from http://www.tns-mi.com/prodAllProducts.htm

Van den Bulck, J., & Beullens, K (2005). Television and music video exposure and adolescent alcohol use while going out. *Alcohol and Alcoholism, 40,* 249–253.

Wakefield, M., Szczypka, G., Terry-McElrath, Y., Emery, S., Flay, B., Chaloupka, F., et al. (2005). Mixed messages on tobacco: Comparative exposure to public health, tobacco company- and pharmaceutical company-sponsored tobacco-related television campaigns in the United States, 1999–2003. *Addiction, 100,* 1875–1883.

Wallace, L. S., Rogers, E. S., Turner, L. W., Keenum, A. J., & Weiss, B. D. (2006). Suitability of written supplemental materials available on the Internet for non-prescription medications. *American Journal of Health-System Pharmacy, 63,* 71–78.

Weissman, J. S., Blumenthal, D., Silk, A. J., Newman, M., Zapert, K., Leitman, R., et al. (2004). Physicians report on patient encounters involving direct-to-consumer advertising. *Health Affairs, 23,* 219–233.

Weissman, J. S., Blumenthal, D., Silk, A. J., Zapert, K., Newman, M., & Leitman, R. (2003). Consumers' reports on the health effects of direct-to-consumer drug advertising. *Health Affairs, 22,* 82–95.

Wellman, R. J., Sugarman, D. B., DiFranza, J. R., & Winickoff, J. P. (2006). The extent to which tobacco marketing and tobacco use in films contribute to children's use of tobacco. *Archives of Pediatric and Adolescent Medicine, 160,* 1285–1296.

Wilkes, M. S., Bell, R. A., & Kravitz, R. L. (2000). Direct-to-consumer prescription drug advertising: Trends, impact, and implications. *Health Affairs, 19,* 110–128.

Wingood, G. M., DiClemente, R. J., Bernhardt, J. M., Harrington, K., Davies, S. L., Robillard, A., et al. (2003). Exposure to rap music videos and African American female adolescents' health. *American Journal of Public Health, 93,* 437–439.

Wright, D., & Pemberton, M. (1999). *Risk and protective factors for adolescent drug use: Findings from the 1999 National Household Survey on Drug Abuse* (DHHS Publication No. SMA 04–3874, Analytic Series A–19). Rockville, MD: Substance Abuse and Mental Health Services Administration, Office of Applied Studies.

CHAPTER 26

ENVIRONMENTAL APPROACHES TO PREVENTING DRINKING AND DRINKING PROBLEMS AMONG YOUTH

Joel W. Grube

Environmental approaches to preventing drinking and drinking problems among youth focus on modifying the context in which drinking occurs through the application of alcohol policy. Broadly defined, alcohol policy includes (a) formal legal and regulatory mechanisms, rules, and procedures for reducing the consumption of alcohol or risky drinking behaviors and (b) enforcement of these measures (Grube, 2007; Grube & Nygaard, 2001, 2005). Alcohol policies can be implemented at many levels, including national (e.g., excise taxes), state (e.g., limitations on retail or wholesale distribution), local (e.g., zoning ordinances), or institutional (e.g., school policies; responsible service practices in stores, bars, and restaurants). The primary purposes of such policies are to deter drinking or reduce availability of alcohol. More recently, prevention policy has begun to focus on harm reduction approaches that attempt to reduce risky drinking rather than overall consumption (Marlatt & Witkiewitz, 2002; Riley & O'Hare, 2000). The primary goal of alcohol policies is to increase the full costs of alcohol to young people, including the opportunity costs required to obtain it, the potential costs for possessing or consuming it, and the potential costs to adults for selling or supplying it to youth (Grube, 2007; Grube & Nygaard, 2001, 2005). Regulatory policies, practices, and enforcement may also reinforce norms against underage drinking or supplying alcohol to underage drinkers (Perry et al., 2002; Toomey, Lenk, & Wagenaar,

2007). This chapter gives a brief overview of the extent of youth drinking and drinking problems. It then presents a review of the literature on alcohol policy and youth to inform policymakers, advocates, and researchers about the current state of knowledge in this area.

ALCOHOL USE AMONG YOUTH

Alcohol is the most commonly used and abused drug by youth in the United States. Although rates of alcohol use by youth have fallen dramatically since the 1980s, consumption remains relatively high. Data from the 2006 Monitoring the Future (MTF) survey, for example, indicated that 73% of all high school seniors have tried drinking at some time in their lives, 67% reported drinking in the past year, and 45% reported doing so in the past 30 days (Johnston, O'Malley, Bachman, & Schulenberg, 2008). The consumption patterns of young drinkers are particularly problematic. Thus, 25% of high school seniors reported heavy episodic drinking (five or more drinks in a row) during the previous 2 weeks and 30% reported being drunk at least once in the past month. That is, 56% of seniors who drank in the past month had at least one occasion of heavy drinking in the previous 2 weeks, and 60% reported being drunk on at least one occasion in the past 30 days. Moreover, alcohol use far surpassed that of tobacco, marijuana, and other illicit drugs. The 2006 MTF data, for example, showed that more

Preparation of this chapter was partially supported by National Institute on Alcohol Abuse and Alcoholism Grants AA014958 and AA06282.

than twice as many youth reported using alcohol as compared with tobacco or marijuana and nearly five times more reported drinking than using other illicit drugs (Figure 26.1).

Drinking by young people is associated with an array of problems. Each year, as many as 5,000 U.S. youth under the age of 21 die as a result of drinking-related motor vehicle crashes, homicides, suicide, and other injuries such as falls, burns, and drowning (Hingson & Kenkel, 2004; National Highway Traffic Safety Administration, 2007; National Institute on Alcohol Abuse and Alcoholism, 2007). Heavy episodic drinking by youth may be particularly closely associated with problem outcomes (Wechsler, Davenport, Dowdall, Moeykens, & Castillo, 1994). Early onset of drinking is also associated with increased likelihood of a broad range of negative consequences later in life such as dependence and abuse, drinking and driving, unwanted or unplanned sex, unintended pregnancy, sexually transmitted infections, violence, and unintentional injury (e.g., Hingson & Kenkel, 2004). Overall, the estimated costs of underage drinking in the United States reach $61.9 billion annually (Miller, Levy, Spicer, & Taylor, 2006). Given

these statistics, preventing drinking and drinking problems among youth remains a high priority.

COMMERCIAL AND SOCIAL AVAILABILITY OF ALCOHOL

Despite a uniform drinking age of 21 years in all 50 states and the District of Columbia, young people still readily obtain alcohol. Data from the 2006 MTF, for example, have shown that 93% of high school seniors report that alcohol is fairly easy or very easy to obtain (Johnston et al., 2008). Purchase surveys have routinely shown that 30% or more of alcohol outlets will sell to underage buyers (e.g., Forster et al., 1994; Forster, Murray, Wolfson, & Wagenaar, 1995; Freisthler, Gruenewald, Treno, & Lee, 2003; Grube, 1997; Paschall, Grube, Black, Flewelling, et al., 2007; Wagenaar, Toomey, & Erickson, 2005). In part, these high rates of sales result from low and inconsistent levels of enforcement (Wagenaar & Wolfson, 1994, 1995). High levels of commercial availability may be one factor in youth drinking. Thus, a recent study combining purchase surveys with school surveys

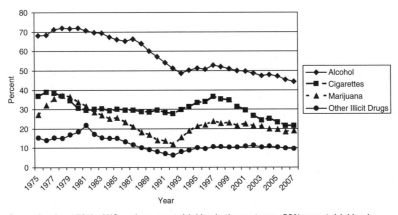

Currently, about 70% of HS seniors report drinking in the past year, 50% report drinking in past month, and nearly 30% drank 5+ drinks in past 2 weeks.

Trends down from highs in early 80s, especially after 1984 when uniform MLDA laws took effect. Leveled out in 90s and has remained stable for the past decade.

Some disturbing trends:
Age of initiation going down. According to NHSDA, age of initiation for individuals of all ages decreased from 17.6 to 15.9 years between 1965 and 1999. Age of initiation related to later dependence and alcohol problems.

Most young drinkers are heavy drinkers—60% of those who drank in the past month report having 5+ drinks in a row in the past two weeks.

FIGURE 26.1. Long-term trends in 30-day alcohol and other drug use among high school seniors: 1975–2007 (Johnston et al., 2008).

found that the school district–level alcohol sales rate was positively related to students' use of commercial alcohol sources and perceived alcohol availability (Paschall, Grube, Black, & Ringwalt, 2007).

Social sources for alcohol may be even more important for youth drinking than are commercial outlets. Data from the 2005 Oregon Healthy Teens survey (Center for Health Statistics, 2005), for example, indicated that 25% of 11th-grade drinkers and 16% of 8th-grade drinkers obtained alcohol from at least one commercial source in the past 30 days. In contrast, 87% 11th-grade drinkers and 81% of 8th-grade drinkers obtained alcohol from at least one social source (Figure 26.2). The most common commercial alcohol sources were grocery stores, convenience stores, gas stations, and liquor stores. The most common social alcohol sources were friends older than age 21, parties, and friends younger than age 21. Successful environmental interventions, then, need to address social and commercial availability of alcohol in communities.

ALCOHOL POLICIES AND YOUTH DRINKING

Nature of the Evidence for Policy Effectiveness

Although randomized controlled trials are generally considered the gold standard for evaluating preventive interventions, they may often be too expensive or impractical in applied settings (Biglan, Ary, & Wagenaar, 2000). This is particularly the case in evaluations of policy interventions for which random assignment of communities, states, or nations to experimental and control conditions may simply not be feasible. In some instances, random assignment would actually work to the detriment of external validity by ignoring the processes through which policy is developed and implemented. As a result of these considerations, alcohol policies are most often evaluated using quasi-experimental designs such as interrupted or multiple-baseline time series. These designs can provide strong evidence for policy effectiveness if there are adequate controls for confounding factors that may co-occur with the policy of interest. The ability to draw conclusions from such studies is enhanced to the extent that there are replications across time or geographical units.

Minimum Drinking Age

In 1984, the National Minimum Drinking Age Act required states to enact a minimum age of 21 years for purchase or public possession of alcohol or risk losing federal highway funds. Since 1987, the minimum legal drinking age (MLDA) in the United States has been 21 years in all 50 states and the District of Columbia. Jurisdictions, however, vary greatly in the scope of the restrictions they place on underage purchase, possession, and consumption of alcohol and on use of fraudulent identification to purchase alcohol (Alcohol Policy

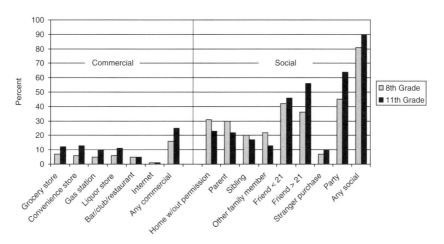

FIGURE 26.2. Use of commercial and social sources of alcohol in past 30 days by Oregon youth (Center for Health Statistics, 2005).

Information System, 2007). For example, some states allow underage drinking to take place in private residences or clubs if a minor is accompanied by a parent.

Despite inconsistencies in MLDA laws, the available studies have shown that increasing MLDA significantly decreased drinking and drinking problems among young people. On the basis of national data from the 1976–1987 MTF survey, it has been concluded that having a minimum drinking age of 21 is associated with a 5.5% lower prevalence of 30-day alcohol use and a 2.8% lower prevalence of heavy alcohol use among high school seniors and recent high school graduates (O'Malley & Wagenaar, 1991). Similarly, increasing the drinking age from 18 resulted in a 13.8% decrease in frequency of 30-day alcohol consumption. An analysis of state-level data has indicated that raising the MLDA to 21 years in the United States reduced alcohol-related crashes by as much as 19% (Voas, Tippetts, & Fell, 2003). A systematic review of 33 evaluations of MLDA laws in the United States, Canada, and Australia found a median decline of 16% in crash-related outcomes for the targeted age groups following passage of laws to increase the MLDA (Shults et al., 2001). Other reviews have reached similar conclusions (Wagenaar & Toomey, 2002). Conversely, a review of available research has indicated that during the 1970s the trend to decrease the MLDA in the United States from 21 to 18 years was associated with a 7% increase in traffic fatalities for the affected age groups (Cook, 2007).

Drinking Among American and European Youth

Although the preponderance of evidence has indicated that the uniform minimum drinking age of 21 has reduced drinking and drinking problems among young people, this policy is sometimes questioned as contributing to irresponsible styles of drinking by making alcohol a forbidden activity and forcing young people to drink in unsupervised contexts (see Engs, 1999; Johnson, 2007). European countries are sometimes held up as examples of contexts in which more liberal drinking age laws and attitudes and consumption in the family context foster more responsible styles of drinking by young peo-

ple. Available data, however, do not support this contention. Figure 26.3 depicts the prevalence of intoxication in the past 30 days taken from two sources: (a) youth 15 years of age from 35 countries that participated in the 2003 European School Project on Alcohol and Other Drugs (Hibell et al., 2004) and (b) the equivalent age group (10th graders) from the 2003 MTF Survey (Johnston, O'Malley, Bachmann, & Schulenberg, 2004). It is clear that lower drinking ages and more liberal drinking cultures alone are not protective factors for heavy drinking among youth. To the contrary, young people from the United States have reported much lower rates of intoxication than youth from the majority of European countries. In fact, the United States is among the countries showing the lowest rates of intoxication. Similarly, youth from most European countries report intoxication at an earlier age than U.S. youth (Figure 26.4). Although the exact mechanism is not clear, early initiation of drinking, and especially regular and heavy drinking, is associated with an array of later problems, including abuse and dependence in adulthood. This relation between early initiation and later problems has been documented in the United States (e.g., Dawson, Goldstein, Chou, Ruan, & Grant, 2008; Grant et al., 2006; Hingson, Heeren, & Winter, 2006), Europe (Jefferis, Power, & Manor, 2005; Pitkänen, Lyyra, & Pulkkinen, 2005; Viner & Taylor, 2007), and other countries (Bonomo, Bowes, Coffey, Carlin, & Patton, 2004; DeWit, Adlaf, Offord, & Ogborne, 2000; Wells, Horwood, & Fergusson, 2004). Overall, then, youth from the United States are less likely to drink, report intoxication, and report early initiation of intoxication than are their European counterparts. As has been noted elsewhere (Cook, 2007), the reduction in availability of alcohol associated with a higher MLDA in the United States apparently outweighs any effect it may have on the appeal of alcohol to youth.

Zero Tolerance

Zero tolerance laws are a special case of minimum drinking age laws that apply a lower legal blood alcohol content (BAC) to drivers under the legal drinking age. These lower limits are usually set at the lowest level that can reliably be detected (e.g.,

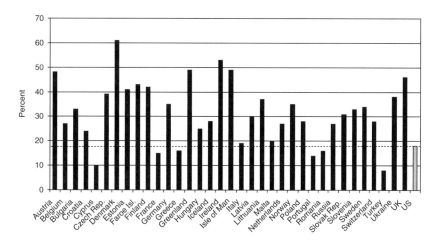

FIGURE 26.3.   Prevalence of being drunk in the past 30 days among 15-year-olds: European countries versus the United States (Hibell et al., 2004; Johnston et al., 2004).

.01%–.02%). Zero tolerance laws have been found to be very effective in reducing underage drinking and driving. In one study, zero tolerance laws were associated with a 19% reduction in self-reported driving after any drinking and a 24% reduction in reported driving after five or more drinks using MTF data (Wagenaar, O'Malley, & LaFond, 2001). The deterrent effects of zero tolerance laws, however, appear to be specific to drinking and driving. No reductions in drinking or heavy drinking were found. More recently, it has been estimated that the implementation of zero tolerance laws in the United States reduced alcohol-related fatal crashes among young

drivers by as much as 24% (Voas, Lange, & Fell, 2003). Similarly, a time series analysis of data from 1982 to 2005 in the United States indicated that implementing zero tolerance laws resulted in a 15% reduction in fatal crashes for young drivers with BACs 0.08% or higher and a 18% reduction in these crashes for young drivers with BACs 0.01% or higher (Dang, 2008). Evidence of the effectiveness of lower BAC limits for young drivers is quite robust and has been reinforced by a review of both U.S. and Australian studies (Shults et al., 2001), which found reductions of between 9% and 24% in fatal crashes associated with the implementation of zero

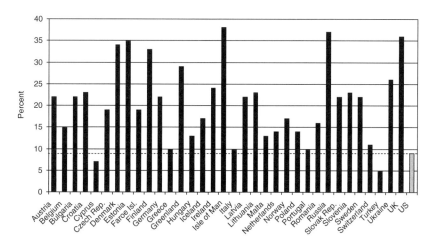

FIGURE 26.4.   Prevalence of first intoxication at age 13 or younger among 15-year-olds: European countries versus the United States (Hibell et al., 2004; Johnston et al., 2004).

tolerance laws. Effective enforcement and awareness of the laws among young people have been identified as key factors in the success of zero tolerance laws (Ferguson, Fields, & Voas, 2000; Hingson, Heeren, & Winter, 1994; Voas, Lange, & Tippetts, 1998). Using media to increase youth's awareness of reduced BAC limits and enforcement efforts may also increase the effectiveness of zero tolerance laws.

Graduated Driver Licensing
Graduated driver licensing laws place restrictions on the circumstances under which young or novice drivers are allowed to drive, such as prohibiting driving during certain hours or driving with other young people in the vehicle. Some graduated driver licensing laws contain zero tolerance provisions. Studies of graduated driver licensing have routinely shown that it is associated with reductions in drinking, motor vehicle crashes, and alcohol-related crashes among young people (Begg & Stephenson, 2003; Langley, Wagenaar, & Begg, 1996; Shope & Molnar, 2003; Shope, Molnar, Elliott, & Waller, 2001). Recent reviews of graduated driver licensing programs have found an overall 20%–40% reduction in crash risk (Hartling et al., 2004; Shope, 2007). In contrast, a few studies (e.g., Masten & Hagge, 2004) have found no effects of graduated licensing on teenage crash rates. Large variations in how graduated driver licensing programs are implemented may account for the mixed findings. An analysis of graduated licensing programs suggested that good programs (based on Insurance Institute for Highway Safety criteria) reduced driver fatalities among 15- to 17-year-olds by 19.4% versus 5.4% for fair programs and less than 1% for marginal programs (Morrisey, Grabowski, Dee, & Campbell, 2006).

Taxation and Price
Research using data from the U.S. National Longitudinal Survey of Youth has suggested that doubling the tax on beer would reduce alcohol consumption among young people by 3% to 6% (Pacula, 1998). Overall, it has been estimated that increasing taxation on alcohol in the United States to keep pace with inflation would lead to a 19% reduction in heavy drinking by youth and a 6% reduction in high-risk drinking (Laixuthai & Chaloupka, 1993).

Although taxation and price increases may be effective prevention strategies, price elasticity may be moderated by social, environmental, and economic factors. As a result, the price sensitivity of alcohol may vary considerably across time, states, and communities, depending on drinking patterns, attitudes, and the presence of other alcohol policies. Studies, for example, have suggested that the relations between taxes on alcohol and alcohol consumption and problems among youth may have weakened in recent years, possibly because of the implementation of the uniform age 21 MLDA and other alcohol policies reducing youth access to alcohol (Dee, 1999; Young & Likens, 2000). Consistent with this hypothesis, a recent study showed that raising either the MLDA or beer taxes in isolation led to fewer youth traffic fatalities (Ponicki, Gruenewald, & LaScala, 2007). A given change in price, however, caused a larger proportional change in fatalities when the MLDA was low than when it was high. Thus, a 10% increase in price was estimated to reduce traffic fatalities among youth by 3.1% if the legal drinking age was 18, but by only 1.9% if the legal drinking age was 21. It was concluded that communities and states with relatively strong existing policies might expect smaller impacts on alcohol-related problems to result from the implementation of new policies than were suggested by prior research, whereas communities with weak policies might expect larger benefits. In addition, price increases may lead to changes in patterns of consumption such as purchasing less expensive beverages without reducing overall consumption (Gruenewald, Millar, Ponicki, & Brinkley, 2000).

Regulation of Sales
Regulation of commercial outlets has been used in various ways, including granting or denying licenses to sell alcohol, restricting hours of sales, restricting the number or density of outlets in a given area, and restricting the types of beverages or container sizes that can be sold. Research evidence for the effectiveness of many of these strategies in reducing drinking by young people is scarce.

Outlet density restrictions. Studies have found significant relations between outlet densities and alcohol consumption (Scribner, Cohen, & Fisher,

2000), violence (Gorman, Labouvie, & Subaiya, 1998; Lipton & Gruenewald, 2002), drinking and driving (Gruenewald, Johnson, & Treno, 2002), and car crashes (Scribner, MacKinnon, & Dwyer, 1994). In one of the few studies focusing on youth (Treno, Grube, & Martin, 2003), on- and off-license outlet density was positively related to frequency of driving after drinking and riding with drinking divers among 16- to 20-year-old youth. Similarly, outlet density surrounding college campuses has also been found to correlate with heavy drinking, frequent drinking, and drinking-related problems among students (Weitzman, Folkman, Folkman, & Wechsler, 2003). Different types of outlets may have distinct effects on problem outcomes. Violence has been found to be positively related to bar density and negatively related to restaurant density (Lipton & Gruenewald, 2002). The opposite relation, however, is true for drinking-and-driving incidents (Gruenewald, Johnson, & Treno, 2002). Although most of the available research is cross-sectional, a recent longitudinal study found that changes in the number of licensed alcohol retail establishments, especially bars and off-premise outlets, were directly related to rates of car crashes and injuries (Treno, Johnson, Remer, & Gruenewald, 2007). No studies, however, appear to have investigated effects of changes in outlet density or zoning ordinances controlling outlet density for purposes of reducing alcohol problems.

Hours of sale. Restricting the days and hours that alcohol sales are allowed is a common policy strategy that is promoted for reducing drinking and drinking-related problems. Generally, greater restrictions have been associated with decreases in drinking and drinking problems, although the findings are mixed. Thus, some studies have failed to find changes in consumption or alcohol-related problems following changes in hours of sale (Graham, McLeod, & Steedman, 1998; McLaughlin & Harrison-Stewart, 1992). Other studies have reported increases in traffic crashes and assaults following extensions of sales hours for bars (Chikritzhs & Stockwell, 2002). A recent study (Duailibi et al., 2007) in the Brazilian city of Diadema, where alcohol sales had been largely unregulated, suggested that a new law prohibiting alcohol sales after 11 p.m.

was related to a decrease of almost nine murders per month. Assaults against women also decreased, but this effect was not significant when underlying trends were controlled. Overall, the evidence is mixed, although it appears that changes in hours of service can influence drinking and drinking-related problems among young people.

Advertising Restrictions

Only a few studies have considered the effects of alcohol advertising restrictions on alcohol consumption or problems. Saffer (1991) investigated the effects of restrictions on broadcast alcohol advertising on alcohol consumption and alcohol problems (liver cirrhosis mortality, motor vehicle fatalities) in 17 European and North American countries. In a series of analyses, he found that countries with partial restrictions on alcohol advertising had lower alcohol consumption than countries with no restrictions. Countries with complete bans had lower consumption rates than countries with partial restrictions. A reanalysis, however, suggested that there was reverse causation, with those countries experiencing low rates of alcohol problems being more likely to adopt bans on alcohol advertising than were countries with high rates of alcohol problems (Young, 1993). More recently, a study of alcohol advertising restrictions in 20 countries over 26 years found that moving from no restrictions to partial restrictions or from partial restrictions to total bans reduced alcohol consumption between 5% and 8% (Saffer & Dave, 2002). Other recent studies, however, have found no effects of advertising bans (Nelson, 2001; Nelson & Young, 2001). Apparently, no studies have investigated the specific effects of advertising restrictions on drinking or drinking problems among young people. The effects of advertising restrictions on young people's drinking are best considered an open question (Grube, 2004; Grube & Waiters, 2005).

Responsible Beverage Sales and Service

Responsible beverage service (RBS) consists of the implementation of a combination of outlet policies (e.g., requiring clerks or servers to check identification for all customers appearing to be under the age of 30) and training (e.g., teaching clerks and servers to recognize altered or false identification). RBS can be implemented at both on-license and off-license establishments. Such programs have been shown to be effective in some circumstances. Thus, RBS has been found to reduce the number of intoxicated patrons leaving a bar (e.g., Dresser & Gliksman, 1998; Gliksman et al., 1993), car crashes (e.g., Holder & Wagenaar, 1994), sales to intoxicated patrons, sales to minors, and incidents of violence surrounding outlets (Wallin, Gripenberg, & Andreasson, 2002; Wallin, Norstrom, & Andreasson, 2003). Voluntary programs appear to be less effective than mandatory programs or programs using incentives such as reduced liability.

Only a handful of studies have directly evaluated the effects of RBS programs on underage drinking and access to alcohol. In one study of off-license RBS, voluntary training for clerks and managers was found to have a negligible effect on sales to minors above and beyond the effects of increased enforcement of underage sales laws (Grube, 1997). Similar results were reported in a second study of increased compliance checks and RBS training for off-license clerks as a part of a community intervention to reduce youth access to alcohol (Wagenaar et al., 2005). A demonstration project implemented in five bars using one-on-one owner and manager training reduced underage sales by 11.5%, although this decrease was not statistically significant (Toomey et al., 2001). Similarly, a study in Australia found that even after training, age identification was rarely checked in bars, although decreases in the number of intoxicated patrons were observed (Lang, Stockwell, Rydon, & Beel, 1998). In contrast, in a study in which random alcohol purchase surveys were conducted in 45 Oregon communities (Paschall, Grube, Black, Flewelling, et al., 2007), buyers appearing to be underage were able to purchase alcohol at 34% of the outlets approached. Purchase rates were highest at convenience (38%) and grocery (36%) stores but were relatively low (14%) at other types of outlets (e.g., liquor and drugstores). Alcohol purchases were less likely at stores that were participating in the Oregon Liquor Control Commission's Responsible Vendor Program. Sales were also less likely when sales clerks asked the purchasers for their IDs, at stores that posted underage alcohol sale warning signs, and when

there were fewer sales clerks present. Sales were not related to clerks' age or gender.

How RBS is implemented and what elements are included in a particular program may be an important determinant of its effectiveness. Policy development and implementation within outlets may be particularly important in determining RBS effectiveness (Saltz, 1997). Research has indicated that establishments with firm and clear policies and a system for monitoring staff compliance are less likely to sell alcohol to minors (Wolfson et al., 1996).

Designated Driver and Safe Rides Programs

Designated driver programs encourage groups of drinkers to select an individual who is not to drink and who can then drive safely. Although designated driver programs are being strongly promoted, there is only limited evidence of their effectiveness. There is some evidence that those who serve as designated drivers are heavier drinkers and more likely to report drinking and driving and riding with drinking drivers than are drinkers who never serve as designated drivers (e.g., Caudill, Harding, & Moore, 2000b). Some studies have indicated that the designated driver is often the person in a group who has consumed the least alcohol, even though that may have been a significant amount (Nygaard, Waiters, Grube, & Keefe, 2003). For instance, a survey study of students in Australia indicated that 26% of those who served as a designated driver reported doing so while feeling the effects of alcohol (Stevenson et al., 2001). Male designated drivers may be particularly likely to drink (Timmerman, Geller, Glindemann, & Fournier, 2003). A systematic review (Ditter et al., 2005) concluded that the available evidence for the effectiveness of designated driver programs was marginal. Overall, population-based campaigns to encourage use of designated drivers resulted in an average 13% increase in drinkers saying they used a designated driver, but no significant change in self-reported drinking and driving or riding with alcohol-impaired drivers. There was limited evidence that designated driver programs implemented in drinking establishments modestly increased the number of patrons reporting being a designated driver and decreased the number of patrons saying they drove after drinking. More recently, a study of a program encouraging groups to designate drivers in advance of drinking, clearly identifying designated drivers (e.g., with a bracelet), and rewarding them for not drinking found substantial increases in the number who moderated their drinking or refrained from consuming alcohol (Lange, Reed, Johnson, & Voas, 2006).

Safe Rides

Safe rides programs offer drinkers low-cost or free transportation as an alternative to driving themselves. As with designated driver programs, there is little available research on their effectiveness. Some evidence has indicated that drinkers use safe rides programs relatively infrequently (Caudill, Harding & Moore, 2000a; Harding, Caudill, Moore, & Frissell, 2001). In one survey study of college students, 44% of those using a safe rides program reported that they would otherwise have driven after drinking (Sarkar, Andreas, & de Faria, 2005). Apparently, however, there is no available evidence regarding the effects of such programs on crash rates or other negative outcomes.

Dramshop Liability

Dramshop liability laws allow individuals injured by a minor who had been drinking or by an intoxicated adult to recover damages from the alcohol retailer who served or sold alcohol to the person causing the injury (Mosher, Toomey, Good, Harwood, & Wagenaar, 2002). Owners and licensees can be held liable for the actions of their employees under most or all dramshop liability laws. Many dramshop liability statutes include a Responsible Business Practices Defense. This provision allows retailers to avoid liability if they can establish that they took reasonable steps to avoid serving minors and obviously intoxicated adults. Key to the defense is evidence that RBS training procedures and policies were fully implemented at the time of the illegal sale or service. Research has suggested that implementation of dramshop liability may lead to significant increases in checking age identification and greater care in service practices (e.g., Sloan, Stout, Whetten-Goldstein, & Liang, 2000). Overall, dramshop liability has been estimated to reduce alcohol-related traffic fatalities

among underage drivers by 3%–4% (Chaloupka, Saffer, & Grossman, 1993).

Social Host Liability

Under social host liability laws, adults who provide alcohol to a minor or serve intoxicated adults in social settings can be sued through civil action for damages or injury caused by that minor or intoxicated adult. There has been very little research on the effectiveness of social host liability laws, and what evidence exists is conflicting. In one study in the United States, social host liability laws were associated with decreases in alcohol-related traffic fatalities among adults but not among minors (Whetten-Goldstein, Sloan, Stout, & Liang, 2000). Social host statutes were not related to single-vehicle nighttime crashes for either group.[1] In a second study, social host liability laws were associated with decreases in reported heavy drinking and in decreases in drinking and driving by lighter drinkers (Stout, Sloan, Liang, & Davies, 2000). The statutes had no effect on drinking and driving by heavier drinkers. The conflicting findings may reflect the lack of a comprehensive program that ensures that social hosts are aware of their potential liability. Although social host liability may send a powerful message, that message must be effectively disseminated before it can have a deterrent effect.

Warning Labels

Warning labels on beverage containers constitute another strategy targeting risky drinking. An early evaluation of warning labels on alcoholic beverage containers in the United States found that about one fifth of respondents to a national survey remembered seeing the warnings 6 months after their introduction (Kaskutas & Greenfield, 1992). Although somewhat greater proportions of key target groups (e.g., heavy drinkers and young men at risk for drunk driving) remembered seeing the labels, no changes in knowledge of the targeted health risks were observed. Similarly, a study of U.S. adolescents found that there were increases in awareness of, exposure to, and memory of the labels after they were implemented, but there were no substantial changes in

---

[1] Nighttime and single-vehicle nighttime crashes are sometimes used as surrogates for alcohol-related crashes because of the high rates of alcohol involvement in such crashes.

alcohol use or beliefs about the risks targeted by the warning (MacKinnon, Pentz, & Stacy, 1993). Overall, there is no evidence that alcoholic beverage warning labels have any discernable effect on drinking or drinking problems among young people.

Keg Registration

Keg registration laws require that the name of a purchaser of a keg of beer be linked to that keg. Keg registration is seen primarily as a tool for prosecuting adults who supply alcohol to young people at parties or for prosecuting retailers who sell kegs to minors. Keg registration laws have become increasingly popular in the United States. There is apparently only a single published study on the effectiveness of these laws. In that study of 97 U.S. communities, it was found that requiring keg registration was significantly and negatively correlated with traffic fatality rates (Cohen, Mason, & Scribner, 2001). The evidence for the effectiveness of keg registration is best considered inconclusive.

School Policies

School policies have long been seen as important tools to prevent and reduce alcohol use by young people. The effectiveness of school policies in reducing alcohol use by students has been addressed in only a few studies. A recent international review concluded that most schools in developed countries have substance use policies in place (Evans-Whipp et al., 2004). These policies, however, differ substantially in terms of comprehensiveness, severity, and focus on abstinence versus harm reduction. Although the evidence was limited, it was concluded that well-implemented school policies may reduce substance use, most notably tobacco use. A further study of school policies in the United States and Australia indicated that strong and consistently enforced policies are related to lower rates of alcohol and other drug use (Evans-Whipp, Bond, Toumbourou, & Catalano, 2007). There was also some evidence that abstinence policies may be more effective than harm reduction policies. These studies, however, largely relied on evidence from correlations.

Recently, interest has grown in randomized drug testing in schools as a prevention tool. A national survey indicated that drug testing in schools is rela-

tively rare, with only about 18% of schools reporting this practice (Yamaguchi, Johnston, & O'Malley, 2003). Using MTF data, no differences were found in levels of drug use among schools with and without testing programs. An evaluation of a random drug-testing program for student athletes that included mandatory counseling and parent notification of positive tests found that the program was related to short-term decreases in illicit and performance-enhancing drug use, but not in alcohol use (Goldberg et al., 2003). In a larger 2-year randomized trial of the same program, student athletes from intervention and control schools did not differ in past-month drug and alcohol use at any of the follow-ups (Goldberg et al., 2007). Some significant reductions were found in past-year combined drug and alcohol use at some follow-ups, but the pattern was not consistent. Overall, the evidence for the effectiveness of drug-testing policies is insufficient. Further research in this area is needed. Interestingly, a large majority of high school and middle school students believe that drug testing would be effective in reducing drug and alcohol use at their schools, but a substantial minority believe such testing is unfair and not a good idea (Evans, Reader, Liss, Wiens, & Roy, 2006). Not surprisingly, students who use drugs or alcohol are less likely to be supportive of drug testing compared with those who do not use drugs or alcohol (Evans et al., 2006; Russell, Jennings, & Classey, 2005).

Enforcement

For deterrence policies, enforcement is a key determinant of effectiveness. The deterrent effect of alcohol policies is affected by their severity, the probability of their imposition, and the swiftness with which they are imposed (Ross, 1982). The probability of being detected and having penalties imposed may be particularly important. Although penalties for many alcohol offenses by youth are severe, they are seldom enforced and therefore can be expected to have only a modest deterrent effect (Hafemeister & Jackson, 2004). Some research, in fact, has suggested that policies that increase the probability of detection and arrest for drinking and driving infractions may have greater effects on alcohol-related traffic fatalities than do policies that increase penalties (Benson, Rasmussen, & Mast, 1999). Similarly, differences in local enforcement of zero tolerance laws have been identified as a key issue in understanding why some programs are less successful than others (Ferguson et al., 2000).

Increasing enforcement against retailers who sell alcohol to minors can have a substantial impact on sales. Grube (1997) found that enforcement of sales laws coupled with media coverage produced a net reduction in sales to minors of 30%–35%. In a study in New Orleans, Louisiana, enforcement of underage sales laws increased compliance with alcohol sales laws from 11% to 39% (Scribner & Cohen, 2001). The greatest gains in compliance occurred among those retailers who had been cited (51%), but substantial gains were also seen for those who were not cited (35%). Decreases in underage sales following increased enforcement may be of limited duration unless routine compliance checks are undertaken. Data from the Complying With the Minimum Drinking Age project showed a 17% decrease in underage sales at off-premise establishments immediately after a compliance check was conducted (Wagenaar et al., 2005). This effect decayed to an 11% decrease 2 weeks following the checks and to a nonsignificant 3% decrease 2 months afterward.

The extent to which such reductions in sales translate into decreases in underage drinking, however, is unknown. Young drinkers may be particularly adept at identifying outlets that continue to sell to minors despite enforcement efforts or may shift to alternative social sources for alcohol. Recent research has examined the relationship between community measures of youth access to alcohol, enforcement of possession laws, and the frequency of youth alcohol use and related problems (Dent, Grube, & Biglan, 2005). The perceived rate of illegal merchant sales in the communities was directly related to 30-day frequency of alcohol use, heavy drinking, using alcohol at school, and drinking and driving. There was also evidence that communities with higher perceived minor-in-possession law enforcement had lower rates of alcohol use and heavy drinking. The use of social and commercial sources in a community expanded and contracted depending on levels of access and enforcement. A

second recent study further investigated possible effects of commercial alcohol availability on high school students' use of commercial and social alcohol sources, perceived ease of obtaining alcohol, and drinking (Paschall, Grube, & Black, 2006). The data for this study were obtained from purchase surveys at 403 off-premise retail establishments and a school survey of 11th graders. Hierarchical linear modeling indicated that the district-level alcohol sales rate was not directly related to students' drinking. However, the associations between students' use of commercial alcohol sources and their drinking behaviors were stronger in districts with higher alcohol sales rates, whereas relationships between use of social alcohol sources and drinking behaviors were diminished in those districts. Thus, commercial alcohol availability may not affect underage drinking directly, but may increase use of commercial alcohol sources and decrease use of social alcohol sources. Additional support for the effect of reducing retail access to alcohol on drinking by adolescents can be obtained from the literature on tobacco control and youth smoking. Most notably, a randomized community trial suggested that increasing retailer compliance with age identification for underage tobacco sales reduced not only tobacco sales to minors and youth smoking, but also underage drinking (Biglan, Ary, Smolkowski, Duncan, & Black, 2000). Other studies of increased enforcement of alcohol sales laws have shown similar results (Barry et al., 2004), although the available evidence is not definitive.

Arrests of minors for possession of alcohol are rare in part because of the burden of prosecuting them and reluctance on the part of law enforcement and courts to enforce criminal penalties in such cases (Wagenaar & Wolfson, 1994). Moreover, because criminal proceedings are often lengthy and removed in time from the infraction, the punishment is seldom swift or certain. Less severe sanctions (e.g., fines, community service, loss of driver's license) may be more likely to be enforced and thus to generate a deterrent effect than would underenforced criminal penalties. Deterrence may also be increased if penalties are imposed administratively through citations issued at the time of apprehension, without requiring court appearances. The size of the fines and length of community service should be sufficiently substantial, however, to register social disapproval and to generate a meaningful deterrent effect.

DISCUSSION

Generally, drinking by young people is normative in the United States. A majority of young people have tried drinking, and substantial numbers are current drinkers. Alcohol consumption by youth, however, is often typified by a pattern of heavy episodic or binge drinking, which is associated with considerable costs both to the individual and to society. It is thus imperative to develop strategies to reduce drinking by youth and the risks associated with it. Although school-based and educational efforts can be effective in some cases, environmental approaches are a necessary component of prevention of alcohol use and problems among youth.

On the basis of the available evidence, the most effective policies appear to be (a) a higher minimum drinking age, (b) zero tolerance laws, (c) taxation or price increases, and (d) graduated licensing. Dramshop and social host liability also appear promising for reducing drinking and drinking-related problems on the basis of studies with the general population, although there is less evidence for their effectiveness specifically with young people. The evidence is growing for the effects of school policies and for outlet license restrictions (e.g., outlet density, hours of sale). There is some empirical support for RBS programs, particularly those that are mandated or motivated by reduction of liability. The evidence on advertising restrictions is conflicting, with some studies showing reductions in consumption and problems and others showing no effects of such policies. Overall, there is little evidence that such restrictions affect youth drinking. Evidence for designated driver and safe rides programs, warning labels, and keg registration as effective strategies for preventing drinking or drinking problems among young people is largely lacking. For many policy strategies, there is not sufficient research to evaluate their effects on drinking by young people. Such research should be conducted to inform policy or at least to evaluate policies as they are implemented.

It is also essential that deterrence policies be enforced and that there be awareness of both the policy and enforcement efforts on the part of the intended targets (e.g., Grube & Nygaard, 2001; Voas et al., 1998). Awareness and knowledge of policies on the part of those charged with enforcement is also important for effective implementation (Findlay, Sheehan, Davey, Brodie, & Rynne, 2002).

Another potentially important element in effective alcohol policy is public support. Law enforcement officers and community leaders may often perceive little popular support for alcohol policies or their enforcement (Wagenaar & Wolfson, 1994). The difficulty of implementing effective policies in the face of public opposition may be considerable. Public support may, in fact, be greater for those policies that are least effective in reducing drinking and drinking problems among youth. Surveys in Canada and the United States, for example, have indicated that public support may be strongest for such interventions as treatment or reducing service to intoxicated patrons in bars (e.g., Giesbrecht & Greenfield, 1999). There is also considerable public support for policies targeting promotions such as providing warning labels and banning or restricting alcohol advertising. There is less support for more demonstrably effective policies targeting access such as increasing the drinking age or increasing taxes. The strategic use of media, however, may help overcome such resistance and elicit public support for effective environmental interventions (e.g., Holder & Treno, 1997).

References

Alcohol Policy Information System. (2007, September 19). *State profiles of underage drinking laws.* Retrieved December 19, 2007, from http://www.alcoholpolicy.niaaa.nih.gov/stateprofiles//index.asp

Barry, R., Edwards, E., Pelletier, A., Brewer, R., Miller, J., Naimi, et al. (2004). Enhanced enforcement of laws to prevent alcohol sales to underage persons—New Hampshire, 1999–2004. *Morbidity and Mortality Weekly Report, 53,* 452–454.

Begg, D., & Stephenson, S. (2003). Graduated driver licensing: The New Zealand experience. *Journal of Safety Research, 34,* 99–105.

Benson, B. L., Rasmussen, D. W., & Mast, B. D. (1999). Deterring drunk driving fatalities: An economics of crime perspective. *International Review of Law Economics, 19,* 205–225.

Biglan, A., Ary, D. V., Smolkowski, K., Duncan, T., & Black, C. (2000). A randomised controlled trial of a community intervention to prevent adolescent tobacco use. *Tobacco Control, 9,* 24–32.

Biglan, A., Ary, D., & Wagenaar, A. C. (2000). The value of time-series experiments for community intervention research. *Prevention Science, 1,* 31–49.

Bonomo, Y. A., Bowes, G., Coffey, C., Carlin, J. B., & Patton, G. C. (2004). Teenage drinking and the onset of alcohol dependence: A cohort study over seven years. *Addiction, 99,* 1520–1528.

Caudill, B. D., Harding, W. M., & Moore, B. A. (2000a). At-risk drinkers use safe ride services to avoid drinking and driving. *Journal of Substance Use, 11,* 149–159.

Caudill, B. D., Harding, W. M., & Moore, B. A. (2000b). DWI prevention: Profiles of drinkers who serve as designated drivers. *Psychology of Addictive Behaviors, 14,* 143–150.

Center for Health Statistics. (2005). *Oregon Healthy Teens Survey, 2005* [Data file]. Retrieved December 16, 2008, from http://www.dhs.state.or.us/dhs/ph/chs/youthsurvey/index.shtml

Chaloupka, F. J., Saffer, H., & Grossman, M. (1993). Alcohol control policies and motor vehicle fatalities. *Journal of Legal Studies, 22,* 161–186.

Chikritzhs, T., & Stockwell, T. (2002). The impact of later trading hours for Australian public houses (hotels) on levels of violence. *Journal of Studies on Alcohol, 63,* 591–599.

Cohen, D. A., Mason, K., & Scribner, R. A. (2001). The population consumption model, alcohol control practices, and alcohol-related traffic fatalities. *Preventive Medicine, 34,* 187–197.

Cook, P. J. (2007). *Paying the tab. The costs and benefits of alcohol control.* Princeton, NJ: Princeton University Press.

Dang, J. N. (2008). *Statistical analysis of alcohol-related driving trends, 1982–2005* (NHTSA Publication No. DOT HS 810 942). Washington, DC: National Highway Traffic Safety Administration.

Dawson, D. A., Goldstein, R. B., Chou, S. P., Ruan, W. J., & Grant, B. F. (2008). Age at first drink and the first incidence of adult-onset DSM-IV alcohol use disorders. *Alcoholism: Clinical and Experimental Research.* Retrieved October 13, 2008, from http://www3.interscience.wiley.com/cgi-bin/fulltext/121428145/PDFSTART

Dee, T. S. (1999). State alcohol policies, teen drinking, and traffic fatalities. *Journal of Public Economics, 72,* 289–315.

Dent, C., Grube, J. W., & Biglan, A. (2005). Community level alcohol availability and enforcement of possession laws as predictors of youth drinking. *Preventive Medicine, 40,* 355–362.

DeWit, D. J., Adlaf, E. M., Offord, D. R., & Ogborne, A. C. (2000). Age at first alcohol use: A risk factor for the development of alcohol disorders. *American Journal of Psychiatry, 157,* 745–750.

Ditter, S. M., Elder, R. W., Shults, R. A., Sleet, D. A., Compton, R., Nichols, J. L., et al. (2005). Effectiveness of designated driver programs for reducing alcohol-impaired driving: A systematic review. *American Journal of Preventive Medicine, 28,* 280–287.

Dresser, J., & Gliksman, L. (1998). Comparing statewide alcohol server training systems. *Pharmacology Biochemistry and Behavior, 61,* 150.

Duailibi, S., Ponicki, W., Grube, J. W., Pinsky, I., Laranjeira, R., & Raw, M. (2007). The effect of restricting opening hours on alcohol-related violence. *American Journal of Public Health, 97,* 2276–2280.

Engs, R. C. (1999). Forbidden fruit (or reasons why drinking age should be lowered). *Vermont Quarterly.* Retrieved December 19, 2007, from http://www.indiana.edu/~engs/articles/fruit.html

Evans, G. D., Reader, S., Liss, H. J., Wiens, A. R., & Roy, A. (2006). Implementation of an aggressive random drug-testing policy in a rural school district: Student attitudes regarding program fairness and effectiveness. *Journal of School Health, 76,* 452–458.

Evans-Whipp, T., Beyers, J. M., Lloyd, S., Lafazia, A. N., Toumbourou, J. W., Arthur, M. W., & Catalano, R. F. (2004). A review of school drug policies and their impact on youth substance use. *Health Promotion International, 19,* 227–234.

Evans-Whipp, T. J., Bond, L., Toumbourou, J. W., & Catalano, R. F. (2007). School, parent, and student perspectives of school drug policies. *Journal of School Health, 77,* 138–146.

Ferguson, S. A., Fields, M., & Voas, R. B. (2000). Enforcement of zero tolerance laws in the United States. In *Proceedings of the 15th International Conference on Alcohol, Drugs, and Traffic Safety.* Borlänge, Sweden: Swedish National Road Administration. Retrieved December 16, 2008, from http://www.icadts.org/proceedings/2000/icadts2000-108.pdf

Findlay, R. A., Sheehan, M. C., Davey, J., Brodie, H., & Rynne, F. (2002). Liquor law enforcement: Policy and practice in Australia. *Drugs: Education, Prevention and Policy, 9,* 85–94.

Forster, J. L., McGovern, P. G., Wagenaar, A. C., Wolfson, M., Perry, C. L., & Anstine, P. S. (1994). The ability of young people to purchase alcohol without age identification in northeastern Minnesota, USA. *Addiction, 89,* 699–705.

Forster, J. L., Murray, D. M., Wolfson, M., & Wagenaar, A. C. (1995). Commercial availability of alcohol to young people: Results of alcohol purchase attempts. *Preventive Medicine, 24,* 342–347.

Freisthler, B., Gruenewald, P. J., Treno, A. J., & Lee, J. (2003). Evaluating alcohol access and the alcohol environment in neighborhood areas. *Alcoholism: Clinical and Experimental Research, 27,* 477–484.

Giesbrecht, N., & Greenfield, T. K. (1999). Public opinions on alcohol policy issues: A comparison of American and Canadian surveys. *Addiction, 94,* 521–531.

Gliksman, L., McKenzie, D., Single, E., Douglas, R., Brunet, S., & Moffatt, K. (1993). Role of alcohol providers in prevention: An evaluation of a server intervention programme. *Addiction, 88,* 1195–1203.

Goldberg, L., Elliot, D. L., MacKinnon, D. P., Moe, E., Kuehl, K. S., Nohre, L., & Lockwood, C. M. (2003). Drug testing athletes to prevent substance use: Background and pilot study results of the SATURN (Student Athlete Testing Using Random Notification) Study. *Journal of Adolescent Health, 32,* 16–25.

Goldberg, L., Elliot, D. L., MacKinnon, D. P., Moe, E. L., Kuehl, K. S., Yoon, M., et al. (2007). Outcomes of a prospective trial of student-athlete drug testing: The Student Athlete Testing Using Random Notification (SATURN) study. *Journal of Adolescent Health, 41,* 421–429.

Gorman, D. M., Labouvie, E. W., & Subaiya, A. P. (1998). Risk of assaultive violence and alcohol availability in New Jersey. *American Journal of Public Health, 88,* 97–100.

Graham, C. A., McLeod, L. S., & Steedman, D. J. (1998). Restricting extensions to permitted licensing hours does not influence the numbers of alcohol or assault-related attendances at an inner city accident and emergency department. *Journal of Accident and Emergency Medicine, 15,* 23–25.

Grant, J. D., Scherrer, J. F., Lynskey, M. T., Lyons, M. J., Eisen, S. A., Tsuang, M. T., et al. (2006). Adolescent alcohol use is a risk factor for adult alcohol and drug dependence: Evidence from a twin design. *Psychological Medicine, 36,* 109–118.

Grube, J. W. (1997). Preventing sales of alcohol to minors: Results from a community trial. *Addiction, 92*(Suppl. 2), S251–S260.

Grube, J. W. (2004). Alcohol in the media: Drinking portrayals, alcohol advertising, and alcohol consumption among youth. In R. Bonnie & M. E. O'Connell (Eds.), *Reducing underage drinking: A collective responsibility, background papers* [CD-ROM]. Washington, DC: National Academies Press.

Grube, J. W. (2007). Alcohol regulation and traffic safety: An overview. *Transportation Research Circular, E-C123,* 13–30. Retrieved December 19, 2007, from http://onlinepubs.trb.org/onlinepubs/circulars/ec123.pdf

Grube, J. W., & Nygaard, P. (2001). Adolescent drinking and alcohol policy, *Contemporary Drug Problems, 28,* 87–131.

Grube, J. W., & Nygaard, P. (2005). Alcohol policy and youth drinking: Overview of effective interventions for young people. In T. Stockwell, P. J. Gruenewald, J. Toumbourou, & W. Loxley (Eds.), *Preventing harmful substance use: The evidence base for policy and practice* (pp. 113–127). New York: Wiley.

Grube, J. W., & Waiters, E. D. (2005). Alcohol in the media: Content and effects on drinking beliefs and behaviors among youth. *Adolescent Medicine Clinics, 16,* 327–343.

Gruenewald, P. J., Johnson, F. W., & Treno, A. J. (2002). Outlets, drinking and driving: A multilevel analysis of availability. *Journal of Studies on Alcohol, 63,* 460–468.

Gruenewald, P. J., Millar, A., Ponicki, W. R., & Brinkley, G. (2000). Physical and economic access to alcohol: The application of geostatistical methods to small area analysis in community settings. In R. A. Wilson & M. C. Dufour (Eds.), *The epidemiology of alcohol problems in small geographic areas* (pp. 163–212). Bethesda, MD: National Institute on Alcohol Abuse and Alcoholism.

Hafemeister, T. L., & Jackson, S. L. (2004). The effectiveness of sanctions and law enforcement practices targeted at underage drinking that does not involve the operation of a motor vehicle. In R. J. Bonnie & M. E. O'Connell (Eds.), *Reducing underage drinking: A collective responsibility, background papers* [CD-ROM]. Washington, DC: National Academies Press.

Harding, W. M., Caudill, B. D., Moore, B. A., & Frissell, K. C. (2001). Do drivers drink more when they use a safe ride? *Journal of Substance Abuse, 13,* 283–290.

Hartling, L., Wiebe, N., Russell, K., Petruk, J., Spinola, C., & Klassen, T. P. (2004). Graduated driver licensing for reducing motor vehicle crashes among young drivers. *Cochrane Database Systematic Reviews, 2,* CD003300.

Hibell, B., Andersson, B., Bjarnason, T., Ahlström, S., Balakireva, O., Kokkevi, A., & Morgan, M. (2004). *The ESPAD report 2003: Alcohol and other drug use among students in 35 European countries.* Stockholm: Swedish Council for Information on Alcohol and Other Drugs.

Hingson, R. W., Heeren, T., & Winter, M. R. (1994). Effects of lower legal blood alcohol limits for young and adult drivers. *Alcohol, Drugs and Driving, 10,* 243–252.

Hingson, R. W., Heeren, T., & Winter, M. R. (2006). Age at drinking onset and alcohol dependence: Age at onset, duration, and severity. *Archives of Pediatrics and Adolescent Medicine, 160,* 739–746.

Hingson, R., & Kenkel, D. (2004). Social, health, and economic consequences of underage drinking. In R. J. Bonnie & M. E. O'Connell (Eds.), *Reducing underage drinking: A collective responsibility* (pp. 351–382). Washington, DC: National Academies Press.

Holder, H. D., & Treno, A. J. (1997). Media advocacy in community prevention: News as a means to enhance policy change. *Addiction, 92*(Suppl. 2), S189–S199.

Holder, H. D., & Wagenaar, A. C. (1994). Mandated server training and reduced alcohol-involved traffic crashes: A time series analysis of the Oregon experience. *Accident Analysis and Prevention, 26,* 89–97.

Jefferis, B. J., Power, C., & Manor, O. (2005). Adolescent drinking level and adult binge drinking in a national birth cohort. *Addiction, 100,* 543–549.

Johnson, A. (2007, December). *Debate on lower drinking age bubbling up. Proponents say current restriction drives teen alcohol use underground.* Retrieved December 19, 2007, from http://www.msnbc.msn.com/id/20249460/

Johnston, L. D., O'Malley, P. M., Bachman, J. G., & Schulenberg, J. E. (2004). *Monitoring the Future national survey results on drug use, 1975–2003. Volume I: Secondary school students* (NIH Publication No. 04-5507). Bethesda, MD: National Institute on Drug Abuse.

Johnston, L. D., O'Malley, P. M., Bachman, J. G., & Schulenberg, J. E. (2008). *Monitoring the Future national survey results on drug use, 1975–2007. Volume I: Secondary school students* (NIH Publication No. 08-6418A). Bethesda, MD: National Institute on Drug Abuse.

Kaskutas, L., & Greenfield, T. K. (1992). First effects of warning labels on alcoholic beverage containers. *Drug and Alcohol Dependence, 31,* 1–14.

Laixuthai, A., & Chaloupka, F. J. (1993). Youth alcohol use and public policy. *Contemporary Policy Issues, 11,* 70–81.

Lang, E., Stockwell, T., Rydon, P., & Beel, A. (1998). Can training bar staff in responsible serving practices reduce alcohol-related harm? *Drug and Alcohol Review, 17,* 39–50.

Lange, J. E., Reed, M. B., Johnson, M. B., & Voas, R. B. (2006). The efficacy of experimental interventions designed to reduce drinking among designated drivers. *Journal of Studies on Alcohol, 67,* 261–268.

Langley, J. D., Wagenaar, A. C., & Begg, D. J. (1996). An evaluation of the New Zealand graduated driver licensing system. *Accident Analysis and Prevention, 28,* 139–146.

Lipton, R., & Gruenewald, P. (2002). Spatial dynamics of violence and alcohol outlets. *Journal of Studies on Alcohol, 63,* 187–195.

MacKinnon, D. P., Pentz, M. A., & Stacy, A. W. (1993). Alcohol warning labels and adolescents: The first year. *American Journal of Public Health, 83,* 585–587.

Marlatt, G. A., & Witkiewitz, K. (2002). Harm reduction approaches to alcohol use: Health promotion, prevention, and treatment. *Addictive Behaviors, 27,* 867–886.

Masten, S. V., & Hagge, R. A. (2004). Evaluation of California's graduated driver licensing program. *Journal of Safety Research, 35,* 523–535.

McLaughlin, K. L., & Harrison-Stewart, A. J. (1992). Effect of a temporary period of relaxed licensing laws on the alcohol consumption of young male drinkers. *International Journal of the Addictions, 27,* 409–423.

Miller, T. R., Levy, D. T., Spicer, R. S., & Taylor, D. M. (2006). Societal costs of underage drinking. *Journal of Studies on Alcohol, 6,* 519–528.

Morrisey, M. A., Grabowski, D. C., Dee, T. S., & Campbell, C. (2006). The strength of graduated drivers licensing programs and fatalities among teen drivers and passengers. *Accident Analysis & Prevention, 38,* 135–141.

Mosher, J. F., Toomey, T. L., Good, C., Harwood, E., & Wagenaar, A. C. (2002). State laws mandating or promoting training programs for alcohol servers and establishment managers: An assessment of statutory and administrative procedures. *Journal of Public Health Policy, 23,* 90–113.

National Highway Traffic Safety Administration. (2007). *Traffic safety facts 2006.* Washington, DC: Department of Transportation.

National Institute on Alcohol Abuse and Alcoholism. (2007, November). *Statistics on underage drinking.* Retrieved December 19, 2007, from http://www.niaaa.nih.gov/AboutNIAAA/NIAAASponsoredPrograms/underage.htm#statistics

Nelson, J. P. (2001). Alcohol advertising and advertising bans: A survey of research methods, results, and policy implications. *Advertising and Differentiated Products, 10,* 239–295.

Nelson, J. P., & Young, D. J. (2001). Do advertising bans work? An international comparison. *International Journal of Advertising, 20,* 273–296.

Nygaard, P., Waiters, E. D., Grube, J. W., & Keefe, D. (2003). Why do they do it? A qualitative study of adolescent drinking and driving. *Substance Use and Misuse, 38,* 835–863.

O'Malley, P. M., & Wagenaar, A. C. (1991). Effects of minimum drinking age laws on alcohol use, related behaviors and traffic crash involvement among American youths: 1976–1987. *Journal of Studies on Alcohol, 52,* 478–491.

Pacula, R. L. (1998). Does increasing the beer tax decrease marijuana consumption? *Journal of Health Economics, 17,* 557–585.

Paschall, M. J., Grube, J. W., & Black, C. (2006). *Commercial alcohol availability, alcohol sources, and underage drinking: A multi-level study.* Berkeley, CA: Prevention Research Center.

Paschall, M. J., Grube, J. W., Black, C., Flewelling, R. L., Ringwalt, C. L., & Biglan, A. (2007). Alcohol outlet characteristics and alcohol sales to youth: Results of alcohol purchase surveys in 45 Oregon communities. *Prevention Science, 8,* 153–159.

Paschall, M. J., Grube, J. W., Black, C. A., & Ringwalt, C. L. (2007). Is commercial alcohol availability related to adolescent alcohol sources and alcohol use? Findings from a multi-level study. *Journal of Adolescent Health, 41,* 168–174.

Perry, C. L., Williams, C. L., Komro, K. A., Veblen-Mortenson, S., Forster, J. L., Bernstein-Lachter, R., et al. (2002). Project Northland high school interventions: Community action to reduce adolescent alcohol use. *Health Education and Behavior, 27,* 29–49.

Pitkänen, T., Lyyra, A. L., & Pulkkinen, L. (2005). Age of onset of drinking and the use of alcohol in adulthood: A follow-up study from age 8–42 for females and males. *Addiction, 100,* 652–61.

Ponicki, W. R., Gruenewald, P. J., & LaScala, E. A. (2007). Joint impacts of minimum legal drinking age and beer taxes on U.S. youth traffic fatalities, 1975 to 2001. *Alcoholism: Clinical and Experimental Research, 31,* 804–813.

Riley, D., & O'Hare, P. (2000). Harm reduction: History, definition, and practice. In J. A. Inciardi & L. D. Harrison (Eds.), *Harm reduction: National and international perspectives* (pp. 1–26), Thousand Oaks, CA: Sage.

Ross, H. L. (1982). *Deterring the drinking driver.* Lexington, MA: Lexington Books.

Russell, B. L., Jennings, B., & Classey, S. (2005). Adolescent attitudes toward random drug testing in schools. *Journal of Drug Education, 35,* 167–184.

Saffer, H. (1991). Alcohol advertising bans and alcohol abuse: An international perspective. *Journal of Health Economics, 10,* 65–79.

Saffer, H., & Dave, D. (2002). Alcohol consumption and alcohol advertising bans. *Applied Economics, 5,* 1325–1334.

Saltz, R. F. (1997). Prevention where alcohol is sold and consumed: Server intervention and responsible beverage service. In M. Plant, E. Single, & T. Stockwell (Eds.), *Alcohol: Minimising the harm* (pp. 72–84). London: Free Association Books.

Sarkar, S., Andreas, M., & de Faria, F. (2005). Who uses safe ride programs: An examination of the dynamics of individuals who use a safe ride program instead of driving home while drunk. *American Journal of Drug and Alcohol Abuse, 31,* 305–325.

Scribner, R. A., & Cohen, D. A. (2001). The effect of enforcement on merchant compliance with the minimum legal drinking age law. *Journal of Drug Issues, 31,* 857–866.

Scribner, R. A., Cohen, D. A., & Fisher, W. (2000). Evidence of a structural effect for alcohol outlet density: A multilevel analysis. *Alcoholism: Clinical and Experimental Research, 24,* 188–195.

Scribner, R. A., MacKinnon, D. P., & Dwyer, J. H. (1994). Alcohol outlet density and motor vehicle crashes in Los Angeles County cities. *Journal of Studies on Alcohol, 55,* 447–453.

Shope, J. T. (2007). Graduated driver licensing: Review of evaluation results since 2002. *Journal of Safety Research, 38,* 165–175.

Shope, J. T., & Molnar, L. J. (2003). Graduated driver licensing in the United States: Evaluation of results from early programs. *Journal of Safety Research, 34,* 63–69.

Shope, J. T., Molnar, L. J., Elliott, M. R., & Waller, P. F. (2001, October 3). Graduated driver licensing in Michigan: Early impact on motor vehicle crashes among 16-year-old drivers. *JAMA, 286,* 1593–1598.

Shults, R. A., Elder, R. W., Sleet, D. A., Nichols, J. L., Alao, M. O., Carande-Kulis, V. G., et al. (2001). Reviews of evidence regarding interventions to reduce alcohol-impaired driving. *American Journal of Preventive Medicine, 21*(Suppl. 1), 66–88.

Sloan, F. A., Stout, E. M., Whetten-Goldstein, K., & Liang, L. (2000). *Drinkers, drivers, and bartenders: Balancing private choices and public accountability.* Chicago: University of Chicago Press.

Stevenson, M., Palamara, P., Rooke, M., Richardson, K., Baker, M., & Baumwol, J. (2001). Drink and drug driving among university students: What's the skipper to do? *Australian and New Zealand Journal of Public Health, 2,* 511–513.

Stout, E. M., Sloan, F. A., Liang, L., & Davies, H. H. (2000). Reducing harmful alcohol-related behaviors: Effective regulatory methods. *Journal of Studies on Alcohol, 61,* 402–412.

Timmerman, M. A., Geller, E. S., Glindemann, K. E., & Fournier, A. K. (2003). Do the designated drivers of college students stay sober? *Journal of Safety Research, 34,* 127–133.

Toomey, T. L., Lenk, K. M., & Wagenaar, A. C. (2007). Environmental policies to reduce college drinking: An update of research findings. *Journal of Studies on Alcohol and Drugs, 68,* 208–219.

Toomey, T. L., Wagenaar, A. C., Gehan, J. P., Kilian, G., Murray, D. M., & Perry, C. L. (2001). Project ARM: Alcohol risk management to prevent sales to underage and intoxicated patrons. *Health Education and Behavior, 28,* 186–199.

Treno, A. J., Grube, J. W., & Martin, S. (2003). Alcohol outlet density as a predictor of youth drinking and driving: A hierarchical analysis. *Alcoholism: Clinical and Experimental Research, 27,* 835–840.

Treno, A. J., Johnson, F. W., Remer, L. G., & Gruenewald, P. J. (2007). The impact of outlet densities on alcohol-related crashes: A spatial panel approach. *Accident Analysis and Prevention, 39,* 894–901.

Viner, R. M. & Taylor, B. (2007). Adult outcomes of binge drinking in adolescence: Findings from a UK national birth cohort. *Journal of Epidemiology and Community Health, 10,* 902–907.

Voas, R. B., Lange, J. E., & Tippetts, A. E. (1998). Enforcement of the zero tolerance law in California: A missed opportunity? In *42nd Annual Proceedings of the Association for the Advancement of Automotive Medicine* (pp. 369–383). Des Plaines, IL: Association for the Advancement of Automotive Medicine.

Voas, R. B., Tippetts, A. S., & Fell, J. C. (2003). Assessing the effectiveness of minimum legal drinking age and zero tolerance laws in the United States. *Accident Analysis & Prevention, 35,* 579–587.

Wagenaar, A. C., O'Malley, P. M., & LaFond, C. (2001). Very low legal BAC limits for young drivers: Effects on drinking, driving, and driving-after-drinking behaviors in 30 states. *American Journal of Public Health, 91,* 801–804.

Wagenaar, A. C., & Toomey, T. L. (2002). Effects of minimum drinking age laws: Review and analyses of the literature from 1960 to 2000. *Journal of Studies on Alcohol, 14*(Suppl.), 206–225.

Wagenaar, A. C., Toomey, T. L., & Erickson, D. J. (2005). Preventing youth access to alcohol: Outcomes from a multi-community time-series trial. *Addiction, 100,* 335–345.

Wagenaar, A. C., & Wolfson, M. (1994). Enforcement of the legal minimum drinking age in the United States. *Journal of Public Health Policy, 15,* 37–53.

Wagenaar, A. C., & Wolfson, M. (1995). Deterring sales and provision of alcohol to minors: A study of enforcement in 295 counties in four states. *Public Health Reports, 110,* 419–427.

Wallin, E., Gripenberg, J., & Andreasson, S. (2002). Too drunk for a beer? A study of overserving in Stockholm. *Addiction, 97,* 901–907.

Wallin, E., Norstrom, T., & Andreasson, S. (2003). Alcohol prevention targeting licensed premises: A study of effects on violence. *Journal of Studies on Alcohol, 64,* 270–277.

Wechsler, H., Davenport, A., Dowdall, G., Moeykens, B., & Castillo, S. (1994, December 7). Health and behavioral consequences of binge drinking in college: A national survey of students at 140 campuses. *JAMA, 272,* 1672–1677.

Weitzman, E. R., Folkman, A., Folkman, K. L., & Wechsler, H. (2003). Relationship of alcohol outlet density to heavy and frequent drinking and drinking-related problems among college students at eight universities. *Health and Place, 9,* 1–6.

Wells, J. E., Horwood, L. J., & Fergusson, D. M. (2004). Drinking patterns in mid-adolescence and psychosocial outcomes in late adolescence and early adulthood. *Addiction, 99,* 1529–1541.

Whetten-Goldstein, K., Sloan, F. A., Stout, E., & Liang, L. (2000). Civil liability, criminal law, and other policies and alcohol-related motor vehicle fatalities in the United States: 1984–1995. *Accident Analysis and Prevention, 32,* 723–733.

Wolfson, M., Toomey, T. L., Murray, D. M., Forster, J. L., Short, B. J., & Wagenaar, A. C. (1996). Alcohol outlet policies and practices concerning sales to underage people. *Addiction, 91,* 589–602.

Yamaguchi, R., Johnston, L. D., & O'Malley, P. M. (2003). Relationship between student illicit drug use and school drug-testing policies. *Journal of School Health, 73,* 159–164.

Young, D. J. (1993). Alcohol advertising bans and alcohol abuse: Comment. *Journal of Health Economics, 12,* 213–228.

Young, D. J., & Likens, T. W. (2000). Alcohol regulation and auto fatalities. *International Review of Law and Economics, 20,* 107–126.

PART VIII

STATISTICAL MODELS
OF DRUG USE ETIOLOGY

CHAPTER 27

THE ROLE OF LATENT CLASS AND MIXTURE MODELS IN SUBSTANCE USE THEORY

Brian P. Flaherty

Mixture models are popular statistical techniques in substance use research and have found broad application in the social and behavioral sciences (McLachlan & Peel, 2000; Titterington, Smith, & Makov, 1985). They form a diverse class of statistical models that allow the inclusion of unobservable subgroups in data. This chapter starts by introducing mixture models and then focuses on the use of one particular type of mixture model, the latent class (LC) model, as a measurement model. Measurement is a very important emphasis for psychology in general, particularly given the use of unobservable constructs like depression and anxiety that are part of everyday linguistic fare. Substance use researchers are also confronted with similar problems not only in the conceptualization of their constructs but also in the delineation of discrete groups of subpopulations on the basis of the measurement of behavior. As researchers consider measurement, they are forced to think about the substantive theory of interest. An application of the LC model to national data on substance use experience is presented. The results of this analysis strongly contrast exploratory and confirmatory modeling and beg the question "What sort of subgroups or latent classes do we expect given our theory?" The chapter ends with a discussion contrasting exploratory and more confirmatory analytic approaches. Measurement in mixture models is also considered.

To quickly provide a sense of mixture models, consider a hypothetical example loosely based on the estimation of the proportion of male and female fish in a population of halibut (Hosmer, 1973). The sex of halibut is not directly observable, but on the basis of previous data it is known that females tend to be larger than males. If multiple size measurements were taken of a random sample of adult halibut, a mixture of two subgroups (corresponding to male and female) could be used to disaggregate the distributions of measurements. For example, we might find that fish in one subgroup tended to be smaller than the fish in the other. On the basis of our knowledge of halibut, we could conclude that the smaller group represents males and the other group represents females. This analysis would also provide estimates of the proportion of each sex in the adult population.

From this brief example, one can see that mixture models are not deterministic but rather probabilistic. That is, small fish are most likely to be male and large fish are most likely to be female. But keep in mind this assignment scheme could be wrong for a particular fish. Additionally, fish in the middle of the distribution are more difficult to classify as male or female (on the basis of the measurements taken). In this way, mixture models accommodate different degrees of uncertainty.

The halibut example highlights some key aspects of mixture models. Associations between measurements are explained by subgroup membership. Not everyone will score exactly the same on some type of standardized measurement, and this variability underlies most measurements of behavior. Along with characterizing the two groups on the basis of size, the analysis provides estimates of the proportion of observations in each group. In the case of the

Preparation of this chapter was supported by National Institute of Drug Abuse Grant R01DA018673.

halibut analysis, the number of classes was known (male and female), but this is often not the case, especially in social and behavioral research in which the waters can be murky and less translucent.

A primary reason for the popularity of LC models is that they allow for different types of people or observations in a population rather than assuming that a single statistical model applies to the entire population. That is, the standard t test, multiple regression, or factor model is assumed to apply to everyone in a particular sample or population, whereas mixture models allow those statistical models to vary by unobserved subgroup membership.

In fact, one can have a mixture of pretty much anything, for example, mixture regression models in which different regression relations between predictors and response hold for different subgroups (DeSarbo & Cron, 1988) or mixture factor models in which subgroups may have potentially different latent factor structures (Lubke & Muthén, 2005). The motivation for mixture models is that one expects unobservable subgroups in the data, and the relations among measured variables may differ among subgroups. As I show in a bit, this becomes a very useful tool when one thinks about the characterization of drug use in a population. Even in a single population of users, there are several different "forms" of drug use (e.g., I don't smoke, I smoke a little, and I smoke a lot); thus, a mixture model could be quite useful in characterizing the different patterns of drug use in a population.

Researchers guided by tremendous substantive interests find mixture models interesting because they are potentially theoretically rich. They offer the flexibility of modeling differences between people that has not typically been possible. Traditional individual differences research has focused on differences among people, but within the context of a fixed model. Thus, a study might find that overall increasing levels of depression are associated with increasing levels of substance use. Thus, people reporting they are more depressed also report more drug use, and this relationship would be cast for all members in the population. In contrast, a mixture approach could identify two groups: one for which this association is positive and another for which it is negative. In the first case, drug use exacerbates depression, whereas

in the second case, the statistical findings follow form with the self-medication hypothesis, in which case drug use ameliorates depression.

One of the simplest mixture models is the LC model (Clogg, 1995; Goodman, 1974; Lanza, Flaherty, & Collins, 2003). It was originally developed in sociology for mixtures of associations among categorical measures. I focus on the traditional LC model, emphasizing its role in measurement and theory, but many of the issues that are highlighted here apply to mixture models even more broadly.

LATENT CLASS MODELS

The LC model is a statistical model for mixtures of categorical data. It can be used to identify homogeneous subgroups in data. The latent classes represent these homogeneous subgroups or types of people. The latent classes are differentiated by the typical item responses expected from members of each LC. The LC model and longitudinal extensions (Collins & Wugalter, 1992; Langeheine & van de Pol, 2002) have been popular in substance use research because interest often centers on types of people, for example, ever tried versus not tried (e.g., Graham, Collins, Wugalter, Chung, & Hansen, 1991). These models have also been popular because substance use etiology research and theory have often conceptualized consumption as discrete stages of use (e.g., Flay, 1993).

The next few sections of this chapter provide a selective overview of the LC model. The goal is to introduce the LC model and highlight aspects of its use that are relevant to the discussion. The chapter is not a complete presentation of the LC model, much less a technical one. Readers seeking more thorough and technical discussions should consult Goodman (1974), Clogg (1995), McCutcheon (1987), Flaherty (2002), Lanza et al. (2003), and a host of references cited therein. An important goal for this chapter is for readers to be able to blend their understanding of LC methodology with some of the more pressing conceptual and theoretical issues in substance use research. The marriage of quantitative methods like LC with substantive efforts will hopefully promote a more refined understanding of etiology.

General Overview of Latent Class Models

As I briefly mentioned in the introduction to this chapter, the LC model was originally developed for categorical data. The general assumption with categorical data is that a respondent is assigned to either one class or category or the other, but not both. Consider a set of questions on a health survey that includes four drug items probing "ever use" (e.g., "Have you ever tried. . . . .") with yes–no responses provided for tobacco, alcohol, marijuana, and cocaine. The data for the LC analysis consist of the cross-tabulation of these four binary items. The cells of this contingency table correspond to response patterns, that is, the set of yes–no responses to the items. Response patterns are the unit of analysis in the LC model and inform us whether a tobacco user also said "yes" to alcohol, marijuana, cocaine, or any of the possible permutations of these responses. Furthermore, each response pattern has an accompanying frequency. In these models, the terms *frequency, proportion,* and *probability* are all somewhat interchangeable. *Frequency* is typically used to refer to the data and *proportion* or *probability* when talking about model estimates. For example, let's say 200 people said "yes" to the tobacco and alcohol items, but the same people said "no" to the marijuana and cocaine items. But perhaps only 12 people said "no" to the tobacco, alcohol, and marijuana items but "yes" to the cocaine item.

In this simple four-item example, there would be a total of $2^4 = 16$ possible response patterns. Statistically, the goal of the LC model is to reproduce the observed response pattern frequencies obtained with a smaller set of parameter estimates. Consider Table 27.1, which presents a hypothetical two-class

model based on the four ever-use items. I use this example to illustrate the two types of parameters in the LC model: LC proportions (or probabilities) and conditional response probabilities.

In Table 27.1, the probability of a "yes" response is given separately for the two LCs. These are the conditional response probabilities, and they quantify how likely members of a particular LC are to make a certain response to an item. Note that the probability of a "no" response is simply $1 - P(\text{yes response} \mid \text{LC})$ when the data are binary. (Data need not be binary for use in the LC model.) We read this probability statement as "one minus the probability of a 'yes' response given a specific LC membership." LC 1 in Table 27.1 might be interpreted as individuals within the sample who have tried predominantly legal substances. Specifically, members of this class are 80% likely to say that they have tried tobacco and 90% likely to indicate having tried alcohol. In contrast, these individuals are only 30% and 2% likely to reply that they have tried marijuana and cocaine, respectively. In the population, 80% of the people are expected to belong to this class.

In contrast, LC 2 represents people with a higher level of substance use experience than LC 1 (see Table 27.1). People in LC 2 are virtually certain to indicate having tried tobacco and alcohol, 70% likely to indicate having tried marijuana, and 30% likely to report past cocaine use. Twenty percent of the population is expected in this class. Assuming this two-class model was a good representation of the data, then we have dramatically reduced the data we need to think about now. Rather than 16 response patterns, we can work with two LCs. This may be a very useful form of data reduction. However, ideally these two LCs are also theoretically interesting. For example, we can ask whether class membership is differentially associated with predictors and outcomes. Is a particular developmental pathway more likely to involve LC 2? Many of the earlier chapters in this handbook address specific risk factors (e.g., temperament, cognition, and expectancies), and one concern addresses whether some of these risk factors differentiate LC membership. If earlier characteristics or experiences were associated with subsequent membership in LC 2, then perhaps prevention efforts can specifically target these individuals and prevent some

---

TABLE 27.1

Hypothetical Two Latent-Class (LC) Model Based on Four Substance Ever-Use Items

| LC | LC proportion | Probability of a yes response conditional on LC membership | | | |
		Tobacco	Alcohol	Marijuana	Cocaine
1	0.8	0.8	0.9	0.3	0.02
2	0.2	0.98	0.99	0.7	0.3

youth from experiencing the deleterious effects associated with their class behaviors (i.e., high drug use). As one can see, this theoretical richness is a significant reason for interest in these models.

In the examples just given, there were two response patterns: 200 people saying "yes" to tobacco and alcohol and "no" to marijuana and cocaine and 12 people saying "no" to everything but cocaine. In a full data set, there would be many other response profiles, some with large accompanying frequencies and others with relatively small frequencies. It is worth considering what happened to those 12 people who indicated no experience with tobacco, alcohol, or marijuana, but some past experience with cocaine. Neither of the two LCs contained in Table 27.1 resembles that pattern of responses.

On the basis of the probability estimates, the LC model reproduces the observed data, much as expected cell probabilities are compared with observed cell probabilities when testing for association in a two-way table. The LC model is just typically much larger. Under an independence hypothesis, the model of independent association along with row and column margins is used to calculate expected cell probabilities. The process is quite similar in the LC model. Along with the structure imposed by the LC model, the model estimates are used to fill in the cell probabilities (frequencies) in the cross-classified table of the measured variables. In a typical unrestricted LC analysis, every response has some probability of being observed, even those that appear quite incongruent with the LCs.

Even though none of the classes in Table 27.1 is characterized solely by past cocaine use, the response profile No, No, No, and Yes to the tobacco, alcohol, marijuana, and cocaine items, respectively, is expected under the model. But what does a response pattern like this represent? Are there people in the population for whom this is a true reflection of their substance use experience? Or would a researcher be likely to regard this response pattern as measurement error or noise? This is an important question, and I return to it later.

Assumptions of the Latent Class Model

The standard LC model is a nonparametric model with relatively few assumptions. The first two of these assumptions are mutual exclusivity and exhaustiveness. In the case of mutual exclusivity, individuals are assumed to belong to one and only one LC. The exhaustive assumption holds that everyone in the population belongs to one of the LCs (i.e., no stragglers). Within-class homogeneity is another assumption of the model. All members of a particular class are assumed to be equally well characterized by the within-class distributions for the measured variables. For example, the last four columns of each row in Table 27.1 are the estimated probabilities for a binomial distribution for each item within a LC. The four "yes" response probabilities are assumed to hold equally as well for all members of LC 1. In other words, these probabilities are assumed to accurately describe the behavior of all members of the class.

The assumption of conditional independence is a common assumption shared by many simple measurement models, such as the exploratory factor model (Comrey, 1992), and the standard LC model uses it as well. Conditional independence implies that once one knows the latent variable score for a given individual, that person's item responses are statistically independent. In the case of the LC model, a latent variable score is the person's LC membership. Therefore, LC membership is assumed to be responsible for all associations among the measured items. The LC model has been generalized to relax conditional independence (Hagenaars, 1988), but these residual covariances between items are not often theoretically motivated and so are not further considered here.

Model Fit and Selection

LC analysis is a model-fitting procedure, like confirmatory factor analysis and structural equation modeling (Bollen & Long, 1989). As I alluded to earlier, the goal of the LC model is to reproduce an observed contingency table. As with many other categorical data methods, the statistical acceptability of the model is determined by comparing the observed frequencies to the model's implied (or expected) frequencies. If the expected frequencies are close to the observed frequencies (i.e., within random sampling variation), then the model is deemed to fit. The likelihood ratio (G^2) and Pearson's chi-square are commonly used fit statistics (Agresti, 1990). Ideally, if the model fits, these two statistics are distributed as chi-square with degrees of freedom equal to the number of possible response patterns minus the number of estimates minus 1.

In discussing model fit, one says "ideally" because data are often sparse. Sparse data have zero frequency counts for some or many response patterns. As data become increasingly sparse, the likelihood ratio statistic or the chi-square statistic is not distributed as chi-square. When data are not sparse and the model fits, the value of these two fit statistics should be close to the degrees of freedom. But when data are sparse, the value of the two fit statistics is typically less than the degrees of freedom. Additionally, it is not currently known how to calculate how much lower the expectation of the distribution is.

As a result, it can sometimes be difficult to evaluate model fit well. If data are sparse, the expected value of the likelihood ratio decreases, but if the model does not fit the data well, the value increases. Therefore, in an LC analysis, the observed value of the likelihood ratio is being pushed in these opposing directions. For these reasons, some recommendations have been to select an interpretable LC solution for which the likelihood ratio value is close to the degrees of freedom (or lower). Other approaches to model fit and selection are cross-validation (Collins, Graham, Long & Hansen, 1994), bootstrapping (Efron & Tibshirani, 1993), and Bayesian simulation or data augmentation (Lanza, Collins, Schafer, & Flaherty, 2005; Rubin & Stern, 1994).

Absolute fit is intended to be an objective measure of how well the model and estimates reproduce the observed data. Very often, researchers also want to compare the relative fit of models. Nested model comparisons are commonly used to make this comparison. A model is nested within another model if the former is a restricted version of the latter model. For example, the more complex model may include a freely estimated parameter, whereas the nested model restricts that parameter estimate somehow (see Flaherty, 2002, and Formann, 1985, 1989, for some discussion of parameter restrictions). The comparison of the models is made with a likelihood ratio difference test. That is, the difference between the likelihood ratio statistics (simpler model minus larger model) is compared with a chi-square distri-

bution with degrees of freedom equal to the difference between the two model degrees of freedom ($df_{simple} - df_{larger}$). Nested model comparisons tend to have fewer total degrees of freedom and do not appear to be as susceptible to the effects of sparse data.

Choosing the Number of Classes

Often, a difficult decision in exploratory LC analyses is the number of classes required. For statistical reasons, models with different numbers of classes cannot be compared with nested model comparisons (Aitkin & Rubin, 1985; Wilks, 1938). Typically, to make this decision researchers have used information criteria like Akaike's information criterion (AIC; Akaike, 1987) or the Bayesian information criterion (BIC; Schwarz, 1978). AIC and BIC attempt to balance model fit with model parsimony. Both statistics are penalized versions of the likelihood ratio, where the penalty term is a function of the number of parameters in the model. In the examples provided in the remainder of this chapter, I focus on the likelihood ratio, AIC, and BIC, three of the most common quantities used when considering the number of classes.

EMPIRICAL ILLUSTRATION

Methamphetamine has become one of the more problematic drugs of abuse for American youth and is associated with both individual harm and substantial social costs (Iritani, Hallfors, & Bauer, 2007). Understanding factors associated with methamphetamine use and developmental pathways that may involve methamphetamine use could be useful in mounting effective prevention efforts. Although cross-sectional data cannot be used to study developmental pathways per se, cumulative (retrospective) histories may point to possibly divergent pathways. Toward this end, I compared past substance use experience of individuals indicating some methamphetamine use with that of individuals who did not indicate any past methamphetamine use. Differences in prevalence patterns (for other drugs) between past methamphetamine users and nonusers could indicate different antecedent experiences that could further inform the knowledge base with regard to etiology and consequences.

Method

This work uses data from the 2004 National Survey of Drug Use and Health (U.S. Department of Health and Human Services, 2005). The National Survey of Drug Use and Health is an annual survey of substance use and related factors, given to a national sample of noninstitutionalized U.S. residents age 12 and older. In the most recent iteration of this survey with publicly available data, the total sample size was 55,602. Forty-eight percent of the sample were male. Furthermore, youth were oversampled in 2004, yielding a sample with about 33% of respondents between age 12 and 17, 33% between age 18 and 25, 10% between age 25 and 34, and 24% of the sample age 35 or older. Sixty-six percent of the sample were non-Hispanic White, 12% were non-Hispanic Black, and 14% were Hispanic. Eight percent of the sample indicated they were of the following racial or ethnic groups: Native American/Alaska Native, Native Hawaiian/other Pacific Islander, Asian, or multiracial.

For the analyses presented here, we are interested in the categorical drug measures for "ever use." In addition to methamphetamine, the other substances and substance classes in this analysis are listed in Table 27.2. All but one of the items used was written along the lines of "Have you ever, even once, used . . . ?" For these items, valid data were coded as "yes" or "no," but "don't know," "refused," or

"skipped" response categories were coded as missing. For hallucinogens, the item used asked about the age at first hallucinogen use. This item was recoded to match the other binary data (ever use). Any age indicating past hallucinogen use was coded as a past use. Nonusers were coded as such, and missing data categories were coded as missing.

Because there is little theory to guide the expected classes of substance use in these data, exploratory LC models were fit for the two different methamphetamine groups separately. For each methamphetamine group, models containing between two and seven classes were fit. Model selection decisions were based on the likelihood ratio statistic, AIC, and BIC. The National Survey of Drug Use and Health includes sampling weights to adjust for oversampling. These were incorporated by reweighting the response pattern frequencies. This analysis did not, however, incorporate the clustered sampling information (e.g., in a household survey people living in the same house are more likely to be behaviorally similar than are people living in different houses).

These analyses were run with a Unix version of the latent transition analysis software I maintain (Collins, Flaherty, Hyatt, & Schafer, 1999). This software uses an expectation maximization algorithm (Dempster, Laird, & Rubin, 1977) to find the maximum likelihood estimates. When fitting LC models, it is often advisable to test the identifiability of the model with multiple sets of random start values. For these analyses, 25 sets of random start values were run for each number of classes. The way this iterative process works, if the majority of the 25 parameter start values ended at the same solution and that solution was clearly better than the rest, that number of classes was considered identified. If many of the 25 sets of start values ended at different solutions or there were two solutions with nearly equal fit but different interpretations, then that number of classes was considered unidentified.

Results of the Latent Class Modeling

About 5% (unweighted $N = 2,465$) of the sample indicated past methamphetamine use. Table 27.2 contains the univariate endorsement probabilities of each of the remaining substances across the entire sample. Alcohol was most prevalent (73%) and heroin was

---

TABLE 27.2

Univariate Endorsement Rates for Ever Trying a Substance or Substance Use Class Across All Respondents From the 2004 National Survey of Drug And Health

Substance (or substance class)	Proportion indicating past experience (%)
Tobacco	58
Alcohol	73
Marijuana	40
Cocaine	12
Inhalants	12
Hallucinogens	14
Analgesics	17
Tranquilizers	8
Sedatives	3
Heroin	1

least prevalent (1%). However, these univariate endorsement rates provide no insight into whether if someone has tried one substance, he or she is also likely to have tried another. These conditional relations are the heart of any LC analysis. In the methamphetamine and nonmethamphetamine groups, there were 286 and 631 response pattern frequencies, respectively.

Model selection for the nonmethamphetamine sample is presented first. Table 27.3 contains the likelihood ratio, AIC, and BIC values for the best model, based on the 25 start values for between two and five classes. Models with six or more classes were not identified. Recall that the likelihood ratio values should be "near" the degrees of freedom. This is not the case in any of the models. However, the data represent more than 53,000 people, and therefore there is far too much statistical power (it would be easy to detect trivial deviations between sample estimates and population parameters as being statistically significant). Because the six-class model was not identified, the five-class model is the best one can do in this exploratory analysis. Also, of the models shown in Table 27.3, AIC and BIC are lowest for the five-class model. The results of this model are presented below.

Model selection information for the subsample with past methamphetamine experience is contained in Table 27.4. In contrast to the nonmethamphetamine group, the likelihood ratio statistic falls well below the degrees of freedom for the three-class model. Because these data are sparse, the expectation of the likelihood ratio is less than the degrees of freedom, but the likelihood ratio value of 751.52 is

TABLE 27.4

Model Fit for Different Numbers of Classes in the Methamphetamine Experience Subgroup

No. classes	df	G^2	AIC	BIC
2	1002	1,198.52	1,240.52	1,362.52
3	991	751.52	815.52	1,001.42
4	980	614.56	700.56	950.37
5	969	501.94	609.94	923.66

Note. G^2 = likelihood ratio; AIC = Akaike information criterion; BIC = Bayesian information criterion.

nearly 240 less than the degrees of freedom. Because it is so much lower than the degrees of freedom, the three-class model was chosen for the methamphetamine subgroup. However, note that both AIC and BIC again indicate that the five-class model is to be preferred.

Let's turn to the five-class nonmethamphetamine model (Figure 27.1). The largest class (46%) had high probabilities of experience with tobacco and alcohol and moderate rates of marijuana (legal and marijuana, denoted by diamonds). They had near-zero probabilities of having ever tried any other substance. The second largest class (32%) had relatively low rates of tobacco or alcohol and near-zero probabilities of experience with any illicit drug (lowest use, denoted by plus signs). The third largest class was much smaller in size (13%) and can be called the popular illicit LC (designated with circles). Members of this class had very high rates of tobacco, alcohol, and marijuana experience and moderate experience with cocaine and hallucinogens. The individuals within this class were about 20% likely to have ever tried inhalants and less likely to have ever tried any of the other drugs. The fourth largest class had the highest use rates across all of the substances and substance use classes (5%; highest use, denoted by a triangle in the figure). The fifth class represented about 4% of the sample and was characterized by relatively high rates of analgesic and tranquilizer use (denoted by an *x*). Members of this class were as likely to have experience with analgesics as were the members of the highest use class. Furthermore, this class had the second highest rate of tranquilizer use. Also, compared with the other classes involving use

TABLE 27.3

Model Fit for Different Numbers of Classes in the Nonmethamphetamine Experience Subgroup

No. classes	df	G^2	AIC	BIC
2	1002	19,599.84	19,641.84	19,828.31
3	991	6,206.7	6,270.7	6,554.84
4	980	3,158.89	3,244.89	3,626.7
5	969	1,815.05	1,923.05	2,402.53

Note. G^2 = likelihood ratio; AIC = Akaike information criterion; BIC = Bayesian information criterion.

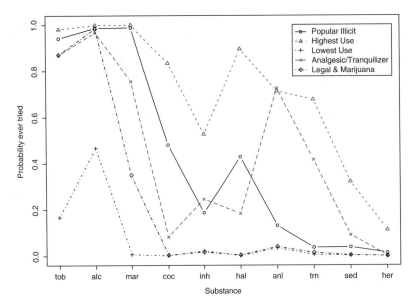

FIGURE 27.1.   Probabilities of a "yes" response to the 10 substance use items for the five latent class model in the nonmethamphetamine sample. Diamonds denote legal and marijuana class; plus signs denote lowest use class; circles denote popular illicit class; triangles denote highest use class; and xs denote analgesics and tranquilizers class. tob = tobacco; alc = alcohol; mar = marijuana; coc = cocaine; inh = inhalants; hal = hallucinogens; anl = analgesics; trn = tranquilizers; sed = sedatives; her = heroin.

of illicit substances, this class had relatively low rates of cocaine and hallucinogen use.

Interestingly, the three classes within the methamphetamine sample paralleled the illicit substance use classes of the nonmethamphetamine sample (Figure 27.2). The salient differences were the magnitudes of the probabilities of experience with the different substances. Among the methamphetamine sample, the largest LC was the popular illicit class (43%; denoted by circles). Consider the differences in magnitude on the cocaine item. In the nonmethamphetamine sample, the probability that someone in the popular illicit class had tried cocaine was less than 50%, but in the methamphetamine sample, that same probability was nearly 90%. The probability of use of every other illicit substance was also higher in the methamphetamine sample. The highest use class (37% of the methamphetamine sample, denoted by triangles in the figure) also had markedly higher probabilities of experience with all the illicit substances.

The third class in the methamphetamine sample was defined by its response profile to the questions about analgesics and tranquilizer use. This class

included 20% of the sample (denoted by xs in the figure). The most striking characteristic of this class is that the probabilities of past experience with analgesics and tranquilizers are markedly lower in this class than they are for the analgesics and tranquilizers class in the nonmethamphetamine sample.

CONCLUSIONS

This chapter describes a comparative LC analysis in a large, nationally representative U.S. sample of noninstitutionalized people age 12 and older. Items measuring substance use experience were analyzed separately for those with and without methamphetamine use experience. A five-class model was presented for the nonmethamphetamine sample, and a three-class model was presented for the methamphetamine sample. Interestingly, the three classes in the methamphetamine sample mirrored the illicit substance use classes in the nonmethamphetamine sample. The fact that essentially the same three substance use classes were found lends some support to their being substantively meaningful behavioral groups in

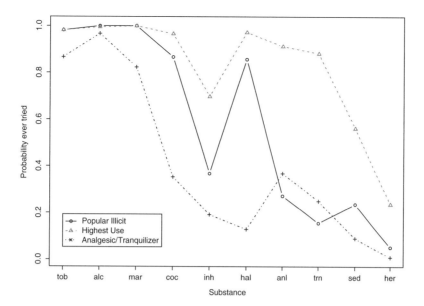

FIGURE 27.2.   Probabilities of a "yes" response to the 10 substance use items for the three latent class model in the methamphetamine sample. Plus signs denote lowest use; circles denote popular illicit; triangles denote highest use. tob = tobacco; alc = alcohol; mar = marijuana; coc = cocaine; inh = inhalants; hal = hallucinogens; anl = analgesics; trn = tranquilizers; sed = sedatives; her = heroin.

the data. However, the original motivation behind this analysis was to see whether methamphetamine experience was associated with different patterns of substance use. Unfortunately, this supposition was not borne out empirically.

The results presented also highlight some of the ambiguity and difficulty involved in model assessment and selection in LC models. It is not uncommon to have different fit and model selection indicators point to different conclusions. It is also not uncommon to encounter empirical underidentification. Undoubtedly, some more technical readers and those familiar with these quantitative methods will feel that the model selection was not done properly. One should use more start values and other checks on the number of classes, such as data augmentation (Lanza et al., 2005) or bootstrapping (Efron & Tibshirani, 1993). However, the criteria focused on here are those most commonly used in the literature. Additionally, another important purpose of this presentation was to draw attention to the difficulty of statistical decision making in light of the diverse behaviors we study. This difficulty exists whether one uses a simple statistical approach such as BIC model comparisons or a more complex

approach such as data augmentation. Both are solely statistical approaches and cannot incorporate substantive knowledge and theoretical expectations.

Statistical decisions are likely to always be difficult in LC and mixture models, just as they can often be in large structural equation models (see chap. 29 of this volume). But they are made much more difficult by the sometimes infrequent use of theory or at the very least reasonable expectations about the number and composition of the classes. Exploratory LC and other mixture models can be very useful for hypothesis generation, but there needs to be simultaneous work in theory development.

To take this one additional step further, consider the empirical example presented in this chapter. How many classes should we expect? A five-class solution was presented for the nonmethamphetamine sample because of identification problems. But perhaps a six- or seven-class model is actually what we want. As more classes are extracted, the size of those classes will get smaller (i.e., fewer people with those specific response profiles, which capture extreme behaviors). How many people should be in a class for us to consider it important? In the nonmethamphetamine sample, there were 631 response patterns. The LC model presented in this chapter represented all those patterns with five discrete classes. One thing to consider is that this may be too few to truly represent the currents underneath the data. The reduced set of classes may gloss over many interesting patterns of behavior (i.e., drug use) in these data. Another important concern with LC methods is where to draw the line when low frequency response patterns should be considered "error" versus when are they worth considering as real phenomena.

As soon as we mention the term *error*, we are forced to think about measurement. One important benefit of theory development is that it forces us to develop a more refined sense of what should be measured and how. Significant amounts of time and effort go into developing scales for research, and many of those scales are designed with a factor model in mind. But the same could be done for LC and mixture models. Most current applications of LC and mixture models simply use the items that are available in the data. In this respect, secondary data analyses, as I have conducted here to illustrate LC methods, can be very informative. But a more informative approach would use the LC approach with a measurement model in mind before the data are collected. In other words, the search for classes should help us refine our target measures and behaviors. As much as the current example exemplified "use" and "nonuse," one could also use "used a little" versus "used a lot" as definitive measures to build a LC model. In this respect, the LC model has been discussed as a psychometric measurement model (Clogg & Manning, 1996; Flaherty, 2002).

The availability of software to fit a large array of mixture models has led to a huge increase in their employment as part of substantive research. These advances are tremendously exciting because of the research possibilities they bring. Learning new statistical and design techniques can lead to new ways of thinking about the different phenomena of interest. But for these LC and mixture models to foster advances in our knowledge, they must be paired with adequate theory, theory that drives the conceptualization of the model, the measures, and the behavior of the investigator. The models cannot be limited by reason, but only by their application to the real world we seek to describe.

References

Agresti, A. (1990). *Categorical data analysis*. New York: Wiley.

Aitkin, M., & Rubin, D. B. (1985). Estimation and hypothesis testing in finite mixture models. *Journal of the Royal Statistical Society, Series B, 47*, 67–75.

Akaike, H. (1987). Factor analysis and AIC. *Psychometrika, 52*, 317–332.

Bollen, K. A., & Long, J. S. (1993). *Testing structural equation models*. Newbury Park, CA: Sage.

Clogg, C. C. (1995). Latent class models. In G. Arminger, C. C. Clogg, & M. E. Sobel (Eds.), *Handbook of statistical modeling for the social and behavioral sciences* (pp. 311–359). New York: Plenum Press.

Clogg, C. C., & Manning, W. D. (1996). Assessing reliability of categorical measurements using latent class models. In A. von Eye & C. C. Clogg (Eds.), *Categorical variables in developmental research: Methods of analysis* (pp. 169–182). San Diego, CA: Academic Press.

Collins, L. M., Flaherty, B. P., Hyatt, S. L., & Schafer, J. L. (1999). *WinLTA user's guide 2.0*. University Park: Pennsylvania State University.

Collins, L. M., Graham, J. W., Long, J. D., & Hansen, W. B. (1994). Cross-validation of latent class models of early substance use onset. *Multivariate Behavioral Research, 29*, 165–183.

Collins, L. M., & Wugalter, S. E. (1992). Latent class models for stage-sequential dynamic latent-variables. *Multivariate Behavioral Research, 27*, 131–157.

Comrey, A. L., & Lee, H. B. (1992). *A first course in factor analysis* (2nd ed.). Hillsdale, NJ: Erlbaum.

Dempster, A. P., Laird, N. M., & Rubin, D. B. (1977). Maximum likelihood from incomplete data via the EM algorithm. *Journal of the Royal Statistical Society, Series B, 39*, 1–38.

DeSarbo, W. S., & Cron, W. L. (1988). A maximum likelihood methodology for clusterwise linear regression. *Journal of Classification, 5*, 249–282.

Efron, B., & Tibshirani, R. J. (1993). *An introduction to the bootstrap*. Boca Raton, FL: Chapman & Hall/CRC.

Flaherty, B. P. (2002). Assessing reliability of categorical substance use measures with latent class analysis. *Drug and Alcohol Dependence, 68*(Suppl. 1), S7–S20.

Flay, B. R. (1993). Youth tobacco use: Risks, patterns, and control. In C. T. Orleans & J. D. Slade (Eds.), *Nicotine addiction: Principles and management*. (pp. 360–384). New York: Oxford University Press.

Formann, A. K. (1985). Constrained latent class models: Theory and applications. *British Journal of Mathematical Psychology, 38*, 87–111.

Formann, A. K. (1989). Constrained latent class models: Some further applications. *British Journal of Mathematical Psychology, 42,* 37–54.

Goodman, L. A. (1974). Exploratory latent structure analysis using both identifiable and unidentifiable models. *Biometrika, 61,* 215–231.

Graham, J. W., Collins, L. M., Wugalter, S. E., Chung, N. K., & Hansen, W. B. (1991). Modeling transitions in latent stage-sequential processes: A substance use prevention example. *Journal of Consulting and Clinical Psychology, 59,* 48–57.

Hagenaars, J. A. (1988). Latent structure models with direct effects between indicators: Local dependence models. *Sociological Methods & Research, 16,* 379–405.

Hosmer, D. W., Jr. (1973). A comparison of iterative maximum likelihood estimates of the parameters of a mixture of two normal distributions under three different types of sample. *Biometrics, 29,* 761–770.

Iritani, B. J., Hallfors, D. D., & Bauer, D. J. (2007). Crystal methamphetamine use among young adults in the USA. *Addiction, 102,* 1102–1113.

Langeheine, R., & van de Pol, F. (2002). Latent markov chains. In J. A. Hagenaars & A. L. McCutcheon (Eds.), *Applied latent class analysis* (pp. 304–341). Cambridge, England: Cambridge University Press.

Lanza, S. T., Collins, L. M., Schafer, J. L., & Flaherty, B. P. (2005). Using data augmentation to obtain standard errors and conduct hypothesis tests in latent class and latent transition analysis. *Psychological Methods, 10,* 84–100.

Lanza, S. T., Flaherty, B. P., & Collins, L. M. (2003). Latent class and latent transition analysis. In J. A. Schinka & W. F. Velicer (Eds.), *Handbook of psychology: Research methods in psychology, Vol. 2.* (pp. 663–685). Hoboken, NJ: Wiley.

Lubke, G. H., & Muthén, B. (2005). Investigating population heterogeneity with factor mixture models. *Psychological Methods, 10,* 21–39.

McCutcheon, A. L. (1987). *Latent class analysis* (Quantitative Applications in the Social Sciences Series No. 64). Thousand Oaks, CA: Sage.

McLachlan, G., & Peel, D. (2000). *Finite mixture models.* New York: Wiley.

Rubin, D. B., & Stern, H. S. (1994). Testing in latent class models using a posterior predictive check distribution. In A. von Eye & C. C. Clogg (Eds.), *Latent variables analysis: Applications for developmental research* (pp. 420–438). Thousand Oaks, CA: Sage.

Schwarz, G. (1978). Estimating the dimension of a model. *Annals of Statistics, 6,* 461–464.

Titterington, D. M., Smith, A. F. M., & Makov, U. E. (1985). *Statistical analysis of finite mixture distributions.* New York: Wiley.

U.S. Department of Health and Human Services, Substance Abuse and Mental Health Services Administration, Office of Applied Studies (2005). *National Survey on Drug Use and Health, 2004* [Computer file]. Retrieved July 14, 2006, from http://www.icpsr.umich.edu/cocoon/ICPSR/STUDY/04373.xml

Wilks, S. S. (1938). The large-sample distribution of the likelihood ratio for testing composite hypotheses. *Annals of Mathematical Statistics, 9,* 60–62.

Chapter 28

A LATENT VARIABLE FRAMEWORK FOR MODELING DRUG USE ETIOLOGY

Terry E. Duncan and Susan C. Duncan

The past few decades have witnessed a gradual shift in conceptual approaches to explicate the etiology of substance use behaviors across the life course (e.g., Sampson, 1988, 1992; Sampson & Laub, 1990). The field has moved away from an emphasis on cross-sectional person-centered approaches toward a wider examination of the developmental nature of behavior over time, person–environment interactions, and the social context as an interactive, interdependent network exerting influence on all its members (e.g., Conger, 1997). This conceptual movement to examine substance use behavior from both a developmental and a social–contextual perspective parallels recent methodological and statistical advances in analytic strategies addressing these complex issues in behavior change. Rather than focusing on interindividual variability within homogeneous populations, analysts are turning to new methods to explore both inter- and intraindividual variability and heterogeneity in substance use growth trajectories, as well as the hierarchical nature of the social environment within which these behaviors unfold (Mehta & West, 2000).

These new analysis techniques have fundamentally altered how researchers conceptualize and study change. Methodology for the study of change has matured sufficiently that researchers are beginning to develop larger methodological and statistical frameworks in which to integrate this knowledge. One such framework incorporating a plethora of analytic techniques appropriate for exploring the etiology of substance use is latent variable growth curve modeling.

A LATENT VARIABLE APPROACH TO MODELING ETIOLOGICAL PROCESSES

The latent variable growth curve modeling approach differs from more traditional fixed effects analytical approaches in at least three important ways. First, it allows modeling of not only the group statistics of interest, but also individual variation about the mean representing interindividual differences in intraindividual growth. Second, and perhaps the most compelling characteristic of latent variable growth curve modeling, is the capacity to estimate and test relationships among latent variables. The isolation of concepts from uniqueness and unreliability of their indicators increases the potential for detecting relationships and obtaining estimates of parameters close to their population values. Finally, the latent variable growth curve modeling approach permits a more comprehensive and flexible approach to research design and data analysis than any other single statistical model for longitudinal data in standard use by social and behavioral researchers.

Example Study

An ongoing longitudinal study of youth alcohol and substance use behavior, "Social Influences on Adolescent Alcohol Use Development," or the ALCOHOL study (for which Susan C. Duncan is

Preparation of this chapter was supported in part by National Institute on Alcohol Abuse and Alcoholism Grant AA11510.

the principal investigator and Terry E. Duncan is coinvestigator), provides an example of research requiring a statistical framework such as latent variable growth curve modeling for combining data from a multitude of sources and contexts. The study's general aim was to test a longitudinal social contextual model of the development of alcohol use and other problem behaviors from preadolescence through adolescence and into young adulthood, incorporating family, peer, and neighborhood influences. Model comparisons across gender and ethnicity (White and African American) were also proposed. Specific aims of the study were

- to examine the developmental progression of alcohol use (onset, escalation, maintenance, and cessation) from ages 9 to 20, using a cohort-sequential design for the accelerated collection of longitudinal data (9-, 11-, and 13-year-old cohorts);
- to examine and clarify the role of family and peer risk and protective factors on the developmental progression of alcohol use and related problem behaviors from ages 9–20;
- to examine, using an interrupted time series latent variable growth curve modeling approach, the etiology of substance use across distinct transition periods (e.g., elementary to middle school, middle school to high school, and high school and the transition to young adulthood);
- to examine the dynamic relationships between adolescent alcohol use, other substance use, and related problem behaviors (e.g., academic failure, antisocial behavior) over time;
- to compare the processes specified within the theoretical social-contextual model across White and African American youth;
- to examine the generalizability and validity of the theoretical model across genders; and
- to investigate the influence of neighborhood contextual characteristics (e.g., demographics, crime rate, drug problems, neighborhood social control and social cohesion) on youth and family alcohol use and related problem behaviors over time.

Data were collected annually for 8 years (1999 to 2007) from residents of a large metropolitan area in the Northwest. The initial sample consisted of

405 youth and families from 58 neighborhoods for which disaggregated data sources (e.g., census, police) were available. Youth were 48.4% female and 50.4% African American. The majority of families were randomly recruited via telephone cold calling. Quotas were established to ensure a final target youth sample with age (9-, 11-, and 13-year-old cohorts), gender (male and female), ethnicity (African American and White), and neighborhood groups equally represented. The three age cohorts were selected so that a long-term longitudinal study could be approximated by combining, in a cohort-sequential model, the temporally overlapping short-term longitudinal assessments from the different cohorts. Thus, with eight yearly assessments, the 9-, 11-, and 13-year-old cohorts could be linked to form a common developmental trajectory spanning a 12-year period from ages 9 to 20. More detailed recruitment information is available in S. C. Duncan, Strycker, Duncan, He, and Stark (2002).

Historically, a number of separate, often multistepped statistical procedures have been required to examine hypotheses arising from complex studies such as this one. Fortunately, in recent years methodologists have extended the latent variable framework to accommodate the increasingly complex research examining the etiology of substance use. As such, the latent variable framework can currently accommodate (a) the accelerated collection of longitudinal data, (b) longitudinal assessments of related behaviors requiring multivariate or higher order specifications of growth and development, (c) multiple populations, (d) unobserved sample heterogeneity, (e) multilevel or hierarchically nested structures, (f) complex sampling schemes, (g) missing data, and (h) power analyses related to all these design features.

A comprehensive treatment of the latent variable approach to studying the etiology of substance use development is not possible in the context of a single chapter. Instead, we focus on several recent advances in latent variable growth curve modeling methodology applicable to the study and treatment of substance use and abuse. We begin by introducing a general approach to growth analyses using a latent variable growth curve modeling specification that allows for varying representations of growth and correlates of change. This section includes informal definitions and interpretations as well as formal specifications for the various model parameters.

Subsequent sections build on this introduction, presenting various extensions to latent variable growth curve modeling that address specific components of standard epidemiological design, such as (a) the accelerated collection of longitudinal data, (b) the inclusion of predictors and sequelae of change, (c) transitions that occur between distinct social-developmental periods and contexts, (d) multivariate or higher order specifications of growth and development, (e) the inclusion of multiple populations, (f) multilevel or hierarchically nested structures, and (g) a brief discussion of analyses incorporating missing data and the use of the latent variable growth curve modeling framework for the estimation of power for these and other complex models.

TYPICAL APPROACHES TO STUDYING CHANGE

Historically, the most prevalent type of longitudinal data in the behavioral and social sciences have been longitudinal panel data consisting of observations made of many individuals across pretest and posttest occasions. Traditional approaches to studying change within this context have been fixed effects analysis of variance (ANOVA) and multiple regression techniques. However, these approaches analyze only mean changes, treating differences among individual participants as error variance. Some of this error variance may contain valuable information about change. Recently, a host of methodological contributions have extended the ability of researchers to describe individual differences and the nature of change over time (e.g., random effects ANOVA, random coefficient modeling, multilevel modeling, and hierarchical linear modeling). A strength of the random effects approaches is that individual differences in growth over time are captured by random coefficients, enabling more realistic modeling of the growth process. A weakness is that statistical modeling within these methods has largely been limited to a single response variable. As such, these methods do not fully accommodate the complexity and analytical

needs of current developmental theories (e.g., Conger, 1997).

A tradition largely independent of analysis of longitudinal data has been conducted within the latent variable structural equation modeling (SEM) framework. Although the estimation procedures are not yet well established for sufficiently general cases, the modeling framework has considerable flexibility to fully examine the types of questions now posited by developmental, prevention, and intervention researchers. Once the random coefficient model has been placed within the latent variable framework, a researcher can then study many general forms of longitudinal analyses. It has been suggested that the development of the latent variable modeling framework is perhaps the most important and influential statistical revolution to have recently occurred in the social and behavioral sciences (Cliff, 1983).

TOWARD AN INTEGRATED DEVELOPMENTAL FRAMEWORK

An appropriate developmental model is one that not only describes a single individual's developmental trajectory but also captures individual differences in these trajectories over time. If, for example, trajectories produced a collection of straight lines for a sample of individuals, the developmental model should reflect individual differences in the slopes and intercepts of those lines. Another critical attribute of the developmental model is the ability to study predictors of individual differences to answer questions about which variables exert important effects on the rate of development. At the same time, the model should be able to capture the vital group statistics in a way that allows the researcher to study development at the group level.

There has been a recent resurgence of interest in statistical models for time-ordered data using SEM. Although time ordering of the data may be useful in drawing causal inferences, without a longitudinal nature to the data that allows for the repeated measurement of the same individual or sets of individuals from one wave to another using the same measure or measures, the data do not permit the measurement or quantification of change. Although methods for analyzing time-ordered and longitudinal data have typically required equal time spacing between assessments for each individual in the sample, advancements in methods for analyzing longitudinal data now allow for growth modeling with data on the basis of random spacing of assessments. Interest in models that have the ability to incorporate information concerning the group or population, as well as information concerning changes in the individual, has reintroduced the formative work of Rao (1958) and Tucker (1958), who promoted the idea that although everyone develops in the same way, individual differences are both meaningful and important. These researchers proposed a partial solution to this problem by constructing a procedure that included unspecified longitudinal growth curves, or functions. One methodology that provides a means of modeling individual differences in growth curves has been termed a latent growth model, or LGM.

Although strongly resembling the classic confirmatory factor analysis, the latent growth factors are actually interpreted as individual differences in attributes of growth trajectories over time (McArdle, 1988). For example, two potentially interesting attributes of growth trajectories are rate of change and initial status. For simple straight-line (i.e., linear) growth models, these are the slope and intercept, respectively. Meredith and Tisak (1990) noted that repeated measures polynomial ANOVA models are actually special cases of latent growth models in which only the factor means are of interest. In contrast, a fully expanded latent growth analysis takes into account both factor means, which correspond to group-level information, and variances, which correspond to individual differences. This combination of the individual and group levels of analysis is unique to the LGM procedure. Heuristically, growth curve methodology can be thought of as consisting of two stages. In the first stage, a regression curve, not necessarily linear, is fitted to the repeated measures of each individual in the sample. In the second stage, the parameters for an individual's curve become the focus of the analysis rather than the original measures.

Thus, the modeling task involves identifying an appropriate growth curve form that will accurately and parsimoniously describe individual development and allow for the study of individual differences in the parameters that control the pattern of growth over time. If, for example, the trajectories were well described by a collection of straight lines for a sample of individuals, the developmental model should reflect individual differences in the slopes and intercepts of those lines. Beyond describing and summarizing growth at the group and individual level, however, the model can also be used to study predictors of individual differences to answer questions about which variables exert important effects on the rate of development. Researchers such as Meredith and Tisak (1990) and McArdle (1988) have extended the basic model to permit the use of current standards in estimation and testing procedures found in SEM programs such as LISREL (Jöreskog & Sörbom, 1993), EQS (Bentler & Wu, 2002), Amos (Arbuckle, 1999), Mx (Neale, 2002), and Mplus (Muthén & Muthén, 1998). Each of these programs offers a full line of model fit statistics and testing procedures that allow for an estimation of how well the implied population model fits the data.

Because latent variable growth curve modeling is carried out using SEM methodology, it shares many of the same strengths and weaknesses with regard to statistical methodology. Strengths of the latent variable growth curve modeling approach include an ability to inferentially test the adequacy of the hypothesized growth form, to incorporate both fixed and time-varying covariates, to correct for measurement error in observed indicators, to incorporate growth on several constructs simultaneously, and to develop from the data a common developmental trajectory, thus ruling out cohort effects. The more commonly cited limitations of SEM programs for estimating LGMs include the assumption of multinormally distributed variables and the necessity of large samples, although recent Monte Carlo simulations have demonstrated that basic LGMs hold up well with relatively small sample sizes (e.g., Muthén & Muthén, 2002). Therefore, the requisite sample size largely depends on the specific empirical context (e.g., psychometric behavior of indicators, amount of missing data, size of effects) and design aspects such as the number of assessment points.

In addition to these concerns, a fundamental assumption of growth curve methodology is that change is systematically related to the passage of time, at least over the time interval of interest (Burchinal & Appelbaum, 1991). Evaluating the extent to which a particular growth model is capable of describing the observed pattern of change with respect to time is an important part of growth model testing. The application of latent variable growth curve modeling within the SEM framework depends, at least ideally, on data that are collected when participants are observed at about the same time and for which the spacing of assessments is the same for all individuals. Longitudinal panel data are typical of this design. Latent variable growth curve modeling can be applied to circumstances in which individuals are not measured at the same time intervals, but specific constraints need to be placed on the models for parameter identification. SEM methodology can still be applied if change in the variables of interest is not related to time. That is, any ordinal variable can be used as the index of the basic function. Time is only one useful possibility. However, if change is not systematically related to the passage of time, the models lose their growth curve interpretations, and studying individual trajectories over time will not be very informative.

SPECIFICATION OF THE LGM

The simplest LGM involves one variable (e.g., a measure of alcohol use) measured the same way at two time points. Two points in time are not ideal for studying development or for using growth curve methodology (Rogosa & Willett, 1985) because the collection of individual trajectories is limited to a collection of straight lines. Although two observations of alcohol use provide information about change, they poorly address some research questions (Rogosa, Brandt, & Zimowski, 1982). For example, two temporally separated observations allow estimation of the amount of change, but it is impossible to study the shape of the developmental trajectory or the rate of change in the individual's alcohol use. The shape of individual development of alcohol use between two observations may be of theoretical interest as either predictor or sequela. Unfortunately, two-wave panel designs preclude testing theories related to the shape

of development. Two-wave designs are appropriate only if the intervening growth process is considered irrelevant or is known to be linear. In general, developmental studies should be planned to include more than two assessment points.

Multiwave data offer important advantages over two-wave data. With more than two observations of each individual separated in time, the validity of the straight-line growth model for the trajectory can be evaluated (e.g., tests for nonlinearity can be performed). In addition, the precision of parameter estimates will tend to increase along with the number of observations for each individual. To introduce the simplest LGM, a model with two time points representing repeated measures of adolescent substance abuse is presented in Figure 28.1.

Intercept

As Figure 28.1 shows, the first factor (F1) is labeled *Intercept*. The intercept is a constant for any given individual across time, hence the fixed values of 1 for factor loadings on the repeated measures. The intercept in this model for a given individual has the same meaning as the intercept of a straight line on a two-dimensional coordinate system: It is the point at which the line intercepts the vertical axis. The Intercept factor presents information in the sample about the mean (Mi) and variance (Di) of

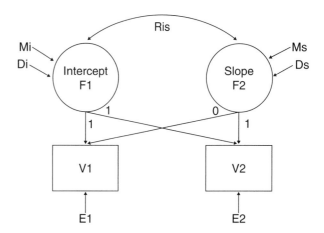

FIGURE 28.1. Representation of a two-factor latent variable growth curve model for two time points. Mi = intercept mean; Di = intercept variance; Ris = covariance of the slope and mean; Ms = slope mean; Ds = slope variance; F1 = Factor 1; F2 = Factor 2; V1 = Variable 1; V2 = Variable 2; E1 = error variance of V1; E2 = error variance of V2.

the collection of intercepts that characterize each individual's substance abuse growth curve.

Slope

The second factor (F2), labeled *Slope,* represents the slope of an individual's substance abuse trajectory. In this case, it is the slope of the straight line determined by the two repeated measures. The Slope factor has a mean (Ms) and variance (Ds) across the whole sample that, like the intercept mean and variance, can be estimated from the data. The two factors, Slope and Intercept, are allowed to covary, Ris, which is represented by the double-headed arrow between the factors. The interpretation of the correlation between the intercept and slope is the same as between static variables. A negative correlation between intercept and slope suggests that individuals with higher factor scores on the intercept tend to have lower factor scores on the slope (e.g., they are changing more slowly relative to others). The correlation between intercept and slope may have an interesting substantive interpretation, or it could point to a more mundane artifact of the outcome scale suggesting ceiling or floor effects, such that if a person starts high he or she is unable, because of scaling restrictions, to grow as much. The error variance terms ($E1, E2$) are shown in the diagram, but to keep the presentation simple, error is assumed to be zero (i.e., $E1 = E2 = 0$).

To identify this model, two slope loadings must be fixed to two different values. Although the choice of loadings is somewhat arbitrary, the Intercept factor is bound to the time scale. Shifting the loadings on the Slope factor alters the scale of time, which affects the interpretation of the Intercept factor mean and variance. The Slope factor mean and variance differ from the Intercept factor mean and variance in that changing the fixed loadings, and thereby changing the time scale, rescales the slope factor mean and variance, in this case by constants. Rescaling by constants does not change the fundamental meaning or affect significance tests of the parameters. It also does not affect the correlations between the slope factor and other predictors in the model.

In the simple two-points-in-time model, there are not enough degrees of freedom to estimate the error variances from the data. The overall model has five estimated parameters (the intercept mean and variance, the slope mean and variance, and the covariance between the intercept and slope), and there are five pieces of known information (two variances, two means, and one covariance) from which to estimate the model. Note that the error variances and the factor loadings for the intercept and slope are not included as estimated parameters in the model because they have been fixed to user-specified values.

If the model has more parameters to estimate than pieces of information in the data (e.g., if we attempted to estimate measurement error in our model), it cannot be uniquely estimated and is therefore not *identified.* Having an unidentified model implies that it is impossible to compute a reasonable estimate for one or more of the model's parameters, indicating that the model should not generally be relied on. If the model can be identified, then it is *just identified,* meaning the model provides a perfect fit to the data using all the available degrees of freedom (as is the case with the model depicted in Figure 28.1).

Unfortunately, there is no way to test or confirm the plausibility of a saturated or just-identified model because saturated models will always provide a perfect fit to the data. If, however, the error variance is known either from prior research or from theoretical considerations, it can be fixed at that value and the model estimated. This would result in positive degrees of freedom (e.g., more unique information in the data than parameters to be estimated) and the ability to provide an adequate test of the hypothesized model. The error variances affect the interpretation of the model parameters by correcting the measured variances for random error. For example, the variance of the substance abuse Slope factor (F2) would be the variance of the difference scores corrected for measurement error, and the variance of the substance abuse Intercept factor (F1) is just the true score variance of *V1.* By expanding the model to include error variance terms, the model parameters retain the same basic interpretations but are now corrected for random measurement error. Model identification is a complex issue that deserves careful consideration and handling (Mulaik et al., 1989).

INTERPRETATION OF THE GROWTH FACTORS

Even with only two time points, the choice of loadings can affect the interpretation of both the Intercept and the Slope factors. Each of the models depicted in Figure 28.2 describes growth over two occasions but varies the centering of time. For example, the model depicted in Figure 28.2a describes growth in substance abuse over two occasions (one

unit of time) where there is a 1-unit increase in mean levels of substance abuse (e.g., $M_{t2} - M_{t1} = 1$).

The selected contrasts rescale the Intercept factor to represent initial status at Time 1 (T1). Because the variables have no measurement error, the mean of the Intercept factor (F1) will equal the mean of the T1 variable ($Mi = 8$). The mean of the Slope factor (F2) will equal the change in terms of differences between T2 and T1 means per one unit of time

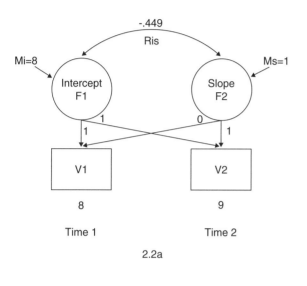

2.2a

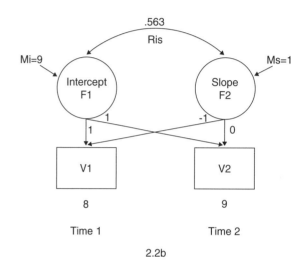

2.2b

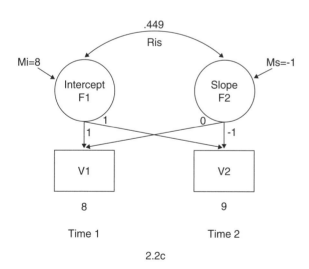

2.2c

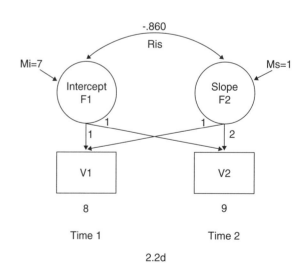

2.2d

FIGURE 28.2. Representation of latent variable growth curve modeling centering and factor interpretation.
A: Representation of the Intercept factor scaled to represent a positive growth trend with initial status at Time 1.
B: Representation of the Intercept factor scaled to represent a positive growth trend with initial status at Time 2.
C: Representation of the Intercept factor scaled to represent a negative growth trend with initial status at Time 1.
D: Representation of the Intercept factor scaled to represent a positive growth trend with initial status at Time 1–1.
Mi = intercept mean; Di = intercept variance; Ris = covariance of the slope and mean; Ms = slope mean; Ds = slope variance; F1 = Factor 1; F2 = Factor 2; V1 = Variable 1; V2 = Variable 2; E1 = error variance of V1; E2 = error variance of V2.

$[(9_{\text{mean at T2}} - 8_{\text{mean at T1}})/1_{\text{unit of time}}]$ or $Ms = 1$. Because the factor loadings represent a positively increasing trend, the Slope factor is interpreted as positive growth, where higher scores on the factor (i.e., factor scores) represent more positive, or greater, increases in substance abuse. The correlation between the Intercept and Slope factors ($r = -.449$) is negative, suggesting that those with greater values on substance abuse at T1 tend to have lower slope scores or less positive growth in substance abuse over time.

Figure 28.2b depicts factor loadings set at values of -1 and 0. Note that the mean for the Intercept factor is no longer initial status at T1 but is now interpreted as status at T2 (e.g., $Mi = 9$). (Note that the variable mean associated with the time point at which the factor loading on the Slope factor is fixed at a value of 0 defines the Intercept factor mean.) The loadings still represent a positively increasing trend; thus, the Slope factor mean is again positive, and higher scores on the factor represent greater increases in substance abuse. Because the interpretation of the Intercept factor has changed, the correlation between the Intercept and Slope factors has also changed ($r = .563$).

Figure 28.2c depicts the same model in which the factor loadings are now fixed at values of 0 and -1. Note that the zero loading for the first variable of the Slope factor allows for the Intercept factor to be once again interpreted as initial status at T1. However, because the loadings on the Slope factor represent a negative trend from T1, the Slope mean is negative (e.g., $Ms = -1$) and higher scores on the Slope factor now represent more negative or greater decreases in substance abuse. Compared with Figure 28.2a, the correlation between the Intercept and Slope is of the same magnitude but now of opposite sign (positive vs. negative).

The choice of factor loadings also allows the researcher to express the Intercept factor as representing a point before or after the time frame encompassed by the data collection. For example, the model depicted in Figure 28.2d represents linear growth emanating from a time point (T1 − 1) before that expressed by the substance abuse data. Here, the zero loading on the Slope factor originates from a T1 − 1 data point, and T1 and T2 are fixed at values of 1

and 2, respectively. Extrapolating the linear trend backward one unit in time yields an Intercept factor mean of $Mi = 7$. Note that the Slope factor mean is still 1 because the model now represents substance abuse change from T1 − 1 to T2, or two units of time, and mean growth in substance abuse from $M_{t1} - 1 = 7$ to $M_{t2} = 9$, or two units of change (note that the change in the interpretation of the Intercept factor again changes the correlation between intercept and slope, $r = -.860$). Although the specification of factor loadings offers the researcher a wide range of modeling possibilities, extrapolation beyond the range of scores used in the estimation of the growth trajectory is not advisable because it assumes that the trajectory continues to be linear when in fact it may be curvilinear.

The ability to posit growth around various time points affords the researcher great latitude when specifying conditional latent variable growth curve models involving various predictors of the growth sequence. For example, in the course of a naturalistic longitudinal study on the course of risk factors and substance abuse outcomes over three time points, the researcher can alternately specify predictors of initial status (T1), average growth (the constant), or the ending or terminal status (T3), in addition to predictors of the growth trend.

REPRESENTING THE SHAPE OF GROWTH OVER TIME

With three or more points in time, the factor loadings carry information about the shape of growth over time that provides the opportunity to test for nonlinear trajectories in substance abuse trajectories across time (e.g., during adolescence). In the example ALCOHOL project, there are up to eight time points, which provides the ability to test for numerous nonlinear trajectories in the data. The most familiar approach to nonlinear trajectories is probably the use of polynomials. The inclusion of quadratic or cubic effects that reflect curvature or piecewise growth trajectories is easily accomplished by including more factors. One factor captures one piece of the curve (trend), and a second factor, with different fixed loadings, captures a different portion of the curve (trend). The factor loadings can then be fixed to represent a quadratic function of the observed time metric.

However, polynomials with squared or higher order terms are not the only way to model nonlinear growth. Other plausible nonlinear growth curves can be modeled with fewer than three factors. The two-factor model can also be used to model unspecified trajectories. For example, if the shapes of the substance abuse trajectories are not known, the data can determine their shape. This could be a starting point from which more specific types of trajectories (e.g., quadratic) are tested. In unspecified models, when there are enough time points to freely estimate factor loadings beyond the two required for identification of the model, the Slope factor is better interpreted as a general shape factor.

COHORT-SEQUENTIAL OR ACCELERATED DESIGNS

Although a true longitudinal design is ideal for modeling the development of behavior, alternative approaches are needed to reduce study time, participant attrition, and the cost of continual participant assessment. Bell (1953) advocated the method of convergence as a means for meeting research needs not satisfied by either longitudinal or cross-sectional methods. This method consists of linking limited, temporally overlapping repeated measurements of independent age cohorts. Figure 28.3 presents a cohort-sequential model from the ALCOHOL study in which 3 years of data from three age cohorts (9, 11, and 13 years) are linked together to form a common developmental trajectory

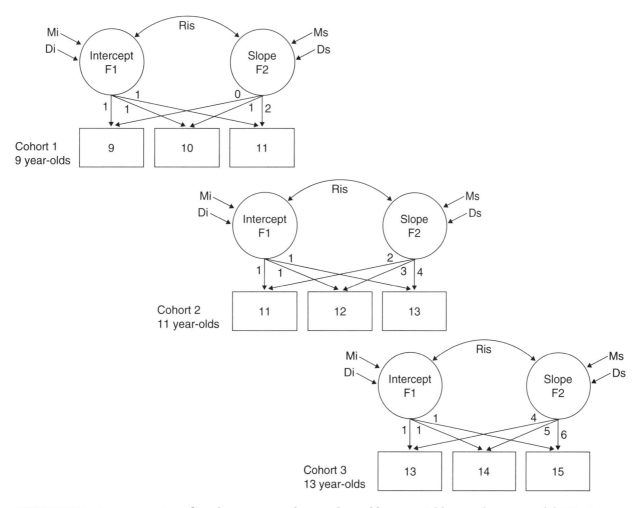

FIGURE 28.3. Representation of a cohort-sequential or accelerated latent variable growth curve model. Mi = intercept mean; Di = intercept variance; Ris = covariance of the slope and mean; Ms = slope mean; Ds = slope variance; F1 = Factor 1; F2 = Factor 2.

of alcohol use spanning a 6-year period (ages 9–15).

This cohort-sequential design links adjacent segments consisting of limited longitudinal data to determine the existence of a common developmental trend, or growth curve (Nesselroade & Baltes, 1979). This technique also allows the researcher to determine whether those trends observed in the repeated observations are corroborated within short time periods for each age cohort. This design approximates a long-term longitudinal study by conducting several short-term longitudinal studies of different age cohorts simultaneously. Although Bell (1953) described the technique as an ad hoc statistical procedure, S. C. Duncan, Duncan, and Hops (1996) demonstrated how it approximated a full longitudinal curve. Recently, a number of researchers (e.g., T. E. Duncan & Duncan, 1995; T. E. Duncan, Duncan, & Hops, 1994; McArdle & Anderson, 1989; McArdle & Hamagami, 1991; Meredith & Tisak, 1990) have demonstrated the usefulness of the accelerated longitudinal design.

INCLUDING PREDICTORS AND SEQUELAE OF CHANGE

Once the shape of growth is determined in the latent variable growth curve model, the parameters of an individual's curve can be used to study predictors of individual differences and answer questions about which variables (e.g., family and/or peer influences) affect the rate of adolescent substance use development and how development influences subsequent behaviors (e.g., transitions to adult roles or subsequent or continued substance use or abuse). Continuous covariates accommodated in an analysis of covariance allow for tests of both continuous predictors of change and change as a predictor, but not for the simultaneous inclusion of change as both an independent and a dependent variable. The ability to use variables simultaneously as independent and dependent variables in the same model, allowing for complex representations of growth and correlates of change, represents a major advantage of the latent variable growth curve model as compared with more traditional approaches.

MODELING TRANSITIONS IN GROWTH AND DEVELOPMENT: INTERRUPTED TIME SERIES MODELS

The traditional latent variable growth curve model focuses on combining the repeatedly measured variables to estimate a single underlying growth trajectory. However, interest sometimes centers on changes in substance abuse during distinct time periods (e.g., transitions between schools or changes observed during treatment and follow-up phases of a treatment outcome trial). Using piecewise growth models, it is possible to subdivide a series of repeated measurements into meaningful segments and summarize growth in each segment. Piecewise growth models provide a means of examining (a) whether rates of change differ as a function of growth period, (b) whether individual variability in rates of change differs between periods of interest, and (c) important predictors of change unique to a particular developmental period. Applications of piecewise latent variable growth curve models can be found in Sayer and Willet (1998) and Wang, Siegal, Falck, Carlson, and Rahman (1999).

This segmenting of the overall series in the latent variable growth curve model spanning distinct developmental periods (e.g., changes observed across treatment and follow-up phases rather than a specific follow-up period) has its corollary with the time series prevention and treatment literature in which the analysis of interest is usually an interrupted time series (ITS). Here, the interruptions correspond to the occurrence of an intervention, and the goal of the analysis is to evaluate the intervention's effect. However, similar to piecewise latent variable growth curve models, ITS LGM analyses can also be specified to evaluate naturally occurring interruptions in a series of observations. For example, the interruption may correspond to distinct time periods or processes not under the researcher's control, such as the normal transition that occurs when students move from middle to high school. In this case, factors related to differences in change in one segment of the overall growth period may differ substantially from those in a different segment. Moreover, rates of change during one period may vary substantially among individuals, whereas in another period they may be fairly homogeneous. The ITS applied within an LGM framework provides the ability to examine various developmental transitions across the life span, which is important for understanding functioning within each stage and adjustments between each critical transition.

In the basic ITS design, measurements of the outcome variable are collected over an extended period of time, with an interruption or transition occurring at a specific point within that period. ITS designs allow for assessments of the onset (i.e., abrupt, gradual) and duration (i.e., permanent, temporary) of change in response to the transition. Moreover, unlike the piecewise approach, which uses a common intercept for both segments of the overall curve, the ITS latent variable growth curve model captures differences in both intercepts and slopes over the two distinct periods.

As can be seen in Figure 28.4, the ITS latent variable growth curve model captures both intercept and slope differences over the two distinct periods (e.g., middle school and high school phases) created by the transition point (e.g., T. E. Duncan & Duncan, 2004). In Figure 28.4, basic terms for the Slope factors at the pre- and posttransition phase (middle school and high school, respectively) were fixed at values of −1, zero, and 1, allowing for interpretation of the pre- (F2) and posttransition (F4)-

phase Slope factors as linear change and the pre- (F1) and posttransition (F3)-level factors as the average levels across the pre- and posttransition periods. The added growth factors (F5 and F6) represent the difference between the pre- and posttransition phases on the average level and slope, respectively. Using equality constraints, the model specifies that common parameters (e.g., means, variances, and covariances) are the same in both middle and high school periods.

MULTIVARIATE AND HIGHER ORDER EXTENSIONS

The previous sections have described how LGMs can be used to model growth as a factor of repeated observations of one variable (e.g., alcohol use). Although development in a single behavior is often of interest, longitudinal studies such as the ALCOHOL study often examine a number of behaviors simultaneously to clarify interrelationships in their development (e.g., multiple substances or problem behaviors). To this end, multivariate or associative longitudinal models may be considered. The univariate longitudinal model is actually a special case of the general multivariate growth curve model. Multivariate LGMs provide a more dynamic view of correlates of change because development in one variable may be

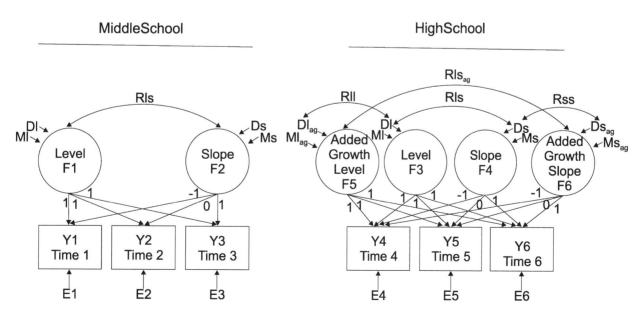

FIGURE 28.4.   Representation of the interrupted time series latent variable growth curve model.

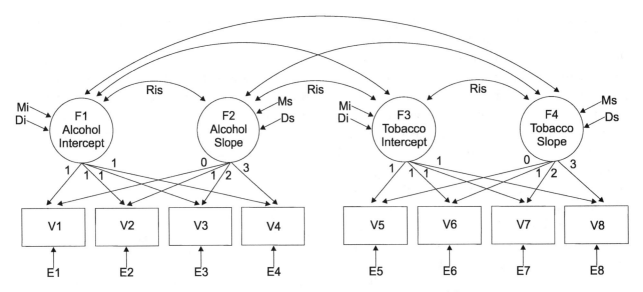

FIGURE 28.5. Representation of the associative latent variable growth curve modeling.

associated with development in another variable. An example of the multivariate LGM for alcohol and tobacco use is shown in Figure 28.5. Associative models are useful in determining the extent to which pairs of behaviors covary over time. In addition, McArdle (1988) suggested two more methods for conducting a multivariate analysis of the relations among numerous behaviors (e.g., alcohol, marijuana, tobacco, and illicit drugs). This second- or higher order multivariate LGM approach includes two alternative methods, a *factor-of-curves* model and a *curve-of-factors* model (McArdle, 1988), which are discussed below in the Full Information Maximum Likelihood Estimation of Multilevel Effects section. Examples of these multivariate models can be found in Curran, Stice, and Chassin (1997); S. C. Duncan and Duncan (1996); S. C. Duncan, Duncan, and Strycker (2001); McArdle (1988); Tisak and Meredith (1990); Wickrama, Lorenz, and Conger (1997); and Hix-Small, Duncan, Duncan, and Okut (2004).

MULTIPLE POPULATIONS AND MODELING BETWEEN-SUBJECTS EFFECTS

In addition to modeling growth for a single population, LGMs also allow researchers to analyze change in behavior among multiple groups (e.g., treatment and control conditions, age, gender). In

the ALCOHOL study, specific aims (the fifth and sixth) included comparing findings across ethnicity (African American and White youth) and genders. Just as repeated measures ANOVA models can be considered special cases of the general LGM, so too can between-subjects repeated measures ANOVAs be considered a special case of the multiple-sample LGM approach.

In the typical LGM application, individuals whose data are being analyzed are assumed to represent a random sample of observations from a single population. However, in practice, this assumption is not always reasonable. A powerful application of the general LGM is in the examination of substance abuse treatment effects within an experimental design. For example, individuals may be identified as belonging to certain groups, such as treatment or control conditions. In this case, it is appropriate to test for the existence of multiple populations (treatment and control) rather than a single population, as well as multiple developmental pathways for each condition rather than a single underlying trajectory for all. Many studies involving multiple populations have examined separate models for each group and compared the results. Unfortunately, such procedures do not allow a test of whether a common developmental model exists and whether there are multiple developmental pathways across groups. Developmental hypotheses involving multiple populations can be evaluated simultaneously provided that data on the same variables over the same developmental period are available in multiple samples. For example, a multiple-sample growth model has clear relevance to randomized control trials in which one group might involve a wait-list control or an alternative treatment condition. In many cases, populations may be indistinguishable as far as the measured variables are concerned. When this occurs, the same population moment matrix describes all populations, and different sample moment matrices obtained from the various samples would simply be estimates of the same single population moment matrix. Growth models generated from the different samples should describe the same underlying developmental process for the population, and the separate models should be identical except for chance variations.

In other cases, the populations may share the same population covariance matrix but differ in the means obtained from the various samples. Growth models generated from these different samples would not be expected to describe the same underlying developmental process for the population, and the separate models would carry unique information concerning the growth trajectories for that population despite identical covariance structures (except for chance variations).

A variety of growth models can be generalized to the simultaneous analysis of substance abuse data from multiple populations. To some extent, population differences can be captured in single-population analyses by representing the different groups as dummy vectors used as time-invariant covariates. However, to achieve more generality in modeling and specificity in the examination of population differences, it is necessary to use the multiple-population approach. Collapsing across different populations (e.g., gender, age, and ethnicity) may mask potential group differences that are important to the study of change. Multiple-sample LGM has the potential to test for similarities and differences in developmental processes across different populations, including differences in levels of behaviors, developmental trajectories, rates of change, and effects of predictors and outcomes. Thus, when data from multiple populations are available, a multiple-

sample LGM is likely to be advantageous in the study of numerous behavioral processes.

Added Growth Models

Conventional longitudinal multiple-population latent variable analyses specify a common growth model in multiple groups, testing for equality of parameters across the different populations. An alternative approach (Muthén & Curran, 1997) particularly applicable to experimental designs is shown in Figure 28.6. Here, an added Growth factor is introduced for one population (e.g., the treatment condition in a program to reduce family substance use). Whereas the first two factors (i.e., Intercept and Slope) are the same for both the control and the treatment groups, the added Growth factor, specified in one group (e.g., treatment condition), represents incremental or decremental growth that is specific to that group. The added Growth factor has a mean (*Mag*) and variance (*Dag*) across the whole sample that, like the intercept and slope

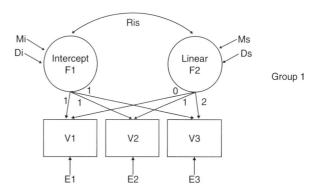

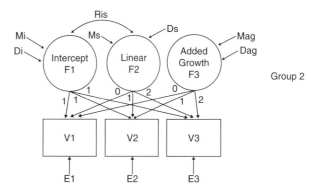

FIGURE 28.6.   Representation of the added growth latent variable growth curve modeling.

mean and variance, can be estimated from the data. In Figure 28.6, the linear Slope factor captures normative growth that is common to both control and treatment groups, whereas the added Growth factor is specified to capture linear differences between the two groups.

For substance abuse researchers, the multiple-sample LGM framework affords a powerful design for detecting differences in program effectiveness by attributes such as subgroup membership. Examples of multiple-sample approaches can be found in T. E. Duncan, Duncan, and Alpert (1997); Jo and Muthén (2001); McArdle, Hamagami, Elias, and Robbins (1991); Muthén and Curran (1997); and Tisak and Tisak (1996).

INCORPORATING EFFECTS OF THE SOCIAL CONTEXT: HIERARCHICAL OR MULTILEVEL DESIGNS

How individuals and social factors operate independently and interactively to shape development can be adequately studied only in the context of longitudinal and hierarchically structured research. There are substance use research designs in which it becomes essential to represent social-contextual effects in the analysis of longitudinal data. In many randomization trials, intact groups such as communities, families, or therapy groups, rather than individuals, are randomly assigned to experimental substance abuse treatments. Moreover, the treatments are administered to these intact groups rather than to individuals. It is assumed, therefore, that the responses of individuals in these groups will be similar by virtue of the experiences they share in those settings (Raudenbush, 1995).

Researchers have struggled for some time with such concepts as hierarchically nested observations, intraclass correlation, unit of analysis, and random rather than fixed effects. Despite the assumption of somewhat homogeneous shared social environments, until recently substance use researchers have possessed few tools to accommodate the interdependence of such data. The absence of hierarchical methodologies for handling interdependence often led researchers to rely on analyses that assumed the data consisted of independent and identically dis-

tributed observations from a simple random sample in a single population. However, analyzing the data as a simple random sample ignores the potential interdependence within social or experimental clusters and increases the possibility of inflated test statistics for estimated parameters and overall model fit. A hierarchical approach to statistical modeling avoids these distortions. The analysis of data that has a hierarchical structure and contains measurements from different levels of the hierarchy requires techniques based on assumptions that are in agreement with the data structure.

New analytic techniques that are more suited to the hierarchical data structure have recently emerged under the labels of hierarchical, or multilevel, models (see, e.g., Goldstein, 1986; Kreft, 1994; Longford, 1987; Muthén & Satorra, 1989; Raudenbush & Bryk, 1988). Appropriate analysis techniques of this kind are now widely available for standard regression and ANOVA situations, but Muthén and Satorra (1989) highlighted the lack of techniques for covariance structure analyses. Just as ANOVA and multiple regression techniques can be considered special cases of the general SEM (Hoyle, 1995), so too can hierarchical linear models be viewed as special cases of the general multilevel covariance structure model. The multilevel covariance analysis approach differs from more traditional hierarchical approaches in its capacity to estimate and test relationships among latent variables. Measurement of substance use is less than precise and fraught with measurement error given the sensitive nature of the data collected. Dissattenuation, accomplished by the isolation of uniqueness and unreliability from a variable's commonality, increases the probability of detecting relationships and obtaining sound estimates of parameters close to their population values. Muthén (1989) discussed the relationships of multilevel SEM to conventional SEM and pointed out the possibility of using conventional SEM software for multilevel SEM.

Full Information Maximum Likelihood Estimation of Multilevel Effects

Full information maximum likelihood (FIML) estimation is an approach to the estimation of missing data that calculates the log likelihood of the data for each observation rather than on the basis of subgroup estimates (e.g., mean substitution). McArdle (1988) presented two full information LGM methods that are appropriate for hierarchical analyses with longitudinal data. Originally formulated to model growth for multiple variables or scales over multiple occasions, these two methods are easily extended to modeling growth for multiple informants over multiple occasions (e.g., longitudinal and hierarchically nested data). These methods are termed the factor-of-curves and curve-of-factors models. The factor-of-curves model can be used to examine whether a higher order factor adequately describes relationships among lower order developmental functions (e.g., intercept and rate of change). The curve-of-factors method, however, can be used to fit a growth curve to factor scores representing what the lower order factors have in common at each point in time. An application of these two methods can be found in S. C. Duncan and Duncan (1996) and S. C. Duncan, Duncan, and Strycker (2001). When there are many clusters of different size (e.g., unbalanced data), full information likelihood growth model estimation can be accomplished using a model-based extension of the multiple group frameworks.

Limited Information Multilevel LGM

Although FIML approaches can be used for multilevel longitudinal data, they can be computationally heavy, and input specifications can be tedious if group sizes are large. Thus, Muthén (1991, 1994) proposed a multilevel covariance analysis approach to analyzing multilevel data using a limited information estimation approach that is simpler to compute than FIML. The multilevel latent growth modeling approach of Muthén (1997) involves two generalizations of the factor-of-curves SEM model: (a) SEM growth modeling as generalized to cluster data and (b) SEM multilevel modeling as generalized to mean structures. Within the latent variable modeling of longitudinal and multilevel data, the total covariance matrix, S_T, is decomposed into two independent components, a between-families covariance matrix, S_B, and a within-families covariance matrix, S_{PW}, or $S_T = S_B + S_{PW}$. The multilevel latent growth model makes use of S_{PW} and S_B simultaneously.

Muthén (1994) showed that the estimator provides full maximum likelihood estimation for bal-

anced data (e.g., hierarchical clusters of the same size) and gives results similar to full maximum likelihood estimation of data that are not too badly unbalanced. Within the Mplus SEM program (Muthén & Muthén, 1998), Muthén's ad hoc approach greatly simplifies model specification for unbalanced hierarchically nested longitudinal data. Thus, with large groups of different sizes, little may be gained by the extra effort of FIML computation. In the multilevel covariance analysis, the total covariance matrix is decomposed into two independent components, a between-level covariance matrix (e.g., family), and a within-level covariance matrix (e.g., individuals or family members). Conventional covariance structure analysis that ignores grouping or clustering assumes that all observations are independent. As in the general LGM framework, the multilevel covariance analysis allows the researcher to specify the hierarchical structure in multiple populations (e.g., treatment and control conditions), to predict changes in treatment outcomes from time-invariant and time-varying covariates, and to use changes in treatment outcomes as predictors of subsequent outcomes.

Developments such as these make possible the specification, estimation, and testing of a variety of complex models involving hierarchically structured longitudinal substance abuse data. T. E. Duncan, Duncan, Alpert, Hops, et al. (1997); T. E. Duncan, Duncan, Li, and Strycker (2001); Khoo and Muthén (2000); and Muthén (1997) all provided additional information regarding applications of the multilevel covariance analysis limited information approach.

Extension of the Multilevel LGM to Four Levels of the Hierarchy

In the ALCOHOL study mentioned previously, analyses include examining the development of alcohol and other substance use over time, among individuals, within families, and within designated neighborhoods, in essence creating a four-level hierarchical model. Figure 28.7 shows one such model in which the hierarchical extension incorporates the full information likelihood growth model factor-of-curves growth structure for both within and between levels within the multilevel latent growth modeling approach (see Figure 28.7). That is, the multilevel

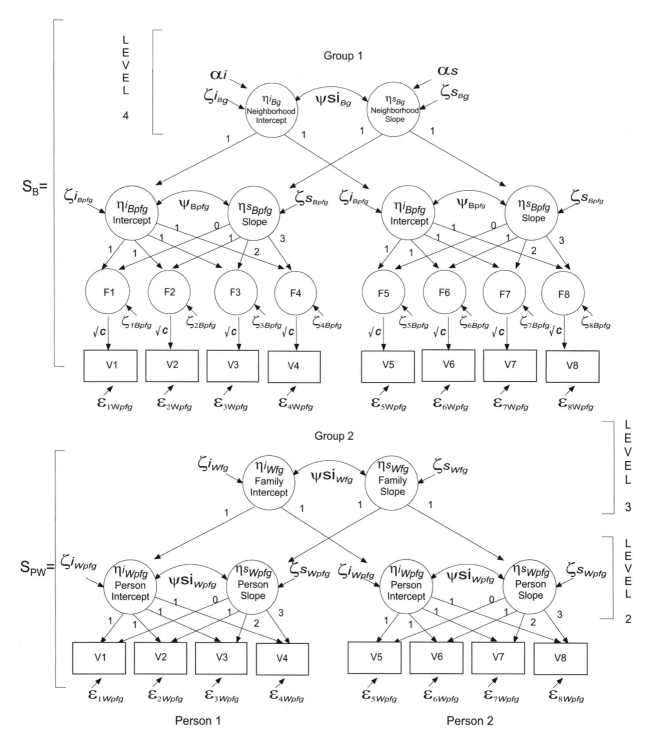

FIGURE 28.7. Representation of the combined full- and limited information four-level latent variable growth curve model.

structure is further decomposed by allowing equations at lower levels (i.e., repeated measures, person, and family) to be accounted for by the Level 4 growth factors, the intercept and slope of the neighborhood geographical areas. Such a model represents how variation in the outcome variable (e.g., substance use) can be allocated across the different levels of the hierarchy.

The four-level data now become

Neighborhood : $g = 1, 2, \ldots, G$

Family : $f = 1, 2, \ldots, F$

Person : $p = 1, 2, \ldots, P$

Time : $t = 1, 2, \ldots, T.$

Assume x_{tpfg} does not vary across persons for a given t ($x_{tpfg} = x_t$), that is, for the tth occasion, all persons have the same x_t. The equations for the four level models are presented below.

Level 1 Model

The equation for modeling Level 1 variation accounts for within-person variation. Let v_{tpfg} represent a vector of measures. Then

$$v_{tpfg} = \eta i_{Wpfg} + \eta s_{Wpfg} + \eta q_{Wpfg} + x_{tpfg} + \varepsilon_{Wtpfg},$$

where x_{tpfg} is a person-level (time-related) variable, ηi_{Wtpfg} represents initial status for person pfg, ηs_{Wpfg} represents the slope for person pfg, ηq_{Wpfg} represents the quadratic trend for person pfg, and ε_{Wtpfg} represents a vector of random errors within person with zero mean and σ^2 variance.

Level 2 Model

Each of the coefficients (ηi_{Wpfg}, ηs_{Wpfg}, and ηq_{Wpf}) in the Level 1 model becomes a random variable in the Level 2 equations. Here, the Level 2 model accounts for variation between persons within family as a function of family-level variation. As such, the model for Level 2 is

$$\eta i_{Wpfg} = \eta i_{Wpfg} + \zeta i_{Wpfg},$$
$$\eta s_{Wpfg} = \eta s_{Wpfg} + \zeta s_{Wpfg}, \text{ and}$$
$$\eta q_{Wpfg} = \eta q_{Wpfg} + \zeta q_{Wpfg},$$

where ηi_{Wfg}, ηs_{Wfg}, and ηq_{Wfg} represent the initial status, mean rate of change, and amount of curvature (quadratic trend), respectively, for family fg at Level 2.

Level 3 Model

The Level 3 model accounts for variation between families within geographic regions. Therefore, variation between families is a function of geographic-level variation. The equations for the Level 3 model are

$$\eta i_{Wfg} = \eta i_{Bg} + \zeta i_{Wfg},$$
$$\eta s_{Wfg} = \eta s_{Bg} + \zeta s_{Wfg}, \text{ and}$$
$$\eta q_{Wfg} = \eta q_{Bg} + \zeta q_{Wfg},$$

where ηi_{Bg}, ηs_{Bg}, and ηq_{Bg} are the initial status, mean rate of change, and quadratic trend for neighborhood level g, respectively.

Level 4 Model

The Level 3 variation just described is further accounted for by the Level 4 equations. Each of the Level 3 coefficients (ηi_{Bg}, ηs_{Bg}, and ηq_{Bg}) becomes a random variable in the Level 4 equations, which have the following form:

$$\eta i_{Bg} = \alpha i + \zeta i_{Bg},$$
$$\eta s_{Bg} = \alpha s + \zeta s_{Bg}, \text{ and}$$
$$\eta q_{Bg} = \alpha q + \zeta q_{Bg},$$

where αi, αs, and αq represent overall neighborhood mean values in initial status, rate of change, and curvature or quadratic trend.

The total variability in the outcome v_{pfg} is decomposed into its four components: Level 1 within-person σ^2 that is broken down into between and within components, Level 2 among persons within families represented by $\tau_{\eta a}$, Level 3 among families within neighborhoods represented by $\tau_{\eta b}$, and Level 4 among neighborhoods represented by $\tau_{\eta c}$. This decomposition of effects also allows us to estimate the proportion of substance use variation that is within persons, among persons within families, among families within neighborhoods, and among neighborhoods. That is, $\sigma^2/(\sigma^2 + \tau_{\eta a} + \tau_{\eta b} + \tau_{\eta c})$ is the proportion of variance within persons; $\tau_{\eta a}/(\sigma^2 +$

$\tau_{\eta a} + \tau_{\eta b} + \tau_{\eta c})$ is the proportion of variance among persons within families; $\tau_{\eta b}/(\sigma^2 + \tau_{\eta a} + \tau_{\eta b} + \tau_{\eta c})$ is the proportion of variance among families within neighborhoods; and $\tau_{\eta c}/(\sigma^2 + \tau_{\eta a} + \tau_{\eta b} + \tau_{\eta c})$ is the proportion of variance among neighborhoods.

The four-level model can be formulated and estimated within the LGM framework. This is achieved by the nesting of the FIML factor-of-curves LGM within the multilevel latent growth modeling approach as represented by the sample covariance structure of $S_B + S_{PW}$. The between-level factors (F1 through F8) represent the neighborhood portion of the individual's repeated measures substance use scores. The first-order LGM structure serves to filter the between-level variance–covariance structure for the neighborhood-level intercept, slope, and quadratic trend factors. The total covariance ($\Sigma_B + \Sigma_W$) differs from the covariance matrix structure ($C\Sigma_B + \Sigma_W$) by the scalar multiplier C (the average neighborhood size) for the between part, necessitating scaling by the square root of C as shown in Figure 28.7.

ADVANTAGES OF THE LGM FRAMEWORK

LGM methodology provides a number of advantages to epidemiological and prevention-oriented substance abuse researchers interested in modeling change over time. The LGM describes a single individual's developmental trajectory and also captures individual differences in these trajectories over time. Moreover, the LGM is able to include predictors of individual differences to answer questions about which variables exert important effects on the rate of development of substance abuse. At the same time, the model is able to capture the important group statistics in a way that allows the researcher to study substance abuse development at the group level. Given more than two assessment points, LGMs are able to test both linear and nonlinear growth functions. When appropriate, the LGM also allows the flexibility of including more than two factors to capture developmental trends through the use of specified growth functions and additional growth factors (e.g., quadratic, exponential, and cubic growth). Another advantage of LGM methodology is its ability to incorporate time-varying covariates. Both static and time-varying variables can be included in models as predictors and outcomes of substance use growth functions, thus

allowing the researcher to address questions related to the antecedents and consequences of substance abuse developmental trends. In practical terms, LGMs offer different opportunities for evaluating the dynamic structure of both intra- and interindividual change and represent a logical progression in the paradigm of behavioral dynamics. In addition to the special cases of the LGM already presented, several other noteworthy extensions are possible.

Incorporating Missing Data in LGMs

Because nearly all longitudinal data-sets suffer from various forms of missing data, analytic techniques must be able to appropriately handle planned missingness as well as missing data resulting from attrition (loss of participants) and omissions (loss of data through nonresponse). From a statistical point of view, the best missing data procedures do several things. First, they take into consideration all available causes of missingness. Second, they use the same statistical model to handle the missing data that is used to perform the desired analysis. For example, if the final model is a latent variable model, the best approach would also use a latent variable model to handle the missing data. Finally, the best procedures provide consistent and efficient parameter estimates. Within LGM, model-based procedures can be used to analyze incomplete data using either multiple-sample SEM or raw maximum likelihood procedures.

Design Issues: Sample Size Selection and Power Estimation

The latent variable method described in this chapter also provides a power estimation framework to aid researchers in making design decisions for a variety of intervention studies. Statistically, the best procedures for power estimation should (a) use the same statistical model for power and sample size estimation as that planned for the desired analysis (e.g., if the final model is a LGM, the best approach for power estimation would also use a LGM), (b) cover the situations most commonly encountered by researchers, (c) be flexible enough to deal with new or unusual situations, (d) allow easy exploration of multiple values of input parameters, and (e) allow estimation of sampling variance from pilot data and from statistics commonly reported in the literature.

Under the latent variable framework for growth modeling, power estimation is directly related to the parameter values of a specified model. The relations among values of the level of significance, measures of effect size, the sample size, and the degrees of freedom are identical to those in more traditional techniques. However, the LGM has the added advantage of accounting for measurement error, thus disattenuating the relations among the variables of interest, which increases reliability, improves power, and reduces sample size requirements. Examples of power analyses conducted within the SEM framework can be found in Muthén and Curran (1997); Muthén and Muthén (2002); T. E. Duncan, Duncan, Strycker, and Li (2002); T. E. Duncan, Duncan, and Strycker (2006); and T. E. Duncan, Duncan, and Li (2003).

LIMITATIONS OF THE LGM

Despite numerous attractions, latent variable growth curve modeling is not always the appropriate analytical choice for substance abuse prevention and treatment research. The more commonly cited limitations of SEM programs for estimating LGM models include multinormally distributed variables and the necessity of large samples. However, it must be noted that recent Monte Carlo simulations have demonstrated that basic LGMs hold up well with relatively small sample sizes (e.g., Muthén & Muthén, 2002). In fitting latent variable models, inferences are made from observed data to the model thought to be generating those observations (Tanaka, 1987). In part, these inferences depend on the degree to which the information in the sample is representative of the same information in the complete population, which in turn depends on the adequacy of the sample size. Therefore, the requisite sample size largely depends on the specific empirical context (e.g., psychometric behavior of indicators, amount of missing data, size of effects) and design aspects such as the number of assessment points.

In terms of modeling flexibility, the LGM is limited in its handling of randomly varying within-subject designs and varied within-person distributions of time-varying covariates having random effects. Although recent software developments have begun to address these limitations (e.g., Muthén &

Muthén, 2003), LGM analyses do not yet allow the flexibility on these issues afforded by the random coefficient approach conducted within the regression framework (Muthén & Curran, 1997).

CONCLUDING REMARKS

The search continues for the best methods to address the complex issues encountered in studies regarding substance use and abuse. As the field of substance abuse research continues to develop, new and more complex research questions will be posed, and these will continue to prompt the development of new statistical methods. Just as there are a plethora of substantive questions posed by substance abuse researchers, so too are there a broad and varied assortment of newly developed statistical methods available to answer these substantive questions. The LGM approach presented here provides a comprehensive and flexible approach to research design and data analysis and provides a powerful tool to assist researchers in their efforts to model development at both inter- and intraindividual levels and to identify important predictors and outcomes of change.

References

Arbuckle, J. L. (1999). *Amos for Windows: Analysis of moment structures* (Version 4.0). Chicago: Small-Waters.

Bell, R. Q. (1953). Convergence: An accelerated longitudinal approach. *Child Development, 24,* 145–152.

Bentler, P. M., & Wu, E. J. C. (2002). *EQS 6 for Windows user's guide.* Encino, CA: Multivariate Software.

Burchinal, M., & Appelbaum, M. I. (1991). Estimating individual developmental functions: Methods and their assumptions. *Child Development, 62,* 23–43.

Cliff, N. (1983). Some cautions concerning the application of causal modeling methods. *Multivariate Behavioral Research, 18,* 115–126.

Conger, R. D. (1997). The social context of substance abuse: A developmental perspective. In E. B. Robertson, Z. Sloboda, G. M. Boyd, L. Beatty, & N. J. Kozel (Eds.), *Rural substance abuse: State of knowledge and issues* (NIDA Research Monograph 168, pp. 6–36). Washington, DC: US Government Printing Office.

Curran, P. J., Stice, E., & Chassin, L. (1997). The relation between adolescent alcohol use and peer alcohol use: A longitudinal random coefficients model. *Journal of Consulting and Clinical Psychology, 65,* 130–140.

Duncan, S. C., & Duncan, T. E. (1996). A multivariate latent growth curve analysis of adolescent substance use. *Structural Equation Modeling, 3,* 323–347.

Duncan, S. C., Duncan, T. E., & Hops, H. (1996). Analysis of longitudinal alcohol use data within accelerated longitudinal designs. *Psychological Measurement, 1,* 236–248.

Duncan, S. C., Duncan, T. E., & Strycker, L. A. (2001). Qualitative and quantitative shifts in adolescent problem behavior development: A cohort-sequential multivariate latent growth modeling approach. *Journal of Psychopathology and Behavioral Assessment, 23,* 43–50.

Duncan, S. C., Strycker, L. A., Duncan, T. E., He, H., & Stark, M. J. (2002). Telephone recruitment of a random stratified African American and White study sample. *Journal of Ethnicity in Substance Abuse, 1,* 57–73.

Duncan, T. E., & Duncan, S. C. (1995). Modeling the processes of development via latent variable growth curve methodology. *Structural Equation Modeling, 2,* 187–213.

Duncan, T. E., & Duncan, S. C. (2004). A latent growth curve modeling approach to pooled interrupted time series analyses. *Journal of Psychopathology and Behavioral Assessment, 26,* 271–278.

Duncan, T. E., Duncan, S. C., & Alpert, A. (1997). Multilevel covariance structure analysis of family substance use across samples and ethnicities. *Journal of Gender, Culture, and Health, 2,* 271–286.

Duncan, T. E., Duncan, S. C., Alpert, A., Hops, H., Stoolmiller, M., & Muthén, B. (1997). Latent variable modeling of longitudinal and multilevel substance use data. *Multivariate Behavioral Research, 32,* 275–318.

Duncan, T. E., Duncan, S. C., & Hops, H. (1994). The effect of family cohesiveness and peer encouragement on the development of adolescent alcohol use: A cohort-sequential approach to the analysis of longitudinal data. *Journal of Studies on Alcohol, 55,* 588–599.

Duncan, T. E., Duncan, S. C., & Li, F. (2003). Power analysis models and methods: A latent variable framework for power estimation and analyses. In Z. Sloboda & W. Bukowski (Eds.), *Handbook of drug abuse prevention* (pp. 609–626). New York: Kluwer Academic/Plenum.

Duncan, T. E., Duncan, S. C., Li, F., & Strycker, L. A. (2001). A comparison of longitudinal multilevel techniques for analyzing adolescent and family alcohol use data. In D. S. Moskowitz & S. L. Hershberger (Eds.), *Modeling intraindividual variability with repeated measures data: Methods and applications* (pp. 171–201). New York: Plenum.

Duncan, T. E., Duncan, S. C., Strycker, L. A., & Li, F. (2002). A latent variable framework for power esti-

mation and analyses within intervention contexts. *Journal of Psychopathology and Behavioral Assessment, 24,* 1–12.

Duncan, T. E., Duncan, S. C., & Strycker, L. A. (2006). *An introduction to latent variable growth curve modeling: Concepts, issues, and applications* (2nd ed.). Mahwah, NJ: Erlbaum.

Goldstein, H. I. (1986). Multilevel mixed linear model analysis using iterative general least squares. *Biometrika, 73,* 43–56.

Hix-Small, H., Duncan, T. E., Duncan, S. C., & Okut, H. (2004). A multivariate associative finite growth mixture modeling approach examining adolescent alcohol and marijuana use. *Journal of Psychopathology and Behavioral Assessment, 26,* 255–270.

Hoyle, R. (1995). The structural equation modeling approach: Basic concepts and fundamental issues. In R. H. Hoyle (Ed.), *Structural equation modeling: Issues and applications* (pp. 1–15). Thousand Oaks, CA: Sage.

Jo, B., & Muthén, B. (2001). Modeling of intervention effects with noncompliance: A latent variable approach for randomized trials. In G. A. Marcoulides & R. E. Schumacker (Eds.), *New developments and techniques in structural equation modeling* (pp. 57–87). Mahwah, NJ: Erlbaum.

Jöreskog, K. G., & Sörbom, D. (1993). *LISREL 8: Structural equation modeling with the SIMPLIS command language.* Chicago: Scientific Software International.

Khoo, S. T., & Muthén, B. (2000). Longitudinal data on families: Growth modeling alternatives. In J. Rose, L. Chassin, C. Presson, & J. Sherman (Eds.), *Multivariate applications in substance use research* (pp. 43–78). Hillsdale, NJ: Erlbaum.

Kreft, I. G. (1994). Multilevel models for hierarchically nested data: Potential applications in substance abuse prevention research. In L. Collins & L. Seitz (Eds.), *Advances in data analysis for prevention intervention research* (NIDA Research Monograph No. 142, pp. 140–183). Washington, DC: U.S. Government Printing Office.

Longford, N. T. (1987). A fast scoring algorithm for maximum likelihood estimation in unbalanced mixed models with nested effects. *Biometrika, 74,* 817–827.

McArdle, J. J. (1988). Dynamic but structural equation modeling of repeated measures data. In R. B. Cattell & J. Nesselroade (Eds.), *Handbook of multivariate experimental psychology* (2nd ed., pp. 561–614). New York: Plenum Press.

McArdle, J. J., & Anderson, E. R. (1989). Latent growth models for research on aging. In L. E. Biren & K. W. Schaie (Eds.), *The handbook of the psychology of aging* (3rd ed., pp. 21–44). San Diego, CA: Academic Press.

McArdle, J. J., & Hamagami, F. (1991). Modeling incomplete longitudinal and cross-sectional data using latent growth structural models. In L. M. Collins & J. C. Horn (Eds.), *Best methods for the analysis of change* (pp. 276–304). Washington, DC: American Psychological Association.

McArdle, J. J., Hamagami, F., Elias, M. F., & Robbins, M. A. (1991). Structural modeling of mixed longitudinal and cross-sectional data. *Experimental Aging Research, 17,* 29–52.

Mehta, P. D., & West, S. G. (2000). Putting the individual back into individual growth curves. *Psychological Methods, 5,* 23–43.

Meredith, W., & Tisak, J. (1990). Latent curve analysis. *Psychometrika, 55,* 107–122.

Mulaik, S. A., James, L. R., Van Alstine, J., Bennett, N., Lind, S., & Stilwill, C. D. (1989). Evaluation of goodness-of-fit indices for structural equation models. *Psychological Bulletin, 105,* 430–445.

Muthén, B. (1989). Latent variable modeling in heterogeneous populations. *Psychometrika, 54,* 557–585.

Muthén, B. (1991). Multilevel factor analysis of class and student achievement components. *Journal of Educational Measurement, 28,* 338–354.

Muthén, B. (1994). Multilevel covariance structure analysis. *Sociological Methods & Research, 22,* 376–398.

Muthén, B. (1997). Latent variable modeling of longitudinal and multilevel data. In A. Raftery (Ed.), *Sociological methodology* (pp. 453–480). Boston: Blackwell.

Muthén, B. O., & Curran, P. J. (1997). General longitudinal modeling of individual differences in experimental designs: A latent variable framework for analysis and power estimation. *Psychological Methods, 2,* 371–402.

Muthén, L. K., & Muthén, B. (1998). *Mplus: User's guide.* Los Angeles: Author.

Muthén, L. K., & Muthén, B. O. (2002). How to use a Monte Carlo study to decide on sample size and determine power. *Structural Equation Modeling, 4,* 599–620.

Muthén, L. K., & Muthén, B. (2003). *Addendum to the Mplus user's guide.* Los Angeles: Author.

Muthén, B., & Satorra, A. (1989). Multilevel aspects of varying parameters in structural models. In R. D. Bock (Ed.), *Multilevel analysis of educational data* (pp. 87–99). San Diego, CA: Academic Press.

Neale, M. C. (2002). *Mx: Statistical modeling.* Richmond: Department of Human Genetics, Medical College of Virginia.

Nesselroade, J. R., & Baltes, P. B. (1979). *Longitudinal research in the study of behavior and development.* New York: Academic Press.

Rao, C. R. (1958). Some statistical methods for comparison of growth curves. *Biometrics, 14,* 1–17.

Raudenbush, S. W. (1995). Statistical models for studying the effects of social context on individual development. In J. Gottman (Ed.), *The analysis of change* (pp. 165–201). Hillsdale, NJ: Erlbaum.

Raudenbush, S., & Bryk, A. (1988). Methodological advances in studying effects of schools and classrooms on student learning. In E. Z. Roth (Ed.), *Review of research in education* (pp. 423–475). Washington, DC: American Educational Research Association.

Rogosa, D. R., Brandt, D., & Zimowski, M. (1982). A growth curve approach to the measure of change. *Psychological Bulletin, 92,* 726–748.

Rogosa, D., & Willett, J. B. (1985). Understanding correlates of change by modeling individual differences in growth. *Psychometrika, 50,* 203–228.

Sampson, R. J. (1988). Local friendship ties and community attachment in mass society: A multilevel systemic model. *American Sociological Review, 53,* 766–779.

Sampson, R. J. (1992). Family management and child development: Insights from social disorganization theory. In J. McCord (Ed.), *Advances in criminological theory. Vol. 3: Facts, frameworks and forecasts* (pp. 63–93). New Brunswick: Transaction.

Sampson, R. J., & Laub, J. H. (1990). Crime and deviance over the life course: The salience of adult social bonds. *American Sociological Review, 55,* 609–627.

Sayer, A. G., & Willet, J. B. (1998). A cross-domain model for growth in adolescent alcohol expectancies. *Multivariate Behavioral Research, 33,* 509–543.

Tanaka, J. S. (1987). How big is big enough? Sample size and goodness of fit in structural equation models with latent variables. *Child Development, 58,* 134–146.

Tisak, J., & Meredith, W. (1990). Descriptive and associative developmental models. In A. von Eye (Ed.), *Statistical methods in developmental research* (Vol. 2, pp. 387–406). San Diego, CA: Academic Press.

Tisak, J., & Tisak, M. S. (1996). Longitudinal models of reliability and validity: A latent curve approach. *Applied Psychological Measurement, 20,* 275–288.

Tucker, L. R. (1958). Determination of parameters of a functional relation by factor analysis. *Psychometrika, 23,* 19–23.

Wang, J., Siegal, H., Falck, R., Carlson, R., & Rahman, A. (1999). Evaluation of HIV risk reduction intervention programs via latent growth curve model. *Evaluation Review: A Journal of Applied Social Research, 23,* 649–663.

Wickrama, K. A. S., Lorenz, F. O., & Conger, R. D. (1997). Parental support and adolescent physical health status: A latent growth-curve analysis. *Journal of Health and Social Behavior, 38,* 149–163.

CHAPTER 29

STRUCTURAL EQUATION MODELING AND DRUG ABUSE ETIOLOGY: A HISTORICAL PERSPECTIVE

Adi Jaffe and Peter M. Bentler

Research into the factors affecting the initiation and progression of drug-taking behavior has had a long and fruitful history. A PsycINFO search conducted in August 2007 revealed that more than 2,500 articles have been published in the area beginning as early as 1912 (Hart, 1912). Since 1960 alone, more than 800 publications have examined early drug use and the variables affecting its onset and development. A variety of interesting theoretical and empirical results based on these publications are reviewed in the numerous chapters of this volume. This chapter focuses on the contribution of structural equation modeling (SEM) to the analysis of data from well-conceived theoretical and empirical studies of drug use etiologies; a specialized type of SEM is the growth curve model, whose role and impact is discussed in chapter 28 of this volume. SEM has become a major methodology in the field primarily because it is ideally suited to handle the complexities that arise in research examining drug use etiology. These include the need to consider many related substantive constructs and constructs to control for confounding or alternative explanations, where, in turn, each may be measured with a variety of indicators such as survey responses. In addition to the complex nature of the analyses, challenges in drug use etiology research include inadequate quantification of key constructs, errors of measurement, missing data, outliers, categorical and non-normally distributed variables, selective and heterogeneous samples, hierarchical sampling plans, and more.

Although all of these can be handled with SEM, only some fundamental ideas can be covered in this chapter. For a more comprehensive, yet still introductory overview of SEM, see Byrne (2006) or Kim and Bentler (2006); for more technical discussions of the methodology, see Hancock and Mueller (2006); Hayashi, Bentler, and Yuan (in press); Lee (2007); or Yuan and Bentler (2007).

We start by discussing the role of experimental and nonexperimental data in the study of drug use etiology. Then, after summarizing a few methodological approaches taken in this research before the advent of SEM as a methodology, we discuss its early implementation in etiology research. We also review the development of SEM itself, with its ability in later years to deal with the type of non-normal data often found in etiological drug use data. To obtain a more detailed look at specific etiological issues studied with SEM, we discuss a few older publications and one recent publication. We conclude with a note on the role of SEM in preventative intervention research and a summary of some promising new developments.

WHY NOT JUST DO EXPERIMENTS?

Before we begin, we want to acknowledge that causal inference is best served in the context of randomized experiments (e.g., Shadish, Cook, & Campbell, 2002). However, in the field of drug abuse etiology, experimentation is rarely a realistic

Preparation of this chapter was supported in part by National Institute on Drug Abuse Grants DA01070 and DA00017.

option. Although experimental manipulations can be used to study certain short-, and long-, term effects of drugs of abuse (Hart, Ward, Haney, Foltin, & Fischman, 2001; J. R. Taylor & Jentsch, 2001; Vanderschuren & Everitt, 2004), they cannot accurately capture the naturalistic process that drives people to use drugs. Because the random assignment of children to levels of prenatal cocaine exposure, childhood drug exposure, or exposure to violence is not an option for obvious ethical reasons, observational studies become necessary tools for studying the influence of these and many other factors on drug use etiology. Even when matched comparison groups are available in observational research, statistical control for unwanted sources of variance is needed to replace control by experimental design and randomization. Furthermore, some central questions on genetic and social inheritance of substance abuse etiology, such as are implemented in twin, cross-generational, family influence, or neighborhood–social disorganization studies, are, by their very nature, hard to pose via randomized experiments. Additionally, fixed status differences, such as gender, sexual orientation, or ethnicity, also cannot be reassigned experimentally. Finally, even if experiments were possible, they only allow for evaluation of direct effects (e.g., X → Y), whereas frequent etiological questions involve mediated effects (such as X → Y → Z) that are difficult but not impossible to handle with alternate methods but are standard fare for structural modeling. All of these limitations have led to the growth of SEM as a methodology for statistical control to replace experimental control. However, its role in etiology research developed slowly across years, as we illustrate with a few selected studies.

One drug use–related area of experimental research that has effectively combined experimental methodology with SEM analysis is that of drug prevention intervention research (Orlando, Ellickson, McCaffrey, & Longshore, 2005; Scheier, Botvin, & Griffin, 2001; Spoth & Redmond, 2002). An obvious exception to the above-mentioned assignment-to-condition problem, prevention research has made excellent use of SEM's ability to assess complex models that often include numerous mediating variables. Although the lion's share of this chapter

is dedicated to the use of SEM in observational research examining the factors associated with early drug use, recent publications making use of this method in prevention research are also mentioned throughout.

RESEARCH ON DRUG USE ETIOLOGY IN PRE-SEM YEARS

Although simple statistical procedures have been used for a long time (e.g., critical ratio analysis; Milton, 1944), many of the earliest publications in the area of drug use etiology relied on case studies and qualitative analyses for their conclusions. By the 1960s, researchers were increasing their use of statistical procedures and using larger sample sizes when presenting their results. Analysis of variance, *t* test, and chi-square statistics were used to reveal differences in Minnesota Multiphasic Personality Inventory personality profiles between drug users and nonusers (McAree, Steffenhagen, & Zheutlin, 1969), male and female drug users (Olson, 1964), and Black and White drug users (Hill, Haertzen, & Glaser, 1960). Statistical advancement in the area continued throughout the 1970s with the use of multiple regression analysis (Jessor, Jessor, & Finney, 1973) and factorial analysis of variance procedures (Lewis & Trickett, 1974). These early examinations expanded our understanding of the differences between drug-using and drug-naïve individuals on variables related to personality, peer relationships, and familial environment. It became clear through this earlier work that the associations between factors of interest were not always direct, but that some factors instead mediated the impact of others in what was clearly becoming viewed as a quite complex mechanism of action. Still, with rare exception (Jessor et al., 1973), most of this earlier work made use of statistical techniques that did not allow for the evaluation of realistically complex models of drug use etiology, but instead focused on the important job of establishing a basic understanding of drug user characteristics.

By the mid- to late 1970s, researchers began untangling the interrelationships among variables known to affect drug use behavior and its initiation. The increased availability and sophistication of computer systems during this time was making statistical innovation and creativity more accessible than ever before. Factor analysis was used to examine the clustering of explanatory variables (Perez, Padilla, Ramirez, Ramirez, & Rodriguez, 1980; Smith & Fogg, 1974), and drug use variables were clustered in an attempt to create a more comprehensive out-come measure (Huba, Wingard, & Bentler, 1979). This statistical grouping of variables was the starting point for what would later be known as latent variables, that is, unobserved factors that are hypothesized to underlie correlated observations. By using partial correlations (Thomas, Petersen, & Zingraff, 1975), multiple classification analysis (Kandel, Treiman, Faust, & Single, 1976), canonical correlations (Huba et al., 1979), and extracted factors in multiple regression analysis (Perez et al., 1980), researchers were able to study not only how specific measured variables directly affect drug use patterns, but also the concurrent relationship among the predictor variables themselves.

Huba, Wingard, and Bentler (1980) used variable clustering to test the effect of participants' drug use (13 variables), adult and peer drug use and supply (14 variables), and general peer characteristics (22 variables) on later drug use. Results indicated that although past drug use and adult and peer support and supply did affect later drug use, general characteristics of the participants' peer group (i.e., their general proclivity for deviance) did not. By clustering related predictor variables, these advances in analysis allowed researchers to reduce the effect of sample-specific measurement variations, focusing instead on more stable shared associations between measures. Much like the relatively greater reliability of a factor over its individual indicators (or a subset of them), the increased consistency of these composite predictors supported the study of more complex causal mechanisms. Kandel et al. (1976) used another clustering-based analytic strategy (i.e., multiple classification analysis) to show support for a stage-based development of drug use, with their relationships to predictors changing as drug use progressed from cigarettes to alcohol and then to marijuana.

In spite of the advances in abilities to study complex mechanisms, these studies were still limited to only single-layer explorations, generally examining the relationship between specific composite-independent variables and other composite-dependent variables. An assessment of multiple relationships simultaneously, in which a variable might be both a dependent variable in one part of a model and also a predictor variable in another part of the model, was not possible, even using the most sophisticated statistical procedures of the time. Path analysis and path diagrams (Wright, 1921, 1934) and the software package LISREL (Jöreskog & Sörbom, 1978) changed this.[1]

SEM: THE EARLY YEARS

As an important precursor to SEM, the 1960s and 1970s saw the rediscovery of Sewell Wright's method of path analysis, which offered a general way to represent complex hypotheses of causal sequences by means of a path diagram. This not only made it possible to present theories related to the flow of variables' influences on other variables, but also, in principle, to use path tracing to generate covariance structure algebra. Additionally, it fostered thinking about constructs, latent variables, or factors as separate from their observed indicators, which contain errors of measurement. Still, the methodology proved impractical until, urged by Goldberger (1971) to join econometrics and psychometrics, Keesling, Wiley, and especially Jöreskog wedded the econometric simultaneous equation model and the psychometric factor analytic measurement models. Jöreskog implemented and fostered the methodology with the LISREL (a copyrighted acronym for linear structural relations) computer program (see Bentler, 1986b).

The LISREL approach called for the specification of a measurement model to relate observed to latent variables and, separately, to relate latent variables to each other by a simultaneous equation model. More important, the parameters of the model could be estimated by a statistically sound method, the method of maximum likelihood, based on the assumption of multivariate normality of the variables. A test of

---

[1] The National Institute on Drug Abuse has been, for several decades, a strong supporter of research on SEM methodology and applications.

model fit and the statistical significance of specific parameters were also made available, for the first time encouraging systematic hypothesis testing with nonexperimental data. The program was quickly put to use by researchers eager for analyses that would allow them to test their theories regarding drug use (Huba, Wingard, & Bentler, 1981; Kandel & Adler, 1982; Krosnick & Judd, 1982).

Huba et al. (1981) used this emerging methodology to compare two popular theories about the progress, and indeed the underlying basis, of drug use. A simplex model, with its sequential progression from use of alcohol, to cannabis, to hard drugs was compared with a common factor model, which allowed for a direct, as well as an indirect, path between alcohol use and the use of hard drugs. Each of the three latent use factors was estimated by using multiple observed variables, with some variables (e.g., liquor, hashish) loading onto more than one factor. Using a sample of 1,634 students drawn from 11 schools in Los Angeles, Huba et al. showed that both models fit the data equally well. In their discussion of the results, the authors suggested that given the essentially equivalent fit and parameters provided by both models in their sample, the question

of which theory is supported by actual behavior may be, in essence, moot. They asserted that both models support the introduction of a "unidimensional representation of involvement in drug use at the next higher order of abstraction" (p. 191). Although no definitive conclusion was available, this early use of an emerging statistical method allowed for an empirical comparison of two theories that until then was impossible.

Almost concurrently, Kandel and Adler (1982) used LISREL to examine the relationship between parental and peer alcohol and drug use, attitudes about marijuana, and self-reported marijuana use. Although grounded in multiple regression, their relatively complex model included not only latent predictors (e.g., parental and own alcohol use, with beer, wine, and hard liquor use as indicators), but also a number of direct and indirect effect estimates that would have been impossible to examine using simpler multiple regression analyses (Figure 29.1). In the model, the authors used six factors as predictors of an adolescent's marijuana use: father's alcohol use, mother's alcohol use, peers' alcohol use, adolescent's alcohol use, peers' marijuana use, and adolescent's marijuana attitudes.

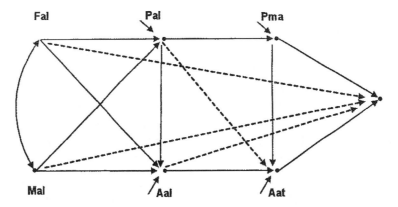

FIGURE 29.1. Kandel and Adler's (1982) representation of interpersonal influences on marijuana use. Solid lines indicate significant coefficients, and dashed lines indicate nonsignificant coefficients. Fal = father's alcohol use; Mal = mother's alcohol use; Pal = peer alcohol use; Aal = adolescent's alcohol use; Pma = peer marijuana use; Aat = adolescent's marijuana attitudes; Ama = adolescent's marijuana use. From "Socialization into marijuana use among French adolescents: A cross-cultural comparison with the United States," by D. B. Kandel, R. Z. Marulies, and M. Davies, 1982, *Journal of Health and Social Behavior, 23*, p. 301. Copyright by the American Sociological Association. Reprinted with permission.

Most factors had two or more observed variables as indicators (e.g., beer, wine, and liquor consumption for parental and self alcohol use variables; legalization attitudes and beliefs regarding marijuana use as being harmful for self-attitudes regarding marijuana), whereas alcohol use by peers and marijuana use by both peers and the target adolescent were only measured using a single indicator. Kandel and Adler (1982) collected their data in France and the United States and analyzed them separately for each of the samples. In addition, they conducted separate analyses for men and women within each of these samples.

The results of this early SEM investigation revealed a number of interesting findings, including a greater effect of parental alcohol use on peer alcohol use in the French versus U.S. sample. In addition, findings indicated that only alcohol use by a parent of the opposite sex significantly affected the adolescent's own use. One of Kandel and Adler's (1982) most interesting findings showed that although the target adolescent's alcohol use did not directly predict his or her marijuana use, it was positively associated with the target adolescent's attitudes about marijuana, which in turn were positively associated with the use of marijuana itself. Furthermore, these attitudes, as well as the adolescent's actual marijuana use, were both positively associated with their peers' use of marijuana. In fact, in the American sample, peer marijuana use was actually a stronger predictor of the target adolescent's marijuana use compared with his or her own attitudes regarding use. Overall, the direct and indirect effects of peer alcohol and marijuana use were shown to be the strongest predictors of actual marijuana use by the adolescent.

These findings reiterated and reinforced previous reports regarding the effect of peer support and supply, parental influence, and internal motivation on drug use (Huba et al., 1979, 1980; Kandel, Margulies, & Davies, 1978; Pomazal & Brown, 1977) but did so in a way that integrated them more fully than ever before. This integration allowed the authors to examine effects (i.e., multiple mediational effects along with multiple direct effects) that would have been more tedious to examine using other methods, but more important, it allowed the reader to examine the influences among these latent factors separately

from the relationships among the variables within each factor. This method, allowing the separation of observed variables from latent factors, therefore made it easier than ever to see the forest for the trees, a feat that can be difficult to accomplish at times.

Despite these incredible advances, the early use of SEM left something to be desired. Tests of factor loadings and intercorrelations, goodness-of-fit statistics, and parameters assessing variance accounted for in each model were inconsistently reported across investigations. In addition, there were methodological issues that remained unclear, such as an appropriate minimal sample size for use in SEM, the effects of violation of distributional assumptions, and so on. This made it difficult to fully evaluate the utility of the analyses and hard to draw conclusions about assessment of model fit. Goodness-of-fit statistics constructed to help assess model quality on a 0–1 scale helped to resolve some of the issues, for example, excessive power because of large sample size (Bentler & Bonett, 1980). Researchers using SEM methodologies adopted the use of goodness-of-fit statistics more widely (McAlister, Krosnick, & Milburn, 1984), although further research on population-based fit indices had yet to be done (e.g., Bentler, 1990a; McDonald, 1989; Steiger, 1998).

ANOTHER APPROACH TO SEM AND ITS APPLICATION TO DRUG USE

It became clear by the middle of the 1980s that the LISREL approach had limitations for the study of drug use etiology. First, the program required knowledge of matrix algebra and Greek characters that proved difficult to learn, and its job interface was hard to use. Second, the model used did not easily lend itself to evaluating hypotheses that did not cleanly fit into the measurement versus simultaneous equation conception. Third, the assumption of multivariate normality necessary for the statistics seemed inappropriate in the drug abuse domain where many variables are highly skewed and kurtotic. Fourth, the modification indices used by LISREL to locate sources of misspecification had no good statistical rationale. These limitations were addressed by the EQS program (Bentler, 1986c) and also, in subsequent years, by LISREL and many other SEM programs.

EQS solved these problems as follows: First, it did not require matrix algebra in its user interface, making it more user friendly, and in later years it also added a graphical interface to allow specification of models via path diagrams. Second, although in its standard form the LISREL model does not allow observed variables to influence other variables or factors, residuals to influence factors, or other specific or nonstandard effects, drug abuse theorizing implies the importance of such effects (Bentler, 1990b; Newcomb, 1994). These effects could be easily specified in the Bentler–Weeks (1980) model used in EQS, which allows any conceivable effect to be included in the model as long as the model itself remains identified. Third, newly developed statistical methods allowing elliptical and arbitrary non-normal distributions for the variables in a model (Bentler, 1983; Bentler & Dijkstra, 1985; Browne, 1984) were made available in EQS, allowing for better use of non-normal data. This aspect of SEM was further bolstered with the later introduction of the Satorra–Bentler (1988, 1994) scaled test statistic, which proved to be more reliable for non-normal data in smaller samples. Finally, the modification index was reconceptualized as a Lagrange multiplier test, allowing standard statistical theory to apply to model modifications (Bentler, 1986a; Sörbom, 1989). Parameter change estimates quickly followed this test refinement (Bentler & Chou, 1993; Kaplan, 1989).

GROWTH OF SEM IN DRUG USE ETIOLOGY RESEARCH

Although only a handful of papers making use of SEM were published in the area of drug use etiology during the early 1980s, dozens were published in the latter half of the same decade. The ability of SEM to untangle complex associations among observed variables made it a natural way to examine large datasets. One such study combined the causal inference benefits of SEM with the temporal sequencing of longitudinal data, allowing for greater certainty in asserting causality than would be prudent using each method separately (Stein, Newcomb, & Bentler, 1987).

The analysis reported in Stein et al. (1987) was conducted with 654 participants from the Los Angeles area who were originally recruited while in junior high school and followed across 9 years. Stein et al. examined the effects of early self-reported, peer (perceived), and adult (perceived) drug use, as well as social conformity, on later drug use and problems associated with the use of drugs. Making use of the new features in EQS, these authors assessed the causal pathways among latent factors across the three observation points and the "within-time" (i.e., concurrent) correlations among latent factors. Figure 29.2 shows the cross-time latent variable influences.

This investigation, like others before it, supported the role of peer and adult drug use in augmenting a participant's use of drugs. However, although the model offered by Stein et al. (1987) revealed significant concurrent associations between self-reported drug use and both adult and peer drug use, it showed a direct "across-time" link only between the perceived adult use factor at Year 5 and target drug use at Year 9. Peer influence on later drug use was reported as being significant only when pertaining to more specific drug use domains (i.e., Year 5 peer cannabis use associated with Year 9 self-reported cannabis use). In addition, the socialization factor of social conformity was found to have a pervasive effect on peer, adult, and self-reported drug use, as well as on its longer term consequences. Last, early exposure to adult use, but not peer use, was linked with problem use in later life. These findings offered some sobering implications regarding early exposure to adult use and its pervasive long-term effects. Analytically, Stein et al. recognized that SEM "made it feasible" (p. 1104) to examine a more comprehensive model than would have been possible using any other method and that this ability to assess both concurrent and longitudinal influences is necessary when examining a syndrome as complex as substance use.

In reporting their results, Stein et al. (1987) provided readers with a more complete assessment of their model than was commonly found. This included a full descriptive assessment of variables used (i.e., mean, standard deviation, skew, and kurtosis) and a confirmatory factor analysis to verify the underlying latent factors and their indicators as

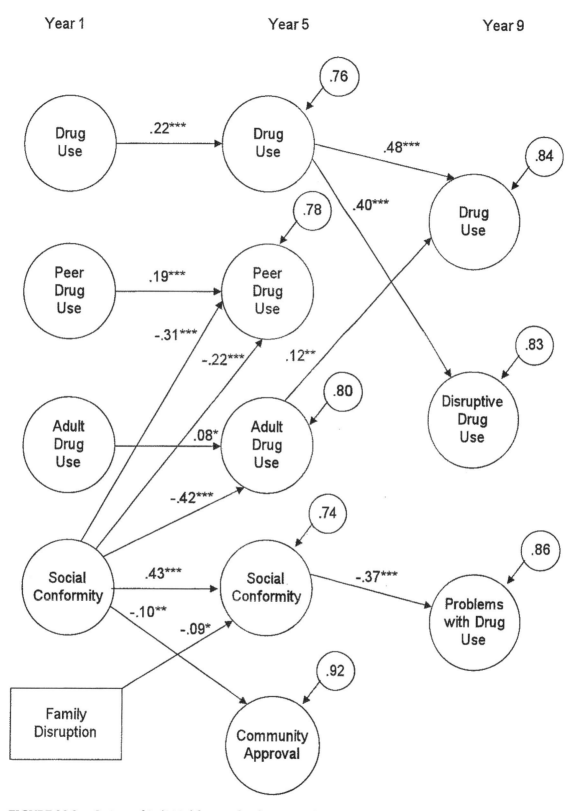

FIGURE 29.2. Stein et al.'s (1987) longitudinal structural equation model testing the effect of adult and peer drug use on later drug use and problems. Significant regression paths between the latent variables in the final structure, or path, model. Regression coefficients are standardized and residual variances are in circles. *$p \leq .05$. **$p \leq .01$. ***$p \leq .001$. From "An 8-Year Study of Multiple Influences on Drug Use and Drug Use Consequences," by J. A. Stein, M. D. Newcomb, and P. M. Bentler, 1987, *Journal of Personality and Social Psychology, 53*, p. 1102. Copyright 1987 by the American Psychological Association.

used in the full SEM model (Table 29.1). The factor loadings in Table 29.1 serve to give meaning to the constructs shown in Figure 29.2.

Although a number of the drug use variables used displayed severe non-normality, Stein et al. (1987) chose to use maximum likelihood estimation methods because performance of the newer distribution-free methods was not known for a

model containing the specified complexity. Additionally, Stein et al. reported on the statistical methods used to improve the initial model (i.e., the Lagrange multiplier test) and augmented standard goodness-of-fit statistics (i.e., chi-square, normed fit index) by significance tests of direct and indirect paths in the model as well as measured variable–latent factor relationships. Last, they used emerging

TABLE 29.1

Stein et al.'s CFA for Latent Factors Used in SEM Model

	Year 1		Year 5		Year 9	
Variable	**SFL**	**RV**	**SFL**	**RV**	**SFL**	**RV**
Drug Use						
Alcohol use	.61[a]	.62	.69[a]	.52	.33[a]	.79
Cannabis use	.78	.39	.90	.19	.64	.51
Hard-drug use	.50	.74	.65	.58	.88	.23
Peer Drug Use						
Peer alcohol use	.81[a]	.35	.78[a]	.38		
Peer cannabis use	.85	.27	.81	.35		
Peer hard-drug use	.69	.52	.80	.36		
Adult Drug Use						
Adult alcohol use	.54[a]	.71	.58[a]	.66		
Adult cannabis use	.68	.53	.72	.40		
Adult hard-drug use	.47	.77	.76	.42		
Social Conformity						
Law abidance	.74[a]	.45	.68[a]	.53		
Liberalism	−.48	.77	−.43	.81		
Religious commitment	.27	.92	.25	.94		
Family Disruption	1.00	0				
Community Approval						
Alcohol			.61[a]	.63		
Cannabis			.99	.01		
Hard drugs			.67	.55		
Disruptive Drug Use						
Alcohol					.27[a]	.93
Cannabis					.63	.60
Hard drugs					.68	.54
Problem Drug Use						
Alcohol					.54[a]	.71
Drugs					.50	.74
Alcohol or drugs					.55	.70

Note. SFL = standardized factor loading. RV = residual variance. All factors significant at *p* < .001. From "An 8-Year Study of Multiple Influences on Drug Use and Drug Use Consequences," by J. A. Stein, M. D. Newcomb, and P. M. Bentler, 1987, *Journal of Personality and Social Psychology, 53,* p. 1100. Copyright 1987 by the American Psychological Association.
[a]Parameter fixed in original model for identification purposes.

standards of presentation, with figures representing latent factors as ovals and observed variables as rectangles. These additions allowed for a more complete examination of many important aspects of a quite complex model that would have been hard to decipher given earlier technology and reporting standards in the SEM literature.

More generally, by this time prominent researchers were calling for the use of structural modeling methods to establish and evaluate more complex, causal, and comprehensive models that go beyond multiple regression and simple path analysis (Zucker & Gomberg, 1986). Researchers in the field were eager to answer the call, putting SEM to use in increasingly more rigorous and creative ways.

MORE RECENT SEM ADVANCES IN DRUG USE ETIOLOGY RESEARCH

Since the mid-1980s, the use of SEM has become standard practice in many examinations related to early drug use. Given the highly adaptable nature of the analyses and the increasing ease of use of the programming interfaces being made available, SEM became available not only to experienced quantitative psychologists but also to more resourceful and enterprising researchers in many related disciplines. This expansion of its user base brought with it more creative utilization of SEM's abilities, including the use of residuals in factors—that is, residual latent change—as predictors of subsequent outcomes (Newcomb, Scheier, & Bentler, 1993), the inclusion of multiple intervening mediators (MacKinnon, 2000; A. B. Taylor, MacKinnon, & Tein, 2007), and as noted earlier, a wider variety of designs and methodologies (Arbuckle, 1996; Duncan et al., 1998; Little, Schnabel, & Baumert, 2000; Muthén, 2001a, 2001b). Developments such as these were fostered by advances in the statistical underpinnings of SEM, which gradually allowed for more complex analyses in their own right, adding latent growth curve modeling, multiple-group analyses, mixture modeling, and multilevel modeling to the proverbial SEM toolbox. Space limits do not allow us to discuss these advances, although some are covered by chapters 27 and 28 of this volume.

To illustrate how far SEM has come since its introduction into the drug use etiology field, we discuss an interesting recent study and note its strengths and weaknesses. In their recent investigation, Pilgrim, Schulenberg, O'Malley, Bachman, and Johnston (2006) put SEM analysis to great use in their investigation of mediation and moderation among factors known to be involved in the development of early substance use. Using a fabulously large, representative, national sample of more than 13,000 students, the authors configured their analyses to address pressing questions regarding the role of parental involvement in the lives of their children and the effects of parenting on school success, recreational activities, and drug use (Figure 29.3). Drawing on earlier research suggesting that poor parenting leads to children's underdeveloped social skills, poor scholastic performance, and eventual acceptance into deviant peer groups where they are exposed to drugs (Hawkins & Weis, 1985; Patterson et al., 1989; Thornberry, 1987, all as cited in Pilgrim et al., 2006), the authors examined the notion that family relationships affect drug use through these mediational processes similarly across ethnicity and gender groups. Such a complex question of interest, involving not only mediation but also moderation (i.e., interaction), multiple indicator, and outcome variables, is ideally suited to SEM.

Pilgrim et al. (2006) used multigroup covariance structure analysis, which allows a similar structural model to be tested on a number of predetermined groups, examining the impact of group membership not only on overall model fit, but also on the important effects within the model. Discovery of significantly different effects between different groups indicates an interaction between model variables and the grouping variable used. Making use of both latent factor predictor variables and outcome variables, Pilgrim et al. took great care in specifying their measurement model before embarking on their latent effects analysis. Four latent predictors were hypothesized (i.e., parental involvement, risk taking, school success, and time with friends), and most were configured with more than two observed variables as indicators. Having three

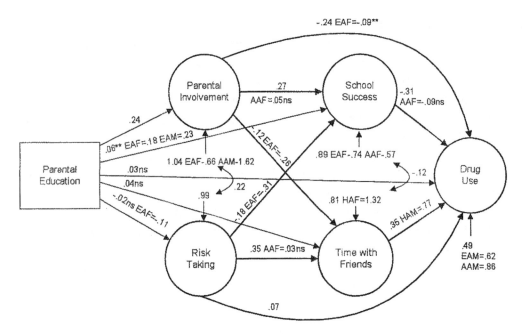

Note: Parental education entered as a control variable .
*p < .05, ** p < -.01. All pathways without an asterisk are significant to p < .001 unless noted "ns"

FIGURE 29.3. Pilgrim et al.'s (2006) mediational model. Six-group structural equation model for eighth grade assessing differences in the mediational impact of school success and time with friends. Note that specified notations on paths show coefficients significantly different from those for the overall sample. Fit indices: χ^2(579, N = 12,715) = 1,438.05, non-normed fit index = .94, comparative fit index = .94, goodness-of-fit index = .95, root-mean-square error of approximation = .04. AA = African American; EA = European American; HA = Hispanic American; F = female; M = male. From "Mediators and moderators of parental involvement on substance use: A national study of adolescents," by C. C. Pilgrim, J. E. Schulenberg, P. M. O'Malley, J. G. Bachman, and L. D. Johnston, 2006, *Prevention Sciences*, 7, p. 84. Copyright 2006 by Springer. Reprinted with permission.

or more indicators per factor helps alleviate model identification problems because at least one indicator per factor must be fixed to determine the scale of the factor. The model also included a measure of parental education as a control variable.

For model estimation and testing, Pilgrim et al. (2006) used both maximum likelihood and a generalized least squares method. Non-normal, highly skewed, and kurtotic data are often encountered when using measures of self-reported drug use. Thus, the authors intended to correct for these distributional anomalies by implementing alternative estimation procedures. However, the generalized least squares method used appears to have been Browne's (1974) normal theory method rather than his asymptotically distribution-free method (Browne, 1984), which would be more appropriate

and could be relied on in this large sample.[2] Still, the authors made great use of a number of fit statistics such as the goodness-of-fit index and root-mean-square error of approximation, which are absolute fit statistics assessing how well the model accounts for the data covariance structure, and the non-normed fit index and comparative fit index, which assess model fit as compared with the null model of uncorrelated variables. In addition, they tested numerous (six) nested models that included different combinations of direct and mediating effects by the proposed predictor factors (Figure 29.4), a

[2] In very large samples, such as this national sample (before division into groups), SEM will have very high power, and almost any effect will be statistically significant and any proposed model may be rejectable statistically regardless of the estimation method chosen. The classic issue of "statistical" versus "practical" significance remains as relevant in SEM as it does in the wider field of applied statistics (Bentler, 1990a).

Only Mediation

Only Direct Effects

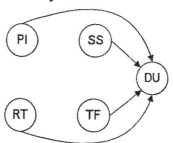

Single Predictor Models

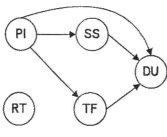

Parental involvement

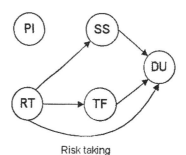

Risk taking

Single Mediator Models

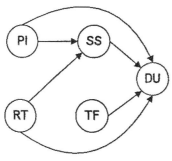

School Success

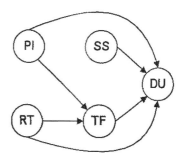

Time with Friends

FIGURE 29.4.   Nested model diagrams from Pilgrim et al. (2006) showing the variations on the final model tested for comparative fit. PI = parental involvement; SS = school success; RT = risk taking; TF = time with friends; DU = drug use. From "Mediators and moderators of parental involvement on substance use: A national study of adolescents," by C. C. Pilgrim, J. E. Schulenberg, P. M. O'Malley, J. G. Bachman, and L. D. Johnston, 2006, *Prevention Sciences, 7,* p. 80. Copyright 2006 by Springer. Reprinted with permission.

commonly used method for simplifying models to achieve a parsimonious model.

Pilgrim et al. (2006) indeed reported that a more restricted model, which includes only the indirect influence of parental involvement and risk-taking behavior (i.e., a model specifying only mediation, the top left model in Figure 29.4), fits nearly as well as the model that also includes these variables' direct effects on drug use. Because the goal of this study was to assess the generalizability of these indirect effects across gender and ethnic group, the observation that the thrust of the above-mentioned variables' influence on drug use was indirect substantiates a relationship that the authors proposed to be broadly applicable.

Taking further caution to ensure the appropriateness of their model, Pilgrim et al. (2006) used cross-validation to assess the adequacy of their model. The technique involved developing and refining a model using a screening sample (i.e., the 1996 cohort) and testing the developed model, unchanged, on an independent calibration sample or samples (i.e., the 1994 and 1995 cohorts). After finding no differences in fit between the three groups, the authors combined the 1994–1995 cohorts for later analyses. Pilgrim et al. also conducted separate analyses on 8th- and 10th-grade data, given a few significant differences in estimated model parameters between the grades. Furthermore, the authors used a six-group SEM analysis to compare the model simultaneously for African American, European American, and Hispanic American boys and girls. Generally, the effects of parental involvement and risk taking were found to be similar for all groups; both factors were significantly predictive of adolescent substance use, with parental involvement inversely related and risk taking positively related to drug use. A small, interesting deviation from this general pattern of results was discovered for 8th-grade African American girls, for whom mediated effects were very small because of highly reduced associations between parental involvement and school success on one hand and risk taking and time spent with friend on the other. Interestingly, this departure disappeared by 10th grade, at which point the African American girls' model provided evidence of mediation similar to the effects observed with all other groups. This pattern of results suggests that

the mediational effect itself may be a developmental phenomenon that is somehow differentially expressed in young African American girls. Overall, however, Pilgrim et al. found that the influence of both parental involvement and risk taking was significantly mediated through school success and time with friends, supporting the appropriateness of a model positing mediation.

Future research can further strengthen Pilgrim et al.'s (2006) ideas. The main conceptual issue, as they noted, is that their main hypotheses imply effects across time, but the models were tested on cross-sectional data, thus limiting statements regarding causation. Some technical enhancements would also provide more information. First, as compared with the pairwise deletion they used to deal with missing data, using direct or casewise maximum likelihood can reduce bias. Second, they used covariance structure analysis and hence could not test for mean differences in their factors across groups, such as intercept or mean differences in drug use by grade or gender. Such effects can be studied using a mean structure model. Third, their database contains students nested within schools, and with a multilevel model it would be possible to disentangle school effects from individual difference effects. But these are minor quibbles with a very nice study. The graphical presentation of results by the authors allowed for a very coherent step-by-step movement from their initial generalized model to later group-specific results. Overall, the analyses presented by Pilgrim et al. helped support and augment an existing theory regarding the role of parental involvement in adolescent substance use initiation and development. Finding that mediational processes are indeed important, and equally so across ethnicity and gender groups, is relevant for intervention design because it suggests that strengthening parental supervision and involvement should help reduce substance use equivalently for all groups.

Indeed, an investigation regarding the role of parents and effective parenting in drug use intervention efforts made use of longitudinal data analyzed using a SEM approach. This model was structured to disentangle the effects of the intervention on effective parenting from its effects on the child's general alcohol-related peer pressure refusal skills (Spoth & Redmond, 2002). Results indicated that not only did the intervention affect a child's refusal skills, but it also affected relevant parental skills, which in turn both directly and indirectly (i.e., through their impact on the child's refusal skills) affected the child's propensity to use alcohol. Similarly, Scheier et al. (2001) have reported that an intervention aimed at improving a child's social competence can play a role in reducing alcohol and cigarette use, and as a consequence multiple drug use, at 1- and 2-year follow-ups.

One of the major strengths of the Spoth and Redmond (2002) and Scheier et al. (2001) studies lies in the authors' use of random assignment (i.e., of schools and/or students) to different intervention conditions. As mentioned earlier, the inability of most drug use–related research to use random assignment not only reduces researchers' ability to assert causal relationships but was also the impetus for much of the thinking behind SEM as a statistical method to minimize errors of inference because of the lack of experimental manipulation. In recent years, SEM has increasingly been used by intervention researchers augmenting their experimental control with statistical methods that enable them to include more variables and assess more complex models. Such research often makes extensive use of longitudinal data, which, like random assignment, helps to clarify the direction of causal influences.

CONCLUSIONS

The overview we have provided of the role of SEM in the study of drug use etiology has necessarily been limited and our presentation focused on basic SEM methods. Still, it should be clear that this statistical method has provided much in the way of expanding knowledge regarding the complex mechanisms involved in the early development of substance use. Yet, drug use data challenge psychologists, statisticians, and quantitative methodologists to expand the capabilities of this relatively new tool to the types of designs and data commonly encountered in this substantive area. Recent developments have provided variants of SEM that are also directly relevant to the study of drug use etiology. Dozens of

subfields of structural modeling, including various methods for dealing with incomplete data including nonignorable missing responses, binary data, Bayesian methods, meta-analysis, nonlinear models, and robust methods, are reviewed in Lee (2007). Additional recent developments that would seem to hold promise for substance abuse etiology research include a wider range of model types (Rabe-Hesketh & Skrondal, 2007); estimation and testing under an alternative (vs. null) hypothesis (Yuan, Hayashi, & Bentler, 2007); combining multiple-group SEM with propensity score methodology to alleviate biases that can occur with standard applications of propensity scores (Hoshino, 2007; Hoshino, Kurata, & Shigemasu, 2006); new developments in models with nonlinear relations and interactions among latent variables (e.g., Klein & Muthén, 2007; Mooijaart, in press); permitting use of an item response theory model in place of the standard linear factor analysis measurement model in structural modeling (Hoshino & Bentler, 2007; Skrondal & Rabe-Hesketh, 2004); new developments in mediational analysis (MacKinnon, 2008); and further extensions of mixture models (Hancock & Samuelsen, 2008).

References

Arbuckle, J. L. (1996). Full information estimation in the presence of incomplete data. In G. A. Marcoulides & R. E. Schumacker (Eds.), *Advanced structural equation modeling: Issues and techniques* (pp. 243–277). Mahwah, NJ: Erlbaum.

Bentler, P. M. (1983). Some contributions to efficient statistics in structural models: Specification and estimation of moment structures. *Psychometrika, 48*, 493–517.

Bentler, P. M. (1986a). *Lagrange Multiplier and Wald tests for EQS and EQS/PC.* Los Angeles: BMDP Statistical Software.

Bentler, P. M. (1986b). Structural modeling and *Psychometrika:* An historical perspective on growth and achievements. *Psychometrika, 51*, 35–51.

Bentler, P. M. (1986c). *Theory and implementation of EQS: A structural equations program.* Los Angeles: BMDP Statistical Software.

Bentler, P. M. (1990a). Comparative fit indexes in structural models. *Psychological Bulletin, 107*, 238–246.

Bentler, P. M. (1990b). Latent variable structural models for separating specific from general effects. In

L. Sechrest, E. Perrin, & J. Bunker (Eds.), *Research methodology: Strengthening causal interpretations of nonexperimental data* (pp. 61–85). Rockville, MD: U.S. Department of Health and Human Services.

Bentler, P. M., & Bonett, D. G. (1980). Significance tests and goodness of fit in the analysis of covariance structures. *Psychological Bulletin, 88,* 588–606.

Bentler, P. M., & Chou, C. P. (1993). Some new covariance structure model improvement statistics. In K. A. Bollen & J. S. Long (Eds.), *Testing structural equation models* (pp. 235–255). Newbury Park: Sage.

Bentler, P. M., & Dijkstra, T. (1985). Efficient estimation via linearization in structural models. In P. R. Krishnaiah (Ed.), *Multivariate analysis VI* (pp. 9–42). Amsterdam: North-Holland.

Bentler, P. M., & Weeks, D. G. (1980). Linear structural equations with latent variables. *Psychometrika, 45,* 289–308.

Browne, M. W. (1974). Generalized least squares estimators in the analysis of covariance structures. *South African Statistical Journal, 8,* 1–24.

Browne, M. W. (1984). Asymptotic distribution-free methods for the analysis of covariance structures. *British Journal of Mathematical and Statistical Psychology, 37,* 62–83.

Byrne, B. M. (2006). *Structural equation modeling with EQS: Basic concepts, applications, and programming* (2nd ed.). Mahwah, NJ: Erlbaum.

Duncan, T. E., Duncan, S. C., Alpert, A., Hops, H., Stoolmiller, M., & Muthén, B. (1998). Latent variable modeling of longitudinal and multilevel substance use data. *Multivariate Behavioral Research, 32,* 275–318.

Goldberger, A. S. (1971). Econometrics and psychometrics: A survey of communalities. *Psychometrika, 36,* 83–107.

Hancock, G. R., & Mueller, R. O. (2006). *Structural equation modeling: A second course.* Greenwich: Information Age.

Hancock, G. R., & Samuelsen, K. M. (Eds.). (2008). *Advances in latent variable mixture models.* Charlotte, NC: Information Age.

Hart, B. (1912). *The psychology of insanity.* New York: Cambridge University Press.

Hart, C. L., Ward, A. S., Haney, M., Foltin, R. W., & Fischman, M. W. (2001). Methamphetamine self-administration by humans. *Psychopharmacology, 157,* 75–81.

Hayashi, K., Bentler, P. M., & Yuan, K.-H. (in press). *Structural equation modeling* (Vol. 27). Amsterdam: Elsevier.

Hill, H. E., Haertzen, C. A., & Glaser, R. (1960). Personality characteristics of narcotic addicts as indicated by the MMPI. *Journal of Genetic Psychology, 62,* 127–139.

Hoshino, T. (2007). Doubly robust-type estimation for covariate adjustment in latent variable modeling. *Psychometrika, 72,* 535–549.

Hoshino, T., & Bentler, P. M. (2007). *The cause of bias in factor score regression and a new practical solution.* Unpublished manuscript, University of Tokyo.

Hoshino, T., Kurata, H., & Shigemasu, K. (2006). A propensity score adjustment for multiple group structural equation modeling. *Psychometrika, 71,* 691–712.

Huba, G. J., Wingard, J. A., & Bentler, P. M. (1979). Beginning adolescent drug use and peer and adult interaction patterns. *Journal of Consulting and Clinical Psychology, 47,* 265–276.

Huba, G. J., Wingard, J. A., & Bentler, P. M. (1980). Longitudinal analysis of the role of peer support, adult models, and peer subcultures in beginning adolescent substance use: An application of setwise canonical correlation methods. *Multivariate Behavioral Research, 15,* 259–279.

Huba, G. J., Wingard, J. A., & Bentler, P. M. (1981). A comparison of two latent variable causal models for adolescent drug use. *Journal of Personality and Social Psychology, 40,* 180–193.

Jessor, R., Jessor, S. L., & Finney, J. (1973). A social psychology of marijuana use: Longitudinal studies of high school and college youth. *Journal of Personality and Social Psychology, 26,* 1–15.

Jöreskog, K. G., & Sörbom, D. (1978). *LISREL IV: Analysis of linear structural relationships by the method of maximum likelihood.* Chicago: National Educational Resources.

Kandel, D. B., & Adler, I. (1982). Socialization into marijuana use among French adolescents: A cross-cultural comparison with the United States. *Journal of Health and Social Behavior, 23,* 295–309.

Kandel, D. B., Margulies, R. Z., & Davies, M. (1978). Analytical strategies for studying transitions into developmental stages. *Sociology of Education, 51,* 162–176.

Kandel, D. B., Treiman, D., Faust, R., & Single, E. (1976). Adolescent involvement in legal and illegal drug use: A multiple classification analysis. *Social Forces, 55,* 438–458.

Kaplan, D. (1989). Model modification in covariance structure analysis: Application of the expected parameter change statistic. *Multivariate Behavioral Research, 24,* 285–305.

Kim, K. H., & Bentler, P. M. (2006). Data modeling: Structural equation modeling. In J. L. Green, G. Camilli, P. B. Elmore, A. Skukauskaite, & E. Grace (Eds.), *Handbook of complementary methods in education research* (pp. 161–175). Mahwah, NJ: Erlbaum.

Klein, A. G., & Muthén, B. O. (2007). Quasi-maximum likelihood estimation of structural equation models with multiple interaction and quadratic effects. *Multivariate Behavioral Research. 42*, 647–673.

Krosnick, J. A., & Judd, C. M. (1982). Transitions in social influence at adolescence: Who induces cigarette smoking. *Developmental Psychology, 18*, 359–368.

Lee, S. Y. (Ed.). (2007). *Handbook of latent variable and related models*. Amsterdam: North-Holland.

Lewis, S. H., & Trickett, E. J. (1974). Correlates of differing patterns of drug use in a high school population. *American Journal of Community Psychology, 2*, 337–350.

Little, T. D., Schnabel, K. U., & Baumert, J. (Eds.). (2000). *Modeling longitudinal and multilevel data: Practical issues, applied approaches, and specific examples.* Mahwah, NJ: Erlbaum.

MacKinnon, D. P. (2000). Contrasts in multiple mediator models. In J. S. Rose (Ed.), *Multivariate applications in substance use research: New methods for new questions* (pp. 141–161). Mahwah, NJ: Erlbaum.

MacKinnon, D. P. (2008). *Introduction to statistical mediation analysis*. Mahwah, NJ: Erlbaum.

McAlister, A. L., Krosnick, J. A., & Milburn, M. A. (1984). Causes of adolescent cigarette smoking: Tests of a structural equation model. *Social Psychology Quarterly, 47*, 24–36.

McAree, C. P., Steffenhagen, R. A., & Zheutlin, L. S. (1969). Personality factors in college drug users. *International Journal of Social Psychiatry, 15*, 102.

McDonald, R. P. (1989). An index of goodness-of-fit based on noncentrality. *Journal of Classification, 6*, 97–103.

Milton, E. O. (1944). A study of 363 cases of institutional behavior problems in a drug addict population. *Journal of General Psychiatry, 31*, 15–22.

Mooijaart, A. (in press). Random polynomial and interaction latent variable models. *Proceedings of the International Meeting of the Psychometric Society, Tokyo, July 2007*.

Muthén, B. (2001a). Latent variable mixture modeling. In G. A. Marcoulides & R. E. Schumacker (Eds.), *New developments and techniques in structural equation modeling* (pp. 1–34). Mahwah, NJ: Erlbaum.

Muthén, B. (2001b). Second-generation structural equation modeling with a combination of categorical and continuous latent variables. In L. M. Collins & A. G. Sayer (Eds.), *New methods for the analysis of change* (pp. 291–322). Washington, DC: American Psychological Association.

Newcomb, M. D. (1994). Drug use and intimate relationships among women and men: Separating specific from general effects in prospective data using structural equation models. *Journal of Consulting and Clinical Psychology, 62*, 463–476.

Newcomb, M. D., Scheier, L. M., & Bentler, P. M. (1993). Effects of adolescent drug use on adult mental health: A prospective study of a community sample. *Experimental and Clinical Psychopharmacology, 1*, 215–241.

Olson, R. W. (1964). MMPI sex differences in narcotic addicts. *Journal of Genetic Psychology, 71*, 257–266.

Orlando, M., Ellickson, P. L., McCaffrey, D. F., & Longshore, D. L. (2005). Mediation analysis of a school-based drug prevention program: Effects of project ALERT. *Prevention Science, 6*, 35–46.

Perez, R., Padilla, A. M., Ramirez, A., Ramirez, R., & Rodriguez, M. (1980). Correlates and changes over time in drug and alcohol use within a barrio population. *American Journal of Community Psychology, 8*, 621–636.

Pilgrim, C. C., Schulenberg, J. E., O'Malley, P. M., Bachman, J. G., & Johnston, L. D. (2006). Mediators and moderators of parental involvement on substance use: A national study of adolescents. *Prevention Science, 7*, 75–89.

Pomazal, R. J., & Brown, J. D. (1977). Understanding drug use motivation: A new look at a current problem. *Journal of Health and Social Behavior, 18*, 212–222.

Rabe-Hesketh, S., & Skrondal, A. (2007). Multilevel and latent variable modeling with composite links and exploded likelihoods. *Psychometrika, 72*, 123–140.

Satorra, A., & Bentler, P. M. (1988). Scaling corrections for chi-square statistics in covariance structure analysis. *Proceedings of the Business and Economic Statistics Section of the American Statistical Association, 36*, 308–313.

Satorra, A., & Bentler, P. M. (1994). Corrections to test statistics and standard errors in covariance structure analysis. In A. von Eye & C. C. Clogg (Eds.), *Latent variables analysis: Applications for developmental research* (pp. 399–419). Thousand Oaks, CA: Sage.

Scheier, L. M., Botvin, G. J., & Griffin, K. W. (2001). Preventive intervention effects on developmental progression in drug use: Structural equation modeling analyses using longitudinal data. *Prevention Science, 2*, 91–112.

Shadish, W. R., Cook, T. D., & Campbell, D. T. (2002). *Experimental and quasi-experimental designs for generalized causal inference*. Boston: Houghton Mifflin.

Skrondal, A., & Rabe-Hesketh, S. (2004). *Generalized latent variable modeling: Multilevel, longitudinal, and structural equation models*. Boca Raton, FL: Chapman & Hall.

Smith, G. M., & Fogg, C. P. (1974). Teenage drug use: A search for causes and consequences. *Personality and Social Psychology Bulletin, 1*, 426–429.

Sörbom, D. (1989). Model modification. *Psychometrika, 54,* 371–384.

Spoth, R. L., & Redmond, C. (2002). Project Family prevention trials based in community-university partnerships: Toward scaled-up preventive interventions. *Prevention Science, 3,* 203–221.

Steiger, J. H. (1998). A note on multiple sample extensions of the RMSEA fit index. *Structural Equation Modeling, 5,* 411–419.

Stein, J. A., Newcomb, M. D., & Bentler, P. M. (1987). An 8-year study of multiple influences on drug use and drug use consequences. *Journal of Personality and Social Psychology, 53,* 1094–1105.

Taylor, A. B., MacKinnon, D. P., & Tein, J. Y. (2007). Tests of the three-path mediated effect. *Organizational Research Methods,* 1–29.

Taylor, J. R., & Jentsch, J. D. (2001). Repeated intermittent administration of psychomotor stimulant drugs alters the acquisition of Pavlovian approach behavior in rats: Differential effects of cocaine, d-amphetamine and 3, 4-methylenedioxymethamphetamine ("ecstasy"). *Biological Psychiatry, 50,* 137–143.

Thomas, C. W., Petersen, D. M., & Zingraff, M. T. (1975). Student drug use: A re-examination of the "hang-loose ethic" hypothesis. *Journal of Health and Social Behavior, 16,* 63–73.

Vanderschuren, L. J. M. J., & Everitt, B. J. (2004, August 12). Drug seeking becomes compulsive after prolonged cocaine self-administration. *Science, 305,* 1017–1019.

Wright, S. (1921). Correlation and causation. *Journal of Agricultural Research, 10,* 557–585.

Wright, S. (1934). The method of path coefficients. *Annals of Mathematical Statistics, 5,* 161–215.

Yuan, K.-H., & Bentler, P. M. (2007). Structural equation modeling. In C. R. Rao & S. Sinharay (Eds.), *Handbook of statistics, 26: Psychometrics* (pp. 297–358). Amsterdam: North-Holland.

Yuan, K.-H., Hayashi, K., & Bentler, P. M. (2007). Normal theory likelihood ratio statistic for mean and covariance structure analysis under alternative hypotheses. *Journal of Multivariate Analysis, 98,* 1262–1282.

Zucker, R. A., & Gomberg, E. S. L. (1986). Etiology of alcoholism reconsidered: The case for a biopsychosocial process. *American Psychologist, 41,* 783–793.

PART IX

FACTORS INVOLVED IN CESSATION

CHAPTER 30

MATURING OUT OF SUBSTANCE USE: THE OTHER SIDE OF ETIOLOGY

Kimberly A. Jochman and Kim Fromme

It is well established that heavy drinking and illicit drug use typically reach their peak between 20 and 25 years of age. Epidemiological evidence from both cross-sectional studies (Cosper & Mozersky, 1968; Substance Abuse and Mental Health Services Administration [SAMHSA], 2005; Vogel-Sprott, 1974; Wechsler, Demone, & Gottlieb, 1978) and longitudinal studies (Fillmore, 1974, 1975; Bachman et al., 2002; Jackson, Sher, Gotham, & Wood, 2001; Labouvie, 1996; Pape & Hammer, 1996; Schulenberg, O'Malley, Bachman, Wadsworth, & Johnston, 1996; Temple & Fillmore, 1985–1986) then supports a noticeable decline in consumption patterns. In contrast, the evidence for cigarette smoking is mixed, with some research finding a peak in smoking in the years following high school, followed by a decline, at least for women (Bachman, Wadsworth, O'Malley, Johnston, & Schulenberg, 1997; Office of Applied Studies, SAMHSA, 1995). Other studies have found that smoking is one of the most stable forms of drug use (Chassin, Presson, Rose, & Sherman, 1996; K. Chen & Kandell, 1995), with few regular smokers quitting successfully (Rose, Chassin, Presson & Sherman, 1996).

Although maturing out of substance use is the norm, a number of individuals will maintain or increase use throughout their adult years. For alcohol use, cross-sectional data indicate that the rates of binge drinking and heavy drinking (binge drinking five or more times in the past 30 days) peak at age 21 and decrease throughout the life span, yet 42% of 24-year-olds, 35% of 26- to 29-year-olds, and 31% of 30- to 34-year-olds still report binge drinking at least once per week, and 14%, 11%, and 9% of participants

in these respective age ranges still report heavy drinking (SAMHSA, 2005). National panel data from the Monitoring the Future study have also shown that nearly 13% of men and 7% of women 35 years of age reported marijuana use in the past month (Merline, O'Malley, Schulenberg, Bachman, & Johnston, 2004). Likewise in this same sample, 6% of men and 3% of women reported using cocaine in the past year. Rates of drug use in the 2006 National Household Survey of Drug Abuse similarly indicated that a substantial percentage of adults ages 30 to 34 continue to smoke cigarettes (36.3% reported past-year use; 32.0% reported past-month use) and marijuana (11.7% reported past-year use; 7.0% reported past-month use; SAMHSA, 2006). Thus, despite the overall decline in substance use with increasing age, a substantial proportion of adults in the United States continue to use illicit drugs, smoke cigarettes, and abuse alcohol.

PROBLEMS ASSOCIATED WITH PERSISTENCE OF SUBSTANCE USE

Although a number of recent studies have suggested that light to moderate levels of drinking throughout the life span have beneficial effects on cardiovascular health (Fuchs et al., 2004; Gronbaek et al., 2000; Marmot, 1984; Moore & Pearson, 1986; Mukamal et al., 2006; but see Naimi, Brown, Brewer, Giles, Mensah, & Serdula, 2005; Shaper, 1990; and Smothers & Bertolucci, 2001, for criticisms of these studies), there is overwhelming evidence that persistence of heavy drinking is associated with a number of negative outcomes. A range of psychological consequences, including poor overall psychological adjustment, unipolar depression, and anxiety disorders, are linked to sustained high levels of alcohol use in young adulthood (Allan, 1995; Perreira & Sloan, 2002; Rehm et al., 2003; Tubman, Vicary, von Eye, & Lerner, 1990). Impaired cognitive functioning, including poor abstraction abilities, attentional capacities, memory, and visual–spatial construction, has also been found in adults who continue to drink heavily (Parker, Parker, Brody, & Schoenberg, 1983; Perreira & Sloan, 2002; Sorrell, Zolnikov, Sharma, & Jinnai, 2006). Furthermore, long-term, heavy consumption of alcohol is associated with a number of medical problems, including predisposition to stroke (Gill et al., 1991; Rehm et al., 2003), various types of cancer (Gutjahr, Gmel, & Rehm, 2001; Rehm et al., 2003), hypertension (Gutjahr et al., 2001; Rehm et al., 2003), cirrhosis and pancreatitis (Gutjahr et al., 2001; Rehm et al., 2003), and liver disease (Blane, 1979).

Similarly, long-term illicit drug use leads to a wide range of problems. For example, long-term cannabis use is associated with amotivational syndrome (Institute of Medicine, 1982; National Institute on Drug Abuse, 1980), depression, and anxiety (Patton et al., 2002; Zammitt, Allebeck, Andreasson, Lundberg, & Lewis, 2002). Chronic, regular use of Ecstasy (methylenedioxymethamphetamine) is associated with a range of neuropsychological problems, including increased behavioral impulsivity and impaired working memory and verbal recall (Morgan, McFie, Fleetwood, & Robinson, 2002). Furthermore, there is an association between stimulant use and diminished overall health throughout the life span, particularly with the use of crack cocaine and combined use of crack cocaine, powder cocaine, and methamphetamine (Falck, Wang, Siegal, & Carlson, 2000; Garrity et al., 2007).

The potential for long-term consequences underscores the need to identify factors that predict those individuals who will or will not mature out of substance use. Because more than 2 decades of research have indicated that the late teens and early 20s are key times when substance use patterns peak, persist, or cease (K. Chen & Kandel, 1995; Johnston, O'Malley, Bachman, & Schulenberg, 2007; Kandel & Logan, 1984), we focus on this developmental period. Termed *emerging adulthood* (Arnett, 2000), this period is also a time of abundant social role transi-

tions that may influence substance use. These social role changes are discussed within the framework of role incompatibility theory (Yamaguchi, 1990) and their impact on maturing out of substance use. We then examine the mediating and moderating influences that peer behavior, demographic factors, and psychological factors have on substance use during these social role changes. Because the majority of the recent literature has focused on maturing out of heavy drinking patterns, our review focuses primarily on alcohol use, but we also include information about the influence of social role changes on other substance use as the existing literature permits.

EMERGING ADULTHOOD AS A CRITICAL TIME FOR CHANGES IN SUBSTANCE USE

Emerging adulthood, which lasts roughly from age 18 to age 25, is a time of increased autonomy relative to adolescence but a freedom from the social roles and responsibilities of adulthood (Arnett, 2000). Perhaps as a consequence, this period coincides with the time that substance use typically peaks and then declines. One of the key features of emerging adulthood is identity exploration, or a time when emerging adults are free to explore a variety of romantic partners, seek new occupations, and develop a view of the world without the constraints that are typically imposed by adult responsibilities (Arnett, 2004). The psychosocial moratorium granted to emerging adults provides certain latitudes and gives them leeway to sample a range of new experiences, including substance use. As emerging adults progress through their 20s, a number of social role changes are possible, including but not limited to marriage, parenthood, and full-time employment. Thus, emerging adults must transition, for example, from being full-time students to employees, from being single to being married, and/or from being responsible for only themselves to being responsible for a family. The abundance of social role changes during this period has implications for changes in substance use that are discussed below.

ROLE INCOMPATIBILITY THEORY

One possible framework for interpreting the impact that social role changes may have on substance use is role incompatibility theory. Kandel and Yamaguchi (Yamaguchi, 1990; Yamaguchi & Kandel, 1985) suggested that individuals strive to minimize incompatibilities between their social roles and their behavior. These authors asserted that maintaining compatibility between social roles and behaviors reduces possible stresses associated with specific role transitions. Consider incompatibilities that may arise between someone who uses marijuana and is preparing for an important milestone such as marriage. Spending the money to purchase and the time to use marijuana diminishes the probability that the time and monetary resources associated with maintaining and supporting a marriage will be fulfilled, thereby increasing the chances that the marriage will dissolve. Yamaguchi and Kandel (1985) reported that marijuana use delays the onset of marriage, supporting the idea that postponement of marriage prevents role incompatibilities and may increase the chances of marital success. The possibility that marijuana use leads to amotivational syndrome (Institute of Medicine, 1982; National Institute on Drug Abuse, 1980), which might also delay commitment to conventional institutions like marriage.

Yamaguchi and Kandel (1985) also suggested that individuals strive to minimize role incompatibilities via two processes. The first is role selection, in which roles that are compatible with a set of behaviors are chosen so that behavioral change can be minimal. For example, the responsibilities associated with a 9-to-5 job may not allow for late-night binge drinking and sleeping off a hangover the next day. A person who wants to maintain this type of lifestyle may select part-time employment or a job with more flexible hours. The second process identified by Yamaguchi and Kandel is role socialization, in which one's behavior is brought into line with the demands of the new social role (Yamaguchi, 1990). For instance, the binge-drinking individual described above may be forced, because of limited employment opportunities and monetary needs, to take or keep a 9-to-5 job. Through role socialization, binge drinking might necessarily be limited to the weekends or the individual may eventually stop drinking altogether. It is likely that the processes of role selection and role socialization operate in tandem rather than in isolation. For example, marriage is associated with lower mari-

juana use both because marijuana use leads to postponement of marriage (role selection) and because marriage increases the propensity to stop marijuana use (role socialization; Yamaguchi & Kandel, 1985).

Labouvie's (1996) work on maturing out has also suggested two mechanisms through which social role changes may influence substance use. Selection of certain environmental settings and peer groups may support or antagonize substance use. In addition, through a process of self-appraisal, an individual might determine that substance use impedes his or her overall life goals and therefore make self-corrections by changing his or her use. On the basis of longitudinal data from the Rutgers Health and Human Development project, Labouvie studied two birth cohorts who were initially tested at ages 15 or 18 and were followed up over a 13-year period. Findings emphasized the tendency to mature out of substance use over time and also supported both selection and self-correction as the mechanisms by which changes in substance use occur.

Taken within the context of role incompatibility theory, it is likely that the social role changes that occur during emerging adulthood will be chosen to correspond with current substance practices (role selection) or will stimulate change in substance use patterns (role socialization), or a combination of the two processes may occur. In the following sections, we discuss findings regarding the effects of marriage, pregnancy, parenthood, and full-time employment on substance use, with special attention paid to processes of role selection, role socialization, and self-correction.

SOCIAL ROLE CHANGES AND SUBSTANCE USE

Marriage

Transitioning from the role of boyfriend or girlfriend to the role of spouse involves increased responsibilities associated with maintaining a relationship and managing a household. Role incompatibility theory therefore predicts that marriage, because of its increased demands and responsibilities, will be associated with a decrease in substance use. In support of this notion, marriage is the most consistently reported factor associated with age-related declines in heavy drinking patterns and illicit drug use (Arnett, 1998; Leonard & Rothbard, 1999; Schulenberg et al., 2005). Entering into marriage is associated with a decrease in heavy drinking, alcohol-related problems, and alcohol use disorders, whereas divorce reverses these changes (Bachman et al., 1997, 2002; Gotham, Sher, & Wood, 2003; Karlamangla, Zhou, Reuben, Greendale, & Moore, 2006; Miller-Tutzauer, Leonard, & Windle, 1991; Schulenberg, O'Malley, et al., 1996). Likewise, marriage is associated with decreases in marijuana, cocaine, and cigarette use (Bachman et al., 1997; Burton, Johnson, Ritter, & Clayton, 1996), a phenomenon termed *the marriage effect*. One study, however, has suggested that the marriage effect on marijuana use is unidirectional, with the wife's use having greater influence on the husband's use (Leonard & Homish, 2005). Husbands are more likely to begin using marijuana if their wives use, but to stop using marijuana if their wives do not. Whereas the marriage effect is rather robust, it is also important to remember that individuals who remain single also mature out of substance use. Marriage simply appears to accelerate the downturn in consumption (Curran, Muthén, & Harford, 1998; Labouvie, 1996).

The timing of marriage is an important factor predicting whether marriage will have a protective effect on drinking. For example, developmentally persistent problem drinkers are less likely to be married than youth-limited problem drinkers or stable low drinkers, but only in the cohort spanning ages 21 to 28 (Bennett, McCrady, Johnson, & Pandina, 1999). The same study showed that marriage is not predictive of heavy drinking patterns in older and younger cohorts. Labouvie (1996) also reported that marriage before the age of 25 is not associated with a decrease in substance use. This age-related effect of marriage is not explained by the length of marriage because those who married in their late 20s show a more immediate decrease in substance use. The timing of marriage may also be an important moderator of the marriage effect on cocaine use because early or late entry into marriage nullifies the effect of marriage on cocaine use (Burton et al., 1996). This compilation of findings suggests there may be a critical period during which the marriage effect on drug use is most likely to occur.

A number of studies have suggested that marriage may not affect drinking in the most alcohol-involved individuals. For example, among both problem drinkers and alcohol-dependent men, marriage is not the most salient factor for predicting changes in drinking levels. Rather, individual predisposing characteristics such as age, income, and education; social predisposing characteristics such as the extensive nature of the heavy alcohol- and drug-using social network and having a family member with an alcohol problem; and problem severity indicators such as age of initiation of regular alcohol use, number of alcohol dependence symptoms, and drug severity are more important than marital status in predicting drinking levels over the subsequent 5 years (Matzger, Delucchi, Weisner, & Ammon, 2004). Additionally, people with alcoholism are more likely to be married to other people with alcoholism than would be expected by chance (Hall, Hesselbrock, & Stabenau, 1983a, 1983b; Jacob & Bremer, 1986), and they are more likely to return to drinking if their spouse is a drinker (Moos, Finney, & Cronkite, 1990). These findings suggest that the marriage effect only holds if the selected mate is not a heavy drinker.

According to role incompatibility theory, the association between marriage and substance use may occur either because individuals have elected not to marry so that they can continue their current substance use patterns or because they decrease their substance use to meet the new demands of marriage. The evidence supporting the position that people with different drinking patterns differentially select into marriage is equivocal (for a review, see Leonard & Rothbard, 1999). Conversely, a variety of longitudinal studies have supported a role socialization effect around the time of marriage (Bachman et al., 1997; Chilcoat & Breslau, 1996; Horwitz, White, & Howell-White, 1996; Miller-Tutzauer et al., 1991). This socialization effect may be especially strong in women, as Leonard and Eiden (1999; Leonard & Mudar, 2003) reported that husbands' drinking at the time of marriage predicted wives' drinking 1 year after marriage but not vice versa.

Although the evidence for a selection effect for entering into marriage is unclear, there is stronger evidence that divorced individuals drink and use drugs and cigarettes more than do married people because their drug use has selected them out of marriage (Bachman et al., 1997, 2002). Heavy alcohol use is a known source of marital conflict that can lead to marital distress and dissolution (Moos et al., 1990; Roberts & Leonard, 1998). There is, however, also evidence in support of a socialization effect of divorce (Bachman et al., 1997; Chilcoat & Breslau, 1996; Horwitz et al., 1996; Temple et al., 1991). Specifically, the stress that accompanies divorce, the diminution of family responsibilities (depending on the presence of children and the gender of the individual), and the restructured social network and patterns of socializing contribute to the increases in substance use following the dissolution of a marriage.

Pregnancy and Parenthood

Transitioning into the role of parent brings with it the enormous new responsibilities associated with caring for a child. A hazardous lifestyle brought about by substance use is in many ways incompatible with the demands of parenting. Indeed, pregnancy is associated with decreased substance use, including alcohol, cigarettes, marijuana, and cocaine (Bachman et al., 1997). Because pregnancy is so closely tied to marriage in the majority of cases, however, these effects are generally better explained by the marriage effect, especially for men. For example, pregnant women show decreased substance use above and beyond decreases associated with marriage, whereas men's substance use is not altered by their wives' pregnancies (Bachman et al., 1997).

Parenthood is also associated with decreased alcohol use, binge drinking, marijuana use, and cocaine use, but these decreases are better explained by the marriage effect for both married men and women (Arnett, 1998; Bachman et al., 1997; Burton et al., 1996; Gotham, Sher, & Wood, 1997). In the case of unmarried parents, mothers decrease their alcohol consumption, whereas fathers do not (Bachman et al., 1997). This is likely related to which parent has custody because custodial parents decrease their alcohol, marijuana, and cocaine use; conversely, noncustodial parents do not, regardless of the sex of the parent (Merline et al., 2004). As role incompatibility theory would suggest, it appears that the responsibilities associated with parenthood rather than parenthood

per se are responsible for the observed decrease in substance use. It should also be noted that even among custodial parents, 29% of fathers whose children lived with them drank heavily in the past 2 weeks, and 1 in 10 men with at least one child living with them reported marijuana use in the past month (Merline et al., 2004). Interestingly, there has been no decrease observed in the abuse of prescription pills in custodial or noncustodial parents (Merline et al., 2004), suggesting that those individuals abusing prescription pills cannot or will not change their behavior to conform to the demands of the role of parenthood.

Employment

Whereas role incompatibility theory suggests that the responsibilities of full-time employment are incompatible with heavy substance use, in fact the relation between full-time employment and substance use is not clear. Some studies have shown that full-time employment decreases alcohol use (Gotham et al., 1997), whereas other studies have found that it increases alcohol use (Temple et al., 1991). Still other studies have found no association between full-time employment and alcohol use (Bachman, O'Malley, & Johnston, 1984; Gotham et al., 2003). Full-time employment after high school is associated with a reduction in the use of some drugs, including marijuana, but an increase in daily smoking (Bachman et al., 1997). As a form of employment, military service is associated with the most distinct changes in substance use, with earlier studies showing higher use among those in the military than among civilians (Segal, 1977; Robins, 1974). More recent studies, however, have suggested that those who join the military have lower drug use but higher use of alcohol and cigarettes than those not in the military (Bray, Marsden, & Peterson, 1991; Kroutil, Bray, & Marsden, 1994).

Although evidence for the effect of employment on substance use is mixed, it appears that social role incompatibility may be important for the most alcohol-involved individuals. Specifically, it appears that people with alcoholism select out of certain employment opportunities rather than change their drinking behavior in accordance with new responsibilities, especially within a certain age range. For example, alcohol dependence in college, but not alcohol abuse or heavy drinking, predicts occupational attainment early after college (Wood, Sher, & McGowan, 2000). This effect appears to be moderated by age because Mullahy and Sindelar (1993) indicated that alcoholism has negative effects on occupational achievement in middle-age men (ages 30–44), but not in younger men (ages 22–29) or older men (ages 60–64).

The relation between unemployment and substance use is similarly not clear, with some studies finding that unemployment decreases use, possibly because of a lack of financial resources (Temple et al., 1991), and others finding that unemployment increases use (Power & Estaugh, 1990). It is possible that this effect is moderated by gender and age, which could account for the discrepant findings. More detail on the conditioned nature of these relations is provided in the Demographic Factors section below.

Social Networks and Changes in Substance Use

Changes in social roles during emerging adulthood inevitably lead to changes in social networks. For example, marriage may lead to an increase in married friends; similarly, friendships with new coworkers are established with commencement of full-time employment. Changes in social networks may have direct or mediated effects on substance use cessation. Whereas the majority of studies that examine social influences on alcohol use have focused on adolescents (see chaps. 20 and 21, this volume), a growing number of studies have suggested that peer influences are related to concurrent drinking throughout the life span. For example, Schulenberg, O'Malley, et al. (1996) reported that time spent with heavy-drinking peers is positively correlated with the frequency of concurrent binge drinking between the ages of 18 and 24. In this same sample, individuals who decreased their marijuana use reported having fewer friends who used marijuana (Schulenberg et al., 2005). Lending further support to the importance of current social networks, student members of Greek organizations drank more than nonfraternity members during college, but these effects were short lived (Sher, Bartholow, & Nanda, 2001). Three years postgraduation there was no difference in drinking behaviors between those who were Greeks and those

who were not, suggesting that alcohol use changes as peer networks change. For cigarettes, social networks appear to be more important determinants of smoking cessation than social role changes or a variety of psychological factors (P.-H. Chen, White, & Pandina, 2001).

Changes in social networks may also mediate the effects of social role changes on substance use, especially in terms of the marriage effect. For example, the marriage-induced decreases in heavy drinking, monthly alcohol use, marijuana use, and cocaine use are mediated by the associated decreases in the number of evenings out following marriage (Bachman et al., 2002). Additionally, marriage is associated with an increase in married friends, a decrease in substance-using friends, and a decrease in the amount of friends characterized as "drinking buddies," in addition to an increased interdependence of spouses' social networks (Kearns & Leonard, 2004; Labouvie, 1996; Leonard & Mudar, 2003). Although it may appear that marriage-related shifts in favor of married, non–substance-using peers partially mediate the effects of marriage on substance use, one study found no relation between peer drinking and couple members' drinking in a married sample (Leonard & Mudar, 2003). Thus, there is mixed support for the idea that social group mediates the marriage effect, but the topic warrants further investigation.

Demographic Factors

Several demographic factors traditionally associated with substance use may moderate the effect of social role changes on substance use. Gender and race and ethnicity are consistently associated with different patterns of substance use. Notwithstanding, evidence for the influence of gender and race and ethnicity on the process of maturing out of substance use is almost exclusively focused on alcohol. Data from studies over the past decade have indicated that both high school and college men consistently drink at higher levels than their female counterparts (SAMHSA, 2006; Schulenberg, Wadsworth, O'Malley, Bachman, & Johnston, 1996), but gender differences are smaller for marijuana use (37% men; 31% women) or other illicit drug use (22% men; 19% women; e.g., Johnston, O'Malley, Bachman, & Schulenberg, 2005). Caucasians consistently drink more alcohol and, with one exception (i.e., crack, ice, and heroin use by Hispanic and Latino youth), use drugs at higher levels than African American and Hispanic individuals (Johnston et al., 2005). By the time they reach their mid-30s, African Americans show lower rates of heavy drinking and marijuana use than Caucasians, but there are no ethnic differences in reported use of cigarettes or cocaine (Merline et al., 2004).

Gender. Even though epidemiological studies of adolescents have suggested a narrowing of the gender gap in recent years (Corbin, Vaughan, & Fromme, 2008; Johnston, O'Malley, Bachman, & Schulenberg, 2006; Wallace et al., 2003), gender has still been a reliable predictor of heavy drinking patterns for most age groups. Men are consistently more likely than women to both initiate and sustain problematic heavy drinking patterns (Bennett et al., 1999; Johnston et al., 2007; SAMHSA, 2006; Schulenberg, O'Malley, et al., 1996) as well as marijuana and cocaine use (Merline et al., 2004), but gender differences are not as apparent for cigarette smoking (Merline et al., 2004). A number of studies have suggested that the observed gender differences are because of differences both in initial rates of use and in maturing out of substance use. For example, the male-to-female ratio for prevalence rates of heavy drinking is lower for emerging adults ages 18 to 25 (approximately 2:1) than it is for adults age 26 and older (approximately 4:1; SAMHSA, 2006). This increase in the male-to-female ratio may be because of an increased likelihood for women to mature out of substance use during emerging adulthood. For example, Jackson et al. (2001) revealed that women are more likely to transition out of large-effect drinking between the ages of 18 and 24. Similarly, in two different articles, Schulenberg, O'Malley, et al. (1996) and Schulenberg, Wadsworth, et al. (1996) showed that among frequent binge drinkers at age 18, women are more likely to decrease their drinking between ages 18 and 24, whereas men are more likely to continue frequent binge drinking. Taken together, these studies suggest that gender differences in maturing out of heavy substance use occur throughout emerging adulthood. Two studies, however, found no differences in the changes in drinking over

time between men and women (Johnstone, Leino, Ager, Ferrer, & Fillmore, 1996; Moore et al., 2005). It is notable that both of these latter studies covered a substantially larger age range than did the studies in support of gender-related differences in drinking trajectories, with Moore et al.'s (2005) participants being ages 25 to 74 at baseline and Johnstone et al.'s (1996) meta-analysis including studies with participants as young as 9 and older than 70. It is therefore possible that emerging adulthood is a particularly sensitive time period for the manifestation of gender effects on maturing out of heavy substance use.

Nolen-Hoeksema and Hilt (2006) invoked both biological and psychosocial explanations to account for the observed gender differences in maturing out of problematic patterns of alcohol use. Among the biological explanations, women may have less of a genetic risk for alcohol use than men. Additionally, women may be more susceptible to the negative physiological effects of chronic heavy alcohol use, such as brain damage, cessation of or irregular menstruation, and sexual dysfunction. In terms of psychosocial explanations, women may anticipate or perceive greater social sanctions against drinking. Additionally, men report more positive alcohol expectancies, whereas women report more negative expectancies (see chap. 8, this volume), and men are more impulsive and display less behavioral control than do women (see chap. 7, this volume).

Another possible explanation for the observed gender differences in maturing out of heavy drinking is that changes in social roles may differentially influence men and women. For example, whereas the majority of studies have shown decreased drinking following marriage for men and women, a few studies have found a decrease in drinking and in alcohol-related problems for women only (Horwitz et al., 1996; Leonard & Mudar, 2003). Additionally, although heavy drinking decreases in both sexes following marriage, general alcohol use decreases with marriage only for women (Bachman et al., 1997). Several explanations could account for these noted differences. On the one hand, it is possible that men are less concerned about role incompatibility within the domain of marriage; on the other hand, it is possible that they perceive less incompatibility between drinking and the responsibilities associated with marriage.

There are other ways to augur support for differential effects of social role changes on men's and women's substance use. For instance, Power and Estaugh's (1990) finding that unemployment increases consumption was largely driven by the men in their sample. Thus, women may not respond to the problems associated with job loss by drinking excessively, as men do. In a slightly different take on this issue, Gotham et al. (1997) reported that the decrease in alcohol use following full-time employment is more pronounced in men than in women. Taken together, these two studies suggest that men's drinking is more susceptible than women's to the effects of employment. It is possible that opposite to the marriage effect, men are either more concerned with role incompatibility in the domain of employment or they perceive greater incompatibility between drinking and the responsibilities associated with their position in the workforce.

Race. The association between race and the maintenance of heavy drinking is less clear than the association between gender and heavy drinking (see chaps. 15–18, this volume, for a complete review of race and ethnicity and substance use etiology). Whereas some studies have suggested that Whites are more likely than racial minorities to mature out of heavy alcohol use, others have suggested an opposite pattern. For example, White men (age 18 and older) are more likely to decrease heavy drinking than are Black and Hispanic men (Caetano & Kaskutas, 1995), and Caetano (1991) reported higher rates of frequent heavy drinking in Black and Hispanic men than in White men in middle age. Conversely, one study found that White men are more likely than non-White men to sustain frequent binge-drinking patterns between the ages of 18 and 24 (Schulenberg, O'Malley, et al., 1996). Additionally, three large-scale epidemiological studies found lower prevalence rates of substance use disorders in Blacks than in Whites in participants age 15 and older (Kip, Peters, & Morrison-Rodriguez, 2002). A number of factors may account for these discrepant findings. A reporting bias view suggests that Blacks may be more likely to underreport substance use disorders compared with Whites because of greater fear of consequences

and possible discomfort with White interviewers (Kip et al., 2002). However, a susceptibility view suggests that Blacks may be more vulnerable to alcohol-related problems even when the frequency of heavy drinking does not differ between the three groups. For instance, Muthén and Muthén (2000) reported that Blacks transition from having the lowest levels of alcohol-related problems at age 25 to the highest levels at age 37, but that they drink heavily with similar frequency to Whites and Hispanics.

Race, like gender, may moderate the effects of social role changes on substance use. In particular, it appears that the protective effect of marriage is more pronounced in Whites than in Blacks. For example, whereas the protective effect of marriage is found for both Blacks and Whites, the effect is significantly stronger in Whites (Curran et al., 1998). Mudar, Kearns, and Leonard (2002) reported a decrease in heavy drinking and alcohol dependence throughout the early marital years in Whites, but the same effect was not apparent in Blacks. This effect may be further moderated by gender because White men and women report fewer alcohol-related problems over the first 2 years of marriage, as do Black women; however, Black men report an increase in alcohol-related problems early in marriage (Mudar et al., 2002). Again, there may be differential sensitivity to the institution of marriage, to drinking within the context of marriage, and to drinking itself, all of which may condition these relations.

Psychological Factors

A number of psychological factors, including personality, alcohol expectancies, and drinking motives, are associated with age-related declines in substance use. To date, there is no evidence supporting or refuting possible interactions between these psychological factors and social role changes. Studies focusing on the impact of these psychological factors on maturing out of substance use are summarized below, and hypotheses regarding potential ways through which these factors may influence the effects of social role changes on substance use are discussed.

Personality Factors

A number of personality factors have been associated with substance use, but they are less well studied than influences on maturing out of substance use. Part III of this volume on cognitive and affective influences attends to a handful of personality factors linked with drug use etiology. In particular, certain aspects of behavioral undercontrol (as defined by Sher & Gotham, 1999; to include sensation seeking, aggressiveness, antisociality, hyperactivity, and impulsivity) appear to be the most reliable personality factors related to alcohol use. Several longitudinal studies have also suggested that individuals reporting high levels of behavioral undercontrol are more likely to demonstrate continued substance use throughout emerging adulthood, and perhaps into later life. For example, developmentally persistent drinkers from adolescence to young adulthood are more likely to show high levels of disinhibition compared with non–problem drinkers and youth-limited drinkers (Bennett et al., 1999). Additionally, young adults who report more sensation-seeking reasons for drinking at the beginning of college are more likely to develop an alcohol use disorder during college and to continue on a chronic course of alcohol use throughout college and after graduation (Sher & Gotham, 1999). The findings of one study suggested that relations between behavioral undercontrol and heavy drinking may be conditioned by gender. Specifically, Schulenberg, Wadsworth, et al. (1996) found that infrequent binge drinkers at age 18 are more likely to increase their frequency of binge drinking between the ages of 18 and 24 if they endorse high levels of risk taking in adolescence, but this relationship was apparent only for women.

Self-efficacy, extraversion, and negative affect are also associated with sustained patterns of heavy alcohol use throughout emerging adulthood. High levels of self-efficacy are associated with maturing out of frequent heavy alcohol use, whereas low levels of self-efficacy are associated with sustained increases in frequent heavy alcohol use between the ages of 18 and 24 (Schulenberg, Wadsworth, et al., 1996). Extraverted individuals are also more likely to sustain heavy alcohol use and experience alcohol-related problems in young adulthood (Gotham et al., 1997; Kilbey, Downey, & Breslau, 1998). Finally, lower positive affect scores in 21- to 30-year-olds predict alcohol use dependence 3.5 years later (Kilbey et al., 1998).

It is unlikely that these personality factors act in isolation to influence trajectories of substance use; however, no single study has examined the role of all four factors and their interactions with each other and with social role changes. One might speculate that individuals high in aspects of behavioral undercontrol lack the self-regulatory capacities for either social role selection or socialization. Nevertheless, it is unclear how self-efficacy, extraversion, and negative affect may interact with social role changes to influence changes in substance use. An additional challenge in studying the interaction of personality factors, social role changes, and substance use is elucidating the direction of causality. For example, if an association was identified among negative affect, marital stress, and substance use, one explanation might be that the negative affect of one partner in the marriage leads to marital stress, which in turn leads to substance use as a coping mechanism. Another possible explanation is that substance use could lead to marital stress, which in turn could lead to negative affect. Clearly, longitudinal data are necessary to fully understand the nature of the relation among personality factors, social role changes, and substance use.

Expectancies and Motives

From adolescence through emerging adulthood, developmentally persistent problem drinkers report more reasons for using alcohol than do youth-limited or non–problem drinkers (Bennett et al., 1999). In addition to the number of reasons for and expectations that arise from drinking, the nature of the reasons and expectations also appears to be an important predictor of maturing out or persistence of heavy drinking patterns. For example, coping and tension reduction motives are associated with persistent heavy drinking, particularly during the post-college years. In one study, undergraduates with primary stress-related drinking motives drank similarly to those with other primary drinking motives, whereas among postgraduates, those with primary stress-related drinking motives drank more in terms of quantity and frequency (Perkins, 1999). Throughout college and 3 years postcollege, tension reduction motives were a stronger predictor of heavy drinking in men compared with women (Rutledge & Sher, 2001), but postgraduate women reported more drinking consequences if they drank for stress-related motives (Perkins, 1999), suggesting that gender and tension reduction motives interact to influence heavy drinking and alcohol-related problems. It is possible that tension reduction motives interact with social role changes, and particularly with individuals' perceptions of social role changes, in predicting substance use. For example, individuals high in tension reduction motives may report more drinking following marriage but only if they find marriage to be stressful. Conversely, individuals better able to manage stress and therefore low in tension reduction motives may report less drinking following marriage.

Social and sexual drinking expectancies, mood enhancement, and drinking to get drunk are also associated with drinking patterns during emerging adulthood. Specifically, expectations of alcohol-induced improvements in mood and social and sexual experiences are predictive of both concurrent and future alcohol-related problems in emerging adulthood (Kilbey et al, 1998; Sher & Gotham, 1999; Stacy, Newcomb, & Bentler, 1991). Additionally, lower endorsement of drinking to get drunk predicts maturing out of frequent binge drinking in both men and women, whereas higher endorsement of drinking to get drunk predicts sustained increases in frequency of binge drinking in men only (Schulenberg, Wadsworth, et al., 1996). Again, it is possible that alcohol expectancies, particularly mood and social enhancement expectancies, may interact with individuals' perceptions of social role changes to predict alcohol use following transitions such as marriage, parenthood, and employment. See chapter 9 for a review of explicit expectancies and motives for substance use.

CONCLUSION

A synthesis of the literature reveals that social role transitions are a formidable influence on substance use, especially during emerging adulthood. Consistent with Yamaguchi and Kandel's (1985) role incompatibility theory, it appears that social role changes such as marriage, parenthood, and employment result in increased responsibilities and therefore prepare the foundation for decreased substance use. In the case of marriage, data support a role socializa-

tion effect for entering into marriage. Those who fail to adequately socialize in this new role, however, may then select out of marriage via divorce. The socialization effects of employment are unclear at this time because of a number of inconsistent findings; however, individuals characterized by heavy alcohol involvement may select out of certain occupational roles that require the most responsibilities.

A number of demographic and psychological factors are associated with maturing out of substance use. One unfortunate feature of the existing body of knowledge, however, is that these factors have been studied in a largely isolated manner. Little is therefore known about possible interactions or the ways in which they condition each other as they influence substance use. For example, one might expect an interaction between social role changes and behavioral undercontrol. In a very simple manner, behavioral undercontrol reflects a regulatory style during both social and nonsocial experiences. Given the amount of regulation (role socialization) required to adapt to the new roles and responsibilities associated with the social role changes that occur during emerging adulthood, it seems reasonable to predict that individuals showing poor control might fare poorly throughout this adjustment period and fail to control their drinking following marriage. Similarly, an interaction between drinking motives, social role changes, and perceptions of these changes might fit this predictive framework. For example, those who drink to cope may fail to gain the upper hand on their drinking or even, in some cases, drink more following a social role change, to the extent that they find this change stressful. To advance research on maturing out from a descriptive to explanatory level, future studies will need to focus on the interaction of these factors to understand why some individuals successfully mature out of, whereas others persist in, problematic substance use.

References

Allan, C. A. (1995). Alcohol problems and anxiety disorders: A critical review. *Alcohol & Alcoholism, 30,* 145–151.

Arnett, J. J. (1998). Risk behavior and family role transitions during the twenties. *Journal of Youth and Adolescence, 27,* 301–320.

Arnett, J. J. (2000). Emerging adulthood: A theory of development from the late teens through the twenties. *American Psychologist, 55,* 469–480.

Arnett, J. J. (2004). *Emerging adulthood: The winding road from the late teens through the twenties.* New York: Oxford University Press.

Bachman, J. G., O'Malley, P. M., & Johnston, L. D. (1984). Drug use among young adults: The impacts of role status and social environment. *Journal of Personality and Social Psychology, 47,* 629–645.

Bachman, J. G., O'Malley, P. M., Schulenberg, J. E., Johnston, L. D., Bryant, A. L., & Merline, A. C. (2002). *The decline of substance use in young adulthood.* Mahwah, NJ: Erlbaum.

Bachman, J. G., Wadsworth, K. N., O'Malley, P. M., Johnston, L. D., & Schulenberg, J. E. (1997). *Smoking, drinking, and drug use in young adulthood: The impacts of new freedoms and new responsibilities.* Hillsdale, NJ: Erlbaum.

Bennett, M. E., McCrady, B. S., Johnson, V., & Pandina, R. J. (1999). Problem drinking from young adulthood to adulthood: Patterns, predictors and outcomes. *Journal of Studies on Alcohol, 60,* 605–614.

Blane, H. T. (1979). Middle-aged alcoholics and young drinkers. In H. T. Blane & M. E. Chafetz (Eds.), *Youth, alcohol, and social policy* (pp. 5–38). New York: Plenum Press.

Bray, R. M., Marsden, M. E., & Peterson, M. R. (1991). Standardized comparisons of the use of alcohol, drugs, and cigarettes among military personnel and civilians. *American Journal of Public Health, 81,* 865–869.

Burton, R. P. D., Johnson, R. J., Ritter, C., & Clayton, R. R. (1996). The effects of role socialization on the initiation of cocaine use: An event history analysis from adolescence into middle adulthood. *Journal of Health and Social Behavior, 37,* 75–90.

Caetano, R. (1991). Findings from the 1984 national survey of alcohol use among U.S. Hispanics. In W. B. Clark & M. E. Hilton (Eds.), *Alcohol in America: Drinking practices and problems* (pp. 293–307). Albany, NY: SUNY Press.

Caetano, R., & Kaskutas, L.-A. (1995). Changes in drinking patterns among Whites, Blacks, and Hispanics, 1984–1992. *Journal of Studies on Alcohol, 56,* 558–565.

Chassin, L., Presson, C. C., Rose, J. S., & Sherman, S. J. (1996). The natural history of cigarette smoking from adolescence to adulthood: Demographic predictors of continuity and change. *Health Psychology, 15,* 478–484.

Chen, K., & Kandel, D. B. (1995). The natural history of drug use from adolescence to the mid-thirties in a general population sample. *American Journal of Public Health, 85,* 41–47.

Chen, P.-H., White, H. R., & Pandina, R. J. (2001). Predictors of smoking cessation from adolescence into young adulthood. *Addictive Behaviors, 26,* 517–529.

Chilcoat, H. D., & Breslau, N. (1996). Alcohol disorders in young adulthood: Effects of transitions into adult roles. *Journal of Health and Social Behavior, 37,* 339–349.

Corbin, W. R., Vaughan, E. L., & Fromme, K. (2008). Ethnic differences and the closing of the sex gap in alcohol use among college bound students. *Psychology of Addictive Behaviors, 22,* 240–248.

Cosper, R., & Mozersky, K. (1968). Social correlates of drinking and driving. *Quarterly Journal of Studies on Alcohol, 4*(Suppl.), 58–117.

Curran, P. J., Muthén, B. O., & Harford, T. C. (1998). The influence of changes in marital status on developmental trajectories of alcohol use in young adults. *Journal of Studies on Alcohol, 59,* 647–658.

Falck, R. S., Wang, J., Siegal, H. A., & Carlson, R. G. (2000). Longitudinal application of the medical outcomes study 36-item short-form health survey with not-in-treatment crack-cocaine users. *Medical Care, 38,* 902–910.

Fillmore, K. M. (1974). Drinking and problem drinking in early adulthood and middle age: An exploratory follow-up study. *Quarterly Journal of Studies on Alcohol, 35,* 819–840.

Fillmore, K. M. (1975). Relationships between specific drinking problems in early adulthood and middle age: An exploratory 20-year follow-up study. *Journal of Studies on Alcohol, 36,* 882–907.

Fuchs, F. D., Chambless, L. E., Folsom, A. R., Eigenbrodt, M. L., Duncan, B. B., Gilbert, A., et al. (2004). Association between alcoholic beverage consumption and incidence of coronary heart disease in Whites and Blacks. *American Journal of Epidemiology, 160,* 466–474.

Garrity, T. F., Leukefeld, C. G., Carlson, R. G., Falck, R. S., Wang, J., & Booth, B. M. (2007). Physical health, illicit drug use, and demographic characteristics in rural stimulant users. *Journal of Rural Health, 23,* 99–107.

Gill, J. S., Shipley, M. J., Tsementzis, S. A., Hornby, R. S., Gill, S. K., Hitchcock, E. R., et al. (1991). Alcohol consumption–A risk factor for hemorrhagic and non-hemorrhagic stroke. *American Journal of Medicine, 90,* 489–497.

Gotham, H. J., Sher, K. J., & Wood, P. K. (1997). Predicting stability and change in frequency of intoxication from the college years to beyond: Individual-difference and role transition variables. *Journal of Abnormal Psychology, 106,* 619–629.

Gotham, H. J., Sher, K. J., & Wood, P. K. (2003). Alcohol involvement and developmental task completion during young adulthood. *Journal of Studies on Alcohol, 64,* 32–42.

Gronbaek, M., Becker, U., Johansen, D., Gottschau, A., Schnohr, P., Hein, H. O., et al. (2000). Type of alcohol consumed and mortality from all causes, coronary heart disease, and cancer. *Annals of Internal Medicine, 133,* 411–419.

Gutjahr, E., Gmel, G., & Rehm, J. (2001). Relation between average alcohol consumption and disease: An overview. *European Addiction Research, 7,* 117–127.

Hall, R. L., Hesselbrock, V. M., & Stabenau, J. R. (1983a). Familial distribution of alcohol use: I. Assortative mating in the parents of alcoholics. *Behavior Genetics, 13,* 361–372.

Hall, R. L., Hesselbrock, V. M., & Stabenau, J. R. (1983b). Familial distribution of alcohol use: II. Assortative mating of alcoholic probands. *Behavior Genetics, 13,* 373–382.

Horwitz, A. V., White, H. R., & Howell-White, S. (1996). Becoming married and mental health: A longitudinal study of a cohort of young adults. *Journal of Marriage and the Family, 58,* 895–907.

Institute of Medicine. (1982). *Marijuana and health.* Washington, DC: National Academies Press.

Jackson, K. J., Sher, K. J., Gotham, H. J., & Wood, P. K. (2001). Transitioning into and out of large-effect drinking in young adulthood. *Journal of Abnormal Psychology, 110,* 378–391.

Jacob, T., & Bremer, D. A. (1986). Assortative mating among men and women alcoholics. *Journal of Studies on Alcohol, 47,* 219–222.

Johnston, L. D., O'Malley, P. M., Bachman, J. G., & Schulenberg, J. E. (2005). *Monitoring the Future national results on adolescent drug use: Overview of key findings 2004* (NIH Publication No. 05-5726) Bethesda, MD: National Institute on Drug Abuse.

Johnston, L. D., O'Malley, P. M., Bachman, J. G., & Schulenberg, J. E. (2006). *Demographic subgroup trends for various licit and illicit drugs, 1975–2005* (Monitoring the Future Occasional Paper No. 63). Ann Arbor, MI: Institute for Social Research. Retrieved December 1, 2007, from http://monitoringthefuture.org/pubs/occpapers/occ63.pdf

Johnston, L. D., O'Malley, P. M., Bachman, J. G., & Schulenberg, J. E. (2007). *Monitoring the Future national survey results on drug use, 1975–2006. Volume II: College students and adults ages 19–45* (NIH Publication No. 07-6206). Bethesda, MD: National Institute on Drug Abuse.

Johnstone, B. M., Leino, E. V., Ager, C. R., Ferrer, H., & Fillmore, K. M. (1996). Determinants of life-course variation in the frequency of alcohol consumption: Meta-analysis of studies from the collaborative alcohol-related longitudinal project. *Journal of Studies on Alcohol, 57,* 494–506.

Kandel, D. B., & Logan, J. A. (1984). Patterns of drug use from adolescence to young adulthood. I: Periods of risk for initiation, continued use, and discontinuation. *American Journal of Public Health, 74,* 660–666.

Karlamangla, A., Zhou, K., Reuben, D., Greendale, G., & Moore, A. (2006). Longitudinal trajectories of heavy drinking in adults in the United States of America. *Addiction, 101,* 91–99.

Kearns, J. N., & Leonard, K. E. (2004). Social networks, structural interdependence, and marital quality over the transition to marriage: A prospective analysis. *Journal of Family Psychology, 18,* 383–395.

Kilbey, M. M., Downey, K., & Breslau, N. (1998). Predicting the emergence and persistence of alcohol dependence among young adults: The role of expectancy and other risk factors. *Experimental and Clinical Psychopharmacology, 6,* 149–156.

Kip, K. E., Peters, R. H., & Morrison-Rodriguez, B. (2002). Commentary on why national epidemiological estimates of substance abuse by race should not be used to estimate prevalence and need for substance abuse services at community and local levels. *American Journal on Drug and Alcohol Abuse, 28,* 545–556.

Kroutil, L. A., Bray, R. M., & Marsden, M. E. (1994). Cigarette smoking in the U.S. military: Findings from the 1992 worldwide survey. *Preventive Medicine: An International Journal Devoted to Practice and Theory, 23,* 521–528.

Labouvie, E. (1996). Maturing out of substance use: Selection and self-correction. *Journal of Drug Issues, 26,* 457–476.

Leonard, K. E., & Eiden, R. D. (1999). Husband's and wife's drinking: Unilateral or bilateral influences among newlyweds in a general population sample. *Journal of Studies on Alcohol, 13*(Suppl.), 130–138.

Leonard, K. E., & Homish, G. G. (2005). Changes in marijuana use over the transition into marriage. *Journal of Drug Issues, 35,* 409–429.

Leonard, K. E., & Mudar, P. (2003). Peer and partner drinking and the transition to marriage: A longitudinal examination of selection and influence processes. *Psychology of Addictive Behaviors, 17,* 115–125.

Leonard, K. E., & Rothbard, J. C. (1999). Alcohol and the marriage effect. *Journal of Studies on Alcohol, 13*(Suppl.), 139–146.

Marmot, M. G. (1984). Alcohol and coronary heart disease. *International Journal of Epidemiology, 13,* 160–166.

Matzger, H., Delucchi, K., Weisner, C., & Ammon, L. (2004). Does marital status predict long-term drinking? Five-year observations of dependent and problem drinkers. *Journal of Studies on Alcohol, 65,* 255–265.

Merline, A. C., O'Malley, P. M., Schulenberg, J. E., Bachman, J. G., & Johnston, L. D. (2004). Substance use among adults 35 years of age: Prevalence, adulthood predictors, and impact of adolescent substance use. *American Journal of Public Health, 94,* 96–102.

Miller-Tutzauer, C., Leonard, K. E., & Windle, M. (1991). Marriage and alcohol use: A longitudinal study of "maturing out." *Journal of Studies on Alcohol, 52,* 434–440.

Moore, A. A., Gould, R., Reuben, D. B., Greendale, G. A., Carter, M. K., Zhou, K., et al. (2005). Longitudinal patterns and predictors of alcohol consumption in the United States. *American Journal of Public Health, 95,* 458–464.

Moore, R. D., & Pearson, T. (1986). Moderate alcohol consumption and coronary heart disease: A review. *Medicine, 65,* 242–267.

Moos, R. H., Finney, J. W., & Cronkite, R. C. (1990). *Alcoholism treatment: Context, process, and outcome.* New York: Oxford University Press.

Morgan, M. J., McFie, L., Fleetwood, L. H., & Robinson, J. A. (2002). Ecstasy (MDMA): Are the psychological problems associated with its use reversed by prolonged abstinence? *Psychopharmacology, 159,* 294–303.

Mudar, P., Kearns, J. N., & Leonard, K. E. (2002). The transition to marriage and changes in alcohol involvement among Black couples and White couples. *Journal of Studies on Alcohol, 63,* 568–576.

Mukamal, K. J., Chung, H., Jenny, N. S., Kuller, L. H., Longstreth, W. T., & Mittleman, M. A., et al. (2006). Alcohol consumption and risk of coronary heart disease in older adults: The cardiovascular health study. *Journal of the American Geriatrics Society, 54,* 30–37.

Mullahy, J., & Sindelar, J. L. (1993). Alcoholism, work, and income. *Journal of Labor Economics, 11,* 494–520.

Muthén, B. O., & Muthén, L. K. (2000). The development of heavy drinking and alcohol-related problems from ages 18 to 37 in a U.S. national sample. *Journal of Studies on Alcohol, 61,* 290–300.

Naimi, T. S., Brown, D. W., Brewer, R. D., Giles, W. H., Mensah, G., & Serdula, M. K. (2005). Cardiovascular risk factors and confounders among nondrinking and moderate-drinking U.S. adults. *American Journal of Preventative Medicine, 28,* 369–373.

National Institute on Drug Abuse. (1980). *Marijuana and health* (8th annual report). Washington, DC: U.S. Government Printing Office.

Nolen-Hoeksema, S., & Hilt, L. (2006). Possible contributors to the gender differences in alcohol use and problems. *Journal of General Psychology, 133,* 357–374.

Office of Applied Studies, Substance Abuse and Mental Health Services Administration. (1995). *National Household Survey on Drug Abuse: Population estimates 1994* (DHHS Publication No. SMA 95-3063). Rockville, MD: Author.

Pape, H., & Hammer, T. (1996). How does young people's alcohol consumption change during the transition to early adulthood? A longitudinal study of changes at aggregate and individual level. *Addiction, 91,* 1345–1357.

Parker, D. A., Parker, E. S., Brody, J. A., & Schoenberg, R. (1983). Alcohol use and cognitive loss among employed men and women. *American Journal of Public Health, 73,* 521–526.

Patton, G. C., Coffey, C., Carlin, J. B., Degenhardt, L., Lynskey, M., & Hall, W. (2002). Cannabis use and mental health in young people: Cohort study. *British Medical Journal, 325,* 1195–1198.

Perkins, W. H. (1999). Stress-motivated drinking in collegiate and post-collegiate young adulthood: Life course and gender patterns. *Journal of Studies on Alcohol, 60,* 219–227.

Perreira, K. M., & Sloan, F. A. (2002). Excess alcohol consumption and health outcomes: A 6-year follow-up of men over age 50 from the health and retirement study. *Addiction, 97,* 301–310.

Power, C., & Estaugh, V. (1990). Employment and drinking in early adulthood: A longitudinal perspective. *British Journal of Addiction, 85,* 487–494.

Rehm, J., Room, R., Graham, K., Monteiro, M., Gmel, G., & Sempos, C. T. (2003). The relationship of average volume of alcohol consumption and patterns of drinking to burden of disease: An overview. *Addiction, 98,* 1209–1228.

Roberts, L. J., & Leonard, K. E. (1998). An empirical typology of drinking partnerships and their relationship to marital functioning and drinking consequences. *Journal of Marriage and the Family, 60,* 515–526.

Robins, L. N. (1974). A follow-up study of Vietnam veterans' drug use. *Journal of Drug Issues, 4,* 61–63.

Rose, J. S., Chassin, L., Presson, C. C., & Sherman, S. J. (1996). Prospective predictors of quit attempts and smoking cessation in young adults. *Health Psychology, 15,* 261–268.

Rutledge, P. C., & Sher, K. J. (2001). Heavy drinking from the freshman year into early young adulthood: The roles of stress, tension-reduction drinking motives, gender, and personality. *Journal of Studies on Alcohol, 62,* 457–466.

Schulenberg, J. E., Merline, A. C., Johnston, L. D., O'Malley, P. M., Bachman, J. G., & Laetz, V. B. (2005). Trajectories of marijuana use during the transition to adulthood: The big picture based on national panel data. *Journal of Drug Issues, 35,* 255–279.

Schulenberg, J., O'Malley, P. M., Bachman, J. G., Wadsworth, K. N., & Johnston, L. D. (1996). Getting drunk and growing up: Trajectories of frequent binge drinking during the transition to young adulthood. *Journal of Studies on Alcohol, 57,* 289–304.

Schulenberg, J., Wadsworth, K. N., O'Malley, P. M., Bachman, J. G., & Johnston, L. D. (1996). Adolescent risk factors for binge drinking during the transition to young adulthood: Variable- and pattern-centered approaches to change. *Developmental Psychology, 32,* 659–674.

Segal, D. R. (1977). Illicit drug use in the U.S. Army. *Sociological Symposium, 18,* 66–83.

Shaper, A. G. (1990). Alcohol and mortality: A review of prospective studies. *British Journal of Addiction, 85,* 837–847.

Sher, K. J., Bartholow, B. D., & Nanda, S. (2001). Short- and long-term effects of fraternity and sorority membership on heavy drinking: A social norms perspective. *Psychology of Addictive Behaviors, 15,* 42–51.

Sher, K. J., & Gotham, H. J. (1999). Pathological alcohol involvement: A developmental disorder of young adulthood. *Development and Psychopathology, 11,* 933–956.

Smothers, B., & Bertolucci, D. (2001). Alcohol consumption and health-promoting behavior in a U.S. household sample: Leisure-time physical activity. *Journal of Studies on Alcohol, 62,* 467–476.

Sorrell, J. H., Zolnikov, B. J., Sharma, A., & Jinnai, I. (2006). Cognitive impairment in people diagnosed with end-stage liver disease evaluated for liver transplantation. *Psychiatry and Clinical Neurosciences, 60,* 174–181.

Stacy, A. W., Newcomb, M. D., & Bentler, P. M. (1991). Cognitive motivation and drug use: A 9-year longitudinal study. *Journal of Abnormal Psychology, 100,* 502–515.

Substance Abuse and Mental Health Services Administration. (2005). *Results from the 2005 National Survey on Drug Use and Health: National findings.* Retrieved June 20, 2007, from http://www.oas.samhsa.gov/NSDUH/2k5NSDUH/2k5results.htm#Ch3

Substance Abuse and Mental Health Services Administration. (2006). *Results from the 2006 National Survey on Drug Use and Health: National findings.* Retrieved December 29, 2007, from http://www.oas.samhsa.gov/NSDUH/2k6NSDUH/tabs/TOC.htm

Temple, M. T., & Fillmore, K. M. (1985–1986). The variability of drinking patterns and problems among young men, age 16–31: A longitudinal study. *International Journal of the Addictions, 20,* 1595–1620.

Temple, M. T., Fillmore, K. M., Hartka, E., Johnstone, B., Leino, E. V., & Motoyoshi, M. (1991). A meta-analysis of change in marital and employment status as predictors of alcohol consumption on a typical occasion. *British Journal of Addiction, 86,* 1269–1281.

Tubman, J. G., Vicary, J. R., von Eye, A., & Lerner, J. V. (1990). Longitudinal substance use and adult adjustment. *Journal of Substance Abuse, 2,* 317–334.

Vogel-Sprott, M. (1974). Defining "light" and "heavy" social drinking: Research implications and hypotheses. *Quarterly Journal of Studies on Alcohol, 35,* 1388–1392.

Wallace, J. A., Bachman, J. G., O'Malley, P. M., Schulenberg, J. E., Cooper, S. M., & Johnston, L. D. (2003). Gender and ethnic differences in smoking, drinking, and illicit drug use among American 8th, 10th, and 12th grade students, 1976–2000. *Addiction, 98,* 225–234.

Wechsler, H., Demone, H. W., & Gottlieb, N. (1978). Drinking patterns of Greater Boston adults: Subgroup differences on the QFV index. *Journal of Studies on Alcohol, 39,* 1158–1165.

Wood, M. D., Sher, K. J., & McGowan, A. K. (2000). Collegiate alcohol involvement and role attainment in early adulthood: Findings from a prospective high-risk study. *Journal of Studies on Alcohol, 61,* 278–289.

Yamaguchi, K. (1990). Drug use and its social covariates from the period of adolescence to young adulthood. In M. Galanter (Ed.), *Recent developments in alcoholism. Volume 8: Combined alcohol and other drug dependence* (pp. 125–144). New York: Plenum Press.

Yamaguchi, K., & Kandel, D. (1985). On the resolution of role incompatibility: A life event history analysis of family roles and marijuana use. *American Journal of Sociology, 90,* 1284–1325.

Zammitt, S., Allebeck, P., Andreasson, S., Lundberg, I., & Lewis, G. (2002). Self-reported cannabis use as a risk factor for schizophrenia in Swedish conscripts of 1969: Historical cohort study. *British Medical Journal, 325,* 1199–1203.

CREATING A BRIDGE BETWEEN ETIOLOGY AND PREVENTION: POLICY AND PRACTICE IMPLICATIONS

TRANSLATING RESEARCH INTO PRACTICE AND PRACTICE INTO RESEARCH FOR DRUG USE PREVENTION

Mary Ann Pentz

All of the chapters in this volume are, in some way, directed toward understanding the etiology of drug use, hence the handbook's title. However, this chapter assumes that—at least with humans and in reference to prevention of drug use rather than of drug abuse or dependence—we cannot accurately predict the etiology of drug use in the individual. At least we cannot do this yet; the advent of genome and brain mapping may change this situation in the near future. Today, however, risk factors in the arena of drug use prevention address the epidemiology of drug use in populations and subgroups of populations. It is with this understanding that I examine the translation of research into practice and vice versa, with an express emphasis on prevention.

Translating the findings of etiological and epidemiological research into widely dispersed consumer-friendly disease prevention messages has been the cornerstone of public health since the 1800s (Fielding et al., 2002). For example, decades of findings from research on risk factors for typhoid fever, diphtheria, and tooth decay have resulted in rapid translation to practice with inoculations, water quality monitoring, and the introduction of fluoride. In contrast, translating etiological and epidemiological research findings to evidence-based prevention programs has been slow getting off the starting block, particularly but not exclusively in the field of drug abuse prevention. Translating research findings on evidence-based drug abuse prevention programs to practice has been even slower.

Several factors may be responsible for this time lag in translation, for example, the relatively longer disease trajectory in drug abuse compared with the trajectory of diseases such as typhoid fever, less definitive individual versus population-based risk factors, and less constant—or politically driven—attention to the problem as a public health problem. Nevertheless, translation of drug abuse etiology, epidemiology, and prevention program research into practice is finally occurring. This emerging field of translation is centered primarily in dissemination research studies. Dissemination is covered briefly in this chapter, with a more thorough review provided by Botvin in chapter 34 of this volume. The translation of practice back into research is also emerging, but the focus at this time is dispersed across efforts representing community-based participatory research, qualitative policy research, and meta-analyses and other types of program reviews, for example, the Cochrane Library's database of reviews of prevention studies (Brown, Berndt, Brinales, Zong, & Bhagwat, 2000). Although the procedure of translation–back-translation is commonplace in other fields, including language translation and engineering, in the field of drug abuse prevention back-translation has been invoked only when a program failure has occurred (e.g., Dishion, McCord, & Poulin, 1999; Weiss et al., 2005). In this chapter, I discuss the translation of practice back into research from the point of view of these efforts and from the point of view that necessary back-translation or feedback should be required at several points in drug abuse prevention programming, not just at the point of dissemination (Ginexi & Hilton, 2006).

In the remainder of this chapter, I present a brief overview of translation in the field of drug abuse prevention. I then consider variations on translation from the perspective of drug use etiology and risk factors, reflecting the overall theme of this handbook. This section is followed by discussion of three prevention trials that represent different steps in translation (one defining translation as Type I to Type II using National Institutes of Health [NIH] terminology, a second defining Type II translation from dissemination into the beginning stages of practice, and a third defining Type II translation as translation of prevention practice from one health risk behavior to another, e.g., from drug use to obesity prevention). The chapter concludes with a proposed 10-step model through which one can categorize progressive research–practice–research translation in the field of drug abuse prevention, along with recommendations for addressing gaps in translation research, particularly that in translation from practice back to research (Green, 2001; Simpson, 2002).

OVERVIEW OF TRANSLATION

An ongoing issue in drug use research (as well as in research in other health risk areas such as obesity) has been the separation of etiological, epidemiological, and prevention research that has often impeded translation of findings from one of these domains to another. There are many reasons for this, among them the lack of a common language, widely differing theoretical models and unique methods by which to frame research, and historically separated funding streams for research in these areas (Pentz, Mares, Schinke, & Rohrbach, 2004). The wide chasm between these disciplines has slowed the development of prevention research. For example, Pentz, Jasuja, Rohrbach, Sussman, and Bardo (2006) searched for risk factors that had successfully been translated from animal etiological studies to human epidemiological studies and that eventually made their way to prevention trials. The only major risk factor that transited these disciplines was sensation seeking. Interestingly, it took almost 30 years to successfully translate etiological and epidemiological research on this one risk factor into effective preventive interventions. Current strategies seek to counteract sensation seeking with decision-making skills or adaptive goal setting or to divert youth high in sen-

sation seeking into more positive behavioral pursuits than drug use.

The separation of research into distinct scientific pursuits—combined with research training that is increasingly becoming inter- and transdisciplinary, shrinking federal budgets for behavioral research, and political pressure to find and disseminate evidence-based prevention strategies into practice—has led to the emerging field of research referred to as *translation*. To add to these pressures, there is now at least one generation of evidence-based drug use prevention programs that are products of years of interpreting and translating epidemiological, methodological, and formative program development studies into viable interventions that have appeared on national registries such as Blueprints (J. Collins et al., 2002; Elliott, 1997), the National Institute on Drug Abuse's (2003) Red Book, and the Center for Substance Abuse Prevention's (2002) National Registry of Effective Programs. Yet, adoption of evidence-based programs and the quality of implementation of these programs—even when they are adopted—are low. For example, Ringwalt et al. (2002) showed that fewer than 30% of schools that were eligible to receive prevention funds for evidence-based prevention programs were actually using an evidence-based program. Halfors and Godette (2002) reported similar results and questioned whether providing federal guidelines or registries of evidence-based programs and funding for them were sufficient to promote their use.

Findings such as these have spurred new epidemiological studies on program dissemination and practice and new prevention studies that are considered dissemination trials. In general, this movement toward dissemination research represents what NIH has referred to as translation from Type I to Type II research (Pentz et al., 2006; Sussman, Valente, Rohrbach, Skara, & Pentz, 2006). However, the development of new epidemiological studies that are expressly designed to identify variables that could be considered risk factors for failure of program dissemination could also be considered a form of back-translation to Type I research, that is, negative findings of prevention dissemination trials in Type II studies that are used to inform further Type I epidemiological studies.

Type I to Type II Translation

A three-volume series of articles in *Evaluation and the Health Professions* provided a thorough examination of the history of translational research, elucidating different phases of research that represent translation (Sussman et al., 2006). Two sets of definitions of translation stemming from those articles are briefly summarized here. First is the set of definitions the National Cancer Institute developed more than 20 years ago to categorize research into five phases: basic research, methods development (hypothesis development), efficacy trials (rigorous experimental prevention trials with high levels of research support and monitoring), effectiveness trials (experimental prevention trials conducted in field settings with relatively lower levels of research support and monitoring), and demonstration, also referred to as technology transfer (prevention service delivery or practice, with no research and little or no evaluation). Etiological and epidemiological research falls within the first two stages, preventative intervention research occupies the third and fourth stages, and practice is assumed to be the fifth.

Since that time, NIH has revised this set of definitions, categorizing research as either Type I or Type II (Rohrbach, Grana, & Sussman, 2006). This is the second set of definitions, the one that is used currently by NIH to classify studies for review, funding, and agency portfolio planning. Type I includes etiological and epidemiological studies on animals and humans that address risk factors, prevention program development, and efficacy and effectiveness trials. Type II is reserved primarily for prevention dissemination research, also referred to as diffusion research. Type II research focuses on how programs are spread, including their adoption, implementation, dissemination, and sustainability. Ironically, because Type II research is exactly that, research, there is no provision for addressing practice or service delivery if it is not evaluated as part of research. A considerable gap exists, then, in our understanding of what translation of research all the way into practice really amounts to. New NIH initiatives, including the funding of centers to translate basic research directly into clinical practice, are intended to fill this gap.

Variations on Translation From a Risk Factor Approach

Several theories and theory-based models have been developed to understand adolescent drug use etiology by means of a risk factor perspective, isolating the influences of risk factors on adolescents in different contexts and discerning whether they operate in either an accumulative fashion or synergistically (e.g., Hawkins, Catalano, & Miller, 1992). Pentz (1999b) outlined an integrative transactional theory (ITT), which posits that 17 risk factors can be clustered into intrapersonal (P), social situational (S), or environmental (E) contexts of influence on adolescent drug use. Within and across contexts, these risk factors are hypothesized to have synergistic relationships over time. The P level, for example, includes prior drug use behavior of the individual, immediate physiological reactions (e.g., feeling high), intentions to use, and prior drug use refusal skills, attitudes, and social support seeking. The S level includes peer and family modeling influences, peer group interactions, social support, and social transition vulnerability (e.g., moving from middle to high school). The E level includes media influences, prevailing community norms, availability of organizational prevention resources (social capital), fiscal resources, school and community policy, and community demographic factors (e.g., poverty status, high mobility rates). Most, but not all, of the P- and S-level risk factors have been translated from epidemiological research into prevention program design and content (Pentz, 2003). With the exception of a handful of community-based prevention trials, none of the E-level factors have been translated from epidemiological research into prevention programs. However, E-level factors have been the main focus of translation of program testing into prevention dissemination research (Pentz, 2007). Translation of epidemiological risk factor research into both program development and program dissemination is discussed next.

Translation of Risk Factors Into Prevention Program Development and Testing

Among P-level risk factors, all but physiological reactions have been incorporated into prevention programs thus far (see, e.g., Pentz, 1999b, 2007; Tobler, 1997). Emerging etiological and epidemiological studies on brain–behavior relationships (e.g., Volkow & Wise, 2005) may change that. For example, recent research has shown synergistic relationships between emotional regulation, sensation seeking, and executive cognitive function and their subsequent impact on physiological reactions to drug use (Riggs, Greenberg, Kusche, & Pentz, 2006). As a result, emotional regulation has been introduced into new drug prevention programs that have been translated from programs aimed at emotional regulation for prevention of conduct problems (e.g., see description of PATHWAYS in the Three Examples of Translation in Prevention Trials section of this chapter).

Among S-level factors, all but transition vulnerability have been directly addressed in drug prevention programs. Epidemiological research on the negative effects of social transition could be translated into the development of booster sessions that are deliberately timed to coincide with these transitions. Thus far, booster sessions have primarily been designed to provide successive, repeated exposure to prevention-based skills, for example, Life Skills Training (see chap. 34, this volume) rather than a bridge or support during times of transition.

Among E-level factors, epidemiological research on media influences has been successfully translated into programs that are designed to counteract these influences (e.g., Pentz, 1999a, 2005a). The introduction to this handbook also mentioned the Office of National Drug Control Policy media campaign, a large, federally sponsored social marketing campaign. Research studies on perceived community drug use norms, low awareness of policy, and low enforcement of policy have been translated into community tobacco interventions to increase awareness and support through youth activism (e.g., tobacco policy study [Forster et al., 1998], TOPP [Pentz, 1999a, 2000], Project Northland [Perry et al., 2002]). Other E-level factors are being addressed only in dissemination trials.

Translation of Risk Factors Into Program Dissemination and Practice

Translation of research into dissemination trials and practice may involve somewhat different sets of P-, S-, and E-level risk factors than have been applied to prevention program development and testing. These risk factors are considered for their potential negative impact on prevention program adoption, implementation, dissemination, and sustainability in a community rather than on drug use per se. At least five community trials and case studies of dissemination research have provided information on these risk factors. They include, but are not limited to, Communities That Care (Feinberg, Greenberg, & Osgood, 2004), PROSPER (Spoth, Greenberg, Bierman, & Redmond, 2004), community readiness (Slater et al., 2005), Steps Toward Effective Prevention (STEP; Pentz, 2005a, 2005b; Pentz, Chou, et al., 2004), and community capacity building (Chinman et al., 2005). Because this area of research is just emerging, the 15 dissemination risk factors described subsequently may not yet represent the full set that could inform successful movement of prevention from research into practice.

At the P level, the prior drug use history of community leaders and prevention program implementers and the fact that they may model drug use can have a negative impact on whether a prevention program is supported and implemented effectively. For example, a community leader who smokes cigarettes might be less inclined to support a no-tobacco-use preventative intervention in the community than would a nonsmoker. The perceived empowerment to promote prevention, as well as the individual organizational skills and prevention attitudes of community leaders and identified prevention program implementers (e.g., teachers, parents, counselors), has an impact on their ability to work effectively in supporting, promoting, and disseminating evidence-based programs in their community (e.g., Feinberg et al., 2004; Jasuja et al., 2005).

At the S level, three risk factors for poor dissemination have emerged thus far: poor social support and interpersonal communication within organizations that are charged with disseminating prevention programs, poor internal functioning (Feinberg et al., 2004; Jasuja et al., 2005), and poor communication networks (Feinberg, Riggs, & Greenberg, 2005; Valente, Chou, & Pentz, 2007).

At the E level, lack of awareness of community policy and negative media influences operating in the community appear to have negative relationships to community progress in adopting prevention programs (Pentz, Mares, et al., 2004). However, in dissemination, *adverse media influences* refers mainly to negative coverage or attention to drug use prevention in the community versus glamorized media images of drug use that serve as the adverse media influence addressed in prevention programs. Similarly, perceived drug use community norms are addressed as one indicator of low community readiness for prevention dissemination rather than as a direct risk factor to be addressed in prevention programs (Feinberg et al., 2004; Slater et al., 2005). Low fiscal resources for prevention and poor organizational capacity are both considered risk factors for poor prevention program dissemination (Chinman et al., 2005; Jasuja et al., 2005; Riggs & Pentz, 2007). Of these concerns, none are currently evaluated in developing prevention programs or testing their efficacy. Finally, although demographic factors have not yet been evaluated other than as covariates, some suggestive evidence indicates that community poverty status outweighs ethnicity and other demographic variables as a risk factor for poor prevention program dissemination (M. Greenberg et al., personal communication, August 2007).

THREE EXAMPLES OF TRANSLATION IN PREVENTION TRIALS

One thing that needs to be recognized is that enumeration of epidemiological risk factors that have informed prevention program testing and prevention program dissemination does not provide concrete examples of how translation actually occurs, nor of the detailed steps involved in successive translation. I use the following three prevention trials to illustrate examples of translation and some of the detailed steps involved.

Type I Translation to the Beginning of Type II Translation: Program Testing to Replication—The Midwestern Prevention Project (Project STAR)

By the mid-1980s, there was a rash of evaluation studies examining the efficacy of drug prevention programs. Among these were Life Skills Training,

ALERT, SMART, SASS, and a few others. Although these programs were proving to be effective, the question arose as to whether more comprehensive drug prevention strategies might be required to produce strong and lasting effects on drug use. The National Institute on Drug Abuse, the National Institute on Alcohol Abuse and Alcoholism, the Center for Substance Abuse Prevention, and other federal agencies raised the possibility that, using comprehensive, community-based heart disease prevention trials as a model (e.g., the Minnesota and Stanford Projects), similar types of interventions might be designed for the purpose of drug use prevention. The Midwestern Prevention Project (MPP), also referred to as Project STAR (Students Taught Awareness and Resistance), was subsequently developed as a multicomponent, community-based program for the prevention of drug use in adolescents and their families to specifically address this question (Pentz et al., 1989; Pentz, Mihalic, & Grotpeter, 1997). The active intervention period of the trial extended from 1985 to 1991, and the original cohorts of early adolescents have been followed into their mid-30s. The experimental research design involved randomly assigning all middle schools within the Kansas City, Missouri, metropolitan area school district to an intervention or delayed-intervention control group. Three years later, all schools within the Indianapolis metropolitan area were randomly assigned in the same manner as part of a replication study.

The STAR intervention had five components: media programming, a school program, a parent program, community organization, and government policy change. Each of the separate components had been tested in other studies in the early to mid-1980s using either randomized or quasi-experimental designs and were found to be effective in changing adolescent drug use attitudes, intentions, and/or behavior. Thus, the separate components had undergone program testing through the efficacy trial phase, but had not been tested together in sequence, tested under effectiveness trial conditions, or even replicated. Thus, the MPP was a prevention trial that incorporated features of an efficacy trial (because the components had not been tested in sequence), an effectiveness trial (the program was organized, implemented, and supervised by local personnel trained by research staff from the University of Southern California), and replication under effectiveness trial conditions. Using NIH terminology for translation, the MPP represented the end of Type I translation.

The MPP represented a planned translation of risk factors, theory, and program concepts from epidemiological and program development research to program testing, as well as translation across stages of research, from Type I efficacy and effectiveness trials to replication, representing the beginning of Type II dissemination research. Translation from research into practice was not a planned design feature of this project, but it did occur as a result of the trial. A few examples of each of these types of translation are summarized here.

First, strategies for counteracting risk factors of peer pressure, misperceived social norms for drug use, risk taking, and parental modeling behavior were translated from the school program to the parent program, mass media programming, and community organization program components. Social learning, problem behavior, and attitudinal theories were translated into one integrative theory, ITT (Pentz, 1999b), which unified the different program components and elaborated their hypothesized synergistic effects.

As described earlier, ITT posits that risk factors can be organized as sets of influences: intrapersonal (P level), social situational (S level), and environmental (E level). At the P level, previous drug use behavior, attitudes toward drug use, intentions to use drugs, personality traits such as sensation seeking, and physiological reactions to drug use experimentation were all translated from epidemiological research into points of discussion in the classroom as part of the school program component. S-level risk factors of actual and perceived pressure, actual and perceived social norms for drug use, and social support for drug use and risk taking were all translated into behavioral skills that youth could learn and practice. E-level risk factors consisting of poor resources for prevention, lack of non–drug use policies, and negative media images of drug use were all translated into campaign and fund-raising activities

that the community organization could implement. Program training concepts of guided participant modeling, from social learning theory (Pentz et al., 1997), were translated for use in training teachers to implement the school program, parents and principals to implement the parent program, community leaders to implement community organization and policy change, and media managers to implement media programming.

Another type of program translation was requested by the Indianapolis site during replication of the MPP, that is, incorporation of violence prevention into the drug prevention program. The request resulted in the development and addition of three optional violence prevention lessons to the school program component. Incorporating this type of request fit in with the overall MPP model of implementation, which required joint planning and decision making between internal (University of Southern California research staff) and external (research site staff) planners (Pentz, Cormack, Flay, Hansen, & Johnson,1986; Pentz et al., 1989). In later research, this type of joint work would be referred to as *community-based participatory research* (Best et al., 2003; Chinman et al., 2004).

Finally, the community organizations that were developed in the MPP were translated into organizations with resources for sustainability after the intervention period ended, and their ongoing work resulted in translation to practice. The Kansas City Drug Abuse Task Force ended its initial work by design in 1991. The Kauffman Foundation took over its responsibilities and disseminated the STAR school program throughout the states of Kansas and Missouri until Mr. Kauffman's death. The Indianapolis Community Advisory Council had several iterations after the MPP intervention period at that site ended in 1991, including integration with the local Red Cross, which continued for almost 10 years. The community advisory council's work resulted in the dissemination of the school and parent program components throughout most of the state of Indiana. This type of translation also represented translation into practice. Unfortunately, research funding for Type II research was not yet available in the early 1990s, therefore dissemination of STAR directly into practice was not systematically evaluated other than counts of the number of requester sites, trainers trained, and student materials distributed. A final example of translation of research into practice is the adoption of STAR by Lycoming County, Pennsylvania. From 1999 to 2000, five rural communities in the county were trained in all STAR program components. Organization, implementation, monitoring, and evaluation were conducted by the Lycoming County Mental Health Coalition, an umbrella organization responsible for supervising drug prevention interventions. Prevention practice of STAR has continued for several years as an institutionalized part of county prevention planning.

Type II to the Beginning of Practice: Program Replication to Dissemination—STEP

Comprehensive, multicomponent, community-based prevention programs such as STAR and Project Northland showed long-term effects on drug use (Pentz, 1998, 1999a; Perry et al., 2002). However, these programs were expensive to implement and labor and time intensive, raising the question of whether these types of prevention programs, now considered evidence based, could be taken to scale (i.e., disseminated) with fewer resources, with a lower drawdown of existing resources, and at a much lower cost. To answer this next question of translation, several new trials were initiated around the beginning of the second millennium. Their express aim included disseminating evidence-based programs on a large scale, using various strategies to leverage existing organizational resources. STEP was one of these, a prevention dissemination trial in which all aspects of organization, implementation, and monitoring were conducted by local community leaders, teachers, and parents who were trained by University of Southern California research staff in a series of relatively low-cost, interactive televised training sessions. The main research question was whether prevention programs that had been tested and replicated with intensive resources, monitoring, and relatively hefty costs could be disseminated widely with more abbreviated training, using existing community resources, implementing community self-monitoring, and at considerably reduced cost.

A total of 24 cities in five states were randomly assigned to one of three conditions: interactive televised training with limited off-site technical assistance, training alone, or a delayed intervention control condition. The research design reflected priorities that had been identified in moving evidence-based programs into the dissemination stage (Pentz, 2004a). Within each of the two intervention conditions, middle schools were randomly assigned to a prevention media literacy program, Media Buzz (Pentz, 2005a). The active intervention period took place between 2000 and 2005. Follow-up of sustainability now continues. Using NIH terminology, STEP represents the beginning of Type II translation (dissemination research on evidence-based programs).

STEP has six intervention components: community organization needs and resources assessment, following the Communities That Care model (Feinberg et al. 2004); community organization training and implementation, based on STAR; media advocacy for community leaders, which is a translation of STAR's media program component; prevention media literacy for adolescents, translated from the media program component from STAR and the media literacy program from TOPP, a tobacco policy program (Pentz, 2005a); the STAR school program; and a parent program translated from Guiding Good Choices, which was derived from Preparing for the Drug Free Years (Park et al., 2000). At the time that the STEP program was funded, the components translated from STAR were considered evidence based, Communities That Care was considered promising, and Guiding Good Choices was about to be classified as evidence based.

STEP represents a planned translation of risk factors, theory, program concepts, and program delivery to dissemination. First, results of community organization and communication research studies were translated into risk factors that could be addressed in the training of community leaders. At the E level, these risk factors included low community readiness or apathy toward prevention, low community awareness of evidence-based prevention programs and support of prevention policy (also considered as readiness indicators), negative local mass media coverage of community drug use problems, and poor organizational capacity to disseminate prevention programs. The ITT theoretical model developed for the MPP was retained to explain drug use development and prevention in adolescents, but a second model was translated from ITT and Rogers's (1995b) diffusion of innovation theory to explain how evidence-based prevention could be disseminated in communities (Pentz, Mares, et al., 2004). This dissemination model included constructs from Rogers's (1995b) theory that could be operationally defined and treated as program mediators in intervention. For example, perceived program diffusion potential is a construct that includes all five of Rogers's (1995a) hypothesized indicators of effective program diffusion: adaptability, relative advantage, compatibility, innovativeness, and trialability (i.e., user friendliness). This construct has thus far been shown to be a significant mediator of STEP effects on youth drug use, even before the introduction of actual programs for youth (Pentz, Riggs, et al, 2008). Program concepts, processes, and materials from the original prevention programs were abbreviated, prepared in manual form, pilot tested, and scripted for use in an interactive televised training format. Delivery methods were translated from live in-person training to off-site, television-based broadcast training, complemented by regular local community organizational meetings devoted to training and implementation.

It could be argued that STEP represents three types of translation. First, the abbreviation of Communities That Care and the MPP for testing in the STEP trial could be considered a tailored replication of these programs. Second, because training was standardized but received individually by broadcast to each community in each state, each community could be considered an independent replication of the STEP intervention. Third, although not part of the research design and not funded as such, results showed evidence of spontaneous dissemination into practice in at least three ways.

When community leaders who were initially trained left their organizations or moved, the STEP organizations recruited new replacement members on their own and requested videotape copies of training so that they could train these new recruits themselves. Additionally, teacher program implementation survey results for both of the school programs (STAR and Media Buzz) showed that 28% of

trained teachers were naturalistically sharing and modeling their training for other teachers after training (Pentz., 2005a, 2005b). Finally, 1 year after active STEP intervention ended, community organizations showed evidence that they were incorporating both the community organizational skills taught in STEP and the youth programs into their existing prevention planning frameworks (Riggs & Pentz, 2007). All of these indicators could be considered evidence of translation into practice.

Type II Back to Type I Translation: Translation of Prevention From Drug Use to Obesity Prevention: PATHWAYS

In 2004, NIH convened a special conference examining potential site-specific approaches to child and adolescent obesity prevention. I was asked to address whether the evidence-based programs used in STAR or similar multicomponent drug prevention programs could be made suitable for obesity prevention, meaning that with little modification program applications could be changed from drug use to obesity (Pentz, 2004b). The response by the investigative team was no, but that there were potentially several risk factors and potential program mediators that were common to both drug use and obesity prevention. The result was the development of a new translational prevention trial, PATHWAYS, with the express purpose of translating two evidence-based prevention programs from other fields, PATHS for violence prevention (Greenberg, 2006; Riggs, Greenberg, et al., 2006) and the STAR school and parent program components for drug use prevention (Pentz et al., 1997), into a viable obesity prevention program for children. Long-term findings from STAR supported this translation, showing that program effects on drug use through the adolescent years had direct and mediated effects on physical activity and body mass index in adulthood (Pentz, Riggs, & Chou, 2008). The research design involved randomization, with 24 elementary schools in two large mixed-ethnicity and Hispanic districts assigned to a 3-year school and parent program or a delayed intervention control condition. Although the trial has yet to commence, early results of a partial pilot have been published and have shown rapid uptake of the program and intentions to change dysregulated eating behavior (Riggs, Kobayakawa-Sakuma, & Pentz, 2007). Dysregulated eating has been linked to low impulse control, lack of emotional regulation, and poor executive cognitive function (decision-making skills), all of which are risk factors for both obesity and drug use.

PATHWAYS has required translation on all fronts: risk factors, theory, program concepts, and program delivery. Translation of risk factors was drawn from research on brain–behavior relationships, particularly the relationships involving affect, executive cognitive function, and behavior (Greenberg, 2006; Riggs, Greenberg, et al., 2006). Some of these putative risk factors are addressed in other chapters of this volume. A basic science model of the endocannabinoid system was also translated to understand how children might first reach for a certain food or a certain physical (or sedentary) activity for its novelty or arousal effect (Volkow & Wise, 2005; Wang, Volkow, Thanos, & Fowler, 2004). This system helps to explain low impulse control, sensation or novelty seeking, arousal as a physiological reaction, low emotional regulation, and poor decision making as P-level risk factors that are common to both dysregulated eating and drug use. Other P-level risk factors were more easily translated, including past behavior, intentions, and attitudes.

At the S level, modeling of eating, food preferences, and physical activity by family members and peers was easily translated from drug use to obesity. Translation of social support, norms, and peer pressure was less clear, partially because drug use is not socially supportive or normative because it is illegal, whereas eating and physical activity—the two primary risk factors for obesity—are legal, normative, and necessary for survival (see Grosbras et al., 2007, regarding peer influences). At the E level, resources for drug prevention have been translated into resources for nutrition programs and aspects of the built environment that support or inhibit physical activity. Media influences and policy are still being examined for their translation potential.

Theory was translated by integrating the cognition–affect–behavior dynamic model from PATHS (Riggs, Greenberg, et al., 2006) and the ITT from STAR (Pentz, 1999b), with P-, S-, and E-level risk factors and program mediators from STAR translated to

obesity. New program mediators were also introduced, including affect awareness and decision-making skills targeted directly toward eating and physical activity.

The original derivative programs, as well as new program mediators, have been translated into program concepts and delivery. For example, the original PATHS program involved multiple grades from kindergarten to sixth, with more than 80 lessons aimed generally at affect, social, and academic competence. PATHWAYS has translated and consolidated the PATHS program into implementation in Grades 4–6, with 30 lessons aimed directly at eating and physical activity practice and the addition of part of the parent program translated from STAR (Riggs, Elfenbaum, & Pentz, 2006). The program is teacher delivered, but teacher training and implementation are based on the more active guided-participant modeling approach used in STAR rather than the didactic approach used in PATHS. Translation also involves converting the STAR parent program to eating, physical activity, and related family rule setting and incorporating this program into the school program in fifth grade.

Not all translation in PATHWAYS is occurring from evidence-based program concepts and delivery methods. Some concepts are new and are being piloted by using a fractional factorial design, appropriate for the pilot phase of preventative interventions (L. Collins, 2008). For example, researchers in the field of obesity have debated whether sugar or fiber should be emphasized in efforts to change eating behavior (Huang & Horlick, 2007). Another concern is whether eating should be emphasized to a greater or lesser extent than physical activity. Both are known as the main proximal risk factors for overweight and obesity, yet there is little research information available on what should be the relative emphasis, sequencing, or even promotion of synergy between the two in a prevention program. These are questions that can be tested in the PATHWAYS pilot by varying the relative emphasis of some lessons on sugar versus fiber and some on eating versus activity while still retaining the aims of controlling impulsive eating behavior and activity choices. An additional new concept is whether and how PATHWAYS can be used by schools to complement or link with other existing prevention activities in schools (e.g., in California, the Health Fitness Zone testing and the California Nutrition Network). Finding ways in which PATHWAYS can be fit into existing school activities represents one aspect of Rogers's (1995a) diffusion principles, compatibility.

A PROPOSED STEPWISE MODEL OF TRANSLATION FROM RESEARCH TO PRACTICE AND BACK

The types of translation that have been discussed thus far, and the examples given from three prevention trials, do not provide a framework that represents a systematic progression of steps in translation, either forward or backward. A 10-step model is proposed here and is shown in Figure 31.1. Collectively, Steps 1 through 5 represent Type I research as currently categorized by NIH, and Steps 6 through 10 represent Type II research. The reciprocal arrows shown between some steps are intended to represent instances of a failure or unexpected result achieved at one step that invites "revisiting" the previous step in an either formative or confirmatory (summative) research study. These arrows represent feedback loops of reciprocal translation (Sneden, Gottlieb-Nudd, Gottlieb, & Huang, 2006). In other words, they can inform each other and can be repeated. Finally, the arrows leading from each of Steps 5 (program testing), 6 (program replication), and 10 (program translation across health risk behaviors) back to Step 1 (etiology and epidemiology research on drug use) indicate the importance that basic research on drug use risk continues to have. The assumption is that some drug use risk factors are not immutable but are subject to secular, market, and political changes (Maibach, Van Duyn, & Bloodgood, 2006). This may be especially important for S- and E-level risk factors.

Step 1 emphasizes continued etiological and epidemiological research on drug use risk. For example, adolescents will not be at equal risk of methamphetamine use if its prevalence is extremely low in some communities and not others. Thus, developing a national or statewide prevention campaign aimed at methamphetamine use as a specific substance may not be effective in some areas. Basic research on rising prevalence rates of substances may help guide further

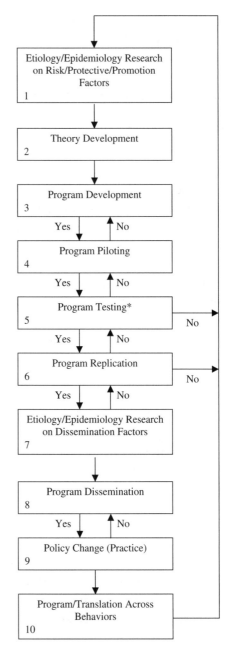

Note. Program testing includes efficacy and effectiveness trials

FIGURE 31.1. **Steps to translating research into practice and practice into research. Program testing includes efficacy and effectiveness trials.**

intervention development. At the same time, and using the same example, S-level risk factors that represent peer use, peer pressure to use, and family use might be redirected back to universal prevention programs that are currently aimed at the most prevalent drugs: tobacco, alcohol, and marijuana. Using another example, recent epidemiological research has found a relatively new social and environmental risk factor for drug use: pressure to achieve academically (Sussman, Pentz, Spruijt-Metz, & Miller, 2007). This pressure has been associated with both increased anxiety among youth and peer pressure to use as study aids drugs that are normally prescribed for attention deficit and hyperactivity disorders.

Step 2 emphasizes continued theory development. Currently, theory development is driven by findings from risk factor research that is moving in at least four new directions. One is extrapolation of theories such as problem behavior theory (Donovan, Jessor, & Costa, 1991) to theories of multiple health risk behaviors, for example, a theory that can explain drug use, obesity, accidental injury, and HIV risk through common underpinnings of the endocannabinoid system and affect–cognition triggers in the brain. Another direction entails refinement of a class of theories referred to as social–ecological or contextual. These theories, among them ITT (Pentz, 1999b), continue to generate hypotheses about how P, S, and E levels of risk relate to each other and affect each other over time. Third is the development of a theory that equally encompasses health promotion and health risk. The social development model (Catalano, Kosterman, Hawkins, Newcomb, & Abbott, 1996) fits this bill, addressing the role of conventional behaviors and school bonding as protective factors against drug use. Izard's (2002) emotion theory, which could be applied to both prevention and health promotion, provides another example of new directions. Finally, the recent NIH initiatives on transdisciplinary approaches to prevention are leading toward the integration of models from fields as diverse as engineering and mathematics with theories that have already been developed in the fields of psychology and public health (e.g., L. Collins, 2008).

Step 3 entails program development. Sussman (2001) articulated six stages that should be followed in program development (see also chap. 33, this volume). One of these, the pooling of relevant activities that can be considered for inclusion in a prevention program, could be revised in the future to include the pooling of program components that have already been tested and shown to be effective in separate prevention studies. These might include a school pro-

gram with a brief at-home visit or a school program followed up with motivational interviewing delivered over the phone or Internet.

Step 4 consists of program piloting, also included in Sussman's (2001) stage model. Although most, if not all, prevention programs have conducted rigorous piloting before a large-scale prevention trial begins, few of these are published or available to other drug use prevention researchers. There are several reasons for this, including reluctance of some journals to publish pilot studies, small sample sizes that may prohibit drawing valid conclusions, and short timelines, which may reduce the possibility of finding any useful outcomes. Yet, increasingly it appears that NIH prefers that a longer program development and pilot period be included in proposed studies to help reduce the possibility of trial failure later on. Results of the pilot can then be used to revise or refine program development before the full and more costly randomized trial begins. For example, the piloting of the PATHWAYS program components of sugar versus fiber should determine which of these should be eliminated or enhanced. The program will be revised accordingly (translation back to Step 3), and if necessary repiloted before the trial begins. A pilot of lessons focusing on emotion that was abbreviated from the original PATHS program has already shown effects on children's intentions to curb impulsive eating (Riggs et al., 2007). The next step includes folding these into the main trial.

Step 5 is program testing in quasi-experimental and experimental studies. For simplification, this step includes both efficacy and effectiveness trials (August et al., 2004). If the program is shown to be effective under tightly controlled research conditions, it can be considered for further replication (Step 6). However, if it fails, there are several options for back-translation to another stage, including repiloting, further program development, or even continued epidemiological research to elucidate risk factors or other program-relevant factors that were not addressed in the program. An example of how this process works is DARE (Drug Abuse Resistance Education), which after several program tests did not show significant effects on drug use. The failure of DARE led some researchers to translate the program back to development and piloting before testing it again. One such study was

DARE PLUS, conducted by Perry et al. (2003). The PLUS version contained a new community activity component. Results of program testing showed that only the PLUS component was effective. Questions remain as to whether there are factors that have not yet been addressed to explain why DARE is not effective. These questions point toward the need for more basic epidemiological research on this widely disseminated program.

Step 6 consists of program replication. The MPP/STAR prevention trial included both program testing and replication in its design. However, in the MPP as well as in most other prevention trials, replication is rarely exact. The addition of optional violence lessons in the MPP replication at the request of prevention experts from the city of Indianapolis represents a replication with some tailoring. Other replications also reflect some tailoring, for example, Life Skills Training replicated under different conditions of program monitoring, such as in the Blueprints replication project (Mihalic & Irwin, 2003). In most cases, continued evidence of effectiveness in a replication study, even if the magnitude of effect differs from the results of the original program test, is considered sufficient to proceed to the next step of examining the epidemiology of prevention dissemination. However, if a replication fails or shows no effect or iatrogenic effects, further research is warranted, translating back to more basic program testing.

Step 7 involves epidemiological research on program dissemination factors. Research has already shown that lack of a school or community prevention coordinator, poor communication between administrators and implementers, poor implementer preparation for training, and poor organizational structure and capacity to promote prevention are all risk factors for poor prevention program dissemination (e.g., Jasuja et al., 2005; Mihalic & Irwin, 2003; Ringwalt et al., 2002). Evidence that any of these risk factors may have operated in a major prevention trial or replication should be grounds for moving back to another replication study, with these risk factors addressed as part of the intervention itself.

Step 8 marks the point of program dissemination. One could argue that replication *is* dissemination, but this model treats the two as slightly different steps in translation into practice. Replication is conducted

with approximately the same amount of vigilance and rigor as an effectiveness trial, or should be. The question remains whether the program will work in new circumstances with less investigative research support. Dissemination is conducted further along in the translational process, with relatively less monitoring of program implementation and greater monitoring of program spread to other settings and implementers (Sloboda & Schildhaus, 2002). The question is now whether a community (or other site) will use the program on its own and how much adaptation is required for successful adoption and implementation (L. Collins, Murphy, & Bierman, 2004). An example is whether evidence-based programs need to be tailored to fit a specific cultural or ethnic group (Dévieux et al., 2005; Pentz, 1995). Dissemination trials, such as those described earlier in this chapter, are starting to yield information on whether dissemination occurs and also on whether it can be sustained with a community's own resources.

Step 9 is policy change and incorporation of prevention into practice (Pentz, 2000). Although not synonymous, the two are considered in the same step because it seems highly unlikely that a prevention program will be incorporated into standard education, health, or public health practice without a policy that sanctions the use of this program in such practice. For example, per capita funds are set aside for the use of evidence-based drug prevention programs as part of the Drug Free Schools and Communities Act of 1986 (Pentz, Mares, et al., 2004). It is important to recognize that the legislative act itself is a policy. The institutionalized use of evidence-based programs in schools is also a policy, one that determines what school prevention practice will be.

Step 10 involves program translation from drug use prevention to other health risk behaviors that may share common risk factors and mediators (Chambers, Taylor, & Potenza, 2003). This is the most recent area of translational research (e.g., Pentz, in press; Riggs et al., 2007; Werch, Moore, DiClemente, Bledsoe, & Jobli, 2005). The new PATHWAYS project provides an acute example. This step logically follows drug prevention policy change and practice. To wit, as health practitioners are trained and become comfortable in implementing drug prevention standards into their practice, a logical next step is to translate these standards to other areas of health for which health practitioners are already responsible in their normal practice. These new health behaviors may include eating (nutrition), physical activity, avoidance of harm, and general promotion of a healthy lifestyle. This last step translates back to the entire sequence as new risk factors and programs are developed that may address these multiple health risk behaviors. Thus, the last directional arrow in Figure 31.1 represents translation of practice back into research.

CONCLUSIONS AND FUTURE DIRECTIONS

Most of the translation of prevention research into practice has occurred within and across Type I and Type II research. Little is known about the actual translation of drug prevention programs into practice, unlike the translation of patient care, diagnostic, and pharmacological intervention research into medical practice, which has received extensive evaluation. This type of translation, and the translation of practice back into research on multiple health risk behaviors, is an area ripe with opportunities for new research. For example, new research studies could evaluate the effectiveness of prevention programs that are delivered in alternative practice settings, such as the physician's or nurse's office, or at point-of-contact settings, such as leisure-time gathering places for school dropouts. Management information systems and other archival records could be compared with dissemination and implementation surveys as alternative measures to evaluate effective prevention program dissemination. Glasgow and Emmons (2007) suggested more research on the connectedness and potential synergy of program components and contexts for delivery. Finally, community-based participatory research studies should develop replicable guidelines by which practitioners help develop drug prevention programs from the perspective of practice realities, in partnership with researchers who contribute to programs from the perspective of theory and research design (e.g., Green & Glasgow, 2006).

References

August, G. J., Winters, K. C., Realmuto, G. M., Tarter, R., Perry, C., & Hektner, J. M. (2004). Moving evidence-based drug abuse prevention programs from basic

science to practice: Bridging the efficacy-effectiveness interface. *Substance Use & Misuse, 39,* 2017–2053.

Best, A., Stokols, D., Green, L. W., Leischow, S., Holmes, B., & Bucholz, K. (2003). An integrative framework for community partnering to translate theory into effective health promotion strategy. *American Journal of Health Promotion, 18,* 168–176.

Brown, C. H., Berndt, D., Brinales, J. M., Zong, X., & Bhagwat, D. (2000). Evaluating the evidence of effectiveness for preventive interventions: Using a registry system to influence policy through science. *Addictive Behaviors, 25,* 955–964.

Catalano, R. F., Kosterman, R., Hawkins, J. D., Newcomb, M. D., & Abbott, R. D. (1996). Modeling the etiology of adolescent substance use: A test of the social development model. *Journal of Drug Issues, 26,* 429–455.

Center for Substance Abuse Prevention. (2002). *SAMHSA model programs: Effective substance abuse and mental health programs for every community.* Retrieved August 14, 2006, from http://www.modelprograms.samhsa.gov/model.htm

Chambers, R. A., Taylor, J. R., & Potenza, M. N. (2003). Developmental neurocircuitry of motivation in adolescence: A critical period of addiction vulnerability. *American Journal of Psychiatry, 160,* 1041–1052.

Chinman, M., Early, D., Ebener, P., Hunter, S., Imm, P., Jenkins, P., et al. (2004). Getting to outcomes: A community-based participatory approach to preventive interventions. *Journal of Interprofessional Care, 18,* 441–443.

Chinman, M., Hannah, G., Wandersman, A., Ebener, P., Hunter, S. B., Imm, P., et al. (2005). Developing a community science research agenda for building community capacity for effective preventive interventions. *American Journal of Community Psychology, 35,* 143–157.

Collins, L. (2008). *Choosing among complete factorial, fractional factorial, and other designs to maximize scientific gain in relation to resources expended.* Manuscript submitted for publication.

Collins, J., Robin, L., Woole, S., Fenley, D., Hunt, P., Taylor, J., et al. (2002). Programs-that-work: CDC's guide to effective programs that reduce health-risk behavior of youth. *Journal of School Health, 72,* 93–99.

Collins, L., Murphy, S. A., & Bierman, K. L. (2004). A conceptual framework for adaptive preventive interventions. *Prevention Science, 5,* 185–196.

Dévieux, J. G., Malow, R. M., Rosenberg, R., Jean-Gilles, M., Samuels, D., Ergon-Pérez, E., et al. (2005). Cultural adaptation in translational research: Field experiences. *Journal of Urban Health, 82,* iii82–iii91.

Dishion, T. J., McCord, J., & Poulin, F. (1999). When interventions harm: Peer groups and problem behavior. *American Psychologist, 54,* 755–764.

Donovan, J. E., Jessor, R., & Costa, F. M. (1991). Adolescent health behavior and conventionality–unconventionality: An extension of problem-behavior theory. *Health Psychology, 10,* 52–61.

Drug-Free Schools and Communities Act of 1986, Pub. L. 99-570, 20 U.S.C. 4601 *et seq.* (1986).

Elliot, D. S. (Ed.). (1997). *Blueprints for violence prevention.* Boulder: Center for the Study and Prevention of Violence, University of Colorado.

Feinberg, M. E., Greenberg, M. T., & Osgood, D. W. (2004). Readiness, functioning, and perceived effectiveness in community prevention coalitions: A study of Communities That Care. *American Journal of Community Psychology, 33,* 163–176.

Feinberg, M. E., Riggs, N. R., & Greenberg, M. T. (2005). Social networks and community prevention coalitions. *Journal of Primary Prevention, 26,* 279–298.

Fielding, J. E., Marks, J. S., Myers, B. W., Nolan, P. A., Rawson, R. D., & Toomey, K. E. (2002). How do we translate science into public health policy and law? *Journal of Law and Medical Ethics, 30,* 22–32.

Forster, J. L., Murray, D. M., Wolfson, M., Blaine, T. M., Wagenaar, A. C., & Hennrikus, D. J. (1998). The effects of community policies to reduce youth access to tobacco. *American Journal of Public Health, 88,* 1193–1198.

Ginexi, E. M., & Hilton, T. F. (2006). What's next for translation research? *Evaluation & the Health Professions, 29,* 334–347.

Glasgow, R. E., & Emmons, K. M. (2007). How can we increase translation of research into practice? Types of evidence needed. *Annual Review of Public Health, 28,* 413–433.

Green, L. W. (2001). From research to "best practices" in other settings and populations. *American Journal of Health Behavior, 25,* 165–178.

Green, L. W., & Glasgow, R. E. (2006). Evaluating the relevance, generalization, and applicability of research: Issues in external validation and translation methodology. *Evaluation & the Health Professions, 29,* 126–153.

Greenberg, M. T. (2006). Promoting resilience in children and youth: Preventive interventions and their interface with neuroscience. *Annals of the New York Academy of Sciences, 1094,* 138–150.

Grosbras, M.-H., Jansen, M., Leonard, G., McIntosh, A., Osswald, K., Poulsen, C., et al. (2007, July 25). Neural mechanisms of resistance to peer influence in early adolescence. *Journal of Neuroscience, 27,* 8040–8045.

Halfors, D., & Godette, D. (2002). Will the "principles of effectiveness" improve prevention practice? Early findings from a diffusion study. *Health Education Research: Theory and Practice, 17,* 461–470.

Hawkins, J. D., Catalano, R. F., & Miller, J. Y. (1992). Risk and protective factors for alcohol and other drug problems in adolescence and early adulthood: Implications for substance abuse prevention. *Psychological Bulletin, 112,* 64–105.

Huang, T. T., & Horlick, M. N. (2007). Trends in childhood obesity research: A brief analysis of NIH-supported efforts. *Journal of Law, Medicine, & Ethics, 35,* 148–153.

Izard, C. E. (2002). Translating emotion theory and research into preventive interventions. *Psychological Bulletin, 128,* 796–824.

Jasuja, G. K., Chou, C. P., Bernstein, K., Wang, E., McClure, M., & Pentz, M. A. (2005). Using structural characteristics of community coalitions to predict progress in adopting evidence-based prevention programs. *Evaluation and Program Planning, 28,* 173–184.

Maibach, E. W., Van Duyn, M. A., & Bloodgood, B. (2006). A marketing perspective on disseminating evidence-based approaches to disease prevention and health promotion. *Preventing Chronic Disease, 3,* A97.

Mihalic, S. F., & Irwin, K. (2003). Blueprints for violence prevention: From research to real world settings—Factors influencing the successful replication of model programs. *Youth Violence and Juvenile Justice, 1,* 307–329.

National Institute on Drug Abuse. (2003). *Preventing drug use among children and adolescents: A research-based guide for parents, educators, and community leaders* (2nd ed., NIH Document No. 04-4212[A]). Bethesda, MD: Author. Retrieved January 28, 2008, from http://www.drugabuse.gov/prevention/prevopen.html

Park, J., Kosterman, R., Hawkins, J. D., Haggerty, K. P., Duncan, T. E., Duncan, S. C., & Spoth, R. (2000). Effects of the "Preparing for the Drug Free Years" curriculum on growth in alcohol use and risk for alcohol use in early adolescence. *Prevention Science, 1,* 125–138.

Pentz, M. A. (1995). Prevention research in multiethnic communities: Developing community support and collaboration and adapting research methods. In G. J. Botvin, S. P. Schinke, & M. A. Orlandi (Eds.), *Drug abuse prevention with multiethnic youth* (pp. 193–214). Thousand Oaks, CA: Sage.

Pentz, M. A. (1998). Preventing drug abuse through the community: Multicomponent programs make the difference. In Z. Sloboda & W. B. Hansen (Eds.), *Putting research to work for the community* (NIDA Research Monograph, NIDA Publication No. 98-4293, pp. 73–86). Washington, DC: U.S. Department of Health and Human Services.

Pentz, M. A. (1999a). Effective prevention programs for tobacco use. *Nicotine & Tobacco Research, 1,* 99–107.

Pentz, M. A. (1999b). Prevention aimed at individuals: An integrative transactional perspective. In B. S. McCrady & E. E. Epstein (Eds.), *Addictions: A comprehensive guidebook* (pp. 555–572). New York: Oxford University Press.

Pentz, M. A. (2000). Institutionalizing community-based prevention through policy change. *Journal of Community Psychology, 28,* 257–270.

Pentz, M. A. (2003). Evidence-based prevention: Characteristics, impact, and future direction. *Journal of Psychoactive Drugs, 35,* 143–152.

Pentz, M. A. (2004a). Applying theory and methods of community-based drug abuse prevention to pediatric obesity prevention. In *Summary report: Site specific approaches: Prevention or management of pediatric obesity* (pp. 97–100). Bethesda, MD: National Institute of Diabetes and Digestive and Kidney Diseases. Retrieved March 23, 2005, http://www.niddk.nih.gov/fund/other/management_pediatric_obesity/SUMMARY_REPORT.pdf

Pentz, M. A. (2004b). Form follows function: Designs for prevention effectiveness and diffusion research. *Prevention Science, 5,* 23–29.

Pentz, M. A. (2005a, May). *Building adolescent competence in prevention media literacy: Early effects of media buzz in Project STEP.* Paper presented at the meeting of the Society for Prevention Research, Washington, DC.

Pentz, M. A. (2005b, May). *Do training dosage and exposure make a difference in community coalition progress in adopting and implementing evidence-based prevention? The Step Diffusion Trial.* Paper presented at the meeting of the Society for Prevention Research, Washington, DC.

Pentz, M. A. (2007). Disseminating effective approaches to drug use prevention. In M. K. Welch-Ross & L. G. Fasig (Eds.), *Handbook on communicating and disseminating behavioral science* (pp. 341–364). Thousand Oaks, CA: Sage.

Pentz, M. A. (in press). Understanding and preventing risks for obesity. In R. DiClemente, R. Crosby, & J. Santelli (Eds.), *Adolescent health: Understanding and preventing risk.* Hoboken, NJ: Wiley.

Pentz, M. A., Cormack, C., Flay, B. R., Hansen, W. B., & Johnson, C. A. (1986). Balancing program and research integrity in community drug abuse prevention: Project STAR approach. *Journal of School Health, 56,* 389–393.

Pentz, M. A., Chou, C. P., McClure, M., Bernstein, K., Mann, D., Ross, L., et al. (2004, May). *Adoption and early implementation of STEP: A multi-state teleconference-based prevention diffusion trial.* Paper presented at the meeting of the Society for Prevention Research, Quebec City, Quebec, Canada.

Pentz, M. A., Dwyer, J. H., MacKinnon, D. P., Flay, B. R., Hansen, W. B., Wang, E. Y. I., et al. (1989, June 9). A multicommunity trial for primary prevention of adolescent drug abuse: Effects on drug use prevalence. *JAMA, 261,* 3259–3266.

Pentz, M. A., Jasuja, G. K., Rohrbach, L. A., Sussman, S., & Bardo, M. (2006). Translation in tobacco and drug abuse prevention/cessation research. *Evaluation and the Health Professions, 29,* 246–271.

Pentz, M. A., Mares, D., Schinke, S., & Rohrbach, L. A. (2004). Political science, public policy, and drug use prevention. *Substance Use & Misuse, 39,* 1821–1865.

Pentz, M. A., Mihalic, S. F., & Grotpeter, J. K. (1997). The Midwestern Prevention Project. In D. S. Elliot (Ed.), *Blueprints for violence prevention.* Boulder: Center for the Study and Prevention of Violence, Institute of Behavioral Science, University of Colorado.

Pentz, M. A., Riggs, N. R., & Chou, C. (2008). *Translating drug abuse prevention to obesity prevention: Long-term effects of a comprehensive community-based trial.* Manuscript submitted for publication.

Pentz, M. A., Riggs, N., Valente, T., Chou, C., McClure, K., Bunce, P., & Hawkins, J. D. (2008). *Mediational effects of community organizational change on changes in youth drug use risk outcomes: Effects of Project STEP.* Manuscript submitted for publication.

Perry, C. L., Komro, K. A., Veblen-Mortenson, S., Bosma, L. M., Farbakhsh, K., Munson, K. A., et al. (2003). A randomized controlled trial of the middle and junior high school D.A.R.E. and D.A.R.E. Plus programs. *Archives of Pediatrics and Adolescent Medicine, 157,* 178–184.

Perry, C. L., Williams, C. L., Komro, K. A., Veblen-Mortenson, S., Stigler, M. H., Munson, K. A., et al. (2002). Project Northland: Long-term outcomes of community action to reduce adolescent alcohol use. *Health Education Research, 17,* 117–132.

Riggs, N. R., Elfenbaum, P., & Pentz, M. A. (2006). Parent program component analysis in a drug abuse prevention trial. *Journal of Adolescent Health, 39,* 66–72.

Riggs, N. R., Greenberg, M. T., Kusché, C. A., & Pentz, M. A. (2006). The mediational role of neurocognition in the behavioral outcomes of a social-emotional prevention program in elementary school students: Effects of the PATHS curriculum. *Prevention Science, 7,* 91–102.

Riggs, N. R., Kobayakawa-Sakuma, K. L., & Pentz, M. A. (2007). Preventing risk for obesity by promoting self-regulation and decision-making skills: Pilot results from the PATHWAYS to Health Program (PATHWAYS). *Evaluation Review, 31,* 287–310.

Riggs, N. R., & Pentz, M. A. (2007, May). *Sustainability of prevention diffusion channels: STEP and next steps.* Paper presented at the meeting of the Society for Prevention Research, Washington, DC.

Ringwalt, C. L., Ennett, S., Vincus, A., Thorne, J., Rohrbach, L. A., & Simons-Rudolph, A. (2002). The prevalence of effective substance use prevention curricula in U.S. middle schools. *Prevention Science, 3,* 257–265.

Rogers, E. M. (1995a). Diffusion of drug abuse prevention programs: Spontaneous diffusion, agenda setting, and reinvention. In T. E. Backer, S. L. David, & G. Saucy (Eds.), *Reviewing the behavioral science knowledge base on technology transfer* (NIDA Research Monograph No. 155, pp. 90–105). Rockville, MD: U.S. Department of Health and Human Services, Public Health Service, National Institutes of Health.

Rogers, E. M. (1995b). *Diffusion of innovations* (4th ed.). New York: Free Press.

Rohrbach, L. A., Grana, R., & Sussman, S. (2006). Type II translation: Transporting prevention interventions from research to real-world settings. *Evaluation & the Health Professions, 29,* 302–333.

Simpson, D. D. (2002). A conceptual framework for transferring research to practice. *Journal of Substance Abuse Treatment, 22,* 171–182.

Slater, M. D., Edwards, R. W., Plested, B. A., Thurman, P. J., Kelly, K. J., Comello, M. L., et al. (2005). Using community readiness key informant assessments in a randomized group prevention trial: Impact of a participatory community-media intervention. *Journal of Community Health, 30,* 39–53.

Sloboda, Z., & Schildhaus, S. (2002). A discussion of the concept of technology transfer of research-based drug "abuse" prevention and treatment interventions. *Substance Use & Misuse, 37,* 1079–1087.

Sneden, G. G., Gottlieb-Nudd, A. S., Gottlieb, N. H., & Huang, P. P. (2006). A feedback model for applied research on tobacco control. *Preventing Chronic Disease, 3,* A65.

Spoth, R., Greenberg, M., Bierman, K., & Redmond, C. (2004). PROSPER community-university partnership model for the public education systems: Capacity-building for evidence-based, competence-building prevention. *Prevention Science, 5,* 31–39.

Sussman, S. (Ed.). (2001). *Handbook of program development for health behavior research and practice.* Thousand Oaks, CA: Sage.

Sussman, S., Pentz, M. A., Spruijt-Metz, D., & Miller, T. (2007). Abuse of "study drugs": Prevalence, consequences, and implications for therapeutic prescription and policy. *Journal of Drug Addiction, Education, and Eradication, 2,* 309–327.

Sussman, S., Valente, T. W., Rohrbach, L., Skara, S., & Pentz, M. A. (2006). Translation in the health professions: Converting science into action. *Evaluation and the Health Professions, 29,* 7–32.

Tobler, N. S. (1997). Meta-analysis of adolescent drug prevention programs: Results of the 1993 meta-analysis. In W. J. Bukoski (Ed.), *Meta-analysis of drug abuse prevention programs* (NIDA Research Monograph 170, pp. 5–68). Rockville, MD: Alcohol, Drug Abuse, and Mental Health Administration, U.S. Department of Health and Human Services.

Valente, T. W., Chou, C. P., & Pentz, M. A. (2007). Community coalition networks as systems: Effects of network change on adoption of evidence-based prevention. *American Journal of Public Health, 97,* 880–886.

Volkow, N. D., & Wise, R. A. (2005). How can drug addiction help us understand obesity? *Nature Neuroscience, 8,* 555–560.

Wang, G. J., Volkow, N. D., Thanos, P. K., & Fowler, J. S. (2004). Similarity between obesity and drug addiction as assessed by neurofunctional imaging: A concept review. *Journal of Addictive Diseases, 23,* 39–53.

Weiss, B., Caron, A., Ball, S., Tapp, J., Johnson, M., & Weisz, J. R. (2005). Iatrogenic effects of group treatment for antisocial youth. *Journal of Consulting and Clinical Psychology, 73,* 1036–1044.

Werch, C., Moore, M. J., DiClemente, C. C., Bledsoe, R., & Jobli, E. (2005). A multihealth behavior intervention integrating physical activity and substance abuse prevention for adolescents. *Prevention Science, 6,* 213–226.

CHAPTER 32

OPERATING CHARACTERISTICS OF PREVENTION PROGRAMS: CONNECTIONS TO DRUG USE ETIOLOGY

William B. Hansen, James Derzon, Linda Dusenbury, Dana Bishop, Karren Campbell, and Aaron Alford

For decades, North American youth have been prolific in their consumption and abuse of substances, including alcohol, tobacco, and marijuana (Johnston, O'Malley, Bachman, & Schulenberg, 2008). The impact of this excessive consumption and its sequelae has driven national policies that focus on promoting abstinence and reducing alcohol, tobacco, and other drug consumption generally. There has been significant funding by the U.S. government to research the extent, causes, and prevention of substance use. Over the years, different federal agencies have been responsible for important research and practical emphases. The National Institute on Drug Abuse has primarily been responsible for research on efficacious prevention programs. Other federal agencies have funded projects targeting program evaluation for community service organizations, faith-based groups, and treatment of mental health and drug abuse as comorbid disorders. Of notable importance has been the funding of a national prevention registry by the Substance Abuse and Mental Health Services Administration (SAMHSA). The registry is a compilation of evidence and practice information encompassing approaches to preventing and treating substance abuse and mental health disorders. The National Registry of Evidence-based Programs and Practices, or NREPP (available at http://nrepp.samhsa.gov), includes programs that have demonstrated effectiveness on the basis of independent scientific reviews held to the highest standard of evidence-based criteria.

One relevant goal of NREPP is to identify substance abuse prevention programs with proven effectiveness. During the years before 2005, more than 1,100 programs were nominated for inclusion in the list of proven programs. Of these, 153 programs were certified for inclusion in the registry on the basis of statistical significance and reviewers' judgments of the scientific merit of experimental and quasi-experimental research submitted in support of the program. Each certified program was classified as *model* (57 programs with demonstrated effectiveness that are ready for dissemination), *effective* (45 programs with demonstrated effectiveness but that are not available for dissemination), or *promising* (51 programs with evidence suggesting effectiveness but lacking sufficient rigor in evaluation methods).

To date, no empirical examination has been conducted of programs included in NREPP. The goal of the analyses reported here is to summarize the measured impact of these programs on reducing substance use and to identify critical features of programs that may account for their success. In the study detailed in this chapter, we use a meta-analytic approach to examine the relationship of program content, dosage, developmental appropriateness, cultural appropriateness, ease of implementation, potential of the program to engage participants, integration of the program across settings, and the program's Institute of Medicine (IOM) classification regarding the impact programs have had on substance use.

Preparation of this chapter was supported in part by Center for Substance Abuse Prevention Contract 277-99-6023.

RATIONALE

Beginning in the mid-1990s, federal agencies responsible for funding research have encouraged local agencies and schools to adopt evidence- or science-based programs. However, in choosing to disseminate programs that have had a demonstrable and statistically significant impact, two legitimate questions arise. First, statistical significance is different from clinically relevant or meaningful change (Jacobson & Truax, 1991). In other words, a program can have an effect determined by statistical reasoning; however, the size of this effect overall may be too insignificant to really make a difference at a policy or practical level. Second, programs can be delivered across many different venues, with different sample composition, ultimately bringing into question the value of the program from a practical point of view. Meta-analysis provides a convenient method for converting disparate effectiveness estimates to the expected percentage of difference in prevalence attributable to an intervention. This information is valuable to local prevention providers for managing expectations of the expected impact of adopting an NREPP-approved substance abuse intervention.

Although fidelity to program implementation—delivering a program as its creator intended—has been cited as important to intervention success (Dusenbury, Brannigan, Falco, & Hansen, 2003), local prevention providers must often balance this call for fidelity with local resources, capacity, and local sensibilities (Backer, 2001). Adapting intervention programs often requires selecting lessons, reducing sessions, and/or modifying content to match cultural competencies (Castro, Barrera, & Martinez, 2004). By identifying the common features across programs that are associated with greater success in preventing and reducing substance use, a meta-analysis can provide initial guidance as to how prevention programming can, should, and (even more important) should not be adapted when meeting local needs.

METHOD

Sample of Programs

We considered programs listed as model and effective by NREPP for inclusion in the study. Programs had to be listed and identified before December 31, 2003. They had to include manuals that would guide implementation. Programs also had to have either published or unpublished reports that documented the impact of the program on alcohol, tobacco, marijuana, or other drug use outcomes. An initial set of 48 programs were identified for inclusion. The complete list of programs can be found in Hansen, Dusenbury, Bishop, and Derzon (2007).

Program Coding

We included an analysis of manuals because only by examining the manual or the protocol can the essential strategic and logistical elements of a program be understood. It is crucial to understand the structure, content, and process by which an intervention is intended to be delivered. Research papers are summaries and are often cryptic in their portrayal of an intervention (Lipsey, 1988, 1997). Brief summaries often give an incomplete description of an intervention or describe program modalities, without sufficient detail for understanding program content and procedures. Finally, program developers' brief descriptions, even when accurate, are often couched in idiosyncratic and highly specialized language, frequently producing an uneven presentation of content materials. These descriptions cannot be relied on to classify a program's components and strategies. Manuals were collected from program developers, systematically evaluated, and rated on the basis of the following criteria.

Program content. Program content refers to the topics addressed in an intervention and can be thought of as the risk factors and protective factors targeted for change. Our goal in reviewing manuals was to identify which content was and was not addressed by each program on the basis of emerging categorization schema that began with earlier reviews of research on program components (Hansen, 1992; Hawkins, Catalano, & Miller, 1992). Overall, we were able to identify 23 definable and distinct content areas. Details about this coding system have been published elsewhere (Hansen et al., 2006). A brief summary is presented here.

We coded the quality and quantity of content in manuals along four primary dimensions: (a) components designed to alter motivations to use drugs, (b) components designed to promote the development of personal competence, (c) components designed to develop interpersonal or social skills, and (d) components designed to change social and environmental characteristics.

- *Motivation*—Motivational approaches are designed to prevent substance use by making it unappealing. These approaches focus on six specific prevention strategies, which consist of components designed to promote (a) antidrug or antideviance attitudes; (b) bonding to school, family, or other positive institution; (c) beliefs about the likelihood of experiencing negative consequences; (d) a commitment to not participate in drug use or other negative behaviors; (e) the adoption of positive normative beliefs about the behavior and attitudes of others; and (f) the development of values that are incongruent with risky behavior.
- *Personal competence*—Personal skills or competence development approaches prevent substance us by promoting the development of self-management skills. These include approaches designed to promote (a) academic skills; (b) decision-making skills and the control of impulsivity; (c) emotional self-regulation for managing anger, anxiety, and stress; (d) goal-setting skills; and (e) self-esteem.
- *Interpersonal and social skills*—Interpersonal and social skills development approaches to substance use prevention focus on developing the ability to deal with social influences. These approaches include strategies to teach (a) assertiveness and resistance skills, (b) media literacy, (c) communication skills, (d) social problem-solving skills, and (e) general social skills needed for social interaction and friendship formation.
- *Social environment*—Social and environmental substance use prevention strategies are designed to improve the social and physical environment. These methods include strategies for (a) limiting availability and access and promoting the enforcement of laws; (b) providing alternatives to drug use; (c) improving classroom management and the use of appropriate discipline and creating positive school environments; (d) improving family management and discipline and fostering positive family environments; (e) increasing

active monitoring and supervision; (f) promoting affiliation with positive peers; and (g) providing access to positive support and involvement in positive activities.

Each program was evaluated on the extent of coverage (quantity) it provided for each content area. Coders rated each program's coverage as providing (a) no coverage, (b) a little or minimal coverage (typically judged as devoting less than one session to the topic), (c) some content (typically judged as devoting one or two sessions to the topic), or (d) extensive coverage (labeled as *a lot* and typically judged on the basis of having three or more sessions devoted to the topic). Each of the 23 content areas was also given a qualitative judgment. We used the following questions to establish a framework for judging quality: "How well did the program address the content area?" "Is it organized in a way that allows the objectives to be achieved?" and "How likely were the program materials to be engaging to participants?" For programs that devoted attention to the content area, a qualitative rating of 2 (*not sufficient*), 3 (*adequate*), or 4 (*outstanding*) was made. If a program did not include content, a rating of 1 (*none*) was made.

Developmental appropriateness. Three ratings were made to describe the developmental appropriateness of each program. First, we rated the age appropriateness of written materials (reading level of worksheets, etc., for students). Second, we rated the age appropriateness of concepts being presented, using terms consistent with Piaget's cognitive–developmental model, such as *complexity, level of detail,* and *social relevance,* to make these judgments. Finally, we made a global rating of the overall age appropriateness of the program. Each rating was made on a 4-point scale: *substandard* (1), *acceptable* (2), *above average* (3), or *outstanding* (4).

Cultural appropriateness. Three ratings about the cultural appropriateness of the program were made. The first included ratings of neutrality. This included such aspects as presenting examples in the program that are not exclusive to a particular group. For this rating, options included *unacceptable* or *acceptable.* Second, cultural specificity was rated ("Does the curriculum address issues of specific cultural groups?"). Response options were *no* and *yes*. Third, we rated cultural adaptability by answering the question "Does the program allow and provide guidance about how to adapt the program for different ethnic groups?" Three options were provided, including whether cultural adaptations were (a) not allowed, (b) allowed but no detail was provided, or (c) allowed and detailed instructions were provided.

Ease of implementation.   We examined and rated curriculum manuals and other program materials on a number of dimensions related to the ease with which the program could be implemented. Specifically, five ratings were made:

- *Preparation time*—The amount of preparation time and effort required was rated as *excessive, extensive, acceptable,* or *minimal.*
- *Layout*—how easy it would be to use the manual. Rating categories included *substandard, acceptable, above average,* or *outstanding.*
- *Quality of instructions*—the level of detail and clarity provided in the manual. Ratings included *not acceptable, acceptable, above average,* or *outstanding.*
- *Structural integration*—how much the program would require the creation of new structures (e.g., a new class). Ratings included *demanding, moderate,* or *easy.*
- *Overall ease*—how well a teacher, facilitator, or other user would be able to implement the program with quality on the basis of what is provided. Ratings included *difficult, acceptable, above average,* or *outstanding.*

Potential of the program to engage participants. We rated five qualities related to the degree to which the program might engage participants (Tobler et al., 2000).

- *Appeal of the program to students*—how likely it is to be fun and engaging to students. Ratings included *dull, acceptable, above average,* or *outstanding.*
- *Structured interactivity*—the extent to which the program includes discussion, small group activities, role-plays, games, and brainstorming. Ratings were *substandard, acceptable, above average,* or *outstanding.*

- *Interactivity prompts*—the extent to which the manual prompts teachers to ask questions of students. Ratings were the same as for structured interactivity.
- *Directions for interactivity*—how well the manual gives directions for discussions, small group activities, role-plays, games, and brainstorming. Ratings were the same as for structured interactivity.
- *Opportunities for practice*—degree to which there are opportunities for practice and application, including such aspects as homework and community service. Ratings were *none or minimally, some,* or *extensively.*

Dosage.   For each program, we calculated the number of sessions. For multiyear programs, we calculated numbers of sessions per year. For programs that allowed implementation across a range of grades or ages of participants, we calculated only number of sessions for one age or grade group. For programs targeting multiple ages, number of sessions was attributed to the earliest year in which they could be delivered. In addition to the number of sessions, we also coded the frequency of sessions (e.g., daily, weekly, monthly).

Integration across settings.   The program was characterized in terms of the degree to which it used any one of several sites for implementation, including school, family, workplace, and the community. For each setting, ratings included *none or minimally* (1), *some* (2), or *extensively* (3). In addition to rating the degree of implementation in each of these settings, we also rated several other characteristics of implementation. In the school setting, these included the degree to which the program encouraged positive changes in the school environment and integration in other areas of the school curriculum. In the workplace setting, these included the degree to which the program encouraged positive changes in the workplace environment and the integration of program content in other areas of the workplace. We also rated the degree to which the program used a balance among multiple settings (school, family, community, and/or workplace) to achieve its outcomes. Programs that used only one setting were classified as exclusive. Expanded programs were primarily delivered in one setting but included others minimally. Extensive programs were primarily delivered in one setting but included others extensively. Finally, balanced programs were delivered in multiple settings with a fair degree of balance across settings.

Institute of Medicine classification. Programs were classified as being universal, selective, or indicated, according to IOM descriptions of these classes (Mrazek & Brown, 1999; Mrazek & Haggerty, 1994). We examined each program and classified it on the basis of the content presented in the manual. Each program was required to have at least one classification; however, it was possible for any given program to have multiple classifications (e.g., universal and selective). In general, universal programs were those presented to a broad population. Selective programs were those that identified and addressed the needs of at-risk individuals or groups as defined by the program itself. Indicated programs were required to include individuals who had previously been diagnosed through clinical or legal assessment as having problematic behavior.

Effect size coding. We gathered as many evaluation reports as possible about each of the 48 target programs. Reports were gathered using information from the SAMHSA model programs Web site (http://modelprograms.samhsa.gov) as it existed in 2004. This list was expanded through literature searches and by contacting program developers and program evaluators.

We scanned research reports to determine whether they contained the statistical information appropriate for meta-analysis. At a minimum, data were considered ready to be coded if they estimated program effects on preventing or reducing alcohol, tobacco, marijuana, or other drug use using main effects analysis or provided data from which main effects could be calculated. Thus, eligible reports included a chi-square, *t* test, or analysis of variance reporting comparisons between a single treatment and control group and posttest means, standard deviations, and sample sizes. Regression statistics, analysis of variance outcomes that modeled multiple pretest covariates, and other complex statistical approaches (i.e., multivariate) that cannot be converted to a common metric were excluded from this synthesis. Data for each of these programs was extracted using standard proce-

dures for calculating effect size (Hedges & Olkin, 1985). The primary statistic calculated was Cohen's *d*, which is calculated using the formula Cohen's $d =$ M1 − M2 / spooled, where *spooled* indicated a pooled standard deviation, or $\sqrt{(s1^2 + s2^2)} / 2$.

Thus, effect size is a standardized measure of how large an impact an intervention had compared with a control group in terms of standard deviations. According to Cohen's (1988) original classification for *d* as an effect size indicator, small effects range from 0.20 to 0.49; medium effects, from 0.50 to 0.79; and large effects, from 0.80 to 2.00. On the basis of prior meta-analyses of substance abuse prevention programs, this may not be a meaningful way to view these programs, which might be suspected to have smaller effect sizes overall. For example, Tobler and Stratton (1997) found that for universal school-based substance abuse prevention programs, the median effect size was .14 and the mean effect size was .20.

Altogether, we assembled 384 research reports. Only 42 reports provided eligible substance use data on 25 of the 48 programs. Reports were excluded for four reasons: (a) Results were reported only in terms of statistical significance, and values of statistical tests were not provided; (b) results were presented in statistical terms that were too complex—regressions and analyses of variance with more than pretest as covariates and parameters obtained from structural equation models; (c) outcomes were based on archival records about substance use–related death and injuries or suspensions from school; and (d) sample size was not sufficiently well documented.

Programs that had coded outcome data included Across Ages, All Stars Core, ATLAS, Brief Alcohol Screening BASICS, brief strategic family therapy, CASASTART, Communities Mobilizing for Change on Alcohol, Coping Power, Family Matters, Good Behavior Game, Guiding Good Choices, Healthy Workplace, Keepin' It REAL, Life Skills Training, multidimensional family therapy, multisystemic therapy, Positive Action, Project Northland, Project Success, Reconnecting Youth, Residential Student Assistance Program, STARS for Families, SOAR, Smoking Cessation Mass Media Intervention, and Social Competence Promotion.

Reports were organized so that they were not only associated with the program they represented but also reflected different studies if multiple studies were appropriate. Effect sizes were therefore tied not only to each program but also nested within studies within programs, if multiple studies were identified.

Overall, we calculated 288 effect sizes. The most sensitive outcome measure for each substance was selected to represent program impact. For example, we considered number of smoking days in the past month more sensitive than any past-month cigarette use. Effect sizes were corrected for small sample bias, and all mean estimates were weighted by the inverse variance of each estimate to reflect the greater confidence associated with larger samples (Hedges & Olkin, 1985). Before synthesis, we aggregated all inverse variance weighted estimates first within study and then within program, so that each program contributed only a single effect size.

In the initial distribution of estimates, two extreme outliers, one positive and one negative, were observed. These were recoded (i.e., Winsorized) with an effect size more likely to represent its true status. Because some studies were much larger than others, the weights associated with the largest studies were similarly recoded to the mean of the weight plus 2 standard deviations. Winsorizing the weights keeps the contribution of the largest studies from overwhelming the contribution of the more typical study (Rivest, 1994).

RESULTS

Overall Effect Size

Overall, the mean effect size for the 25 SAMHSA programs that measured substance use outcomes was .141 with a standard error of .016 (see Figure 32.1). Although the overall effect size is relatively small compared with Cohen's standard, these results are comparable to those reported in Tobler and Stratton's (1997) earlier meta-analysis.

Although the average impact of NREPP programs varied by type of substance use measured, the differences were not significant. As can be seen in Table 32.1, somewhat larger average effect sizes were seen among programs that measured tobacco and marijuana outcomes. Alcohol was associated with the smallest average impact.

Motivation-Focused Program Content

Table 32.2 presents the degree to which each of the motivation-focused content areas was included among

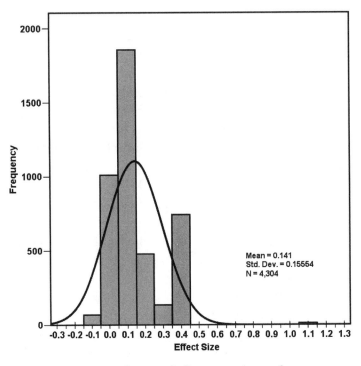

FIGURE 32.1. Distribution of effect sizes observed.

TABLE 32.1

Effect Sizes of Measured Outcomes

Substance	n	Mean effect size	SE	−95% CI	+95% CI
Tobacco	9	0.140	0.023	0.096	0.184
Alcohol	16	0.084	0.017	0.050	0.118
Marijuana	9	0.140	0.027	0.088	0.193
Other drugs	10	0.113	0.028	0.057	0.169

Note. CI = confidence interval.

the sample of 48 programs and their correspondence with the different programs' measured impact on substance use. Overall, the most common program content included in these programs was a focus on beliefs about consequences with almost three quarters of programs (73%) addressing these beliefs some or a lot on the basis of an analysis of program manuals. Slightly more than half of the programs (52%) addressed attitudes, and slightly fewer than half of the programs addressed normative beliefs (46%). About 4 in 10 programs addressed commitment (42%) and bonding (42%); only 1 in 4 programs (25%) addressed values or values incongruence.

TABLE 32.2

Outcomes Associated With Content

Content area	Number including Some n	Number including Some %	Number including A lot n	Number including A lot %	Correlations with effect size Quantity	Correlations with effect size Quality	Correlations with effect size Quantity × Quality
Motivation							
Attitudes	15	31	10	21	0.427	0.499	0.436
Beliefs about consequences	19	40	16	33	0.148	0.024	0.241
Bonding	8	17	12	25	0.033	0.331	0.053
Commitment	13	27	7	15	0.276	0.402	0.294
Normative beliefs	16	33	6	13	0.142	−0.198	0.139
Values incongruence	9	19	3	6	−0.039	0.018	−0.037
Personal skills							
Academic skills	4	8	8	17	0.363	0.128	0.363
Decision-making skills	13	27	11	23	−0.084	−0.088	−0.062
Emotional self-regulation	12	25	14	29	0.178	0.131	0.176
Goal setting	8	17	12	25	0.220	0.344	0.227
Self-esteem	7	15	2	4	0.025	.	0.011
Social skills							
Communication skills	10	21	12	25	0.133	0.144	0.123
Media literacy	13	27	3	6	−0.216	−0.152	−0.165
Resistance skills	19	40	13	27	−0.344	−0.421	−0.327
Social problem-solving skills	7	15	9	19	0.047	0.065	0.046
Social skills	10	21	8	17	0.065	−0.430	0.115
Environment							
Access, availability, and enforcement	2	4	6	13	−0.139	−0.767	−0.149
Alternatives	6	13	4	8	0.285	0.221	0.269
Classroom management	5	10	4	8	0.350	−0.311	0.350
Family management	4	8	13	27	−0.037	0.179	−0.013
Monitoring	4	8	7	15	0.081	0.150	0.071
Positive peer affiliation	8	17	3	6	0.307	0.050	0.261
Social support/involvement	8	17	4	8	0.368	0.182	0.402

Correlations with effect size can be used to explore the extent to which content areas are associated with program success. When correlations are strong and positive, programs that achieved greater effectiveness gave more attention to this content area. Because all programs included in NREPP had demonstrated effectiveness, this restriction of range likely makes these correlations a conservative test of which program features account for effectiveness.

Both the extent to which programs focused on building anti–substance use attitudes and the quality of their approach were important to achieving large reductions in substance use. Well-designed programs that gave attention to building commitments had larger effects than did those that did not include this component. Placing an extensive emphasis on building bonding between children and positive social institutions was not as crucial for success as having a method for promoting bonding that was well designed and soundly articulated.

Programs did not have a large effect on reducing substance use when they focused on building beliefs about consequences unless both quantity and high quality of programming were present. Providing sufficient content and having a well-crafted intervention were both required to produce desired outcome.

The remaining content areas, including improving normative beliefs and focusing attention on the lack of fit between personal values and substance use, were not strongly correlated with the size of effects observed.

Personal Skills Program Content

Table 32.2 also presents findings about programs that develop personal skills. The most common personal skills content included in programs was related to developing competence at emotional self-regulation, including stress, anxiety, and anger management. Just over half of the programs (54%) included this type of instruction. Decision-making skills were taught in half (50%) of the programs. Four in 10 programs (42%) included instruction about setting and achieving goals, 1 in 4 programs (25%) addressed building academic skills and competence, and very few programs addressed self-esteem (19%).

Program efforts to improve personal skills from two areas were correlated with improved substance use outcomes. The more attention given to improving academic skills, the more effective the program. Academic skill improvement programs did not need to be especially well designed to achieve this effect. Furthermore, programs that taught students how to make and set goals, particularly when well designed, had larger effects.

Having more or better instruction to develop skills for dealing with anxiety, stress, or anger was only weakly associated with increased program effectiveness. Giving greater attention to improving self-esteem had no effect on increased effectiveness; lack of variance in the quality with which programs improved self-esteem precludes testing the association of quality with outcome achieved. Neither the quality nor the quantity of decision-making skills programming was associated with program effectiveness.

Social Skills Program Content

Table 32.2 presents findings about social skills approaches. Two thirds of programs (67%) included some form of resistance skills training. Almost half of the programs (46%) included a component addressing the development of interpersonal communication skills. About one third of programs included an emphasis on general social skills development (38%), media literacy skills (32%), or social problem-solving skills (34%).

None of the social skills program content areas were strongly associated with effect size magnitude. Indeed, addressing resistance skills extensively and with high-quality programming was associated with decreased effectiveness. After beliefs about consequences, resistance skill training was the most popular content area addressed by the studies. Given the popularity of this approach, these findings suggest that its value for reducing substance use should be reconsidered. Similarly, the more and better a program addressed media literacy, the smaller the effect.

Environment-Focused Program Content

Compared with the other content areas, relatively few programs incorporated environmental strategies for prevention (see Table 32.2). The most popular of the environmental approaches, promoting positive family management and discipline practices, was incorporated in just more than one third (35%) of the programs. Providing additional social support was a part of one quarter (25%) of the programs. Promoting parental monitoring (23%), providing for opportunities for associating with positive peers (23%), and providing for positive alternatives (21%) were included in fewer than one quarter of the programs. Finally, strategies for reducing access and availability and increasing the enforcement of laws regarding the possession and sale of substances (17%) and providing training to improve classroom management (18%) were seen in fewer than one in five programs.

Despite their rarity, many environmental approaches were associated with increased program effectiveness. Programs that provided increased opportunities for social support and for positive involvement in the community increased effectiveness, especially when they were well designed.

Extensive training to help teachers promote positive school climates and cultures and to manage classrooms also produced more effective outcomes. Interestingly, classroom management programs that were designed well resulted in less effective outcomes; nonetheless, when considered jointly, positive outcomes were still obtained. Providing quality opportunities for positive peer affiliation and providing extensive and quality materials and/or activities as an alternative to drug use were each associated with increased program effectiveness.

Interestingly, among these programs environmental approaches that stressed limiting access and availability and increasing the enforcement of laws were associated with reduced effectiveness, particularly those that were well designed. These findings are counterintuitive at some level and should not be interpreted to mean that these programs were not effective. However, relative to other programs, interventions that stressed these components performed less well in terms of the magnitude of effect they produced.

A Classification of Program Types

Program developers typically create interventions that address multiple content areas. Indeed, except for environmental programs that address access, availability, and enforcement (which were considered one content area), nearly all NREPP programs include content from multiple areas. The average program addresses 8.5 content areas ($SD = 4.3$) some or a lot.

In a previously published article (Hansen et al., 2007), we reported the results of a principal-components factor analysis that determined which content areas were associated with each other. Seven groups of programs resulted: (a) programs that stressed skills-building approaches (decision-making skills, emotional self-regulation, social skills, communication skills, social problem-solving skills, and resistance skills); (b) environmental approaches that stressed access, availability, and enforcement; (c) approaches that stressed affiliation (family management, monitoring, bonding, and positive peer affiliation); (d) approaches for dealing with social influences (resistance skills, developing media literacy, strengthening beliefs about consequences, and improving attitudes); (e) programs that provided opportunity and support (goal-setting skills, alternatives, and social support, as well as self-esteem and values incongruence); (f) approaches that emphasized supporting schools and creating positive school experiences (academic skills, classroom management, and association with positive peers); and (g) programs that emphasized promoting positive motivations (commitment, normative beliefs, and values incongruence). Factor scores were calculated for each program and were correlated with aggregated effect size estimates (see Table 32.3). The factor most strongly correlated with increasing effectiveness was Factor 5, which included content associated with developing positive schools. These programs placed an emphasis on building academic skills such as studying, reading, and completing homework and

TABLE 32.3

Correlations Between Factors and Effect Size

Factor	r
Positive schools (Factor 5)	.427
Support, goals, and alternatives (Factor 4)	.358
Affiliation (Factor 2)	.127
Skills versus environment (Factor 1)	−.159
Motivation (Factor 6)	.115
Social influence (Factor 3)	.080

TABLE 32.4

Reliability and Interrelationships Among Program Design Features

Variable	α	1	2	3	4	5
1. Content quality		—				
2. Developmental appropriateness	.870	.603	—			
3. Cultural appropriateness	.867	−.048	.121	—		
4. Ease of implementation	.801	.292	.470	−.011	—	
5. Engaging to students	.850	.430	.519	.361	.465	—

provided teachers and administrators with tools for improving the quality of the school environment. These programs also provided opportunities to develop friendships with others who have positive attitudes and behaviors. Generally, these programs were more effective than programs that featured other content.

Programs that addressed support, goal setting, and alternatives were also highly effective; the more programs included these components, the larger the substance abuse prevention outcome. It is likely that these programs' success was because of their emphasis on providing opportunities for positive social support and involvement, engaging alternatives to substance use, and encouraging goal setting. The negative correlation on Factor 1 suggests that programs that emphasized personal and social skills were generally less effective, particularly when compared with those that emphasized limiting access and availability and increasing enforcement.

Program Design Features

Because they are related to general design features, quality, developmental appropriateness, cultural appropriateness, ease of implementation, and the potential of the program to engage participants are worth considering together.

The rating category of quality consisted of the average of ratings of quality across all content areas for which a program had developed an intervention. The remaining four measures (developmental appropriateness, cultural appropriateness, ease of implementation, and the potential of the program to engage participants) were structured as scales, with items averaged to form the scale score. Table 32.4

presents Cronbach's alpha coefficients when individual items were combined as scales. As can be seen, all scales had excellent internal estimates of consistency. With the exception of cultural appropriateness, measures tended to be highly related.

When examined as correlates of effect size (see Table 32.5), three design features predicted the magnitude of effect. Notably, programs that were engaging to students and that were developmentally and culturally appropriate increased their potential to be effective. Quality of content and ease of implementation were not predictive of effect size.

Intensity of Delivery

Because intensity consists of categorical measures, we assessed it separately. As can be seen in Table 32.6, more frequent implementation was clearly superior. Daily implementation during the course of the intervention and varied implementation—typically once or more per week—was superior to weekly and monthly schedules of implementation. There were essentially no effects if the schedule for implementation was not specified.

TABLE 32.5

Correlations of Program Design Features With Effect Size

Design feature	r
Engaging to students	.299
Developmental appropriateness	.280
Cultural appropriateness	.271
Content quality	−.007
Ease of implementation	−.068

Tab. 4

606

TABLE 32.6

Effect Size Associated With Frequency
of Program Delivery

Frequency	n	Mean effect size	SE	−95% CI	+95% CI
Daily	5	0.2686	0.0473	0.1758	0.3614
Varied	7	0.2868	0.0374	0.2135	0.3601
Weekly	7	0.1283	0.0225	0.0843	0.1724
Monthly	2	0.0946	0.0527	−0.0087	0.1978
Not specified	4	−0.0081	0.0353	−0.0774	0.0612

Note. CI = confidence interval.

Dosage

Dosage captures participants' exposure to intervention and is often considered a critical design feature in achieving effectiveness. From program manuals, we were able to code several measures of dosage, including the total number of sessions, the average number of sessions per year, and the number of years spanned by the program. These items were not highly correlated with each other and lacked the internal consistency needed to create a reliable scale.

Interestingly, and counter to much of the attention it has received, effect size was not correlated with any of our primary measures of dosage. The correlation between effect size and total number of sessions was .011. The correlation between effect size and the average number of sessions per year was .052. The correlation between effect size and the number of years spanned by a program was −.032. Table 32.7 presents the results when programs with more than 15 sessions (in all years) were compared with those with 15 or fewer sessions. A small but not statistically meaningful difference can be seen.

Target Age

Programs were generally age specific in terms of the age of participants for which they were intended. Target age was defined by the corresponding grade level of the target participant, irrespective of whether the program was delivered in a school setting. The average program claimed to have a total of 61.4 sessions ($SD = 158.3$). There were structural differences in the programs targeting younger versus older participants. Programs that targeted elementary school age participants had, on average, more sessions ($M = 121.3$, $SD = 239.4$) than did either programs that targeted middle school age participants ($M = 31.7$, $SD = 44.4$) or programs that targeted high school age participants ($M = 15.7$, $SD = 15.2$).

The age at which programs started was correlated at .160 with effect size; the age at which programs ended was correlated at .203; the average age was correlated at .193. Thus, programs were slightly more effective for older than for younger participants. Similarly, effect sizes were different for programs that targeted elementary, middle school, and high school age participants. Generally, programs targeting elementary school age participants had the smallest effect sizes and those that targeted high school age participants had the largest effect sizes, but these differences were not significant (see Table 32.8).

Effectiveness Within and Across Settings

The analyses presented in Table 32.9 summarize observed effects when school was considered as the setting for implementation. In all three analyses, using school as the setting for implementation was more effective than when school was excluded. Moreover, the more a program focused on changing school climate and culture, the more effective it became. Similarly, programs were more effective

TABLE 32.7

Effect Size Associated With Number of Sessions

No.	n	Mean effect size	SE	−95% CI	+95% CI
Fewer than 15 sessions	10	0.161	0.061	0.042	0.281
15 or more sessions	15	0.216	0.073	0.073	0.358

Note. CI = confidence interval.

TABLE 32.8

Effect Size Resulting From Target Age
of Participant

Target age	n	Mean effect size	SE	−95% CI	+95% CI
Not elementary	18	0.218	0.065	0.091	0.345
Elementary	7	0.132	0.057	0.019	0.244
Not middle school	12	0.189	0.058	0.075	0.302
Middle school	13	0.199	0.081	0.040	0.357
Not high school	17	0.177	0.069	0.043	0.311
High school	8	0.230	0.055	0.122	0.338

Note. CI = confidence interval.

when they included content that was delivered across multiple class settings.

Table 32.10 presents findings that resulted when the family was examined as a setting for implementation. Generally speaking, programs that included some family involvement—but not extensive family involvement—performed better than programs that either ignored the family or were extensively family focused.

Table 32.11 presents findings from analyses that included community as an implementation setting. In both the analysis that examined the use of community resources and communitywide implementation, relatively smaller overall effect sizes were observed.

Effect sizes were only available for a single workplace program. Because of the paucity of evidence for

the effectiveness of programs in these settings, comparisons cannot be presented.

Table 32.12 presents findings about the degree to which programs were judged to focus narrowly, involving only one setting (exclusive), or more broadly, involving multiple settings for implementation (expanded, extensive, or balanced). Only one program was judged to be balanced, in this case involving school, family, and community. This program had a comparatively large effect size, but it is difficult to generalize because it was limited to one case. Programs judged to have extensive cross-setting integration had the smallest average effect size, although it should be noted that none of the classifications had extremely small effects and all more or less had effect sizes that reflected the overall observed mean.

Institute of Medicine Classification

Finally, we examined the IOM classification of programs (see Table 32.13). Most of the programs included in our analysis were universal. Two programs were selective. Four programs were indicated. Six programs had multiple target populations: Two focused on both universal and selective populations, and four addressed selective and indicated populations. On one hand, overall, programs that addressed indicated, combined universal and selective, or combined selective and indicated programs performed most effectively. On the other hand, the two programs classified as being only selective did not perform well. The programs clas-

TABLE 32.9

Effect Size Resulting From Implementation in Schools

Comparison	n	Mean effect size	SE	−95% CI	+95% CI
School implementation					
None	7	0.029	0.029	−0.028	0.086
Extensive	18	0.184	0.018	0.149	0.219
School change					
None	17	0.113	0.018	0.077	0.149
Little	4	0.170	0.035	0.102	0.239
Extensive	4	0.272	0.046	0.182	0.363
School integration					
None	20	0.120	0.017	0.088	0.153
Extensive	5	0.260	0.040	0.182	0.337

Note. CI = confidence interval.

TABLE 32.10

Effect Size Resulting From Implementation in Families

Family implementation	n	Mean effect size	SE	−95% CI	+95% CI
None	8	0.135	0.020	0.096	0.173
Some	6	0.206	0.047	0.114	0.297
Extensive	11	0.130	0.029	0.074	0.186

Note. CI = confidence interval.

sified only as universal performed slightly below the overall average.

Methodological Considerations

The number of effect sizes per program varied, ranging from 1 to 60 with a mean 11.3 effect sizes per program and an *SD* of 13.9. Sample sizes also differed greatly among programs. The average enrollment in analyzed studies was 757 participants, with a range of 59 to 7,721 and an *SD* of 1,011. We used regression to examine the relative contribution of each sample size on observed effect sizes. When regressed, the effect of sample size clearly contributed most to determining the size of effects ($\beta = .481$, $p \leq .0001$), although the number of effect sizes provided by a program also predicted the size of the effect ($\beta = .150$, $p = .21$). Essentially, smaller studies yielded larger effect sizes. Similarly, programs that reported more effect sizes generally had smaller effect sizes on average.

DISCUSSION

NREPP represents a significant advance in the field of prevention. The creation of this registry

has been the first systematic attempt at providing substance abuse prevention and mental health promotion programs with objective certification of effectiveness. The results of this analysis provide evidence that may be useful for understanding which strategies may have the greatest potential for effectiveness when considering which approaches to prevention communities might wish to adopt.

NREPP programs had almost universally positive effects in reducing alcohol, tobacco, marijuana, or other drug use. The average effect size was similar to those in other meta-analyses of prevention; however, programs showed significant variability in their impact, suggesting that some programs produce larger effects than others. The range of effect sizes observed was bounded by zero on the small side and .40 on the large side.

Program Content

Program content figured pivotally as a predictor of the magnitude of a program's substance use outcomes. Eight of the 23 content areas were positively and at least moderately correlated ($rs > .200$) with the size of effect produced. These included programs that placed an emphasis on (a) promoting antidrug attitudes, (b) giving young people increased support from others and engaging them in positive activities in their communities, (c) promoting positive academic skills, (d) helping teachers manage their classrooms, (e) developing positive peer affiliations, (f) providing young people with positive alternatives, (g) helping participants develop strong commitments to avoid substance use, and (h) helping participants develop and achieve personal goals. In general, the more emphasis a program placed on

TABLE 32.11

Effect Size Resulting From Implementation in Communities

Community Implementation	n	Mean Effect Size	SE	−95% CI	+95% CI
No community implementation	18	0.201	0.022	0.159	0.243
Extensive community implementation	7	0.081	0.022	0.039	0.123
No communitywide change	21	0.206	0.021	0.166	0.246
Extensive communitywide change	4	0.061	0.023	0.016	0.106

Note. CI = confidence interval.

TABLE 32.12

Effect Size Resulting From the Degree of Integration Across School, Family, Community, and Workplace Settings

Degree of integration	*n*	Mean effect size	*SE*	−95% CI	+95% CI
Exclusive	11	0.148	0.021	0.108	0.188
Expanded	3	0.186	0.063	0.063	0.308
Extensive	10	0.117	0.026	0.067	0.167
Balanced	1	0.211	0.090	0.035	0.387

Note. CI = confidence interval.

each of these elements, the larger the effect on substance use. At a minimum, communities may wish to adopt these types of programs. Communities may ultimately benefit by adopting programs that complement one another by targeting multiple content areas.

Several content areas were negatively correlated with substance use outcomes; the more programs emphasized these approaches, the smaller the effect size. Negatively correlated content included programs that focused on (a) resistance skills training, (b) promoting literacy of media messages about alcohol and drugs, (c) reducing access and availability and increasing enforcement, (d) providing decision-making skills training, (e) increasing incongruence

---

TABLE 32.13

Effect Size Associated With Institute of Medicine Classifications

Classification	*n*	Mean effect size	*SE*	−95% CI	+95% CI
Universal	13	0.103	0.017	0.069	0.137
Selective	2	−0.026	0.104	−0.230	0.177
Indicated	4	0.316	0.098	0.124	0.508
Universal and selective	2	0.312	0.049	0.216	0.408
Selective and indicated	4	0.303	0.054	0.196	0.409

Note. CI = confidence interval.

between personally held values and substance use, and (f) promoting family rules, discipline, and management. Simply interpreting these findings as providing support for positively correlated approaches and as grounds for avoiding negatively correlated approaches is not fully warranted. All of the programs included in this analysis had demonstrated their effectiveness in reducing and preventing substance use. At issue is how large an impact was demonstrated and what aspects of these programs were associated with its effects. There are many reasons for small effects. Programs that feature content that is negatively associated with effect size may wish to give attention to how these program components work.

Although central to estimating a program's impact, the magnitude of the effect size obtained is only one measure of a program's worth, and the value of a program to a community extends beyond this single measure of effectiveness. An inexpensive and easily disseminated intervention with a small effect size that is broadly implemented may produce greater community impact than a more effective intervention that affects fewer people (Derzon & Lipsey, 2002). There may be some temptation to similarly interpret approaches that were negatively correlated with effect size as program strategies to be avoided. However, there must be a caveat to both interpretations. For example, consider programs that address reducing youth's access to alcohol through enforcement and restricted availability. These programs are likely to have relatively small effect sizes in part because they are communitywide efforts. They involve large numbers of people, and the intervention is only indirectly targeted at individuals. Nonetheless, the number of people within a community who may be affected is likely to be very large. The overall effect on a community may certainly be worth the effort. Furthermore, access reduction programs may affect profound outcomes that were not included in analyses, such as deaths and injuries resulting from accidents and violence. The negative correlation between content area and effect size does not mean programs of that type are having contraindicated effects, only that the impact is less than that of alternative approaches.

Viewed another way, programs that focus on individuals may have large effect sizes, but because they are focused on relatively few people within a community, they may not have much of an effect on drug use in the community as a whole. Overall, when selecting content area for adoption, communities should balance the estimated impact of the prevention strategy with consideration of the scope and cost of the intervention strategy adopted. Moreover, we should emphasize that the results of these analyses are not definitive. Programs were not randomly assigned to implement different components, and nearly all programs included both elements with the potential to augment and elements with the potential to suppress effectiveness. The evidence summarized here can only document which program features are associated with greater program effectiveness among programs already deemed effective. There are no "pure" programs, and it is likely that measured effectiveness results from program options, sample features, and the research methods used to assess effectiveness (Lipsey, 1997).

Program Design Features

Several program design features were strongly correlated with positive outcomes. Programs that were engaging to students and those that reflected developmental and cultural appropriateness were associated with larger effect sizes. These findings fit with expectations (Tobler & Stratton, 1997). Selecting programs that provide extensive opportunities for interactivity and training facilitators to fulfill the interactive potential of the programs they implement may be expected to augment prevention effectiveness.

Our findings suggest that developmentally appropriate programs were more successful. A number of programs were judged to be too advanced for the intended population, a problem more likely to occur with programs that target younger populations. Similarly, culturally sensitive programs have been widely advocated (Castro et al., 2004). Programs that provided guidance about how to adapt the program for cultural groups or that addressed specific issues of cultural groups as part of the program were likely to be more successful.

Ease of implementation and the overall quality with which content was addressed were not correlated with magnitude of effect. It should be remembered, however, that once programs are disseminated,

the quality with which they are written and the ease with which they may be implemented may both be important for determining the degree to which fidelity can be maintained. Thus, even though these measures were not predictors of effectiveness for studies that were examined, they may become important considerations once programs are disseminated.

Intensity of Delivery

Programs that were delivered more frequently were also more effective. Programs that were delivered on a daily basis and programs that were delivered on what was coded as a varied schedule were highly effective. Typically, varied scheduling was at least weekly, allowing multiple meetings per week but not usually requiring daily implementation. In contrast, programs that called for weekly and monthly implementation produced smaller effect sizes. The logic of these findings is compelling—programs are most effective when they are delivered frequently. Young people probably need continuity in the messages they receive, and respond only to messages to which they have sufficient exposure to get their attention. Communities should seek programs that allow a schedule of frequent implementation. Programs that do not require at least weekly implementation may be augmented with supplementary activities or may be combined with other programs to provide a reasonably intense type of intervention.

Dosage

Given the importance of the frequency with which programs were delivered, it is interesting that dosage was not correlated with effect size. It has been accepted as commonsense wisdom that the more intervention a program provides, the more effective it will be. This hypothesis was not supported by the results observed. The total number of sessions, the average number of sessions per year, or the number of years spanned by the program did not predict effectiveness.

There are several possible explanations for this observation. First, it is doubtful that the lack of relationship can be attributed to single-session programs being as effective as programs that had large numbers of sessions. There was only one single-session program identified, and it was classified as single session primarily because it was a communitywide effort that had no defined number of sessions per se. One possible explanation for the lack of correlation between number of sessions and effect size is that some programs that had extensive dosage requirements did not require frequent interactions, whereas others had fewer dosage requirements but more frequent interaction. A second reasonable explanation is that programs that provide a large number of sessions did not necessarily provide full implementation of all sessions. Programs with a large number of sessions often allow implementers to choose which to implement. A third plausible explanation is that some programs may have many sessions, but these sessions may be shorter. Finally, it may be the case that there is a threshold that must be met, but that after the threshold number of sessions becomes less important. Indeed, we found that programs with more than 15 sessions were generally more effective than programs with 15 or fewer sessions, suggesting this may be the case.

Target Age

Programs that targeted elementary school children, even though they generally had more sessions, were less effective than programs that targeted high school age participants. It is likely that these results reflect a statistical boundary effect. That is, there is very little substance use among elementary school age children. Prevention programs that target younger students primarily seek to delay onset. Effect sizes are therefore highly dependent on changes in behavior of a control group. Without this change in control group, effect sizes are diminished because participants generally cannot reduce use. This restriction of range unavoidably reduces effect size. However, programs targeting older populations increasingly focus on encouraging reductions in use. Because use among controls may continue to escalate during this period, the effect size can benefit from both increased use among controls and decreased use among treated participants.

Effectiveness Within and Across Settings

School-based programs are among the most widely disseminated programs in the registry. The effectiveness of the school-based programs warrants a continued emphasis on using this setting. However, it has been relatively rare for programs to seek to create schoolwide change or to integrate prevention concepts beyond the delivery of a packaged program. Efforts to extend programming to improve school culture and engage the entire staff in promoting prevention goals have clear added benefits and should be pursued.

Programs were most effective when they included some family component but were not exclusively focused on the family. The lack of effectiveness of programs that focus extensively on families may be because some of these programs target highly dysfunctional families in which changing behavior may be more challenging. These families may have embedded risks that programs will have a difficult time removing.

Programs that had extensive community implementation and that intended extensive communitywide change generally did not produce large effects. However, it may be that community efforts have the benefit of making changes on an entire population. School programs, family programs, and workplace programs target smaller numbers of individuals. It is difficult to compare highly effective programs that target small numbers with programs of less overall effectiveness that change entire communities.

There were few programs that focused broadly, involving multiple settings for implementation. Most programs focused on one setting exclusively or expanded their approach to include extensive focus in two of the four possible settings. There were also few programs that had a primary focus in one setting and some, but rather limited, exposure in a second setting. A commonsense notion that has guided prevention during the past decades is that programs should extend their influences so that all players—schools, community centers and agencies, workplaces, and families—should cooperate in prevention. The single program that achieved a balanced rating showed a larger effect size than did more narrowly focused programs. To the extent that this program represents this ideal, there is some evidence that this approach should be emphasized, although increasing scope may strain local resources and may require greater coordination of services than more focused prevention programming.

Coordination may, in itself, be a difficult goal to achieve. Only 1 of the 25 programs purported to do so. The limited evidence for coordinated approaches should not, however, be taken as lack of support for the approach. Evaluating such coordinated efforts is expensive, and evaluation designs that allow all elements to be independently tested are few. It may be that on this topic, communities will find it easier than researchers to engage a broad spectrum of the community in prevention. Communities may be able to launch coordinated efforts, particularly if they feel less pressure to provide experimentally valid results and if various components can be phased in over time. There is a great deal to learn about such efforts.

Institute of Medicine Classification

Finally, programs that addressed indicated, combined universal and selective, or combined selective and indicated programs were most effective at reducing substance use. Programs that were only universal or that were only selective failed to have a large impact on substance use. Indeed, the programs that were only classified as selective essentially had no observed effect. It should be emphasized that our coding of IOM classification did not match the coding presented on the SAMHSA Web site. Our initial concern is that programs may not be correctly classified. Manuals are not required and, for the list on which our analyses were based, were not examined as part of the NREPP review process. (A revised NREPP review system that does examine materials has subsequently been adopted.) NREPP as implemented before 2004 did not produce an IOM classification as part of review. Therefore, a great deal of the information provided for classification comes from program developers, who may have varied understanding of the basis for classification. Indeed, as far as we can tell, there is no sanctioned method for classifying programs that has been developed.

The fact that multiple classifications can be attributed to a program may serve to confuse the initial intent of this classification system. It is difficult to imagine what a program would need to do to qualify for all three classifications, yet some programs in the registry do just that. We felt confident in allowing for two simultaneous classifications. Indeed, those that received multiple classifications did extremely well in terms of producing outcomes. It may well be that programs that adopt methods for addressing different risk groups either simultaneously (i.e., through programming that appeals to or can be addressed to multiple groups) or differentially (i.e., separate programming for each group but packaged together) may be efficient for effectiveness.

Methodological Limitations

By nature, all registries will contain diverse programs, many of which may not be directly comparable with each other. In this analysis, only 48 of the 153 certified programs provided manuals, and of these only 25 provided unconditioned estimates of their effectiveness in reducing substance-using behavior. These numbers are somewhat disappointing; however, such numbers are typical of meta-analyses. The reasons for the small numbers are primarily because (a) promising programs were excluded, (b) programs that did not have substance abuse as an outcome were excluded, (c) programs that did not have manuals were excluded, and (d) in the case of programs that were otherwise included for manual analysis, programs that did not have outcomes coded for effect size were excluded.

This latter point is crucial because it applies to approximately half the programs that might have been included in this analysis. The critical difference between having programs that met NREPP criteria but did not meet our criteria for coding was primarily based on the kind of data reported. Even though NREPP requires statistical evidence to qualify for inclusion, the standard of exactly what statistical evidence is required has not been specified. Meta-analysis has strict criteria for which data can be included. Ironically, the types of data required for meta-analysis (main effects analysis) are simpler than those often required for peer-reviewed research reports (e.g., theory-testing analyses).

Other general problems with finding sufficient data included the unavailability of research reports, the unavailability of manuals (particularly for programs on the effective list that are not intended for dissemination), and studies that did not collect behavioral measures or that did not use a standard pretest–posttest, treatment–control group design.

In sum, even among generally effective programs, certain program components and features are associated with greater program effectiveness. Because these features show consistency across multiple independent implementations, it is likely that they contribute to program success, but at what level and in what combination is not estimable from this analysis. Moreover, given that programs or approaches are effective, selecting strategies to increase the overall impact of the program in reducing substance use needs to be balanced against the resources and support for their implementation. Achieving buy-in for a strategy that marginally improves program effectiveness may cause more rancor than result. A less effective intervention strategy easily disseminated to a broad population may produce greater reductions in substance use than more effective strategies that target fewer individuals. Nonetheless, given the evidence summarized in this analysis, adopting strategies that are negatively correlated with effectiveness shifts the burden of proof that these strategies represent good community choices to those who would advocate their adoption.

References

An asterisk indicates that the study was included in the meta-analysis.

Backer, T. E. (2001). *Finding the balance—Program fidelity and adaptation in substance abuse prevention: A state-of-the-art review*. Rockville, MD: Center for Substance Abuse Prevention.

Baker, J. A., Kamphaus, R. W., Horne, A. M., & Winsor, A. P. (2006). Evidence for population-based perspectives on children's behavioral adjustment and needs for service delivery in schools. *School Psychology Review, 35*, 31–46.

Castro, F. G., Barrera, M., & Martinez, C. R. (2004). The cultural adaptation of prevention interventions: Resolving tensions between fidelity and fit. *Prevention Science, 5*, 41–45.

Cohen, J. (1988). *Statistical power analysis for the behavioral sciences* (2nd ed.). Hillsdale, NJ: Erlbaum.

Derzon, J. H., & Lipsey, M. W. (2002). A meta-analysis of the effectiveness of mass communication for changing substance use knowledge, attitudes, and behavior.

In W. D. Crano (Ed.), *Mass media and drug prevention: Classic and contemporary theories and research* (pp. 231–258). Mahwah, NJ: Erlbaum.

Dusenbury, L., Brannigan, R., Falco, M., & Hansen, W. B. (2003). A review of research on fidelity of implementation: Implications for drug abuse prevention in school settings. *Health Education Research, 18*, 237–256.

*Flynn, B. S., Worden, J. K., Secker-Walker, R. H., Chir, B., Pirie, P. L., Badger, G. J., et al. (1997). Long-term responses to higher and lower risk youths to smoking prevention interventions. *Preventive Medicine, 26*, 389–394.

*Flynn, B. S., Worden, J. K., Secker-Walker, R. H., Pirie, P. L., Badger, G. J., Carpenter, J. H., et al. (1994). Mass media and school interventions for cigarette smoking prevention: Effects 2 years after completion. *American Journal of Public Health, 84*, 1148–1150.

*Goldberg, L., Elliot, D. L., Clarke, G., MacKinnon, D. P., Moe E., & Cheong, J. (2000). The Adolescents Training and Learning to Avoid Steroids Program: Preventing drug use and promoting health behaviors. *Archives of Pediatrics and Adolescent Medicine, 154*, 332–338.

Hansen, W. B. (1992). School-based substance abuse prevention: A review of the state of the art curriculum 1980–1990. *Health Education Research, 7*, 403–430.

Hansen, W. B., Dusenbury, L., Bishop, D., & Derzon, J. H. (2007). Substance abuse prevention program content: Systematizing the classification of what programs target for change. *Health Education Research, 22*, 351–360.

*Hansen, W. B., & Graham, J. W. (1991). Preventing alcohol, marijuana, and cigarette use among adolescents: Peer pressure resistance training vs. establishing conservative norms. *Preventive Medicine, 20*, 414–430.

*Hansen, W. B., Malotte, C. K., & Fielding, J. E. (1988). Evaluation of a tobacco and alcohol abuse prevention curriculum for adolescents. *Health Educational Quarterly, 15*, 93–114.

*Harrington, N. G., Giles, S. M., Hoyle, R. H., Feeney, G. J., & Yungbluth, S. C. (2001). Evaluation of the All Stars character education and problem behavior prevention program: Pretest-posttest effects on mediator and outcome variables for middle school students. *Health Education & Behavior, 28*, 533–546.

*Hawkins, J. D., Catalano, R. F., Kosterman, R., Abbott, R., & Hill, K. G. (1999). Preventing adolescent health-risk behaviors by strengthening protection during childhood. *Archives of Pediatric and Adolescent Behavior, 153*, 226–234.

Hawkins, J. D., Catalano, R. F., & Miller, J. Y. (1992). Risk and protective factors for alcohol and other drug problems in adolescence and early adulthood: Implications for substance abuse prevention. *Psychological Bulletin, 112,* 64–105.

*Hawkins, J. D., Catalano, R. F., Morrison, D. M., Abbott, R. D., & Day, L. E. (1992). The Seattle Social Development Project: Effects of the first four years on protective factors and problem behaviors. In J. McCord & R. Tremblay (Eds.), *The prevention of antisocial behavior in children* (pp. 139–161). New York: Guilford Press.

Hedges, L. V., & Olkin, I. (1985). *Statistical methods for meta-analysis.* New York: Academic Press.

*Henggeler, S. W., Clingempeel, W. G., Brondino, M. J., & Pickrel, S. G. (2002). Four-year follow-up of multisystemic therapy with substance-abusing and substance-dependent juvenile offenders. *Journal of the American Academy of Child & Adolescent Psychiatry, 41,* 868–874.

*Henggeler, S. W., Rowland, M. D., Randall, J., Ward, D. M., Pickrel, S. G., Cunningham, P. B., et al. (1999). Home based multisystemic therapy as an alternative to the hospitalization of youths in psychiatric crisis: Clinical outcomes. *Journal of the American Academy of Child & Adolescent Psychiatry, 38,* 1331–1339.

Jacobson, N. S., & Truax, P. (1991). Clinical significance: A statistical approach to defining meaningful change in psychotherapy research. *Journal of Consulting and Clinical Psychology, 59,* 12–19.

Johnston, L. D., O'Malley, P. M., Bachman, J. G., & Schulenberg, J. E. (2008). *Monitoring the Future national survey results on drug use, 1975–2007. Volume 1: Secondary school students* (NIH Publication No. 08-6418A). Bethesda, MD: National Institute on Drug Abuse.

*Kellam, S. G., & Anthony, J. C. (1998). Targeting early antecedents to prevent tobacco smoking: Findings from an epidemiologically based field trial. *American Journal of Public Health, 88,* 1490–1495.

Lipsey, M. W. (1988). Reports on topic areas: Practice and malpractice in evaluation research. *American Journal of Evaluation, 9,* 5–24.

Lipsey, M. W. (1997). What can you build with thousands of bricks? Musings on the cumulation of knowledge in program evaluation. *New Directions for Evaluation, 76,* 7–24.

*Lochman, J. E., & Wells, K. C. (2002). The Coping Power program at the middle-school transition: Universal and indicated prevention effects. *Psychology of Addictive Behaviors, 16*(4, Suppl.), S40–S54.

*LoSciuto, L., & Taylor, A. S. (2000). *Across ages: An intergenerational approach to drug prevention.* Unpublished manuscript.

*Marlatt, G. A., Baer, J. S., Kivlahan, D. R., Dimeff, L. A., Larimer, M. E., Quigley, L. A., et al. (1998). Screening and brief intervention for high-risk college student drinkers: Results from a 2-year follow-up assessment. *Journal of Consulting and Clinical Psychology, 66,* 604–615.

*Marsiglia, F. F., Kulis, S., Dustman, P., & Nieri, T. (2002). *Final report: Keepin' it REAL prevention curriculum implementation.* Unpublished manuscript.

*McCormick, B., & Aseltine, R. H. (2000). *Final report: Across Ages.* Unpublished manuscript.

*McNeal, R. B., Hansen, W. B., Harrington, N. G., & Giles S. M. (2004). How All Stars works: An examination of program effects on mediating variables. *Health Education & Behavior, 31,* 165–178.

*Morehouse, E., & Tobler, N. S. (2000). Preventing and reducing substance use among institutionalized adolescents. *Adolescence, 3,* 1–28.

Mrazek, P. J., & Brown, C. H. (1999). *An evidence-based literature review regarding outcomes in psychosocial and early intervention in young children* (Final Report). Toronto: Invest in Kids Foundation.

Mrazek, P. J., & Haggerty, R. J. (Eds.). (1994). *Reducing risks for mental disorders: Frontiers for preventive intervention research.* Washington, DC: National Academies Press.

Nutt, D., King, L. A., Saulsbury, W., & Blakemore, C. (2007). Development of a rational scale to assess the harm of drugs of potential misuse. *Lancet, 369,* 1047–1053.

*Pentz, M. A., Dwyer, J. H., MacKinnon, D. P., Flay, B. R., Phil, D., Hansen, W. B., et al. (1989, June 9). A multicommunity trial for primary prevention of adolescent drug abuse: Effects on drug use prevalence. *JAMA, 261,* 3259–3266.

*Perry, C., Williams, C., Veblen-Mortenson, S., Toomey, T., Komro, K., Anstine, P., et al. (1996). Project Northland: Outcomes of a community-wide alcohol use prevention program during early adolescence. *American Journal of Public Health, 86,* 956–965.

Rivest, L. P. (1994). Statistical properties of Winsorized means for skewed distributions. *Biometrika, 81,* 373–383. doi: 10.1093/biomet/81.2.373

*Santisteban, D. A., Coatsworth, J. D., Perez-Vidal, A., Kurtines, W. M., Schwartz, S. J., LaPerriere, A., & Szapocznik, J. (2003). Efficacy of brief strategic family therapy in modifying Hispanic adolescent behavior problems and substance use. *Journal of Family Psychology, 17,* 121–133.

*Smith, C., & Kennedy, S. D. (1991a). *Final impact evaluation of the friendly persuasion program of girls incorporated.* Unpublished manuscript.

*Smith, C., & Kennedy, S. D. (1991b). *Final impact evaluation of the friendly persuasion targeted substance abuse education program of girls incorporated.* Unpublished manuscript.

*Spoth, R. L., Redmond, C., & Shin, C. (2001) Randomized trial of brief family interventions for general populations: Adolescent substance use outcomes 4 years following baseline. *Journal of Consulting and Clinical Psychology, 69,* 1–15.

*Spoth, R. L., Redmond, C., Trudeau, L., & Shin, C. (2002). Longitudinal substance initiation outcomes for a universal preventive intervention combining family and school programs. *Psychology of Addictive Behaviors, 16,* 129–134.

Tobler, N. S., Roona, M. R., Ochshorn, P., Marshall, D. G., Streke, A. V., & Stackpole, K. M. (2000). School-based adolescent drug prevention programs: 1998 meta-analysis. *Journal of Primary Prevention, 20,* 275–336.

Tobler, N. S., & Stratton, H. H. (1997). Effectiveness of school-based drug prevention programs: A meta-analysis of the research. *Journal of Primary Prevention, 18,* 71–128.

*Wagenaar, A. C., Murray, D. M., Gehan, J. P., Wolfson, M., Forster, J. L., Toomey, T. L., et al. (2000). Communities mobilizing for change on alcohol: Outcomes from a randomized community trial. *Journal of Studies on Alcohol, 61,* 1–11.

*Werch, C. E., Pappas, D. M., Carlson, J. M., Edgemon, P., Sinder, J. A., & DiClemente, C. C. (2000). Evaluation of a brief alcohol prevention program for urban school youth. *American Journal of Health Behavior, 24,* 120–131.

CHAPTER 33

COGNITIVE MISPERCEPTIONS AND DRUG MISUSE

Steve Sussman

Addiction has been referred to as a problem of perception, and it is a concern recognized by members of the recovery movement and those conducting research on drug abuse (Alcoholics Anonymous, 1976; Chuck C., 1984; Ellis & Harper, 1975; Glynn, Levanthal, & Hirshman, 1994; Gorski, 1989; Johnson, 1980; Meichenbaum, 1977; Sussman, Earleywine, et al., 2004; Twerski, 1997). For example, Twerski (1997) discussed the thinking of drug abusers as exhibiting various distortions of thought. He believed that recognition and remediation of such cognitive distortions need to come from outside the addict, that the addict may block out certain facts that must be provided by others. However, exactly how selective learning of information occurs, and how it is that subsequent, more accurate, potentially corrective information is not incorporated adequately into one's cognitive repertoire, is generally not described. A better understanding of the formation and maintenance of cognitive misperceptions can come from an integration of several literatures: recovery movement, critical thinking (philosophy), social and cognitive psychology, health psychology, clinical psychology, health behavior research, and sociology. By examining cognitive misperception–related phenomena within these diverse literatures, types of cognitive variables may be inferred that are relevant to an understanding of the processes underlying the formation and maintenance of addictions.

To begin with, cognitive misperceptions are created that might make drug use an attractive option to a perceiver. "Cognition information" errors may facilitate one's interest in experimenting with drugs. Such errors may make drug use appear to be a statis-

tically normative, acceptable, or subjectively desirable behavior. Once an individual begins drug use, subjective effects of the drugs and peripheral experiences may reinforce continued use. Both explicit and implicit cognitive processes may lead the user to automatically tie use behavior to a variety of cues and outcomes that facilitate continued use (Stacy & Ames, 2001). Over time, drug use is paired with negative consequences; however, corrective information is not deeply processed, and drug misuse behavior does not change. Certainly, corrective information would need to compete with already prelearned information (Sussman & Unger, 2004; Wiers, de Jong, Havermans, & Jelicic, 2004). An individual's cognitive processing limits may deter successful competition with already learned information.

Second, there may also be cognitive processes that actively deter learning new information. For instance, an individual may be driven to maintain belief–behavior congruence. In this situation, an individual uses cognitive processes—which distance the perceiver from incongruence between his or her beliefs and behavior, perhaps to keep incongruent information from consciousness—or uses logical-appearing processes that more directly attempt to maintain congruence between behavior (drug misuse) and one's beliefs. In a related vein, one may distort the context of one's lifestyle to normalize one's behavior (situational–contextual distortions).

In the following sections of this chapter, I briefly summarize each of these possible sources of cognitive bias. First, I describe cognitive information error formation. Next, I describe the cognitive processes (explicit and implicit) that occur during the development of a behavioral relationship with drug use and cognitive processing limits. These two cognitive variables may facilitate development of a stable pattern of drug misuse. Then, I discuss belief–behavior congruence processes, including distancing and other means to maintain congruence (e.g., logical fallacies). I then discuss situational–contextual distortion perspectives as a framework for cognitive bias in drug use. These latter two types of cognitive variables may help maintain a stable pattern of drug misuse. Finally, I suggest approaches to counteract cognitive information errors, cognitive variables associated with the development of a behavioral relationship with drug use, belief–behavior congruence, and situational–contextual distortions.

Cognitive Information Errors

It is patently clear that people prefer to live with certainty; individuals base their ascertainment of predictability and control in life on their own subjective experiences. People's subjective experiences become familiar and entrenched as the "taken-for-granted" world (Schutz & Luckman, 1973). Representativeness heuristics involve basing judgments on one's experiential schema of how familiar to a standard a case appears to be. Availability heuristics involve basing judgments on one's experiential schema of how easily the case comes to mind. Both types of heuristics involve cognitive processes that fail to rely on further evidence. Thus, errors of frequency or importance occur for rare or vivid stimuli (Kahneman, 2003), sometimes regardless of the distinctiveness of the stimuli within the encoding context (McConnell, Sherman, & Hamilton, 1994).

Specific theories in health behavior research that have been used to explain these phenomena include the false consensus effect (Sherman, Presson, Chassin, Corty, & Olshavsky, 1983), illusory correlation (McConnell et al., 1994), implicit cognition theory (Stacy & Ames, 2001), and unrealistic optimism (Weinstein, 1982, 1987). The false consensus effect captures a tendency to believe that one's own attitudes or behaviors are more prevalent than they actually are. Illusory correlation as applied to behavioral phenomena refers to a tendency to overestimate the co-occurrence of two infrequent events or objects, perhaps because of processing mechanisms

related to the relatively novelty of their co-occurrence (e.g., drug use behavior and very novel pleasurable events [peak experiences]). Implicit cognition theory describes in part the tendency to bias one's automatic outcome associations of the consequences of one's behavior because of its past repeated associations with positive consequences. Unrealistic optimism is the tendency to perceive that one's chances of suffering an (unexpected or undesired) disease is less than is actually the case. Together, the cognitive experiences described by these theories may tend to normalize people's estimates of drug use frequency or appropriateness, leading them to infer that their behavior will result in greater pleasure than is actually indicated by repeated experience and furthermore leading people to discount the likelihood of negative consequences to the self from drug use.

There are several specific examples of how cognitive information errors occur among those at risk of participation in unhealthy lifestyles. Pertaining to errors in frequency estimation, relative overestimation of drug use prevalence, relative overestimation of peer approval of drug use, and relative underestimation of personal risk for negative drug use consequences may lead to (or stem from) problem drug use (MacKinnon et al., 1991; Sussman et al., 1988; Weinstein, 1982, 1987). Relative overestimation of the normative frequency of a person's attitudes and behavior (false consensus) may differ by health area and may serve positive and negative functions for health (e.g., in the case of depression, this cognitive process may serve a self-protective function; Tabachnik, Crocker, & Alloy, 1983). In the arena of drug abuse, false consensus serves a self-destructive function (e.g., Sherman et al., 1983; Sussman et al., 1988). These frequency errors tend to result from selective exposure to others who use drugs, a tendency to more firmly process vivid stimuli, and motivational distortions that conform to one's recent behavior (e.g., Sherman et al., 1983; Sussman et al., 1988).

Moreover, biased recall may result merely from repeated memory associations (e.g., Stacy & Ames, 2001). For example, mere familiarity with statements about drug effects, whether they are provided as statements of myth or fact, may alter outcome expectancies regarding drug use effects consistent with previously learned statements or behavior. Myths may subsequently become interpreted as facts, reinforcing previously pleasurable subjective effects of drug use experiences.

Limits in Cognitive Processing and Drug Use

Two general cognitive processing systems operate during the development of a behavioral relationship with drug use: explicit cognitive processes, including executive functioning; and implicit cognitive processes. These two cognitive systems operate together to direct one's behavior as a behavioral relationship with drug use is forming. Executive function processes operate to solve abstract problems and involve deliberation and planning as part of the control over behavior. These processes detect changes in performance as a function of continued drug use. Decrements in performance may become recognized and logically attributed to drug use if deliberately processed (Sussman & Unger, 2004).

Implicit cognitive processes involve automatically activated (rapid, efficient, and preconscious) cognitions that can sometimes be manifested in one's conscious stream of thought (if unfiltered), as opposed to deliberate, controlled processing of information. As such, implicit cognition changes rapidly and is not easily subject to introspection. Implicit cognitive processes act more on a store of information that includes the previous pleasurable effects of drug use and the memory of decrements in current performance as a function of drug use. Interestingly, explicit and implicit cognitive systems are likely to interact and take on different roles regarding the contemplation and performance of a behavior. An individual may observe him- or herself acting out of impulse and know that the behavior is self-defeating (executive function), yet keep doing it anyway (implicit cognition). In this instance, an individual is acting on implicit cognition, and his or her executive function is acting as the observer. It is possible for one to resist drug use by structuring one's time (executive function), although thoughts of drug use and pleasure may spontaneously keep coming to mind (implicit cognition). In this case, executive function is the actor and implicit cognition is the observer. Certainly, contextual factors

serve as stimuli that may influence the relative operation strength of explicit or implicit cognition. Stimuli that tend to evoke pleasurable drug-related memories may tend to influence implicit cognition, whereas stimuli that tend to evoke awareness of negative effects of drug use on current performance may tend to influence explicit cognition, at least until explicit cognitive information later becomes stored as implicit cognitive information (Alcoholics Anonymous, 1976; Stacy & Ames, 2001; Sussman & Unger, 2004; Wiers et al., 2004).

Corrective executive operations are impaired by time pressure, concurrent (multiple) task demands, mood fluctuation, or avoidance of the desire or tendency to plan events (Kahneman, 2003; Matthys & Lochman, 2005). That is, corrective operations are impaired by cognitive processing limits. People act to the limits of their behavioral repertoire and their knowledge of behavioral choices. One may or may not be fully aware of living in a world of "free operants" (Epstein, 1992). In other words, an individual may not be aware that he or she can make several choices to obtain satisfactory life outcomes. This lack of awareness may come from different sources. First, a person may be unable to comprehend subtle information or to otherwise interact effectively enough with others so as to obtain needed information. Second, a person may have difficulty keeping two or more options in working memory (Stacy & Ames, 2001). Third, he or she may have difficulty generating and weighing alternatives (Matthys & Lochman, 2005). Finally, a person may have difficulty making decisions related to initiating behavioral change. If a person does attempt to initiate change, he or she may have difficulty observing the impact of his or her behaviors on others (decision making regarding matching of behavior to context).

Belief–Behavior Congruence

People prefer to live in harmony, striking a balance between their beliefs and behavior, at least that brought into their awareness. Twerski (1997) asserted that addicts engage in perceptual distancing. According to this formulation, the tendency to distort or discount time and daily experience would insulate a person who exhibits self-destructive behaviors from the consequences of the behavior to self and others.

Such perceptual distancing would create a strong barrier against change. According to Twerski, drug addicts think in terms of brief chunks of time. Thus, they may believe that change should happen quickly. For example, stopping use for a month may feel like a very long time to an addict, even though life course changes actually occur much more slowly. A second characteristic, according to Twerski, is that potential addicts may view their experiences as not genuine. The characteristics Twerski described may also be reconceptualized as categories of logical fallacies (e.g., Downes, 1995–2001; Ellis & Harper, 1975; Kahane, 1990; Sussman, Dent, & Stacy, 1996; Twerski, 1997). Three types of fallacies are particularly pertinent. One major set of fallacies is *fallacies of distraction,* whereby processing insufficient information results in poor decisions (e.g., misuse of *or, not, if–then,* or *and* operators; you are either an alcoholic or you are not, and if you are alcoholic then you will tend to be homeless). Not going into treatment because of where it is located (an example provided by Twerski) might be attributed to an addict or drug user who fails to consider all the potential treatment locations. A second major set of fallacies is *causal fallacies,* in which the identification of the cause of a behavior or event is misplaced (e.g., stress causes smoking vs. smoking causes one to feel stress; others complain so one has to drink vs. one drinks and that leads others to complain). A third major set of fallacies is *fallacies of ambiguity,* in which phrases are used unclearly or inconsistently. For example, a person may think, "I am sober today, so I am not an alcoholic" rather than "I am sober today, but usually I am drunk." As a second example, an individual may think, "I used to be dishonest [lying], and now I quit drinking. Going into treatment would make me dishonest again because I am not drinking" (e.g., Twerski, 1997). Once again, implementing these fallacies may provide a cognitive–perceptual distance separating the perceiver from his or her self-destructive behavior.

An individual may actively attempt to maintain belief–behavior congruence. Awareness of equivocation or discrepancy in one's beliefs or desires leads to a tendency to want to eliminate the inconsistency (Miller & Rollnick, 1991). Two classic social psychological theories are relevant to the belief–behavior

discrepancy. Balance theory argues that a person seeks to achieve consistency regarding the polarity (positive or negative) of relations with others, oneself, and one's own beliefs (Heider, 1958). If a person's beliefs are inconsistent with his or her sense of self or with whom he or she forms a relationship or an attitude about, the person may be motivated to change the belief, modify his or her sense of self, or alter the relationship. Of course, although balanced situations might be relatively easy to remember, they will not necessarily be pleasant unless the polarities created are all positive (West & Wicklund, 1980). Drug users may perceptually distance themselves so as to ignore a cognitive imbalance, or they may change their beliefs to become more favorable toward drug use so as to maintain a relationship with another drug user.

A second approach, cognitive dissonance theory, argues that people are motivated to perceive a consistency between their decisions–behaviors and cognitions–beliefs. To make cognitions more consistent with decision behavior, a person might discount the importance of his or her thoughts, change them, or add new, consonant cognitions or beliefs (Festinger, 1957). It is possible that discounting one's cognitions is similar to perceptual distancing, and new consonant cognitions may be supplied to support one's drug use.

Contextual–Situational Distortions

An individual generally likes to perceive his or her lifestyle as normal, appropriate, and fun or optimal. This opens the door for people to interpret the contexts within which they exist so as to normalize life experience. There are at least three examples of notions that apply to situational distortions. One is mystification theory, which states that meanings of behavior may become confounded or distorted because of subjective effects interpreted within contexts (Lennard, Epstein, Bernstein, & Ransom, 1971). The process of mystification involves defining issues and situations in such a way as to obscure their most basic and important features. In one's social world, behaviors previously defined as normal may become defined as not normal (e.g., mild social anxiety), and drugs may be perceived as the optimal means to fix this behavior. Drugs may achieve their effects by bypassing meaning and means such that the experiential outcome is not the real outcome (e.g., drug-induced relaxation is not the same as learning to become more at ease in social situations by learning social skills). Also, the effects of drugs are derived not only by the pharmacological qualities of the drug but also by beliefs about the drug and the social context within which drug use occurs (Zinberg, 1984). Thus, it is understandable that a variety of myths regarding drug use and its effects can be widely disseminated. For example, a person may view him- or herself as having formed meaningful friendships with others just because they used drugs together in a social context (Ames, Sussman, & Dent, 1999; Sussman, Dent, & Stacy, 1996).

Another example of mystification is that applied to "getting used to" a drug. There are some drugs that create immediate physical problems with first or subsequent use. Initial use of cigarettes, for example, usually makes people feel sick, makes their stomach queasy, and makes them cough. Ecstasy causes jaw clenching, hyperthermia, profuse sweating, and headaches. Other drugs (opiate derivatives) can induce vomiting, sickness, and constipation. Over time, these negative consequences abate, and individuals also learn from their drug-using peers that they will eventually "accommodate" to these nasty side effects. In general, rather than getting used to the drug, one is suffering increasing tolerance to the drug, a sign of addiction.

A second related concept derives from perceived effects theory (Smith, 1980). Most acts are intended to benefit the actor, and some consequences of drug use may be grossly misperceived but may explain initiation of drug use because they appear to benefit the actor. For example, one may reinterpret a negative consequence of drug use (e.g., losing one's car in a parking lot) as being positive (e.g., funny). Also, one may interpret a positive consequence of drug use (e.g., spending time with another person) as being more positive than it really is (e.g., true love, meaningful friendship). As use escalates, greater distortions of reality may justify continued use and abuse.

A third theory, delinquent subcultures, has a strong foothold in sociology, including differential association theory (Sutherland, 1929) and related variants highlighting deviant peer bonding. The

basic notion of delinquent subcultures is that differential socialization may lead to group norms that serve to rationalize problem behavior (Akers, Krohn, Lanza-Kaduce, & Radosevich, 1979; Cohen, 1955). These rationalizations, however, reflect norms that exist in opposition to dominant social values and occur in distinctly subcultural groups. Cohen (1955), and several of his contemporaries who were sociologists (e.g., Bordua, 1962), argued that certain youth subcultures engaged in problem behaviors as a result of a gross reaction against middle-class society, as an expression of a general negativism, and because they found such activities to be a great deal of fun in the short run.

There are several variants of the deviant subcultures theory. One such variant is neutralization theory. A modification of Cohen's (1955) perspective, this approach asserts that people who exhibit problem behavior do internalize dominant social norms. However, norms are viewed as qualified guides for action, limited by situational variables (e.g., killing during war is okay; Agnew & Peters, 1986; Dodder & Hughes, 1993; Shields & Whitehall, 1994; Sykes & Matza, 1957). Techniques of neutralization include denial of responsibility (e.g., beyond one's control), denial of injury, denial of the victim (e.g., deserved it), condemnation of the condemners (e.g., as hypocrites), and appeal to higher authorities (e.g., loyalty to people or causes).

Work on deviant talk has explored the development of deviant interactions underlying such subcultural groups. Deviant or rule-breaking talk is defined as utterances that contain antisocial or norm-breaking elements. Talk about stealing, lying, aggression, illegal acts, favorable depictions of drug use (i.e., talk about "being bad"), swearing and rude or offensive gestures, removing clothes ("being bad"), and positive reactions to rule-breaking behavior (e.g., laughing) are exemplars of rule-breaking topics and deviancy training. Although many youth engage in rule-breaking behavior, those who become more deeply absorbed in such talk are at increased risk for future problem behavior (Granic & Dishion, 2003). Time spent with deviant peers, positive reactions among deviant peers to rule-breaking behavior, and processes in which deviant youth act to attract attention from lower risk peers are all aspects of deviancy training that lead to subsequent increases in drug use (Dishion, 2000; Dishion, Poulin, & Burraston, 2001; Poulin, Dishion, & Burraston, 2001).

CORRECTIVE STRATEGIES

A cognitive misperceptions view suggests that individuals can develop steadfast positive beliefs about drug use through social learning processes (Bandura, 1986), through subjective experience (Stacy & Ames, 2001) or because of peculiarities of learned behavior–outcome memory associations (Sussman, Dent, & Stacy, 1996). One good illustration of memory associations entails how marijuana use might be justified to regularly co-occur with driving a car. In this example, an individual links marijuana use to slowing down (i.e., relaxing) and safe driving to slowing down, which could engender a cognitive information error that marijuana use leads to safe driving (marijuana use equals slowing down, safe driving equals slowing down, hence marijuana use equals safe driving). This association fosters a logical fallacy. Cognitive processing of a favorable relationship among marijuana use, driving, and perceived safety may solidify to the extent that no car accidents initially occur while driving under the influence of marijuana. Cognitive processing limits may interfere with the ability to process that although marijuana use might lead a person to drive slower, the same individual might also feel drowsy or experience a dangerously slower reaction time (Sussman, Stacy, et al., 1996). One may also believe that one should drive safely, so marijuana use is a good drug to use, and at the same time drive more safely (belief–behavior congruence). Finally, one may view people who deter marijuana users from driving as uninformed villains (contextual–situational distortion). Several strategies have been developed to counteract the litany of cognitive information errors, cognitive processing limits, belief–behavior congruence, and contextual–situational distortions that promote drug use.

Cognitive Information Errors

There are several examples of how prevention programs can counteract cognitive information errors.

As one example, overestimations of drug use prevalence may be counteracted by an overestimate reduction prevention activity. In this activity, teens are polled on their perceptions of the number of peers who use drugs and also on their own behavior. They are presented with a comparison of their own perception (e.g., that 74% and 46% of their peers have used marijuana and LSD in the last week, respectively) and their own polled behavior (e.g., only 12% of youth at regular high schools used marijuana in the past week, only 28% of youth who attend alternative high schools [at-risk youth] used marijuana in the past week, and only 1% reported use of LSD in the past week in either type of school environment; Sussman et al., 1995; Sussman, Craig, & Moss, 2002). By understanding that they tend to overestimate others' use, youth realize that not everyone is using drugs and that they do not need to use drugs to fit in with peers. The intended result of such a program to correct misperceptions is that teens will reduce their prevalence estimates.

In addition to this strategy, preventative modalities can also counteract cognitive information error–related myth formation through the use of elaborative processing (Stacy & Ames, 2001). Sussman, Craig, and Moss (2002) provided an operational definition for this process in a drug abuse prevention curriculum. First, one discusses the kernel of truth in the myth, and then one discusses why the myth is a myth. For example, one may discuss the myth of using drugs to protect oneself from life stresses. The kernel of truth here suggests that some individuals will feel protected for at least a short time period. However, the myth is a fabrication because one is able to think less clearly and is more likely to become victimized and incur greater stresses.

Cognitive Processing Limits

As the consequences of use begin to take effect, many drug experimenters stop use. The literature on natural recovery posits that the majority of people who begin to use a range of psychoactive substances cease consumption on their own (Sussman & Ames, 2001). The number and types of consequences that a person can incur increase as one grows older (e.g., job and family), and many teen drug misusers will quit use as they reach adulthood because they perceive that they have different priorities or have more to lose. However, cognitive factors also operate to maintain drug use as a lifestyle behavior. A person may have acquired a lifestyle schema that involves obtaining and using a drug under numerous life circumstances. Giving up drug use may conflict with the thoughts and skills a person has nurtured in response to primary daily activities and social networks structured around drug use. The person is an expert in communications regarding the drug, and thoughts of pleasurable drug use may continually pop into mind (Stacy & Ames, 2001). It may take many annual cycles before the person can adjust to not using drugs each day, and these annual cycles may be needed to create a new implicit cognitive thought flow that does not evoke thoughts about drug use on certain occasions. For example, a person may need to cycle through February 2nd three or four times before he or she no longer links February 2nd as a day on which drugs were used. Thus, merely experiencing life over a long period of time without using drugs would be sufficient to create new memory networks that might be protective against future drug use.

Of course, people may desire more direct methods to change their thinking and behavior. Practice (in the form of behavioral rehearsal) in decision making–related activity appears essential to drug use prevention and cessation programs (e.g., Fiore et al., 2000; Sussman, Earleywine, et al., 2004). Practice in decision making using hypothetical scenarios can assist one in remediating difficulties by sorting out options and planning self-constructive action. For example, one should practice generating multiple solutions, considering the costs and benefits of each solution to self and others, selecting a maximally beneficial solution, making a commitment to follow through with the solution, and reevaluating multiple solutions contingent on satisfaction with the selected solution's outcome. As a person continues to use various decision-making steps, the executive function processes involved will become more automatic and solidify in memory.

Belief–Behavior Congruence

People may engage in self-destructive behaviors, even those that might be contrary to their basic beliefs

about themselves, because they often do not think about how their beliefs and different behaviors relate. Belief–behavior discrepancies can be brought to awareness to help people not engage in self-destructive behavior. For example, there are at least four examples of education formats that have attempted to make teens aware of their own discrepancies and reduce them through potentially healthful action. One such application is stereotyping remediation. Among teens, in-group and out-group stereotyping may exist (Fishkin et al., 1993). The notion here is that in-group members perceive out-group members as more extreme and homogeneous than they actually are. For example, high school and college youth are well aware that they are perceived by younger peers or older adults as more uniformly extreme or deviant ("wild") than they actually are. This stereotyping can become a self-fulfilling prophecy if people conform to such stereotypes. Alternatively, awareness of the stereotype can lead to people's counteracting it by taking on less obtrusive action and informing others of their decision to opt for healthful pursuits.

In summary, the logic of stereotyping remediation is as follows:

1. One notes that others (older teens) think one is a loser, deviant, or stoner (using adjectives list sheet).
2. One appreciates that older teens are somewhat deviant but not that bad (using adjectives list sheet).
3. One (an older teen) concludes that one should either give in to a self-fulfilling prophecy or rebel against it.

A second example is derived from attitudinal perspective theory (Upshaw & Ostrom, 1984), another theory harvested from social psychology. The theory posits that a person's attitudes about behaviors or events have two different aspects. First, an individual holds a general attitudinal perspective (e.g., as a moderate). Separately, he or she also holds specific attitudes about behaviors or events (e.g., believing that certain drugs should be legal). It is possible that the individual's general attitude about him- or herself may appear contradictory with his or her specific attitude. If the individual is confronted with the discrepancy, he or she will tend to try to reduce it, which in the present context could lead to specific anti–drug use statements. The "logic" of attitudinal perspectives remediation is as follows:

1. One recognizes that one holds a general self-attitude that one is characteristically a moderate (not extreme, but balanced and reasonable) type of person.
2. One also recognizes a specific attitude that risky behavior (e.g., regular recreational drug use) is viewed as radical by youth (an extreme stance against the norm).
3. One (an older teen) concludes that one should view oneself as a radical type of person or not engage in the specific behavior (abuse drugs).

A third example is derived from a "health as a value" notion (Lau, Hartman, & Ware, 1986; Ritt-Olson et al., 2004; Sussman et al., 1993; Sussman, Earleywine, et al., 2004). This notion suggests that the more a person values health, the more likely that person is to refrain from health-compromising behaviors. This cognitive construction may moderate the effects of one's perceived control over health and act as a motive for engaging in healthy behavior. For example, if people place importance on good health to better help them achieve life goals, they may be motivated to avoid drugs. More specifically, a person may desire goals (e.g., good grades), know he or she needs good health to achieve these goals, and be educated to recognize that drug use may interfere with goal attainment and that therefore he or she needs to change either goal attainment or drug use. The logic of instilling health as a value is as follows:

1. One considers what one wants to accomplish in the future.
2. One considers whether one's health is important to accomplish these goals. (One is likely to agree.)
3. One considers whether a self-destructive pattern of behavior (e.g., drug abuse) can interfere with one's health. (One is likely to agree.)
4. One concludes that one should give up one's goals or not engage or continue to engage in the self-destructive behavior (e.g., abusing drugs).

A fourth example is evident in motivational interviewing. Motivational interviewing is a thera-peutic tool to induce change in a brief period of time. Eight strategies are identified to motivate the individual to change behavior (Miller & Rollnick, 1991). These strategies are (a) giving advice, through which the problem is identified, the need for change is clarified, and specific change is encouraged; (b) removing impediments to change, which are mastered through effective problem solving; (c) providing choices, an important antecedent of voluntary commitment to change; (d) decreasing desirability of the continuation of present behavior by making its costs explicit; (e) providing empathy regarding the struggle to change; (f) providing behavioral feedback; (g) clarifying goals, especially confronting the individual with discrepancies between his or her future goals and present behavior (perhaps the most important aspect of motivation-enhanced programming); and finally (h) in active helping, demonstrating genuine interest in the client's change process.

Contextual–Situational Distortions

Mystification may be counteracted by direct confrontation of the mystification process. For example, with cigarette smoking, one may be taught that getting sick at first is a bodily warning signal that one is inhaling poisons. The cessation of getting sick does not arise from acclimating to cigarette use (i.e., the taste of nicotine and smoke inhalation); rather, the failing of these signals constitutes the beginning of tolerance. To impart this message, one tobacco use prevention curriculum instructs teens to read cards and to take on roles at different stages of use from trial to experimental, regular, and abuse (e.g., see Glynn, Levanthal, & Hirschman, 1985; Sussman, Barovich, et al., 2004).

An example of a means to counteract drug-related experiences from perceived effects theory includes the use of humorous cartoons that can be discussed in a group situation (Sussman, Craig, & Moss, 2002). In one such cartoon, the actor comments on how funny it was when she was arrested, took a drug test, was handcuffed and booked, and asked for a retake of the mug shot. The reinterpretation of a very negative social and legal situation is made clear, and a realization of the cognitive misperception is made explicit.

Appeals to personal responsibility and clarification of the negative consequences are essential to combating neutralization techniques. Use of psychodramas or "talk shows" can assist in accomplishing healthy changes. For example, in a "marijuana panel" talk show in Project Towards No Drug Abuse (Sussman, Craig, & Moss, 2002), various panelists report their experiences. Scripts are provided to all participants in the group. Participants volunteer to take on various roles, and they can work off the scripts. Participants in this activity serve either as other panelists or as audience members. An ex-marijuana abuser reports that he or she "used to smoke weed everyday. It became a problem." The abuser says,

> I felt like I couldn't make it through the day without at least one joint. I depended on marijuana to make me feel better. All I wanted to do was to be high and not think about anything. I told myself, and everyone else, that I did it because I was stressed. A lot of the jobs are asking for drug tests. I don't want to miss out on a job that I really want because of using weed. It's not worth it. Since I quit, I feel better. I have more energy and I'm finally taking care of the things in my life.

In this script, the marijuana abuser mentions that he or she used to blame continual marijuana use on stress, the neutralization technique of denial of responsibility. Then the person makes an appeal to personal responsibility and clarifies personal consequences suffered as a result of marijuana use. This may reduce the tendency to use neutralization techniques among all participants in this activity.

INTEGRATION AND CONCLUSIONS

A Model of the Self-Destructive Process

These four cognitive misperception processes provide a unique perspective of the self-destructive process, which may operate across the life-span. Information distortions may lead to retention of "facts" that are in truth not accurate (e.g., marijuana improves one's driving safety). Limitations in cognitive processing permit solidification of cognitive information errors. Inaccurate facts may lead to the perception of belief–behavior congruence (e.g., one believes in safe driving–marijuana use can help). Situational

distortions may operate to maintain a sense of certainty regarding one's behavioral processing of beliefs about one's world (e.g., bad people persecute and vilify marijuana users; one must go around these people to be able to drive more safely). The combination of these factors leads to, and composes, one's "addictive thinking."

Young children who tend to blame others in conflict situations, who appear hypersensitive regarding fulfillment of immediate needs (e.g., food and comfort), and who are not grounded in ongoing supportive and educative interactions with significant other adults are relatively likely to resort to acting out as a means of expressing their dissatisfaction (Kellam et al., 1989; Shedler & Block, 1990). They may tend to perceive that their acting-out behavior is appropriate (cognitive information errors); their executive functions may elicit perseveration of ultimately self-defeating behavior; by blaming others, they may tend to show belief–behavior congruence; and their alignment with other such youth may indicate creation of a contextual distortion (Matthys & Lochman, 2005).

Young teens who are curious regarding solution to their sense of dysregulation and who are approached by other teens who share a similar curiosity may seek out or yield to offers to try drugs or engage in other risky behaviors (Sussman et al, 1995). Drug prevalence overestimates, difficulties in decision making, alienation beliefs, and identification with other at-risk youth are facets of the four types of cognitive misperceptions that operate in young teens (Sussman, Dent, & McCuller, 2000).

Older teens solidify a sense of self and become more resistant to direct influence. They also tend to live in heterosexual contexts and are less mutually dependent on peers. Intrapersonal motivations become more important (Sussman, Earleywine, et al., 2004) and tend to dominate as a precipitant of risky or health behaviors throughout adulthood. Likewise, for emerging adults fear or lack of hope that one will be able to satisfactorily settle down into adult roles is a driving source of pressure that might lead one to resort to drug use or other self-destructive behavior. In both of these age groups, cognitive information errors (e.g., false consensus effect, unrealistic optimism), cognitive processing limitations in terms of the tendency to engage in overlearned albeit self-defeating behavior, belief–behavior congruence maintenance (e.g., perceived effects), and contextual distortions (e.g., hanging out in bars) all help to solidify and maintain drug use behavior.

For older adults, one's purview of life may include achievement of a subjective sense of wisdom versus a subjective sense of despair (Erickson, 1968), as shaped by social–environmental experiences such as amount of free time, lack of structure, and number of significant others remaining in one's social circles. Here, too, the same four types of cognitive variable may influence drug misuse among elderly people. In each of these developmental periods, one may seek out available resources, take a logical consideration of options, and make decisions that are fulfilling to self and others. Alternatively, one may begin or continue to process information in potentially distorted ways.

Counteracting the Self-Destructive Process: A Taxonomy

To translate the information we obtain from etiology to effective preventative strategies, the field needs to develop a taxonomic classification of drug abuse prevention strategies. These would detail program strategies as a function of type of programming (e.g., universal, selective, indicated) or other factors (e.g., stage of development, modality of implementation) as a start. Just as Mendelov's table of chemical elements lays out the distinguishing qualities of each element, integrative descriptive work is a reasonable starting point for program-based theoretical development (Sussman & Sussman, 2001). Certainly, across any type of programming some common features are likely to apply, including trust building among facilitator and participants, facts about the health behavior and information about the consequences, knowledge of high-risk situations, general social communication skills or enhancement, decision making, and interactive learning. Also, some programming might be intrinsically universal, such as making a public commitment (as opposed to a private commitment) and normative restructuring or a reduction in prevalence overestimates (in which most of the population demonstrates healthy lifestyles). Targeted programming appears to involve

strategies that make use of equivocation; motivate change; instruct cognitive and behavioral coping, including mood management; and provide information on recovering from damage already experienced by not pursuing a healthy course of behavior (e.g., Sussman & Ames, 2001). Certainly, age-specific counteraction of the four types of cognitive variable presented herein, which likely overlap with type of programming (targeted programs are relatively likely to be applied to older teens and emerging adults), should be considered in such a taxonomy and could advance prevention–cessation science.

Final Comments: A Prevention Strategy That Operates on All Four Cognitive Processes

The four cognitive misperception–related processes discussed compose four process modalities as a result of their discussion in distinct research and popular literatures. This does not mean that these processes may necessarily be different. For example, cognitive information errors could be accounted for in part by errors in recall related to one's implicit cognition associational network. Certainly, the other three types of cognitive processes are constituents of implicit or explicit cognitive processes, the latter being general categories of cognition. (The interplay of implicit and explicit cognition and processing limits was the emphasis of the discussion of implicit–explicit processing here.) One could argue that all cognitive misperceptions are the result of cognitive processing limits. Rather than enter into a whole variety of arguments, in this chapter I outlined a taxonomy of cognitive misperception processes that includes information from both applied and basic research. Certainly, much additional work is needed and will provide clarification over time on the input provided in this chapter.

I also described a variety of preventative strategies. A single type of strategy that might counteract multiple cognitive misperceptions at one time would be more economical. One potential candidate strategy is conscientiousness. *Conscientiousness* refers to a propensity to follow socially prescribed norms of behavior (e.g., social responsibility, tradition, or virtue), to be goal directed (e.g., industriousness), and to delay gratification (e.g., constraint, order, or self-control). In a review of studies resulting from a database search on consciousness-related terms and health-related behavior, Bogg and Roberts (2004) engaged in a meta-analysis and quantitatively synthesized data from 194 studies. They found that conscientiousness-related traits were negatively related to all risky health-related behaviors uncovered (e.g., drug use, unhealthy eating, risky driving, risky sex, violence) and positively related to all beneficial health-related behaviors (e.g., job attainment, exercise, healthy eating). Although Bogg and Roberts did not provide an overall theoretical explanation of why these relations should exist, it appears that social responsibility beliefs, a desire to contribute to the workforce and to others, and a willingness to sacrifice immediate pleasure are consistently related to health and unhealthy behavior. Also, although Bogg and Roberts took a trait perspective in their discussion of conscientiousness, this construct is central to the recovery movement and many public works strategies (community service; Alcoholics Anonymous, 1976; Swisher & Hu, 1983). There is an old saying in the recovery movement: When the light is green, go; when the light is red, learn. Perhaps a willingness to be restrained enough to learn the best ways to live out situations is what helps people to be the most healthy. Also, in providing service to a group one may bypass one's own individual miswiring.

References

Agnew, R., & Peters, A. A. R. (1986). The techniques of neutralization: An analysis of predisposing and situational factors. *Criminal Justice and Behavior, 13,* 81–97.

Akers, R. L., Krohn, M. D., Lanza-Kaduce, L., & Radosevich, M. (1979). Social learning and deviant behavior: A specific test of a general theory. *American Sociological Review, 44,* 636–655.

Alcoholics Anonymous (3rd ed.). (1976). New York: Alcoholics Anonymous World Services.

Ames, S. L., Sussman, S., & Dent, C. W. (1999) Pro-drug use myths and competing constructs in the prediction of substance use among youth at continuation high schools: A one-year prospective study. *Personality and Individual Differences, 26,* 987–1003.

Bandura, A. (1986). *Social foundations of thought and action: A social cognitive theory.* Englewood Cliffs, NJ: Prentice Hall.

Bogg, T., & Roberts, B. W. (2004). Conscientiousness and health-related behaviors: A meta-analysis of the leading behavioral contributors to mortality. *Psychological Bulletin, 130,* 887–919.

Bordua, D. J. (1962). Some comments on theories of group delinquency. *Sociological Inquiry, 32,* 245–260.

Chuck C. (1984). *A new pair of glasses.* Irvine, CA: New-Look.

Cohen, A. K. (1955). *Delinquent boys: The culture of the gang.* New York: Free Press.

Dishion, T. J. (2000). Cross-setting consistency in early adolescent psychopathology: Deviant friendships and problem sequelae. *Journal of Personality, 68,* 1109–1126.

Dishion, T. J., Poulin, F., & Burraston, B. (2001). Peer group dynamics associated with iatrogenic effects in group interventions with high-risk young adolescents. In C. A. Erdley & D. W. Nargle (Eds.), *The role of friendship in psychological adjustment: New directions for child and adolescent development* (pp. 79–92). New York: Jossey-Bass.

Dodder, R. A. & Hughes, S. P. (1993). Neutralization of drinking behavior. *Deviant Behavior: An Interdisciplinary Journal, 14,* 65–79.

Downes, S. (1995–2001). *Stephen's guide to the logical fallacies.* Retrieved November 24, 2008, from http://onegoodmove.org/fallacy/welcome.htm

Ellis, A., & Harper, R. A. (1975). *A guide to rational living.* North Hollywood, CA: Wilshire.

Epstein, L. H. (1992). Role of behavior theory in behavioral medicine. *Journal of Consulting and Clinical Psychology, 4,* 493–498.

Erickson, E. H. (1968). *Identity, youth and crisis.* New York: W. W. Norton.

Festinger, L. (1957). *A theory of cognitive dissonance.* Stanford, CA: Stanford University Press.

Fiore, M. C., Bailey, W. C., Cohen, S. J., Dorfman, S. F., Goldstein, M. G., Gritz, E. R., et al. (2000). *Treating tobacco use and dependence: Clinical practice guideline.* Rockville, MD: U.S. Department of Health and Human Services, Public Health Service.

Fishkin, S. A., Sussman, S., Stacy, A. W., Dent, C. W., Burton, D., & Flay, B. R. (1993). Ingroup versus outgroup perceptions of the characteristics of high-risk youth: Negative stereotyping. *Journal of Applied Social Psychology, 23,* 1051–1068.

Glynn, K., Levanthal, H., & Hirschman, R. (1985). A cognitive developmental approach to smoking prevention. In C. S. Bell & R. Battjes (Eds.), *Prevention research: Deterring drug abuse among children and adolescents* (NIDA Research Monograph 63, pp. 130–152). Rockville, MD: National Institute on Drug Abuse.

Gorski, T. T. (1989). *Passages through recovery.* San Francisco: Harper & Row.

Granic, I., & Dishion, T. J. (2003). Deviant talk in adolescent friendships: A step toward measuring a pathogenic attractor process. *Social Development, 12,* 314–334.

Heider, F. (1958). *The psychology of interpersonal relations.* New York: Wiley.

Johnson, V. E. (1980). *I'll quit tomorrow: A practical guide to alcoholism treatment.* San Francisco: Harper & Row.

Kahane, H. (1990). *Logic and philosophy: A modern introduction.* Belmont, CA: Wadsworth.

Kahneman, D. (2003). A perspective on judgment and choice: Mapping bounded rationality. *American Psychologist, 58,* 697–720.

Kellam, S., Ialongo, N., Brown, H., Laudolff, J., Mirsky, A., Anthony, J., et al. (1989). Attention problems in first grade and shy and aggressive behaviors as antecedents to later heavy or inhibited substance use. In L. S. Harris (Ed.), *Problems of drug dependence 1989: Proceedings of the 51st Annual Scientific Meeting* (NIDA Research Monograph 95, pp. 368–369). Rockville, MD: National Institute on Drug Abuse.

Lau, R. R., Hartman, K. A., & Ware, J. E. (1986). Health as a value: Methodological and theoretical considerations. *Health Psychology, 5,* 25–43.

Lennard, H. L., Epstein, L. J., Bernstein, A., & Ransom, D. C. (1971). *Mystification & drug misuse.* New York: Jossey-Bass.

MacKinnon, D. P., Johnson, C. A., Pentz, M. A., Dwyer, J. H., Hansen, W. B., Flay, B. R., & Wang, E. Y. I. (1991). Mediating mechanisms in a school-based drug prevention program: First year effects of the Midwestern Prevention Project. *Health Psychology, 10,* 164–172.

Matthys, W., & Lochman, J. E. (2005). Social problem solving in aggressive children. In M. McMurran & J. McGuire (Eds.), *Social problem solving and offenders* (pp. 51–66). Chichester, England: Wiley.

McConnell, A. R., Sherman, S. J., & Hamilton, D. L. (1994). Illusory correlation in the perception of groups: An extension of the distinctiveness-based account. *Journal of Personality and Social Psychology, 67,* 414–429.

Meichenbaum, D. (1977). *Cognitive behavior modification: An integrative approach.* New York: Plenum.

Miller, W. R., & Rollnick, S. (1991). *Motivational interviewing: Preparing people to change addictive behavior.* New York: Guilford Press.

Poulin, F., Dishion, T. J., & Burraston, B. (2001). Three-year iatrogenic effects associated with aggregating high-risk adolescents in cognitive-behavioral preventive interventions. *Applied Developmental Science, 5,* 214–224.

Ritt-Olson, A., Milam, J., Unger, J. B., Trinidad, D., Teran, L., Dent, C. W., & Sussman, S. (2004). The protective influence of spirituality and health-as-a-value against monthly substance abuse among adolescents varying in risk. *Journal of Adolescent Health, 34,* 192–199.

Schutz, A., & Luckmann, T. (1973). *The structure of the life world.* Evanston, IL: Northwestern University Press.

Shedler, J., & Block, J. (1990). Adolescent drug use and psychological health: A longitudinal inquiry. *American Psychologist 45,* 612–630.

Sherman, S. J., Presson, C. C., Chassin, L., Corty, E., & Olshavsky, R. (1983). The false consensus effect in estimates of smoking prevalence: Underlying mechanisms. *Personality and Social Psychology Bulletin, 9,* 197–207.

Shields, I. W., & Whitehall, G. C. (1994). Neutralization and delinquency among teenagers. *Criminal Justice and Behavior, 21,* 223–235.

Smith, G. M. (1980). Perceived effects of substance use: A general theory. In D. J. Lettieri, M. Sayers, & H. W. Pearson (Eds.), *Theories on drug abuse: Selected contemporary perspectives* (NIDA Research Monograph 30, pp. 50–58). Rockville, MD: National Institute on Drug Abuse.

Stacy, A. W., & Ames, S. L. (2001). Implicit cognition theory in drug use and driving under the influence interventions. In S. Sussman (Ed.), *Handbook of program development in health behavior research and practice* (pp. 107–130). Thousand Oaks, CA: Sage.

Sussman, S., & Ames, S. L. (2001). *The social psychology of drug abuse.* Birmingham, England: Open University Press.

Sussman, S., Barovich, M., Hahn, G., Abrams, C., Selski, E., & Craig, S. (2004). *Project TNT—Towards No Tobacco Use teacher's guide* (2nd ed.). Santa Cruz, CA: ETR Associates.

Sussman, S., Craig, S., & Moss, M. A. (2002). Project TND—Towards No Drug Abuse teacher's manual. Los Angeles: University of Southern California.

Sussman, S., Dent, C. W., & McCuller, W. J. (2000). Group self-identification as a prospective predictor of drug use and violence in high-risk youth. *Psychology of Addictive Behaviors, 14,* 192–196.

Sussman, S., Dent, C. W., Mestel-Rauch, J. S., Johnson, C. A., Hansen, W. B., & Flay, B. R. (1988). Adolescent nonsmokers, triers, and regular smokers' estimates of cigarette smoking prevalence: When do overestimates occur and by whom? *Journal of Applied Social Psychology, 18,* 537–551.

Sussman, S., Dent, C. W., Simon, T. S., Stacy, A. W., Burton, D., & Flay, B. R. (1993). Identification of which high risk youth smoke cigarettes regularly. *Health Values, 17,* 42–53.

Sussman, S., Dent, C. W., Simon, T. R., Stacy, A. W., Galaif, E. R., Moss, M. A., et al. (1995). Immediate impact of social influence-oriented substance abuse prevention curricula in traditional and continuation high schools. *Drugs and Society, 8,* 65–81.

Sussman, S., Dent, C. W., & Stacy, A. W. (1996). The relations of pro-drug-use myths with self-reported drug use among youth at continuation high schools. *Journal of Applied Social Psychology, 26,* 2014–2037.

Sussman, S., Earleywine, M., Wills, T. A, Cody, C., Biglan, A., Dent, C. W., & Newcomb, M. D. (2004). What are the implications of a motivation-skills-decision making approach on drug abuse prevention? Is this a transdisciplinary fusion approach? *Substance Use & Misuse, 10–12,* 1971–2017.

Sussman, S., Stacy, A. W., Dent, C. W., Simon, T. R., & Johnson, C. A. (1996). Marijuana use: Current issues and new research directions. *Journal of Drug Issues, 26,* 693–726.

Sussman, S., & Sussman, A. N. (2001). Praxis in health behavior program development. In S. Sussman (Ed.), *Handbook of program development in health behavior research and practice* (pp. 79–97). Thousand Oaks, CA: Sage.

Sussman, S., & Unger, J. B. (2004). A "drug abuse" theoretical integration: A transdisciplinary speculation. *Substance Use & Misuse, 39,* 2055–2069.

Sutherland, E. (1929). *Principles of criminology* (3rd ed.). Philadelphia: J. B. Lippincott.

Swisher, J. D., & Hu, T. W. (1983). Alternatives to drug abuse: Some are and some are not. In T. J. Glynn, C. G. Leukefeld, & J. P. Ludford (Eds.), *Preventing adolescent drug abuse: Intervention strategies* (NIDA Research Monograph 47, pp 141–153). Rockville, MD: National Institute on Drug Abuse.

Sykes, G., & Matza, D. (1957). Techniques of neutralization: A theory of delinquency. *American Sociological Review, 22,* 664–670.

Tabachnik, N., Crocker, J., & Alloy, L. B. (1983). Depression, social comparison, and the false consensus effect. *Journal of Personality and Social Psychology, 45,* 688–699.

Twerski, A. J. (1997). *Addictive thinking.* Center City, MN: Hazelden.

Upshaw, H. S., & Ostrom, T. M. (1984). Psychological perspective in attitude research. In J. R. Eiser (Ed.), *Attitudinal judgment* (pp. 23–42). New York: Springer-Verlag.

Weinstein, N. D. (1982). Unrealistic optimism about susceptibility to health problems. *Journal of Behavioral Medicine, 10,* 481–500.

Weinstein, N. D. (1987). Unrealistic optimism about susceptibility to health problems: Conclusions from a community-wide sample. *Journal of Behavioral Medicine, 10,* 481–500.

West, S. G., & Wicklund, R. A. (1980). *A primer of social psychological theories.* Monterey, CA: Brooks/Cole.

Wiers, R. W., de Jong, P. J., Havermans, R., & Jelicic, M. (2004). How to change implicit drug use-related cognitions in prevention: A transdisciplinary integration of findings from experimental psychopathology, social cognition, memory and experimental learning psychology. *Substance Use & Misuse, 39,* 1625–1684.

Zinberg, N. E. (1984). *Drug, set, and setting: The basis for controlled intoxicant use.* New Haven, CT: Yale University Press.

CHAPTER 34

ADVANCES IN THE SCIENCE AND PRACTICE OF PREVENTION: TARGETING INDIVIDUAL-LEVEL ETIOLOGIC FACTORS AND THE CHALLENGE OF GOING TO SCALE

Gilbert J. Botvin and Kenneth W. Griffin

The accumulation of research over the past quarter century or so has led to important advances in the etiology and prevention of a growing number of health problems. What once appeared to be disparate findings in largely unrelated areas have now come together into the exciting new field of prevention science. The quality of prevention research and the impressive progress in the field of prevention science have been well documented through scholarly reviews of the prevention literature (Dodge, 2001; Kelly & Kalichman, 2002; Lochman & van den Steenhoven, 2002; Roth & Brooks-Gunn, 2003; Tobler & Stratton, 1997) and expert consensus panels (e.g., the American Psychological Association Task Force on Prevention, the Center for Substance Abuse Prevention's National Registry of Effective Programs, and the U.S. Department of Education Expert Panel on Safe and Drug Free Schools). Although the focus of this volume is on the etiology and prevention of drug use, it has become evident that there is a growing convergence in the broader field of prevention science in terms of shared methods and theories, similar etiologic factors and developmental trajectories, and commonalities among effective intervention approaches. In this chapter, we review the growth in prevention as a scientific enterprise, discuss advances in drug abuse prevention research, and identify current challenges and future directions related to both drug abuse prevention and the wider field of prevention science.

DEVELOPMENT OF PREVENTION SCIENCE

Interest in prevention has increased markedly over the past 25 years as health professionals and the general public have come to recognize that many contemporary health problems are preventable. As interest in prevention has grown, there has been a corresponding increase in prevention research—in terms of both etiology and the development of evidence-based prevention programs and policies. Prevention research has targeted a diversity of problems (e.g., tobacco, alcohol, and drug abuse; HIV/AIDS; teen pregnancy; aggression and violence; mental health) and populations (e.g., youth and adults, students and parents, racial and ethnic subgroups); has been conducted in a variety of settings (e.g., schools, home, workplace, and communities); and has used a range of intervention modalities (e.g., involving the school, family, community, and environmental policies) along the prevention spectrum, including universal, selective, and indicated approaches. Prevention research has progressed from investigations of developmental epidemiology and etiology to small-scale efficacy studies and large-scale randomized trials testing preventive interventions.

Early prevention research was largely problem centered or disease specific. For example, research concerning the prevention of cigarette smoking, drug abuse, HIV/AIDS, and mental health problems developed in separate scientific silos. However, over time it became increasingly clear that researchers were often focused on similar sets of etiologic factors, relying on similar theoretical perspectives, using shared research methods, and confronting very similar research challenges. The defining features of contemporary prevention science are high-quality empirical research using rigorous and well-established scientific methods, careful hypothesis testing, and the systematic accumulation of knowledge in a manner consistent with other areas of science. As in the biomedical sciences, the gold standard for studies testing therapeutic or preventive interventions is the randomized controlled trial. As the field of prevention science has grown, new knowledge in prevention has accumulated at an ever-faster pace.

In the United States, prevention research uses the same peer review system as and a lion's share of funding comes from the same sources as biomedical research—the National Institutes of Health—including the National Cancer Institute, the National Institute on Drug Abuse, the National Institute of Mental Health, the National Institute on Alcohol Abuse and Alcoholism, the National Institute of Child Health and Human Development, and the National Heart, Blood, and Lung Institute—and the Centers for Disease Control and Prevention. Some prevention research has also been funded by the National Science Foundation and the U.S. Justice Department's Office of Juvenile Justice and Delinquency Prevention. Moreover, prevention research has been forged in the crucible of the scientific peer review process, starting with the rigorous review of National Institutes of Health grant applications and extending to the review of research findings for publication in top scientific journals.

One indication of the vitality and robustness of any field is the level of scientific activity taking place. Although the field of prevention science is made up of researchers trained in a variety of disciplines (e.g., sociology, psychology, medicine, epidemiology, statistics) with their own journals and conferences, they have come together in a little more than a decade to form a multidisciplinary professional organization (the Society for Prevention Research) focused exclusively on prevention science. The society has its own annual conference and its own high-quality, peer-reviewed journal (*Prevention Science*). The annual meeting of the Society for Prevention Research has provided an international

forum for more than 200 presentations in 10 years, discussing new developments in prevention science from around the world in the areas of epidemiology, etiology, demonstration projects, policy research, natural experiments, efficacy and effectiveness trials, and studies of the diffusion of evidence-based prevention.

As this handbook so nicely demonstrates, a great deal of high-quality research has been conducted concerning the etiology of drug abuse and other maladaptive or health-compromising behaviors. However, in addition to the accumulation of knowledge in etiology, the field of prevention science is contributing to a new generation of evidence-based approaches and policies that, if widely used, offer the potential to reduce the mortality and morbidity associated with a number of major health problems such as heart disease, cancer, HIV/AIDS, and chronic obstructive lung disease that are now viewed as being largely preventable. Cigarette smoking, the single most important preventable cause of death and disability, is responsible for more than 430,000 premature deaths each year (U.S. Department of Health and Human Services, 1998). Given the public health need to reduce mortality and morbidity associated with health behaviors such as cigarette smoking and the growing body of prevention research, government agencies have convened expert panels to identify the most effective interventions available as a guide to practitioners and policymakers. These lists of evidence-based exemplary or model programs have been widely disseminated and are transforming the practice of prevention throughout the country.

ADVANCES IN DRUG ABUSE PREVENTION RESEARCH

Research concerning the etiology and prevention of tobacco, alcohol, and illicit drug abuse has been an area of considerable activity over the past 25 years. Because of the high morbidity and mortality associated with the early and continued use of tobacco, alcohol, and illicit drugs, reducing the use of these substances among American youth is a major public health goal and a priority for federal, state, and local governments. The development and dissemination of effective intervention approaches for preventing drug use are a critical part of the federal government's national drug control policy (Office of National Drug Control Policy, 1997). These preventive interventions have taken different forms, including intervention activities conducted within schools, families, and communities; mass media public service announcements; policy initiatives such as required health warning labels on cigarettes and alcohol; changes in school rules (i.e., zero-tolerance policies); and laws and regulations such as increased cigarette taxes and minimum purchasing age requirements. Notwithstanding the urgent public health imperative to reduce drug use and its associated deleterious consequences, the empirical evidence for the efficacy of particular approaches is stronger for some than for others.

Scientific knowledge regarding the etiology and prevention of adolescent drug use has increased markedly in recent years. Risk and protective factors for early-stage drug use have been identified (for reviews, see Hawkins, Catalano, & Miller, 1992; Scheier, 2001). The onset and escalation of various forms of drug use and the developmental progression to abuse result from a complex interaction of a number of etiologic factors including cognitive, attitudinal, social, personality, pharmacological, biological, and developmental factors (e.g., Cicchetti & Luthar, 1999; Jessor & Jessor, 1977; Swadi, 1999). Moreover, drug use progresses in a well-defined sequence (Kandel, 2002; Kandel, Yamaguchi, & Chen, 1992), beginning in the early stages with cigarettes and alcohol and progressing somewhat later to the use of marijuana. The use of opiates, hallucinogens, and other illicit drugs typically occurs still later in the sequence of drug use behaviors. Given this general pattern of drug use initiation and escalation, the aim of most prevention programs involving adolescents is to deter or delay early-stage use on the assumption that this will disrupt the developmental progression of drug use and ultimately translate into reductions in drug abuse.

Because adolescence marks the beginning of a critical period of increased risk, most interventions to reduce youth drug use target middle school or junior high school students to deter initial experimentation. For this target population, prevention programs typically focus on tobacco, alcohol, and marijuana because these are not only the most widely used substances in our society but also because experimentation with these substances occurs during the early stages of drug use and abuse. Developing effective drug abuse prevention programs is important not only because of their potential to reduce morbidity and mortality related to alcohol, tobacco, and marijuana use, it is also important because preventing early use of these gateway substances may delay, reduce, or prevent the use of other drugs further along the developmental progression, along with the multiple negative outcomes associated with drug abuse (Newcomb & Bentler, 1988).

LINKING ETIOLOGY AND PREVENTION

Many of the most effective behavioral interventions in the field of prevention science have stemmed from systematic advances in knowledge. This typically begins with a thorough understanding of the epidemiology and etiology of a behavior that contributes to one or more social or health problems. As the scientific knowledge base describing the epidemiology of the problematic behavior expands, so too does our understanding of the context in which it occurs and the populations that are at highest risk. Findings about the short- and long-term consequences of health risk behaviors help us understand and articulate the harm they present to individuals and society. The accumulation of research on risk and protective factors is critical in the development of relevant psychosocial theory regarding etiology. Conceptual models based on etiology findings can in turn be used as the basis for developing theory-driven preventive interventions. Finally, testing such interventions using rigorous scientific methods, including an examination of hypothesized mediating mechanisms, can further inform our conceptual models for etiology and prevention.

In the 1970s, a growing body of research on the epidemiology and etiology of adolescent smoking showed that experimentation with cigarette smoking often occurs during early adolescence among one's peer group and that prosmoking social influences play a key role. The first psychosocial approaches to the prevention of adolescent smoking were developed and tested. Research by Evans (1976) and his colleagues focused on teaching adolescents to recognize the sources of these influences and on teaching skills to refuse offers to smoke. This research led to development of the social resistance model of prevention, a conceptual model that incorporated key social risk factors for smoking (and later, for other substances) such as exposure to prosmoking social influences from peers, adult role models who smoke, and persuasive advertising appeals and media portrayals encouraging smoking. This conceptual model incorporated key concepts from Bandura's (1977) social learning theory in the process of smoking initiation, such as the important roles of modeling, imitation, reinforcement, and vicarious learning. In subsequent years, a variety of prevention programs based on the social resistance model were developed that taught students how to recognize and resist negative social influences to engage in smoking and other drug use, particularly peer pressure.

In the 1980s, social psychological theory and research have suggested that certain psychological characteristics determine the extent to which individuals are susceptible to social influence (e.g., an external locus of control, low self-esteem, lack of self-confidence, and anxiety) and that some of these same characteristics are associated with cigarette smoking. Etiologic models of smoking began to incorporate key concepts of Jessor and Jessor's (1977) problem behavior theory, which proposed that proneness to problem behavior can be explained by a variety of psychological variables such as values, expectations, beliefs, and attitudes that support the behavior; the specific psychological meaning or function of the behavior (e.g., rejection of conventional norms or expression of independence from parental control); and personality factors such as sensitivity to social criticism, higher alienation, lower self-esteem, and greater tolerance of deviance. Thus, the onset of cigarette smoking during early adolescence appeared to be the result of both social and psychological factors: Social influences promote cigarette smoking, and specific individual characteristics related to poor social and personal competence increase susceptibility to internal and external pressures to smoke (Botvin, 2000; Flay, 1987).

TARGETING INDIVIDUAL-LEVEL ETIOLOGIC FACTORS

Our own prevention research has centered on a universal, school-based prevention approach to adolescent drug abuse prevention that incorporates elements of social learning and problem behavior theory. The Life Skills Training (LST) approach has been carefully and extensively tested over the past 25 years. It was originally developed to prevent cigarette smoking (Botvin & Eng, 1980). LST was designed to modify perceived tobacco use norms, decrease social influences to smoke cigarettes, and increase personal and social competence to address key social and psychological factors related to smoking onset. Over time, different studies have replicated and extended the efficacy of LST with cigarette smoking and tested its potential for preventing other forms of substance use and health risk behaviors. Research has also tested its efficacy with different types of program providers, under different intervention conditions, and with different populations. Our prevention and etiology research has been driven by a conceptual etiologic model (see Figure 34.1) that illustrates the role of social and psychological factors in the etiology of adolescent substance use, the contextual factors in which these etiologic processes operate, and how LST is designed to influence key etiologic determinants.

The LST approach is one of the most extensively tested school-based drug abuse prevention programs. To date, the effectiveness of LST has been tested in 14 separate cohort studies conducted by scientists at the Cornell Medical College, Institute for Prevention Research, resulting in 25 peer-reviewed outcome studies. Table 34.1 summarizes the study designs, sample descriptions, and primary outcomes. These studies, ranging from small-scale efficacy studies to large-scale effectiveness trials, all used randomized controlled research designs. The scope and methodological sophistication of these studies increased, as did the sample sizes (in terms of both students and schools), the racial and ethnic diversity of study populations, and the length of follow up. The effectiveness of LST has been tested by external researchers in four additional cohorts of students, with results published in six additional peer-

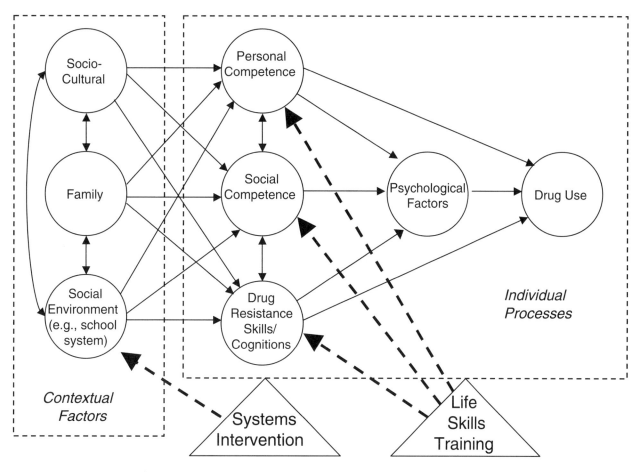

FIGURE 34.1. Model of individual and contextual factors in adolescent drug use and targets of intervention.

reviewed outcome studies, which are also included in Table 34.1.

The studies mentioned in the table were designed to systematically address important research issues with implications for theory and practice. The research fueling these studies tested hypotheses relating to (a) the effectiveness of the LST approach (targeting an array of individual-level risk and protective factors, including normative expectations, resistance skills, and generic personal and social skills) for preventing cigarette smoking; (b) the effectiveness of this approach on use of alcohol, marijuana, and other illicit drugs; (c) the effectiveness of different types of program providers; (d) the durability of prevention effects; (e) the extent to which "booster sessions" can help sustain or enhance initial prevention effects; (f) the effectiveness of this approach with different populations (e.g., White, African American, and Hispanic youth); (g) the relationship between implementation fidelity and effectiveness; (h) whether the

prevention of early-stage ("experimental") substance use can disrupt the developmental progression to more serious forms of substance use (e.g., pack-a-day cigarette smoking, binge drinking, use of illicit drugs other than marijuana, or polydrug use); (i) the impact of the LST approach on other health behaviors (e.g., aggression, violence, delinquency, risky driving, HIV/ AIDS risk behaviors) with minimal modification; and (j) the mediating mechanisms of effective preventive interventions such as LST. Taken together, these studies have not only consistently demonstrated that the LST approach can decrease the use of tobacco, alcohol, marijuana, and other drugs, but they have also contributed to the science of prevention by providing information about these and other research questions important to prevention.

Small-Scale Efficacy Trials

The LST approach was originally developed as a smoking prevention program, and the initial research

TABLE 34.1

Studies Testing the Effects of Life Skills Training on Substance Use and Related Outcomes

Authors, year published, journal	Dataset / cohort[1]	Study design — Randomized trial	Efficacy trial	Effectiveness trial	# of schools	# of LST sessions[2]	Years of follow-up[3]	Sample description — Number of students	Predominantly white	Predominantly minority	Urban	Suburban	Rural	Outcome analysis[4] — Effects on smoking	Effects on alcohol use	Effects on marijuana use	Effects on other drugs	Effects on related problem behaviors	Notes
Botvin et al. 1980, Prev Med	1	•	•		2	10	0	281	•			•		•	na	na	na	na	smoking among white suburban youth
Botvin et al. 1980, J School Health	1	•	•		2	10	.25	281	•			•		•	na	na	na	na	follow-up of cohort 1
Botvin et al. 1982, Prev Med	2	•	•		2	12	1	426	•			•		•	na	na	na	na	examination of one-year effects
Botvin et al. 1983, J Behav Med	3	•	•		7	15	1	902	•			•		•	na	na	na	na	examination of different providers
Botvin et al. 1984, Addict Behav	4	•	•		10	20	0	1311	•			•		•	•	•	na	na	extension to alcohol and marijuana
Botvin et al. 1984, J Stud Alc	5	•	•		2	20	1	239	•			•		na	•	na	na	na	extension to alcohol
Botvin et al. 1989, J Behav Med	6	•	•		8	15	0	471		•	•			•	na	na	na	na	smoking among Hispanic youth
Botvin et al. 1989, Public Health Rep	7	•	•		9	12	0	608		•	•			•	na	na	na	na	smoking among Black youth
Botvin et al. 1990, Addict Behav	4	•	•		10	30	1	998	•			•		•	•	•	na	na	follow-up of cohort 4
Botvin et al. 1990, J Consult Clin Psychol	8	•		•	56	30	2	3684	•			•		•	•	•	na	na	effectiveness trial, White youth

Study	No.	v1	v2	v3	N	Description
Botvin et al. 1992, Health Psychol	9	47	15	0	3153	smoking among Hispanic youth
Botvin et al. 1994, Psych Addict Behav	10	6	15	0	639	minority youth, generic vs cultural program
Botvin et al. 1995, Psych Addict Behav	10	6	23	2	456	follow-up of cohort 10
Botvin et al. 1995, JAMA	8	56	30	6	3597	6 year follow-up of cohort 8
Botvin et al. 1997, JCASA	11	7	30	0	721	multiple drug use, minority youth
Botvin et al. 1999, JAMWA	12	29	25	1	2209	effectiveness trial, minority girls smoking
Botvin et al. 2000, Addict Behav	8	56	30	6	447	illicit drug follow-up of cohort 8
Botvin et al. 2001, Prev Sci	12	29	25	1	3621	effectiveness trial, minority youth
Botvin et al. 2001, Psych Addict Behav	12	29	25	2	3041	binge drinking, follow-up of cohort 12
Scheier et al. 2001, Prev Sci	8	56	30	5	2288	examination of disrupting gateway use
Spoth et al. 2002, Psych Addict Behav [5]	13	24	30	1	1115	effectiveness trial, rural youth
Botvin et al. 2003, JCASA	14	20	24	0	1090	elementary school version
Griffin et al. 2003, Prev Med	12	29	25	1	758	high risk youth, follow-up of cohort 12
Trudeau et al. 2003, Prev Sci	13	24	30	1.5	847	rural youth, follow-up
Fraguela et al., 2003, PIS	15	5	16	4	1029	students in Spain
Zollinger et al. 2003, J School Health	16	16	15	2	1598	students in Indiana
Griffin et al. 2004, Prev Sci	8	56	30	6	2042	follow-up of cohort 8, risky driving
Spoth et al. 2005, Psych Addict Behav [5]	13	36	15	2	1109	effectiveness trial, rural youth
Spoth et al. 2006, Arch Ped Adol Med [5]	17	36	20	5.5	398	effectiveness trial, rural youth
Griffin et al. 2006, Prev Sci	8	56	30	6	2042	follow-up of cohort 8, HIV risk behavior
Botvin et al., 2006, Prev Sci	18	41	18	0	4858	extension to violence and delinquency

Note. 1) Publications with same number represent studies on same cohort of students; 2) In first two studies listed, intervention was provided to students in 8th, 9th, and 10th grades; In the last study listed, intervention was provided to students in the 6th grade; In all other studies by Cornell or Iowa State researchers, the intervention was first provided in 7th grade; 3) Years of follow-up after posttest assessment; 4) na = outcome not assessed; 5) Results presented are for LST only vs. control condition was conducted in suburban schools with predominantly White, middle-class populations. This research consisted of several small-scale studies testing the short-term effects of the intervention on cigarette smoking and related risk factors. These studies randomized between two and seven schools to experimental conditions with sample sizes ranging from nearly 300 students to more than 900 students. Findings demonstrated that this prevention approach effectively reduced cigarette smoking among students who received the program as compared with control students who did not. Results from these studies provided preliminary evidence for the efficacy of the LST approach for preventing cigarette smoking at the initial posttest (e.g., Botvin & Eng, 1980; Botvin, Eng, & Williams, 1980), and findings from two other early studies indicated that the effects on smoking lasted for up to a year after the completion of the program (Botvin & Eng, 1982; Botvin, Renick, & Baker, 1983). These initial studies focused on the efficacy of LST when first delivered to students in the 7th through 10th grades and when implemented using different delivery formats and different program providers. Findings indicated that the prevention approach is equally as effective when taught by teachers, peer leaders, and health educators. They also indicated that the durability of prevention effects can be increased by adding booster sessions after the initial year of intervention (Botvin et al., 1983). Additional research demonstrated that the LST approach could also reduce alcohol and marijuana use (e.g., Botvin, Baker, Botvin, Filazzola, & Millman, 1984; Botvin, Baker, Renick, Filazzola, & Botvin, 1984). These initial studies were among the first randomized, school-based prevention studies to show consistent behavioral effects on adolescent substance use.

Effectiveness With Minority Youth

LST was subsequently tested with racial and ethnic minority youth in several efficacy trials involving predominantly African American and Hispanic students from urban junior high schools, initially to assess its impact on cigarette smoking. Prevention effects were observed for smoking among two samples of Hispanic youth (Botvin, Dusenbury, Baker, James-Ortiz, & Kerner, 1989; Botvin et al.,

1992) and a sample of African American youth (Botvin, Batson, et al., 1989). A study was conducted comparing two skills-based interventions, one generic and one culturally adapted by incorporating inner city and multicultural narrative and references (Botvin, Schinke, Epstein, & Diaz, 1994). At the posttest assessment, there were no effects on drug behavior, but both programs effectively reduced intentions to drink alcohol among students receiving the intervention relative to the control group. A follow-up of this study assessed students 2 years after the posttest (Botvin, Schinke, Epstein, Diaz, & Botvin, 1995) and found that both interventions reduced alcohol use. Taken together, findings suggested that although generic skills training approaches can be effective for a variety of youth populations, cultural tailoring can further increase effectiveness. An additional study found that LST reduced alcohol, tobacco, marijuana, and polydrug use in an inner-city minority sample (Botvin, Epstein, Baker, Diaz, & Ifill-Williams, 1997).

Large-Scale Effectiveness Trials

More recent studies involving LST have focused on the long-term effects on drug use, effects on more serious levels of drug involvement including illicit drug use, and examination of mediating mechanisms. The evaluation designs have become increasingly sophisticated with time, including two large-scale, multisite, randomized controlled trials with long-term follow-up, one with suburban White youth (Botvin et al., 1995) and a second with inner-city minority youth (Botvin, Griffin, Diaz, & Ifill-Williams, 2001a).

In the first large-scale randomized trial (Botvin, Baker, et al., 1995), 56 schools in New York State were randomly assigned to experimental and control conditions. Students in the prevention condition received the intervention in the 7th grade and booster sessions in the 8th and 9th grades. Long-term follow-up data were collected at the end of 12th grade. This study was designed to test several hypotheses, including (a) whether a school-based, prevention approach implemented during middle school would produce prevention effects on drug use at the end of high school; (b) whether a prevention approach targeting early-stage drug use would reduce one or more forms of more serious (later-stage) drug use such as heavy (pack-a-day) smoking, heavy (binge) drinking, drunkenness, and multiple (polydrug) use; and (c) whether higher implementation fidelity would produce stronger prevention effects. The first two hypotheses were testable by using data from the full follow-up sample. The third hypothesis was testable using a fidelity subsample (operationally defined as students exposed to 60% or more of the intervention on the basis of classroom observations).

Results indicated that there were significant prevention effects on cigarette smoking, alcohol abuse (drunkenness), and polydrug use (tobacco, alcohol, and marijuana use) among students in the full follow-up sample exposed to the LST intervention relative to controls. The strongest prevention effects were observed in this study for students exposed to at least 60% of the prevention program (fidelity sample). At the end of high school, the fidelity sample had significantly lower rates than controls on nearly every measure of tobacco, alcohol, marijuana, and polydrug use. In fact, nearly every comparison (16 out of 18) between the fidelity LST sample and controls was significant. Additional data from a random subsample that completed a survey to assess illicit drug use approximately 6 months later found that there were lower levels of overall illicit drug use and lower levels of use for hallucinogens, heroin, and other narcotics for LST students relative to controls (Botvin et al., 2000). In a separate study, a series of structural equation models examined participants on the basis of distinctions between pretest use or nonuse of alcohol and cigarettes in an attempt to discern whether the prevention program disrupted the onset of gateway substance use (Scheier, Botvin, & Griffin, 2001). Findings showed prevention effects on multiple drug use that were mediated in part by improvements in social competence, demonstrating the utility of targeting more than one gateway substance to prevent escalation of drug involvement.

A second large-scale randomized trial tested the effectiveness of LST among inner-city minority youth in New York City attending 29 urban middle schools. Results at the posttest and 1-year follow-up indicated that those who received the prevention program reported less smoking, alcohol use, inhalant use, and polydrug use relative to controls who did not receive the intervention (Botvin, Griffin, Diaz, & Ifill-Williams, 2001a). Additional analyses with this cohort showed that the LST approach reduced binge drinking (five or more drinks per drinking occasion) among inner-city, minority youth by more than 50% at both the 1-year and 2-year follow-up assessments (Botvin, Griffin, Diaz, & Ifill-Williams, 2001b). Research with this data set examined the impact of LST on high-risk youth (students who had poor grades in school and friends who engage in substance use). Results showed that high-risk students who received the LST program were less likely to engage in smoking, drinking, inhalant use, or polydrug use as compared with similarly matched controls (Griffin, Botvin, Nichols, & Doyle, 2003).

Independent Research Testing LST

Several studies conducted by other research groups have provided additional support for the LST approach. Researchers at Iowa State University examined the effectiveness of LST among rural youth as part of a large-scale NIH-funded effectiveness trial. An initial study examined the impact of LST when provided with and without a family-based prevention program supplementing the school program (Spoth, Redmond, Trudeau, and Shin, 2002). Significant prevention effects were found for both conditions, with stronger effects found for students who received both LST and a family-based preventive intervention. However, significant behavioral effects were also observed between the LST group and the control group for marijuana use assessed 1 year after the end of the intervention. A second study measured students 6 months later (Trudeau, Spoth, Lillehoj, Redmond, & Wickrama, 2003) and found that students in the LST condition had less growth in substance use initiation (measured by rates of smoking, drinking, and marijuana use) as compared with the control group students. A third study examining the long-term impact of LST alone and LST plus a family-based prevention program found decreased rates of methamphetamine use for both conditions relative to controls at the 4.5-year and 5.5-year follow-up assessments (Spoth, Clair, Shin, & Redmond, 2006).

An additional study evaluated the effectiveness of LST with Indiana students in Grades 6–8. Survey data from 1,598 students were used to compare tobacco use behavior, attitudes, and knowledge of those exposed to the program with those not exposed. Results showed that relative to controls, there were significantly fewer current smokers among the LST students and more students indicating an intention to remain smoke free. Students in the LST condition were more knowledgeable about the health effects of smoking and more likely to refuse a cigarette if offered one (Zollinger et al., 2003). A research group in Spain conducted a fifth independent study testing the LST approach. This 4-year longitudinal study involved 1,029 students from five secondary schools. Initial prevention effects were found for cigarette smoking and alcohol use, followed later by the emergence of effects for the use of other drugs, such as cannabis, tranquilizers, or amphetamines (Fraguela, Martin, & Trinanes, 2003).

Taken together, these studies provide strong evidence of the effectiveness of the LST approach with White suburban youth, minority urban youth, and White rural youth. Of the studies summarized here and presented in Table 34.1, 20 showed an impact on tobacco use, 15 showed an impact on alcohol use, 10 showed an impact on marijuana use, and several others showed an impact on other drug use outcomes. These findings illustrate that the effects of LST on alcohol and marijuana use have been reported independently from effects of the intervention on smoking.

Impact on Other Health Behaviors

Several studies have also examined the impact of the LST approach on other health behaviors. Many health risk behaviors tend to cluster together—that is, the same individuals are often at risk for multiple health problems (Biglan, Brennan, Foster, & Holder, 2004). In addition to being highly associated with one another, many health risk behaviors share common or overlapping sets of etiologic factors. This suggests the possibility that a single broad-spectrum prevention approach targeting these etiologic factors may have an impact on multiple health risk behaviors. This hypothesis has been tested in several studies using the LST approach. In addition to demonstrating

that the LST approach can prevent the use of tobacco, alcohol, marijuana, and other illicit drugs, research has also found that LST can significantly reduce risky driving (Griffin, Botvin, & Nichols, 2004) and violence and delinquency (Botvin, Griffin, & Nichols, 2006) and significantly lower HIV/AIDS risk behaviors (Griffin, Botvin, & Nichols, 2006).

METHODOLOGICAL STRENGTHS

As described earlier, there is a large body of research demonstrating the effects of LST on tobacco, alcohol, other drug use, and related risk behaviors. This body of work has many an important methodological strengths worth noting. All of the studies by Cornell or Iowa State researchers used randomized controlled designs with entire schools randomized to intervention or control conditions. This was done to control for potential biases such as contamination across conditions and other threats to internal validity. In the larger effectiveness trials of LST, schools were blocked on relevant covariates before random assignment, on factors such as school-level smoking rates, reading levels, and percentage of minority students. This type of randomized block design was implemented to minimize pretest differences and produce equivalent intervention and control groups before the intervention. In fact, LST studies have demonstrated that the intervention and control groups were equivalent on demographic characteristics and behavioral outcome measures; in a few instances in which pretest differences were found, they were statistically controlled to reduce any bias. Another methodological strength of the LST studies is that the research methods, materials, and assessment procedures have been standardized and have used detailed written protocols in data collection and program implementation procedures. Survey instruments have been tested for reliability and validity and shown to have good psychometric properties. Data collection protocols emphasized procedures used to maintain confidentiality to enhance the truthfulness of responses. Biological or biochemical indicators of behavior have been collected simultaneously with survey data to enhance the validity of the self-report data and were shown to validate the self-report measures. Data collectors with racial and ethnic backgrounds similar to those of study participants have been used, and all have been trained using standardized protocols to maintain the high quality of data collected. Additional strengths of the LST research include lengthy follow-up of participants after the end of the intervention and the use of appropriate data analysis techniques. We have followed students for several years after they received LST and have been successful in retaining a high proportion of participants in follow-up assessments. Attrition of participants has been examined and shown to be similar across intervention and control groups, and attrition analyses of high-risk youth have also shown similar rates across conditions. Finally, statistical techniques that account for school-level clustering effects have been used in the larger effectiveness trials of LST, either by conducting the analysis at the school level or by using techniques that control for clustering effects such as generalized estimating equations.

TESTING THE CONCEPTUAL MODEL

Figure 34.1 shows a conceptual model of individual and contextual factors in the etiology of adolescent drug use and demonstrates how interventions such as LST target individual-level mediators and how broader systems-level interventions can target contextual factors such as the school system. Individual- or student-level processes are illustrated in the box on the right-hand side, depicting the mediating mechanisms through which competence skills and drug resistance skills are protective (via a number of potential psychological factors). Competence is conceptualized as a specific set of social and self-management skills hypothesized to lead to a variety of positive developmental and mental health outcomes, thus fostering resilience. Second, the flow from left to right shows that multiple contextual factors—including the social environment (e.g., school system), family, and sociocultural influences—influence skills and behavioral outcomes. Third, the LST program is designed to influence social and personal competence skills and drug-related refusal skills and cognitions (effects on hypothesized mediators are

represented in Figure 34.1 by the dotted arrows from LST), whereas additional intervention at the systems level may help to address barriers to implementation at the school level. These variables represent key mediators through which interventions are hypothesized to influence drug use behavior, as well as explain the continued use of evidence-based prevention programs over time.

Etiologic Studies on the Protective Effects of Competence Skills

In this section, we review etiology studies, guided by the model in Figure 34.1, that provide evidence for the mediating mechanisms through which competence skills protect adolescents from drug abuse. These studies of normative development resulted from using control group participants in the prevention trials to explore the roles of psychosocial influences and personal characteristics (i.e., competence skills) in the etiology of adolescent substance use. Our research on mediating etiologic mechanisms has shown that the protective role of competence skills in the development of adolescent substance use can be explained by (a) increased psychological well-being, (b) reduced positive expectancies regarding the social benefits of drug use, and (c) increased refusal assertiveness and refusal efficacy.

Three studies examined the relationships among competence skills, psychological distress and well-being, and substance use during the junior high school years. Psychological distress and well-being were specified as distinct mediators because research has suggested that positive and negative affect are to some extent independent (e.g., Russell & Carroll, 1999). In the first study of predominantly White suburban students attending junior high schools in upstate New York, we found that greater competence skills were associated with less subsequent distress and greater well-being and that well-being was associated with less subsequent substance use but that distress did not predict later substance use (Griffin, Scheier, Botvin, & Diaz, 2001). Further analyses indicated that the effect of personal competence skills on later drug use was fully mediated by greater psychological well-being. The findings illustrate that well-being (i.e., affective regulation) plays a central role in mediating the relationship between early competence skills and decreased later use of tobacco, alcohol, and marijuana. A second study replicated this general finding in a predominantly Black inner-city sample during early adolescence (Griffin, Botvin, Scheier, Epstein, & Diaz, 2002), and a third found that competence skills predicted later well-being, which was in turn protective in terms of alcohol use in a multiethnic, predominantly Hispanic sample (Epstein, Griffin, & Botvin, 2002). These studies offer compelling evidence that competence skills promote resilience against early-stage substance use in part by enhancing psychological well-being.

We have also examined whether competent youth are less likely to use drugs because they perceive fewer social benefits of substance use. One study consisting of rural youth attending junior high schools in a midwestern state found that social competence had a direct protective effect on substance use; youth who were more socially confident and assertive and had better communication skills reported less smoking and drinking (Griffin, Epstein, Botvin, & Spoth, 2001). Further analyses revealed that the protective effect of social competence on substance use was fully mediated by higher perceived social benefits of drug use (i.e., positive expectancies). This general finding was replicated in a sample of inner-city minority youth focusing on the perceived social benefits of smoking (Epstein, Griffin, & Botvin, 2000a). Findings of this study indicated that low competency (reflected by poor decision-making skills and low personal efficacy) was associated with positive beliefs in the benefits of smoking, which was associated with increased smoking behavior over time. Taken together, these findings suggest that young people lacking social competence skills smoke and drink alcohol because they believe these behaviors convey social status and have important social benefits. In other words, these youth believe smoking will make them cool, grown up, and admired by their peers. Prevention programs that teach youth social skills (assertiveness and interpersonal skills) may reduce substance use by improving social competence and providing youth with more adaptive means of gaining approval from others.

We have also examined the extent to which general social and personal competence skills

(measured by decision-making skills and perceived self-efficacy) provide barriers to drug use because they enable young people to draw on specific drug refusal skills. One study found that good general competence skills predicted higher drug refusal assertiveness, and this greater assertiveness predicted less smoking at the 2-year follow-up (Epstein et al., 2000a). A second study showed that more general competence skills enabled young people to better enact alcohol-specific refusal assertiveness skills, which was in turn associated with less subsequent alcohol use (Epstein, Griffin, & Botvin, 2000b). We also found that general media resistance skills were protective for alcohol use over time, in part because youth with these skills were better able to implement specific drug refusal skill techniques (Epstein & Botvin, 2008). These studies suggest that by teaching general social and personal competence skills, young people are better prepared to use advantageous personal and social skills related to reduced substance use.

Taken together, these findings suggest that a broad range of social and personal competence skills are protective in a variety of ways and that competence enhancement prevention programs such as LST may work in part by increasing well-being, reducing positive expectancies regarding the social benefits of substance use, and increasing drug-specific refusal skills among youth. Although progress has been made in investigating these risk-targeting mechanisms, new etiologic models that incorporate additional mediating constructs need to be developed and tested. Along these lines, research is needed that expands on individual-level risk and protective factors within the broader context of family, sociocultural, and social environmental influences, and work is needed to test whether existing and new potential hypothesized mediators are influenced by prevention programs such as LST.

ADDRESSING THE CHALLENGE OF GOING TO SCALE

A central theme throughout this handbook is that there has been significant progress in our understanding of the etiology and prevention of adolescent drug abuse over the past 25 years. As the chapters in this section of the handbook detail, the field of drug abuse prevention has produced a number of effective research-based intervention programs that have been shown in rigorous evaluation studies to prevent the onset and escalation of alcohol, tobacco, and other drug use during adolescence. As the scientific literature has grown, so too has a sense of optimism about the potential of prevention. However, although the number of research-based prevention programs has increased in recent years, a gap remains in what we know about how to effectively translate these programs into practice and take evidence-based prevention to scale (Botvin, 2004).

Promoting the Use of Evidence-Based Approaches

The exciting progress that has been made in prevention and the accumulation of scientific evidence supporting specific prevention approaches has stimulated efforts to disseminate the most effective approaches to influence prevention practice and ultimately ameliorate the health and social problems being targeted. These efforts are already beginning to transform the way prevention is conducted throughout the country. Instead of developing and implementing prevention programs based on intuition, there is a growing trend toward the use of evidence-based approaches. The transformation currently underway in prevention is largely the result of science-to-practice initiatives by several leading government agencies to identify and promote the use of prevention approaches for which there is credible empirical evidence of effectiveness. Federal agencies with missions related to prevention such as the Center for Substance Abuse Prevention, the U.S. Department of Education's Safe and Drug Free Schools program, and the U.S. Department of Justice's Office of Juvenile Justice and Delinquency Prevention, as well as the National Institute on Drug Abuse and the Centers for Disease Control and Prevention, have all developed initiatives intended to influence prevention practice by promoting evidence-based prevention approaches. These agencies have identified effective prevention programs and policies, published lists of model or exemplary programs, and conducted conferences to disseminate information on what works. In addition, three practice-oriented agencies (Center for Substance Abuse Prevention, Office of Juvenile Justice and Delinquency Prevention, and Safe and Drug Free Schools) have provided funding to support large-scale adoption and implementation of evidence-based prevention programs.

These efforts have had a growing impact on prevention practice throughout this country. However, despite these efforts, we are still at the beginning of the diffusion process; estimates have suggested that fewer than 30% of schools in the United States are implementing evidence-based programs (Ringwalt, Vincus, Ennett, Johnson, & Rohrbach, 2002). To foster continued adoption, prevention programs will need to be further refined to increase their simplicity, flexibility, and ease of use. At the same time, research needs to be conducted to identify malleable factors influencing adoption, implementation, and institutionalization.

Diffusion of Innovation

A theoretical model that is useful for conceptualizing the process of bringing effective programs to scale is the diffusion of innovations model developed by Rogers (1995). Diffusion of innovation has been described as the process by which new knowledge is "communicated through specific channels over time among members of a social system" (Rogers, 1995, p. 5), and this model represents a useful starting point for developing strategies to encourage organizations and individuals to adopt efficacious programs and practices. The process of diffusing innovations can be divided into four stages: dissemination, adoption, implementation, and maintenance. According to Rogers, *dissemination* refers to the process by which effective innovations are spread or distributed, *adoption* refers to the decision processes by which organizations decide to use an innovation, *implementation* refers to the degree to which the program is delivered with fidelity to its original design, and *maintenance,* or *sustainability,* refers to how a program is institutionalized over time. Research is needed on each stage of the diffusion process so that the public health benefits of evidence-based prevention programs can be realized. In fact, now that effective programs have been developed, surmounting the many challenges of going to scale is an important next step for the field of prevention to consider (Botvin, 2004).

Implementation Fidelity

As evidence-based prevention programs have been disseminated, adopted, and implemented on an increasingly larger scale, it has become evident that implementation in real-world settings may diverge considerably from implementation efforts witnessed in the research trials that established the programs' effectiveness. First, not all students may be exposed to the prevention program. Although this may occur for a variety of reasons, the most common reason for school-based prevention programs relates to absenteeism—students who are absent from class or school on days when the prevention program is taught will not receive the full benefit of the program. Because high-risk students tend to have higher rates of absenteeism from school or school dropout, the very students who need effective prevention programs the most may have limited exposure to them.

Second, program providers (teachers, peers, or prevention specialists) may not adhere to the program content and procedures. Although it seems obvious that decreased exposure to a prevention program will undermine its effectiveness with unexposed students, it may not seem quite as obvious to administrators and program providers that failure to implement a prevention program as designed will undermine effectiveness. Yet, there is good reason to believe that if prevention programs are not implemented with adequate fidelity, their effectiveness will be compromised. In fact, research has shown that high implementation fidelity leads to superior outcomes, and poor fidelity leads to decreased effectiveness (Elliott & Mihalic, 2004). Still, difficulties in achieving high fidelity are widely reported in field settings, and concerns about fidelity and its potential impact on effectiveness are heightened by empirical findings (Gottfredson & Gottfredson, 2002). This raises the specter that as evidence-based prevention programs are taken to scale, they may not result in the outcomes expected because of poor fidelity in schools or other natural settings.

Fidelity often suffers in real-world settings like schools for a number of reasons. Many of these reasons seem foreign to those who work in these settings. Furthermore, the same reasons are not entirely recognized or sufficiently appreciated by prevention researchers. First, evidence-based prevention programs may not be adequately standardized through easy-to-follow prevention materials (e.g., provider manuals, participant workbooks, handouts, CDs, DVDs). Second, implementation fidelity may be less than adequate because of a lack of training and support. Program providers may lack the skills, motivation, or knowledge necessary to implement a particular evidence-based program. Providers often need some degree of in-service training to help them understand the conceptual framework, logic model, or rationale for a new prevention approach. In-service training for prevention programs can take the form of a live 1- or 2-day provider training workshop. More recently, training has been offered in self-study formats such as on DVDs or as a Web-based online course. Training can not only provide individuals who will be implementing new programs with the skills and knowledge that they need, but it can also engender a sense of enthusiasm, motivation, and self-efficacy that together offer the potential for increasing implementation fidelity. In addition to training before implementation, technical assistance and ongoing support is often helpful, particularly in the 1st year of installing a new prevention program. Providers often encounter problems that they did not foresee or that were not adequately covered during an in-service training. Therefore, some technical assistance mechanism may be needed to provide support after implementation is underway, ranging from Web-based support (a list of frequently asked questions, electronic bulletin boards, e-mail consultation) to telephone and on-site support.

Low fidelity in school settings may occur for other reasons that are unique to schools. These include limited resources, classroom overcrowding, classroom management and disciplinary problems, low teacher morale and burnout, multiple competing demands, and insufficient time because of an increased emphasis on basic academic subject areas and preparation for standardized testing. Research is therefore necessary to increase our understanding of the various obstacles that may arise independently in the school, affecting implementation fidelity, and how to recognize and surmount them.

Adaptation

In contrast to the failure, inability, or unwillingness of a prevention provider to implement a new program with fidelity, programs may be deliberately modified by local educators or prevention practitioners. These modifications are usually an effort to adapt the program to fit real or perceived local needs. These adaptations may involve adding, modifying, or deleting existing material. Adaptations may also be made because the site does not have a thorough understanding of the program and its underlying causal mechanism or for practical reasons, such as insufficient class time because of mandates related to traditional academic subject areas and standardized testing.

One of the most common reasons for adapting a prevention program involves efforts to tailor a program to a particular culture or population, particularly an ethnic minority population. Castro, Barrera, and Martinez (2004) presented a compelling case for adaptations designed to render prevention programs more appropriate to ethnic and racial minority populations. In some instances, they argued, there may actually be a cultural mismatch between a particular program and the population of students receiving the program. Such a mismatch might undermine the effectiveness of the program, hamper implementation, and emerge as a barrier to institutionalization. In other situations, improving the fit of prevention programs offers the potential of increasing buy-in, perceived relevance, and the likelihood that programs will be maintained beyond the period of use following its initial adoption. Observations that some degree of adaptation may be viewed by program providers as necessary to improve the cultural fit between prevention programs and students have been supported by research showing that teachers working with minority populations were more likely to adapt prevention curricula in an effort to make them more culturally appropriate for their students (Ringwalt et al., 2004).

Adaptation Versus Fidelity

Thus, a major challenge that needs to be confronted as evidence-based prevention programs are taken to scale concerns the natural tension between fidelity and adaptation. Some have argued that any local adaptation of a program reduces its effectiveness (Elliott & Mihalic, 2004). Our own research with the LST program provides support for placing an emphasis on fidelity. We found that the most powerful prevention effects were obtained for students whose teachers adhered more closely to the procedures and content contained in the LST program materials (Botvin, Baker, et al., 1995). Elliott and Mihalic (2004) argued forcefully that every effort should be made to promote a high degree of implementation fidelity and preserve program integrity. However, practitioners often make the case that it is unrealistic to expect that prevention programs will be implemented with high fidelity and that efforts to promote fidelity are unlikely to succeed. Elliott and Mihalic countered this argument using evidence from the Blueprints Violence and Drug Abuse Prevention Initiative. They made the case that evidence-based prevention programs can be implemented on a wide scale with both high fidelity and sustainability. They also argued that contrary to the conventional wisdom, the implicit assumptions underlying the various arguments for adaptation are not supported by existing data. The bottom line from their perspective is that if prevention programs are not implemented with fidelity, they are not likely to be effective.

Others have suggested that some degree of program change is inevitable and that such "reinvention" (Rogers, 1995) may be necessary to match the program with its audience. Rogers (1995) and other proponents of this strategy have suggested that significant reinvention of programs is necessary to preserve program effectiveness. Rogers also argued that programs that are adaptable and flexible are more likely to be adopted and institutionalized, suggesting that "programming in" adaptations can increase buy in, ownership, and fit to local community needs and characteristics. Adaptation permits greater inclusion of local contextual information in the implementation process, and fidelity recognizes the importance of the relationship between conducting a particular preventive intervention "as tested" and its documented outcomes.

Still, a note of caution is warranted. Adapting evidence-based prevention programs by deleting material carries with it the risk of inadvertently deleting one or more essential elements of the preventive intervention and undermining its effectiveness. Similarly, adapting proven programs by adding untested material or modifying elements has the potential to undermine effectiveness by including material that may inadvertently actually increase drug abuse risk. The greater the number of modifications present, the greater the likelihood that key components linked to effectiveness will be changed. Furthermore, modifying or adding components to a program can present a serious threat to program fidelity if the modification or addition consists of elements that have been found to be harmful to or ineffective with youth, such as scare tactics in drug or violence prevention (Botvin, 2004).

The pursuit of implementation fidelity offers the benefit of improved effectiveness, whereas adaptation may offer potential benefits such as tailoring programs to local needs, increasing cultural relevance, and increasing acceptability and buy in. In addition, evidence-based prevention programs may be less likely to be adopted, implemented, and sustained over time if they are perceived to be low in flexibility and adaptability.

Therefore, it is critical to the field that we acknowledge and reconcile the natural tension between fidelity and adaptation. Both are essential elements of prevention program design and are best addressed by a planned, organized, and systematic approach. One approach to dealing with the issue of cultural tailoring without jeopardizing program effectiveness by undermining program integrity is to develop prevention programs that build in adaptation to enhance program fit while also maximizing fidelity and effectiveness (Castro et al., 2004). Currently, there is considerable controversy concerning the extent to which evidence-based programs should be adapted, but little empirical evidence to guide practitioners.

More research is clearly needed to determine how to implement programs with fidelity on a large scale in a way that will have an impact on local, state, or national rates of violence and drug use. Given the reality that at least some teachers adapt prevention programs, Ringwalt et al. (2004) suggested that developers should learn more about how teachers

are modifying their programs and incorporate these modifications in their curricula wherever possible. Research is also necessary to identify how to ensure that prevention programs meet the needs of the students receiving them. Castro et al. (2004) suggested that future research should expand current prevention models to include cultural variables and adaptation issues (see also chap. 16, this volume). Therefore, further research is needed to understand the nature and degree of adaptation to evidence-based prevention likely to occur in real-world settings and the relative tradeoffs associated with adaptation and fidelity with respect to effectiveness and to adoption, implementation, and sustainability.

Institutional Support Structures

The widespread dissemination of evidence-based programs that has occurred over the past decade is likely to continue in the years ahead. Coincident with the continued dissemination of evidence-based programs, it is crucial that prevention research focus on issues related to optimizing greater program integration at the school and community levels. On a practice level, it is important to identify appropriate structures and systems for dissemination, training, technical assistance and ongoing support, program integration across developmental stages and the prevention–treatment continuum of care, and the institutionalization and sustainability of prevention programs.

The public school system is perhaps the most often used institutional structure for prevention in the United States. It consists of a national network of schools containing most of the target population that prevention researchers and practitioners hope to reach. Another national network that may be appropriate as a dissemination and support structure for evidence-based prevention is the Cooperative Extension System, which consists of land-grant universities in virtually every county of every U.S. state. Spoth, Greenberg, Bierman, and Redmond (2004) proposed a partnership model that offers the potential for building capacity for diffusion of evidence-based prevention programs through the Cooperative Extension System. This approach involves the integration of two different delivery systems: the Cooperative Extension System of land-grant universities and the public school system. The Cooperative Extension System and the public school system have independent, multilevel program delivery networks reaching every community or district in the country. Such a model offers considerable potential as a delivery system with extensive penetration to promote the dissemination, adoption, implementation, and institutionalization of evidence-based prevention.

FUTURE DIRECTIONS

Despite the impressive progress made in the field of prevention in recent years, considerably more work is needed to advance both the science and the practice of prevention. Research is needed to enhance our understanding of the etiology of drug use and related health risk behaviors. Research is also needed to further refine existing prevention models and to explore the development of new and potentially more powerful approaches. Consistent with the theme of this volume, future research should strengthen the linkage between etiology and prevention. Efforts to refine existing prevention approaches or to develop new approaches are likely to be most successful if they are firmly grounded in etiology research.

Although efficacy research will remain important for testing these new approaches, shifting the emphasis from efficacy research to effectiveness research in real-world settings will facilitate the integration of research and practice and promote the adoption and sustained use of prevention programs that are tested and proven effective.

Little is known about the barriers to implementing evidence-based programs with fidelity and how to surmount them. As readers will glean from this chapter, this is a critical area of inquiry. Without a better understanding of these and other issues relating to implementation of prevention programs in real-world settings, it will be difficult to achieve the public health goals that have driven the development of prevention science. Another important issue warranting further research concerns whether adaptation is necessary to make prevention programs suitable to different populations. Similarly, research is needed to determine how or whether evidence based prevention programs can be adapted without undermining their effectiveness. Finally,

research is needed to identify or develop effective institutional structures for promoting the adoption, implementation, and sustained use of evidence-based prevention.

SUMMARY AND CONCLUSIONS

There have been important advances in prevention research over the past 25 years, and the field of prevention science has grown rapidly. The defining features of contemporary prevention science are high-quality empirical research using rigorous and well-established scientific methods, careful hypothesis testing, and the systematic accumulation of knowledge in a manner consistent with other areas of science. A new generation of evidence-based prevention approaches and policies has been developed and, if widely used, offers the potential to reduce the mortality and morbidity associated with a number of major health and social problems.

In the field of drug abuse prevention, substantial progress has been made in developing effective evidence-based intervention programs for adolescents and young adults. With respect to LST, the accumulation of findings from careful and rigorous research provides compelling evidence that LST reduces tobacco, alcohol, and marijuana use. There has been impressive growth in the field of prevention science overall and major advances in the field of drug abuse prevention in particular. Knowledge concerning the etiology of tobacco, alcohol, and illicit drug abuse has increased markedly, and there has been steady accumulation of evidence demonstrating the effectiveness of a variety of preventive interventions. Nonetheless, for the field of prevention science to continue advancing, it is essential that we continue to view our work critically, subject our theories to repeated examination, improve the effectiveness of preventive interventions through a greater linkage with etiology research, and confront the challenges associated with taking evidence-based prevention to scale.

References

Bandura, A. (1977). *Social learning theory*. Englewood Cliffs, NJ: Prentice Hall.

Biglan, A., Brennan, P. A., Foster, S. L., & Holder, H. D. (2004). *Helping adolescents at risk: Prevention of multiple problem behaviors*. New York: Guilford Press.

Botvin, G. J. (2000). Preventing drug abuse in schools: Social and competence enhancement approaches targeting individual-level etiological factors. *Addictive Behaviors, 25,* 887–897.

Botvin, G. J. (2004). Advancing prevention science and practice: Challenges, critical issues, and future directions. *Prevention Science, 5,* 69–72.

Botvin, G. J., Baker, E., Botvin, E. M., Filazzola, A. D., & Millman, R. B. (1984). Prevention of alcohol misuse through the development of personal and social competence: A pilot study. *Journal of Studies on Alcohol, 45,* 550–552.

Botvin, G. J., Baker, E., Dusenbury, L., Botvin, E. M., & Diaz, T. (1995, April 12). Long-term follow-up results of a randomized drug abuse prevention trial in a White middle-class population. *JAMA, 273,* 1106–1112.

Botvin, G. J., Baker, E., Dusenbury, L., Tortu, S., & Botvin, E. M. (1990). Preventing adolescent drug abuse through a multimodal cognitive–behavioral approach: Results of a 3-year study. *Journal of Consulting and Clinical Psychology, 58,* 437–446.

Botvin, G. J., Baker, E., Filazzola, A., & Botvin, E. M. (1990). A cognitive-behavioral approach to substance abuse prevention: A one-year follow-up. *Addictive Behaviors, 15,* 47–63.

Botvin, G. J., Baker, E., Renick, N., Filazzola, A. D., & Botvin, E. M. (1984). A cognitive-behavioral approach to substance abuse prevention. *Addictive Behaviors, 9,* 137–147.

Botvin, G. J., Batson, H., Witts-Vitale, S., Bess, V., Baker, E., & Dusenbury, L. (1989). A psychosocial approach to smoking prevention for urban Black youth. *Public Health Reports, 104,* 573–582.

Botvin, G. J., Dusenbury, L., Baker, E., James-Ortiz, S., Botvin, E. M., & Kerner, J. (1992). Smoking prevention among urban minority youth: Assessing effects on outcome and mediating variables. *Health Psychology, 11,* 290–299.

Botvin, G. J., Dusenbury, L., Baker, E., James-Ortiz, S., & Kerner, J. (1989). A skills training approach to smoking prevention among Hispanic youth. *Journal of Behavioral Medicine, 12,* 279–296.

Botvin, G. J., & Eng, A. (1980). A comprehensive school-based smoking prevention program. *Journal of School Health, 50,* 209–213.

Botvin, G. J., & Eng, A. (1982). The efficacy of a multi-component approach to the prevention of cigarette smoking. *Preventive Medicine, 11,* 199–211.

Botvin, G. J., Eng, A., & Williams, C. L. (1980). Preventing the onset of cigarette smoking through life skills training. *Preventive Medicine, 9,* 135–143.

Botvin, G. J., Epstein, J. A., Baker, E., Diaz, T., & Ifill-Williams, M. (1997). School-based drug abuse prevention with inner-city minority youth. *Journal of Child & Adolescent Substance Abuse, 6,* 5–20.

Botvin, G. J., Griffin, K. W., Diaz, T., & Ifill-Williams, M. (2001a). Drug abuse prevention among minority adolescents: One-year follow-up of a school-based preventive intervention. *Prevention Science, 2,* 1–13.

Botvin, G. J., Griffin, K. W., Diaz, T., & Ifill-Williams, M. (2001b). Preventing binge drinking during early adolescence: One- and two-year follow-up of a school-based preventive intervention. *Psychology of Addictive Behaviors, 15,* 360–365.

Botvin, G. J., Griffin, K. W., Diaz, T., Miller, N., & Ifill-Williams, M. (1999). Smoking initiation and escalation in early adolescent girls: One-year follow-up of a school-based prevention intervention for minority youth. *Journal of the American Medical Women's Association, 54,* 139–143.

Botvin, G. J., Griffin, K. W., Diaz, T., Scheier, L. M., Williams, C., & Epstein, J. A. (2000). Preventing illicit drug use in adolescents: Long-term follow-up data from a randomized control trial of a school population. *Addictive Behaviors, 5,* 769–774.

Botvin, G. J., Griffin, K. W., & Nichols, T. R. (2006). Preventing youth violence and delinquency through a universal school-based prevention approach. *Prevention Science, 7,* 403–408.

Botvin, G. J., Griffin, K. W., Paul, E., & Macaulay, A. P. (2003). Preventing tobacco and alcohol use among elementary school students through Life Skills Training. *Journal of Child & Adolescent Substance Abuse, 12,* 1–17.

Botvin, G. J., Renick, N. L., & Baker, E. (1983). The effects of scheduling format and booster sessions on a broad-spectrum psychosocial smoking prevention program. *Journal of Behavioral Medicine, 6,* 359–379.

Botvin, G. J., Schinke, S. P., Epstein, J. A., & Diaz, T. (1994). The effectiveness of culturally focused and generic skills training approaches to alcohol and drug abuse prevention among minority youth. *Psychology of Addictive Behaviors, 8,* 116–127.

Botvin, G. J., Schinke, S. P., Epstein, J. A., Diaz, T., & Botvin, E. M. (1995). Effectiveness of culturally focused and generic skills training approaches to alcohol and drug abuse prevention among minority adolescents: Two-year follow-up results. *Psychology of Addictive Behaviors, 9,* 183–194.

Castro, F. G., Barrera, M., & Martinez, C. R. (2004). The cultural adaptation of prevention interventions: Resolving tensions between fidelity and fit. *Prevention Science, 5,* 41–45.

Cicchetti, D., & Luthar, S. S. (1999). Developmental approaches to substance use and abuse. *Development & Psychopathology, 11,* 655–656.

Dodge, K. A. (2001). The science of youth violence prevention: Progressing from developmental epidemiology to efficacy to effectiveness to public policy. *American Journal of Preventive Medicine, 20,* 63–70.

Elliott, D. S., & Mihalic, S. (2004). Issues in disseminating and replicating effective prevention programs. *Prevention Science, 5,* 47–53.

Epstein, J. A., & Botvin, G. J. (2008). Media resistance skills and drug skill refusal techniques: What is their relationship with alcohol use among inner-city adolescents? *Addictive Behaviors, 33,* 528–537.

Epstein, J. A., Griffin, K. W., & Botvin, G. J. (2000a). A model of smoking among inner-city adolescents: The role of personal competence and perceived benefits of smoking. *Preventive Medicine, 31,* 107–114.

Epstein, J. A., Griffin, K. W., & Botvin, G. J. (2000b). Competence skills help deter smoking among inner-city adolescents. *Tobacco Control, 9,* 33–39.

Epstein, J. A., Griffin, K. W., & Botvin, G. J. (2002). Positive impact of competence skills and psychological wellness in protecting inner-city adolescents from alcohol use. *Prevention Science, 3,* 95–104.

Evans, R. I. (1976). Smoking in children: Developing a social psychological strategy of deterrence. *Preventive Medicine, 5,* 122–127.

Flay, B. R. (1987). Social psychological approaches to smoking prevention: Review and recommendations. *Advances in Health Education and Promotion, 2,* 121–180.

Fraguela, J. A., Martin, A. L., & Trinanes, E. A. (2003). Drug-abuse prevention in the school: Four-year follow-up of a programme. *Psychology in Spain, 7,* 29–38.

Gottfredson, D. C., & Gottfredson, G. D. (2002). Quality of school-based prevention programs: Results from a national survey. *Journal of Research on Crime and Delinquency, 39,* 3–35.

Griffin, K. W., Botvin, G. J., & Nichols, T. R. (2004). Long-term follow-up effects of a school-based drug abuse prevention program on adolescent risky driving. *Prevention Science, 5,* 207–212.

Griffin, K. W., Botvin, G. J., & Nichols, T. R. (2006). Effects of a school-based drug abuse prevention program for adolescents on HIV risk behaviors in young adulthood. *Prevention Science, 7,* 103–112.

Griffin, K. W., Botvin, G. J., Nichols, T. R., & Doyle, M. M. (2003). Effectiveness of a universal drug abuse prevention approach for youth at high risk for substance use initiation. *Preventive Medicine, 36,* 1–7.

Griffin, K. W., Botvin, G. J., Scheier, L. M., Epstein, J. A., & Diaz, T. (2002). Personal competence skills, distress, and well-being as determinants of substance use in a predominantly minority urban adolescent sample. *Prevention Science, 3,* 23–33.

Griffin, K. W., Epstein, J. A., Botvin, G. J., & Spoth, R. L. (2001). Social competence and substance use among rural youth: Mediating role of social benefit expectancies of use. *Journal of Youth and Adolescence, 30,* 485–498.

Griffin, K. W., Scheier, L. M., Botvin, G. J., & Diaz, T. (2001). The protective role of personal competence skills in adolescent substance use: Psychological well-being as a mediating factor. *Psychology of Addictive Behaviors, 15,* 194–203.

Hawkins, J. D., Catalano, R. F., & Miller, J. Y. (1992). Risk and protective factors for alcohol and other drug problems in adolescence and early adulthood: Implications for substance abuse prevention. *Psychological Bulletin, 112,* 64 105.

Jessor, R., & Jessor, S. L. (1977). *Problem behavior and psychosocial development: A longitudinal study of youth.* New York: Academic Press.

Kandel, D. (2002). *Examining the gateway hypothesis: Stages and pathways of drug involvement.* New York: Cambridge University Press.

Kandel, D. B., Yamaguchi, K., & Chen, K. (1992). Stages of progression in drug involvement from adolescence to adulthood: Further evidence for the gateway theory. *Journal of Studies on Alcohol, 53,* 447–457.

Kelly, J. A., & Kalichman, S. C. (2002). Behavioral research in HIV/AIDS primary and secondary prevention: Recent advances and future directions. *Journal of Consulting and Clinical Psychology, 70,* 626–639.

Lochman, J. E., & van den Steenhoven, A. (2002). Family-based approaches to substance abuse prevention. *Journal of Primary Prevention, 23,* 49–114.

Newcomb, M. D., & Bentler, P. M. (1988). *Consequences of adolescent drug use: Impact on the lives of young adults.* New York: Sage.

Office of National Drug Control Policy. (1997). *The National Drug Control Strategy, 1997* (Document NCJ163915). Washington, DC: Executive Office of the President.

Ringwalt, C. L., Vincus, A., Ennett, S., Johnson, R., & Rohrbach, R. L. (2004). Reasons for teachers' adaptation of substance use prevention curricula in schools with non-White student population. *Prevention Science, 5,* 61–67.

Rogers, E. M. (1995). *Diffusion of innovations* (4th ed.). New York: Free Press.

Roth, J. L., & Brooks-Gunn, J. (2003). Youth development programs: risk, prevention and policy. *Journal of Adolescent Health, 32,* 170–182.

Russell, J. A, & Carroll, J. M. (1999). On the bipolarity of positive and negative affect. *Psychological Bulletin, 125,* 3–30.

Scheier, L. M. (2001). Etiologic studies of adolescent drug use: A compendium of data resources and their implications for prevention. *Journal of Primary Prevention, 22,* 125–168.

Scheier, L. M., Botvin, G. J., & Griffin, K. W. (2001). Preventive intervention effects on developmental progression in drug use: Structural equation modeling analyses using longitudinal data. *Prevention Science, 2,* 89–100.

Spoth, R. L., Clair, S., Shin, C., & Redmond, C. (2006). Long-term effects of universal preventive interventions on methamphetamine use among adolescents. *Archives of Pediatric & Adolescent Medicine, 160,* 876–882.

Spoth, R. L., Greenberg, M., Bierman, K., & Redmond, C. (2004). PROSPER community-university partnership model for public education systems: Capacity-building for evidence-based, competence-building prevention. *Prevention Science, 5,* 31–39.

Spoth, R. L., Randall, G., Shin, C., & Redmond, C. (2005). Randomized study of combined universal family and school preventive interventions: Patterns of long-term effects on initiation, regular use, and weekly drunkenness. *Psychology of Addictive Behaviors, 19,* 372–381.

Spoth, R. L., Redmond, C., Trudeau, L., & Shin, C. (2002). Longitudinal substance initiation outcomes for a universal preventive intervention combining family and school programs. *Psychology of Addictive Behaviors, 16,* 129–134.

Swadi, H. (1999). Individual risk factors for adolescent substance use. *Drug and Alcohol Dependence, 55,* 209–224.

Tobler, N. S., & Stratton, H. H. (1997). Effectiveness of school-based drug prevention programs: A meta-analysis of the research. *Journal of Primary Prevention, 18,* 71–128.

Trudeau, L., Spoth, R. L., Lillehoj, C., Redmond, C., & Wickrama, K. (2003). Effects of a preventive intervention on adolescent substance use initiation, expectancies, and refusal intentions. *Prevention Science, 4,* 109–122.

U.S. Department of Health and Human Services. (1998). *Tobacco use among us racial/ethnic minority groups: A report of the surgeon general.* Atlanta, GA: Centers for Disease Control and Prevention, Office on Smoking and Health.

Zollinger, T. W., Saywell, R. M., Muegge, C. M., Wooldrige, J. S., Cummings, S. F., & Caine, V. A. (2003). Impact of the Life Skills Training curriculum on middle school students tobacco use in Marion County, Indiana, 1997–2000. *Journal of School Health, 73,* 338–346.

CONCLUDING REMARKS: MUSHING ALONG IN THE FROZEN TUNDRA WITHOUT A MAP

Lawrence M. Scheier

The Iditarod Trail Sled Dog Race started in 1925 as an emergency medical relief effort to transport serum for the treatment of diphtheria following an outbreak in Nome, Alaska. The serum was available in Anchorage and was brought to Nome by a succession of 20 mushers and their sled dogs, who rode different legs of the trail covering roughly 1,000 miles of the most barren, frozen tundra in Alaska.

The Iditarod dogsled race, which began officially in 1973 as an organized sledding competition, commemorates the medical relief expedition and represents one of the most challenging confrontations between humans and the wild. Stories abound of mushers riding with their dogs through arctic storms, experiencing whipping gale-force winds, and describing physically challenging and heroic encounters with wild moose, caribou, and packs of wolves. In the event that a competitor gets lost during whiteout conditions, it is usually the dogs that inevitably sniff out a trail. The love and respect held by mushers for their dogs has been a trademark of many stories about the Iditarod (Frederic, 2006; Price, 2008). Chronicles of the race recall how several competitors fell through sea ice cracks into the freezing water beneath. With no one else around for assistance, it was the dogs that saved the competitors' lives, pulling them out of the water before hypothermia set in, leading to likely death.

The Iditarod race is unique among competitions and represents a prime example of how people can set out with a laudable goal and venture forth into the unknown; face down challenges that may seem daunting, even insurmountable; and eventually emerge with a new understanding of the world and a revised vision of the self. A discussion of the history of this race and the fierce competition it represents provides a fitting way to frame the conclusion of this handbook. Like any journey, there have been significant milestones along the route that have pointed readers in a singular direction, toward the conclusion. Having now read through the handbook, readers should recognize that the study of drug use stands at a crossroads, with pathways leading in many different directions.

WHAT WE DO KNOW FROM LOOKING AT THE MAP?

At the start, the handbook briefly outlined a philosophical discussion of causation because such a discussion helped to shape the journey, to provide a sense of where the journey began and where it might take readers. Another signpost encountered in some of the early chapters was the need for a unified theory of causation in drug use etiology, and various chapter contributors also entertained the possibility that drug use is part of an experiential reality best characterized by multiplicity. As the handbook shows, drug use etiology researchers have accumulated a considerable body of knowledge focusing on a wide range of risk factors that seem to cause drug use. Although we cannot entertain the possibility of finding a reducible set of causes, there seem to be several themes worth exploring.

One of the more compelling themes that surfaces in the handbook suggests that there are many different perspectives used to explain drug use by youth. I said in the Preface that if there are a thousand drug users, there are as many pathways to drug use. Each youth who begins using drugs has his or her own story, and the various handbook contributors have recounted these different tales. Every chapter reflects a perspective, structured to cross-fertilize ideas from diverse disciplines and reflecting the different ways in which we each view drug use. This combined scholarly effort is perhaps the unique perspective that differentiates this handbook from anything previously published. What links all of the contributors together is not only that our ideas are bound in the same volume but also our commitment to scientific reasoning and a critical investment in the pursuit of knowledge about human behavior. In effect, drug use is one instantiation of behavior that captured our interest, but the real goal was to lay out some type of bridge spanning the subjective and the objective and find a common language to describe and sustain this connection (Jessor, 1981).

As the various chapters unfolded, we also came to realize that the study of drug use etiology has benefited from a rich and active history of scientific exploration, tinged with public concern. This is not a form of dialectical materialism; rather, it is an admonition to look more carefully at the collective effort that provides the foundation of our theories. The rich history of drug use etiology derives from the ardent efforts of our predecessors and continues to take shape in our current work. This is the perspective we build, the web of beliefs that drives etiology researchers to find the causes of drug use, provide substantive meaning to various determinants, and embody these reasons in effective prevention programs. As chapter 2 by Campbell relayed, perspective is colored by many forces including but not limited to history, politics, and public interest, all of which help formulate an epistemic culture and shape our view of drug use.

Chapter 3 by Glantz clarified the touchstone issues faced by etiology researchers, detailing the need for a common language as a prelude to creating relevant and meaningful theory. Before scientists even explicate theory, a period of questioning and reality testing precedes their inquiry. During this time, scientists sift through mounds of historical information, often searching for milestones to mark the correct path. In the case of drug use etiology, one

critical moment is the search for a phenotype. This search is of paramount importance because it suggests that drug use etiology is both the impetus and the destination. Clarification of what makes drug use etiology a scientific phenomenon is virtually the reason why we embark on a journey. Only by realizing that people's very human nature is part of the problem can science really frame the touchstone issues.

At this point, readers should quickly come to grasp that the most important take-home message in the handbook is that perspective is really about the marriage of ideas, the dialogue required to be creative, and the appropriateness of the theories used to explain reality. More than a decade ago, several authors noted that the field was characterized by the absence of a clear, comprehensive, and coherent picture of the causes of early-stage drug use (Petraitis, Flay, & Miller, 1995). Petraitis et al. (1995) went on to note that the utility of this vast accumulation of information on drug use etiology is hampered by a lack of integration and organization. One limitation in the field, noted in the handbook, is the absence of any formal discourse between different disciplines. For instance, sociologists proffer theories of deviance as explanations of drug use, whereas psychologists prefer models that accentuate cognitions (beliefs) and social influences. As should be patently clear after reading this handbook, it does little good to consider differential association theory (Sutherland, 1939) in the absence of a more refined understanding of the social influences that encompass peer selection (e.g., Fisher & Bauman, 1988) and peer socialization (Oetting & Beauvais, 1987). Once a youth decides to bond with less conventional peers, he or she has made a choice to eventually act on cognitive input, reifying a social cognitive basis to the underlying mechanisms (e.g., Akers, Krohn, Lanza-Kaduce, & Radosevich, 1979).

It should also not go unnoticed that Sutherland's (1939) emphasis on small, informal groups that are typically less conventional in behavior and thus more attractive to disenfranchised youth still begets the importance of social learning. Where we encounter a problem in devising unified etiology models is that some models highlight beliefs generated inside the head of the youth as proximal to drug use, whereas others emphasize role models and significant others outside the youth as being responsible for drug use. As several chapters in the handbook jointly chorused, we still lack a precise explanation of how youth capture these influences as part of their cognitive machinery. There is some clout to this concern, given the persistent question of why one youth becomes a drug user while another youth, experiencing quite similar influences, adopts a more conventional, antidrug lifestyle. One could speculate, consistent with the argument put forth by social control theory (Elliott, Huizinga, & Ageton, 1985), that at some point, disenfranchised youth become economically minded and engage a cost–benefit analysis, which helps them decide whether moving away from a conventional group and toward another, more deviant group will result in loss of status or bearing. Given the absence of any formal mechanism to address the incorporation of a wide range of social influences, and the limited knowledge we possess that specifically undresses the concept of reasoned action, it is better to see the two views not as incommensurate, but rather as complementary.

INTEGRATING DEVELOPMENTAL MILESTONES INTO THE PICTURE

Science is for the most part a social enterprise, one that takes shape as a conversation between human beings seeking a meaningful and systematic way to clarify the truth. As we engage in this dialogue, we must always keep in mind that we are one step removed, through perception, from the reality we seek to describe. Reality is essentially a social construction woven together as a fabric of ideation resulting from a continual stream of mental activity. Part of our mental fabrication of reality is made up of stored experiences (remembrances), and another portion is based on new information garnered from daily interactions with others. As the search for structure meaningful to the self broadens during adolescence and youth become intrigued by their constructions of reality, many develop the belief that drugs are a tool that can bring them closer to others, lessen any imprecision stemming from their cognitive machinations, and create a more meaningful

sense of self. Therefore, it should come as no surprise that adolescent drug use is functional and mired in a search for meaning. This search for meaning is derived in part from the gap between adolescents' image of themselves as physically capable and biologically primed for adult roles and the true social roles made available to them by society (Csikszentmihalyi & Schneider, 2000; Moffitt, 1993).

Chapter 4 by Griffin portrayed adolescence as a collage of developmental milestones, with a select few instigating drug use as a means of assuaging the painful experiences of identity formation and achieving autonomy. The hallmarks of this period center on individuation and strivings for autonomy but also include sexual exploration, testing limits, and a noticeable shifting in demands placed on the adolescent. Whether or not we tacitly accept the term *sturm und drang* (Arnett, 1999; Offer & Offer, 1975) used to characterize this period, it is still a time of remarkable personal challenge that witnesses a major overhaul of social relations. Chapter 4 also elucidated the fact that rapid acceleration of drug use seems to be associated with several major transitions, including those stimulated by puberty and entrance to high school, the workforce, and college. As Jochman and Fromme pointed out in chapter 30 on maturing out of drug experiences, deceleration of drug use seems to be centered around milestones of adulthood including marriage, bearing and rearing children, and employment. If one could synthesize the processes leading to early-stage drug use with those stimulating cessation, it would become apparent that drug use is essentially depicted as a form of autonomous expression resulting from spillover from the experience of incongruity.

BEGINNING TO SKETCH OUT THE PICTURE

As readers progressed through the handbook, other themes dealt with the sources of influence that shape the lives of youth. The mainstays of influence consist of their peers, family (including siblings), school friends, teachers, and other significant adult authority figures (administrators, athletic coaches,

community leaders, clergy, and adult role models).
Through their interactions, these social agents of
change press on youth new cognitions consisting of
beliefs, attitudes, and behavioral standards (both
anti- and prosocial) that pave the way toward intentions and willingness to engage in health-promoting
or health-compromising behaviors. There are a
number of theoretical mechanisms that link these
sources of influence with the behaviors of the focal
adolescent. As discussed in chapter 5, there has been
a proliferation of models to account for the precise
mechanism of influence, many of which appear at
some level to reflect the importance of learning and
cognition. This signpost along the journey was reinforced by four excellent chapters elucidating the
role of self-regulation, outcome expectancies, associative memory, and affective learning processes.

In chapter 7, Wills and Ainette painted a picture
of drug use as reflecting problems of self-regulation
and poor behavioral control. Their chapter provides
an epigenetic view of human behavior, with suggestions that early behavior canalizes later development, just like a diesel-powered locomotive running
on a long, winding track toward its destination.
Some of the points raised in this chapter suggest that
early stylistic forms of behavior, particularly those
that capture relations between the individual and his
or her world, morph into self-regulatory mechanisms that predict drug use. The evidence shows
that distractible, restless children who have problems approaching new people and adapting to novel
stimuli are vulnerable to using drugs when they
reach adolescence. The risk conveyed by early
behaviors is modeled on the basis of a progressive
unfolding of learned response contingencies; however, in reality there is an underlying commonality
or substrate on which this change arises. In an epigenetic framework, development is not experienced
as an interrupted flow of discrete points across the
life span but rather as a continuum with change
meted out in terms of self-expression. No matter
that a researcher points out some developmental
inflection called early childhood or adolescence,
there is always a solid core of identity we call *self*
that remains part of the fabric of our mental world.

Expectancies appear as one of the more prominent mechanisms of interest reflecting a glimmering

sheen of cognition that binds the internal subjective
world with external influences. One highlight of
Patel and Fromme's chapter on expectancies (chap. 8)
was the notion that we have significantly moved
away from drive reduction theories to consider mental explanations of the reasons why people drink
and use drugs. In applying expectancy theory, we
have elaborated a more complex cognitive model
that infers that people weigh or evaluate the implications of drinking or drug use. In essence, youth ask
themselves what they will get from drinking or drug
use as opposed to what they will not get. At the
same time, youth deliberate about reasons to use
drugs and drink (motives) and juxtapose these
along with their perception of what is acceptable
and prevalent among their peer group.

One of the more prominent modes of framing
the way humans cogitate and organize their mental
activity involves a dual-processing view of cognition. In this view, two systems coordinate learning
or acquisition of drug-related behaviors, one focusing on rapid, efficient, heuristic (implicit) processing
in which decisions may be based on affect or on
socially reactive-type thinking and the other reflecting a more controlled, deliberative (explicit) system
that involves conscious choice, reflection, and reasoned thought. It is interesting that self-concept
research has coined the term *confederacy of selves* to
capture the possible multiple selves that make up
our mental operations (Hart, 1988). The two systems of mental processing outlined in the handbook
quite possibly provide a means to unravel this confederacy. A benefit to studying automaticity and reasoned thinking is the push it gives psychologists to
consider alternatives to Skinner's radical behaviorism and introduce mental explanations like conscious
choice as a means of understanding the basis for
human behavior (Bargh & Ferguson, 2000).

Research on dual processing emphasizing associative cues and memory functions that underlay
behavior really points toward the role of inhibitory
and decision functions in prevention efforts. If peer
influences behave like associative cues or constitute
neural chaining effects to propel youth toward risky
behaviors, teaching them resistance skills and cognitive restructuring may be protective at some level of
thinking. Arguably, any reference to dual processing

and associative memory mechanisms has to consider the work of Neisser (1976) and Mowrer (1960), both of whom addressed the concepts of self and personal meaning in terms of cognition and symbolic thinking. The chapters that propose dual-processing models of drug use etiology are therefore fine tuning "how the world meets the mind" and incrementally adding to our knowledge of the cognitive enterprise we call *self*.

As readers have come to understand from digesting the contents of this handbook, our human experience rests on certain principles that reflect our day-to-day interactions, the way we feel about each other, and the way we feel about ourselves. Toward this end, Kassel and colleagues (chap. 10) explored the role of affect and feelings in drug use, reminding us that we are always seeking to calibrate, if not alter, our human experience. This latter phenomenon was what William James (1890/1950) outlined in *Principles of Psychology* as self-understanding, the search for a deeper level of intuitive knowledge that surfaces in nearly every study of adolescence. As the story on affect unfolds, emotional lability arising from drug use is reinforcing, representing what the authors term the *affective payoff* of drugs. If we are looking for cause, perhaps it is the unsettling cognitive, emotional, and social growth of adolescence that requires amelioration for healthy mental tone, or youth become a puddle of nerves. There is, in the authors' own words, some intuitive appeal to this argument because of the rapid hormonal, biological, and pubertal-based changes that occur in the early part of adolescence. If readers reflect back on the earlier statement about incongruity, regulation of mood by drugs is nothing more or less than a search for homeostasis.

A second source of support for a dual-process view of drug use comes from the reformulated model of negative reinforcement. As Kassel and his colleagues explain, the creeping sense of negative affect that accompanies dropping levels of drug-induced euphoria is detected preconsciously. The resultant attentional bias encourages the individual to use drugs as a means of staving off withdrawal and associated negative mood. This leads to a dual-system view of hot and cold information processing involving affective regulation. The mind behaves one way to move

toward relief and then seeks a different affective modality to stave off troubled cognitions that interfere with relief.

In terms of our own cognition, we are difficult and complex creatures with numerous variations on behavior that make finding a single cause for our actions difficult, if not impossible. This complexity was duly noted in chapter 12 by Sher and colleagues, who suggested that there is much that goes on under the hood. Searching under the hood has brought recognition of new terms, including *hedonic tone, incentive sensitization, wanting,* and *allostatic processes,* all of which can help clarify the differences between normal and disordered drinking and drug use. For those vested in etiology, this is quite helpful because it frames a stronger picture of the processes underlying the fine gradations between use and abuse, even though readers still have to march through a thicket of crowded lexical description.

FAMILIAL LIABILITY AND GENETIC INFLUENCES

Although the handbook clearly articulates a focus on social cognitive influences and underlying mental substrates of drug use, there is also another side of the equation involving familial and genetic influences. Many readers will say that genetics is about biology and alleles over which we have no control, short of engaging in purposeful social eugenics. A different view suggests that genetics can be informative by helping to clarify familial vulnerability and giving credence to individual differences in subjective reactions (tolerance and level of response) that arise from drug consumption. People do vary in their responses to alcohol, and this variability is not environmentally determined or predictive of later dependence. Thus, an important component of the handbook recognizes that there is a biological or genetic substrate to individual differences that plays a role in etiology. Several chapters addressed more formally the concept of substrates that may guide vulnerability to drug use. The notion that chromosomal regions or genes with specific phenotypic expression may be linked to substance use disorders is no different than a social psychologist saying some specific feature of social cognition drives drug use.

Both the constructivist view and the genetic or heritability view deserve equal attention (although this makes for dubious assertions by each camp). As Hasin and Katz reminded us in chapter 13, enzymes (alcohol dehydrogenase and aldehyde dehydrogenase) are used to metabolize alcohol, for instance, and control or regulation of these enzymes may be heritable. It is conceivable that the location of a specific allele on a particular chromosome is part of familial heritability and influences metabolism. Moreover, receptor sensitivity (excitability and plasticity) to drug effects can be heritable, as demonstrated in a slew of studies using data from the Collaborative Study on the Genetics of Alcoholism. In the end, the field grows from realizing that genetic influences on synapses and brain–behavior mechanisms (i.e., sensitivity of brain–reward systems) are one feature of the larger etiology picture that needs to be considered along with other influences that derive from the social milieu.

Two other chapters in the handbook tackled the notion of liability, invoking arguments from the use–abuse distinction to clear the air. In a much earlier and influential work, Richard Clayton (1992) spoke to the problems etiology encounters stemming from the inability to cleanly differentiate use from abuse. In fact, he spelled out for drug researchers that although there was much focus on initiation to drugs, perhaps the most compelling focus should be on when recreational and experimental use transitions into more protracted (excessive) and possibly harmful use (what is now termed *abuse*). Understanding what promulgates these transitions provides theoretical strength to the field. Furthermore, Clayton suggested that conceptual quagmires still dominate the field. For instance, there is the dilemma of "chipping." To put this into perspective, chippers defy theoretical explanation and likewise defy classification. Chippers rarely develop the telltale signs of dependence, yet their use, albeit infrequent or sporadic, never abates. On the basis of the various perspectives regarding consumption patterns, chronic exposure as evidenced by chippers should inevitably lead to abuse. Invariably, those supporting a pharmacological model would argue that frequency, quantity, or intensity of use should be the ruler used to measure the use–abuse distinc-

tion (Vogel-Sprott, 1974). A careful examination of the substance use disorders classification system of the *Diagnostic and Statistical Manual of Mental Disorders* (4th ed.; American Psychiatric Association, 1994) shows that some of the hallmark criteria constituting dependence, including withdrawal and tolerance, are symptoms consonant with frequent use. As the chapters in Part IV highlight, solutions to this problem may require additional blending of epidemiology, etiology, and theory so that we have a clearer picture of the distinction between use and abuse.

UNDERSTANDING HOW RACE AND CULTURE CONTRIBUTE TO DRUG USE

Although it is common to think of cognition as being buried inside the head, there is also the specter of more encompassing spheres of influence reflecting larger social institutions that are also partially responsible for our behavior. One sphere in particular, addressed in the handbook, attends to the role of race and culture. The concepts of race, ethnic identity, and culture came under considerable scrutiny owing to the specialized expertise of the contributors. Their focus has been to discern the relative effects of race or culture on drug use, moving beyond simple epidemiological frameworks to encompass broader thinking about mechanisms of causation. The several chapters on this subject all concluded that race and culture are fuzzy constructs and have led to considerable confusion in the research community. On the plus side, the consensus among these chapter contributors is that the field is currently poised to reframe questions about race and culture with greater precision. As these authors collectively pointed out, the question of race (to exemplify only this point) is really about whether being Black matters. In other words, the perceptions of life that resonate inside the head of the Black teenager should be the focus of etiology, not his or her skin color.

Support for this contention comes from studies that accentuate race differences in etiology as a matter of intrapersonal vulnerability (e.g., Ellickson & Morton, 1999; Griffin, Scheier, Botvin, & Diaz, 2000). These initial findings suggest that cognition is what differentiates youth in their susceptibility, elements of which include goal setting, decision making, and perceived personal and social competence. Despite peering in from the outside and discerning subgroup variation, the focus of these and related studies resonates around processes resident inside the black box. Some of the components of vulnerability to the early stages of drug use revolve around acculturation and the stress experienced by constantly moving between two cultures. Racial minority youth who move effortlessly between cultural mores may acquire certain behaviors of the dominant group, which through modeling and socialization can induce higher levels of drug use (i.e., changes in normative influences), whereas those youth who stay closer to their roots may be less inclined to deviate from conventional norms for that group. An interesting and fairly consistent observation is that Black and Hispanic youth who acculturate to White mores report higher rates of drug use, owing perhaps to an assimilation of deviant social values. Chapter 18 by Gibbons and colleagues painted a very clear picture that perceived racial discrimination can promulgate "behavioral willingness" to engage in deviant acts as a palliative coping mechanism. Black youth engage in drug use as a means of assuaging their anger, an anger that stems from feelings of isolation, dehumanization, and the absence of authentic being. Once this anger sets in and takes hold of their behavioral choices, normative social influences reinforce that other youth in the same predicament feel the same way. The despair creates a "racial homophilic" response that results in deviant subgroup bonding and rejection of conventional mores. It should thus come as no surprise to readers that race is a complex matter and requires more detailed examination to tease apart the causal mechanisms underlying race-specific vulnerability to drug use. Notwithstanding, evidence is accruing that culture plays some role in determining behavior.

QUESTIONS OF INFLUENCE: WHO HOLDS THE KEY?

Readers also learned that parental influence wanes considerably in adolescence and that peers become a focal source of influence. Several chapters in the

handbook addressed the different theoretical mechanisms that promulgate peer influence, suggesting that in some cases peers socialize drug use through normative and attitudinal pressures, whereas in other instances a selection mechanism operates to pull youth toward like-minded others. Dissection of these mechanisms harks back to an earlier claim made by philosophers that people are other directed, operating with looking-glass selves. This type of thinking accentuates conformity disposition stemming from both upward and downward social comparison as perhaps the single biggest push or influence in people's lives (Brown, Clasen, & Eicher, 1986; Cialdini & Trost, 1998; Wills, 1992).

A more careful look at the peer and family influence literatures shows that drug use corrects an imbalance and that in fact, drug use remediates discord between the private world and the publicly viewed self (Seltzer, 1989). In this manner, the process of peer rejection is just the tip of the iceberg, obscuring underneath a maelstrom of coercive family activity and felt rejection that erodes the basis for developing a positive sense of self. Consistent with this, we must recognize the importance of peer susceptibility in the larger scheme of identity formation (Erikson, 1968). Peers serve a developmental socializing function, with cliques and friendship networks representing a natural milieu for identity reflection (Hartup, 1989). Some of us are more and some of us are less susceptible to peer influences, and we should probably leave it for personality theorists to argue why (McGuire, 1968). We should also recollect the argument that although drug use is solipsistic in action, it truly remains a social activity. Here again, an older theoretical position suggests that social comparison drives formation of a self through accurate evaluation of others (Festinger, 1954; Festinger, Schachter, & Back, 1950).

LOCATION IS EVERYTHING!

A second theme that surfaced in the handbook acknowledged the individual as an agent of social change but then introduced another layer of social interaction, including the environment. As history reveals, methodological individualism was for a long time the dominant approach to studying drug use, emphasizing that the causes of drug use resonate within the individual. This blatant disregard of social institutions prompted Durkheim (1893/1997) to look more closely at social facts, encouraging his colleagues to consider that macro-level influences are proxies for chains that bind us collectively and cognitively to social structures. Fast forward a hundred years, and one encounters the work of Felner and Felner (1990), which highlighted the concept of developmentally hazardous environments that transact with the individual to create maladaptive functioning. This point was highlighted in chapter 6 by Anthony, who used an elegant statistical model based in epidemiology to show that Black–White differences in crack cocaine abuse disappear when controlling for socially shared local area characteristics in racially mixed neighborhoods. Studies of this nature throw light on causal mechanisms involved with drug use etiology and illuminate the reality that location (and possibly contagion) does matter.

Studying structural indicators and large social forces including schools, communities, and neighborhoods should augment our understanding of whether factors like poverty, social class, residential turmoil, and social or physical decay meaningfully contribute to drug use. Along these lines, several chapters explored various characteristics of the neighborhood, schools, community, and even the media with an eye toward assessing how variability in these institutions influences individual behavior. Inclusion of this body of work was a throwback to Bronfenbrenner (1986) and others who cautioned us not to ignore these forces as our investigative efforts narrowed down to individual–family interactions. Again, the precise mechanisms or conduits through which large environmental influences express themselves or leave their imprint on behavior may escape the fine-tooth comb of our measurement tools, but following a careful reading of these chapters, readers now recognize that there is a larger sphere of influence pressing on individual behavior. More important, the ruminations of sociologists (as Richard Clayton pointed out in the Introduction) and those in other disciplines (economics and anthropology) teach us that differences in larger social institutions and the conditions created by

individuals interacting with these institutions are somehow also responsible for drug use.

One important point to come from discussions of context is to realize that scholars of drug use etiology may need to retool their thinking to incorporate the notion of dependency that exists between the forces that operate to stimulate entry into drug use. Peer influences do not exert themselves in a vacuum; rather, they are often encountered in and around school environments, at parks during free time, or as part of extracurricular activities. Consider the number of youth who initiate to alcohol use on Friday nights before or after high school football games. Likewise, there are innumerable instances in which youth initiate to cigarette smoking or drinking alcohol at parties held in someone's house while the parents are out of town or out of sight. Chapter 26 by Grube especially highlighted the sources of underage environmental influences and reinforced the strengths of well-constructed, community-supported policies that can disrupt these influences.

FOCUS ON MECHANISMS OF CHANGE

I was very fortunate to be able to include in this volume several eminent scholars whose work embodies an appreciation of statistical methods for theory testing. Their arduous efforts to provide the latest information in modeling provide a basis to address some of the most pressing questions facing drug use etiology, including prediction in a multivariable framework, estimating behavioral heterogeneity, and assessment of change. Change is a very interesting concept from a philosophical point of view. Arguably, if something changes, it is no longer what it was. In other words, when youth undergo developmental change, the question arises as to whether they leave behind some sense of self and acquire a new identity or whether there is a continual blending or progressive refinement of selves (e.g., Markus & Kunda, 1986). Do we ever strip ourselves of the initial impetus, or do we rather experience a gradual morphing that leaves residual pieces reflecting earlier selves?

This is an interesting question to drug use researchers invested in longitudinal prediction and particularly to investigators who rely on measures of earlier functioning to predict later behaviors. Should we even expect that early measures of one form of behavior will be efficient predictors of later and more evolved behaviors? This type of thinking has probative value and has been the basis for criticisms of autoregressive methods in panel designs that parse stability variance but fail to appropriately model change (Rogosa, 1979). The type of statistical modeling outlined by these three contributors to the handbook represents a very powerful tool to resolve these and related questions. The study of drug use etiology really reinforces the demand for statistical solutions to these problems because as Flaherty pointed out in chapter 27, even among initiates there is wide variation in the first signal event (i.e., smoking a first cigarette), progression of drug use (i.e., alcohol leading to cigarettes or vice versa, as gateway studies have shown), and the type of drugs used (alcohol, cigarettes, marijuana, pills, to name a few). To think of these various possible etiological routes as a single homogeneous group (i.e., initiates) is somewhat problematic.

Flaherty's chapter 27 directed our attention to newer latent class analysis methods, which can model uncertainty in the data (conditional relations based on response profiles) and capture subgroup homogeneity where there is much apparent behavioral heterogeneity. Chapter 28 by Terry and Susan Duncan showed that correctly specified random coefficient models enable the testing of developmental hypotheses modeling trajectories of behavior. This statistical tool helps to chart the rate of developing behavior and determine whether certain factors calibrate or modify the course of development. In addition, the levels of influence become a focal concern as researchers grapple with large forces resident in neighborhoods and smaller loci tapping genetic influences. Modeling multilevel data provides a nuance that reflects scientific interest in developing ecologically valid models.

Chapter 29 by Jaffe and Bentler provided an overarching framework showcasing the strengths of structural equation modeling when combined with theory testing. Nearly 3 decades ago, Bentler (1978) reminded the field that a significant focus of psychology and even of drug use etiology was discovering and manipulating unobserved processes. Scientists

examining concepts like abuse or dependence are, as he suggested, speculating up until the point at which theory fits the data using an appropriate methodology. Added to the use of latent constructs, developmental theory then requires explicit statements of causation, postulating how one construct influences another. The resulting structural equation model provides a framework for relating observational data to theory via simultaneous hypothesis testing. Taken as a whole, the wonderful opportunity presented by recent technical advances in modeling provides a chance for researchers to sift through the enormous pool of risk factors linked etiologically with drug use behavior and progressively eliminate those characterized by unreliability, temporal dissipation, or inefficient prediction. The end result provides much better characterization of the different types of drug users, different etiologic pathways, different drug types, and different ways in which drug use manifests consequences.

TOWARD A UNIFIED CONCEPT OF CAUSATION

If anything, this handbook should help readers learn that scientists invoke a very special argot to express their knowledge about youthful drug users. As editor, one goal I made clear to all the contributing authors was that they strive for clarity in their terminology and not offer obfuscating text that would confuse readers. Our very specialized lexicon can be frustrating at times and a hindrance to efforts at unification. One of the recurring themes in the handbook is that we are in dire need of a distillation process whereby we reduce our language to a more manageable set of terms that strives for clarification. In fact, we need more precise means to connect our theories to empirical observations without further linguistic digression. That message was made clear to the individual chapter authors when I responded during the review process, "This term is not clear; is there another way to say this?" One author even suggested that I used a bait-and-switch tactic: asking authors to wander freely through content issues and then on further consideration asking them to separate the wheat from the chaff. Although this tactic may seem heavy handed, it worked, and the contributors responded with greater clarity, providing a means to link their ideas and language with what we already know. It should be patently clear that instead of an endless parade of new terms, we need to have better theories.

One recurrent theme readers encountered in the handbook is that drug use etiology is truly a reflection of the melting pot syndrome, having borrowed from many disciplines, including sociology, epidemiology, psychology, medicine, anthropology, and behavioral science, among others. This collage of disciplines is what led Jessor (1991) to suggest creating a "developmental behavioral science," moving away from parochial models of psychology steeped in traditional learning theory to more inclusive models that draw on a more complete knowledge of the multitude of forces that influence development over time. The real issue, as we pursue a unified theory or develop a concerted approach, is that we agree to collaborate and that we initiate this within a climate of trust and cooperation.

Most important, we must agree not to accept intellectual tyranny so that a single set of ideas remains prevalent despite questions arising from contraindicating evidence. A unified theory must bring together the disparate pieces of evidence and seamlessly sew them together into a fabric of understanding. The goal is to avoid reductionism and inspire creativity (Bohm & Peat, 1987). This may require that we find truth in varied disciplines such as genetics, psychology, sociology, anthropology, biology, philosophy, and history. One way to create a positive forum for an open exchange is to rid ourselves of the notion that drug use results from a fixed cause. In the Preface to this handbook, I alluded to the fact that resorting to an absolute authority does not bode well. Flexing our scholastic muscles with respect to finding the single cause of drug use may not be profitable given the proliferation of theories and the different vantage points researchers take when addressing drug use etiology. A better way to learn about etiology requires juxtaposing different theories against each other rather than against a fixed standard. In combination with this approach, policymakers, legislators, and those controlling the scientific purse strings need to be more democratic in the way in which they fund studies of etiology, giving precedence to creativity and rich ideas as

opposed to maintaining or rewarding the reigning scientific zeitgeist (Feyerabend, 1975). If a better grasp of cultural influences in drug use etiology is needed to improve the functionality of prevention, society is far behind the eight ball with regard to its understanding of these processes. Only in the past decade has the scientific community really emphasized the role of culture in health disparity, and to this end, many researchers and clinicians alike are still embroiled in significant debate about what precisely is culture.

There may be other roadblocks that impede the journey toward unification. For instance, although prevention experts have collectively agreed on copacetic standards of excellence (Flay et al., 2005) and refined their conceptualization of accountability, etiology has lagged considerably behind. In other words, we do not have a workable gauge or benchmark of what is satisfactory in terms of theoretical prediction. An exhaustive review of the literature, partly accomplished in this handbook, would show a paucity of empirical studies that account for large amounts of variance in specified drug outcomes. The studies are not poorly conceived; they actually identify critical risk mechanisms (as opposed to markers) that spring from our own intuition of what causes drug use. The real question at hand is whether they are ecologically valid given in some cases the overly simplified exposition of a very complex set of etiologic mechanisms. If we accept the pleadings of the critical rationalist perspective for just a moment, many theories would be overthrown or at least set aside as new and more parsimonious theories emerge and prove more worthy in terms of falsifiability (Popper, 1963). The criteria for testable theories have to at a minimum include logical coherence, prediction, explanation, intuitiveness, and simplicity.

There is a point at which the return on a theory has diminishing potential, particularly as the theory gains in complexity. The probability of a highly complex theory's being accurate goes down as the theory becomes more cumbersome. Problem behavior theory fits this bill, given that it is replete with interactions and conditional predictions between the three specified systems—person, environment, and behavior. We should be able to develop firm axioms and postulates from theory; however, the poor performance of several theoretical statements leads to weak assertions and inconsistent effects (Blalock, 1969). As a leading proponent of critical rationalism, Popper (1963) was also concerned with testability and corroboration, and these two functions need to be incorporated into the scheme of things. As a scientific body, etiology needs to mandate that the exclusion of a theory from the fold comes only as a result of tests that weaken the theory on the basis of its application in real-world settings. To do this—and this is a major step—we need to agree on common measures across multiple studies, thus making verifiability a primary goal of science.

Naturally, there are instances in which a formal system of assessment might not fit the goals of a particular study or a study seeks to refine existing measures as a departure from current knowledge. But for the most part, researchers need to blend existing measures rather than create them *de novo*. Pooling our psychometric resources into a repository will enable us to confirm the utility of constructs across diverse populations and configure risk mechanisms made up of the same observed measures. Again, in the interests of refutation, we can then determine whether risk operates in the same manner for different groups (e.g., Griffin et al., 2000). It is essential to establish whether a measure operates in a similar fashion for different groups as well as maintains developmental constancy from year to year or wave to wave. Comparisons across groups or within groups across time are fraught with difficulty if the measures used are not quantitatively identical (Drasgow & Kanfer, 1985). The restriction of equivalence across time infers that the meaning of the construct remains developmentally constant (i.e., the model is stationary). The restriction of equivalence across groups infers that the construct behaves identically for the two groups. Consider that most prevention field trials rely on random assignment but that the overall sampling methods are somewhat arbitrary. Even with random assignment, we cannot be assured of invariance across groups. Thus, it is essential to show that a particular model can be generalized to the population and that underlying constructs being measured are equivalent in form, for instance, between treatment and control groups (Marsh & Hocevar, 1985;

Pentz & Chou, 1994). Etiology researchers can learn from this premise by estimating equivalent measurement models for gender, race, and age groups, for example, and verifying a common measurement structure that reflects comparability across subpopulations (Byrne, Shavelson, & Muthén, 1989; Widaman & Reise, 1997). Structural invariance for parameters of interest in the model then becomes the basis for making unambiguous assertions about model fit in different groups, under contrived conditions, or in unique applications.

One other way etiology researchers can improve the value of their scientific endeavor is to choose common analytic approaches to elucidating how risk operates. More of the literature should emphasize validation and refutation rather than choking up the publication avenues with needless empirical stories. The distinction of moderators and mediators nicely illuminates this concern (Baron & Kenny, 1986). Many well-constructed examples abound of researchers specifying one or both mechanisms to build etiology models (Abel, 1996; Bukowski & Adams, 2005; Grube, Chen, Madden, & Morgan, 1995; Kung & Farrell, 2001). Even on a larger front, the same temptation to mix analysis modes exists when testing broader psychological theory (e.g., Frazier, Tix, & Barron, 2004; Hoyle & Robinson, 2003; Kraemer, Stice, Kazdin, Offord, & Kupfer, 2001; Quittner & Glueckauf, 1990). There is even a line of empirical inquiry in drug use etiology exemplifying moderated mediation, which represents a mediating relation that is conditioned on the basis of some third variable (Cleveland et al., 2005; Pilgrim, Schulenberg, O'Malley, Bachman, & Johnston, 2006).

Although both moderation and mediation deal fundamentally with alteration of statistical relationships, they go about defining this in different ways. Mediation is focused more on establishing pathways that embody generation of risk, whereas moderation is more concerned with establishing the conditions of risk based on "when" and "for whom." Positing both moderation and mediation as accounting for explanatory mechanisms creates a conundrum, given that we have no idea which is the superior explanatory form. Granted, there are clearly certain situations in which an investigator wants to test mediation and then ask the question of whether this process works differently for certain groups. In the case of interventions, for example, it makes sense to query whether social skills mediate program effects on drug outcomes and then turn to address whether the intervention worked more efficaciously for boys or girls, Blacks or Whites, or youth with high or low self-esteem.

What would be helpful for the field, overall, would be for investigators to choose a prevailing dominant risk mechanism to account for youthful drug use.[1] Such dominance is based on the strength of findings using analytic proofs that comport with theory. Following Popper's (1963) falsification hypothesis, we can then eliminate the weaker models on the basis of their poor empirical fit to the data. Stacy, Newcomb, and Bentler (1991) did precisely this when they contrasted moderation and mediation with data emphasizing drunk driving, ultimately selecting the model that best accentuated theory and fit the data. Conversely, Chassin, Pillow, Curran, Molina, and Barrera (1993) tested three distinct forms of mediation to account for the process linking parental alcoholism with youthful drug use. One of the three approaches fit the data better and was ultimately used to explain behavior. This approach is more consistent with the aims of refutation, seeking to build valid theories, and would have the effect of eliminating weaker models, eventually discovering the more dominant mechanism that can become the focus of prevention activities.

These and other standards will eventually percolate into the common pool of techniques researchers use to gain greater scientific precision. However, there also has to be a push from scientists to enact specific benchmarks that encompass technique and communication, outlining a template for the necessary and sufficient conditions of professional work. The rigor required to ensure utilization of common measures and encourage common modeling strategies needs to be an indelible feature of grant and

journal reviews and incorporated into other means of knowledge diffusion.

ON THE MAKINGS OF A PARADIGM SHIFT

At the very heart of this handbook is the rumination that perhaps the field is ripe for a paradigm shift. Thomas Kuhn's (1962) classic work *The Structure of Scientific Revolutions* was meant to elucidate the forces that operate to influence science and scientific thinking, not to criticize the actual discoveries of science. In this respect, Kuhn talked about "normal science," reflecting the organized day-to-day means we use to link observation with theory. This discussion gave way to the forces that move science from one precipice of understanding to another. Kuhn used the term *paradigm* as a means of understanding how science moves from one interpretation of reality to another, as a force that influences the shifting tides of knowledge. Paradigms encompass the way in which we investigate the world, outlining in quasi-philosophical terms the way information proceeds from the laboratory to the layman. What is important for readers to glean from Kuhn's insight is that the various anomalies and crises that prompt radical shifts in the processes underlying scientific discovery are currently operating to stimulate a paradigm shift in drug use etiology.

Several chapters in the handbook gave notice of this pending transformation. In particular, Stacy and colleagues' chapter 9 provided a fresh look at the essential nature of information processing underlying drug use etiology. Their chapter focused on spontaneous cognitive processes that represent a form of decoding information that deviates from the reflective, rule-governed, more controlled way in which we process reality. In the spontaneous mode, we process information automatically, in a rapid and efficient manner that is perhaps undetected by the self or at the very least free from social desirability. The unconscious mode allows us to survive in a maelstrom of mental activity and does not require vigilance to each and every presenting stimulus. As Stacy and colleagues artfully pointed out, this type of processing may be the root cause of drug use and addiction, where cues and triggers meander into the deepest recesses of our thought without our really

---

[1] There are many other examples that could have been used to illustrate the moderator–mediator distinction (problem). For instance, the role of peer influence has also been cited as both a moderator (Stacy, Newcomb, & Bentler, 1992) and a mediator (Yanovitzky, 2005), owing to the fact that researchers are not precisely sure how exchanges with peers result in the formation of attitudes, beliefs, intentions, or behavior. Chapter 21 of this volume also reviews empirical findings showcasing peer social influence functions as a mediator of other external forces.

knowing it. The way spontaneously activated memories work, governed by the principles of association, and the way in which a drug user becomes conditioned to various stimuli and vulnerable to associations, requires that we develop health prevention interventions along the same lines. In essence, if this is the way we process information, then we need to change the way we measure information processing so that there is a greater correspondence between our science and reality. Whether scientists want to acknowledge this or not, a change in the way all of us see the world is the basis for a paradigm shift.

Stacy and colleagues admonished the field to take a more careful look at what is gained from using self-report as opposed to indirect tests of cognition that avoid social desirability and self-reflection. At some point, consumers of research must realize that the framework of scientific inquiry is slowly changing. If an investigator asks a drug user whether specific cues that prompt consumption exist, he or she will naturally say, "Sure." However, the precise nature of these cues as components of cognition is somewhat obscure given current scientific methods. More important, it is hard for the user to locate the precise manner in which these cues influence his or her everyday thinking. Notwithstanding, the discovery of mental triggers that presage consumption and that fall below users' conscious radar screen paves the way for treatment professionals to intervene by showing users promising ways to avoid making these associations. Readers are urged to recognize that the paradigm shift exists on two levels: the scientist who uses new measures and invokes new arguments and the drug user who is told there are new ways of looking at the self. Both views count in the estimation of whether we have advanced our science.

THE BONDS THAT TETHER PREVENTION TO ETIOLOGY

It is only natural that a handbook on drug use etiology seeks a modicum of practicality in a world so consumed with eradicating disease. That is, the handbook is covered with a patina of functionality, and this decision at the very outset created the opportunity to include an entire section dealing with prevention. As many contributing authors

noted, the problem of drug abuse is rooted in use, and readers familiar with the three tiers of prevention (primary, secondary, and tertiary) should easily grasp that all primary prevention must begin at the basic level of early experimentation, a point at which nonusers deliberate over their first sip of alcohol, smoking their first cigarette or marijuana joint, or consuming pills to get high. Added then to the classic use–abuse dichotomy discussed at length by several authors in the handbook, readers must now consider a third level of consumption termed *recreational* or *experimental use*. It should come as no surprise from reading these materials that if society wants to make headway in the War on Drugs, a good place to gain a firm beachhead is eradicating early experimentation.

Although this emphasis is a laudatory goal, some problems in exercising the principles of prevention remain, and the four chapters in the final section dealt with these unresolved issues. First and foremost is the translation of research into practice, the methods through which we take information on causality and put it inside the glove of prevention. As Pentz points out in chapter 31, the focus of the public health agenda has always emphasized making headway with etiology and epidemiology for the sole purpose of eradicating disease. Whether we are fighting tooth decay or heart disease, research on causation has to filter into viable prevention modalities, and that is the work of translation. Even with the recent codification by the National Institutes of Health of the translation process, scientists still face a steep uphill climb with drug use given that there are multiple causal agents and multiple outcomes and no single prevention effort has proven more effective than another. What Pentz outlined is a systematic means to create a bridge between theoretical disciplines, establishing new inroads from translation-to-practice efforts, and a means to widen the horizon of sustainable prevention goals.

Second, prevention faces dire straits in identifying and unraveling the active ingredients in multicomponent prevention trials. There is a pressing question that reinforces the need to uncover the biggest bang for the buck. In chapter 32, Hansen and colleagues did a wonderful job of helping readers find their way through this thicket, using empirical examples of programs that can be dissected into manageable working pieces. Their comprehensive and systematic exploration of what makes model programs work helps consumers grapple with difficult decisions owing to the popularity of certain programs that just do not make the grade. Surprisingly, programs promoting school achievement and bonding to school were relatively more successful than other highly touted skills programs. Perhaps the cultural milieu of schools provides the perfect venue for instilling behavior change given its pro-achievement and conformist environment. In chapter 34, Botvin and Griffin addressed a third focus, taking programs to scale and the efficacy–effectiveness–dissemination paradigm that now governs the drug prevention research community (Flay et al., 2005). Their chapter deftly addressed the issues of diffusion and technology transfer and whether preventive interventions sculpted and shaped around intensive research efforts can be adapted to various community settings while still retaining their original significance.

In an effort to reinforce the importance of cognition in constructing reality, Sussman (chap. 33) examined the basis for how youth make a realistic appraisal of their drinking and drug use. Some of the concepts proffered by the *Diagnostic and Statistical Manual of Mental Disorders* (fourth ed.; American Psychiatric Association, 1994) nosological classification, such as impaired control and denial, are part of clinical lore but still exist on shaky psychometric grounds. Tied in with these concepts, Sussman reviewed the literature on imprecision, errors of judgment, cognitive distortions, and erroneous beliefs as a source of drug-related behaviors. One fascinating concept readers got to explore was pluralistic ignorance, suggesting that people may share widely held beliefs despite their inaccurate nature. In other words, people will strive for a consensus even though a careful look at their own behavior confirms they are making a cognitive error or miscalculation. Some other crucial ideas contained in the handbook emphasize that most people also operate under the third-person hypothesis, thinking that everyone but them is getting duped. Prevention is also hampered by the fact that people think that their own thoughts are unique and that nobody shares them. This makes it harder to discuss prevailing injunctive

norms to youth when they inform researchers that each person holds his or her own behavioral standard.

The work of Prentice and Miller (1993) is very interesting in this regard. These authors proposed a model of behavior that tries to explain what happens when there are discrepancies in attitudes and norms. Much of their thinking was preceded by Sherif's (1936) early laboratory studies of the autokinetic phenomenon (visually tracking a light beam displayed in a darkened room). Sherif found that most people modified their answers regarding the light beam's position in accordance with group standards rather than retaining their own answers, which may actually have been more accurate. These and other studies accentuate certain mechanisms for transmitting norms as part of social reality. In general, people go a long way to conform to a norm regardless of whether that norm is considered adaptive or correct. If we think about this, many youth find themselves at odds with the current behavioral standards, particularly if they are not doing well in school, lack certain social graces, or just do not fit in well with the larger peer crowd. The ambiguity of their position or social status within the larger peer crowd instigates feelings of social anomie and sparks a downward drift, propelling the youth to move away from social stigma toward social acceptance. Movement away from the behavioral standards of the more popular (and perhaps more conventional) crowd toward deviant norms may actually result from prestige seeking and go a long way toward explaining why youth choose drug-abusing friends (see also Festinger's [1954] social comparison theory).

TAKING STOCK

At this point, we have reached the end of our journey, and the handbook must come to a close. Perhaps the most important means of evaluating the handbook is to address whether it responds to the major concerns that have been outlined in the field. One starting point is to take the prescient view outlined by Petraitis et al. (1995) as a litmus test of where the field finds itself currently situated and then query where the field needs to go. It follows then to address whether the handbook has touched on the issues raised by those authors almost 13 years ago. First and foremost, contributors to this volume followed suit and provided a means to organize the pieces of the puzzle. Rather than looking at major theories (Petraitis et al. examined a total of 14), the authors aligned themselves more along the lines of the tactic chosen by Hawkins, Catalano, and Miller (1992), who refreshingly looked at the major risk and protective factors in drug use etiology and discussed their implications for prevention.[2] The handbook contributors carved out several areas of concern that have been the focus of drug use etiology and addressed the major issues or challenges confronting the field. As the handbook progressed, the various authors contrasted views within each domain (e.g., implicit vs. explicit) and provided arguments that helped to extend our knowledge base with respect to poorly defined concepts and constructs.

The contributors to the handbook also took on additional onus by pushing the event horizon, pointing out the directions the field should take and speculating on whether these different pathways were fit to travel. The handbook thus serves not so much as a map revealing the destination, but more as a compass pointing us in the right direction. This functional role and the metaphor of the Iditarod remind readers that the journey of a thousand miles begins with the first step. As with any journey of considerable distance, especially through such treacherous terrain as the Iditarod, readers should be cautious in their preparations. In their haste to follow the data, many researchers often lose sight of the theoretical imperatives that guide our field. More important, readers should not lose sight of the social dialogue that forms the basis of science, the norms or conventions that dictate the manner of scientific inquiry, and the ways in which science molds itself somehow to reflect the political and/or social interests of the people. Drug use etiology is not insulated from this constant doubting and the practice of how scientific decisions are made. In this respect, a piece of the

handbook waxes philosophical and asks pertinent questions about where the field should be heading.

WILL SCIENCE PROVIDE THE ANSWER TO DRUG USE?

There is another more philosophical side to the continuing crisis of drug use that warrants attention. John Horgan's (1996) fascinating and compelling book *The End of Science* contains a compendium of interviews and informal chats with some of the world's most prestigious and illustrious scientists, philosophers, and pragmatists. The interviews focus on whether science has brought us any closer to finding The Answer, representing a panoramic intellectual assessment touching on "why are we here," "what is consciousness," "how did life begin," and other fascinating intellectual riddles of the universe. Of the many troubling themes that percolate to the surface of Horgan's writing, he carefully admonishes readers to recognize that science unravels mysteries in a very coherent and systematic fashion. Ever the optimist, Horgan believes that given enough time and resources, science can and will provide answers to important questions.

There is a lesson that springs forth from this advice for drug use etiology researchers. Over a considerably extended period of time, perhaps more than a single person's lifetime, it is increasingly apparent that drug use etiology research has shifted its emphasis from psychosocial studies examining internal motivations such as self-control, self-regulation, and self-esteem (Scheier, Botvin, Griffin, & Diaz, 2000; Wills, 1994; Wills & Stoolmiller, 2002) to brain imaging research that can uncover neural substrates of addiction (Fowler, Volkow, Kassed, & Chang, 2007; Volkow, Fowler, & Wang, 2002). Given enough time and resources, and a certain modicum of creative insight, we can, one hopes, integrate the concepts and methods from diverse disciplines, creating the template for a unified model.

Horgan (1996) admonished readers to realize that truth may lie outside the bounds of science and that all our efforts are for naught unless we rest comfortably with the notion that the goal of science is to improve our lives through utility. A richer understanding of the compelling reasons why youth use

---

[2] Arguably, we did follow suit with respect to the classification system offered by Petraitis et al. (1995). To wit, I included in the handbook sections that attend to normative influences (peers and family), cultural or attitudinal influences (race, culture, and ethnicity), and intrapersonal influences (temperament, self-control, expectancy, and affect). However, impetus for our table of contents and thus the formal content of the handbook was contrived in a slightly different manner.

drugs may eventually create a society absent these destructive and costly behaviors. Twenty years ago, a study examining the relative influence of peers and family on drug use was considered exemplary. Today, the same study delves deeper into the matryoshka doll in which ideas have become folded into one another. Peers, for instance, are not the "reason" youth do drugs, they are part of the social nexus that gives meaning to drug use. The better framework is to tease apart the relative meaning of different social networks within larger peer circles and discern their relative influence on drug use. The many innovations of science are making it possible to refine our understanding of the basic processes that are part and parcel of our mental and physical landscape. One must keep in mind, however, that as much as laboratory rats can help us develop a much richer appreciation for the role of learning in drug addiction, they cannot participate in focus groups and neither can they tell us the principal reasons, motivations, and causes that drove them to use drugs. I say this because where science ends or comes to a screeching halt because of technical limitations, hope begins anew and should compel us forward.

References

Abel, M. H. (1996). Self-esteem: Moderator or mediator between perceived stress and expectancy of success. *Psychological Reports, 79*, 635–641.

Akers, R. L., Krohn, M. D., Lanza-Kaduce, L., & Radosevich, M. (1979). Social learning and deviant behavior: A specific test of a general theory. *American Sociological Review, 44*, 636–655.

American Psychiatric Association. (1994). *Diagnostic and statistical manual of mental disorders* (4th ed.). Washington, DC: Author.

Arnett, J. A. (1999). Adolescent storm and stress, reconsidered. *American Psychologist, 54*, 317–326.

Bandura, A. (1997). *Self-efficacy: The exercise of control.* New York: W. H. Freeman.

Bargh, J. A., & Ferguson, M. J. (2000). Beyond behaviorism: On the automaticity of higher mental processes. *Psychological Bulletin, 126*, 925–945.

Baron, R. M., & Kenny, D. A. (1986). The moderator-mediator variable distinction in social psychological research: Conceptual, strategic and statistical consideration. *Journal of Personality and Social Psychology, 51*, 1173–1182.

Bentler, P. M. (1978). The interdependence of theory, methodology, and empirical data: Causal modeling as an approach to construct validation. In D. B. Kandel (Ed.), *Longitudinal research on drug use: Empirical findings and methodological issues* (pp. 267–302). Washington, DC: Hemisphere.

Blalock, H. M. (1969). *Theory construction: From verbal to mathematical formulations.* Englewood Cliffs, NJ: Prentice Hall.

Bohm, D., & Peat, F. D. (1987). *Science, order, and creativity: A dramatic new look at the creative roots of science and life.* New York: Bantam Books.

Bronfenbrenner, U. (1986). Ecology of the family as a context for human development. *Developmental Psychology, 22*, 723–742.

Brown, B. B., Clasen, D. R., & Eicher, S. A. (1986). Perceptions of peer pressure, peer conformity dispositions, and self-reported behavior among adolescents. *Developmental Psychology, 22*, 521–530.

Bukowski, W. M., & Adams, R. (2005). Peer relationships and psychopathology: Markers, moderators, mediators, mechanisms, and meanings. *Journal of Clinical Child and Adolescent Psychology, 34*, 3–10.

Byrne, B. M., Shavelson, R. J., & Muthén, B. (1989). Testing for the equivalence of factor covariance and mean structures: The issue of partial measurement invariance. *Psychological Bulletin, 105*, 456–466.

Chassin, L., Pillow, D. R., Curran, P. J., Molina, B. S. G., & Barrera, M., Jr. (1993). Relation of parental alcoholism to early adolescent substance use: A test of three mediating mechanisms. *Journal of Abnormal Psychology, 102*, 3–19.

Cialdini, R. B., & Trost, M. R. (1998). Social influence: Social norms, conformity, and compliance. In D. T. Gilbert, S. T. Fiske, & G. Lindzey (Eds.), *The handbook of social psychology* (Vol. II, pp. 151–192). Boston: McGraw-Hill.

Clayton, R. (1992). Transitions in drug use: Risk and protective factors. In M. Glantz & R. Pickens (Eds.), *Vulnerability to drug abuse* (pp. 15–51). Washington, DC: American Psychological Association.

Cleveland, M. J., Gibbons, F. X., Gerrard, M., Pomery, E. A., & Brody, G. H. (2005). The impact of parenting on risk cognitions and risk behavior: A study of mediation and moderation in a panel of African American adolescents. *Child Development, 76*, 900–916.

Csikszentmihalyi, M., & Schneider, B. (2000). *Becoming adult: How teenagers prepare for the world of work.* New York: Basic Books.

Drasgow, F., & Kanfer, R. (1985). Equivalence of psychological measurement in heterogeneous populations. *Journal of Applied Psychology, 70*, 662–680.

Durkheim, E. (1997). *The division of labor in society* (J. P. Smith, Trans.). New York: Free Press. (Original work published 1893)

Ellickson, P. L., & Morton, S. C. (1999). Identifying adolescents at risk for hard drug use. Racial/ethnic variations. *Journal of Adolescent Health, 25,* 382–395.

Elliott, D. S., Huizinga, D., & Ageton, S. S. (1985). *Explaining delinquency and drug use.* Beverly Hills, CA: Sage.

Erikson, E. H. (1968). *Identity, youth, and crisis.* New York: W. W. Norton.

Felner, R. D., & Felner, T. Y. (1990). Primary prevention programs in the educational context: A transactional ecological framework and analysis. In L. Bond & B. Compas (Eds.), *Primary prevention in the schools* (pp. 116–131). Beverly Hills, CA: Sage.

Festinger, L. (1954). A theory of social comparison processes. *Human Relations, 5,* 117–139.

Festinger, L., Schachter, S., & Back, K. (1950). *Social pressures in informal groups.* New York: Harper.

Feyerabend, P. (1975). *Against method: Outline of an anarchistic theory of knowledge.* Atlantic Highlands, NJ: Humanities Press.

Fisher, L. A., & Bauman, K. E. (1988). Influence and selection in the friend-adolescent relationship. Findings from studies of adolescent smoking and drinking. *Journal of Applied Social Psychology, 18,* 289–314.

Flay, B. R., Biglan, A., Boruch, R. F., Castro, F. G., Gottfredson, D., Kellam, S., et al. (2005). Standards of evidence: Criteria for efficacy, effectiveness and dissemination. *Prevention Science, 6,* 151–175.

Fowler, J. S., Volkow, M. D., Kassed, C. A., & Chang, L. (2007). Imaging the addicted human brain. *Science & Practices Perspectives, 3,* 4–16.

Frazier, P. A., Tix, A. P., & Barron, K. E. (2004). Testing moderator and mediator effects in counseling psychology research. *Journal of Counseling Psychology, 51,* 115–134.

Frederic, L. (2006). *Running with champions: A midlife journey on the Iditarod trail.* Anchorage: Alaska Northwest Books.

Griffin, K. W., Scheier, L. M., Botvin, G. J., & Diaz, T. (2000). Ethnic and gender differences in psychosocial risk, protection, and adolescent alcohol use. *Prevention Science, 1,* 199–212.

Grube, J. W., Chen, M. J., Madden, P., & Morgan, M. (1995). Predicting adolescent drinking from alcohol expectancy values: A comparison of additive, interactive, and nonlinear models. *Journal of Applied Social Psychology, 25,* 839–857.

Hart, D. (1988). The adolescent self-concept in social context. In D. K. Lapsley & F. C. Power (Eds.), *Self, ego, and identity: Integrative approaches* (pp. 71–90). New York: Springer.

Hartup, W. W. (1989). Social relationships and their developmental significance. *American Psychologist, 44,* 120–126.

Hawkins, J. D., Catalano, R. F., & Miller, J. Y. (1992). Risk and protective factors for alcohol and other drug problems in adolescence and early adulthood: Implications for substance abuse prevention. *Psychological Bulletin, 112,* 64–105.

Horgan, J. (1996). *The end of science: Facing the limits of knowledge in the twilight of the scientific age.* New York: Broadway Books.

Hoyle, R. H., & Robinson, J. I. (2003). Mediated and moderated effects in social psychological research: Measurement, design, and analysis issues. In C. Sansone, C. Morf, & A. T. Panter (Eds.), *Handbook of methods in social psychology* (pp. 213–233). Thousand Oaks, CA: Sage.

James, W. (1950). *The principles of psychology* (Vols. 1 and 2). New York: Dover. (Original work published 1890)

Jessor, R. (1981). The perceived environment in psychological theory and research. In D. Magnusson (Ed.), *Toward a psychology of situations: An interactional perspective* (pp. 297–317). Hillsdale, NJ: Erlbaum

Jessor, R. (1991). Behavioral science: An emerging paradigm for social inquiry? In R. Jessor (Ed.), *Perspectives on behavioral science: The Colorado lectures* (pp. 309–316). Boulder, CO: Westview Press.

Jessor, R., & Jessor, S. L. (1977). *Problem behavior and psychosocial development.* New York: Academic Press.

Kraemer, H. C., Stice, E., Kazdin, A., Offord, D., & Kupfer, D. (2001). How do risk factors work together? Mediators, moderators, and independent, overlapping, and proxy risk factors. *American Journal of Psychiatry, 158,* 848–856.

Kuhn, T. S. (1962). *The structure of scientific revolutions.* Chicago: University of Chicago Press.

Kung, E. M., & Farrell, A. D. (2001). The role of parents and peers in early adolescent substance use: An examination of mediating and moderating effects. *Journal of Child and Family Studies, 9,* 509–528.

Markus, H., & Kunda, Z. (1986). Stability and malleability of the self-concept. *Journal of Personality and Social Psychology, 51,* 858–866.

Marsh, H. W., & Hocevar, D. (1985). Application of confirmatory factor analysis to the study of self-concept: First- and higher order factor models and their invariance across groups. *Psychological Bulletin, 97,* 562–582.

McGuire, W. (1968). Personality and susceptibility to social influence. In E. F. Borgatta & W. W. Lambert (Eds.), *Handbook of personality theory and research* (pp. 1130–1187). Chicago: Rand McNally.

Moffit, T. E. (1993). Adolescence-limited and life-course-persistent antisocial behavior: A developmental taxonomy. *Psychological Review, 100,* 674–701.

Mowrer, O. H. (1960). *Learning theory and the symbolic processes.* New York: Wiley.

Neisser, U. (1976). *Cognition and reality.* San Francisco: Freeman.

Oetting, E. R., & Beauvais, F. (1987). Peer cluster theory, socialization characteristics, and adolescent drug use: A path analysis. *Journal of Counseling Psychology, 34,* 205–213.

Offer, D., & Offer, J. B. (1975). *From teenage to young manhood: A psychological study.* New York: Basic Books.

Pentz, M. A., & Chou, C.-P. (1994). Measurement invariance in longitudinal clinical research assuming change from development and intervention. *Journal of Consulting and Clinical Psychology, 62,* 450–462.

Petraitis, J., Flay, B. R., & Miller, T. Q. (1995). Theories of adolescent substance use: Organizing pieces in the puzzle. *Psychological Bulletin, 117,* 67–86.

Pilgrim, C. C., Schulenberg, J. E., O'Malley, P. M., Bachman, J. G., & Johnston, L. D. (2006). Mediators and moderators of parental involvement on substance use: A national study of adolescents. *Prevention Science, 7,* 75–89.

Popper, K. (1963). *Conjectures and refutations: The growth of scientific knowledge.* London: Routledge Classics.

Prentice, D. A., & Miller, D. T. (1993). Pluralistic ignorance and alcohol use on campus: Some consequences of misperceiving the social norm. *Journal of Personality and Social Psychology, 64,* 243–256.

Price, J. (2008). *Backstage Iditarod.* Wasilla, AK: Sunhusky Productions.

Quittner, A. L., & Glueckauf, R. L. (1990). Chronic parenting stress: Moderating versus mediating effects of social support. *Journal of Personality and Social Psychology, 59,* 1266–1278.

Rogosa, D. (1979). Causal models in longitudinal research: Rationale, formulation, and interpretation. In J. R. Nesselroade & P. B. Baltes (Eds.), *Longitudinal research in the study of behavior and development* (pp. 263–302). New York: Academic Press.

Scheier, L. M., Botvin, G. J., Griffin, K. W., & Diaz, T. (2000). Dynamic growth models of self-esteem and adolescent alcohol use. *Journal of Early Adolescence, 20,* 178–209.

Seltzer, V. C. (1989). *The psychosocial worlds of the adolescent: Public and private.* New York: Wiley.

Sherif, M. (1936). *The psychology of social norms.* New York: Harper.

Stacy, A. W., Newcomb, M. D., & Bentler, P. M. (1991). Personality, problem drinking, and drunk driving: Mediating, moderating, and direct-effect models. *Journal of Personality and Social Psychology, 60,* 795–811.

Stacy, A. W., Newcomb, M. D., & Bentler, P. M. (1992). Interactive and higher-order effects of social influences on drug use. *Journal of Health and Social Behavior, 33,* 226–241.

Sutherland, E. H. (1939). *Principles of criminology* (3rd ed.). Philadelphia: J. B. Lippincott.

Vogel-Sprott, M. (1974). Defining "light" and "heavy" social drinking: Research implications and hypotheses. *Quarterly Journal of Studies on Alcohol, 35,* 1388–1392.

Volkow, N., Fowler, J., & Wang, G.-J. (2002). Role of dopamine in drug reinforcement and addiction in humans: Results from imaging studies. *Behavioral Pharmacology, 13,* 355–366.

Widaman, K. F., & Reise, S. P. (1997). Exploring the measurement invariance of psychological instruments: Applications in the substance use domain. In K. J. Bryant, M. Windle, & S. G. West (Eds.), *The science of prevention: Methodological advances from alcohol and substance abuse research* (pp. 281–324). Washington, DC: American Psychological Association.

Wills, T. A. (1992). Social comparison and self change. In J. Fisher, J. Chinksy, Y. Klar, & A. Nadler (Eds.), *Self-change: Social-psychological and clinical perspectives* (pp. 231–252). New York: Springer-Verlag.

Wills, T. A. (1994). Self-esteem and perceived control in adolescent substance use: Comparative tests in concurrent and prospective analyses. *Psychology of Addictive Behaviors, 8,* 223–234.

Wills, T. A., & Stoolmiller, M. (2002). The role of self-control in early escalation of substance use. *Journal of Consulting and Clinical Psychology, 70,* 986–997.

Yanovitzky, I. (2005). Sensation seeking and adolescent drug use: The mediating role of association with deviant peers and pro-drug discussions. *Health Communications, 17,* 67–89.

Index

National Youth Anti-Drug Media
      Campaign, xix–xx
Native Americans
      alcohol reactions of, 252
      ethnic identity among, 342
      and historical trauma, 329
      research with, 328, 334
      studies including, 39
Natural experiments, 427
Natural history approach, 40, 120
Naturally rewarding behaviors, 170–171
ND. *See* Neurobehavioral disinhibition
Negation, xxii
Negative affect (NA), 186, 348–349, 573
Negative emotionality, 128, 132, 136, 211
Negative reinforcement model, 185,
      188–190
Neighborhood clusters, 425
Neighborhood disadvantage and
      deterioration, 462
Neighborhood disorder, 435–436
Neighborhood influences on substance
      use, 423–441
      mechanisms of, 432–437
      methods of studying, 424–427
      socioeconomic status, 427–432
Neighborhood matching, 118
Neighborhood risk, 465–466
Neighborhoods, 23, 118–119, 446.
            See also Chicago Household Survey
Neighborhood units, 425
NESARC study. *See* National
      Epidemiologic Study of Alcohol
      Related Conditions study
Nested case control studies, 19, 22
Nested designs, 424–425
Nested model comparisons, 517
Nested models, 556–558
Neural cell adhesion molecule 1, 254–255
Neural connections, 171
Neurobehavioral disinhibition (ND), 60,
      211–212
Neurodevelopment, 209–219
      endophenotypes in, 212–217
      and environment, 218–219
      and heritable risks, 210–211
      and psychological dysregulation,
            211–212
      and risky behaviors, 217–218
Neurotic character disorders, 35
Neurotransmitters systems, 254–256
Neutralization theory, 621
News media depictions, of substance use,
      480, 482–485
News Scan, 335

New York City Bureau of Social Hygiene,
      30, 31, 33
New York City Narcotic Clinic, 33
New York Longitudinal Study, 129
NIAAA. *See* National Institute of Alcohol
      Abuse and Alcoholism
Nicotine dependence, 254–255
NIDA. *See* National Institute on Drug Abuse
NIH. *See* National Institutes of Health
NIMH. *See* National Institute of Mental
      Health
1960s social revolution, 39–40, 97, 305
Nixon administration, 40
NLAES (National Longitudinal Alcohol
      Epidemiology Survey), 270
Nonmedical use of prescription drugs, 79,
      80, 482
Nonoptimal decisions, 166–167
"Normal science," 662
Normative perceptions, 101
Norms
      community, 585
      models of, 158–159
      perceived, 157–158, 393, 406–407
      research on, 389–390
Noscapine, xix
Novelty seeking, 129, 130
NREPP. *See* National Registry of
      Evidence-based Programs and
      Practices
NREPP review process, 613
NSDUH. *See* National Survey on Drug Use
      and Health
Nucleus accumbens, 171, 216, 218

Obesity prevention program, 588–590
Obsessive–compulsive disorder, 231
Odds ratios (ORs), 274
O'Donnell, J. A., 40–41
Office of National Drug Control Policy
      (ONDCP), xx, 485–486
Omnibus Drug Initiative Act, xx
ONDCP (Office of National Drug
      Control Policy), xx
ONDCP media campaign, 584
Opiate addiction, 30–33
Opiate Addiction (Lindesmith), 37
Opiate derivatives, 621
Opiate users, 33
"Opium Addiction in Chicago"
      (Bingham), 37
Opium poppy, xix
"Opium problem," 31
The Opium Problem (Terry and Pellens),
      31–32

Opium use, among Chinese laborers, 29, 30
Opponent processes, 229
Opponent-process model, 188–189
Opponent-process theory, 229, 230
Oppositional culture, 312–313
OPRM1 (mu-opioid receptor gene), 256
Oregon Liquor Control Commission, 500
Organism–context relations, xviin.1
ORs (odds ratios), 274
Orthogonal acculturation model, 311–312
"Other directed," xvii
"Out-of-body" experiences, 81
Outsiders (Becker), 37
Over-the-counter drugs, 81, 484
Oxycodone, xix

P300 amplitude, reduced, 212–213
PA (positive affect), 186
Pacific Islanders, research with, 328
Panic attacks, 122
Papaverine, xix
Paradigm, 662
Paradigm for drug use etiology, 308, 310
Paradigm shifts, 45–46
Parental attitudes, 370–371, 374, 410–411
Parental authority, 368
Parental coaching, 367–372
      and coping processes, 371–372
      emotional tone/content of, 370–371
      summary of coaching pathway, 372
Parental disapproval, 370–371
Parental influences
      as environmental factor in SUD
            development, 218–219
      peer influence as moderator of,
            411–412
      and racial discrimination, 351, 353, 354
      on substance use/abuse/dependence,
            250–251
Parental involvement, 218, 555–559, 608
Parental modeling, 157, 367, 372–374
Parental monitoring, 218, 250, 251, 342,
      375, 434–435, 569, 605
Parental supervision, 218
Parental support, 411–412
Parental values, 371, 374
Parent–child communication, 368–370
Parenthood
      social role changes with, 569
      and substance use, 88
Parenting in the Drug Free Years
      prevention program, 196
Parenting practices, 295, 318–319, 411
Parenting style, 250, 251, 375, 411

desistence, 65–66
heterogeneity, 56–57
intermediary constructs, 59–61
multiple determinants, 55–56
pathways, 64
progressions, 64–65
risk/protective factors, 62–64
subtypes, 57
terms used in, 51–52
trajectories, 64
vulnerability, 61–62
TRA. *See* Theory of reasoned action
Traditionalism, modernism vs., 307–309,
313–314
Traffic fatalities, xxi, 496. *See also* Motor
vehicle crashes, alcohol-related
Training
of program providers, 644
of researchers, 331–332
Trajectories, of substance use, 64, 341–344
Transitions in activated states, 170
Translating research into practice and
practice into research, 582–585
Translating research into practice and
practice into research (for drug
use prevention), 581–593
MPP example, 585–587
overview of, 582–585
PATHWAYS example, 588–590
in prevention trial examples, 585–590
risk factor approach to, 583
of risk factors into prevention program
development/testing, 583–584
of risk factors into program
dissemination/practice, 584–585
STEP example, 587–588
stepwise model of, 590–593
Type I to Type II, 583
Trauma, 218
Treatment, growing enrollment in, xxi
Truth Anti-Tobacco Campaign, 477,
485, 486
Truth campaigns, 485
Tuberculosis, 21
Tuskegee syphilis study, 331
Twins-reared apart designs, 24
Twin studies (of substance dependence),
253
Two-factor model of etiological processes,
127–141
behavioral or emotional control, 138
and cognitive content sources, 138–139

as dual-process approach, 140
high reward sensitivity vs. poor,
139–140
implications for prevention, 140–141
self-control affects exposure to
proximal factors, 134–141
self-control and substance use,
132–134
temperament as a substrate for
self-control, 130–132
temperament dimensions, 127–130
Two-parent families, 412
Type I studies, 583
Type I to Type II translation, 583,
585–587
Type I–Type A subtype, 57
Type II studies, 583
Type II to practice translation, 587–588
Type II to Type I back-translation,
588–590
Type II–Type B subtype, 57

Underage drinking, costs of, 494
Underage drinking laws, 249
Unemployment
and African American substance
use, 343
and substance use, 433–434, 572
Unequal Treatment (Smedley, Stith,
& Nelson), 326
Unintentional injuries, 326
Universality of theory, 104–106
Universal laws, 98
University of Chicago, 36, 37, 463
University of Michigan, 330–331
Unrealistic optimism, 618
Urban areas, 298, 299, 409–410
U.S. Census Bureau, 117, 271
U.S. Congress, 326
U.S. Public Health Service, 29, 30, 45
U.S. Public Health Service Narcotic
Farm, 34
U.S. Public Health Service Narcotics
Hospitals, 36, 38
U.S. Supreme Court, 426

Vaillant, George, 38
Valence–arousal model, 186
Ventral striatum, 169
Vicious associations, 33

Vicodin, xix
Vietnam soldiers, 29, 40
Violence, 499
Violence prevention, 586
Virginia Slims, 478
Volstead Act. *See* National Prohibition
Act of 1919
Vulnerability, 44, 51, 61–62
Vygotsky, L. S., xvii

"Wanting" (drugs), 190, 230
Warning labels, 479, 501–502
War on Drugs, xix, xx, 327
Well-being, 641–642
White matter development, 213–215
Wisdom, 626
Withdrawal-relief model, 188
Within-subject designs, 191
Wolfe, Tom, 97
Wong, F. Y., 335
Woodlawn study, 9
Working memory, 173, 174

Yale Center of Alcohol Studies, 37
Yale Laboratory of Applied Physiology,
37
Yale Plan Clinics, 37
Yonkers project, 426–427
Young adulthood
defined, 404
developmental changes in, 74
peer socialization/selection during,
404–405
Young adult substance use, 73–89
changes in, 74
decline during young adulthood,
87–88
developmental framework for, 81–88
and life-span epidemiology of
substance use, 74–78
progression of, 83–88
types of, 78–81
Young Men and Drugs (NIDA), 40, 41
Youth in Transition Study, 42, 75
Youth in Transition survey, 97
Youth organizations, 433
Youth Risk Behavior Survey, 77, 271

Zero tolerance laws, 496–498, 503

About the Editor

Lawrence M. Scheier is president of LARS Research Institute, Inc., a Nevada-based not-for-profit company offering a full line of research services encompassing health promotion, program evaluation, program development, and behavioral science technology transfer. He is also adjunct professor of psychiatry in the School of Medicine at Washington University St. Louis and voluntary associate professor at the Weill Medical College, Cornell University, affiliated with the Department of Public Health, Division of Prevention and Health Behavior, Institute for Prevention Research. Dr. Scheier received a BA in psychology from Duke University in 1978, an MA in psychology from New York University in 1983, and a PhD in educational psychology and technology from the University of Southern California in 1988. He is a developmental psychologist whose research emphasizes the causes and consequences of drug use and evaluation of programs that promote positive youth adaptation. His specific interests include the role of social cognition in health behaviors, identity formation, self-concept, and risk and protective factors that nurture developmental change. For the past 20 years he has examined the efficacy of several school- and community-based drug prevention programs. He uses multivariate and causal modeling strategies with longitudinal data to examine factors that influence growth and change in normal development as well as investigating programmatic change through drug abuse prevention programs. He has received funding from various federal agencies and engaged the private business sector in research on youth health. He resides in Las Vegas, Nevada, where he pursues an active lifestyle and raises his two teenage daughters.